The Middle East

16th Edition

Sara Miller McCune founded SAGE Publishing in 1965 to support the dissemination of usable knowledge and educate a global community. SAGE publishes more than 1000 journals and over 600 new books each year, spanning a wide range of subject areas. Our growing selection of library products includes archives, data, case studies, and video. SAGE remains majority owned by our founder and after her lifetime will become owned by a charitable trust that secures the company's continued independence.

Los Angeles | London | New Delhi | Singapore | Washington DC | Melbourne

The Middle East

16th Edition

Edited by Ellen Lust

University of Gothenburg

Foreword by Marwan Muasher

FOR INFORMATION:

CQ Press
An Imprint of SAGE Publications, Inc.
2455 Teller Road
Thousand Oaks, California 91320
E-mail: order@sagepub.com

SAGE Publications Ltd.
1 Oliver's Yard
55 City Road
London, EC1Y 1SP
United Kingdom

SAGE Publications India Pvt. Ltd.
B 1/I 1 Mohan Cooperative Industrial Area
Mathura Road, New Delhi 110 044
India

SAGE Publications Asia-Pacific Pte. Ltd.
18 Cross Street #10-10/11/12
China Square Central
Singapore 048423

Printed in the United States of America

Library of Congress Control Number: 2022919438

ISBN: 978-1-0718-4446-5

This book is printed on acid-free paper.

Acquisitions Editor: Christy Sadler

Product Associate: Kat Wallace

Production Editor: Vijayakumar

Copy Editor: Benny Willy Stephen

Typesetter: diacriTech

Cover Designer: Janet Kiesel

23 24 25 26 10 9 8 7 6 5 4 3 2 1

BRIEF CONTENTS

DETAILED CONTENTS

Chapter 13 Israel   **501**

Lihi Ben Shitrit

Chapter 23 Sudan   **773**

Liv Tønnessen

BOXES, FIGURES, TABLES, AND MAPS

BOXES

FIGURES

TABLES

MAPS

ABOUT THE EDITOR

Ellen Lust is a Professor in the Department of Political Science and the Founding Director of the Program on Governance and Local Development, first at Yale University (2013–2016) and then at the University of Gothenburg (2015–present). She received her MA in Modern Middle East and North African Studies (1993) and PhD in Political Science (1997) from the University of Michigan. Before joining the faculty at the University of Gothenburg, she taught at Rice University (1997–1999) and then moved to Yale University (2000–2015), where she was on the faculty of the Department of Political Science and served as the Chair of the Council on Middle East Studies, spearheading the establishment of the BA degree and MA certificate program in Modern Middle East Studies. Ellen has conducted research and engaged in policy dialogue across the Middle East, including Egypt, Jordan, Libya, Malawi, Morocco, Palestine, Syria, and Tunisia, as well as in sub-Saharan Africa. She has served as an advisor and consultant to such organizations as the UNDP, UN Democracy Fund, The World Bank, USAID, Carter Center, Freedom House, and NDI. Ellen has authored numerous books and articles, including *Structuring Contestation in the Arab World* (Cambridge University Press, 2005); *Political Participation in the Middle East and North Africa* (Lynne Rienner, 2008), coedited with Saloua Zerhouni; *Taking to the Streets: Activism and the Arab Uprisings* (Johns Hopkins University Press, 2014), coedited with Lina Khatib; and *Trust, Voice, and Incentives: Learning from Local Successes in Service Delivery in the Middle East and North Africa* (World Bank, 2015) in collaboration with Hana Brixi and Michael Woolcock; and *Everyday Choices: The Role of Competing Authorities and Social Institutions in Politics and Development* (Cambridge University Press, 2022). Her research has been supported by foundations such as the Hicham Alaoui Foundation, the US National Science Foundation, Social Science Research Council, FORMAS, and the Swedish Research Council.

CONTRIBUTORS

LAHOUARI ADDI, author of the chapter on Algeria, is an Emeritus Professor of Sociology at Sciences Po Lyon, University of Lyon, France. He is a member of the Research Centre Triangle, UMR CNRS 5206. Addi has published many books and papers on Algeria, among them are *L'Algérie et la démocratie* (Editions La Découverte, 1995), *Les Mutations de la Société Algérienne* (Editions La Découverte, 1999), and *Sociologie et Anthropologie chez Pierre Bourdieu* (blog, 2002). His most recent books are *Deux anthropologues au Maghreb: Ernest Gellner et Clifford Geertz* (Les Editions des Archives Contemporaines, Paris, 2013), *Radical Arab Nationalism and Political Islam* (Georgetown University Press, 2017), and *The Crisis of Religious Muslim Discourse: The Necessary Shift from Plato to Kant* (Routledge, 2021).

HESHAM AL-AWADI, author of the chapter of Kuwait, is Professor of History and International Relations at the American University of Kuwait. His recent publications include *The History of Slaves in the Arabian Gulf* (in Arabic) (Dar Altanweer, 2021) and *The Muslim Brothers in Pursuit of Legitimacy: Power and Political Islam in Egypt Under Mubarak* (I. B. Tauris, 2014).

MEHRZAD BOROUJERDI, author of the chapter on Iran, is the Vice Provost and Dean of the College of Arts, Sciences, and Education at Missouri University of Science and Technology. He is the author of *Iranian Intellectuals and the West: The Tormented Triumph of Nativism* (Syracuse University Press, 1996), coauthor of *Post-revolutionary Iran: A Political Handbook* (Syracuse University Press, 2018), and editor of *Mirror for the Muslim Prince: Islam and Theory of Statecraft* (Syracuse University Press, 2013).

LAURIE A. BRAND, author of the chapter on Jordan, is Professor Emerita of Political Science and International Relations and Middle East Studies at the University of Southern California. She is a former president of the Middle East Studies Association, whose Committee on Academic Freedom she has chaired since 2007, a four-time Fulbright scholar to the Middle East and North Africa, and a Carnegie Corporation scholar from 2008 to 2010. She is the author of *Palestinians in the Arab World* (Columbia University Press, 1988), *Jordan's Inter-Arab Relations* (Columbia University Press, 1994), *Women, the State and Political Liberalization* (Columbia University Press, 1998), *Citizens Abroad: States and Emigration in the Middle East and North Africa* (Cambridge University Press, 2006), and *Official Stories: Politics and National Narratives in Egypt and Algeria* (Stanford University Press, 2014).

MELANI CAMMETT is Clarence Dillon Professor of International Affairs in the Department of Government and Director of the Weatherhead Center for International Affairs at Harvard University. She also holds a secondary faculty appointment at the Harvard T.H. Chan School of Public Health. Cammett's books include *The Oxford Handbook on Politics in Muslim Societies* (coedited with Pauline Jones, Oxford University Press, 2021), *Compassionate Communalism: Welfare and Sectarianism in Lebanon* (Cornell University Press 2014), which won the American Political Science Association (APSA) Giovanni Sartori Book Award and the Honorable Mention for the APSA Gregory Luebbert Book Award; *A Political Economy of the Middle East* (coauthored with Ishac Diwan, Alan Richards, and John Waterbury, Westview Press 2015); *The Politics of Non-State Social Welfare in the Global South* (co-edited with Lauren Morris MacLean, Cornell University Press 2014), which received the Honorable Mention for the ARNOVA book award; and *Globalization and Business Politics in North Africa* (Cambridge University Press 2007). Her current research explores peace and reconciliation after ethnoreligious conflict, the politics of social service delivery, and the historical roots of economic and social development, primarily in the Middle East. Cammett has published numerous articles in academic and policy journals, consults for development policy organizations, and is the recipient of various fellowships and awards.

BENOIT CHALLAND, coauthor of the chapter on Palestine, is Associate Professor of Sociology at the New School for Social Research, New York. His research focuses on civil society in Palestine and Tunisia, Marxist theory, and European identity. He has taught at the *Scuola Normale Superiore* (Florence), New York University, and the University of Fribourg (CH). He is the author, among others, of *Palestinian Civil Society: Foreign Donors and the Power to Promote and Exclude* (Routledge, 2009), and guest editor of a special issue of *Constellations* on social theory and the 2011 Arab Uprisings. He also coedited with F. Bicchi and S. Heydemann, *The Struggle for Influence in the Middle East: The Arab Uprisings and Foreign Assistance* (Routledge, 2017). With Chiara Bottici, he has coauthored two books: *Imagining Europe: Myth, Memory, Identity* (Cambridge University Press, 2013) and *The Myth of the Clash of Civilizations* (Routledge, 2010), and has coedited the collection of essays *The Politics of Imagination* (Routledge, 2011).

JULIA CHOUCAIR-VIZOSO, author of the chapter on Iraq, is a political scientist with expertise in comparative politics, governance structures, environmental politics, and the contemporary Middle East. She is a Senior Fellow at the Arab Reform Initiative, Managing Editor at the Lebanese publication *The Public Source*, and Adjunct Professor at IE University in Madrid. She was previously Vice Chair of the Center for Middle Eastern Studies at the University of California, Berkeley, and Associate at the Carnegie Endowment for International Peace in Washington, DC. She holds a PhD in Political Science from Yale University.

ISHAC DIWAN directs the Development and Globalization Program at the CEPREMAP (Centre pour la Recherche Economique et ses Applications) at the Paris School of Economics and teaches economics at the Ecole Normale Superieure. He is also in charge of the Political Economy program of the Economic Research Forum, an association of Middle East social scientists. Ishac has previously held positions at NYU, Columbia University, and the Harvard Kennedy School and worked for the World Bank from 1987 to 2011. His current research focuses on the political economy of the Middle East and broader development and international financial issues. He is widely published in a variety of journals (see https://ishacdiwan.com/), and his recent (coauthored) books include *A Political Economy of the Middle East* (Westview Press 2015); and *Crony Capitalism in the Middle East* (Oxford University Press 2019).

MINE EDER, author of the chapter on Turkey, is Professor of Political Science and International Relations at Boğaziçi University in Istanbul, Turkey. Her work explores different dimensions of Turkey's political economy, including regionalism, welfare reform, poverty, informality, and migrant incorporation. Her most recent study focuses on various aspects of urban transformation in Istanbul, analyzing dynamics of gentrification, contested urban encounters, and challenges of living together. Her research has been published in journals such as *Political Geography, International Journal of Urban and Regional Research, Middle Eastern Studies*, and *Middle East Law and Governance.*

MICHAEL GASPER, author of the chapter on the making of the modern Middle East, teaches at Occidental College in Los Angeles, California. He coedited, with Michael Bonine and Abbas Amanat, *Is There a Middle East? The Evolution of a Geopolitical Concept* (Stanford University Press, 2011) and is the author of *The Power of Representation: Publics, Peasants and Islam in Egypt* (Stanford University Press, 2009). He is finishing a manuscript *Re-Thinking Secularism and Sectarianism in the Lebanese Civil War (1975–1991).*

MICHAEL HERB, author of the chapter on the lower Gulf states, is Professor of Political Science at Georgia State University and serves as department chair. His work focuses on Gulf politics, monarchism, and the resource curse. He is the author of *The Wages of Oil: Parliaments and Economic Development in Kuwait and the UAE* (Cornell University Press, 2014) and *All in the Family: Absolutism, Revolution, and Democracy in the Middle Eastern Monarchies* (SUNY, 1999). He has twice won Fulbright awards to study in Kuwait.

STEVEN HEYDEMANN holds the Janet Wright Ketcham 1953 Chair in Middle East Studies at Smith College, with a joint appointment in the Department of Government. He is also a nonresident senior fellow in the Center for Middle East Policy of the Brookings Institution. From 2007 to 2015, he held several leadership positions at the US Institute of Peace in Washington, DC, including vice president of applied research on conflict and senior adviser for the Middle East. Heydemann is a political scientist who specializes in the comparative politics and the political economy of the Middle East. His interests include authoritarian governance, conflict and postconflict reconstruction, economic development, social policy, political and economic reform, and civil society. He has published in, among others, *World Development, Journal of Democracy,* and *Daedalus.* He has also authored several books, the most recent being *Middle East Authoritarianisms: Governance, Contestation, and Regime Resilience in Syria and Iran* (coedited with Reinoud Leenders, Stanford University Press 2013).

RAYMOND HINNEBUSCH, author of the chapter on Syria, is Professor of International Relations and Middle East Politics at the University of St. Andrews in Scotland and is director of the Centre for Syrian Studies. Among his publications on Syria are *Authoritarian Power and State Formation in Baathist Syria: Army, Party, and Peasant* (Westview Press, 1990), *The Syrian-Iranian Alliance: Middle Powers in a Penetrated Regional System* (with Anoushiravan Ehteshami, Routledge, 1997), *Syria: Revolution from Above* (Routledge, 2001), *Syria: From Reform to Revolt* (co-edited with Tina Zintl, Syracuse University Press, 2013), *The Syrian Uprising: Domestic Origins and Early Trajectory* (coedited with Omar Imady, Routledge, 2018) and *The War for Syria: Regional and International Dimensions of the Syrian Uprising* (coedited with Adham Saouli, Routledge 2020).

INTISSAR KHERIGI is an associate researcher at the Center for International Relations (CERI), Sciences Po University, Paris. She holds a PhD in Political Science from Sciences Po University in Paris, with a focus on the politics of decentralization reforms in postrevolution Tunisia. Her research focuses on local governance and decentralization reforms in the Arab world. She holds a Bachelors in Law from the University of Cambridge and a Masters in Human Rights from the London School of Economics and Political Science.

ROBERT LEE, coauthor of the chapter on religion, society and politics in the Middle East, is Professor Emeritus of Political Science at Colorado College, where he taught courses in comparative politics and international relations. He is the author of *Overcoming Tradition and Modernity: The Search for Islamic Authenticity* (Westview, 1997) and *Religion and Politics in the Middle East* (Westview, 2009).

MARC LYNCH, author of the chapter on international relations, is Professor of Political Science and Director of the Middle East Studies Program at the Elliott School of International Affairs at George Washington University. He is author of *Voices of the New Arab Public* (Columbia University Press2006), *The Arab Uprising* (Public Affairs, 2012), and *The New Arab Wars* (Public Affairs, 2016). He is also Director of the Project on Middle East Political Science, contributing editor for the *Washington Post's* Monkey Cage political science blog, and editor of the series *Columbia Studies in Middle East Politics*.

DRISS MAGHRAOUI, coauthor of the chapter on Morocco, is Associate Professor of History and International Relations with the School of Humanities and Social Sciences at Al Akhawayn University in Ifrane, Morocco. He is the coeditor of "Reforms in the Arab World: The Experience of Morocco" (*Mediterranean Politics*) and the editor of *Revisiting the*

Colonial Past in Morocco (Routledge, 2013). His most recent publications include "Searching for Normalization: The Party of Justice and Development in Morocco" in Chernov and Mecham's *Strategies and Behavior of Islamist Political Parties: Comparative Lessons from Asia and the Middle East* (University of Pennsylvania Press, 2014), "The Moroccan 'Effort de Guerre' in the Second World War" in Byfield's *Africa and The Second World War* (Cambridge University Press, 2015), "Obedience, Civil Resistance, and Dispersed Solidarities" in Roberts, Willis, McCarthy, and Ash's *Civil Resistance in the Arab Spring: Triumphs and Disasters* (Oxford University Press, 2016), "The ambiguity of Citizenship and the Quest for Rights in Morocco" in Meijer, Sater and Babar's *Routledge Handbook of Citizenship in the Middle East and North Africa* (Routledge, 2020) and "Le Maroc comme "communauté imagine" à travers le journal Al-Istiqlal 1950–1960, in Kenbib's *Pour une Maison de l'Histoire du Maroc*, (Academie du Royaume du Maroc, 2020).

RABAB EL MAHDI, author of the chapter on political participation, is an Associate Professor of Political Science at The American University in Cairo. Her work focuses on contentious politics and social movements. Her publications include the edited volumes *Arab Spring in Egypt: Revolution and Beyond* (with Bahgat Korany, 2012) and *Egypt: The Moment of Change* (with Philip Marfleet, 2009), as well as a number of book chapters and journal articles on labor movements, the feminist question in Egypt, and youth mobilization. She is also the founder and director of AUC's research project, Alternative Policy Solutions (APS).

TAREK MASOUD, author of the chapter on Egypt, teaches at Harvard University's John F. Kennedy School of Government. He is the author of *Counting Islam: Religion, Class, and Elections in Egypt* (Cambridge University Press, 2014), coauthor of *The Arab Spring: Pathways of Repression and Reform* (with Jason Brownlee and Andrew Reynolds, Oxford University Press, 2015) and coeditor of *Democracy in Hard Places* (with Scott Mainwaring, Oxford University Press, 2022).

VALENTINE M. MOGHADAM is Professor of Sociology and International Affairs at Northeastern University, Boston. Born in Tehran, Iran, Professor Moghadam received her higher education in Canada and the United States. In addition to her academic career, Moghadam has been coordinator of the research program on women and development at the UNU's WIDER Institute (Helsinki, 1990–1995) and a section chief for gender equality and development in UNESCO's Social and Human Sciences Sector (Paris, 2004–2006). In Fall 2021, she was in residence at the US Library of Congress as Kluge Chair in the Countries and Cultures of the South. Her areas of research include globalization, transnational social movements and feminist networks, economic citizenship, and gender and development in the Middle East and North Africa. Among her many publications, Moghadam is author of *Modernizing Women: Gender and Social Change in the Middle East* (first published 1993; second edition 2003; revised and updated third edition Fall 2013); *Globalizing Women: Transnational Feminist Networks* (2005), which won the American Political Science Association's Victoria Schuck award for best book on women and politics for 2005; and *Globalization and Social Movements: The*

Populist Challenge and Democratic Alternatives (2020). She has edited seven books, including *Empowering Women after the Arab Spring* (2016, with Marwa Shalaby). *After the Arab Uprisings: Progress and Stagnation in the Middle East and North Africa,* coauthored with Shamiran Mako, was published in July 2021 by Cambridge University Press.

JACOB MUNDY, author of the chapter of Libya, is an associate professor and director of the Peace and Conflict Studies Program at Colgate University, where he also contributes to the program in Middle Eastern and Islamic Studies. His research examines the intersection of armed conflicts, foreign interventions, and political-economy in North Africa. He has conducted field research in Algeria, Libya, Morocco, and Western Sahara, and he was a Fulbright Professor in Tunisia during the 2018–2019 academic year. His book *Libya* was published by Polity Press in 2018.

SARAH G. PHILLIPS, author of the chapter on Yemen, is an associate professor in the Department of Government and International Relations at The University of Sydney. Her research draws from years of in-depth fieldwork and focuses on international intervention in the Global South, knowledge production about conflict-affected states, and nonstate governance, with a geographic focus on the Middle East and sub-Saharan Africa. Her publications include *When There Was No Aid: War and Peace in Somaliland* (Cornell University Press, 2020), *Yemen and Politics of Permanent Crisis* (Adelphi Paper Series, 2011), and *Yemen's Democracy Experiment in Regional Perspective* (Palgrave Macmillan, 2008).

PAUL SALEM, author of the chapter on Lebanon, is president of The Middle East Institute in Washington, DC. Salem is the editor and author of a number of books, including *Escaping the Conflict Trap: Toward Ending Civil Wars in the Middle East* (coeditor with Ross Harrison, MEI 2019); *From Chaos to Cooperation: Toward Regional Order in the Middle East* (coeditor with Ross Harrison, MEI 2017); *Winning the Battle, Losing the War: Addressing the Conditions that Fuel Armed Non State Actors* (coeditor with Charles Lister, MEI 2019); *Broken Orders: The Causes and Consequences of the Arab Uprisings* (in Arabic, Dar Annahar, 2013), *Bitter Legacy: Ideology and Politics in the Arab World* (Syracuse, 1994), *Conflict Resolution in the Arab World* (editor AUB, 1997). Prior to joining MEI, Salem was the Founding Director of the Carnegie Middle East Center in Beirut (2006–2013), the Director of the Fares Foundation (1989–1999), and the founding director of the Lebanese Center for Policy Studies (1989–1999). He received his BA, MA, and PhD in Political Science from Harvard University and taught at the American University of Beirut.

LIHI BEN SHITRIT, author of the chapter on Israel and coauthor of the chapter on religion, society, and politics in the Middle East, is an associate professor at the School of Public and International Affairs, University of Georgia, Athens. Her research focuses on religion, politics, and gender in the Middle East. She is the author of *Righteous Transgressions: Women's Activism on the Israeli and Palestinian Religious Right* (Princeton University Press, 2015) and *Women and the Holy City: The Struggle over Jerusalem's Sacred Space* (Cambridge University Press, 2020).

DINA AL SOWAYEL, author of the chapter on Saudi Arabia, is Associate Director of Women's Studies at the University of Houston in Texas. She received her MA and PhD from Rice University in Political Science and her JD from the University of Houston. Her BA is from Wellesley College. Al Sowayel teaches a variety of courses in the history department, including History of the Modern Middle East, State and Society in the Middle East, Women and Islam, A History of Islam, War in the Middle East, and A History of the Palestine–Israeli Conflict. She also takes students to the Arab and Muslim world annually.

ALAA TARTIR, coauthor of the chapter on Palestine, is a researcher and academic coordinator at the Graduate Institute of International and Development Studies (IHEID) in Geneva, Switzerland. Tartir is also a Global Fellow at the Peace Research Institute Oslo (PRIO), a Policy and Program Advisor to Al-Shabaka: The Palestinian Policy Network, and a research associate at the Centre on Conflict, Development and Peacebuilding (CCDP) at IHEID. Among other positions, Tartir was a visiting professor at Paris School of International Affairs (PSIA), Sciences Po, a postdoctoral fellow at the Geneva Centre for Security Policy (GCSP), and a researcher in international development studies at the London School of Economics and Political Science (LSE), where he earned his PhD. Tartir is the author of *Policing Palestine: Securitising Peace and Criminalising Resistance in the West Bank* (Pluto Press, 2022), the editor of *Outsourcing Repression: Israeli-Palestinian Security Coordination* (AMEC, 2019), the co-editor of *Palestine and Rule of Power: Local Dissent vs. International Governance* (Palgrave Macmillan, 2019), and the coeditor of *Political Economy of Palestine: Critical, Interdisciplinary, and Decolonial Perspectives* (Palgrave Macmillan, 2021). Tartir can be followed on Twitter (@alaatartir), and his publications can be accessed at www.alaatartir.com.

MARK TESSLER, author of the chapter on the Israeli–Palestinian conflict, is Samuel J. Eldersveld Collegiate Professor of political science at the University of Michigan, where from 2005 to 2013 he also served as vice provost for international affairs. Tessler is the author or coauthor of sixteen books and more than 150 scholarly articles dealing with the Middle East and North Africa, including the award-winning *A History of the Israeli-Palestinian Conflict* (Indiana University Press, 2009), upon which his chapter draws. He is one of the few US scholars to have attended university and lived for extended periods in both the Arab world and Israel. Among Tessler's other books are *Public Opinion in the Middle East: Survey Research and the Political Orientations of Ordinary Citizens* (Indiana University Press, 2011); *Islam and Politics in the Middle East: Explaining the Views of Ordinary Citizens* (Indiana University Press, 2015); *Religious Minorities in Non-Secular Middle Eastern and North African States* (New York: Palgrave MacMillan, 2020); and *Social Science Research in the Arab World and Beyond: A Guide for Students, Instructors and Researchers* (Springer, 2022). Tessler is also cofounder and coprincipal investigator of the Arab Barometer Survey project, which was established in 2006 and through seven waves has carried out 68 surveys in sixteen countries and conducted face-to-face interviews with more than one hundred thousand men and women. His work on political Islam has been supported by a Carnegie Scholar award.

SALOUA ZERHOUNI, coauthor of the chapter on Morocco, is a professor at Mohammed V University in Rabat, where she was vice dean for scientific research and cooperation. She has taught in several universities and *grandes écoles*, such as the University of Michigan in the United States and Sciences Po Bordeaux in France. Between 2001 and 2003, she worked as an associate researcher at the German Institute for International and Security Affairs in Berlin (SWP), where she contributed to a study on "Elite Change in the Arab World." Previously, as part of a Fulbright scholarship, she was visiting researcher at Georgetown University. Zerhouni has publications on Moroccan elites, democratization and its limits, the Moroccan parliament, elections, Islamist parties, and youth and political participation. She is coeditor with Ellen Lust-Okar of *Political Participation in the Middle East* (Lynne Rienner, 2008). Saloua Zerhouni is a cofounder and currently the president of the Moroccan think-tank, Rabat Social Studies Institute (RSSI).

FOREWORD

MARWAN MUASHER, VICE PRESIDENT FOR STUDIES, THE CARNEGIE ENDOWMENT FOR INTERNATIONAL PEACE

More than a decade since the Arab uprisings began, the region continues to suffer from the same problems that led to these uprisings in the first place: a continued lack of good governance by most countries of the region, and an equally continuous denial by these countries that the old tools they used to keep social peace are quickly losing their effectiveness. In the absence of a political will to use new tools of political and social inclusion, buildi effective political institutions and move away from patronage systems and toward meritocracy, the status quo in the Arab world is precarious. In the short run, it might be kept artificially stable by force or financial means where available, but it will not do so indefinitely.

The year 2021 witnessed a major retreat in democracy across the Arab world, perhaps in line with a worldwide retreat democracy is currently witnessing. The big disappointment is, of course, Tunisia, which until recently still held the hope that the different societal and political forces can agree on new social contracts, settle their differences peacefully, and build systems of checks and balances. The elected President Saied's dictatorial power grab dashed hopes of many across the Arab world who looked at Tunisia as a model that the rest of the region could aspire to follow. At the time of this writing, it is not clear whether Saied's move will permanently dictate Tunisia's future. Civil society and the public at large are showing signs of disillusionment with a president who claims he wants to uphold constitutional principles but acts otherwise.

The future of democracy darkened elsewhere as well. In Sudan, which was part of a second wave of Arab uprisings in 2019 (when Algeria, Iraq, and Lebanon also witnessed popular uprisings to demand good governance and an end to corruption), the military moved to grab all power, despite an earlier agreement to share this power with civilians. And Lebanon, after a large popular uprising in October 2019 against a dysfunctional, sectarian, and highly corrupt system, became a clearly failed state. It suffered from a political stalemate and an economic catastrophe, precisely because the sectarian pillars of the political system continued to refuse necessary steps to reverse the economic situation and thereby allow international support to become feasible.

Meanwhile, the situation in the Palestinian occupied territories worsened considerably. The clashes in May between the Palestinians and the Israelis, brought about by the Israeli move to evict Palestinians forcibly out of their homes in the Jerusalem suburbs of Sheikh Jarrah and Silwan, and the ensuing war on Gaza point to several important conclusions.

The international community is no longer able to ignore Israeli human rights violations under cover that a promised and elusive two-state solution would make attention to these violations moot. The new, post-Oslo generation of Palestinians trusts neither that Israel will ever withdraw from occupied Palestinian territories and allow for the emergence of a credible Palestinian state, nor that its own government acts in the interests of the Palestinian people. The violation of rights for Palestinians under occupation as well as for those Palestinians who are Israeli citizens, particularly with the passage of a basic law that views Israel as the nation-state of the Jewish people and disregards the more than 20 percent of Israel's citizens who are not Jewish, has unified Palestinians inside Israel and those under occupation. It has also led many human rights organizations to label Israel with the hitherto taboo word: Israel's biggest human rights organization, B'Tselem, and Human Rights Watch have both accused Israel of becoming an apartheid state.

That label was unthinkable by the international community only a few years ago. Today, that view of Israel is shared widely. A recent poll of 521 Middle East experts, conducted by Shibley Telhami of the University of Maryland and Marc Lynch of George Washington University, came to the same conclusion. A majority, 52 percent, said that a two-state solution was no longer viable, while a full 77 percent of the respondents predicted a one-state reality akin to apartheid if a two-state solution is no longer possible.

The Abrahamic Accords, peace treaties signed by Israel and four Arab states—the UAE, Bahrain, Morocco, and Sudan—did not help the cause of peace. The Accords were touted as historic steps towards advancing the peace process, but it is clear that they were signed to push purely bilateral interests. In the meantime, the unintended consequence is that they have helped kill any chance for a two-state solution by violating the land-for-peace principle as well as that of an Arab consensus stipulated in the Arab Peace Initiative of 2002, which promised Israel total peace with all Arab countries in return for total withdrawal. It is becoming clear today that the Arab Peace Initiative is dead, along with any prospects for a two-state solution.

A new alternative to peacemaking is emerging, one that is calling for a rights-based approach. This approach, adopted by several respected international organizations, including Carnegie, is in line with the views of a new generation of Palestinians. It argues that focus should shift from one on the shape of a solution (e.g., two-states or one-state) to one that upholds equal rights for all, Palestinians and Israelis alike, regardless of whatever shape the two sides agree on at the end. Absent that, the international community would be supporting apartheid.

It is important to note that the United States engagement in the Palestinian–Israeli conflict, and the Middle East more generally, has waned notably in recent years. The United States' interest in the Middle East diminished since the aftermath of the Gulf war in 2003 convinced most Americans of the folly of foreign military intervention, and the Biden administration has further shifted focus away from the region. The clashes between Israelis and Palestinians in May only cemented the view that the current end game for the United States is to achieve a long-term truce between the two sides that would miraculously preserve the conditions for a two-state solution, but not more. There are no attempts today to restart negotiations between the two sides, which have anyway lost all credibility among most Palestinians and perhaps many Israelis as well. The United State's growing energy independence has further contributed to this new shift, even if many allies of the United States still depend on Middle East oil. The vacuum left by the United States has so far been filled by countries such as Russia, China, Iran, and Turkey, all with authoritarian tendencies that are not likely to aid the cause of political reform in the region.

The one exception to the United States's lack of interest in the region is a renewal of an Iranian nuclear deal. The Obama administration ignored Iran's interference in the Arab region, as it calculated that it would be impossible to reach a deal if that issue was part of negotiations. More people in the region, including in Israel, are convinced today that President's Trump withdrawal from the deal was unwise. As of this writing, the chances for a new deal are dwindling, and the repercussions for the region are dire.

Does this mean that the region is doomed? That the Arab uprisings are for naught? That peace will never come?

Not really. I have argued since the start of the Arab uprisings in 2010/2011 that the status quo was not sustainable and that we are at the start of a historic transformation process that will take decades to unfold. As long as the challenges of the Arab world persist—authoritarianism and lack of good governance, patronage economic systems based on oil, persistent unemployment made worse by COVID-19, and lack of citizen equality before the law regardless of gender, ethnic or religious origin—the region will witness successive waves of uprisings until these challenges are properly addressed. As long as most Arab countries insist on relying on the outdated and dwindling tools of security and financial means to keep social peace without addressing the underlying causes of instability, the region will not know either stability or prosperity. Either the Arab world internalizes the need for inclusion, equality before the law, and productivity as the new tools to ensure prosperity, or it will face even worse times. And so long as peace efforts are not directed at finding a solution between the occupier and the occupied, and do not insist on ending violations of Palestinians' human rights, no peace will come to the region, even if the Abrahamic accords were extended to cover most Arab states.

There are new challenges as well. Climate change is creeping to the center of the region's radar screen. It is a challenge that has been ignored for long. Not anymore. The water dispute between Egypt and Ethiopia is at least partly driven by climate change and increased surface evaporation from reservoirs in Egypt. The region also hosts half of the world refugees today, posing unprecedented economic, security, and identity challenges.

These issues and more will be discussed in this volume. I have attempted to describe some of these major challenges within an overall framework that will continue to define the region for years to come. I hope you will find this volume informative and insightful.

Marwan Muasher

ACKNOWLEDGMENTS

I am extremely grateful to the authors who agreed to participate in this project and did so with energy and dedication. They make writing the chapters look easy, but in reality, providing well-written, rich, detailed discussions of the themes and countries is a difficult task. Without their dedication to the project and to expanding our understanding of the Middle East more generally, this book simply would not be. The book also benefits from the insight of reviewers, who have highlighted the strengths of the previous editions and pointed to areas that we might improve. Thanks are due to all of them: Heba F. El-Shazli, George Mason University; Peter B. Heller, Manhattan College; Sally J. Howard, Concord University; George K. Keteku, State University of New York, Westchester Community College; Robert Lee, Colorado College; Jalil Roshandel, East Carolina University; Filiz Otuco Ruhm, Plymouth State University; Yusurf Sarfati, Illinois State University; and Jacqueline M. Sievert, Bowling Green State University. In addition, my gratitude goes to Christy Sadler and SAGE/CQ Press for shepherding the project from beginning to end. I am also extremely grateful to Hanna Andersson, Jennifer Bergman, and Mina Ghassaban Kjellén for research assistance, and to Rose Shaber-Twedt, who helped to keep the project in order and on track. I also thank the Department of Political Science at the University of Gothenburg and the Swedish Research Council, which provided me support during this project. These individuals and institutions make a sometimes-difficult task not only possible, but enjoyable.

INTRODUCTION

The Middle East and North Africa (MENA) is a region both diverse and unified. The upheavals that began in 2010 reflected the intricate connections between peoples and states of the MENA region. Demonstrations in Tunisia that led President Ben Ali to flee the country in January 2011 rippled across the region. Citizens from Egypt to Oman, seeing Tunisia's events as a cue that they, too, could overthrow long-standing authoritarian leaders, took to the streets. So, too, nearly a decade later, the region once again witnessed sociopolitical conflict and political instability, with uprisings in Algeria, Lebanon, and the Sudan. Results varied. After 2011, for instance, leaders in Tunisia, Egypt, Libya, and Yemen were overthrown; Libya, Syria, and Yemen deteriorated into civil war; while incumbents in Algeria, Morocco, Jordan, and the Gulf remained entrenched. Far from isolated incidents, changes in one country impacted and was impacted by neighbors, near and far. Refugees fled, placing new burdens on countries such as Lebanon, Jordan, Turkey, Iraq, and Tunisia, as well as the West; transnational radical movements expanded, challenging the very existence of states in Iraq and Syria; and money and resources flowed from one country to another in attempts to influence the region's dynamics. A region long associated with Islam, Israel, oil, and authoritarianism came to be associated with revolution, civil war, refugees, and radical extremism, but it remained a region united, despite its diversity.

The diversity of the MENA region existed before the 21st century, and it will continue to do so long after as well. The region is vast, spanning from Morocco in the west, through the countries of North Africa, to Turkey in the north, and to Iran and the Arabian Peninsula in the east. And it contains a range of historical, political, and social factors that both unite the region and make each country within it distinct and complex.

The sixteenth edition of *The Middle East* explores these unifying and distinguishing factors. It introduces readers to the MENA in its domestic, regional, and international contexts, examining the societies and politics of the region and the challenges facing the people living there. It asks how the trajectories of these countries have differed and the factors that have driven differences in the social and economic development, politics, and regional and international relations of countries across the region.

The chapters in the book's Overview section introduce readers to the key forces that shape the region—its common history, the types of institutions and governing arrangements at play, the role of religion, avenues citizens use to make demands on the state, societal changes, political economy, and regional and international relations among states. The seventeen country profile chapters that follow give readers a detailed look at each of the region's countries, examining the particular effects of those same forces in each country's context.

The chapter authors collectively bring a wealth of experience and perspectives to the analysis of the MENA today. They include anthropologists, historians, political scientists, and sociologists drawn from Australia, Europe, the Middle East, North Africa, and the United States. Each of the chapters provides a comprehensive, accessible, and balanced look at the region. Readers who are encountering the field for the first time can come away with a strong sense of the factors common to the MENA as well as an appreciation for the enormous diversity across the region, while more seasoned students of the Middle East can benefit significantly from the insights and expertise offered here. To fully appreciate the range of insights and information contained in the sixteenth edition, and to orient readers to the coverage of the book, we briefly consider the themes discussed in the pages that follow and then turn to a more detailed look at this edition's organization and features.

OVERVIEW OF THEMES

The volume opens by exploring how the historical experiences and identities that tie countries of the region together began centuries ago. As Michael Gasper explains in Chapter 1, the spread of Islam after its emergence during the 7th century in present-day Saudi Arabia was accompanied by the spread of the Arabic language and the development of an Arab identity. It also led to the establishment of a series of Islamic empires. These took various shapes and influenced the peoples living across this vast region differently, but they nevertheless helped to create a common historical experience that shapes the region today.

By the 20th century, the MENA was increasingly engaged with the West. The most important factor driving European interest in the Middle East during this period was geography. Located between Europe and today's India and China, the Middle East became a particularly important passageway for Europeans trading with the East. The opening of the Suez Canal in 1869 linked the Mediterranean Sea and the Red Sea, creating a direct sea route between Europe and Asia and eliminating the need to circle Africa. The Middle East (and the Ottoman Empire that ruled much of the area in the late 19th century) also became increasingly important as a buffer zone between the French, the British, and the growing Russian power. In short, the region was strategically important long before the discovery of oil and establishment of Israel, two factors many cite as driving the West's interest in the region today.

The establishment of Israel as a Jewish state in 1948 also impacted the region. In Chapter 2, Mark Tessler shows that, instead of a centuries-old and inevitable conflict, the process of establishing modern-day Israel and the ensuing Arab–Israeli conflict was a late 19th- and early 20th-century phenomenon, driven by both international forces and domestic factors. The existence of Israel has attracted international attention, created a nexus of conflict in the region, and exacerbated domestic political tensions, particularly in neighboring states. Domestic social structures and the political forces of states within the region have combined to yield very different reactions to, and engagements with, Israel, but it also served to draw the region together in shared struggles, if not always common cause.

Thus, the development of the Middle East was driven in part by relation to the West. Indeed, *Middle East* is a Eurocentric term. The term arose around the turn of the 20th century, as Europeans stepped up their economic and political interests and interventions in the region, and was used to designate the region east of Europe and midway to the Far East. The fact that we call the region the "Middle East"—and that those within the region have largely adopted this label—demonstrates both the extent to which a common identity has been established over the centuries and the indelible influence that outside forces, and particularly the West, have had on the region. However, although historical experience and strategic location between East and West have shaped the Middle East, they have done so in different ways, in different places, and at different times across the region.

The diverse historical, social, and economic influences contribute to a range of political regimes and citizen engagement that is also more varied than often supposed. In Chapter 3, we see that although weak states, authoritarian regimes, and ineffective institutions have hindered development in the region, there is important variation in the region's states, regimes, and institutions. The tendency to characterize the Middle East as a bastion of authoritarianism overlooks democratic competition in Israel, Lebanon, Turkey, and the Palestinian Authority; ignores the broad array of political arrangements even among authoritarian regimes; and misses variation in the strength of MENA states—that is, their ability to accomplish state goals. The first two decades of the 21st century continue to demonstrate the region's diversity. Some regimes weathered the storm of the 2011 Arab Uprisings, while others transitioned peacefully and still others fell into civil war. The same is true a decade later, as countries such as Algeria, Lebanon, and Sudan, which earlier saw stability, have witnessed disruption. These patterns of change brought into stark relief important differences in state strength; the role of political regimes, especially that of monarchies and dominant-party regimes; and various institutions, such as the media, military, and political parties.

Regimes also differ significantly in the ways in which they incorporate religion. Asked to describe people of the MENA, many focus on Arab Muslim culture. The majority of inhabitants of the MENA are indeed Muslim, but the majority of the world's Muslims does not live in the Middle East.[1] In fact, Egypt, the country with the largest Muslim population in the Middle East, is only the fifth largest country with a predominantly Muslim society in the world today. Moreover, while societies of most countries in the region are predominantly Muslim, they are not uniformly so. The Middle East is the birthplace of the three major monotheistic religions— Judaism, Christianity, and Islam—and adherents of all three religions (and others as well) continue to live there. Even among Muslims in the region, there are intense differences in doctrine, as well as in the ways religion and politics intertwine. The dominant distinction is between Shiite and Sunni Muslims, but the picture is complicated by important theological distinctions within each sect, combined with varied practices of Islam that emerged as Islam spread across the region, arrived at different times, and met different cultures. In short, Muslims in MENA societies practice Islam in very different ways, hold competing notions of how Islam should be incorporated into the state, and live in states that incorporate Islam to greater and lesser extents into their regimes. Moreover, as Lee and Ben Shitrit skillfully demonstrate, the variation among adherents, and the role of religion in politics, is not limited to Muslims in the Middle East. Jewish populations are equally diverse, and the role of different religious schools on politics is as important in Israel as in the states with predominantly Muslim societies. There is a great deal of variation in how religion is incorporated into politics. That is true both in its use as an ideology and as a tool for mobilizing opposition forces, as well as religious cooptation by incumbent regimes to maintain order and stability.

Understanding the nature of states and institutions, and the incorporation of religion in politics, provides a basis for examining political participation in the region. In Chapter 5, Rabab El Mahdi explores the various forms of political participation in the region, ranging from participation in formal politics, through elections and political parties, to civil society organizations, social movements, violence, and 'everyday' politics. She considers how citizens view the institutions associated with these venues (e.g., political parties, parliaments, and CSOs), as well as their priorities. Many remain critical of their countries' conditions and skeptical of their institutions. They also remain politically engaged, however, in part facilitated by changes in technology, such as the spread of satellite television, Internet, and cellular telephones. These technologies provide not only spaces of communication and interaction but also the means to shape political identities and promote mobilization, particularly among the youth. In the face of authoritarianism, weak institutions, and political constraints, they often lead to mobilization outside of formal political institutions.

The participation described in Chapter 5 both reflects and contributes to societal changes. Perhaps one of the most misleading aspects of how the MENA is conventionally portrayed is in its tendency to portray societies as static and timelessly bound to traditional roles—think images of Arabs in long-flowing robes and riding camels through the desert (à la scenes from the film *Lawrence of Arabia*) or of women covered head to toe in black and quietly serving tea. Such accounts are seriously misleading. Many Middle Easterners are Arabs, the region is also home to peoples from a wide range of ethnic and linguistic identities; Arabs, Turks, and Persians—the major groups in the region—live alongside Azeris, Turkmen, and Amazighs, to name only a few. Moreover, if given the opportunity to visit the region, one finds not only spectacular deserts but also beautiful beaches, towering mountains, lush woodlands, and fruitful plains; small towns and open spaces but also sprawling metropolises and high-rise apartments; and people in traditional dress drinking tea at home but also men and women fashionably dressed, working in advanced medicine, with new technologies and other "modern" fields.

As Valentine M. Moghadam explores in Chapter 6, MENA societies have experienced major changes both in the provision of such services as health and education and also in changing norms and values regarding gender roles, human rights, and the role of religion in politics. In some cases, this has resulted in significant legal changes. As Driss Maghraoui and Saloua Zerhouni explore, in Morocco, the mobilization of the women's movement united with the will of the monarchy to create a new family code that enhanced the status of women in 2003; and as Hesham Al Awadi shows, in Kuwait, the monarchy responded to long-standing appeals by women for greater political incorporation, leading to the expansion of political rights in 2005. Even in Saudi Arabia, a kingdom perhaps most intensely stereotyped as being conservative, Dina Al Sowayel describes the major social and political changes afoot. Change is often uneven—with some members in societies adapting new mechanisms, changing attitudes and opinions, and pressing for greater social change than others. But it is also widespread across the region.

The region's economies are no more static and homogenous than its societies. There is a tendency to characterize MENA economies as oil dependent and traditional. Melani Cammett, Ishac Diwan, and Steven Heydemann's discussion of the region's political economy in Chapter 7 shows, however, that neither of these assumptions is true. Countries in the region vary greatly in their degree of oil dependency. Some states, including not only those in the Gulf but also Algeria, Iran, Iraq, and Libya, are highly oil dependent, and oil stimulates the migration of unemployed workers and the distribution of remittances from non-oil-producing states in the region as well. This has both economic and political impacts. But it is not the whole story.

The states in the region differ significantly in their level of industrialization, their economic policies, and the resultant patterns of human development. Even among oil-dependent countries, there is enormous variation. Studies comparing the Persian Gulf states, Algeria, Libya, Kuwait, and Saudi Arabia demonstrate how different the political arrangements and resultant dynamics can be, even among oil-dependent countries. Cammett, Diwan, and Heydemann provide a theoretical framework that helps students make sense of the diversity across the region. The chapter also draws attention to the fact that the presence of oil does not imply stagnation. Indeed, the oil-rich states in the Gulf have seen striking innovation in areas such as architecture and education, and across the region, there have been dramatic changes in the nature of integration in the global economy, the degree of state intervention in the market, and the economic conditions of the individuals living there.

Finally, while the region's strategic location—including the establishment of Israel and the presence of oil—have shaped the Middle East, they have not impacted all societies and countries equally. As Lihi Ben Shitrit highlights, some of the changing relations with neighboring states drive, and are driven by, changes in Israeli society and politics over time. The same can be said of the Palestinian Authority; Alaa Tartir and Benoît Challand remind us that not only has the conflict affected Palestinians, but their internal social and political dynamics have structured their engagement with Israel, surrounding states, and the international forces. Palestinians, too, have agency.

Similarly, a closer look at Israel's closest neighbors—Egypt, Jordan, Lebanon, and Syria—reveals enormous diversity in their relations with Israel. Perhaps most notably, Jordan and Egypt have established peace treaties with Israel (albeit creating a rather cold peace), while the Syrian and Lebanese conflicts continue. Laurie A. Brand's discussion of Jordan, however, demonstrates that the impact of Israel's establishment on the societies and politics of its neighboring states can be complex. The 1948 Arab–Israeli war led not only to the opportunity for King Abdallah to expand his Hashemite kingdom but also to the influx of Palestinian refugees, which created fissures in Jordanian society and challenged the monarchy. Indeed, until today, the socioeconomic development and political stability of Jordan remain intricately connected to Palestinian–Israeli relations across the Jordan River.

Moreover, as Marc Lynch shows in Chapter 8, the MENA has witnessed significant changes in its regional and international relations. States in the region enjoy greater bargaining power vis-à-vis the West in bi- and multipolar eras (most notably during the Cold War and presently) than unipolar eras (such as that which immediately followed the Cold War). Syria provides a case in point. As Raymond Hinnebusch argues, President Hafiz al-Asad's choices to join the US-led coalition against Iraq in the 1990 to 1991 war and then join the Madrid peace talks aimed at solving the Arab–Israeli conflict were largely pragmatic ones. He understood that with the end of the Cold War and the loss of his country's powerful backer, the Soviet Union, he faced new constraints and opportunities, and he shifted Syrian foreign policy in response to them. As the United States found itself embroiled in the war in Iraq and Afghanistan, losing ground to Russia and China, Syria's ability to counter US demands once again rose. Indeed, as President Bashar al-Asad faced escalating conflict and international pressure in 2011–2012, it was the reemerging bipolar environment and resistance from China and Russia that stymied Western efforts to intervene. The continued fragmentation of political power in the region and further afield has even led to recent efforts to bring Bashar al-Asad in from isolation.

Importantly, although many view the region as constantly embroiled in conflict, conflict is neither constant nor uniformly present across the region. Marc Lynch argues in Chapter 8 that the region is not as war prone as often portrayed. Interstate wars are relatively rare, and those that existed have until recently been centered primarily around two axes: the Arab–Israeli conflict and Iraq. These axes of conflict have, at times, expanded to include a number of peripheral actors, and, indeed, the Lebanese civil war can be seen in part as playing out the Arab–Israeli conflict on Lebanese soil. Generally, however, conflict has been localized, centered on the Levant. Given the regional identity that binds the region together, the resolution of the conflicts—particularly the Palestinian–Israeli conflict—is often seen as a broader Middle Eastern enterprise. As the power structure of regional politics has shifted over time, the leading forces in this enterprise have also changed. Contrary to the notion of a conflict-ridden Middle East, much of the region has remained relatively peaceful.

In short, the Middle East is a diverse, vibrant, changing region, which poses challenges and opportunities not only for the international system but, of course, for the people living there. Indeed, this is perhaps never before as true as it is today, as citizens across the region continue to renegotiate their relations with the state, doing so in the midst of a changing regional and international order. Understanding the forces at play is critical for those attempting to make sense of this region in flux.

Looked at closely, we find that most of the conventional wisdom that Westerners hold about the region has some basis in fact: The historical experiences of the rise of Islam and the interaction with the West have left a lasting legacy on the region; societies are largely Arab Muslim; the majority of states in the region are ruled by authoritarian regimes with restricted room for political participation; and regional and international relations are shaped by the region's strategic location, the presence of Israel, and oil.

Yet the reality is also much more complex: The historical influences of Islam and interaction with the West were varied and sometimes left contradictory legacies across the region; the development of predominantly Arab Muslim societies took place over time and through interaction with diverse local cultures, leaving societies that are best understood as a patchwork of ethnicities, religions, and traditions; ruling regimes, their political economies, and citizens' engagement in politics take a variety of forms; and far from a region engaged in endless conflict fueled by oil, the Middle East is better understood as relatively stable, with sets of conflicts by which states are variously affected and in which they differentially engage. Understanding the complexity of the region is the first step to recognizing the conditions for people living there, assessing the challenges and opportunities they face, and formulating effective policies.

ORGANIZATION AND KEY FEATURES OF THE BOOK

This new edition draws on and retains the strengths of *The Middle East* that have set the textbook apart from other treatments of the region. It continues to provide a wealth of information on regional trends and country studies, giving students and policymakers both theoretically important and policy-relevant insights into the region. Like earlier editions, this volume is also divided into two parts. The first, the Overview section, provides readers thematic overviews of the Middle East that introduce them to major issues that inform studies of the region, including the general trends, important exceptions, and a review of theoretical approaches and concepts. The second, the Profiles section, presents comprehensive studies of individual countries. The country studies in the Profiles section continue to be structured to fit closely to the thematic chapters in the Overview section, with each covering the history of state formation, societal transformations, religion and politics, political economy, domestic institutions, political participation, domestic conflict, and regional and international relations.

The sixteenth edition of *The Middle East* is also significantly revised. Chapters throughout the volume have been fully updated to take into account domestic, regional, and international changes in the past three years. A country study of Sudan has also been added to the sixteenth edition, providing an insightful overview of its background and contemporary challenges. Authors continue to streamline the chapters, making them less daunting to students.

The book maintains pedagogical features aimed at enhancing readers' appreciation of both the continuity and diversity within the Middle East. The symmetry between the Overview and Profiles sections is designed to lend flexibility to instructors. Readers can turn to specific sections of country chapters to gain a deeper understanding of the issues, and teachers can easily assign country profiles to supplement reading on thematic issues. Maps, figures, tables, and boxes help readers easily digest a wealth of information. The book begins with a full-color map on the inside front cover showing the region's geography, supplemented by additional maps in the chapter openers of each country profile that remind readers of where the country fits within the broader Middle East. The twenty-eight maps in the Overview and Profile chapters provide critical information about the boundaries, resources, and other features of each country.

Finally, this edition includes twenty-four photographs, some of which have been taken by contributing authors. The photographs reinforce key points in the chapters and provide insight into the politics and society of these states. The volume encourages readers to pursue further study. Both thematic chapters and country studies are supplemented by reference notes and authors' suggestions for further reading.

In short, the goal of this volume is to give readers an entry point into understanding a vibrant, exciting region: the Middle East. The material provided is aimed at making information accessible while encouraging further study. The hope is that a better understanding of this vitally important region will not only help readers comprehend more fully the world around them but also recognize and formulate policies that can more successfully map onto the Middle East. A wealth of information from a variety of sources—the hallmark of *The Middle East* series—is a first step in this direction.

OVERVIEW

1 | THE MAKING OF THE MODERN MIDDLE EAST

Michael Gasper

The modern Middle East emerged out of a variety of social, cultural, and political transformations. While the degree of these transformations differed from place to place, they produced comparable historical experiences, social structures, cultural norms, and political tensions across the region. The region's 19th- and 20th-century encounters with the West—out of which the term "Middle East" emerged—created a shared sense of identification across the region.

At the same time, elements of this common identity date back to earlier events such as the spread of Islam in the 7th century CE. Islam spread remarkably quickly in the early period, with Muslims establishing large empires, converting populations to Islam, and spreading the Arabic language and culture.[1] The Abbasid, Umayyad, and later the Ottoman, Safavid, and Qajar empires extended across a vast territory, stretching from North Africa to the Persian Gulf. These empires established a memory of "greatness," a time of Islamic empires that rivaled the West.

By the 18th century, the two major political entities in the Middle East, the Ottoman Empire (centered in what is today the Republic of Turkey) and Safavid/Qajar Persia (centered in what is today the Islamic Republic of Iran), enjoyed relative strength and security. The Ottoman Empire was a vast multiethnic, multilingual, and multireligious polity that at its peak stretched from central Europe all the way to Yemen and across North Africa to Morocco. It compared favorably with the expanse of the Roman Empire at its height. The Safavid/Qajar domains stretched from the Caucasus to what is today Afghanistan, and they too hosted a myriad of different ethnicities and religions.

The 19th century saw a number of challenges to Ottoman and Qajar power. The resulting pressures convinced the Ottomans and to a lesser degree the Persian Qajars to undertake substantial political and economic reform during the course of the 19th century. These reforms were accompanied by cultural and religious modernization movements that generated new intellectual and ideological perspectives for the people of the region.

In the 20th century, World War I (1914–1918) was a cataclysmic event in the Middle East. It resulted in a redrawing of the map of the entire area and laid the foundation for a series of rivalries and conflicts that reverberate up until the present day. Anticolonialism, nationalism, and the rise of the United States and the Soviet Union as superpowers after World War II added new dimensions to these questions. Finally, the increasing importance of the politics and economics of oil and the regional role of the states that produce it emerged as a major question in the last decades of the 20th century and into the 21st.

THE OTTOMAN AND SAFAVID EMPIRES

The Ottomans

The infamous Mongol invasion of 1258 CE completely disrupted the political and social worlds of the Middle East. The Ottoman state emerged out of the wholesale changes and dislocations wrought by this event. Eventually based in Istanbul, the Empire became a major world power and ruled over much of the Middle East for centuries. The Ottomans descended from Turkish-speaking Muslim tribes that fled the Mongol invaders between 1100 and 1300 CE. Osman I, head of a tribe known for its horsemanship and martial culture, established the Ottoman dynasty around 1300 in the northwestern corner of Anatolia (the central plateau of modern Turkey) on the frontier with the Byzantine Empire. The word *Ottoman* is derived from his name.

By the beginning of the 16th century, Osman's descendants had built an empire that stretched from western Asia to North Africa to southeast Europe. Ottoman armies in 1529 and again in 1683 laid siege to the Habsburg capital of Vienna, and they controlled much of the Middle East and the Balkans as well as vast areas around the Black Sea until the beginning of the 20th century. The Ottomans could not control their vast territory through force alone. Indeed, one of the most remarkable features of Ottoman rule was its ability to insert itself into local power dynamics to achieve a measure of security and stability.[2] In the Balkans, for example, the Ottomans ended the dominance of feudal lords and limited the growth of church lands. Both moves proved very popular within the majority Eastern Orthodox Christian communities that detested their former Habsburg and Hungarian Catholic rulers.

The Ottoman sultans (rulers) built a large standing army that successfully dampened the threat of political fragmentation, a constant problem in large, premodern, military patronage empires. The janissaries (from the Turkish *yeniçeri*, or new soldier), or infantry force, were a professional, full-time force that wore distinctive uniforms and were paid even during peacetime. Initially, the janissaries consisted of Christian boys enslaved at a young age through a system called the *devshirme* (*devşirme*). The Ottoman sultans adopted this system early in the history of the empire to prevent the emergence of rivals from among the Turkish noble and warrior classes. The *devshirme* levy was imposed every four years on non-Muslims in the Balkans. Each locality provided a certain number of boys who were taken from their families, converted to Islam, and trained to serve the Ottoman state—theoretically, they were loyal to the person of the sultan. Those with greater intellectual abilities staffed the large bureaucracy throughout the empire, reaching the highest offices in the state. Thus, slavery represented an odd form of upward mobility for the rural poor of the Balkans. Much of the administrative and military elite of the Ottoman Empire was made up of slaves, or Mamluks, of the sultan. They were, in fact, a privileged caste who could profit handsomely from their position in the state hierarchy. Taken from their villages and educated far away, they were theoretically cut off from their families. In practice, however, they often maintained links to their families and found ways to advance their relatives' interests.

MAP 1.1 ■ The Expansion of the Ottoman Empire

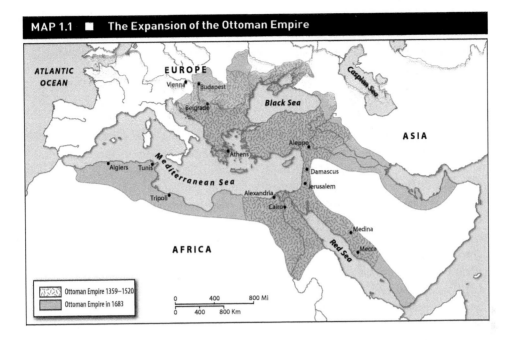

PHOTO 1.1 Süleymaniye Mosque

Muhammed Enes Yldrm/Anadolu Agency/Getty Images

In addition to a large standing army, the Ottoman military was also innovative in its use of firearms. The Ottoman infantry and cavalry units became legendary for their effective use of gunpowder weapons (such as muskets and cannons) in the conquest of Constantinople in 1453. The Ottomans became the first successful "gunpowder empire"; the Safavids of Persia and the Mughals of India soon followed suit. In an effort to project this power and authority, the Ottomans developed a predilection for architectural grandness. They built stunning mosques and other magnificent edifices throughout their realm, and visitors to Istanbul still marvel at the splendid monuments built by Ottoman architects.

The Safavids

To the east, another state grew into a rival of the Ottomans. The Safavid Empire had its roots in the Azerbaijan region of Iran, and its rulers, like the Ottomans, were of Turkic descent. The king, Shah Ismail I, who reigned until 1524, established the Safavid dynasty in 1501 with his capital in Tabriz, and declared himself shah (sovereign). The Safavids spread from Azerbaijan to unite the lands of Persia for the first time in nearly a thousand years. The borders that Ismail eventually established still define Iran today. To undermine the power of elite Turkic clans, Shah Ismail I established a Persian-speaking bureaucracy and built a conscript slave army made up of peoples from the Caucasus. In contrast to the Ottomans, Shah Ismail made Islam a centerpiece of his authority, declaring that the shah was the shadow of God on earth. Importantly, he decreed that Shi'i Islam would become the state religion, and this generated an enduring identification with Shi'ism in Iran. Ismail compelled all of his subjects to embrace Shi'i Islam and abandon Sunni Islam. Sunni clerics (*ulema*) were given the choice to convert or face exile or death. In contrast to the Ottoman religious authorities, who were incorporated into the state structure, the *ulema* remained independent in Safavid (and later Qajar) Iran. In Shi'i Persia, the religious establishment grew into a formidable and separate center of power. After the 1979 Iranian Revolution, the *ulema* became the main power brokers in the Islamic Republic of Iran.

Iran's Shi'i identity and its imperial ambitions were sources of friction with the Sunni Ottoman sultans. Between the 16th and 17th centuries Safavid/Ottoman relations existed in a constant state of tension. Indeed, the presence of this ambitious and expansionist Shi'i regime on its eastern frontier drove Ottoman conquerors south into the Arab heartlands of the Middle East rather than eastward into Persia and central Asia. In the late 16th century, reacting to a series of military defeats at the hands of the Ottomans, Shah Abbas I (reigned 1587–1629) undertook a number of reforms to strengthen the Safavid state. Following the Ottoman lead, he rebuilt a large standing army of slave conscripts and adopted the use of gunpowder weapons. Shah Abbas I also bolstered the state bureaucracy in an effort to increase tax revenues to pay for these military reforms. The new army, organized with the idea of matching the strength of the Ottoman janissaries, enabled Abbas to secure the frontiers and to recover territories the Safavids had lost to the rival Ottomans. For a time, Abbas I's armies won control over parts of Iraq, Afghanistan, Armenia, and eastern Turkey. Abbas helped finance his army, a reenergized bureaucracy, and a new capital by facilitating commercial relationships between European merchants and local Armenians. Commodities such as carpets and other textiles as well as porcelain found their way to markets around Europe.

The reign of Abbas I in the first two decades of the 17th century was the high point of Safavid power. A lack of leadership and resolve among the later shahs left the Safavid Empire without an effective army and with a weak central government by the end of the 17th century. The Safavid state soon collapsed, and more than a hundred years passed before the Qajar dynasty reunited Iran under a single ruler again.

PHOTO 1.2 Safavid manuscript. Detail from illustration of Gayumars and his court from the *Shāhnamah* (Book of Kings) by Firdawsī. Sixteenth century (British Museum).

British Library/GRANGER.

Ottoman Society

Ottoman society varied a great deal across its vast expanse and over the course of its 6 centuries of existence. Thus, this section should be read as merely an approximation of how Ottoman society functioned. Until the 1820s, the multiethnic, multireligious Ottoman society was organized hierarchically on a system of social and legal differentiation based on communal religious identity, with the largest group, Sunni Muslims, at the tip of the pyramid. The guiding social-legal principle of premodern and early modern Ottoman society was that of administration based on a universally recognized hierarchy of identities rather than the modern notion of equality among citizens.[3] There were no citizens as such; there were only Ottoman subjects of the sultan. The modern notion that the general population would have duties, responsibilities, and rights as well as an obligation to share in governance through voting, jury duty, or other tasks did exist at the time. The idea of universal citizenship and equality came to the Middle East in the late 19th century. Nevertheless, this social pyramid was flexible to the extent that non-Muslims often achieved preeminent positions both in the state structure and in commerce. The Phanariot Greeks of Istanbul, for example, supplied the empire with translators and diplomats and consequently enjoyed great prestige.[4]

In theory (especially in the later centuries of Ottoman rule), the social-legal structure of the Empire was roughly organized by *millet* (pronounced mil-lét). A *millet* was a religious group officially recognized by the Ottoman authorities and granted a degree of communal autonomy. The leader of the *millet* reported directly to the sultan, who appointed him after consultation with the *millet*'s leading personalities. Each *millet* could use its own language, establish charitable and social institutions, collect taxes for the imperial treasury, and operate its own religious courts.[5] The competency of such courts extended to personal status (marriage, inheritance, family relations) and sumptuary laws (laws that regulated dress, public comportment, and preparation of food, among other behaviors). State courts adjudicated in areas of public security, crime, and other areas not covered by religious law. These courts applied Ottoman legislation or *qanun* in their rulings. In practice, therefore, a series of local religious courts with no relationship to one another oversaw the daily life routines of individuals and families, while another court system acted as the arbiter of the general society.

Gender relations were patriarchal but also based on a notion of complementarity. Certain tasks, such as economic production, were the purview of men, and other areas, such as child-rearing and the management of the household, were women's responsibility. This general outline varied according to social class and communal identity. For example, gender roles tended to be more flexible among the poor than among the ruling elite. Urban women worked in markets and textile workshops, while rural women worked in the fields alongside the males of the family. Women also tended animals and saw to the affairs of the household when men were conscripted into military service or drafted into levies to repair or construct agricultural canals and roads.

In urban society, public life—that is, life outside of the home—was divided along gender lines. To a great extent, social space was largely homosocial; in other words, people of the same gender socialized together. Strict separation along gender lines was thought to be the best way of maintaining the moral and social order. Gender separation led to misunderstanding on the part

MAP 1.2 ■ The Safavid Empire

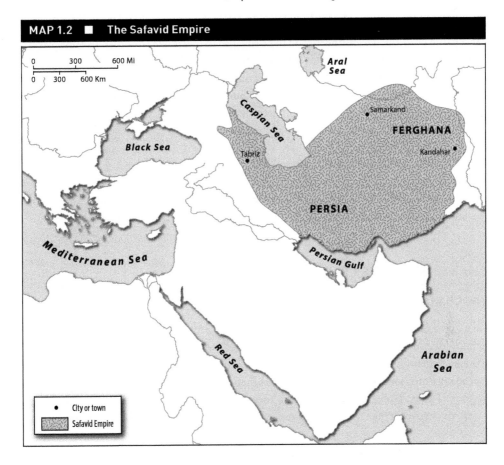

of some Western travelers about the notion of the harem. Some wrongly believed that women were locked away in a harem, and the image of women imprisoned in a luxurious golden cage persists in the popular imagination to this day. Some wealthy urban households did make efforts to seclude the family's women, but the fact is that this sort of lifestyle was unknown among the vast majority of the population. The harem was merely the part of a large house or villa open only to immediate family members. Social life with people from outside the family was conducted in more public sitting rooms. Of course, almost no one in Ottoman society possessed the financial wherewithal to live in such a home; for all intents and purposes, the idea was unknown to the general population. This began to change in the 19th century with the emergence of new middle classes. While historians sometimes argue that this class was more "Westernized" than the traditional Ottoman elite, many of its members imitated some of the old guard's cultural practices; as a consequence, the practice of seclusion became more, not less, widespread with the proliferation of Western education and tastes in the late 19th and early 20th centuries.[6]

Society was arranged hierarchically, with each stratum undertaking tasks thought to be essential for the maintenance of society. Many trades were organized into guilds in order to ensure proper taxation as well as to regulate competition and quality of work. Carpenters, tanners, smiths, peasants, sharecroppers, servants, and even those working in sex trades (such as dancers and prostitutes) were understood to be engaged in trades like any other. In some places, prostitutes were organized into guilds similar to those in other lines of work.

In a political and social sense, society consisted of rulers and ruled. The ruling caste comprised the leaders of the military, the chief bureaucrats, and the religious authorities or the *ulema*. Despite the social hierarchies, markets and coffeehouses were open to people of all classes. Residents in a particular quarter of a city or in a smaller town's central market gathered to conduct business and to socialize. Markets and the coffeehouses usually located near them were places where traveling merchants and others would discuss news and developments from other regions. Coffeehouses were also sites of relaxation, socializing, and entertainment. The Ottoman authorities understood the potential for political agitation in markets and coffeehouses, and they placed informants in them to keep them apprised of what was discussed.[7]

CHANGING CONTEXTS

The Challenge of the West

Even as the Ottomans lay siege to the Habsburg capital of Vienna in 1683, the center of power in the West had already shifted from the Mediterranean to the North Atlantic. Benefiting from the vast riches of the New World, technological advances, and increasing economic output, ascendant European powers caught up to and then surpassed the Ottomans' military might. England, France, Holland, Spain, Portugal, and soon Russia increasingly exerted economic and political pressure on the Ottoman government (or the Sublime Porte, or Porte, as it was known in the West).

The initial push was provided by the wealth brought to Europe from the Americas beginning in the 16th century. The huge influx of silver from South American mines set off an inflationary cycle in the Ottoman lands. As the value of silver decreased with the increase in supply, prices for the products and goods and services purchased with silver coins necessarily increased. Smuggling became a major problem as merchants sought to avoid increased customs duties and to profit from the suddenly more valuable raw materials such as Balkan lumber. These developments resulted in lower Ottoman tax receipts, major security issues, and an increase in corruption. All had a corrosive effect on the state.

The so-called Capitulations treaties that date from the 16th century were a testament to Ottoman strength that vanished so quickly in the 17th and 18th centuries. Ottoman rulers sought to encourage foreign merchants' activities in the Ottoman domains, and thus, these treaties offered favorable conditions to European merchants doing business in Ottoman lands such as offering extraterritoriality (immunity from Ottoman law) and favorable customs duties. Consular courts set up by the various embassies adjudicated cases between European merchants exempt from Ottoman law. This legal immunity meant that these foreign merchants paid almost no taxes. Initially, the treaties enabled the empire to obtain goods and maintain a positive relationship with other European states. As the balance of power shifted away from the Ottomans, however, these concerns paled in comparison to the depredation caused by the treaties. Europeans flooded local markets with finished goods, devastating the Ottoman merchant class. Adjusting to these changed circumstances, local merchants began to acquire foreign citizenship in order to enjoy the advantages of the Capitulations. In doing so, many became local agents of foreign trading houses. In addition, the Europeans used these treaties and the economic power they provided to exert political pressure on Ottomans.

The question of the treatment of minorities in the Ottoman Empire was another tactic that European powers used to bring pressure on the Porte. In claiming that minorities were denied equal rights, European critics ignored the fact that there was no notion of rights in Ottoman law for any subjects of the sultan. This did not stop the major European powers from asserting that they would "protect" a particular group from discrimination and persecution. Orthodox Christians and Armenians became the patrons of Russia, and the French and Austrians looked after the interests of Catholics, while the British sponsored the Greeks in their war of independence in the 1820s and later declared Ottoman Protestants and then Jews to be under British protection.

With economic and political pressure mounting, the Ottoman Empire suffered through a long period of crisis that began at the end of the 18th century. The newly ascendant Russian Empire defeated the sultan's armies on several occasions beginning in 1774, and the Ottomans were forced to cede wide swathes of territory around the Black Sea. The French invaded and occupied the Ottoman province of Egypt in 1798. Egypt's Mamluk rulers had become increasingly remote from the Porte over the course of the 18th century, but they continued to send tribute to Istanbul up until the time of the French campaign. Meanwhile, the Balkans became restive with the rise of Greek and Serbian nationalist movements. The Serbs achieved de facto independence in 1817, and the Greeks gained independence with British help in 1830. Finally, the French conquered and annexed the province of Algeria in 1830.

Napoleon's Invasion of Egypt and Reaction

In 1798, Napoleon Bonaparte landed a French expeditionary force of twenty-five thousand troops on the northern coast of Egypt. Napoleon hoped to cut British supply lines to India. He also viewed the conquest of Egypt in historical terms, seeing himself as a new Alexander the Great. Along with his army, Napoleon brought a group of experts, or *savants*, who were tasked with studying Egypt's people, history, and archaeology and thereby to provide assistance to the French occupiers. At the outset of the occupation, these savants tried to establish legitimacy for French rule by claiming the French had arrived merely to remove Ottoman oppression. They also tried to camouflage the fact that Egypt's new French rulers were non-Muslims. They posted notices in appallingly bad Arabic around Cairo not only informing the populace that the French meant them no harm but also implying that Napoleon himself was a Muslim.[8] These notices and other attempts by the French to legitimate their rule failed. Consequently, despite quick victories over the antiquated tactics and weaponry of the Mamluk cavalry, the French never succeeded in stabilizing their rule throughout much of the country. British ships soon transported Ottoman troops to Egypt, and this, combined with popular resistance, led the French to sue for peace. They departed Egypt in 1801 leaving little trace of their brief occupation.

By the end of the 18th century, the main question for the Great Powers was no longer how to defend themselves against Ottoman expansion; instead, it was how to deal with an Ottoman

Empire that was not keeping up with its neighbors' growing strength. This was the "Eastern Question" that dominated European international relations for more than a hundred years until the end of World War I. Any change of status of the Ottoman Empire was seen as almost inevitably benefiting the interests of one European state over the interests of another, potentially upsetting the carefully maintained balance of power. Thus, those seeking to change the status quo, in particular the Russians, did their utmost to undermine the Ottoman state. Meanwhile, those invested in the status quo, in particular Britain and Hapsburg Austria, supported the sultan whenever convenient.

Egypt: Mehmet Ali

An indirect consequence of the French campaign in Egypt was the emergence of Mehmet Ali (in Arabic, Muhammad Ali). Mehmet came to Egypt as part of the Ottoman force sent to dislodge the French. Within a few years, this ambitious Mamluk officer from Albania had established himself as the de facto ruler of Egypt. Through a combination of political skill and ruthlessness, Mehmet Ali established a ruling dynasty that would endure until 1952. He then set about building a strong, centralized state by bringing tax collection and other functions under his direct control. Wanting to expand from Egypt, Mehmet built a formidable military machine with its own industrial base. He also established modern schools, sent promising students abroad to complete their studies, and brought in foreign advisers and experts to train military officers and to teach at new scientific and technical institutes.

He paid for these elaborate reforms by setting up agricultural monopolies. The Egyptian state essentially became the only merchant in the entire country licensed to buy and sell agricultural commodities. Mehmet Ali compelled peasants to grow export crops and sell them to his government at low prices. In 1820, he introduced the cultivation of long-staple cotton. Egypt soon became famous for high-quality cotton that English mills bought up in large amounts. The immense wealth this created provided Mehmet Ali the necessary capital to build the Egyptian state and his army. The Egyptian government also undertook a number of steps to increase agricultural production, including building roads, irrigation canals, dams, and waterworks. Cotton cultivation proved, however, to be as much of a curse as a blessing. During the last third of the 19th century, Egypt's overreliance on cotton as a source of income led not only to increased hardship for its peasant producers but also to devastating financial crisis, breakdown of the state, and, ultimately, to British occupation.

In any case, Mehmet Ali's army of Egyptian conscripts conquered Sudan, the Arabian Peninsula, and then the eastern Mediterranean through Syria, and for a time, it threatened the Ottoman heartland of Anatolia and Istanbul itself. It seemed as though Egypt might even supplant the Ottoman Empire as the major power in the East. However, just as they had done against Napoleon in 1801, the British (with Austrian help) came to the Ottomans' rescue and confronted the Albanian's Egyptian army in 1840. Mehmet Ali was forced not only to withdraw from Syria but also to accept the Treaty of London of 1840 that included the British-Ottoman Commercial Convention forbidding monopolies in the Ottoman Empire. The treaty deprived him of the ability to raise the enormous sums of capital that had funded his reforms, and it also limited the Egyptian army to 18,000 troops from its previous 130,000. In return for Mehmet Ali's withdrawal from Syria and signing this treaty that effectively put an end to his short-lived mini empire, the sultan declared Mehmet Ali's family the hereditary rulers of Egypt. Indeed, Mehmet Ali's heirs remained in power until the 1952 military coup led by Gamal Abdel Nasser.

The Tanzimat Reforms

From at least the end of the 18th century, Ottoman rulers recognized that drastic administrative and organizational changes in the empire were necessary. However, stubborn resistance from entrenched interests hobbled the first steps toward change. For example, the janissaries, once the heart of the Ottoman army, had become less a military force and more a political lobby in Istanbul. Their military effectiveness declined precipitously after the end of the 17th century. By the beginning of the 19th century, they were completely outside of the sultan's control and more interested in pursuing the good life than in protecting the empire's borders. In 1808, Sultan Selim III paid with his life when he attempted to abolish the janissaries; however, his son and successor, Mahmud II, planned carefully for years and successfully disbanded the janissaries in 1826.

Any resistance to change that existed in Ottoman-ruling circles disappeared with the shock caused by Mehmet Ali's march to the doorsteps of Istanbul.[9] No one in a position of authority could now doubt the imperative of fundamental change. Mahmud II's successor, Abdülmecid I (Abd al-Majid I), introduced a series of major reforms that came to be called the Tanzimat (Reorganization). What had once been a strength of Ottoman administration and governance—its practice of making allowances for local custom and tradition—had become a major liability. The Ottomans' Western European rivals ruled over states with relatively centralized, uniform administrative regimes that promoted a single economic policy. The Ottoman Empire's propensity toward local autonomy, in contrast, handicapped efforts to formulate coherent economic strategies across the entire realm. It was abundantly clear to Abdülmecid I, his successor Abdülaziz I (Abd al-Aziz I), and even more so to their advisers such as Mehmet Fuad Pasha, Mustafa Reshid Pasha, Ahmed Shefik Mithat Pasha, and Mehmet Emin Ali Pasha that this situation needed to be rectified.

Historian James Gelvin terms the sort of reform strategy the Ottomans undertook as *defensive developmentalism*.[10] Ottoman rulers attempted to modernize the state by centralizing power in order to maintain their position and to stave off revolutionary change. They wanted to reproduce the modern, efficient European state model in the Ottoman Empire. This would enable them to manage and tax their population more efficiently and in turn provide the necessary capital to undertake ambitious reforms. The Ottoman reform program bore some resemblance to that of Mehmet Ali's in Egypt. Like their rebellious Egyptian governor, the Ottoman sultans aimed to improve security, concentrate power in the central government, build a more stable economic base, and guarantee sufficient income for government coffers to pay for their development plans. Unlike Mehmet Ali, however, who had brought his reform program to a fairly homogeneous population living in a contiguous geographic area, the Ottoman reformers faced the much more onerous task of trying to implement fundamental change across a multilingual and multiethnic empire that spanned three continents.

The question of security was paramount to the reformers as corruption and porous borders weakened the economic foundation of the empire. They tackled this complex problem with administrative reforms and by rebuilding the armed forces and upgrading the empire's communication and transportation infrastructure. They built vast road, railroad, and telegraph networks that crisscrossed the empire. These improvements enabled Istanbul to act quickly to quell disturbances and to confront internal challengers to the Ottoman center. This, in combination with more professionalized and efficient policing throughout the empire, led to increased security, making it possible for the state to extend its writ to outlying areas such as Syria and Palestine, which had often suffered from raiding and general lawlessness.

A rationalized and modernized bureaucracy required qualified and educated officials; thus, the Ottomans expended a great deal of effort to modernize education. They established new kinds of primary and secondary schools throughout the empire. In Istanbul, they opened a modern university, as well as medical, veterinary, and engineering schools. They also established an institute to train the bureaucrats who were to implement the Tanzimat reforms. The Ottomans also created modern military academies for infantry and naval officers and other technical schools for munitions experts, engineers, and military doctors.

Legal reform represented another priority for the Tanzimat reformers. They took a number of steps to rationalize the complicated and multilayered Ottoman legal system. For example, the Ottoman Land Code of 1858 and Land Registration Law of 1859 codified, standardized, and modernized land ownership rules that varied widely from place to place throughout the empire. Reformers then introduced a modified French civil code that restricted the brief of Islamic law. These moves brought the Ottoman legal regime in line with those operating in Western Europe. The hope was that these steps would help Ottoman merchants compete with their European competitors. Unfortunately, legal reform also made it easier for European merchants to do business locally. It did nothing to stem the tide of European finished goods pouring in; nor did it change the fact that the Ottoman Empire was merely a source of raw materials for Western European manufacturers. All of this deepened the Ottoman's marginal economic position in the emergent global economy.

The scale of the reforms was staggering and extremely expensive. To fund the Tanzimat, the sultans took out a series of loans beginning in 1854. Given the vast sums required and the relatively limited ways the Ottomans could raise the funds necessary to meet their obligations, it is hardly surprising that the Porte soon found itself in dire financial straits, and by the mid-1870s, bankruptcy loomed. In 1881, European creditors forced the Sultan into accepting a financial oversight body called the Ottoman Public Debt Commission made up of representatives of British, French, Dutch, and other nations' bondholders, and it had extraordinary power to use tax payments to reimburse foreign investors. With the debt commission, the Ottoman Empire essentially ceded control of its finances to Western Europeans.

Legal Reform and Ottomanism

Legal reform had far-reaching consequences beyond the economic sphere. With the Hatt-i Hümayun decree of 1856 and the Nationality Law of 1869, the Ottomans undertook one of the most sweeping social and legal reforms of the Tanzimat period. They completely restructured the *millet* system and its multiple status hierarchies and, in its place, inaugurated a form of modern protocitizenship. All individuals were accorded the same legal status regardless of religious identity. This step raised new questions of collective belonging and identity. How would the Ottomans replace the multiple sectarian identities of the past with a single modern form of identity? Did the diverse populations of the Ottoman lands comprise a single people? One response to these questions was through the promotion of a kind of protonationalism called *Osmanlılık* (Ottomanism), which stressed that all citizens were equal members of the same political community and bound together by a common allegiance to the state. This notion of universal political community was supposed to transcend religious and regional identity. One early 20th-century reformer put it this way:

> Henceforth we are all brothers. There are no longer Bulgars, Greeks, Romanians, Jews, Muslims; under the same blue sky we are all equal, we glory in being Ottomans.[11]

Equality did not prove to be very popular. Equality politicized difference in ways that had not been seen before. This was true among Muslims and non-Muslims alike. Some Muslims, especially among the elite, felt they were losing privileges justified by their status as the majority of the population. At the same time, some Christians objected to the new definition of equality and protocitizenship because of the duties it imposed upon them—in particular, military conscription. Indeed, conscription was so unpopular that the Ottoman authorities eventually permitted Christians to buy their way out of military service. This concession then created great resentment among Muslims, who were not granted this right.

Equality and a universal legal definition of the individual in effect created the idea of a "minority." Instead of a discrete community with its own hierarchy and therefore its own privileged elites, all members of the seventeen recognized *millets* became part of the larger pool of Ottoman citizens. This new status deprived the well-connected within each *millet* of their privileged position; moreover, the Christian population in general became a minority within a predominantly Muslim empire. The relationship of Christians to the state was changed as their former collective autonomy was replaced by the individual's direct relationship to the state. Influence in these changed circumstances no longer depended solely on status within an identity group; now it depended on numbers. This new legal framework compelled elites to seek sufficient numbers of supporters for the state to take notice. Partly as a consequence, popular appeal to sectarian and national identity in order to mobilize large groups of people replaced the older, more "polite" form of the politics of notables.[12]

The new legal regime left almost everyone dissatisfied. The Ottoman world became politicized in ways it had not been before.[13] This led to the emergence of political tensions that plagued the empire during its final decades and led to its final dissolution after World War I. The irony is that measures intended to promote equality resulted in sharpened divisions between Christians and Muslims and others. These divisions then fed latent nationalist tendencies, which were in turn fomented by the empire's enemies in Moscow, Vienna, and elsewhere.

The End of the Tanzimat

The last of the Tanzimat reforms was the promulgation of the first Ottoman constitution in 1876 and the election of the first Ottoman parliament in 1877. A new sultan, Abdülhamid II (Abdul Hamid II), ascended to the throne in August 1876. Many assumed that he was another liberal reformer. But dismayed at what he saw as the dissolution of the empire, Abdülhamid II suspended the constitution, dismissed or pushed aside the reformers, and reversed the devolution of the sultan's absolute power to other state institutions. Yet, even as he reversed some of the political reforms, he continued other aspects of the Tanzimat, such as the modernization of the communication and transportation infrastructure and educational reform.[14]

Abdülhamid II became well known for emphasizing the Islamic character of the Ottoman Empire and using the title of caliph rather than sultan. Beginning in the 16th century, the Ottomans had claimed descent from the family of the Prophet, but this had been generally viewed as a convenience and hardly taken seriously by the sultans themselves or anyone else for centuries. Abdülhamid II's focus on the Islamic character of the Ottoman Empire thus was not a turn back to the past but rather a completely new departure. The importance he accorded the Islamic aspects of Ottoman identity contrasted with what he saw as creeping Western influence and interference in Ottoman lands. He was convinced that the political reforms of the Tanzimat era had only aggravated these problems.

Abdülhamid II's Islamic Ottomanism potentially appealed to Muslims, whose communal identity was no longer validated by the now-revamped *millet* system. Indeed, nascent forms of pan-Islamic thought were already circulating in intellectual circles around the Muslim world. With Britain, France, Holland, and Russia ruling over so much of the world's Muslim population, thinkers throughout the Muslim lands argued that political unity was the only way to resist further domination. Aware of this, Abdülhamid II hoped to capitalize on this idea in his efforts to build support for his besieged regime. Perhaps an indication of the success of his efforts was the fact that his reign is associated with a dramatic expansion of the secret police and the use of informants and spies to keep tabs on the public. Likewise, his government suppressed dissidents such as Arab nationalists with great vigor, but Abdülhamid II reserved the harshest treatment for Armenians who were perceived as a "fifth column" that might ally with the rival Russians to the north. Consequently, Armenians faced moments of extreme state-sanctioned violence in the mid-1890s and once again in 1909.[15]

Reforms in Qajar Persia

Qajar Persia, like the Ottoman Empire, gradually succumbed to the pressure of the Great Powers. By the end of the 19th century, the Qajar state was in disarray. The shah had little direct authority outside of the capital, Tehran. The Qajars relied on farmed-out tax collection to various fief holders and ruled not through a central administration or through coercion but rather through the shah's balancing tribal, clan, and ethnic factions against one another. To offset the power of the Shi'i *ulema*, the Qajars created genealogies that linked them to Shi'i imams, presented themselves as the protectors of Shi'i Islam, and made very public shows of their piety and support for shrines in Mashhad and Samarra. Nevertheless, as was the case with the Ottoman Empire, the lack of central authority resulted in the growing influence of European powers, primarily the Russians in the north and the British in the south, who bypassed the shah's government altogether by signing treaties with various tribal leaders and regional notables.

The shah Nasser al-Din attempted some reforms during the 19th century. In 1852, he opened a school staffed mostly with teachers from France to train personnel for the military and for the bureaucracy. Beginning in the 1860s, he tried to extend his reach outside of the capital by building telegraph lines and a postal service across the country. Then in 1879, he created a new military force called the Cossack Brigade, officered by Russians. These moves did little to stem the decline of Qajar power. Indeed, at the turn of the 20th century, most of the tribal confederations grew more autonomous and had greater military capability than the central state.

To reverse the dissolution of their authority, the Qajars, like the Ottomans, contemplated a program of defensive developmentalism. Of course, this entailed raising more revenue, but the state could not collect taxes more efficiently because it lacked both a bureaucracy and an effective military to impose its writ. Consequently, Nasser al-Din borrowed money and sold concessions to foreigners to raise funds. In the 1870s, he began selling the rights to build a communications infrastructure (railroads, telegraph lines, roads, and dams) to European investors who would then pocket most of the proceeds. This paved the way for his successor, Mozaffar al-Din, to grant the famous D'Arcy oil concession in 1905 that surrendered much of Iran's oil wealth to the British for decades. Despite their efforts, the Qajars could not hold off the Russians and the British. Around the turn of the century, the two Great Powers essentially divided the country into two spheres of influence, with the Russians dominating in the north and the British in the south. At the same time, the state was unable to repay British and Russian loans, and a Belgian-administered financial oversight board was put in place. Economic distress caused in part by foreign economic encroachment led to growing dissatisfaction among the bazaar merchants and the *ulema*. These groups together rebelled in 1906 and forced Mozaffar al-Din to accept a constitution. However, Persia's new constitution did not solve the basic problem of a weak state. As a result, the next two decades witnessed increasing anarchy and civil war. Order was not restored until the 1920s with the emergence of Reza Khan.

European Encroachment Elsewhere in the Middle East

From the later part of the 19th century until World War I, the entire Middle East experienced deepening European influence and domination. Often, this involvement began with crushing debt, leading to financial crises that Europeans took upon themselves to "resolve." In other cases, European powers simply wanted to build colonial empires.

In Egypt during the second half of the 19th century, for example, Mehmet Ali's successors undertook a number of large infrastructure projects to expand agricultural production. The most spectacular was the opening of the Suez Canal in 1869. The Egyptian government secured loans from European creditors that it intended to pay off with the proceeds from expanded cotton cultivation. A spike in world cotton prices during the US Civil War (caused by the blockade of the Confederate states by the Union Army) spurred the hopes of substantial returns for cotton growers. Cotton prices soon collapsed, however, and Egypt found itself on the verge of bankruptcy. In 1876, European creditors took control of Egypt's finances, and the resentment this generated precipitated a rebellion. In 1882, an Egyptian army colonel, Ahmad Urabi, led a revolt that aimed to remove foreign influence from Egypt. The British put down the rebels in the summer of 1882 and occupied Egypt and Sudan, where British troops remained until 1952 and 1956, respectively.

With the exception of Morocco, Libya and the area known collectively as the Maghreb (Algeria, Tunisia, and Morocco) had been part of the Ottoman order for centuries. As was often the case in much of the Ottoman periphery, the reach of Istanbul was often tenuous at best. In general, these territories were ruled over by semiindependent Ottoman-appointed governors (Deys or Beys) whose tenure depended on skillfully managing relations with different elements of elites such as tribal leaders, Sufi shaykhs, and merchants in coastal cities. North Africa's population spoke Arabic and Berber (Tamazight) and was predominantly Muslim, although there were Jewish communities in a number of cities across the region.[16] Merchants and craftsmen made up the urban population along the coast and in inland market towns. Tribal formations and pastoralists dominated the countryside, and Sufi Islam played an important role in the organization of society and the legitimization of authority.

All of North Africa came under control of European colonial powers beginning in the first third of the 19th century. In 1830, after the famous "fly swatter" incident when the Ottoman ruler of Algiers, Hussein Dey, slapped the French consul, Pierre Duval, during a disagreement about French debts, the French occupied the city. Thus began a campaign of conquest that, due to determined local resistance, required forty years to complete. In 1848, France declared Algeria an integral part of France and divided it into three administrative units, or *départements*. Algeria's legal status as part of France came to a bloody end with the Algerian War of Independence in the 1950s and 1960s. Through the 1860s and 1870s, the Ottoman province of Tunisia experienced a financial and debt crisis not unlike that of Egypt. Just as in Egypt, foreign creditors came to control Tunisian finances; then, the French army occupied the country and added Tunisia to its official North African colonial portfolio in 1881 when it declared Tunisia a protectorate under the pretext that Algerian rebels used the territory for sanctuary. In Morocco, after a period of tension caused by conflicting French and German colonial ambitions and after the collapse of Morocco's finances, it too fell to European rule. The French and the Spanish (who were granted a strip of land along the Mediterranean coast) occupied and then divided Morocco into two protectorates in 1912. Italy, too, desired a foothold in North Africa, and in 1911, Italy invaded Ottoman Libya. After two decades of local resistance, the Italians succeeded in combining the Ottoman provinces of Tripolitania, Cyrenaica, and Fezzan into a single colony in the mid-1930s. Libya remained a colonial possession of Italy until after World War II, when the United Nations declared that it should become independent.

The Ottomans lost other territories during this period; for instance, in southern Arabia, the British chipped off pieces of Yemen, such as the Aden Protectorate. The British established a line of protectorates and principalities from Kuwait to Yemen by throwing their support behind cooperative local families who, in return, they recognized as rulers of small statelets. Many of these families remain in power today. During the course of the 19th century, Britain installed the families that currently rule Bahrain, Kuwait, Oman, Qatar, and the principalities that came together as the United Arab Emirates in 1971.

Originally, the British saw these ruling families and the small states they controlled as a way to maintain trading privileges and to keep the shipping lanes to India free of piracy. With the discovery of oil, these small semicolonies took on more direct importance. For example, Kuwait had been merely a coastal town known for its pearl divers and fishermen. In 1913, the British forced the Ottoman government to recognize the Sabah family as the rulers of the city of

Kuwait and the surrounding area. After World War I, the British declared Kuwait an independent British protectorate, controlling it until 1961. British Petroleum received a lucrative concession after oil was discovered in the emirate in 1934, and within two decades, Kuwait became one of the largest oil exporters in the region.

Cultural Renaissance: Social and Religious Reform

The reforms of the 19th and 20th centuries set in motion far-reaching cultural and social changes that continue to reverberate today. In building educational institutions to officer armies and staff modern bureaucracies, the Ottomans, Qajars, and others helped create a new literate stratum not associated with religious institutions. Western missionaries also contributed to this development through the schools they established during the course of the 19th and early 20th centuries. While Christian missionaries had little success in converting the local Muslim and Jewish populations, the schools they set up played a significant role in producing a modern, educated intelligentsia. From primary and secondary schools to modern postsecondary institutions such as the Syrian Protestant College (American University of Beirut), Robert College of Istanbul (Boğaziçi University), and then the American University in Cairo, missionary schools had a role in producing many important Middle Eastern intellectuals of the nineteenth and twentieth centuries.

The graduates of the state and missionary schools were the force behind far-reaching cultural and intellectual movements that began to crystallize during the second half of the 19th century. What first began as a series of critical questions blossomed into a full-fledged cultural renaissance as many in the region sought to answer how the Middle East, North Africa, and indeed most of the Muslim world came to be dominated by the Great Powers. Intellectuals began to ask questions about themselves, their societies, and their future: How did this happen? Is there something wrong with us? How can we change these circumstances? This questioning inaugurated an intensely creative period in the region's cultural history and was instrumental in producing many of the ideological currents later translated into the nationalist and Islamist politics of the 20th century. Two extremely influential trends were the Arabic Nahda (or literary renaissance; there were Turkish- and Persian-language counterparts) and the Islamic Modernist or Islamic Reform movement.

The Nahda—the Arabic literary renaissance—refers to a cultural phenomenon that began around the middle of the 19th century and drew to a close around the middle of the 20th century. The Nahda began as a revival movement in Arabic literature that sought to rejuvenate Arabic letters and music. Figures such as the Egyptian Rifa'a Rafi' al-Tahtawi and the Lebanese Butrus al-Bustani were leaders in the movement to modernize Arabic. Many of those associated with this literary movement also became advocates of Arab nationalism. The progression was logical. Men and women of letters such as the Lebanese May Ziade and the Egyptian Malak Hifni Nasif began their quest to revive Arabic by developing new forms of prose and poetry. This led them to study the history of classical Arabic letters. In their view a parallel existed between what they perceived as a decline of Arabic letters and the stagnation of Arab society. It was not long before some traced this stagnation to Ottoman hegemony. These theories evolved into a political prescription: Arab society could not move forward until it threw off the yoke of "Turkish" dominance. It was no coincidence that these thoughts crystallized at a time when Abdülhamid II's government began to press Turkification of the Ottoman Empire. This nascent Arab nationalism was given a further boost after the Young Turk coup of 1908 brought an even more extreme Turko-centric leadership into power.

The emergence of the newspaper was a significant factor in the Nahda. Newspapers were an incubator of discussions and political ideas, allowing Arabic speakers from across the region to engage with one another in ways that had heretofore been impossible. One can favorably compare the emergence of the newspaper in the Arabic-speaking world to the invention of the Internet to get a sense of the magnitude of this development. . The first newspapers, little more than government newsletters or gazettes, appeared in the first half of the 19th century. By the 1880s, however, with the emergence of capitalist print culture, newspapers had become widespread. A growing audience of voracious readers created a market for the new literary products.[17] Newspapers were important laboratories for linguistic experimentation with simplified forms of expression, grammar, and punctuation. Traditional forms of prose (such as rhyming prose) gave way to sentence structure and syntactical style more recognizable to the modern reader. But newspapers were also the primary conduit for new ideas written in this new, simplified idiom of Arabic. Newspapers helped to manifest the idea of an Arabic-speaking community, and in this sense, they helped create the idea of an Arab world that had not existed before.

MAP 1.3 ■ The Shrinking of the Ottoman Empire

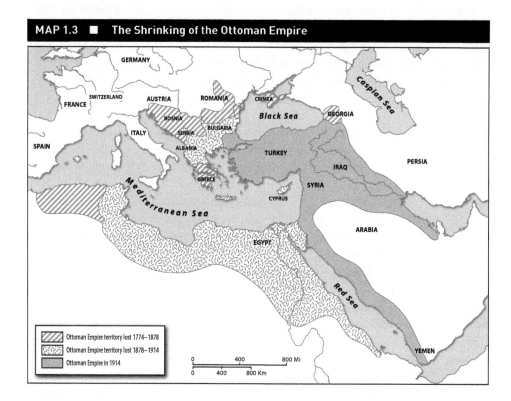

This new forum inevitably led to new forms of solidarity across the Arab world, and it also helped fuel a vibrant culture of research and critique. This in turn led to a greater interest in a variety of questions related to culture, identity, history, and social reform. Indeed, newspapers became the preferred method by which social reformers detailed their ideas, communicated with their fellow travelers, and challenged their opponents. The newspaper was the vehicle for the sustained debate over the status of women at the turn of the century. The controversy followed the publication of Egyptian lawyer Qasim Amin's books *The Liberation of Women* (1899) and *The New Woman* (1900). Every major newspaper and public figure weighed in on the topic.[18] Qasim Amin called for the elimination of the full-face veil, the education of girls, and reform of marriage practices. For these views, some condemned him as a "Westernizer." Reformers were sensitive to the charge made by some of their opponents that they were advocates of Westernization. Thus, important figures, especially those who were not men of religion, such as Qasim Amin, Abdallah al-Nadim, and Muhammad Kurd 'Ali, were very careful to explain that their calls for women's rights, education, and social and political change were aimed at reform and advancement of Muslim society and not its destruction. The Islamic reformer Rashid Rida spoke for many when he called the uncritical adoption of all things European a dangerous form of imitation that led only to cultural obliteration.

Islamic Modernism

Another important current of thought spurred by the ethos of reform and the culture of debate during the late 19th and early 20th centuries was the Islamic reform movement, or the Islamic modernist movement. The influence of the luminaries of the movement, the Iranian Jamal al-Din al-Afghani, the Egyptian Muhammad Abduh, and the Syrian Rashid Rida, continues almost a century after the death of the last of them. Their writing and activism shaped a major rethinking of the practice of Islam on a scale that compares with that of the Protestant Reformation in 16th-century Europe. Islamic modernists reread the canon of Islamic thought in light of the changed circumstances of the modern world, the challenge of colonialism, and the cultural power of the West. The era in which they wrote was unlike any other in Islamic history. Most of the Muslim world was either colonized or dominated in other ways by the non-Muslim European states.

As was the case with social reformers, newspapers and other kinds of periodicals were the preferred technology for transmitting their ideas. Jamal al-Din al-Afghani provided financial support to a number of newspapers, and among his many devotees were some of the most prominent journalists and editors of the era. Rashid Rida studied to be a religious scholar in Syria before going to Cairo. There, he became a journalist and essayist, founding the legendary Islamic reform journal, *al-Manar*. Muhammad Abduh had a regular column in *al-Manar*, and his writing appeared often in other newspapers.

Islamic modernists were not only in conversation with other Muslims but also with the many European commentators discoursing about Islam and the state of the Muslim world. Many of these Europeans were connected to, or were supporters of, the colonial enterprise, and they thought that only through enlightened European intervention and guidance could the Muslim world emerge from what they saw as its stupor. In many cases, Islamic reformers and their European interlocutors agreed on the diagnosis about what ailed the Muslim world. Both groups used the word *backward* to describe its general condition, and they agreed that ignorance and superstition were by-products of the intellectual isolation of Muslims. Likewise, they concurred with the suggestion that Islam was stagnant because too many Muslims mindlessly repeated what they had been taught. In addition, they both decried religious scholars at some of the major centers of Islamic learning who opposed any call for change or modernization.

European critics of Islam and Islamic modernists saw the same problems, but they differed markedly in their analyses about the source of the problems and how to overcome them. Simply put, Europeans argued that Islam was the major problem facing Muslim society, while Islamic reformers countered that Muslims were the source of society's difficulties. Indeed, Islamic reformers asserted that Islam was the solution rather than the problem: Muslim society began to decline, the reformers argued, when Muslims strayed from the true essence of Islam. They had distorted its true meaning and its simple practice, and only by returning to the faith of the first generations of Muslims, the so-called *al-salaf al-salih* (the pious ancestors), could Muslims reverse the corrosion of their civilization. Because of their emphasis on the experience of the *al-salaf al-salih*, modernists were sometimes called *salifiyun* and their movement *salafiyya*.

Islamic modernists pinned the blame for "distortions" in Islamic practice on the role played by Muslim clerics whose views supported centuries of repressive rule. The modernists argued that those clerics of the past had become an entrenched interest group that gave more importance to loyalty and obedience to rulers than to following God's law. These earlier clerics had declared all major questions of Islamic law settled and advised Muslims that they needed only to imitate precedent. Islamic modernists saw this not only as a prescription for suicidal rigidity but as a violation of the basic tenets of Islamic law. Because of the history of despotism and its deleterious effects on Islamic practice, Islamic reformers became strong advocates of representative government. Colonial domination by non-Muslims made this all the more imperative for them.

The cure for the illnesses of backwardness and foreign domination lay in a return to the original teachings of Islam and to the reimplementation of its simple message. They argued that Muslims must seek the answers to contemporary problems through the use of reason derived from the Islamic tradition. For them, there were no answers either in "blind imitation" of the past or in "blind imitation" of the West. The solutions to their problems would be found in Islam. Islamic modernism offered a dynamic picture of Islamic law and thought. For reformers, the universality of Islamic law meant that it was appropriate for every time and place and could never be "settled" because every era is unique. Muslims of every generation must seek answers in the Qur'an and other foundational texts to meet the challenges of their age. In this sense, they advocated for a methodology of Islamic rational practice rather than a specific set of rulings.

They argued that Muslims must be taught how to seek answers within Islam and not outside of it. Superstition entered Islam because Muslims had borrowed from other traditions. Reformers cited ecstatic mysticism with its "wild" chanting, self-flagellation, and saint worship as an example of this sort of dangerous syncretism. Such practices contradicted Islam's strict monotheism because they were akin to Muslims seeking divine intercession of human, or worse, other godly figures. If Muslims learned to think rationally, they would never partake in such rituals. Consequently, education was the centerpiece of Islamic modernism. Reformers campaigned for modern education for both men and women. They asked, "How can women be expected to raise upright children if they are slaves to superstition?" They also were strong advocates for scientific and technical education, as this knowledge would help Muslims build a modern society.

Religious and social reformers had much in common. Whether in the Arab East, Egypt, Istanbul, or elsewhere reformers sought to reconcile what they saw as the positive elements of European society—scientific and technical knowledge, new economic practices, democratic political institutions, and freedom of expression—with what they believed was essential to Muslim or Eastern society. Both trends contained elements of cultural translation as reformers of all stripes self-consciously and unapologetically borrowed from the West, but in ways they felt most appropriate for their own societies. In so doing, they viewed themselves as taking these new forms and implanting them in an Eastern or Muslim cultural and religious context that would produce a fusion that was true to Islam and to the culture, history, and mores of the East.

THE NEW MIDDLE EAST

The Ottoman Empire in the Post-Tanzimat Period and World War I

The map of the Middle East was completely redrawn as a result of World War I. The only pre-war border in the region that remained essentially unchanged was that between Iran and what became the Turkish Republic. These changes had extraordinary effects on the region's entire population, upsetting centuries of commercial, social, political, and cultural ties. The effects of these wholesale changes still reverberate nearly a century later.

The 20th century began with the Ottoman state facing a multitude of external and internal problems, including dissent throughout the provinces and among reformers unhappy with the absolutist rule of Abdülhamid II. The reformers believed that Abdülhamid II had moved the Ottoman state backward by suspending the constitution in 1878 and by using religious rhetoric to prop up his authority. He was deposed in 1908 by a group of reformers known as the Young Turks in a revolt that started as a military insurrection in the Balkans and eventually moved to Istanbul.[19] After the coup, power moved from the older Ottoman institutions to the newly formed Committee of Union and Progress (CUP) that the Young Turks established. Across the Ottoman Empire's ethnic and religious communities, groups of new leaders modeled on the Young Turks replaced the traditional leaderships. The new leaders did not possess the same allegiance to the Ottoman state and its institutions as the traditional elite. The stage was set for the rise of nationalist movements throughout the empire.

The end of the 19th century also saw a shift in the British attitude toward the Ottomans. Throughout the 19th century, Britain had viewed the empire as a strategic asset because it acted as a buffer between the Mediterranean and the Russians, whom the British viewed as their most immediate threat. The only ports the Russians could use year-round were in the Black Sea, and this required them to pass through Ottoman-controlled sea-lanes whenever they wanted to reach the Mediterranean sea. However, toward the end of the 19th century the rise of Germany began to concern British strategists more than Russia. Consequently, support that Britain had given the Ottoman Empire throughout the 19th century no longer seemed necessary. Instead of looking for ways to preserve the Ottoman Empire, Britain now contemplated the best way to carve it up.

When the CUP government in Istanbul threw its support behind Germany and the Central Powers in World War I, the die was cast. Britain now had a green light to begin dismantling the Empire. In 1914, Britain declared the Ottoman province of Egypt a protectorate of the British Crown, independent of the Ottoman Empire for the first time in four hundred years. The British deposed the khedive, Abbas II, the Egyptian head of state, and chose the pliant Hussein Kamel from among the descendants of Mehmet Ali and gave him the title of sultan of Egypt.

After two years, the war in Europe had been fought to the bloody stalemate and wholesale slaughter of trench warfare. Worried about troubling signs of unrest in Russia, the British sought ways to keep the Russians in the war. At the outset of hostilities, the Russian military had inflicted a crushing defeat on the Ottoman army in the east. The Ottoman forces were completely wiped out not by enemy bullets but by the catastrophically inadequate supply lines set by the Ottoman commander, Enver Pasha. This defeat led Enver to seek a scapegoat for his mismanaged and ill-advised plan to march through the Caucasus during the dead of winter. He accused the region's Armenians of actively supporting the Russians and, beginning in April 1915, used the crisis as an excuse to deport the entire Armenian population in eastern Anatolia. This precipitated what is now referred to as the Armenian Genocide and resulted in as many as one million deaths. Less than two years later, however, the Russians seemed to be the ones wavering. The British were convinced that they could knock the Ottomans out of the war and, by doing so, alleviate the pressure on the bogged-down Russian-led eastern front. This thinking led to the disastrous campaign on the Gallipoli Peninsula southwest of Istanbul in 1915–1916. After nine months of bloody fighting, the British withdrew in ignominious defeat, and the Ottomans had their first war hero. The Ottoman commander, Mustafa Kemal, devised strategies that frustrated all attempts by the British to break out of their beachhead. Mustafa Kemal, who later became known as Atatürk, would make an even bigger name for himself after World War I as the leader of the new Turkish Republic.

Contradictory British Promises

After their defeat at Gallipoli, the British sought other ways to undermine the Ottoman military. British armies moved from Basra in Iraq toward Baghdad and from Cairo toward Palestine. They also responded positively to the promise of Hussein bin Ali (aka the Sharif or Guardian of Mecca) to revolt against his Ottoman overlords in exchange for British guarantees for an Arab kingdom after the war. The British were willing to support Hussein's aspirations as long as they coincided with their own strategic interests. British advisers, including Thomas Edward (T. E.) Lawrence, later known as Lawrence of Arabia, aided the rebellion. Throwing in their lot with the British would make Hussein and his three sons Faisal, Abdallah, and Ali pivotal figures in the history of the Middle East.

British interests in the Middle East at the time could be summarized by two words: *oil* and *India*. Oil had become a strategic asset a little more than a decade before World War I, when the Royal Navy switched from coal to oil. The British never wavered in their quest to control the oil fields of Iraq in any postwar settlement. Since the opening of the Suez Canal in 1869, British strategic planning in the Mediterranean was fixated on the need to protect the supply lines to British India.

Henry McMahon, the British high commissioner in Cairo, and Sharif Hussein exchanged a series of letters in 1915 and 1916, the content of which later became a source of much trouble. Hussein understood the letters to say that the British pledged that the Arabian Peninsula and the Arab lands of the Eastern Mediterranean (except what is now Lebanon) would be granted independence as an Arab kingdom in return for Hussein organizing a rebellion against the Ottomans. McMahon, however, was intentionally vague so as not to restrict British maneuverability. The Arab Revolt nevertheless commenced soon after and was led by Hussein's son, Faisal.

In May 1916, about a month after making their pledges to Hussein, the British, French, and Russians completed other postwar settlement agreements. The Sykes–Picot Agreement violated the spirit if not the letter of the Hussein-McMahon correspondence. The French and British agreed to divide much of the Middle East between them. The British received most of Iraq and the lands of the Persian Gulf, while the French would control Syria, Lebanon, and parts of Anatolia. The fate of Palestine would be decided later through consultation with other allies and other concerned parties, including Hussein. The actual borders of the spheres of influence of the parties to the Sykes–Picot Agreement were to be delineated at a later time. In a separate agreement, Russia would realize its long-held desire to have access to the Mediterranean from the Black Sea, as the Russians would gain control of Istanbul, the Bosporus, and the Dardanelles as well as the Armenian lands to the east. However, this agreement was not honored because mounting Russian losses and the general misery of the Russian population resulted in Russia's 1917 revolution. Russia soon dropped out of the war and signed a peace treaty with the Ottomans.

If all of this were not already complicated enough, the British made one additional set of promises about how conquered Ottoman land would be divided. On November 2, 1917, an advertisement appeared in the newspaper *Times of London* that soon became a source of resentment and scorn among Britain's Arab allies in the Middle East. The Balfour Declaration, as it became known, was a note signed by Arthur James Balfour, the British foreign secretary, and addressed to the banker Lord Walter Rothschild. The simple four-line announcement pledged British support for a Jewish "national home" in Palestine. The Balfour Declaration was the culmination of a massive lobbying campaign by the influential Polish-born chemist Chaim Weizmann. Weizmann was widely known in London's power circles, and he had an important role in British munitions production. He also had a gift for political lobbying and networking, and he convinced British politicians to regard the small Jewish nationalist movement, Zionism, as a potential British ally in the Middle East.

The Balfour Declaration was a sign of British desperation. Britain was deeply troubled by the prospect of a collapse of the French army after a mutiny in its infantry divisions. Some in Her Majesty's government even believed that if Britain seemed positively disposed toward the Zionists in Palestine, the government might convince the Jews in the Russian revolutionary government to remain in the war. The Bolsheviks not only rebuffed this idea but also made a

MAP 1.4 ■ The Sykes–Picot Agreement and the Mandates

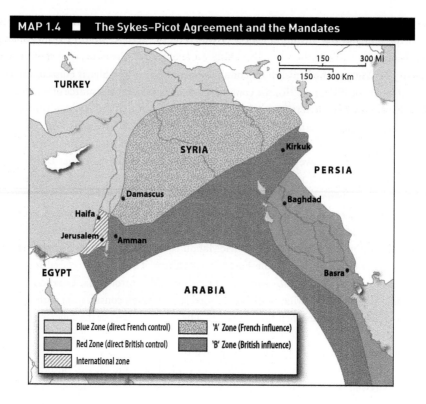

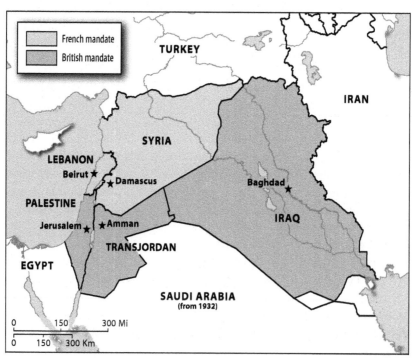

mockery of it by releasing the details of the Sykes–Picot Agreement, the contents of which infuriated Britain's Arab allies. In the end, the French stayed in the war, and the British managed to convince Greece to join the allies by making yet another promise of postwar spoils from the carcass of the Ottoman Empire.

The End of the War and the Mandate System

The end of World War I signaled the beginning of a new era in the Middle East. The peace treaties that followed the armistice introduced a new term into the lexicon of international relations: the *mandate*. A mandate was essentially a colony by another name. It was given an international legal fig leaf by its authorization through the newly organized League of Nations. The people of mandated territories were deemed unable to "stand by themselves under the strenuous conditions of the modern world." The state designated as the "Mandatory Power" would provide "administrative advice and assistance" until the people of the mandate could "stand alone." Just when that time would be was not specified.

The 1923 Treaty of Lausanne formalized the mandate system, and it recognized the borders of the new Turkish Republic. This ended any hope for independent Kurdish and Armenian states as part of the Great War settlement. The British received mandates in Palestine, Transjordan, and Iraq. The French, who had appended some Syrian territory to the Mount Lebanon area in 1920, creating a larger Christian-dominated entity, were granted mandatory power over Syria and over this new Greater Lebanon. The new lines drawn on the post–World War I maps of the Middle East effectively divided a contiguous area into discrete entities. These new borders disrupted commercial ties that had existed for centuries and placed unprecedented restrictions on the movement of people and the flow of goods around the region. The economies of these individual mandates became increasingly oriented toward the mandatory power and away from their immediate neighbors. The mandate system's multiple jurisdictions replaced the central Ottoman political and legal structure throughout the Middle East.

Administering the new territories necessitated establishing individual governments and other institutions of state. New borders created an assortment of regimes and forms of local administration that imposed new kinds of responsibilities and legal sanctions on the peoples of the various mandates. As a consequence, new kinds of loyalties and identities began to take hold among locals. While the idea of a Greater Syrian Arab nation encompassing Syria, Lebanon, Jordan, Palestine/Israel, and parts of Iraq, Turkey, and Iran continued to have a powerful hold on some, it was not long before ideological rivals in the form of Iraqi, Syrian, or Palestinian nationalism came to vie for the hearts and minds of locals as well.[20]

The British and Mandate Iraq

The case of Iraq is representative. Although much of the area that became the mandate had been known as Iraq for millennia, the new entity combined three Ottoman administrative units: Mosul, Baghdad, and Basra. The population of the mandate was diverse, with a majority of Shi'i Muslim Arabs, a sizable minority of Sunni Muslim Arabs, along with Assyrian and Armenian Christians, and a large, ancient Jewish community in Baghdad. Complicating matters even more were the many ethnic groups such as Turkmen and the large number of Kurds in the north around Mosul. In addition, the experience of Iraq during late Ottoman times was such that the Tanzimat and post-Tanzimat era reforms had little effect outside of the largest cities. Iraq had been on the margins of Ottoman society, and the presence of the central government had never been very pronounced.

The establishment of the British mandate government and its powerful security forces signaled an abrupt change. The new British-run administration in Baghdad imposed its will through military force, especially by using the new technology of airpower.[21] Local objections took a variety of forms. Arab nationalism had found fertile ground among the literate urban classes. These groups objected to the semicolonial rule implied by the mandate and sought outright independence. The lower middle classes and small merchants resented military conscription and the tax collection apparatus of the new government. Regional elites objected to the centralized power the British built in Baghdad, seeing it as a direct assault on their local prerogatives. The British were oblivious to these concerns, and their heavy-handedness touched off a major rebellion in 1920 that joined together many segments of Iraqi society, including tribal confederations and urban notables. Although the rebellion was suppressed, it signaled the emergence of what later became Iraqi nationalism. In the wake of the 1920 rebellion, the British established separate legal and administrative regimes for the cities and for the countryside. In the semiautonomous Kurdish north, the British devolved administrative and legal authority to Kurdish tribal leaders and other important figures such as Sufi shaykhs in exchange for pledges of loyalty.

Britain encountered great financial difficulty in the postwar era. Therefore, the British looked for a cost-effective style of indirect rule for their new possessions. They handed the reins of state to friendly leaders who signed treaties favorable to British commercial interests and backed them with British military power. Faisal, the British-installed king of Iraq, for example, granted a seventy-five-year oil concession in 1925. In the early 1920s, the British granted a limited form of independence to Iraq, Transjordan, and Egypt. These "sovereign" states did not control their militaries, their borders, or their foreign affairs, and they granted Britain the right to maintain troops on their soil.

Britain came to depend on Sharif Hussein bin Ali and his sons to maintain its new colonies in the Middle East. At the outset, the ambitious Sharif Hussein hoped to lead an Arab kingdom himself, and he even declared himself caliph in 1924. His grand scheme did not come to fruition as his ambitions rankled the Al Saud family of Riyadh, with whom he had fought a few years earlier. In 1924, the House of Saud attacked Hussein's British-backed kingdom of the Hejaz and forced Hussein into exile. A few years later, the Al Sauds also deposed Hussein's third son, Ali, and incorporated the entire kingdom of the Hejaz into their territory. At that point, the British merely shifted their support from the hapless Ali to the House of Saud.

Hussein's other sons were more fortunate. In 1920, the Syrian National Congress declared Hussein's son Faisal king of Syria. The French, who had been promised the Syrian mandate, objected, and they deposed Faisal five months later. The British, still reeling from the Iraqi revolt of 1920, hoped Faisal could bring legitimacy to "independent" Iraq and installed him as king of Iraq in 1921. The British subsequently named Faisal's brother Abdallah the king of Transjordan (Jordan).

Mandate Palestine and Zionism

The question of Palestine had its own unique complications and would significantly shape the region, from the early 20th century to today. While known as Palestine during Ottoman times, the area was divided between several administrative units belonging to the province of Beirut. Muslims, Christians, and people who were later called "Palestinian Jews" (to differentiate them from European Jewish immigrants who had begun arriving around the turn of the 20th century) populated the area. On the eve of World War I, the total population of Palestine was approximately 850,000—about 750,000 were Muslims and Christians; 85,000 were Jews; and the remainder were made up of Ottoman troops and officials and Europeans of various nationalities. A detailed examination of the Israeli-Palestinian conflict is found in Chapter 2, as well as in the chapters on Israel and Palestine in this volume. Given the importance of the mandate in shaping the region, however, a brief overview is in order here.

Zionism in Europe

Before we examine the Palestine mandate, it is necessary to say a few words about the background of the Zionist movement and its prewar history and presence in Palestine. Zionism is a form of Jewish nationalism, the roots of which go back to central and eastern Europe. In response to a history of oppression punctuated by periods of extreme violence, Jews of those European regions began to despair about their future. In response, increasing numbers of Jews chose to immigrate to the United States and elsewhere. Others, such as the Russian Leon Pinsker, suggested in 1882 that, just as the Jews would never be accepted in eastern Europe, it was only a matter of time before every host nation would reject them. This was the predicament articulated in the so-called Jewish Question: Could Jews ever be accepted as Jews in a nation made up of non-Jews? No, responded Zionists, arguing that Jews must therefore have their own nation-state.

Zionism was very much an eastern-European phenomenon at its inception, but this changed in the last years of the 19th century. In 1897, Vienna-based Jewish journalist Theodor Herzl published *The Jewish State*. Herzl had become convinced that Jews could never be safe from oppression except through the "restoration of the Jewish state." For Herzl, a nonreligious Jew, the Jewish Question was not a religious question but a political one. For him, it was a simple formula: Jews were not French, nor were they German, nor were they Dutch. As such, France, Germany, and Holland could never fully assimilate them.

Herzl was neither the first nor the most articulate to make this argument. He was a skilled publicist, however, and he brought the Zionist message to Jews around the world. He was also a tireless organizer. Through his efforts, the first international Zionist conference was convened in Basel, Switzerland, in 1897. There, he proposed that Jews should endeavor to obtain "sovereignty over a portion of the globe large enough for the rightful requirements of a nation." After some disagreement about where that "portion of the globe" should be, the conferees founded an organization to assist Jews in immigrating to Palestine, which began in earnest shortly after the Basel conference.

The Beginning of Zionism in Palestine

The Zionists were unsuccessful in acquiring a large footprint for their community during the first decades of the 20th century. The small numbers of settlers had very little impact on the area. Thus, for the rural Palestinian population the early Zionist settlements were little more than a curiosity. Later, with the advent of Zionist agricultural estates, Palestinians found work as laborers on these settlements. The early Zionist planters were more than willing to hire Palestinians because it was more economical to hire local labor at lower wages than immigrant Jewish workers who demanded wages more in line with those in Europe.

Nevertheless, there was some resistance to the Zionist presence from the beginning because of the question of land. Palestinian peasants often did not own the land they worked; according to local practice, when a new landlord took over a piece of land it was understood that the peasants would simply work for the new landowners. In contrast with this practice, when Zionist immigrants bought the land they sometimes tried to expel the peasant renters. Peasants objected to being removed from land that they had rented for decades. Tensions also developed between the Palestinian population and the newly arrived Zionists in cities. Resentment toward them emanated from small merchants and artisans, who were weary of the Zionist competition. As in other places in the Ottoman Empire, the fact that these new arrivals often had the protection of foreign governments—because of the Capitulations—intensified this resentment. In addition, these new arrivals were wealthier than the local Palestinians. The Palestinians also grew suspicious of what they perceived as the Zionists' aloofness. The Zionists set up their own institutions and organizations and seemed uninterested in becoming part of local society.

Upper- and middle-class Palestinians soon joined peasants and lower-middle-class artisans and merchants in their discomfort with the growing Zionist presence. Before the end of the first decade of the 20th century, local newspapers voiced their opposition to land transfers to the "foreigners." With the greater freedom of expression that came with the 1908 Young Turk coup, criticism of the central government for allowing Zionist immigration became widespread. Some of this anger took the form of Arab nationalist agitation against the local "Turkish" officials for aiding Zionist land purchases . Newspaper editors and journalists in Palestine began to write more frequently about the expropriation of peasant land and the lack of concern shown by Ottoman authorities toward the local Palestinian population. In the second decade of the 20th century, this criticism spread to the newspapers of Beirut and Damascus. This growing discontent took on an Arab nationalist tone as the CUP government of the Young Turks was depicted as ineffectual and unconcerned with the fate of the Arab population of the Ottoman Empire. By the outbreak of World War I, the land question in Palestine had become a central issue in Arab nationalist grievances against the Young Turks. It was one of the factors that led to widespread support of the anti-Ottoman Arab Revolt during World War I.

Zionists and Palestinians in the British Mandate

When the British took over their mandate in Palestine in 1920, they found brewing tensions between the Palestinians and Zionists. These tensions were compounded by the Balfour Declaration, which created a general feeling of distrust toward British intentions in Palestine and throughout the entire region. These doubts were certainly not assuaged by the fact that the preamble of the League of Nations Charter for the Palestine mandate included the text of the 1917 Balfour Declaration. Thus, this short statement that began its life as a newspaper advertisement became a legal document with the backing of the Great Powers.

The British and Palestinians did not get off to a good start, and things soon worsened. When the British set up their mandate authority, they chose Herbert Samuel, a dedicated Zionist, as the first high commissioner of Palestine. British mandate policies recalled the Ottoman *millet* system, with each religious community treated as a single unit. Funds from the mandate authority were distributed on a community basis—not according to population, but as a proportion of taxes collected from each community. Members of the Zionist community, or *yishuv*, received a much greater percentage of government funding because they earned higher wages and therefore paid more in taxes. Each community was to have its own executive that would represent the collective interests to the British authorities. The Zionists had already set up an organization, known as the Jewish Agency, as their de facto government, and it represented the yishuv to the British mandate authorities. The Palestinians had no such local administration, so they were at an immediate disadvantage in petitioning British officials. Two early attempts by the British to set up a representative body of all the communities did not succeed. The Palestinians rejected the first plan because it gave disproportionate representation to the yishuv. They rejected the second because the British authorities forbade the body from discussing the issues most important to the Palestinians: Jewish immigration and land sales to Zionists.

Violence broke out intermittently even before the official declaration of the mandate. On November 2, 1918, fights flared in Jerusalem on the one-year anniversary of the Balfour Declaration. In 1920, only weeks after Faisal's short-lived Arab kingdom emerged in Damascus, riots erupted after a local religious occasion was transformed into a celebration of Arab nationalism. In 1921, May Day riots began as clashes between Jews in Tel Aviv, but soon local Palestinians were drawn in, and then violence spread to Jaffa and Jerusalem. In the ensuing rioting, Palestinians killed dozens of Jews, and British soldiers gunned down a large number of Palestinians. The volatility of the situation led the British to issue their first policy study or "white paper" on the question of Palestine in 1922. British investigators concluded that resentment toward the Zionists and the perceived British favoritism toward the yishuv was the primary cause of the violence. At the same time, the white paper re-endorsed both the British commitment to the Balfour Declaration and the continuation of Jewish immigration to Palestine. The yishuv welcomed the report while the Palestinians repudiated it.

Underlying tensions exploded again in the 1929 Western Wall clashes. These disturbances began when a group of Zionists tried to change some of the conventions regarding the use of space around the highly contested Western Wall–al-Aqsa Mosque complex, an area that both Muslims and Jews view as sacred. Quickly, this dispute became a clash between supporters of Zionism and Arab nationalism. An orgy of violence erupted in several towns that resulted in 250 dead Palestinians and Zionists. The Jewish community of Hebron suffered tremendously and was not rebuilt until after the Israeli occupation of the West Bank in 1967.

The wanton violence of this event led the British to produce another investigative report about Palestine. This 1930 report essentially absolved the Palestinian leadership of responsibility and put the blame on increasing anger toward Zionist immigration and the ways in which the Zionists were acquiring land. Another report issued less than a year later made the case even stronger. As a consequence, some British officials called for restricting Jewish immigration to Palestine. This drew the ire of the Zionists in London, and Chaim Weizmann pressured the British prime minister into releasing a letter that rejected these reports and dismissed any notion of restricting Jewish immigration.

The Arab Revolt of 1936

During the mandate period Palestinians were frustrated at what they saw as British partiality toward the Zionists. This set the stage for the Great Arab Revolt of 1936–1939. The aftermath of this revolt transformed the dynamics of the Palestine question forever. During the mid-1930s, tensions were high and needed only a spark to set off a conflagration. There were two such sparks in 1935. The first was the discovery, in October 1935, of a ship carrying arms for the military arm of the Zionist movement, the Haganah. Many Palestinians accused the British of turning a blind eye to Zionist arms imports The second was the killing of Shaykh Izz al-Din al-Qassam in 1935. Al-Qassam was born in Syria but came to Palestine after fleeing the French in the wake of the collapse of Faisal's Arab kingdom in 1920. He worked with the urban poor in shantytowns but also traveled widely in the countryside. He was a well-known figure whose populist nationalism drew on religious imagery. Al-Qassam also preached the importance of military organization and helped set up an armed group called the Black Hand. His importance as an organizer, agitator, and militant brought him to the attention of the British, who ambushed and killed him in November 1935. Open rebellion was now just a matter of time.

The rebellion began in April 1936 in Nablus as a series of attacks and counterattacks between Palestinians and Zionists . The British called for a state of emergency, and then the Palestinian leadership headed by Hajj Amin al-Husseini called for a general strike. This in turn led to a generalized rebellion against the British and the Zionists. The British tried to force merchants to open their shops, and they also brought strikebreakers to mines and large industrial enterprises. As a result, the level of violence rose dramatically. The Palestinian leadership then called for a boycott of Jewish products and businesses and adopted a policy of noncooperation with British authorities. Fissures within Palestinian society came to the fore as some traditional leaders, fearing increasing economic damage to their interests, began to take a more conciliatory approach toward the British. Meanwhile, militant elements from among the lower social classes pushed for more radical and violent methods of resistance.

After months of clashes, the British convened a commission to study the troubled state of their Palestine mandate. War was brewing in Europe, and the British could ill afford to spare large numbers of troops to keep the peace in a small colony on the Mediterranean. The resulting Peel Commission report succeeded in nothing except fueling the most violent round of fighting. The report concluded that the mandate as constituted was unworkable and a clash between "national" communities inevitable. Then, it went on to suggest partition for the first time. It recommended that 80 percent of Palestine be set aside for the Palestinians and 20 percent for the Zionists. The Palestinian community reacted strongly against the report. Many in middle-class leadership positions and virtually every local leader rejected the proposal because of what they saw as its fundamental unfairness. According to the partition plan, the Zionists would receive the most fertile lands of Palestine in areas where Arab land ownership was four times greater than that of the Zionists. Furthermore, Palestine would not be independent; instead, it would be linked politically to Britain's closest ally in the area, King Abdallah of Transjordan. Zionist leaders such as Chaim Weizmann and David Ben-Gurion tentatively accepted the idea of partition as a first step toward acquiring all of Palestine. Nevertheless, because of the vehemence of the Palestinian rejection and the upsurge in fighting after partition proposals were made public, the British were forced to repudiate it.

From the summer of 1937 and until it was finally put down in January 1939, the Great Arab Revolt shifted to the countryside and became more violent. By 1938, there were perhaps ten thousand insurgents. In this stage of the rebellion, traditional notable figures gave way to a new stratum of grassroots leadership who controlled the local "popular committees" that determined tactics and strategies. The appearance of these local figures marked something of a social revolution within Palestinian society. Indeed, after the emergence of this new leadership, the rebellion took a more radical approach to social questions within Palestinian society itself. The insurgents now not only targeted British and Zionist interests but also attacked privilege among Palestinians, obliging wealthy Palestinians to "donate" to the nationalist cause. In the countryside, the rebels attacked large landowners and threatened moneylenders. In the cities and towns, they warned landlords not to try to collect rents. Meanwhile, middle-class urbanites were compelled to wear the Palestinian scarf, or *kaffiyeh* (also known as the *hatta*), as a sign of solidarity, transforming this traditional peasant garment into a national symbol. As the rebellion dragged on, criminal elements also took advantage of the chaotic security situation, and brigandage became a constant worry. Inevitably, wealthy Palestinians began to flee. Many left for Beirut or Cairo, leaving Palestinian society further depleted economically and politically. The Palestinian economy was devastated by the rebellion and especially by the anarchy and criminality that became so prominent in its last stages.

Through spring and summer 1938, the insurgents controlled the central highlands, as well as many towns and cities. In October 1938, the British moved twenty thousand troops to Palestine just after reaching the Munich agreement with Nazi Germany that cleared the way for the occupation of Czechoslovakia. With war looming in Europe, the British were determined to do anything necessary to calm the situation in Palestine. Accordingly, their counterinsurgency campaign was brutal, with tactics that included the destruction of whole villages, assassinations, and the employment of Zionist "night squads" to perform some of the more unsavory tasks for the British.

With one eye on the situation in Europe and the other on pro-German demonstrations in Arab capitals, the British policymakers became very uneasy. They began to search for ways to extract themselves from the morass of Palestine. Trying to curry favor with the Arab world, the British released yet another policy study in 1939. It called for a limit of seventy-five thousand Jewish immigrants for five years and then a total moratorium. The white paper of 1939 also promised that only with Palestinian acquiescence would the British allow the establishment of a Jewish state. This, in turn, infuriated the Zionists.

The events of 1936–1939 had far-reaching consequences. The British no longer wanted to deal with Palestinian leaders such as Hajj Amin al-Husseini, especially after he fled to Nazi

Germany. Instead, they tried to negotiate the Palestine question with Egyptians, Iraqis, Saudi Arabians, Transjordanians, and Yemenis. It was another thirty years before the Palestinians would once again gain the ability to speak for themselves and nearly sixty years before Palestinians and Israelis would hold face-to-face negotiations. Perhaps paradoxically, the rebellion was also a catalyst for the emergence of popular Palestinian nationalism. Large segments of the Palestinian public joined in the nationalist cause for the first time through strikes, demonstrations, boycotts, and combat. At the same time, the rebellion was an economic and social disaster for Palestinian society. Many wealthy and educated Palestinians fled the violence, depriving Palestinian society of an important mediating group. Years of fighting left many exhausted, and whatever military capabilities the community possessed at the beginning of the revolt in 1936 were destroyed during the British counterinsurgency campaign. As a result, the Palestinians were at a major disadvantage when the war for Palestine started seven years later.

Palestine Mandate After World War II

On the Zionist side, the diplomatic approach to the British championed by the London-based Chaim Weizmann came under increased pressure after the release of the 1939 white paper. Zionist leaders in Palestine such as David Ben-Gurion favored a more confrontational approach and were deeply concerned about the legacy of the white paper in postwar Palestine. Other more radical elements among the Zionists chose to confront the British militarily right away; these radicals were the so-called revisionists. They wanted to revise the Balfour Declaration's promise of a Jewish national home west of the Jordan River by claiming the area to the east—that is, Transjordan—as well.

During the 1940s, the United States stepped into the question for the first time since the Versailles Conference in 1919. In 1942, American Zionists called for the United States to back the call for a Jewish national home in Palestine. Then, immediately after the war, President Harry Truman pressured the British to admit European Jewish refugees to Palestine on humanitarian grounds. The British feared the powder keg of Palestine was on the verge of detonation. They were right. As expected, soon after the end of World War II, the British sought a quick exit from what one minister called the "millstone around our neck" that Palestine had become. By 1947, nearly one hundred thousand British soldiers were in Palestine trying to keep the peace. This was more than in all of India for a place a tiny fraction of the size.

Two irreconcilable positions defined the immediate postwar situation. Zionist representatives refused to participate in any conference or negotiation where partition was not the starting point. Meanwhile, the Palestinians rejected on principle all suggestions about partitioning Palestine into two separate states. Palestinians called for a single secular state and an end to Jewish immigration. Their argument was simple: They made up 70 percent of Palestine's population, and it was manifestly unfair to divide the land for the sake of a minority.

The War for Palestine

In early 1947, with no deal in sight, the British announced that they would withdraw from Palestine in May 1948. On November 29, 1947, the United Nations voted in favor of partition. Immediately after the vote, the war for Palestine began. From December 1947 until May

1948, war between the Zionist Haganah (soon to be renamed the Israel Defense Forces [IDF]) and Palestinian irregulars raged in Palestine. Then, when the British withdrew in May 1948, the Zionists declared Israel an independent state, and units from the Egyptian, Syrian, Iraqi, and Saudi Arabian armies invaded. This fighting went on until mid-1949. Fortunately for the Israelis, these Arab armies not only lacked a unified command structure; they also did not have unified war aims in mind. Indeed, they were as opposed to one another as they were to the new state of Israel.

Each of the Arab factions had its own reasons for becoming involved in the war, and very few of them had to do with the Palestinian right to self-determination. Egypt and Saudi Arabia did not trust the so-called Hashemite "axis" of Iraq and Transjordan. They knew King Abdallah wanted to prevent the emergence of an independent Arab state on his western border and was in contact with the Israelis on how best to carve up the area. Transjordan's Arab Legion was the best-trained fighting force in the Arab world, and with the exception of some fighting around Jerusalem, barely participated in the war. By prior agreement with Zionist leaders, King Abdallah's men occupied central Palestine, the area that has come to be called the West Bank. The Egyptians supported the Palestinians only to the extent that they opposed King Abdallah. The Egyptians also hoped that they could use any territory they captured as a bargaining chip in negotiations about the future of the British army in Egypt. After some early losses, the Israelis pushed these armies back. By midsummer of 1948, with the exception of the Gaza Strip and the West Bank, the Israeli forces had taken all of the land set aside for both the Jewish and Palestinian states. The war officially ended with the armistice agreements of 1949.

The Arab–Israeli war resulted in the establishment of the state of Israel and crushing defeat for the Arab armies—even more so for the Palestinians, who have come to refer to the war as the *nakba*, or catastrophe. Approximately 750,000 Palestinians were displaced and expelled through a combination of fear, compulsion, and psychological pressure on the part of the IDF. Out of a prewar population of nearly 900,000, only about 133,000 Palestinians remained within the borders of Israel.

STATES, NATIONS, AND DEBATES ABOUT THE WAY FORWARD

In the region, the processes of state- and nation-building were two of the most notable features of the post–World War I period and, indeed, in the first two-thirds of the 20th century. The decades after World War I also saw a transition to mass politics with political mobilization and agitation centered around anticolonial nationalism. It began in Syria, Iraq, Palestine, and Egypt and spread to almost every other country in the region to some degree. The period also saw the emergence of new political entities, which required the development of new institutions, practices, and identities.

The late 1930s and 1940s saw the rise of elite-led nationalist parties more often narrowly focused on the interests of their supporters—urban professionals from large, landowning families, big-business owners, and elements of the old Ottoman elites (the Turkish Republic was an exception in this regard). These groups wanted merely to take the reins of the colonial mandate, or protectorate state, leaving intact the extant social structure. They feared popular democratic rule and its threat of social revolution, and they showed little or no interest in the problems faced by the vast majority of the populations. The myopia of elite nationalists opened the door to movements from the lower social classes.

Communist parties, various Arab nationalisms, ethno-nationalisms, groups inspired by the Italian Fascists and Franco's Spanish Falange movement, and Islamist parties all drew supporters from groups alienated from elite nationalism: the peasantry, the growing labor sector, small-business owners, tradespeople, and other marginalized ethnic and religious groups. They formed the basis of Ba'thist support in Syria, Iraq, and Lebanon; Nasserist Arab socialism throughout the entire Arab world; communist parties in Egypt, Iraq, Syria, Iran, Turkey, and North Africa; the Muslim Brotherhood in Egypt and its branches elsewhere in the region; and also groups such as Young Egypt and the Phalange Party of Lebanon.

The interwar period also witnessed the beginning of the cultural struggle between the self-described secular modernists and those claiming to stand for the preservation of Eastern and/or Islamic tradition. The opening salvo in this face-off began in Egypt with controversies around two books written by respected intellectuals. Ali Abdel Raziq, an Islamic scholar, published his *Islam and the Foundations of Governance* [*Al-Islam Wa Usul Al-Hukm*] in 1925. He argued that there existed no Islamic textual support for the idea of the caliphate. His book appeared just after the Turkish Republic was officially abolishing the office of caliph and declaring itself a secular state based on a modified Swiss legal code, causing much consternation throughout the Muslim world. A year later, Taha Hussein, a Cairo University literature professor and well-known author, published *On Pre-Islamic Poetry* [*Fi al-Shi'r al-Jahali*], which some read as expressing doubt about the authenticity of the Qur'an. Both of these authors were accused of attacking Islam, and protracted and inconclusive public debates and legal moves followed. Taha Hussein championed the idea that Egypt's Mediterranean heritage should be the source of inspiration for overcoming the country's "backwardness." He became a symbol for a form of modernization that his critics described as Western-style secularism.

The other pole of these culture wars was personified by Hassan al-Banna and the organization he founded, the Muslim Brotherhood. He and his successors argued that Muslims must look to the leaders of the Islamic past for guidance. Nevertheless, theirs was not a call for a *return* to the past. Indeed, they became strong advocates for adopting Western technology and science and modern education for boys and girls.

In any case, these two "opposing camps" had much in common. They shared the view that Egypt and indeed the entire Muslim world was plagued by backwardness compared with Europe. They both called for political and cultural independence and sought to modernize Egyptian society by adapting appropriate elements of Western civilization while preserving Egyptian identity. These culture wars added two new elements to 19th century reformism: popular nationalism and an emphasis on social justice. Over the course of the 20th these elements increasingly became part of a new era of mass politics and state building.

As we have seen, the map of the post–World War I Middle East was populated with semicolonial political entities called mandates. Iraq, Jordan (Transjordan), Syria, Israel (Palestine), and Lebanon all began their lives as mandates. But this map also shows other new states, such as the Republic of Turkey, Pahlavi Iran, and Saudi Arabia, that emerged out of the wreckage of the old Middle East.

Every political entity in the region was new (see Table 1.1). Almost without exception, governmental and legal structures, institutions, and practices had to be created from scratch. All of the states in the region ratified constitutions that delineated the limits of governmental power and defined the rights and responsibilities of the citizenry. In addition, elections were held in most countries. These practices produced at least an illusion of a modern state and mass participation, even if they would become little more than window dressing for authoritarian regimes.

TABLE 1.1 ■ Dates of Independence of Middle Eastern and North African Countries		
Country	**Date of Independence**	**Former Colonial Holding Power**
Algeria	1962	France
Bahrain	1971	Great Britain
Egypt	1922	Great Britain
Iran	1925	None; Qajar dynasty
Iraq	1932	Great Britain
Israel	1948	Great Britain
Jordan	1946	Great Britain
Kuwait	1961	Great Britain
Lebanon	1943	France
Libya	1951	Italy, France, Great Britain
Morocco	1956	France, Spain
Oman	1951	British Protectorate
Qatar	1971	Great Britain
Saudi Arabia	1932	None
Sudan	1956	Great Britain de facto (de jure Anglo-Egyptian)
Syria	1946	France
Tunisia	1956	France
Turkey	1923	None; Ottoman Empire
United Arab Emirates	1971	Great Britain
Yemen	1967	Great Britain

Source: Author's data.

These structures were planned and designed with the aim of inculcating a national consciousness, a sense of "modernity" and national pride. For example, public schools and the military imparted nationalist ideologies (and in some cases, such as Iran, taught the national language) to students and conscripts. Museums were dedicated to national history and culture; sporting clubs and competitions were instituted at the local and national level; institutes for the study of national folklore and folk customs were established. The new states became more deeply involved in the daily lives of their populations while self-consciously using this power to sanction modern ways of life. They did this through such things as outlawing traditional dress and compelling the use of one national, and therefore "modern," language while forbidding the use of others; by using the most ordinary forms of surveillance, such as licensing, permits, zoning laws, and identification documents; and by using, of course, an expanded and more efficient security apparatus. Employment in the public sector was another way that these states induced a sense of loyalty from the population. The bureaucracy was not only a source of patronage but also a tie between people's personal interests and the maintenance of the regime. All of this helped generate a sense of national identity and belonging where none had existed before.

The Birth of the Turkish Republic

The birth of the modern Republic of Turkey upon the ruins of the Ottoman Empire was not without severe labor pains. In the peace negotiations after World War I, the victors demanded their recompense in the form of Ottoman territory. The sultan reluctantly signed the Treaty of Sèvres in 1920, ceding huge swathes of territory to Britain, Italy, Greece, and France and tacitly agreeing to the establishment of Kurdish and Armenian states on former Ottoman territory. The sultan also agreed to relinquish control of the waterways between the Black Sea and the Mediterranean. Only a small Turkish rump state would remain from the lands of the once-vast Ottoman Empire. Nationalist sentiment was enflamed throughout Turkey.

For nearly two years prior to Sèvres, however, nationalist leaders were planning a new direction for postwar Turkey. From their base in Ankara, the Turkish nationalists quickly rejected the Sèvres treaty and established a parliament, the Grand National Assembly. The nationalist government denied that the sultan possessed the authority to sign the treaty because he no longer represented the Turkish people. The Grand National Assembly soon voted to abolish the office of the sultan, whose collaboration with the Entente powers deprived him of whatever semblance of legitimacy he might have once had. In the subsequent Turkish war of independence, fighting erupted between nationalist forces and British, Armenian, French, and especially Greek armies in the east, southwest, and south of the country.

Mustafa Kemal, the hero of the Gallipoli campaign, was one of the major figures behind the nationalist movement. He organized the nationalist army and directed the insurgency against the Entente forces. Fighting raged off and on until 1922 when the Entente powers no longer had the stomach to continue. They admitted defeat and agreed to renegotiate the postwar settlement.

The Treaty of Lausanne of July 1923 recognized the legitimacy of the nationalist government and delineated the borders of the new Turkish state. The Turkish Republic was declared in

October 1923. After more than 600 years, the Ottoman state had ceased to exist. International recognition of the Turkish Republic was the beginning of a new era in modern Turkish history. It signaled another stage in the top-down, state-led transformation process that began with the Ottoman Tanzimat eighty years earlier. In this stage, the nationalist government transformed the former heartland of the Ottoman Empire into a secular republic. Like the transformations of the 19th century, this process was neither seamless nor without violence.

The early history of the Turkish Republic is almost inseparable from its founder, Mustafa Kemal. The provisional government in Ankara chose him as its president during the war for independence in 1920. During the course of the next few decades, he became the most important Turkish political figure of the 20th century. Kemal created a model of secular populist nationalism that guided Turkey in the transition from "Ottomanism" to "Turkishness." His program, which became known as Kemalism, was a conscious effort to break with the Ottoman past and replace it with a modern, nationalist, and secular consciousness. He moved the capital from the old imperial center of Istanbul to the central Anatolian city of Ankara. Kemal also acted to impose a strict separation of religion and state and to remove all vestiges of Ottoman efforts to harness religious legitimacy for the regime. Through the use of state edict, Kemal's government tried to remove religion from the public sphere. The office of caliphate was abolished in 1924, and a modified Swiss legal code replaced Islamic law in 1926. The new state replaced the Muslim calendar with the Gregorian calendar and adopted Sunday as the official weekly holiday instead of Friday, as was traditional in Muslim societies.

Kemalism projected a populist vision of Turkish nationalism. Kemal presented himself as a man of the people, and the new Turkish Republic declared universal suffrage for all adult citizens, male and female. The state was interested in more than promoting populist republicanism; however, it sought to reproduce its vision of modernity in every citizen. The Kemalist state outlawed clothing that hinted at regional, ethnic, or religious identity. Women were forbidden from wearing the Muslim veil on state property. In 1928, the Turkish language was "purified" and modernized. Arabic words were removed from the language, and the Arabic script was replaced with a Latin alphabet. In 1934, citizens were obliged to use Turkish surnames, eschewing the traditional practice of children simply taking their fathers' first names as second names and the names of their paternal grandfathers as third names. No longer were people in Turkey going to be known as Mehmet son of Ahmet son of Murad. It was at this time that by an act of parliament Mustafa Kemal became Mustafa Kemal *Atatürk*, or Father of the Turks. Banning traditional customs does not stamp out identity, however; and this move pointed to the deep suspicion that came to mark Republican Turkey's view of its minorities, particularly its Kurdish population.

A centerpiece of Kemalist nationalism was its emphasis on Turkishness. This left little or no room for minorities. Among strident nationalists, even the act of acknowledging the presence of minorities seemed to call into question the validity of the idea of the Turkish nation. Consequently, the history of non-Turkish peoples in the new republic has not been a happy one. While not nearly as bad as their previous experience under the Ottomans, Armenians continued to face discrimination well into the republican period as well. The ethnically distinct Kurdish population who live in the southeast of the country faced the greatest difficulties in the new era. Kurds speak an Indo-European language from the Iranian branch that is far more similar to Farsi than it is to Turkish. At one point after World War I, there was some momentum to create a Kurdish mandate and eventually a state, but resistance from the Great Powers, who would have had to cede parts of their newly won territories, scuttled those plans. Kurds saw their traditional homelands split between four states: Turkey, Syria, Iraq, and Iran.

To say that there have been problems between the Republic of Turkey and its Kurdish population is an understatement. For decades, Turkey relentlessly suppressed Kurdish language and culture. The legislation outlawing traditional dress in Turkey was aimed primarily at the Kurds, and until recently, it was illegal to teach or even speak Kurdish in Turkey. Turkey would not even admit that Kurds existed; for decades, state media routinely referred to them as "mountain Turks."

In the 1980s, the Kurdistan Workers Party (PKK) launched an insurgency against the Turkish state, seeking greater cultural and political rights, including an autonomous Kurdistan region in Turkey. The Turkish military responded with a ferocious counterinsurgency campaign that led to the deaths of nearly forty thousand people, most of them Turkish Kurdish civilians, and the displacement of more than three million Kurds from southeastern Turkey.

Beginning in 2004, the Turkish government, bowing to long-standing demands, permitted Kurdish-language radio and television programs. Political rights, however, continued to be circumscribed by a constitution that outlaws ethnically based political parties. There was a brief glimmer of hope on the Kurdish question around 2013 when Recep Tayyip Erdoğan's government began talks with Kurdish militants. However, the spillover of the Syrian Civil War put an end to this process and, in 2015, led the Turkish government to launch a new campaign of political repression against its Kurdish citizens.

Reza Khan and the Pahlavi Regime

Post–World War I Iranian history has some parallels with Turkey's history. Iran suffered foreign intervention and was also invaded and partially occupied. After the war, the British occupied the southern half of the country, while a Soviet-led army moved toward Tehran from the north. With Persia's leadership either paralyzed or openly collaborating with the occupying forces, an ambitious army officer attacked the old regime and eventually set the country on a path toward fundamental change.

During the first two decades of the 20th century, the British sought access to Persian oil while the British–Russian understanding regarding their respective spheres of influence continued undisturbed. After World War I, the British feared that the Soviet Union would try to install a friendly government in Persia. Consequently, the British became heavily involved in supporting Persian resistance against the Soviet-backed invasion in 1920 and 1921. They chose an officer of the Persian Cossacks named Reza Khan to be the Iranian face of their efforts. After Reza Khan and his forces succeeded in pushing back the Soviet-sponsored forces, he set his sights on a much higher goal. In 1925, he deposed the last of the Qajar Shahs and declared himself Shah of the new "Pahlavi" dynasty. Reza Shah was independent minded, and one of his first acts was to refuse the terms of the much-despised Anglo-Persian Agreement of 1919 that would have made the whole of Persia a de facto British protectorate.

Over the next fifteen years, through a combination of brute force, clientelism, and political savvy, Reza Shah built the rudiments of a centralized, modern state. There are some similarities between Reza Shah's modernizing programs and those of Mustafa Kemal in Turkey. As was the case in Turkey, much of the shah's initial base of support was in the military. Reza Shah secured the loyalty of the military through generous financial inducements to the officer corps. Army officers received excellent benefits and were provided with opportunities for personal enrichment in return for their service. The Conscription Law of 1925 provided new recruits for the security forces, whose size was increased from around 20,000 in 1925 to 127,000 fifteen years later. The expanded army and the paramilitary forces in turn played a pivotal role in the extension of state authority throughout the entire country for the first time in its long history. At the same time, the shah established a number of new ministries while thoroughly modernizing those that his government had inherited. He built a bureaucracy of some ninety thousand civil servants by 1941. Improved security and efficient administration enabled the central government to collect taxes and customs duties throughout the country. These new funds, along with the income from oil sales, provided much of the revenue necessary for the shah's reforms.

Reza Shah undertook wide-reaching legal and social reforms that, as in Kemalist Turkey, were imposed by government decree. These reforms aimed at modernizing the country and building a sense of Iranian nationalism. Legal reform brought a new secular judiciary to Iran. The state adopted French law in 1928 and all but eliminated the public role of the *ulema* and religious institutions. The shah decreed that all Iranians should take family names, and he chose Pahlavi for himself. Pahlavi was the name of an ancient form of the Persian language and evoked its classical literary and imperial traditions. Therefore, it should come as no surprise that the shah's version of linguistic reform did not consist of imposing a Latin script, as had been done in Turkey, but rather involved "purifying" the Persian language by removing all so-called foreign words.

Reza Shah, like Atatürk before him, focused much attention on the gender question and on dress in an effort to build a sense of national unity. In 1936, Iran banned the wearing of the veil, and Iranian officials were encouraged to appear at all public functions with their unveiled wives in tow. Gender separation in cafés and cinemas was outlawed. Reza Shah, however, was no advocate of women's equality. Even as he promoted a form of state feminism in the battle against "backwardness," he offered little in the way of political or social rights to women. Women never gained suffrage, divorce was almost impossible for them to obtain, and polygamy continued to be permitted even after the adoption of the French civil code. In the shah's eyes, state diktats on gender issues, dress, and personal grooming were not an infringement of personal rights but a means to produce a modern Iranian people. Therefore, men too were subject to the brief of the shah's intrusive vision. The state compelled men to wear Western-style clothes and hats. Any headgear that hinted at one's occupation or identity was outlawed, as were all tribal or traditional clothes. Reza Shah's "Pahlavi cap" eventually gave way to a fedora-type hat that men were encouraged to wear. In addition, men were aggressively discouraged from growing beards, and only neatly trimmed moustaches were deemed acceptable.

Despite their many similarities, the nationalist modernizing projects of interwar Turkey and Iran had significant differences. In contrast with Atatürk, who sought to distance his new republic from its Ottoman past, the shah drew on the cultural heritage of pre-Islamic Iran in conjuring his vision of modernity. Thus, he changed the name of the country from Persia to Iran. Likewise, he replaced the Muslim lunar calendar with an Iranian calendar, which begins on March 21. The name the shah chose for his dynasty, Pahlavi, also harkened back meant to pre-Islamic times. In addition, Reza Shah eschewed the populism of Atatürk. He self-consciously wrapped himself in regal spectacle meant to evoke the splendor of ancient Iranian kings. In any case, any populist airs he might have put on would have been contradicted by both the substantial wealth he amassed and his lavish and ostentatious lifestyle.

In another departure from the Turkish case, Reza Shah made no effort to institute a republican regime. In Pahlavi Iran, legislative elections were insignificant events because the parliament, or *majles*, exercised little real power. Almost from the beginning, Reza Shah's Iran began to take on characteristics of an authoritarian state. The shah paid little heed to the constitution, imposed strict media censorship, and abolished political parties and trade unions at will. Political opponents faced arrest and sometimes execution. Nevertheless, although he did not hesitate to use coercion to achieve his aims, the shah was also skillful in the use of patronage to build support. He appointed political cronies to important positions in the state bureaucracy or within his myriad personal enterprises.

While Reza Shah's regime adopted policies aimed at linguistic "Persianization," in contrast to Turkey, it did not take a suspicious or hostile approach to its "minority" populations. Iran's population was and remains ethnically and linguistically very diverse. By one count, there are more than seventy languages spoken in Iran. The vast majority of these are usually classified as either Iranian (such as Farsi and Kurdish) or Turkic (such as Azeri and Turkmen), but there are also Arabic, Armenian, and Assyrian speakers in Iran. While Shi'i Muslims form the largest religious group, there are large numbers of Sunni Muslims as well as Armenian and Assyrian Christians and Jews.

Despite his efforts at state- and nation-building, the main economic jewel in the country—the Anglo-Iranian Oil Company (AIOC, later called British Petroleum)—remained largely outside his control. Frustrated with the situation, the shah tried to wrest increased rents from the AIOC. This did not please the British, who were already becoming disenchanted with their man in Tehran. Then, the shah committed the fatal mistake of making friendly overtures to the Germans during World War II. The British and Soviets deposed him and placed his twenty-one-year-old son, Mohammad Reza, on the throne in 1941.

The beginning of young Mohammad Reza Shah's rule was marked by the return of the landed elites to power through their control of the majles. The late 1940s and early 1950s was a period of rising discontent and nationalist agitation. The Soviets, now occupying the north and hoping to expand the territory they controlled, encouraged Kurdish nationalists to establish their own short-lived Republic of Mahabad in 1945. In 1951, even as the inexperienced young shah was seeking some way to step out from behind the domination of the majles, he was obliged to accept a popular nationalist prime minister, Mohammad Mossadeq. This set in motion a series of events that some believe was later a decisive factor in the Islamic Revolution in 1979.

In 1951, Mossadeq nationalized (in other words, put under Iranian state control) the AIOC, enraging Britain. As a consequence, Britain, the United States, and the shah plotted to remove the Mossadeq government by force. In late August 1953, the US Central Intelligence Agency, with the help of a group of Iranian military officers, staged a coup against the popularly elected Iranian prime minister. The shah was returned to power, and then he made his move against the majles and against all his political opponents. With the help of the American FBI and the Israeli Mossad, he built his notorious state security organization, SAVAK, and began to construct the absolutist state that would become the hallmark of his rule by the 1970s. The legacy of British and US involvement in Iranian domestic affairs and the taint that this put on Mohammad Shah was a major part of antishah agitation in the run-up to the Islamic Revolution twenty-five years later in 1979.

In 1961, Mohammad Shah launched what he called the White Revolution, which he hoped would increase support for his regime and prevent a "Red Revolution" (i.e., communist take-over). The White Revolution was in essence a top-down reform initiative consisting of such measures as land reform and increased spending on public health and education. The reforms failed to satisfy expectations of the urban working and middle classes, did little to alleviate rural poverty, and alienated some of the Shah's supporters among rural landowners. All in all, the reforms succeeded in little more than generating resentment toward the Shah, and with an increasing monopoly of state power, avenues for expressing discontent were increasingly circumscribed. Indeed, by 1975 Mohammad Reza Shah had created a one-party state (his Resurgence Party was the only legal party), based largely on a cult of personality.

The Founding of the Kingdom of Saudi Arabia

The modern state of Saudi Arabia emerged out of a long-running series of tribal wars in the Arabian Peninsula. Beginning in the first years of the 20th century, the historically powerful Al Saud family of the town of Riyadh in the Nejd, or central highlands, sought to extend its dominance throughout the peninsula. The Saudis and their main fighting force, the Ikhwan (a group inspired by the idea of purifying the Arabian Peninsula through imposing their austere understanding of Islam), vanquished their neighboring rivals one by one. By 1926, ibn Saud, the sultan of the Nejd, and his Ikhwan had brought all but one of his rivals to heel. Only the British-supported Hashemite family of Hussein ibn Ali in the western part of the Arabian Peninsula, or the Hejaz stood in their way. As we saw earlier, the British had promised the Hashemites a kingdom in Arabia in return for their service during World War I. Nevertheless, when the British saw the writing on the wall, however, they deftly transferred their support from their protégés to the Al Saud clan. In 1932, after uniting the entire peninsula, Abdul al-Aziz ibn Saud proclaimed the kingdom of Saudi Arabia with himself as king, thus becoming monarch of the only country in the world named after a family.

Oil was discovered in the kingdom during the mid-1930s, but it was only after World War II that commercial exploitation of oil began in earnest. US oil companies assisted by the US government displaced the British as the main suitors for the right to access this oil wealth. In 1933, ibn Saud granted the first oil concession to the Arabian American Oil Company (Aramco).

Aramco was a consortium, or joint venture, made up of the companies that later became Shell, Exxon, Mobil, Chevron, Gulf, Texaco, and British Petroleum.

Aramco developed a close relationship with Saudi rulers by transferring vast sums of money to them and undertaking the immense task of building a state where none had existed previously. Until the mid-1940s, Saudi Arabia was basically a confederation of tribes and small towns on the coast or built around oases. Beginning in the late 1940s, Aramco and major US defense contractors, such as the Bechtel Brothers, undertook a variety of development activities throughout the new country. Because of the sheer volume of projects in which they were involved, ranging from road and airport building to setting up a telephone network to establishing air transport, one scholar referred to Aramco as the de facto "Ministry of Public Works."[22] In short, Aramco created the entire transportation and extraction infrastructure necessary for oil exportation. US oil executives were fond of describing the Aramco-Saudi relationship as a "third way." They boasted that the Aramco model was neither socialist radicalism nor an example of colonial exploitation. For them, it was a capitalist partnership in which both sides benefited. Meanwhile, Abdul al-Aziz ibn Saud used the Ikhwan to attack his internal enemies who sought a more equitable relationship with Aramco and those calling for more democratic politics. For example, the Saudis set the Ikhwan against "anti-Islamic" workers' movements in the mid-1950s.

Post–1948 Egypt and the Rise of Nasserism

The repercussions of the Arab defeat in the war for Palestine in 1948 reverberated throughout the Arab world. In Egypt, many ordinary citizens saw the monarchy as complicit in the defeat; moreover, Egyptians regarded the country's so-called liberal era of the previous two decades as an abject failure. Neither the charade of parliamentary elections nor the power struggles among the tiny ruling elite brought relief from grinding poverty for most Egyptians. The country's rulers seemed oblivious to growing landlessness among peasants as well as the lack of education and opportunity available to Egyptians in general.

Even more ominous for the king was that the military was disenchanted with what it considered a lack of support for the war effort in Palestine and the continuing presence of British troops in the Suez Canal Zone stoked nationalist resentment. Egyptian guerrillas began to clash with British forces in 1951, and this led to the January 1952 Black Sunday fire in Cairo that targeted foreign-owned businesses, hotels, nightclubs, and bars. The general chaos of this period set the stage for the July 1952 coup that toppled the Egyptian monarchy.

The old regime was swept away by the so-called Free Officers who had grown impatient with the king's inability to negotiate a British withdrawal (the 1952 coup began a period of military rule that continues to this day with the exception of Mohamad Morsi's popularly elected government in 2012–2013). Soon after deposing and exiling the king, the Free Officers created the Revolutionary Command Council (RCC) as the main governing institution in the country. Lieutenant Colonel Gamal Abdel Nasser soon emerged as the major force in the new regime.

Nasser, the new Egyptian ruler, implemented a series of reforms that remade Egyptian society. These domestic reforms and the foreign policy of the new regime came to be known as Nasserism. Nasserism was populist and vaguely socialist. Nasser introduced land reform that restricted the amount of land a single family could hold, and the new government nationalized banking, insurance, large manufacturing, and other industries. The Nasserist state built a mass education system and opened universities to large numbers of Egyptians for the first time. A greatly expanded public sector guaranteed employment for university graduates, and the state offered vastly improved health services to many millions. One of the achievements of Nasserism was the creation of a wide and viable middle class for the first time in modern Egyptian history. Nasser adopted a foreign policy of aggressive anti-imperialism and nonalignment, which meant that he endeavored to steer a course between the Eastern and Western blocs of the Cold War. Regionally, Nasser expressed support for the Palestinian cause and espoused a commitment to Arab nationalism. Arab nationalist fervor was such that Egypt and Syria briefly merged as the United Arab Republic from 1958 to 1961.

Gamal Abdel Nasser was more than just the leader of a coup that toppled a moribund and corrupt monarchy in Egypt. This charismatic young leader projected a great sense of optimism about the future. He proffered an ideology that inspired people in the Arab world for decades. Many in Egypt, the Arab world, and even throughout much of the postcolonial world saw in Nasserism the dawning of a new age when the have-nots of the world would finally receive their due. His place in history was confirmed by the Suez Crisis (known in Egypt as the Tripartite Aggression) of 1956.

In July 1956, Nasser nationalized the Suez Canal that had been British-controlled since 1875. This move was met with wild enthusiasm and national pride throughout Egypt. Even though Nasser pledged to compensate the canal's foreign stockholders, the British government was incensed. Almost immediately, the British began to build an alliance to attack Egypt. France, angry about Nasser's support for the Algerian revolution, and Israel, concerned about the threat of such a charismatic leader on its southern border, both signed on. In late October 1956, the three allies attacked Egypt. The Egyptian military was defeated rather quickly, and the Egyptian cities of Port Said and Port Fouad were heavily damaged.

The United States reacted with anger, however, and in cooperation with the Soviet Union compelled the British, French, and Israelis to withdraw. After 1956, the United States replaced Great Britain as the dominant Western power in the region. In addition, the Israeli Defense Forces' (IDF) performance during the Suez crisis erased any doubt about Israel's military supremacy among regional powers. Moreover, through an agreement reached with the French before the hostilities commenced, the Israelis procured a nuclear reactor that they subsequently used to produce material for their substantial (although officially unacknowledged) stockpile of nuclear weapons.[23] In the immediate wake of the crisis, however, Egypt held on to the canal, and Nasser was hailed throughout the Arab world as a champion against the old imperial powers.

Syria, Jordan, and Iraq: Turmoil and Change After 1948

Syria and Transjordan became independent states in 1946. Two years later, both were drawn into the Arab–Israeli war for Palestine, and both experienced a period of turmoil following the events of 1948.

In Syria, there was little consensus within the political class that inherited the mandate state from the French. As in Egypt, the military did not forgive the civilian leaders of the country for what they perceived as a lack of commitment to the war for Palestine. In 1949 alone, there were three military coups. This was the beginning of more than twenty years of political instability, with nearly twenty different governments and the drafting of multiple constitutions. In 1958, the military, fearing that a full-fledged communist takeover would be the alternative, embraced unification with Egypt. The United Arab Republic, as the unified state was called, fell apart three years later following another military coup in Syria. The Syrians and Egyptians spent most of the 1960s in an Arab cold war, with each trying to establish its credentials as the true champion of Arab nationalism. At the same time, stability in Syria remained elusive, with Syria experiencing successive coups, until the young air force commander and Ba'thist Hafiz al-Asad seized power in 1970, and upon his death al-Asad's son Bashar became ruler in 2000.[24]

The War for Palestine also had important ramifications for the former British mandate of Transjordan. In return for his unwavering loyalty, the British gave Transjordan's King Abdallah a yearly stipend, and a British army officer led the armed forces until 1956. During the war in 1948, King Abdallah's Arab Legion, the best trained and equipped of the Arab armies, fought only briefly against the Israelis. Jordan's main goals in the war consisted of preventing the establishment of an independent Palestinian state and seizing control of central Palestine. Zionist leaders ceded the area to Abdallah in exchange for his not getting involved in the fighting elsewhere. In 1949, Abdallah annexed central Palestine and discouraged the use of the word *Palestine* in his kingdom. As a consequence, central Palestine eventually became known as the West Bank (of the Jordan River). He also changed the name of Transjordan to the Hashemite Kingdom of Jordan. In 1951, a Palestinian, unhappy with the king's dealings with Zionist leaders, assassinated him in Jerusalem.

Abdallah's son Talal ascended to the throne but was deposed shortly afterward in favor of his own son Hussein bin Talal. After the 1956 Suez crisis, the Hashemite Kingdoms of Jordan and Iraq came together in a confederation called the Arab Federation of Iraq and Jordan, hoping to offset the growing power of Egypt's Gamal Abdel Nasser and his own newly declared United Arab Republic with Syria. Their wariness of the Egyptian leader and his influence in the region was well founded, as the Iraqi Hashemite monarchy was overthrown in a violent coup in July of 1958 by army officers who modeled themselves on Nasser's Free Officers. The coup leader, Colonel Abdel Karim Qasim, initially allied himself with Nasser's Arab nationalism. As an ally (and cousin) of the deposed king, Jordan's King Hussein found himself in a precarious position, and the British brought troops to the country under US air cover to protect his regime. Hussein, who ruled until 1999, continued to receive British (and later US) subventions and, like his grandfather Abdallah, remained unpopular with many Jordanian Palestinians, who eventually comprised about half of the country's population.

In Iraq, the Qasim government soon took a more independent line and adopted a hybrid Iraqi Arab nationalist position. These ideological commitments, combined with a low tolerance for opposition, led the postrevolutionary Iraqi state into almost constant strife with Kurdish nationalists. After failing to convince Qasim's revolutionary government to fulfill its commitment to Kurdish regional autonomy, Kurdish leader Mustafa Barzani led his militia, the Peshmerga, in rebellion against the Baghdad government. Fighting raged from 1961 to 1970, until the Ba'thist government, which took power in a coup in 1968, agreed to another autonomy plan. When the Ba'thists proved to be as insincere as Qasim's government had been about autonomy, a second rebellion broke out in 1974. The Kurds rebelled again in the 1980s and in the 1990s. Only in the aftermath of the US-led invasion of Iraq in 2003 did Iraqi Kurdistan finally gain officially recognized status in the new federal system. However, the autonomy of Iraqi Kurdistan was severely restricted, first by the emergence of the Islamic State in northern Iraq in 2014 and then since 2017 after a series of missteps by the Kurdish Regional Government (KRG), including the loss of its main oil fields to the central government.

North Africa After 1948 and Toward Independence

North Africa did not play a direct role in the events of 1948; however, its history during the 1950s and 1960s has much in common with the history of the Arab states that did, with one major exception: The North African countries achieved their independence later than the countries in the Arab East. Nevertheless, in postindependence Algeria and Tunisia and later in Libya, new military-backed leaders implemented sweeping social and economic reforms. Their foreign policy tended toward Arab nationalism, although Tunisia's first president, Habib Bourguiba, remained a thorn in Nasser's side during the 1960s. Libya and, to a lesser extent, independent Algeria used their oil to support a variety of nationalist and leftist movements in the Arab world.

Libya was granted independence in 1949 and ruled by King Idris I (Sayyid Muhammad Idris) until 1969. The country remained extremely poor and underdeveloped, even after oil was discovered in the late 1950s. In 1969, a military coup modeled on that of Egypt toppled the monarchy. The coup planners, a group of army officers who emulated Egypt's Free Officers, named Colonel Muammar al-Qadhafi as chairman. He remained the head of state until 2011, when he was deposed and killed in an uprising supported by NATO airpower. In the early days of the Qadhafi government there was talk about unification with Egypt, but that soon faded. Instead, Qadhafi used Libya's oil wealth to build a centralized, modern state and to fund radical Arab nationalist and leftist movements throughout the Arab world. He became a major source of financial support for the Palestine Liberation Organization (PLO) in the early 1970s. Like the rest of the military-run Arab states, Qadhafi's government became more repressive with time.

In Algeria, the National Liberation Front (FLN) launched a war of independence against France in 1954. The French refused to grant what they considered an integral part of France the right to secede. The ensuing Algerian war of independence was a protracted and bloody affair, with more than five hundred thousand Algerian deaths and tens of thousands of French soldiers and civilians killed. In 1962, France reluctantly granted Algeria independence. In the postindependence era, FLN-led Algeria started down a road of socialist-style central planning. The state became increasingly authoritarian, and its foreign policy remained anti-imperialist and openly supportive of the Palestinian cause.

Tunisia gained its independence from France in 1956 and was declared a republic in 1957. Despite its democratic façade, the new government never countenanced political opposition or even debate. From 1957 to 2011, there were only two presidents, and elections meant little or nothing. Tunisia's first president, Habib Bourguiba, initiated intensive reform and modernization programs that have been compared with those of Mustafa Kemal in Turkey for their emphasis on secularism and women's emancipation. Like Egypt, Tunisia experimented with quasi-socialist economic planning in the 1960s, and, as in Egypt, abandoned socialism in the 1970s. Throughout the 1960s, Bourguiba and Nasser were rivals for the sympathies of the Arab public. After Egypt signed a peace treaty with Israel in 1979, the League of Arab States moved its headquarters from Cairo to Tunis. Zine al-Abidine Ben Ali replaced Bourguiba in a bloodless coup in 1987.

The French (and the Spanish in the northern Rif region) ruled over Morocco from 1912 to 1956. The French governed their protectorate indirectly through the Alaouite sultans and favored tribal and Sufi figures. As in other French colonies, French farmers and factory and mine owners enjoyed tax policies and government support that created great advantages for them. This, combined with France's obdurate refusal to grant even the most basic political rights, gave impetus to a burgeoning anticolonial nationalism in the interwar period. By the early 1950s, Moroccan nationalist leaders persuaded Sultan Muhammad V to adopt their cause. The French, still determined to hold on to their North African possession, exiled the increasingly defiant Muhammad V for rejecting a dual sovereignty plan in 1953. However, within two years the French had to yield, as popular pressure nearly boiled over into open revolt. In 1956, the French recognized Moroccan independence, and shortly thereafter, Muhammad V was proclaimed king.

Muhammad V's son, Hassan II, upon ascending to the throne soon became an absolute monarch through patronage and the policing and surveillance power of the state, despite Morocco's formal constitutional structure. The 1960s witnessed political violence and repression, with regime opponents jailed, exiled, and disappeared. In the 1980s, International Monetary Fund–mandated privatization policies increased income disparity, deepening poverty for many on the margins. Predictably, the 1980s and 1990s were decades of growing political opposition, protest, and government repression. In 1999, there were high hopes that Morocco's new king, Muhammad VI, would undertake fundamental reforms. With the exception of a few minor initiatives, after two decades on the throne these hopes have yet to be realized.

AL-NAKSA AND ITS RAMIFICATIONS

The June 1967 War and the End of Nasserism

The June 1967 War caused a major upheaval in the region, the reverberations of which still echo. Throughout the 1960s, tensions increased between Israel and its Arab neighbors. The Israeli policy of massive retaliation for attacks by Palestinian guerrillas or anything it considered a breach of its borders created instability in the region, especially in Jordan and later Lebanon. Meanwhile, Syria and Israel engaged in periodic artillery duels over demilitarized areas between the two states.

The Suez crisis of 1956 had clearly demonstrated that the Arab armies were no match for Israel's military might. Nevertheless, Nasser and the other Arab leaders continued to confront Israel putatively in defense of the Palestinians. They did so in order to pressure rival Arab states and to curry favor with their own populations, who were increasingly disenchanted with political repression and the material progress that the military regimes had failed to provide. Because support for the Palestinian cause was so strong among the general Arab populations, the regimes cynically channeled domestic political criticism toward the Palestine issue. Likewise, the Arab regimes regularly accused one another of not showing real commitment to the Palestinians.

The June 1967 War, or the *naksa* (the Setback) as it is known in the Arab world, resulted from a fundamental misreading of the military-political situation by the Arab states in general and Gamal Abdel Nasser in particular. Nasser hoped that through a game of brinkmanship he could force the United States to rein in Israeli attacks on Jordan and Syria. He assumed that the United States and the Soviet Union would not permit a war in the Middle East. There is also some evidence that he thought Israel wanted to avoid a war, at least for the moment. He was badly mistaken on both counts. In the spring of 1967 at a particularly tense moment, Nasser asked for the removal of UN observers between Egyptian and Israeli forces in the Sinai and announced a blockade of the Israeli port on the Red Sea. He did not expect Israel to attack, and in any case, he was confident that the superpowers would prevent a regional explosion. In this way, he would be seen as standing up to the main regional power—Israel—without any real risk. His gambit failed disastrously. The Israelis struck on June 5, 1967. Within hours, the Israeli surprise attack destroyed the Egyptian, Syrian, and Jordanian air forces on the ground. Without air cover, the Arab armies were defenseless, and by June 11, Israeli infantry units had occupied the whole of the Sinai Peninsula, the West Bank, the Gaza Strip, and the Golan Heights.

In just six days, Israeli-controlled territory quadrupled in size, and Israel occupied new territory with one million Palestinian residents. The Arab world was devastated. Nasser submitted his resignation immediately but withdrew it after huge, government-backed demonstrations expressed support for him. In the wake of the defeat, Nasser was forced to reconcile with King Hussein of Jordan, seek financial support from his Saudi rivals, and accept large quantities of Soviet armaments that essentially put him in the Soviet camp in the Cold War. The Israeli victory in 1967 marked the twilight of Nasser's dominance over the political scene in the Arab world. Soon, more radical Arab nationalist, leftist, and Islamist political groups vied for the hearts and minds of the Arab public.

Although not tied directly to the events of 1967, in Iraq Ahmed Hasan al-Bakr, with his deputy Saddam Hussein, led the Ba'th party to power in a bloodless coup in 1968. In consolidating their position, the Ba'thists systematically eliminated all their internal opponents and negotiated an end to the insurgency in the Kurdish north. In 1979, Saddam Hussein forced an aged and ailing al-Bakr into retirement, and within a year, Hussein's Iraq launched a disastrous war with the Islamic Republic of Iran that lasted nearly eight years and resulted in more than a million deaths.

Radical Palestinian Nationalism

For Palestinians, 1967 represented a turning point in their quest to achieve their own state. The military defeat of Egypt, Syria, and Jordan set the stage for a new phase of direct Palestinian participation in the question of Palestine. A younger, more radical leadership inspired by anti-colonial struggles in Algeria and Vietnam called on Palestinians, for the first time since 1948, to take up the fight for a homeland themselves. This new revolutionary spirit resonated both inside and outside of the Middle East, and it pushed the entire political orientation in the region to the Left. The June 1967 War had led radicals to conclude that the Arab states possessed neither the capability nor the desire to win them a homeland and that Israel would respond only to the language of force. No Israeli government would come to the negotiating table willingly. They recognized Israel as invincible militarily, but reasoned that Palestinian resistance could inflict enough pain to compel Israel to bargain.

The PLO became the vehicle through which Palestinians came to articulate their own collective aspirations. This was not always the case. Nasser was instrumental in the formation of the PLO in 1964, and he chose as the organization's first leader the lawyer Ahmad al-Shuqayri, who had previously worked for Aramco and the Saudi government. The PLO was an umbrella group made up of a number of different Palestinian resistance movements. Nasser hoped to control Palestinian resistance through the PLO. He sought to avoid any Palestinian provocations that might lead to direct confrontation with Israel. The defeat of 1967 changed all of this. The guerrilla leader, Yasir Arafat of the Fatah (Palestine Liberation Movement) faction, parlayed Palestinian frustration into his election as chairman of the PLO in 1969. The PLO, based in the Jordanian capital Amman, began to attack Israel in the West Bank and then within Israel itself. This prompted conflict between the Palestinians and Jordanian regime, ultimately culminating in Black September (see Box 1.1).

However, the fractious nature of Palestinian politics and the basic Palestinian condition of being dispersed across a region divided by all-but-impassable borders made unity a hard-to-achieve ideal. In addition, a number of Arab states—Libya, Iraq, Saudi Arabia, Kuwait—funded individual factions of the Palestinians, some within the PLO and some outside of the organization. This funding came with strings attached, and this too had centrifugal consequences for Palestinian unity. The Palestinian question was a way for Middle Eastern regimes to fight proxy wars. Thus, the Iraqis might fund a group opposed to factions supported by Syria; Syria and Iraq both might support radical Palestinian factions opposed to the Jordanian regime; while Kuwait and Saudi Arabia supported the PLO with the understanding that the group would do nothing to harm the Jordanian monarchy. The many permutations of this logic and its manifestations in practice are too numerous to detail here. One can say that, ultimately, just as the Arab states never had a united position on Palestine, the Palestinians, funded by various regimes, often worked at cross-purposes because of their own ideological differences as well as those between their paymasters.

BOX 1.1

BLACK SEPTEMBER

In the wake of the June 1967 War, Palestinian guerrilla groups began to fight in earnest against Israel. Egypt, Syria, and the rest of the Arab states feared military confrontation with Israel. As 1967 clearly demonstrated, their fears were well founded. They sought to curb Palestinians' attacks on Israel and instead to exploit the Palestine question in their domestic and regional political maneuvering.

In the late 1960s, Jordan's King Hussein became increasingly wary of the radical regimes on his Iraqi and Syrian borders. Meanwhile, these regimes supported Palestinian groups united in little else than their disdain for the Hashemite monarch, whom they saw as a stooge for the imperialist West and its local ally, Israel. By 1970, Hussein became worried about the stability of his regime in the wake of Palestinian raids on Israel and the massive Israeli reprisals they inevitably provoked. While PLO Chairman Arafat was well aware that his funding from the Gulf states was contingent upon avoiding conflict with King Hussein, radical Palestinian factions supported by Syria and Iraq sought to topple the Hashemite monarchy. The situation in Jordan came to a head in September 1970. After a series of provocative moves designed to undermine the Jordanian regime, King Hussein moved against the PLO in a confrontation known as Black September. Thousands of Palestinian civilians lost their lives in several rounds of fighting. Nasser negotiated an agreement to end the conflict, although he died unexpectedly the day after completing it.

Following Black September, the PLO moved its headquarters and its base of operations to Lebanon. The events of September 1970 also led to the emergence of the Black September terrorist group, whose first act was to kill the Jordanian interior minister who had been the architect of the Black September violence. The group is much better known for its infamous attack on the Olympic Village in Munich, Germany, in 1972, which led to the deaths of thirteen Israeli athletes and coaches during a botched German rescue operation.

The October War and the First Peace Treaty

In the aftermath of the June 1967 War, the UN Security Council agreed on Resolution 242. This resolution, which enshrined the notion of land for peace, became the basis of all subsequent peace initiatives. Not surprisingly, there exists strong disagreement about what this short document says. This confusion was not accidental. The English version of the resolution is more ambiguous than the French and Arabic versions. The author of the resolution, the British UN representative Lord Caradon, called the wording "constructive ambiguity." The resolution called for Israel to withdraw "from territories occupied in the recent conflict." The Arabic and French versions have a definite article before the word "territories." That little word makes a world of difference in interpretation. The Arab states and Israel have argued about this for fifty years. Israel understands the resolution as requiring it to withdraw from "territories"—that is, some territory but not all of *the* territories. In other words, Israel need not withdraw from all of the territory it captured in 1967 to satisfy the conditions of the resolution. The Arab states argued for a long time that Israel must vacate all of the territory captured in 1967. For their part, the Palestinians rejected UN Security Council Resolution 242 outright for the simple reason that it refers to them not as a national group seeking a state, but only as refugees.

In the aftermath of their defeat, the Arab states reconciled themselves to the fact that Israel was there to stay. In the summer of 1967, the League of Arab States adopted a resolution that has come to be known as the *Three NOs*. In it, the members of the League affirmed that there would be no negotiation with Israel, no peace with Israel, and no recognition of Israel. However, the resolution was also a tacit recognition that the Arab–Israeli conflict had shifted from a question of the destruction or removal of Israel to the inescapable conclusion that Israel was not leaving. They adjusted their aims accordingly by seeking to regain the territory they lost in 1967. Meanwhile, the Palestinian cause more than ever became a tool by which these states manipulated regional political questions or attempted to draw superpower interest to their parochial concerns.

The Arab states were clearly not powerful enough to defeat Israel militarily. However, this realization did not bring hostilities between the Arab states and Israel to an end. Instead, the Arabs merely altered their tactics a bit to keep pressure on the Israeli military. Between 1967 and 1970, Israel and Egypt fought the so-called War of Attrition across the Suez Canal. In reality, this was a series of artillery duels and aerial attacks on each other's fixed positions. The Egyptian cities of Ismailia and Suez were constantly under attack and were heavily damaged, and eventually, their entire populations of nearly a million were evacuated. At the same time, Syria encouraged Palestinian guerrilla attacks across Israel's northern border and in the West Bank.

Then in October 1973, Egypt and Syria launched an attack on Israel. The Egyptian forces crossed the Suez Canal and overwhelmed the Israeli defenses while Syrian armor also achieved initial success on the Golan Heights. However, the Egyptian infantry units abruptly halted their advance eight miles into the occupied Sinai. In so doing, the Egyptian president, Anwar al-Sadat, was demonstrating his desire only for the return of the occupied Sinai and not the destruction of Israel. He hoped at this point that the superpowers would intervene and bring about negotiations. The Syrians, not having been privy to Sadat's plans, were baffled. This soon gave way to feelings of betrayal, as the Israelis were now free to concentrate all of their firepower on the Syrian front in the Golan Heights. The United States undertook a massive airlift to resupply Israeli forces, and the ensuing Israeli counterattack devastated the Syrian forces and pushed them back across the 1967 cease-fire line. Israel then turned its full attention to the Egyptian front. The Israelis crossed the Suez Canal and besieged the Egyptian army defending Cairo. At this point, the superpowers became involved. They brokered the cease-fire and withdrawal agreements that ended the immediate hostilities.

The agreements that came out of the October War of 1973 eventually led to the signing of the 1979 Camp David Accords between Israel and Egypt. The beginning of the process came with Egyptian president Sadat's visit to Jerusalem in 1977. Two years later, the two states signed a peace treaty ending their thirty-year state of war. The Israelis agreed to give up the Sinai Peninsula in return for full diplomatic relations. This agreement officially delinked Egypt from the Palestinian issue. The treaty was extremely unpopular in Egypt and the Arab world. Egypt was expelled from the League of Arab States, and the League moved its headquarters from Cairo to Tunis. Ultimately, the treaty led to Sadat's assassination two years later.

Internally, Israel witnessed a major transformation of its political culture in the 1970s. The Israeli electorate's perception that the Israeli military was unprepared for the 1973 war accelerated this change. In the 1977 parliamentary elections, the Labor Party's monopoly of power came to an end with the victory of Menachem Begin's revisionist Zionist Likud Party. The "earthquake election" signaled the rise of non-European Jews as a major political force in Israel. These so-called Eastern Jews resented what they saw as preferential treatment for European Jews in Israel. The right-wing parties had courted these voters for decades, and it began to pay off by the 1970s. With a Likud prime minister, a more strident rhetoric emanated from the Israeli government toward the Palestinians. This did not seem to augur well for those seeking peace; however, it was the Likud government under Begin that signed the first peace treaty with an Arab state in 1979.

The War Moves to Lebanon

Paradoxically, the Likud government also seemed willing to use force on a greater scale than its predecessors. For example, as was the case in Jordan, Palestinians began to attack Israel from Lebanese territory after 1967, and, just as in Jordan, this brought massive Israeli retaliation. The Israelis argued that these actions were justified because they were in response to Palestinian provocations or undertaken to preempt attacks. Israeli forces engaged in constant fighting in southern Lebanon, with incursions a regular occurrence. Between 1968 and 1975, Israel bombarded Lebanon more than four thousand times and undertook nearly 350 incursions into Lebanese territory. In the midst of Lebanon's violent civil war, Israel launched major invasions of its northern neighbor in 1978 and again in 1982. The Israelis hoped to remove Palestinian guerrillas from the border area from where they staged attacks on Israel. After the invasion of 1978, the Israelis set up a Lebanese proxy force to protect their northern border.

The second invasion in June 1982 was much more substantial and even led to the brief occupation of parts of the Lebanese capital, Beirut. After more than two months of fighting and thousands of Lebanese casualties, the United States brokered a deal for the withdrawal of the PLO and Palestinian fighters from Lebanon. Immediately following the departure of the PLO, the Israeli government, working with its allies within the right-wing Christian camp, sought to install a new pro-Israeli government on Lebanon that would sign a peace treaty. Israel coerced the Lebanese parliament to elect its candidate, Bashir Gemayal, as president. The Israeli goals of a PLO withdrawal from Lebanon and a peace treaty with Lebanon seemed within reach. However, days before the new president was to take office, he was assassinated by a bomb planted by allies of the Syrian government. In the aftermath of his death, Gemayal's Christian supporters took their revenge on defenseless Palestinian civilians. Over the course of two days, Israeli troops allowed Gemayal's militia to enter the Palestinian refugee camps of Sabra and Shatila, where they killed between 2,000 and 3,500 people. The massacres caused such revulsion in Israel that the defense minister, Ariel Sharon, was forced to resign.

The events of summer 1982 also set the stage for the disastrous US and French involvement in Lebanon. After Israel laid siege to Beirut for more than two months, the United States along with France and Italy contributed troops to the newly formed multinational force (MNF) to supervise the removal of the PLO fighters and to provide security to the Palestinian civilian population left behind. The MNF inexplicably withdrew two weeks before scheduled, setting the stage for the horrors of Sabra and Shatila. After the massacres, the MNF returned to Beirut, where it would stay for another year and a half. During the next few months, US and French armies became directly involved in the civil war on the side of the Christian right. The headquarters of the US Marines and the French paratroopers serving in the MNF were destroyed by simultaneous bomb blasts a little more than a year later, resulting in the deaths of more than three hundred military personnel. The United States soon withdrew ignominiously. The Lebanese civil war continued for nearly eight years after the US and French withdrawals.

The civil war was an extremely complex affair. In reality, it was a series of wars that lasted from 1975 until 1990 and resulted in the complete breakdown of the Lebanese state. From its inception in the 1940s, Lebanon had a weak central government with a decentralized power structure that resembled something close to the late Ottoman *millet* system in miniature. Much of the authority normally associated with the modern state devolved onto the seventeen recognized sectarian religious groups. Unfortunately, this also meant that the state did not enjoy a monopoly of arms. A number of militias and sectarian parties trained and carried weapons openly. According to the 1943 National Pact (a power-sharing formula worked out by the Lebanese elite shortly before independence), government positions were distributed according to a sectarian formula. Thus, the all-powerful president was required to be a Maronite Christian, the prime minister a Sunni Muslim, and the speaker of the parliament a Shi'a, while parliamentary seats were divided according to a six-to-five ratio in favor of the Christian minority. All of the ministries and units of the government as well as civil service positions were likewise distributed. This odd formula was inherently unstable, and civil disturbance and political violence were common. The country suffered through a brief civil war in 1958 that resulted in the landing of US Marines on Lebanese soil.

After the PLO moved its headquarters from Amman to Beirut in 1970, the situation in Lebanon became even more unstable. Pressure to abolish the sectarian system came up against an entrenched class of wealthy families that rejected any change. By the mid-1970s, tensions had reached a boiling point, and in April 1975, the situation exploded. The war began as a showdown between leftist nationalist forces allied with the Palestinians against right-wing, predominantly Christian forces seeking to preserve their privileged position and resentful of the Palestinian presence. The war quickly became far more complex. The fighting unleashed social forces marginalized by the sectarian system maneuvering to better their collective social and economic positions. The war then mutated into a series of intersectarian and intrasectarian struggles. This situation was made even more complex by the many outside powers that became involved directly and indirectly. A partial list of these actors includes Syria, Israel, Iraq, Libya, Saudi Arabia and the Gulf states, Iran, the United States, France, Italy, and the Soviet Union. Finally, in 1990, Syria, with the acquiescence of the United States, France, and Israel, imposed a settlement through the Taif Agreement that amended and further entrenched the sectarian formula established in 1943.

The First Intifada and the First Gulf War

In 1987, the intensification of Israeli repression and a lack of basic services such as electricity and water finally exploded into a major uprising of the Palestinians in the West Bank and Gaza; it has become known as the *intifada* (this literally means "shaking off," but it is also used to mean "insurrection"). The uprising began spontaneously after a traffic accident at an Israeli army checkpoint. Soon, Palestinians were boycotting Israeli products, engaging in mass strikes and demonstrations, and cheering groups of stone-throwing youth confronting heavily armed

Israeli troops. The intifada signaled the emergence of new grassroots leaders in the occupied territories. The PLO leadership had moved to Tunis after the 1982 withdrawal from Beirut, and many saw them as remote and unresponsive to the situation in the West Bank and Gaza. The PLO leadership tried to make itself relevant after the outbreak of the revolt, but the intifada continued to be guided by local leaders in so-called popular committees.

The intifada resulted in about one thousand Palestinian deaths while fifty-six Israelis died. Tens of thousands Palestinians were injured and arrested. The uprising was also a public relations disaster for the Israelis as the prime minister announced a series of brutal policies, such as the intentional breaking of bones by Israeli soldiers of anyone suspected of throwing stones. The Israelis also began to give passive support to a local offshoot of the Muslim Brotherhood by allowing the group to receive funding from the Gulf states. Israel hoped that the religious activists associated with this group would be less troublesome than the secular nationalists of the PLO. In this, they were badly mistaken. Even if at first the plan seemed to work, as Hamas (the Islamic Resistance Movement) activists criticized secular nationalists and attacked female political leaders of the PLO, they soon became an even bigger problem for Israel.[25] The intifada lasted from 1987 to 1993, and it demonstrated in excruciating detail to many Israelis the high moral and economic costs of the occupation. Israeli soldiers in heavy battle gear riding in tanks and armored personnel carriers seemed to be locked in never-ending battles with defiant stone-throwing Palestinian youths, while Israel's economy suffered from labor shortages and other problems caused by the intifada. Given all of this, it is not surprising that the first Israel-PLO agreement, the Oslo Accords of 1993, came about as a direct result of the intifada.

One of the most significant events of the 1990s in Middle Eastern history came on the heels of the end of the Lebanese civil war and the Palestinian intifada. In 1991, Saddam Hussein's armies invaded and occupied Kuwait. Fearing for the West's access to the region's oil, the United States cobbled together a broad coalition to remove the Iraqis. The Gulf War, which lasted just one hundred hours, pitted the United States against Iraq only three years after the two nations had been allies during Saddam Hussein's war on Iran that lasted from 1980 to 1988. The coalition victory over Iraq in 1991 left Saddam Hussein in power but brought eleven years of severe economic sanctions on Iraq until the United States finally removed Hussein from power in the aftermath of the 2003 invasion.

It was also during the Gulf War, the United States set up a number of military bases in the Arabian Peninsula. These bases eventually became a rallying point for anti-American Islamist militants led by Osama bin Laden and his al-Qa'ida organization, who demanded that these bases be closed. Later, the presence of these bases was one of al-Qa'ida's stated reasons for the 9/11 attacks.

The Oil-Producing States

An important feature of Middle East history during the past century was the emergence and rising importance of the Middle Eastern oil-producing states such as Iran, Iraq, Saudi Arabia, Kuwait, Algeria, Libya, the United Arab Emirates, Bahrain, and Qatar.

The oil-producing states are sometimes referred to as "rentier states." This means that their revenues are derived from sources other than taxation of the local population. In such circumstances, the state has a propensity to become a dispenser of patronage. Instead of developing a governing consensus, the state merely pays the population—or, more likely, an important constituency—for its loyalty. Because there is little need for rulers to respond to the demands for greater openness, rentier states have a strong tendency to be undemocratic. This general framework more or less describes a number of the oil-producing states throughout the region: They have vast oil wealth, provide extensive subsidies and material support to key populations, have very little governmental transparency and few democratic institutions, and are ruled by small oligarchies and/or military cliques.

Through most of the 20th century, international oil companies worked in the region through the consortium model. With this approach, a group of companies would pool their resources under a single name; Aramco of Saudi Arabia was the best known of the consortia. Consortia bought the rights to exploit oil fields for terms of a half-century or more. Over time, they came to control the entirety of oil drilling and production in the region. They paid the oil states rent in exchange for monopoly rights over exploration and production. These consortium (and the earlier concessions) agreements enabled the largest of the oil companies, the so-called seven sisters, to control the industry prior to 1973.

Persia granted the first oil concession to Britain in 1901. William Knox D'Arcy, a British explorer, gained the right to "obtain, exploit, develop, carry away and sell" petroleum and petroleum products from Persia in exchange for £40,000 as well as 16 percent of the annual profits to be paid to the Qajar monarchs. The British government bought the concession from D'Arcy and created the Anglo-Iranian Oil Company (AIOC), which eventually became British Petroleum or BP. The agreement was extremely profitable. By 1923, BP was receiving upward of £40 million per year in revenue while the Iranian government received around £5 million. D'Arcy's agreement with the Persian monarchy became the model for subsequent oil concessions. Local rulers, often put in power and sustained by British and later US support, granted a number of these concessions.

During the 1950s and 1960s, some states attempted to amend the concession agreements under which multinational oil companies and their consortia controlled the oil wealth in the region. Saudi Arabia and Iran were able to gain 50 percent of profits in the 1950s; however, full local control did not come until much later. Iraq was the first state to successfully nationalize its petroleum sector in 1972.

Oil Politics and Neoliberal Reforms

During the 1960s, Nasser-inspired Arab nationalists savaged the Saudis and the other oil states in the Gulf. They accused the monarchs of being backward, regressive tools of Western imperialism. Domestic support in their countries for Nasser and other radical voices convinced these rulers of the need to counter these attacks. Accordingly, they began to take a higher profile in diplomatic questions concerning the entire Arab world. This approach entailed fostering anti-Nasserist political movements and sentiments whenever they could. The mutual antagonism played out in the 1962–1970 Yemeni civil war where Saudi Arabia and Egypt became directly involved on opposite sides. The criticism of the Gulf oil states as pawns of the West became even more acute with the radicalization of Arab politics after Arab defeat in June 1967. One of the ways they sought to quiet their critics was through providing generous financial support to the more moderate elements in the PLO. The other way was through supporting conservative religious movements throughout the region.

The prominence of the oil-producing states grew exponentially after the October 1973 War. The Organization of Petroleum Exporting Countries (OPEC; the cartel made up of many of the world's oil-exporting states) had sought to raise prices long before the October War, and Western support for Israel became a convenient pretext for a dramatic price increase. The Arab members of OPEC then began a five-month oil embargo to protest the US airlift of military supplies to Israel that not only resulted in long gasoline lines on Main Street USA but was also a financial windfall for the oil exporters. At about the same time, the monarchies of the Gulf began to emphasize their Islamic bona fides, actively portraying themselves as the guardians of Islam. Saudi Arabia and Kuwait encouraged Islamic missionary activity, emphasizing conservative religious thought throughout the Arab and wider Muslim worlds. The effect of this has been manifest in the growth of the influence of the Muslim Brotherhood and the rise of "salafist" or ultraconservative groups. The United States saw this as a positive development because it viewed such religious activity as nonpolitical; moreover, seen through the lens of the Cold War, religious activism seemed to provide a popular platform for anticommunism.

Outside of the oil-producing states, the optimism of the early 1960s gave way to stagnation and decline by the mid-1970s. The Nasserist Arab socialism and regionwide state-capitalist programs had run out of steam. An inefficient and nepotistic management culture ruled over a huge public sector of increasingly alienated workers. Middle Eastern governments could no longer promise a decent living to quickly expanding populations, and real incomes decreased rapidly. The resultant discontent manifested itself in an invigorated Left that called for greater social justice and more democratic political institutions, as well as in energized Gulf-supported Islamism that began to proclaim that "Islam is the solution." At the same time, a number of regimes took steps toward liberalizing their economies. These policies entailed cutting back on spending for social programs and food subsidies upon which people had come to depend. Liberalization failed to stem the tide of inflation, underemployment, and economic hardship that was quickly bankrupting the middle classes. This was an explosive combination, and eventually, something had to give.

Egypt's experience illustrates this process. In the mid-1970s, Anwar al-Sadat, Gamal Abdel Nasser's successor, put an end to the quasisocialist policies of his predecessor. He enacted a series of reforms intended to move the Egyptian economy toward capitalism. Sadat, hoping to spur economic growth and create new jobs for a rapidly growing population, opened the economy to foreign investment. He also hoped to parlay his economic liberalization plans into new loans from the International Monetary Fund and the World Bank to help reduce Egypt's huge foreign debt. Collectively, these reforms were known as *infitah*, or opening.

Egypt's path toward liberalization included the privatization of state-owned companies (which often led to the dismissal of large numbers of workers) and cutbacks on food subsidies in an effort to decrease government spending. These policies created great resentment because they resulted in intense inflation and gave rise to a group of investors who profited handsomely from their insider position within the ruling elite. Real wages did not keep up with rising prices, and much of the salaried middle class (formerly one of the main bases of support for the regime) was forced to work at several jobs to make ends meet. The dire economic situation engendered new forms of petty corruption that increased the general feeling of disorientation. It seemed as if anything and everything was for sale at the right price. Discontent rose, and unrest spread around the country. In 1977 after the government slashed subsidies for basic food staples, President Sadat sent the army into the streets in Cairo and other cities to quell a series of violent confrontations between protesters and the police.

Islamic Militancy, 9/11, and the Second Gulf War

In the 1970s and 1980s, increasing numbers of people gravitated toward a diverse genre of political activism, often analytically abridged under the rubric of "Islamism." On one level, the roots of these trends recall the 19th-century Islamic modernist movement's emphasis on the importance of adopting a critical stance toward the practice of Islam and on reforming society through education. At the same time, some Islamist movements also bear a family resemblance to 20th-century ideologies that emphasize anti-imperialism, mass social and political engagement, and, in some cases, calls to revolutionary violence. Events such as the 1979 Islamic Revolution in Iran and the US-organized anti-Soviet insurgency in Afghanistan were seminal events in the history of Islamism and its transformation into a significant part of the region's political imagination.

   In 1970s Iran, Mohammad Reza Shah (along with his friends in the West) was oblivious to the many signs of widespread discontent. The last decade and a half of the shah's rule was defined by a series of hard-to-fathom missteps in the face of building dissatisfaction and opposition. His regime became more, not less, autocratic. In 1975, for example, in the face of budding hostility and calls for greater political freedoms, the shah eliminated the two legal political parties and established a one-party state. At about the same time, he declared himself the "spiritual leader" of Iran and in so doing seemed to be engaging in a frontal assault on the powerful clergy who protested vociferously, claiming the shah was seeking to "nationalize" religion. Meanwhile, the merchants from the traditional markets or bazaars, who were allied with the clergy, also felt threatened by the shah's moves to impose new laws and labor regulations implemented by what they saw as draconian methods. By 1977, demonstrations and protests were spreading throughout the country. Then inexplicably in January 1978, a government newspaper ran an editorial insulting the most popular cleric, the exiled Ayatollah Ruhallah Khomeini, which resulted in antishah demonstrations and the police use of deadly force. This began an escalation against the regime that eventually led to the shah's ouster. Over and over, antishah demonstrators were met with deadly force by security forces, and then mourners for the slain would organize even bigger marches that were attacked, resulting in more deaths, and so on. In early December 1978, massive demonstrations and a general strike against the shah sealed his fate. Millions of antishah protestors in the streets of Tehran were proof that the military had lost its appetite for killing Iranian civilians, that the urban middle classes had abandoned the shah, and that court patronage had become meaningless. The shah departed Iran in January 1979 for a "vacation," and Khomeini returned from more than twenty years of exile about two weeks later.

In April 1979, nearly 99 percent of the Iranian electorate approved a referendum to replace the Pahlavi monarchy with an Islamic Republic. Ayatollah Khomeini became Iran's first postrevolutionary leader. The success of what became known as the Islamic Revolution inspired like-minded activists around the world who saw it as a victory for both Islam and anti-imperialism. The shah had seemed to be among the most secure leaders in the whole region. The Iranian military was powerful, well trained, and seemingly loyal to the head of state. But popular discontent resulting from extremely uneven economic development, the shah's perceived aloofness from ordinary Iranians, and his ostentatious lifestyle quickly overwhelmed the regime. In the end, Muhammad Reza Shah's pride and joy, the military, stood by as the Iranian people forced him into exile.

Iran was not the only state that grew more autocratic in the 1970s. Regimes throughout the region silenced domestic opponents, especially those objecting to economic liberalization. Rulers from North Africa to the Persian Gulf were simultaneously committed to opening their economies and shutting down political dissent. They viewed the Left, which appealed to large segments of the population (especially youth), as a threat. In response, some encouraged Islam-inspired political movements as a counterweight. At the outset, Islamic activists seemed more interested in preaching and in the minutiae of religious questions than in the politics of economic liberalization. In addition, they attacked secular leftists for "aping" the communist atheism of the West.

The appeal to Islamists turned out to be misguided as militants turned on their sponsors throughout the region. In Egypt, an Islamist militant organization, hoping to ignite a general uprising, tried to seize a military school in Cairo in 1974. Then in 1977, another group kidnapped and killed a former Egyptian government minister. In 1979 in Saudi Arabia, in an event that shocked the Muslim world, Islamist militants opposed to the Saudi monarchy seized the Grand Mosque in Mecca. Saudi troops regained control after nearly three weeks of ferocious fighting with the help of advisers from the French special forces Groupe d'Intervention de la Gendarmerie Nationale.[26] In 1981, another militant organization infiltrated the Egyptian army and assassinated President Sadat at a military parade. Meanwhile in Syria after several years of a violent Islamist insurgency, the government, with the help of Soviet advisers, launched an all-out assault on the insurgent stronghold in the city of Hama in 1982. Some have estimated that as many as thirty thousand people died in the assault.

These events did not seem to dampen US support for Islamic militancy in the period before and just after the Soviet invasion of Afghanistan in 1979. Under President Jimmy Carter, the United States began the biggest covert operation in its history, funneling money and arms and providing training through Pakistan to Afghans fighting the Soviet invaders. The United States even commissioned the writing of a booklet to encourage "freedom fighters" to travel to Afghanistan and join in the jihad against the "atheist communist" regime. Throughout the 1980s, US funding for the insurgency grew enormously. Governments in Egypt, Syria, Morocco, Tunisia, Algeria, and the Gulf states saw the campaign against the Soviets as a golden opportunity to encourage troublesome malcontents to travel to Afghanistan to fight against the infidel invaders. A wealthy Saudi citizen named Osama bin Laden helped facilitate the travel and training of some of the fighters. These young men gained valuable fighting experience that they would later put to use against their own regimes as well as against the United States in the 1990s and 2000s.

Just as Iran's Islamic Revolution in 1979 energized Muslim militants around the region, so too did the insurgency against the Soviet occupation of Afghanistan. The US-funded campaign succeeded in forcing the Soviet Union to withdraw from Afghanistan in 1989. Then later, after an extended period of internecine fighting, a group sponsored by Pakistani military intelligence—the Taliban—triumphed over its rivals and established a government in Kabul in 1996. While the Taliban government was toppled by the United States after the attacks of September 11, 2001, in the ensuing twenty years, the United States failed to eliminate the movement. Indeed, after President Joe Biden announced the United States would withdrew its forces in 2021, the Taliban quickly regained control over the entire country.

After the Soviet withdrawal from Afghanistan in 1989, some of the radicalized fighters, the so-called Afghan Arabs, returned to their home countries where they launched their own insurgencies. The 1990s saw Islamist militant activity in Egypt, Saudi Arabia, Libya, Tunisia, Algeria, Morocco, Jordan, and beyond.

In the midst of the turmoil and social dislocation caused by the combination of economic liberalization, these Islamist insurgencies, and government-led counterinsurgency campaigns, there emerged an important cultural phenomenon that its devotees sometimes called the Islamic awakening, or *al-Sahwa al-Islamiya*. Some analysts view this complex social and cultural movement and Islamist militancy as a single phenomenon, using terms such as *Islamic fundamentalism* or *political Islam*. However, by lumping together a large number of tendencies and groups with diverse orientations, aims, and national histories, such terms obscure much more than they illuminate. Indeed, depending on how one defines *fundamental*, the term *Islamic fundamentalists* could include almost all who consider themselves practicing Muslims. The neologism *political Islam* is equally fraught because much of the activity of the Islamic awakening was not oriented toward creating an Islamic political entity. For example, many of those participating in Islamic piety movements understood themselves endeavoring to make society more Islamic through the reform of everyday practice of individual believers.[27]

To be sure, there is also a wide array of Islamist political groups, but one should be very wary of labeling legal political parties and extremist militant organizations under the same rubric, *political Islam*. The Muslim Brothers in Jordan and (until 2013) Egypt, the Islamic Salvation Front in Algeria, Hamas in Palestine, and Hizballah in Lebanon all participated successfully in electoral processes in their countries. A more useful criterion would distinguish between reformist groups working within the legal framework of the state and those employing violent tactics and terrorism to achieve their aims. Of the latter, there are roughly two types: those seeking to establish an Islamic state or to change the political orientation of a particular national state, such as the Islamic Group in Egypt during the 1990s, and those, such as al-Qa'ida, that seek to undermine the entire global sociopolitical economic regime.

In the 1990s, this latter type, many of whom were associated with the anti-Soviet insurgency in Afghanistan, came to the fore. These militants viewed their victory as a historic turning point, the significance of which became manifest only a few years later when the Soviet Union fell apart. This idea continues to inspire those in the fight against the United States, that their actions might topple a second superpower. Using their Afghanistan experience as a model, instead of mobilizing large numbers of followers in a revolutionary tide to topple a national government, they formed themselves into small and unattached units and employed violent tactics to bring about what they hoped would be the collapse of the entire international system. Thus, in the mid-1990s, they began to strike the main pillars of the international system, the United States and its allies. A series of attacks followed against US interests in Saudi Arabia, Yemen, and the United States in New York in 1993 and then most dramatically again in New York and Washington, DC, on September 11, 2001.

Like the US-backed jihad against the Soviet Union in the 1980s, the US response to the attacks of September 11, 2001, fomented an even more violent manifestation of Islamic extremism. After 9/11, the United States launched military operations in Afghanistan and removed the Taliban government because it refused to hand over the al-Qaʻida leaders responsible for the attacks. Then, in what the US government at the time claimed was a further response, President George W. Bush authorized a US-led invasion of Iraq in 2003. The fighting ended quickly, but the mismanaged occupation created a power vacuum in which violent anarchy reigned supreme and multiple insurgencies raged across Iraq.

Evolving out of the ensuing chaos, the group that became ISIS (or, the Islamic State in Iraq and Syria) adopted a hybrid form of Islamist extremism. Like Osama bin Laden's al-Qaʻida, ISIS rejected any semblance of conformity to the international order, but its disdain for national borders was merely a step in its quest to establish a "caliphate" that would eventually encompass the entire Muslim world. ISIS militants exploded onto the world scene in 2014 and quickly captured a wide expanse of territory across Iraq and Syria.

Rebellion, Civil War, ISIS, and US Intervention

Surprising experts and laypeople alike, 2011 and 2012 saw masses of protesters pouring into the streets across the Arab world, demanding fundamental change. Despite the shock at the time, such phenomena were not unprecedented in Arab countries. For example, in 1985, massive protests in Sudan led to the overthrow of its autocratic ruler Jafar Numayri and in 2019 a similar event occurred there as Omar al-Bashir, another Sudanese despot, was ousted after nearly a year of peaceful demonstrations and mass mobilization. However, the difference in 2011 was how these popular protests and their slogans moved across borders so quickly. In case after case, entrenched rulers, taken by surprise and unaccustomed to domestic opposition, refused to grant major concessions. Their intransigence only hardened the resolve of demonstrators in the streets, and soon, calls for revolution replaced those for reform. The sobriquet *Arab Spring* referred not so much to a particular season of the year but rather to the hope for long-delayed political transformation and social and cultural renewal. In actual fact, many of the seminal events of the Arab Spring occurred in the winter of 2010–2011.[28]

The spark that set the Arab world on fire emerged from the most unlikely of sources: a desperate individual act in a provincial town in what was thought to be one of the most stable countries in the region. On December 17, 2010, in Sidi Bouzid, a dusty town of forty thousand in central Tunisia, a street vendor named Muhammad Bouazizi set himself on fire in front of the town hall. Fed up with constant police harassment and despondent about his bleak future prospects, Bouazizi acted out of frustration and anger. Solidarity protests broke out immediately in Sidi Bouzid and soon engulfed the entire country. Muhammad Bouazizi's life and death became potent symbols for a whole generation constrained by repressive political systems and meager economic prospects. Within days, Tunisia was in open, peaceful revolt, with increasing numbers of demonstrators standing steadfast in the face of police violence. On January 14, 2011, a little over a month after Bouazizi's self-immolation, Tunisia's president Zine al-Abidine Ben Ali fled with his family to Saudi Arabia. Almost simultaneously, protests broke out from the Maghreb to the Persian Gulf as protesters in one country after another borrowed the most popular chants of the Tunisian revolutionaries: *al-sha'ab yurid isqat al-nizam*—"The people want to bring down the regime"—and *silmiya, silmiya*—"Peaceful, peaceful." Mass protests began in Egypt during the last week of January 2011. The besieged Egyptian President Hosni Mubarak called the army into the streets, but as was the case in Tunisia, the army declared its neutrality and refused to shoot at demonstrators. On February 11, 2011, after weeks of sustained protest, Mubarak too was forced to step down.

The jubilation of those months soon gave way to despair. Fast-moving events across the region did not augur well for a democratic transition, and regional and international interventions dimmed prospects for democracy. For example, when huge protests threatened the absolute monarchy in Bahrain, a Persian Gulf state that houses the US Naval Forces Central Command and the US Naval Fifth Fleet, its embattled king (whose forebears have ruled for more than two hundred years) invited the Saudi armed forces to invade the country and crush the peaceful antigovernment demonstrations. At almost the same time, the eastern Libyan city of Benghazi rebelled against the Tripoli-based government of Muammar al-Qadhafi and declared itself "liberated." With Libyan forces bearing down on the city, NATO initiated an air campaign, ostensibly to protect civilians. Whatever its initial purpose, the air campaign soon became a full-scale assault on the Libyan armed forces and was the decisive factor in the end of Qadhafi's rule and his death on October 20, 2011. Unfortunately, the Obama administration and its European allies had not learned the lessons of the 2003 Iraq fiasco (see below), and without any proper postwar planning, Libya soon fell into a state of violent, febrile anarchy, punctuated by murderous score-settling, collective punishment, and attacks on those whose darker skin color was evidence enough of their support or opposition to some faction or another. Even a decade after the end of the Qadhafi regime, Libya remained without a functioning state, with several governments claiming legitimacy and fractious militia politics generating disorder, constant fighting, and great bloodshed among civilians.

Then there are the civil wars in Yemen and Syria. In 2011, huge demonstrations in Yemen called for the end of the thirty-three-year rule of Ali Abdallah Salih. Saudi Arabia and the United States, fearing greater instability in a notoriously unstable country, began to press Salih to transfer power to one of his deputies. After months of foot-dragging, Salih's vice president, Abdo Rabbuh Mansur al-Hadi, became president, "winning" a single-candidate election. Many of Yemen's youthful rebels and some political factions, including the Houthi Movement from the Sa'dah Governate, refused to recognize al-Hadi. The Houthis mobilized their militia and quickly took the two largest cities, the capital Sana'a and Aden, from Yemeni forces loyal to al-Hadi, who was eventually forced to flee to Saudi Arabia. In spring 2015, Saudi Arabia, accusing the Houthis of receiving Iranian support, began an air campaign (with the United States providing intelligence and logistical support) in support of al-Hadi's exiled government. Subsequently as the Saudi-led coalition blockaded Yemen by land, sea, and air, the situation for civilians in the poorest country in the region became desperate, with millions threatened with starvation and disease.

Meanwhile, in 2011, an armed rebellion broke out in Syria after security forces in the city of Daraa killed a number of demonstrators opposed to the more-than-four-decade rule of the al-Asad family. There were three factors that set the Syrian revolt apart from the others at the time: (1) Syria's proximity to Israel, (2) its role as part of the "resistance" to the United States and its main Middle Eastern allies (Israel and Saudi Arabia), and (3) the rise of ISIS and its success in exploiting the vacuum created by civil war to take over large swathes of the country. From the outset, regime opponents drew on the first two factors to lobby for outside military intervention (what some referred to as the "Libyan Option") at the United Nations. However, with two allies of Syria's president Bashar al-Asad (Russia and China) in a position to block any such move on the UN Security Council, this strategy only succeeded in pulling Syria inexorably toward an abyss. Indeed, the civil war in Syria quickly devolved into a regional and global proxy war, with the Saudis, Qataris, Turkey, the CIA, and the US Defense Department all backing different factions. For all intents and purposes, the anti-Asad forces on the ground consisted of Islamist militias, including al-Qa'ida's local franchise. For a time, there was talk of building a "Free Syrian Army" as a secular alternative to the Islamists; despite astronomical sums spent by the United States, Britain, and others, these efforts came to naught. In 2014, the entry of ISIS into Syria ratcheted up the violence exponentially in a conflict already marked by wanton savagery on a mass scale. With so many external opponents underwriting a plethora of opposition groups and with Turkey openly facilitating the movement of Islamist fighters across its shared border into Syria, it was unclear if the Syrian government would survive. However, the war took a decisive turn in the regime's favor when in September 2015 Vladimir Putin committed the Russian military to propping up the teetering Asad government. The Syrian army, backed by Russian airpower and Iran-supported militias from Lebanon and Iraq, turned the tide of the war over the next three years, methodically recapturing rebel-held territories in a vicious war of attrition. By 2021, the only rebel holdouts remained in the Idlib province under the protection of the Turkish military.

Since the dissolution of the Soviet Union, one of the primary factors in the history of the Middle East has been the unrivaled power of the United States to impose its will on regional actors. Large US military interventions began with the First Gulf War of 1990 and continued after 9/11—first in Afghanistan and subsequently in the Second Gulf War of 2003. The United States justified its invasion and occupation of Iraq by alleging that Saddam Hussein's government had contact with the perpetrators of the attacks on New York and Washington, DC, and that the Iraqis had resumed their outlawed weapons of mass destruction (WMD) program. Because of the unsubstantiated nature of these assertions, the United States was unable to convince some of its major allies and the UN to approve the Iraq invasion (both of the allegations turned out to be false). Thus, the United States—without UN approval and with limited support around the world—invaded Iraq and deposed Saddam Hussein.

This proved to be the easiest part of Operation Iraqi Freedom. The country soon descended into chaos, as the US occupying forces were ill-prepared to carry out their mission. The Coalition Provisional Authority, as the occupation administration was known, acted in ad hoc and ill-conceived ways. One of its most glaring mistakes was disbanding the Iraqi army without warning and thereby depriving one hundred thousand armed men their livelihood. Not surprisingly, a very violent anti-US insurgency soon developed, as did a horrifying sectarian bloodbath replete with a campaign of ethnic cleansing that eliminated areas with mixed Sunni/Shi'i Muslim populations, to say nothing of mass exodus of Iraqi Christians from the country. As the US finally began pulling out its troops in 2011, Iraq descended even deeper into maelstrom of chaos as a result of political stalemate, rampant corruption, economic collapse, and continuing violence.

Making matters worse, in the midst of the violence and political disorder ravaging the country, ISIS swept across northern Iraq in 2014. Despite being vastly outnumbered, ISIS militants captured huge amounts of territory from an Iraqi army that offered almost no resistance. Mosul, Iraq's second largest city with a population of over 1.5 million, defended by three divisions of the Iraqi army fell to just 800 ISIS fighters. At its peak in 2015 the Islamic State controlled an area in Northern Syria and Iraq about the size of the United Kingdom and ruled over nearly 11 million people.

In 2014, seeking to push back against ISIS, the Obama administration tasked the US military with providing air power in support of ground forces from the predominately Kurdish Syrian Democratic Forces (SDF) in Syria and the Iraqi army along with Iran-backed Shi'ite militias in Iraq. By 2017, the Islamic State had crumbled under the weight of this military campaign, although its militants continued to carry out attacks throughout the Middle East, Afghanistan, and elsewhere. Nevertheless, the defeat of the Islamic State did not signal an end to US military intervention in the region. US "anti-terror" operations continue to expand from the Middle East into South Asia, East Africa, and the Sahel region of Africa. Each new entanglement seems to metastasize into another apparently endless series of operations involving small numbers of American forces or the use of US drones, missiles, or aircraft. Ultimately, the violence and political upheaval across the region from Libya to Iraq to Yemen to Syria and beyond caused ripples across the globe, creating the worst refugee crisis in Europe since World War II and driving the rise of right-wing, anti-immigrant politicians across the entire world.

Will the United States reconsider its use of military power in the Middle East? While President Donald Trump promised to scale back US military involvements abroad, he did little to translate this promise into action—unless we count his administration abandoning the Kurdish SDF after its defeat of ISIS in Syria. Indeed, as a presidential candidate in 2016, Trump pledged to end US "forever wars" like that in Afghanistan, but it was the Biden administration in 2021 that withdrew American forces from that country. In addition, the Trump administration declared it would no longer honor the 2013 so-called Iran Nuclear Agreement. Was this a prelude to the next US-led war in the region? While Biden-as-candidate signaled he would return to the agreement, this seemed increasingly unlikely to happen as negotiations dragged on into 2022.

With respect to the Palestine Question too, Trump—despite some campaign rhetoric to the contrary—was quick to endorse the most uncompromising right-wing positions ever adopted by an Israeli government. After moving the American Embassy from Tel Aviv to Jerusalem, his administration tried to sidestep the Palestine issue completely by sponsoring the Abraham Accords which saw the United Arab Emirates and Bahrain (later joined by Sudan and Morocco) sign peace treaties and open full diplomatic relations with Israel. While Israel supporters in the US and abroad heralded this gambit, it did little to address the primary cause of the conflict—that millions of Palestinians continue to live under Israeli occupation. As for the Biden administration's initial approach to the Palestine question, beyond a few peripheral moves, it undertook no significant steps to distance itself from the previous administration's Palestine policy. Thus, the jury is still out about whether the US government will reconsider an approach to the Middle East that depends upon the use of force while providing unwavering support to regional powers seemingly uninterested in addressing the most vexing, long-running problems plaguing the region.

CONCLUSION

No one can deny that the history of the Middle East for the past two centuries was profoundly affected by the rise of Western European economic and military power. The Ottoman Tanzimat and the more equivocal reforms of the Qajar shahs were, at least in part, driven by unease about the burgeoning hegemony of Europe. The rise of the West, however, is not the entire story. Events largely driven by internal dynamics, such as Mehmet Ali's short-lived Egyptian empire, come to mind. Important cultural movements such as the Nahda and Islamic modernism, too, have roots that reach back to the region's precolonial history. Even the long-term consequences of events authored in Europe, such as the cataclysm of World War I, played out on social, cultural, and economic fields already well established. For example, the creation of new states in the region, such as Iraq and Syria, did not erase extant social and historical dynamics; it merely reoriented their trajectories. The old regimes did not simply disappear; they blended into the new contexts.

That said, the redrawn post–World War I map of the region, anticolonial nationalist movements, and the emergence of independent states during the course of the first half of the 20th century ushered in a new Middle East. Elites and charismatic figures armed with new kinds of political ideologies appealed to populations within and without these individual political entities. Arab nationalism, Arab socialism, Islamism, and a myriad of local nationalisms vied for the loyalty of the region's peoples. Top-down reform promulgated by individual strongmen such as Turkey's Mustafa Kemal or Iran's Reza Shah Pahlavi as well as authoritarian military regimes became the norm—so too did inter-Arab rivalries or cold wars involving Nasserist Egypt; Hashemite Jordan; and Iraq, Saudi Arabia, and Syria. The establishment of the state of Israel and the subsequent Arab–Israeli conflict produced momentous events with long-term consequences. The 1948 Arab–Israeli war, the 1956 Suez Crisis, the June 1967 War, the October

1973 War, the Egypt–Israel peace treaty, and the question of a Palestinian state all continue to weigh on the region in some way.

The founding of the stridently secular Turkish Republic in 1923 certainly raised new perspectives on the public place of Islam, but the genealogy of these questions can be traced to the mid-19th century. Nevertheless, the issue did not disappear over the course of the next century, achieving new relevance beginning with the rise of Islamist militancy in the 1970s, the 1979 Islamic revolution in Iran, and the blossoming of the Islamic awakening of recent the past decades. It again came to the fore in the immediate aftermath of the Arab Spring, in which Islamist-oriented parties and movements played a major role. But the question of the public place of Islam does not exist within a historical vacuum; the contexts in which it arises are populated with a range of historical factors. For example, in Egypt's heady early days of revolution Mohammad Morsi of the Muslim Brothers' Freedom and Justice Party became Egypt's first (and only) freely elected president in 2012. However, Morsi was deposed by a military coup a little more than a year later. In its aftermath, the Egyptian armed forces outlawed the Muslim Brothers and once again instituted a type of military-led dictatorship that harkened back to the 1950s and 1960s. In the same way, in Tunisia's postrevolutionary parliamentary system the Islamist Ennahdha Party and its leader, Rachid al-Ghannouchi, was one of the major players. However, Tunisia's democratic experiment too seemed to come to an end in summer 2021 when Kais Saied, the largely ceremonial president of the Republic, in a move reminiscent of nearly every post-World War II despot in the Arab world, citing corruption and the failure of the political class to address major problems, suspended parliament and claimed the power to rule by personal decree. Indeed, even in "secular" Turkey, the neo-Islamist Justice and Development Party (AKP) led by Recep Tayyip Erdoğan has used the majoritarian power of its overwhelming electoral dominance to force through amendments to the constitution and steer the Republic away from its supposedly strict secular origins. In a controversial referendum in 2017, Turkey scrapped its parliamentary system and put in its place a strong presidential system. President Erdoğan's ethnonationalist rhetoric and policies now recall those of the early "secular" Turkish republic.

Finally, the last few decades were marked by popular frustration with the lack of economic opportunity, the near absence of the right to free political expression, and most recently, the consequences of the COVID-19 crisis. These frustrations, combined with the increasing violence largely perpetrated or encouraged by outsiders that has marked the region's history for decades, may offer us a vantage point from which to make sense of the emergence of extreme militant groups such as ISIS and the horrifying violence that has shattered a number of states in the region and set millions of refugees on the move. It also might offer some insight into the failure of the other attempts at change such as the Arab Spring. For example, in Tunisia, Kais Saied's 2021 suspension of the parliament was initially popular among demonstrators protesting the country's scandalous failure in combatting the COVID-19 pandemic. In Tunisia and the Middle East (as in the rest of the world), the COVID-19 pandemic disproportionately affected poorer, marginalized populations; these were the very same populations who took to the streets during the Arab Spring of 2010. Public health systems across the region, suffering from years of neglect and underfunding, collapsed. A lack of basic medical supplies (such as oxygen in hospitals), the failure to set up efficient vaccination programs, and the subsequent shutdowns and economic disruptions created public outrage and led once again to large demonstrations denouncing the political elite with the same slogans of 2010. Political unrest spread across the region and governments from Egypt, Jordan, Algeria, Morocco, Lebanon, and elsewhere found themselves under fire. While one can be excused for looking at the recent history of disorder and rancor with dismay, perhaps the continuing willingness of Middle Easterners to take to the streets to protest peacefully, offers a more optimistic imagining of the future. For, despite the intense and persistent problems across the Middle East, the region's inhabitants, by taking to the streets, are demonstrating their belief that collectively they have the capacity to shape their own destiny.

SUGGESTED READINGS

Abrahamian, Ervand. *A History of Modern Iran.* 2nd ed. New York, NY: Cambridge University Press, 2018.

Anderson, Betty S. *A History of the Modern Middle East: Rulers, Rebels, and Rogue.* Stanford, CA: Stanford University Press, 2016.

Bardawil, Fadi A. *Revolution and Disenchantment: Arab Marxism and the Binds of Emancipation.* Durham, NC: Duke University Press, 2020.

Campos, Michelle. *Ottoman Brothers: Muslims, Christians, and Jews in Early Twentieth-Century Palestine.* Stanford, CA: Stanford University Press, 2011.

Faroqhi, Suraiya. *Suraiya Subjects of the Sultan : Culture and Daily Life in the Ottoman Empire,* 2nd ed. New York, NY: I.B. Tauris, 2005.

Gelvin, James. *The Modern Middle East: A History.* 5th ed. New York, NY: Oxford University Press, 2020.

Greene, Molly. *A Shared World: Christians and Muslims in the Early Modern Mediterranean.* Princeton, NJ: Princeton University Press, 2000.

Guirguis, Laure, ed. *The Arab Lefts: Histories and Legacies, 1950s–1970s.* Edinburgh: Edinburgh University Press, 2020.

Hanioğlu, M. Şükrü. *A Brief History of the Late Ottoman Empire.* Princeton NJ: Princeton University Press, 2010.

Hannoum, Abdelmajid. *The Invention of the Maghreb: Between Africa and the Middle East.* New York, NY: Cambridge University Press, 2021.

Kamaly, Hossein. *God and Man in Tehran Contending Visions of the Divine From the Qajars to the Islamic Republic.* New York, NY: Columbia University Press, 2018.

Lockman, Zachary. *Contending Visions of the Middle East: The History and Politics of Orientalism.* 2nd ed. Cambridge: Cambridge University Press, 2009.

Mitchell, Timothy. *Carbon Democracy: Political Power in the Age of Oil.* New York, NY: Verso, 2011.

Philliou, Christine M. *Biography of an Empire Governing Ottomans in an Age of Revolution*. Berkeley, CA: University of California Press, 2010.

Rouighi, Ramzi. *Inventing the Berbers: History and Ideology in the Maghrib*. Philadelphia, PA: University of Pennsylvania Press, 2019.

Schreier, Joshua. *Arabs of the Jewish Faith: The Civilizing Mission in Colonial Algeria*. New Brunswick, NJ: Rutgers University Press, 2010.

Sharkey, Heather J. *A History of Muslims, Christians, and Jews in the Middle East*. New York, NY: Cambridge University Press, 2017.

Surkis, Judith. *Sex, Law, and Sovereignty in French Algeria, 1830–1930*. Ithaca, NY: Cornell University Press, 2019.

2 THE ISRAELI–PALESTINIAN CONFLICT

Mark Tessler[1]

Many assume, quite mistakenly, that the Israeli–Palestinian conflict is a centuries-old feud based on ancient religious antagonisms between Jews and Muslims. This is not correct. The circumstances of Jews in Muslim lands were for the most part proper; indeed, Muslim–Jewish relations were often cordial and friendly. There were instances of hostility or even violence directed at Jewish minorities, but these were the exception; in general, Jews fared much better in the Muslim world than they did in the Christian West. The Israeli–Palestinian conflict did not take shape until the end of the 19th century. Slow to emerge even then, it resulted from claims to the same territory by competing nationalist movements.

EMERGENCE OF THE CONFLICT

In making the case for a Jewish national home in Palestine, Zionists begin by pointing to the existence of Jewish kingdoms in the territory during biblical times. Biblical record and archaeological evidence indicate that the Jews conquered and began to settle in Palestine, known in the Bible as the land of Canaan, during the 13th century before the Christian era (BCE). Moses had given the Israelites political organization and led them out of Egypt, bringing them to the country's borders. Thereafter, under Joshua, they initiated a prolonged military campaign in which they gradually took control of the territory and made it their home. By the 12th century BCE, the period of Judges, the Jews were firmly established in ancient Palestine, and the area of their control included substantial tracts of territory on both sides of the Jordan River. This was the center of Hebrew life until the Jews were driven from the territory by the Romans in the 1st century of the Christian era (CE).

Religious Zionists add that their claim reflects not only the national history of the Jewish people but also a promise by God to one day return the Jews to Eretz Yisrael, the historic Land of Israel. This belief that an ingathering of the exiles is part of God's plan is the foundation of classical religious Zionism, which has animated the prayers and aspirations of believing Jews since the Romans destroyed the Second Jewish Temple in Jerusalem and drove the Jews from the country. As expressed by one modern-day Zionist, "The Jewish people has never ceased to assert its right, its title, to the Land of Israel. This continuous, uninterrupted insistence, an intimate ingredient of Jewish consciousness, is at the core of Jewish history."[2] Similarly, as another maintains:

> Despite the loss of political independence and the dispersion of the Jewish people, the true home of the Jews remained Jerusalem and the Land of Israel; the idea of eventual return from the four corners of the earth was never abandoned.[3]

Zionists insist that this historic national consciousness and belief that Palestine was the Jewish homeland gives Jews political rights in present-day Palestine. According to one Zionist writer, "If ever a right has been maintained by unrelenting insistence on the claim, it was the Jewish right to Palestine."[4]

Palestinians, by contrast, insist that they are the indigenous population of the country and that their superior political rights to the territory derive, at least in part, from their uninterrupted residence in the disputed territory. They claim descent from the earliest-known inhabitants of the territory, the Canaanites and the Philistines, the latter having given Palestine its biblical name. It is believed that the Canaanites entered the area around 3000 BCE. Palestinians therefore assert that the country belongs to them, not to the Jews. They argue that the Jews, whatever might have been their experience in biblical times or the beliefs to which they clung "in exile" during the postbiblical period, cannot suddenly reappear after an absence of almost two thousand years and announce to the people who have been living in Palestine during all that time that they, the Jews, are the country's rightful owners. The following statement is a typical expression of this assertion of Palestinian rights. It was given by Palestinian officials to the Anglo-American Committee of Inquiry established in 1946, prior to Israeli independence, in response to the escalating conflict between Arabs and Jews in Palestine:

> The whole Arab people is unalterably opposed to the attempt to impose Jewish immigration and settlement upon it, and ultimately to establish a Jewish state in Palestine. Its opposition is based primarily upon right. The Arabs of Palestine are descendants of the indigenous inhabitants of the country, who have been in occupation of it since the beginning of history; they cannot agree that it is right to subject an indigenous population against its will to alien immigration, whose claim is based upon a historical connection which ceased effectively many centuries ago.[5]

There was little conflict as long as Jewish political thought was animated by *classical religious* Zionism. Believing that their return to the Land of Israel would take place with the coming of the Messiah, Jews viewed themselves as needing only to wait patiently and faithfully for the unfolding of God's plan. The Jewish posture was thus one of passivity, or patient anticipation, the only requirement being that Jews keep the faith and reaffirm a conviction that they were a people living in exile and would eventually be reunited and restored to their land. Accordingly, prior to the modern period, most Jews did not believe it was appropriate to initiate steps toward the reconstruction of their national home in Palestine. On the contrary, such action would indicate a loss of faith and the absence of a willingness to wait for the Creator's plan to unfold in its own divinely ordained fashion, and this, as a consequence, would rupture the covenant between God and the Jewish people and make illogical and illegitimate any proclamations of Jewish nationhood or any assertion of a continuing tie between Diaspora Jewry and the Land of Israel. The most Jews might do would be to live in a fashion pleasing to the Creator in the hope that this might hasten the onset of the Messianic age, if in fact the Day of Redemption was not preordained and was thus amenable to modification. Thus, as notes a prominent Israeli scholar, the Jews' link to Palestine, for all its emotional and religious ardor,

> did not change the praxis of Jewish life in the Diaspora. . . . The belief in the Return to Zion never disappeared, but the historical record shows that on the whole Jews did not relate to the vision of the Return in a more active way than most Christians viewed the Second Coming.[6]

These classical Zionist conceptions provided little motivation for a Jewish return to Palestine. As explained, it would have been heretical for Jews to arrogate unto themselves the work of God, to believe that they need not await the unfolding of the divine plan but rather could take into their own hands the fulfillment of a destiny for which they considered themselves chosen by the Creator. Thus, although there was an unbroken Jewish presence in Palestine from the destruction of the Second Commonwealth until the modern era, and although there were also periods of renaissance among the Jews in Palestine, during the early years of Ottoman rule in the 16th century, for example, the number of Jews residing in Palestine after the 2nd century never constituted more than a small proportion either of the country's overall population or of world Jewry. At the beginning of the 19th century, there were roughly five thousand Jews in the territory of present-day Palestine, which had a total population of perhaps 250,000. Most of these Jews lived in Jerusalem, with smaller numbers in Safed, Tiberius, and Hebron. These communities were populated by religious Jews who viewed their presence in the Holy Land as having spiritual but not political significance; most had no thought of contributing to the realization of political or nationalist objectives. Nor were these communities self-sufficient. They were supported in substantial measure by donations from Jews in the Diaspora.

Given their small numbers and apolitical character, there was little conflict between these Jews and the larger Muslim and Christian Arab populations of Palestine. This quietism was also a reflection of the traditional character of Palestinian society. From the rise of Islam in the 7th century and for the next five hundred years, Palestine was incorporated sequentially into the Umayyad, Abbasid, and Fatimid empires, which ruled their vast territories from Baghdad, Damascus, and Cairo, respectively. Palestine was a peripheral region in these larger structures, without a unified administration or a clear and overarching political identity. This continued to be the situation following the fall of the Fatimid Empire in the late 12th century. First under the Ayyubis and then the Mamluks, Egypt and the Fertile Crescent were governed from Cairo until the Ottoman Turks took control of most of the Arab world, including Palestine, early in the 16th century. Palestine remained part of the Ottoman Empire, ruled from Constantinople, until the end of World War I. During all of this period, or at least until the late 19th century, Palestinian society was largely immobilized; it was on the political, economic, and intellectual periphery of larger empires, by which it was for the most part neglected, and thus, overall, a relative backwater. Moreover, the country suffered not only from the neglect of its absentee governors but also from the absence of progressive local leadership and an indigenous reform movement. As discussed in Chapter 1, modernist and protonationalist movements did emerge in a number of Arab countries, the most important of which was Egypt, early in the 19th century. Moreover, the development that these movements introduced involved changes in many fields, including military affairs, government, taxation, agriculture, industry, and, above all, education. As a British journalist in Alexandria wrote in 1876, "Egypt is a marvelous instance of progress. She has advanced as much in seventy years as many other countries have done in five hundred."[7] But many Arab societies were largely untouched by these developments, and Palestine was among these. In contrast with Egypt, Tunisia, and western Syria, where these modernist currents were most pronounced, Palestine, like many other Arab lands, did not until much later witness the emergence of significant indigenous efforts at economic development, educational innovation, or administrative reform.

The situation began to change during the latter years of the 19th century and the first years of the 20th century. Although slowly at first, relations between Jews and Arabs in Palestine became more complex during this period, and they eventually became much more difficult. In part, this reflected the diffusion of political and social currents from neighboring Arab countries, which in turn contributed to the gradual emergence among Palestine's Arab population of new social classes, of institutions dedicated to development and reform, and, a few years later, of debates about the country's political identity and future. Of even greater significance, however, was the emergence of *modern political* Zionism, which slowly displaced classical religious Zionist thought with the view that the Jewish people need not wait for the Creator to act but should themselves organize the return to the Holy Land and establish the Jewish national home in Palestine.

Modern political Zionism began as an intellectual movement in Europe, stimulated by the broader currents of emancipation and reform that emerged first in western Europe and later in Russia and eastern Europe during the course of the 19th century. As a result of these developments, many European countries extended to Jews political rights and economic opportunities that had previously been denied, and this in turn produced new intellectual currents and passionate debates among Jews themselves. Some traditional Jews, fearing assimilation and a loss of faith, called on their coreligionists to reject the new opportunities and remain apart from mainstream European society. At the other end of the ideological spectrum were those who called for an unreserved embrace of the new currents, while still others, taking an intermediate position, sought compartmentalization, what some described as being a Jew inside the home and a European outside. The latter two trends welcomed the changing situation and sought to embrace, admittedly to varying degrees and in different ways, the political reforms they brought. The broader intellectual movement of which they were a part was known as the *haskalah*, or Jewish Enlightenment.

In this intellectual climate, there emerged a number of writers who placed emphasis on the national and political aspects of Jewish peoplehood and who thus became the ideological precursors of modern political Zionism. It is not always possible to associate *maskalim*, as adherents of the *haskalah* were known, with a particular normative position. The movement had no unifying organization or structure, and it incorporated different schools of thought and varying points of view about the issues of the day. As one scholar notes, "The ideas current among, and promoted by, adherents [of the *haskalah*] were rarely formulated with consistency and were often mutually exclusive."[8] Nevertheless, there were Jewish intellectuals who clearly articulated modern Zionist themes during this period. These men for some time remained a small minority among the educated and middle-class Jews who addressed themselves to the concerns of a new age. Furthermore, they reaped scorn from more orthodox and traditional Jewish leaders, who condemned their political brand of Zionism as heresy and who insisted upon the Jews' historical understanding that the return to Zion was a destiny to be fulfilled by God and not by man. But there were, nonetheless, Jewish writers of prominence who proclaimed that the Jews were a nation in the modern sense, who called on the Jewish people to assert their national rights, and who saw the reconstruction of Jewish society in Palestine as the key element in a nationalist program of action. Articulating these themes, they added modern political Zionism to the expanding range of Jewish responses that were called up by the revolutionary character of the times.

The first wave of Jewish immigration to Palestine began in 1882. It was organized by a student group in Kharkov, Russia, that took the name *Bilu*, derived from the passage in Isaiah that reads, "Bet Yaakov lechu ve nelcha" (O House of Jacob, come ye, and let us go). The group was motivated not only by the intellectual currents of the day but equally, if not more so, by the anti-Semitism that reappeared in eastern Europe during the latter part of the 19th century. Virulent anti-Jewish pogroms broke out in 1881, bringing disaster to hundreds of thousands of Jews and dashing the illusions of Jewish intellectuals who had been inclined to view anti-Semitism as a vestige of an earlier era, grounded in a lack of education and in religious fanaticism and destined to slowly fade away as European society continued to evolve. The impact of the pogroms and the devastation they brought as well as the positive attraction of the modern Zionist idea, and the connection between the two, are reflected in the manifesto issued by the Bilu group:

> Sleepest thou, O our nation? What hast thou been doing until 1882? Sleeping and dreaming the false dream of assimilation. . . . Now, thank God, thou art awakened from thy slothful slumber. The pogroms have awakened thee from thy charmed sleep. . . . What do we want . . . a home in our country. It was given to us by the mercy of God; it is ours as registered in the archives of history.

A key event during this period was the publication by Theodor Herzl of *The Jewish State*, which set forth the case for modern political Zionism and called upon Jews to work for the establishment of a Jewish homeland in Palestine. Herzl, a highly assimilated Jew from Vienna, was a journalist stationed in Paris, and he became increasingly disturbed about the growth of anti-Semitism in France toward the end of the century. The critical episode in Herzl's conversion to Zionism was the trial and conviction of Alfred Dreyfus, a Jew who had risen to a position of importance in the French army and who, in 1894, was falsely accused of spying for Germany. This event, and the angry mob that greeted Dreyfus's conviction with shouts of "Down with the Jews," confirmed Herzl's growing belief that if anti-Semitism could rear its head even in France, the center of European progress and enlightenment, it would never fully disappear, and, there-fore, assimilation was never truly an option for the Jews.

Following publication of *The Jewish State* in 1896, Herzl worked to pull together disparate Zionist groups and create an international structure to support Jewish colonization in Palestine. The First Zionist Congress, convened at Herzl's urging and held in Basel, Switzerland, in 1897, was attended by more than two hundred individuals, some representing local Jewish communi-ties and Zionist societies in various countries. The meeting resulted both in the adoption of a formal program and in the establishment of the Zionist Organization, thereby initiating the transformation of modern political Zionism from a diffuse and disorganized ideological ten-dency into an international movement with a coherent platform and institutional structure. As explained by one Zionist historian,

> Prior to the Congress the spectacle is largely one of disunity, incoherence, painfully slow progress—or none at all—confusion of ideas, dearth of leadership, and, above all, no set policy and no forum in which a set policy can be hammered out and formally adopted. Before the Congress there is, as it were, proto-Zionism.

By contrast, after the Basel meeting, "there is Zionism proper."[9] Other Zionist congresses followed, held at regular one- or two-year intervals. Among the other Zionist institutions cre-ated during this period were the Jewish Colonial Trust and the Jewish National Fund. The former, established in London in 1899, became the first bank of the Zionist Organization. The latter, created in 1901 at the Fifth Congress of the Zionist Organization, was devoted to pur-chasing and developing land for Jewish settlement in Palestine.

Waves of Jewish immigration to Palestine, known as *aliyot* from the Hebrew word for ascent, continued during the ensuing decades. At the turn of the century, there were almost fifty thousand Jews in Palestine, most of whom came from Russia and eastern Europe; by the outbreak of World War I in 1914, the number had increased to roughly eighty-five thousand; and by 1931, according to the census of that year, the population of Palestine was about one mil-lion, including 175,000 Jews, 760,000 Muslims, and 89,000 Christians.[10] Agriculture was the backbone of the new community, partly reflecting a drive for Zionist self-sufficiency, but there were also efforts to create a modern urban population and an industrial base. The city of Tel Aviv was founded in 1909 as a garden suburb of Jaffa, and by 1931, only 27 percent of Palestine's Jews lived in communities classified as rural.

The Jewish community in Palestine, known as the *yishuv*, also established a wide range of institutions designed not only to serve but also to unite its expanding population. In 1904, for example, a Hebrew-language teacher-training institute was opened in Jerusalem, and in the same year, the Jewish Telegraph Agency and the Habimah Theater were established. Bezalel School of Art opened in Jerusalem two years later; several Hebrew-language daily newspa-pers began publication in 1908; and construction began on a technical university in Haifa, to become the Technion in 1912. At a meeting of Palestine Jews in Jaffa in 1918, agreement was reached on governing the *yishuv*. There would be an elected assembly of delegates, Asefat Hanivharim, and a national council, Va'ad Leumi. In 1920, the general union of Jewish work-ers in Palestine, the Histraduth, was established; and within a decade, the union's sick fund was maintaining clinics in five cities and thirty-three rural centers and operating two hospitals and two nursing homes. In 1925, Hebrew University was founded in Jerusalem. As a result of these developments, the *yishuv* soon possessed virtually all of the institutions and agencies that would later provide the infrastructure for the Israeli state. And with its growing population and increasing complexity and sophistication, the *yishuv* gradually displaced Europe as the center of Zionist activity.

Although the proportion of Jews among Palestine's population rose steadily during the first half of the 20th century, the Arabs remained the overwhelming majority. In 1930, they still constituted over 80 percent of the country's inhabitants, and as late as 1940, they accounted for almost 70 percent. Moreover, the absolute size of the Arab population grew steadily during this period. In part as a result of improvements in health care, the Palestinian Arab population grew at an annual rate that averaged almost 3 percent between 1922 and 1945, enabling it to nearly double during these years. In many respects, especially during the first part of this period, Palestinian Arab society remained traditional. Residing in approximately 850 small villages, peasants made up nearly two-thirds of the population. At the other end of the socioeconomic spectrum was a small corps of wealthy, extended Muslim families. These powerful clans dominated the country's political economy and constituted a kind of Palestinian aristocracy; based in the major towns but with extensive landholdings, they sat atop a national pyramid of patron–client relationships. It is estimated that in 1920 the estates of these upper-class urban families occupied nearly one-quarter of the total land in Palestine.

Palestinian society nevertheless experienced important changes during the first decades of the 20th century. New newspapers, journals, and political associations appeared in the years before World War I, showing that Palestine was to at least some degree affected by the same intellectual and political forces that were associated with the Arab awakening elsewhere. While the country continued to lag far behind Egypt and a few other centers of modernization and nationalist agitation, there was a clearly visible rise in political consciousness and concern about the future. Between 1908 and 1914, five new Arabic-language newspapers appeared, including *al-Quds*, published in Jerusalem, and *al-Asma'i*, published in Jaffa. The latter frequently criticized Zionist settlers, resentful, in particular, of the privileges that foreign immigrants enjoyed under the legal capitulations granted by the Ottoman Empire. Among the organizations that sprang up during the same period were the Orthodox Renaissance Society, the Ottoman Patriotic Society, and the Economic and Commercial Company. Few of these associations possessed more than limited institutional strength. They met only intermittently, had a short radius of influence, and ultimately proved to be short-lived. Nevertheless, the presence of these organizations was another indication of the Arab awakening inside Palestine. In addition to concerning themselves with business matters or sectarian affairs, their programs represented, as did articles in the new newspapers, early expressions both of local Arab patriotism and nationalist sentiment and of a growing anti-Zionist orientation. Indeed, although Palestinian opposition to the expanding Jewish presence did not emerge as a full-blown phenomenon but, instead, grew incrementally during this period, almost all of the Arab arguments against Zionism that were later to become familiar were expressed in Palestine in the years before World War I.

Developments of this sort accelerated in the years following World War I. The first Western-style union, the Palestine Arab Workers Society, was founded in Haifa in 1925, and a few years later, it opened branches in Jaffa and Jerusalem. New middle-class organizations were established as well, including various Arab chambers of commerce and the Palestine Arab Bar Association. There were also Arab women's societies in Jerusalem, Jaffa, Haifa, and a few other cities. Led by the wives of prominent political figures, these societies' programs and activities sought to help the needy, to promote educational and cultural advancement, and to build support for Palestinian political causes. The first Palestine Arab Women's Congress was convened in Jerusalem in 1929. All in all, thirty to forty clubs sprang up in Palestine after World War I, two of which were of particular political importance. One was the Muslim–Christian Association, which was led by older politicians associated with the most notable families of Arab Palestine and had branches in a number of cities. Among the planks in its political platform was firm opposition to Zionist immigration and to the creation of a Jewish national home in Palestine. The other was the Supreme Muslim Council. Led by al-Hajj Amin al-Husayni, the mufti of Jerusalem, the council's declared purpose was the supervision of Muslim affairs, especially in matters pertaining to the administration of religious trusts and shari'a courts. In addition, however, it soon became an important vehicle for the articulation of Palestinian opposition to the Zionist project.

The political map of Palestine changed after World War I. The Ottoman Empire was dismantled following the Turkish defeat in the war, with most of its provinces in the Arab Middle East divided between the British and the French; this involved three significant and interrelated developments concerning Palestine. First, despite Arab objections, Britain established itself as the colonial power in the country and was granted a "mandate" in Palestine by the League of Nations in 1922. Palestinians had hoped that independence would follow the end of Ottoman rule, even as they debated among themselves whether or not this should be as a province in an independent Syrian Arab state. In November 1918, for example, six patriotic and religious societies and more than one hundred prominent individuals addressed a petition to British military authorities in which they proclaimed their affinity with Syria.[11] In February 1919, delegates at a meeting of the Jerusalem and Jaffa Muslim–Christian societies adopted a platform that not only expressed opposition to Zionism but also called for unity with Syria, stating, "We consider Palestine as part of Arab Syria as it has never been separated from it at any time."[12] But postwar diplomacy produced neither Palestinian independence nor unity with Syria nor even Syrian independence as the French became the colonial power in that country. Mandatory arrangements were nonetheless conceived as transitional, to be in place while the country prepared, presumably with British assistance, for its eventual independence. The relevant provision from the league's resolution, adopted in July 1922, stated,

> Certain communities formerly belonging to the Turkish Empire have reached a stage of development where their existence as independent nations can be provisionally recognized subject to the rendering of administrative advice and assistance by a Mandatory power until such time as they are able to stand alone.

The second significant development was the incorporation of the Balfour Declaration into the mandatory instrument. The declaration was issued in 1917 by Lord Balfour, the British foreign secretary, and its key provision stated,

His Majesty's Government view with favor the establishment in Palestine of a national home for the Jewish people, and will use their best endeavors to facilitate the achievement of this object, it being clearly understood that nothing shall be done which may prejudice the civil and religious rights of existing non-Jewish communities in Palestine, or the rights and political status enjoyed by Jews in any other country.

Issued in response both to Zionist lobbying in Britain and to Britain's own war needs and strategic calculations, the declaration was strongly denounced by Palestinians and other Arabs. Not only did it indicate British support for Zionism; it also contravened a promise to support Arab independence after the war that the British had made two years earlier. This promise was recorded in an exchange of letters in 1915 between Hussein, the sharif of Mecca and an important British ally during the war, and Sir Henry McMahon, the British high commissioner in Egypt. In this correspondence, McMahon stated that "Great Britain is prepared to recognize and support the independence of the Arabs in all the regions within all the limits demanded by the Sharif of Mecca." Although Britain attempted to explain away the contradictions between its various statements, the situation was clarified after the war, and Palestinians were disturbed not only that the promise of independence had not been honored but also that the Balfour Declaration, reflecting Britain's sympathy for the Zionist project, had been reaffirmed through its inclusion in the preamble of the mandatory instrument for Palestine. The preamble also contained language giving explicit recognition "to the historical connection of the Jewish people with Palestine and to the grounds for reconstituting their national home in that country." Among the various articles of the mandatory instrument was a provision declaring that "the Administration of Palestine . . . shall facilitate Jewish immigration under suitable conditions and shall encourage . . . close settlement by Jews on the land, including State lands and waste lands not required for public purposes."[13]

The third development was the fixing of Palestine's borders and, specifically, the creation of separate mandates for Palestine and Transjordan (see Chapter 1, Map 1.4). Under its general mandatory authority and with approval from the League of Nations, Great Britain established Transjordan as a semiautonomous state on the east side of the Jordan River. The British hoped by this action to reduce opposition from the Arabs, and for this purpose, too, they recognized Abdallah ibn Hussein, a son of the sharif of Mecca, as leader of this state. This established the Hashemite dynasty in Transjordan, later to become Jordan. Unlike other British policies, these actions were bitterly denounced by the Zionists, whose territorial aspirations included land to the east of the river, and the Jews were particularly angry when Britain closed Transjordan to Jewish immigration and settlement. Although the Zionists claimed that the Balfour Declaration recognized their right to construct a national home on both sides of the Jordan River, the terms of the mandate specified that the provisions of the Balfour Declaration, and of other clauses supportive of Zionism, need not apply in the territory east of the river. These developments led to the creation in 1925 of a new Zionist party, the Revisionist Party, which took its name from the party's demand that the mandate be revised to recognize Jewish rights on both sides of the Jordan River. Labor Zionists had been and remained the dominant political faction in Zionist politics. But the emergence of the Revisionist Party, led by Vladimir Jabotinsky, added a new and more militant element to the Zionist political map.

CONSOLIDATION OF THE CONFLICT

Against this background, conflict between Palestinian Arabs and the country's growing Jewish population was probably inevitable, and not long after the war, there were indeed significant confrontations and disturbances. Clashes between the two communities resulted in violence as early as 1920. In April of that year, there was an Arab assault on Jews in Jerusalem. After two days of rioting, five Jews had been killed and more than two hundred had been injured, while four Arabs had been killed and twenty-one had been injured. In May 1921, much more serious and widespread disturbances took place. Anti-Jewish riots began in Jaffa and were followed by attacks in Rehovoth, Petach Tikva, Hadera, and other Jewish towns. Forty-seven Jews were killed and 140 wounded; Arab casualties were forty-eight dead and seventy-three wounded, mostly caused by British action to suppress the rioting. After a period of relative calm, there was new violence in August 1929, beginning with an Arab attack on Jews shouting nationalist slogans at the Western Wall in Jerusalem and followed by clashes elsewhere in the city and in other Palestinian towns. The worst violence took place in Hebron and Safed, with sixty-seven Jews killed in Hebron and eighteen killed in Safed. Overall, these events resulted in the deaths of 133 Jews and 116 Arabs, with 339 Jews and 232 Arabs wounded. Most Jews were killed by Arabs, while most Arabs were killed by security forces under British command. In each case, Jews pointed out, correctly, that the violence had begun with unprovoked attacks by Arabs. Arabs responded, understandably from their perspective, that the focus should not be on the immediate episodes but rather on the root causes of the disturbances and that these involved the steadily expanding and increasingly unwelcome Jewish presence in Palestine.

The most important issue fueling Arab anger at this time was Jewish immigration. Zionists point to five identifiable waves of immigration, beginning, as noted, with that of the Bilu group in 1882. Each wave was larger than the preceding one, with the last beginning in the 1930s and composed primarily of those who were able to escape the growing Nazi menace in Europe. By 1945, approximately 550,000 Jews lived in Palestine, constituting roughly 31 percent of the country's population. Jewish land purchases were a related Arab complaint. The total amount of land acquired by the Jews was limited. It constituted no more than seven percent of mandatory Palestine on the eve of Israeli independence in 1948. Furthermore, much of the land, often of poor quality, was purchased from willing absentee Arab landlords, sometimes at inflated prices. Nevertheless, some of these sales resulted in the displacement of Arab tenant farmers and contributed to a growing class of landless and embittered Palestinian peasants. Land acquisition thus reinforced the Arab concerns about Jewish immigration, leading many to conclude that their country was in danger of being taken over by the newly arrived Jews.

The contribution of these concerns to the violence in Palestine was documented by a British commission of inquiry following the disturbances of May 1921. Directed by Sir Thomas Haycraft, the chief justice of Palestine, the commission placed the blame on anti-Zionist sentiment among the Arabs and also on a widespread belief among the Palestinians that Great Britain was favoring the Jews and according them too much authority. The report did denounce the Arabs as the aggressors. It also strongly criticized the police for failing to contain the violence. Nevertheless, the underlying problem on which the Haycraft Commission placed emphasis was of a different character. It concluded that "the fundamental cause of the Jaffa riots and

MAP 2.1   ■   Jewish Land Ownership in Palestine, 1947

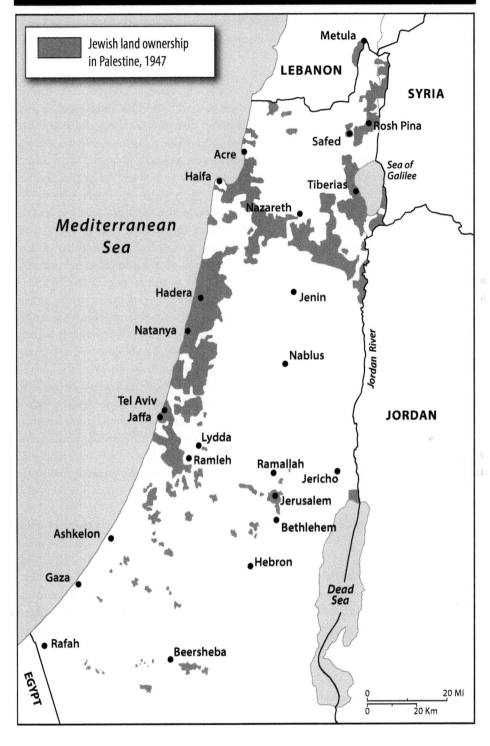

the subsequent acts of violence was a feeling among the Arabs of discontent with, and hostility to, the Jews, due to political and economic causes, and connected with Jewish immigration."[14]

The Zionists, as expected, rejected these conclusions. They insisted Arab anti-Zionism, at least among ordinary Palestinians, was being deliberately fostered and manipulated by self-serving Palestinian leaders. The latter, they charged, were fearful that the introduction of modern and Western ideas would undermine the feudal social and political structure that supported their privileged positions. Although there may well have been a measure of accuracy in these contentions, the Haycraft Commission refused to draw from them any suggestion that the riots would not have occurred "had it not been for incitement by the notables, effendis and sheikhs." According to the commission's report, "the people participate with the leaders, because they feel that their political and material interests are identical."[15]

Despite the deteriorating situation, interpersonal relations between Arabs and Jews in Palestine were not uniformly hostile during this period. Some leaders and intellectuals in the two communities carried on personal friendships. It was also common for Arabs and Jews in rural communities to visit one another and attend weddings, circumcisions, and so forth in each other's villages; and even after the violence of 1929, such relationships did not entirely disappear. A British commission investigating these disturbances observed in 1930, for example, that "it . . . is very noticeable in traveling through the villages to see the friendliness of the relations which exist between Arab and Jew. It is quite a common sight to see an Arab sitting on the veranda of a Jewish house."[16] Nevertheless, such relationships became increasingly rare over the course of the interwar period as the incompatibility of Arab and Zionist objectives in Palestine, and the fact that the two peoples were on an apparently unavoidable collision course, became steadily more evident and eroded any possibility of compromise.

As institutions and enterprises that brought Jews and Arabs together became increasingly rare and for the most part marginal within both communities, two essentially separate societies emerged in Palestine. Both developed and became more complex, with the *yishuv* continuing to grow in numbers and becoming increasingly modern and self-sufficient, and Palestinian society, despite the persistence of traditional leadership patterns, becoming more mobilized, integrated, and politically conscious. But with each community evolving according to its distinct dynamic and rhythm, all of the momentum pushed toward continuing confrontation and violence.

A new and more sustained round of disturbances began in 1936, starting with a call by Arab leaders for a general strike "until the British Government introduces a basic change in its present policy which will manifest itself in the stoppage of Jewish immigration."[17] Six Palestinian political factions formed the Higher Arab Committee at this time to coordinate strike activities, and this in turn brought endorsements from the Arab mayors of eighteen towns and petitions of support signed by hundreds of senior- and middle-level civil servants. Thousands of workers subsequently left their jobs, and numerous businesses were shut down. There was also considerable violence associated with these events. A demonstration in Haifa in May turned into a riot, for example, with demonstrators attacking police and security forces firing into the crowd and killing several persons. By the middle of June, the British reported that they had arrested more than 2,500 persons in connection with various disturbances. The general strike formally ended in October, but the country had by this time entered a period of prolonged disorder. Commonly known as the "Arab Revolt," clashes continued intermittently until 1939, when interrupted by World War II. After the war, the pattern of civil conflict resumed.

These events brought increased visibility to the Palestinian cause. Despite the Zionist contention that popular anti-Jewish sentiment was for the most part manufactured and manipulated by Arab leaders, the Arab Revolt left little doubt that there was widespread opposition to Zionism among the indigenous inhabitants of Palestine. The cost-benefit ratio was not entirely favorable to the Palestinians, however. The disturbances were highly disruptive to the Palestinian economy and social order, and they succeeded neither in slowing Jewish immigration nor in bringing a change in British policy.

These disturbances led the British to establish another commission of inquiry—the Peel Commission, which submitted a comprehensive and balanced report in 1937. Among its major findings was the conclusion that the unrest of 1936 had been caused by "the desire of the Arabs for national independence" and by "their hatred and fear of the establishment of the Jewish National Home." The report added, moreover, that these were "the same underlying causes as those which brought about the disturbances of 1920, 1921, 1929 and 1933," and also that they were the *only* underlying causes, all other factors being "complementary or subsidiary." The commission then offered a bold proposal for the future of Palestine. "An irrepressible conflict has arisen between two national communities within the bounds of one small country," the commission report stated. "About 1,000,000 Arabs are in strife, open or latent, with some 400,000 Jews. There is no common ground between them."[18] Therefore, the mandate should be terminated and, in order that each national community might govern itself, the territory of Palestine should be partitioned. More specifically, the Peel Commission proposed creation of a small Jewish state. The territory suggested for this state included the coastal plain, though not the port cities of Jaffa, Haifa, and Acre, and most of the Galilee. The remaining territory, with the exception of a corridor from Jaffa to Jerusalem, which was to remain under British control, would be given over to the Palestinians. The commission also envisioned an exchange of populations in connection with partition, which for the most part would involve the resettlement of Arabs living within territory proposed for the Jewish state.

Although partition was a logical response to the deepening conflict, the Peel Commission's report was rejected by the protagonists. Zionists judged that their state would possess an inadequate amount of territory, and they also refused to accept the loss of Palestine's most important cities. The Twentieth Zionist Congress, held in Zurich in August 1937, thus passed a resolution declaring that "the scheme of partition put forward . . . is unacceptable." The congress did not reject the principle of partition, however, and in fact welcomed the Peel Commission's recognition that creation of a Jewish state was desirable. Wisely choosing to regard this critical aspect of the commission's recommendations as an important opportunity, it empowered the Zionist executive "to enter into negotiations with a view to ascertaining the precise terms of His Majesty's Government for the proposed establishment of a Jewish State."[19] In contrast to the careful and politically calculated response of the Zionists, the Arab Higher Committee rejected the Peel Commission's proposal totally and unequivocally. Al-Hajj Amin, head of the committee, as well as other Palestinian spokesmen proclaimed that Britain had neither the authority nor the right to partition Palestinian territory. Faced with this opposition, Britain allowed the Peel Commission proposal to die after a year of unproductive negotiations.

Communal conflict diminished during the war but thereafter resumed with more intensity than ever, leading the British, who were increasingly unable to keep order, to formally and publicly acknowledge in February 1947 what had long been evident: that it was not within London's power to impose a settlement in Palestine. The British government then announced that it would turn the matter over to the United Nations, the successor to the League of Nations on whose behalf Britain was, in theory at least, exercising the mandate. The UN accepted the return of the mandate, and in May, the world body established an eleven-member Special Committee on Palestine (UNSCOP) to assess the situation and make recommendations.

The UNSCOP submitted its report at the end of August. It contained both a majority and a minority proposal. The majority endorsed the idea of partition but added several new features. First, the division of territory differed from that proposed by the Peel Commission, giving more territory to the Jews but with each state having three noncontiguous regions that many considered impractical. Second, the majority proposed that the two states establish by treaty a formal economic union and then added that the independence of neither state should be recognized until such a treaty had been signed. Finally, this proposal envisioned the establishment of an international enclave surrounding Jerusalem and extending as far south as Bethlehem. The minority proposal derived its inspiration from the idea of binationalism and called for the Arab and Jewish political communities to be united within a federal political structure. Under this proposal, the federal government would have full powers in such areas as defense, foreign relations, finance, and immigration.

The Arabs rejected both of these proposals. They adhered to their long-held position that Palestine was an integral part of the Arab world and that from the beginning its indigenous inhabitants had opposed the creation in their country of a Jewish national home. An image often presented by Palestinian spokesmen was that of an occupied house. Arguing that the Jews had entered and then occupied the house of the Palestinians, as it were, against the will of the Palestinians and with the aid of European colonial powers, they asked, rhetorically, how can someone pretend that he is reasonable because he is content to steal only half of another person's house, or label as *fanatic* the owner of the house who resists this theft? The Palestinians and other Arabs also insisted that the United Nations, a body created and controlled by the United States and Europe, had no right to grant the Zionists any portion of their territory. In what was to become a familiar Arab charge, they insisted that the Western world was seeking to salve its conscience for the atrocities of the war and was paying its own debt to the Jewish people with someone else's land.

The Zionists, by contrast, after initial hesitation declared their willingness to accept the recommendations of the majority. The Jewish Agency, which represented world Jewry in the effort to establish a Jewish national home in Palestine, termed the Zionist state that would be created by implementation of the UNSCOP proposals "an indispensable minimum," on the basis of which the Jews were prepared to surrender their claims to the rest of Palestine. In responding to Arab charges, Zionists insisted that Jews as well as Arabs had legitimate rights in Palestine, rights that derived from the Jewish people's historic ties to the land and that had in fact been recognized by the international community at least since the time of the Balfour Declaration. They also pointed out that their movement and its program neither began with the war nor derived their legitimacy from the Holocaust. Thus, they insisted, partition was a reasonable and fair solution—indeed, the only

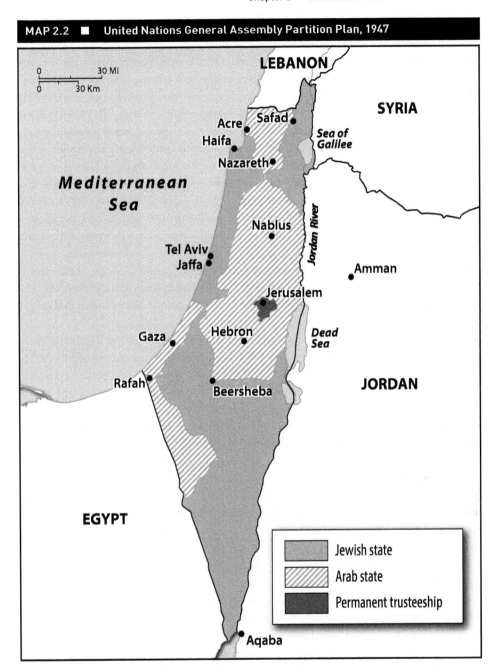

MAP 2.2 ■   United Nations General Assembly Partition Plan, 1947

logical solution—to the conflict in Palestine. Adding that the conflict, whatever its history, had reached the point when compromise was essential and that there was no body more capable of taking the lead in this matter than the United Nations, the Zionist Organization deployed what political influence it possessed in support of the partition plan recommended by the UNSCOP majority. The UN General Assembly endorsed the partition resolution, Resolution 181, on November 29, 1947.

War broke out in Palestine almost as soon as the UN passed the partition resolution. Arab leaders declared that they considered the partition resolution to be "null and void" and that it would not be respected by the Palestinian people. Thus, with Britain preparing to withdraw its military forces from Palestine, the Palestinians raised a guerrilla army, which was soon augmented by the arrival of six thousand to seven thousand volunteers from neighboring Arab countries. The Arab forces achieved a number of early successes, but the tide of the war had turned by April 1948, with the Zionist military force, the Haganah, scoring a succession of victories and gaining control of most of the territory allocated to the Jewish state by the United Nations. In accordance with the Haganah's master plan, *Tochnit Dalet* (Plan D), Jewish forces also launched operations that eventually brought control of some of the areas the UN had allocated for an Arab state in Palestine.[20]

The mandate was to be terminated on May 15, and as the date approached, the Zionists assembled the provisional National Council. This body in turn elected a thirteen-member provisional government, with David Ben-Gurion as its prime minister and defense minister. On May 14, the council assembled in Tel Aviv and proclaimed the establishment of the state of Israel in that portion of Palestine that the United Nations had allocated for a Jewish state. The new country was immediately recognized by the United States, the Soviet Union, and others. With these events, the state of Israel came into existence.

The war nonetheless continued for another eight months, and by the time it ended, both the political map and the demographic character of Palestine had changed dramatically. First, the Palestine Arab state envisioned by the United Nations partition resolution did not come into existence. Much of the territory envisioned for the Palestinian state was occupied by Zionist forces and became a permanent part of the state of Israel. The largest remaining block, the West Bank, was held by Transjordanian forces at the end of the war and was formally annexed in 1950, at which point Transjordan became the kingdom of Jordan. What remained was the small Gaza Strip, which Egypt continued to occupy as a military district. These territorial arrangements became the permanent borders of the new Jewish state, on the bases of which Israel signed armistice agreements with its Arab neighbors in 1949. The division of Jerusalem was also part of the new territorial status quo. With Zionist and Transjordanian forces occupying different areas of the city at the end of the war, and thereafter separated by a strip of no-man's-land running north to south, East Jerusalem became part of Jordan, and West Jerusalem became part of Israel.

Second, the bulk of the Palestinian population left the country. Approximately 750,000 Arab men, women, and children either fled or were expelled from the country, making Jews the majority and transforming the Palestinians into stateless refugees. Although Jews and Arabs have long disagreed strenuously about the reasons for this exodus, which Palestinians call the *nakba*, or catastrophe, there is little doubt that many Palestinians were deliberately removed by Zionist forces from areas that became part of the state of Israel, including those originally intended for the Palestinian state. The best evidence suggests that three phases may be used to describe this exodus.[21] During the early months of the conflict, from the partition resolution through March or early April of 1948, it appears that Palestinians fled primarily in response to the fighting itself. Most were middle- and upper-class Palestinians who possessed the resources to support themselves while away from home and who almost certainly believed their absence would be temporary. They were not, for the most part,

MAP 2.3 ■ The Armistice Lines of 1949

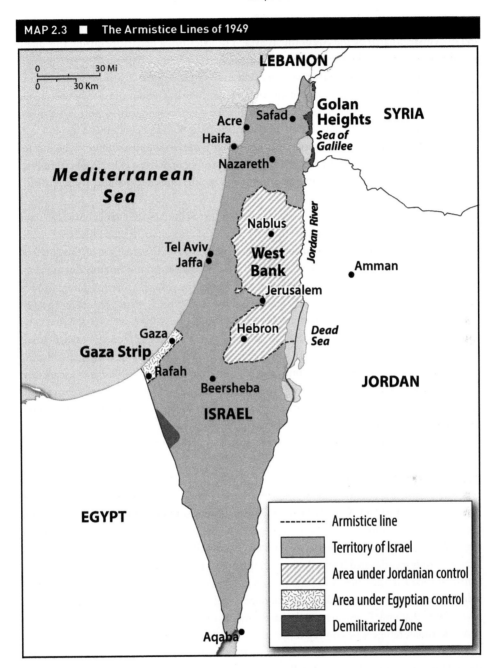

motivated either by Zionist intimidation or by Arab calls for them to leave but rather by a straightforward desire to distance themselves from wartime perils.

The refugee story became more complex after this period. Atrocities committed by Jewish forces, including a massacre at Deir Yassin in April, were an important stimulus to the intensifying Palestinian exodus. Although such episodes were relatively few in number, they contributed to Palestinian fears, especially as accounts of them were often embellished and then disseminated by the Arabs themselves. The Palestinian departure during this phase was also a consequence of Zionist military offensives. The first goal of these operations was to block the advance of armies from neighboring Arab states. Yet the Israeli military's Plan D also provided for the expulsion of civilian Arab populations in areas deemed to have strategic significance. This was not a consistent and coordinated Zionist policy. By summer 1948, however, Israeli leaders seem to have become consciously aware of the benefits that would result from the departure of the Palestinians, and, accordingly, decisions and actions by mainstream Zionist leaders were sometimes taken with the explicit intent of driving Palestinians from their towns and villages. This is illustrated by a campaign in July 1948 to expel the Arabs of Lydda and Ramleh.

During the concluding phase of the conflict in the fall of 1948, there appears to have been a more widespread and explicit understanding that it was in Israel's interest to facilitate the Arabs' departure. Thus, military operations in the southern part of the country, conducted in October and November, left almost no Palestinian communities in place behind the advancing Israeli lines. This was not always the case, even at this late date. For example, Arab villages in the Galilee, conquered in late October, were left intact. In addition, more generally, the Palestinian exodus had by this time assumed its own dynamic, and strong-arm tactics were often unnecessary; the mere arrival of Jewish forces was sometimes sufficient to provoke Arab flight. In any event, as a result of these developments during 1947 and 1948, celebrated by Jews but described by Palestinians as *al-naqba*, the catastrophe, Palestinians emerged from the war as stateless refugees. Most took up residence, usually in refugee camps, in the West Bank, the Gaza Strip, Lebanon, Transjordan, and Syria. Only about 160,000 remained in Israel, becoming non-Jewish citizens of the new Jewish state.

THE ARAB STATE DIMENSION

The situation that prevailed following Israeli independence in 1948 defined the character of the Arab–Israeli conflict for the next two decades. Having no state and dispersed among neighboring Arab countries, the Palestinians were no longer a significant political force. Opposition to Israel was thus spearheaded by the Arab states, for a time transforming the Zionist–Palestinian conflict inside Palestine into a regional, interstate Israel–Arab conflict. With leadership provided by Egypt, the Arabs refused to recognize Israel and continued to deny its legitimacy, proclaiming that only Palestinian Arabs have national rights in Palestine. They also demanded that Palestinian refugees be allowed to return to their homes in the territory from which they had been evicted. Israelis rejected these arguments and demands, of course. They reaffirmed the right of the Jews to a homeland in Palestine, emphasizing their historic and religious ties to the land. With respect to the refugee question, they argued that they bore little responsibility for the Palestinian exodus, especially since, they insisted, there would have been no exodus had the Palestinians accepted UN General Assembly Resolution 181 instead of going to war. Their contention, understandable from the Zionist perspective, was that the return of hundreds of thousands of Palestinians to what was now Israel would undermine and perhaps destroy the Jewish character of the state. Compensation and resettlement was the only realistic solution to the refugee problem, they insisted.

With no agreement on these two basic issues—Israel's right to exist and the Palestinian refugee problem—the Arab–Israeli conflict settled into a familiar pattern of charge and countercharge during the 1950s and 1960s. There were also armed confrontations during this period. In 1956, following an Egyptian blockade of Eilat, Israel's port city on the Red Sea, Israel, with help from Britain and France, attacked Egypt and scored a military if not a political victory in what became known as the Sinai–Suez War. It is notable that the Egyptian president, Gamal Abdel Nasser, had initially sought to explore the possibilities for peace with Israel in order that the energy and resources of his government might be devoted without distraction to domestic development.[22] Indeed, there were private contacts between Egyptian and Israeli officials during the first part of 1954. Any possibility that these contacts might have led to a breakthrough soon disappeared, however, as a result of events in Israel, in Egypt, and in the Egyptian-controlled Gaza Strip.

The Israeli action that did the greatest damage to hopes for an accommodation was a sabotage scheme planned in secret by Defense Ministry operatives and put into operation in July 1954. The plan was to use Israeli agents and about a dozen locally recruited Egyptian Jews to plant bombs and set fires at various public buildings in Cairo and Alexandria, including libraries of the United States Information Service. The purpose was to create anti-Egyptian sentiment in the United States at a time when Nasser's government was seeking arms and assistance from Washington and was also hoping to enlist US support in negotiations with Great Britain over military bases in the Suez Canal Zone. The plot was uncovered, however, and the majority of the participants were captured and tried. Surprised and angered by this Israeli action, Egypt immediately terminated its contacts with the Jewish state. In Israel, the episode was known as the "Lavon Affair," after the name of the defense minister, Pinhas Lavon, and it was followed by a bitter and politically disruptive argument about responsibility for the operation in Egypt.

Other events heightened tension between Israel and Egypt. Britain had long maintained troops along the Suez Canal, but in October 1954, Cairo and London reached agreement that these British forces would be withdrawn by the summer of 1956. Israeli ships had not been permitted to pass through the canal; but Israeli officials, who had been insisting on their country's right to use the waterway, worried that Egypt would oppose this more vehemently than ever and also that the British evacuation might bring new restrictions on the passage of non-Israeli ships bound for the Jewish state. Thus, in September, the Israeli government decided to test Egypt's intentions by sending a ship, the *Bat Galim*, into the Suez Canal, whereupon it was seized by Egyptian authorities. Coming in the wake of the Israeli-sponsored sabotage operation in Egypt, this pushed Egypt and Israel further along the road toward armed confrontation.

The Gaza Strip provided the arena for a third set of developments leading to the Sinai–Suez War. Palestinian guerrillas had for several years occasionally crossed into Israel from refugee camps in Gaza in order to commit acts of sabotage and harassment. Pipelines were cut and roads were mined in typical operations. Israelis blamed Palestinians for these attacks, but some also argued that Egypt's control of Gaza made Cairo at least partly responsible. There was disagreement at the time, even in Israel, about both the extent of these guerrilla raids and the degree to which they were abetted by Egypt. Nevertheless, insisting that the pattern of infiltration was intolerable, the government in Jerusalem adopted a deterrent strategy based on retaliatory strikes that were far more severe than the original provocations. The most massive Israeli strike occurred in February 1955; during the operation, Israeli forces ambushed an Egyptian military convoy and, according to Cairo, killed thirty-eight Egyptians and wounded sixty-two others. This brought to a definitive end whatever remained of the possibility for a rapprochement between Nasser's government and leaders of the Jewish state.

Determined to resist what it considered to be extremism and provocation on Israel's part, Cairo undertook to respond in kind. In the summer of 1955, it began to organize and equip squads of Palestinian commandos, known as *fedayeen*, and to send these units across the Gaza border into Israel. Guerrilla raids were often aimed at civilian targets. In addition, in September 1955 Egypt used its control of Sharm al-Shaykh at the southern tip of the Sinai Peninsula to close the Strait of Tiran, which leads into the Red Sea, to all shipping in and out of the southern Israeli port of Eilat. This was a casus belli as far as Israel was concerned, and in response, the government in Jerusalem prepared for war. Israel found willing allies in Britain and France, each of which had its own reasons for opposing some of Nasser's policies. On October 29, 1956, the Israeli Defense Forces (IDF) invaded Sinai and attacked positions of the Egyptian army. The next day, France and Britain vetoed Security Council resolutions calling upon Israel to leave Egypt without delay, and the day after that, French and British planes dropped bombs on Egyptian airfields. By early November, Israel had occupied the Gaza Strip and strategic locations throughout the Sinai Peninsula, including Sharm al-Shaykh, while France and Britain landed paratroopers and occupied the Suez Canal Zone. The confrontation, usually known as the Sinai–Suez War, ended in a complete military victory for Israel and its allies. For Egypt, which was forced to accept a ceasefire with foreign troops occupying large portions of its territory, the war was a humiliating military defeat.

Despite its military victory, Israel's political situation after the war was far from advantageous. On the one hand, the terms under which Israel withdrew its forces from the Sinai Peninsula and Gaza Strip were skewed in favor of Egypt. The United Nations established an international peace-keeping force, the United Nations Emergency Force (UNEF), to take up positions in the territory from which Israel withdrew and to act as a buffer between Israel and Egypt. But the arrangement specified that the UNEF could remain in place only as long as Egypt agreed and that it must be composed of troops from countries acceptable to Cairo. Furthermore, the Israeli withdrawal was not accompanied by a nonbelligerency agreement, as Israel had sought. Israeli calls for assurances that the withdrawal of its troops would not be followed by new Egyptian provocations were for the most part brushed aside by UN officials. On the other hand, the Suez Canal remained closed to Israeli shipping. Egypt's nationalization of the canal also enabled Nasser to claim that he stood up to British and French imperialism and brought an end to the last vestiges of colonialism in Egypt, thereby increasing his prominence and influence in inter-Arab and third-world circles. All of this left Jerusalem with little to show for its military victory, whereas significant political gains had been realized by Egypt and Nasser.

Another legacy of the war was Egypt's determination to rebuild its army in order to confront Israel from a position of strength should there be military conflict in the future. Despite the Israeli withdrawal, Egyptian officials worried after the war that Jerusalem might have expansionist impulses. They noted with concern, for example, that Ben-Gurion had declared after the invasion of Sinai that "our forces did not infringe upon the territory of the land of Egypt" and that the Sinai Peninsula "has been liberated by the Israeli army."[23] The Egyptians were therefore eager to prepare for whatever confrontations the future might bring, and in this, Cairo found a willing ally in the Soviet Union. The delivery of Soviet arms soon brought a considerable increase in the strength of Egypt's military forces. These developments, too, helped to shape the political order that emerged in the Middle East after the Sinai–Suez War—an order, as it turned out, that a decade later brought a new war between Israel and its Arab neighbors: the June 1967 War.

The decade between 1957 and 1967 saw Syria emerge as another important element in the Arab–Israeli equation. Syria joined with Egypt in February 1958 to form the United Arab Republic; and although the experiment in political unification lasted only until September 1961, Damascus became an increasingly important player in inter-Arab politics and in the Arab–Israeli conflict. In contrast to the border between Israel and Egypt, where 3,400 UNEF troops were assigned to keep peace, the frontier between Syria and Israel was the scene of frequent clashes. Syria sometimes fired on Israeli farmers working land claimed by the Arabs, for example, and Jerusalem periodically launched retaliatory strikes. Israeli and Syrian forces also sometimes traded fire directly across the demilitarized zone.

The regime in Damascus became increasingly militant and ideologically opposed to compromise with Zionism during this period, and from the Israeli point of view, this was the major cause of the tension along the Israeli–Syrian border. From the Syrian perspective, however, Israeli provocations were the source of the problem. Damascus charged that while Israel cultivated land in the demilitarized zone between the two countries, it frequently employed border police to prevent Arabs from doing the same. Syria also charged that Israel was illegally denying use of the Sea of Galilee to Syrians and Palestinians. Although the lake lies wholly within the Jewish state, its northeastern shore defines the border between Israel and Syria; and Damascus claimed that Arabs living along the sea were therefore entitled to fish in the lake without interference from Jerusalem. Finally, in what eventually became the most important source of tension, Syria objected vehemently to an Israeli plan to draw large quantities of water from the Sea of Galilee for irrigation and industrial development inside the Jewish state. This plan was of concern not only to Syria but to other Arab states as well, and in 1960, the Arab League called it "an act of aggression against the Arabs, which justifies collective Arab defense."[24]

Various Palestinian organizations also appeared on the scene about this time and involved themselves in both inter-Arab politics and the conflict between the Arab states and Israel. There were a number of clandestine and small-scale guerrilla movements, the most important of which was Fatah, led by Yasir Arafat. Fatah is an acronym for the Palestinian National Liberation Movement [*Harakat al-Tahrir al-Filastini*], the order of the initials being reversed. In addition, the Palestine Liberation Organization (PLO) was established during this period. The PLO was actually a creation of the Arab states, established at the January 1964 Arab summit meeting in Cairo in order not only to demonstrate support for the Palestinians but also, and equally, to co-opt the Palestinian resistance movement and prevent the guerrilla organizations from drawing the Arab states into a war with Israel. Fatah and other Palestinian groups were thus extremely cautious in their dealings with the PLO, rightly regarding it as an agent of Nasser and other Arab leaders rather than an independent voice for the Palestinian cause.

Although it would play a critical role after 1967 when the Palestinian dimension returned to center stage in the Arab–Israeli conflict, the PLO was not an important participant in the Arab struggle against Israel during the first years of its existence. It did establish a Palestine Liberation Army, with units based in Egypt, Syria, and Iraq, but the force was kept under tight control and was not a major factor in the escalating tension. By contrast, Fatah and other Palestinian guerrilla groups began to carry out raids against Israeli targets. By the end of 1964, they had decided to break with the PLO; and during 1966 and the first months of 1967, operating primarily from Jordan but with active Syrian support, Fatah carried out commando operations against the Jewish state. Damascus also sponsored guerrilla raids against Israel by other Palestinian commando groups.

By themselves, these raids were no more than a minor irritant for Israel. But reinforced by occasional Syrian military actions and a steady barrage of propaganda emanating from Damascus, guerrilla raids fostered a climate of uncertainty in the Jewish state. Many Israelis became convinced that Syria was laying the foundation for a full-scale guerrilla war, and as public concern mounted, the government in Jerusalem debated the pros and cons of a major attack against Syria. In the meantime, driven by what one analyst called "a nearly irresistible determination to react,"[25] Israel carried out a number of strikes in response to Fatah raids launched from Jordan. In November 1966, for example, Israeli forces invaded the West Bank in the region south of Hebron and carried out a major attack on the towns of as-Samu, Jimba, and Khirbet Karkay. This large-scale military operation, the most extensive since the Sinai–Suez War, resulted in the deaths of several Jordanian civilians and a larger number of Jordanian military personnel, as well as extensive property damage.

Against this background, Egypt signed a mutual defense pact with Syria in November 1966. Cairo entered into the agreement largely in hopes of restraining Damascus and reducing the chances of a major Arab–Israeli confrontation. But the Syrians would not permit Egyptian troops to be stationed on their soil, thus leaving Cairo with only limited ability to control Syrian behavior. Moreover, the agreement gave Damascus the ability to control Egyptian behavior. By sufficiently provoking Israel, the Syrians could elicit a military response from Jerusalem, and this in turn would drag Egypt into a war with the Jewish state.

Continuing Fatah raids against Israel added to the tension in early 1967, as did clashes between Israel and Syria. In April, for example, a conflict over the cultivation of disputed lands in the Israeli–Syrian demilitarized zone led to a major engagement. Following an exchange of fire between forces on the ground, Israel and Syria both sent planes into the air, and six Syrian MIG aircraft were shot down in a dogfight over Mount Hermon. Each side blamed the other for initiating the incident, and Syria also condemned Egypt for failing to come to its aid.

In another critical development, the Soviet Union informed Syria and Egypt on May 13 that its intelligence assessments indicated the presence of Israeli troops massing near the Syrian frontier. This information turned out to be false, raising questions about Soviet motivation.[26] A common view is that the Russians knowingly and deliberately passed false information to the Arabs. According to one assessment, the Soviets wanted Nasser to commit his forces in Sinai in order to deter the Israelis from attacking the regime in Damascus.[27] Alternatively, some analysts suggest that the Russians may have believed the reports they delivered. In any event, the reports were taken seriously by the Arabs and helped to solidify their conviction that an invasion of Syria was imminent.

The final act in the drift toward war opened on May 16, when Egyptian authorities declared a state of emergency and instructed the UNEF to withdraw from Sinai in order that its positions might be occupied by the armed forces of Egypt. Because Cairo was fully within its rights in ordering the UN force out of Egyptian territory, the UN complied three days later, removing the buffer that had separated Egypt and Israel since 1956 and instantly transforming the Israeli–Egyptian border into a second focus of concern. Regardless of what may or may not have been Jerusalem's prior intentions, the prospects for an armed conflict between Israel and Egypt, as well as between Israel and Syria, increased significantly with the departure of the UNEF.

There was little disagreement that Nasser's government was acting with proper authority; the UNEF's presence in Egypt had from the beginning been subject to the approval of the government in Cairo. But many, especially in Israel, argued that the UN secretary-general, U Thant, should not have so speedily complied with the demand and should rather have temporized in order to provide time for a diplomatic intervention. Some argued, for example, that he might have insisted that he needed time to consult the Security Council about a possible threat to international peace.

There were also differing opinions about the intentions of Nasser himself. Pro-Israeli and some other sources assert that the Egyptian leader was eager to confront Israel, both to avenge the military defeat his country had sustained in 1956 and also to solidify his claims to leadership in the Arab world. Others, including many neutral as well as pro-Arab analysts, argue that the Egyptian president was for the most part overtaken by events and perhaps to a degree by his own rhetoric; he thus found himself moving inexorably toward a confrontation he in fact would have preferred to avoid. As one student of Egypt suggests, "It is very probable that Nasser himself believed he would have more time to think out his next move and was surprised by U Thant's quick compliance."[28]

After the UNEF departed, Egyptian troops moved up to the frontier. They were also now in unrestricted control of Sharm al-Shaykh at the southern tip of the Sinai Peninsula, and Nasser on May 23 used his forces there to close the Strait of Tiran to Israeli shipping. Those who believe Cairo was not seeking war assert that Nasser took this step without the guidance of a master plan, or even careful premeditation, having in effect been pressured to do so by the escalating tension in the region more generally. As leader of the most powerful Arab state, however, he could hardly refrain from imposing a blockade on Israel at a time when Jerusalem was thought to be planning an attack on his Syrian allies, to whose defense he was committed by formal treaty obligations. Yet in taking this step, Nasser and other Egyptian leaders understood that it would be considered a casus belli by Israel. Indeed, a number of senior Egyptian officials rightly concluded at the time that closing the strait to Israel made war inevitable.

The Israeli cabinet met in emergency session in response to these developments, agreeing that closure of the Strait of Tiran could not be tolerated but initially considering diplomatic as well as military options for reopening the waterway. Then, on June 5 Israel carried out a devastating strike against its Arab neighbors. With awesome precision, Israeli planes attacked the airfields of Egypt and other Arab states. More than 350 Arab bombers and fighter planes were knocked out within the first two days of the war, along with several dozen transport aircraft. On the ground, Israeli forces pushed into Sinai and Gaza on the Egyptian front and into East Jerusalem and the West Bank on the Jordanian front. The main battles with the Syrians were fought on the Golan Heights, overlooking the Upper Galilee. Despite stiff resistance in some areas, the Israelis pushed forward on all fronts and were soon in control of large stretches of Arab territory.

The war was a crushing defeat for the Arabs, and by June 10, Egypt, Syria, and Jordan had all agreed to cease-fire arrangements. Some sources put the number of Arab soldiers killed as high as twenty thousand, although estimates vary widely. There were 766 soldiers killed on the Israeli side.

The impact of the June 1967 War cannot be overstated. It introduced critical new elements into the Arab–Israeli conflict, including a revival of concern with its central Palestinian dimension. Since Israel's victory left it in possession of land that had previously been part of Egypt, Jordan, or Syria, or controlled by Egypt in the case of the Gaza Strip, the most immediate result of the June 1967 War was a change in the territorial status quo.

The area under Israeli control at the end of the fighting included five Arab territories: the Sinai Peninsula, the Gaza Strip, the West Bank, East Jerusalem, and the Golan Heights. Two of these territories, the Sinai Peninsula and the Gaza Strip, were captured from Egypt. The Sinai is a vast region but is sparsely populated, owing primarily to its inhospitable mountainous and desert terrain. Unlike Sinai, Gaza was not an integral part of Egypt but rather a portion of Palestine that had come under Cairo's administrative control as a result of the 1947–1948 war. Small and densely populated, the precise opposite of Sinai, its landmass is only 140 square miles, but in 1967, the tiny territory was home to a population of about 360,000, almost 90 percent of whom were Palestinian refugees from the 1947–1948 war.

Another territory that came under Israeli control as a result of the June 1967 War was the West Bank, which some Israelis prefer to call by the biblical names of Judea and Samaria. The West Bank, which is about one-quarter as large as pre-1967 Israel, was left in Jordanian hands at the conclusion of the 1947–1948 war. It was formally annexed by the Hashemite kingdom in 1950, and Israeli officials insist that it would have remained a part of Jordan had King Hussein not entered the June 1967 War in support of Egypt and Syria. Capture of the West Bank, along with Gaza, gave Israel control over all of the territory that had been allocated for Jewish and Palestinian states under the United Nations partition resolution of 1947—the territory between the Mediterranean Sea and the Jordan River from which the international community had once sought to carve both a state for Jews and a state for Palestinian Arabs.

As in the case of the Gaza Strip, Israel's capture of the West Bank had demographic as well as territorial implications. It not only extended the Jewish state's control over the land of Palestine; it also placed hundreds of thousands of additional Palestinian Arabs under Israeli military administration. In 1950, the population of the West Bank was composed of about 400,000 indigenous Palestinians who had not left their homes as a result of the 1947–1948 war and approximately 250,000 more who were refugees from other parts of Palestine. By June 1967, the West Bank's population had grown to approximately 900,000, but about one-quarter of this number fled eastward across the Jordan River during and shortly after the fighting, many becoming refugees for the second time. This meant that after the war not only did Israel control all of the land that had been allocated for a Palestinian state but also that more than one million Palestinians were living in the territories Israel had recently captured and now occupied.

East Jerusalem was an integral part of the West Bank prior to 1967, but Israel almost immediately gave the city a legal status different from that of other occupied territories and took action to separate it from the rest of the West Bank. Although a number of foreign powers, including the United States, spoke out against any permanent change in the legal and political circumstances of the occupied territories, Israel was determined that there should be no return to the status quo ante in East Jerusalem. Thus, without debate, the Knesset (parliament) empowered the minister of the interior to apply Israeli law and administration "in any area of Palestine to be determined by decree," and the next day, the government used this power to proclaim the unification of Jerusalem. The Israeli and Jordanian sections of the city were merged into a single municipality under Israeli control, and the borders of the new municipality were enlarged to include Mount Scopus, the Mount of Olives, and several adjacent Arab villages. All of the barriers and military installations that had separated the two halves of the city since 1948 were thereafter removed.

The Golan Heights, captured from Syria, is the final piece of territory that Israel occupied as a result of the war. The Golan is a forty-five-mile-long plateau that lies immediately to the east and rises sharply above Israel's Upper Galilee. An integral part of Syria, the Golan had a population of about 120,000 before the war, the vast majority of whom were Syrian citizens. Not being a part of Palestine, the Golan Heights, like the Sinai Peninsula, derives much of its significance for the Arab–Israeli conflict from its potential strategic value in any future armed conflict. From an elevation averaging two thousand feet, the Golan dominates the entire northern "finger" of Israel stretching up to the border with Lebanon.

The June 1967 War gave the world community new determination to address the Arab–Israeli conflict, and international efforts at mediation, centered principally at the United Nations, began within days of the cessation of hostilities. On July 4, responding to Israel's annexation of Jerusalem, the General Assembly passed a resolution declaring any alteration of the city's status to be without validity and calling on the Jewish state to rescind the measures it had already taken. On June 30, a draft resolution was circulated by a group of Latin American countries. It called for Israeli withdrawal from Arab territories captured in the war, an end to the state of belligerence, freedom of navigation in international waterways, and a full solution to the Palestinian refugee problem. Both Israel and the United States opposed the resolution because it did not call for Arab recognition of the Jewish state.

Diplomatic activity resumed in the fall, with the United Nations Security Council becoming the principal arena. Slow to start, the political bargaining became increasingly intense and complicated in October and November, with various draft resolutions presented and debated. The compromise resolution that was finally adopted on November 22, 1967, was UN Security Council Resolution (UNSCR) 242; and despite the important disagreements it papered over, reflecting what is sometimes described as "constructive ambiguity," it became and has remained the most significant UN resolution pertaining to the conflict after the UN partition resolution

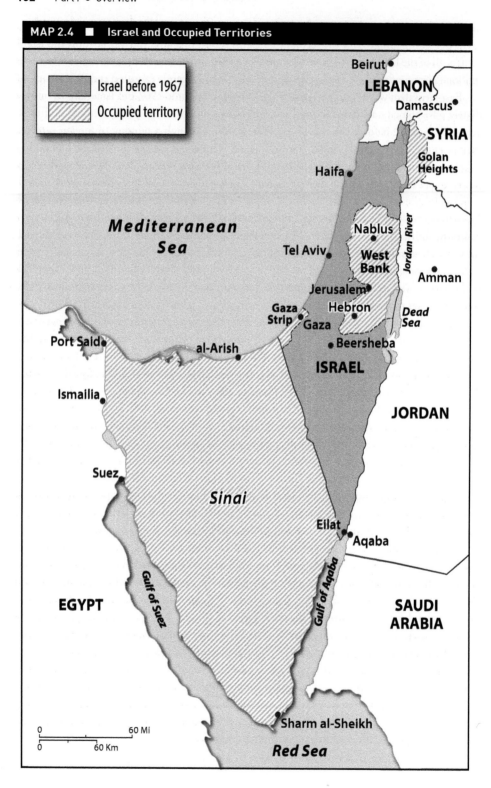

MAP 2.4 ■   Israel and Occupied Territories

of 1947. Emphasizing the inadmissibility of the acquisition of territory by war, the key provisions of UNSCR 242 call for (1) the withdrawal of Israeli armed forces from territories occupied in the recent conflict; (2) the termination of all claims or states of belligerency and respect for and acknowledgment of the sovereignty, territorial integrity, and political independence of every state in the area; (3) the guarantee of freedom of navigation through international waterways in the area; and (4) a just settlement of the refugee problem.

Although UNSCR 242 was endorsed by Israel, Egypt, and Jordan, and eventually by Syria as well, the parties had different interpretations of what had been agreed to and how the resolution should be implemented. The Arab states believed that implementation must begin with Israel's withdrawal from the territory it had captured, whereas Israel said it could not be expected to relinquish territory until the Arabs had ended the state of belligerency and recognized Israel. Distrustful of each other, each side argued that it would not be the first to surrender the elements that gave it leverage since its adversary would then have little incentive to fulfill, or to fulfill completely, its part of the bargain.

Even more important were the competing interpretations of the provision calling for Israel to withdraw from "territories" occupied in the recent conflict. The Arabs pressed, unsuccessfully, for language stating that Israel should withdraw from "all territories," or at least "the territories," which would have made it clear that the UN was calling for a full withdrawal—a withdrawal to the borders prevailing before the war. The United States would not agree to this, however, and so the Security Council resolution spoke only, and ambiguously, of "territories." The Arabs and many other observers claimed that the intent of the resolution was nonetheless clear: that Israel was indeed expected to surrender all of the Arab territory it had captured in the June 1967 War—that this was the price, and a fair price, for peace with the Arabs. Yet as Israeli spokespersons pointed out, the Arabs had sought to have this made explicit in the resolution and, having failed, agreed to endorse it nevertheless. As expressed by Abba Eban, at the time the Israeli foreign minister, "For us, the resolution says what it says; it does not say that which it has specifically and consciously avoided saying."[29]

Subsequent diplomatic efforts aimed to break the impasse, including efforts that focused on a step-by-step approach and reciprocal confidence-building measures. The thought was that despite their differing interpretations, both sides had agreed on the principles; therefore, the constructive ambiguity of UNSCR 242 might be the basis for productive negotiations. The most important of these efforts was the mission of Gunnar Jarring, a seasoned Swedish diplomat with prior experience in the Middle East, and Jarring's efforts did narrow the political distance between Israel and its Arab neighbors. For example, Egypt and Jordan abandoned their insistence that Israel withdraw from captured Arab territory before peace talks could begin, and they accepted the idea that the exchange of peace for land envisioned in UNSCR 242 could be carried out simultaneously, rather than in stages that had to begin with an Israeli withdrawal.[30] The Jarring mission nevertheless did not achieve a breakthrough, and it came to an end in April 1969, having made no real progress. Although constructive ambiguity had temporarily papered over the gap between the positions of Jerusalem on the one hand and those of Cairo and Amman on the other, thus enabling the passage of UNSCR 242, critical differences between the parties came to the fore as soon as negotiations began.

REEMERGENCE OF THE PALESTINIAN DIMENSION

The Palestinian question in the late 1960s was generally perceived as a refugee issue, as a problem involving displaced individuals in need of relief and rehabilitation; thus, consistent with its reliance on constructive ambiguity, UNSCR 242 had contented itself to call in the vaguest possible terms for a just settlement of the refugee problem. To the Arabs, however, and especially to the Palestinians themselves, the problem was one of statelessness. Even those who supported other aspects of UNSCR 242, as they interpreted these provisions, called this the "greatest fallacy" of the resolution.

The absence of help from the international community notwithstanding, Arafat and other Fatah activists continued their grassroots organizational efforts. They made little headway in the West Bank, thwarted in part by a local leadership class with ties to the Hashemite regime in Amman and, even more, by Israel's tough and effective security apparatus. By contrast, they were able to establish a political presence in the towns and especially in the refugee camps of the East Bank.[31] Swelled by new recruits attracted by the activism of the Palestinians in the wake of the crushing defeat of the Arabs in the June 1967 War, Fatah established a political department to coordinate its activities and to produce newspapers and booklets for distribution through its growing network of local committees. The movement also undertook to provide an expanding range of social services, establishing, for example, a number of clinics and healthcare projects. Although their scope and effectiveness should not be overstated, these activities helped to mobilize the Palestinian population and gave substance to the guerrillas' claim that they alone were working on behalf of the Palestinian cause.

Led by Fatah, the guerrilla organizations were now in a position to challenge the existing leadership of the Palestine Liberation Organization (PLO). They charged, correctly, that the PLO was the artificial creation of Arab governments seeking to prevent meaningful resistance and that its leadership had been selected not for their nationalist credentials but for their subservience to Nasser and other Arab heads of state. At the fourth Palestine National Council (PNC), held in Cairo in July 1968, Fatah and the other guerrilla movements obtained almost half of the 100 seats on the council. Fatah easily dominated the fifth PNC and emerged from the meeting with control of the PLO's key institutions, completing the guerrilla group's capture of the organization. In effect, a new, more representative, and more authentic PLO had been created. The Executive Committee was dominated by Fatah and its sympathizers, as there remained only one holdover from the old PLO. Yasir Arafat was elected chairman of the committee.

The institutional development of the PLO was accompanied by an important evolution of the organization's ideology. Despairing of effective assistance from Arab governments and determined that the Palestinian people should in any event speak for themselves in international affairs, the PLO's immediate concern was to make clear that the Palestinians required more than "a just settlement of the refugee problem," as UNSCR 242 had stated, and that there could be no resolution of the conflict with Israel without an end to Palestinian statelessness.

Beyond this core principle, Palestinians aligned their ideology with that of radical Arab intellectuals who, in the wake of the defeat in the June 1967 War, were questioning religious, cultural, and political traditions and calling for far-reaching reform. These areas, they argued, were at the root of Arab weakness and Israeli strength. According to one prominent Arab scholar, the Arabs were defeated because they lacked "the enemy's social organization, his sense of individual freedom, his lack of subjugation, despite all appearances, to any form of finalism or absolutism."[32] According to another,

> We must realize that the societies that modernized did so only after they rebelled against their history, tradition and values. . . . We must ask our religious heritage what it can do for us in our present and future. . . . If it cannot do much for us we must abandon it.[33]

Secularism was a key plank in the revolutionary platform of these intellectuals, and the concept appealed to the Palestinians for several reasons. With a substantial Christian minority in its ranks, the conduct of politics without reference to religion would both promote the unity of the Palestinian people and encourage the emergence of political processes that were progressive and truly egalitarian. The notion might also have public relations value, especially in the secular West, while at the same time shining a light on what Palestinians regarded as the discrimination, if not indeed the racism, inherent in Israel's character as a Jewish state. Accordingly, the Palestinians advanced what is sometimes called the "de-Zionization" proposal: that the Jewish state of Israel be replaced by a secular and nondenominational state in which Jews and Palestinian Arabs would all be citizens and live together as equals.

In January 1969, the Central Committee of Fatah adopted a declaration proclaiming that "the final objective of its [Fatah's] struggle is the restoration of the independent, democratic State of Palestine, all of whose citizens will enjoy equal rights regardless of their religion." Several months later, Fatah's chairman, Yasir Arafat, repeated these points, saying that the PLO offered an enlightened alternative to the Jews in Palestine:

> The creation of a democratic Palestinian state for all those who wish to live in peace on the land of peace . . . an independent, progressive, democratic State of Palestine, which will guarantee equal rights to all its citizens, regardless of race or religion.

Israelis and supporters of the Jewish state responded to the PLO's de-Zionization proposal in a predictable manner. Many argued that the Palestinians were not sincerely committed to their vision of Arab–Jewish rapprochement but rather had deliberately devised a strategy of propaganda and public relations calculated to appeal to Western audiences. Many also asserted that the PLO vision was fraught with ambiguities and contradictions, making it, whether put forth with sincerity or not, an unsatisfactory foundation for thinking about peace. Among other things, supporters of Israel argued that it was for Jews, not Palestinians, to determine the character of their political community: If the PLO were sincere in its insistence that every people has a right to self-determination, which was the basis for its repeated claim that this right could not be denied to the Palestinians, then surely it was for Jews themselves to define the political requirements of the Jewish people and to answer any questions that might arise about the relationship between Judaism and Zionism. Palestinians might reasonably complain that as a consequence of Zionism their own political rights had been abridged, but many Israelis argued that Palestinians could not plausibly assert that they know better than the Jews how Jewish political life should be structured or that they, the enemies of Zionism, have the right to determine whether the concepts of Jewish nationalism and Jewish statehood are or are not legitimate. Such an assertion would run directly counter to the principle of self-determination, in whose name the PLO had rejected not only Israeli efforts to deny the legitimacy of Palestinian nationalism but even attempts by the United Nations to specify the just requirements of the Palestinian people.

These institutional and ideological developments within the ranks of the PLO did not move the Arab–Israeli conflict nearer to a solution or convince many Israelis that the road to peace lay in the creation of a democratic and secular state. They did, however, alter international perceptions of the conflict in significant ways. They returned the attention of diplomats and would-be peacemakers to the Palestinian dimension of the conflict and forced an awareness, and ultimately an acceptance, of the Palestinians' demand that they be represented by men and women of their own choosing. These developments also contributed to a modified perception of the Palestinians themselves, who, as the PLO intended, were now increasingly viewed as a stateless people with a legitimate political agenda rather than a collection of displaced individuals requiring humanitarian assistance. This important evolution in the way the world saw the Arab–Israeli conflict can be traced directly to the political and ideological transformations that took place in the Palestinian community after the June 1967 War.

Although the restructuring of the PLO and the organization's ideological evolution brought growing recognition that the Palestinian problem formed the core of the Arab–Israeli conflict, the confrontation between Israel and the Arab states remained a pressing concern in the aftermath of the June 1967 War. Particularly significant were the hostilities between Israel and Egypt during this period, with dozens of armed exchanges and Nasser publicly acknowledging that his country had initiated a "war of attrition" against Jerusalem.

Egypt's declared objective in the war of attrition was to destroy the defensive fortifications that Israel had built on the eastern side of the Suez Canal, at the edge of the occupied Sinai Peninsula. The war dragged on from fall 1968 through summer 1970 as Israel responded with harsh retaliatory actions and Egypt then appealed to the Soviet Union for assistance. Early in 1970, approximately 1,500 Soviet personnel arrived in Egypt with advanced anti-aircraft equipment, including new SAM-3 missiles, and the momentum of the conflict for a time shifted in favor of Egypt. In March, April, and May of 1970, sixty-four Israelis were killed, 155 more were wounded, and six were taken prisoner. Then in mid-June, the United States proposed to Israel, Egypt, and Jordan that they accept a cease-fire. The US administration hoped that a reduction in hostilities between Egypt and Israel would check the growing Soviet influence in the region, and by including Jordan, the United States hoped to commit King Hussein to putting an end to raids by Palestinian guerrillas who opposed any settlement based on UNSCR 242. President Nasser accepted the US proposal after consulting with the Russians, and shortly thereafter, Israel agreed to the plan as well, bringing an end to the costly and prolonged war of attrition.

Additional tension during this period resulted from Palestinian commando raids launched against Israel from the East Bank. According to one Israeli source, these raids represented almost half of all the hostile acts carried out against the Jewish state in 1968 and 1969.[34] Israel responded with retaliatory strikes, and this put pressure on Jordan to confront the Palestinians and put an end to the attacks, including attacks on Israeli targets abroad that were planned from

Palestinian strongholds in Jordan. There was an even more important dimension to the growing conflict between the Jordanian government and the Palestinians, however. Many of the social and political institutions set up by the reorganized PLO had their headquarters in Jordan, and the Palestinian organization took control of many of the refugee camps in the country. In addition, not only did the PLO assume responsibility for organizing and administering life in the camps, but well-armed militia units patrolled the streets of Amman where, in order to demonstrate the power and independence of the guerrilla groups, they stopped pedestrians to examine identity papers and sometimes even directed traffic. Steadily encroaching on the prerogatives of the Jordanian state, the Palestinians were described by one analyst as "appealing to the people over the head of the government."[35]

King Hussein for a time seemed uncertain about how to respond to this challenge from the PLO. Throughout 1969 and the first half of 1970, his government avoided an all-out military confrontation with the Palestinians, but this came to an end in September. Led by the leftist Popular Front for the Liberation of Palestine (PFLP), the Palestinians dramatically escalated the stakes in what had been a war of relatively low intensity. PFLP agents made two unsuccessful attempts to assassinate the king early in September. A few days later, the same organization carried out a spectacular series of four airline hijackings. In an act intended as a symbolic attack on Jordanian sovereignty, two of the planes, one American and one Swiss, were flown to a little-used airstrip in the Jordanian desert, where their crew and passengers were held for four days. The Jordanians then responded with an assault designed to put an end to the challenge from the PLO. With their light weapons, the Palestinians had no chance against the disciplined, tank-backed troops of the Jordanian army, and the result during eleven days of fighting was a bloody and disastrous rout for the Palestinians, thousands of whom were killed. The official Jordanian estimate was 1,500 killed, although this figure is almost certainly too low. The fighting finally came to an end on September 27, when, in response to the PLO's desperate situation, Nasser persuaded King Hussein to accept a ceasefire. Sometimes described as the civil war in Jordan, Palestinians often refer to this deadly month as "Black September."

The military defeat handed to the PLO by the Jordanian army left the Palestinian organization in disarray. Although it still had a solid base of operations in Lebanon, from which it gradually rebuilt itself and eventually assumed a position of prominence on the international diplomatic stage, there was a possibility in the early 1970s that the resistance movement might disappear altogether. Palestinian leaders acknowledged that the PLO was on the verge of collapse during this period. "Not only were its military units defeated and fragmented," one of them wrote, but "the political and social work of the previous three years was practically destroyed."[36] This situation reduced Israeli concern about an external challenge from the PLO and allowed Jerusalem to focus its thinking about the Palestinians on the occupied West Bank and Gaza, territories that had been administered by Israel since the war of June 1967 and that in the early 1970s were inhabited by 700,000 and 350,000 Palestinians, respectively.

But even as Israel was formulating its policy toward the occupied territories and debating their future, the country received a severe shock from an unexpected quarter, one that indicated that the Palestinian dimension of the Arab–Israeli conflict had not yet made the attitudes and behavior of the Arab states a secondary consideration. On October 6, 1973, which was Yom Kippur, the Day of Atonement, the holiest day in the Jewish calendar, Egypt and Syria launched coordinated attacks on Israeli positions in the Sinai Peninsula and on the Golan Heights, taking the IDF completely by surprise and scoring important victories in the early days of the fighting. Thus began what Israelis call the Yom Kippur War, which is often called the Ramadan War by the Arabs because it occurred during Ramadan, the holiest month in the Islamic calendar and a month of fasting. The success of the Egyptian and Syrian attacks reflected careful and effective planning and coordination between the two Arab countries, as well as the skill and bravery with which both Egyptian and Syrian soldiers fought. Also, on both fronts, Arab fortunes were significantly enhanced by the failure of Israeli intelligence to give advance warning and, in some instances, by the complacency and inadequate organization that characterized Israel's forward bases.

Although these Arab military accomplishments were without parallel in any of the previous Arab-Israeli wars and were a justifiable source of pride to the Egyptians and the Syrians, the IDF was able to contain the threat on both fronts within several days and thereafter initiate a series of successful counterattacks. Many Israeli soldiers displayed bravery and even heroism during the difficult early days of the fighting. In addition, Israel was aided during the critical early stage of the war by Egypt's decision to consolidate its positions in western Sinai rather than to advance eastward, which enabled the IDF to use more of its resources against the Syrians on the Golan. The Syrian attack was accordingly broken on October 9, and thereafter, it was the Israelis who were moving forward. After this point, with Syria on the defensive, Israel was also able to concentrate more of its forces in the Sinai Peninsula, eventually knocking out hundreds of Egyptian tanks and routing the Egyptian army. Israel also received critical assistance from the United States in the form of a full-scale airlift of military equipment, and this, too, played a major role in the eventual outcome of the October 1973 War.

While the war left Israel in an advantageous military position, the country was nonetheless badly shaken. The intelligence failures of the IDF and associated battlefield losses during the first days of the fighting raised deep doubts about the country's military establishment. Furthermore, the somber mood in the Jewish state was greatly intensified by the heavy casualties that had been sustained. Much public anger was directed at Golda Meir and Moshe Dayan, prime minister and defense minister, respectively, and these sentiments were clearly visible during the Knesset elections that took place in December. The long-dominant Labor Party of Meir and Dayan was aggressively challenged by the right-wing Likud Union, which included in its platform the permanent retention of the West Bank and Gaza. Likud and two smaller opposition factions increased their representation by 50 percent in the balloting, capturing 39 of the assembly's 120 seats.

The mood in the Arab states was different. Despite their military defeat, they—not the Israelis—reaped the political benefits of the war. Recognition of this apparent anomaly was yet another factor contributing to the gloom in Israel. Political gains were made in particular by Anwar al-Sadat, Nasser's vice president who had become president of his country following the Egyptian leader's death in 1970. Prior to the 1973 war, Sadat, like other Arab leaders, had been derided for inaction and charged with a failure to end the humiliation imposed on his country by its disastrous defeat in the war of June 1967. During and after the 1973 war, by contrast, the Egyptian president was hailed at home for taking action to end the lethargy and defeatism that had reigned in Arab capitals since 1967. In the months that followed, Sadat was also welcomed on the international scene as an effective political strategist who had designed and implemented a plan to break the deadlock in the Arab–Israeli conflict.

It also soon became apparent that Sadat had carefully related his military actions to political objectives and that, from the Egyptian point of view, the October 1973 War had been part of a more elaborate plan that at its core was political and diplomatic. The Egyptian president had never intended more than a limited military operation; he had sought only to recapture enough Egyptian territory to show the Israelis that their forces were not invincible and, accordingly, that the Jewish state's security lay not in maintaining a territorial buffer but in seeking good relations with its neighbors. It is for this reason that Egyptian troops had not sought to drive eastward after their successful invasion of Sinai. Sadat continued this strategy in the immediate postwar period by improving relations with the United States and by working with the Americans to secure a partial Israeli withdrawal from the Sinai Peninsula, hoping to obtain through political action the breakthrough he had failed to achieve by military means. Having emerged from the war as a man of initiative and vision—a world statesman—he sought to consolidate and further enhance his new political status by demonstrating that his strategy would produce movement in the direction of an Israeli return to the pre-1967 borders.

The major international diplomatic initiative of the mid-1970s was undertaken by Henry Kissinger, at the time both the US secretary of state and President Richard Nixon's assistant for national security affairs. Having received signals that Egypt and Syria were now ready for compromise, and reasoning that Israel's postwar political troubles might lead Jerusalem to be more flexible on the issue of territorial withdrawal, Kissinger undertook an extended mission that subsequently came to be known as "shuttle diplomacy."

Tirelessly traveling back and forth between Jerusalem, Cairo, and Damascus, Kissinger eventually secured limited Israeli pullbacks in Sinai and the Golan Heights in return for a reduction in Egyptian and Syrian belligerency toward the Jewish state. Under agreements signed by Cairo and Jerusalem in January 1974 and September 1975, Israel relinquished a significant portion of Sinai. In return, the disengagement agreement specified that nonmilitary cargoes destined for or coming from Israel would be permitted to pass through the Suez Canal. Israel also obtained from Kissinger a promise that the United States would not recognize or negotiate with the PLO unless that organization explicitly accepted UNSCR 242 and thereby recognized the Jewish state's right to exist. The agreement with Syria was signed in May 1974. In return for Israeli withdrawal from a portion of the Golan Heights, the Syrian president, Hafiz al-Asad, promised to prevent Palestinian guerrillas from using Syrian territory to attack Israel.

An even more significant development, and one that again had Anwar al-Sadat occupying center stage, occurred two years later. Moreover, this development brought a new relationship between Egypt and Israel and solidified the evolution of the conflict from one in which the Arab state dimension had become preeminent to one in which the relationship between Israel and the Palestinians was again recognized as the core issue. This evolution was already well underway, of course, notwithstanding the war of attrition and the war of October 1973; and during this period, it was also pushed forward by developments both among Palestinians and within Israel.

Following its defeat in the civil war in Jordan, the PLO rebuilt its base in Lebanon, and by the mid-1970s, it had established a strong political and institutional foundation and initiated an increasingly successful international diplomatic campaign. Both the Arab League and the Organization of the Islamic Conference recognized the PLO as the "sole legitimate representative" of the Palestine people at this time. This was significant, in part, because it meant that the PLO, rather than King Hussein, was held to represent Palestinians in the occupied West Bank, almost all of whom were Jordanian citizens. The Non-Aligned Movement also adopted a resolution recognizing the PLO as the sole legitimate representative of the Palestinians, indicating that the PLO's campaign was bearing fruit beyond Arab and Islamic circles, and the movement also called on members to break off diplomatic relations with Israel. Yet another important accomplishment was Arafat's official visit to the Soviet Union in August 1974, during which the Soviets, too, agreed that the PLO alone represented the Palestinians. The culmination of this diplomatic campaign came in November, when Arafat was invited to address the United Nations General Assembly. The decision to invite the PLO to participate in the assembly's deliberations of the Palestine question was approved by a 105 to 4 vote, with twenty abstentions.

There was also an evolution of the PLO's ideological orientation during this period. Although it did not formally renounce the democratic secular state proposal, the twelfth PNC meeting, held in Cairo in 1974, adopted a ten-point program calling for the Palestinian revolution to be implemented in stages, which was widely understood to mean the PLO would now set as its immediate objective the creation of a Palestinian state in the West Bank and Gaza Strip. This was the first official expression of a willingness to accept anything less than the liberation of all of Palestine, leading many to conclude that a basis for compromise had been established. Indeed, observers pointed out that the phrase "liberation of Palestine," so prominent in the PLO's National Charter, had been replaced in the text of the program by the much more ambiguous "liberation of Palestinian land." In addition, in another significant departure from earlier PLO thinking, the 1974 PNC meeting accepted the possibility of political dialogue between a Palestinian state in the liberated territories and progressive- and peace-oriented forces in Israel.

Most Israelis dismissed these changes as distinctions without differences. They insisted that the idea of stages showed the PLO to be as committed as ever to the destruction of the Jewish state, and some Palestinian leaders who had supported the ten-point program declared that the establishment of a democratic state over the whole of Palestine did indeed remain their long-term objective. The impression that a change in PLO thinking had taken place nonetheless persisted, with many Palestinians and others arguing that what was declared to be an intermediate stage today might well be accepted tomorrow as the basis for a permanent solution.

These moderating trends were more prominently in evidence at the thirteenth PNC meeting, convened in March 1977. Although the details were left unspecified, the program represented a clear victory for Fatah and its supporters, including mainstream nationalists in the West Bank and Gaza Strip, and a defeat for the more uncompromising factions of the Palestinian left. These moderate and nationalist elements favored the pursuit of Palestinian goals through political rather than military action, placed emphasis on the establishment of an independent state alongside Israel, and even suggested that this state might form political alliances with progressive elements in Israel. As for the idea of a democratic secular state in all of Palestine, the proposal was not repudiated but was increasingly understood by Palestinians as a distant objective that would only be achieved, if at all, through natural, historical evolution. Thus, as summarized by one analyst, the significance of the thirteenth PNC meeting is this:

> After a three-year struggle, it was the "moderates" who had won in the PLO. By agreeing to participate in the peace process and endorse the idea of a Palestinian state [alongside Israel], the PLO appeared to be taking its full place in an international search for a settlement of the conflict.[37]

Ideological developments and gains in the international diplomatic arena were matched by an evolution of the political situation in the West Bank and Gaza Strip. Despite Israeli and Jordanian efforts to limit its influence, the PLO was growing steadily more popular among the Palestinian inhabitants of the occupied territories. Moreover, in the West Bank a new generation of pro-PLO political leaders emerged to rival the class of notables tied to Jordan, who had been dominant before 1967.

These trends were encouraged by Israeli policies that restricted the activities of Palestinian officials in order to prevent the emergence of an all–West Bank leadership. They were also encouraged by the expansion of quasi-political associations, such as labor unions and student movements, outside the control of the traditional elite. Each of these developments provided opportunities for the emergence of new and more nationalist-oriented political forces. Finally, and equally important, the expansion of opportunities for Palestinians to work in Israel weakened the position of established notable families. By 1974, approximately one-third of the West Bank labor force was employed in Israel; and, whatever the balance of benefits and disadvantages of such employment for individual workers, an important consequence was a reduction in their dependence on West Bank landowners and businesspeople, the backbone of the traditional political class. The magnitude and significance of the political shift taking place among Palestinians in the West Bank and Gaza were reflected in the West Bank municipal elections of April 1976, in which pro-PLO candidates defeated incumbents and gained control of the mayor's office and the Municipal Council in Nablus, Hebron, Ramallah, and eleven other towns.

As a result of these developments, the position of the PLO was radically different from what it had been only five or six years earlier. It had been possible to argue in 1970 and 1971, in the wake of the Jordanian civil war, that the revival of the Palestine resistance movement after June 1967 had run its course and that the PLO would now return to the periphery of the Arab–Israeli conflict. By 1976 or 1977, and probably as early as 1974 or 1975, it was evident that such assessments had been extremely premature. The PLO had achieved wide recognition in the international diplomatic arena, and a new generation of political leaders identified with the Palestinian organization had emerged in the West Bank and Gaza. The PLO had also built a formidable political infrastructure in Lebanon, effectively governing the large Palestinian population in that country and presiding over what some described as an autonomous ministate.

The evolution of the conflict was also shaped by Israel's policies toward the territories it had captured in the June 1967 War, particularly the West Bank and Gaza, which are part of historic Palestine. Israel maintained that its acquisition of the West Bank, Gaza, and other territories had been the result of a war forced on it by Arab belligerency; it was not, Israel insisted, the consequence of any deliberate plan to expand the borders of the Jewish state. Yet the government took steps almost immediately to alter the territorial status quo. First and most important, there was a deliberate effort to divide East Jerusalem from the rest of the West Bank, of which it had been an integral part prior to the June 1967 War. The part of the city formerly belonging to Jordan was merged with West Jerusalem shortly after the war, creating a unified municipal administration governed by Israeli law, and the borders of the new municipality were then expanded to the north, east, and south. The government also began to construct Jewish neighborhoods in former Arab areas, some of which were explicitly designed to give newly acquired sections of the city a more Jewish character and some of which were intended to create a physical barrier between East Jerusalem and the rest of the West Bank.

Israeli actions in the other captured territories were much more limited, and they were also the subject of disagreement among Israelis. Beginning in 1968, small Israeli paramilitary settlements were established in the Jordan Valley along the eastern perimeter of the West Bank. They were constructed for the purpose of preventing Palestinian commandos from infiltrating from the East Bank, and presumably, they could be dismantled should conditions later permit Israel to withdraw from the occupied territories in return for peace. Over time, however, the Jordan Valley settlements developed a solid economic foundation based on commercial agriculture, which provided a rationale for their maintenance and expansion that transcended the military objectives that had led to their creation.

Settlement activity after the June 1967 War was also undertaken by Israelis who were committed to permanent retention of the West Bank and Gaza. These Israelis referred to the former territory by the biblical designations of Judea and Samaria, terms chosen for the deliberate purpose of asserting that the territorial claims of the Jews predate those of the Arabs. In contrast with the Jordan Valley settlements, which were established for purposes relating to military security, these civilian communities were constructed by Israeli civilians with the intention that they would create a Jewish demographic presence in the occupied areas and lead eventually to the exercise of Israeli sovereignty over Judea, Samaria, and Gaza. The first initiative of these Israelis, who are often described as the "settler movement," was the construction of Qiryat Arba, a religious community adjacent to the West Bank city of Hebron.

These two sets of settlement activities reflect a division of opinion about the occupied territories, particularly about the West Bank and Gaza, that emerged after the June 1967 War and became one of the most important and contentious issues in Israeli politics during the 1970s. The centrist and politically dominant Labor Party endorsed the "land for peace" principle in UNSCR 242. There were debates within the party and among its supporters about whether Israel should relinquish all or simply most of the West Bank and Gaza, but the Labor-led government never argued that all or even most of the territory should be retained permanently by the Jewish state. The country's official position was that the UN resolution gave Israel international justification for maintaining its control of the territories, but only as long as the Arab governments persisted in their refusal to make peace. According to a report prepared by the Ministry of Defense, UNSCR 242 "confirmed Israel's right to administer the captured territories [but only] until the cease-fire was superseded by a 'just and lasting peace' arrived at between Israel and her neighbors."[38]

As noted, the Likud Union had become the most important opposition party in Israel, especially after the December 1973 election, and Likud and its supporters took a very different approach to the West Bank and Gaza. Aligned with the settler movement and various factions on the political right, Likud argued that the West Bank and Gaza were part of the historic "Land of Israel" and should be permanently retained by the Jewish state, even if the Arabs offered the country peace in return. Likud's improving political fortunes in the mid-1970s were helped by the blame for losses in the 1973 war that much of the public placed on the Labor government and its leaders. Likud also benefited greatly from demographic changes taking place in Israel. Jews whose families had emigrated from Middle Eastern countries during the decade following Israeli independence had become an increasingly significant proportion of Israel's Jewish population, and these "Afro-Asian" Israeli Jews increasingly gave their votes to Likud. The partisan attachments of this segment of the population were shaped by a variety of factors, but prominent among these was a belief that they or their families had been poorly treated by the Labor government at the time of their arrival in Israel.[39] Accordingly, although predisposed in many cases to be sympathetic to Likud's foreign policy positions, these Israelis were often casting their votes against Labor as much as for Likud.

The culmination of Likud's ascent came in the Israeli election of May 1977. Likud won 43 seats to Labor's 32, and the party's leader, Menachem Begin, then formed a cabinet and assumed the premiership. This was the first time since the founding of the state that the government had not been under the control of Labor, leading some to describe the election results as a political earthquake. During the electoral campaign, Likud had issued a straightforward call for retention of the West Bank and Gaza Strip, whereas Labor, as in the past, had reaffirmed its commitment to UNSCR 242 and championed the principle of territorial compromise. Likud emphasized the strategic significance of the West Bank and Gaza, discussing the Sinai Peninsula and Golan Heights in this context as well and stating that its approach to all of the occupied territories was guided by Israel's need for secure and defensible borders. But its attitude toward the West Bank and Gaza also reflected other considerations—ones that were central to the party's ideology. Affirming that Judea and Samaria and the Gaza district were integral parts of the historic Land of Israel, Likud also justified its insistence on retaining these territories on historical and religious grounds and rejected returning to the Arabs even those regions with no military value. The party maintained that foreign (meaning "non-Jewish") sovereignty should not be reestablished over any part of the West Bank and Gaza, adding as a corollary that the right of Jews to live in any part of these territories was not a subject for negotiation.[40]

Consistent with this ideological commitment, the new Likud-led government set out almost immediately to establish a vastly expanded network of Jewish settlements and interests in the West Bank and other occupied territories. Critics of the policy often described this as "creating facts," meaning that the political and demographic situation in the territories was deliberately being transformed in order to establish a new set of realities, to create a situation that would reduce, and possibly eliminate, any chance of an Israeli withdrawal in the future. Prime Minister Begin proclaimed in this connection that there would never again be a political division between the Jordan River and the Mediterranean Sea.

There had been settlement activity under previous Labor governments, of course, primarily in the Jordan Valley, but on a limited scale in other areas as well. At the time Likud came to power in May 1977, approximately four thousand Israeli Jews were living in the West Bank, excluding East Jerusalem. By the end of 1977, more than five thousand Jewish settlers lived in the West Bank, and the number rose to 7,500, 10,000, and 12,500 during the following three years, with the actual number of settlements more than doubling by the end of 1980. The numbers also increased for the other occupied territories. By late 1980, there were twenty-six Jewish settlements on the Golan Heights, with about 6,500 people; thirteen settlements in northern Sinai, with approximately six thousand people; and seven hundred Israelis in three settlements in the Gaza Strip. In addition, the Begin government expanded the geographic locus of its settlement activities in the West Bank. Whereas Labor had deliberately discouraged the construction of Jewish communities in the central hilly areas where most Palestinians live, Likud made the heavily populated highlands the principal focus of its colonization efforts.

The Israeli election was not the only earthquake of 1977. In November of that year after several months of behind-the-scenes negotiations, Egypt's president, Anwar al-Sadat, traveled to Jerusalem and in a speech to the Knesset offered the Israelis a formula that he considered to be the basis for a fair and lasting end to the conflict. As president of the largest and most powerful Arab country, which only four years earlier had launched a surprise attack and inflicted heavy casualties on the Jewish state, al-Sadat was making a dramatic gesture and offering a potential breakthrough as he spoke to the most important political body in Israel. He told the Israelis that Egypt was ready for peace. He added, however, that his country did not seek a separate peace with Israel and that a resolution of the conflict would require complete withdrawal from Arab territories captured in 1967. Al-Sadat also emphasized the centrality of the Palestinian dimension of the conflict, stating that peace would be impossible without a solution to the Palestinian problem, even if peace between Israel and all the confrontation states were achieved. In one passage, he told the Israeli assembly that "it is no use to refrain from recognizing the Palestinian people and their right to statehood."

Al-Sadat's visit to Jerusalem set off a new round of diplomatic activity, in which the United States as well as Egypt and Israel were heavily involved, and that eventually led to the historic summit meeting at Camp David in September 1978. With continued prodding from the US president, Jimmy Carter, Anwar al-Sadat and Menachem Begin and their respective teams engaged in difficult and often-tense negotiations for almost two weeks. They eventually agreed on two "frameworks," which were then signed in a public ceremony. The first, the "Framework for the Conclusion of a Peace Treaty between Egypt and Israel," set forth a detailed formula for resolving bilateral issues and arriving at a peace treaty between the two countries. The second, the "Framework for Peace in the Middle East," dealt with the rights of the Palestinians and the future of the West Bank and Gaza. This framework offered only a general blueprint; it was characterized by broad guidelines, deferred decisions, and language amenable to differing interpretations, at best reflecting the kind of constructive ambiguity that in the past had failed to provide a basis for productive negotiations.

Despite some sticking points, bilateral relations between Egypt and Israel evolved satisfactorily following the Camp David summit. The two countries signed a formal peace treaty in March 1979, and during the next two years, Israel dismantled its settlements in northern

Sinai and completed its withdrawal from the peninsula. There was also progress during this period on the normalization of relations. As early as the summer of 1979, Egypt was visited by delegations of Israeli business leaders, university professors, and others. The first group of Israeli tourists also traveled to Egypt at this time, and they were met upon their arrival by welcome signs in Hebrew. Travel in the other direction brought Egyptian businesspeople, industrialists, and senior government officials to Israel; in addition, the two countries coordinated tourist exchanges and made plans for several joint ventures. These were stunning accomplishments, and despite some continuing problems and misunderstandings between Egypt and Israel, they constituted a significant, indeed revolutionary, development in the Arab–Israeli conflict, further reducing the importance of the Arab state dimension and focusing attention even more sharply on the conflict's core Palestinian dimension.

ISRAEL AND THE TERRITORIES

Unfortunately, the story of the Camp David framework dealing with the West Bank and Gaza is unlike that of the framework dealing with peace between Egypt and Israel. The framework called for negotiations about the final status of these territories to be based on the provisions and principles of UNSCR 242 and specified that the solution resulting from these talks must recognize the legitimate rights of the Palestinian people and their just requirements. The framework also envisioned a transitional period, not to exceed five years, during which time the final status of the West Bank and Gaza would be determined. During this period, inhabitants of these territories were to have "full autonomy," with the Israeli military government and its civilian administration being withdrawn as soon as "a Self-Governing Authority (Administrative Council)" could be freely elected by the inhabitants of the West Bank and Gaza. Jordan would be invited to join with Egypt and Israel in negotiating these arrangements, it being specified that the delegations of Jordan and Egypt could include Palestinians from the West Bank and Gaza or other Palestinians as mutually agreed.

These "autonomy talks," as they were informally known, soon reached an impasse; and after waiting three months, consistent with Israel's interpretation of what had been promised at Camp David, the Begin government resumed the construction of new settlements in the West Bank and Gaza. In October 1978, the World Zionist Organization presented a plan, accepted by the government in Jerusalem as a guide to its own action, for raising the number of Jewish settlers in the West Bank to one hundred thousand by 1983. This would involve approximately twenty-seven thousand families, approximately ten thousand to be accommodated through the expansion of existing settlements and the remainder to be located in some fifty new settlements specifically proposed by the plan. In response to these developments, as well as the failure to reach agreement on any substantive or even procedural issues pertaining to the West Bank and Gaza, al-Sadat unilaterally suspended the autonomy talks in May 1980.

With Egypt's increasing disengagement from the conflict, the most important events of the 1980s involved the political and diplomatic competition and also the violent confrontations between Israel and the Palestinians. The PLO continued its diplomatic campaign from its base in Lebanon, where it had also become a key player in Lebanese domestic politics. Palestinian officials repeated their readiness for a political settlement based on compromise and, focusing on Israeli settlement activity, insisted that the Jewish state was the intransigent party. For their part, Israeli representatives insisted that the PLO remained a terrorist organization dedicated to the destruction of the Jewish state. They pointed to the 1968 PLO charter and other early hard-line documents that had not been formally repudiated, stating as well that Arafat and other Palestinian leaders often said different things to different audiences. There was validity to the arguments and interpretations advanced by both Israeli and PLO spokespersons, but international diplomatic opinion nonetheless increasingly lined up on the side of the Palestinian organization. In European diplomatic circles, for example, criticism of Israel's settlement drive increased, and many judged the evolution of PLO thinking to be more significant than a failure to remove all ambiguities and conditionalities from its recent declarations. Also persuasive, apparently, were Palestinian claims that hard-line statements by Fatah and other mainstream PLO leaders were increasingly rare and, in any event, designed only to fend off extremist critics and create room to maneuver.

Developments among Palestinians in the occupied territories lent additional credibility to the PLO's claim to be ready for a political settlement and also to the PLO's insistence that it was the sole legitimate representative of the Palestinian people. Palestinians in the West Bank and Gaza were now being led by a new generation of men with an explicitly nationalist orientation, men who openly identified with the PLO and who declared their opposition to both the Israeli occupation and the autonomy scheme that had emerged from the Camp David summit. At the same time, many stated without hesitation that they were prepared to accept the existence of Israel—and, specifically, Israel as a Jewish state—in return for the exercise of Palestinian self-determination and the establishment of an independent Palestinian state alongside Israel. As noted, some of these men had come to power in the relatively democratic election of 1976, which gave them an important measure of legitimacy and made it possible to gauge the political preferences of Palestinians in the territories more generally.

Standing in opposition to the PLO and the Palestinians of the West Bank and Gaza was the Israeli government, led by Likud and actively supported by other nationalist and religious factions on the right side of the political spectrum. No matter how vigorous Palestinian resistance might be and no matter how plausible in the eyes of outside observers the political solution for which Palestinians and other Arabs now claimed to be ready might be, these Israelis were determined that the future of the West Bank and Gaza would be shaped exclusively by their own ideological vision. Furthermore, they were in the midst of an intense campaign to transform the political, economic, and demographic character of the West Bank and Gaza, and from their point of view, they were having considerable success in their drive to translate vision into reality.

Not all Israelis shared this vision. Indeed, the country was deeply divided on questions relating to the West Bank and Gaza. Many leaders and supporters of the centrist Labor Party, as well as those affiliated with other centrist and leftist political factions, argued, often passionately, that permanent retention of the West Bank and Gaza was not in Israel's interest and that, in fact, it would be extremely detrimental to the Jewish state. Not only would this make more remote, and possibly remove permanently, any chance of peace with the Arabs; it would also leave Israel with a large non-Jewish population, whose existence was likely to force the country to choose, impossibly and with no acceptable outcome, between its Jewish character and its democratic character.

This choice could be avoided if most Palestinians in the territories could be induced, or forced, to leave the West Bank and Gaza for other Arab lands, a policy of "transfer" that was advocated by some groups on the extreme political right. But transfer, with its implications of ethnic cleansing, was strongly rejected on both moral and political grounds by the overwhelming majority of Israelis. Thus, retention of the West Bank and Gaza and the extension of Israeli sovereignty to these territories would require Israel to decide whether to grant citizenship to the Palestinian inhabitants of the territories. If citizenship were not awarded, so that these Palestinians became "subjects" with only local-level political rights, the country would cease to be a democracy. Israeli Jews and those Palestinians who were citizens of pre-1967 Israel would possess political rights denied, legally and by official design, to the West Bank and Gaza Palestinians who now lived in "greater Israel." Alternatively, if these Palestinians were granted citizenship in order to preserve the country's democratic character, non-Jews would be a large part of the country's citizenry; and given the higher birthrate among Arabs compared with the birthrate among Jews, non-Jews within a generation might constitute the majority of the population and be in a position to pass legislation that would abolish the laws and policies that institutionalize Israel's connection to Judaism and Jews throughout the world. Israeli opponents of retaining the territories called this the "demographic issue."

Although the political weight of Labor and other domestic opponents of the Likud-led government was considerable, Likud retained its supremacy in the Israeli election of June 1981, albeit by a narrow margin, and this brought an acceleration of Israeli settlement activity. Menachem Begin appointed Ariel Sharon, a hard-line former general, as minister of defense. As minister of agriculture in the previous Begin cabinet, Sharon had emerged as a powerful force within the government and played a leading role in formulating and implementing Israel's policies in the occupied territories. Now, at the Defense Ministry he was able to dominate the army as well as government policy, and this gave him responsibility for the Israeli military government that ruled the West Bank and Gaza.

Bitter confrontations between Israelis and Palestinians in the territories emerged in this environment, and Israel's annexation of the Golan Heights in December 1981 contributed further to Arab anger. The Golan had been captured from Syria in the June 1967 War; and although the territory had no ideological significance for the Jewish state as it is not considered part of the historic Land of Israel, it was judged to be of major strategic importance. Both Labor and Likud governments had built settlements in the territory. A motivation for the Begin government's annexation of the Golan was to defuse criticism from right-wing elements that were pressing the prime minister to renege on his promise to relinquish those portions of the Sinai Peninsula that Israel still controlled. Whatever the motivations, the extension of Israeli law to the Golan Heights added to the tension. In addition to the understandable condemnation from Syria and other states, a general strike was called by Syrian Druze residents of the Golan. The Israeli military's use of coercion and collective punishment in an effort to break the strike and to force the Druze to accept Israeli identification cards only exacerbated the situation.

The most important confrontations were in the West Bank and Gaza, where Palestinian resistance and Israel's response brought broad and sustained disturbances in spring 1982. These began when an Israeli official was beaten by Palestinian students at Birzeit University near Ramallah in February, after which Israeli authorities closed the school for two months, and protest demonstrations were then organized at other West Bank universities. Agitation grew more intense in the weeks that followed, and in addition to demonstrations and protest marches, there were general strikes in many areas, including East Jerusalem, and incidents in which young Palestinians threw stones at Israeli soldiers and Jewish civilians traveling in the occupied territories. The clashes that erupted during this period were the most intense and prolonged of any that had occurred since Israel took control of the West Bank and Gaza in 1967.

Both the Israeli and Palestinian press provided vivid accounts of these clashes, giving attention not only to Palestinian activism but also to the forceful and sometimes lethal response of the Israeli military. Regular features in April and May were articles with titles such as "Boy Dies as Violence Sweeps Gaza, W. Bank," "Two Arabs Killed as Troops Disperse Riots," "Youth Shot after Stonings in Bethlehem Area Village," and "Girl Pupil Killed during Gaza Strip School Riot."[41] Describing the overall situation in a May 12 editorial titled "Road to Nowhere," the *Jerusalem Post* wrote that "this little war has emerged as nasty, brutish and hopeless." Another editorial, prompted by a press conference at which six Israeli reserve officers recounted their experiences while serving in the occupied territories, described the situation as "depressing when it was not hair-raising." Thus with a scope and intensity unmatched during the previous fifteen years of Israeli occupation, the West Bank and Gaza exploded in the spring of 1982, making it all the more evident that even a positive evolution of relations between Israel and Egypt would not bring peace in the absence of a solution to the Palestinian dimension of the conflict.

The Israeli actions to which Palestinians were responding in the spring of 1982 included not only the settlement drive of the Begin and Sharon government but also the lawlessness and vigilantism of elements within the organized Israeli settler movement. Not only were there a number of incidents in which Palestinians were attacked by Jewish settlers, but the lenient treatment that Israeli authorities gave to the perpetrators was an additional source of Palestinian anger. In March 1982, for example, an Arab teenager from the village of Sinjal was shot and killed by an Israeli resident of a nearby settlement. The settler was detained briefly but released a few days later, and the case against him was subsequently dropped. According to an Israeli government inquiry into settler violence against Palestinians in the West Bank, headed by Deputy Attorney General Yehudit Karp, there were a total fifteen such incidents during April and May, all of which involved either death or injury as a result of shootings.[42] There were also instances of Jewish settlers throwing hand grenades at Arab homes, automobiles, and even schools in several locations.

Israeli authorities responded to the unrest not only by confronting demonstrators in the streets but also by seeking to undermine Palestinian political institutions. This included the dismissal of a number of elected mayors of West Bank towns, beginning with Ibrahim Tawil of al-Bireh and followed by Bassam Shaka of Nablus and Karim Khalaf of Ramallah. Both Shaka and Khalaf were outspoken supporters of the PLO, and both had been wounded in 1980 in attacks carried out by an underground Jewish settler group calling itself "Terror Against

Terror." The Israelis said that the mayors' refusal to cooperate with the civilian administration provided a legal basis for their removal, accusing them as well of helping to incite strikes and demonstrations.

A logical extension of Israel's campaign against PLO influence in the West Bank and Gaza was a desire to inflict damage on the PLO itself through an attack on the organization's base in Lebanon. Prime Minister Begin and Defense Minister Sharon, as well as others in the Likud government, considered the PLO to be the source of most of Jerusalem's troubles in the occupied territories. As a US State Department official put the matter at the time, "The Israeli government believes it has a Palestinian problem because of the PLO; not that it has a PLO problem because of the Palestinians."[43] The conclusion that Begin and Sharon deduced from their analysis was that if Israel could force the PLO to curtail its encouragement of resistance in the West Bank and Gaza, either by weakening the organization or by teaching it that its actions were not cost-free, Palestinians in the territories would accommodate themselves to a political future in which the West Bank and Gaza were part of the Jewish state. To Begin and Sharon, suppressing Palestinian nationalism in the West Bank and Gaza and inflicting a military and political defeat on the PLO in Lebanon were thus two interrelated aspects of a single political strategy.

Israeli troops entered Lebanon in force on June 6, 1982. Amid charges and denials about whether the PLO fighters in southern Lebanon had been shelling towns in northern Israel, Begin and Sharon had told the cabinet that the purpose of the invasion was to establish a forty-kilometer security zone north of the Lebanon–Israel border. The IDF swept into southern Lebanon with a huge force of almost eighty thousand men and 1,240 tanks. There was fierce fighting in some areas, with the stiffest resistance to the invasion offered not by the PLO's semiregular units but by the home guard forces of a number of Palestinian refugee camps. The Israelis nonetheless reached their objective in less than forty-eight hours. On June 8, at almost the same time that Begin was repeating to the Knesset that Israel's objectives in Lebanon were limited, Israeli forces reached a line forty kilometers from the country's northern border.

But it turned out that Israel's objectives in Lebanon were not limited, and Israeli forces did not stop upon achieving the invasion's declared objective. Instead, the IDF pushed northward and eastward and encircled Beirut in the west. Sharon had kept the cabinet in the dark about his true intentions, but he now revealed that he had always planned to expand the operation and articulated two broad goals for the mission: the elimination of the PLO as a military and a political threat and the installation of a friendly, unified, and Christian-dominated government in Lebanon.

Beyond calling for the establishment of a new political order in Lebanon, an objective that was not achieved, supporters of the expanded operation argued that crushing the PLO was the key to reaching an accommodation with Palestinians. Israeli spokespersons had long maintained that PLO intransigence was the major obstacle to an expansion of the peace process begun at Camp David. Equally important, the Begin government blamed the PLO for the disturbances in the West Bank and Gaza in spring 1982, alleging that the PLO had directed resistance to the occupation and intimidated Palestinians interested in compromise. Israel's expanded operation in Lebanon was designed to change this. With its fighting forces either captured, killed, or dispersed and with its independent political base destroyed, the organization would no longer be able to carry out operations against the Jewish state. Nor, in the Israeli analysis, would the PLO be able to impose its will on the Palestinian people and, most critically, on the inhabitants of the occupied territories.

Although some Israelis were persuaded by the government's case for an expansion of the war, others doubted the wisdom of such action; accordingly, a full-fledged political debate was raging in the Jewish state by the latter part of June 1982.[44] Critics raised two particular concerns: one relating to costs associated with the war and a second to the feasibility of Israel's expanded objectives. With respect to costs, the greatest preoccupation was the steadily growing number of Israeli casualties. With respect to feasibility, Likud's critics repeated what they had been saying for some time: Israel's policies, as much as or even more than PLO rejectionism, were what was producing unrest in the West Bank and Gaza. Without Israeli recognition of Palestinian rights, these critics asserted, resistance in the territories would continue, regardless of the outcome of the fighting in Lebanon. With such recognition, in contrast, many Palestinians would accept the principle of reconciliation with Israel, thereby making the war irrelevant in bringing mainstream Palestinians to the bargaining table.

As the expanded campaign evolved during July and August, Sharon ordered an escalation of the IDF's attacks on PLO positions in Beirut, which culminated with saturation bombing and shelling by the Israeli navy from offshore positions. Israeli firepower was directed not only at buildings used by the PLO in the center of Beirut but at Palestinian refugee camps as well. Casualty figures vary widely, but the number of Palestinians and Lebanese killed or wounded during the entire campaign is in the thousands—more than ten thousand by some estimates—with many more rendered homeless.[45] With the PLO defeated, Arafat left Lebanon at the end of August, departing by sea along with about eight thousand PLO guerrillas. Another six thousand fighters, including Syrian soldiers as well as members of the Palestine Liberation Army, left by land. The PLO then reestablished its headquarters in Tunis.

A tragic postscript to the Israeli–PLO war in Lebanon was written from September 16 to September 18. During this period, with Israeli knowledge and possibly approval, forces of the Lebanese Christian Phalange Party entered Sabra and Shatila, two large, adjacent Palestinian refugee camps on the outskirts of Beirut, and carried out a massacre of hundreds of civilians, many of them women and children.

An Israeli commission of inquiry established after the massacre, the Kahan Commission, found that Israeli authorities had permitted Phalange forces to enter Sabra and Shatila without giving proper consideration to the danger of a massacre, which, under the circumstances, they "were obligated to foresee as probable." The commission also saw fit to make recommendations concerning responsibility and punishment, reserving its harshest judgments for Ariel Sharon. It charged the defense minister with "personal responsibility" because he had not ordered "appropriate measures for preventing or reducing the chances of a massacre." It also called upon Sharon to draw "the appropriate personal conclusions," meaning that he should resign, and it added that if he refused to do so the prime minister should consider removing him from office.[46] In the end, Sharon refused to resign, and, as a compromise, Begin relieved him of the defense portfolio but allowed him to remain in the cabinet.

The war in Lebanon was followed by a number of US and Arab diplomatic initiatives. On September 1, 1982, the day that the last PLO guerrillas departed from Beirut, the US president,

Ronald Reagan, introduced a peace plan. It placed emphasis on continuing US support for Israel. In addition, however, in what appeared to be an important evolution in US policy, it also spoke of the "legitimate rights of the Palestinians," specifying that these rights are political in character and acknowledging that the Palestinian problem is "more than a question of refugees." This was quickly followed by a plan put forward by Arab leaders meeting in Fez, Morocco. Frequently described as the "Fez Plan," it proposed a "two-state solution" based on Israeli withdrawal from all Arab territories occupied in 1967 and removal of the Israeli settlements in these territories.

Although they gave rise to extended diplomatic activity, neither the Reagan plan nor the Fez plan produced any lasting agreements or led to any significant changes on the ground in the occupied territories. The Fez plan was nonetheless significant for its embrace of the notion of partition, committing Arab countries to the proposition that both a Jewish state and an Arab state should be established in Palestine. This reflected a continuing evolution and clarification, and also the moderation, of Arab thinking about the basis for an accommodation with Israel.

This evolving acceptance of a two-state solution was also present among Palestinians. While the PLO mainstream had been greatly weakened by the war in Lebanon and, hence, was more vulnerable to interference by Arab governments allied with Palestinian rejectionists, PLO losses in Lebanon dealt an even harsher blow to the rejectionist camp. One Palestinian scholar explained that, prior to the war, rejectionists within the PLO possessed something approaching a veto over PLO decisions, a power incommensurate with their actual size. But the demise of the PLO's independent base in Lebanon destroyed many of the institutional arrangements that had been the power base of radicals and leftists, reducing their ability to impose limits on the policies pursued by Fatah and the PLO mainstream.[47]

The PLO's defeat in Lebanon also enhanced the political weight of the West Bank and Gaza in intra-Palestinian politics. At the grassroots level, Palestinians in the occupied territories became the PLO's most important and politically influential constituency, and this in turn brought greater support for the more moderate ideological orientation that had long been dominant among these Palestinians.

Also on the agenda in the aftermath of the war was the relationship between Israel and Lebanon. Israel attempted to persuade Lebanon to sign a peace treaty, and an accord ending the state of war between the two countries and committing Israel to withdraw all of its armed forces from the country was signed in May 1983. The accord was stillborn, however. The withdrawal of Israeli troops was conditional upon removal of the Syrian forces in Lebanon, something that was not about to take place. Even more important, the agreement was denounced in Lebanon as the product of Israel's illegal and unjustified invasion and as an unacceptable reward for an aggressor that had brought death and destruction to the country. For this reason, the accord was never submitted to the Lebanese parliament for ratification.

Finally, there was the issue of the Israeli troops that remained in Lebanon after the war. With few gains and high costs, the war, or at least the expanded operation, had become highly unpopular in Israel. Moreover, Israelis continued to be killed and wounded in Lebanon, with losses now the result of attacks by Lebanese, not Palestinians. This led to limited pullbacks in 1982 and 1983 and to a significant redeployment in the summer of 1985. Israel kept forces in southern Lebanon, however, in order to police a narrow security zone immediately north of the Israeli–Lebanese border. Israel also created a local militia, the South Lebanese Army, to assist in this policing function. The situation thus settled into a tense status quo marked by Israel's continuing occupation of a portion of Lebanese territory.

None of this was a basis for celebration in Israel. On the contrary, the country's mood was unhappy and troubled, and this was reflected in the unexpected retirement of Menachem Begin. Late in August 1983, despondent over the country's losses in Lebanon as well as the death of his wife the preceding spring, Begin announced that he would step down as the country's prime minister; he formally submitted his resignation two weeks later. Moreover, he retired from public view as well as public life, remaining in his Jerusalem apartment, refusing all requests for interviews, and playing no part in the affairs of either the nation or the political party he had previously led. He was replaced by Yitzhak Shamir, a Likud stalwart who differed greatly from Begin in style and personality but was no less committed to the expansion of settlements and the concept of greater Israel.

THE INTIFADA

Diplomatic efforts continued during the mid-1980s but produced no results of consequence. Instead, while the diplomats talked, the situation continued to deteriorate for Palestinians in the territories. Israeli settlement activity in the West Bank and Gaza continued and intensified during these years. The number of Jewish settlers in the occupied territories stood at almost sixty thousand in the fall of 1986, whereas it had been about twenty thousand four years earlier. These figures do not include East Jerusalem. Moreover, numbers tell only part of the story. The government allocated approximately $300 million for infrastructure projects in support of the settler movement.

Israel also continued its efforts to weaken those Palestinian institutions in the territories that it judged to be sources of opposition and resistance. Palestinian universities were frequently closed, for example, on the grounds that instead of pursuing their education, students were engaging in political activities and organizing opposition to the occupation. Other Israeli actions, which by summer 1985 were routinely described as an "Iron Fist" policy, included deportations, press censorship, and such forms of collective punishment as curfews and the demolition of homes. This was the situation when Israel was led by Labor as well as Likud. The 1984 elections had produced a virtual tie between Likud and Labor, and the two parties then formed a national unity government and agreed that the premiership should rotate between Shimon Peres of Labor and Yitzhak Shamir of Likud. Peres took the first term, and the defense minister at this time was Yitzhak Rabin of Labor; but although Peres, Rabin, and their party advocated territorial compromise and the exchange of land for peace, there was no appreciable change in Israel's actions in the occupied territories.

Finally, growing tension in the West Bank and Gaza resulted not only from the actions of the Israeli government but also from confrontations between an increasingly frustrated and angry Palestinian population and an increasingly emboldened and aggressive Jewish settler movement. In the spring of 1987, for example, there was a spiral of violence that began when a petrol bomb thrown at an Israeli vehicle in the West Bank town of Qalqilya resulted in the death of a Jewish woman. Settlers took revenge by carrying out a rampage through the town, breaking windows and uprooting trees in what the May 23, 1987, *Jerusalem Post* described as a "vigilante orgy." In the weeks that followed, there were additional raids by Jewish settlers and numerous clashes between stone-throwing Palestinian youths and Israeli soldiers. By mid-1987, these confrontations had become so common that they almost ceased to be newsworthy.

All of this produced a steadily deteriorating and increasingly hopeless situation from the viewpoint of the 1.5 or 1.6 million Palestinians residing in the West Bank and Gaza. A careful Palestinian American scholar who visited the territories at this time offered the following description:

> Gaza resembles a pressure-cooker ready to explode. In this "forgotten corner of Palestine," one witnesses overcrowding, poverty, hatred, violence, oppression, poor sanitation, anger, frustration, drugs and crime. The Palestinian population is daily becoming more resentful and rebellious. The military occupation responds by becoming more insecure and oppressive.[48]

The situation in the West Bank was only slightly less grim, with Israeli as well as Palestinian analysts reporting that the tension had become palpable. As expressed in October 1987 by a correspondent for the *Jerusalem Post*, "You can feel the tension. . . . Fear, suspicion and growing hatred have replaced any hope of dialogue between Israelis and Palestinians."[49]

Under pressure and in the absence of any prospect that diplomatic efforts by either the PLO, Egypt, Jordan, the United States, or Israeli advocates of territorial compromise would bring an end to the occupation of their homeland, Palestinians were searching in 1987 for ways to change the political momentum and resist Israeli expansion. And then in December 1987, spontaneous and widespread protest demonstrations erupted throughout the territories. The spark that ignited the disturbances was an accident at the Israeli military checkpoint at the north end of the Gaza Strip. An IDF tank transport vehicle crashed into a line of cars and vans filled with men from Gaza who were returning home after a day of work in Israel, killing four and seriously injuring seven others. The funerals that night for three of the deceased quickly turned into a massive demonstration.

In the days and weeks that followed, there were protests and civil disobedience on a scale that exceeded anything seen in the territories since the beginning of the occupation in 1967. Moreover, spontaneous outbursts of anger and efforts at resistance rapidly coalesced into a coordinated uprising embracing virtually all sectors of Palestinian society, a rebellion that some compared to the revolt of 1936–1939 and that soon became known as the *intifada*, literally translated as the "shaking off."

The intifada was marked by a new determination among Palestinians and by daring action on the part of youthful protesters taking to the streets in the West Bank and Gaza. According to one report based on two visits to Israel and the occupied territories during the first half of 1988,

> Even Israelis with little sympathy for the Palestinian cause sometimes say they have a new respect for their enemy . . . and one occasionally hears comments [from Israelis] to the effect that these are not the craven and cowardly Arabs described in our propaganda

MAP 2.5   ■   Israeli Settlements in the West Bank, 1982

Legend:
- ○ Settlements established before 1977
- ● Settlements established after 1977
- ■ Major Arab towns

Reihan
Ginat
Jenin
Mevo Dotan
Sanur
Irit
Mehola
Tulkarm
Shomron
Elon Moreh
Qedumim
Nablus
Brakha
Hamra
Qalqilya
Alfei Menashe
Qarnel Shomron
Argaman
Ma'aleh Shomron
Emmanuel
Mekhora
Yaqir
Netafim
Tapuah
Massu'a
Elqana
Ariel
Gittit
Beit Abba
Shiloh
Ma'aleh Ephraim
Shlomtzion
Ateret
Tomer
Netiv Hagdud
Gilgal
Ofra
Ramallah
Beit El
Rimonim
Givat Ze'ev
Jericho
Mitzpeh Jericho
Beit Ha'arava
Jerusalem
Ma'aie Adumim
Almog
ISRAEL
Har Gilo
Bethlehem
Efrat
Kfar Etzion
Migdal Oz
Mitzpe Shalem
Telem
Ma'aleh Amos
Qiryat Arba
Adora
Hebron
Yaqin
Negohot
Karmel
Eshkolot
Zohar

Mediterranean Sea

Jordan River

JORDAN

Dead Sea

0   10 Mi
0   10 Km

but young men with the courage of their convictions, willing to stand before our soldiers and risk their lives in order to give voice to their demands.[50]

This new assertiveness was repeatedly displayed as protest activities expanded in both scope and intensity during the months that followed. Demonstrations began in the refugee camps but soon spread to major towns and thereafter to the roughly five hundred villages of the West Bank. Demonstrators chanted slogans, raised Palestinian flags, and threw stones at Israeli soldiers who sought to disperse them. Young Palestinians also frequently threw stones at Israeli vehicles, including those of Israeli civilians traveling in the occupied territories. Makeshift roadblocks were erected in a further attempt to disrupt normal circulation, especially at the entrances to villages or in urban neighborhoods that the Palestinians sought to prevent Israelis from entering. These roadblocks were constructed of rocks or, occasionally, of burning tires; and although they sometimes inconvenienced local inhabitants as much as Israelis, they represented an effort to wrest control of the streets from occupation authorities and were accordingly left in place.

Emerging patterns of organization and leadership constituted a particularly important feature of the intifada, and one that also helped to set the uprising apart from prior Palestinian efforts to arrest Israel's drive into the West Bank and Gaza. The political institutions that crystallized to give direction to the intifada and to deal with the problems and opportunities it created included both popular neighborhood committees and a unified national leadership structure. Furthermore, at both the local level and beyond, the new institutions were to a large extent led by the members of a new political generation.

As soon as they recognized the coordinated and sustained character of the Palestinian uprising, Israeli leaders declared their intention to suppress the intifada. Primary responsibility for achieving this objective fell to Yitzhak Rabin, the minister of defense in the national unity government that had been established after the parliamentary elections of 1984. In addition to detaining and deporting suspected activists, Israel undertook to suppress Palestinian protest demonstrations, and when necessary, it dispersed demonstrators by firing live ammunition. Rabin and most other Israeli leaders justified these actions by saying that the Palestinians had left them no alternative. Yet the intifada continued and, if anything, grew more intense, even as the number of Palestinian demonstrators shot by Israeli soldiers increased.

All of this violence was in addition to the severe administrative measures that Israel employed in its effort to contain the intifada. Universities were closed by Israeli authorities until further notice, for example, although several institutions managed to hold some classes in secret. Many primary and secondary schools were also shut for prolonged periods. Dozens of homes were blown up by Israeli troops, usually because it was believed that someone who lived there had thrown stones at Israeli soldiers. In addition, entire communities were placed under curfew, sometimes for a week or more, preventing people from leaving their homes at any time, even to obtain food. As with school closings and the demolition of homes, curfews are a form of collective punishment that falls heavily not only on protesters but also on men and women who have not taken part in protest-related activities. The fifty-five thousand residents of Jabaliya refugee camp in Gaza, for example, spent about two hundred days under curfew between the beginning of the intifada and June 1989. The continuing deportation of suspected activists was another administrative measure designed to suppress the uprising. Finally, thousands of Palestinians were arrested and detained, some for prolonged periods and the overwhelming majority without trial. In February 1989, Rabin announced that 22,000 Palestinians had been detained since the beginning of the intifada and that 6,200 were being held in administrative detention at that time. Palestinian and some US sources put the figures even higher.

These measures were not uniformly applauded in Israel. Many Israelis, including some in the military, were disturbed by the tactics being employed to suppress the uprising. In one denunciation that received wide public attention, the prime minister was told by troops in January 1988 that they were very disturbed by the IDF's behavior. Shamir was inspecting IDF operations in the northern West Bank city of Nablus and stopped to talk to a group of soldiers who, to his consternation, told him in extremely strong terms that young Israelis were not raised on universal values and respect for human rights only to be sent to the occupied territories to commit violence unrestrained by the rule of law. The political and military establishments "have no idea what really goes on in the territories," one soldier told him, while another stated, with reporters present, that he had to "beat innocent people" every day.[51]

The Israeli government nonetheless remained determined to crush the uprising, and this determination did not diminish as the intifada entered its second and then its third year. "The nation can bear the burden no matter how long the revolt goes on," Rabin declared in December 1989. Furthermore, he specified that "we will continue with all the measures that we used for the first years, including the confrontations, the hitting, the arresting, the introduction of the plastic bullet, the rubber bullet and the curfews on a large scale."[52]

Palestinians under occupation were seeking by the rebellion that began in December 1987 to send a message to Israel and the world. The content of this message, made explicit in the conversations between Palestinian intellectuals and the large number of foreign journalists who flocked to the region to report on the spreading disturbances, can be summed up simply: We exist and have political rights, and there will be no peace until these rights are recognized.

The Israeli public was the most important audience to which the Palestinians' message was addressed. In the debates and discussions inside Israel, Prime Minister Shamir and others on the political right had frequently argued that most Palestinians in the occupied territories were actually content to live under Israeli rule. Asserting that the material conditions of most inhabitants of the West Bank and Gaza had improved significantly since 1967, Likud leaders told the Israeli public that only a few radicals affiliated with the PLO called for Israeli withdrawal. The vast majority of the Palestinian population, by contrast, was said to recognize and appreciate the improvement in their standard of living that had accompanied occupation and accordingly, for the future, to seek no more than local or regional autonomy under continuing Israeli rule.

A related Likud claim was that continuing occupation of the West Bank and Gaza was without significant costs from the Israeli point of view. Shamir and like-minded Israelis insisted that the Palestinian inhabitants of these territories did not constitute a serious obstacle to developing these areas in accordance with the design of Israelis committed to territorial maximalism. Palestinian acquiescence, they asserted, meant there would be few burdens associated with the maintenance of order and little to prevent ordinary Israeli citizens from conducting themselves in the West Bank and Gaza as if they were in their own country.

The intifada was intended to show these assertions to be myths in a way that could not be explained away by apologists for the occupation. In other words, the Palestinian uprising sought to send the Israeli public a message to the effect that the parties of the political Right were either ignorant about the situation in the West Bank and Gaza or, more probable, deliberately seeking to mislead the people of Israel. Palestinians sought to leave no room for doubt about their implacable opposition to occupation and also to foster in Israel a recognition that the course charted by the country's leaders was a costly one, which was not in the interest of the Jewish state. This message was particularly important in view of the deep political divisions that existed within Israel, with the public bombarded by conflicting claims from Labor and Likud and with many ordinary Israelis trying to determine which party's vision of the country's future was the wisest and most realistic.

Evidence that the Palestinians' message was having an impact in Israel was offered by a significant change in the way that most Israelis looked at the West Bank and Gaza after December 1987, a change often described as the resurrection of the "Green Line" in Israeli political consciousness. The Green Line refers to the pre-1967 border separating Israel from its Arab neighbors, and during the twenty years between the June 1967 War and the outbreak of the intifada, those parts of the Green Line running between the West Bank and Gaza on one side and Israel on the other had become nearly invisible to many Israelis. Israelis frequently traveled through the West Bank to get from one part of Israel to another or took their cars to garages in Gaza or drove to Jericho for a casual meal in one of the city's oasis restaurants. This gave many and perhaps most Israelis the sense of a natural connection between their country and these areas. Indeed, by the end of 1987 a majority of Israel's population was too young even to remember a time when the West Bank and Gaza were not under their country's control. As a result, while the West Bank and Gaza were not quite seen as Israel itself, neither did they appear to many Israelis to be part of another, foreign country.

The intifada transformed these perceptions, leading most Israelis to regard the West Bank and Gaza as zones of insecurity that should be avoided as much as possible. As Yitzhak Rabin himself explained in September 1988 when he was asked to comment on the fact that the number of Israelis killed in the territories had actually declined since the beginning of the uprising, "Jews simply don't visit the territories as they used to. No one's wandering around the garages of Gaza any more these days."[53] The resurrection of the Green Line was similarly evident in the effective "redivision" of Jerusalem. In the words of an authority on walking tours in the city, "Before the intifada, all the routes of the hikes I wrote about were over the Green Line. . . . [But] today the Green Line is my map of fear."[54] Thus in the judgment of yet another Israeli analyst, writing in December 1989,

> Perhaps the most conspicuous result of the intifada has been the restoration of Israel's pre-1967 border, the famous Green Line, which disappeared from Israeli maps and consciousness as early as 1968. . . . [Today] the West Bank and Gaza are seen as foreign territories inhabited by a hostile population, whose stone-throwing youngsters are ready to die—and do—in their quest for freedom.[55]

The intifada had an equally significant impact on political discourse in Israel. On the political right, some began to think about removal of the Palestinians from the West Bank and Gaza, which was a disturbing but nonetheless logical response to the Palestinian uprising from the perspective of those committed to territorial maximalism. If Israel were indeed to retain the territories, and if it were the case, as the intifada itself proclaimed, that the Palestinians would never submit to Israeli rule, then it was not a very big logical leap to arrive at the view that the Palestinians should be pressured, or if necessary forced, to leave the occupied areas for a neighboring Arab country.

Of much greater consequence, however, was the degree to which the intifada strengthened the arguments of Israeli supporters of territorial compromise. With many Israelis reexamining commonly held assumptions about the costs and benefits of retaining the territories, the arguments of those who had long insisted that retention of the territories was not in Israel's interest were increasingly finding a receptive audience in the Jewish state. The new realism in debates about the West Bank and Gaza also led a growing number of Israelis to call for talks with the PLO, which was illegal at the time.

Moreover, in addition to the traditional arguments of the Center and the Left—that refusal to withdraw from the occupied territories removed what possibility might exist for peace with the Arabs, as well as the "demographic issue," which pointed out that extending Israeli sovereignty to territories inhabited by 1.5 million Palestinians would threaten either the country's Jewish character or its democratic character—doubts were now being raised, in military as well as civilian circles, about the strategic value of the West Bank and Gaza. Indeed, many suggested that the territories might be a security liability rather than a security asset. A May 1989 poll by the newspaper *Yediot Ahronot*, for example, reported that 75 percent to 80 percent of the IDF's reserve officers believed that withdrawing from the West Bank and Gaza involved fewer security risks than remaining in these territories.

The message that Palestinians sought to send by means of the intifada was addressed to a variety of audiences; in addition to Israel, these included US policymakers and the US public. Palestinians were disturbed by Washington's apparent indifference to the deteriorating situation in the occupied territories and hoped the uprising would force Americans to look at the Israeli–Palestinian conflict in a new light. And with Americans seeing violent Israeli–Palestinian confrontations on their television sets virtually every evening, the intifada did appear to be having an impact on US public opinion. In January 1989, a *New York Times*-CBS poll found that 64 percent of the Americans surveyed favored contacts with the PLO, in contrast with 23 percent who were opposed. The same poll found that only 28 percent judged Israel to be willing to make "real concessions" for peace, whereas 52 percent did not think that Israel was genuinely interested in compromise.

The intifada also had something to say to the rulers of Arab states. By seizing the initiative and launching their own attempt to shake off the occupation, Palestinians were in effect declaring that the lethargy and self-absorption of Arab leaders left ordinary men and women with no choice but to take matters into their own hands. This message also reminded Arab leaders that Palestinians were not the only Arabs unhappy with the status quo. With many Arab countries ruled by inefficient, corrupt, or authoritarian regimes, and with many Arab leaders and elites largely preoccupied with their own power and privilege, or at least widely perceived to be thus preoccupied, the intifada demonstrated that there were limits to the patience and passivity of the Arab rank and file and that it was not inconceivable that popular rebellions would break out elsewhere.

Among individual Arab states, Jordan was the most sensitive to developments in the occupied territories, and it was King Hussein who took the most dramatic action in response to the intifada. On July 31, 1988, the king made a televised address in which he officially relinquished his country's claims to the West Bank, declaring that "the independent Palestinian state will be established on the occupied Palestinian land, after it is liberated, God willing."

Beyond seeking to make the occupied territories difficult to govern and showing that Palestinians, not Israelis, controlled events on the ground, Palestinians sought to send a second message to the Israeli public, again going over the heads of the government, as it were. To show that territorial compromise not only was in Israel's interest but was in fact a viable option, the Palestine National Assembly, meeting in Algiers in November 1988, explicitly endorsed UN resolutions 181 and 242 and declared its willingness to resolve the conflict on the basis of an independent Palestinian state in the West Bank and Gaza living alongside Israel in its pre-1967 borders.

This declaration was aimed in particular at Israelis who might favor territorial compromise in principle but who doubted that this would in fact bring peace. And the message appeared to be having an impact. While Israeli government spokespersons insisted that the Palestinian organization was sincere neither about renouncing terrorism nor about recognizing Israel, support for a dialogue with the PLO continued to grow in the Jewish state. A March 1989 poll found that 58 percent of those surveyed disagreed with the proposition that Palestinians want a "Palestinian state plus all of Israel in the long run," meaning that much of the Israeli public believed there to be a basis for negotiating with the PLO; and, accordingly, 62 percent said they expected Israeli–PLO talks within five years.[56]

The intifada continued with varying but essentially sustained intensity for the next two years, or even longer by some assessments. Toward the end of this period, the uprising became less organized and lost much of its initial direction and discipline. There was even Palestinian-against-Palestinian violence in the final stages, with charges of collaborating with Israeli security forces sometimes used as a pretext for attacks that were in reality motivated by personal grievances and rivalries. Nevertheless, the intifada was a watershed event. On the one hand, it galvanized Palestinians, helped to foster a significant evolution of the PLO's official position, and consolidated a shift in the center of attention from Palestinian leaders in exile to on-the-ground Palestinians who had stood up to the Israelis and carried the uprising forward. On the other, it shifted the political center of gravity in Israel, not removing the country's sharp ideological divisions but strengthening advocates of territorial compromise and helping to lay a foundation for the peace process that would soon take shape. As explained in mid-1989 by Ze'ev Schiff, one of Israel's most highly regarded analysts of military and security affairs, the intifada "has shattered a static situation that Israel has consistently sought to preserve.... It has led to the unavoidable conclusion that there can be no end to the Arab-Israeli conflict without a resolution of the conflict between Israel and the Palestinians."[57]

THE OSLO PEACE PROCESS

A number of diplomatic initiatives in 1989 and 1990 sought to capitalize on the momentum generated by the intifada and the PLO's endorsement of a two-state solution. These included a substantive dialogue between the PLO and the United States, which previously had refused to recognize or talk to the Palestinian organization, as well as peace plans presented by Egypt, the United States, and the Israeli government. None produced tangible results, however; and then in summer 1990, world attention abruptly shifted from the Israeli–Palestinian conflict to a new crisis in the Persian Gulf. On August 2, 1990, Iraq under Saddam Hussein invaded Kuwait, and early in 1991, the United States led a massive and successful military campaign to oust Iraqi forces and restore the Kuwaiti monarchy. Many Palestinians supported Saddam Hussein in the war, in part because he represented an alternative to the political status quo in the region and in part because he championed the Palestinian cause and even fired missiles at Israel.

The Gulf War had an impact on the Israeli–Palestinian conflict in at least two important ways. First, because most Palestinians had supported Iraq, Kuwait as well as Saudi Arabia and several other Arab states suspended the important financial and political support they had been providing to the PLO. This significantly weakened the Palestinian organization, which had been heavily dependent on the Gulf for its budget. Second, in part to show that its intervention on behalf of oil-rich Kuwait had not been motivated solely by petroleum interests, the United States launched a diplomatic initiative that moved the Palestine question back to center stage on the region's political agenda. In a speech before a joint session of Congress in March 1991, President George H. W. Bush coupled his declaration of an end to hostilities against Iraq with the announcement of a new US effort to achieve Arab–Israeli peace on the basis of UNSCR 242 and an exchange of land for peace.

The Bush administration quickly followed up, with Secretary of State James Baker making frequent trips to the Middle East in the spring and summer of 1991. Signaling a change in the pro-Israel policies of the Reagan years, Baker called on Israel to end the expansion of Jewish settlements in the occupied territories. Famously, he told the Shamir government that the administration would not support providing Israel with $10 billion in loan guarantees for the absorption of immigrants from the former Soviet Union if the building of settlements continued.

The culmination of the US diplomatic initiative was the 1991 Middle East Peace Conference in Madrid, convened in late October with cosponsorship by the Soviet Union and usually known simply as the Madrid Peace Conference. The meeting was attended by Israeli, Egyptian, Syrian, and Lebanese delegations, as well as a joint Jordanian–Palestinian delegation in which the Palestinian team was essentially independent. Also present were the Saudi Arabian ambassador to the United States and the secretary-general of the Gulf Cooperation Council (GCC). The talks, begun at Madrid, continued in Washington and elsewhere throughout 1992 and the first half of 1993. Although no important agreements were reached, the fact that Israeli and Arab representatives were meeting and discussing substantive issues was itself a significant development. Particularly encouraging was the spectacle of Israeli officials negotiating with Palestinians from the occupied territories who were in direct contact with PLO leaders in Tunis.

Another important development that further changed the political landscape during this period was the Labor Party's victory in the Israeli parliamentary election of June 1992. Although narrow, reflecting the continuing political divisions within the Jewish state, Labor's victory was widely interpreted as giving Yitzhak Rabin, the new prime minister, a mandate to seek an accord with the Palestinians. Indeed, the June 1992 balloting is sometimes described as Israel's "intifada election," meaning that it was shaped in substantial measure by the messages directed at the Israeli public by the Palestinian uprising and the PLO peace initiative. Labor's principal coalition partner in the government that now came to power was the peace-oriented Meretz bloc, with the relatively dovish Shas Party supplying the remaining votes necessary for a parliamentary majority.

This was the situation in August 1993 when the world learned that secret negotiations between officials of the Israeli government and the PLO had been taking place in Norway for several months. Even more dramatic was the news that the two sides had reached agreement on a Declaration of Principles, often called the "Oslo Accords," that held out the possibility of a revolutionary breakthrough in the long-standing conflict. The declaration's preamble recorded the parties' hope for the future; it stated that it was time for Israelis and Palestinians to end "decades of confrontation and conflict, recognize their mutual legitimate and political rights, and strive to live in peaceful coexistence and mutual dignity and security to achieve a just, lasting and comprehensive peace settlement and historic reconciliation." The declaration was signed on September 13, 1993, at a ceremony at the White House in Washington. Israeli prime minister Yitzhak Rabin and PLO chair Yasir Arafat both spoke movingly, and Rabin then accepted the hand extended to him by Arafat.

Although important obstacles remained on the road to peace, the Declaration of Principles generated hope throughout the Middle East and beyond and introduced significant changes into the dynamic of the Israeli–Palestinian conflict. In line with agreed-upon interim arrangements, Israeli forces withdrew from Gaza and the Jericho area in May 1994, and Palestinians assumed administrative responsibility for the two territories. An Egyptian helicopter then flew Arafat from Cairo to Gaza, where he had decided to establish his permanent residence. Before departing, the Palestinian leader declared, "Now I am returning to the first free Palestinian lands." After Arafat arrived in Gaza, while right-wing Israelis protested in Jerusalem, he delivered to a waiting crowd of two hundred thousand Palestinians a triumphant address from the balcony of the former headquarters of the Israeli military governor.

In addition to this "Gaza and Jericho First" plan, the interim accords outlined provisions for Palestinian self-rule in other parts of the West Bank. Specifically, it called for the establishment of a Palestinian Interim Self-Government Authority, which would take the form of an elected council and would govern during a transition period not to exceed five years. This council was to be elected no later than July 13, 1994, by which time the modalities of the balloting were to have been negotiated, as were structure, size, and powers of the council and the transfer of responsibilities from the Israeli military government and its civil administration.

Finally, the Israeli–PLO accords specified that negotiations to resolve final status issues should commence no later than two years after the Israeli withdrawal from Gaza and Jericho, at which time the transition period would begin. These negotiations were to cover all outstanding issues, including Jerusalem, refugees, settlements, security, borders, and relations with other neighbors. The transitional period, which was not to exceed five years, would end with the conclusion of a "permanent settlement based on Security Council Resolutions 242 and 338." UNSCR 338, adopted during the war of October 1973, called on the parties to terminate all military activity and implement UNSCR 242 immediately after the ceasefire.

Many Israelis and Palestinians doubted the sincerity of the other side's commitments. Many Palestinians also complained that the Declaration of Principles did not require a halt to Israeli settlement activity in the West Bank and Gaza. Nor did it explicitly promise that negotiations would lead to the creation of a Palestinian state. As expressed by one Palestinian leader from Gaza, who favored compromise but viewed the accords as one-sided and flawed, the agreement "is phrased in terms of generalities that leave room for wide interpretations. . . . It seems to me that we are trying to read into it what is not there."[58]

Despite this kind of skepticism, as well as the determined opposition of some Israelis and some Palestinians, there was unprecedented movement in the direction of peace during 1994 and 1995. Israeli–Palestinian negotiations during this period culminated in Washington on September 28, 1995, with Arafat and Rabin signing the "Oslo Interim Agreement," often described as "Oslo II." Provisions of the agreement dealt in detail with the redeployment of Israeli military forces and the transfer of power and responsibility to the Palestinian Authority (PA) and subsequently to an elected Palestinian Council. With respect to deployment, the agreement delineated three categories of territory. In Area A, which included the major cities of the West Bank as well as Jericho and Gaza, Palestinians were to have both civilian and security control. In Area B, which included most smaller towns, villages, refugee camps, and hamlets, Palestinians were to exercise administrative authority, with Israel retaining overall security responsibility. In Area C, which included Israeli settlements, military bases, and state lands, Israel retained sole control over both civilian and military affairs. Areas A and B together constituted about 27 percent of the West Bank, exclusive of East Jerusalem, and gave the PA responsibility for about 97 percent of the Palestinian population of Gaza and the West Bank, again exclusive of East Jerusalem (see Chapter 20, Map 20.1).

Oslo II also dealt with the institutions that would govern the areas over which Palestinians exercised authority. These included a Palestinian Council and an Executive Authority, with the council and the chairman of the Executive Authority, or president, constituting the Palestinian Interim Self-Government Authority. Both the council and the president were to be elected directly and simultaneously by the Palestinian people of the West Bank, Jerusalem, and Gaza Strip, and these elections took place on January 20, 1996. With turnout heavy and monitors pronouncing the balloting to be generally free and fair, the results were a decisive victory for Arafat and Fatah. The Palestinian leader received 88 percent of the vote for the post of chairman of the Executive Authority. Fatah, for its part, won 68 of the council's 88 seats, 21 of these going to candidates who supported the faction but had run as independents.

The Israeli redeployment and the establishment of a Palestinian Interim Self-Government Authority were not the only important accomplishments during the hopeful years of 1994 and

1995. There was also a significant change in Israel's relations with the broader Arab world. With Israel recognized by the PLO, a number of Arab countries were now willing to deal with the Jewish state, and new contacts were established almost immediately after the Declaration of Principles was signed. In October 1994, Israel and Jordan signed a peace treaty, making Jordan the second Arab country, Egypt being the first, to formally declare itself at peace with the Jewish state. Israel also established important cooperative relations or joint projects with Morocco, Tunisia, Qatar, and Oman at this time. In addition, Saudi Arabia and other GCC countries ended their boycott of Israel; more generally, the Arab states ended their practice of challenging Israeli credentials at the United Nations. Israel, for its part, supported Oman's bid for a seat on the UN Security Council, this being the first time Israel had supported an Arab country seeking membership on the council.

Nor was cooperation limited to state-to-state relations. In Jerusalem and Tel Aviv, in Arab capitals, and in Europe, Arab and Israeli businesspeople and others met to discuss a wide range of joint ventures and collaborations. A sense of the momentum that had been generated is conveyed in the following excerpt from a May 1994 *International Herald Tribune* article, titled "When Former Enemies Turn Business Partners":

> Israel's transition from pariah to potential partner is most evident in the overtures to Israel by Arab governments and businessmen seeking potentially lucrative deals. Since September, Israeli officials have received VIP treatment in Qatar, Oman, Tunisia and Morocco. Qatar is studying how to supply Israel with natural gas. Egypt has launched discussions on a joint oil refinery, and officials talk of eventually linking Arab and Israeli electricity grids. . . . Millionaire businessmen from Saudi Arabia, Kuwait, Qatar and Bahrain [are] jetting off to London, Paris, and Cairo to meet Israelis, while Jordanians, Egyptians and Lebanese are rushing to Jerusalem for similar contacts.[59]

While business and commerce were at the heart of most of these contacts, it was understood, especially in Israel, that the noneconomic benefits of business deals, joint ventures, and development projects were no less important. Of equal or perhaps even greater value was their contribution to the normalization of Arab–Israeli relations. Economic linkages and cooperative ventures would give each side proof of the other's good intentions, thereby contributing to the psychology of peace and accelerating its momentum. They would also establish a network of shared interests, thus discouraging any resumption of hostilities and interlocking the new economic and security regimes that appeared to be sprouting in the region.

This was not the whole story of this period, however. Against the hope and optimism generated by what became known as the Oslo peace process stood the continuation of Israel's settlement drive and a cycle of violence that usually began with attacks on Israeli civilians by Palestinian extremists opposed to an accommodation with the Jewish state, followed by harsh and sometimes excessive reprisals by Israel. With respect to settlements, while the number of Israelis living in the occupied territories (exclusive of East Jerusalem) had already grown to 105,000 by the beginning of 1993, settlement activity did not slow; if anything, it accelerated after the signing of the Oslo Accords. By spring 1996, there were 145,000 Israelis living in these territories. With respect to violence, Israelis were particularly disturbed by the growing number of suicide bomb attacks against civilian targets in Israel, for the most part carried out by Hamas (*H.arakat al-Muqāwamah al-'Islāmiyyah*), an Islamist political movement that had grown up in recent years. In 1994 and 1995, these and other attacks, including those directed at civilian and military targets in the West Bank and Gaza, killed 120 Israelis. Also contributing to the violence were attacks on Palestinians by Israeli settlers.

These trends reinforced the fear of each side that the other side was not serious. For Palestinians, the Israeli government appeared to lack the ability and perhaps even the will and desire to confront the settlers and, as had been expected, to limit settlement expansion and preserve the status quo in the West Bank and Gaza until final status negotiations. For Israelis, the PA appeared to lack the ability and perhaps even the will and desire to put an end to the violence that was claiming Israeli lives. There were thus competing trends in late 1995: one extremely hopeful but another that raised fears that the Oslo process might unravel.

The tragic assassination of Yitzhak Rabin on November 4, 1995, marked the beginning of a new phase of the Oslo process. Rabin was shot by Yigal Amir, a young religious Jew and former yeshiva student, following a rally in Tel Aviv in support of the Oslo Accords. Amir had made plans to assassinate Rabin on two previous occasions, although these were never implemented, and he expressed satisfaction upon hearing that his attack had killed the prime minister. In his view, Rabin deserved to die for his willingness to withdraw from parts of the Land of Israel, which he considered a betrayal of the Jewish people.

Shimon Peres, a veteran Labor Party politician who at the time was foreign minister, assumed the premiership upon Rabin's death, and in February, he called for new elections, which were held in May. The election, which was marked by an especially bitter campaign, pitted Peres against Benjamin Netanyahu, the leader of Likud. By a slender margin, 50.5 percent to 49.5 percent, Netanyahu emerged the victor and became prime minister. The coalition government formed by Netanyahu included Knesset members from Likud and religious and other parties from the Center and the Right.

Although he had opposed the Oslo Accords, Netanyahu stated that his government would respect agreements made by the previous government. At the same time, he insisted that he would do only what was clearly required, embracing the letter but not the spirit of the interim agreement, and that he would demand strict Palestinian compliance with all relevant provisions. Netanyahu also had little interest in halting or even slowing the expansion of Jewish settlements in the West Bank and Gaza. His government restored the financial incentives offered to settlers that had been canceled by Labor and authorized settlement expansion in the central part of the West Bank, which had been opposed by Labor. More than four thousand new housing units were built during his time as prime minister.

All of this reinforced Palestinian doubts about the peace process, but Israeli actions were not the only Palestinian complaints. Many Palestinians were also disappointed at the autocratic way in which Arafat and the PA governed the areas over which they had authority. As described by a prominent Palestinian analyst, Arafat "was egocentric, reveled in attention, and was jealous of rivals. He worked tirelessly to keep all the strings controlling Palestinian politics, particularly the financial ones, in his hands alone."[60] There were also growing complaints about corruption within the Palestinian leadership and administration. According to opinion polls, the proportion of Palestinians concerned about corruption was 49 percent in September 1996, 61 percent in March 1998, and 71 percent in June 1999.

The failure of the peace process to halt or even slow Israel's settlement drive, as well as mounting dissatisfaction with Arafat's leadership, contributed to the growing popularity of Hamas, and to a lesser extent Islamic Jihad, another political faction operating under the banner of Islam. Although these were still minority movements, a growing number of Palestinians were receptive to their message that peace with Israel was neither possible nor desirable and that "armed struggle" was the only way to secure Palestinian rights. By late 1998, approximately 20 percent of Palestinians in the West Bank and Gaza were telling pollsters that Hamas and Islamic Jihad were their preferred political factions.[61] The Islamist movement was also building a grassroots organization, laying the foundation for a more serious challenge in the future, especially if Arafat was unable to obtain meaningful concessions from Israel and unwilling to deliver honest and effective government.

In January 1999, amid mounting political discontent in Israel, not only among those dissatisfied with the meager accomplishments of the peace process but also among those to the right of Netanyahu, the Knesset voted to dissolve itself and hold new elections. The Labor Party was led at this time by Ehud Barak, one of the most decorated soldiers in the history of Israel, and Barak's election campaign emphasized the need for a breakthrough in the peace process and also the withdrawal of the Israeli troops remaining in southern Lebanon. The election was held in May, and the result was a decisive victory for Barak and Labor over Netanyahu and Likud.

Upon becoming Israel's tenth prime minister, Barak moved quickly on his agenda, displaying the straightforward and goal-oriented style of a military officer. There was a flurry of diplomatic activity during the remainder of 1999 and the first half of 2000. This period saw the first Israeli–Palestinian talks addressed to final status issues, as well as a short-lived effort by Israel and Syria to reach a peace agreement and, as Barak had promised, the withdrawal of Israeli forces from southern Lebanon. Barak's election also brought increased US involvement in the Israeli–Palestinian conflict. In July 1999, for example, Secretary of State Madeleine Albright coordinated a meeting between Arafat and Barak at the Egyptian resort of Sharm al-Shaykh, where the Israeli and Palestinian leaders signed a document devoted to the implementation of outstanding commitments and agreements. Also notable at this time was President Bill Clinton's strong personal interest and involvement in the Israeli–Palestinian peace process.

Despite the flurry of diplomatic activity, progress on the ground was limited, and by 2000, both Barak and Clinton had concluded that a summit meeting offered the only possibility for a breakthrough. Clinton was in the last months of his presidency, and having already invested heavily in the Middle East peace process, he hoped that his legacy would include an Israeli–Palestinian accord. Barak believed that only at a summit devoted to final status issues could the two sides make concessions that were not only difficult and painful but also potentially explosive at home. The Palestinians did not share the US and Israeli eagerness for a summit; in fact, they strongly opposed the idea, insisting that they would not have time to prepare adequately and that continued negotiations were required if the summit, when held, were to have any chance of success. Pressed by the United States, however, and with Clinton assuring Arafat that the Palestinians would not be blamed if the summit ended in failure, the Palestinian leader was unable to refuse the Americans, and the summit opened at Camp David on July 11, 2000.

The overriding final status issues facing the Israelis and Palestinians at Camp David were borders and settlements (which were interrelated), Jerusalem, refugees, and security. Each of these issues would have to be satisfactorily resolved if there were to be a two-state solution that brought the Israeli–Palestinian conflict to an end. With respect to borders, the question was the extent to which Israel would withdraw from the West Bank and Gaza, allowing all or at least most of this territory to be the basis for a Palestinian state, and to what extent Israel would dismantle Jewish settlements in order to make this possible. Palestinians claimed that by recognizing Israel in its pre-1967 borders they had already agreed that the Jewish state would occupy 78 percent of historic Palestine, and they thus insisted that they could not accept less than the remaining 22 percent for their own state. Indeed, they claimed that a territorial compromise on the basis of the pre-1967 borders was implicit in the Oslo Accords. For its part, Israel sought to retain at least some of the West Bank and to reach agreement on a border that would allow the largest-possible number of settlements to be annexed to the Jewish state and the smallest-possible number of settlements to be dismantled because they would otherwise be in the territory of the Palestinian state.

With respect to Jerusalem, the question was the extent to which the city would be redivided on the basis of the pre-1967 borders so that the Palestinians would have all of East Jerusalem as their capital, or whether the borders would be redrawn to reflect the fact that Israel had unified the city after 1967 and since that time had built new neighborhoods and municipal institutions that virtually erased the old boundaries. Furthermore, apart from the question of how to distribute Israeli and Palestinian sovereignty across the various and intertwined Jewish and Arab neighborhoods in the eastern part of the city, there would also have to be agreement about the exercise of sovereignty over places having religious significance for both Jews and Muslims. Of particular importance in this connection was the Temple Mount/Haram al-Sharif, which neither side was prepared to see fall under the sovereign control of the other.

The refugee question concerned the rights and future of Palestinians who had left or been driven from their homes during the 1947–1948 war, many of whom, with their offspring, had lived in neighboring countries, frequently in refugee camps, since that time. The Palestinians insisted that Israel recognize the refugees' "right of return"—their right to return to the communities, now in Israel, they had left in 1947 and 1948. They also called for reparations, to include compensation not only for individuals but also for the property abandoned by the refugees, and they argued that claims for these reparations should be addressed solely to Israel. The refugee question was thus a *political* issue for the Palestinians, and they insisted that Israel's recognition of its responsibility for creating the refugee problem would be a historic gesture—one that was necessary for Israeli–Palestinian peace.

The Israelis, by contrast, insisted on addressing the issue as a *humanitarian* concern. They were unwilling to recognize the Palestinians' right of return, arguing that Israel's Jewish character would be compromised should a significant number of non-Jews be added to the country's population. Already Muslim and Christian Arabs constituted about 20 percent of Israel's citizens. From the Israeli perspective, the solution to the refugee issue thus lay in compensation and resettlement. No more than a small number of refugees would be permitted to return to Israel, and this would be within the framework of family reunification. The rest would be able either to move to the Palestinian state or, should they prefer, to receive assistance in relocating elsewhere.

After two weeks of complicated, difficult, and ultimately unsuccessful negotiations, the Camp David summit ended on July 25, 2000, with no agreement on any of the key issues. Nor was there agreement after the summit about exactly what had been offered by each side and, in particular, about who was responsible for the failure to reach agreement on any of the final status issues (see Box 2.1).

With distrust already heightened by the failure of the Camp David summit, the situation in the West Bank and Gaza deteriorated quickly, and an escalating cycle of violence, often called the "al-Aqsa intifada," took shape in the fall of 2000. Helping to ignite the violence in late September was a provocative and controversial visit to the Temple Mount/Haram al-Sharif by Ariel Sharon, who had assumed the leadership of Likud following Netanyahu's electoral defeat in 1999. There is dispute about Sharon's motives for this visit. Sharon himself declared that his purpose was to examine archaeological sites following work by Muslim authorities in an area of historic importance to Jews. Others suggested that his objectives were more political, both to shore up support within Likud against a possible challenge from Netanyahu and to pressure Barak and reduce any chance of a compromise with the Palestinians on control of the holy sites.

Whatever his motivation, or combination of motivations, the visit helped to touch off a cycle of violence that continued throughout the fall and then through 2001, 2002, and beyond. Although the visit itself was completed without incident, clashes soon followed as young Palestinians threw stones at Israeli police, who in return fired tear gas and rubber bullets at the protesters. Rioting later broke out in East Jerusalem and Ramallah, and confrontations continued and became more lethal in the days that followed. By the end of the month, the disturbances had spread to almost all Palestinian towns in the West Bank and Gaza, with twelve Palestinians killed and more than five hundred wounded. Small numbers of IDF troops were also wounded during this period. Palestinian and Israeli deaths resulting from the violence during 2001 were 469 and 191, respectively. The next year was even more lethal; the numbers for 2002 were 1,032 and 321, respectively.

As with the Camp David summit, there are competing narratives about who was responsible for the outbreak of the al-Aqsa intifada. Although it seems clear that Sharon's action was a catalyst, some Israeli accounts contend that the visit merely gave the Palestinians an excuse to launch a campaign of violence that had in fact been planned in advance. A variation on this Israeli narrative is that although the uprising may not have been planned in advance, Palestinian leaders, and Arafat in particular, concluded that it served their interest, and they therefore made no attempt to restrain it once it was under way. For Palestinians, however, the disturbances were simply an understandable response to the deteriorating conditions and hopelessness that characterized life under occupation. Given this situation, it was predictable; and indeed the Palestinians had predicted it and had warned Israeli authorities in advance that Sharon's visit would bring protests that could easily lead to violence.

What was left of the Oslo peace process played out against the background of the al-Aqsa intifada, often called the second intifada, in late 2000 and early 2001. Diplomatic initiatives were renewed during these months, including meetings that brought Barak and Arafat together in Paris and Sharm al-Shaykh and even in Barak's home. The most important events during this period were meetings at the White House in December 2000 and at Taba, Egypt, in late January 2001. Bill Clinton presented what became known as the "Clinton Parameters" at the December White House meeting. These spelled out what the US president, and many others, considered to be a fair and realistic compromise on each of the issues that had divided Israelis and Palestinians at Camp David, and this led some analysts to suggest that had Clinton presented these at Camp David the summit might have turned out differently.

BOX 2.1

COMPETING NARRATIVES OVER THE JULY 2000 CAMP DAVID SUMMIT

Although there is a general consensus on the broad outlines of the positions and proposals that were advanced, there are competing narratives about exactly what transpired at Camp David in July 2000.[62]

One narrative reflects the Israeli position, which also received support from Bill Clinton and some US analysts. It holds that Israel made unprecedented and indeed revolutionary concessions at Camp David. For example, Barak crossed traditional Israeli red lines by agreeing to Palestinian sovereignty in the Jordan Valley and some parts of Jerusalem. More generally, as expressed by Barak himself, for the first time in the history of this conflict, the Palestinians were offered . . . an independent contiguous state in more than 90 percent of the West Bank and in 100 percent of the Gaza Strip, access to neighboring Arab countries, the right of return for Palestinian refugees to any place in the Palestinian state, massive international assistance and even a hold in a part of Jerusalem that would become the Palestinian capital.

Thus, according to this narrative, the summit failed not because of any deficiencies in what the Israelis offered but rather because the Palestinians, and Arafat in particular, were not seriously interested in concluding a peace agreement. After describing what the Israelis offered, Barak stated that "Arafat refused to accept all this as a basis for negotiations and [later] deliberately opted for terror. That is the whole story."[63]

Another narrative, advanced not only by Palestinians but also by some US and Israeli analysts, puts forward two interrelated arguments: that there were serious shortcomings in what the Israelis offered, even if the proposals did break new ground from the Israeli perspective; and that responsibility for the failure to conclude an agreement does not rest solely with Arafat and the Palestinians. Furthermore, many of these analysts contend that the summit was followed by a campaign of disinformation and spin, led by Israeli and US allies of Barak, regarding Israel's "generous offer" and Arafat's "rejectionism." According to Robert Malley, a member of the US team at Camp David, "The largely one-sided accounts spread in the period immediately after Camp David have had a very damaging effect." Malley additionally asserts, however, that these accounts "have been widely discredited over time."[64]

The substance of this second narrative identifies what its advocates consider serious deficiencies in the Israeli proposals offered at Camp David. Specifically, the borders proposed by Israel made a significant portion of the West Bank and most of East Jerusalem a permanent part of the Jewish state; Israel refused to accept Muslim sovereignty over the Temple Mount/Haram al-Sharif in return for Palestinian recognition of Jewish sovereignty over the Western Wall; Israel insisted on de facto control of the Jordan Valley for an extended period, thereby reducing further the proportion of historic Palestine controlled by the Palestinian state; Israel also insisted on retaining two slender land corridors running from pre-1967 Israel in the west to the Jordan Valley in the east, thus dividing the Palestinian state into three noncontiguous blocks, in addition to Gaza; and not only did Israel refuse the return of a significant number of Palestinian refugees to the territory they left in 1947 and 1948, but the Israelis at Camp David also refused even to acknowledge Israel's responsibility for the refugee problem.

Those who support this narrative do not necessarily contend that the failure of the summit rests solely with the limitations of Israel's proposals. Many acknowledge that the Palestinians did not do an adequate job of advancing counterproposals and that Clinton and the Americans were too closely aligned with the Israelis and should have done more to fashion compromise proposals. Overall, as Malley writes in this connection, "All three sides are to be indicted for their conduct" at Camp David, including the Palestinians, but the summit did not fail because of Palestinian rejectionism. "If there is one myth that has to be put to rest," he contends, it is that the US-backed Israeli offer was something that any Palestinian could have accepted. One should not excuse the Palestinians' passivity or unhelpful posture at Camp David. But the simple and inescapable truth is that there was no deal at Camp David that Arafat, Abu Mazen, Dahlan, or any other Palestinian in his right mind could have accepted.[65]

The Taba meeting took place without US participation. George W. Bush had won the US election of November 2000, and the new US president decided that his administration would not get involved in the Arab–Israeli conflict. The discussions at Taba were nonetheless substantive and productive, and at their conclusion, the parties issued a joint statement saying they had made significant progress even though important gaps remained. The talks concluded shortly before elections were to be held in Israel, and the final communiqué stated that "the sides declare that they have never been closer to reaching an agreement and it is thus our shared belief that the remaining gaps could be bridged with the resumption of negotiations following the Israeli elections."[66]

The elections held on February 6 resulted in a crushing defeat for Barak and Labor and a decisive victory for Sharon and Likud. Sharon received 62.39 percent of the vote, winning by the largest margin ever in Israeli politics. During the electoral campaign, the Likud leader had made clear that his government would have no interest in talks with the Palestinians under the conditions prevailing in the West Bank and Gaza. Thus, if there is a specific date on which the Oslo peace process can be said to have completed its run, it would be February 6, 2001.

NEW ACTORS, CONTINUING CONFLICT

The post-Oslo period was marked not only by the absence of Israeli–Palestinian negotiations but also by a deteriorating situation on the ground. On the one hand, the settler population in the West Bank and Gaza continued to grow and received increased support from the government.

On the other hand, the al-Aqsa intifada continued and became ever more deadly. Thus, whereas there had been something of a contest between hope and doubt during the early years of the Oslo process—when a sense of genuine opportunity competed with a history of distrust and for a few years it even looked like hope was the more justified sentiment—the landscape of the Israeli–Palestinian conflict in 2001 was bleak, angry, and moving in a direction that brought satisfaction only to those who opposed the historic compromise promised by the Declaration of Principles.

Approximately 193,000 Israeli settlers were living in the West Bank, exclusive of East Jerusalem, at the beginning of 2001, and the number increased steadily in the years that followed. According to a report based on a 2004 Israeli government database, 38.8 percent of the West Bank land on which settlements were built was listed as "private Palestinian land," much of it secured illegally for settlement purposes.[67] The settler population also grew in Gaza and East Jerusalem during this period. In Gaza, the number of settlers increased by 18 percent after Sharon became prime minister, from about 6,700 in early 2001 to about 7,900 in August 2005, when the settlers were evacuated. The number of Israelis living in East Jerusalem in areas captured in the June 1967 War increased from 172,000 to 184,000 between the beginning of 2001 and the end of 2005 (see Chapter 20, Map 20.1).

The troubled situation on the ground was also the result of the expanding and increasingly lethal violence associated with the al-Aqsa intifada. Whether condemned as "pure terrorism" by Israelis or defended by some Palestinians as "armed struggle" against a determined and deepening occupation, the al-Aqsa intifada did not resemble the popular mass uprising of the first intifada, in which most Palestinians pursued a strategy of nonviolent resistance. With murderous attacks on civilian targets inside Israel, as well as armed assaults on both soldiers and settlers in the occupied territories, the al-Aqsa intifada had the character of a guerrilla war. By the end of 2004, 905 Israelis had been killed by Palestinians, with the largest number of deaths (443) resulting from suicide bomb attacks against civilians in Israel.

If the total number of Israelis killed by Palestinians from 2001 to 2004 was 905, the number of Palestinians killed by Israelis during the same period was more than three times as high: 469 in 2001, 1,032 in 2002, 588 in 2003, and 821 in 2004, for a total of 2,910. Most of these deaths were the result of Israeli military action, although fifty-five Palestinians were killed by settlers. It was inevitable, and understandable, that Israel would respond to the violent assaults by Palestinians and that Israelis would be particularly outraged by the attacks carried out not in the occupied territories but against civilian targets in the country itself. Many observers nonetheless judged the Israeli response to be excessive, and some, including some Israeli analysts, suggested that IDF aggressiveness might have helped to shape the violent character of the intifada. This was also the conclusion of a fact-finding committee led by former US Senator George Mitchell. The Mitchell committee additionally concluded that the al-Aqsa intifada had not been planned in advance, as Israel charged. And again, as stated in a report written by prominent Israeli scholars and published in 2005 by the Teddy Kollek Center for Jerusalem

Studies, "The IDF's excessive reaction might have... transformed the popular uprising into a full-fledged armed conflict."[68]

Among the strategies Israel employed in an effort to suppress the intifada was Operation Defensive Shield, launched in late March 2002. The operation brought about the reoccupation of the West Bank by the Israeli forces and was intended to undermine the PA as well as to suppress the violence—related objectives in the judgment of the Sharon government. In what became the largest IDF operation in the West Bank since the June 1967 War, armored units moved into major Palestinian cities for the purpose, as Sharon told the Knesset, of capturing terrorists, their dispatchers, and those who support them; confiscating weapons intended for use against Israeli citizens; and destroying the facilities used to produce weapons. Strict and extended curfews were placed on Palestinian communities during the operation, leading human rights organizations to complain that Israel was practicing collective punishment. The fiercest fighting associated with the operation was in Jenin and its refugee camp, considered by Israel to be a center of Palestinian terrorism. Operation Defensive Shield was officially terminated on April 21, 2002, but the occupation of areas under PA authority continued, as did the violence that brought about a steadily increasing number of Israeli and Palestinian deaths.

With suicide bombings inside Israel continuing in the weeks and months after Operation Defensive Shield, the Sharon government in June 2002 began the construction of what it termed a security barrier (and what critics called a separation wall) in an effort to prevent terrorists from entering Israel from the West Bank. The barrier was to consist of an electrified fence in most sections, with barbed wire, trenches, cameras, and sensors running alongside. In some areas, it was to involve high concrete walls with fortified guard towers. Designed to seal off the West Bank and projected to be more than four hundred miles long when completed, the barrier was to run through Palestinian territory, roughly following the Green Line but also cutting eastward in order to place settlements on the Israeli side of the divide wherever possible. The barrier was strongly condemned by Palestinians, in part because its projected route placed almost 15 percent of the West Bank and the villages in this territory on the Israeli side of the barrier. In some instances, it also divided Palestinian communities or separated Palestinian farmers from their fields and made it difficult for them to market their produce to other parts of the West Bank. If Israelis sought to barricade themselves inside a wall, the Palestinians argued, the wall should be built on Israeli land rather than along a route that imposed new hardships on many Palestinians and confiscated Palestinian land.

The barrier was also controversial in Israel, in ways that transcended the traditional ideological differences between the Right and the Left. Sharon, like many on the Right, had initially opposed the construction of a barrier, despite the popularity of the idea among the Israeli public, because it would divide the Land of Israel and separate not only Palestinians but also many settlers from the Jewish state. Thus, the project was originally proposed by Labor and the Left, rather than Likud and the Right, as a response to Palestinian terrorism. Sharon embraced the concept in the aftermath of Operation Defensive Shield, but the plan remained a divisive issue on the right side of the political spectrum—not only because of its potential territorial implications but also because it might send the message that the intifada had succeeded in forcing Israel to make unilateral concessions.

Four initiatives aimed at reviving the peace process were put forward in 2002 and 2003 in an effort to reverse the deteriorating spiral of events on the ground. Two were well-intentioned but ultimately short-lived Israeli–Palestinian efforts. The first of these was a petition drive initiated in March 2002 by Ami Ayalon, former head of Israel's General Security Services, and Sari Nusseibeh, a prominent Palestinian intellectual and president of al-Quds University in East Jerusalem. The petition called for a two-state solution and the resolution of final status issues along the lines set forth in the Clinton Parameters and the understandings reached at Taba the year before. By late summer 2005, 254,000 Israelis and 161,000 Palestinians had signed the petition. The second Israeli–Palestinian effort was the product of a small working group led by Yossi Beilin, who had been the minister of justice in the Barak government, and Yasir Abd Rabbo, who at the time was the PA's minister of information. The document produced by the group, known as a "Geneva accord" because of support provided by the Swiss government, was introduced at a signing ceremony in Jordan in October 2003. It also drew on the Clinton Parameters and the discussions at Taba but went into more detail than the Ayalon–Nusseibeh proposal.

One of the two remaining initiatives during this period was a Saudi Arabian proposal introduced at an Arab League summit in March 2002. The proposal advocated a two-state solution and offered Israel not only peace with the Arabs but also full and normal relations. In return, it called upon Israel to return to its pre-1967 borders and agree to the establishment of a Palestinian state in the West Bank and Gaza, with East Jerusalem as its capital. The Arab League summit, with all twenty-two member states represented, approved the proposal unanimously but added the provision of a "just solution to the Palestinian refugee problem" to be agreed upon in accordance with relevant United Nations resolutions.

Finally, there was an international initiative. Called the "Road Map for Peace," or simply the "road map," it was put forward in April 2002 by the United States, the European Union, Russia, and the United Nations, frequently designated "the quartet" in diplomatic circles. The road map put forward a three-stage plan: first, through May 2003, ending violence, normalizing Palestinian life, and building Palestinian institutions; second, from June to December 2003, a transition to an independent Palestinian state with provisional borders and attributes of sovereignty; and third, a permanent status and end of conflict agreement to be completed during 2004 and 2005.

None of the documents and plans put forward in 2002 and 2003 brought changes on the ground or led to a resumption of peace talks. Other post-Oslo developments, by contrast, altered the political landscape in both Israel and the Palestinian territories. In January 2003, the Likud coalition won an overwhelming victory in the Israeli general election, enabling Sharon to form a new center-right government. Of even more immediate consequence was a change in Palestinian politics. In November 2004, Yasir Arafat fell ill, and after being taken to France for treatment, the seventy-five-year-old Palestinian leader fell into a coma and died. Following Arafat's death, Mahmoud Abbas, commonly known as Abu Mazen, became head of the PLO, which in theory continued to represent Palestinians throughout the world. Abbas was also elected president of the Palestinian Authority in January 2005. As a member of Arafat's inner circle, Abbas represented continuity in Palestinian leadership. At the same time, he was known as someone who favored negotiations with Israel and who considered the use of violence in the name of "armed struggle" and "resistance" to be detrimental to the Palestinian cause.

Palestinian politics at this time was also marked by the emergence of a "young guard," younger members of Fatah who had not been in exile with Arafat and had earned their nationalist credentials during the first intifada or in Israeli jails. These Palestinians complained about the cronyism and corruption of the PA under Arafat. The most prominent member of the young guard was Marwan Barghouti, who had been in prison in Israel since 2002. In late 2004, Barghouti declared that he would run against Abbas in the presidential election, although he subsequently withdrew after receiving assurances that the younger generation would be given more influence in the future.

The young guard was not the only challenge facing Abbas. Of greater and more immediate concern were relations with Hamas, which had gained significantly in popularity during the al-Aqsa intifada. The growing influence of Hamas became increasingly consequential as the Palestinians moved toward elections for a new legislative council, which were scheduled for January 2006. Israeli politics also saw transformative developments during this period. Early in 2004, Sharon shocked both supporters and opponents by announcing "a change in the deployment of settlements, which will reduce as much as possible the number of Israelis located in the heart of the Palestinian population," and he then indicated that the key element of the new policy would be Israel's total pullout from the Gaza Strip, not only redeploying the IDF but also relocating the settlers and dismantling the settlements.

The proposed pullout from Gaza divided the political Right in Israel and brought bitter criticism from many in Sharon's coalition. The prime minister nevertheless pushed ahead, and the pullout began in August 2005, with the IDF forcibly removing those settlers who insisted on remaining in Gaza and then demolishing their residences. The removal of all Israeli civilian and military personnel and the demolition of all residential buildings were completed by mid-September. Opponents of the withdrawal had hoped the pullout would prove to be something of a national trauma, sufficiently difficult and divisive to discourage any consideration of dismantling additional settlements in the future. In fact, however, despite angry denunciations on the political Right and determined resistance by some settlers, the evacuation for the most part went smoothly. In explaining and seeking to justify the withdrawal, Sharon stated that defending the Gaza settlements had become unacceptably difficult and costly, whereas the pullout would facilitate engagement with the enemy, when needed, and improve Israel's security. The conclusion reached by Palestinians was, accordingly, that armed struggle was more effective than negotiation in securing Israel's withdrawal from occupied territory.

The withdrawal was also a tacit admission that retention of the West Bank and Gaza involved a demographic challenge. The argument, whose implications Sharon and Likud had always refused to accept, is that Arabs would soon outnumber Jews in Israel, the West Bank, and Gaza, taken together, and that permanent retention of the occupied territories would, therefore, make Jews a minority in the Land of Israel. According to this argument, this situation would present Israel with an impossible choice: either deny political rights to a permanent Palestinian majority, in which case the country would cease to be democratic, or grant citizenship and equality to the Palestinians, in which case the country would not remain Jewish. Sharon's spokesperson said in this connection that Israel "must draw its borders so it has a clear Jewish majority, ensuring that it is both a Jewish and democratic state. Staying in Gaza goes against those goals."[69]

Palestinians, for their part, welcomed the Israeli withdrawal from Gaza, and many also drew the conclusion that confrontation rather than negotiation seemed to be the best way to obtain territorial concessions from the Jewish state. But Palestinians also had important complaints and reservations. They complained about the unilateral character of Israel's action. The absence of Palestinian involvement, they contended, worked against a smooth and orderly transfer of authority to the PA, which might lead to instability in the future. In addition, many pointed out that the withdrawal hardly made Gaza independent since Israel retained control of its sea and airspace and most land access routes. Indeed, the disengagement plan itself specified that Israel "will guard and monitor the external land perimeter of the Gaza Strip, will continue to maintain exclusive authority in Gaza air space, and will continue to exercise security activity in the sea off the coast of the Gaza Strip."

Many Palestinians also distrusted Sharon's motives, arguing that he was pulling Israel out of Gaza in order to remove security and demographic challenges that might exert pressure for greater territorial concessions elsewhere. According to this analysis, the Gaza pullout was not a step on the road to territorial compromise. On the contrary, by withdrawing from Gaza with its roughly then 1.4 million Palestinians, Sharon was sacrificing seventeen Israeli settlements in order to retain the West Bank, or at least most of it.

Whatever the relative explanatory power of the various factors that shaped Sharon's decision to evacuate the settlements in Gaza, his action split the Right in Israel and dramatically changed the country's partisan landscape. With continuing opposition to his policies in Likud and with new elections scheduled for March 2006, Sharon formed a new political party, Kadima, in order to have a freer hand in pursuing his policy of unilateral disengagement should the new party succeed in the forthcoming election. A number of Sharon's allies in Likud followed him into Kadima, including Ehud Olmert. Shimon Peres, at the time vice premier in Sharon's beleaguered coalition, stated that he would leave the Labor Party and join the prime minister's next government, should he be elected.

Early in January 2006, the seventy-seven-year-old Sharon suffered a massive brain hemorrhage and subsequently lapsed into a prolonged coma. With the prime minister incapacitated, presumably permanently, Olmert assumed the leadership of Kadima as the party prepared for elections and as Israeli politics entered the post-Sharon era. Sharon's program of unilateral disengagement was a central plank in the party's campaign platform. It specified that the borders to be drawn by Israel would be determined according to three rules: inclusion of areas necessary for Israel's security; inclusion of places sacred to the Jewish religion, and first and foremost a united Jerusalem; and inclusion of a maximum number of settlers, with a stress on settlement blocs. The election gave Kadima 29 seats in the new parliament, with Labor finishing second and winning 19 seats; this enabled Olmert to form a new centrist-governing coalition.

In the meantime, elections for the Palestinian Legislative Council in January 2006 had introduced equally significant changes into Palestinian political life. With a turnout of 78 percent and the balloting pronounced to be free and fair by both international and local observers, the Palestinian public handed a decisive and unexpected victory to Hamas. The party's lists, presented to voters under the label of Change and Reform, captured 74 of the Council's 132 seats. Fatah, by contrast, won 45 seats. Of the remaining 13 seats, four went to independent candidates backed by Hamas, three went to the Popular Front, two went to an alliance of the Democratic Front and several other small factions, two went to the Independent Palestine list, and two went to the Third Way list of Hanan Ashrawi and Salam Fayyad.

A variety of factors contributed to the Hamas victory. Prominent among these was dissatisfaction with Fatah and the leadership of the PA. There was broad dissatisfaction with the PA, and hence with Fatah, because it had failed to win concessions from Israel or even slow Israeli settlement activity, despite more than a decade of peace negotiations. Hamas, by contrast, was given credit for the resistance that had forced Israel to dismantle settlements and withdraw from Gaza, the only time the Jewish state had ever relinquished Palestinian territory. Probably even more important, the PA's corruption and cronyism hurt Fatah candidates, whereas Hamas won appreciation from the public for its operation of schools, orphanages, mosques, clinics, and soup kitchens. About 90 percent of Hamas' estimated annual budget of $70 million was spent on social, welfare, cultural, and educational activities, delivering services that the government often failed to provide.

In addition to emphasizing social justice and internal political reform, the Hamas electoral platform also declared, "Historic Palestine is part of the Arab and Islamic land and its ownership by the Palestinian people is a right that does not diminish over time. No military or legal measures will change that right." Accordingly, there were immediate questions in Israel about the degree to which Palestinians who voted for Hamas were endorsing the party's rejection of territorial compromise and a two-state solution. In fact, however, public opinion polls taken at the time of the election showed only a weak correlation between partisan preference and attitudes toward Israel and the peace process. A poll taken by the Palestinian Center for Policy and Survey Research (PCPSR) two weeks after the election, for example, reported that 40 percent of Hamas voters supported the peace process and only 30 percent opposed it, so it concluded that the victory of Hamas "should not be interpreted as a vote against the peace process." A PCPSR poll taken a month later reported that 75 percent of the Palestinian public wanted Hamas to conduct peace negotiations with Israel, while only 22 percent were opposed to such negotiations.

These developments from 2004 to 2006 swept away the status quo that had been in place for decades. For both Palestinians and Israelis, there were consequential changes in leadership and in the partisan map of parties and factions. And on the ground, Israel's unilateral withdrawal from Gaza meant that the status quo in the occupied territories had changed as well. Subsequent events played out against this background and brought continuing tension and fresh confrontation. Following its success in the Palestinian elections of January 2006, Hamas invited Fatah to join it in a national unity cabinet. Abbas and Fatah declined, however, in large part because Hamas refused to accept international agreements previously signed by the PA, without which negotiations with Israel would be impossible. The situation became much more tense in April 2006 when PA security forces, most of whom were members of Fatah, clashed in

Gaza with forces loyal to Hamas and the latter eventually, in June 2007, seized control of the territory. Thereafter, Gaza and the West Bank had separate and competing administrations. Importantly, the Hamas take-over of Gaza led Israel to significantly intensify its blockade of the territory.

Israel held elections for a new Knesset in March 2006, and the balloting confirmed the political primacy of Kadima, now led by Ehud Olmert. In December, Olmert began negotiations with PA president Mahmud Abbas, and over the course of 2007 and much of 2008, the two leaders developed many creative ideas and significantly narrowed the gap between them on key issues, including security, borders, Jerusalem, and refugees. Despite the promise of these negotiations, however, and while both Olmert and Abbas later made statements to the effect that they were "very close," negotiations ended in September 2008 without a final agreement after Abbas withdrew his support for a plan he had helped to negotiate.[70]

In the meantime, the newly elected Olmert government almost immediately faced serious challenges on other fronts. In July 2006, Hezbollah fired rockets at towns south of the Israel–Lebanon border and then attacked two IDF vehicles patrolling on the Israeli side of the frontier, killing three soldiers and kidnapping two others. Israel's need to respond to this provocation was understandable, but at least some observers believed that the situation could have been resolved through diplomacy; and many, in any event, judged the IDF's military response to be disproportionate and excessive. Israel's military operation, which included massive air strikes and artillery fire, caused extensive loss of life and damage to the Lebanese infrastructure. Yet, the result after thirty-four days of fighting was a stalemate, not an Israeli victory.

Violent confrontations at this time were not limited to Israel's war with Hezbollah. Increasingly accurate missile attacks on southern Israeli towns from Gaza caused tension to rise further. By May 2007, four Israelis had been killed and eighty-four had been injured. Hamas argued that the intensifying Israeli blockade of Gaza justified these attacks, but the attacks were intolerable for Israel, and the Jewish state responded with massive retaliatory strikes. During the fall of 2006, Israeli actions killed more than three hundred Palestinians. In December 2008, the Palestinian organization intensified its campaign of rocket attacks on Israeli communities, and Israel again responded with devastating air raids, this time followed by a ground assault in January 2009. The Israeli operation, "Operation Cast Lead," killed more than one thousand Palestinians, most of whom were civilians, according to Israeli human rights organizations. It also caused extensive damage to both government and civilian buildings.

The death and destruction in Gaza brought a predictable array of charges and counter-charges. Israelis argued that their military operation was both necessary and justified. They pointed out that the actions of Hamas had initiated the confrontation, and they bitterly observed that the international community, now eager to condemn Israel for defending itself, had not responded to Israel's repeated complaints about Hamas's provocations and its own consistent warnings that its patience in the face of these attacks was limited. Israelis also charged that Hamas had launched many of its missile attacks from areas with a dense civilian population and that this, not any Israeli desire to punish the people of Gaza, was the main reason for the large number of civilian deaths.

Palestinians and some international observers offered a different assessment. While not necessarily defending Hamas, they argued that the root of the problem lay in the Israeli blockade of Gaza and, more generally, in Israel's refusal to offer the Palestinians a serious alternative to armed struggle. In addition, even those who expressed sympathy for the Israeli position often judged the Jewish state's action to have been disproportionate and significantly beyond what could be justified. These arguments were rekindled in the fall of 2009 when the "Report of the United Nations Fact Finding Mission on the Gaza Conflict" was submitted. The mission was headed by Richard Goldstone, former judge of the Constitutional Court of South Africa and former prosecutor of the international criminal tribunals for the former Yugoslavia and Rwanda. The Goldstone report condemned both Hamas and Israel, but it was much more critical of Israel. It condemned Israel in particular for failing to take the actions needed to prevent the widespread loss of civilian life. Subsequently, while continuing to be critical of Israel's actions on the ground, Goldstone stirred new controversy in April 2011 when, in a *Washington Post* opinion article, he distanced himself from some of the report's conclusions and endorsed the Israeli position that Palestinian deaths had not been the result of deliberate policy.

The fighting between Israel and Hamas in Gaza was replayed in fall 2012 and again in summer 2014. The 2014 clashes brought death and destruction that exceeded even that of the Israel–Hamas "war" of January 2009. Responding to Hamas rocket attacks and the use by Hamas of tunnels to carry out raids or to attack or kidnap Israelis, the IDF launched Operation Protective Edge. Air strikes were accompanied by the entrance into Gaza of Israeli troops. By the time a ceasefire was accepted in late August, more than 2,100 Palestinians had been killed, the majority of whom were civilians, and seventy Israelis, sixty-four of whom were soldiers, had lost their lives. There was also extensive damage to housing and infrastructure in Gaza. As in the past, there were bitter arguments about the legitimacy of Hamas' attacks on Israel, particularly since the faction's rockets were not aimed at specific military targets, and about the legitimacy and proportionality of the Israeli response.

Israel held elections for a new Knesset in February 2009 against the background of the earlier wars between Israel and Hamas; and Likud, once again led by Benjamin Netanyahu, was victorious. Netanyahu and Likud prevailed again in the elections of January 2013, this time presenting a common list with Yisrael Beitanu, a secular right-wing party. Kadima received only two seats, in large part because the leader of the party who followed Olmert, Tzipi Livni, had left to form a new political party.

In the Palestinian political arena, Fatah and Hamas worked during this period, with uneven results, to end their four-year rift. Meeting in Cairo in talks brokered by Egypt, Abbas and Hamas leader Khaled Meshal signed a "Reconciliation Pact" in May 2011. The pact called for an interim government to administer both the West Bank and Gaza Strip and to prepare for presidential and parliamentary elections within a year. Talks aimed at implementing the agreement made only limited progress, however, and although further agreements were signed in Doha in February 2012 and in Cairo in May of the same year, skeptical observers were right to predict that there would be neither a unity government nor new elections.

The second decade of the 21st century brought not only continuing domestic political challenges for Israelis and Palestinians but also regional developments that introduced additional uncertainties. One source of tension was Iran's increasingly effective efforts to produce weapons-grade nuclear materials. Israel and its supporters insisted that Iran could not be allowed to acquire nuclear weapons, raising the prospect of an Israeli attack on Iranian facilities if international sanctions failed to bring a change of course in Tehran.

Perhaps the most important sources of regional uncertainty during the first years of the 2010s were associated with what became known as the "Arab Spring," which involved massive antigovernment protests in a number of countries and led to the fall of long-standing authoritarian regimes in Tunisia, Egypt, Libya, and Yemen. The change of regime in Egypt was of particular concern, especially after a candidate affiliated with the Islamist Muslim Brotherhood, Muhammad Morsi, became the country's first democratically elected president in June 2012. While promising to respect Egypt's international engagements, including its peace treaty with Israel, and while also helping to broker a ceasefire between Hamas and Israel when the two were on the brink of war in November 2012, Morsi and his party were much more critical of Israel than had been the Mubarak government, and this raised the possibility of a change in the Egyptian–Israeli relationship.

There were also diplomatic initiatives during these years. The election of a new American president, Barack Obama, brought hopes that the United States would work to revive the Israel–Palestinian peace process. In May 2011, Obama made an especially strong speech in which he called for a Palestinian state based on Israel's pre-1967 borders. Then in July 2013, following Obama's reelection the previous November, the new US secretary of state, John Kerry, launched a peace initiative that involved numerous meetings with Israeli and Palestinian leaders, as well as direct meetings between Palestinian and Israeli officials. The initiative never made significant or sustained progress, however, despite Kerry's determination and very substantial commitment. With each side blaming the other, and with some blaming the United States as well, Kerry reluctantly abandoned his quest nine months after it had begun.[71]

The Palestinians undertook diplomatic initiatives of their own during this period. In fall 2011, Mahmoud Abbas declared that Palestine would seek to become a full member of the United Nations, thereby giving it access to additional channels through which to put pressure on Israel and the United States. The Palestinians had a meaningful measure of success in November 2012 when they sought, and received, recognition by the UN General Assembly. By a vote of 138 to 9, with forty-one abstentions and with the United States among the dissenters, the assembly passed a resolution upgrading Palestine to a "nonmember observer state" at the United Nations.

An additional dimension of the Palestinians' international campaign in support of their cause is the Boycott, Divestment, and Sanctions Movement, popularly known as BDS. Claiming inspiration from the campaign to end apartheid in South Africa, the BDS movement was initiated in 2005 by a coalition of Palestinian nongovernmental organizations (NGOs); and since that time, it has evolved into a global campaign with support in many countries. It calls for divestment from Israeli companies, or at least those that do work in the occupied territories, and the boycott of Israeli activities and institutions, including Israeli universities. The movement has been strongly criticized by Israel and its supporters, who argue that many of its advocates are motivated by anti-Semitism and also that it seeks to undermine Israel's right to exist, not only to pressure the Jewish state into withdrawing from the West Bank and East Jerusalem.[72] The effectiveness of BDS has also been questioned. Nevertheless, the movement has continued to gain support in some quarters, particularly in Europe and on some American university campuses. In November 2015, for example, the European Union mandated that there be identifying labels on Israeli products manufactured in the West Bank and exported to Europe. Some companies, like Ben & Jerry's ice cream, stated that they would no longer sell their products in occupied Palestinian territory.

A PARADIGM SHIFT?

Developments during the last years of the 2010s brought significant changes but also left prospects for an Israeli–Palestinian accord as remote as ever. Likud scored a decisive victory in the Knesset elections of March 2015, and Israeli settlement activity continued to surge under the right-wing government led by Benjamin Netanyahu. By early 2018, the number of Israeli settlers in the West Bank was about 438,000, with another 209,000 Jewish Israelis living in East Jerusalem. By early 2021, the figures had grown to about 475,000 and 220,000, respectively.

The election of Donald Trump as US president in November 2015 brought increased American support for Israel and its occupation policies. Particularly significant and symbolic was Trump's decision to move the American Embassy in Israel from Tel Aviv to Jerusalem, something that past presidents, both Republican and Democratic, had been unwilling to do. The new American Embassy opened in May 2018, and as the new American ambassador to Israel, Trump appointed a man who endorsed and had financially supported Israeli settlement activity in the West Bank. Other Trump actions hostile to the Palestinians included an end to American aid to the PA, which was about $60 million annually and was used primarily to support Palestinian security services. In fall 2018, Trump also ordered closure of the PLO office in Washington.

There were new confrontations between Israel and Hamas in the spring of 2018. Beginning in March, Palestinians in Gaza began a series of protest demonstrations near the territory's border with Israel. The protests were organized by independent activists but had the support of Hamas. While organizers stated that the demonstrations were to commemorate the *nakba* and affirm the Palestinian refugees' right of return, demonstrators were also protesting Israel's deepening blockade of Gaza. On May 14, as the day of Israeli independence and the Palestinian *nakba* approached, protesters massed along the border and some tried to cross into Israel. Israeli soldiers responded by firing at the protesters; and according to Palestinian sources, fifty-eight were killed and more than one thousand were wounded. In summer 2018, Israel imposed additional restrictions on the entry of goods into Gaza and blocked all delivery of fuel and gas.

Apart from the periodic flare-ups of violence, an admixture of anger, resignation, and steadfastness marked Palestinian life in Gaza. To many Israelis, Gaza is a base for terrorism. To many Palestinians, however, Gaza is an open-air prison.

Among Palestinians in general, and especially among West Bank Palestinians, anger was fueled not only by the deepening occupation and expansion of Israeli settlements but also by discontent with the Palestinian Authority under the leadership of Mahmoud Abbas and by the continuing division between Fatah and Hamas. A poll in December 2016 reported, for example, that two-thirds of the Palestinian public believed a two-state solution to the conflict with Israel was no longer possible, and about the same proportion wanted Abbas to resign. In October 2017, Fatah and Hamas agreed to a "reconciliation" arrangement that gave Fatah civilian control in the Gaza Strip, but an April 2018 poll found that only one-third of those surveyed were satisfied with the performance of the reconciliation government. And again, two-thirds wanted Abbas to resign.[73]

New questions about the future of Palestinian leadership presented themselves in the spring of 2021. Hamas at this time changed its status from leader of the resistance and representative of the interests of the Gaza Strip to leader of the resistance and representative of the interests of all Palestinian people in their relations with the Israeli occupation. As reported by Palestinian political scientist Khalil Shikaki, a majority of Palestinians in the occupied territories believe Hamas to be more deserving than Fatah of representing and leading the Palestinian people. Nevertheless, Shikaki concluded, it remains to be seen whether Hamas can actually do this and really even wishes to do so.[74]

New political dynamics were emerging in Israel as well. One of these was increased support for centrist political parties, coming primarily from voters who had previously voted for a party of the Left, but also, though to a lesser extent, for a party of the Right. This gave rise to an electoral standoff between centrist parties and right-wing parties, particularly Likud, making it difficult for either to put together a governing coalition. Two elections in 2019 and one in 2020 were indecisive for this reason. The results of the March 2021 election, the fourth in two years, were not dissimilar, but this time parties across the political spectrum that shared only a dislike of Benjamin Netanyahu joined together to make yet another election unnecessary and to deny Netanyahu the possibility of another term as prime minister. Notably, too, for the first time, an Arab party was a member of the governing coalition. It remained to be seen whether, as many predicted in mid-2021, this "coalition of opposites" would break apart before very long and make another election necessary after all. And indeed, defections in spring 2022 left the unwieldy coalition without a parliamentary majority, and in June the coalition's leaders introduced a bill calling for new elections, to be held in November.

Another development with significant implications is the Israeli parliament's passage, in July 2018, of the controversial "Jewish Nation-State Law." The law makes Israel, first and foremost, the state of the Jewish people, wherever they may reside, and only thereafter the state of its citizens. The law specifically states that the right to exercise national self-determination in the State of Israel is unique to the Jewish people. The legislation is a "basic law," giving it the strength of a constitutional amendment; a basic law cannot be amended except by another basic law enacted by the parliament.

Those potentially most disadvantaged by the law are Israel's Palestinian Arab citizens. Although many would argue that the nation-state law merely codified, or further codified, what was already the situation—that Palestinian Arab citizens of Israel were already second-class citizens, the law nevertheless strengthened the divide between Jewish and Arab members of the Israeli political community. For example, Arabic lost its status as a language of state and was downgraded to "special status." It is in this context, in part, that in 2021 there were confrontations, sometimes lethal, between Jewish and Arab residents of Israel's mixed cities. Palestinian Israelis were not alone in complaining about the nation-state law. The law was also denounced by many centrist and left-leaning Jewish Israelis. There were vehement denunciations from some American Jews as well. As head of the US-based Union for Reform Judaism stated shortly after the nation-state law was passed, "The damage that will be done by this new nation-state law to the legitimacy of the Zionist vision … is enormous."[75]

The nation-state law also has implications for the occupied territories and Israel's conflict with the Palestinians. It codifies as basic law the positions of Israel's political Right. It declares that Jerusalem is the complete and united capital of Israel, that the development of Jewish settlement is a national value, and that the land of Israel is the historic homeland of the Jewish people. As has frequently been pointed out, permanent retention of the West Bank will force Israel to decide whether the territory's Palestinian inhabitants will have political rights. Giving these rights will preserve Israel's democratic character but dilute its Jewish character. Denying these rights will preserve the country's Jewish character but not its democratic character. The nation-state law suggests that many Jewish Israelis have already decided what they are intent on preserving, the country's Jewish character, and what they are willing to sacrifice, the country's democracy.

Donald Trump claimed during his campaign for the American presidency in 2015 that he would present a plan to end the Arab–Israeli conflict, and he continued promising to present a peace plan after he was elected. Many were skeptical that Trump would have anything constructive to offer since the actions of his administration were decidedly pro-Israeli and anti-Palestinian. Late in January 2020, as he began the last year of his presidency, Trump unveiled the long-promised plan, entitled "Peace to Prosperity: A Vision to Improve the Lives of the Palestinian and Israeli People." As expected, the plan favored Israel. Israeli Prime Minister Benjamin Netanyahu accompanied Trump when he presented the plan at a White House press conference. No Palestinian official was present.

The political dimension of Trump's plan envisioned Israeli annexation of the Jordan Valley and other parts of the West Bank, together totaling roughly 30 percent of the territory. The remaining noncontiguous enclaves were to be the basis of a Palestinian "state," which would not come into existence until Israel and the United States certified that the Palestinians had met certain conditions. These include total demilitarization and abandonment of actions against Israel at the United Nations and elsewhere in the international arena. The Trump plan did not provide for a Palestinian capital in East Jerusalem; it proposed instead that the capital be located in an Arab neighborhood, or refugee camp, on the outskirts of the city.

As expected, the Palestinians vigorously denounced the plan, calling it an American–Israeli conspiracy to deny the Palestinian people its political rights. Interestingly, and despite effusive praise from the Netanyahu government, the plan was vehemently denounced by the Yesha

Council, which represents Jewish Settlements in the West Bank. By supporting the establishment of a Palestinian state, however fragmented and enfeebled it might be, Trump and his advisors had, according to the council, demonstrated that they do not support Israel's security and settlement interests and are not true friends of Israel.

There was also an economic dimension to Trump's plan. In the hope of persuading Palestinians to accept the plan's unfavorable political terms, it states, ambiguously, that "The Trump Economic Plan" would "facilitate more than $50 billion in new investment over ten years." Palestinian initiatives involving internal economic, legal, and educational reforms, the plan continued, would "unleash the economic potential of the Palestinian people."

The Abraham Accords, although separate from the Trump peace plan, are an additional element of the Trump administration's actions aimed at resolving the conflict between Israel and its Arab neighbors. Led by the president's son-in-law, Jared Kushner, and with the initiative also pushed forward by the United Arab Emirates ambassador to the United States, Yousef Al-Otaiba, US brokered consultations led to a friendship treaty between Israel and the UAE. Signed in September 2020, the agreement was entitled, "Abraham Accords Peace Agreement: Treaty of Peace, Diplomatic Relations and Full Normalization between the United Arab Emirates and the State of Israel." A parallel treaty between Israel and Bahrain was signed at the same time; Sudan and Israel signed an agreement to normalize relations the following month; and Israel and Morocco reached a similar agreement in December. The four agreements are often known collectively as the Abraham Accords.

The Trump administration offered concessions to incentivize the Arab countries to normalize relations with Israel. The United States agreed to sell advanced F-35 aircraft to the UAE, to lift Sudan's designation as a state sponsor of terrorism, and to recognize Moroccan sovereignty in the Western Sahara. These countries might not have signed on to the Abraham Accords without these incentives. On the other hand, at least in the case of the UAE and Morocco, there were already well-developed, albeit unofficial, connections with Israel. Reflecting their own embrace of accords, thousands of Israelis traveled to the UAE for tourism or business as soon as flights were available.

The Trump peace plan and the Abraham Accords raise questions that will be answered in the months and years ahead. Most important is whether a durable peace can be achieved without an agreement with the Palestinians. Will the political dimension of the Trump plan be implemented, with Israel annexing large parts of the West Bank? If so, how will the Palestinians respond? It is very unlikely that they will agree, albeit grudgingly, to see their struggle for statehood realized in the fragmented political entity proposed by the Trump plan. But will they then find ways to resist; if so, will this bring protests by Arab publics; and should such protests be widespread and intense, would this force Morocco and Sudan, and possibly also Bahrain and perhaps even the UAE, to move away from normalized relations with Israel?

The contours of Palestinian resistance will be shaped not only by Israeli actions but also by the structure and personnel of Palestinian leadership, which, as discussed, may change in the coming days. American policies and actions will help to shape the future as well. Trump's successor, Joe Biden, has already restored aid to the PA. Much remains to be determined, but it is at least possible that the Israeli–Palestinian conflict and Israel's place in the Middle East will change to a degree not seen since the early days of the Oslo Accords. Maybe there will be a paradigm shift. Or maybe, more likely, the familiar and unhappy dynamics of the Israeli–Palestinian conflict will reassert themselves. Students of the conflict will need to stay tuned.

SUGGESTED READINGS

Abu-Lughod, Ibrahim, ed. *The Transformation of Palestine: Essays on the Origin and Development of the Arab-Israeli Conflict*. Evanston, IL: Northwestern University Press, 1971.

Anziska, Seth. *Preventing Palestine: A Political History from Camp David to Oslo*. Princeton, NJ: Princeton University Press, 2018.

Avineri, Shlomo. *The Making of Modern Zionism: The Intellectual Origins of the Jewish State*. New York, NY: Basic Books, 1981.

Brenner, Michael. *In Search of Israel: The History of an Idea*. Princeton, NJ: Princeton University Press, 2018.

Brynen, Rex, ed. *Echoes of the Intifada: Regional Repercussions of the Palestinian-Israeli Conflict*. Boulder, CO: Westview Press, 1991.

Gordis, Daniel. *Israel: A Concise History of a Nation Reborn*. New York, NY: Harper Collins, 2016.

Enderlin, Charles. *Shattered Dreams: The Failure of the Peace Process in the Middle East, 1995–2002*. New York, NY: Other Press, 2003.

Feldman, Shai, Shikaki Khalil, and Monem Said Aly Abdel. *Arabs and Israelis: Conflict and Peacemaking in the Middle East*. New York, NY: Palgrave Macmillan, 2013.

Hurewitz, Jacob Coleman. *The Struggle for Palestine*. New York, NY: Schocken Books, 1976.

Khalidi, Rashid. *Palestinian Identity: The Construction of Modern National Consciousness*. New York, NY: Columbia University Press, 2009.

Khalidi, Rashid. *The Hundred Years' War on Palestine: A History of Settler Colonialism and Resistance, 1917–2017*. New York, NY: Metropolitan Books Henry Holt, 2020.

Kurtzer, Daniel, ed. *Pathways to Peace: America and the Arab-Israeli Conflict*. New York, NY: Palgrave Macmillan, 2012.

Laqueur, Walter. *A History of Zionism*. New York, NY: Schocken Books, 1976.

Lesch, Ann Mosley, and Tessler Mark. *Israel, Egypt and the Palestinians: From Camp David to Intifada*. Bloomington, IA: Indiana University Press, 1989.

Malek, Cate, and Hoke Mateo. *Palestine Speaks: Narratives of Life Under Occupation*. San Francisco, CA: Voice of Witness, 2014.

Maoz, Zeev. *Defending the Holy Land: A Critical Analysis of Israel's Security and Foreign Policy*. Ann Arbor, MI: University of Michigan Press, 2006.

Morris, Benny. *Righteous Victims: A History of the Zionist-Arab Conflict, 1881–2001*. New York, NY: Vintage, 2001.

Morris, Benny. *The Birth of the Palestinian Refugee Problem, 1947–1949*. Cambridge: Cambridge University Press, 1987.

Rabinovich, Itamar. *Waging Peace: Israel and the Arabs, 1948–2003*. Princeton, NJ: Princeton University Press, 2004.

Ross, Dennis. *Doomed to Succeed: The U.S.-Israel Relationship from Truman to Obama*. New York, NY: Farrar, Staus and Giroux, 2015.

Rotberg, Robert, ed. *Israeli and Palestinian Narratives of Conflict: History's Double Helix.* Bloomington, IA: Indiana University Press, 2006.

Sahliyeh, Emile. *In Search of Leadership: West Bank Politics since 1967.* Washington, DC: Brookings Institution Press, 1987.

Said, Edward. *The Question of Palestine.* New York, NY: Vintage Books, 1992.

Shamir, Jacob, and Shikaki Khalil. *Palestinian and Israeli Public Opinion: The Public Imperative in the Second Intifada.* Bloomington, IA: Indiana University Press, 2010.

Shlaim, Avi. *The Iron Wall: Israel and the Arab World.* New York, NY: W. W. Norton, 2001.

Tessler, Mark. *A History of the Israeli-Palestinian Conflict.* Bloomington, IA: Indiana University Press, 2009.

Tessler, Mark. *Religious Minorities in Non-Secular Middle Eastern and North African States.* New York, NY: Palgrave MacMillan, 2020.

3 STATES AND INSTITUTIONS

Ellen Lust[1]

As discussed in Chapter 1, in the decades following World War II, those living in the area comprising the Middle East and North Africa (MENA) moved from being ruled by expansive, Islamic empires to being under the control of European mandates to, finally, being citizens of independent states. At least in theory, Syrians, Tunisians, and others were to govern themselves, managing their own society's problems and development. But as we will see in subsequent chapters, in many cases societies have often fallen short of achieving optimal outcomes; they suffer sectarian strife (Chapter 4), limitations on political participation (Chapter 5), social inequalities (Chapter 6), stalled economic development (Chapter 7), and international and regional interference (Chapter 8). In part, this is because much of the region is marked by weak state development and a lack of institutions that depersonalize and depoliticize the distribution of goods and services. This limits societies' ability to use resources efficiently, granting opportunities to all.

This chapter presents three interrelated ways to understand the states and institutions that affect governance in the MENA region today. First, the chapter examines the strength of MENA states—their ability to affect the daily lives of citizens, influence the distribution of resources, and implement public policies that improve the living conditions for society as a whole. Most states in the region are weak, making it difficult for governments to respond to citizens' demands and improve their lives. Second, the chapter considers regime type. Even after the Arab uprisings of the 21st century (both those that began in 2010–2011 and others that emerged nearly a decade later), authoritarian regimes remain prevalent in the MENA region. Consequently, political processes often divert resources away from social development and toward narrow coalitions of ruling elites. Third, the chapter examines key state institutions, including legislatures, political parties, judiciaries, and the media. In the MENA, these institutions tend to be captured by small circles of elites, leading to suboptimal outcomes. The chapter describes these three factors—weak states, authoritarian regimes, and ineffective institutions, explores why these are found throughout much of the region, and considers possibilities for change. The chapter ends by discussing two questions commonly raised with regard to the region: What explains the endurance of regimes in the face of discontent? And why has liberal democracy been so elusive?

THE STATE

Max Weber conceptualized the state as "a human community that (successfully) claims the monopoly on the legitimate use of physical force within a given territory."[2] There are three important components of this definition. First, the state has *defined territorial boundaries*, presumably enjoying control over the entire area within the boundaries. Second, the state has *legitimacy*—that is, the acceptance of the community's *right* to govern, which in the 20th century can be enjoyed, and contested, on two levels: within the domestic community (those living within the boundaries of the state) and among actors in the international community (other states within the international system).[3] Finally, the state has a *monopoly* on the use of force. The use of force by the military, police, or other arms of the state is generally viewed as a legitimate means of keeping order, while the use of force by paramilitary groups, vigilantes, or gangs—at times also intended to keep order—is not.

Ideally, the modern state system is constituted of strong nation-states—that is, countries in which nationalism (a socially constructed identity that leads a group of people to see themselves as belonging to a shared community) and state boundaries overlap, and states enjoy sovereignty over territory within established borders. Further explained, these are states in which "coercion-wielding organizations that are distinct from households and kinship groups . . . exercise power over all other organizations within substantial territories."[4] Strong states are able to extract resources from populations and implement policies that benefit society as a whole rather than subnational populations (e.g., families, tribes, or other distinct subnational groups). A strong sense of nationalism makes it easier for them to do so.

Weak States in the MENA Region

States in the MENA have often failed to live up to these ideals on a number of counts. Both international and domestic forces have challenged states' legitimate right to rule. In many cases, social groups—often based on ethnicity, sectarianism, or kinship—captured state institutions, using them to benefit themselves rather than society as a whole. This undermined the establishment of an autonomous state that is capable of acting and formulating policies independent of the interests of specific groups or classes. Elsewhere, social groups have found ways to circumvent the state, avoiding the attempts of the state apparatus to govern and maintain order according to local customs and institutions. At times, groups negotiate the boundaries of state influence with those in power, leaving entire areas out of the reach of state authorities.

These problems are not unique to the MENA region. In a cross-regional study of state-building, Joel Migdal pointed out the problems that emerge in the context of "strong societies, weak states."[5] Ruling elites remain in power without developing the ability to extract resources, maintain order, and affect the daily lives of citizens or promote economic and social development, and he argued that they do so by establishing agreements—tacit or explicit—with local elites that effectively grant them control over spaces. The result is a sort of Swiss-cheese arrangement in which the state has control over some areas but is relatively absent in others.

This is also not to say that state-building, and even the attendant development of nation-states (e.g., of shared identity of a community congruent with state boundaries), has been entirely absent in the MENA region. Citizens today appear to identify with the state more than they did when it was established in the 20th century. During the 1950s, Arabs often took to the streets, calling for the establishment of pan-Arab states and challenging the legitimacy of newly founded states. In contrast, during the more recent Arab uprisings, Egyptians, Libyans, Tunisians, and others made claims on state leaders as "nationals," demanding their rights as citizens. That said, however, the rise of the so-called Islamic State of Iraq and Syria (ISIS), the resurgence of Kurdish movements, and others that draw into question the existing state system show that the state—and particularly the nation-state—remains weak. Conflicts still often center on demands by sectarian, ethnic, regional, and kin-based communities.

Many argue that MENA states are not simply fragile, but failed. Failed states often have the trappings of state institutions (e.g., government ministries, legislatures, and heads of state), but they have lost important aspects of statehood, such as physical control over the territory and legitimate decision-making authority.[6] Failed states receive a great deal of international attention both because they are unable to provide services and security to their people and because they are viewed as a threat to international security. Uncontrolled territory gives transnational terrorist movements room to maneuver, while the lack of development arguably provides a base of potential recruits for such movements.

A large number of MENA states today are seen to be at high risk for state collapse and the emergence of violence, as Map 3.1 shows. The 2022 Fragile States Index (FSI) rated Yemen the first, Libya the twenty-first, and Iraq the twenty-third most fragile states in the world, with South Sudan and Syria tied at third.[7] All of these countries are affected by civil conflict. The FSI gives most of the other countries in the region a "warning" status, with only Israel, Kuwait, Oman, Qatar, and the UAE considered "stable." This is particularly disconcerting as the most fragile states are countries with some of the largest populations: Yemen, Syria, Sudan, and Iraq.[8] Millions of people live in states that cannot maintain security and guide socioeconomic development effectively.

Moreover, there is little reason to expect conditions to improve in these already fragile states. The pressures of conflicts in Iraq and Syria are abating somewhat, but they continue to affect their neighbors. For instance, the movement of Syrian refugees into Jordan and Lebanon has slowed, but both countries continue to host significant Syrian populations; in 2021, Jordan had about 670,000 registered Syrian refugees (in a population of approximately 10 million Jordanians), while Lebanon had approximately 850,000 registered Syrian refugees (in a population of approximately 6.8 million Lebanese).[9] The US withdrawal from Afghanistan and the Taliban takeover also affected state stability across the region. It created a new refugee crisis, affecting Iran and, to a lesser extent, Turkey, and it also may embolden similarly minded groups across the region.[10] These pressures combine with the pressures from the coronavirus pandemic, falling oil prices, and domestic mismanagement to exacerbate economic inequalities, further deteriorate public services, and foster polarization among domestic factions,[11] thus creating conditions for further instability and violence.

Fragile and failed states face common challenges, but there are also important differences among them. For instance, Yemen has long been a classical weak state—unable to control territory, implement social and economic politics, and promote development; in 2010, just before the Arab uprisings, the FSI ranked Yemen the world's fifteenth-most fragile state. As one analyst explained, "Those in the countryside [are] unconcerned about national government. They have neither contributed to, nor been affected by, central decisions." Rather than attempting to regulate and control social forces, the Yemeni state adopted "policies of inclusion, accommodation and incorporation toward local strongmen in order to maintain social stability and regulate daily life."[12] At times, this strategy fails, and the country erupts in violence. This was the case after 2011, when Yemen faced threats from al-Qaida in the Arabian Peninsula (AQAP), from a secessionist movement (al-Hirak) in the former South Yemen, from the Houthi movement in the north, from armed Yemeni tribes, and finally, from international intervention. The crisis

MAP 3.1 ■ **Fragile States Index for Middle Eastern and North African States, 2021**

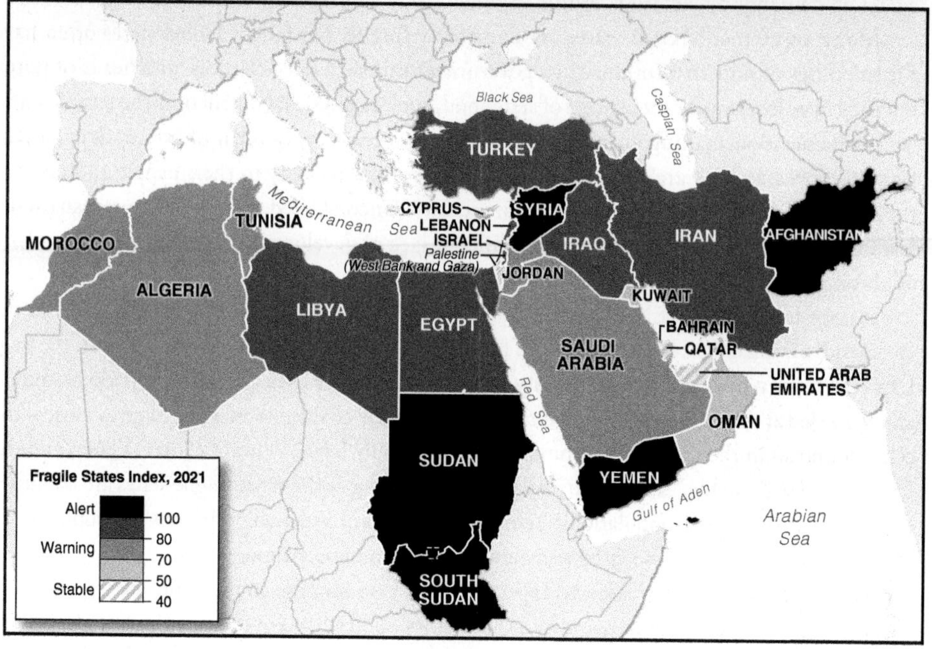

Source: Data available at http://fundforpeace.org/fsi/excel/ (accessed June 20, 2022)

has placed enormous costs on the population: By 2021, an estimated 80 percent of the population (or 24 million Yemenis) required some form of humanitarian assistance, and over half of these (or 14.3 million) were in need of acute assistance.[13]

Syria represents a case of civil war within a midperforming state. Before 2011, Syria ranked forty-eighth in the world on the FSI.[14] It provided health, education, and other services; in fact, Syria's health system was highly regarded in the Arab world. Yet it also suffered cronyism, corruption, and state capture, which contributed to the war. As discussed in Chapter 7, years of war destroyed hospitals, schools, and other public infrastructure; spurred the flight of doctors and teachers; and undermined the state's control over territory.[15] President Bashar al-Asad and those around him attempted to shore up their regime by claiming to be the sole defenders of Syrian sovereignty, maintaining the bureaucracy (including paying bureaucrats and public servants, even those under occupied territory), and attempting to monopolize service provision (requiring that humanitarian aid be channeled through the government and reportedly destroying hospitals, schools, and other services in opposition-controlled areas).[16] The ability to portray the Syrian state as intact, combined with support from Iran and Russia, appears to have been instrumental in helping the Asad regime survive the civil war.[17] Arguably, the Syrian conflict may not have erupted had the state been strong in 2011; nevertheless, the case reminds us that even when states are flawed, ruling elites can benefit from the state apparatus during conflict.

A third lesson about state failure is found in the case of Lebanon. Lebanon lacks territorial control, is unable to provide services, and frequently has fallen into civil war. The World Bank thus designates Lebanon as a "Fragile and Conflict-affected Situation," given its institutional and social fragility. Yet, until recently, the Lebanese have enjoyed good socioeconomic conditions, particularly by regional standards. It has been an upper-middle-income country, and, as the World Economic Forum notes, has consistently "punched above its weight"[18] in terms of development and global competitiveness. Such achievements were the result of a vibrant private sector; as the economist Sami Nader put it, in Lebanon the "private education soars, public education sinks."[19] Arguably, however, the weak state has contributed, and limited its ability to respond, to social and economic pressures. As discussed in Box 3.1, the result is an extraordinary social and economic crisis, which the World Bank dubbed the "Deliberate Depression," considering it among the top ten, and possibly top three, worst crises since the mid-19th century.[20]

BOX 3.1

LEBANON'S WEAK STATE AND THE EMERGENCE OF CRISIS

PHOTO 3.1 Bombing of the Rafic Hariri Airport following escalation between Hezbollah and the Israeli military.

Fadel Itani/NurPhoto via Getty Images

Lebanon has experienced a series of problems associated with weak state institutions. It collapsed into civil war from 1975 to 1990, was dominated by Syria from 1990 to 2005, and has witnessed sectarian tensions and unstable governing coalitions. Indeed, for long periods of time Lebanon has failed to have a sitting president or legitimate parliament. It also lacks a monopoly on the legitimate use of force. Two events—the 2006 war with Israel and the socioeconomic crisis emerging since 2019—illustrate the Lebanese state's failure.

The 2006 war with Israel demonstrates the Lebanese state's failure to monopolize the legitimate use of force within its borders, to maintain territorial control, and to stand as the sole representative of the Lebanese people when engaging with other states. The various labels attached to the war—the "July War," the "Second Lebanese War," or the "2006 Israel-Hezbollah War"—reflect the limited role of the Lebanese state. The war—which would last thirty-four days, cost thousands of lives, and create enormous financial setbacks—was initiated not through military escalation between states but by the engagement of a Lebanese nonstate actor and the Israeli military. The conflict began on July 12, 2006, when Hezbollah (primarily a Shiite Lebanese resistance movement with strongholds in southern Lebanon and ties to Syria and Iran) escalated the long-running conflict with Israel by ambushing two Israeli Humvees patrolling the Israeli side of the border. Lebanon claimed that this was an action of Hezbollah and not of the Lebanese government, but the Israeli government escalated its attacks. Most notably, on July 13, 2006, the Israeli military bombed the Rafic Hariri International Airport in the center of Beirut as the Lebanese government adamantly denied support for Hezbollah. The weakness of the Lebanese state was on full display: It was unable to contain Hezbollah, which effectively had engaged in a foreign policy decision outside government control.

The 2021 'Deliberate Depression' demonstrates how little had changed since 2006. The crisis became apparent in 2019, but the roots of the crisis run much deeper. Years earlier, the Lebanese government had set an official exchange rate (1,507 lira for $1), one that became more difficult to sustain after tourism and investment declined following the 2011 Arab uprisings, civil war in Syria, and refugee crisis. The full implications went largely unnoticed, however, until 2019, when Lebanon faced a triple crisis. First, the government sought to raise taxes, including a tax on WhatsApp, raising citizens' ire and lowering the interest from investors abroad. Second, like the rest of the world, Lebanon confronted the coronavirus pandemic and the subsequent decline in tourism, which typically made up 18 percent of Lebanon's GDP. Third, in August 2020, the country faced a port explosion in Beirut that not only killed two hundred, injured thousands, and destroyed neighborhoods, but also highlighted the government's ineptitude.[21] The explosion prompted the government's resignation; and the inability of elites to find compromise and put the national interests above their own led to a stalemate. Not until September 2021, over a year after the resignation, was the billionaire Najib Mikati able to form a government. In the meantime, the Lebanese lira devalued 90 percent; inflation was in triple digits; citizens went without water, electricity, and medicine; sectarian tensions rose; and those who could, fled the country.

Before we consider why states remain fragile, it is important to note that some critics object to the concepts of failed and fragile states. They argue that these concepts lack a coherent definition and operationalization and thus fail to extend scientific knowledge. Moreover, they argue, the World Bank, the European Union, G7+, and other organizations use the designation of states as *failed* or *fragile* as a justification for intervention. Critics see the designation as an "attempt by state powers to describe reality in accordance with their foreign policy priorities."[22] Such points are well taken but do not belie the fact that in many cases, the entities that govern do not possess many characteristics of statehood.

Challenges of State-Building

Scholars and development specialists have moved from assuming that state-building is a relatively natural process (a belief prevalent in the 1950s and 1960s) to expressing great concern over "failed" and "fragile" states.[23] But how do we understand the failure to build strong states? What drives fragility?

There are two basic theories of state-building. The first views the state as a social contract between individuals who seek security. The state thus develops to maintain order and grant protection, and the relationship between citizens and the state is one of relative cooperation.[24] The second perspective is that states develop as the outcome of war-making by competing groups that seek to expand their control over territories and extract resources.[25] Victors attempt to establish authority in an effort to extract resources from those within the territories under their control, thus developing taxation; to protect human and material resources and establish order, thus establishing security; and to reduce the costs of ruling by gaining domestic and international legitimacy of their rights to control over this territory.

One explanation for the weakness of MENA states lies in the challenges of postcolonial state-building. State-building was a much different process in the MENA than it was in the West. In Europe, state-building took place during an extended period of conflict between warring factions, roughly between 1000 and 1800 CE. The conflicts were bloody and destructive, but they arguably also fostered the development of nationalism and strong states. In contrast, in the MENA modern states emerged out of conflict between elites vying for power in a much more compact period, roughly during the last one hundred years. Consequently, state borders were established, but they did not necessarily result in nation-states. Identities did not match the contours of new states but instead tended to be on either larger or smaller territorial units.[26] Rather than seeing themselves as "Syrian," "Tunisian," or "Iraqi," for instance, many saw themselves as "Arabs" or "Muslims" (and were, therefore, attracted to pan-Arab and pan-Islamic movements) or as "Shi'a," "Kurdish," or "Aleppan," members of smaller sectarian, ethnic, or geographic communities. New leaders attempted to develop national identities through flags, anthems, stamps, rallies, and other performances of "nation" in the hope of shoring up their legitimacy, but they also often relied on subnational allegiances for support. The resurfacing of these identities in the face of state collapse that we see, for example, in Iraq, Libya, and Syria demonstrate the limited success of these efforts.

A second difficulty has been the intervention of powerful third parties.[27] External actors—most notably Britain, France, Russia, and the United States, but other states, nonstate actors, and multinational organizations as well—have often stepped in to bolster one side over another or to quash conflict altogether. Invested in maintaining the international state system, they have sought to reinforce territorial boundaries, shoring up central authorities in the face of secessionist movements or working to undermine the establishment of larger, more powerful entities (for example, the United Arab Republic, a greater Saudi Arabia, greater Syria or, more recently, Iraq's annexation of Kuwait). This is not to say that MENA elites were puppets in the hands of the international forces. Elites vying for power in MENA states often managed to thwart external actors, to play them off against one another, or to use their support for their own purposes. For instance, the ruling Al Thani in Qatar showed savvy in first allying with the British and gaining local authority before strategically joining Saudi Arabia once it seemed more beneficial; they even went so far as converting to Wahhabism to show allegiance. Domestic elites had agency, but powerful external forces invested in maintaining an international state system created opportunities and constraints that shaped their actions.

Importantly, in some countries, states developed more organically, as they had in the West. Iran and Turkey were founded on the centers of the fallen Qajar and Ottoman empires, respectively. The empires had been weakened, and when Reza Shah Pahlavi and Mustafa Kemal Atatürk came to power in the 1920s in Iran and Turkey, respectively, they worked to establish a new national identity and modern, Western-oriented state systems. At the same time, however, they benefited from the institutional structures that had been established in these seats of empire. Saudi Arabia, too, developed differently, with the Al Saud family establishing control over the territory that gained international recognition as an independent state in 1932.[28] In Iran, Turkey, and Saudi Arabia, ruling elites benefited from an institutional system and historical experience that helped in the development of state-building, although Western support still played an important role in keeping Western-oriented leaders in power.

A third complication in the state-building process has been the ability of incumbent rulers to rely on external rents to remain in power. They are able to obtain the resources necessary to defend their position without extracting resources from the people within their states. The sources of rents vary. Oil provides important sources of income, undermining state-building efforts. Strategic rents—or direct support from members of the international community to incumbents who are situated in particularly strategic locations—can play a similar role. Egypt and Jordan, for example, have both benefited from their strategically important locations as frontline states with Israel, receiving significant aid from the United States. Such rents can allow rulers to maintain their position while providing little space for voice and accountability.

REGIME TYPES

Many scholars and policymakers focus on regime type rather than state strength. Some emphasize prospects for democracy, which they view as intrinsically better at promoting life and liberty and positively associated with good governance and socioeconomic development.[29] Another set of scholarship considers differences within regime types, particularly distinguishing between authoritarian regimes. This section defines regimes and then examines the nature of regimes in the MENA region, the challenges they face, the strategies that incumbents use to maintain the regime, and the possibilities for regime change.

What Is a Regime?

Regimes should be understood as the set of formal and informal rules (institutions) that are used to select leaders and policies. Regimes thus determine the relative power and relationships among different actors within the governing system as well as how efficiently and for whose benefit resources are used. Regimes are relatively durable. They change, but it takes more than a change in a single rule or actor to alter regimes. Indeed, while it is quite clear that Libya and Tunisia witnessed regime change in 2011, the case of Egypt seemed initially more tenuous, as the military—and many former Mubarak allies—retained significant power. The extent of change was even more ambiguous in Yemen: although former president Ali Abdallah Salih was removed from power after decades in office, the former vice president under Salih, Abd Rabbuh Mansur Hadi, was elected in an uncontested presidential election that, initially, ushered in little fundamental change.

We need to distinguish between regimes and individuals in power. Many use the term *regime* to denote the leaders in power or, similarly, the period during which certain leaders are in power—that is, they refer to the "Mubarak regime" in Egypt or the "Asad regime" in Syria. Compare this with discussions of US politics, for instance, which focus on the "Bush administration" or the "Obama administration." The assumption is that in the United States the rules remain the same although those in power to administer the rules may change, while in Egypt and Syria political rules and institutions are presumably determined—almost embodied—by the leaders themselves.

Yet using *regime* to refer to the individuals in power is misleading. One can find great continuity in a country's regime even when leaders change. For example, the transition from Egyptian president Gamal Abdel Nasser to Anwar al-Sadat altered the ruling elite in Egypt but was not a significant change in regime. At other times, the underlying rules of the game can change quite significantly while the leader remains in power. Thus, President Ali Abdallah Salih, president of the Yemen Arab Republic since 1978, continued to rule Yemen even after the unification in 1990, when not only the borders but also the rules of the game that governed politics in both the former People's Democratic Republic of Yemen and the Yemen Arab Republic altered significantly.

Regimes in the MENA Region

The MENA region has long been characterized by resilient authoritarianism. When much of the rest of the world experienced what is now called the "third wave" of democratization, the region saw much less change (see Figure 3.1). This remained true even after the Arab uprisings. Attempts at democratization in most countries where regimes fell—Libya, Egypt, and Yemen—have failed. Of these countries, only Tunisia initially enjoyed relatively stable democratic processes. Even there, in the context of economic decline and instability, talk turned from optimistic proclamations of an "Arab spring" to gloomy discussions of "Arab winter," and finally in July 2021, to steps by Tunisian President Kais Saied to sack the prime minister, disband the elected parliament, suspend parts of the constitutions and take steps toward one-man rule.[30] Authoritarian regimes, with long-standing leaders, continue to dominate the region. (See Figure 3.1, Table 3.1, and Box 3.2.)

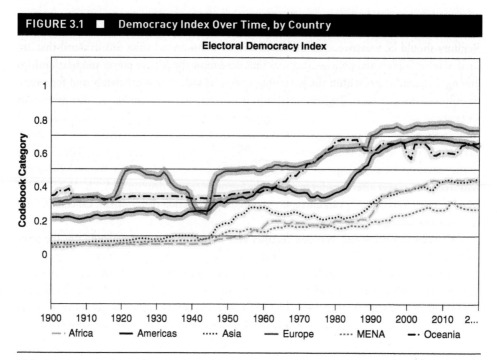

FIGURE 3.1 ■ Democracy Index Over Time, by Country

Electoral Democracy Index

Legend: — · Africa — Americas ····· Asia — Europe ···· MENA —· Oceania

Michael Coppedge et al. 2021. "V-Dem Dataset v11.1" Varieties of Democracy Project. https://doi.org/10.23696/vdemds21

TABLE 3.1 ■ Longevity of Rulers in the Middle East and North Africa, as of November 2021

Country	Date of ascendance	Current leader (years in office)	Previous leader (years in office)
Authoritarian Republics			
Algeria	December 19, 2019	President Abdelmadjid Tebboune (2 years, 10 months)	Acting President Abdelkader Bensalah (8 months)
Egypt	June 8, 2014	President Abdel Fattah el-Sisi (8 years, 4 months)	Acting President Adly Mansour (11 months)
Syria	July 17, 2000	President Bashar al-Asad (22 years, 3 months)	President Hafiz al-Asad (29 years, 3 months)
Monarchies			
Bahrain	March 6, 1999	Shaykh Hamad bin Issa Al Khalifa (23 years, 7 months)	Shaykh Isa bin Salman Al Khalifa (37 years, 6 months)

TABLE 3.1 ■ Longevity of Rulers in the Middle East and North Africa, as of November 2021 (*Continued*)

Country	Date of ascendance	Current leader (years in office)	Previous leader (years in office)
Jordan	February 7, 1999	King Abdallah II (23 years, 8 months)	King Hussein (46 years, 5 months)
Kuwait	September 30, 2020	Shaykh Nawaf Al-Ahmad Al-Jaber Al-Sabah (2 years, 1 month)	Shaykh Sabah Al-Ahmad Al-Jaber Al-Sabah (14 years, 8 months)
Morocco	July 23, 1999	King Muhammad VI (23 years, 3 months)	King Hassan II (38 years, 4 months)
Oman	January 11, 2020	Sultan Haitham bin Tariq Al Said (2 years, 9 months)	Sultan Qabus bin Said Al Said (49 years, 2 months)
Qatar	June 25, 2013	Shaykh Tamim bin Hamad al Thani (9 years, 4 months)	Shaykh Hamad bin Khalifa Al Thani (18 years)
Saudi Arabia	January 23, 2015	King Salman bin Abdul Aziz Al Saud (7 years, 9 months)	King Abdallah bin Abdul Aziz Al Saud (9 years, 5 months)
United Arab Emirates	May 14, 2022	Shaykh Mohamed bin Zayid Al Nuhayyan (5 months)	Shaykh Khalifa bin Zayid Al Nuhayyan (17 years, 6 months)
Quasi Democracies			
Iraq	October 17, 2022	President Abdul Latif Rashid (less than 1 month)	President Barham Salih (4 years)
	October 13, 2022	Prime Minister Mohammed Shia' Al Sudani (less than 1 month)	Prime Minister Mustafa Al-Kadhimi (2 years, 5 months)
Israel	July 7, 2021	Issac Herzog (1 year, 7 months)	President Reuven Rivlin (7 years)
	July 1, 2022	Prime Minister Yair Lapid (4 months)	Prime Minister Naftali Bennet (1 year, 1 month)
Lebanon	October 31, 2016	Acting President Michel Aoun (5 years, 11 months)	No direct predecessor
	September 10, 2021	Prime Minister Najib Mikati (1 year, 1 month)	Prime Minister Hassan Diab (1 year, 8 months)
Libya	March 15, 2021	Prime Minister Abdul Hamid Dbeibeh (1 year, 7 months)	Prime Minister Fayez al-Sarraj (5 years)

(*Continued*)

TABLE 3.1 ■ Longevity of Rulers in the Middle East and North Africa, as of November 2021 (Continued)

Country	Date of ascendance	Current leader (years in office)	Previous leader (years in office)
Turkey	August 28, 2014	President Recep Tayyip Erdoğan (8 years, 1 month)	President Abdallah Gül (7 years)
	N/A	Prime Minister position abolished June 2018	Prime Minister Binali Yıldırım (2 years, 1 month)
Tunisia	October 23, 2019	President Kais Saied (3 years)	President Beji Caid Essebsi (4 years, 7 months)
Yemen	April 7, 2022	Chairman of the Presidential Leadership Council, Rashad Muhammad Al-Alimi (6 months)	President Abd Rabbuh Mansur Hadi (10 years, 1 month) (transferred executive powers to the Chairman of the Presidential Leadership Council in April 2022)
Islamic Republic			
Iran	June 4, 1989	Supreme Leader Ali Hosseini Khamenei (33 years, 5 months)	Supreme Leader Ruhollah Mousavi Khomeini (9 years, 6 months)
	August 3, 2021	President Ebrahim Raisi (1 year, 2 months)	President Hassan Rouhani (8 years)

Source: Author's records, November 2021.

BOX 3.2

CLASSIFYING REGIMES

There are many different ways to classify regimes. Some focus on the degree of freedom and inclusion of everyday citizens in politics. For instance, Robert Dahl's classic book, *Polyarchy*, classified regimes according to the degree of contestation and participation, with closed hegemonies at one end of the spectrum and polyarchies at the other.[1] More recent scholarship on hybrid regimes (e.g., regimes that are nondemocratic yet allow for significant freedom and contestation) or advocates of ranking systems such as that employed by Freedom House take this approach as well.[2] A second perspective considers the sociological basis of rulers and their supporters. Barrington Moore's seminal study, *Social Origins of Dictatorship and Democracy*, considered how class relations could underpin the development of different regime types.[3] Subsequent scholars distinguish, for instance, peasant-military alliances from urban bourgeoisie or military rule and consider this as a basis for distinguishing regimes.[4] A third approach emphasizes the nature of executive power, focusing on patrimonialist or sultanistic regimes (e.g., regimes in which all power flows directly from the leader). A fourth view focuses on institutional arrangements. This approach dates back to Aristotle, who distinguished among regimes with one, few, and many rulers. The emphasis on institutions may be particularly appealing because rules of the game may be more malleable than factors such as resource endowments or the sociological basis of ruling coalitions.

Scholars (including Aristotle) often combine institutional arrangements with other factors. Two recent and influential coding schemes demonstrate this. Barbara Geddes and her colleagues created a typology that combines institutional structures and a focus on actors who emphasize "control over access to power and influence," thus distinguishing among military, personalist, and single-party regimes.[5] Emphasizing the institutional rules of the regime, Jose Cheibub, Jennifer Gandhi, and James Vreeland set forth a typology that distinguishes among parliamentary, semipresidential, and presidential democracies[6] and monarchic, military, and civilian dictatorships.

It is worth noting that the distinction between civilian and military dictatorships may not be as clear-cut as the typology suggests. For instance, Bjørnskov and Rode (building from Cheibub, Gandhi, and Vreeland) consider Algeria to be a civilian dictatorship while they viewed Egypt, even before 2011, as a military dictatorship. However, as Lahouari Addi explains in Chapter 9, the military plays a significant role in Algeria, while in Egypt the military played a key role in overthrowing President Mubarak in 2011, despite the fact that Mubarak hailed from the military himself. Yet more importantly, there is quite a bit of disagreement over the classification of regimes. In the previous example in 2010, while Cheibub, Gandhi, and Vreeland classified Algeria as a civilian and Egypt as a military dictatorship, respectively, Geddes, Wright, and Frantz[7] characterized Algeria as a military regime and Egypt as a party-personal-military hybrid. Moreover, regimes that are apparently similar in one coding scheme are viewed as distinct in another. For instance, Bjørnskov and Rode and Magaloni et al. view Lebanon and Libya as similar regimes, while Varieties of Democracy see them as distinct. It is important for students of politics to keep this in mind when using these indicators and to employ robustness checks across different datasets when undertaking research.[8]

---

[1] Robert Dahl, *Polyarchy: Participation and Opposition* (New Haven: Yale University Press, 1971).

[2] Larry Diamond, "Thinking about Hybrid Regimes," *Journal of Democracy* 13, no. 2 (2002): 21–35; Steven Levitsky and Lucan Way, "The Rise of Competitive Authoritarianism," *Journal of Democracy* 13, no. 2 (2002): 51–65.

[3] Barrington Moore, *Social Origins of Dictatorship and Democracy* (Boston, MA: Beacon Press, 1966). On the Middle East, see also Haim Gerber, *Social Origins of the Modern Middle East* (Boulder, CO: Lynne Rienner, 1994).

[4] H. E. Chehabi and Juan J. Linz, eds., *Sultanistic Regimes* (Baltimore, MD: Johns Hopkins University Press, 1998); Juan J. Linz, *Totalitarian and Authoritarian Regimes* (Boulder, CO: Lynne Rienner, 2000); Gero Erdmann and Ulf Engel, "Neopatrimonialism Reconsidered: Critical Review and Elaboration of an Elusive Concept," *Journal of Commonwealth and Comparative Politics* 45, no. 1 (February 2007): 95–119.

[5] Barbara Geddes, "What Do We Know about Democratization after Twenty Years?" *Annual Review of Political Science* 2 (June 1999): 123.

[6] A democracy is presidential if the government is not responsible to the legislative assembly, and it is parliamentary if it is. It is semipresidential if it is responsible to the legislative assembly, but there is an elected head of state with a fixed term in office.

[7] Barbara Geddes, Joseph Wright, and Erica Frantz, "Autocratic Breakdown and Regime Transitions: A New Data Set," *Perspectives on Politics* 12, no. 2 (2014): 313–31.

[8] For more discussion, see Hans Lueders and Ellen Lust, "Multiple Measurements, Elusive Agreement, and Unstable Outcomes in the Study of Regime Change," *Journal of Politics* 80, no. 2 (April 2018): 736–41.

Despite the tendency of MENA regimes to be authoritarian, there is important variation in regimes of the region. It is wrong to presume, as is often done, that the entire MENA region is nondemocratic (and destined to remain so). It is also problematic to think that the only important distinction between regimes is that which separates democracies from autocracies. Institutional arrangements that distinguish autocracies from each other and those that do similarly in democracies are also consequential. There are many ways to characterize regimes, as described in Table 3.2.

TABLE 3.2 ■ Classification of MENA Regimes				
	Classification Scheme			
Country	**Christian Bjørnskov and Martin Rode (2018)+**	**Magaloni et al. (end of 2012)**	**Freedom House (2021)**	**Varieties of Democracy, Regimes of the World (RoW) 2017**
Algeria	Civilian dictatorship	Multiparty autocracy	Not free	Electoral autocracy
Bahrain	Royal dictatorship	Monarchy	Not free	Closed autocracy
Egypt	Military dictatorship	Multiparty autocracy	Not free	Electoral autocracy
Iran	Civilian dictatorship	Single-party autocracy	Not free	Electoral autocracy
Iraq	Military dictatorship	Multiparty autocracy	Not free	Electoral autocracy
Israel	Parliamentary democracy	Democracy	Free	Liberal democracy
Jordan	Royal dictatorship	Monarchy	Not free	Closed autocracy
Kuwait	Royal dictatorship	Monarchy	Partly free	Closed autocracy
Lebanon	Civilian dictatorship	Multiparty autocracy	Partly free	Electoral autocracy
Libya	Civilian dictatorship	Multiparty autocracy	Not free	Closed autocracy
Morocco	Royal dictatorship	Monarchy	Partly free	Closed autocracy
Oman	Royal dictatorship	Monarchy	Not free	Closed autocracy
Palestine	N/A	N/A	Gaza Strip: Not free West Bank: Not free	Gaza Strip: Closed autocracy West Bank: Electoral autocracy
Qatar	Royal dictatorship	Monarchy	Not free	Closed autocracy

TABLE 3.2 ■ Classification of MENA Regimes (*Continued*)

	Classification Scheme			
Country	Christian Bjørnskov and Martin Rode (2018)[+]	Magaloni et al. (end of 2012)	Freedom House (2021)	Varieties of Democracy, Regimes of the World (RoW) 2017
Saudi Arabia	Royal dictatorship	Monarchy	Not free	Closed autocracy
South Sudan	Military dictatorship	Multiparty autocracy	Not free	Closed autocracy
Sudan	Military dictatorship	Multiparty autocracy	Not free	Closed autocracy
Syria	Military dictatorship	Military	Not free	Closed autocracy
Tunisia	Presidential democracy	Multiparty autocracy	Free	Electoral democracy
Turkey	Civilian dictatorship (Mixed democratic)	Democracy	Not free	Electoral autocracy
United Arab Emirates	Royal dictatorship	Monarchy	Not free	Closed autocracy
Yemen	Military dictatorship	Multiparty autocracy	Not free	Closed autocracy

Note: [+] Classification in parentheses denotes coding in 2012 for the case in which classification changed from 2012, in order to afford comparison with the coding in Magaloni et al.

Sources:

1. Bjørnskov, Christian and Rode, Martin, Regime Types and Regime Change: A New Dataset (August 18, 2018). Available at SSRN: https://ssrn.com/abstract=3234263 or http://dx.doi.org/10.2139/ssrn.3234263 http://www.christianbjoernskov.com/wp-content/uploads/2018/03/Codebook-BR-dataset.pdf Regime category coding follows Cheibub, Ghandi, and Vreeland (2010): Parliamentary Democracies, Mixed Democracies (with weak presidents), Presidential Democracies, Civilian Autocracies, Military Dictatorships, and Royal Dictatorships.

2. Magaloni, Beatriz, Jonathan Chu, and Eric Min. 2013. Autocracies of the World, 1950-2012 (Version 1.0). Dataset, Stanford University. https://fsi-live.s3.us-west-1.amazonaws.com/s3fs-public/res/Codebook.pdf Coding: Monarchy, Military, Single Party Autocracy, Multiparty Autocracy, Democracy.

3. Freedom House, "Freedom in the World 2018," https://freedomhouse.org/sites/default/files/FH_FITW_Report_2018_Final_SinglePage.pdf Coding, according to Freedom House: "Each country and territory is assigned between 0 and 4 points on a series of 25 indicators, for an aggregate score of up to 100. These scores are used to determine two numerical ratings of 1 representing the most free conditions and 7 the least free. A country or territory's political rights and civil liberties ratings then determine whether it has an overall status of Free, Partly Free, or Not Free."

4. Lührmann, Anna & Tannenberg, Marcus & Lindberg, Staffan. (2018). Regimes of the World (RoW): Opening New Avenues for the Comparative Study of Political Regimes. Politics and Governance. https://www.v-dem.net/files/5/Regimes%20of%20the%20World%20-%20Final.pdf Coppedge, M., Gerring, J., Lindberg, S. I., Skaaning, S.-E., Teorell, J., Altman, D., . . . Staton, J. (2017a). V-Dem codebook v7.1. Gothenburg: Varieties of Democracy (V-Dem) Project.

In this section, we take an institutional approach. We examine variations in regime type, considering commonalities among regimes of the same type as well as their differences. We focus on the historical evolution of MENA regimes, their bases of support, the strategy of rule, and sources of threat to incumbent elites.

Monarchies

The contemporary MENA hosts more monarchies than any other region, and the majority of the world's absolute monarchies. Monarchies are distinguished by the fact that hereditary rule is the legitimate form of transfer for executive power, and they thus rely on family networks to determine succession. It is not always the oldest male family member who assumes power (in other words, primogeniture is not a universal rule), but when succession is not determined by birth order, potential ascendants must be a member of the family and vetted by other family members in order to take the throne. In absolute monarchies, the throne comes with enormous power. Unlike the constitutional monarchies found in much of Europe today—where law, constitutions, and democratically elected parliaments constrain kings and queens—in the absolute monarchies of the MENA region, rulers enjoy relatively unconstrained sovereignty.

Emergence of Monarchies

As Lisa Anderson has argued, MENA monarchies are not relics of an ancient past or an extension of historical caliphates. Instead, they are 19th- and 20th-century institutions much more suited for and resilient to the strains of contemporary rule than one may first expect.[31] As states obtained independence in the 20th-century MENA, the vast majority of them came to be ruled by hereditary monarchs. In many cases, kings—backed by Western powers—inherited the state at independence. In Egypt, for instance, the ruling family was of direct descent from Mehmet Ali (in Arabic, Muhammad Ali), who had been given control over Egypt in return for withdrawing his threat to the Ottoman sultan during the 1840 pacification of the Levant (see Chapter 1). By the early 20th century, Egypt had fallen into debt and was increasingly dependent on the British, for whom the Egyptian ruling family provided a convenient, loyal ally. Similar arrangements existed in Iraq and Jordan, where Hashemite kingdoms were established in the wake of World War I as a "consolation prize" for Sharif Hussein, whose ambitions to gain a greater Arab kingdom the Europeans curtailed. In Tunisia, Libya, and small Gulf states, ruling families emerged from families who had worked closely with their French, Italian, and British protectors, respectively. Even in Morocco, Saudi Arabia, and Iran, where leaders emerged more independently, the ruling families sought French, British, and, later, US support.

Bases of Support

Monarchs derive power from several sources. They enjoy formal institutional guarantees of immunity vis-à-vis their subjects. For example, Article 54 of Kuwait's constitution states that the "Emir is the Head of the State. His person is immune and inviolable." Monarchs hold similarly expansive powers in Morocco and Jordan, despite constitutional reforms taken in the wake of the Arab uprisings. Morocco's 2011 constitution defines the king as "commander of the faithful" and head of state (Article 41), assures that the "person of the king inviolable, and respect is due to him" and provides him immunity (Article 46).[32] Similarly, Article 30 of the Jordanian constitution dictates that "the King is the Head of the State and is immune from any liability and responsibility."

Monarchs sit above parliaments, where they exist. Parliamentarians often take an oath of allegiance not only to the state but also to the king. Kings can dismiss cabinets, parliaments, and ministers swiftly and without legal recourse, discussion, debate, or deliberation;[33] and, when necessary, they can pass legislation by decree. Moreover, the elected representatives' subordinate position is clearly demonstrated through the members' oaths. For instance, in the Jordanian constitution, Article 80 specifies the member's oath as, "I swear by Almighty God to be loyal to the King and to the country, uphold the Constitution, serve the Nation and conscientiously perform the duties entrusted to me."

Monarchs also derive power from historical, hereditary, religious, and procedural legitimacy. Legitimacy is difficult to see or measure, but it is potentially powerful. Think of it as the "discount rate" of rule achieved when people believe that the rulers have the right to govern. Monarchs tend to emphasize legitimacy of the royal family, often in terms of historical legitimacy or a unique relationship with God (for example, the commander of the faithful in Morocco, the custodian of the two holy mosques in Saudi Arabia, and the descendant of the Prophet Muhammad in Jordan). We should not overestimate the role of legitimacy in maintaining rule, and one can question whether it is legitimacy or other factors, such as oil rents or repression, which keep rulers in power. Yet an example from Morocco helps to illustrate how religious legitimacy can provide support. On July 10, 1971, the Moroccan military reacted to the growing national unrest by mounting a coup attempt during a party at the king's palace in Skhirat. The king, invoking his role as commander of the faithful, asked the dissident troops to join him in prayer. The troops—apparently reminded of the king's special status—abandoned their cause.[34]

Importantly, a popular mandate is not a source of legitimacy in monarchies, and palace politics are thus isolated from participatory politics. In Jordan and Morocco, members of the royal family do not run for parliamentary seats; and in Kuwait, the al-Sabahs can neither vote nor run for seats in the National Assembly.[35] In short, monarchs in the contemporary MENA enjoy a status more akin to the divine right of rulers in medieval Europe than to contemporary European royalty, but they nonetheless need to maintain support in order to rule.

Strategies of Rule

Monarchs have devised a set of strategies of rule by which they garner support and attempt to contain potential opposition. These include the rules governing the distribution of key positions within the system, as well as divide-and-rule strategies and controlled liberalization. We find considerable variation in the rules governing the distribution of power, but rather similar attempts to divide-and-rule and undertake political liberalization when necessary.

Some monarchies have devised dynastic systems that help stabilize their regime. In dynastic monarchies, the top government positions, including cabinet portfolios, the military, and other leading posts, are reserved for members of the ruling family, while in nondynastic monarchies, members outside the ruling families hold the key portfolios. As Michael Herb points out, this creates very different incentives for members of the ruling family and inner circles of government to remain loyal to the ruler.[36] In dynasties, members of the royal family are heavily invested in maintaining the regime. They may disagree over the direction of foreign policy, succession, or other key issues, but they ultimately find ways to compromise and maintain their family rule rather than risk losing control.[37] Family members benefit in nondynasties as well, but they are less likely to see their personal success as fundamentally tied to maintaining the dynasty. Moreover, those who hold these key positions can often imagine doing well in another regime because their position is not dependent on their bloodline. In short, it is easier to buy the loyalty of members of the ruling family—who believe their options are limited if the family loses power—than it is to buy the loyalty of powerful elites who are not closely tied to the regime.

Monarchs also employ a divide-and-rule strategy to overcome threats. They benefit from emphasizing political competition and division rather than popular unity and thus foster social and ideological divisions. By doing so, they establish themselves as a crucial "moderator" among competing forces. As Alan Richards and John Waterbury explain,

> What the monarchs want is a plethora of interests, tribal, ethnic, professional, class based, and partisan, whose competition for public patronage they can arbitrate. None of these elements can be allowed to become too powerful or wealthy, and the monarch will police and repress or entice and divide.[38]

Thus, monarchies tend to exacerbate divisions among various groups in the population, such as those between citizens and noncitizens in Kuwait, citizens of East Bank and Palestinian origin in Jordan,[39] or Amazighs, and Arabs in Morocco. They also promote divisions in and among parties in order to keep them weak and divided.

Monarchs can employ controlled liberalization in the hope of depressing opposition, and they can do so in a manner that promotes their importance in the political system. By bringing the various parties together to form national pacts, as seen in the Jordanian National Charter (Mithaq al-Watani), the Moroccan constitutional reforms of 1972, and the Jiddah Compact, monarchs both appear to grant concessions and reinforce their role as supreme arbitrator. Rex Brynen, Bahgat Korany, and Paul Noble conclude: "What is interesting about the monarchies is that they appear to be in a position to establish many of these rules and to thereby act simultaneously as both interested players and far-from-impartial umpires in the political reform process."[40]

One-Party Regimes: Single-Party and Dominant-Party Types

One-party regimes are also prevalent in the MENA, and we find them in two types: single-party and dominant-party regimes. Single-party regimes have a "vanguard party" that officially dominates political power. Smaller parties sometimes are allowed to participate in politics if they accept the ruling party's role and rules, but they have little power. Dominant-party regimes allow for the participation of multiple parties and theoretically permit alternation in power; however, the dominant party monopolizes power. It makes the rules of the game, determines who is permitted to compete, and enjoys disproportionate control over resources. Thus, single- and dominant-party regimes have much in common.

Pathways to One-Party Regimes

By the end of the 20th century, one-party regimes had emerged across much of the region. They came to power via three historical pathways: emergence through revolution, military coups, and transitions between dominant- and single-party regimes. Exploring these paths illuminates distinctions between these regimes and also suggests that the civilian-military distinction may not be particularly helpful, at least not in the contemporary MENA. In other regions, such as Latin America, militaries that came to power often ruled collectively through military juntas. In the MENA, military rulers have tended to establish one-party regimes.

The first set of one-party regimes emerged from struggles for independence. In a study of 169 countries covering the period from 1950 through 2006, Beatriz Magaloni and Ruth Kricheli found that 28.36 percent of one-party regimes were established after periods of anarchy, including independence wars.[41] Forty years earlier, Samuel Huntington examined the emergence of one-party regimes from independence movements, arguing that "the more intense and prolonged the struggle and the deeper its ideological commitment, the greater the political stability of the one-party system."[42] In the MENA, such regimes emerged in Tunisia and Algeria, following the independence struggles against the French which helped establish the national movements that emerged into ruling parties: the Destour (Constitutional) Party in Tunisia (which later became the Neo-Destour Party) and the National Liberation Front (FLN) in Algeria. In these cases, party structures were established before independence.

The second pathway to one-party regimes was emergence through military coups, sometimes in partnership with political parties. Again, this is fairly common; Magaloni and Kricheli found that military dictatorships led to the founding of 33.33 percent of dominant-party regimes and 23.33 percent of single-party regimes. In Iraq and Syria, for instance, military leaders who were the major force behind the regime transformations were loosely allied with the leaders of the Ba'ath Party. The regimes transformed into Ba'athist regimes, and party structures came to play an important role in politics. In other cases, most notably Egypt, the military took power and sought to establish a dominant party as a means of control. Doing so was not necessarily easy. Egyptian president Gamal Abdel Nasser struggled to establish a ruling party. He first established the Egyptian National Union in 1957 (five years after the Free Officers revolution) and then renamed it the Arab Socialist Union in 1962 in one of many efforts to revitalize the party system.

The third means of transition in MENA one-party states has been the shift from single-party to dominant-party regimes, and vice versa. When ruling elites found themselves under attack, they sometimes chose to open space for opposition parties, allowing them greater freedom of participation; when they became more secure, they constricted the political space once again. Globally, 63.33 percent of dominant-party regimes from 1950 through 2006 transitioned to single-party regimes, and 25.33 percent of single-party regimes transitioned to dominant-party regimes.[43]

Egypt illustrates the transition from a single-party to a dominant-party regime. Following the assassination of President Anwar al-Sadat in 1981, the newly inaugurated president, Hosni Mubarak, allowed multiparty elections for the national legislature while he simultaneously clamped down on Islamist opposition. In 2005, facing regional instability, opposition, and concerns about regime succession, he called the first multiparty elections for the presidency. The Egyptian system went from one in which there was a vanguard party to one in which several parties compete, but until the fall of Mubarak in 2011, the governing National Democratic Party enjoyed clear dominance.

Bases of Support

Ruling elites in one-party systems may seem to have unlimited power, but their legitimacy is closely tied to maintaining the appearance of popular support. Unlike monarchs, who sit above the fray of participatory politics, presidents' legitimacy is based largely on their ability to represent the people. They thus often promote state-led development or a nationalist or anti-imperial project to shore up their regime. It is important that the ruling party be seen as embodying the will of the people.

Institutional structures reflect this. Presidents are generally not granted the special privileges and isolation from popular politics that monarchs enjoy. For example, Tunisia's constitution under President Zine al-Abidine Ben Ali mentioned neither executive immunity nor scrutiny. Members of parliament took oaths of allegiance to the state, but not to the head of state.[44] Legislatures also generally have more *formal* authority than their counterparts in the monarchies.[45] In reality, however, presidents often gain extraconstitutional powers by declaring a state of emergency and by utilizing their control over resources to ensure that legislatures are packed with supporters.

Strategies of Rule

One-party regimes take a different approach than monarchies to shore up their regime. Building ruling parties and legislatures is itself a strategy of rule and one that scholars have consistently found makes regimes more durable.[46] In addition, when necessary, ruling elites turn to political liberalization in an attempt to strengthen their regime in times of crisis. As we shall see, however, the logic of one-party regimes makes such liberalization a more difficult tactic than it is in monarchies.

Three points should be kept in mind as we discuss the role of ruling parties. First, one must remember that many of the efforts to establish ruling parties were made between the 1950s and the 1970s when the Soviet Union was a major power and socialist-oriented, state-led development was a widely accepted strategy for newly independent states. In many ways, the enthusiasm for one-party regimes mirrored that for democracies in the 1990s. The function of political parties was to mobilize resources and channel activities in solving the twin problems of governance and development that plagued the new states; it was not to provide an arena for political competition. Second, not all governing elites have invested equally in developing the ruling party, and nowhere in the MENA did ruling parties achieve the organizational strength that they did in communist China, Mexico, or the USSR. Third, and relatedly, politics became increasingly personalized in these regimes. The Baathist revolution in Syria, for example, evolved toward the personalistic regime of Saddam Hussein in Iraq, and of Hafiz al-Asad, and subsequently his son Bashar, in Syria. In Tunisia, Bourguiba and then Ben Ali dominated the ruling party, called first the Neo-Destour and then the Constitutional Democratic Assembly (RCD). The personal leadership of the president and the president's closest associates became far more important in determining the distribution of resources within society than the organizational structures and internal politics of the ruling party. This is not unusual: examining leadership changes in nondemocratic states that took place between 1946 and 2008, Anne Meng[47] finds that the majority of parties do not survive their leader's demise. Strong ruling parties may be the exception, rather than the rule.

Nevertheless, the establishment of party organizations may help sustain authoritarian regimes. Parties do this first by helping to alleviate internal conflict among elites. The party can also provide a source of recruitment and socialization for emerging elites, giving them space within the existing regime. Ruling parties, and the legislatures associated with them, also provide an arena for the distribution of patronage and the co-optation of elites. Furthermore, they can be a mechanism through which demands are voiced—within boundaries—and limited policy concessions can be made. Finally, they can provide a mechanism through which mass support can be mobilized. This can help to tie citizens (particularly in the rural areas) to the regime, and the party also provides a base of support that can be mobilized in the face of potential threats to the regime.[48]

Political parties—and the accompanying legislatures and elections—serve to reduce the pressures on ruling elites, but they also tie presidents to participatory institutions. This may make attempts at controlled liberalization more difficult for dominant party elites than for monarchs. In contrast to the monarchs who direct political liberalization from above the fray, presidents must compete in popular politics. Thus, during liberalization, presidents must compete in elections (albeit as participants who hold the reins of power) and risk the chance of being overthrown. Consequently, there is reason to believe that liberalization is more difficult for presidents and that it calls for different tactics. There is also reason to believe that allowing greater space for freedom of speech, association, and engagement in elections entails more risks in the early years of liberalization[49]; elections may create opportunities for the opposition to mobilize successfully, rather than providing a mechanism for cooptation and stabilization. Thus, presidents face the risk of creating a political system in which competing forces will emerge as they attempt to develop a system that strengthens their own party and weakens opponents.

Military Regimes

The MENA region also hosts military regimes, in which military officers take power and rule. The prevalence of military regimes depends, in part, on how one defines these regimes. As Geddes, Wright, and Frantz argue, there are three usages of the term *military regime*. The most inclusive simply refers to an autocracy led by a military officer.[50] As Magaloni puts it, "The key distinctive trait of military regimes is that the armed forces control access to the principal positions of power," and even if political parties exist, "the dictator and his critical ruling coalition share power through the institution of the armed forces rather than the party."[51] In this view, Egypt under Mubarak and Tunisia under Ben Ali were military regimes. A second perspective focuses on the role of the military as an institution; military regimes are those in which a military *junta*, or organization, rules. For instance, Egypt under General Neguib, following the Free Officers revolution, was a military regime but Mubarak's Egypt was not. A third type, which they call the "military strongman," exists when power is held in the hands of a single military officer. Syria under Asad or Egypt under Nasser or Sisi are examples of such regimes.

Strategies of Rule: The Emergence and Evolution of Military Regimes

It may seem relatively easy to identify the emergence of a military regime, but the ways by which they come into power and evolve can make them much more difficult to detect than one might expect. Military regimes emerge when officers take power. These are often dramatic events, such as military tanks rolling through the streets of the capital city or officers taking over means of communication. It could also be a military declaration to "restore order," particularly after people have taken to the streets in protest. Such was the case on July 3, 2013, when General Sisi, flanked by Egyptian notables across the political spectrum, declared President Morsi's removal. The debate then ensued over whether or not this was a military coup.

Similar ambiguities arise as military regimes evolve. Military officers may choose to build a ruling party, as Nasser did in Egypt, or to establish a multiparty system, as Ataturk did in Turkey. They may also consolidate personal power, as did Hafez al-Asad in Syria, Muammar Ghaddafi in Libya, and Abdel Fatah el-Sisi (to date) in Egypt. Barbara Geddes argues that military leaders prefer to consolidate personal power,[52] but it is not clear under what conditions they can wrest control from other military leaders. Indeed, these are interesting questions to be studied. It is clear, however, that these institutional changes make it much more difficult to identify military regimes than one may expect.

Challenges and Implications

Military regimes appear brittle. In her classic 1999 study, Geddes found that military regimes were the least durable, although they were more likely to extricate themselves from rule through elections or other "uncoerced" means. It appeared that military leaders were less able to withstand the challenges of collective rule and more likely to return to the barracks. Although it was not the focus of her study, it was also possible that those leaders who succeeded in overcoming these challenges did so by transitioning to personalistic or party rule. These were no longer "military regimes" in her early classification, but the leaders had nevertheless remained in power—that is, there were two ways for military juntas to overcome their challenges, either by relinquishing power or by consolidating it through a personalist or party regime.

Distinguishing military regimes that rule collectively from those in which the military officer concentrates power in his own hands sheds important light on the nature of the military rule. Indeed, Nam Kyu Kim and Alex Kroeger test the differences between collectivist military regimes, or military juntas, and personalist military regimes on a global dataset of regime transitions. They find that a regime that rules through a military collective, which Geddes and her colleagues call a "military regime," is more likely to be short-lived, extricate itself from rule without conflict, and have a better chance at establishing democracy. A regime that is ruled through a military strongman, on the other hand, is likely to be ousted through uprisings or invasions and to usher in another era of autocracy.[53]

This has important lessons for understanding the trajectories of regimes in the MENA. Egypt's Mubarak and Libya's Ghaddafi could be understood as military strongmen. In this view, it was unsurprising that these leaders' tenure resulted in an uprising. The current Sisi regime is in the process of consolidating power. If Sisi continues to consolidate a personalistic regime, the likelihood of the military choosing to withdraw from power peacefully is low and the prospects for democracy dim.

Islamic Republic

The Islamic Republic of Iran is a unique regime in the region, incorporating elements of monarchic and republican rule. Iran's institutional arrangements were intended to shape revolutionary change after the 1979 overthrow of Western-oriented Mohammad Reza Shah Pahlavi. The regime is best known as the world's only Shiite theocracy. It has been an explicit, revolutionary attempt to create a regime based on Islam.

Institutionally, the Islamic Republic of Iran has a dual-government structure: One side includes the popularly elected executive and legislative branches, while the second includes unelected bodies aimed at guarding the Islamic nature of the regime. In Chapter 11, Mehrzad Boroujerdi discusses the regime in more detail, but what is critical to note is that the unelected leadership is more powerful than the elected bodies—that is, the supreme leader is more powerful than the president; the Guardian Council and the Expediency Council play more important roles than the parliament. This is well illustrated by the simple fact that candidates for the parliament and presidency must be first vetted by the Guardian Council. No one who would violate what is deemed as legitimate for an Islamic republic can run for office, let alone win.

Within these limits, however, there has generally been a great deal of competition, transparency, and accountability. The mechanisms that we often associate with good governance in democracies are not entirely absent in Iran, nor are they fully assured. The elections of the summer of 2009, in which there was significant contestation over the extent to which the balloting was free and fair and the subsequent electoral results were legitimate, clearly illustrate the limitations of the regime. The contestation curtailed daily progress and development, bringing the regime to deal with upheaval long after the polls had closed.

Importantly, while the ruling elites in Iran purposefully attempted to fashion a distinct regime, the Iranian regime has some elements of monarchic rule. Like monarchies, the clerical rule is based on religious legitimacy. Moreover, the clerics stand above the fray of participatory politics and thus can manage a more open arena of political competition. Moreover, although it is based on an Islamic model, the details of the model and the mechanisms of rule are themselves often contested. The regime is thus less unique than it may initially appear.

Quasi Democracies

The MENA is also home to regimes that, either currently or recently, fit the *procedural* or *minimalist* view of democracy. Each falls short of liberal democracy in important ways, and as shown in Table 3.2, analysts may disagree about applying the label *democracy* to the regime. Nevertheless, Israel, Lebanon, Tunisia (at least until 2022), and Turkey (until around 2015) may be described as quasi-democracies.

Before examining the nature of democracies in the region, it is useful to note that these cases illustrate the distinction between regime type, state strength, and political stability. Democracies, like strong states and political stability, are believed to enhance governance. Many thus mistakenly conclude that these three factors go hand in hand. Yet the countries discussed here have very different levels of state strength and political stability. Israel is a relatively strong, stable state; Lebanon is weak and unstable; and Tunisia has a relatively strong state but unstable regime. In short, it is important to keep in mind that regime type, state strength, and stability are separate factors.

Emergence of Quasi Democracies

As Dankwart Rustow reminded us long ago, democracy can be born out of hotly contested "family feuds," wherein the bargain of democracy is preferred to the near uncertainty of political conflict. For him, it was primarily a domestic conflict that mattered. When individuals see themselves as part of the same community (e.g., nationalism is developed) but have divergent preferences, they can create democratic institutions that allow them to resolve differences in the short run and maintain the chance to win in the future.[54] Yet in much of the MENA region, international forces have played an important role in shaping institutions.

In some cases, the international influences have been primarily through demonstration effects, wherein ideals of successful arrangements in the West encouraged the adoption of democratic institutions. For instance, Israel was a settler state, with many of its founding leaders coming from democratic states in Western Europe. Often considered the only liberal democratic regime in the region, it strove to be a "Jewish, democratic state" since its establishment in 1948, developing a vibrant party system, civil society, and freedom of speech, press, and association, as well as an active and influential parliament. The formation of the Turkish Republic in 1923 was formed in part out of emulation of the West. Mustafa Kemal, a military officer who took the name of Atatürk (Father of the Turks), was determined to establish a modern, secular, Western-oriented regime in the seat of the former Ottoman Empire. In the 20th century, Turkey evolved toward democracy, albeit with a series of military interruptions. The 1924 constitution (and more than twenty subsequent versions) established Turkey as a parliamentary system, with an elected president, parliament, prime minister, and an independent judiciary. The extent of competition steadily increased in Turkey, with an initial period of single-party dominance followed by a multiparty period after World War II. More recently, Turkey has witnessed a remarkable centralization of power in the hands of President Recep Tayyip Erdoğan, increasingly drawing into question whether Turkey is accurately described as a "democracy" (see Chapter 25).

Exposure to the West also played a role in the establishment of a democratic system in Lebanon. Lebanon developed a confessional, semipresidential democracy. It is confessional because it is a system that is established to guarantee representation to various groups in society (an arrangement called *consociationalism*, which is sometimes seen as a solution for social tensions in deeply divided societies) and one in which the divisions and representational guarantees are based on religious sect. It is semipresidential because it holds elections for a president, as well as parliament with a prime minister.

Both confessionalism and semipresidentialism are often critiqued as systems that are highly volatile and fragile, but at the time the system was instituted, it seemed a reasonable solution to the conflict between Lebanese sectarian groups over the nature and boundaries of the Lebanese state. Christian Maronites strongly preferred that Lebanon remain an independent entity with French support, while Sunni Muslims advocated Lebanese unification with Syria. The result was a compromise solution embodied in the National Pact: Lebanon was to be an independent country (*not* unified with Syria) with an Arab (*not* French) orientation, but the institutional arrangements would guarantee protection of both Muslim and Christian interests. The president would be a Maronite Christian, the prime minister a Sunni Muslim, the speaker of the house a Shiite, and the distribution of parliamentary seats would be in a ratio of six to five between Christians and Muslims. The ratio reflected the population distribution shown in the 1934 census, the last to be taken in Lebanon.

Strategies of Rule

The strategies of rule in democracies have received less attention than those of autocracies. In part, this may be because there is an implicit assumption that democracies rule by the will of the people, which removes strategies of rule somewhat from consideration. Yet elites in democracies make efforts to maintain democratic regimes in the face of challenges.

One strategy is institutional reform. For instance, in Iraq the 2005 Constitution recognized an Iraqi Kurdistan as an autonomous region, thus alleviating tensions between Kurds and Arabs. Similarly, federalism has been proposed in Libya as a solution to regional tensions, although it failed to be instituted. As already discussed, Lebanon designed a confessional system to assure competing communal groups representation, and it established a dual legal system with both civil and religious courts in order to guarantee individuals the right to adjudicate personal matters in accordance with their religion. These institutions facilitated the installation of democracy, although division of political power along sectarian lines also exacerbated tensions between them.

Even where democratic institutions are established, they are often fragile. Israel and Lebanon face instability and the threat of heightened conflict, and each fails to guarantee free competition and equal participation in decision-making. Turkey has recognized a new constitution that strengthens the role of the presidency, has withdrawn freedoms and liberties, and is considered by most to be no longer democratic. Even Tunisia, the "success story" of the Arab uprisings, faces instability and the threat of autocracy.

KEY INSTITUTIONS

A third strand of scholarship on the region focuses on key institutions within regimes, particularly those associated with democracy: legislatures and political parties, judiciaries, and the media. In this section, we give a brief overview of the role that these institutions are expected to play and the variation in their performance in the MENA region.

Before turning to these institutions, it is important to consider whether they are even meaningful in authoritarian regimes. Many argue they are not, and certainly, it is true that these institutions do not fully determine the distribution of resources. In the MENA, as elsewhere, one must look at players and political practices outside the formal political sphere in order to understand politics. However, even in authoritarian regimes, elites both in and out of power debate constitutional amendments that shape executive-legislative relations, argue over electoral rules, critique laws governing the press and publication, and push back against restrictions on political parties. They do so because these institutions matter.[55]

Legislatures

Ideally, legislatures perform four core functions. They provide a mechanism through which the demands of different constituencies within societies are represented and competing ideas contested. They shape public policy through crafting, vetting, and passing legislation. Legislatures oversee the executive branch, ideally to ensure both vertical accountability of rulers to the ruled and horizontal accountability of other government agencies to the legislature. And finally, throughout the world, legislators provide constituency service.[56] Strong legislatures are potentially important tools for establishing effective governance.[57]

Yet legislatures in much of the region are weak or absent. In one-party regimes, the legislature is closely tied to the regime's legitimacy; eliminating legislatures is thus politically costly for the ruling party, but incumbents use electoral rules and political manipulation to ensure that the legislature is comprised primarily of members from the ruling party. In monarchies, legitimacy is not closely tied to the performance of a ruling party, so it is less politically costly to rule without functioning legislatures. Both Jordan and Morocco have experienced long stretches of time when the parliament was disbanded; Qatar elected its first parliament only in 2013; and as of 2021, Saudi Arabia had a consultative assembly, which could propose laws to the king and his cabinet, but not an elected legislature. One might expect that quasi-democracies would have strong, functioning legislatures, but even here, we find weaknesses. Lebanon, for instance, postponed legislative elections from 2009 to 2018, leading many to argue during that time that the sitting parliament lacked legitimacy.

Where legislatures do exist, they are often highly constrained. Many have no significant input into the formation of government. This is true even in nominally parliamentary monarchies, where members of parliament (MPs) should, technically, influence the choice of prime minister and the government. For example, in Jordan the king appoints the prime minister, who then appoints the government. In Morocco, since 2011, the king must choose the prime minister from the party holding the most parliamentary seats, and the parliament can give a vote of no confidence on the government. However, the fact that kings can dissolve the government and parliament at any time puts parliament in a weak position. Similarly, in one-party regimes parliaments can and have been restricted by declaring emergency powers. Moreover, in some cases the legislature can only debate those laws that have been presented to it. In other cases, the lower house may propose legislation, but an appointed upper house holds veto power.

MENA legislators are often poorly equipped to meet the tasks of legislation. Many legislatures have low incumbency rates due in part to weak and fragmented party systems, discussed later in this chapter.[58] Legislators often have little or no policymaking experience and lack competent staff, efficient technology, and organizational structures that allow them to form committees, draft legislation, or provide oversight of the executive. At the same time, legislators often benefit directly from their positions, making them less willing to challenge the system. Holding office brings prestige and personal benefits such as cars, drivers, direct access to the government bureaucracy that doles out public contracts, and often immunity from prosecution. These perks can be enormously lucrative. For instance, a businessman may use his connections with the ministries to bypass import duties, to obtain preferential treatment, or to win bids for public contracts worth huge sums of money.[59]

Citizens also tend to reward legislators who focus on providing them with personal services, rather than lawmaking and executive oversight. Where there is little bureaucratic transparency, accomplishing seemingly simple bureaucratic tasks—obtaining licenses or building permits, for example—requires not simply finding the right government office, filling out forms, and paying a fee, but often finding the right person to exert personal influence on one's behalf.[60] Given legislators' contacts with government, their ability to (threaten to) use the floor of the legislature, and their access to media to call into question officials' performance if they don't respond, legislators are particularly well placed to perform these tasks. Consequently, some refer to the legislators as *na'ib khidma* (service deputies), charged with providing services rather than legislating or overseeing the executive.

In short, for many, parliament is a service organization, not a legislative body, and elections are a competition over access to a pool of state resources, not struggles over policymaking or the rules of the game. Voters want legislators who can deliver the goods and services. Legislators, recognizing that their success is tied to meeting such needs, have little incentive to push for reforms that would expand the legislative powers and enhance accountability.

Political Parties and Party Systems

Political parties and party systems can also be key institutions. Strong political parties are characterized by programmatic platforms that reflect relative agreement of members over policy bundles; close ties and communication with the citizens; avenues for democratic leadership, decision-making, and mobility within the party; financial resources; and a fair degree of party stability and longevity.[61] Strong party systems are characterized by moderate fragmentation (neither too many nor too few parties), low polarization (parties not spread too widely across the political spectrum), and high institutionalization (stable, depersonalized, and embedded within the system).[62]

Yet many MENA countries contain weak political parties. In monarchies such as Jordan and Morocco, this may not be surprising. The monarch does not rely on a strong political party to legitimize his rule. That political parties are weak in democracies is somewhat more surprising since elections and political parties are intimately tied to determining the highest political offices. Here too, however, the political-party system suffers from personalization, as in Lebanon. Perhaps most surprising is the fact that the one-party states often suffer from weak parties. This is true not only of opposition parties but also of the ruling party. Those who want to succeed professionally or to obtain political perks are virtually required to be party members in countries like Syria. However, these parties are more intent on mobilizing support for the regime than on providing venues for transmitting preferences, facilitating turnover of political elites, and influencing policy. In the decades after these regimes were established, the ideological and programmatic bases of the parties were undermined, and the core organizational structures withered.[63] Parties functioned mainly as a mechanism for elite control. Thus even in transitioning regimes, the vast majority of parties (with the notable exception of Islamist parties that were closely linked to service-providing organizations) had difficulty providing a conduit of information between elites and masses and failed to mobilize the masses effectively.

Political party systems are also weak in much of the MENA. Existing parties fragment into new parties, parties disappear, or ruling elites ban parties from politics and encourage others to take their place. This party system fluidity may at first seem to reflect a vibrant political system, but it really demonstrates the system's fragility. It also makes it difficult for citizens to recognize and trust the parties. In fact, in the MENA, citizens often recognize political parties by their leaders and cliques rather than by their platforms and policy positions.

There are several reasons for this. In authoritarian regimes, elites intent on crushing the opposition thwart party development. Incumbents often shape and implement political party laws in a manner that excludes or weakens potential contenders, at times using rules to drive a wedge between political parties that are given legal status (and thus have an opportunity to access state resources) and those that are not. Where political parties are uniformly permitted or excluded from the political system, the parties are more likely to cooperate, demand greater political reforms, and experience somewhat more stable systems. Where some are included but others excluded, such cooperation between political parties is much less likely.[64] Finally, the weak role that parliaments play also undermines political parties and the party system. Party labels signal policy preferences, which are important when policymaking is at stake. However, where parliaments play a limited role in policymaking, voters pay little attention to political parties and party platforms, and party leaders have no incentive to develop them. Parties and party systems remain underdeveloped.

Judiciary

An independent judiciary and strong rule of law may play an important role in ensuring human rights, securing property rights, and providing responsive governance. Thomas Carothers defined *rule of law* as "a system in which the laws are public knowledge, are clear in meaning, and apply equally to everyone." Establishing a strong rule of law, he argued, is "a way of pushing patronage-ridden government institutions to better performance, reigning in elected but still only haphazardly law-abiding politicians, and curbing the continued violation of human rights that has characterized many new democracies."[65] Similarly, one Egyptian activist argued, "We cannot aspire to have reform without an independent judiciary. . . It is the first and most important block in the reform process."[66]

The MENA region has a great deal of variation in the Rule of Law and in the locus of rights.[67] Countries such as Algeria, Egypt, Iran, Lebanon, and the Palestinian Authority have judiciaries that are often closely tied to and dependent on the ruling elite. Indeed, in such cases, judiciaries may play an important role, helping ruling elites route out threats from "insiders."[68] Elsewhere, as in Iraq, Libya, Syria, and Yemen, where the reach of the state is limited, nonstate forces often mete out justice. Finally, in a case such as the UAE, the country scores high in rule of law, but rights are extended fully only to those who are UAE citizens—approximately 10 percent of those living in the territory.[69]

Judicial independence can vary over time, shaped by political forces. In Egypt, for instance, courts became notably more independent during the three decades preceding Mubarak's fall. The Supreme Constitutional Court increased the number of rulings it issued from one ruling in 1980, when it upheld the government position, to more than thirty rulings in 2000, two-thirds of which found government decrees unconstitutional.[70] Tamir Moustafa argues that extending judicial independence, at least initially, served President Mubarak's needs. The ruling elite, seeking to provide for credible protection of property rights in an era of economic liberalization and to rein in the corruption and indiscipline of an increasingly unwieldy bureaucracy, could benefit from shifting potentially difficult and polarizing decisions into the courts that were seen as independent.[71] As Tarek Masoud explains in Chapter 10, the post-Mubarak period saw a marked decline in the judiciary's reputation and, ultimately, its independence. President Morsi limited the judiciary's oversight abilities through constitutional amendments, and President Sisi has continued to control its purview. Similar rollbacks in judicial independence have been witnessed in Turkey as well. Strengthening rule of law is important, but even where advances are made, they can be reversed.

Media

A well-functioning, independent media can play an important role in providing transparency and constraining ruling elites. Often called the "fourth pillar of democracy," the media can be the watchdog over the checks-and-balances system among executives, judiciaries, and legislatures. It can sound the alarm in response to abuses of power and ultimately help reduce the possibilities and prevalence of corruption.

Media in much of the MENA became considerably more vibrant in the 21st century, owing in part to technological changes. The increased use of satellite television, radio, and the Internet provided important channels of alternative information that were not previously available and helped to create a new public sphere.[72] It gave voice to opposition forces and, in the eyes of some, played an instrumental role in mobilizing the uprisings. Yet the Arab uprisings that began in 2011 occurred earliest and with the most force in the MENA countries where Internet usage was least widespread.[73] It was long-standing grievances—not new media—that brought citizens into the streets to demand change.[74]

The media in much of the region remains restricted. Press and publication laws often set the boundaries within which journalists must act—not writing slanderous or treasonous material, for instance; they do not specify what kinds of material are deemed to cross the red lines. These interpretations are left to the authorities, who are closely tied to the ruling elites. It is also difficult for journalists to demand reforms. Laws governing association and state control over the media as well as press associations limit journalists' abilities to act collectively. The situation is complicated by the fact that some journalists working within the country are rewarded handsomely for their close association with and support for the ruling elite, while the same closeness between the regime and journalism undermines linkages with external associations.

UNDERSTANDING REGIME BREAKDOWN AND REFORM

Let us conclude by considering two important, interrelated questions: First, why and when do regimes break down? And second, what explains the nature of the regimes that arise in their place, or as it is more frequently put, why is the region so resistant to (liberal) democracy?

What Explains Regime Breakdown?

Explanations for why increased discontent leads to conflict and regime breakdown in some countries and not others center on four factors: economic factors, regime type, Islam, and external factors. As we turn to each of these, it is important to remember that these are not necessarily mutually exclusive. The breakdown in any country may be a combination of economic factors and the regime, for instance. Moreover, when we consider regime breakdown, we should be aware that we are examining a probabilistic event. There is a great deal of uncertainty and chance affecting when protesters take to the streets, military coups succeed, and regimes are overturned. The questions we ask regard what makes regime breakdown *more or less likely*, and the explanations we examine are *probabilistic, not deterministic*.

Economic Factors

Economic factors are generally understood to affect the breakdown of authoritarianism in three ways. First, economic development, including industrialization, urbanization, and rising standards of living, can spur demands for reform.[75] Second, economic crises can increase discontent in society, making it easier for members of a political opposition to challenge incumbent author-itarian regimes.[76] Third, economic resources, and particularly rents obtained from oil, strategic aid, or other resources, can strengthen incumbent elites. They can avoid the need to extract taxes, thus diminishing demands for taxation; can distribute goods and services to society; and can develop a strong security apparatus to repress potential opposition.[77]

This third explanation is often singled out as the most important factor explaining which regimes were destabilized during the 2011 uprisings. Jason Brownlee, Tarek Masoud, and Andrew Reynolds argue that oil was one of two necessary factors that stabilized some regimes during the uprisings (the other factor, dynastic rule, will be discussed shortly).[78] Determined to keep their populations from joining in the spreading demands for political reform, Gulf mon-archs handed out fistfuls of funds. At least in the short run, they succeeded everywhere but in Bahrain, where economic coffers were less endowed and the Shi'a–Sunni divide is politicized.

Regime Type

As discussed earlier, another set of explanations for regime durability or breakdown is situated in the nature of the authoritarian regime. Barbara Geddes turned scholars' attention to the importance of regime type in 1999 when she found that single-party regimes are more stable than military regimes or personalistic dictatorships.[79] The mechanism at work is a matter of debate. Some point to the ability of ruling parties to solve intra-elite conflict,[80] while others argue that parliaments (often associated with one-party states) provided a mechanism of coop-tation and "controlled bargaining" with potential oppositions.[81] More recently, scholars have argued that it is revolutionary regimes, which come into power through "conflicts triggered by efforts to carry out radical social change" and subsequently build highly cohesive coalitions, that are extremely durable.[82] A similar argument about the cohesion of ruling elites is heard with regard to monarchies.[83]

There does appear to be a relationship between regime type and the ability of regimes to survive the recent uprisings. This is seen in Table 3.3, which examines the relation-ship between regime type and levels of popular unrest since 2010. The table suggests that one-party regimes proved brittle. This stands in contrast to prevailing wisdom that one-party regimes are resilient. It may be explained by the weak political parties and tendency toward personalism in the aging regimes.[84] In some of these cases, a contradiction emerged between these leaders' impulse to ensure the succession of power to their sons, a process referred to as "dynastic republicanism," and the logic of a regime whose legitimacy was based on participa-tory institutions.[85] Egypt's president Hosni Mubarak, Yemen's president Ali Abdallah Salih, and Libya's Qadhafi' were intent on ensuring that their sons—Gamal Mubarak, Ahmad Salih, and Saif Qadhafi', respectively—replace them. Many military and other long-standing regime supporters saw the leaders' political maneuvering, aimed at achieving these goals, as simply unacceptable. Because legitimacy is closely tied to ruling parties and electoral insti-tutions in these regimes, the personalization of power undermined the very institutions on which the regime relied.[86]

In contrast, most monarchies saw little mobilization in this period, and where more sub-stantial uprisings took place—in Oman and Bahrain—they were ended without regime

TABLE 3.3 ■ Regime Type and Challenges Against Regimes, 2011–2021[+]				
	Little mobilization	Partial mobilization	Mass mobilization	Violent unrest
Monarchy	Qatar Saudi Arabia UAE	Jordan Kuwait Morocco	Oman Bahrain Morocco (2017–2018)	
One-party (republican)	Algeria (2010–2011)		**Egypt** **Tunisia** **Yemen** **Algeria (2019–2021)** **Sudan (2018–2021)** Turkey (2013)	Syria Yemen
Revolutionary experiment				**Libya (2011)**
Competitive	Lebanon (2010–2011) Iraq (2010–2011) Palestine	Libya (2020)	**Lebanon (2019–2020)** **Iraq (2019)** Iran (2016–2021)	

[+] Challenges are coded as follows. All mobilization refers to challenges against the regime (i.e., not economic protests alone). Little mobilization refers to cases in which protests are held by fewer than 1000 protesters and not sustained over weeks; partial mobilization refers to cases in which the largest protest has more than 1000 protesters but mobilization is not sustained over weeks, mass mobilization refers to cases in which mobilization by more than 1000 protesters is sustained over weeks, and violent unrest refers to cases in which there are protests with a significant level of violence or civil war.

Source: Author's records.

Note: Bold denotes cases in which the incumbent was removed from power.

change.[87] Some scholars argue that the reason for this lies in the fact that the ruling coalition, particularly in dynastic monarchies, depends on the regime's survival and is thus more likely to remain cohesive.[88] Others call attention to the fact that monarchs can promote democracy while remaining in power; this strengthens reformers, who seek democratization under the king, over radicals, who would seek to overthrow the king, and it divides and weakens opposition movements.[89] A third explanation turns our attention to the role that cultural norms, and the legitimacy of monarchs, can play in depressing mobilization.[90] A final one, in line with the argument advanced earlier, is that there was no discord between shoring up personal power and strengthening a regime based on hereditary legitimacy.

Not all scholars agree that these factors explain the stability of monarchies. Greg Gause and Sean Yom argue that three "strategic decisions" explain their resistance: the ability of resource-rich monarchs to offer their populations incentives to remain quiescent; the regime's ability to draw domestic support from long-cultivated, cross-cutting coalitions of support; and external support from international actors committed to the regime's stability.[91] At least two of these factors were present in all MENA monarchies. Certainly, these factors make change less likely, but they do not make monarchies immune to pressures. In fact, Bahrain experienced serious challenges that may have led to very different outcomes in the absence of foreign intervention.

Quasi-democracies were also notably resilient during the 2011 uprisings, although many of these have more recently experienced unrest. Palestinians took to the streets to express frustration over the Hamas-Fatah division; hundreds of thousands of Israelis mobilized to demand better economic and social conditions; Turkey saw demonstrations aimed at protecting democratic liberties as well as increased Kurdish unrest in the southwest; and the Lebanese, too, saw sectarian mobilization, fueled in part by the growing instability in Syria. Yet, in most cases, demands were primarily focused on the need for changes in policies and maintaining liberties, not on the downfall of the regime. Even imperfect democracies seemed more capable of staving off more fundamental ruptures than one-party regimes.

Finally, some scholars argue that we need to pay attention to other characteristics of regimes to understand authoritarian endurance. For instance, one can focus on the level of institutionalization of the military or nature of social ties underpinning the regime. As Eva Bellin points out, when the military is professionalized, as it was in Tunisia and to a lesser extent Egypt, it is less likely to shoot on protesters to repress unrest. In contrast, Bellin notes that when the military is

> organized along patrimonial lines, where military leaders are linked to regime elites through bonds of blood or sect or ethnicity, where career advancement is governed by cronyism and political loyalty rather than merit, where the distinction between public and private is blurred and, consequently, where economic corruption, cronyism, and predation is pervasive [the military is much more likely to repress protesters brutally].[92]

As the civil war in Syria demonstrates, such conditions do not entirely eliminate the possibility of protest or even regime breakdown. They may, however, make it less likely.

Islam

Many see the predominance of Islam in the MENA region as the reason for so little regime change in the region. The argument is often set forth with an emphasis on the prospects for democracy, as discussed below. Yet, Islam can also be seen as a factor that reinforces existing regimes.

One explanation focuses on the relationship between Islam and a patriarchal society, arguing that Islam fosters a culture that represses citizens' participation. As we will see in Chapter 5, neither civil society organizations nor mobilization is a new phenomenon in the region,[93] and the 2011 uprisings demonstrated that mobilization was possible, even in highly religious, patriarchal societies such as that found in Libya.

A more nuanced explanation suggests that Islam provides authoritarian rulers with a particularly compelling, symbolic repertoire by which to legitimize their rule. This is particularly true in monarchies where the king's legitimacy is based in part on religious authority. Thus, for instance, Madawi Al-Rasheed argues that the Saudi monarchy was able to conflate obedience to the state with the notion of being a good Muslim, helping to reinforce its rule.[94] Certainly, regimes that are most explicitly based on religious legitimacy were less likely to break down, but it is not clear whether they survived because they could invoke religious legitimacy or due to other reasons previously discussed. Moreover, incumbent rulers are not the only ones who can use Islam to reinforce their claims on political authority; opposition forces can do so as well.

A third explanation focuses on the relationship between opposition and ruling elites and the relative power between them. Scholars have long paid particular attention to the relationships between elites engaged in competition over the rules of the game[95] and to changes in the political conditions that alter the ability of leaders on both sides to create networks, mobilize support, and frame their concerns as they engage in this struggle.[96] Where radical forces are too strong, reforms are often stalled.[97] Moderate forces in the ruling elite are reluctant to form coalitions with the radical opposition, fearing the consequences of change. Indeed, when it appears that radicals may be able to claim the playing field if the status quo changes, even moderate opposition forces are unwilling to side with radicals. Importantly, the decisions of these actors are driven by the perception of the different actors' goals and relative strengths. The belief that radical opponents are strong and unyielding undermines the possibility of change, whether or not such beliefs are empirically correct.

Applying this logic to the MENA suggests that the *belief* that the MENA contains strong, radical, antidemocratic, Islamist forces can undermine pressures for change. It is not Islam as a set of beliefs that affects the likelihood of change, but rather the belief about the nature and strength of Islamist political movements that matters. If democratically oriented, secularist forces and their international sympathizers fear the ascendency of Islamists, they can prefer the authoritarian regime in power over the possibility of an Islamist alternative.[98] In the period leading up to the 2011 Arab uprisings, the decline of the radical jihadi movement, incorporation of some Islamists into the formal political system, and cooperation between Islamist and secularist opposition over such issues as the Palestinian–Israeli conflict and the US intervention in Iraq led to the diminishing of fear between secularists and Islamists.[99] The resurgence of radical jihadi forces in the form of ISIS, Ansar al-Sharia, and other groups, combined with the experience of Muslim Brotherhood rule in Egypt, may have the opposite effect, making non-Islamist opposition less willing to challenge their regimes.

Regional and International Forces

External forces also influence the possibility of regime change. Two sets of arguments are put forth to explain the stability of regimes in the region: first, the strategic importance of many countries in the region, which explains why external actors are often reticent to see regime change in the region; and second, the neighborhood effects, wherein changes in neighboring states provide more or less of an impetus for actors to rally for regime change.

It has long been recognized that the geopolitics of the region, and particularly on the presence of Israel, affect the MENA region. Some argue that authoritarian leaders used the protracted Arab–Israeli conflict to justify building a large military apparatus, maintaining martial law, and repressing the people. Yet while ruling elites have used the language of the conflict to justify the strong militaries and emergency rule, it is not clear that their people are always—or even usually—convinced by their arguments. Indeed, even in regimes that lie far from the conflict (and where the military conflict with Israel provides little justification for maintaining repressive regimes), one finds long-standing authoritarian regimes.

Others argue that external actors support authoritarian regimes in order to protect their own interests. Rather colorfully, Shaykh Fadlallah claims that the United States has

> pressed Arab rulers into service as watchdogs for their policies and interests in the Islamic world. Consequently, Muslims are repressed by other Muslims. The Egyptians are being beaten by the Egyptian regime, and the Algerians are beaten by the Algerian regime, so the United States does not have to dirty its hands.[100]

Many citizens in the region are highly skeptical that the United States acts to promote democracy in the region.

The belief that powerful international players were not necessarily interested in democracy promotion may quash mobilization from below as well. Amaney Jamal, for instance, argued that citizens support authoritarian regimes because they fear that an alternative, likely Islamist, regime would lose US support and endanger state security.[101] Turning attention from citizens to democracy promoters, Sarah Bush argued that in an effort to maintain their ability to operate within authoritarian regimes and facing little alternative pressure from donors, democracy promoters turned to "tamer" forms of aid that ultimately shored up—or at least failed to undermine—authoritarian regimes.[102]

The 2011 uprisings demonstrated that foreign influence does not fully explain the persistence of authoritarianism. Perhaps the most important evidence in this regard was the fall of the Mubarak regime. The United States would have preferred that the region's largest aid recipient, most influential regional partner, and neighbor to Israel would have remained under control of Mubarak, and when the uprisings began, the United States worked hard to portray Mubarak as a reformer and stabilize the regime. Yet the United States has never controlled political change in the region as completely as proponents of this perspective suggest. The failure to support the shah of Iran and to maintain a quiescent alliance with Saddam Hussein also shows that the United States does not fully determine the region's politics. In short, even if the United States had not promoted democratization in the MENA region as enthusiastically and consistently as it does elsewhere, it also cannot ensure its allies' stability.

Regional actors may also affect the likelihood of regime change. The spread of unrest across the region since 2011 could be understood as the result of four effects: first, the demonstration effect, by which citizens in other countries "learn" that change is possible, and second, the diffusion effect, by which transnational networks facilitate the conscious dissemination of frames and tactics. This is more likely to occur when citizens identify strongly across countries; thus, shared Arab language and culture (reinforced by satellite and Internet media) facilitated the spread of unrest across the region.[103] Third is the result of direct intervention, particularly by regional players (e.g., states, the Gulf Cooperation Council [GCC], and other regional organizations) that choose to intervene in the domestic politics of their neighbors, partly in an effort to assure stability at home (see Marc Lynch's Chapter 8 for further discussion). Fourth is the spillover effect from changes in the neighboring states, most notably through the deterioration of border control as neighboring regimes' grip on the state weakens and in the influx of refugees from neighboring conflicts, such as that seen in Libya, Syria, Iraq, and Yemen after 2011.

Importantly, international and regional forces can act either to promote or prevent regime change. For instance, intervention in the uprising in Bahrain promoted regime stability, while it promoted regime overthrow in Libya and prolonged conflict in Syria. So, too, the uprising in Tunisia, Egypt, and Syria initially encouraged Jordanians to take to the streets in 2011, yet by 2018, the increasing authoritarianism in Egypt and violent conflict in Syria convinced them to stay home. It is important to look closely at these factors on a case-by-case basis.

In short, the Arab uprisings tested arguments about the persistence of authoritarian regimes in the Arab world and also provided new evidence and insights into the scholarship on regime breakdown. The nearly unthinkable became reality when first Ben Ali, then Mubarak, Qadhafi', and Salih were pushed from power. They exited in different ways in each case and with different results, but they shook the belief that the Arab world was destined to endure aging authoritarian regimes. Oil, Islam, and Israel may influence the likelihood that individual authoritarian regimes endure, but none of these factors make MENA regimes entirely immune from breakdown.

PROSPECTS FOR DEMOCRACY?

Scholars have long sought to understand why the region appeared so resistant to liberal democracy. Before 2011, scholars of the Arab world, in particular, focused on understanding "enduring authoritarianism." Why, they asked, did authoritarian regimes in the region persist, despite escalating social and economic crises,[104] while those in Eastern Europe and the former Soviet Union, sub-Saharan Africa, and Latin America underwent democratization? After a brief moment of optimism following the uprisings, first in 2011 and then nearly a decade later, the question once again rose to the surface. In a global context of democratic backsliding and instability, the region may not appear as anomalous today as it did during the third wave of democratization, but many still ask, Why does democracy remain so elusive?

Before we answer this question, two points are in order. First, the region lacks a stable, liberal democracy in a well-functioning state, but contrary to conventional wisdom, it does contain electoral democracies—even Arab ones. Second, while it is important to consider the prospects for democracy in the region, this is not the only significant question to ask regarding regimes in the region. There are interesting questions about the politics of authoritarian regimes and how these regimes transition from one form of authoritarianism to another that deserve study, even if a goal is to foster democracy.

Economic Factors

There are two ways in which economic conditions may affect the establishment or consolidation of democracy. The first focuses on the relationship between economic development and democracy. As discussed earlier, modernization theorists such as Seymour Martin Lipset argued that economic growth would create demands for inclusion, ultimately fostering democracy.[105] More recent scholars nuanced this argument, most notably with Adam Przeworski and his colleagues arguing that development made democratic *consolidation*, not democratization, likely. While it is important to recognize this argument, it is unlikely to explain the lack of democracy in the MENA region. In general, the region consists of middle-income countries, far more developed than their counterparts in sub-Saharan Africa. If democracy is possible in poor countries of Africa, it should be possible in the MENA region.

A second way that economic factors may affect democracy is found in the nature of assets and income distribution. Scholars argue that when assets are immobile and income unequal, it is difficult to establish a stable democracy;[106] the obstacles may be particularly high in oil-based economies, where stakes are high.[107] Conflict over oil rents and the ability of incumbent elites to use oil wealth to buy support can undermine nascent democratic institutions. And in the MENA region, this appears to be the case. The conflicts in Libya and Iraq, for instance, are closely linked to the struggles over oil. Indeed, fighting often takes place around and over oil fields, and the destruction of oil pipelines becomes a strategy of war.[108]

Importantly, the impact of oil in undermining democracy, or sustaining authoritarianism, is a matter of debate. Indeed, even proponents of the argument recognize that it does not fully explain regime stability and the lack of democracy in the MENA region.[109] Moreover, Ben Smith and David Waldner review the scholarly literature and make a compelling argument that the generalized understanding of the political resource curse—or the argument that oil wealth precludes democracy—is both more diverse and less consistent than often portrayed. Moreover, they argue, it is based largely on historically contingent conditions in the MENA region; globally, oil has very different effects in Africa, Latin America, Southeast Asia, and the Middle East.[110]

Religion and Democracy

Another set of explanations for the failure to develop strong, stable democracies centers on the relationship between religion and the state. Some believe that Islam and democracy are simply incompatible. Focusing on both the doctrine and organization of Islam, Huntington famously argued that democracy and Islam are incompatible because "no distinction exists between religion and politics or between the spiritual and the secular, and political participation was historically an alien concept."[111] There are several problems with this argument. First, it assumes that all Muslims identify, first and foremost, as *Muslims* (rather than with ethnic groups, regions, and economic classes, for instance), an assumption that is rarely made of Christians in the West. This perspective also suggests that there is a single, monolithic interpretation of Islam, ignoring various strains within Islam and the competition among them. Finally, the argument that for Muslims "political participation was historically an alien concept"[112] is also incorrect both historically and currently. The first caliph, Abu Bakr, reportedly told the people in the 7th century that they had the power to remove him if he failed to act according to God's laws,[113] which is strikingly democratic. Today as well, Islamic parties in such countries as Malaysia and Indonesia take an active role in democratic governance. Moreover, there is considerable support for democracy among Muslims in the Arab world.[114]

A second way to understand the impact of Islam on democracy focuses on polarization. The polarization between Islamist and non-Islamist forces may explain not only the unwillingness of regime opponents to take to the streets (as discussed earlier) but also the failure of these forces to make the compromises necessary for democracy. Alfred Stepan has postulated that democracy requires "twin tolerations," wherein, first, religious individuals agree to act in accordance with man-made laws and, second, officials allow individuals to express their values and practice their beliefs freely, as long as they do so in a manner that respects other citizens' rights and the law.[115] He credits Tunisia's successful transition to date with its ability to practice these twin tolerations. In contrast, Egypt's failed attempt to establish democracy after the fall of Mubarak may be understood, at least in part, as the outcome of stark differences over views regarding the role of religion in the state.[116]

Even in more long-standing democracies in the region, the tension between religion and the state challenges democracy. The struggle between secularists and Islamists long undermined democracy in Turkey. In the early period of the republic, Atatürk's secularist vision took the upper hand, repressing rights of more religious Muslims to express their views and practice religion freely. This gradually changed, such that today the struggle between secularism and Islamism continues, with Islamists having the upper hand. In each case, rights and liberties are curtailed for opponents out of fear of the other, arguably contributing to democracy's demise.

The issue of religion and the state undermines democracy in Israel as well. The tension between Israel as a Jewish state and Israel as a democratic state is arguably the greatest challenge to its democracy. Arabs, who make up about 20 percent of the population inside what is known as the Green Line, are given Israeli citizenship and voting rights and have even formed political parties and sat in the Knesset. Yet their citizenship is curtailed, perhaps most notably in their inability to serve in the military, which is a major source of social mobility in Israel, their loyalty is sometimes drawn into question, and they find themselves the target of discussions over the "Arab problem" in Israel. That is, even Jewish Israelis recognize that Israel cannot, in the long run, simultaneously safeguard Israel's identity as a Jewish state and be fully democratic. There is a fundamental contradiction between the definition of *democracy* in a multireligious society and the maintenance of a Jewish state. The tension not only divides Palestinian citizens of Israel from Israeli Jews but also creates fissures among Israeli Jews as well.

International and Regional Actors

Regional and international actors can also undermine democracy. Given their own strategic goals, external actors can challenge democracies by aiding domestic contenders in sometimes-violent struggles or by engaging directly in internal affairs. It is always difficult to know what would have been in the absence of interventions, but arguably, they have at times undermined MENA countries' prospects for democracy. These include actions aimed at overthrowing democratically elected leaders, such as Iran's Prime Minister Mossadeq or the Palestinian Hamas, or those in support of authoritarian leaders, outlined earlier.

The prospects for democracy appear particularly bleak for countries surrounded by authoritarian regimes. Some argue that there is a "neighborhood effect" for democracies, wherein countries surrounded by autocracies are less likely to democratize.[117] This seemed at work after the Arab uprisings, as oil-rich monarchies, in particular, sought to stave off regime change and democratization in the region. Given this, strong liberal democracies may be difficult to establish in the MENA today.

Longue-Duree Arguments

A final set of arguments for why democracy is absent in the MENA focuses on historical factors, not contemporary conditions. In many ways, the foundation of these arguments is the same factors outlined previously: economic factors, religion, and international forces. The difference, however, is that all are based on the notion that divergent paths taken centuries ago explain contemporary outcomes.

Some focus on the role of financing and state-building. For instance, Blaydes and Cheney argue that the nature of military establishments in 16th-century Europe and the Muslim world explains the divergence in regime types today. European rulers relied on land grants to support their military, thereby establishing a feudal society, while Muslim leaders had a military force raised from slaves. Consequently, European leaders enjoyed a loyal military but found themselves constrained by a rising feudal nobility, while the Muslim rulers were put at risk of undisciplined militaries but remained unconstrained—that is, feudalism promoted democracy in Europe but not the Muslim world.[118] For Rothstein and Broms, it is "temple financing" that explains the divergence between medieval Europe and the Middle East. In Europe, churches financed themselves by gathering tithes from the people, while in the Muslim world, Islamic waqfs worked akin to financial foundations. Where there was no financing from below, there was similarly no need to develop responsive institutions. This argument echoes the "no democracy without taxation" argument put forth by scholars who focus on oil, but it seeks the antecedents of autocracy centuries earlier.[119]

Others consider international actors. For instance, Hariri argues that differences in colonial penetration account for "Middle Eastern and Muslim Exceptionalism." As did Blaydes and Cheney, he sees the early Muslim empire as fiscally and militarily stronger than other regions. He asserts, however, the effect was that the colonial expansion was less able to penetrate these areas. Consequently, there were fewer settlers from the West who had "communication and communion" with Europeans and weaker institutional legacies.[120] The result, again, was democracy where Europeans had a strong presence but not in the Muslim Middle East.

These accounts are intriguing, but they also are problematic. Explanations for contemporary divergence in regimes must account not only for the correlation between these factors and present outcomes but also for instances in between—that is, the feudal system, taxation, or colonial success should account not only for a difference across regions in democracy today but for a divergence (or lack thereof) in interwar Europe and the region or elsewhere. Moreover, the underlying reasoning should follow for countries and regions outside the sample, traveling to Latin America, Asia, and elsewhere. And finally, they raise an important concern: If the outcomes of choices regarding military recruitment, financing, or colonial success are so permanent, and intervening choices of such little consequence, what are the prospects for countries as they go forward? These theories, though intriguing, give us very little guidance.

CONCLUSION

The MENA region has some particular characteristics that seem to undermine state-building, democratization, and institutional reform. One has been the prevalence and strength of Islam. There is little reason to believe that Muslims in the MENA region are unable to establish strong states or democracies, as they have done elsewhere. However, there is reason to believe that the presence of political Islam may affect the possibilities of democratization and pressures for institutional reform. When prodemocratic forces inside and outside the country step down their demands for reform out of fear that Islamists may be a Trojan horse, pretending to embrace democracy only until they hold the reins of power, the prospects for reform are dim. Similarly, when they seek external support against Islamist forces in transitional processes, the necessary democratic bargains will be less likely to emerge.

A second challenge has been the strategic location of the region. Its position—previously a major trade route to the East but now as a region seated atop massive oil reserves, located at the crossroads of the cold war, and one that includes Israel—has prompted international forces to invest enormous amounts of energy and resources into shoring up dependable leaders. They have tended to give incumbents the means to remain in power without building strong states, often rewarding them for repressing public opinion when it would advocate policies they find unacceptable. In doing so, regional and international forces not only accept the authoritarian nature of the leaders but often help to reinforce these tendencies. Moreover, the support that they offer leaders undercuts the needs for leaders to establish bargains with their citizens and thus arguably promotes a weak state.

Oil also appears to undermine state-building and political reform. Oil sales provide an easy source of revenue that can be invested in education, health, and other social policies, but this revenue also reduces the state's need to tax citizens. This may help maintain authoritarian leaders and impede development of strong states.

Not only do oil, Islam, and international support affect the three facets of governance, but policies aimed at strengthening states, promoting democracy, and reforming institutions are equally entwined. Programs intended to promote effective governance often focus on one facet of development, and they use different strategies. Thus, for instance, programs aimed at strengthening states may focus on such factors as education and civic training. The approach is to help shape citizen–state engagement and extend state legitimacy and its mandate, which often requires long-term, relatively indirect interventions. Other programs are aimed at strengthening parliaments, political parties, and other institutions associated with increasing accountability, improving transparency, and, ultimately, promoting democracy. In this case, training programs and technical changes can help increase institutional capacity. It may appear far easier to address problems one institution at a time, focusing on legislative strengthening, the rule of law, political parties, and the media. Yet without addressing the broader issues of state-building, a focus on institutions—or even democratization—may have limited impact.

Solutions, as the problems themselves, must be seen as part of an interrelated whole, each being conditioned by and impacting the possibilities of others' success. Programs aimed at strengthening parliaments, the media, political parties, and judiciaries are likely to be successful only insofar as they are associated with broader changes in the mandates of institutions and changing executive-legislative relations. Strong, democratic institutions may be ultimately necessary if legislatures, parties, courts, and the media are to function effectively. At the same time, regimes are limited in the absence of state strength. Democratization, even if successful, may improve the living conditions for citizens only if the state is strong enough to govern. Strong states may lead to effective governance when the state not only acts upon citizens but incorporates them into decision-making processes. Improving governance is a messy, complicated process, but this messiness must be recognized if the lives of citizens are to improve. The challenges are daunting, but not insurmountable.

SUGGESTED READINGS

Angrist, Michele Penner. *Party Building in the Modern Middle East*. Seattle, WA: University of Washington Press, 2006.

Ayubi, Nazih N. M. *Over-Stating the Arab State: Politics and Society in the Middle East*. New York, NY: I. B. Tauris, 1995.

Brownlee, Jason. *Authoritarianism in an Age of Democratization*. New York, NY: Cambridge University Press, 2007.

Corstange, Daniel. *The Price of a Vote in the Middle East: Clientelism and Communal Politics in Lebanon and Yemen*. Cambridge: Cambridge University Press, 2017.

Herb, Michael. *The Wages of Oil: Parliaments and Economic Development in Kuwait and the UAE*. Ithaca, NY: Cornell University Press, 2014.

Luciani, Giacomo, ed. *The Arab State*. London: Routledge, 1990.

Lust-Okar, Ellen. *Structuring Conflict in the Arab World: Incumbents, Opponents, and Institutions*. New York, NY: Cambridge University Press, 2005.

Masoud, Tarek. *Counting Islam: Religion, Class, and Elections in Egypt*. Cambridge: Cambridge University Press, June 2014.

Moustafa, Tamir. *The Struggle for Constitutional Power: Law, Politics and Economic Development in Egypt*. New York, NY: Cambridge University Press, 2007.

Salame, Ghassan, ed. *The Foundations of the Arab State*. London: Routledge, 2002.

4 RELIGION, SOCIETY, AND POLITICS IN THE MIDDLE EAST

Robert Lee and Lihi Ben Shitrit

Middle Eastern societies appear more religious today than they did fifty years ago. Here and there, radical Islamist groups threaten governments and civilians. In countries where the Arab Spring unseated dictatorships, Islamist parties emerged to dominate elections and compete for power. Coptic Christians worried about their status in an Egypt governed by Islamists, and Syrian Christians, not to mention Alawites, fretted about their position as minorities in a new Syria governed by Sunnis. Religion appears in the name of the Islamic Republic of Iran, and Israel regards itself as a Jewish state. Students beginning to study the Israel-Palestine conflict often assume it is essentially the continuation of an age-old struggle between Judaism and Islam. Global television transmissions from the Middle East occasioned by public demonstrations or aimed at portraying daily life show heavy proportions of the population in dress that they or others may interpret as religious.

It is not surprising, then, that Westerners tend to see religion as a dominant force in the society and politics of the region—a more prominent aspect of life there than it is in the United States or in Europe. This Western perception is not new. European academics of the nineteenth and twentieth centuries—those who came to be known as "Orientalists" for their knowledge of Middle Eastern languages and societies—emphasized the contrast between the rationalism of the Enlightenment in the West and the mysticism of the East. When Napoleon invaded Egypt, he pretended to be Muslim, so confident was he that proclamations of fidelity to Islam would be sufficient to win popular support for him and his troops. Europe always saw the Ottoman Empire as primarily Turkish and Muslim, even though it included substantial populations that were neither; religious minorities reached out to Europe for support against their own governments, and religious mystics drew the attention of Europeans with their dances, music, rituals, and excesses. In the Orientalist vision of things, as expressed in literature, textual analysis, accounts by travelers, social interaction, and works of art, Western secularism contrasted with the religiosity of the East.

There is some truth in these perceptions of both past and present, but we argue that the influence of religion on the region is more subtle, more selective, and less determinate than commonly thought. The Middle East is, indeed, home to the world's three most prominent monotheistic religions—a place where remnants of still-older religious traditions have left important marks and where sectarian splits have created a bewildering diversity of religious minorities. It is a region where most constitutions identify a state religion and where both governments and opposition groups invoke religious themes to muster support. It is a region where religious community has been an important aspect of personal identity, sometimes congruent with ethnic, local, and political identities and sometimes in conflict with them. But religion everywhere is shaped and reshaped by human interactions; it is an evolving phenomenon, forged by environments, political entities, social structures, individual actions, and the flow of events. The advent of European imperialism, the fall of the Ottoman Empire, the emergence of independent nation-states in the 20th century, the creation of the state of Israel, the attacks of September 11, 2001—all have profoundly altered the role, significance, and structure of the religions themselves. Transformative through its spiritual impact and social dynamism, religion has also been transformed by context and events. Religion matters, but perhaps not in the ways and to the degree that many Westerners imagine.

What we mean by religion is not merely scriptures, beliefs, and rituals. Every major religious tradition has given rise to a set of understandings and interpretations that have evolved, sometimes as a result of disputation, sometimes in response to geographical dispersion, and sometimes in response to political and social circumstances. To speak of Judaism, Christianity, or Islam as though they comprised single sets of scriptures, beliefs, and rituals is thus misleading.

Understood as a social phenomenon, religion includes the communities that have emerged under the leadership of priests, *ulema*, rabbis, shaykhs, and shaykhas, some claiming divine guidance, others offering only scholarly wisdom and advice on moral law. As literacy has spread beyond the world of religious scholars, laypeople without special training have entered the field to interpret scripture and organize believers in the pursuit of social and political goals. Early Zionists were interested in national more than spiritual redemption, but the notion of Zion came from Jewish tradition. Hasan al-Banna, founder of the Muslim Brotherhood (MB) in Egypt, used religion to fashion a nationalist organization. Zionists and Islamistsnecessarily fall within our definition of religion, though neither movement was purely or even primarily religious. A single religion gives rise to an unlimited set of group identities. Moreover, believers engage in behaviors that they see as religious, such as putting amulets on babies to protect them from evil spirits or visiting the tombs of saints, activities that some monotheists may see as heretical and offensive. A broad definition of a religion includes what people believe and do in the name of that religion.

It is common to assert that the Middle East is a part of the Muslim world or to speak of countries in the area as Islamic. While Muslims constitute a majority in most countries of the region, the term Muslim world obscures enormous variation in the social and political impact of Islam and wrongly implies the existence of a vast, homogeneous, transnational entity extending from West Africa to Indonesia. Most states in the area identify in some measure with Islam, but only three—the Islamic Republic of Iran, the Islamic Republic of Afghanistan, and the Islamic Republic of Pakistan—include religion in their formal titles. By current convention, the word Islamic suggests direct inspiration from religion, as in Islamic ritual or Islamic art; Muslim states are those where the majority of citizens are Muslims, those who submit to God; and Islamists are those groups and individuals who invoke Islam in their pursuit of social or political ends, according to prevailing academic conventions. Writers often refer to the activities of Islamists as "political Islam" and call that fraction of Islamists who endorse the use of violence in their cause "radical Islamists."[1] We will use Islamists to refer to Muslims who are committed to the social and political applications of Islam but label as Islamic the groups and associations they organize in the name of Islam.

RELIGIOUS DIVERSITY

The population of the Middle East including North Africa (MENA) is 93 percent Muslim, and includes about 20 percent, or about 340 million of 1.75 billion, of the world's Muslims in 2015.[2] But great diversity exists both within the religion of Islam as it is practiced in the area and among the non-Muslims that make up about 7 percent of the population of the region.[3] The main division within Islam is between Sunni Muslims and Shi'i Muslims. The origin of this split dates back to the contestation over the succession of the Prophet Muhammad following his death in 632 CE. Shi'i Muslims believe that leadership should have passed to Ali ibn Abi Talib, the Prophet's cousin and husband of the Prophet's daughter Fatima. According to Shi'i doctrine, Muhammad's direct descendants through the line of Ali are the only rightful rulers of the Muslim community (*umma*).

The Prophet was succeeded by three of his companions (Abu Bakr, Umar, and Uthman) before Ali became the caliph following the assassination of Uthman. Ali's reign was brief and violently contested. After Ali's assassination at the hands of a hard-line Muslim faction in 661, Muawiya, who had earlier waged a battle against Ali for control of the emerging Islamic community, came to power and established the Umayyad dynasty. Hussein, Ali's second son, led a rebellion against the Umayyads but was defeated and killed in 680 in the city of Karbala in Iraq, becoming a martyr honored by Shi'a to this day. Shi'a believe that certain descendants of Ali, called Imams, were deprived of their rightful claim to leadership by the ruling dynasties that have held power over the Muslim world since the death of Ali. In the Twelver version of Shi'i doctrine, the twelfth Imam, al-Mahdi, is believed to have gone into occultation—a temporary absence or disappearance—in 874 and is expected to return to reign over the *umma* in the future.

Sunni Muslims are those who have accepted the four rightly guided successors to Muhammad as well as subsequent rulers of the community not related to the Prophet by blood. Sunnis constitute the majority of Muslims in the Middle East today, but some countries in the region, such as Iran, Iraq, Lebanon, and Bahrain, have majority- or plurality-Shi'i populations. While Twelvers dominate Shi'ism, other sects prominent in the Middle East include Ismailis and Zaidis, who hold different interpretations of the imamate's line of succession; the ruling Alawites in today's Syria; and the Alevis in Turkey, who combine Sunni and Shi'i traditions. Sunnis make up an estimated 80 percent of the Muslim community in the Middle East,[4] but they do not constitute a monolith. Practices and interpretations of religious law differ throughout the Sunni countries of the Middle East. Among Sunnis, there are four main traditions of Islamic jurisprudence: the Hanafi, Shafi'i, Maliki, and Hanbali schools. The Shi'a differ by sect and within sects in their interpretations of the Qur'an and the sunna, which is the custom of Muhammad and his righteous companions and a foundation for all Muslims of Islamic law.

Sufism constitutes an important tendency within both Sunni and Shi'i versions of Islam, further diversifying religious practice; it offers a more mystical approach to religious experience and focuses on prayer, meditation, and ecstatic rituals that are meant to induce closeness with God. Sufism's syncretic ability to draw on local, non-Islamic traditions has made it especially popular in Asia and Africa and has helped the spread of Islam in these regions. In several countries Sufi organizations have exercised political influence; the Sanusiyya order in Libya, whose leader won U.N. support to become king of Libya after the end of Italian colonialism, would be one example.

With Arab migrations and expansions to the north, east, and west, Muslims came to control territories largely populated by Christians, Jews, and Zoroastrians, as well as by followers of various polytheistic Near Eastern religions in Arabia, the Byzantine Empire, and Sasanian Iran. Much of today's religious diversity in the MENA is a result of the pre-Islamic religious demography of the region. Muslim rule in the region was significantly more tolerant of religious diversity than the empires it replaced. Designated as *dhimmis*—tolerated religious minorities— by Muslim regimes, Jews and Christians enjoyed the right to continue their religious practice. They were not, however, equal to Muslims. Non-Muslims were required to pay a special poll tax (*jizyah*) and faced special restrictions, such as, for example, restrictions on the size of their places of worship relative to Muslim sites. Religious minorities were second-class subjects, but they enjoyed significant accommodations. Jewish communities, for instance, did not suffer the severe limitations and persecution experienced by Jews in Europe. Muslim-ruled Spain and Iraq became centers of flourishing Jewish culture and scholarship, and after their expulsion from Spain in 1492, many Jews fled to the eastern Mediterranean and established their homes in territories governed by the Ottoman Empire. The Ottomans developed a pattern of rule (the *millet* system) that accorded Greek Orthodox Christians, Armenian Christians, and Jews official autonomy to manage their own communities and their internal religious affairs.

In the 20th and 21st centuries, the number of Jews and Christians in Muslim-majority countries in the region has diminished. Opposition to Zionism in the early 20th century led to violent attacks against Jewish communities in several Muslim countries, which were followed by both expulsions and wide-scale emigration of Jews to Israel and elsewhere. The once flourishing Jewish communities of Egypt, Iraq, Morocco, Tunisia, Libya, Iran, and Syria have all but disappeared. In Morocco, which has the largest Jewish population in an Arab country, the community counts only three to four thousand members. The non-Arab states of Iran and Turkey retain larger Jewish communities—about fifteen[5] thousand each—but their size and influence relative to the wider populations are minuscule. The creation of Israel and subsequent waves of Jewish immigration from Europe and Russia (described in Chapter 2) have, however, increased the total number of Jews in the region. There were about 7 million people who identify themselves as Jews in the state of Israel (in a total population of about 8.8 million in July 2021).[6] A multitude of Christian communities also have a small presence in the region. These include Orthodox, Roman Catholic, and Protestant groups. Their relative numbers, however, have declined as a result of emigration and higher Muslim birth rates. The largest concentrations of Christians relative to the size of the country are in Egypt, where Christians, mostly Copts, make up between 5 percent and 10 percent of the population, and in Lebanon, where Christian groups constitute about a third of the population. In Syria before the uprising that began in 2011, about 10 percent of the population was thought to be Christian, but the proportion may be only a fourth of that in 2021.[7] Other religious communities, including Druze, Bahá'ís, Hindus, and Buddhists, maintain a small presence in the region.

Although still significantly diverse, the Middle East is no longer the haven of religious tolerance it once was. The constitutions of all the countries in the region today, except for Turkey,

Lebanon, and Israel, affirm that the country's religion is Islam, or that the ruler must be a Muslim, or both. Israel, in this respect, is not so different. It does not have a constitution, but its declaration of independence proclaims the country a "Jewish democratic state." The preference for a state religion at times leads to discrimination against minority religions and to limitations on freedom of religion. By one system of ranking, the Middle Eastern states offer less religious freedom than any other region of the world.[8] Communal conflict, though often motivated by political rather than religious interests, has pitted religious communities against one another in political competition and at times in outbreaks of violence. In the 20thand 21st centuries, confessional politics have become salient in countries with significant religious minorities, including Lebanon, Israel, Iraq, Syria, and Bahrain.

The Muslim population worldwide is increasing at a higher rate than that of non-Muslims, especially in sub-Saharan Africa; fertility rates of Middle Eastern Muslims are slightly higher than those of non-Muslims, and rising emigration by religious minorities has contributed to a growing gap in the growth rates of majority and minorities.[9] The recent violence in Iraq and Syria along with conflict in other countries have led to considerable population change in the region, especially with the targeting of religious minorities by groups such as the Islamic State in Iraq and Syria, or ISIS, which may further diminish their numbers in the region. However, the Pew Center reports that "there is little reliable data to measure overall regional shifts in the last few years."[10] The growth rates of Sunni and Shi'i populations appear to be equal, but lower fertility rates in Iran, with the largest concentration of Shi'i Muslims in the region, might mean that the Sunni population will increase slightly in relative size. As for prospects of greater religious freedoms and diminishing levels of confessional tensions, the Arab Spring of 2011 initially promised a more democratic future together with greater respect for individual freedom and rights. Instead, postrevolutionary politics have produced disorder, repression, and even anarchy accompanied by sharp sectarian conflict in several countries. Only Tunisia appeared to be on the path toward liberal democracy until 2021 when even that country seemed to be sliding back toward authoritarian rule.

RELIGIOSITY

Middle Easterners have long seemed highly religious to Western observers. Europeans of the 19th century who traveled in the area or who participated in European military and economic offensives equated the Middle East with the religion-centeredness of medieval Europe. While God was "withdrawing from the world" as a result of the Enlightenment and European intellectuals were abandoning Christianity and exploring notions of nihilism, Muslims seemed set in patterns of regular prayer, mosque attendance, dervish orders, local saint cultures, backwardness, and superstition. Scholars analyzed religious texts and posited an Islam opposed in its essential nature to the sort of creativity and innovation that increasingly marked European societies. European social scientists believed ever more fervently in the idea of progress or modernization and in the idea that progress necessarily depended upon the secularization of society.

Many Middle Eastern leaders of the 20th century embraced these ideas. Mustapha Kemal Atatürk, the founder of modern Turkey; Gamal Abdel Nasser, the leader of Egypt from 1952 to

1970; Reza Shah and his son Mohammed Reza Shah Pahlavi in Iran, from 1925 to 1979; Habib Bourguiba, the founder and president of the Republic of Tunisia from 1956 to 1987—all sought to liberate their fellow citizens from the religious practices and beliefs they thought inhibited economic growth. Without opposing Islam itself, they sought to reduce and reform its impact on society and politics in ways consistent with Western liberal theory. Working with those same theories, Western scholars studying the Middle East between World War II and the Six-Day War of 1967 tended to concur that religion was losing its hold in the region.

Then religious revival swept the Middle East and to some extent the world as a whole. Student movements once steeped in leftist ideology began to speak the language of Islam. Girls whose mothers and even grandmothers had abandoned the veil suddenly began to dress in more conservative fashion. Young people flocked to support Islamist movements, most of them peaceful, some of them violent, in protest against authoritarian governments and against the materialism and secularism of Western societies. The Gulf states, once viewed as hypocritical or hyperconservative, suddenly seemed to be leaders not only in their prosperity but in their conservative Muslim attitudes. One image of contemporary Egypt is that of air-conditioned shopping malls drawing wealthy, bourgeois women whose stylish and fashionable Islamic dress seems intended to temper materialism with piety. The Middle East appeared much more religious in 2020 than it did in 1960.

By some measures, Middle Easterners do seem more religious than their Western counterparts, but by other standards, the differences do not appear great. For example, individuals from a number of Middle Eastern countries who were asked to evaluate the importance of God in their lives on a scale of 1–10 responded overwhelmingly with "10," which is equivalent to "very important" (see Figure 4.1). The percentage responding "very important" topped 90 percent in Algeria, Egypt, Iraq, Iran, Jordan, Libya, Qatar, Saudi Arabia, and Yemen in at least one wave of the World Values Survey (WVS). Turks and Tunisians were only slightly less inclined to accord God such importance in their lives. In contrast, fewer than 60 percent of Americans, Lebanese, and Israelis said God was "very important" to them.

When respondents from Middle Eastern countries were asked whether they considered themselves "religious persons," the contrasts were not as great (see Figure 4.2), and the results showed greater inconsistency year to year. Americans were as willing to call themselves "religious persons" as citizens of several countries in the MENA, including Saudi Arabia, which is often thought to be especially devout. Egypt, Jordan, Morocco, and Qatar registered the highest percentages on this measure of religiosity. Sharp variations in the survey results from wave to wave in Algeria, Lebanon, and Iraq suggest the difficulty of sampling in these countries or, alternatively, sharp changes in the way people responding to local or regional contexts interpret the term religious person. Note that the WVS does not revisit the same individuals over time. Many questions remain the same from one wave of surveys to the next, but different people are responding.

Middle Easterners may pray more than Westerners; mainstream Islamic doctrine does, after all, call upon believers to pray five times a day. A question asked only in Iran (2000) sought to compare the ideal with reality: "How often do you perform the prescribed five prayers of Islam?" Nearly half the sample said they perform all five prayers every day, and another 40 percent indicated that they pray more than once a week.[11] Only 4 percent said they never prayed. In Turkey, Morocco, Iraq, and Iran, people were asked how often they prayed outside of religious

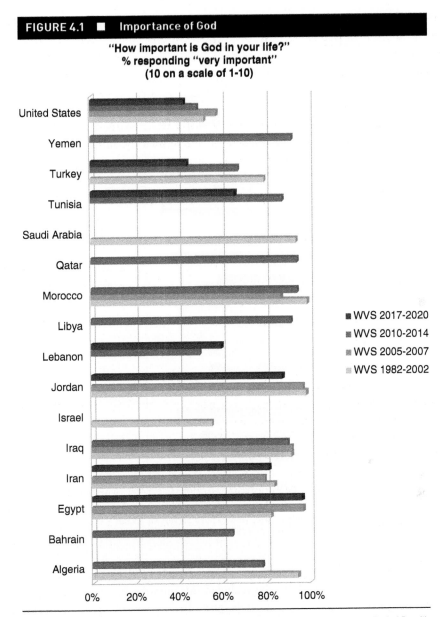

FIGURE 4.1 ■ Importance of God

"How important is God in your life?"
% responding "very important"
(10 on a scale of 1-10)

Legend:
- WVS 2017-2020
- WVS 2010-2014
- WVS 2005-2007
- WVS 1982-2002

Source: Inglehart, R., C., et al. (eds.). 2014. *World Values Survey: All Rounds - Country-Pooled Datafile Version*: http://www.worldvaluessurvey.org/WVSDocumentationWVL.jsp. Madrid: JD Systems Institute.

services. The percentages reporting that they prayed every day or at least once a week ranged from 60 percent in Iran to 94 percent in Iraq. The figure was 71 percent for respondents in the United States. Thus, by the response to one question in the survey, 60 percent of Iranians pray outside religious services at least once a week; the response to the other question suggests that 90 percent of Iranians pray more than once a week in some fashion or other.[12]

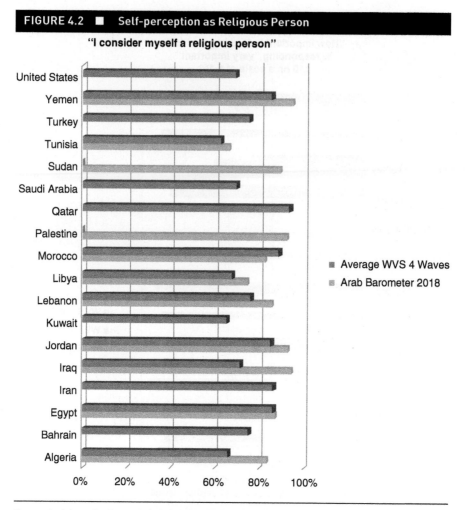

FIGURE 4.2 ■ Self-perception as Religious Person

"I consider myself a religious person"

Legend:
■ Average WVS 4 Waves
■ Arab Barometer 2018

Source: Inglehart, R., C., et al. (eds.). 2014. *World Values Survey: All Rounds - Country-Pooled Datafile Version:* http://www.worldvaluessurvey.org/WVSDocumentationWVL.jsp. Madrid: JD Systems Institute.

If one measures religiosity by attendance at religious services, the Middle East does not look extraordinary. The WVS has included this question in a number of its instruments: "Apart from weddings and funerals, how often do you attend religious services?" Interviewers have proposed these possible responses: "More than once a week, once a week, once a month, only on special [named] holy days, other specific holy days, once a year, less often, never or practically never" (see Figure 4.3). It is not, of course, self-evident that "attending religious services" has the same meaning in Muslim countries as it does in the non-Muslim world. The United States, Algeria, Egypt (except on one survey), Lebanon, Turkey, Morocco, and Tunisia all stood at about the same level, with 40 percent to 50 percent of respondents saying they attended religious services at least once a week. The

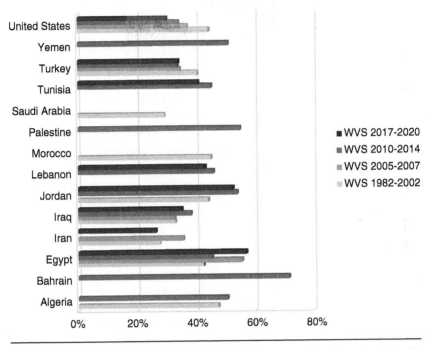

FIGURE 4.3 ■ Reported Frequency of Prayer

"How often do you attend religious services?"
% who say once a week or more

Legend:
- WVS 2017-2020
- WVS 2010-2014
- WVS 2005-2007
- WVS 1982-2002

Source: Inglehart, R., C., et al. (eds.). 2014. *World Values Survey: All Rounds - Country-Pooled Datafile Version:* http://www.worldvaluessurvey.org/WVSDocumentationWVL.jsp. Madrid: JD Systems Institute.

proportion of Iraqis, Iranians, and Saudis who said they attended services was lower than 40 percent.[13] The Saudi result seems to coincide with the relatively small number of Saudis who consider themselves "religious persons." In the latest wave of the WVS, more than 50 percent of the respondents from Bahrain, Jordan, Palestine, and Yemen reported that they attend services at least once a week.

Only the United States figured in all four waves. Israel, Bahrain, Saudi Arabia, Yemen, and Qatar were included once. Source: World Values Surveys, four waves.

Answers for the WVS question: "religious person," "not a religious person," "atheist." Averages for the WVS reflect only the first response. Only the United States figured in all four waves. Waves are 1982–2002; 2005-2007; 2010–2014; and 2017–2020. Answers for the Arab Barometer: "religious," "somewhat religious," and "not religious." Percentages here are sum of the first two responses.

The United States, Egypt, Iraq, and Turkey were included in all these four waves of the WVS.

Religion is a polarizing force in Israel, with ultra-Orthodox (Haredim, 8 percent of the country's population) and secular (Hiloni, 40 percent) representing the two opposite ends of the spectrum. Orthodox (Dati, 10 percent) and Traditional (Masorti, 23 percent) Jews fall in between in religious observance and political attitudes.[14] Relatively few Jewish Israelis say that they try to follow all religious traditions, and relatively few say they follow none. Many think of themselves as secular, even if they light candles on religious occasions. Many see themselves as religious without necessarily following Orthodox prescriptions about diet and behavior. Whether the glass of religious observance is half full or half empty has long been a debate in Israeli sociology.[15] Religious Jews, especially settlers in the West Bank, deplore the lack of commitment of many Israelis to the defense of lands linked to important sites of biblical history, while many secular Jews criticize the state's concessions to the demands of the Orthodox and ultra-Orthodox. Pew Research finds Muslims in Israel more observant of religious traditions than Jews but less observant than Muslims in other states of the region.

Religiosity is important for the outcomes it may produce. One might imagine that higher religiosity in a society correlates with greater respect for religious leadership, with a tendency to join Islamist organizations or religious parties, with intolerance toward minority religions, with seeing international conflict in religious terms, with the incidence of radicalism, and with believing that religion is a significant reason for conflict between East and West. There is some evidence for these propositions, but it is not overwhelming. For example, respondents who say that religion is "very important" in their lives (10 on a scale of 10) have somewhat greater confidence in religious leadership than respondents who claim it is "less important." These two questions were included in the WVS in Algeria, Egypt, Iran, Iraq, Jordan, Morocco, Saudi Arabia, and Turkey between 2000 and 2002. About 58 percent of those who hold religion "very important" in their lives have a "great deal" of confidence in religious leaders, whereas only 28 percent of those who see religion as somewhat less important or not important at all have a "great deal" of confidence.[16] "In many countries Muslims who pray several times a day are more likely to support making shari'a official law than are Muslims who pray less frequently," but the percentage of Muslims who favor shari'a law varies widely from one country to another.[17]

High levels of religiosity may pose problems of tolerance, especially where Islam is the religion of an overwhelming majority. Turks, Egyptians, Moroccans, and Jordanians are much more inclined than US respondents to say that they mistrust people of another religion. (see Figure 4.4) The percentages run from 20 in the United States to about 60 in Egypt and Turkey, 67 in Jordan, and 77 in Morocco.[18] In earlier versions of the WVS, respondents were asked if there were particular types of people they might not like to have as neighbors. One-fifth of the Iranian respondents named "people of a different religion"; twice that many people responded that way in Saudi Arabia.[19] In 2009, the Gallup organization asked for a reaction to this statement: "I would not object to a person of a different religious faith moving next door." Gallup asked respondents to agree or disagree on a scale of 1 (strongly disagree) to 5 (strongly agree). Three-fourths of Egyptians and two-thirds of Lebanese respondents said they strongly agreed, but the countries of the Gulf Cooperation Council, which were the focus of the Gallup study, ranged from 18 percent of strong agreement in Saudi Arabia to 39 percent in Bahrain. The study speculated that these results reflected the degree of contact with other religions: the less the

FIGURE 4.4   ■   Intolerance Toward Other Religions

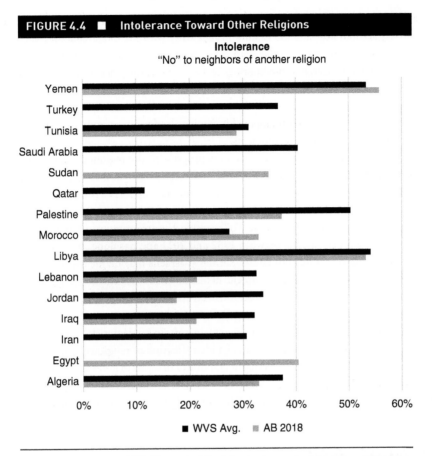

Intolerance
"No" to neighbors of another religion

■ WVS Avg.   ▨ AB 2018

Source: Arab Barometer 2018: "For each of the following types of people, please tell me how much you would like having people from this group as your neighbors." Percent of respondents responding "Strongly dislike" and "dislike." WVS: average of four waves: "On this list are various groups of people. Could you please mention any that you would not like to have as neighbors?" Percent mentioning neighbors of another religion.

contact, the less likely that citizens would welcome a neighbor of another faith.[20] By that theory, Saudi responses reflected the country's willful isolation. Might the relative isolation of Yemen, Libya and Palestine help explain the survey results represented in Figure 4.4?

On the basis of forty-four surveys conducted in fifteen Arab countries from 2002 to 2011, Mark Tessler concluded that about 60 percent to 65 percent of the Muslim respondents are religious by a combination of standards, and 10 percent to 15 percent do not pray frequently, read the Qur'an, identify themselves primarily with religion, and care not whether their children marry within the religion.[21] The remaining 20 percent to 30 percent fall in between. Persons of greater personal religiosity are more likely than others to believe Islam should play a significant role in political life, but the surveys show sharp disagreements about the appropriate relationship between religion and politics.[22]

There is, of course, variation across countries and over time. Egypt, a country long reputed to be relatively secular, now appears to rank in religiosity with the monarchies of the Arabian Peninsula. Israelis appear more secular than other peoples in the region but nonetheless support political parties dedicated to maintaining and enhancing the place of religion in the society. Iran defines itself as an Islamic republic, but the available survey data do not suggest that Iranians are more religious as individuals than are other Middle Easterners. Religiosity does not seem to correlate convincingly with support for religious leadership or conviction that religious leadership would help resolve social problems.

As for whether high levels of religiosity slow progress in the region, the jury is still out. The Islamist groups holding power (as in Turkey) or exercising great influence (as in Tunisia) see themselves as modernizing forces. They invoke religious support in the name of economic improvement and democratic reform. Their opponents, warning of impending danger, attack Islamic organizations but not Islam per se. For example, the government of Egypt attacked the Muslim Brotherhood periodically between 1952 and 2011 and has done so again since 2013, all the time insisting that it defends Islam. Similarly, Israelis may blame the ultra-Orthodox for obstructing progress but the government demands that Palestinians recognize Israel as a "Jewish state." For a country at the postindustrial stage of development, the United States exhibits remarkably high levels of religiosity. Religiosity does not seem to have impeded progress or promoted it, but religiosity may help explain certain characteristics of American culture: its emphasis on morality in public life, its identification of religious organizations with democracy, and its tendency to see international politics in terms of good and evil. But relying on religiosity to account for concrete American behavior at either the individual level or that of the nation would be hazardous, indeed. The same might be said of the Middle East.

STATE AND RELIGION

States in the Western world and in East Asia have tended to dissociate religious activities from those of the state. France adheres to a conception of *laïcité* that reaches beyond the doctrine dear to constitutional theory in the United States, separation of church and state. The French make exceptions to *laïcité* by adhering to religious holidays and subsidizing religious schools, and the American separation of church and state does not prevent candidates for the presidency from proclaiming their religious views or presidents from invoking God in almost every speech. Some Western states have official religions (England, for example), but even such states permit nonofficial religious organizations and sustain legal equality of all citizens with regard to religion. Nowhere is there complete separation of religion and politics; rather, there exists a variety of national relationships between state and religion that might be categorized according to several variables, including the official status of a religion, state subsidies for religion, rules for religious schools, and protection of religious minorities.

Many in the West tend to exaggerate the degree of separation between church and state in their own countries, contrasting that separation with what they perceive as the conjuncture of state and religion in the Middle Eastern region. "There is no separation of religion and state in

Islam," runs the common dictum. It is not clear whether that statement refers to the Qur'anic message itself, to the early years of Muslim experience when Muhammad was still alive, to the Umayyad and Abbasid caliphates, to the Ottoman Empire, or to contemporary Middle Eastern states. The statement probably applies most accurately to the period from 620 to 632, when Muhammad governed a small but growing community centered in Medina. After 632, the fissures began to appear. Middle Eastern states may tend to be more involved with religion than states in the West, but the enormous variation in that involvement, both in degree and in kind, makes it clear that religion and state are not identical anywhere. The variation among countries is inconsistent with the idea that Islam itself determines the relationship between religion and state. If it did, then the religion-state relationship would be identical across the states that define Islam as their official religion, but this is scarcely the case. Several states, including Lebanon and Turkey, do not proclaim Islam as the official religion, even though Muslims constitute a majority. And then there is the Jewish state, Israel. There are as many patterns as there are states; the problem is to make sense of similarities and differences.

One scholar has created an index of government involvement in religion (GIR) and coded all nation-states worldwide on five factors that combine to form the index. Table 4.1 orders Middle Eastern states according to their ranking on the index. The five factors are "the official role of religion in the state; whether the state restricts or gives preferential treatment to some or all religions; restrictions placed on minority religious practices; regulation of all religion or the majority religion; whether the state legislates religion."[23] The range of the index, from 22.17 for Lebanon to 77.56 for Saudi Arabia, suggests the enormity of variation. The presence of Saudi Arabia and Iran at the top of the table, with Israel and Lebanon at the bottom, causes little surprise to someone familiar with those political systems. Perhaps more startling is the presence of Egypt and Jordan near the top. Both countries appear to be relatively secular but quite different from each other: One is a monarchy that invokes religious heritage, the other a republic long governed by a secularly inclined military establishment. The commonality is that both have undergone considerable influence from Islamic groups.

Most countries of the Middle East fall into a relatively small, eight-point interval on the GIR index, from the United Arab Emirates at 54.70 to Kuwait at 46.82 (see Table 4.1). Yet the range of relationships within that set of countries is large. Turkey and Tunisia, for example, have tried to prevent religion from playing a major role in public life, and to do so, they have sought to manage official religious practices. Even since the advent of an Islamist-led government in Turkey in 2002 and the uprising in the spring of 2011 in Tunisia, which temporarily brought an Islamist government to power, those states have largely pursued policies they deem secular. Their policies contrast with those of the Persian Gulf states, which have generally embraced religious law as the foundation of their legislation.

The ranking of states on this index should not be interpreted as suggesting that religion is unimportant in the politics of Syria, Bahrain, Israel, and Lebanon. Quite the contrary, power has resided with the Shi'i-oriented Alawite minority in Syria and the Sunni minority in Bahrain. The unrest of 2011 and 2012 in those countries took on a religious dimension as the minority elites sought to defend their privileged positions. The Christian minority in Syria hesitated to join the insurrection for fear that Sunni Islamists would win control of the country and suppress

TABLE 4.1 ■ Religion and State in the Middle East

Country	GIR Index	Rank by GIR	Official Religion	Largest Religious Group	Percentage of Largest Religious Group[s]	Largest Religious Minority	Percentage of Largest Religious Minority	Number of Minority Groups With 5 Percent of Population
Saudi Arabia	77.56	1	Yes	Sunni	82–87	Shiite	10–15	1
Iran	66.59	2	Yes	Shiite	90–95	Sunni	4–9	1
Egypt	62.92	3	Yes	Sunni	90–95	Christian	5–10	1
Jordan	60.51	4	Yes	Sunni	92*	Christian	6*	1
UAE	54.70	5	Yes	Sunni	65	Shiite	11	3
Tunisia	53.73	6	Yes	Sunni	99	Christian	1	0
Iraq	53.66	7	Yes	Shiite	65–70	Sunni	30–35	1
Algeria	53.35	8	Yes	Sunni	98	Christian	<1	0
Qatar	52.90	9	Yes	Sunni	78	Shiite	10	0
Morocco	51.86	10	Yes	Sunni	99.0	Christian	<1	0
Western Sahara	49.36	11	Yes	Sunni	99	—	—	0
Yemen	48.41	12	Yes	Sunni	54–59	Shiite	35–40	1
Libya	48.13	13	Yes	Sunni	90.0	Ibadi	7.0	1
Turkey	47.21	14	No	Sunni	83–88	Alevi	10–15	1

TABLE 4.1 ■ Religion and State in the Middle East (*Continued*)

Country	GIR Index	Rank by GIR	Official Religion	Largest Religious Group	Percentage of Largest Religious Group(s)	Largest Religious Minority	Percentage of Largest Religious Minority	Number of Minority Groups With 5 Percent of Population
Oman	46.23	15	Yes	Ibadi	48–53**	Sunni	45–50**	1
Kuwait	46.82	16	Yes	Sunni	70–75	Shiite	20–25	1
Syria	43.69	17	No	Sunni	72–77	Alawi	15–20	2
Bahrain	39.89	18	Yes	Shiite	65–75	Sunni	6–16	2
Israel	36.84	19	No	Jewish	76*	Muslim	17	1
Lebanon	22.17	20	No	Sunni	27.0***	Shiite	27.0***	4

Sources: Columns 1–3: Jonathan Fox, A World Survey of Religion and the State (New York, NY: Cambridge University Press, 2008), 219; other columns from "Mapping the Global Muslim Population," Pew Research Center, October 2009, except where indicated. See also "The Global Religious Landscape," Pew Research Center, December 2012. All percentages are estimates based on total populations, not just the number of citizens. Sunni, Shi'a, Ibadi, Druze, and Alawite are varieties or offshoots of Islam; CIA World Factbook; Marc Valeri, Oman: Politics and Society in the Qaboos State (New York, NY: Columbia University Press, 2009), 127–128; In Lebanon, Muslims may constitute about 54 percent of the population, Christians 39 percent. The government recognizes four Muslim groups, twelve Christian, one Druze, and one Jewish. "Lebanon," US Department of State, International Religious Freedom Report, 2010.

* CIA World Factbook.

** Marc Valeri, *Oman: Politics and Society in the Qaboos State* (New York, NY: Columbia University Press, 2009), 127–28.

*** In Lebanon, Muslims may constitute about 54 percent of the population and Christians 39 percent. The government recognizes four Muslim groups, twelve Christian, one Druze, and one Jewish. "Lebanon," US Department of State, International Religious Freedom Report, 2010.

both Christians and Alawites. The tolerance of minorities has translated into rule by minorities in those two states. In Lebanon, the political system depends upon the confessional makeup of the country. Seats in the one-house legislature are apportioned according to religious confession. The state does not try to manipulate the practice of its multiple religions, but religion plays a decisive role in the allocation of political positions. In Israel, religion exerts its force through political parties and through advantages accorded Orthodox Judaism by a state that calls itself Jewish.

Identity

One way in which states in the area distinguish themselves is by the degree of emphasis on religion in national identity. Three states stand out for their dependence on religion in this sense: Iran, Saudi Arabia, and Israel.

The Pahlavi dynasty that ruled Iran from 1925 until the revolution in 1979 invoked pre-Islamic glories by celebrating the 2,500th anniversary of the Peacock Throne in 1971. The dynasty ran afoul, though, of a politicized element of the clerical class led by Ayatollah Ruhollah Khomeini. It was Khomeini who articulated a theory of Shi'i governance in the absence of the hidden twelfth Imam believed by Iranian Shia to be the last legitimate successor to the Prophet. It was Khomeini who led the revolution and authorized a constitution based partly on his own theory. The constitution of 1979 makes Islam the official religion and details the role of Islam in defining the purposes of the state, the meaning of morality, the process of legislation, and more. Although many Iranians supported the revolution to oppose the authoritarianism of the shah and hoped for a more democratic regime to replace it, the rulers of postrevolutionary Iran have emphasized their success in overthrowing secularism and establishing a new order based on Islam. Islam has become the official foundation of the state's identity.

As discussed in Chapter 1, the linkage of the Saud family with Islam dates from the eighteenth century, when a relatively minor religious figure, Muhammad ibn Abd al-Wahhab, allied himself with Muhammad ibn Saud and helped solidify Saudi control of the Najd region, the center of the Arabian Peninsula. The first Saudi state fell to Egyptian-Ottoman conquest in the early 19th century; a second state arose and fell in the latter part of that century; and a third state arose under the leadership of Abdel Aziz ibn Saud, again in alliance with the descendants and followers of Ibn Abd al-Wahhab. By seizing control of the Hijaz region in 1925, the Saudi ruler became the protector of the holy places in Mecca and Medina, and the kingdom became the principal sponsor and organizer of the annual pilgrimage—a business that now attracts about three million tourists a year. The Saud family has identified itself with Muslim causes, such as the liberation of Jerusalem from Israeli rule and the liberation of Afghanistan from Soviet domination; it propagates its version of Islam via the airwaves and via funding for foreign and transnational Islamic groups. The first article of Saudi basic law reads, "The Kingdom of Saudi Arabia is a sovereign Arab Islamic state with Islam as its religion; God's Book and the Sunna of His Prophet... are its constitution, Arabic is its language, and Riyadh is its capital." The regime depends upon the legitimacy of a ruling family, but the ruling family depends on Islam for its right to rule. However, changes in Saudi Arabia under King Salman long opposed by religious officials suggest a potential lessening of that dependence.

In Israel, the question of religion so bedeviled the founders that they could not agree upon a constitution. That is, while there was no dispute that Israel should be a Jewish state as proclaimed in its declaration of independence, many early Zionists saw themselves as champions of the Jews as a people but not Judaism as a religion. Still, Israel took a name and adopted symbols linked to Jewish tradition. The state reached an agreement with Orthodox and ultra-Orthodox Jews about Jewish holidays, respect for the Sabbath, Kashrut (religious dietary rules) in state institutions, the automatic absorption of Jewish immigrants, and many other matters related to religion. For some Israelis, the state is Jewish because a majority of its citizens are Jewish; if non-Jews eventually became a majority through annexation of the Arab populations of the West Bank and Gaza, then it would no longer be a Jewish state in this view. As a Jewish state, Israel has solicited support from the worldwide Jewish diaspora; it often speaks up on behalf of discrimination against Jews everywhere, even though individual leaders of the state do not necessarily see themselves or their duties as religious.

The emergence of the Islamic State in 2013 violated the boundaries of Syria and Iraq established by the imperial powers after World War I. It also threatened Iran and Saudi Arabia, which tend to see themselves as Islamic states—one Shi'i and the other Sunni—and as the power brokers of the region. In its young history, the Islamic State appeared to have outdone all rivals in its authoritarianism, militancy, cruelty, and intolerance. Nowhere else in the region is the linkage between religion and identity of the country as strong as it is in these cases, but in two other states—Jordan and Morocco—leaders claim special ties to religion. The Moroccan king calls himself "Commander of the Faithful," a title adopted by the second successor to the Prophet, Umar, and used by the leaders of the Muslim community until the end of the 7th century and beyond.[24] The king of Morocco claims to be Sharifian, a descendant of the Prophet Muhammad, and the king of Jordan comes from a family that traces its lineage to the clan of the Prophet, the clan of Hashim. Both monarchs lead religious services and speak on religious occasions. Because the Sunni tradition offers no clear theory of governance, leaders calling themselves caliphs, sultans, amirs, shaykhs, or kings have asserted their authority and sought legitimating support from the scholarly community, the *ulema*. The Saud family, in alliance with Wahhabi *ulema*, best exemplifies this mutual dependence; the Jordanian and Moroccan rulers fall into that tradition, as do the rulers of the smaller states along the Persian Gulf.

Morality and Legislation

Religious ideas about morality underpin legislation in all countries. Several Muslim states of the Middle East commit themselves in their constitutions to follow legal rules developed within the Islamic tradition, rules known collectively as the shari'a. Saudi Arabia and Iran make the strongest commitments in this regard. Article 23 of Saudi basic law proclaims: "The state protects Islam; it implements its shari'a; it orders people to do right and shun evil; it fulfills the duty regarding God's call." The Iranian constitution declares: "All civil, penal, financial, economic, administrative, cultural, military, political, and other laws and regulations must be based on Islamic criteria." Egypt makes the shari'a "the principal source of legislation," the Kuwaiti constitution refers to the shari'a as a "main source of legislation," and the other Persian Gulf states subscribe to a similar formula. The Iraqi constitution adopted after

American occupation specifies that "no law contradicting the established provisions of Islam may be established."

Such provisions might suggest a uniformity of legislation among these states, but uniformity there is not—not in the significance attached to constitutions, and not in the interpretation of those clauses. What constitutes Islamic law is a matter of disagreement not just between Shi'a and Sunnis but within the separate Shi'i and Sunni traditions. Elaborated at great length in many different versions, now as in the past, the shari'a is the product of human efforts to define God's will for human beings. While the word shari'a is often translated as "holy law," its status is nonetheless quite different from that of the Qur'an, which Muslims regard as the word of God. The great legal scholars of the medieval period worked from the Qur'an, which provides relatively little basis for law, and from the *sunna* of the Prophet. While the *sunna* originally referred to how things were done in the time of the Prophet, the lawyers came to identify it with a set of documents—the *hadith* literature—reporting what the Prophet or his companions had said or done. The development of law thus depended heavily on a filtering of the *ahadith* (plural of *hadith*) to sift the fraudulent messages from those regarded as reliable and then on interpreting these *ahadith* according to a set of principles. There emerged four primary schools of law within the Sunni tradition, marked by the application of somewhat different principles and by differential reliance on the *hadith* literature. While each school of Sunni legal thought bears the name of its founder, many scholars contributed and continue to contribute to the development of each of them. Shi'a have their own collections of *hadith* and a legal tradition elaborated over the centuries. For these reasons, uniform endorsement of the shari'a does not mean uniformity of legislation.

Most Muslim countries of the Middle East distinguish between matters subject to the jurisdiction of civil courts and those reserved for judgment by religious courts. States often assign personal and family matters such as apostasy, marriage, divorce, inheritance, and property rights to the shari'a system. The religious courts have typically treated women as subordinate to men and subject to some measure of segregation. Unlike most other countries in the region, Iran and Saudi Arabia also extend the jurisdiction of religious law beyond personal status matters. These countries both depend on a morality police to make sure that the rules of the shari'a (as they interpret them) are enforced. The morals police (*mutawwain*) can warn or arrest men or women they judge to be dressed immodestly; raid parties where alcohol is being served; and, in Saudia Arabia until recently, stop women who are driving automobiles. The Saudis have made great strides with the education of women but insist that females must not interact in schools, public places, or even the workplace with males who are not relatives. No other Muslim country engages in such effort and expense to segregate the sexes. In Iran, a higher percentage of women now work outside the home than before the revolution, and women outnumber men in the university system. The Iranians do not insist on segregation—only on standards of dress for women appearing in public. Showing too much hair can get a woman in trouble.

The other countries of the Persian Gulf region share the conservative tendencies of Saudi Arabia and Iran but in less rigid fashion. Far from minimizing a foreign military presence and discouraging foreign tourism, as did Saudi Arabia until very recently, several other Gulf states have welcomed American bases (Kuwait, Bahrain, Qatar) and the tourist trade (Abu Dhabi).

Without objecting to coeducation, these countries have subsidized American universities to establish branches there. In Kuwait, women have acquired the right to vote; in Bahrain, they have participated in protests. Iraqi women, who made great strides toward equal treatment under the Ba'thist regime between 1968 and the beginning of the Iran-Iraq war in 1980, have found themselves disadvantaged by almost thirty years of war and sanctions. The religiously oriented Shi'i parties that have won power in postwar Iraq seem more inclined to implement shari'a law than did the Ba'thist government of the 1970s.

Among the Muslim countries of the Middle East, Turkey, Tunisia, and Lebanon occupy the secular end of the spectrum. Turkey abolished the shari'a court system under the leadership of Mustapha Kemal Atatürk. Convinced that religious forces stood in the way of Turkish progress, he opened the way for women to step into the public realm and urged them to dress in Western fashion. Already in the 1920s, newspapers pictured young Turkish women in ball gowns and bathing suits. Eventually, Turkey outlawed the wearing of the veil (even headscarves) for women and beards for men in public places. Tunisia adopted a Code of Personal Status shortly after independence in 1956, a set of laws that established the equality of men and women in virtually every domain except that of property ownership. The founder of the Tunisian Republic, Habib Bourguiba, saw himself as someone empowered to adapt the shari'a to the needs of the modern age. His successor as president of Tunisia, Ben Ali, never wavered from his support for the Code of Personal Status, even though he succumbed to the Islamizing pressures of the 1980s and 1990s by building new mosques and issuing elegant editions of the Qur'an. After the overthrow of Ben Ali, the electoral success of an Islamic party, Ennahda, caused concern among secularists about the protection of gender equality. In Turkey, while the government of Recep Tayyip Erdoğan brought Islamists to power and encouraged Islamizing tendencies in the country as a whole, it also enhanced the liberty of women to dress as they wish in universities and other public places. The strength of Christianity in Lebanon makes it unlikely that any government would seek to impose shari'a rules.

To sum up, Islam alone cannot explain the diverse ways that Muslim governments implement the shari'a in these countries. Authoritarian governments have not been uniform in their approaches, and there is no certainty that democratization of these same countries would produce uniform attitudes toward shari'a.

Islam and Judaism are similar in the degree to which law has been fundamental to both—that is, while Christianity has emphasized belief as the primary criterion of adherence, Islam and Judaism have emphasized conformity to rules governing behavior. Just as the shari'a constitutes an issue for Muslim states, so the Jewish law, the *halakha*, represents a problem for the state of Israel. From the beginning of the state, legislation proposed by the cabinet, approved by the Knesset, and enforced by the courts has taken precedence over the *halakha*. The assassin of Prime Minister Yitzhak Rabin in 1995 claimed Rabin was violating Jewish law by proposing to trade land for peace with Palestinian Arabs. Israeli courts negated the assassin's claims and those of rabbis who had been denouncing Rabin's intentions.

Aspects of Jewish law have found their way into the civil code in Israel through the work of religious parties in the Knesset. Orthodox and ultra-Orthodox parties, essential to coalition governments, have been able to influence budgets and advance legislation to protect yeshivas, religious education more generally, the definition of Israeli citizenship, and the authority of Orthodox rabbis. Democratic politics in Israel, reflecting the impact of immigrants from the Middle East, have pushed the state toward privilege for the religiously driven settler movements and the ultra-Orthodox. It is the court system, and especially the Supreme Court, that has most systematically championed notions of equality between the sexes and among religious groups, often challenging religious interpretations.

Efforts to implement religious law raise questions about equality of citizenship. What is the position of a non-Muslim in a Muslim state or the status of a non-Jew in a Jewish state? At the extreme, religious minorities may be excluded from the body politic. That is the case of the Bahá'í faith in Iran and atheists in a number of countries. Some countries assert the freedom of belief but then make it a capital offense to abandon Islam (apostasy). In Muslim-majority countries, members of other religions of "the book"—Christians, Jews, and Zoroastrians—rate better treatment than those of other persuasions. In Saudi Arabia, the Wahhabi movement has treated even non-Wahhabi Muslims—Shi'a, Sufis of all sorts, Sunnis who practice figurative art or who make music—as the enemy. The Saudis stand for not just Islam but a particular kind of Islam, Wahhabism, which has been intolerant of other visions and other religions from its beginnings in the 18th century.

State Regulation

States of the Middle East differ in the degree to which they have wrapped their nationalism in religion. They differ in the extent to which they invoke religious law to support their legislation and policies. They differ to a lesser extent in the ways that they seek to organize and control religious institutions. With few exceptions, the Muslim states have undermined the economic autonomy of religious establishments, made religious scholars into employees of the state, transformed mosques into state institutions, organized and regulated the annual pilgrimage to Mecca and national religious celebrations in the month of Ramadan, and ensured the propagation of religion in the public schools. Lebanon, where no single religion enjoys official status or even a dominant position, looks exceptional among the Muslim states. In Lebanon and Israel, the state has not so much colonized religion as religion has colonized the state. Arab publics dedicated to democratization in their countries seem deeply divided on whether future governments should be secular or linked to Islam.[25]

State control of religion, though stronger in some states than others, has become the prevailing pattern, and state control always implies ambivalence. The state provides means and resources, but it also imposes restrictions. The typical Muslim state of the Middle East seeks the legitimacy that voluntary religious support could potentially provide, but it does not grant a degree of autonomy that could threaten the state's legitimacy and crystalize opposition. It does not want religious education to be independent of state control and standards, but it supports religious institutions and education, thereby putting itself at the forefront of an apparent surge in religiosity if only to undermine the potential for extremists to exploit this religiosity and resort to violence against the state. The typical state uses—the word *uses* is itself ambivalent—religion to promote citizenship and loyalty.

The ambivalence extends to the use of state power to enforce religious principles, as in Iran and Saudi Arabia. Is the primary objective public morality, or is it control for the sake of political authority?

Even the celebration of Ramadan, a month of spiritual renewal, social interaction, and fasting, depends in part upon the state and redounds to the advantage of the state.[26] State-owned media capture enormous audiences as families gather with friends to break the daily fast. In general, programming emphasizes prayers and readings from the Qur'an as sundown nears, but then with deference paid to the appropriate religious sentiments, it shifts toward entertainment. Sometimes the state network produces original dramas with Ramadan as the setting, but often, the network rebroadcasts foreign productions that galvanize audiences but do not necessarily please religious authorities. Music, dancing, dramas featuring romantic dalliance, conspicuous consumption—all can evoke protest even as they draw spectators. Religion serves as the appetizer, state-sponsored spectacle as the main course.

Two states of the Middle East, Lebanon and Israel, constitute exceptions to this pattern of state control. In these relatively democratic systems, the flow of influence has been from religious groups toward the state. In both cases, the religious makeup of the population has conditioned the nature and function of the state. Religious diversity prevents both states from proclaiming an official religion and exploiting religion for political purposes, as do most states in the region. Muslims probably constitute a majority in contemporary Lebanon, but they are split among Sunnis, Shi'a, and Druze, whom some Muslims regard as post-Islamic. The Christian camp divides into Maronites (Roman Catholic), Greek Catholic, Greek Orthodox, and Armenian. To proclaim any religious tradition as the official one would alienate significant minorities. In Israel, the Labor-Settlement movement that built the state resisted the adoption of a constitution that would have recognized Judaism as the state religion. Immigration from Middle Eastern countries has strengthened the religious parties in Israel, but even now, the adoption of an official religion would alienate an important part of the political spectrum in Israel. Religiously oriented parties have never been dominant in Israel, but they have exercised a critical voice in almost every political coalition.

In Israel, state involvement in religion goes well beyond the entanglement of state and religion in Lebanon because the religious parties dominate elements of the Israeli state. But religion is less central in Israel than in Lebanon because voters are not obliged to vote for candidates segregated by religious preference. Most Israeli voters choose parties that are primarily secular in orientation. The Left tends to be the most critical of religion, but even the Right, though perhaps more observant of religious traditions, has traditionally put security above religion. The main effect of the confessional system in Lebanon has been government paralysis in the face of pressing problems. The Israeli government has preserved its capacity to act in the case of crisis on matters unrelated to religion and state. However, on issues involving the tug of war between the religious and the secular, Israel has made very little headway.

RELIGION AND CIVIL SOCIETY

From the 1970s to the first decade of the 21st century, religious movements have become the most effective force in civil society and oppositional politics in the Middle East. With the decline of formerly dominant ideologies such as Arab nationalism, socialism, and secularism that promised to solve the various social, economic, political, and security challenges plaguing the region, advocates of religiously based remedies for the ills of their societies found a receptive market for their untested prescription of an ideal Islamic society. The Arab defeat by Israel in the 1967 Six-Day War signaled the death of secular Arab nationalism personified in the figure of Egyptian president Gamal Abdel Nasser. Later, the oppressive and corrupt nature of Middle Eastern regimes, their inability to deliver on promised socioeconomic advances for their populations, and their reliance on Western backers led to further disillusionment with the ideologies associated with these regimes and frustration with the political realities of the region. In 1979, the Iranian Islamic Revolution that ousted the oppressive US-backed shah of Iran demonstrated the potential power of religious organizing. Finally, the demise of the Soviet Union deprived leftist oppositional actors of their material and ideological wellspring. Combined with the intolerance of authoritarian leaders for any significant oppositional activity and their harsh persecution of political activists, these trends led to the weakening of socialist, secular, and liberal avenues for political organizing. The increased reliance of secular and liberal nongovernmental organizations on foreign donor funding often discredited them as viable challengers to Western-backed regimes (see Chapter 8).

In this context, various strands of the Islamic movements that have maintained a grassroots presence in almost all countries in the region have come to represent the most sustainable and potentially transformative alternative to the dominant political configurations in the Middle East. The unrepresentativeness of most governments in the region makes assessing the political strength of Islamic movements a speculative exercise, but when governments have permitted free and fair elections—for example, in Turkey from 2002 to 2018; the Palestinian Authority in 2006; Tunisia in 2011 and 2014; and Egypt at the end of 2011—parties affiliated with Islamic movements have often done very well in comparison with other contenders.

It is imprudent to speak of Islamic movements—or Islamists, as members of such movements are often called—as if they belong to a monolithic trend with identical iterations in the varied contexts of the different countries of the Middle East and North Africa. Though they share a particular historical and ideological genealogy and employ a similar religious vocabulary, Islamic movements across the region reflect the specific realities of the countries in which they operate. It is important, however, to recognize both the shared features of Islamic movements throughout the region and their evolutionary divergence in important respects. A common feature of many Islamic movements is their commitment to affording Islam a greater place in the individual lives of Muslims, in the public life of Muslim communities, and in the formal institutions of Muslim-majority states. In this respect, these movements are not different from religious movements of other faiths; similar efforts are common among Jewish, Christian, Hindu, and other religious activists around the world. Where Islamic groups and movements differ enormously is in the interpretation of "Islam"; the extent of, or need for, its incorporation into individual, public, and institutional life; and the method by which this might be achieved.

The notion that Islam could provide the solution to modern challenges faced by Muslim communities dates back to the 18th century when Muslim reformers started to respond to their encounters with the West. Reformers saw these encounters as exposing the weakness and disadvantage of the Muslim world in comparison with a modernizing, scientifically, and technologically advanced West; they stressed the need for change if the Muslim world were to catch up and successfully compete with Western powers (see Box 4.1 for an overview). A majority of their successors around the Muslim world would also subscribe, as a matter of practicality, to the idea that movements must operate within specific national contexts. Rather than trying to unify the *umma* or reestablish the caliphate, most contemporary Islamic movements work to reform their own societies and states.

BOX 4.1

MODERN RELIGIOUS REFORMERS

Modern religious reformers, such as Jamal al-Din al-Afghani (1838–1897) and Muhammad Abduh (1849–1905), sought to establish the compatibility of Islam with scientific and rational thought, with technological advancement, and with the social and political realities of modern life. The Muslim world lagged behind the West, they argued, because it had deviated from true Islam. According to them, this deviation grew from the blind following of tradition as developed by Islamic religious scholars (*ulema*) over the centuries. Instead of unthinking acceptance of religious authority, the reformers argued for personal interpretation (*ijtihad*) of the sacred religious sources—the Qur'an and the *sunna* (the practice of the Prophet and his companions)—in a way that would make them accord with modern life and deliver the Muslim world from what the reformers considered a state of "backwardness." Rashid Rida (1865–1935), a disciple of Abduh, continued on the path of reform, but with a more anti-Western stance than his mentor. Rida advocated an Islamic state ruled by Islamic law (shari'a) as the solution to the many problems facing the Muslim world, among which confrontation with the West and with Westernization figured prominently. The term *salafi*, or the *salafiyya* movement, which turns to the righteous religious forefathers (*al-salaf al-salih*) for models of correct conduct, refers to the reformist movement inspired by Abduh and developed into a more conservative tendency by Rida. Though the modern reformers called for the unity of the Muslim *umma*, they generally acknowledged the rising popularity of nationalism and the reality of distinct Muslim states.

One of the most influential contemporary movements, the Society of the Muslim Brothers, was founded by Hasan al-Banna (1906–1949), a schoolteacher in Egypt. The Muslim Brotherhood, founded in 1928, felt the influence of Abduh and Rida. According to al-Banna's vision, the Muslim Brothers aimed to reform Egyptian society in order to bring it closer to Islam. He argued, however, that before state institutions could be reformed to better accord with Islamic law the practice and morals of individuals and society would need to become more Islamic. The Muslim Brothers engaged in welfare and educational work; established hospitals, mosques, and schools; and quickly drew a significant following. By 1949, the Muslim Brothers had established two thousand branches and enrolled almost five hundred thousand members across Egypt.[27] The vision of the Muslim Brothers also extended beyond Egypt; they fostered affiliated societies in Palestine, Jordan, Syria, Yemen, and elsewhere. Many of the most influential Islamic opposition movements in the region today are the ideological offspring of the Egyptian Muslim Brothers.

Originally supportive of Gamal Abdel Nasser's coming to power in 1952, the Egyptian Muslim Brothers soon took issue with the Nasser government. In the context of opposition to Nasser and his repression of the organization, the writings of the Brothers' chief ideologue, Sayyid Qutb (1906–1966), became a major force in the movement in the 1950s and 1960s. In militant publications, Qutb denounced the West and nominal, hypocritical Muslim rulers in terms that suggested "true" Muslims would be justified in using violence to achieve an Islamic state. From the South Asian Islamic scholar Mawlana Mawdudi, Qutb adopted the modern application of the concept of *jahiliyya*—the pre-Islamic age of ignorance—and used it to describe contemporary Muslim societies and all other regimes he considered to be the propagators of ignorance. Qutb popularized two important ideological themes: the concept of excommunication (*takfir*) of political rivals, and the importance of *jihad*, which he interpreted as the uncompromising struggle against unjust rulers for the sake of implementing God's sovereignty. President Nasser's government imprisoned, released, rearrested, tried, and ultimately hanged Qutb for his writings, making him a martyr of the radical cause. Radical Islamic groups in Egypt and elsewhere in the Sunni world later seized upon Qutb's ideas to rationalize violent action, including the assassination of President Anwar al-Sadat of Egypt in 1981.

Most contemporary Islamic movements have included both the reformist and the more militant strands of their ideological forbearers. Contentious relations with authoritarian regimes in the region have often determined which of these strands, moderate or extremist, enjoyed greater prominence in different periods. In general, however, the bulk of activism by the most popular Islamic movements has been aimed at reforming society and politics by reviving and popularizing religious practice, engaging in social welfare work, and creating viable opposition to incumbent authoritarian regimes, rather than in militant revolutionary action. Very roughly, the activism of contemporary Islamic movements falls into three categories. The first is religious and social work. The second is political activity, often through an affiliated political party. The third is paramilitary violence, which is a main feature of only some of these movements. The Palestinian Hamas and the Lebanese Hizbullah, for example, both have their own well-equipped military wings. Unlike most other Islamic movements, however, these two organizations have operated within a context of foreign occupation and have usually maintained military capabilities, at least officially, for the sake of resisting occupation rather than imposing their Islamic vision on their own societies. Some Islamic movements have also been implicated in acts of violence, but usually, it has been smaller, breakaway radical organizations that have responded to state repression by violently attacking representatives of the regime, their fellow citizens, or even foreigners, as was the case, for example, with the most radical groups in Egypt and in Algeria during the 1990s. However, with the turmoil, repression, and violence that have followed the events of the popular Arab uprisings of 2011, militant Islamist militias have come to increasingly fill the chaotic vacuum that opened in parts of Syria, Iraq, Yemen, Libya, and in the Sinai in Egypt.

Religious and Social Activism

Reforming society, the objective of many Islamic movements starts with individual and community-wide efforts to live by Islamic values and cultivate Islamic virtues. These encompass both religious and social practices. Islamic movements have therefore worked to build mosques, promote religious education, offer religious lessons for children and adults, and make religious practice a more central aspect of the everyday lives of Muslims. In addition, the provision of social services has been an integral part of these movements' efforts. Dedicated to the notion that "Islam is the solution" for the problems of modern states and societies, the offshoot organizations of the Muslim Brothers in Egypt, Palestine, Jordan, Yemen, and elsewhere have established health clinics, hospitals, and schools, as well as a plethora of charities that offer material aid to the poor. Social welfare work has helped Islamic movements demonstrate the power of Islamic commitment as well as offer alternative institutions to those run by the un-Islamic state. Moreover, with the shrinking of state investment in social welfare that has characterized the structural adjustment and economic liberalization policies of the 1980s and 1990s (see Chapter 3), Islamic charity has come to fill the gap in social services. Exact figures are not available, but the number and influence of Islamic social institutions is considerable. For example, studies estimated that by 2003 there were 2,457 Islamic voluntary associations in Egypt and that 70 percent of the two thousand nongovernmental associations in Yemen were Islamic. In Jordan, the largest association to run schools, kindergartens, health clinics, and hospitals is the Islamic Center Charity Society, which is affiliated with the Muslim Brothers.[28] In the Palestinian territories, Islamic charities ran an estimated 40 percent of all social institutions in the West Bank and Gaza in the year 2000.[29] By 2003, 65 percent of primary and middle schools in Gaza were Islamic, and the Hamas-affiliated Islamic Society in Gaza, alongside other Islamic charities, financially supported at least 120,000 individuals on a monthly basis.[30]

Charitable activity, which has a long history in the Middle East, has not been confined to institutions directly affiliated with Islamic political movements. Many independent Islamic charities operating in the region have no official ties to movements such as the Muslim Brothers. Nevertheless, taken together, diverse religious charities, associations, and institutions help further the agenda of contemporary political Islamic movements in several ways. First, they demonstrate Islam's power in alleviating some of the socioeconomic challenges experienced by many in the region. They also highlight the state's inability to adequately provide these services and advertise religious activism as a viable alternative. Second, through affiliated welfare institutions, activists gain access to potential recruits among the poor and the lower-middle classes. However, Islamic social institutions do not necessarily serve as venues for religious indoctrination or direct political recruitment of the poor.[31] Many Islamic institutions, run by middle-class professionals and attuned to middle-class needs, help build horizontal middle-class networks and create environments in which the Islamic movements can effectively carry out their work.[32] Third, religious welfare institutions—sometimes explicitly, sometimes unintentionally—help make the vocabulary and mode of action of Islamic movements resonate more effectively with the users of these services. Finally, the fact that Islamic charities and institutions provide vital services makes it difficult for states to shut down their activities.

Islamic organizations have drawn attention for the scale of their charitable endeavors in an age of diminishing state services, but they are not unique. The Jewish ultra-Orthodox Shas movement in Israel, for example, runs an extensive network of kindergartens, schools, charities, and welfare institutions across the country that supports thousands of families. In Egypt, the Coptic Church provides an associational life and social services that help preserve and enhance the identity of a minority community.[33] Nonreligious organizations providing social services have also proliferated. In addition, following the 2013 coup in Egypt, which ousted President Morsi of the Muslim Brothers, unprecedented levels of repression and the strict outlawing of the Brotherhoods have undermined much of the charitable work and infrastructure of Islamic social activism associated with the movement. Scholars who have been doubtful about the political effectiveness of Islamists' social services provision now call for reevaluation of the connection between religious charitable work and political mobilization, especially given the swiftness with which many Egyptians turned against the Brotherhood following its brief stay in power.[34]

Political Participation

Most states in the region have restricted political participation by opposition groups. Even under these limiting conditions, Islamic movements have been able to organize and compete effectively in electoral politics to the extent permitted by the state. Islamic movements have run candidates in elections for professional associations, labor unions, and student councils. A 2010 study found that, when allowed to participate in parliamentary elections, Islamists have run in 140 different elections since 1970, either through an affiliated political party, by fielding independent candidates, or in coalition with other parties.[35] This track record reflects the willingness of many Islamic movements to play by democratic rules and submit to the will of their people, even when these rules are severely slanted against them by authoritarian restrictions, manipulation, and rigging.

Despite this track record of participation, liberal and secular actors in the region, as well as Western policymakers, have been suspicious of the sincerity of the democratic commitment professed by Islamic movements. This suspicion stems from two assumptions. The first is that Islamists simply use the democratic political game as a tactical means for gaining power, after which, critics fear, they will abolish the same democratic system that had brought them to power and will seek to establish a theocratic state similar to the Iranian model. Such anxieties were among the reasons secular opposition groups, with approval from France and the United States, supported the military abortion of the Algerian election process following a first-round victory by the Islamic Salvation Front (FIS) in 1991. Critics of Islamic movements also cite the violent clashes between Palestinian Hamas and Fatah that followed the electoral victory of Hamas in 2006 and the subsequent takeover of Gaza by Hamas as a reason to doubt the democratic commitment of Islamic movements. Authoritarian regimes invoke the fear that these movements adhere to democratic principles only to win power—"one person, one vote, one time"[36] is the slogan—to justify their reluctance to implement liberalizing political reforms. Fear of Islamists' authoritarianism may also help explain the support of large segments of the Egyptian population for the military coup against the government of the Muslim Brotherhood in 2013. Though hardly enjoying democratic credentials themselves, authoritarian governments try to convince both the secular opposition and the West that "the devil you know—the regime— is better than the devil you don't know—the Islamic contenders."[37] These fears, however, are largely speculative. The few examples often used in support of such arguments fail to address the integral part that incumbent regimes or their affiliates in the military, security services, and the bureaucracy have played in instigating and propagating the upheavals that followed these contested elections.

Scholars debate whether participation by Islamists in the electoral process might lead to the moderation of hard-line ideologies.[38] Jillian Schwedler defines moderation as

> [a] process of change that might be described as movement along a continuum from radical to moderate, whereby a move away from more exclusionary practices (of the sort that view all alternative perspectives as illegitimate and thus dangerous) equates to an increase in moderation.[39]

The exigencies of running in election, some scholars argue, create incentives for Islamists to moderate their positions. For example, in order to win seats, Islamists must appeal to diverse voters, including those who do not necessarily subscribe to their religious agenda.[40] In some cases, they must also cooperate and even create coalitions with opposition forces that hold views directly opposed to an Islamist ideology, such as secular and socialist or communist groups.[41] Inclusion of Islamists in the democratic process can also give rise to internal debates about strategy within the movements between hard-liners and moderates or between the older and younger generations.[42] Inclusion may also prevent radicalization by offering legitimate forms of participation to Islamists and others who are critical of the existing political situation in their countries and are committed to changing it.

While some scholars argue that inclusion leads to moderation, others think that the causal direction is actually the reverse and that the ideological moderation of Islamists leads them to seek participation and not the other way around. During the late 1990s and early 2000s, for example, Islamists in Turkey, Egypt, and Morocco moderated their political stances, advocating participation and compromise instead of revolutionary overhaul of the political system, even under conditions of exclusion or the absence of meaningful democratic reforms.[43] Some scholars argue that, in fact, this moderation by Islamists and their inclusion or even co-optation by authoritarian regimes might have the paradoxical effect of reducing the pressure on authoritarian incumbents to pursue genuine democratic reform.[44] However, there is some evidence that inclusion is strongly associated with political liberalization. As Islamists participate in the political game more openly, they become less of an "unknown threat" to other, mostly secular, opposition groups and therefore cease to be the "Islamist menace" that authoritarian regimes can use to defer reforms.[45]

Whether inclusion leads to behavioral moderation or ideological moderation leads to participation, it appears that religious parties in the Middle East generally abide by democratic rules when given the opportunity to do so. For instance, when Islamic parties have competed in elections that required a quota for women candidates, as in elections in the Palestinian Authority, Jordan, and Tunisia, they did not contest the rule and fielded women as candidates.

Israel's experience offers an important lesson as well. Religious parties have freely participated in Israeli elections from the establishment of the state. Since the late 1990s, religious parties have held almost a fourth of the seats in the Israeli parliament, the Knesset. These parties have exerted their significant power to maintain and strengthen the religious character of the state, but they have not sought to abolish the democratic system itself and have continued to participate in repeated elections. The case of the Turkish Justice and Development Party (AKP) serves as still another indicator of how Islamic parties might perform after winning free democratic elections. In power since 2002, the AKP had removed all reference to religion in its party platform by 2011, referring to itself simply as a "conservative" party. At the same time, President Erdoğan of Turkey worked to consolidate his power in increasingly authoritarian ways. His brutal repression of political opponents, including other Islamist groups like the Gülen movement, bore more resemblance to the actions of other authoritarian leaders in the region—secular or religious—than it did to the implementation of a uniquely "Islamic" model.

Even if many Islamic movements are at least somewhat committed to procedural democracy, some critics see their agenda of increasing the role of religion in public life and state institutions as inherently incompatible with liberal democratic principles. Islamic parties often mention in their electoral platforms and their campaigns that they intend to ensure that shari'a assumes its proper role. They usually leave unspecified both the extent to which shari'a law would be implemented and the procedure by which this would be achieved.[46] Critics fear that the interpretation of shari'a law pursued by Islamic parties could undermine women's rights, the rights of minorities, freedom of expression, and freedom of religion. The Freedom and Justice Party, affiliated with the Egyptian Muslim Brothers, for example, mentioned in its 2011 election platform that it would support international human rights conventions "so long as they are not contrary to the principles of Islamic law."[47] Similarly, the provisional constitution adopted in Tunisia after the revolution of the Arab Spring requires that the head of state be Muslim.[48] While concerns about Islamic movements for their lack of adherence to liberal democratic values are not unfounded, it is also important to keep in mind that the record of authoritarian incumbents in the protection of civil, political, and human rights is poor. For instance, in most Middle Eastern countries, including non-Muslim Israel, religious law already governs many personal status matters such as marriage, divorce, and citizenship with provisions that discriminate against women. A non-liberal approach to rights is common to incumbent regimes, Islamist contenders, and, possibly, the majority of people in the region.

As Figure 4.5 shows, contemporary Islamic parties often perform well in elections that are relatively free and fair. In some elections in Palestine, Egypt, Tunisia, Turkey, Morocco, and Lebanon, Islamic parties or coalitions led by Islamic parties won more seats than other contenders. Why do Islamists seem to do relatively well in elections? The most widespread popular perception is that Islamists succeed in the ballot boxes because the poor, who benefit from Islamic social services, tend to support them.[49] But more recent studies point in other directions. Tarek Masoud[50] and Janine Clark,[51] for example, find that Islamist movements are generally run by and appeal to the educated, professional middle classes who are less concerned with economic need and more interested in social and political change. Other scholars suggest that Islamists do well because they have several organizational advantages over other opposition contenders.

FIGURE 4.5   ■   Seats Won by Islamic Parties/Coalitions in Selected Recent Elections (Percentage of Parliament Seats)

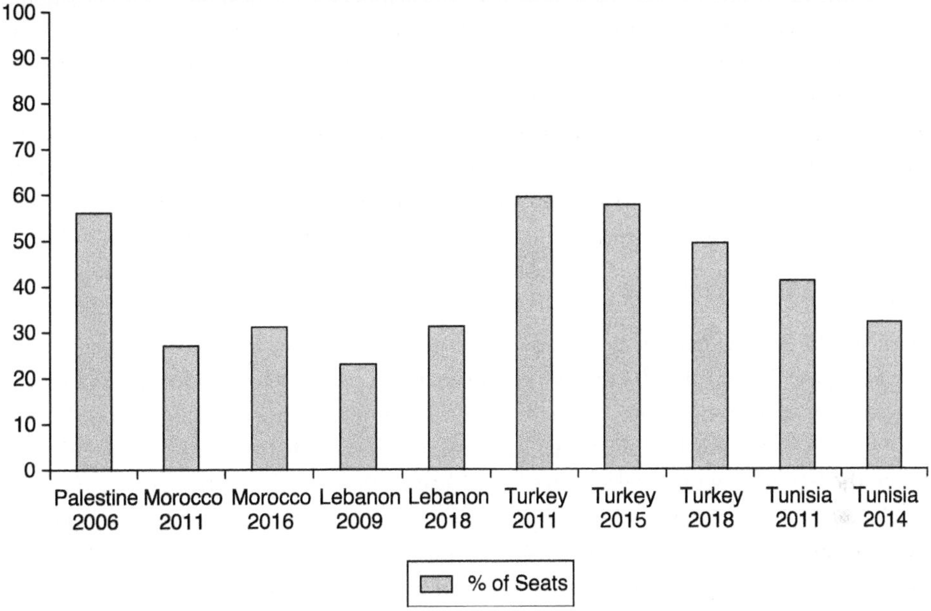

Source: Compiled from Inter-Parliamentary Union data, http://www.ipu.org and other news sources.

From their extensive experience in the management of vast networks of social services, Islamic movements possess logistical skills, experience, and presence that is superior to what any other opposition group might muster. They also have better resources as they mobilize devoted volunteers and Islamic charity—*zakat*—while their secular civil society competitors rely on salaried positions and limited donations from the international community and appear tainted through their association with the West (see Chapter 8). A vote for an Islamic party is therefore not always a vote for an Islamizing agenda. Because they are often the most organized alternative to undemocratic and corrupt incumbents, Islamic parties at times also win protest votes from citizens who do not share the religious commitments of the parties. Yet after they are elected and confronted with the burdens of governance, Islamists tend to lose the support of protest voters, as has been the case, for example, with the Muslim Brothers in Egypt, Ennahda in Tunisia, and Hamas in Palestine.

Partly to counter the appeal of Islamists, authoritarian incumbents in the region have in their turn also attempted to bolster the religious credentials of their regimes by employing so-called moderate religious rhetoric and supporting loyal religious education and religious institutions. Their actions have further contributed to the ascendance of religious discourse in the public sphere. It is yet unclear whether this last phenomenon has helped boost support for Islamists by rendering their religious vocabulary the most dominant one in the public square, or whether, on the contrary, as other scholars argue, this has led to greater disillusionment with religious rhetoric.[52]

Momentarily, the Arab Spring promised a more democratic political process in the Middle East that would permit scholars to better estimate popular support for religious parties measured through their electoral performance. It could have also given us an opportunity to observe how Islamists perform in power or in governing coalitions across the region. However, the aftermath of the uprisings has been characterized across the region—except for Tunisia—by increased political violence, repression, and conflict, which make formal politics again a largely unrepresentative reflection of popular political preferences.

Contextualizing Violence

In the media and the popular imagination, the specter of violence hovers over Islamic movements. Especially since the 9/11 attacks, violent action by groups who self-identify as Islamic is perceived as senseless, irrational, and indiscriminate. Groups such as Al-Qaʿida and ISIS, and their brutal violence provided additional, gruesome material for this narrative. For analytic purposes, the Islamic groups that do engage in violence can be divided into three types, although overlap or transition from one form of group to another also occurs in response to changing political contexts. The first type includes nationalist movements engaged in an armed conflict against a foreign occupier. The most well-known and popular among these are Hamas and Hizbullah. The second type involves small, radical groups that use violence against oppressive authoritarian governments in their own countries. These are usually isolated, clandestine militias that do not enjoy mass support. Their violence tends to flare up when state repression increases and no peaceful avenues for change seem available. It is also often short-lived, as violence against civilians tends to alienate local populations. Finally, the third group includes transnational terrorist networks such as al-Qaʿida, and more recently the Islamic State, that employ indiscriminate violence in the service of abstract causes and use domestic conflicts and weak states to further their transnational agendas. Complicating matters, many of these various groups—from nationalists to transnational jihadists—often receive support from authoritarian governments in the region as part of the latter's regional geopolitical interests.

Islamic nationalists resort to violence essentially against external occupiers rather than against internal secular rivals. However, the fact that they maintain their own militias makes internal political competition riskier for their opponents; the threat of internal violence remains a possibility. Hamas developed out of the Palestinian branch of the Muslim Brothers that, until the outbreak of the *intifada* (uprising) in 1987 against the Israeli occupation, was primarily engaged in religious and social work. In the 1980s, Hamas combined its commitment to promoting an Islamic society with the cause of liberating Palestine, couching the latter in religious terms and adopting a discourse of religious jihad against the foreign occupier. For Hamas, regaining Muslim control of Palestine became a religious duty. In the 1990s, Hamas executed attacks, including suicide missions, against Israeli military and civilian targets, killing many and contributing, alongside Israeli violations, to the death of the Oslo peace process, which had begun in 1993. Faced with retaliation from both the Israeli army and the Palestinian Authority, Hamas turned back to focus on its religious and social activities in the late 1990s. The outbreak of the second intifada in 2000, which triggered severe violence from Israel and from secular Palestinian factions under the leadership of Fatah, brought Hamas back into the armed struggle against Israel. Hamas has maintained that it endorses violence only to end Israeli occupation and not to impose its religious vision on Palestinians. In 2006, Hamas participated in the national election of the Palestinian Legislative Council, signaling its intention to become a legitimate political party that participates in the democratic game. Its unexpected victory in the election led to a short-lived unity government with Fatah, which soon disintegrated as a result of internal rifts and external pressures. In the aftermath of the disintegration, violent clashes between Fatah and Hamas ensued; Hamas took control of the Gaza Strip in 2007, while Fatah dominated the West Bank. In 2021, nearly fifteen years later, the Fatah-Hamas split between the West Bank and Gaza still persisted.

Armed nationalist Islamic movements can destabilize a country, but their resistance to occupation, their vast social services, and their reputation for honesty in a context of widespread corruption means that they continue to enjoy significant popularity in some places. In Lebanon, the armed group Hizbullah was established to resist the Israeli occupation of southern Lebanon that began in 1982. Building on a network of religious and social services it provided for the underprivileged and underrepresented Shi'i community of Lebanon, Hizbullah became not only a religious resistance militia but also a popular representative of Shi'a in Lebanon. In 1989, with the end of the civil war that had raged in Lebanon since 1975, the Taif Accords stipulated the disarming of Lebanese militias but exempted Hizbullah, thus permitting Hizbullah to continue its resistance against the Israeli occupation of southern Lebanon. By 2000, Israel withdrew from the south in what Hizbullah considered a victory of its armed resistance. Despite the absence of direct occupation, Hizbullah maintained its arms for the stated purpose of continued defense against potential Israeli attacks and for the liberation of a small disputed area, the Shabaa Farms, still under Israeli control. It also participated in Lebanese elections and has become one of the strongest political parties in the country. Like Hamas, however, Hizbullah's military capacities, thought to be greater than those of the Lebanese army, contributed to internal instability; the Lebanese state, like the Palestinian Authority, did not monopolize the means of violence. In 2006, Hizbullah's kidnapping of two Israeli soldiers led to a devastating Israeli attack on Lebanon that targeted civilian infrastructure and caused massive destruction. In 2008, Hizbullah forces took control over downtown Beirut in a show of military might that was meant to intimidate internal political rivals. Though resolved without violence, the incident demonstrated that Hizbullah's weapons could, under certain circumstances, be used internally. These nationalist groups garner material support from regional players as well, further destabilizing domestic politics. Hizbullah has historically received tremendous military support from Iran and Syria, and in turn has dragged Lebanon into the Syrian conflict post 2011. Hamas has been variously funded by Iran, Syria, and Qatar, which have assisted the organization for reasons that are not strictly about genuine support for the Palestinian people. It is important to note, however, that in the cases of Palestine and Lebanon, non-Islamic factions, including the dominant secular groups, have also used force internally to fight political rivals and have been supported by various external players.

Radical revolutionary organizations constitute the second type of Islamic groups that have resorted to violence. They have sought to replace what they consider insufficiently Islamic governments by violent means. These groups have been relatively small and have garnered limited support in their countries. Moreover, such groups have resorted to violence not simply as a result of their radical ideology but in response to actions of the state. Their violence has often been brief, suppressed by the state, and even renounced by their own leadership. Militant activities in Egypt and Algeria in the 1990s, which were among the most visible and violent instances of radical Islamic insurgencies, demonstrate these three aspects of Islamic militant violence.

In the 1990s, the radical group al-Gama'a al-Islamiyya, which advocated the establishment of a purely Islamic state, executed vicious attacks against government representatives, Egyptian civilians, and in extreme cases, foreign tourists. Earlier, the group had cooperated in the assassination of Egyptian president Anwar al-Sadat, but in the 1990s, its violence greatly intensified. Between 1992 and 1997, it was responsible for 1,442 deaths and 1,799 injuries.[53] These attacks came in response to the increased repressiveness of the Egyptian regime, which closed off alternatives to legitimate, nonviolent contestation of the status quo. The regime also arrested and imprisoned Islamist activists, without discrimination between moderates and radicals, contributing to the frustration of many activists and their turn to violence.[54] Rising violence by al-Gama'a, and in particular its gruesome massacre of foreign tourists at Luxor in 1997, which hurt the Egyptian tourist industry, quickly turned many sympathizers away from the group. In addition, unrelenting retaliation by the state decimated the organization's military capacities and available personnel. Later in 1997, the Gama'a declared a unilateral ceasefire and began a process of deradicalization that included publishing twenty-five volumes by Gama'a leaders, who denounced violence and advocated a nonviolent religious and political ideology.[55] Since the 2013 military coup under now-Egyptian president Abdel Fattah el-Sisi, the intensification of the state's brutal repression of Islamists of all kinds—from the moderates to the more radical—has created a new round of militant radicalization that may mirror the events of the 1990s.

In Algeria, the military coup that followed the Islamic FIS victory in the 1991 election brought severe repression of Islamic activism. In 1992, thousands of FIS activists were arrested, and by 1996, half of the 43,737 prisoners in Algeria's 116 prisons were held on charges of terrorism.[56] "The gravest development, however, was the almost daily killing of Islamists, either through manhunts or clashes during searches. Many human rights organizations condemned the military regime's use of torture, 'disappearances,' and the extrajudicial killing of suspected Islamists."[57]

One result was a radicalization of Islamic activists, who increasingly turned to armed resistance in the Islamic Salvation Army (AIS), the military wing of the FIS, and in more extreme groups such as the Armed Islamic Group (GIA). The armed uprising quickly deteriorated into indiscriminate violence against civilians and threw Algeria into a bloody civil war. As in Egypt, the loss of civilian life in the widespread violence, alongside effective violent repression by the state, eventually brought an end to the insurrection. In 1997, the AIS declared a unilateral ceasefire, which signaled the return of many Islamist activists to nonviolent activity.[58]

Transnational terrorist networks such as al-Qa'ida and ISIS make up the third type of Islamic group given to violence. The scale of their attacks against Western targets and the brutality of their violence against Shi'a, other religious minorities, and ideological rivals have drawn international attention. Although such transnational networks have recruited from among the ranks of radical Islamic groups in the Middle East, their objectives and mode of operation are distinct from those of Islamic nationalists and radical local revolutionaries. Local groups restrict their activism to their own country and aim at regime change rather than international upheaval. Transnational terrorist networks such as al-Qa'ida, like the local groups, also hope to establish an Islamic state or states but believe that in order to overturn existing regimes they must also target the Western powers that lend material and military support to these regimes. Their ideology, influenced by the writings of Sayyid Qutb, rests on the idea of offensive jihad and is captured in the now-famous document of 1998 titled "Jihad against the Jews and the Crusaders" and attributed to Osama bin Laden. The document asserts that

> [to] kill the Americans and their allies—civilian and military—is an individual duty incumbent upon every Muslim in all countries, in order to liberate the al-Aqsa Mosque and the holy mosque from their grip, so that their armies leave all the territory of Islam, defeated, broken and unable to threaten any Muslim.[59]

Egyptian radicals such as Ayman al-Zawahiri of the Islamic jihad organization, Omar Abdel-Rahman of al-Gamaa al-Islamiyya, Saudi ideologists such as Osama bin Laden, and fighters from other Arab countries met in the 1980s during the Islamic resistance campaign—supported by the United States—against the Soviet incursion into Afghanistan. After their victory over the Soviet Union, armed veterans of the Afghan campaign returned to their countries with the message of transnational jihad. Heavy and effective repression in Egypt, Algeria, and elsewhere led them to move their fight to other international arenas such as Bosnia, Kosovo, Kashmir, and Chechnya and to weak states such as Pakistan, Yemen, and later Iraq, Syria, and Libya. The name *al-Qa'ida* has become a sort of a franchise that independent radical groups around the world adopt in their struggle for a plethora of different objectives.[60] In the aftermath of the 2011 Arab uprisings or Arab Spring, al-Qa'ida subsidiaries such as Jabhat al-Nusra in Syria and al-Qa'ida in Iraq, later known as ISIS, began to employ a new method—the conquering and administration of territories.

Most notorious among these groups was ISIS, which focused on the occupation and administration of territory, the erasure of national borders, and the extreme persecution of religious minorities as well as rival Sunni groups. ISIS traced its origins to al-Qa'ida in Iraq, a subsidiary of al-Qa'ida since 2003 under the leadership of Jordanian militant Abu Musab al-Zarqawi. As early as 2005, Ayman al-Zawahiri, an al-Qa'ida leader, warned al-Zarqawi that his indiscriminate violence against Muslims and particularly his atrocities against Shi'a were harmful to the jihadi cause. Under the leadership of Abu Bakr al-Baghdadi since 2010, ISIS gained strength through alliances with former Ba'athists leaders and military officers as well as the recruitment of disgruntled Iraqi Sunnis feeling increasingly marginalized by the policies of Iraq's former prime minister Nuri al-Maliki. The group also expanded its operations into Syria with the onset of the civil war there. In 2013, however, ISIS's demand to merge with Jabhat al-Nusra in Syria and the group's extreme brutality have led al-Qa'ida to disassociate itself from the group.[61] In 2014, ISIS arguably became the most powerful terrorist group in the region. Using the expertise of former Ba'thists and the recruitment of thousands of foreign fighters, it was able to gain control over large swaths of territory in Iraq, including Mosul, Iraq's second-largest city, and in Syria. With military equipment it captured from the Iraqi army, a stream of revenue—from oil fields under its control, ransoms, and taxes—and an effective social media presence that drew foreign recruits, ISIS briefly appeared as a formidable threat. It quickly provoked mobilization of an international coalition that through airstrikes largely decimated the organization. The response reconfigured international alliances because the United States, Russia, and Iran considered ISIS a common enemy. With respect to religion, its extreme theology that included the expulsion and killing of religious minorities, the resurrection of the institution of slavery, and severe social repression had appalled the majority of Muslims across the world, even as it found some resonance among small numbers of disaffected, mainly young Muslims inspired by its purported reestablishment of a mythical Islamic caliphate.[62] In the aftermath of this episode, it became clear that ISIS benefitted more than anything else the interests of authoritarian regimes in the region. The extreme "Islamist" menace enabled every stripe of dictator—from Asad to Sisi—to intensify the crackdown on all religious (and nonreligious) opposition. The idea that the Middle East's options are either the "devil you know" in the form of incumbent authoritarians or a worse devil in the form of ISIS helped to bolster authoritarian regimes and fortify international support for them from both the West and Russia.

Despite their dominance of media attention, transnational terrorist networks and local radical groups together represent only a small minority of Islamist activists and cannot compete with the more mainstream social and political Islamic groups in terms of popularity and support. Nonviolent transnational Islamic activism enjoys significantly greater support and influence in the Middle East than the networks dedicated to violence. Transnational Islamic activism promotes the spread of religious knowledge through the influence of popular religious authorities—such as the religious scholar Yousef al-Qaradawi—and the use of the Internet and satellite television channels such as al-Jazeera. Transnational Islamic charity networks and growing lines of communication between religious activists in the Middle East and the wider Muslim world, Europe, and the United States appear to be gaining in significance at a time when the violent groups are relegated to failed states or territories without effective government. The Organization of Islamic Cooperation (OIC),[63] for example, an intergovernmental body with fifty-seven member states that serves as a sort of UN of the Muslim world, has also exerted efforts to create a forum for international Muslim solidarity.

CONCLUSION

Scholars writing about the Middle East between World War II and the Iranian Revolution of 1979 paid scant attention to religion as a dynamic factor in the region. They emphasized the importance of understanding religion as an enduring aspect of culture, but one that seemed to be diminishing in importance with an acceleration of social, economic, and political change. The ascendant ideologies of liberalism, socialism, Zionism, and Arabism were predominantly secular, although some forms of Arabism and Zionism evoked religious commitment. Already after the Six-Day War of 1967 and especially after the Iranian Revolution of 1979, religion began to attract more attention. In the third decade of the 21st-century, religion seems central to much that is happening in the region. States rely on it for identity and legitimacy; civil organizations use it to goad members into action; radical groups engage in violence in the name of religion; and individual Middle Easterners appear more committed to religion than in previous generations. The increased centrality of religion has not, however, resulted in a significant political change in the region. Islamic groups have challenged regimes in both violent and non-violent ways, but in doing so, they have necessarily reinforced the nation-state framework at the expense of the *umma*, the community of all believers—Osama bin Laden, al-Qaʻida, and ISIS notwithstanding.

These developments confirm that religion is a dynamic rather than a static force in the region. Human beings continually reshape their religions, claiming all the while that it is religious belief that impels them to do so. Understood in the broadest sense, Islam is not what it was a century ago; neither is Judaism or Christianity, for that matter. Citizens of this region have availed themselves of religion for social and political purposes in ways previous generations would not have imagined, transforming the nature of religion in the process. It is not a certainty that this trend will continue. Neither is it a certainty that this trend will come to be seen as a temporary deviation from the long-term pattern of secularization, as some modernization theorists think it will. To extrapolate from contemporary events is hazardous.[64]

SUGGESTED READINGS

François, Burgat. *Islamism in the Shadow of Al-Qaeda*. Austin, TX: University of Texas Press, 2008.

Clark, Janine A. *Islam, Charity, and Activism: Middle-Class Networks and Social Welfare in Egypt, Jordan, and Yemen*. Bloomington, IA: Indiana University Press, 2003.

Cesari, Jocelyne. *The awakening of Muslim democracy: Religion, modernity, and the state*. Cambridge: Cambridge University Press, 2014.

Karagiannis, Emmanuel. *The New Political Islam: Human Rights, Democracy, and Justice*. Philadelphia, PA: University of Pennsylvania Press, 2017.

Lee, Robert D. *Religion and Politics in the Middle East: Identity, Ideology, Institutions, and Attitudes*. London: Routledge, 2018.

March, Andrew F. *The Caliphate of Man*. Cambridge, MA: Harvard University Press, 2019.

Monshipouri, Mahmood. *Muslims in Global Politics: Identities, Interests, and Human Rights*. Philadelphia, PA: University of Pennsylvania Press, 2011.

Roy, Sara. *Hamas and Civil Society in Gaza: Engaging the Islamist Social Sector*. Princeton, NJ: Princeton University Press, 2011.

Shehata, Samer, ed. *Islamist Politics in the Middle East: Movements and Change*. London: Routledge, 2012.

Tessler, Mark. *Islam and Politics in the Middle East: Explaining the Views of Ordinary Citizens*. Bloomington, IA: Indiana University Press, 2015.

5 CITIZENS' PARTICIPATION

Actors, Arenas, and Dilemmas

Rabab El-Mahdi[1]

Political participation is multifaceted, its dynamics shaped by the present context as well as historical factors. As in other regions of the world, citizens in the Middle East and North Africa (MENA) participate through formal and informal venues—some more obvious than others. The most evident formal channels include participation in elections or through Civil Society Organizations (CSOs), including nongovernmental organizations (NGOs), trade unions, and associations. Yet, much of the recent political activity in the MENA has also emerged through social movements, engaging in a plethora of collective actions, and even more through informal and often overlooked venues of participation, such as joke-making, social media discussions, and cafe conversations. All are significant features of political life in the region.

This chapter focuses on the different forms of citizens' participation. It highlights some of the main historical factors that have shaped participation—namely, the rise of the postcolonial state, the changing social contract governing state–society relations, and the political economy of neoliberal reforms. Country-specific factors decide the form and magnitude of citizen's participation, creating unique challenges for political action, but the MENA also displays regional trends. This chapter highlights these regional trends and interrogates commonly held assumptions on political participation, both formal and informal.

The chapter proceeds as follows. The first section examines the most easily recognized and formal type of participation through political parties and elections. The second section turns to participation through civil society and its different organizations, assessing claims over its potential and limitations. The third section focuses on social movements and direct collective action including violent movements. The chapter then moves to discuss some of the less obvious but more common forms of participation; how seemingly apolitical activities within informal venues form an important type of political participation in the region. Next, it considers the impact of changing communications technologies on potential engagement in the region. The chapter concludes with an examination of how patterns of political engagement across the region might be changing in the aftermath of the Arab Uprisings and the COVID-19 pandemic.

POLITICAL PARTIES AND ELECTIONS

Elections are the most obvious arena for direct political engagement. Through political parties, citizens articulate their interests, mobilize votes, and allocate support to certain policy positions and interest groups. The role political parties play in the different MENA countries varies, depending on parties' historical evolution and the present political system in each country. Despite variations, however, two historical features are found across MENA countries with multiparty systems[2]: First, following independence in the second half of the 20th century, regimes often only allowed pro-regime parties, such as the National Liberation Front (FLN) in Algeria, the Ba'thist Party in Syria and Iraq, and the Neo-Destour in Tunisia or banned them altogether as in the former Libyan Jamahiriya, Egypt, until the later 1970s and the Gulf monarchies. The postcolonial state–society social contract, crudely summarized, was "economic rights in return for political participation" or "bread for freedom" in addition to a lot of rhetoric on national independence. Second, in the majority of countries in the region (except for Lebanon, Israel, Turkey, Sudan, and Morocco), holding competitive multiparty elections is a relatively recent experience. By the late 1980s, in the face of economic crises and pressures for structural adjustments, many regimes allowed for some political opening and liberalization. This led to the entry of new political parties and, at face value, competitive parliamentary elections.

Elections Under Authoritarianism

Rather than a sign of burgeoning democracy, holding multiparty elections has often been a survival strategy, or what Holger Albrecht and Oliver Schlumberger call a strategy of adaptation for authoritarian regimes.[3] In other words, elections can help maintain the stability of authoritarian regimes. They allow leaders to manage political elites by bringing them into the political process, thus keeping them accountable to the existing regime[4] and moderating dissent and deradicalizing the opposition.[5] Political parties channel dissent, making it easier for authoritarian regimes to assess discontent among the population. At the same time, authoritarian regimes often manipulate elections, or the rules that govern them, so that outcomes of the electoral process result in added legitimacy and domestic credibility for leaders in power.[6]

Thus, in the end, most national elections in the MENA have ended up reinforcing, rather than undermining, authoritarian regimes. In no small part, this result owes thanks to clientelist bargains between constituents and elites, and between elites and the state. Under these regimes, elites compete over special access to a limited set of state resources, which they can then distribute to their clients and maintain their positions of power. Political parties tend to have a pro-regime bias because, more often than not, they are rewarded for catering to the regime, and it is these benefits that keep party constituents happy. Opposition leaders are often coopted by the regime. The activities of opposition parties are restricted or hindered; elections are commonly rigged so that opposition parties obtain few seats in parliament; and to exacerbate these disparities, channels through which to launch complaints of electoral harassment or wrongdoing have been limited or—depending on the context—entirely nonexistent.

Once they gain access to parliament, the ability of political parties to influence policy remains limited owing to limited executive oversight of the legislative body. Authoritarian rulers "wall off"

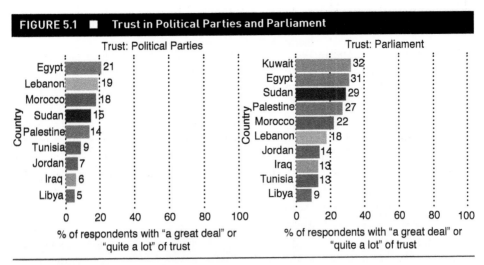

FIGURE 5.1 ■ Trust in Political Parties and Parliament

Source: Arab Barometer data. Used with permission.

the executive branch so that no act of legislature can transform the system. In much of the region, the cabinet is appointed from outside the parliament, and it must approve all legislation passed in assemblies. The executive is not accountable to the elected parliament or legislative body.

Hence, it is not surprising that citizens' trust in the institutions associated with elections is low. We see this in Figure 5.1. As discussed in Chapter 3, such lukewarm trust in political parties across the region can be attributed to the ineffectual roles political parties have played in parliaments, a result of low parliamentary autonomy and efficacy. Trust in elected councils of representatives (parliaments) as institutions does not fare much better. MENA citizens rank them as the second-least trusted institution—after political parties.

Subsequently, voting patterns must be understood in relation to such limitations of parties and parliaments in the region, and the consequent lack of trust in both. Voter turnout in many of the Arab countries of MENA is not simply a sign of citizens' political engagement or apathy in the absolute. It is shaped by contextual factors.

Participation in Elections

Three factors have to be considered when assessing citizens' participation in elections: the players, the process, and the context. Regarding the players, as discussed above, the political elite are mostly coopted by the regime, and the majority of citizens (for good reasons) do not trust the political parties. In terms of the process, most regimes use direct and indirect methods to control electoral outcomes. This ranges from blatant rigging of results through changing numbers, ballot-box stuffing, and coerced mass voting to obstructing registration and impeding access to casting votes, either forcefully or through administrative measures. Having the discretion to decide on the rules of the game, regimes also use gerrymandering, with tactics like "cracking" and "packing" constituencies and choosing the electoral system that best serves their interests (plurality, majoritarian, proportional, or semi-proportional). Given these different forms of

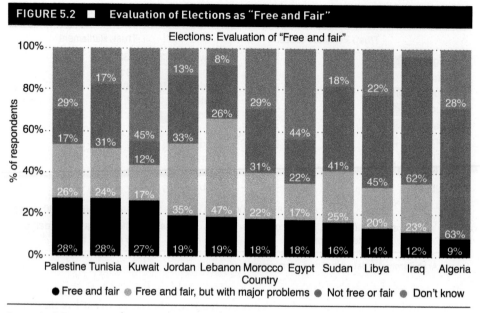

FIGURE 5.2   ■   Evaluation of Elections as "Free and Fair"

Source: Arab Baraometer data. Used with permission.

manipulation, it is not a surprise that only a minority of citizens in Arab countries believe in the integrity of the process in their respective countries (see Figure 5.2).

Perceptions of the electoral processes, its players, and outcomes affect voting behavior and turnout. Under these circumstances, citizens do not necessarily possess democratic aspirations or policy preferences when they vote; instead, they hope to leverage more benefits from existing regimes. Under this system of "competitive clientelism," as Ellen Lust calls it, voting revolves around patronage, with constituents determining their voting preference based on their perception of who can and will deliver the goods to them.[7] Those individuals with personal relations to candidates are more likely to vote, as they anticipate that they are more likely to benefit from the candidate's patronage. Occasionally, these voting behaviors are portrayed as "irrational," or as evidence of a lesser mentality that is also used to explain away the lack of democracy in the region. Others use the characteristics of these systems to juxtapose, and indeed pit against one another, traditional forms of societal organization (such as tribalism) and modern systems of political organization. However, a closer look lends itself to understanding such voting patterns as perfectly rational, given the limitations of electoral systems in these countries and the realistic expectations of what electoral participation can achieve.

Examining voter turnout figures provides some additional insights. Figure 5.3 shows two sets of voter turnout data for each country: on the left is the official government-reported figure for turnout of voting-age population (extracted from the International Institute for Democracy and Electoral Assistance—IDEA), and on the right is the self-reported figure from the 2018–2019 Wave V Arab Barometer (AB) survey.[8] The first point to note is the discrepancy between the officially reported figures on elections and self-reported voter turnout. Some of the discrepancy can be attributed to the difference in the kind of data, one being exact figures and the other

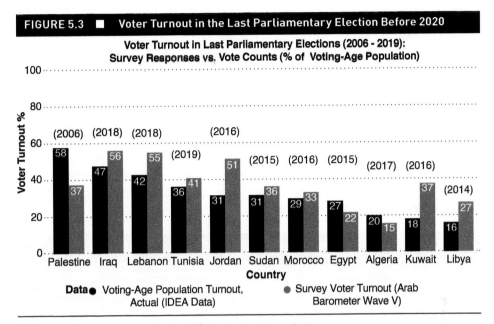

FIGURE 5.3 ■ Voter Turnout in the Last Parliamentary Election Before 2020

Source: Arab Barometer Wave V (2018–2019) data. Used with permission.

being respondent-reported turnout. In some cases, like Palestine, the interval between the most recent election and the fielding of the AB survey is more than twelve years; many respondents were not eligible to vote in the last election. In addition, the official figures correspond with the voting-age population (VAP) and not the voting-eligible population (VEP) of each country, while the survey data do not make this distinction. Finally, survey methodologists have found there is a tendency for respondents to overreport voting in national surveys although the extent of overreporting may vary based on the social and political context. Social desirability, or the respondent's belief that there is a "right answer" and interest in pleasing the interviewer, may help to explain this phenomenon.[9] Students of elections in the MENA region need to draw on various sources of information to understand who votes. Given the lack of transparency in most of these countries, they need to cross-examine official figures; at the same time, they also need to consider the potential drawbacks of self-reported turnout.

The second feature is that one cannot infer direct correlations between levels of trust in the parties, parliaments, and elections, on the one hand, and levels of participation, on the other. This is evident when comparing the data shown earlier in Figures 5.1 and 5.2, with that in Figure 5.3. For example, Iraq shows one of the highest voter participation rates and yet ranks among the lowest countries in terms of trust in both players and the process. This warns against mechanical assumptions about turnout. Voting, like any human behavior, is much more complex than to be determined by one factor. Moreover, it encourages the investigation of other confounding variables, particularly the structural and contextual conditions that could influence behavior—for example, the state of security during elections, dominating narratives, shifting political opportunities, the candidates themselves, and so on.

The impact of changing context is most evident when examining the fluctuation of voter turnout within the same country across time (Table 5.1). For example, after the Arab uprisings of 2011, countries like Egypt and Tunisia witnessed a surge in the number of new political parties following the easing of restrictions on registering and participating in political parties, or as in the case of Libya, saw party formation for the first time. Emerging from authoritarian contexts, most of these parties did not have well-developed political platforms with wide appeal nor an understanding of the dynamics of electoral competition.[10] Yet, the context was encouraging, and people were highly mobilized. Despite the weakness of political parties, we see a huge spike in voter turnout, for example, in Egypt. Turnout increased from 16.16 percent in December 2010 to 54.99 percent in the first parliamentary elections following the popular uprising (December 2011–January 2012).

TABLE 5.1 ■ Officially Reported Voting-Age Population (VAP) Turnout in Parliamentary Elections

Country	Year	VAP Turnout%	Country	Year	VAP Turnout %
Algeria	2021	19.53 %	Kuwait	2020	16.72 %
	2017	31.65 %		2016	17.77 %
	2012	38.70 %		2013	12.17 %
Egypt	2020	28.82 %	Lebanon	2012	12.93 %
	2015	27.46 %	Libya	2018	42.45 %
	2012	54.99 %		2009	66.34 %
	2010	16.16 %		2014	15.64 %
Iraq	2018	47.38 %	Morocco	2012	48.72 %
	2014	76.81 %		2016	29.19 %
	2010	70.12 %		2011	28.65 %
Jordan	2020	21.13 %	Palestine	2006	57.65 %
	2016	31.13 %	Sudan	2015	30.97 %
	2013	34.11 %	Tunisia	2010	64.11 %
	2010	33.88 %		2019	35.85 %
	2014	45.39 %			
	2011	53.90 %			

Source: Data extracted from *International Institute for Democracy and Electoral Assistance:* "Voter Turnout Database" (Accessed on 31 August 2021)

This changed as the postuprising euphoria led to disillusionment. In Tunisia VAP turnout declined from 53.90% in 2011 to 35.85% in 2019. In Libya, turnout was a sweeping 48.72% in the first competitive elections that the country had ever witnessed, declining to 15.64% just two years later. Again, the deteriorating security situation, civil strife, and disappointment in new political actors clearly impacted the turnout.

Political Participation and the Prospects for Democratization

Public opinion surveys have often shown that MENA citizens are more concerned about the economy and corruption that plague their political systems than they are about democracy. Just like the majority of individuals in other regions, MENA citizens prioritize economic issues as the most important problems facing their countries. They also show concerns over security, terrorism, and stability. In contrast, as shown in Table 5.2, few citizens rank "achieving democracy" as one of the top two challenges facing their countries.

TABLE 5.2 ■ Percentage of Respondents Who Identified Each Challenge as Most or Second-Most Important to Their Country[11]							
	Country						
Category	Algeria	Egypt	Jordan	Lebanon	Morocco	Palestine	Tunisia
Economic	69,6%	60,5%	91,7%	72,0%	42,2%	69,6%	72,6%
Financial	48,2%	12,8%	58,1%	31,5%	19,4%	35,7%	26,4%
Democracy	6,1%	4,8%	1,1%	8,1%	4,7%	4,8%	2,6%
Stability	10,0%	8,0%	2,6%	14,2%	5,9%	22,6%	8,9%
Foreign interference	5,8%	8,1%	5,1%	12,7%	3,9%	17,5%	3,8%
Religious extremism	3,0%	13,3%	1,8%	6,9%	3,5%	5,9%	4,5%
Terrorism	3,2%	33,7%	5,1%	5,4%	3,0%	5,3%	30,4%
Services	40,1%	33,9%	15,0%	34,3%	38,4%	8,3%	10,6%
Security	3,9%	9,3%	2,5%	6,4%	7,9%	12,3%	11,7%
Political	7,1%	2,9%	2,0%	6,7%	4,9%	16,1%	15,8%
Other	1,0%	7,1%	8,8%	1,5%	55,9%	1,5%	8,0%
DK	2,2%	5,7%	6,3%	0,0%	10,2%	0,5%	4,9%
(N)	4626 (200%)	4780 (200%)	4740 (200%)	4800 (200%)	4782 (200%)	4898 (200%)	4370 (200%)

Source: Arab Barometer Wave V (2018–2019) data.

In a similar vein, across the region, we find that citizens express a much higher trust in security organs as compared to political institutions such as parties and parliaments. When asked about their trust in public institutions, MENA citizens overwhelmingly relayed that they trust security institutions a great deal or quite a lot (see Figure 5.4), penning the police and the armed forces as the most trustworthy institutions in the region.

Taken together, the prioritization of economic issues over concerns for democracy and political issues, along with trust in security apparatus over democratic institutions, have been taken to suggest an implicit preference for authoritarianism by the majority of citizens in these MENA countries. Some scholars have taken this as support for the "cultural affinity" argument, claiming that the majority of MENA countries are authoritarian because citizens in these countries—whether because of Islam or other cultural reasons—do not value democracy. Among these, some have gone on to claim that these citizens prefer their despotic leaders.[12]

This interpretation not only carries a clear cultural bias, but is also ahistorical, based on selective reading of data. That citizens prioritize material needs, as symbolized by economic issues, is part of the basic human instinct for survival; individuals anywhere would need to guarantee a living before they are expected to worry about the quality of that life. It is important to note that in data presented in Table 5.1, citizens were asked about the most pressing issues in a region, where the extreme poverty rate has risen from 3.8 percent in 2015 to 7.2 percent in 2018.[13] Moreover, as of 2018, 20.3 percent of citizens in the MENA region are vulnerable to extreme poverty, living at or below US$3.20, and 45 percent of the population live at or below US$5.50.[14] These citizens were not asked to make a choice between economic and political aspirations within a long wishlist in which democracy came at the bottom. Rather, they were asked to identify only two top issues without any prompt from enumerators.

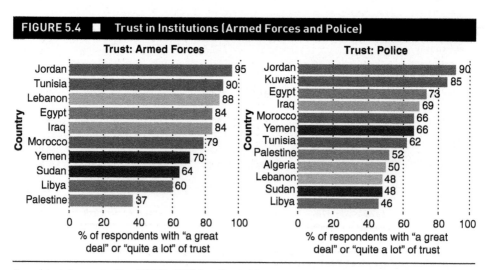

FIGURE 5.4 ■ Trust in Institutions (Armed Forces and Police)

Source: Arab Barometer Wave V (2018–2019) data. Used with permission.

Similarly, citizens' trust in institutions such as the police and the military mirrors their greater concern for security, their very tangible fears in one of the last regions in the world fraught by war, civil strife, and different forms of terrorism. Such trust also must be understood in relative terms, taking into account the historically weak performance of parties and parliaments (as discussed earlier) and the postcolonial legacy in the region. This is not only the impact of 20th-century colonial mandates but also modern extensions of this legacy; the American invasion of Iraq, Israeli occupation of Palestinian territories, transnational efforts to manipulate local happenings (mercenaries in the Libyan conflict, for example, from Russia and Syria), and so on. Within this context, anxiety toward occupations, military invasions, and protracted armed conflict (Libya, Syria, and Yemen) is very present in citizens' minds across the region.

That said, MENA citizens continue to support democracy. This was very evident in the slogan of the Arab Uprisings calling for both "bread" and "freedom" and further confirmed through survey data. When asked if the statement "Democracy is always preferable to any other kind of government" was closest to their own opinion, the majority of citizens in twelve Arab countries agreed as shown in Figure 5.5: Preferred Form of Government. Those supporting nondemocratic systems as the regime of choice ranged from a meager 7 percent of those surveyed in Jordan to the highest 31 percent in Algeria, which is still a smaller percentage than those supporting democracy in the same country.[15]

Similarly, Jordanians, Tunisians, and Lebanese continue to have high confidence in the democratic system. Eighty-five and eighty-three percent of Jordanians and Lebanese, respectively, agreed or strongly agreed with the statement that "democratic systems may have problems, yet they are better than other systems." Across all countries surveyed in Wave V of the

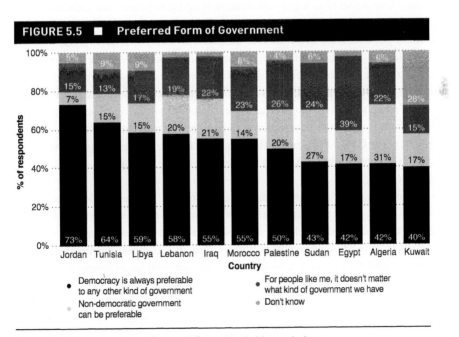

FIGURE 5.5 ■ Preferred Form of Government

Legend:
- Democracy is always preferable to any other kind of government
- Non-democratic government can be preferable
- For people like me, it doesn't matter what kind of government we have
- Don't know

Source: Arab Barometer Wave V (2018–2019) data. Used with permission.

Arab Barometer, the vast majority (72 percent) of respondents agreed or strongly agreed with this statement.[16]

CIVIL SOCIETY

Civil society is a term that has been popular not only with academics but also with government officials, aid workers, international agencies, and a wide variety of other professions. Yet it remains a term that is contested. It is often referred to as the "third sector," separate from the state and from the market or business. It is the sphere of associational activity that is commonly understood as being central to the democratization process. Taking the dominant conceptualization of the term, this chapter defines civil society as those voluntary groups, associations, or organizations that are engaged in nonstate activities and that through their activities, either directly or indirectly, redefine the boundaries between state and society by increasing the separation between the two. However, in the MENA, many scholars also include mosques and discussion groups as part of civil society as these, too, perform many of the organizational functions more typically included in definitions of civil society.

Civil Society's Democratizing Effect

Since the 1990s many social scientists have been adamant about how civil society contributes to and is a prerequisite for democratization. They offer four different propositions to explain the relationship between associational life fostered through civil engagement and democracy. The first claim is that civic organizations serve as agents of democratic socialization, increasing members' support for democratic institutions, and generating such values as moderation and tolerance, which are important for deliberation. Larry Diamond posits that members who participate in civic organizations are more likely to learn about the importance of tolerance, pluralism, and respect for the law.[17] In *Democracy in America*, Alexis de Tocqueville attributes the success of US democracy to the country's rich associational life. Associations serve as "schools for civic virtue," he wrote. Habits of association foster patterns of civility important for successful democracies.[18] However, this positive correlation is derived from a specific set of CSOs. It dismisses the possibility of other forms of right-wing CSOs, such as the Tea Party or Right for America or ultraconservative Salafi groups who do not promote such values.

A second claim is that associational life can effectively increase the levels of social capital among members—that is, trust and norms of reciprocity become well established in organizations and thus increase the likelihood of cooperation *outside* of these groups, between members of society. In *Making Democracy Work*, Robert Putnam argues that membership in horizontal voluntary associations enhances social capital (interpersonal trust) necessary for cooperative ventures in greater society, which in turn leads people to "stand up to city hall" or engage in other forms of behavior that provide a basis for better government performance. Putnam correlates the density of horizontal voluntary associations with strong and effective local government: "strong society; strong state."[19] The overlooked caveats here are that first, there has to be a "city hall" or equivalent institution and second, the repercussions for standing up to government institutions or calling for accountability or change have to be bearable. Such necessary positive conditions also undermine the existence of negative social capital, such as solidarity that leads to nepotism, for example.[20]

A third claim is that associations foster democracy by mobilizing ordinary citizens into the political process. In the pluralist tradition, associations are critical for representation of a diversity of interests in the public sphere.[21] For example, business associations vis-a-vis workers' unions vis-a-vis the state. However, in nondemocratic settings, these associations can be, and have been, coopted by the state, as in the trade unions in Egypt. They can also become vehicles for fostering clientelistic relationships and even sectarianism, as in the case in Lebanon.

The fourth claim is that civic associations that have substantial memberships can place the necessary constraints on authoritarian governing structures. Civic organizations can serve as key sites for citizen mobilization and expression. Associations can serve as counterweights to centralized governing apparatuses by mobilizing sectors of society to oppose authoritarian tendencies.[22] This concept has been at the heart of much of the literature on mobilization, opposition–regime relations, social movements, and revolutions, which is discussed in the following section.

The Evolution of Civil Society in the MENA

Contrary to conventional wisdom, there is a rich history of civil society in the MENA. During the colonial period, the working-class and middle-class professional and student associations galvanized civil society activity as a means of mobilizing toward independence.[23] These associations were vital in training and producing national leadership. After independence, and under the authoritarian regimes that followed in the region, civil society persisted but was severely contained. Most MENA regimes instituted projects of state corporatism to manage participation and foster development. In such cases, particularly in the 1960s and 1970s, regimes directed political participation through state-controlled civil society actors.

The perils of autonomous organization were too much for regimes to take. Civil society activity, not directly linked to the goals of regimes, was drastically curbed. Under the postcolonial social contract, these states had a monopoly on political mobilization in return for citizen's socioeconomic mobility and welfare. By creating spaces where political activity was tolerated, regimes attempted to micromanage the content and form of political participation. In return, pro-regime segments received perquisites and benefits. For example, in Egypt, Iraq, Syria, Sudan, and Algeria, the very rich tapestry of organizations which came to the fore during the national struggle for independence, including student and feminist organizations, trade unions, and professional associations, were soon banned. These governments created unitary trade unions to absorb the workers' movement in some countries, and at other times created what came to be paradoxically known as GNGOs (Governmental Nongovernmental Organizations), sponsored by the First Ladies or other members of the ruling families.

However, by the 1990s, the postindependence social contract was eroding; these states could not uphold the economic part of the deal and hence had to allow for some forms of CSOs.[24] The pressures of neoliberal economic tenets and years of stagnation were taking their toll on these countries. As the material grievances of citizens increased, so did the urgency of addressing these realities. In many instances, regimes allowed civic associations that could help cope with the worsening economic conditions. Thus, charitable CSOs began to grow in number. After the economic reforms of this period, for example, the Moroccan state recognized that resources often used to appease the public were in gradual decline. Allowing the emergence of civic associations, the regime rationalized, would place more of the financial burden of demands on civil society actors.[25] Given the value of social solidarity in these societies, CSOs rose to this challenge, filling the vacuum left by state withdrawal as much as possible and providing medical and educational services, child care, and even financial support to large sectors of the population. This success is reflected in citizens' perceptions of these organizations as shown in Figure 5.6.

Many of the new civic associations that sprang up to address growing economic needs were dominated by Islamist actors across the region. Some argue that this service provision by Islamist groups contributed directly and indirectly to their electoral successes—not simply through vote-buying, but rather through the trust they built in local communities and the reputations they garnered for being capable of addressing people's problems.[26]

The 1980s and 1990s also witnessed the growth of professional associations. This was a direct result of the growing levels of education across the region. These associations include

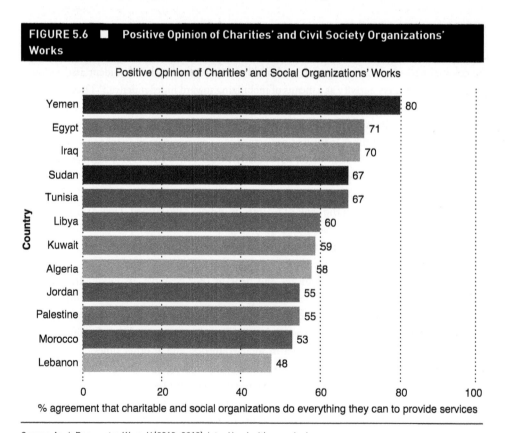

FIGURE 5.6 ■ Positive Opinion of Charities' and Civil Society Organizations' Works

Positive Opinion of Charities' and Social Organizations' Works

Country	% agreement
Yemen	80
Egypt	71
Iraq	70
Sudan	67
Tunisia	67
Libya	60
Kuwait	59
Algeria	58
Jordan	55
Palestine	55
Morocco	53
Lebanon	48

% agreement that charitable and social organizations do everything they can to provide services

Source: Arab Barometer Wave V (2018–2019) data. Used with permission.

lawyers' societies, medical associations, and other professional groupings. In the absence of a free media and fully representative parliaments, the sector of professional associations provided a forum for open political engagement and discussion.[27] It also introduced a plethora of rights-based NGOs. Human rights groups in Egypt emerged in the late 1980s and mushroomed over the following two decades. Women's rights groups, for example, became active in Morocco, Iran, Lebanon, and even Saudi Arabia, where they have formed civil society networks calling for changes in personal status laws (in the cases of Iran, Morocco, and Lebanon) and in electoral law (asking for women's enfranchisement in Saudi Arabia). The variety of CSOs attending to different facets of citizens' needs, whether through direct services or advocating for the rights of different groups, had a positive impact on citizens' trust in civil society. Figure 5.7 shows the high levels of trust that citizens have in CSOs, a stark contrast to the levels of trust in political parties and parliaments (see Figure 5.1).

This remains true even of countries in the bottom quartile. Those surveyed in Tunisia, Libya, and Lebanon report the lowest regional levels of trust in CSOs. Yet they still have comparatively greater trust in civil society than they do in parties and parliaments (see Figure 5.1 regarding trust in parties and parliaments).

Thus, despite attempts at curtailing civic activity, civil society in the MENA was relatively robust at the dawn of the Arab uprisings. Organizations working across different sectors incorporated citizens in different capacities, either as members, volunteers, or beneficiaries. These included

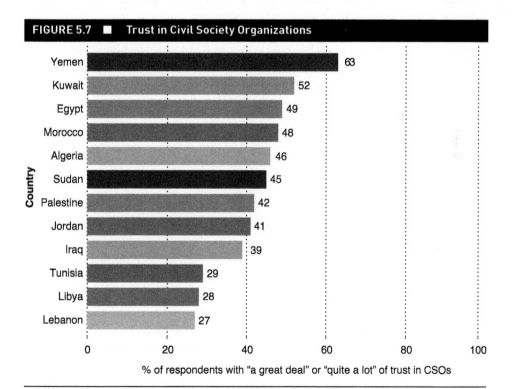

FIGURE 5.7 ■ Trust in Civil Society Organizations

% of respondents with "a great deal" or "quite a lot" of trust in CSOs

Country	Value
Yemen	63
Kuwait	52
Egypt	49
Morocco	48
Algeria	46
Sudan	45
Palestine	42
Jordan	41
Iraq	39
Tunisia	29
Libya	28
Lebanon	27

Source: Arab Barometer Wave V (2018–2019) data. Used with permission.

professional associations, business groups, trade unions, private societies, social clubs, sporting clubs, youth centers, as well as a sizable proportion of NGOs focused on charity, development, and a variety of other causes. Hence, it is no surprise that the Union Générale Tunisienne du Travail (Tunisian General Labor Union) in Tunisia played a significant role in mobilizing for the ouster of the regime. Local human rights organizations, whether in Bahrain, Yemen, Egypt, or Morocco, played an important role in exposing regime violations during and in the aftermath of the protests.

Challenges and Opportunities for Civil Society After the Uprisings

Civil society now faces a number of challenges different from those of the previous authoritarian era of pre-2011. This is true in all MENA countries, whether they were part of the first wave of uprisings in 2011(Libya, Yemen, Egypt, Tunisia, Syria, and Bahrain) or the second wave in 2019 (Algeria, Sudan, Iraq, and Lebanon), or were those which remained relatively stable despite some upheavals (Turkey, Iran, Morocco, and Jordan). In Yemen, Syria, and Libya there is a dire humanitarian situation with multiple human rights abuses and almost absent security in some areas, characteristic of times of war and civil strife. Prolonged and acute crises of governance in Tunisia and Lebanon, respectively, blur the boundaries between the role of CSOs versus the government toward citizens—how can citizens organize in civil society associations and advocate in conditions where there are no clear authorities? In such a context, civil society rises to try to fill the traditional roles of the state. In countries like Egypt, where a new form of authoritarianism presides, CSOs have either been completely crushed or coopted by the state. Whereas in Jordan, Morocco, Iran, and Turkey, civic associations still find themselves having to navigate a web of restrictions, in the latter two to a heightened degree than before.

And in all cases these organizations have to negotiate their principles against the overwhelming need for resources and the shifting parameters (by the government) to keep their programs alive. With the crushing of Islamist CSOs in many countries, the increased economic and physical hurdles posed by COVID-19 and its on-going effects and the declining international pressure on regimes curtailing freedoms of expression and association (in countries such as Israel, Turkey, Iran, Egypt, and the Gulf), it is difficult to think of civil society as a potential repository for impending democratic transitions, as some argue.

MOVEMENTS AND COLLECTIVE ACTION

Citizens also engage in multiple forms of collective action, both in public and in private, which comes to constitute the broad theme of contentious politics. Sidney Tarrow defines contentious politics as, "collective activity on the part of claimants—or those who claim to represent them—relying at least in part on noninstitutional forms of interaction with elites, opponents, or the state."[28] This includes a wide range of actors and actions. Wars, revolutions, rebellions, social movements, industrial conflict, feuds, riots, banditry, shaming ceremonies, and many more forms of collective struggle potentially qualify as contentious politics.[29] However, this section will focus on two prominent forms of participation within that broader terrain of contentious politics, being the most visible in MENA: namely, social movements and violent political groups. "Social movements" are defined as sustained challenges to authority in the name of a disadvantaged population living under the jurisdiction or influence of those powerholders, which can be the state or society or a combination of the two.[30] Violent movements are defined as those mainly employing violence to achieve political goals.

Even though the world only took notice of contentious politics in the MENA during major events such as the Iranian revolution in 1978–79, the Arab Uprisings in 2011, or the more recent events in Algeria, Lebanon, and Sudan, the region has been fraught with different forms of collective action before and in between these major events. Labor protests in Egypt in 1977 which came to be known as the Bread Riots, the Hama uprising in Syria in 1982, and the Kurdish uprising in Iraq in 1991 are just a few of these episodes of contention and collective action. More recently, the pro-Palestine and antiwar protests of 2000–2003 saw major mobilization across the region and were in a way a prelude to the Arab Uprisings.

Mobilization in Contemporary Social Movements

Social movements have been prevalent across the MENA, and social networks form an important component of those movements. The uprisings in 2011 took the world by surprise, but academics and policymakers could have avoided being caught off guard had they been paying attention to rising mobilization in the preceding decade. Across the region, mass mobilization in support of the second Palestinian Intifadah and against the American invasion of Iraq marked the first years of the new millennium. This was followed by prodemocracy mobilization and the rise of some movements such as Kifaya (Enough) in Egypt and the Green Movement in Iran.[31] The region also witnessed collective movements by the urban poor, labor, and other class actions; labor strikes in Egypt in 2006–2008, the Gafsa protests in Tunis in 2008, and protests in Algeria in 2010, to name a few.

Youth networks were also active, often using social media to highlight issues of political and economic importance, blogs, and later Facebook to bring people together and to mobilize. These included the youth campaigns that emerged in Egypt between 2004 and 2011 to push for democratization and those in Morocco to address the issue of unemployment. According to Al-Khatib and Clark, "(T)he combination of online and offline methods of mobilization used by Egyptian activists since 2004 helped inspire activists across the region. Using the media—first, blogs and then social media—to publicize demands and organize protests became prevalent as witnessed in various anti-regime protests in Tunisia in 2008,[32] during the Green Movement in Iran in 2009—where people protested against what they perceived as the fraudulent reelection of Mahmoud Ahmadinejad as president—and during the Arab Spring."[33]

In 2011, in Tunisia, Egypt, Bahrain, Libya, Yemen, and Syria and later in Israel, that summer, mass mobilization emerged, demanding political change. This was followed by Turkey in 2013. In the region, this wave of contentious politics and the movements that carried it through shared many characteristics and tactics. As one author describing the Gezi Park occupation movement put it, "it was not a peaceful 'non-violent' insurrection, but an 'anti-violent' resistance… protesters did not respond in economic, ideological, or doctrinal terms to state violence, they developed new forms of resistance drawing on the resources of humor, irony, and pluralism" (p.247).[34] This was one of the main features characterizing the mobilization of the social movements of 2011. Similarly, these events combined economic and political demands, material and lifestyle interests.

In terms of organization, the movements had several characteristics in common. First, they were diffuse in terms of the distribution of power among their diverse members. Their demands, actions, and platforms were grassroots-based, as opposed to being directed by leaders from above. In many cases, the movements either had diffuse leadership or were leaderless. Second, their members came together because of their agreement on a common cause, as opposed to official political party affiliation or being ideologically motivated. Third, these were temporary networks, rather than permanent organizations. Many scholars celebrated these features, arguing that successful mobilization is not solely the product of centralized organization and that, rather, leaderlessness can even be a source of strength.[35] However, in celebrating the horizontality, democratization, and temporality of these movements, many overlooked what later proved to be fatal weaknesses. After 2011, not having solid organizational structures was one among several reasons that these uprisings dissolved into civil strife (e.g., Syria, Libya, and Yemen) were completely crushed before achieving their goals (e.g., Bahrain, Israel, and Turkey), or had their temporary successes quickly reversed (e.g., Egypt).

Despite their common demands, tactics, and organizational features, these movements used different frames and repertoires of contention.[36] For instance, women's rights groups in different countries may mobilize over similar issues, but the way their demands are articulated and the activities they use to achieve their ends vary. Women's rights groups in Yemen, for example, often employ a religious framework in the way they define themselves and their demands (invoking Islam as a religion of equality between men and women), while most women's rights groups in Lebanon do not. Moreover, in addition to mobilizing in the formal political sphere (e.g., through lobbying of parliament to change personal status laws, as done by Lebanese

PHOTO 5.1 Demonstration against the authoritarian government in Cairo (Jan. 25, 2011)

Source: MOHAMMED ABED/AFP via Getty Images

PHOTO 5.2 "When We Stand Together We Can Do More." Demonstrators rally near the military headquarters in Khartoum, Sudan, in April 2019. The Sudanese protest movement on Monday welcomed the "positive steps" taken by the ruling military council, which held talks over the weekend with the opposition leaders and released some political prisoners.

Source: Sari Omer/Flickr

PHOTO 5.3 İstiklâl Caddesi, Taksim Square—Gezi Park Protests, İstanbul

Source: By Alan Hilditch from Cleethorpes, North East Lincolnshire - İstiklâl Caddesi, Taksim Square - Gezi Park Protests, İstanbul, CC BY 2.0, https://commons.wikimedia.org/w/index.php?curid=26615751

women's groups), mobilization can take place in the cultural sphere through symbolic action (e.g., the Egyptian Kifaya movement staging a vigil and wearing Black following mass assaults on women activists in May 2005).[37] This variation in action depends on, and comes in response to, the different local political contexts.

The short-lived euphoria following the 2011 uprisings soon gave way to pessimism. However, just as analysts were trying to explain the disappearance of mobilization, a second wave of mass protests erupted in Sudan, Algeria, and Lebanon.[38]

A key dimension of all the uprisings was that they were popular protests by citizens reclaiming their sense of dignity, who came together not just from organized networks but also from informal networks. A significant number of protesters did not belong to organized groups. Similarly, the rigid boundaries between religious and nonreligious movements, as well as different actors from civil society were temporarily suspended. So, while existing social movement paradigms are certainly useful for understanding the dynamics of political participation during the Arab uprisings, they cannot explain the full dimensions of this phenomenon. Rather, scholars need to take the Arab uprisings as a moment to further advance the study of contentious politics.

Political Engagement Through Violence

Sadly, other forms of informal political engagement in the MENA, as elsewhere, include violence against the state and sometimes against society. When analyzing violent movements in the region, a number of factors have to be taken into consideration.

First is the issue of labeling and the use of the term *terrorism*. The term *terrorism* was coined to describe the "systematic inducement of fear and anxiety to control and direct a civilian population."[39] In that sense, there is discussion to be had about whether some forms of state violence should be labeled as terrorism. Control through inducement of fear and anxiety is not limited to the actions of private citizens and nonstate organizations. Moreover, the use of the term must be historicized, as it has often been used politically by adversaries to stigmatize one another. In that context, most national liberation movements such the FLN in Algeria have been labeled terrorist organizations at some point. At present the debate on whether Hamas is a resistance movement or terrorist cell, and the battle by the Egyptian regime to internationally recognize the Muslim Brotherhood as a terrorist organization, are two examples of the controversies and political significance surrounding the use of the term.

Second is the diversity of groups and movements using violence as a means of participation, which makes it difficult to put them under one label. These groups differ in terms of their goals, targets, worldview, models of organization, strategies, and tactics. Even seemingly very similar movements such as the Islamic State (IS) and Al-Qaeda, both categorized as radical Islamist extremist groups, are critical of each other, have different outlooks and strategies, and employ different tactics. Similarly, the recent attacks of August 2021 in Afghanistan were directed by the ISIS branch that is critical of and seeks to challenge the Taliban movement. As is discussed in Chapter 4 on religion, society, and politics and in the individual country chapters in this book, these are just a few of the marked differences between groups that choose to operate outside of formal political avenues and informal pathways.

Third is the fact that the use of violence for political purposes is not a monopoly of so-called Islamist movements. Historically, some Leftist organizations across the world have employed violence as their principal means of participation. Currently some secular, Right-wing, white-supremacist movements also engage in terrorist "lone-wolf" attacks.

Finally, such movements are by definition not mass-based. More often violence represents the disaffection of a fragment of society which takes it upon themselves to act "on the behalf of a majority unaware of its plight, unwilling to take action to remedy grievances, or unable to express dissent."[40] Figure 5.8 shows the small percentages of respondents who engaged in violence in different countries of the region, with the exceptions of Yemen and Sudan. Given that Yemen is in a state of civil war and Sudan just recently emerged from prolonged civil strife, these high percentages are expected. Furthermore, when these data are compared to those engaged in peaceful protests and other forms of nonviolent actions, it is clear how marginal violent means of participation are among the general population.

These groups may be marginal in terms of size, but they inflict a disproportionately high human cost on societies; consequently, scholars from different disciplines have been studying the facets of these movements. These scholars consider how and why individuals participate in violence, and how best to combat them.[41] In doing so, analysts adopt a range of approaches, from microsociological perspectives, which outline individual social and psychological profiles of participants, to macro-level systems approaches, which view violence as a symptom and identify structural causes, economic, political, or cultural explanations for the emergence of these movements. Unfortunately, some of this literature tends to start from Orientalist assumptions and tautologically confirm them. Yet, despite variation, the common agreement in the literature is that such movements are prompted by perceived grievances for

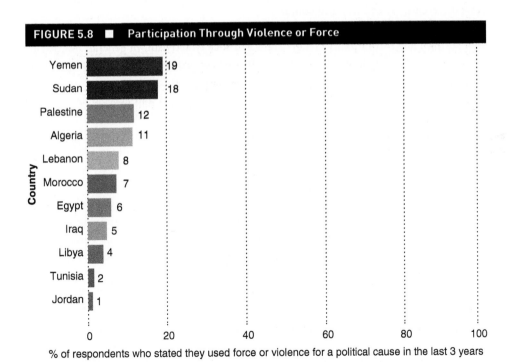

FIGURE 5.8   ■   Participation Through Violence or Force

Source: Arab Barometer Wave V (2018–2019) data. Used with permission.

which participants cannot identify effective channels to address. However, it is important to understand that both the grievances and the effectiveness of means are subjective, and many factors determine whether individually or collectively such perceptions would lead to instrumentalized violence.

INFORMAL PARTICIPATION: THE UNACCOUNTED

For the most part, political participation is predominantly taken to signify electoral competition, voting, collective direct action, and to a lesser extent some of the forms of civic action examined earlier. However, there are other forms of participation that are equally political but remain under-appreciated. This kind of political participation takes place in everyday life, through informal networks and institutions that include family structures, kinship networks, and different communal institutions. Informal political participation includes political discussion groups in the home as well as more organized discussion forums. This form of participation also includes actions ranging from what James Scott labeled "weapons of the weak," or coveted forms of resistance such as joke-making, to what Assef Bayat calls "quiet encroachment," whereby citizens as part of survival mechanisms take over public spaces, bend, or reinvent the rules. This is a fairly common form of participation in the Middle East, even though it manifests differently by country and context.

Political parties are weak, and in some cases nonexistent. CSOs are commonly prohibited from any sort of political activism. Civil society activism, in general, has become increasingly risky for those who take part. In this context, informal political participation offers opportunities for free speech and association outside the eyes and ears of the state, allowing citizens to remain within the bounds of legal and acceptable activities. Likewise, informal political activities do not demand or require an explicit political stance. Participants may view their activities as social, economic, political, or equally all three. Thus, the popularity and strength of informal political participation lies in the fact that it is woven into the daily social and economic lives of citizens and is, therefore, an inexorable part of the social fabric.

Some of these forms of participation are not necessarily aimed at or against the state. Rather, their *raison d'etre* extends to building solidarities among citizens and sustaining a sense of national or local community. Informal participation is in that sense political. Through informal "avenues of participation," as Diane Singerman calls them, and other forums, participants critically discuss public policy in ways they cannot do in the formal political sphere, contribute to the creation of new ways of thinking about politics, and construct informal pathways that impact policy, citizenship, and community-building. Similarly, informal political participation is never far from formal political participation, and it forms the often-invisible backbone of social and political change such as the type witnessed in the Arab Uprisings. Yet, the intent of informal political participation is not necessarily mass political change as was attempted in 2011. In fact, many participants in these discussion groups and networks may not even view their own actions as political.

How Can Social Gatherings Be Political?

Qat chews are an example of a common and important type of informal political participation in Yemen. Qat chews are gatherings in which people come together to engage in the traditional practice of chewing leaves of the qat plant, a stimulant that produces effects similar to caffeine. People meet to discuss social problems, political issues, or literary matters. They often entail a formal presentation about some issue of interest. Others begin with the reading aloud of a newspaper article. Still others are less formal with a general discussion of a variety of issues.[42] As Lisa Wedeen explains, social gatherings such as qat chews are political in at least three senses.[43] First of all, people share information about political events and discuss their significance publicly at qat chews. They promote political engagement and critical debate, and as such are not only political acts but ones that are inherently democratic. Second, qat chews are forums in which power relationships between elites and constituencies are negotiated. Representatives of the village, electoral district, or local group are held responsible for their actions at qat chews and must respond to the needs of participants. Third, during some qat chews actual policy decisions are made; political parties and parliamentary committees, for example, may hold their meetings, discuss events, and make policy changes. Similarly, political activists organize rallies at some qat chews. Even if informal gatherings such as qat chews do not directly or immediately lead to free and fair contested elections or to regime change, they are sites of political debate where issues of accountability, citizenship, and contemporary affairs are discussed and negotiated.[44] These are important political acts particularly in authoritarian regimes where political debate and criticism are at best ineffective or at worst illegal and dangerous.

Diwaniyyas in the Gulf states, such as Kuwait, similarly are important "mini-parliaments" where the informal/formal and private/public intertwine.[45] Much like qat chews, *diwaniyyas* are sites of traditional culture, daily social life, and political activity. The term *diwaniyya* refers both to the place where social gatherings occur inside the house and to the activity of assembling. In Arabic, the word *majlis* means the place of sitting, and in Kuwait, as in many of the other Gulf states, the place of sitting—the room used for (men's) social gatherings—is called the *diwan*. Today, there are male, female, and mixed *diwaniyyas*. Signaling their importance, in many cases separate structures, explicitly to host *diwaniyyas*, are built outside the house. While many *diwaniyyas* are for family and friends to socialize and talk business and politics, others can be quite specialized in terms of attendees and subjects discussed. Mary Ann Tetreault points out, as *diwaniyyas* are in the home and in that strict sense in the private sphere, they can be held without the government permits that other meetings ("public" meetings) require.[46] Although *diwaniyyas* are generally not banned, largely because it is very difficult for the government to do so, the Kuwaiti government has arrested the leaders of particularly influential oppositional *diwaniyyas* and has tried to restrict their influence.

Prominent intellectuals and activists hold diwaniyyas after major political decisions and events, to which members of parliament are commonly invited. The political influence of a diwaniyya depends on current events, the activism of those attending the diwaniyya, and the political orientation of the owner of the diwaniyya.[47] The important interface between formal and informal political participation in Kuwait is perhaps best seen in the role the *diwaniyya* played in reinstating Kuwait's parliament in 1990. When the Amir banned political parties and dissolved parliament in 1985, members of parliament and intellectuals began holding what soon was called the Monday *Diwaniyya* (as it was held each Monday) in order to express their outrage and, most importantly, to demand the reinstatement of parliament. The Monday *Diwaniyya* became so large that loudspeakers had to be used for all those in attendance to hear. Despite police efforts to stop the Monday *Diwaniyya*, it continued to take place and to draw crowds. Eventually, the Monday *Diwaniyya* led to a dialogue and the reestablishment of the parliament.[48]

In Saudi Arabia, we also see citizens increasingly engaging in discussion forums. In contrast to *diwaniyyas*, discussion forums, called *muntada*, are not social gatherings in the home. Rather, they are large, scheduled lectures on specific topics. One of the first discussion groups in Saudi Arabia was the Tuesday Forum, established by a former leader of the main Shi'i opposition movement in 2000. The lectures and discussions are posted online following the forum, reaching a much-wider audience than those in attendance. Discussion forums are helping to create a culture of dialogue and debate in Saudi Arabia even if their audiences are limited to intellectuals and the educated. Thus, their potential for social and political change is not lost on authorities who commonly ban discussion forums for periods of time.

Even in countries with comparatively greater freedom of the press, regimes consider informal gatherings as politically threatening. In Jordan, the king has spoken out harshly against political salons. (*Political salons* is the term given to the after-dinner gatherings that take place in private homes throughout Jordan and particularly in the capital, Amman.) In some cases, political salons are more organized, outside the home, and more akin to discussion forums. On more than one occasion, when the "chattering class" has become too critical of the king's policies, particularly the reversal of many of the political liberties and democratic rights that had

PHOTO 5.4 **"Ultras Martyrs** شهداء الألتراس" graffiti commemorating Ultras Ahlawy martyrs killed in Port Said جرافيتي في الزمالك

Source: Ultras Martyrs شهداء الألتراس/Flickr, CC BY 2.0, https://commons.wikimedia.org/w/index.php?curid=26615751

been gained during the 1990s, the king has criticized the salons, calling them "mafias" that must be stopped.[49]

In Egypt, the football fan groups known as Ultras came to play a significant role in combating the different regimes. They were one of the major actors in the mobilization that preceded and followed the seminal "Day of Revolt" on January 25, 2011 in Egypt. Estimated at one million members, the Director of Security of Cairo Stadium described them as "the most disciplined group after the armed forces."[50] Appearing in 2007, what started with the Zamalek's Ultras White Knights, Ultras 'Ahlāwī, and Ismaīlī Ultras Blue Dragons, and smaller regional clubs such as Port Said's Ultras Māsrī, came to the limelight when a series of clashes with security forces began both in football stadiums and on the streets. Having been known for confronting the police on football-related matters, their first visible political engagement on a nonfootball-related event was on January 25, 2011. They participated individually and not as a group, but they identified themselves to other protestors as "ultras" and were the only ones able to navigate their way against police violence, saving many veteran political activists as well as first-time protestors. Over the course of the following couple of years, as one scholar put it, the Ultras became "a source of hope for some Egyptians alienated by military rule and the Muslim Brotherhood government."[51]

How Are Networks Political?

It is not only through discussion and debate that Arab citizens engage in informal political participation. Multiple works, though limited, show how networks of urban poor, women, and religious groups are political actors that compete with other actors for power, legitimacy, and resources. Even some well-known political actors such as the Muslim Brotherhood in Egypt, Hezbollah in Lebanon, Hamas in Palestine, and the Salafis in many countries are actually nurtured by participants, donations, and citizens' loyalties that arise from seemingly nonpolitical networks.

For example, Diane Singerman's groundbreaking work on Cairo's urban poor under Mubarak shows how the urban poor participate in politics through the creation and mobilization of informal networks. These networks begin with the family unit and intersect with formal institutions and representatives of the state. In their efforts to ensure the maintenance and reproduction of the family, the urban poor, particularly the female heads of families, create vast networks of connections and exchanges that weave in and out of the extended family and neighborhood, informal savings associations, day care and literacy centers, health clinics, food cooperatives, local businesses, mosques, markets and schools, marriage brokers, private charitable and voluntary associations, workplaces, the army, ministries, and the offices of members of parliament. These networks are created to secure basic needs such as food, employment, and education and to gain credit, access services, choose a spouse, arbitrate conflict, etc. In doing so, they shape and encourage the political, social, and cultural norms of the community.[52]

Asef Bayat similarly argues that people across the MENA engage in political acts, particularly acts resisting the state, through their actions in everyday life.[53] The Tunisian street vendor, Muhammad Bouazizi, whose altercation with a policewoman and consequent self-immolation triggered the Tunisian revolution, is an example of the millions of people in the MENA who make up the "urban subaltern." These are the men and women on the margins of society—the unemployed, the working poor, the disenfranchised—who are forced to work illegally as street vendors, beggars, or prostitutes in the public spaces of cities. These people, the urban subaltern, live in constant insecurity and tension with the authorities of the state. This tension may result in fines, bribes, assault, or jail. As Bayat points out, the urban subaltern also develops solidarity through individuals' lived experiences and daily confrontations with the state.

Bayat calls such groups of people "social non-movements" to emphasize their lack of organized structure. Social nonmovements include nonmovements of the poor to claim rights to use public spaces. Nonmovements do not put organized direct pressure on the government as social movements do. They do not push for political reform. Their actions are done by individuals to ensure their daily activities and are often not regarded as political acts by the state. But by doing so, they slowly change the status quo.[54] The encroachment on the status quo "begins with little political meaning attached to it," but it can turn into a collective/political struggle if people's "gains are threatened."[55]

Networks may also strengthen social bonds and create a sense of community bound by a worldview in a manner somewhat similar to qat chews discussed earlier. In her research on Islamic charities in Egypt, Yemen, and Jordan, Janine Clark finds that networks of shared meaning are created through the provision of charity—raising donations, contacting funders, distributing aid, or providing medical care. The act of participating in charity activities brings different networks together. Communities of participants internalize and promote a particular set of values in these networks.[56] Clark finds that what makes Islamic charities "Islamic" and what makes working with the charity political is the feeling of solidarity, of a mission, of teamwork among those who work in the charity and its associated networks. Clark's research on women's Qur'anic study groups in Yemen similarly demonstrates how social networks have important political dimensions.[57] While many Yemeni women attend qat chews, others participate in Qur'anic study groups. At a Qur'anic study group or *nadwa*, women gather in a home to read passages from the Qur'an and discuss themes important to the practice of Islam. These are social gatherings that bring friends and women from different social networks together on a weekly basis. By participating in *nadwas* and the networks in which they are embedded, women gradually may develop new worldviews that are more in line with the Islamist movement, become active in an Islamist-sponsored charity, or may join the Islamist political party.

Gwenn Okruhlik's research on the Islamist movement in Saudi Arabia provides an excellent example of how informal political participation in the home and mosque becomes formal political participation.[58] Okruhlik's research questions how a powerful Islamist movement arose to challenge the regime under conditions of authoritarianism and in a society where concern to protect the family reputation is paramount. The Islamist movement first emerged during the first Gulf War (1990–1991) when US troops were stationed on Saudi soil. This followed an Islamic resurgence in the 1980s, in Saudi Arabia. Several nonpolitical informal Islamist groups were established during this time, advocating for a spiritual awakening. They were not involved in oppositional politics against the regime. The Gulf War transformed these loose underground nonpolitical groups into an organized and explicitly political

PHOTO 5.5 "Forbidden" by ICY and SOT, Valiasr Street-Tehran

Source: Kamyar Adl/Flickr,, CC BY 2.0, https://commons.wikimedia.org/w/index.php?curid=26615751

movement that called for the overthrow of the ruling family. Sermons and discussions in the mosque and home created alternative historical narratives that resonated with people and empowered them to confront the authoritarian state.[59] Family networks were vital to disseminate information and to mobilize support underground.[60] In 1992, under pressure from the Islamist movement, the king created a Consultative Council comprising Saudi citizens to advise him and other political reforms.

So, too, are networks of artists, writers, intellectuals, and bloggers active all over the MENA, producing works that contest the ruling regimes. In Syria, following the death of Hafez Al-Assad in 2000, intellectuals, artists, and writers created what came to be known as the "Damascus Spring." Numerous *muntadayāt* (salons or forums) of like-minded people met in private houses and discussed political matters and wider social issues. Its manifesto known as the Statement of 99 and calling on the regime to end its repressive measures was drafted and signed by film directors, artists, and nonpolitical public figures.[61] Similarly, the network of bloggers and youth who have a strong virtual presence became an indispensable asset in exposing the Egyptian regime pre-2011. With the uprisings, journalists, cartoonists, and graffiti artists capitalized on their existing informal networks to support collective mobilization through their professional skills and talents. In Iran, for example, conceptual artists and filmmakers are prolific in creating products that critique the political status quo of the Islamic Republic and around which an oppositional discourse galvanizes.

NEW CHANNELS OF POLITICAL PARTICIPATION?

For many, the Arab uprisings demonstrated the increasing importance of new channels of participation. The argument put forward by many was that satellite television and online and social media, as well as text messaging, provide "new sources of information, often beyond the regime's control" and create "new venues for participation, often engaging individuals who were previously not politically active."[62] Dubbed as the "Facebook revolution" and Revolution 2.0, the uprisings of 2011 seemed to confirm this point. However, while it is partially true that these technologies are changing communication patterns among citizens and facilitating their participation in public affairs, the assumption that this holds a necessarily positive impact on democratization has to be reevaluated.

Significant change in the media in the Middle East dates back to at least 1996 with the birth of *al-Jazeera*, the MENA's first 24-hour satellite news channel. The channel's reporting stood in sharp contrast to the customary MENA television landscape. It broadcasted political views that often criticized the behaviors of several MENA governments, leading many scholars to characterize the emergence of satellite television as supporting the move toward democratization in the MENA.[63] The credibility of satellite news as potent opposition to state-driven narratives was bolstered following the coverage of key events in the region, such as the Iraq war of 2003; the Israeli attacks on Lebanon in 2006 and Gaza in 2009; and the uprisings in Egypt, Yemen, and Syria in 2011. Importantly reporting was not only framed through live coverage by al-Jazeera anchors and correspondents but also shaped through the channel's reliance on user-generated videos sent by "citizen journalists" for broadcast.[64] Like satellite television, many believed that the Internet challenges the monopoly on state information through increased information sharing and the broadcasting of individual opinion. Some scholars have argued that use of the Internet and other modern technologies (examples of "horizontal communications") would, as Augustus Richard Norton claimed, eventually produce the "slow retreat of authoritarianism in the Muslim world."[65]

Despite low penetration rates at first (see Figure 5.9), ever since the Internet was introduced in these countries, ruling elites have attempted to find ways to control what people could and could not view on it. The fears were twofold: First, there was fear of "political subversion," and second, the religious and conservative segments of the population feared that Internet access would "undermine 'traditional' values." To limit Internet access, individual states took different approaches; in Saudi Arabia, for example, the regime "opted for a high-cost, high-tech solution, while Iraq under Saddam Hussein surrounded Internet use with barely-penetrable bureaucracy."[66]

The Internet and even text messaging have been central in communicating calls for collective mobilization, and varying forms of formal and informal e-networks over time have proved important for strengthening and extending political and social ties. In the mid-2000s, blogging arose as a key platform for the airing of dissident views and political demands, and for holding the state accountable. In Iran and Egypt in particular, blogs were used to expose human rights abuses, criticize state hegemony, and connect young people who aspired to change their societies and political systems from within. Mobile phones acted as supplementary tools in this process.

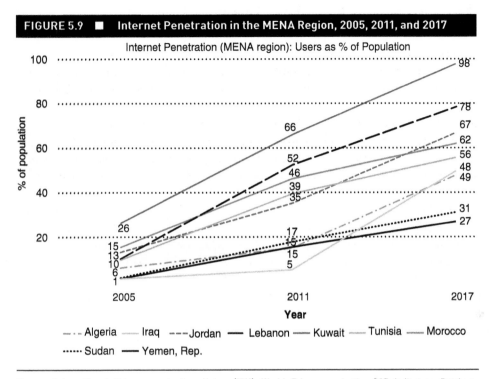

FIGURE 5.9 ■ Internet Penetration in the MENA Region, 2005, 2011, and 2017

Internet Penetration (MENA region): Users as % of Population

Legend: Algeria, Iraq, Jordan, Lebanon, Kuwait, Tunisia, Morocco, Sudan, Yemen, Rep.

Source: International Telecommunication Union (ITU) *World Telecommunications/ICT Indicators Database.* Accessed on 30 August 2021.

By the late 2000s, the rise of social media further enhanced the potential of new technologies to act as political participation tools. Social media sites like Twitter and Facebook allowed citizens to document events and actions by the state, from police beatings to election fraud, and disseminate news about state misbehavior. Visual evidence in the form of photographs and videos was sent not just to their immediate networks but also globally, supporting citizen journalism. In 2012, Facebook usership in the MENA region reached approximately forty million user accounts. Likewise, circa 2011, an estimated three million individuals in the Middle East used Twitter, and consumption of YouTube hit 167 million daily views.[67] Citizen journalism, in-country networks, and transnational linkages themselves later became ways through which the Internet and mobile phones could be used to coordinate public action on the street. The 2011 uprisings were also examples of how new technologies could be used hand-in-hand with public action as tools of political participation. In Egypt, a Facebook page originally created in 2010 by youth to protest the unlawful killing of a young man, Khaled Said, at the hands of the police, evolved into a platform calling for government accountability. This quickly grew, engendering Egyptians in the country and abroad to discuss Egypt's political future as the country prepared for new parliamentary and presidential elections in 2010 and 2011. The page *We Are All Khaled Said* became a space to mobilize for antiregime demonstrations, the biggest of which sparked the revolution of January 25. In Syria, YouTube became a key medium for people to document the assaults by the regime on Syrian people and towns at the beginning of its civil

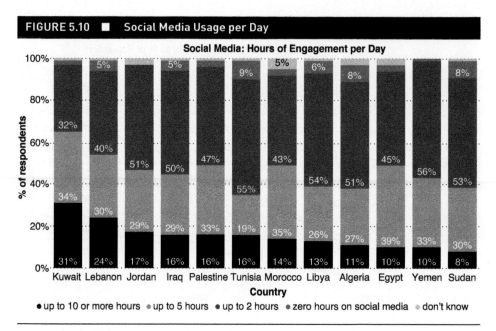

FIGURE 5.10 ■ Social Media Usage per Day

Social Media: Hours of Engagement per Day

Source: Arab Barometer Wave V (2018–2019) data. Used with permission.

unrest. As such, social media platforms became a tool for informal opposition movements and networks to engage in public action.[68]

With even further variegation of social media platforms such as Instagram, TikTok, and Clubhouse and more increased internet penetration, available data are showing more intense citizen engagement on these platforms. As Figure 5.10 shows, less than 10% of respondents in any of the surveyed countries do not spend any time daily on social media.

While this might not be equally applicable throughout each of these countries, given the huge economic disparity and unequal access to services, along with generational and gender variations, it is still indicative of a global trend which the region has not missed. This ease of access to mobile phones with cameras and wide-ranging possibilities have allowed citizens to individually and collectively push forward for changes even under repressive conditions. From antiharassment campaigns such as Assault Police in Egypt to LGBTQ networks in Iran and Saudi Arabia, these changes in communication technologies have prompted optimism surrounding the possibility of progressive changes in the region, both in terms of individual freedoms and even regime change; still, it remains important to reassess the contextual assumptions and possible responses, and pushback, to using this tool for reform.

Three important caveats have to be made here. First, governments of the region also learned the power of social media. Regimes' responses to dissidents expressing unfavorable opinions about the state on the web demonstrate the seriousness with which regional governments take the Internet as a medium for disseminating public opinion. Surveillance and censorship, outright arrests, and even shutting down the Internet have become all-too-common tactics of MENA regimes. This included persecution of citizens posting nonpolitical content on TikTok in Egypt, for example, under the pretense of combating obscenity. As a result, the assumption that these new technologies subvert regime control and hence lower the cost of participation in authoritarian settings should not be overestimated. Second, these tools do not always have a positive impact on collective mobilization. Interestingly, in the cases of the Egyptian mobilization of January 2011 and the Sudanese protests of 2019, internet shutdowns and the cutting off of communication channels coincided with more mobilization.[69] Similar to Gil Scott-Heron's "The Revolution Will Not be Televised," continued variation in terms of the timing and intensity of protest movements across the region, regardless of access to social media or web-based communications, suggests that people do not join just because they participate on social media platforms. Finally, as Marc Lynch points out, social media has proven to be just as capable of transmitting negative and divisive ideas and images as it had been at spreading revolutionary ones.[70] In post-2013 Egypt, for example, Twitter and Facebook contributed to the growing hostility between Islamists and liberals. These caveats are not specific to the region but are shared with other parts of the world, for example, internet control in China or fake news, and the use of social media to propagate false messages and incite violence in the United States.

CONCLUSION

Much of the MENA remains largely authoritarian, but this does not signify a lack of involvement among the region's populations. The 2011 and 2019 uprisings are a testimony to the political engagement of these populations. Citizens employ a variety of modes to better advocate their interests and concerns and to improve their living conditions both economically and politically. The forms of citizen participation present a rich tapestry that is not limited to the "mosque" or the "ballot box," the two overly examined arenas of participation in the region. These different forms are not always as visible as mass street protests in Tahrir square in Cairo, nor as loud as explosions in Al-Reqah and Baghdad; rather, most of the time they are quiet interactions that do not capture the media's attention. It is the entirety of these different forms of participation—visible and not—that shape the terrain for constructs such as the state, the regime, and the aggregate society.

Hence, when examining political participation, one has to question the definition of the "political" and its boundaries versus the non- and the a-political; such boundaries are much more fluid and porous than many assume. Many forms of networks, groups, and everyday acts that do not start out with political intent, end up having significant political implications. Similarly, questioning divisions between the private and the public—recognized early on by the feminist movement—is imperative to understanding political participation in the MENA region, as much as anywhere else. As discussed above, many acts and forums that start in the protected private space of homes have spillover effects into the public sphere. Finally, the clear demarcation of the collective versus the individual has to be understood as dynamic and ever changing, just like people's perceptions, identities, and priorities are, all of which are integral to their participation.

SUGGESTED READINGS

Singerman, Diane. *Avenues of Participation*. Princeton, NJ: Princeton University Press, 1995.

Beinin, Joel, and Vairel Frédéric. *Social Movements, Mobilization, and Contestation in the Middle East and North Africa: Second Edition*. Stanford, CA: Stanford University Press, 2013.

Cavatorta, Francesco, and Storm Lise. *Political Parties in the Arab World: Continuity and Change*. Edinburgh: Edinburgh University Press, 2018.

Frédéric, Volpi, and A. Clark Janine. *Network Mobilization Dynamics in Uncertain Times in the Middle East and North Africa*. London: Routledge Press, 2019.

Brownlee, Jason, E. Masoud Tarek, and Reynolds Andrew. *The Arab Spring: Pathways of Repression and Reform: First ed.* New York, NY; Oxford: Oxford University Press, 2015.

6 SOCIAL CHANGE IN THE MIDDLE EAST

Valentine M. Moghadam

Sociologists have long studied social change, or societal transformation, in terms of changes to a society's production system and its social order. Depending on the historical period, this entails examining structures and relations at micro (household, kinship, family), meso (organizations, formal institutions, and networks), and macro (systems and relations of production and distribution) levels of analysis. More specifically, and certainly for the modern period, sociologists explore societal effects of revolutions, state formation, industrialization, urbanization, mass education, and demographic transitions, as well as social movements, cultural values and attitudes, migration, and global ties. These are, in fact, interrelated phenomena that influence each other and may be grouped under the umbrella term *modernization*. Although there has been an implicit understanding in the modernization literature that such changes occur under conditions of capitalism, significant social changes have taken place under socialist conditions (consider the former Soviet Union as well as communist-era China, Cuba, and Vietnam).[1]

Social change may come about rapidly and dramatically, as in the wake of a social revolution or a purposive state-led development strategy, or more gradually, as in longer-term processes of industrialization, urbanization, educational attainment, and normative shifts. The expansion of education, especially for women, generates decreasing fertility rates, higher age at marriage, shifts in family structure and dynamics, and changing attitudes, aspirations, and behaviors. In recent decades, aspects of globalization such as the introduction and widespread adoption of social media platforms have enabled rapid communication and information exchange, facilitating the organization and mobilization of dissent—as occurred during the Green Protests in Iran in summer 2009, the 2011 Arab Spring, Turkey's 2013 Gezi Park protests, and the 2019 protest wave in Algeria, Iraq, Lebanon, and elsewhere. Social media also have been used for artistic or political self-expression, which, in turn, reflects wider changes in cultural attitudes, values, and norms, as was observed with the 2022 protests in Iran after the death in police custody of a young woman arrested for "inadequate hijab."

Social change may also come about in the aftermath of war or armed conflict. For example, in addition to changing the world's political map, World War I and World War II enabled women's suffrage in Europe and the United States and claims-making by women's organizations that culminated in the global feminist wave of the 1970s. Postconflict democratic transitions in certain parts of the Global South helped launch the "quota revolution" that has increased women's political representation across the world.[2] In the wake of the Arab Spring protests, Algeria and Tunisia became part of the group of countries with a 30 percent or higher proportion of women in parliament. Wars also have had destructive effects, often undoing years or even decades of modernization and positive social change and creating new problems. World War I destroyed the Ottoman Empire (as it did the Austro-Hungarian Empire), changing borders, generating refugees and population resettlements, and creating new states. It also entrenched the European colonial presence in the Middle East and North Africa (MENA). World War II enabled the continued spread of nationalist movements, some of which came into conflict with each other, in part as a reflection of Cold War dynamics. The 2003 US/UK invasion of Iraq not only destabilized Iraq and resulted in years of occupation, terrorism, and political dysfunction, but it also presaged further instability and insecurity in the MENA region, including the destabilization of Libya (in 2011) and Syria (since 2011), the growth of the transnational terrorist group ISIS, and the Saudi-UAE bombing campaign and blockade on Yemen (since 2015). The May 2021 Israeli military assault on Gaza set back years of infrastructural development—and this in the midst of the COVID-19 pandemic. In the case of the MENA region, it is difficult to envision positive social change through war, whether for a country's female population, its institutions, or its economic capacity.

Over the past 2 centuries, the MENA region has experienced considerable social change. The early 20th century saw constitutionalism, nation-building, and colonialism. The 1950s through the 1970s represented a period of postcolonial state-building, state-led socioeconomic development, and left-wing movements. The 1980s were characterized by "structural adjustment" policies as well as the expansion of Islamist movements. The 1990s until 2011 had features of limited political liberalization, competing social movements of Islamists and women's rights advocates, neoliberalization, and subregional conflicts. The Arab Spring and political change in Tunisia, Egypt, Libya, and Yemen initially launched those countries on a path of democratic transition, while Morocco, which had started a slower, more gradual transition in 1998, approved constitutional changes in the referendum of July 2011, which limited some of the vast powers of the king. By 2013, however, Libya had descended into a failed state while Egypt had reverted to military-led authoritarianism. The destabilization of Libya and the internationalized conflict in Syria generated a massive wave of migrants and refugees to neighboring countries and to Europe. The Saudi-UAE assault on Yemen created what the UN and an array of international organizations called a humanitarian catastrophe.

The one positive outcome of the Arab Spring protests, Tunisia, was building democratic institutions in the first decade after the uprising, but also suffering from deteriorating economic conditions. The social changes wrought by the Arab Spring have been a source of scholarly debate, with some underscoring its "modest harvest," others pointing to authoritarian resilience, others emphasizing the absence of revolutionaries as the reason for defeat, and yet others noting cultural changes and positive shifts in value orientations. Throughout, the global context has been important to the regional and country-specific changes that have occurred in MENA.[3]

This chapter traces some of the key elements of social change that have accompanied modernization in MENA, with references to the likely societal effects of the region's conflicts and the pandemic. It begins by providing an overview of social structural changes over time, including class and labor force formation. This is followed by an examination of the role of population growth, urbanization, and education. It continues with a look at changes in family structure and the role of women's organizations in debates on, and reforms to, family law. Related to these changes have been shifts in cultural attitudes and values, as reflected in various surveys.

The chapter concludes with a discussion of the dynamic processes through which both the social conditions and the arena for future contestations over change take place, with references to gender relations, women's mobilizations, and how the short-term effects of COVID-19 may shape societal demands and public policies.

Three theoretical perspectives frame the chapter conceptually. The first is world polity theory, which helps explain the spread and consequences of "modern" institutions, norms, and networks in the region. Second is world-systems theory, which posits a hierarchical global system of markets and states led by a hegemon within which MENA's oil and arms purchases play important roles in global capital accumulation and certain states face geopolitical challenges.[4] A feminist lens rounds out the analysis by highlighting the gendered nature of states, institutions, movements, and social relations.

SOCIAL CHANGE AND SOCIAL STRUCTURE

As in other regions, MENA countries are linked to world society through involvement in multilateral agencies and international nongovernmental organizations (INGOs), treaty obligations, and access to new computer technologies and social media. The adoption of Western-style education systems and other forms of "institutional isomorphism" similarly has enabled norm diffusion—for human rights, women's rights, and democracy—and demands for sociopolitical change. At the same time, location in the economic zones of the contemporary capitalist world-system—whether the periphery (Yemen, Oman, the West Bank and Gaza, Morocco) or semiperiphery (Israel, Iran, Turkey), along with the vast differences in resource endowments (the oil-rich and labor-importing United Arab Emirates [UAE] and Qatar compared with low-income and labor-exporting Syria and Morocco)—have had implications for economic and social development and for state capacity. Relations with the world-system's hegemon matter: the United States supplies Saudi Arabia and Israel with massive military and diplomatic support, while Iran and Syria are subjected to harsh economic sanctions. Configurations of power at global, regional, and national levels shape the opportunity structure for social movements and collective action by nonstate actors.

As various chapters in this volume show in more detail, MENA countries differ in their historical evolution, social composition, economic structures, and state forms. All were once under some form of colonial rule except for Iran (which nonetheless experienced Russian and British intervention in the 19th century), Turkey (which was itself a colonial power until the end of World War I), Israel (a settler-colonial state), and Saudi Arabia. All the countries are predominantly Arab except Iran, Israel, and Turkey, and all have majority Muslim populations except for Israel. Most Muslim countries are largely Sunni, except for Iran, which is Shi'a; Bahrain, which has a Shi'i majority; and Iraq and Lebanon, where Sunni and Shi'i populations are roughly equal. Some of the countries have sizable Christian (Lebanon, Egypt, Syria) or small Jewish (Morocco, Tunisia, and especially Iran) minority populations; others (Iran, Iraq, Morocco) are ethnically and linguistically diverse. Some have had strong working-class movements and trade unions (Iran, Egypt, Tunisia, Turkey) or large communist organizations (Iran, Egypt, southern Yemen, the Palestinians).

Across the region, the development of skills (human capital formation), the depth and scope of industrialization, integration into the global economy, standards of living and welfare, and women's participation and rights are varied. MENA countries are not among the poorest or most unequal in the world, but they exhibit forms of social stratification that are both familiar and distinctive. Privilege or disadvantage is determined by class, gender, ethnicity, and national origin, while religious affiliation is another significant social marker.

Politically, the regime types range from theocratic monarchies (Saudi Arabia) to secular republics (Turkey and Tunisia). Until 1992, the kingdom of Saudi Arabia had no formal constitution apart from the Qur'an and the shari'a, the Islamic legal code. Many of the states in the Middle East experienced legitimacy problems, which became acute in the 1980s when Islamist movements spread across the region. The 1990s saw the beginnings of political liberalization, but for the most part, the process stalled, and many MENA states remained authoritarian, with limited citizen participation.[5]

Much has been written about the authoritarian, patrimonial, or rentier nature of the MENA state (see also Chapter 4). The term *neopatriarchal state*, adopted from Hisham Sharabi, is a useful umbrella term for the various state types in MENA, especially in connection with how gender and family are structured in the region.[6] In the neopatriarchal state, unlike liberal or social democratic societies, the family, rather than the individual, constitutes the universal building block of the community, and religion is bound to power and state authority. The neopatriarchal state and the patriarchal family reflect and reinforce each other, although both have been subject to challenges due to women's educational attainment and labor force participation, as well as civil society organizations and new social movements. The neopatriarchal state retains control over the population through authoritarian means but crucially through the codification of women's second-class citizenship in the region's conservative family laws. As demonstrated later in this chapter, significant change has occurred in this regard, with a shift in the gender regime observed in at least two MENA countries.

In the 1950s and 1960s, the urbanization trend that accompanied state-led economic development and modernization strategies initially saw a drop in women's labor force participation, as households moved from rural areas and agricultural production to urban areas and (male) engagement in industrial production. (This is a pattern sometimes known as "housewife-ization.") At the same time, postcolonial institution-building changed social structures and social relations, creating new occupations and professions for the growing modern middle class and working class as well as transnational migrant communities. As new jobs emerged in the service and industrial sectors, niches were found for female employment. Through policies that some scholars have termed *state feminism,* Tunisian women saw legal reforms and opportunities for higher-education attainment and jobs in the growing public sector.[7] There and elsewhere, educated women secured jobs in teaching, healthcare, and to a lesser degree public administration; in some countries more than others, the manufacturing sector drew women workers. During the period of rapid growth, governments instituted protective legislation for working mothers, such as paid maternity leave and workplace nurseries. Egypt had a policy of guaranteeing public sector jobs to graduates of secondary schools and universities; Morocco's scheme provided "temporary employment" to graduates. Through these policies, the public sectors in countries such as Egypt, Jordan, and Algeria absorbed about 50 percent of the formal labor force, and public sector workers enjoyed social insurance programs that were adopted from international models.

Such social policies, along with advances for women, formed part of the general trend toward modernization.[8] Nonetheless, most citizens were found in agrarian production or traditional commercial activities. As a result, the family remained the key institution of the MENA social welfare regime and neopatriarchal state during the oil boom era. As long as the oil revenues remained buoyant and the economy kept up its growth, informal family transfers and worker remittances played an important role in maintaining economic security for parts of the population that were excluded from the formal social welfare system.[9] Whether in the informal or formal sector, the breadwinners were predominantly men.

This leads to the question of why MENA women remained a small proportion of the nonagricultural labor force until well into the new century, and even today compared with other world regions. A significant reason lies in the region's political economy: the centrality of the oil sector and the relatively high wages enjoyed by male workers during the state-building and oil boom era. Oil-based growth and capital-intensive industrial production limited female labor supply and demand.[10] Higher wages earned by men served to limit the supply of job-seeking women during the oil boom years; indeed, research by Massoud Karshenas on manufacturing-wage trends showed that workers' wages were higher in most MENA countries than they were in Asian countries such as Indonesia, Korea, and Malaysia. Ece Kocabicak offers another explanation: women's historic separation from the means of production, specifically their exclusion from land ownership, had ripple effects over time, marginalizing them from the formal labor force.[11] Women's exclusion from gainful employment reinforced "the patriarchal gender contract"—the implicit and often explicit agreement that men are the breadwinners and are responsible for financially maintaining wives, children, and elderly parents, and women are wives, mothers, homemakers, and caregivers.[12] In turn, the patriarchal gender contract was inscribed in the region's family laws, which render women minors and under the supervision of male kin. Both political economy and formal institutions served to reproduce conservative social norms and the traditional sexual division of labor.

The oil boom era came to an end in the mid-1980s, in the midst of the Iran–Iraq war (1980–1988). In the late 1970s and into the early part of the next decade, many developing countries experienced indebtedness, in part because of the sudden increase in interest rates, and were compelled to accept austerity measures and "structural adjustment" policies as a condition for new loans from the IMF and World Bank. The regional oil economy protected many MENA countries, but by the 1990s, a combination of declining oil prices, mismanagement of economic resources, expensive and destructive conflicts, and the return or expulsion of labor migrants led to economic stagnation, indebtedness, and high unemployment in many countries. Attempts to preserve employment during the long period of retrenchment led to substantial wage erosion in all the countries in the region.[13] Structural adjustment policy prescriptions to reduce the government's wage bill meant that public sectors no longer hired as expansively as they had before, and a strategy to avoid outright layoffs was wage deterioration or encouragement of early retirement.

One of the casualties of the end of the oil boom, as well as intraregional political disputes, was the intraregional labor flow, affecting expatriate Arabs working in the Gulf sheikhdoms. The return of expatriate workers had mixed socioeconomic effects. In some cases, returnees contributed to a boom in the construction industry and in small businesses (especially in Jordan), but in other cases, they faced unemployment, slow absorption into the local labor market, or poverty. The latter was especially acute for Yemenis, who were largely unskilled workers unable to find employment at home. The Gulf states replaced Arab workers with South and Southeast Asians.

The result of these developments—the end of the oil boom, the introduction of structural adjustment, the return of labor migration, and the new discourses and policies of privatization, "flexible" labor markets, and entrepreneurship—was a considerable decline in household incomes and a substantial increase in unemployment. Although adult men were affected, women and youth began to face the greatest difficulty finding jobs.

Another development worth mentioning is the expansion of Islamic fundamentalist movements as well as movements for political Islam (see also Chapter 5). The conservative turn in MENA has been extensively analyzed, with the identification of such factors as the demonstration effect of Iran's Islamic revolution; Saudi Arabia's export of the Wahhabi ideology through its worldwide construction of mosques and madrasses; Arab migrant workers' adoption of that ideology during their employment stay in Saudi Arabia and other Gulf sheikhdoms; US support for the tribal-Islamist uprising in Afghanistan in the 1980s; popular anger over the nonresolution of the Israeli–Palestinian problem; frustration over unemployment and rising living costs following the adoption of privatization and liberalization policies; reunification of Yemen in 1990 and the end of the socialist experiment in the south. In turn, Islamist movements took advantage of those and similar opportunities to mobilize financial, human, and organizational resources to grow their social base and challenge regimes. In some cases, regimes fought or repressed the Islamist movements, especially when acts of terrorism were carried out in the 1980s and 1990s, as occurred in Egypt, Algeria, Jordan, and Tunisia. But regimes also accommodated Islamist movements by introducing or strengthening Muslim family law (as in Egypt in 1985) and allowing the construction of numerous unsupervised mosques. Conservatism, Salafism, and attachment to the Islamist agenda thus spread across many populations. In Egypt, veiling became increasingly widespread within the female population, and in Jordan, the Muslim Brotherhood Islamist party consistently won seats in parliamentary elections, blocking liberal reforms.[14]

As the forces of globalization expanded in the 1990s and states followed international trends in privatization and liberalization, new socioeconomic relations began to be forged.[15] Foreign direct investment flowed to Morocco, Tunisia, and the Gulf states, creating new jobs for workers and the middle class. The globalizing business classes of countries such as Turkey, Egypt, Lebanon, and the Gulf states became part of what sociologists Leslie Sklair and William Robinson have termed the *transnational capitalist class*, with a stake in global flows of financial and industrial capital.[16] However, neither a coherent vision nor a comprehensive strategy of development succeeded the previous models of economic and social development. Aspects of the globalization process such as links to world society through the Internet and transnational advocacy networks were dynamic and liberating, but other aspects contributed to the growing inequalities and income gaps in the region. The shift to the neoliberal model of privatization, liberalization, and labor market flexibilization exacerbated the unemployment problem, especially for women and young graduates. Women's unemployment rates soared, indicative of the growth of the population of job-seeking women in a context of real economic need as well as women's rising educational attainment and changing aspirations. In most countries, unemployment benefits and social insurance—if they were in place at all—were not available to new entrants to the labor market, who were the majority of the registered unemployed in most countries. Economic restructuring and demographic pressures created new inequalities and groups of "new poor."[17] Moreover, conflicts in Palestine and Iraq created or exacerbated poverty.

Conflicts in the region have led to another significant change in the MENA region. Demographer Philippe Fargues has referred to "demographic Islamization," by which he means the declining numbers of non-Muslims—including those populations of Christians and Jews that predated the Muslim conquest—in countries including Iran, Iraq, Egypt, Lebanon, and Syria. What he calls "the golden age for Christian demography" was found during the era of the Ottoman Empire, when several MENA countries were a vibrant mix of religious, ethnic, and linguistic communities. Turkey itself had a Christian population of nearly 20 percent in 1914. That dwindled to 2.5 percent in 1927, the result of the massacre of Armenians, the removal of Greeks, and the departure of other Christians. By 1991, the population of Christians in Turkey was just 0.2 percent.[18]

The Jewish community has shrunk considerably. The formation of the state of Israel led to the displacement of Jews from Iraq, where they had been a large and prominent presence since Biblical times; in the 1950s and 1960s, North Africa lost much of its Jewish population to emigration to Israel or France. Egypt's surge of nationalism in the early 1950s, following the 1952 "Free Officers' Revolution" that ended the monarchy, may have set the country on a path of social development, but it also marked the beginning of the end of "cosmopolitan Alexandria." Members of Alexandria's foreign community and Egyptian Jews left the country after the enactment of regulations that paved the way for the arrests of citizens without charge, seizure of their businesses, and nationalization of their assets. In Iran, the Islamic Revolution changed the country's demographic makeup. Iran still has the largest Jewish population in MENA outside of Israel, but many Iranian Jews—along with Christians, Baha'is, Zoroastrians, and secular Muslims—left Iran during the revolution or in the years afterward.

Regarding the Christian populations, Fargues provides data to show that Lebanon's Christian population declined from about 55 percent in 1956 to 43 percent in 1998, due mainly to the Lebanese civil war and outmigration. The significant decline of the population of Christian Palestinians is attributed to a combination of the pressures of living in Israel, fears of Islamization, and the lack of employment opportunities. One of the many tragic outcomes of the 2003 US invasion and occupation of Iraq was the displacement of the country's minorities, especially its once large Christian population. The enforcement of veiling and the banning of alcohol by vigilante Islamists forced the departure of numerous Christian Iraqis, primarily to safe areas in Jordan and Syria.[19] Later, many Christian Iraqis as well as Palestinians who had sought refuge in Syria faced another crisis. One aspect of the internationalized civil conflict in

Syria has been sectarian violence, in which antiregime Sunni Muslims—aided by foreign fighters, Turkey, Saudi Arabia, Qatar, and the UAE—have targeted Christians. This included the armed takeover by ISIS of the ancient Syrian Christian town of Maaloula.

Other factors for the declining numbers of religious minorities are intermarriage and international migration. For the region as a whole, challenges to non-Muslim communities that have led to emigration (forced or free) include xenophobic nationalisms, political Islam, conflicts and wars leading to sectarian violence, and the absence of jobs. For all these reasons, the proportion of Christians in the Middle East's population has declined from 13.6 percent in 1910 to 4.2 percent in 2010 and is expected to fall to just 3.6 percent by 2025.[20] An irony of history and of demography is that as Europe and North America have become more multicultural, with Muslim residents and citizens demanding more rights, the MENA region has become less multicultural, with Christians on the defensive or departing altogether. The 2021 visit to Iraq by Pope Francis may have heartened the remaining Christians, but it is unlikely to reverse the trend of a community in decline.

This overview of regional transformations over the past century sets the stage for a more detailed look at key social change processes, including the pandemic's effects. We begin with sociodemographic processes and their connection to urbanization, and we end with social reforms and women's rights movements.

URBANIZATION AND POPULATION GROWTH

As seen in Table 6.1, MENA's population and urbanization growth has been steady and, in some cases, dramatic. Between 1950 and 2010, mortality rates dropped and fertility rates remained high; indeed, until relatively recently, high population growth rates in the MENA were second only to those in sub-Saharan Africa. MENA's annual population growth reached a peak of 3 percent around 1980, while the growth rate for the world reached its peak of 2 percent annually more than a decade earlier.[21] The region's high fertility rates resulted in the "youth bulge" that was evident during the mass social protests in Iran in 2009 and in the Arab countries in 2011.[22] Fertility rates have been falling across the region (see discussion below), and the elderly population will likely grow in the next two decades, necessitating social policies appropriate to the new population dynamics, especially in the growing urban areas.

In 1990, MENA had only about twenty cities with populations of more than one million; thirty years later, there are more than forty such cities. Cairo, Tehran, Istanbul are megacities, followed by Baghdad, with about 8.7 million residents. The next largest cities are Riyadh (6.5 million), Ankara (5.2 million), Alexandria (about 5 million), and Jeddah, Ismir, and Amman (roughly 4 million). Cities with between two and three million inhabitants include Algiers, Dubai City, Kuwait City, Morocco's Casablanca and Rabat, and Iran's cities of Isfahan, Mashad, and Shiraz.[23] Istanbul's population of 12.5 million in 2014 increased with the inflow of Syrian migrants. The same can be said of Amman and Beirut, whose populations in 2014 were 1.3 million and 2.2 million, respectively. Conversely, Syria's cities—Aleppo, Homs, and Hama in particular—have seen depopulation due to the conflict and refugee outflow.[24] Indeed, as Table 6.1 shows, Syria's total population declined from 20.4 million in 2010 to 18.5 in 2015 and 17.07 in 2019.

TABLE 6.1 ■ Population and Urbanization in the Middle East and North Africa						
	Total Population (Millions)			*Percentage Urban*			
Country	1950	2010	2019	1950	1980	2010	2019
Algeria	8.75	35.5	43.053	22.2	43.5	72	73.189
Bahrain	0.116	1.26	1.641	64.4	86.1	88.6	89.394
Egypt	21.5	81.1	100.39	31.9	43.9	43.4	42.73
Iran	17.414	74	82.913	27.5	49.7	68.9	75.391
Iraq	5.72	31.7	39.309	35.1	65.5	66.5	70.678
Israel	1.26	7.42	9.05	71	88.6	91.8	92.501
Jordan	0.449	6.19	10.10	37	59.9	82.5	91.203
Kuwait	0.152	2.74	4.207	61.5	94.8	98.2	100
Lebanon	1.44	4.23	6.855	32	73.7	87.1	88.758
Libya	1.03	6.36	6.77	19.5	70.1	77.6	80.393
Morocco	8.95	32	36.47	26.2	41.2	56.7	62.994
Oman	0.456	2.8	4.97	8.6	47.6	73.2	85.443
Qatar	0.025	1.76	2.832	79.2	89.4	98.7	99.188
Saudi Arabia	3.12	27.5	34.27	21	65.9	82.1	84.065
Syria	3.54	20.4	17.07	30.6	46.7	55.7	54.821
Tunisia	3.53	10.5	11.694	32.3	50.6	66.1	69.254
Turkey	21.5	72.8	83.43	24.8	43.8	70.5	75.63
United Arab Emirates	.07	7.51	9.77	54.5	80.7	84	86.789
West Bank and Gaza	.932	4.04	4.685	37.3	62.4	74.1	76.44
Yemen	4.32	24	29.161	5.8	16.5	31.7	37.273

Sources: UN Dept. of Economic and Social Affairs, World Urbanization Prospects, "2011 Revision" and "2014 Revision"; 2015 figures from World Bank, World Development Indicators 2017, 11–14.

Urbanization is a central aspect of social change and economic development, with cities playing a key role in globalization. Urban planning, including the construction of squares such as Cairo's famous Tahrir Square, has been central to modernization and development. Additional factors and forces affect urbanization. Rural-to-urban migration and the growth of cities are usually fueled by "push" and "pull" factors: the push of population pressure on natural resources and the lack of economic opportunity in the rural areas, and the pull of perceived economic opportunity and a better lifestyle in the big cities. Urbanization has implications—both positive and negative—for social structure and class relations, gender relations, normative change, and health. Work is typically less arduous in cities than in rural agrarian areas, but urban labor markets cannot absorb all workers, leading to informality, unemployment, or underemployment. Public and private services are more extensive in cities than in rural areas, but population growth puts pressure on quality and cost. Public space, once the exclusive domain of men, is now also occupied by women, though not necessarily without risk. Still, gender mixing on the streets, in schools, and at workplaces can help change attitudes, values, and behaviors. Urban-based collective action, advocacy, and activism expand, but so do state surveillance and repressive methods.

MENA has experienced rapid rates of urbanization and population growth, and although countries are at different levels of urbanization, the majority of the region's inhabitants now reside in urban areas. By 2018, the Arab region alone was 61 percent urbanized, more so than the world average of 54 percent. Cairo is among the world's 10th largest megacities and shares their problems: extremely high population densities, severe shortages of housing and services, and lack of regulation of construction and urban development. There and elsewhere in MENA, urban economies cannot absorb their large populations, leading to unemployment, underemployment, and poverty (see next section). Other problems include a shortage of clean drinking water, the growth of slums or shantytowns, polluted air, water shortage, inadequate waste disposal systems, power shortages, and noise pollution.

The most rapid growth in MENA's urbanization occurred in the oil-exporting countries, doubling in Iran and Iraq between 1950 and 1985 and in the Persian Gulf sheikhdoms between 1960 and 1980.[25] Among countries not already highly urbanized, the slowest rate of urbanization was in Egypt; its urban share increased from 32 percent in 1950 to 43 percent in 2015. Yemen is the least urbanized country in the region, whereas Kuwait, Qatar, and Bahrain are essentially city-states. In the case of Israel, immigration by Jews from other countries contributed to the growth of Tel Aviv and Jerusalem. In the small, oil-rich Gulf Cooperation Council (GCC) countries, importation of foreign labor for the construction boom contributed to urban growth.

The city of Dubai experienced spectacular urban growth in the 1990s and 2000s, which other Gulf states have sought to replicate. In the 1950s, the once-thriving trade and pearling center had a faltering economy. From the late 1960s through the 1970s, Dubai's leaders invested revenue from the emirate's newly discovered modest oil reserves in seaport and airport infrastructure to further develop the emirate as a trade hub. Migrants from nearby South Asia, other MENA states, and beyond settled in the city, and by 1980, its population was 276,000, up from about 60,000 when the first census was conducted in 1968. In the 1990s and the first decade of the 21st century, further growth and diversification were pursued through development of free zones, tourism, and the emirate's famed real estate and construction boom. In 2010, approximately 1.5 million people lived in Dubai, the vast majority of whom were not citizens and more than 70 percent were men. Dubai's population continued to grow rapidly and was estimated to be 2.68 million in 2018. Gulf cities have become increasingly cosmopolitan, multicultural hubs, sparking concerns and debates among some citizens about the erosion of local culture and identity, as well as mimicry and monumentalism.[26] The Gulf example also raises questions about social relations and rights in such cities, where most inhabitants are noncitizens, often living in a state of what Syed Ali has termed "permanent impermanence," and where social and cultural life transcend the boundaries of the national state.

A very different example of urbanization and its social consequences comes from Alexandria, the ancient Egyptian city and the country's largest after teeming Cairo. Alexandria boasts Greco-Roman monuments and colonial-era buildings. The notable Alexandria Library was built in 2002 on what is believed to be the site of its ancient predecessor, the Royal Library of Alexandria, and plans were underway to build an underwater museum that would show-case the submerged remnants of Cleopatra's palace. As one report explains, until the mid-1990s Alexandria was a popular summer destination for well-to-do Egyptian vacationers. However, decades of state neglect, population growth, beach erosion, and heavy pollution left their mark on the city. As Alexandria grew more dilapidated and congested, the country's elites moved west, spending their summers at the pristine beach resorts farther along the coast. Alexandria's public beaches became the preserve of the less privileged, though these still charge an entrance fee. The Alexandria Chamber of Travel Agencies then signed agreements with Greece, Cyprus, and Italy to promote the city as a tourist destination in the hope of increasing the inflow of tour-ists from the three Mediterranean states. Plans were put in place to build additional hotels and protect female tourists from sexual harassment at the beaches.[27] The 2020 pandemic, however, put those plans on hold, and the city suffered job and income losses. The same occurred across tourism destinations in the region.

Environmental and health costs to urban overdevelopment are increasingly obvious. Tehran's urban development, including new highways and housing complexes, not only expanded the city limits but also exacerbated pollution and traffic jams. In May 2013, mass protests erupted in Istanbul over plans to bulldoze a central park—one of the very few left in Istanbul—to make way for new building construction. The Gezi Park protesters were met with tear gas by police and eventually dispersed; construction went ahead. In Cairo and other cities in Egypt, the cutting down of trees to make way for new urban projects has angered the public and led members of parliament to call for new measures to protect Egypt's dwindling urban green spaces.[28] Urban sprawl and density displace natural habitat, generate pollution, and facilitate the spread of disease, as was observed in MENA and across the world with COVID-19 in 2020–21. The construction craze in GCC countries, for example, led to the proliferation of migrant workers housed in densely-packed dormitories. ESCWA tracking data showed that in the first few months of the 2020 pandemic, Saudi Arabia and Qatar had the largest numbers of COVID-19 cases in MENA, primarily affecting migrant workers.[29]

Nonetheless, governments continue to engage in urban prestige projects that seem to com-pete in size, scale, and cost. Dubai produced the world's tallest building, the Burj Khalifa. In October 2020, Algeria inaugurated the world's third largest mosque; a mega-mosque in Istanbul's Taksim Square opened in May 2021 on the anniversary of the 2013 Gezi Park protests. Turkey's other megaprojects—costly and controversial—include a new airport in Istanbul, one of the world's largest; a third bridge across the Bosphorus, due for completion in

2022; the Istanbul Canal, meant to reduce the volume of ships using the Bosphorus; and the Istanbul Tunnel Project, intended for both cars and metro to reduce Istanbul's notorious traffic jams. Several of the Turkish megaprojects are public–private partnerships, which have been criticized for cronyism.[30]

The demographic transition, which entails changes in health, mortality, and fertility, has driven population dynamics. The region's average infant mortality rate was as high as 200 per 1,000 live births in 1955; by 1990, it had fallen to about 50 per 1,000 live births. In 2000, it was down to 34—still higher than Latin America, the Caribbean, eastern Asia, Europe, and Central Asia, but lower than southern Asia and sub-Saharan Africa. For individual countries, the changes in infant, child, and maternal mortality occurred rapidly and dramatically. For example, in 1960 Tunisia had an infant mortality rate of 159, and its under-age-five child mortality rate was 255. In the 1980s, these declined to 58 and 83, respectively. By 2000, the rate of infant mortality had dropped to just 30, and in 2012, it was 14.[31] Iran similarly saw impressive achievements in the health of children as well as of mothers during the 1990s. Indeed, maternal mortality rates have dropped throughout the region; according to the 2016 *Human Development Report*, they were highest in Morocco and Yemen, with rates of 121 and 385 per 100,000 live births, respectively. Life expectancy varies; the regional average for Arab states (this does not include Israel, Iran, or Turkey) rose from fifty-two years in the early 1970s to nearly seventy-two in 2018. Most MENA countries had life expectancy rates of between seventy-two and seventy-seven years (Israel's was 82.8 years); lower rates were found in Iraq (70.5) and Yemen (sixty-six).[32]

MENA fertility rates began falling in the late 20th century, especially among young, educated women in urban areas. For the region as a whole, the total fertility rate (expected number of births per woman) dropped from 7 children per woman in the 1950s to 4.8 in 1990 and declined further to about 3.6 in 2001; in 2010, it was down to 2.8 children. Iran's total fertility rate declined during the 1970s but increased during the 1980s following the Iranian revolution. Iran's population growth rate of the 1980s is attributed to the pronatalist policies of the new Islamic regime, which banned contraceptives and encouraged marriage and family formation, but it may also be a result of rural fertility behavior, which was slow to decline during the 1970s. As late as 1988, the government reported 5.6 births per woman. With the reversal of the pronatalist policy following the results of the 1986 census and the introduction of an aggressive family planning campaign after 1988, fertility declined dramatically.[33] In the new century, the total fertility rate hovered at replacement level—between a reported 2.1 and 1.8 children per woman. (See Table 6.2 on fertility rates and marriage age.)

Jordan's demographic transition has followed a different pattern. Fertility rates declined through the 1990s but then stalled at around 3.7 births per woman—much higher than the replacement rate—for about a decade in the 2000s. In other words, for "women born between 1975 and 1995, the trends in age at first marriage and first birth were essentially flat." Since 2010, there has been a resumed decline, with 2.8 births per Jordanian woman in 2018. The median age at marriage has risen very slowly from 22 to 23 and median age at first birth from 24 to 25.[34]

The MENA fertility decline is attributed to women's educational attainment and the rising age at first marriage as well as government family planning programs. And yet in both Iran and Turkey, fertility decline has alarmed the authorities. In Turkey, President Erdoğan called on

TABLE 6.2 ■ Fertility Rates and Ages at Marriage in the Middle East and North Africa					
	Total Fertility Rate			Mean Age at Marriage (2002–2020)	
Country	1970–1975	1990–1995	2018	Male	Female
Algeria	7.4[a]	4.1	3.0	33.0	30
Bahrain	6.7	3.4	2.0	30.0	26
Egypt	5.4	3.9	3.3	—	22.7
Iran	6.4	4	2.1	26.8	23.5
Iraq	7.1	5.8	3.7	—	22.8
Israel	3.9	2.9	3.1	29.1	26.2
Jordan	7.6	5.1	2.8	—	24.7
Kuwait	6.7	3.2	2.1	28.5	27.5
Lebanon	4.6	3	2.1	32.3	28.3
Libya	6.8	4.1	2.2	33.9	31.2
Morocco	5.9[a]	3.7	2.4	31.2	26.4
Oman	9.3[c]	6.3	2.9	28.1	24.8
Qatar	4.5[d]	4.1	3.5	27.3	25.4
Saudi Arabia	6.5[d]	5.4	2.3	27.2	24.6
Syria	7.7	4.9	2.8	29.3	25.4
Tunisia	6.1	3.1	2.2	32.6	28.7
Turkey	5.7	2.9	2.1	—	24.2
United Arab Emirates	8.2[c]	3.9	1.4	26.8	25.3
West Bank and Gaza	7.5	6.5	3.6	—	—
Yemen	8.5[a]	7.7	3.8	25.4	22.2

Sources: Fertility rates: 1970–1975: "World Fertility Patterns 2007," UN Population Division, March 2008; 1990–1995, 2005–2014: *Human Development Report*, United Nations, various years, http://hdr.undp.org/en/statistics/data/. Mean age at marriage: "Statistical Indicators on Men and Women," United Nations, http://unstats.un.org/unsd/demographic/products/indwm/tab2b.htm

a. Data are from 1977.

b. Data are from 1997.

c. Data are from 1983.

d. Data are from 1985.

married women to have at least three children; in Iran, the authorities have terminated the family planning program. One concern is the old age dependency rate, which is expected to rise in Iran, Turkey, and several other MENA countries; currently, it is highest in Lebanon.[35]

Decades of high birth rates, nonetheless, have helped to keep the population of Middle Eastern countries young. According to the 2009 *Arab Human Development Report* (AHDR), some 35 percent of the region's population was younger than fifteen years of age, whereas only 4 percent was older than sixty-five; some 60 percent of the population of Arab states was below age twenty-five.[36] In Iran, in 2009 about 70 percent of the population was below age thirty-five. Iraq, the West Bank and Gaza, and Yemen retain high fertility and very young populations (median age in Gaza is 17.4 years, Yemen 19.8, and Iraq 20.2; compared to Tunisia's 32, Iran's 30.8, and Israel's 30.1), which correlates with poverty, poor schooling, conflicts, and patriarchal values. The existence of a large population of young people has economic and political implications. Young people tend to experience high rates of unemployment and may engage in social protest either for jobs, housing, and income or for cultural change and freedoms; young men also may constitute a recruiting base for Islamist movements or radical campaigns.[37] The MENA population is expected to swell to 576 million by 2025—more than double the current size. Given the aridity of much of the region, the growing numbers will place increasing demands on water and agricultural land; urban services, currently strained, will need to be vastly expanded and improved. Other challenges will be job creation and mechanisms for political inclusion.

The challenges are exacerbated by continued conflict and displacement, and the economic effects of the pandemic. The refugee camps of Jordan, Lebanon, and Turkey are home to some four million Syrians. According to 2018 figures, over six million Syrians suffer internal displacement (down from eight million in 2014), while just over six million Syrians are refugees.[38] Apart from the multifaceted humanitarian crisis of the internationalized civil conflict—along with internal displacement and refugee outflow—is the question of how depopulation has affected urban centers and city life in Syria and Iraq. Even cities that have been spared conflict and war face difficulties that have only worsened due to the economic and social effects of the pandemic. The effects include revenue losses and thus GDP declines; firm closures and job and income losses, especially for citizens in the private sector and in small and medium-sized enterprises; severe strains on the social infrastructure, especially hospitals; and education setbacks due to closures and lockdowns.

LABOR FORCE GROWTH, EMPLOYMENT CHALLENGES, AND INCOME INEQUALITIES

Labor force statistics in the region are not always reliable, and women's economic activity outside the formal and modern sector has tended to be underestimated. National and international data sets often present inconsistent figures for female labor force participation (FLFP). Data from both the International Labour Organization (ILO) and the World Bank show that for MENA, average FLFP is about 25 percent, compared to a world average of nearly 50 percent. The female share of the total nonagricultural salaried workforce is very small, at around 23 percent.[39] The higher rates of FLFP found in the GCC countries include the migrant female labor force. Even so, in the GCC as in other MENA countries, analysts have documented many legal barriers to women's employment.[40]

In most MENA countries, the measured female workforce is concentrated in the service sector, even though in some of the larger countries, a considerable proportion of the female, economically active population, remains rooted in agriculture. Among the GCC countries, there is greater involvement in agriculture in Oman and Saudi Arabia, but more on the part of men than of women; and other than Oman, the vast majority of the GCC female workforce (nationals) is found in public sector employment. Asian women workers perform service work considered culturally inappropriate for native women. Only in Morocco and Tunisia are large percentages of the female workforce involved in the industrial (manufacturing) sector, particularly in the garment industry.

Throughout the region, university-educated women have higher FLFP than do less-educated women. Married women have weak labor force attachment, and female unemployment rates are very high. Reasons include the contraction of public sector jobs, the absence of women-friendly work environments in the private sector, the fear of sexual harassment, employer responsibility for paid maternity leave, and the dearth of child care centers and preschool facilities.[41] These issues may also explain the low FLFP among women with secondary schooling or less. For women from working class or lower-middle-class households in particular, the private sector's instability, long hours, and lack of support structures for working mothers may constitute a disincentive to employment.[42]

In all countries, the male workforce is more evenly distributed across the sectors and more likely to be found in modern occupations. Salaried work remains a predominantly male domain in the region, but women have been moving into new occupations and professions that are in line with economic globalization trends: call centers (especially in Morocco); global banking and financial services; insurance agencies; consulting firms catering to foreign businesses; offices of international organizations, banks, and foundations; and high-end tourist shops.[43]

Despite these changes, however, unemployment in the region is high, as can be seen in Table 6.3, hovering around an average of 10 percent in 2015. Contributing factors include urban population growth, contraction of public sector jobs, and lack of formal-sector job growth in the private sector. Urban unemployment rates began increasing in the 1980s and reached highs of 10 percent–18 percent in Algeria, Tunisia, Egypt, Jordan, Iran, Turkey, and Yemen.[44] In the 1990s, female unemployment rates soared to highs of 25 percent, indicating a growing supply of job-seeking women in a situation of limited demand for them. World Bank and ILO figures for 2019 show very high youth unemployment rates (ages 15–24), with a regional average of 29.4 percent; the average for young women, however, was 45 percent. The highest unemployment rates for young women were found in Iraq, Saudi Arabia, West Bank and Gaza, and Libya (62.6 percent–68.4 percent), Algeria, Syria, Jordan, and Egypt (45.5 percent–53.3 percent), Yemen, Oman, Iran, and Tunisia (34.1 percent–38.2 percent). The figures reveal that what Moghadam termed in 1995 the "feminization of unemployment" remains a defining feature of the urban labor markets of the MENA region.[45]

TABLE 6.3 ■ Labor Force, Selected Countries in the Middle East and North Africa					
	Labor Force Participation Rate, Ages 15 and Older, 2015 (Percentage)			Unemployment Rate, 2015 (Percentage)		
Country	Total	Female	Male	Total	Female	Male
Algeria	41	15	67	11.2	16.7	10.0
Bahrain	72	44	87	1.2	3.8	0.5
Egypt	48	22	74	13	26.1	9.1
Iran	43	15	70	11	19.3	9.3
Iraq	47	18	75	7.7	13.2	6.4
Israel	64	59	70	5.3	5.4	5.1
Jordan	39	14	64	13.1	22.7	11.0
Kuwait	70	49	86	2.2	3.1	1.8
Lebanon	47	23	71	6.1	7.4	5.8
Libya	52	26	79	18.4	26.9	15.6
Morocco	49	25	74	9.7	10.4	9.4
Oman	70	30	87	15.8	32	13.3
Qatar	88	59	95	0.2	0.8	0.1
Saudi Arabia	56	22	79	5.6	21.7	2.4
Syria	42	12	71	14.6	39.3	10.4
Tunisia	47	25	71	15.2	21.5	13.0
Turkey	51	31	72	10.2	12.5	9.2
United Arab Emirates	81	42	93	2.1	5.5	1.6
West Bank and Gaza	45	19	71	25.9	39.0	22.5
Yemen	38	6	69	13.1	25.6	12.0

Source: World Development Indicators, World Bank.

The low FLFP rates in MENA (along with the low average rate of female parliamentary representation) are largely what bring down the MENA region in global rankings of gender equality/inequality. A recent study of "gender regime clusters" in the Global South showed that the MENA region ranked within the highest clusters because of good indicators on women's educational attainment and health, but in the lowest clusters because of poor indicators on women's employment and on parliamentary representation.[46]

The closure of schools, businesses, and other enterprises due to the COVID-19 pandemic increased unemployment rates. Workers in the informal sector and in small- and medium-sized businesses (SMEs) were hit the hardest. A June 2020 OECD report cited a Tunisian official that women's informal labor in agriculture and as domestic workers made them especially vulnerable to job losses and that "most women-led SMEs are closed because of the crisis."[47] Egypt's unemployment rate rose to a near two-year high, with women's unemployment rate, at 16.2 percent, nearly double that of men's.[48] Arab Barometer data found more job loss by women than men in the five countries surveyed. Another study found that by November 2020, total unemployment rates in Morocco were 30 percent, in Tunisia 22 percent, and in Egypt 9 percent. However, they were much worse for women: 52 percent in Morocco, 41 percent in Tunisia, and 16 percent in Egypt.[49] Such high rates are disproportionate to the (low) FLFP rates and represent a reversal of women's gains in economic participation and empowerment.

Poverty and Inequality

There has been considerable improvement over time in standards of living in the MENA region—as measured by life expectancy, infant mortality, maternal mortality, age at first marriage, fertility rates, literacy, and school enrollments, along with access to safe water, adequate sanitation facilities, and social protection. The UNDP's *Human Development Report 2016* showed the region progressing over time from the lower to the upper end of "medium human development," though below East Asia and the Pacific and especially Latin America and the Caribbean. Most of the MENA countries are classified as "high human development" in the datasets. Conflict, however, has adversely affected ranking. As noted at the outset of this chapter, conflicts in Iraq, Libya, Palestine, Syria, and Yemen have been destructive of physical infrastructure, labor markets, public services, human capital, and of course lives. The sanctions regime imposed on Iran and enforced by the United States has distorted prices and labor markets, exacerbating unemployment, inflation, and poverty. Syria and Libya dropped from *medium* human development in 2014 to *low* in the 2018 ranking, now joining Yemen, according to the 2018 edition on indices and indicators.[50] It will take those countries decades to move up the human development ladder, and this regression in human development ranking vividly confirms that conflict and war can undo years and decades of modernization. Conflict and war also create *new poor* categories or exacerbate existing poverty. At the same time, the presence of poverty even in an ostensibly *very high* human development country such as Saudi Arabia may be regarded as a puzzle to be explored. (As the *Human Development Report 2016* notes and numerous social science studies demonstrate, poverty is also a developed country problem, typically associated with insufficient redistributive policies or corrupt governance.)

According to the World Bank and United Nations Economic and Social Commission for West Asia (ESCWA), the number of poor people in MENA increased from an estimated sixty million in 1985 to seventy-three million in 1990, or from 30.6 percent to 33.1 percent of the total population. Poverty assessments prepared by the World Bank, which were derived from surveys of living standards undertaken in the 1990s, revealed growing poverty in Egypt and

Jordan and the emergence of an urban "working poor" in Tunisia and Morocco. Poverty was largely rural in Egypt and Jordan. The rural poor were small landholders and tenants, landless agricultural workers, and pastoralists, but the urban poor in Egypt included the unemployed and female-headed households. In Lebanon, the main factors behind the increase in the incidence of poverty and rising inequalities was the civil war of the 1980s and the misguided economic policies of the 1990s, including tax write-offs for large firms engaged in the country's reconstruction and the absence of any property taxes. The ESCWA report singled out the absence of government social spending and "unjust wealth distribution" as the factors behind the rise in nutritional deficiencies, lack of sanitation in poor areas, and lowering of teaching and health standards.[51]

In the case of Iraq, war and economic sanctions worsened the situation of the poor and created new poverty-stricken groups. The destruction of Iraq's infrastructure by US-led bombings in January 1991 and again in March and April 2003, the shortage of medical supplies and foodstuffs caused by the longstanding sanctions regime, and the collapse of public services following the 2003 invasion served to transform a country that was once urbanized, mechanized, and prosperous. By 2012, Iraq's poverty headcount (the percentage of the population living under the national poverty line) was 20 percent–23 percent. Yemen had the largest number of poor as a proportion of its overall population: In 2005, 35 percent lived below the poverty line, and nearly half lived on less than two US dollars per day. The situation has deteriorated even further since the 2015 Saudi-UAE assault, which all but destroyed the country's infrastructure and generated widespread cholera.

As seen in Table 6.4, poverty is most severe in Yemen. Government responses vary, but in Iran, poverty reduction steps include an unconditional and universal cash transfer, introduced in December 2010 when Iran ended its energy and bread subsidies. Monthly, each citizen receives the equivalent of $40, and some 95 percent of households are covered. As a result, the proportion of individuals living in poverty declined from 22.5 percent to 10.6 percent although inflation has been lowering the real value of the transfer.[52] In all countries—because of gender differences in employment and income, and for older women, lower literacy and educational attainment—women are especially vulnerable to poverty during periods of economic difficulty or in the event of divorce, abandonment, or widowhood.[53] Conflicts in the region have exacerbated women's vulnerability. Indeed, a joint ESCWA-UN Habitat report found the following:

> Although most Arab countries reduced extreme poverty during the timeframe of the Millennium Development Goals (MDGs), conflict, and wide-scale displacement to urban areas have contributed to increased relative poverty or absolute poverty since 2010.... [T]he average poverty incidence in the Arab region, based on national poverty lines, rose from 22.7 percent in 1990 to 23.4 percent in 2012.[54]

The same may be said of achieving the current Sustainable Development Goals, given the persistence of conflict as well as the effects of the pandemic.

Economic theory holds that income inequality widens at early stages of economic development and levels off at later stages, when poverty also falls.[55] Neoliberal capitalist globalization has generated rising income inequality even in once relatively egalitarian Western societies. (In

TABLE 6.4 ■ Poverty and Inequality in the Middle East and North Africa				
Country	Population Living Below the National Poverty Line (%, 2007–2018)	Income Share Held by Poorest 40 Percent of Population (%, 2010–2017)	Population Living on Less Than US$1.9 per Day (%, 2007–2017)	Gini Index (2010–2017)
Algeria	5.5	23.1	0.5	27.6
Egypt	27.8	21.9	1.3	31.8
Iraq	18.9	21.9	2.5	29.5
Iran	—	16.6	--	40.0
Israel	—	15.7	--	39.0
Jordan	14.4	20.3	0.1	33.7
Lebanon	--	20.6	--	31.8
Morocco	4.8	17.4	1.0	39.5
Palestine, state of	29.2	--	1.0	33.7
Syria	35.2	—		--
Tunisia	15.2	20.1	0.3	32.8
Turkey	14.4	15.6	0.4	41.9
Yemen	54.4	18.8	18.8	36.7

Notes: Gini: data for the GCC states and Libya.

—: Data not available.

By way of comparison, Gini coefficient is 41.5 in the United States, 46.6 in Chile, 53.3 in Brazil.

Source: Data for percentage of population living below the national poverty line: Human Development Report 2016, United Nations Development Report, Table 6 and World Bank DataBank (for Turkey only); data for percentage of population living on less than two US dollars per day: Human Development Report, United Nations Development Programme, various years, http://hdr.undp.org/en/statistics/data/; all other data from "Key Development Data and Statistics," World Bank, 2000–2006. Note: Data for Algeria, Bahrain, Kuwait, Lebanon, Libya, Oman, Qatar, Saudi Arabi, United Arab Emirates, the West Bank, and Gaza are not available.

Western capitalist states, especially the United States, wealth and income inequality widened during the pandemic.) In MENA, some studies have found moderate and even declining levels of income inequality along with widespread societal perceptions of rising inequality; such studies distinguish between income inequality, wealth inequality, inequality of opportunity, and so on. Some experts dispute this and provide evidence to show that income and wealth inequality are much wider in MENA than is assumed in much of the literature (though not by citizens, who report perceptions of much greater income and wealth inequality).[56] As seen in Table 6.4, income shares held by the poorest 40 percent are low in Iran, Israel, Morocco, and Turkey; these also are the countries with the widest income inequality, as measured by the Gini coefficient. Algeria appears to be the least unequal.

In the large and diversified economies—especially Turkey and Iran but also including Morocco and Tunisia—income inequalities allow those from the upper-middle classes to enjoy very comfortable lives while the lower-income groups struggle. In their 2018 study of four countries, including Egypt, Jordan, and Tunisia, Vladimir Hlasny and Shireen Al-Azzawi found "significant wealth gaps, especially across urban-rural and educated-uneducated divides and between demographic groups," as well as "increasing polarisation of wealth ownership in Egypt, with the poorest 5 percent of households experiencing declining wealth." Studies of the distribution of income and consumption expenditures that find modest degrees of inequality in the MENA region, the authors argue, overlook households' stock of productive and non-productive assets, which increase living standards and economic inequality across households and are related to their present and future earnings. Other scholars confirm that Arab countries are caught in an inequality trap, calling on governments to adopt more effective taxation, including a progressive inheritance tax regime. UN ESCWA—having identified wealth and income assets across the region—advocates a solidarity wealth tax for the benefit of the middle-income countries.[57]

High military expenditures have impeded progress in human development and redistributive policies. US allies in MENA invest in defense at levels that are very high by global standards. In 2005 through 2006, Israel, Saudi Arabia, Qatar, Iraq, Jordan, Oman, and Yemen topped a global ranking of countries by percentage of gross domestic product (GDP) allocated to military expenditures.[58] World Bank figures for 2015 show that at 7.7 percent of GDP, the MENA region had the highest military expenditures of all world regions; the figures ranged from a low of 2.3 percent of GDP in Iran to a whopping 13 percent–14 percent of GDP in Oman and Saudi Arabia.[59] Negative effects of high military spending are evident in countries with weak economies and involvement in conflicts; Yemen's high military spending throughout the period of 2000–2010 is a vivid example of misallocated resources when one considers its levels of poverty, maternal mortality, and adolescent fertility. As Paul Collier has shown, war prevents or sets back development; as Gregory Hooks argues, wars impede the formation of developmental states (defined in Amartya Sen's terms as welfarist states pursuing human capabilities). Others have shown a positive relationship between income inequality and share of military expenditures in the central government budget.[60] In general, high military expenditure crowds out social spending and seems to encourage war-making.

ADVANCES IN EDUCATION

Education has served a central role in the development of modern states globally, and world society theorists have highlighted the role of education in both reinforcing and contributing to world culture.[61] Education is now widely considered a basic right, the provision of which has become essential for both state legitimacy and economic growth. It also plays a key role in nation-building efforts, providing a vehicle for cohering shared collective memory and identity. In the Levant and North Africa, the expansion of education was a cornerstone of state-building efforts during the postindependence period; in the Gulf monarchies, education developed alongside rising oil wealth.[62] In Iran, investments in universities and public schools as well as the growth of an array of private and international schools constituted an essential feature of the state's modernization drive from the 1950s to the 1970s. During the era of state-building and modernization, the university system was a key institution to produce public sector employees, including the country's needed teachers, university professors, health workers, and public administrators. (In many cases, the children of the elites attended university in Europe, but many also gravitated toward the American University of Beirut.) Unemployment was almost unheard of for university graduates, who constituted the growing middle class and professional-managerial cadre.

Education systems, along with the knowledge and methods of learning that they impart, are shaped by sociopolitical and cultural contexts and may be sites of contestation over ideological and political interests, national identity, religiosity, and political authority. As Monica Ringer notes, education's presumed neutrality hides a "competition for hegemony amongst political, social, historical, cultural, and religious actors." School curricula can be used to shape collective memory, assert a hegemonic interpretation of historical events, or obscure the contributions and experiences of some actors. Educational institutions also may reinforce inequalities of class, gender, religion, or ethnicity. In a study of Jordan's education system, Betty Anderson examines the content of textbooks over time, tracing the development of national identity. This national identity, she argues, was supported through particular interpretations of regional history and politics. Bradley Cook argues that Egyptian educational institutions are dominated by an elite minority who enforce their preference for secular education, whereas a majority of Egyptians express a preference for a greater role for Islam in public education.[63] In Saudi Arabia, where sex segregation in education remains the norm, girls' education, until 2002, was overseen by religious authorities rather than the Ministry of Education.[64] Average time devoted to religious studies in MENA is more than twice the 5 percent average for OECD countries.[65] These examples highlight the ways in which education is molded by particular interests and the ways that diverse agendas have shaped educational institutions, pedagogy, and curriculum across countries.

In standardized measures such as literacy, enrollment ratios, and mean years of schooling, MENA educational levels have risen significantly during the past six decades, especially after compulsory schooling was instituted. Women's enrollments and completion have been impressive and correlate with higher rates of female labor force participation. Years of schooling have increased from a very low base. In the mid-20th century, literacy rates ranged from 30 percent to 62 percent, and women's literacy rates were at roughly half those of men. According to data from UNESCO's Institute for Statistics and the World Bank's *World Development Indicators*, by 2009, overall literacy rates had almost doubled, reaching between 56 percent and 95 percent. Literacy tends to spread more rapidly in urban areas; with their significant rural populations, Morocco, Yemen, and Egypt had the lowest adult literacy rates in MENA, at 56 percent, 62 percent, and 66 percent, respectively.[66] Adult women's literacy levels still lag behind those of men in nearly all MENA states.

In 1970, primary school enrollments were very low in Oman, Morocco, and Saudi Arabia; there and elsewhere, the gender gaps were very wide. Today, enrollments are nearly universal across the region, with a reported 94 percent completion rate in 2015, according to the UNESCO database. Mean years of schooling vary across the region but for some countries have risen dramatically, though they might fall behind the expected years of schooling. In 1960, the average number of years of schooling among individuals over age fifteen in MENA ranged from 0.61 in Tunisia to a high of 2.9 in Kuwait. By 2000, the average had risen to a regional mean of 5.4 years. Yemen had the lowest reported years of schooling at 2.9, whereas Kuwait and Jordan had the highest at 7.1 and 6.9, respectively. By 2018, mean years of schooling were highest in Israel (13 years), but at 10 and 11 in the UAE, Oman, Iran, and Jordan, they were on a par with Argentina, Chile, Italy, and Belgium.[67] Much of this growth has been driven by increases in secondary school enrollment.

Secondary school enrollment ratios across the region increased from an average of 22 percent in 1970 to about 71 percent in 2018, according to World Bank and UNESCO data. As seen in Figure 6.1, secondary school enrollments are high in most countries, with women's enrollments exceeding men's in Algeria, Bahrain, Israel, Jordan, Kuwait, Libya, Tunisia, and Palestine. The lowest enrollment rates (60 percent or below) are in Iraq, Lebanon, Syria, and Yemen, with the greatest gender gaps favoring men in Iraq and Yemen.

In 1970, tertiary enrollment was below 10 percent in most of the region and at its highest at 21 percent in Lebanon, but it has expanded since then. Between 2005 and 2010,

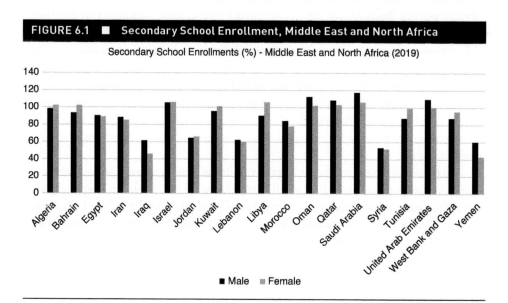

FIGURE 6.1 ■ Secondary School Enrollment, Middle East and North Africa

Secondary School Enrollments (%) - Middle East and North Africa (2019)

■ Male ■ Female

Sources: World Bank, School enrollment, secondary (% net) - Middle East & North Africa | Data (worldbank.org) (male), School enrollment, secondary, female (% gross) - Middle East & North Africa | Data (worldbank.org) (female); School enrollment, tertiary, male (% gross) - Middle East & North Africa | Data (worldbank.org) (male), School enrollment, tertiary, female (% gross) - Middle East & North Africa | Data (worldbank.org).

Israel had the highest tertiary enrollment rate of any MENA state at 58 percent, followed by Libya and Turkey with enrollment rates of 56 percent; the lowest percentage was found in Yemen at 11 percent. By 2016, Qatari women were enrolled in university at a far higher rate than men, reaching a gross enrollment ratio of 47 percent, compared to just 6 percent for men; this is a gap that has only grown (see Figure 6.2). Tunisia has had female tertiary enrollments of over 40 percent since 2008, considerably higher than men's. In Iran, women's tertiary enrollments began to exceed those of men in 2001 and rose to 67 percent in 2015, but by then, men's enrollment rates also had increased considerably.[68] In contrast, Egypt, Lebanon, and especially Iraq and Yemen perform poorly on tertiary enrollments.

Improvements in regional education levels have not been reflected in economic indicators, such as higher macrolevel productivity or GDP per capita or employability of graduates. MENA states as a whole lag behind East Asia and Latin America in metrics such as average years of schooling and test scores. The fifteen participating MENA states fared below international averages on the international standardized *Trends in International Mathematics and Sciences Study* in 2007 and more recently. Lueders and Lust find that education outcomes in the GCC rentier states fall below those of other states at similar levels of development because of guaranteed jobs in the public sector, a major employer of nationals.[69]

Resources allotted to education have been frequently mismanaged and increasingly stretched. Examining the so-called education-employment mismatch, analysts have argued that rote learning and the absence of independent studies, development of critical thinking, internships and cooperative education programs, or collaborations with universities around the world have left students poorly prepared for either the "knowledge economy" or market needs. The privatization of schooling seems not to have improved quality.

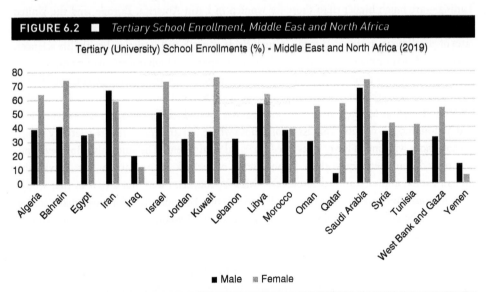

FIGURE 6.2 ■ *Tertiary School Enrollment, Middle East and North Africa*

Tertiary (University) School Enrollments (%) - Middle East and North Africa (2019)

■ Male ■ Female

Sources: World Bank, School enrollment, secondary (% net) - Middle East & North Africa | Data (worldbank.org) (male), School enrollment, secondary, female (% gross) - Middle East & North Africa | Data (worldbank.org) (female); School enrollment, tertiary, male (% gross) - Middle East & North Africa | Data (worldbank.org) (male), School enrollment, tertiary, female (% gross) - Middle East & North Africa | Data (worldbank.org).

Parallel to state-funded universities are private universities in Egypt, Lebanon, Jordan, Morocco, and Turkey. The quality varies considerably, as does the relative autonomy of private institutions from state interference. The expansion of Gulf universities has been accompanied by the increasing adoption of US models, a function of globalization and internationalization trends in higher education, as well as a function of Gulf states' military and economic alliances with the United States. (Still, Lueders and Lust find that citizen students in those Gulf universities perform less well in math and sciences than do the foreign students enrolled there.) The expansion of private education, thus, should not necessarily be viewed as expansion of opportunities for quality education. Indeed, Egyptian sociologist Ghada Barsoum shows that the proliferation of private learning institutions in Egypt is regarded by many young people as an "easy route" that presumably leads to a government job. The objective, she argues, is credential-seeking for status and jobs in a neoliberal era, and she concludes that "easy education in private universities is a waste of the precious resources of lower-achieving students and their families." Writing about Tunisia, Mongi Boughzala and colleagues similarly note that the emergence of private higher education institutions has not improved the quality of educational outcomes. Hicham Araoui and Robert Springborg note that education in the Arab world is deregionalizing, as proportionately ever fewer Arabs have educational experiences in other Arab countries; they also highlight the deficits of many of the new private institutions.[70]

In Iran, by contrast, the sole privately run institution of higher education is Azad University. The most highly regarded and competitive university remains the state-funded University of Tehran; graduates of engineering and related technical fields of Tehran and Sharif universities populate PhD programs in the United States.

MENA women's enrollments in the sciences—for example, in Morocco, Oman, and Tunisia—are much higher than those for women in Latin America, Europe, and the United States, according to a UN report. Tunisian women graduate students, for example, have high rates of enrollments and exceed men's in such fields as math and statistics, health, life sciences, physics, and environmental protection.[71] Still, they experience high unemployment rates.

In many MENA countries, the high rates of unemployment among college-educated youth, and especially educated young women, suggest the presence of a demand-side problem of labor absorption. A study for the World Bank showed that "overeducation" is common in diverse low- and middle-income country contexts, both those where tertiary graduates are relatively plentiful and those with much lower rates of educational attainment. The study also finds evidence that overeducated tertiary workers do not use all of their skills, potentially wasting valuable human capital and educational resources.[72] MENA countries were not a part of that study's cross-national comparisons, but the overall findings may be applicable. Although many studies emphasize the education-employment mismatch, university-educated young people who are unemployed, underemployed, or moving from one temporary gig to another represent a waste of human capital.

The personal and social returns of education to women cannot be overemphasized, even when accounting for the unemployment rates. Female circumcision remains widely practiced in Egypt, though not in families with college-educated mothers. Iranian sociologist Golnar Mehran points out that following the Iranian revolution, sex segregation became compulsory, textbooks were revised to reflect traditional ideas about gender, and female students were increasingly directed into specializations deemed gender appropriate. Schools were intended as vehicles for the creation of the "New Muslim Woman," and women's enrollment and completion rates grew. But education provided a platform for women's increased political awareness, civic activism, and changing aspirations.[73] Women's equal or even greater educational attainment across the region does not indicate the achievement of gender equality, but it does signal a growing pool of educated women who are likely to challenge their second-class citizenship in the family and in the society at large, as occurred in autumn 2022 across Iran.

One by-product of the spread of education, closely tied to globalization's technological advances, has been growing access to and use of the Internet—and not only for educational purposes. In the 1990s, mobile phones and satellite TV spread throughout the region, while the new century saw the expansion first of Internet cafés and then the new social networking sites. Young people in particular began making extensive use of them for purposes of personal self-expression (e.g., blogs), connections with friends and family, and knowledge of events elsewhere in the region and around the world. Eventually, the Internet facilitated engagement with the public sphere, "virtual activism," and—especially in connection with the Iranian Green Protests and then the Arab Spring—political mobilization, recruitment, and coordination of protest activity. On the eve of the Arab Spring outbreak, use of social media was most common among young men in the region. In 2011, male Facebook users outnumbered female users by a margin of 2:1 and greater in most MENA countries. But that changed, with widespread use of Facebook by women not only for connections with family and friends but also for discussion of social and political issues, as has become common in Tunisia. Mobile phone usage surged; in 2019, subscriptions per 100 people exceeded 100 almost everywhere but Iraq, Jordan, Lebanon, Libya, Turkey, and Yemen. The Internet penetration rate for the Middle East, at 75 percent in 2021, was higher than the global rate of 65.6 percent; however, the rates in Egypt, Iraq, Palestine, Syria, and Yemen were lower than the world average.[74] During the pandemic's enforced school closures, the Internet became increasingly important as an educational tool, although not every household had sufficient access.

In summary, advances in educational attainment and their societal impacts have been impressive, but more attention should be directed to ensuring broader access to quality learning and to adequate educational facilities and tools. The region has experienced declining educational quality, increasingly stretched resources, and concerns about the relevance of available education for gainful employment, national growth, development, and international competitiveness. For the children of lower-income families, in particular, the 2020 pandemic-related school closures likely worsened learning outcomes.

THE FAMILY, FAMILY LAW, AND SEXUALITY

Modernization and its entailments—urbanization, schooling, the opening up of public spaces to women, links with world society—have affected the traditional family and prescribed gender roles. Whereas family structures in the MENA region once was described as extended, patrilineal, patrilocal, patriarchal, endogamous, and occasionally polygynous, there have been dramatic changes in the structure of the family and the role of women within it. The nuclear family now predominates. In urbanized countries of the region, and apart from Saudi Arabia and other Gulf monarchies, polygyny has become a statistically insignificant family form. Only Turkey and Tunisia have banned polygyny outright, but monogamy is the norm in the region, and the 2004 reform of family law in Morocco made it very difficult for a man to obtain a second wife.

As noted, early marriage is becoming rare as educational attainment rates increase and young women and men interact with each other in universities, workplaces, and other public spaces. Before 1970, women in the region commonly married in their teens and early twenties. Today, the average age of marriage for women in the region has shifted to the mid-twenties, and the average age for men is three to five years higher. As marriage patterns are influenced by urbanization, urban youth marry later in all countries.

There are some exceptions to the general pattern of rising age at first marriage and lowered fertility. Teenage marriage continues in the poorest countries, the rural areas, and among the most conservative households. A 2005 study found that more than 15 percent of women married before age 20 in Yemen, Oman, parts of Egypt, and Gaza. More recent studies show higher rates for Yemen (32 percent) and Egypt (17.4 percent).[75] Early marriages have been reported among the Syrian refugee populations in Jordan and Lebanon. Whereas just under one in ten Jordanian girls married before age 18, the rate for Syrian refugee girls was about two in ten.[76] In 2015, according to the World Bank, the adolescent fertility rate (births per 1,000 women aged 15–19) was just 7 in Tunisia and 10 in Algeria (and 28.4 in Turkey) but as high as 51 in Egypt, 58 in the West Bank and Gaza, 61 in Yemen, and an astonishing 85 in Iraq. To put these figures in a comparative perspective, most advanced industrialized countries, along with China and South Korea, have single-digit figures for adolescent fertility; alone among the rich industrialized countries, the US rate in 2015 was 23 (it declined to 17.3 in 2019). The numbers were—and remain—much higher in Latin America, the Caribeean, and especially in sub-Saharan Africa.[77]

The rising marriage age is associated with positive outcomes such as higher educational attainment and decreasing birthrates, but it may also signal the impact of economic constraints on desired family formation. Weak regional labor markets are forcing increasing numbers of women and men in the region to delay marriage or remain unmarried.[78] In some cases, young men postpone marriage because they face job insecurity or lack a diploma to guarantee access to desired jobs. Women, faced with the pragmatic necessity to count on themselves instead of relying on a rich husband, further their formal education.

In Iran, the legal age of marriage for girls was lowered to puberty after the revolution; at the turn of the 21st century, after many parliamentary debates, it was finally increased to thirteen, but the mean age at first marriage for women is now twenty-four.[79] The surge in unmarried young people and the fear of illicit sex led some clerical and lay authorities to encourage "temporary marriage" (*muta'a* in Arabic, *sigheh* in Persian), which is a contractual arrangement for licit sexual relations under Shi'i interpretation of shari'a law. Temporary marriage is, however, highly unpopular in middle-class society, which associates it with legalized prostitution. Instead, as Iranian American anthropologist Pardis Mahdavi has explained, young people rebel through unorthodox modes of dress and hairstyles and by holding parties, dancing, drinking alcohol, and "kissing our boyfriends in the park." As such, young people are comporting their resistance and in ways that suggest a kind of sexual or generational revolution, according to Mahdavi. Mixed groups of young Iranians go on camping trips that also allow them both to interact with the opposite sex and enjoy nature.[80] In Tunisia, likewise, in the 1990s only 3 percent of young women ages fifteen to nineteen had been "ever married"; subsequently, the average age at first marriage rose dramatically, reaching twenty-nine years for women in 2004. According to one feminist organization, the Association Tunisienne des Femmes Démocrates, social realities required that the issue of sexual rights be addressed.[81] Indeed, a conference on the subject of sexual and reproductive rights, organized by the Femmes Démocrates and the Turkey-based feminist group Women for Women's Human Rights–New Ways, took place in Tunis in November 2006, providing early evidence, among other things, of the growing assertiveness of the women's rights movement.

The late Moroccan sociologist Fatima Mernissi famously argued that the idea of a young, unmarried woman was completely novel in the Muslim world, for the concept of patriarchal honor is built around the idea of virginity, which reduces a woman's role to its sexual dimension: reproduction within an early marriage.[82] The notion of a menstruating and unmarried woman is so alien to the Muslim family system, Mernissi added, that it is either unimaginable or necessarily linked with *fitna*—moral and social disorder. The unimaginable is now a reality.

Such social changes are significant, but they are not embraced by all segments of a society. Conservative forces in the state apparatus and in civil society contest changes to traditional norms, institutions, and relationships. Thus, the family remains a potent cultural trope, with conservative discourses frequently tying women's family roles to cultural, religious, and societal cohesion. Although changes in sexual behavior have been observed among the young in Tehran, Istanbul, and Tunis, virginity remains an important cultural asset, and hymenoplasty may be performed prior to marriage.[83] In small towns and rural settings, family honor depends in great measure on the virginity and good conduct of the women in the family. The control of the sexual behavior of women and girls remains a preoccupation and a patriarchal legacy.

Options exist for married women and some young women. In Tunisia, medical abortion is legal and has been performed in hospitals since 1973. Muslim religious leaders in a number of MENA countries have issued *fatwa*, declaring that abortion is permitted under certain circumstances, such as fetal anomaly, rape, and if the pregnancy poses a threat to the mother's life and health.[84]

Sylvia Walby distinguishes between the "private patriarchy" of the premodern family and social order and the "public patriarchy" of the state and the labor market in industrial societies. In his work on South Korea, John Lie has identified agrarian patriarchy and patriarchal capitalism. Others have used the term *patriarchy* more strictly so that patriarchal society is cast as a precapitalist social formation that historically has existed in varying forms in Europe and Asia, with a particular kinship structure that favors endogamy.[85] In the patrilocally extended household—which is typical of the peasantry in agrarian societies—property, residence, and descent proceed through the male line (patrilineality), and endogamy is the preferred reproductive strategy, maintained typically through cousin marriage, along with polygyny. The senior man has authority over everyone else in the family, including younger men, and women are subject to control and subordination. Childbearing is the central female labor activity.

"Classic patriarchy" or "private patriarchy" has been dissolving under the weight of modernization and development, but we continue to see the patriarchal legacy in both the public sphere of states and markets and private sphere of the family. Political power remains firmly in masculine hands, and labor markets and businesses are dominated by men. The patriarchal legacy is seen in practices such as adolescent marriage of girls, son preference, compulsory veiling, cousin marriage, sexual control of females, and honor killings. It is also inscribed in family laws that increasingly are regarded as anachronistic by much of the female population and activist generation.

Feminist critiques of Muslim family law have focused on the civil and political aspects of women's forgone human rights and second-class citizenship.[86] The Iranian winner of the 2003 Nobel Peace Prize, Shirin Ebadi—who is a veteran lawyer and served as a judge prior to the Islamic revolution—has pointed out the injustice and absurdity of a legal system whereby her testimony in court would count only if supplemented by that of one other woman, whereas the testimony of a man, even if illiterate, would stand alone. But—as noted earlier in this chapter—family law also has implications for women's socioeconomic participation and rights and may have been a contributing factor to the low female economic activity found across the region.[87]

Muslim family law is predicated on the principle of patrilineality, which confers privileges and authority to male kin, as well as the responsibility to maintain their wives and children. Brothers inherit more than sisters do, and a deceased man's brothers or uncles have a greater claim on his property than does his widow. The groom offers a *mahr* (dower) to the prospective bride and must provide for her; in turn, he expects obedience. Provisions regarding obedience, maintenance, and inheritance presume that wives are economic dependents, thus perpetuating the patriarchal gender contract. In many MENA countries, the concept of *wilaya*, or male guardianship, means that women are required to obtain the permission of father, husband, or other male guardian to undertake travel, including business travel. In Iran and Jordan, a husband has the legal right to forbid his wife (or unmarried daughter) to seek employment or continue in a job. Although wives—at least those who are educated and politically aware—may stipulate in their marriage contracts the condition that they be allowed to work, many wives make no such stipulations, and courts have been known to side with the husband when the issue is contested.[88] In some countries, certain occupations and professions, notably that of judge, are off-limits to women. Muslim family law also affects other policies, such as the inability of wives married to nonnationals to obtain legal citizenship for their children, let alone their husbands, although the Maghreb has seen progress.[89]

Muslim family law is at odds with long-standing discourses about the need to integrate women in development. It also contravenes the equality provisions of constitutions and those articles in the labor laws that describe an array of rights and benefits to women workers. For example, while social security policies make the widow the beneficiary of a deceased employee, in Muslim family law the paternal line has the main claim to a deceased male's wealth. Egypt's policymakers defer to shari'a law; thus, inherited pensions are divided according to Islamic law, with a widow receiving no more than one-quarter or one-eighth of the pension if there are children.

Muslim family law may be seen not only as a premodern or prefeminist code for the regulation of family relations but also as a way of retaining family support systems in the absence of a fully functioning welfare state predicated on concepts of citizen contributions and entitlements. The welfare of wives and children remains the responsibility of the father or the husband. When a woman seeks a divorce or is divorced, her maintenance comes not in the form of any transfers from the state and even less in the form of employment-generating or affirmative-action policies; it comes instead in the form of the *mahr* that is owed to her by her husband, and any assets that she may have brought into the marriage.

Algeria's first codified family law of 1984 became the subject of much feminist contestation, with family law reform remaining the focus of the women's rights movement ever since. The timing of the 2005 amendments may have been influenced by Morocco's 2004 family law reform, but they were seen as insufficient. Algerian women's organizations continue to protest Article 11, stipulating that the woman conclude her marriage contract in the presence of her *wali*, or guardian, as witness. The practice of guardianship places Algerian women in a subordinate role in the family—despite the fact that fully one-third of judges and members of parliament are women. (At a May 2003 meeting in Helsinki, Finland, attended by the present author, Algeria's then minister of women's affairs publicly commented on the absurdity of this requirement.) However, in 2019, only 19 percent of Algeria's total labor force was female.

Social changes have rendered Muslim family law an outdated institution and social policy. The growth of a population of educated and employed women with aspirations to full social participation and equal rights of citizenship has led to dynamic women's movements and campaigns for repeal of discriminatory laws—specifically for reform of family laws. One such campaign was spearheaded by the Collectif 95 Maghreb-Egalité. In a 2003 book that was subsequently translated into English, the authors point out that among the many reasons why Muslim family law is in need of reform is its divergence from the social realities and actual family dynamics of many countries, where women must seek work to augment the family budget and where women are increasingly looking after their elderly parents.[90] In Morocco, a decade-long campaign by women's rights activists and a political opening in 1998 led to the reform of the highly patriarchal Mudawana in 2004.[91] In Iran, the One Million Signatures Campaign was launched in 2007, though almost immediately it faced state repression. A meeting in Kuala Lumpur in February 2009 brought together "Islamic feminists" to form a transnational network called Musawah and craft a set of arguments that would bolster their case for reform. Advocacy includes the adoption of equal inheritance for male and female kin.

In the wake of the Arab Spring, there were fears that newly empowered Islamists would seek to undo the gains made by women's rights advocates and their allies, including abrogation of family law reforms. Egypt's salafists, for example, called for the repeal of women's rights to divorce, lowering the age of marriage from eighteen to fourteen, decriminalizing female circumcision, and the enforcement of shari'a law. In Libya, among the first statements issued by the Western-supported head of the National Transitional Council was that polygamy would be restored. In Tunisia, Islamist women began appearing openly in *niqab*, but feminists mobilized to thwart any attempted changes to their legal status. *"Ne touche pas à mes acquis"* was a prominent slogan chanted and inscribed on placards held by Tunisian women of diverse generations during the postrevolutionary transitional period.

Morocco's much-lauded family law reform of 2004 and the 2011 constitutional amendments have improved women's legal status, but Moroccan scholar Fatima Sadiqi reports that women's economic empowerment has not improved, especially for working-class, poor, and rural women, along with female-headed households. Social norms, she notes, appear to "constitute the biggest hurdle in the implementation of the Moudawana" (Morocco's family law). Although some changes were made to the inheritance law, rural women often give up their already unequal share to male relatives.[92] In the countryside, she adds, women still face difficulty in securing loans because they often do not have bank accounts or assets in their names. On the positive side, Morocco recently appointed women to the profession of *adoul*—marriage officers under Muslim law, authorized to write legal acts, such as for marriage or inheritance. Some eight hundred new *adouls* of both sexes were recruited in October 2018.

DYNAMICS OF SOCIAL CHANGE: SHIFTS IN THE GENDER REGIME?

Changes to women's legal status and social positions depend in part on the dynamics of global civil society, social movements, and advocacy networks, as well as on broader regional and international processes. Citizens come together in voluntary associations, professional organizations, and all manner of NGOs, social movements, and INGOs—some of which may be at philosophical and political odds with each other—to struggle with each other and the state over the distribution of power and resources (see also Chapter 5). How these competing interests and conflicts are resolved depends on the nature of the state, the balance of social power, the strength of democratic institutions, and the types of links to world society; in turn, the resolutions reshape the political and social actors and institutions. As a closer examination of the women's movement shows, the result is a dynamic process, altering both social conditions and the broader institutional arenas within which new struggles take place.

For the most part, political power remains firmly ensconced in male hands. Yemen's Tawakul Karman may have won the 2011 Nobel Peace Prize (sharing it with Ellen Johnson-Sirleaf, president of Liberia, and her countrywoman Leymah Gbowee), but as the 2005 *AHDR* noted, despite the presence of eighty-seven women's associations in Yemen, the proportion of women in decision-making positions did not exceed 6 percent, while their share of parliamentary seats was less than 0.5 percent.[93] The *AHDR* called the establishment of the Arab Women's Organization (AWO), which was launched in 2002, a form of tokenism, given that it was not provided the resources or the authority to influence broader decision-making, much less take part in decisions pertaining to economic development or peace and security.

Elsewhere, women's political participation and representation have grown, the result of both global and local forces. The global women's rights agenda and the UN conferences of the 1990s—especially the 1994 International Conference on Population and Development, which took place in Cairo, and the 1995 Beijing Conference on Women—prompted the proliferation of women's organizations and women-led NGOs in the Middle East. Whereas the 1950s through the 1970s saw women involved almost exclusively in either official women's organizations or charitable associations, the 1990s saw the expansion of many types of women's organizations. Growing state conservatism in some countries forced women's organizations and feminist leaders to assume a more independent stance than they had before. Rising educational attainment and smaller family size freed up women's time for civic and political engagement, allowing them to staff or establish NGOs, advocate for women's equality and rights, and participate in an array of campaigns. Even ultraconservative societies such as in Bahrain, Kuwait, and Saudi Arabia have felt pressure, as activists demand that women receive their rights as full citizens. This includes the right to take part in the political process.

In the 2019 global listing of parliaments by percentage of female members, Arab states ranked second-lowest as a region, with an average of 18.6 percent female representation compared with a global average of 24 percent. This was nonetheless a notable improvement over the 2010 rankings, when the region's average was only 9.6 percent. Half of MENA states ranked in the bottom third globally, anchored by Yemen and Oman. Tunisia topped the MENA list, followed by Israel, Algeria, and Iraq. Following the October 2019 parliamentary elections, Tunisian women's proportion of parliamentary seats fell to 26.3 (57 out of 217 seats), above the world average of 25.5 percent but lower than in the years following the Arab Spring. Still, it did very well on the *Global Gender Gap Report's* 2020 political empowerment ranking of 152 countries; at number 67, Tunisia surpassed the United States (86), Greece (87), Turkey (109), and Hungary (139).

Several MENA countries have adopted quotas to enhance women's political representation, in line with international trends. Even Gulf sheikhdoms without normal parliamentary systems and direct elections have seen increases in women's political representation; the UAE had a 50 percent female share in 2021, although the women representatives are appointed (as in Saudi Arabia). As seen in Table 6.5, only a few countries have legislated or voluntary candidate quotas (to be applied by political parties) while more have reserved seats for women, and nine countries have not adopted quotas at all. Still, according to the Arab Barometer's fifth wave, large majorities in nearly all countries surveyed support a women's quota.[94]

TABLE 6.5 ■ Types of Quotas adopted, by MENA Country (2021)	
Type of Quota	**Country**
Legislative quotas	Algeria, Libya, Tunisia, Palestine
Voluntary party quotas	Israel, Turkey
Reserved seats	Egypt, Iraq, Jordan, Morocco
Appointed seats/reserved seats	Saudi Arabia, UAE

Note: Countries with parliamentary elections but no quotas include Iran, Kuwait, Lebanon, Syria.

Source: https://www.idea.int/data-tools/data/gender-quotas/country-view/97/35, accessed June 2021

TABLE 6.6 ■ Female Parliamentary Representation, 2012, 2021, by Country and Type of Quota

Country	Female Representation (%)		Type of Quota
	2012	2021	
Algeria	25.6	8.1	Legislative quota
Bahrain	18.8	15.0	None
Egypt	2.2	27.4	Reserved seats
Iran	3.1	5.6	None
Iraq	25.2	26.4	Reserved seats
Israel	20.0	26.7	Voluntary party quota
Jordan	11.1	11.5	Reserved seats
Kuwait	6.3	1.5	None
Lebanon	3.1	4.7	None
Libya	16.5	16.0 (2014)	Legislative quota
Morocco	11.0	20.5	Reserved seats
Oman	9.6	2.3	None
Palestine, State of	13 (2006)	13 (2006)	Legislative quota
Qatar	0.1	9.8	None
Saudi Arabia	0.1	19.9	Reserved seats, appointed
Syria	12.0	11.2	None
Tunisia	26.7	26.3	Legislative quota
Turkey	14.2	17.3	Voluntary party quota
United Arab Emirates	17.5	50	Reserved seats, appointed
Yemen	0.7	0.3	None

Sources: 2012: UNDP, *Human Development Report 2013,* Table 4; 2021: Interparliamentary Union, https://data.ipu.org/women-ranking?month=1&year=2021 accessed June 2021.

Table 6.6 illustrates the wide variation in MENA women's *descriptive representation* and the positive effect of quotas. A salient point is that women's *substantive representation*—the capacity to promote women's rights or introduce bills that would benefit women materially—remains underresearched for the region. Still, some studies are instructive. Hanane Darhour and Drude Dahlerup describe the successful campaigns for a quota law in Morocco, the result of women's mobilizations and ties with members of the progressive political parties. In Iran's reformist-dominated sixth parliament, V. M. Moghadam and Fatemeh Haghighatjoo argue, the very small numbers of women representatives were "overactive" in advocating for women's participation and rights; in that parliament and subsequently, female representatives succeeded in raising the marriage age and introduced a bill to protect women from domestic violence. Marwa Shalaby and Laila Elimam show that women parliamentarians take an active part in parliamentary debates and discussions and are members of various legislative committees, though not necessarily the "power committees."[95]

Women's education correlates with both employment and involvement in professional and civic associations, and it is also a powerful predictor of activism for women's rights. Civil society thus becomes an arena more amenable to women's activism and a venue through which they can more easily access decision-making positions. Indeed, women have become visible in civil society organizations—including those focused on human rights and environmental protection—and professional associations of lawyers, judges, educators, artists, and health-workers. In both Tunisia and Morocco, women have led the main employers' associations. In Tunisia, several "feminist syndicalists" are members of both women's rights organizations and the country's large trade union, the UGTT.

The main form of women's civil society participation is found in women's own organizations such as Morocco's Association Démocratique des Femmes Marocaines, Algeria's SOS Femmes en Détresse, Iran's Cultural Center for Women and the Change for Equality Campaign, Tunisia's Association Tunisienne des Femmes Démocrates, and Turkey's Women for Women's Human Rights–New Ways. In the wake of the 2011 Egyptian uprising and revelations of extensive sexual harassment and abuse by police, military, and marauding males, feminists established the online and offline campaign HarassMap. All such movements, organizations, and campaigns have been spearheaded by educated women—most of them also professionals in an array of fields. It is in their own organizations that critically minded, educated women can establish their authority, take part in decision-making, engage with various publics, and exercise their political and social rights.

In so doing, they are also expanding the terrain of democratic civil society and helping to enact legal and policy reforms. Among the recent accomplishments have been the 2014 law against sexual harassment in Egypt; the strengthening of antidomestic violence laws in Algeria and Tunisia; the lifting by governments in Morocco and Tunisia of reservations to the UN Convention on the Elimination of All Forms of Discrimination against Women (CEDAW); the adoption of equal nationality rights for women by the Arab League in October 2017, following reforms in Algeria, Egypt, Morocco, and Tunisia; and the repeal in 2017–18 of marry-your-rapist laws in Algeria, Jordan, Lebanon, Morocco, Palestine, Tunisia. In Iran in 2018, women's rights advocates awaited parliamentary adoption of a landmark "Provision of Security for Women Bill," which expands the legal definition of violence against women but which faced criticism from conservatives. In Saudi Arabia a major reform was to allow women to drive, in 2018.

Another form of MENA women's participation in civil society is through cinema and literary efforts, including the publication of books, journals, and films. Morocco's Edition le Fennec has produced numerous books on women's rights issues as well as many literary works by women. Throughout the 1990s, the very lively women's press in Iran acted as a stand-in for an organized women's movement, until the movement burst onto the national scene in 2005. Shahla Lahiji's Roshangaran Press has published important feminist works as well as historical studies, while the Cultural Center of Women, organized by Noushin Ahmadi-Khorassani and others, has produced feminist analyses, calendars, compendiums, and journals. Filmmaker Rakhshan Bani-Etemad continues to focus on women's lives. Feminist newspapers are produced in Turkey, and the Women's Library in Istanbul contains research and documentation on women and gender issues. *Al-Raida*, a quarterly feminist journal of the Institute for Women's Studies in the Arab World, of the Lebanese American University, has published issues since 1976 on topics such as women in Arab cinema, women and the war in Lebanon, women and work, violence against women, sexuality, and criminality. Tunisia, arguably the most progressive MENA country, has seen the burgeoning of women's cultural production in art, literature, blogs, and cinema, especially in the wake of the Arab Spring and the lifting of political restrictions. The hard-hitting film *Beauty* by Tunisian filmmaker Kaouther Ben Hania boldly takes on the sexual abuse of women and reenacts the real-life 2012 rape of "Meriam" by a group of policemen. The combination of women's cultural production, advocacy efforts, mobilizing structures, access to various media, and engagement with various publics has been referred to by Moghadam and Sadiqi as a gradual feminization of the public sphere in the Middle East.[96]

Like other progressive civil society actors, Middle Eastern feminists are often caught between repressive or unresponsive states and fundamentalist or radical Islamists. As nonviolent groups with limited leverage, they can only watch in despair as extremists wreak havoc in the region. Cognizant, however, that the state is an unavoidable institutional actor, they make claims on the state for the improvement of their legal status and social positions, or they insist that the state live up to commitments and implement the conventions that it has signed—notably CEDAW. Where domestic coalition-building to advance their goals is difficult, women's rights activists appeal to transnational advocacy groups, transnational feminist networks, and the UN's global women's rights agenda, with its panoply of international conventions, declarations, and norms.

The relationship among women's education, employment, and civic engagement is clear. While some have suggested that the "NGO-ization" of the women's movement in Arab countries represents cooptation by the state,[97] a more plausible hypothesis is that participation in NGOs, and especially in women's rights organizations, has contributed to civil society and the development of civic skills necessary for democracy-building—as was seen in Tunisia and to a lesser degree in Morocco following the Arab Spring. For these reasons, the public gender regimes in Tunisia and Morocco are transitioning from the long-standing neopatriarchal form to a more modernized "conservative" model of gender relations.[98]

AFTER THE ARAB SPRING: CHANGES IN ATTITUDES AND VALUE ORIENTATIONS

Changes in values and attitudes, often discerned from surveys and opinion polls, may accompany broader social changes or be reflective of a society's cultural and normative shifts. Attitudes, values, and norms are variable across social groups and certainly across time, but survey research seeks to capture societal attitudes at a given moment while different rounds will enable comparisons over time. For MENA, the primary data are available from the World Value Survey (WVS), the Arab Barometer, the Arab Human Development Report, and national sources. As noted at the start of this chapter, scholars have approached the changes wrought by the 2011 Arab Spring in rather different ways, with some emphasizing authoritarian resilience, others analyzing the new conflicts that have arisen, and yet others examining changes in value orientation. Many scholars have long described the MENA region as beset by patriarchal, conservative, and religious values and practices, though as this chapter has shown and as survey research confirms, cultural changes have occurred. In particular, young people, employed women, men married to employed women, and the older generation raised during the postcolonial state-building and developmentalist era can be expected to hold more egalitarian or liberal values.[99]

An example of normative change, assisted by the power of social media, comes from Iran, described by Iranian journalist Saied Jafari. On June 13, 2018, just before Iran's national soccer team played in the World Cup, a huge poster was displayed in one of Tehran's main squares. It depicted a group of men, with each individual representing a different ethnicity in Iran, standing side by side and holding up a golden trophy. It did not feature a single woman. This sparked a social media backlash of such magnitude, Jafari writes, that two days later the poster was taken down and replaced with another that included women. Moreover a World Cup TV ad by the Iranian branch of Samsung showed members of a family watching soccer, with the men following the game and cheering while the women looked after the children. "The ad was harshly criticized on social media and created a very negative atmosphere for Samsung," writes Jafari. The company responded to critics by posting an explanation in Persian on its official Instagram page in an attempt to calm sentiments while deflecting accusations of being antiwoman.[100]

In another reflection of cultural change, as discerned from the WVS 7th wave (conducted between 2017 and 2020), some 44 percent of Iranians disagreed/strongly disagreed that men are better political leaders; nearly 64 percent agreed/strongly agreed that women having the same rights as men is an essential characteristic of democracy; fully 68 percent had a great deal/a lot of confidence in the women's movement/organizations; and a whopping 93 percent agreed that it was never justifiable for a man to beat his wife. For other countries, too, some WVS responses are especially promising. On the question of whether equal rights for women are an essential characteristic of democracy, a majority of respondents agreed: 57.6 percent in Turkey; and 53 percent in Lebanon, Jordan, and Iraq. In all countries surveyed but Egypt and Iraq, the majority agreed that it was never justifiable for parents to beat their children, with the highest rate found among Iranian respondents (77.3 percent).

And yet attitudes can be affected, and hardened, by macroeconomic difficulties and macropolitical changes. Veronica Kostenko and Eduard Ponarin analyzed gender values and social change in the thirteen Arab societies surveyed in Wave 3 of the Arab Barometer Project.[101] They constructed an index compiled from expressed attitudes to the following statements: A married woman can work outside of home; in general, men are better in political leadership; and university education is more important for boys. The region as a whole still has far less gender egalitarian value orientation than is the case in other world regions. Specifically, the authors find that support for gender egalitarianism generally grows among the youngest generations of the conservative states—that is, those countries with no experience of "secular" regimes, although the growth in support is from a very low level. On the other hand, the countries that have had experience of secular nationalist regimes—Egypt, Palestine, former South Yemen, and Tunisia—show a decline from a relatively high level of egalitarian attitudes among younger cohorts. Iraq, which had an "Arab socialist" form of secular nationalism, now ranks the lowest among all the countries surveyed. Kostenko and Ponarin attribute this to changes in political regimes and the spread of conservative values by oil-rich Gulf states such as Saudi Arabia, although the disastrous effects of the United States–led invasion surely has played a role in the hardening of identities and values in Iraq. For Tunisia, the decline may be attributed to both the influence of the Islamist party made possible by democratization and the difficult economic conditions that the country has faced in recent years. The uncertainty of labor markets and high unemployment rates also may explain why the publics in all MENA countries answer that when jobs are scarce, men have more right to a job than do women. That preference may have been reinforced by the (un)employment effects of the pandemic and rising prices of food, fuel, and fertilizer.

Economic difficulties and the persistence of conflicts also likely explain why most of the publics surveyed in the WVS 7th wave prioritized equality and security over freedom. Only in Tunisia—which embarked on a democratic transition after 2011—were the respondents split on the importance of freedom vs equality, with 50.8 percent favoring freedom over 45.9 percent favoring equality. Taken together, 80 percent of respondents in all seven countries prioritized security over freedom. In Egypt, Iran, Iraq, Jordan, Lebanon, and Tunisia, respondents overwhelmingly agreed that terrorism was never justified, whether for political, ideological, or religious reasons, and that political violence was never justified. (The two questions were not posed in Turkey.)

In his analysis of survey data in Egypt from 2011 to 2016, sociologist Mansoor Moaddel finds most support for secular politics among those with higher socioeconomic status, younger, urban, more tolerant of both gender equality and other religions, and less concerned with Western cultural invasion. Framed by his concept of historical change occurring through "cultural episodes," Moaddel's findings lead him to be more optimistic about future cultural shifts in the wake of the Arab Spring, although he concedes that persistent conservative views on gender equality constitute a barrier to full democratization.[102]

Gender Dynamics of the Pandemic

Could the advances in attitudes and values that have accompanied women's rising participation and rights stall or regress as a result of the socioeconomic effects of the COVID-19 pandemic? In 2020, international organizations were predicting declining human development and poverty for MENA, especially within working-class and rural communities, and for those in the informal sector and small businesses. A June 2020 OECD report cited a Tunisian official that women's informal labor in agriculture and as domestic workers made them especially vulnerable to job losses and that "most women-led SMEs are closed because of the crisis." Youth unemployment rates would increase. A 2020 ESCWA policy brief estimated that out of some 1.7 million jobs that would be lost in the Arab region, fully 700,000 of them would be women's jobs. Labor-exporting MENA countries—among them Egypt, Jordan, and Lebanon—would experience rising unemployment and related effects of return migration and cessation of remittances. Tourist-destination countries would suffer, along with the workers and enterprises involved in the tourism sector.

By the end of the year and into 2021, most of the predictions had materialized. Early on, some Tunisian and Moroccan sources reported increases in domestic violence in the months following the pandemic's start and the lockdowns. Egypt's unemployment rate rose to a near two-year high, with women's unemployment rate, at 16.2 percent, nearly double that of men's. Arab Barometer data found more job loss by women than men in the five countries surveyed. Another study found that by November 2020, total unemployment rates in Morocco were 30 percent, in Tunisia 22 percent, and in Egypt 9 percent. However, they were much worse for women: 52 percent in Morocco; 41 percent in Tunisia, and 16 percent in Egypt.[103] GDP declined almost everywhere; many firms—mostly small- and medium-sized businesses—experienced financial distress or closed; household incomes fell.[104] GCC countries were largely spared the worst effects of the pandemic, although their migrant workers were not, but elsewhere in the region, the pandemic's worst effects were on lower-income working households. School closures hit working women in at least three ways: loss of jobs for lower-paid or unskilled women; intensification of household labor during lockdowns; and early retirement or decision to leave the labor market because of increased care work. Even so, 2021 Arab Barometer data seem not to have found increases in domestic violence rates; indeed, respondents in Algeria reported more family unity.[105]

CONCLUSION

This chapter has surveyed some of the main elements of social change in the MENA region: social structural dynamics; urbanization and rising educational attainment; the demographic transition, the emergence of social movements and civil society organizations calling for broader citizen participation and rights; and value orientations. As has been demonstrated, MENA societies are more varied and vibrant than is often recognized. In the postcolonial or developmentalist era, "state feminism" in countries such as Egypt, Turkey, and especially Tunisia helped create two generations of women with aspirations for employment, empowerment, and activism. The effects of feminist advocacy, along with increasing female educational attainment and women's public roles, clearly manifest themselves in attitudinal changes among segments of current populations. Given women's continued education attainment, employment, civil society activism, cultural production, and political representation, we can expect more changes in government policy, the law, and societal attitudes.

Nevertheless, patriarchal values emerge within new generations or remain resilient among certain older segments of the population—particularly in the context of the spread of Islamist ideology, the continued occupation in Palestine, the destabilization of states, and economic setbacks. If the year 2011 began with hopes for a better future, subsequent years have generated soberer sentiments. The Arab Spring did not achieve the goal of increased socioeconomic rights that citizens called for in Egypt, Tunisia, Morocco, and elsewhere; it was decidedly not a thoroughgoing revolution.[106] It did launch Tunisia on a democratic transition, but the past decade has been turbulent and lacking in robust international support. Most MENA countries continue to face formidable problems: social inequalities, economic difficulties, physical insecurity, interstate hostilities, and the ever-present threat of external military intervention. This is why most of the publics surveyed in the WVS 7th wave prioritized equality and security over freedom. Indeed, the social changes that have occurred in the MENA region have been neither linear nor uniform, as the region is internally differentiated and many factors and forces impinge upon the pace, quality, and direction of change.

In 2020–21, and to mitigate the poverty effects of the pandemic, governments provided cash transfers, food distribution, food price controls, unemployment benefits, waiver of utility bills, and childcare support. These stop-gap measures need to become part of a larger program for social and economic development.[107] In particular, if women are to return to the labor force, institutional reforms will be needed: family law reform, enforcement of antidiscrimination and antiviolence laws, decent jobs, statutory paid maternity leave, and a nationwide network of preschool facilities to generate jobs and enable maternal employment. Social dialogues about the need for paid paternity leaves may help accelerate change in gender relations at micro and meso levels and the gender regime at the macro level. What remains to be seen is whether the socioeconomic effects of the pandemic - along with the fallout from the 2022 Russia-Ukraine-NATO war, which includes rising prices and shortage of wheat - will compel governments to reassess priorities and increase investments in public services, employment generation, and citizen empowerment for a sustainable future.

SUGGESTED READINGS

Alaoui, Hicham, and Springborg Robert, eds. *The Political Economy of Education in the Arab World.* Boulder, CO: Lynne Rienner Publishers, 2021.

Butenschøn, Nils A, and Meijer Roel, eds. *The Middle East in Transition: The Centrality of Citizenship.* Cheltenham: Edward Elgar, 2018.

Chamlou, Nadereh, and Karshenas Massoud, eds. *Women, Work, and Welfare in the Middle East and North Africa.* London: Imperial College Press, 2016.

Joseph, Suad, ed. *Gender and Citizenship in the Middle East.* Syracuse, NY: Syracuse University Press, 2000.

Karshenas, Massoud, and M. Moghadam Valentine. "Female Labour Force Participation and Women's Employment: Puzzles, Problems, and Research,". In *The Routledge Handbook of Middle East Economics.* Edited by Hakimian Hassan. London: Routledge, 2021.

7 THE POLITICAL ECONOMY OF DEVELOPMENT IN THE MIDDLE EAST

Melani Cammett, Ishac Diwan, and Steven Heydemann

In the past decade, economic performance has been disappointing in the Middle Eastern and North African (MENA) regions. Several countries were hit by the political chaos that followed the uprisings of 2011, and by the fall in international oil prices after 2015. COVID-19 made economic and social conditions worse after 2019. To appease a roiling street, and to alleviate the social and economic burdens brought about by the pandemic, governments borrowed heavily to finance increased spending. The recent shocks to the global economy in 2022 made things much worse, as international food and energy prices went up sharply and global interest rates rose. But by now, fiscal deficits and public debts have reached unsustainable levels in many countries, and especially in the energy-importing countries. This ushers in an era of forced austerity and sociopolitical instability.

Already in 2011, the "Arab Spring" had highlighted the profound economic grievances of citizens in Middle Eastern countries. In the uprisings, protestors condemned their leaders for the lack of jobs, unequal distribution of wealth, and the dominant role of crony capitalist networks across the region. To be sure, the Arab protests and revolutions—like all social movements—resulted from more than economic injustices, both real and perceived. Economic factors, however, constitute a necessary component of any explanation for the Arab Spring. At a minimum, the Arab uprisings demonstrated that it is difficult to separate the economic and political roots of the ongoing developments in the MENA region.

There are broad similarities in the economic challenges facing MENA countries, but also important variation. With few exceptions, historical experiences of colonial rule that consolidated varieties of dependent development heavily influenced the political economies of the region. After World War II (WWII), newly independent governments addressed the negative economic and social legacies of colonialism through state-centric development strategies that reflected the economic orthodoxies of the postwar era, including the rapid expansion of public sectors, import substitution industrialization, state regulation of economic activity, and in Egypt, Iraq, Syria, and Algeria, extensive nationalization of industry and large landholdings. In subsequent decades, additional similarities emerged: dependence on the international prices of oil; regional migration and large flows of remittances; geopolitical linkages with increased interventions by Gulf Cooperation Council (GCC) countries, Turkey, and Iran; and common social values carried by a shared culture and media. These similarities also extend to the fragility of the current political, social, and economic conditions, and the problems of high youth unemployment, limited opportunities for socioeconomic advancement, eroding systems of social protection, and underperforming economies witnessed across the region.

At the same time, however, the region encompasses countries with widely divergent economic structures and development trajectories. It is home to some of the richest countries in the world, including the United Arab Emirates (UAE), Saudi Arabia, and the other oil-rich monarchies of the Gulf, and some of the poorest, such as Yemen, where a brutal war that began in 2014 has led to a full-blown humanitarian disaster. Consider the striking contrast between the UAE, where oil wealth has fueled a massive real estate boom, including the construction of an indoor ski slope and hotels built on man-made islands in the shape of a palm tree (see image on p. 565), and nearby Yemen, where over 70 percent of the population lived below the poverty line in 2020, and 55 percent of women are illiterate. It is, thus, important to balance an understanding of the features that are widely shared by MENA countries with a keen appreciation for cross-national variation.

This chapter aims to highlight—and try to explain—both similarities and differences. It introduces the distinct types of political economies found in the Middle East and traces the record of economic development in different clusters of countries.[1] Since WWII, when most Middle Eastern countries either gained independence from colonial rule or consolidated their status as independent states, countries in the region experienced many similarities in their development trajectories, but their governments also faced some divergent initial starting conditions. These resulted in some differences in the political and economic strategies they adopted.

The chapter opens by describing various indicators of economic development and applying these measures to the contemporary Middle East, differentiating between countries that have low, middle, and large levels of oil rents per capita. The chapter then traces the record of economic growth and development across these distinct political economies in different historical periods, including the WWII period, the golden age of economic prosperity during the 1960s and 1970s, and the period of economic crisis and increased integration into the global economy from the 1980s onward. After describing the array of economic challenges facing most Middle Eastern countries in the contemporary period, the chapter briefly reviews diverse explanations for relative underdevelopment in the region. It concludes with considerations about the current socioeconomic situation in the region and what it suggests about possible future developments.

MEASURING DEVELOPMENT IN THE MIDDLE EAST

Before delving into the different pathways of economic development found in the Middle East, it is necessary to define *development*. Traditional views of development focus on income and economic growth, which the World Bank defines as an expansion in a country's overall economy measured as the percentage increase in the gross domestic product (GDP) in a single year. Economic growth can occur in different ways, including the use of more physical, human, or natural resources, or the application of the same resources in more efficient or productive ways.

In turn, economic growth is presumed to lead to higher per capita income and improvement in average living standards in the population.

Economic Growth and GDP

Standard economic classifications of countries focus on per capita income.[2] Table 7.1 provides a snapshot of the MENA economies in 2018.[3] As the table shows, per capita income varies widely within the Middle East. Oil wealth is a key point of differentiation. All high-income countries—Bahrain, Kuwait, Oman, Qatar, Saudi Arabia, and the UAE—have high levels of oil dependence. Population size is also an important factor in classifying income levels in the region. In our typology, countries with high oil endowments and low indigenous or citizen populations are part of the high-oil country (HOC) group. Countries with high oil dependence and large populations, such as Algeria and Iran, fall in the lower-middle-income group, despite their valuable natural resource endowments, and are classified as the middle-oil country (MOC) group.[4] The remaining lower-middle-income countries (LMICs)—the low-oil country (LOC) group—export a relatively low volume of hydrocarbons, or none at all, and tend to have high populations. Box 7.1 discusses the usefulness and limits of this classification.

BOX 7.1

CLASSIFYING THE MENA COUNTRIES

If the analyst does not classify the MENA countries by some analytical grouping, the analysis becomes overly complex—it is certainly clearer to compare performance in three or four subgroups than among a long list of countries. There are various methods used in the literature: geographical grouping (Middle East/North Africa/GCC); income level (rich, middle income, poor); and political regimes (how autocratic/democratic).

In this chapter, as in our 2015 edition of *A Political Economy of the Middle East*, we chose to use the level of oil per capita in a country as the organizing principle for our classification (high, middle, and low oil per capita).

There are drawbacks and advantages in this, as in any, classification. To be sure, this taxonomy is only suggestive, and its boundaries are porous. Libya, for example, and present-day Saudi Arabia, could be classified as high or medium oil, depending on where we put the precise cut-off point. Similarly, Syria or Yemen could belong to the middle or low oil categories, and some countries could be moved from one category to another over time (Sudan is an example). At a more conceptual level, non-oil "rents," such as geopolitical, or relating to other natural resources (phosphates, for example), can play the same sociopolitical role as oil rents. Nevertheless, the main advantage is that there do seem to be important similarities, both political and economic, between the countries in each category, and important differences between these three categories.

Importantly, however, we do not claim in what follows that the amount of oil per capita "causes" these similarities and differences. It is equally possible that other factors cause countries to be governed in particular ways, and determine at the same time how much of their oil reserves they are able to develop—think of the differences, for example, between Saudi Arabia and Iraq, both of which are endowed with similar levels of reserves.

TABLE 7.1 ■ Gross Domestic Product, Oil Rents, and Country Classifications in the MENA Region, 2018

	GDP (In Billions of Current US Dollars (2018))	Population (In Millions) 2018	Oil Rent (In Billions of 2018 Dollars)	Oil Rent per Capita (in 2018 dollars)	Oil Rent (% of GDP) in 2018	GDP per Capita
Labor Poor Resource Rich	**1702.77**	**63.33**	**430.62**	**6,810.32**	**25.13**	**50,610.98**
Bahrain	37.65	1.57	0.87	555.00	2.31	47,353.12
Kuwait	140.65	4.14	59.71	14,432.96	42.46	51,708.25
Libya	52.61	6.68	22.32	3,342.16	42.43	15,383.83
Oman	79.79	4.83	21.43	4,436.86	26.86	29,289.61
Qatar	183.33	2.78	30.41	10,931.42	16.59	93,186.26
Saudi Arabia	786.52	33.70	225.83	6,701.27	28.71	48,756.19
United Arab Emirates	422.22	9.63	70.04	7,272.54	16.59	68,599.62
Labor Abundant Resource Rich	**910.24**	**249.67**	**203.22**	**707.39**	**17.17**	**10,226.09**
Algeria	175.41	42.23	27.67	655.20	15.77	11,925.80
Iran, Islamic Rep.	454.00	81.80	71.03	868.37	15.65	13,800.02
Iraq	224.23	38.43	101.79	2,648.42	45.39	10,919.77
Sudan	33.13	41.80	2.11	50.58	6.38	4,258.78
Syrian Arab Republic	–	16.91	–	–		
Yemen, Rep.	23.49	28.50	0.62	21.80	2.65	
Labor Abundant Resource Poor	**521.75**	**167.39**	**14.21**	**37.06**	**1.31**	**10,502.29**
Egypt, Arab Rep.	249.71	98.42	13.19	133.97	5.28	11,643.22

TABLE 7.1 ■ Gross Domestic Product, Oil Rents, and Country Classifications in the MENA Region, 2018 (*Continue*)						
	GDP (In Billions of Current US Dollars (2018))	Population (In Millions) 2018	Oil Rent (In Billions of 2018 Dollars)	Oil Rent per Capita (in 2018 dollars)	Oil Rent (% of GDP) in 2018	GDP per Capita
Jordan	42.93	9.96	0.00	0.05	0.00	10,266.92
Lebanon	54.96	6.85	–	–	–	15,992.32
Morocco	118.10	36.03	0.01	0.22	0.01	7,613.14
Tunisia	39.77	11.57	1.02	88.15	2.56	11,025.99
West Bank and Gaza	16.28	4.57	–	–	–	6,472.12
OECD Economies						
Israel	370.59	8.88	0.01	0.96	0.00	41,469.55
Turkey	778.38	82.32	0.87	10.58	0.11	28,831.93
Overall MENA	**4,283.73**	**571.59**	**648.93**	**2,483.36**	**13.49**	**27,815.60**

Source: World Bank, World Bank Institute (WBI) data; International Monetary Fund (IMF), World Economic Outlook (WEO).

How does the growth of GDP in the MENA region (excluding Israel and Turkey) compare with the rest of the world over the *longue durée*, say since 1960, shortly after most of these countries gained independence? In the last edition, we reported that the regional performance during the fifty years between 1960 and 2010 was modest by world standards, with average per capita GDP growth of 2.3 percent (over all countries and years), comparable to the average of LMICs around the world, higher than sub-Saharan Africa, Eastern and central Europe, and Latin America, but below East Asia and South Asia. We now have data for the additional decade 2010–2019, which was marked by lower growth in the region. When evaluated over the past sixty years, the performance of the broad Middle East region seems even more modest, with an average growth rate of per capita GDP of only 1.7 percent per year. This is below the global LMIC average and close to the performance of Eastern Europe and Latin America.

This relatively poor performance of the region as whole is surprising given its favorable geographical position between the East and West, and that it has benefited from large oil revenues over time. However, these averages hide more than they reveal as GDP growth rates have varied a lot across types of countries and over time. Four broad remarks can be made about variations in growth rates over longer cycles.

First, economic performance varied quite a lot among the three types of political economies, as is apparent in Table 7.2. At 1.5 percent per capita growth per year on average, the HOC group did not come out highest: its overall GDP did grow very fast, at a remarkable five percent per year over the past sixty years; however, its population also grew very fast, both because of fast demographic growth and because of the massive importation of foreign labor. This performance is not too surprising given the huge contribution of oil wealth to this growth, but it does stand in sharp contrast with the notion of a "resource curse" (see Oil and the "Resource Curse" section). More surprisingly, it is the LOC group that comes out first at 2.4 percent growth per capita on average, with the LMICs' long-term performance a close second. The MOC group,

TABLE 7.2 ■ Economic Growth in the MENA Region and in Other Regions, 1960–2010			
	1960–2019	1960–2019	1960–2010
Countries	Mean GDP, per capita growth (%)	Mean Standard Deviation (%)	Mean GDP, per capita growth (%)
East Asia and Pacific	5.57	3.49	5.60
South Asia	3.06	2.54	2.86
Latin America and Caribbean	1.66	2.26	1.76
Sub-Saharan Africa	0.70	2.54	0.84
Europe and Central Asia	1.65	4.71	1.31
Low income	0.65	2.37	0.90
Lower middle income	2.26	2.02	2.44
Upper middle income	3.21	2.04	3.18
Middle East and North Africa	1.18	4.74	2.28
HOC	1.55	4.23	2.08
MOC	−0.40	4.60	1.30
LOC	2.37	3.29	2.80
Israel	2.57	1.57	2.77
Turkey	2.77	0.56	2.54

Source: World Bank Indicators https://databank.worldbank.org/source/world-development-indicators

which is rich in both oil and people, comes in a distant third place, at slightly negative average growth per capita per year—indicating de-development over time. This group of countries seems to have been hit hard by the oil curse, even though these countries were once believed to show the greatest promise, as they could combine oil wealth with a large population to develop into industrial giants. Iraq, Iran, and Algeria all had such promise and plans, but they got mired in internal and external conflicts that ended up destroying assets and undermining their economic potential. The recent collapse of the Syrian economy has further lowered this average over the last decade.

This brings us to our second point, which is about the huge variability of growth over time, and its relation to the fluctuation of oil prices and, in some cases, to agricultural output. The standard deviation of growth measures how likely growth is to deviate in any given year, either larger or smaller than the mean growth over the period. As can be seen in Table 7.2, the standard deviation of GDP per capita growth in the MENA region is among the highest in the world, especially among the oil-producing countries of the HOC and MOC groupings. This variability is in good part a result of the dependence of the region on oil revenues—oil prices are determined by international markets and have themselves shown a great deal of variability over time, with two marked periods of booms (followed by busts): during 1973–1982, and during 2000–2014 (see Figure 7.1). The very large variability of oil revenues has led to a parallel variability of growth episodes across periods, especially in the HOCs and MOCs. This is a

FIGURE 7.1 ■ Oil Prices and Oil Revenues

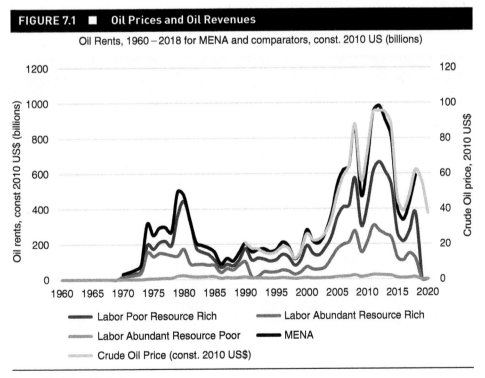

Oil Rents, 1960 – 2018 for MENA and comparators, const. 2010 US (billions)

Source: World Bank Indicators

defining dimension of growth in the region. HOC economies experienced spectacular increases in growth during boom years in world oil markets, but the group also shows an extremely variable growth rate.

The countries in the LOC group are also indirectly affected by oil price variability, albeit in lesser ways. This is because of the close relation between their economies and those of the oil-producing countries. Economic integration in the MENA region has happened largely through the movement of people to the GCC and the remittances they send back to their home countries; labor flows into the GCC from countries with larger populations and high rates of unemployment; and flows of capital out of the GCC into economies across the Middle East in the form of aid and investments.[5] This stands in contrast to a low level of market integration, with the movement of goods between countries remaining low, largely due to similarities in their production structures, the high levels of protectionism practiced in many countries, and a lack of market dynamism.[6] The importance of labor remittances in the LOC economies can be seen in Figure 7.2. In many MENA countries, they make a large contribution to incomes, well above the global average, as a long history of migration, conflict and political instability, and fast growth in the GCC have contributed to the exceptionally high rate of labor migration. The importance of remittances in national economies is especially large in Jordan, Lebanon, and Palestine, constituting on average between 10 and 18 percent of GDP over the past fifty years. In Egypt, Lebanon, Sudan, Yemen, and Syria (although no reliable data are available for the last two countries), remittances also constitute a central contribution to the economy, becoming even more important in the conflict-affected states of the region.

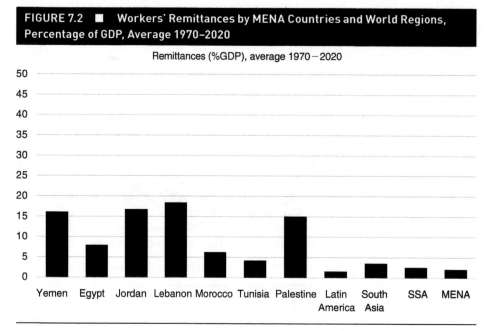

FIGURE 7.2   ■   Workers' Remittances by MENA Countries and World Regions, Percentage of GDP, Average 1970–2020

Source: World Bank Indicators

Third, an important reason for the variability of growth over time and countries relates to the socioeconomic adjustments in growth strategy that much of the region experienced as countries moved from state-led growth to market-oriented economies around the 1990s (this is in addition to the effects of various conflicts which have devastated the economies of particular countries). The period with the lowest economic growth rate was somewhere in the 1980s–1990s, when most of the countries experienced a "lost decade." For the LOCs in particular, per capita growth over the 1980s was zero on average, the lowest decadal performance in their history. Moreover, as we argue later in this chapter, what happened then on the economic, social, and political fronts, including the roll-back of the state and the shift to market economies, has initiated social and economic processes that ultimately contributed to the 2011 uprisings. Paradoxically, the second worst period in terms of growth is the postuprising decade, which ended with the COVID-19 pandemic in 2020–2021.

Finally, another reason for the growth variability is conflict and insecurity. The MOC growth averages in particular have been deeply reduced by devastating wars in Iraq and Iran during the 1980s, Iraq during the 2000s, and intrastate conflicts in Libya, Iraq, Syria, and Yemen during the past decade. Spillover effects of these conflicts have weighed heavily on Jordan and Lebanon as a result of large-scale displacement from Syria. Insecurity has also affected Algeria, Palestine, and Lebanon in various periods (see Table 7.3).

Social Development

The level and growth of per capita gross domestic product capture some important aspects of development and tend to be highly correlated with other measures of development. Indicators based solely on the economy are not sufficient, however. Economic growth can occur without development—that is, economies can grow in the aggregate, but the average person may be no better off. Average income-based approaches neglect distributional issues, or how income is actually dispersed within a given society. If income distribution is highly skewed, economic growth does not automatically trickle down in the form of jobs and social services.

One key aspect of human development in which the region is clearly lacking is gender equality. Studies based on opinion polls have consistently shown that one of the most striking particularities of the region is its high degree of patriarchal values whereby households tend to be organized around a patriarchal bargain.[7] In such an environment, women have lower levels of agency than in other parts of the world and acquire a lower level of education than males, fertility (and population growth) remains high, and female participation in the labor market remains limited. Indeed, female labor force participation in the MENA region is the lowest in the world, as less than 25 percent of women of working age actually work outside the home. Moreover, little progress has been achieved over the past decades in this regard, including among women with higher levels of education, as evident in Figure 7.3.

Thus, understanding development requires more attention to its social dimensions. In 1990, the United Nations Development Programme (UNDP) started to publish its annual *UN Human Development Report* (HDR), which provides its own measure of development—the Human Development Index (HDI). Designed to capture social aspects of development, the HDI provides an aggregate measure of the living conditions of the population across different countries and includes

TABLE 7.3	■	Growth of Gross Domestic Product in MENA, by Decade						

Countries	1961–1970	1971–1980	1981–1990	1991–2000	2001–2010	2011–2019	Std dev 1960–2010	1960–2019	1960–2010
HOCs	**8.22**	**2.56**	**–1.67**	**0.96**	**0.33**	**0.51**	**4.23**	**1.55**	**2.08**
Bahrain	4.20	4.70	–1.49	2.92	–0.94	0.13	2.90	2.38	1.88
Kuwait	2.50	–3.10	–3.12	–1.58	1.92	–1.77	2.72	–0.86	–0.68
Libya	–	–	0.20	1.78	2.32	5.19	1.10	3.16	1.43
Oman	18.62	1.10	4.28	2.64	2.65	–2.35	7.22	4.49	5.86
Qatar	–	–	–	–	0.84	–0.68	0.00	0.08	0.84
Saudi Arabia	4.77	7.86	–5.23	0.55	0.13	0.75	4.98	1.47	1.62
United Arab Emirates	11.00	2.26	–4.66	–0.56	–4.63	2.27	6.47	1.13	0.68
MOCs	**3.02**	**3.88**	**–6.47**	**3.98**	**2.06**	**–8.87**	**4.60**	**–0.40**	**1.30**
Algeria	2.08	3.07	–0.21	–0.18	2.22	0.54	1.50	1.25	1.40
Iran, Islamic Rep.	8.31	0.86	–1.15	1.99	3.79	–1.00	3.59	2.13	2.76
Iraq	3.20	8.00	–30.00	14.92	–1.53	2.20	17.27	–0.54	–1.08
Sudan	–0.77	0.70	–0.11	3.13	4.39	2.48	2.20	1.64	1.47
Syrian Arab Republic	2.29	6.76	–0.87	2.46	2.37	–45.00	2.72	–6.16	2.60
Yemen, Rep.	0.00	0.00	0.00	1.59	1.14	n.a	0.32	–0.78	1.36
LOCs	**3.03**	**6.16**	**0.00**	**2.44**	**2.38**	**0.22**	**3.29**	**2.37**	**2.80**
Egypt, Arab Rep.	2.82	4.32	3.04	2.50	2.97	1.45	0.70	2.85	3.13
Jordan	–	11.74	–1.58	0.99	3.89	–1.28	5.77	2.29	3.76
Lebanon	4.00	7.00	–9.10	4.61	3.93	–3.18	6.38	1.21	2.09
Morocco	2.09	2.65	1.52	1.00	3.80	2.01	1.08	2.18	2.21
Tunisia	3.21	5.14	1.11	3.10	3.46	0.70	1.43	2.79	3.20

(Continued)

TABLE 7.3 ■ Growth of Gross Domestic Product in MENA, by Decade (*Continue*)									
Countries	1961–1970	1971–1980	1981–1990	1991–2000	2001–2010	2011–2019	Std dev 1960–2010	1960–2019	1960–2010
West Bank and Gaza	0.00	6.10	5.00	2.47	–3.74	1.61	4.39	1.91	2.46
OECD									
Israel	5.26	2.99	1.76	2.67	1.17	1.56	1.57	**2.57**	2.77
Turkey	3.01	1.89	3.14	2.07	2.62	3.91	0.56	**2.77**	2.54
Overall MENA	**4.76**	**4.20**	**–2.71**	**2.46**	**1.59**	**–2.71**	**4.04**	**1.18**	**2.30**

Source: World Bank Indicators

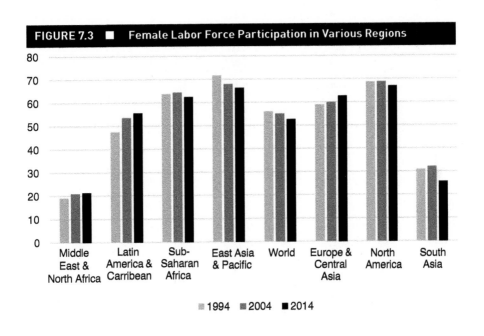

FIGURE 7.3 ■ Female Labor Force Participation in Various Regions

Legend: 1994 2004 2014

Source: International Labor Organization (2016)

measures of health and access to health care services, nutrition levels, life expectancy at birth, adult literacy and mean years of schooling, gender equality, access to basic infrastructure such as water and sanitation, real per capita income adjusted for the differing purchasing power parity of each country's currency, and the percentage of the population living below the poverty line.

Every year, the *HDR* divides countries by HDI rankings into *very high, high, medium*, and *low* human development. In the 2020 report, most Arab countries fell into the *medium* or *high* category (see Table 7.4), despite poor overall rankings in specific indicators, including female participation in the workforce.

To understand the reason for the contrast between rather good social outcomes and rather poor economic performance, it is important to realize that policies implemented by postindependence governments, including high social expenditures and public sector employment,

TABLE 7.4 ■ Human Development Index Rankings: Middle East and North Africa, 2019

	Country	Score	Rank	Category
HOC	Bahrain	0.815	44	Very high
	Kuwait	0.814	46	Very high
	Libya	0.784	55	High
	Oman	0.783	56	High
	Qatar	0.851	31	Very high
	Saudi Arabia	0.836	34	Very high
	UAE	0.827	40	Very high
MOC	Algeria	0.717	93	High
	Iran	0.749	75	High
	Iraq	0.642	120	Medium
	Syria	0.658	118	Medium
	Yemen	0.5	154	Low
LOC	Egypt	0.682	110	Medium
	Jordan	0.745	77	High
	Lebanon	0.765	65	High
	Morocco	0.617	129	Medium
	Palestine	0.686	107	Medium
	Tunisia	0.721	90	High
OECD	Turkey	0.759	69	High
	Israel			

Source: UNDP http://hdr.undp.org/en/countries

explain the relatively high rankings of the region with respect to human development. Indeed, this contrast underpins much of the grievances in the region, as the youth tend to be underemployed relative to their skill levels and their expectations.

Cross-regional comparisons illustrate the importance of government spending in MENA economies, but also of its decline since the 1980s. As Figure 7.4 shows, state spending as a percentage of GDP in the Middle East still outstrips the global average. But it is also evident that there are two distinct periods, one from about 1965 to the mid-1980s, the second from the mid-1980s to the present. In the 1960s and 1970s, across the region, new ruling elites emphasized economic and social development in response to neglect by colonial authorities. Public expenditures rose to between 40 and 50 percent of GDP throughout the region (and up to 60 percent in Egypt). But after the adjustments of the 1980s–1990s, and the fall of oil prices, there was a massive roll-back of the state, with the size of government falling in the three types of countries toward 30 percent of GDP. These trends explain the slowdown in the progress in the HDR index in more recent times. There was more recently a new rise in public expenditure during the second oil boom, triggered in part by governments in the wake of the Arab

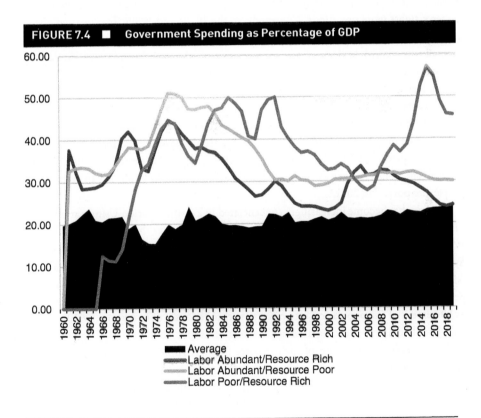

FIGURE 7.4 ■ Government Spending as Percentage of GDP

Legend:
- Average
- Labor Abundant/Resource Rich
- Labor Abundant/Resource Poor
- Labor Poor/Resource Rich

Note: Average is Middle Income Countries' average.

Source: World Bank Indicators

Spring protests to temper the spread of mass mobilization. This was especially the case in GCC countries, but could be observed in milder ways throughout the region, for example, in Jordan, Oman, and Egypt, in the form of some renewed hiring in the public sector, but especially of rising energy subsidies.

A more disaggregated look at the region, however, shows significant variation in human development. As would be expected, the HOC countries of the Gulf have higher HDI rankings and are clustered in the *very high* and *high* human development categories. Conversely, the lower-income countries in the LOC and MOC categories, with larger populations and higher poverty levels, tend to have lower human development rankings. Although there is substantial variation on HDI measures within these two groups of political economies, lower-income countries, such as Egypt, Morocco, and Yemen, have lower rates. At the same time, there are some exceptions to the correlation between income and social indicators. For example, the Palestinian territories have high literacy rates, despite poor economic conditions as a result of protracted conflict and the Israeli occupation discussed in the next section. This is largely due to the importance Palestinians attach to education as the primary means of upward mobility in the face of few other opportunities and because protracted conflict and instability have made property rights more precarious. Conversely, in the 1970s and 1980s, Iraq boasted one of the most educated and skilled populations in the region, but war and international sanctions contributed to a marked decline in Iraqi literacy rates and other social conditions. Similarly, social indicators have declined precipitously in Syria with the outbreak of the civil war in 2011 and the massive humanitarian crisis that has ensued.

In recent years, the Arab region's poverty belt started to grow very fast, especially as a result of the rise in conflict and insecurity. The United Nations Economic and Social Commission for Western Asia (ESCWA) estimates the regional headcount poverty ratio for the non-Gulf countries at 29.2 percent in 2019 (101.4 million people)—up from 22.8 percent in 2010 (66.4 million people). The ESCWA also estimates that COVID-19-related shocks pushed an extra 16 million people into poverty in 2021.[8]

Poverty has become increasingly concentrated in a few territories. Using national poverty lines, 56 percent of the region's poor live in the eight countries that are now classified by the World Bank as "fragile and conflict-affected": Iraq, Lebanon, the West Bank and Gaza, and Syria in the Levant; Somalia, Sudan, and Yemen in the Horn of Africa; and Libya in North Africa. Poverty rates now stand at around 70 percent in Yemen, 50 percent in Sudan, and 80 percent in Syria. In Lebanon, the economic and financial crisis of 2019 has pushed as much as 50 percent of the population into poverty within the span of two years. By 2021, Lebanon was described as experiencing among the worst economic collapse of any country since the mid-19th century. As a result of their massive impoverishment, Syria, Yemen, and Somalia are among the top five largest UN humanitarian operations in the world, and humanitarian assistance to Arab countries represented 59 percent of the total funding committed toward UN-coordinated humanitarian appeals in 2019. More than 30 million people in the region are in need of basic food support to *survive*. Internally displaced persons (IDPs) in the region constitute 47 percent of global IDPs.

THE ECONOMIC COSTS OF WAR AND CONFLICT

The Middle East has been at the epicenter of geopolitical struggles for decades and is the site of multiple protracted regional crises. These include the Israeli–Palestinian conflict, the Lebanese civil war, civil war in Yemen, conflicts in Iraq, the civil war and humanitarian crisis in Sudan, and more recently in Syria, state breakdown in Libya and Yemen, mass violence committed by extremist groups such as ISIS, and ongoing struggles between various Middle Eastern states and armed oppositions. In addition to physical and psychological destruction on the individual and societal levels, war and conflict have enormous economic costs, including the collapse of national markets, mass displacement, increased food insecurity, and, as seen in the previous section, rising poverty levels.

For instance, war and civil conflict have taken a serious toll on economic and social conditions in Iraq. In the 1970s, Iraq was considered the most developed country in the Middle East and ranked as an upper-middle-income country in the World Bank's classification. The educational and health systems were among the best in the region, and Iraq scored high marks on almost all well-being indicators, such as infant mortality, school enrollment, nutrition, income, and employment. Conflict followed by sanctions imposed on Iraq after the first Gulf war in 1990–1991 led to a marked decrease in well-being. Civil war in the aftermath of the US invasion of Iraq and the overthrow of Saddam Hussein in 2003 also took an enormous toll on the Iraqi population, with estimates of hundreds of thousands of Iraqi noncombatant deaths. The rise of ISIS, and the war against it between 2014 and 2018, also led to enormous death and destruction.

Iraqis have also suffered economically because "ethnic cleansing" has led to forced displacement for many and added to the human toll of Iraq's conflicts. Civil conflict has also harmed the economy by undercutting oil drilling and shipping operations, damaging essential infrastructure, deterring private long-term investment, and contributing to the flight of many of the country's educated professionals.

Since 2019, the situation has become more stable, although car bombings and other forms of violence remain a daily fact of life for many Iraqis, but economic consequences remain. Postconflict political economies are conducive to corruption, criminality, and the expansion of conflict-based economic networks. In Iraq, as in other conflict-affected states, black market operations have flourished and new economic networks with connections linking nonstate armed groups and militias with political elites have profited from wartime economic orders. A wave of protests in 2019 against poor government performance and pervasive corruption was brutally suppressed by security forces, often by units affiliated with nonstate, pro-Iranian militias. These events reinforced perceptions of instability and vulnerability among Iraqis.

The civil war in Syria has had even more devastating effects. Economic and social conditions exhibit features similar to those in Iraq and other conflict countries, if on a potentially unprecedented scale. The government's harsh crackdown on peaceful protests in March 2011 turned into a full-blown war with an enormous toll on human life and infrastructure. According to the Syrian Observatory for Human Rights, more than 320,000 people died in the Syrian civil war between March 2011 and June 2015, and more than 1.5 million people were wounded.

The conflict also led to massive displacement of the Syrian population with about six million Syrians seeking refuge in other countries (principally in Lebanon, Jordan, and Turkey) and about eight million people displaced within Syria. The war has also resulted in the large-scale destruction of social service infrastructure and the breakdown of the economy. The domestic economy has contracted significantly (estimated at 50 percent, see Table 7.3), and extreme poverty is widespread.

Social indicators provide a more concrete sense of the indirect effects of the war. Iraq now ranks at the bottom on a range of well-being indicators, and for these measures, it now stands on par with the poorest countries in sub-Saharan Africa and Asia.[9] Iraq witnessed a decline in public health and educational outcomes from the 1980s through the first half of the 2000s. This is particularly striking in light of an overall regional trend toward improvement in basic social indicators, even in the face of economic downturn. Health and educational outcomes have also deteriorated markedly in Syria. The relatively strong health care infrastructure Syria built in the decades prior to the conflict is now devastated in significant portions of the country. Before the conflict, life expectancy in Syria was high (74 in 2005), compared to many neighboring countries, but these achievements have experienced dramatic declines, dropping to 70 on average in 2015. For males, life expectancy dropped from 72 to 64 years.

The situation in Yemen has been similarly bleak since the onset of civil war in 2014. Agriculture and oil production have collapsed, and more than 55 percent of health facilities have been destroyed. Poverty rates are above 75 percent and malnutrition is rampant. In 2020, despite the continued conflict and ongoing crises, there was also a sharp drop in humanitarian support for Yemen. More than 60 percent of the UN humanitarian appeal was funded in 2019, but this collapsed to 30 percent in 2020 as many donors became preoccupied with domestic problems relating to the COVID-19 pandemic and GCC donor countries disengaged. Lower availability of foreign exchange reserves is leading to devaluation, inflation, and higher food prices. With foreign exchange reserves nearly exhausted, famine is a real possibility.

As discussed in Chapter 21, the Palestinian economy has undergone a progressive process of "de-development" since the late 1980s.[10] Growth rates fluctuated widely over time, as a result of insecurity and a decline in external support. Per capita GNI fell from 1996 to 2005, grew in the West Bank between 2003 and 2013, stagnated since 2016, and deteriorated sharply in 2020-2021. Over time, the Palestinian economy has become increasingly dependent on foreign aid. Poverty levels have risen steadily, despite the high educational attainment of the population. The Palestinian economy's productive base has been progressively "hollowed out."

Multiple factors have spurred Palestinian de-development. The primary and most proximate cause is the policy of Israeli closure of the territories and attacks on Gaza. Periodic closures hinder trade and labor flows. Israeli attacks on Gaza (in 2008, 2012, 2014, 2021) have introduced additional hardship, loss of life, destruction of property, and infrastructure. These restrictions have reduced access to land, water, and telecommunications infrastructure and impeded the formulation of a stable investment horizon that would enable private investors to calculate risk.[11] Local entrepreneurs are also entirely dependent on Israeli authorities to allow imports of inputs and final product exports through borders. Closure not only limits or shuts down Palestinian trade channels but also severs the links between the Israeli and Palestinian economies, which became tightly intertwined after 1967, when Palestinian employment became highly dependent on labor markets in Israel. Ironically, de-development accelerated after the 1993 signing of the Oslo Accords, which were designed to establish a framework for a comprehensive peace between Israel and the Palestinians (see Chapter 2).

The chapter thus far has provided a snapshot of Middle Eastern development indicators in the contemporary period. The next section traces the development trajectories of different types of political economies within the region from independence to the present. Focusing on industrialization strategies and social policy, this discussion provides a picture of shared challenges that postindependence governments in the Middle East confronted, elements of similarity in the policies they adopted in response, but also the crucial variations that have contributed to divergence in the economic and social trajectories of Middle Eastern countries in recent decades.

DEVELOPMENT PATHS IN THE MIDDLE EAST

Most Middle Eastern countries did not become independent states until the mid-20th century. Among the first order of business for postindependence elites was economic development and the establishment of national institutions. In the decades after independence, the political economies of Middle Eastern countries developed in strikingly similar ways, despite some divergences in their political characteristics. This section provides an overview of phases of development policy in distinct Middle Eastern political economy groups from about the 1950s to the present.

The Construction of National Economies in the Interwar Period

With the fall of the Ottoman Empire and the establishment of the Republic of Turkey in 1923, European colonial powers took direct control of much of the region, dividing former Ottoman provinces among them.[12] The Sykes–Picot Agreement, which the British and French negotiated secretly during World War I, created colonial protectorates, establishing British control over Iraq, Palestine, and Transjordan and French control over Syria and Lebanon. The territories of the Gulf were loosely ruled by prominent families and tribal leaders and, with the exception of Saudi Arabia, were largely under British control through a series of treaties signed in the late nineteenth and early twentieth centuries between the British and various shaykhdoms. Full independence was only achieved in the Gulf in 1971. In North Africa, France had a longer record of colonial rule, with the occupation and subsequent incorporation of Algeria into France in 1830 and the establishment of protectorates in Morocco and Tunisia in 1913 and 1881, respectively.

As discussed in Chapter 1, during the latter period of Ottoman rule, some regions and communities in the Ottoman Empire were increasingly integrated into the global economy in part through capitulations, or preferential relationships between minority communities and European governments. Colonial rule integrated these territories more directly in global markets controlled by European powers and established a basis for the creation of national economies with fixed borders, national systems of taxation, and tariffs and other trade barriers. These institutions brought about large-scale changes in the regional economy, which had previously enjoyed virtually free exchange within the territories of the Ottoman Empire.

The colonial period left important legacies for subsequent development trajectories, and in some countries laid the foundations for a nascent industrial sector. Colonialism in the Middle East, whether British or French, followed the same general principles. Colonial authorities tended to dominate local industry and invested little in local economies, expecting the colonized protostates to balance their own budgets and devoting few resources to welfare and public works. Local currencies were also closely tied to those of the colonial powers, facilitating trade while increasing the vulnerability of the colonized economies to global market fluctuations. Similar patterns in the administrative mechanisms of colonial rule also emerged: Throughout the region, colonial authorities relied heavily on alliances with tribal elites, large landowners, and nascent industrialists to consolidate their control.

Despite these shared patterns, the precise nature of colonial involvement in the territories varied across the region. The French invested most heavily in North Africa, where they established significant settler communities. In these countries, colonial expatriate investors founded industrial firms and controlled the major farms and agricultural enterprises. French workers were even employed in some urban industrial enterprises. The relative vibrancy of North African labor movements during the colonial period and in the first decades after independence was partly due to the exposure to unionization that indigenous workers gained through contact with their French counterparts. Although these patterns of French investment in the region ensured that the North African economies remained dependent on France and granted preferential treatment to French investors and workers, colonial authorities also invested in infrastructure and public services.

In the East, the British and French colonial authorities also transformed local economies, but they did not own land, nor did they establish resident communities to the same degree as in North Africa. The British effectively took control of Egypt in 1881 and established a formal protectorate in 1914. By this time, European investors had established some factories that largely targeted the domestic market, but British economic interests centered largely on cotton exports. As was true throughout the region, colonial domination granted little or no indigenous control over economic policymaking, and therefore few protective trade barriers designed to spur the rise of local industry were instituted under colonial rule. During the Great Depression, however, increased protectionism enabled more local investors to establish manufacturing enterprises.

In the British and French mandates in the East, including Palestine, Transjordan, Iraq, Lebanon, and Syria, colonial economic control operated in similar ways. Large-scale manufacturing was dominated by foreign investors, usually from the colonizing country, while the bulk of the local economy remained heavily agrarian and low income. In Jordan and Iraq, where much of the population was nomadic and rural, little industrial and agricultural development occurred during this period, particularly in Jordan. The discovery of oil in Iraq in the 1930s provided more resources but did little to stimulate industrialization. In Syria and Greater Lebanon, which encompassed many former Ottoman provinces, the French had established close economic and cultural ties with certain Christian communities, particularly the

Maronites, prior to the establishment of the Mandate. As in the French protectorates of North Africa, however, most of the Syrian and Lebanese economies remained primarily agricultural; a significant manufacturing base did not develop, and French investment did not benefit most of the population.

In Palestine, the influx of Jewish settlers provided an additional dimension to the economic impact of colonialism. Thanks to financial and infrastructural support from Britain and the community's own resources and skills, the Jews in Palestine constructed a relatively prosperous and industrially developed subeconomy within the British mandate. In Arab areas, however, infrastructure was generally less developed; agricultural techniques were not as productive, and industrial development lagged.

Until the discovery of oil in the 1930s, the Gulf economies were dominated by fishing, pearl diving, and in the case of Saudi Arabia earnings from the pilgrimage to Mecca. The Gulf shaykhdoms had virtually no manufacturing base or agricultural production, apart from date harvesting. Many contained significant Indian merchant communities, which received British legal protection. The discovery of oil brought an influx of foreign oil companies, which developed close relationships with ruling families, although significant royalties did not begin to flow until the late 1930s and 1940s.

Unlike most Arab countries, Turkey and Iran were never directly colonized by the European powers. Nonetheless, capitulations and high foreign debt ensured Turkish and Iranian dependence on Europe. After the establishment of an independent state in 1923, Turkey began to promote the local industrial sector, channeling funds through state-owned banks to encourage business development. In the 1930s, Turkey adopted an etatist economic approach, or policies that entailed extensive government intervention in the economy and the promotion of domestic industry through subsidies and protective barriers. As a result, Turkey had a more substantial industrial base than other Middle Eastern countries on the eve of WWII. In adopting state-led development, Turkey's leader, Mustafa Kemal Attaturk, was a pioneer in the region and served as a model for the Arab states in the post–WWII period. In Iran, Colonel Reza Khan, who became Shah in 1925 and founded the Pahlavi "dynasty," embarked on a nation-building initiative which entailed the growth of the state bureaucracy and military. As in Turkey, and reflecting the influence of Attaturk as a model, the Shah's government adopted etatist policies, established public enterprises in diverse industries, and invested in infrastructure and industry.[13]

The Great Depression and, later, WWII were extremely disruptive to the region but had the side effect of boosting domestic manufacturing. As most states in the Middle East protected themselves from the global downturn by instituting import barriers, local industry and even agriculture expanded. During the war, the disruption of trade routes permitted local manufacturing and processing factories to emerge to compensate for the sharp reduction in consumer imports. At the same time, colonial authorities instituted some policies to promote local industry as a way to support the war effort, creating a legacy of state intervention in the economy that was further consolidated in the post–WW II period. Still, the countries of the region remained vulnerable to global market fluctuations and remained fundamentally low-income, agrarian economies.

1950s–1970s: From Import Substitution Industrialization to Adjustment

In the post–WWII period, Middle Eastern countries established distinct political economies that nonetheless reflected variations around broadly shared strategies of state-led economic and social development. These strategies varied depending on a country's specific resource endowments, human capital development, structural features, regime type, and patterns of state-society relations. Yet they reflected the orthodoxies of the period concerning how late-developing, postcolonial countries could meet the economic challenges they faced.

In all countries, the state's role in the economy ballooned, as manifested in the creation of state-owned enterprises, public investment, and the growth of government bureaucracies. In some cases, such as Algeria, Egypt, Iraq, and Syria, state expansion was financed in part through the nationalization of assets held by preindependence economic elites, notably large landowners and industrialists. The non-oil countries tended to institute policies to support local production. The oil countries initially intervened less in domestic production, given the dominant role of oil in their economies and their minimal industrial bases.

These different political economies were associated with distinct types of economic policies. Oil supplied the resources needed for public social provision, and varied state economic ideologies shaped the nature of these arrangements. Countries with little or no oil or other natural resources adopted populist rhetoric and quasi-socialist principles for organizing the economy, including tight regulation of the private sector. Among these countries however, traditional monarchies were guided by a more liberal economic ideology in which private business was expected to play an important role in the economy, while countries dominated by new revolutionary republican regimes saw the traditional elites from the private sector as a threat. But even in the monarchies there was recognition of the sharp limits of private sectors and the need for the state to create conditions for private sector development.

In the postwar period, countries in almost all developing regions, including the Middle East, adopted import substitution industrialization (ISI) as a strategy for economic development. ISI involves a set of trade and economic policies aimed at reducing dependence on foreign imports and substituting foreign with domestically produced goods. To promote national industry and industrialization, ISI policy instruments include tariff barriers, quotas on imports, and, at times, the nationalization of industries. ISI also has ramifications for domestic social structures by fostering the rise of a domestic industrial bourgeoisie oriented toward the local market and the emergence of a local industrial working class, which benefits from relatively high wages in the formal sector and constitutes an important consumer base for domestic production. Populist policies such as consumer price subsidies on staple goods also constituted an important form of state welfare.

During the period from 1950s to the 1970s, these policies produced in most countries an economic expansion that has been unmatched ever since. As a result, much of the region experienced a marked shift in the sectoral structure of the economy, with fast growth in employment and production in manufacturing and a decline of agriculture. At the same time, the public sector grew dramatically with the establishment of state-owned enterprises and vast public investment.[14] But ISI ultimately faced serious challenges in the Middle East—and in most developing countries—because it failed to generate sufficient foreign exchange, a problem that especially plagued the non-oil economies that could not benefit from the sale of oil on world markets.

For varying durations, all of the single-party republics adopted quasi-socialist strategies of legitimation, including Egypt (1957–1974), Algeria (1962–1989), Tunisia (1962–1969), Syria (1963–1990s), and Iraq (1963–1990s). When these policies were initiated, many republics were allied with the Soviet Union, which helped to inspire the adoption of planning and the expansion of the public sector. The new leaders of the republics instituted land reform policies, transferring land held by colonial authorities, settlers, and local landed elites to less privileged strata. They also developed or expanded public health and education systems. Social contracts in these countries took the form of "authoritarian bargains": with the wave of postcolonial nationalizations and the establishment of state-owned enterprises, civil service and parastatal workers gained job security and a range of social protections, but they were expected to be politically docile.

The republics differed in the extent to which they made populism and "Arab socialism" the centerpiece of their rhetoric and actually instituted populist policies. Egypt under President Gamal Abdel Nasser (1956–1970) and Syria during the initial phase of Ba'athist rule from 1963 to 1970 exhibited a particularly strong commitment to populism, while Tunisia turned away from its quasi-socialist experiment earlier than the other republics. In the case of Algeria, oil wealth greatly aided populist policies, particularly during spikes in world oil prices, which helped to postpone the problems that tend to arise with ISI strategies.

As the prototypical example of Arab socialism, the case of Egypt is illustrative. When the Free Officers took over in a coup in 1952 (see Chapter 10), the state instituted a major shift in economic policy. Land reform was designed to undercut the power of large landholders and spur more investment in industry as the first step, although in practice little land was actually redistributed. State relations with the private sector were antagonistic—the nationalization of major banks, insurance companies, shipping companies, and other key industries exacerbated tensions between the state and business. The economic weight of State Owned Enterprises (SOEs) was particularly important, with public enterprises accounting for about 60 percent of manufacturing value added. By the end of Nasser's rule, economic stagnation was growing, contributing to mounting popular disaffection. ISI had not successfully bred a productive, revenue-generating manufacturing sector capable of propelling larger development. In this context, Nasser's successor, Anwar Sadat, moved away from Arab socialism toward *infitah*, or economic opening, which involved a limited liberalization of foreign trade. In practice, the main result of *infitah* was the creation a new export–import class, but the policy had little effect on stimulating private industrial development.

As in Egypt, the other republican middle-oil countries were borne out of violent political processes that put at the helm groups that espoused radical departures from the past—embodied, for example, in Ba'athist ideology in Iraq and Syria and socialism in Algeria. In Iraq and Algeria, oil initially supported a more benign form of autocratic rule, within a modernist nationalistic phase of rapid development, industrialization, and urbanization. The second more violent and repressive form emerged later, after the industrialization drives of the 1960s and 1970s ended in failure, which, coupled with the humiliating defeat of 1967 for the front-line states, put into question the core legitimacy of these regimes. Oil allowed these states to finance large armies and security forces and also to remain somewhat independent of foreign patrons.[15] These countries did not come to see the development of the private sector as an attractive alternative to state-led development, as it threatened regime durability at its core. In many of these countries, when the state retreated, it was replaced by a very narrow form of cronyism, closely associated with the regime and with rising levels of political repression.

In some cases, foreign adventurism was a means to attempt to replenish "strategic rents."[16] Iraq, coming out of the war with Iran with a huge foreign debt and decimated infrastructure, sought to invade Kuwait as a way to shore up its economy, with dramatic consequences for the Iraqi people. Iraq lost most of its oil revenues during its war with Iran and again when it was under sanctions. In both cases, the country had to undergo wrenching and socially calamitous adjustment periods. Syria's participation in the international coalition to push Iraq out of Kuwait was a transparent yet successful bid to generate strategic rents during a period of weak economic performance. In Algeria, the attempt to reform after the first oil shock contributed to the outbreak of the civil war of the 1990s, which still marks the sociopolitical scene today. Under the guise of increased repression and the fight against Islamists, army interests have come to dominate a repressed private sector. In Syria, economic stagnation led to selective economic reforms that included among their effects reduced public investment in the country's poorer regions. Economic pressures also created a motivation to exploit Syria's intervention in Lebanon's civil war in 1976 as a means to extract rents and beef up the regime of Hafez al-Assad in Damascus. In Yemen, the fight over newly discovered oil fueled a civil war and led to the subsequent forced unification of the country in 1990.

From their establishment as independent states, Jordan and Morocco had adopted more liberal economic rhetoric, which privileged the private sector as the driver of development. But despite ideological and policy differences, the public sector was equally important across the non-oil monarchies and single-party republics, with the state as the main source of investment and a major employer. In Jordan, the domestic private sector, which is largely of Palestinian origin, was mainly involved in sectors with low barriers to entry, such as light manufacturing and exports of agricultural goods. In Morocco, SOEs, special investment agencies and holding companies linked to the palace, controlled large portions of the economy, while all major private interests enjoyed close ties with the monarchy. During the early 1970s, a series of investment codes and economic policies, including "Moroccanization" laws that transferred majority ownership of domestic firms to indigenous capital, further promoted local private industry.

The oil monarchies of the Gulf pursued a different development trajectory. With oil dominating their economies and minimal or no manufacturing bases beyond joint ventures with foreign companies in petrochemicals, there was little need to adopt protectionist trade regimes aimed at promoting local industry. Furthermore, with the exception of Saudi Arabia, the indigenous population was too small to warrant an ISI approach. The quadrupling of world oil prices in 1973 provided rulers with the resources to fund generous social programs, which granted citizens free or heavily subsidized health care, schooling, housing, and other benefits, as well as preferential access to secure government employment. It also enabled the Gulf states to launch ambitious infrastructure development programs. Foreign labor was imported on a massive scale to build the national infrastructure and to fill jobs in expanding service sectors. The oil monarchies also established numerous state-owned enterprises in all key sectors of their economies.[17] The presence of comprehensive welfare benefits had political implications: By catering to the needs of the population, they undercut the potential impetus for citizens to oppose their rulers and prevented the rise of an indigenous working class that could mobilize in opposition to the authoritarian monarchies.

Prior to the 1979 Islamic Revolution, Iran could be classified as an oil monarchy, albeit one with a far higher population than those of the Gulf oil monarchies. After 1941, when the Allied Powers helped install Mohammad Reza Shah Pahlavi on the Iranian throne, Iran's economic strategy gradually evolved to rely on oil exports and ISI. In the 1960s and 1970s, the Shah exercised increasingly tight authority over Iranian society. This control was reflected in patterns of state intervention in the economy and growing tensions between the monarchy and traditional elements of the private sector centered in the bazaars of Tehran and other cities. While the state maintained control over heavy industry, the private sector focused on lighter manufacturing and other specialized industries, at times in cooperation with foreign capital.[18] Many of these firms were nationalized after the Iranian revolution of 1979 that instituted an Islamic republic.

1980 TO 2011: THE RETREAT OF THE STATE AND RISE OF CRONY CAPITALISM

By the late 1970s, the golden age of growth had stalled in the Middle East. Most countries in the region began to feel the limits of ISI, which failed to generate sufficient foreign exchange and foster competitive industries. But unlike countries in Latin America and sub-Saharan Africa that initiated adjustment programs in the 1980s, most countries in the MENA region were able to delay reforms. The region as a whole earned more revenues, thanks to oil and regional labor remittances, than other developing regions. Many countries also borrowed resources externally to finance growing deficits. By the late-1980s, however, adjustment became inevitable as fiscal and balance of payment deficits continued to grow, external debt became increasingly more costly to refinance, while the failure of ISI and a drop in international oil prices piled up the pressure on many MENA economies. In many non-oil economies, it was the emergence of full-blown balance-of-payments crises which compelled them to sign on to stabilization and structural adjustment programs (SAPs) with international financial institutions (IFIs), including the International Monetary Fund (IMF) and the World Bank (see Box 7.2).

BOX 7.2

ECONOMIC LIBERALIZATION, STABILIZATION, AND STRUCTURAL ADJUSTMENT

In the 1980s and 1990s, the IFIs—and particularly the World Bank, International Monetary Fund (IMF), and US Treasury Department—reached a consensus on the appropriate policy prescriptions for reforming and reviving economies throughout the developing world. These policies, often referred to as the "Washington Consensus," were designed to decrease the state's role in the economy, promote private sector-led development strategies, and reduce "distortions" in the economy created by government interventions in fiscal and monetary policy. While the Washington Consensus remained an ideal type that was never fully or rigidly implemented in the Middle East, countries with large macroeconomic imbalances, in part resulting from their ISI experiences, were encouraged and even pressured to adopt stabilization followed by structural adjustment policies.

- Stabilization aims to restore macroeconomic balance by stemming inflation and reducing government deficits through higher taxes and reduced spending, in some cases involving cuts of consumer subsidies.

- Structural adjustment focuses on long-term, more microeconomic change in the economy. The SAPs intend to make as many goods and services available for sale through the market as possible, rather than through government allocation, subsidies, import licensing, output quotas, ration shops, government agencies, and public enterprises. Structural adjustment is sometimes referred to as "liberalization" or "deregulation."

By the late 1990s, however, it became evident that the results of stabilization and SAPs were disappointing. Most countries were able to gradually stabilize their internal and external accounts, largely by shrinking the size of the state and reducing imports. However, they were much less keen on liberalizing their economies. In the minds of many analysts, the implementation of structural change was not politically appealing to political leaders, as they faced overwhelming opposition from almost all societal groups, including from organized labor concentrated in SOEs and from economic elites, both of whom have long profited from cozy ties to the state, and have served as the main social support for most Middle Eastern rulers. Reforms also increased economic insecurity—and the deepening of economic grievances—among the region's large middle classes, which had benefited from public support for education, housing, energy and food subsidies, and employment guarantees for college graduates.

Countries that had undergone stabilization programs grew faster after the "lost decade" from the mid-1980s to the mid-1990s, but growth was not inclusive, and the chasm between politically connected firms and the informal market expanded. Some countries experienced painful contractions in consumption with dire consequences for the population, particularly after the reduction or elimination of consumer subsidies and social programs. As a result, the IFIs incorporated greater emphasis on social safety nets and antipoverty programs, although critics claimed that these revisions were little more than window dressing.

The main resource-poor Middle Eastern countries to sign on to economic reform programs with the support of the IFIs were Egypt, Jordan, Morocco, and Tunisia.[19] All four countries experienced mounting debt burdens, albeit to varying degrees, in the lead-up to the adoption of economic liberalization programs. Figure 7.5 shows the rise in total debt as a percentage of GDP in the four countries in the 1980s and 1990s, and its subsequent decline when external debts were reduced in the context of structural adjustment programs. As the figure shows, Tunisia experienced the lowest debt burden of all countries and, therefore, undertook economic reform from a position of relative strength. Jordan faced a particularly high debt burden, which spiked as a result of the first Gulf war when Jordan's perceived support for Iraq compelled some of its

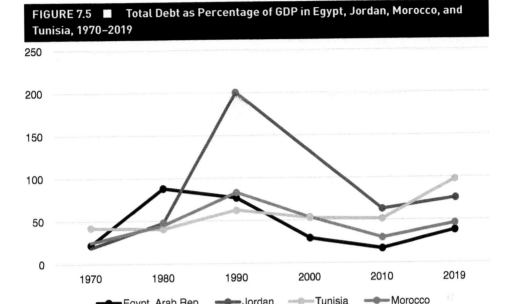

FIGURE 7.5 ■ Total Debt as Percentage of GDP in Egypt, Jordan, Morocco, and Tunisia, 1970–2019

regional and global allies to reduce external assistance. In all cases, trade liberalization, including reductions in trade taxes and tariff barriers, the gradual elimination of quotas and import licenses, and overall deregulation of the economy and privatization were central goals. Yet the actual record of economic reform has varied from country to country.

Economic liberalization in the Middle East has had a mixed record at best. Among the LOC economies, which were compelled to adopt structural adjustment programs due to their lack of resource wealth, growth trajectories varied. In Table 7.3, it is possible to observe the divergence in performance between Egypt, Jordan, Morocco, and Tunisia. Growth rates have been erratic, particularly in Jordan, given its dependence on external rents, and Morocco, which is highly sensitive to drought, among other factors. In the 2000s, growth rates steadily increased in Egypt, reaching a high point in 2008.

Economic restructuring has generally come with enormous social costs and failed to bring benefits to much of the population. Two main critiques have been raised. First, the economic adjustment programs reduced the size and role of the state, including in the provision of essential health, education, social protection, and infrastructural services. This has disproportionately harmed the poor, and reduced social mobility. Persistent poverty and widespread concerns about downward social mobility among middle classes and educated youth constitute an important backdrop to uprisings across the region. Moderate growth in the years leading up to the uprisings raised popular expectations and aspirations including among the middle class, yet economic performance continued to disappoint.[20] Second, the liberalization of markets and new emphasis on private sector development was unbalanced, benefiting disproportionately economic elites that supported regimes in place.[21] In the absence of dynamic markets, economies became increasingly divided between small connected formal private sectors and growing unregulated informal economies. As a result, economic growth remained modest post-liberalization, leading to a rise in unemployment and underemployment, while at the same time, crony capitalists became billionaires.

Economic and social policies that fostered crony capitalism, aggravated inequality, and pushed growing numbers of people into positions of economic precarity eroded the social contracts on which regimes had relied to maintain social stability. The spread of new communications technologies, including both the internet and more widely accessible satellite TV networks such as Aljazeera based in Qatar amplified public awareness of corruption and the abusive treatment of citizens at the hands of indifferent authorities. Several countries experienced increasing levels of public protest during the 2000s, including in Egypt.

In response, regimes struggled to adapt existing models of governance to navigate demands for continued market-oriented reforms with the social and economic effects of declining redistribution. Across the region, regimes undertook projects of authoritarian upgrading(Heydemann 2004) to cope with rising popular discontent. In Syria, these efforts were branded as a transition to a "social-market" economy, emphasizing the regime's intent balance commitments to the traditional social base of the Ba'ath Party with the interests of an increasingly predatory crony elite. In Egypt, Jordan, Yemen, and Morocco, regimes appropriated the rhetoric of political reform and increased tolerance of opposition movements, typically Islamist movements, to bolster their standing. In Egypt's parliamentary elections of 2005, candidates affiliated with the Muslim Brotherhood won 88 of 454 seats to constitute the largest opposition bloc. Moderate Islamist parties fared well in elections in Jordan, Yemen, and Morocco as well during this period.

Cosmetic reforms, however, did little to mitigate the conditions of middle classes and the urban poor. The fall in the quality of public services and the lack of opportunities for youth amidst the growing wealth of the few were the leading causes of anger that led to the uprisings of 2011.[22]

The Roll-Back of the State

Notwithstanding differences in their official economic ideologies and the composition of their ruling coalitions, most governments in the region had invested significantly in social services after independence. When fiscal crises hit countries across the region in the 1980s and 1990s, however, not all countries were able to sustain these investments. Table 7.5 depicts the share of government expenditures devoted to health and education for MENA countries in the three different political economy types at peak and bottom levels of government spending, which vary by country.[23]

In general, as resources contracted, government spending on health and education has been less affected in the region as a whole than expenditures on other areas, falling from about eight percent to six percent of GDP. In the MOC countries, however, it fell the most precipitously, from 6.5 percent to 3.8 percent, an extraordinarily low level. The declines in the budgets for health and education led to less progress in human development and a decline in the quality of services, especially those going to the poor who cannot afford to purchase medical care and schooling in the burgeoning private sector. Most countries of the region therefore experienced setbacks in their HDI indicators.

TABLE 7.5 ■ Public Spending on Health and Education (as a Percentage of GDP) in MENA Countries at Their Peak and Bottom Levels, Various Years

	Peak Expenditure	Peak Date	Bottom Expenditure	Bottom Date
HOC	**9.5**		**6.5**	
Bahrain	7.9	1986	5.4	2000
Kuwait	11.2	1986	5.6	2007
Oman	8.6	1986	6.6	1997
Saudi Arabia	10.2	1987	8.5	1995
MOC	**6.5**		**3.8**	
Iran	9.9	1980	5.6	1991
Syria	3.0	1980	2.0	1990
LOC	**6.9**		**5.7**	
Egypt	6.5	1982	5.5	1998
Jordan	5.3	1980	6.2	1992
Lebanon	N/A	1994	2.7	2011
Morocco	7.8	1981	6.9	1996
Tunisia	7.9	1984	7.1	1998
Other	**7.1**		**7.7**	
Israel	9.6	1983	11.8	2011
Turkey	4.6	1997	3.7	1998

Source: Ishac Diwan and Tarik Akin. 2015. "Fifty Years of Fiscal Policy in the Arab Region." Economic Research Forum (ERF) Working Paper No. 914. Cairo, Egypt: Economic Research Forum, May 2015.

The Rise of Crony Capitalism and Informality

Market reforms do not occur in a political vacuum.[24] Across the MENA region, well-connected elites monopolized economic opportunities as governments "liberalized" their economies. By the end of the first decade of the 2000s, it was clear that economic reforms had failed to transform the region. A principal weakness of the new economic regimes that emerged was the low demand for skilled workers. Governments stopped hiring, but they were not replaced by strong private sectors. Looking at the structure of employment in the region (Figure 7.6), one sees that the size of the formal private sector in the region remained marginal—a mere 10 percent to 15 percent of the labor force in Morocco, Tunisia, Egypt, and much lower figures in Iraq and Yemen. Moreover, unemployment, especially among educated youth, remained high, as the few good jobs created went to the "connected," while other educated youth had to either remain unemployed (Figure 7.7) or move to the poorer informal economy, a sentiment reflected in popular perceptions that good jobs depend on connections, or *wasta*, rather than hard work.

The lack of dynamism of the private sector is also seen in its low rates of investment. The idea of state retrenchment was to make resources available for the private sector to invest according to price signals. But as public sector investment collapsed (Figure 7.3), private investment

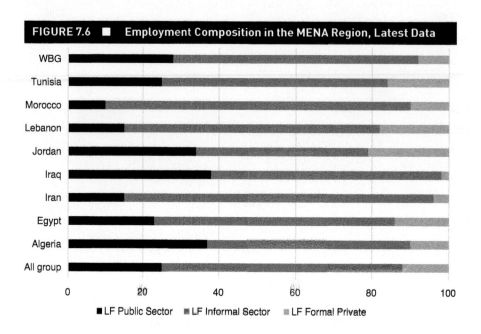

FIGURE 7.6 ■ Employment Composition in the MENA Region, Latest Data

■ LF Public Sector ■ LF Informal Sector ■ LF Formal Private

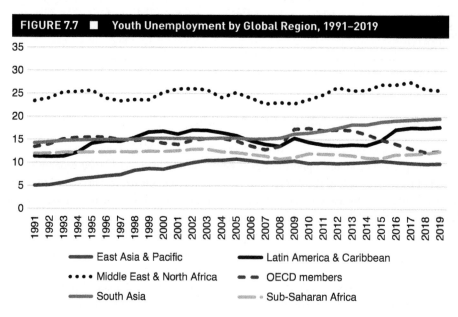

FIGURE 7.7 ■ Youth Unemployment by Global Region, 1991–2019

━━ East Asia & Pacific ━━ Latin America & Caribbean
•••• Middle East & North Africa ━ ━ OECD members
━━ South Asia ━ Sub-Saharan Africa

did not rise sufficiently to take up the slack (Table 7.6). Indeed, by 2010, the private investment to GDP ratio in these countries was at a mere 18.7 percent, about five percent more than in the 1970s, but not sufficiently high to compensate for the roll-back of the state, and not enough to create the types and numbers of jobs needed in the region. Except in Lebanon, coming out of its long civil war, total investment actually decreased everywhere. The performance of Egypt, where private investment remained around ten percent of GDP in the 2000s, and of Jordan and Morocco, where it was slightly higher, but close to its historical levels, were particularly disappointing.

A central question is why the Arab states' economies underperformed. Economists have argued that reforms have not gone far enough, that economies remained dominated by monopolies, and that the market mechanism was not allowed to force innovation and productivity

TABLE 7.6 ■	Private Investment by Decade				
Country	*Private Investment*				
	1970–1980	*1981–1990*	*1991–2000*	*2001–2010*	*2011–2019*
HOCs	9.69	9.21	9.01	12.40	14.40
Bahrain	10.29	12.77	14.82	19.37	22.97
Kuwait	1.53	3.99	6.36	8.55	11.68
Oman	6.61	4.23	4.65	9.44	11.02
Saudi Arabia		6.47	6.91	11.09	12.71
UAE	20.33	18.59	12.30	13.55	13.63
MOCs	12.52	11.11	13.28	13.15	12.95
Algeria	27.59	17.69	15.23	n.a	n.a
Iran	22.58	20.91	21.06	22.06	17.53
Sudan	2.66	6.77	10.51	16.86	14.63
Syria	6.06	9.76	12.01	7.04	n.a
Yemen		2.91	7.23	6.64	6.69
LOCs	3.70	8.60	13.61	16.96	15.11
Egypt	0.00	10.69	8.46	10.14	7.87
Jordan	7.76	15.55	18.63	19.24	16.09
Lebanon	0.00	3.07	24.71	20.57	21.36
Tunisia	10.74	13.69	16.27	17.91	15.2

Source: World Bank Indicators

gains through the process of competition (Diwan, Malik, and Atiyas 2019). Political scientists have focused their attention on the rise of "networks of privilege" and "crony capitalists" with political connections to regimes in place, which have come to dominate the (formal) economy because of their support for regimes, as opposed to their superior economic performance (Heydeman 2004, Henry and Springborg 2010).

In Egypt, the rise of what came to be termed "crony capitalism" accelerated in the 2010s with the "businessmen" cabinet headed by Ahmad Nazif (2004–2011). In Tunisia, the Ben Ali and Trabelsi families monopolized business opportunities and even expropriated the real estate and business holdings of wealthy elites. Similar stories about favoritism and insiders abound in Syria, Libya, Yemen, and Algeria, where political cronies and military elites seemed to control large chunks of the private sector (Alley 2010; Haddad 2012; Sayigh 2020, Tlemcani 1999).

Economic reforms posed existential challenges to the ruling elites. For all the autocratic rulers in the region, a main concern, given that there was little political reform in parallel, was to maintain their political control in contexts in which they were loosening their hold over important instruments of governance and patronage—ranging from ownership of SOEs, to large public investment budgets, large civil services, with significant implications for those who had benefited from postindependence social contracts and weakening constraints on potential sources of opposition. Cronyism entailed practices such as the granting of monopoly rights to the rulers' close associates, the selling of public firms and land at reduced prices, the manipulation of the financial markets for the benefits of a few insiders, and the extension of legal impunity to privileged insiders who engaged in formally illicit economic activities. These practices were the central mechanisms that resolved the contradictions created by the gradual liberalization of the region's economies in environments where political power remained highly autocratic, allowing regimes that confronted growing economic pressures to redefine the rules of the game by building alliances with business elites in ways that permitted them to dominate the business sector and use it as a new source of patronage and predation.

For large segments of the population, cronyism and corruption, both petty and grand, became increasingly seen as the hallmark of economic liberalism and the source of many ills, including the job deficit, the rise in inequality, and the perpetuation of authoritarian rule. Indeed, the perceived corruption of the political and business elites was a driving force of popular discontent that led to the uprisings of 2011.

DEVELOPMENT CHALLENGES IN THE MIDDLE EAST

Economists generally agree on the proximate causes of underdevelopment in the Middle East—weak integration in the global economy, low levels of investment, lack of technology transfer, industrial noncompetitiveness, high levels of government ownership and investment, the low quality of education, and the high costs of doing business.[25] But these factors are symptoms of deeper causes. The Arab Human Development Report (AHDR), first published by the UN Development Program's Arab Fund for Economic and Social Development in 2002, points to broader development failures. Written by Arab scholars and practitioners, the AHDR emphasized not only the low levels of per capita income in the region relative to its potential but also declining productivity, low innovation and underdeveloped research capabilities, poor health and educational outcomes, enormous gender inequality, and persistent authoritarianism. Critics point to the AHDR's apparent adoption of a Western democratization agenda, reluctance to blame external intervention for negative socioeconomic outcomes in the region, and deeply embedded clientelism and patrimonialism within states as factors that perpetuate the status quo.[26] Nonetheless, there is a broad consensus both within and beyond the region that the well-being of citizens of Middle Eastern countries had declined in the period from the 1980s to the onset of mass protests in late 2010 in Tunisia.

Competing explanations for this persistent underdevelopment range from innate and relatively fixed cultural characteristics to the nature of resource endowments, and the role of political institutions. The next section highlights the strengths and weaknesses of these perspectives.

Islam and Economic Development

In searching for features specific to the Middle East that can explain persistent underdevelopment, some point to the predominance of Islam. They argue that Islam leads to unresponsive authoritarian governments, obstacles to independent reasoning, and the absence of a rational secular mindset, which impedes capitalist economic development.[27] Timur Kuran has pointed out that particular institutions in Islamic economics, such as the prohibition against *riba*, or interest, and *zakat*, or almsgiving, as religious obligations could limit capital accumulation.[28]

Arguments linking Islamic beliefs and traditions with underdevelopment can be critiqued on both theoretical and empirical lines. Economic growth is variable over time, and culture and religion, which evolve very slowly, are unlikely to account for this variation. As already noted, predominantly Muslim countries such as Egypt and Jordan have experienced shifting growth rates in a relatively short time frame. Furthermore, countries such as Indonesia and Malaysia, which are also predominantly Muslim, have enjoyed sustained periods of high growth. More broadly, cross-national statistical analyses show that countries with predominantly Muslim populations are not associated with poor growth.

A more nuanced argument centered on Islamic institutions rather than religion also faces theoretical and empirical contradictions. It is conceivable that Islamic institutions have negative effects on development that are erased by the positive effects of other Islamic or non-Islamic institutions in Middle Eastern countries, or that there has been sufficient convergence in institutions and policies in recent years so the negative effects of Islamic institutions have diminished. Economic historians argue that it is in fact alternative factors and not Islam that explain the relative decline of the Ottoman Empire from the 16th century onward. In particular, the strong and highly centralized Ottoman state deterred the rise of an independent entrepreneurial sector and prioritized welfare over economic growth and capital accumulation.[29]

For centuries, the Islamic world outperformed the non-Islamic world, indicating that there is nothing about Islam per se that renders it incompatible with growth. Rather than focusing on Islam or features of Islamic societies, many scholars thus emphasize other explanations for underdevelopment in the Middle East.

Oil and the "Resource Curse"

A prominent explanation for the relative underdevelopment of Middle Eastern countries focuses on the "curse" of oil wealth. This argument refers to the fact that resource abundance is correlated with poor economic performance, unbalanced growth, weak state institutions, and authoritarianism, among other ills. In its economic dimensions, the resource curse centers on the concept of the "Dutch Disease," or the theory that an increase in revenues from natural resources will lead to a decline in a country's industrial sector by raising the exchange rate, which makes the manufacturing sector less competitive. Similarly, states that rely on oil or other forms of windfall profits for a large portion of their revenues are deemed rentier states, which derive their income from nonproductive enterprise. These states concentrate their efforts on distributing wealth to the population, often to buy social peace and preempt greater societal demands for accountability and participation, rather than fostering the conditions for the productive generation of wealth in their societies.[30]

The resource curse provides a theoretically compelling explanation for underdevelopment, particularly in the oil-exporting countries. Yet when viewed from a larger historical and comparative perspective, there are strong reasons to be skeptical of this argument. Oil-rich countries experience more volatile growth rates and underperform with respect to their own wealth endowments, but their long-term growth rates are no slower than those of non-oil economies.[31] Norway and Indonesia, major oil exporters, and Botswana, which has vast mineral deposits, have managed to escape the alleged inevitability of the resource curse, and have also managed to attain sustained records of economic growth.

In the literature on the political economy of development, it has become virtually axiomatic that weak state institutions limit the prospects for economic development because state agencies direct resources to productive sectors and facilitate a climate conducive to investment.[32] Yet recent research questions the alleged negative repercussions of oil wealth on state institutional quality: Oil wealth does not diminish state strength but rather requires governments to perform exceptionally well in order to manage windfall profits effectively. Even among resource-rich countries, economic and social outcomes vary substantially across high- and low-population oil exporters. The low-population HOC oil exporters (whether measured on an aggregate or a per capita basis) had enough resources to placate opposition, and as a result they actually encouraged private sector involvement.[33] As noted earlier, within the Middle East the resource curse has really afflicted the MOCs, which experienced significantly lower growth rates. These critiques of the resource curse argument suggest that oil wealth in and of itself does not explain by itself poor and uneven economic performance in the Middle East.

The "Governance Gap"

Increasingly, explanations for poor economic performance focus on governance. Inclusive and accountable governance is presumed to produce positive developmental outcomes by increasing popular participation and influence on policymaking, thereby increasing the effectiveness of governance and the probability that policies serving the welfare of the people will be enacted. With growing emphasis on private sector-led development, good governance has attained increased importance. Respect for the rule of law and property rights are critical for firms, which require assurances before they will invest that their assets will not be expropriated and have a chance of reaping good returns. Arbitrary enforcement of laws and regulations on the other hand is a deterrent to private investment.

Beyond the challenges posed by natural-resource wealth, oil endowments may have contributed to poor economic performance in less direct ways. Oil wealth, which has spread indirectly throughout the region through foreign aid, investment flows, and remittance earnings, facilitated the establishment of an interventionist and redistributive development model. This model is characterized by a comprehensive state role in the provision of welfare and social services, the repression of the private sector, and the suppression of contestation in the political arena.[34] Aided by resource wealth, then, rulers established bargains or social contracts with their citizens—authoritarian bargains—that entailed generous state social programs for citizens in exchange for political quiescence. In spite of some similarities, the nature of these social contracts, however, shows some variation across the distinct types of political economies, reflecting differences in patterns of governance across the different types of MENA political economies.

The major source of the governance gaps between most countries in the Middle East and other regions are the lack of public accountability to the population, and citizen access to political and civic rights. Figure 7.8 shows that while there is variation among MENA's three types of political economies with respect to some governance indicators, the indicator for "voice and accountability," which measures the extent to which a country's citizens can freely select their

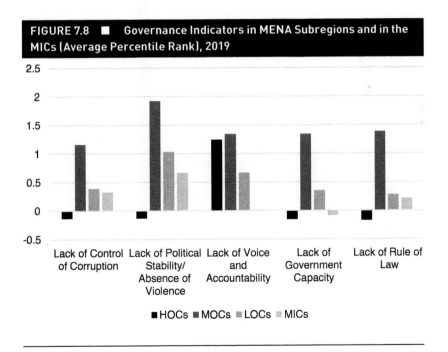

FIGURE 7.8   ■   Governance Indicators in MENA Subregions and in the MICs (Average Percentile Rank), 2019

■ HOCs ■ MOCs ■ LOCs ■ MICs

Source: Kaufman et al. (2020)

government, as well as freedom of expression, freedom of association, and a free media is low across all groups and way below the middle income average.

The other indicators—for the rule of law, government effectiveness, and control of corruption—tend to be highest in the HOCs, followed by the LOCs, and then, at a distance, by the MOCs, which tend to score below the MIC group. This confirms again that it is this group of countries that have been hit most by the resource curse. The differences among the two types of oil-dependent economies is thus large: in the HOCs, governments compensate for limited accountability by providing public goods to maintain citizen satisfaction. In the MOCs, more limited oil resources are instead used to beef up security services to enforce their elites' privileged access to economic opportunities.

Political, economic, and social rights are integral to achieving human development, yet according to many reports, the Arab world is particularly deficient in political freedom. The AHDR reports (2002, 2003, and 2004) condemn low levels of freedom and tie them to poor economic outcomes, such as the failure to create the human capital needed to compete effectively in globalized markets. As Figure 7.9 shows, even after the Arab uprisings, the Middle East hosts the largest number of authoritarian regimes, as measured by Polity IV data on levels of democracy, in comparison with other global regions.

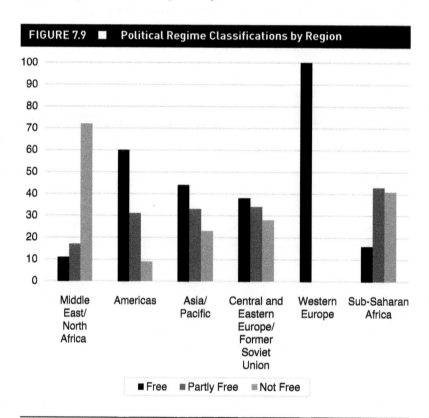

FIGURE 7.9 ■ Political Regime Classifications by Region

Source: Freedom House, "Freedom in the World 2020"

The relative dearth of political freedom and failure to uphold the rule of law inhibit the formulation and implementation of policies that benefit the public good, rather than private interests. Corruption and bureaucratic red tape deter the levels of private and foreign investment needed to sustain economic growth and ultimately inhibit further integration of Middle Eastern countries into the global economy.[35]

Arguments linking poor governance or authoritarianism with relative underdevelopment in the Middle East are compelling. However, the origins of corruption, lack of transparency, and weak state institutions in Middle Eastern political economies deserve much more systematic analysis. Scholars of development increasingly view effective extractive, regulatory, and administrative institutions as critical to development,[36] and, hence, explaining the roots of effective and ineffective state institutions is paramount. Recent studies point to the historical roots of capable state and societal institutions in postcolonial countries and trace the effects of colonialism on subsequent development outcomes.[37] In the Middle East, however, relatively little is known about the precise impact of Ottoman and colonial institutions on the evolution of state institutions and forms of economic management in postindependence states. These protracted colonial experiences disrupted and altered existing economic and social practices in the region and, therefore, shaped growth and development trajectories in the long run.

FUTURE PROSPECTS

The Arab Spring was a major instance of postindependence eruption of anger across the region, where societies voiced loudly their desire for dignity and demanded to participate in the shaping of their future. The effects of the uprisings will continue to reverberate and ripple across the region for years to come. But ten years after 2011 the region's economy is at a historic low. The decade of the 2010s was lost in political maneuvering to fill the political void created by the uprisings, and most countries witnessed regress on both the governance and economic fronts. Political protests continue to occasionally take place in Morocco, Tunisia, Egypt, Jordan, Syria, and Iraq. In 2019, just before COVID-19 hit, the region witnessed a second wave of revolts, which started in Sudan, followed by the Algerian Hirak, and then by massive uprisings in Iraq and Lebanon. While COVID-19 froze these ongoing social movements up to the time of this writing, its economic impact and what it reveals about the true nature of state capacity and economic resilience are issues that could further inflame popular contestation.

By 2020, as the COVID-19 pandemic began, social grievances were as high as ever. No country has managed yet to overcome the deep structural weaknesses that led to the uprisings in the first place, and the challenges have only grown in complexity since. Growth fell to close to zero on a per capita basis, for the 2010s decade, even when Syria is left out of the average (see Table 7.3)—this is very similar to the lost decade of the 1980s.

The collapse of oil prices in the mid-2010s, coming on the heels of the long second oil boom (2000–2014) has left oil producers with large imbalances, and hit the rest of the region through lower remittances, and reduced FDI and official assistance from GCC countries. Oil revenue in the region as a whole fell from about $1 trillion a year, to about $400 billion, with tentative signs of a limited recovery in oil prices at the start of the current decade. While the old slogan of "diversification" again rolls across the region, the harsh reality is that most governments are more focused on balancing their books than on structural change. In 2020, GDP shrank by seven percent for the region. Coming out of the COVID-19 "crisis atop a crisis," most of the regions' economies are on an unsustainable path, with a fast disappearing fiscal space that presages financial crises to come, only foreshadowed by Lebanon's collapse, with Iraq, Tunisia, Jordan, and Oman at great risk given their heightened financial vulnerability (see Table 7.7).

On the governance side, ruling regimes have fought back fiercely after 2011. Instead of a democratic transformation and a "new social contract," the region has witnessed civil wars in four countries, army takeovers in Egypt, Sudan, and Algeria, and a generalized movement of autocratic renewal. In many countries, military budgets went up, even as resources became more constrained. Even as some presidents changed, the willingness of ruling regimes to inflict great harm on their populations in order to survive became all too evident. The only "democracy" to emerge, in Tunisia, became mired in a state power fragmentation that resulted in a presidential takeover of politics in 2021. Tunisia's trajectory demonstrates, that fragile new democracies do not bring short-term salvation—at best, they can take years to nurture effective governance.

In addition to civil wars in three countries, and deepening repression in Egypt, Sudan, Tunisia, and Algeria, the region remains characterized by high levels of social instability. Geopolitical changes, with diplomatic and military disengagement by the United States, a more interventionist Russia, and vastly heightened competition between the largest economies for regional influence (Turkey, Saudi Arabia, and Iran), including through direct military interventions, have added complexity, as political vacuums have been filled by proxy fights—in Syria, Yemen, Libya, but also to some extent, in Lebanon, Iraq, Palestine, and Sudan. The mounting polarization around a Sunni–Shia divide, Iran's continuing rise as a regional power, and the

TABLE 7.7 ■ Fiscal Gap (2019) and Public Debt as a Share of GDP (2020)		
	Fiscal Gap/GDP 2019	**Public Debt/GDP 2020**
All group	**-6.0**	**81.6**
Algeria	-9.7	57.2
Egypt	-7.4	86.6
Iran	-5.6	45.4
Iraq	0.9	68.3
Jordan	-6.0	88.4
Lebanon	-10.7	182.8
Morocco	-.1	76.9
Tunisia	-3.9	84.8
WBG	-7.4	44.2

Source: IMF, Regional Economic Outlook

recent peace moves between Israel and the Gulf via the so-called "Abraham Accords" are reshaping the geopolitical foundations of the region. A civil war in Yemen with extensive regional involvement by Saudi Arabia and the UAE, which seek to counter alleged Iranian interference in support of insurgent forces, has included large-scale bombing campaigns that have taken a distressing civilian toll. Following the outbreak of violent conflict in Libya, oil output collapsed for a time. State institutions also collapsed, political violence remains pervasive, and extremist groups have established control over parts of the national territory. Syria has been devastated with a staggering death toll and millions of internally displaced people and refugees. The Syrian economy has been crippled for decades to come, with the costs of reconstruction estimated in the hundreds of billions of dollars.

Below, we review recent development and political economy challenges facing some of the countries of the region at the time of writing.

Egypt

In Egypt, President Sisi has managed a successful security and macroeconomic stabilization since coming to power in 2013, but his success is built on weak foundations. The Egyptian armed forces struggle to contain violent extremist groups in the Sinai region, while imposing a reign of terror over local communities. Economically, Sisi has relied on the military and the public sector to become the engines of growth and he has been unable, or unwilling, to elicit a private sector supply response. While GDP growth has improved after the maxi-devaluation of 2016 (at about 2 percent to 3 percent per capita per year), reforms have come at a great social cost with poverty increasing. There are three main sources of vulnerability that expose Egypt to a possible blowout: a macrostabilization with no private sector supply response, the militarization of its economy and the weakening of its civilian component, and the absence of a pressure valve and political space to absorb the deteriorating social conditions and rise of discontent.[38]

In spite of the steep devaluation in 2016, the private sector supply response did not materialize. Imports shrank, but exports did not rise—they now stand at only six percent of GDP, as low as in the 1980s. The current performance of the private sector is also at an all-time low. Private investment is only at six percent of GDP— even lower than during Nasser's socialist period. The causes of the low level of private investment are many and include fierce competition by the military economy. Indeed, the expansion of the military economy is one of the more remarkable features of the Sisi era. Since 2013, the armed forces have taken a high-profile lead in managing huge public infrastructure and housing projects, including an expansion of the Suez Canal and the construction of an entirely new administrative capital east of Cairo. Military factories that used to manufacture military equipment are now producing consumer goods, delivering health care, importing basic food commodities and medical supplies, extracting and processing natural resources, and reclaiming land for cultivation and agri-business (much of which they also do). In doing so, the military competes head-to-head with private firms. On the third tension (social aspects), unlike the past, poverty has been rising, even by official figures (from 18 percent to 28 percent of the population, at the PPP$3.5/day line, between 2015 and 2018). At the same time, the Sisi regime has closed down any civic space. The initial crackdown after Sisi seized power in 2013 targeted the

Muslim Brotherhood, but very quickly, repression reached an ever-widening range of journalists, activists, and protesters (under the pretext that they threaten public order or national security).

On both economic and social grounds then, Egypt's stability now appears brittle—resilient on the surface but fragile underneath. Challenges may not rise to a level that would force a change in regime, but the potential for grievances to mobilize a new wave of oppositional activism is high. In order to make Egypt's growth path more resilient, some of the economic and social tensions will need to start being released. Accumulating foreign debt to push the problems away will only compound existing imbalances to the point of becoming insurmountable in the future. The central question then becomes that of the regime's willingness to widen participation in political affairs and, relatedly, to get the private sector to play a more central and dynamic role in the economy.

Indeed, during the summer of 2022, Egypt's international debt was downgraded, followed by large amount of capital flight. To stabilize financial markets, the domestic currency was depreciated, and the domestic interest rate was increased. In parallel, Egypt has started to negotiate a new program with the IMF. The choices became starker: either the country will go through more painful austerity, or it will engage in serious structural reforms that can unshackle the private sector, including reforms that hurt the military economy.

Tunisia

The Tunisian economy is not in good shape either. Its economy was hit early on after the 2011 revolution by several negative shocks, including a collapse in tourism, the loss of the Libyan market, and a fall in the production of phosphates and oil, due to badly managed work-related disputes in SOEs. With social demands unleashed by the revolution, and a more competitive political system, expansionary fiscal policy has been unabated since. On the positive side, successive governments did manage to reduce poverty and inequality, especially in rural areas where it is highest. Overall, poverty fell from 20.5 percent to 15.2 percent of the population between 2010 and 2015, and inequality, as measured by the Gini coefficient, also fell over the same period from 40.4 to 36.5.

But like in Egypt, the country's financial situation has become unsustainable. Between 2011 and 2019, public expenditures rose from 24 to 30 percent of GDP, while tax revenues remained flat. The civil service wage bill rose to a level much higher than that of comparable countries. External debt has shot up from about 40 percent to 100 percent of GDP between 2010 and 2020. In the immediate future, some measures of fiscal stabilization will thus be necessary. These economic weaknesses can be largely related to the particular political developments that took place, notably the rise of the politics of consensus, which may have been essential from a political point of view but have paralyzed the ability to address important economic challenges facing the country.[39] While compromise and power-sharing helped Tunisia avoid some of the political pitfalls that affected other countries, from an economic perspective the politics of consensus led to myopia and inaction.[40] Neither of the two major parties wanted to pay the price of significant economic reforms, including austerity measures, given the low probability of benefiting from the resulting improvements in the future, as both felt they were in a weak position—the liberal Nidaa Party because of its internal divisions, and the Islamist Ennahdha Party because of the deteriorating regional situation (especially after the 2013 coup in Egypt). The elections of 2019 penalized both parties as President Saed, a populist jurist, was overwhelmingly elected. In August 2021, he dismissed the Government and Parliament, and he then followed up by engineering constitutional reforms to centralize power and roll back the recent democratic gains. Whether he is able to address the festering economic crisis remains, at the time of writing, an open question.

By the summer of 2022, Tunisia lost access to the international financial market, and it had to start negotiating with the IMF for a new rescue program. Already, the powerful labor union warned against austerity measures. Whether new economic policies can be taken by the authorities to increase economic growth, using the new powers of the Presidency, to grow out of its current problems was uncertain given the rise in political risk.

Saudi Arabia

The oil-producing countries of the region now face the twin challenges of having to stabilize their internal and external balances in the face of a large macroeconomic shock and reform their economic structures to create new sources of growth to complement their still overly dominant oil sectors. Cutting expenditures while also switching to higher levels of investment is no easy task, as it doubly reduces consumption among citizens, with only the promise of a distant better future to compensate.

The specificities of the current shock are its extraordinary size (on average, a 50 percent fall in oil prices after 2015), the fact that it comes on the heels of a long period of high prices (2000–2014), and the continued possibility of a return to lower oil prices in the future. Between 2016 and 2019, the fiscal deficit was reduced by slashing public investment and instituting a VAT. The harder challenge has been to create good jobs that can attract Saudi youth to seek employment outside the public sector. Expanding the national labor force participation and its productivity would allow for huge gains because the national labor force is grossly underemployed.[41] Currently, only 35 percent of the working-age population is employed, and such employment falls heavily in low productivity government jobs.[42] Low national participation rates are largely the result of extremely low participation of women—although men's participation is not high by international standards either. To encourage national labor to work in the private sector, the wages paid by private firms need to go up, increased investment is needed in technology so that productivity rises in ways commensurate with the higher level of education among Saudi youth, and additional restrictions on expat labor will be required over time.[43]

Algeria

In Algeria, oil revenues have fallen from 34 percent of GDP in 2015 to 20 percent in 2019, but still represent 60 percent of government revenues and 94 percent of exports. The state now spends a third of revenues on the army (the second largest in Africa after Egypt). The government also massively subsidizes consumption (25 percent of GDP), even as the fiscal deficit has shot to double digits and foreign exchange reserves are bleeding. At the same time, the private sector remains heavily repressed, as firms have little access to finance and face a complex web of regulations.

The post-Bouteflika regime has not undertaken any meaningful reforms. Opinion surveys show that the level of confidence in the government collapsed right after the fall in the price of oil, as feelings of economic insecurity increased significantly. Algerians understand that the post–civil war clientelistic model cannot be sustained forever, and the opposition Hirak movement testifies to their anger at the lack of credible reforms. The recent rise in oil revenues in 2022, and the increased interest by Europe jn diversifying the sources of its gas supply, gave the authorities additional means to double up on clientelism as a strategy of power preservation.

Iraq

Iraq depends even more heavily on oil, which accounts for 99 percent of exports, 90 percent of government revenue, and 60 percent of GDP. The post-2003 order has structured access to state resources, public office, and political mobilization along ethnosectarian lines, controlled by a narrow political elite. Instead of rebuilding a country devastated by wars, oil revenues were used to expand clientelism. The public wage bill accounts for 51 percent of spending, electricity is 91 percent subsidized, and an estimated 25 percent of public funds get wasted in corruption. At the same time, most of the private sector is informal and labor force participation is among the lowest in the world. The Popular Mobilization Forces, nonstate armed actors, have reached into all sectors of the economy. Meanwhile, fiscal space is closing, and the country needed to borrow $100 billion in 2020 just to pay its public wage bill. Like Algerians, young revolutionaries in Iraq understood that without change in politics and policies, their future prospects are bleak—a quarter of the population is already living in poverty.

Sudan

In September 2019, after months of popular uprising, Sudan's first civilian cabinet in 30 years was sworn in. As of this writing, it continues to oversee a power sharing agreement between the military and the pro-democracy movement, in a fragile transition to a more democratic order. But the secession of the South in 2011 still haunts the country. This led to a collapse in oil revenues—from 16 percent of GDP in 2007, to less than one percent in 2017. Between 2007 and 2017, President Al-Bashir reduced public expenditures massively—from 21 to 10 percent of GDP, while military spending, which rose during the oil boom, remained untouched. During the 2019 uprisings, which led to a coup that removed Al-Bashir, the revolutionaries wanted the army out of power but were forced to compromise. The county's economic problems are daunting, with inflation running at 200 percent, driven by large deficits that are monetized. Civil-service wages are just three percent of GDP, and core government services have all but collapsed. A transition coalition between the military and the revolutionaries—had managed to reach a debt reduction deal with its international creditors allowing it to receive international support. The attempt by the revolutionaries to roll back the power of the military backfired, with the army launching a coup to retake all the levers of power in 2021. The revolution, however, is far from over, as the revolutionaries now refuse to compromise and insist that the army relinquish all powers. At the same time, huge challenges lurk ahead: regional insurgencies must be extinguished, the security sector needs deep reform, and the economy must be revived.

Lebanon

In October 2019, widespread protests erupted across Lebanon in the midst of rapidly deteriorating economic conditions. To stop its economic free fall would have required addressing three simultaneous crises: balance of payment, fiscal, and banking. In the best of circumstances, it would be difficult for a normal government to put together the type of complex recovery plan needed to deal with these multiple challenges. The longstanding power sharing mechanism between sectarian oligarchs in Lebanon rendered the task far more difficult.

Because much of the public debt is internal, and largely owed to the banking sector, the sudden halt of capital inflows led to a rapid economic deterioration after 2019. Banks ceased normal functions and private firms became starved for liquidity, loans, and imports, bringing economic activity to a standstill. The recession is rapidly growing in scale with estimations of a 40 percent fall of GDP by 2021. Businesses went bankrupt, and unemployment rose rapidly. Annual inflation ran at around 100 percent, and an 80 percent currency devaluation on the parallel market sharply reduced real wages. The devastating Beirut port blast in 2020 and the COVID-19 health crisis complicated the situation further. Within a year, poverty expanded dramatically, reaching an estimated 50 percent of the population, and there are, at the time of writing, shortages in basic goods as well as fuel and medicine. The crisis has prompted a major outflow of highly skilled labor, further undermining prospects for the country's recovery.

The crisis was eminently predictable, but no corrective action was taken by the political elite to prevent it. The principal tenets of the now defunct old model were attracting external capital by maintaining high interest rates and a fixed dollar peg. Capital flowed, largely from the Lebanese Diaspora into the country's banks to the tune of 20 percent of GDP on average over the past three decades. These flows in turn allowed the state to maintain a loose fiscal policy. Capital inflows started to weaken around 2015, and eventually dried out in 2019 as depositors lost trust in the country's ability to repay, leading to a run on banks and on the national currency. The important point is that there was little economic growth to justify such large borrowing. Economic growth was modest until 2010 for a country catching up after a civil war (5.7 percent between 1995 and 2011), and much too low after the start of the Syrian war (about 1.7 percent between 2011 and 2019) to sustain high capital inflows for long. The modest growth performance can be related to the loss of competitiveness generated by an overvalued exchange rate and the policy of high interest rates, both of which depressed investments in the real economy. Corruption and poor infrastructure further increased the cost of doing business. The eruption of the Syria conflict in 2011 accelerated the decline as exports to the GCC were hit by border closures. By 2015, funding from the GCC fell as Lebanon came to be considered a Hezbollah stronghold by GCC countries. It was becoming increasingly apparent that without proactive measures to address the significant debt overhang, the economy was on the road to an inevitable collapse.

A financial crisis of this amplitude is complex to manage, requiring that different policies be implemented in parallel as part of a comprehensive strategy, including deep cuts in public debt, fiscal consolidation, anti-corruption measures, a more flexible exchange rate, and the reorganization of the banking sector. A conservative estimate puts the losses that need to be distributed nationally at two to three times current GDP. A serious recovery plan that tackles the imbalances of the past would be able to garner foreign support, which would greatly increase its chances of success. In normal circumstances, the reform program would adopt an IMF-led umbrella to gain international credibility. Nearly three years into the crisis, however, the political class still struggles to form a stable government, let alone come up with a comprehensive and credible plan to initiate an economic recovery.

CONCLUSION

Regardless of the causes and nature of underdevelopment in the Middle East, the stakes are high, particularly for ordinary people throughout the region. The large-scale rollback of the state in the 1980s and 1990s has marked politics and economic change in the Middle East ever since. In order to stabilize the political situation in the face of mounting opposition, rulers liberalized their economies reluctantly and selectively. Resorting to divide-and-rule strategies, rulers have relied on a combination of selective subsidies and repression as well as fear mongering about political Islam, leading to increasingly fragile and narrow-governing coalitions.[44] In so doing, the old regimes reinvented themselves as market-friendly but in highly discriminatory ways, creating new rents that accrued through privileges and exclusion. As a result, economic growth was far less inclusive than in the past, much of the private sector became informal, monopolies and *wasta* rather than competitive markets became the rule, little trickle down occurred, and inequalities rose. Although the economies of the region began to expand again after the "lost decade" of the 1980s and 1990s, growth was neither inclusive nor sufficient to drive major economic transformation.

Having managed to survive their first major economic challenge in the 1980s, autocratic regimes are now back to square one. But an economic rebound is even harder to engineer now than in the 1980s. The decline in oil revenues after 2015, coming on the heels of a long oil boom, created economic and social challenges that exporters continue to experience even as oil prices recover. Over time, there has been further de-industrialization. Private investment is depressed in many countries by rising political risk. Export growth is more challenging in a slow-growing global economy. And remittances, which remain a lifeline for millions around the region, are on a secular decline as the GCC seeks to replace migrants with nationals. The COVID-19 pandemic further depressed remittances to cash-strapped economies. The global economy has entered into a period of stagflation in 2022, bringing in increased financial pressure on over-indebted MENA countries, and especially on the oil importers. The main sources of external financing are becoming more sensitive to economic performance: bilateral creditors are more budget-constrained at a time when geopolitical rents are eroding. Some countries that were too large to fail are becoming too large to bail. And a good portion of external debt is now owed to financial markets, where interest rates are rising, and new liquidity is becoming much more scarce.

As in the 1980s, the interactions between policies and polities present autocratic regimes with a difficult dilemma. While stabilization and adjustment are needed to rescue weakened authoritarian rule, when pushed too far, they now elicit strong opposition from below that risks weakening authority. How political elites react depends on history, events on the ground, and also, on what external actors do. Some regimes will resist opening up, fearing change and popular retribution, while others may support marginal changes in the hope of consolidating their rule by selectively broadening their support base. The future of polities is thus on a knife-edge and highly uncertain. Against the possibility of improved social coordination, there are negative loops that threaten to create vicious circles of decay and chaos. All that we can say is that in the future some states may emerge stronger, and some much weaker; some may end up more democratic, and some more autocratic; but only those that improve their governance system and generate more trust among their citizens will be able to pave a road toward longer-term progress.

SUGGESTED READINGS

Cammett, Melani, Ishac Diwan, Alan Richards, and John Waterbury. *A Political Economy of the Middle East*. 4th ed. Boulder, CO: Westview Press, 2015.

Ishac, Diwan, Adeel Malik, and Izak Atiyas, eds. *Crony Capitalism in the Middle East*. Oxford: Oxford University Press, 2019.

Hanieh, Adam. *Lineages of Revolt: Issues of Contemporary Capitalism in the Middle East*. Chicago, IL: Haymarket Books, 2013.

Henry, Clement M, and Robert Springborg. *Globalization and the Politics of Development in the Middle East*. Cambridge: Cambridge University Press, 2010.

Hertog, Steffen, Giacomo Luciani, and Marc Valeri, eds. *Business Politics in the Middle East*. London: Hurst & Company, 2013.

Heydemann, Steven, ed. *Networks of Privilege in the Middle East: The Politics of Economic Reform Revisited*. New York, NY: Palgrave Macmillan, 2004.

Karshenas, Massoud, and Valentine Moghadam, eds. *Social Policy in the Middle East: Economic, Political and Gender Dynamics*. New York, NY: Palgrave Macmillan, 2006.

Owen, Roger. *State, Power and Politics in the Making of the Modern Middle East*. 3rd ed. London: Routledge, 2004.

United Nations Development Programme. *Arab Human Development Report*. New York, NY: UNDP, 2002, 2003, 2004, 2005, 2009, 2015, 2016.

World Bank. *Better Governance for Development in the Middle East and North Africa: Enhancing Inclusiveness and Accountability*. Washington, DC: World Bank, 2003.

World Bank. Opening Doors: Gender Equality and Development in the Middle East and North Africa, Washington, DC: World Bank, 2013.

World Bank. *Inclusion and Resilience: The Way Forward for Social Safety Nets in the Middle East and North Africa*. Washington, DC: World Bank, 2013.

8 INTERNATIONAL RELATIONS

Marc Lynch

The Arab Spring unleashed dramatic changes in the international relations of the Middle East. Wars in Syria, Yemen, Iraq, and Libya attracted intense international intervention while unleashing waves of refugees, shattering states, and empowering extremist movements. Traditionally powerful states such as Egypt and Syria receded from the diplomatic scene, while Iran, Turkey, and Gulf states intervened across the region in support of friendly regimes and against rivals. Nonstate Islamist actors such as the Muslim Brotherhood and the self-proclaimed Islamic State took unprecedented international roles. A US-led coalition negotiated a pathbreaking nuclear agreement with Iran only to see the United States later walk away from the deal. Key Arab states worked increasingly closely with Israel against Iran despite the absence of progress on the Palestinian–Israeli peace process. Gulf states ostensibly consumed by the threat posed by Iran divided their own ranks when the United Arab Emirates (UAE) and Saudi Arabia led a blockade of Qatar.

The region's current political turmoil may seem exceptionally complex, but such patterns are far from unique. In the 1950s, the regional struggle known as the "Arab Cold War" saw the fall of multiple governments to popular protests and military coup, the rise of pan-Arabism as a powerful transnational force, the voluntary merger between Egypt and Syria, and a lengthy Egyptian military intervention in Yemen. Nearly thirty years later, the Iranian revolution in 1979 upended the US-led alliance system in the Gulf, set off a revolutionary wave across much of the region, and led to an Iraqi invasion and eight long years of devastating war, just as Egypt realigned with the United States and Israel. The end of the Cold War in 1989 led to the Iraqi invasion of Kuwait, the launch of the Arab–Israeli peace process, and the dramatic introduction of large-scale, semipermanent US military presence in the Gulf. The mid-2000s were shaped by the US invasion and occupation of Iraq, inconclusive war between Israel and Hezbullah, spiraling sectarianism and terrorism, and tentative moves toward an Israeli–Gulf alignment against Iran.

Not everything in the international relations of the Middle East is so turbulent, however. There have been long periods of continuity and often unappreciated zones of stability. The Palestinian issue has occupied a central role in regional politics since at least the creation of the state of Israel in 1948. Negotiations toward a two-state solution have been ongoing for three decades, while the peace between Egypt and Israel has lasted more than forty years. The United States has maintained a dominant position in the Gulf and the Levant since 1991, enjoying robust alliances with almost every state in the Middle East other than Iran and Syria. Conflict between Iran and both Israel and its Arab neighbors has been a constant since the 1979 Islamic Revolution.

These patterns of regional alliances and power struggles in the Middle East have long been fertile ground for theorists in the field of international relations. For some, Middle Eastern regional politics are characterized by a uniquely high level of identity, ideology, and religious concerns. Arabs or Muslims, in this view, have a distinctive political culture that leads them to respect only force or makes them exceptionally susceptible to radical ideological appeals. For others, the region is the epitome of cold-blooded realpolitik, shaped by little more than the survival calculations of authoritarian leaders who bow to public opinion only when absolutely forced to do so. Which view is right—and when? How do the states of the Middle East formulate their foreign policies? Are there consistent patterns of regional international relations? What might change them?

A range of widely accepted theoretical approaches to the international politics of the Middle East offers radically different answers to such questions. Realism, the dominant theory in international relations, argues that Middle Eastern states are fundamentally rational actors competing for power in a hostile, anarchic environment shaped by the constant threat of war.[1] A variant of realism—called regime security—agrees with other scholars of realism about the hostile environment, but contends that the primary concern of Arab leaders is their own survival in power against both internal and external threats.[2] A political economy school of thought emphasizes the role of oil and of the historical construction of distinctive state forms.[3] A constructivist approach focuses on the role of ideas, identity, and ideology in shaping the dynamics and patterns of regional politics—with hostility toward Israel or conflict with Iran, for instance, shaped as much by identity as by security or power concerns.[4]

These theoretical differences have important real-world implications. Whether Iran is understood fundamentally as a realist actor, as a unified state rationally pursuing self-interest in an anarchic and high-risk environment, or as an ideologically motivated actor pursuing power in the name of Islamic revolution matters a great deal in deciding how to respond to its pursuit of a nuclear program. The Iranian pursuit of a nuclear weapons program might be seen as the logical move of a regional great power in a competitive environment (realism), a gamble aimed at preserving the survival of a regime threatened at home and abroad (regime security), or an expression of a distinctive revolutionary ideology (constructivism). Each perspective would point to fundamentally different policies toward Iran.

Iraq offers another example. Whether Iraq embarked on so many wars in the 1980s and 1990s because of Saddam Hussein's unique worldview and ideology or because of Iraq's difficult power position between Iran, the Gulf, and Israel matters a lot for deciding whether invading Iraq to change the regime would fundamentally change regional politics. The realist may read the Iraqi invasion of Kuwait in 1990 as a response to a rapidly shifting global and regional balance of power in which Iraq seized an opportunity to increase its power but miscalculated the international response. A constructivist may see the same decision as a function of the Ba'thist ideology of Iraq's leadership or of its bid to reshape the norms of the Arab order. But for the regime security theorist, the invasion may have primarily been about Saddam's perception of threats to his own survival, both internal and external—a desperate bid to escape a closing trap rather than an aggressive bid for hegemony. Which of these explanations best accounts for the behavior of key players clearly matters for our understanding of regional politics and for how best to respond to regional events at the policy level.

While some are most impressed by the timeless, recurring patterns of behavior in the Middle East, at least some patterns of alliances and competition have changed dramatically over the years. Egypt and Israel went from fierce enemies to reliable allies, while Iran shifted from being America's closest regional ally to its most potent adversary.[5] The occupation of Iraq in 2003 removed one of the central players in the regional balance of power from the equation. In 2020, several Arab Gulf states which had long insisted that normal relations with Israel would depend upon the creation of a Palestinian state signed the Abraham Accords despite the absence of any meaningful peace process.

The lines of contention have also changed. The Arab Cold War of the 1950s pitted Arab nationalists against conservative, Western-backed Arab states, and the various would-be leaders of Arab nationalism against each other in vicious political warfare.[6] During the 1970s, more of a realpolitik dynamic set in as states established their internal dominance over domestic opponents and normalized their relations with one another. Egypt, which fought multiple wars against Israel and led the regional campaign against it for decades, made peace with its enemy, and the two states became close strategic allies. In the 1980s, most of the Arab world backed Iraq against Iran—but Syria, one of the most avowedly Arabist of states, sided with Iran against its Ba'thist rival. But in 1990, those same Arab states largely supported the US-led war against Iraq to liberate Kuwait.

The 1990s were shaped by US unipolarity, stewardship of the Arab–Israeli peace process, and maintenance of "dual containment" of both Iraq and Iran. Since September 11, 2001, the US invasion of Iraq and the so-called global war on terror have been accompanied by a renewed cold war between a US-Saudi camp and an Iranian resistance camp. The struggle over Iran's nuclear weapons program seemed to have finally been resolved in 2015 with the negotiation of the Joint Comprehensive Plan of Action, but it resurged in 2018 with the US withdrawal from the agreement. The Arab uprisings of 2011 triggered multiple wars and political interventions that featured different lines of conflict and cooperation: Qatar, Saudi Arabia, and Turkey against Iran in Syria; Qatar and Turkey against the UAE and Egypt in Libya.

Which matters more: the persistence of basic patterns such as the pursuit of regime survival or the enduring risk of war and domestic subversion? What best explains these patterns: changes in the international and regional balance of power; new ideas and identities; or the shifting domestic capacity and political stability of states?

This chapter proceeds as follows. First, it lays out some of the key conceptual and theoretical issues that lie at the heart of any systematic analysis of regional international politics. After considering what, if anything, might make the Middle East unique compared with other parts of the world, the first section analyzes the nature of anarchy in the Middle East, the nature of power, the importance of domestic political and security concerns relative to international concerns, and the role of identity and the importance of transnational actors. The chapter then offers a brief overview of the major players in regional politics, highlighting their power potential and their foreign policy proclivities over the years, and looks in some detail at the changing role of the United States and other international actors. Third, the chapter shows the different patterns of regional politics across historical periods—the Arab Cold War of the 1950s and 1960s, the state-dominated politics of the 1970s and 1980s, the post–Cold War period of the 1990s, the post–9/11 period of the invasion of Iraq, and the turbulent world shaped by the Arab uprisings that began in 2011. Finally, it considers the potential for stability or change in the post–Arab uprisings Middle East.

CONCEPTUALIZING THE INTERNATIONAL RELATIONS OF THE MIDDLE EAST

International relations theory builds upon the insight that foreign policy and important political outcomes are shaped not only by the internal politics of states but also by the structure within which those states are embedded. International structures, defined in terms of the distribution of power, threat, identities, and institutions, have their own distinctive logic that must be understood on their own terms. While domestic politics and individual leaders are important, they are insufficient for understanding alliance choices, the initiation of wars, patterns of economic aid, or the conclusion of peace agreements. This section outlines the key dimensions of international structure, including the ordering principle of anarchy and the variety of international institutions, the distribution of power among its components, the embeddedness of the regional order within a broader international order, and the logic of the security dilemma.

In one sense, the international relations of the Middle East are no different from those of any other world region. The states of the Middle East, as in every regional system, compete with one another for power, security, and influence in an environment that is formally anarchic. The possibility of war and the prevalence of both internal and external challenges to regime stability structures the foreign policy choices of these states. In this intensely competitive environment, Middle Eastern states must ensure their own survival, whether through the formation of foreign alliances or the mobilization of domestic resources. The nature of those threats has changed dramatically over the years, as authoritarian regimes and state structures have hardened, the international environment has transformed, and the ideological stakes have been redefined. The upsurge of popular mobilization in 2011, which toppled several long-sitting Arab rulers and pushed others into civil war, exacerbated those perceptions of threat.

There are several ways in which the IR of the Middle East systematically differs from the conventional expectations of IR theory, however.[7] First, the Middle East has always been a highly penetrated region, with great power competition shaping regional order and state security more than in many other parts of the world. Second, Middle Eastern states are more likely to prioritize regime survival over state interests than general IR theory would assume. Third, even Realists recognize that transnational identities have higher salience in the Middle East. Finally, oil uniquely structures regional political economy and the relationship between the region and the global system.

Anarchy and Institutions

International relations theory generally begins with the concept of anarchy. This does not mean chaos; it means the absence of any central authority able to legitimately make and enforce agreements. Anarchy means that war is always possible, even if unlikely, and therefore, every state must above all else be concerned with providing for its own security and survival. States in such an environment can never count on others, even their closest allies, to provide for security because no commitment can be enforced, and self-interest must dominate regardless of intentions or affinity. Realism is not a theory of foreign policy, but rather what might be called a 'system dominant' theory: the system forces states to prioritize their own security and national interests over ideology, morality, or domestic preferences, or else risk severe consequences. For example, Realism may struggle to explain why Kuwait refused to make concessions to Iraq in the summer of 1990 despite a clear military threat, but it can explain why that choice led to it being overrun by Iraq until saved by a US-led intervention.

For IR realists, ideology, identity, and public discourse are a mask for the underlying state interests and pursuit of power and should not be taken at anything close to face value. Domestic political systems are not particularly important, and democracy would make little difference because ultimately states are forced by the structure of the system to pursue similar strategies. In the end, it should not especially matter to the realist whether Iraq is ruled by a totalitarian Sunni (Saddam Hussein) or by a democratically elected Shi'a (Nuri al-Maliki) because Iraq remains in the same structural position in the region and will have no choice but to balance against its many powerful neighbors.

Not all anarchy is created equal, however. Recent international relations scholarship has introduced variations in the structural nature of anarchy, with variations in the institutional environment, in the degree of hierarchy, and in the surrounding culture. In densely institutionalized international environments such as the European Union (EU), war becomes exceedingly unlikely and ceases to be a primary motivation for states; international politics then take on many of the characteristics of domestic politics.[8] Constructivists such as Alexander Wendt have further argued that anarchies have distinctive cultures in which the likelihood of war varies dramatically, independent of anarchy. A region with recent experience of war, borders that cannot easily be defended, few shared institutions, autocratic governments, or irredentist movements will face a more acute risk of war—which then can become a self-fulfilling prophecy.

The Middle East remains one of the most realist parts of the world, with a high risk of war, deep mistrust, and fierce competitiveness. The region's international institutions are notoriously weak and ineffectual. There is nothing to prevent war, which means that states must always prepare for its possibility. And the tense, suspicious, conflict-ridden nature of the region means that the implications of anarchy should be particularly intense, with states highly attuned to changes in the balance of power and to emergent threats. There are few institutions to mitigate this problem: the Middle East remains highly state centric, with few signs of a willingness to surrender control to international institutions in order to achieve the benefits of economic or political integration.[9] The Arab League has never been an efficacious organization in any meaningful sense. The institution of the Arab Summit, regularly bringing together Arab heads of state to confer on regional issues, is more significant but has no real institutional component. The Gulf Cooperation Council (GCC) for years offered some limited coordination mechanisms for the Gulf states, but efforts to transform it into a vehicle for economic and political integration have routinely failed—and in 2017, the GCC proved unable to mediate the competition between its member states Qatar, Saudi Arabia, and the UAE.

These conditions exacerbate the security dilemma—meaning the unintended consequences of the search for security under anarchy.[10] The security dilemma does not refer simply to the prosaic fact of insecurity or competition. It refers to a perverse logic in which the search for security through increased military power becomes self-defeating as others feel threatened and arm themselves in response. Israel's efforts to provide for its own security, for example, have led it to adopt a range of hawkish, militaristic policies toward its Arab neighbors that then generated a self-fulfilling prophecy of hostility and mistrust. The security dilemma explains why states so often find themselves spiraling into unnecessary wars and find it so hard to break these cycles of conflict.

International and Regional Orders

This anarchy is tempered to some degree by the unusually high level of international involvement in the region. The Middle Eastern regional system is deeply embedded in the wider international environment because of its oil and its geopolitical centrality. As early as 1959, Leonard Binder described the region as a "subordinate regional system," whose dynamics were fundamentally shaped by the interests of relations with outside powers. Throughout the Cold War, the Soviet Union and the United States identified the region as a crucial battlefield of a global struggle—meaning that few local conflicts could remain truly local, and all actors contemplating war knew that the great powers would eventually step in to impose a cease-fire. Israel's war effort in 1967 revolved heavily around avoiding American calls for restraint, while Egyptian decisions to launch war against Israel in 1973 was driven in large part by an effort to engage US support in the peace talks to follow.[11] Since the end of the Cold War, the US role as the primary international patron of almost every state in the region has rendered it virtually impossible to analyze the region's international relations in isolation from the growing direct role of the United States.[12] From 1990 until relatively recently, the Gulf region looked more like a US imperium than like a true anarchy.[13]

The nature of the relationship between the global and the regional is complex, however. Local actors pursue their own interests but within a playing field shaped by the global distribution of power and institutional order. It is important to see the ways in which global structure shapes these local decisions and dynamics, which might otherwise appear unrelated. During the Cold War, there was a tendency to view many of the region's developments through a global lens, leading to crucial misunderstandings of the importance of local dynamics. US hegemony after 1990 alleviated the effects of anarchy, as it could play the role of interlocutor between potentially hostile states, providing security guarantees to mitigate the pressures of security dilemma dynamics and blocking escalation toward war. The relative decline of the United States over the last decade and the growing role of competitors such as Russia have reintroduced uncertainty about and competition over the international role in the Middle East (Box 8.1).[14]

BOX 8.1

REGIONAL INSTITUTIONS

Arab Summit. Beginning in 1964, meetings of the Arab Summit have brought together the heads of state of the member countries of the League of Arab States to discuss issues of regional interest. There have been thirty-one summit meetings, including a number of emergency summits held at moments of crisis. Meetings of the Arab Summit, rather than meetings of the Arab League, have been the most important location for the formulation of common Arab political positions and for the airing of intra-Arab political conflicts. Among the most important Arab Summit meetings have been Khartoum (1967), which formulated the collective response to the June 1967 War; Rabat (1974), which declared the Palestine Liberation Organization to be the sole legitimate representative of the Palestinian people; Cairo (1990), which decided to support the United States in its opposition to the Iraqi invasion of Kuwait; and Beirut (2002), which endorsed the Saudi peace plan as a solution for the Arab–Israeli conflict.

Gulf Cooperation Council. Created in 1981, the GCC comprises six wealthy Arab Gulf states (Bahrain, Kuwait, Oman, Qatar, Saudi Arabia, and the UAE). Although technically a trade bloc and an economic cooperation zone, the GCC has primarily been a political and security organization designed to coordinate a response to more powerful neighbors such as Iraq and (especially) Iran. After decades of relative success, the GCC was disrupted in 2017 by the blockade of Qatar, led by Saudi Arabia and the UAE, and has largely ceased to function as an international organization.

League of Arab States. Established in 1945 with six members, the Arab League is a formal international organization composed of all states that identify as Arab (formally, with Arabic being the mother tongue of the majority of the population). It currently has twenty-two members. Based in Cairo, it hosts a number of technical agencies promoting inter-Arab cooperation, but it has little formal authority or power.

Organization of the Petroleum Exporting Countries (OPEC). Formed in 1960, OPEC includes both Middle Eastern and non–Middle Eastern states. A cartel designed to coordinate petroleum policy among its member states, OPEC has achieved notable successes in its history, especially the 1973 oil embargo that contributed to dramatically increasing the price of oil. OPEC has been plagued, however, by persistent cheating by countries that produce in excess of their quotas in order to maximize their revenues, and it has struggled in the face of changes in the global oil markets.

The most fundamental characteristic of any international system is its polarity, the number of great powers competing for influence in the region. In the years before the Cold War, the Middle East was profoundly shaped by the multipolar struggle between European great powers. During the Cold War, this resolved into a bipolar structure, with two great powers defining the terms of foreign policy possibility. After the collapse of the Soviet Union, the United States emerged as the sole great power in a unipolar system. Since 2011, American primacy has faded, while Russia and China have taken on greater roles, creating an ambiguous system that is no longer unipolar but not yet truly multipolar. Each of these structures has distinctive dynamics that help to explain a great many patterns that might otherwise seem to have idiosyncratic causes.

The Middle East during the age of multipolarity was a key site of the "great game," profoundly shaped by the European global competition for power and influence. As Chapter 1 details, colonialism entered the Middle East over the course of centuries of such competition. The decline of the Ottoman Empire was manifested by the steady intrusion of European powers into its realm, culminating in the cataclysmic events of World War I. The international system in the Middle East is a product of the resolution of that war, most obviously with the drawing of the borders of the Levant and its division into British and French spheres of influence. The post–World War I period was shaped by nationalist struggles against European colonial rule and the emergence of new forms of Arab nationalism defined by anticolonial resistance.

The resolution of World War II and the crystallization of the Cold War decisively changed the international structure, with crucial implications for the Middle East. By the late 1940s, international politics had settled into a tense bipolar struggle between the Western and Soviet blocs. Maintaining the regular flow of oil from the Gulf became a vital national interest for the United States and a key to the reconstruction of Europe's economy. The Suez crisis of 1956 marked a decisive transition from multipolarity to bipolarity in the Middle East. Britain and France conspired with Israel to seize the Suez Canal in a bid to defeat Egyptian President Gamal Abdel Nasser and restore the former colonial powers to a leading position in regional affairs. The United States, concerned primarily about losing vital Arab states to Soviet influence and about asserting its own primacy within the Western alliance, forced its allies to withdraw. This established US primacy and demonstrated the overwhelming priority of the global Cold War over local political interests. Over the following years, France, consumed by the escalating Algerian war for independence, receded as a Middle Eastern power. Britain retained its bases in the Gulf until 1971 before finally ceding that role as well.

During the Cold War, regional states could maneuver between the two competing blocs in search of military, political, and economic support. Nasser, for example, expertly played the United States and the Soviet Union against each other in the 1950s, gaining food aid and support for the Aswan Dam from the West while obtaining arms from Czechoslovakia. Each superpower was closely attuned to the possible defection of its local allies and to the possibility of disrupting the other's alliances. The mutual Security Council vetoes by the two superpowers sharply limited the ability of the United Nations to act. The zero-sum logic of bipolarity meant that the loss of an ally rebounded to the benefit of the other pole, even if the defector did not join the rival bloc: The 1958 Iraqi revolution, for instance, benefited the Soviet bloc by removing a major Western ally even though the successive governments that followed did not become reliable Soviet clients. Egypt's decision to seek peace with Israel in 1979 shifted a key Soviet ally into the American camp. While regular norms of interaction evolved over time, there were moments of real crisis, as in 1973 when the two superpowers came to the brink of nuclear confrontation over the Israeli–Egyptian war in the Sinai.

The unipolarity that followed the collapse of the Soviet Union created an entirely different structural context for regional international relations. With only one superpower, all roads led through Washington, forcing all regional states to choose between becoming part of the US-led system or to be designated as rogue states subject to international sanctions and threat of war. With no Soviet countervailing power, the direct US presence in the region rapidly expanded. American efforts in the 1990s to contain both Iran and Iraq required a massively expanded direct military presence and the consolidation of an extensive network of military bases. It also supervised the Arab–Israeli peace process, which offered not just a potential resolution of that long-running conflict but a route into the American-led system for states such as Syria and for the PLO, as well as a vehicle for sustaining simultaneous alliance with both Israel and its ostensible Arab enemies. By the mid-2000s, almost every state in the Middle East had aligned with the United States, with the sole remaining exceptions being Iran and Syria (following the failure of nearly a decade of US-backed peace negotiations with Israel).

After 9/11, the system remained unipolar, but US policy in the region dramatically changed. Rather than remaining a status quo power working to preserve a regional order, the United States became a revisionist power actively working to change the regional balance of power and the broader regional political culture. The invasion of Iraq removed one of the major regional powers, creating a vacuum filled by Iran, US forces, and a mélange of insurgent groups. The global war on terror and the Bush administration's "Freedom Agenda" drastically expanded the American role within the domestic politics and institutions of its regional allies, disrupting long-standing accommodations with the survival strategies of those regimes. The Israeli–Palestinian peace process was downgraded in US policy in comparison to the management of the occupation of Iraq, the regional confrontation with Iran, and the struggle against Islamist terrorism.

On the eve of the Arab uprisings, the United States remained a unipolar power, but its dominance had faded. Scarred by the occupation of Iraq, the interminable war on terror, and the ramifications of the global financial crisis, Washington sought to step back from its regional commitments. Its withdrawal from Iraq, pursuit of a nuclear accord with Iran, refusal to engage militarily in Syria's war, and mixed response to the Arab uprisings further disrupted its regional alliances, with America's regional allies increasingly expressing doubts about the credibility of its security guarantees. The overall international system could not yet be described as bipolar or multipolar, however, despite rising Chinese influence and resurgent Russian confrontationalism. It would be more accurate to describe the global balance of power as uncertain and less predictable than in the past, with greater questions about the nature of US commitments and capabilities driving new foreign policy tactics by many regional states.[15]

The Elements of Power

What counts for power in the Middle East? Traditionally, military capabilities have been seen as the ultimate source of power in international affairs. The Middle East suggests a more complex definition. The role of external powers discussed earlier somewhat mediates the direct relevance of military capabilities. Economic capabilities, especially oil, have been critical in defining power relations, as have ideological appeals. Media platforms, such as satellite television stations like Qatar's Al-Jazeera, are a crucial form of power projection. So is alignment with a powerful transnational network, such as Qatar and Turkey's ties to the Muslim Brotherhood or Iran's relationship with Shi'a militias. A relationship with an external power can also increase the power of a local actor. Jordan, for instance, parlayed a close relationship with the United States into outsized influence in the region.

In an odd twist—not a coincidence, in the belief of most Arab nationalists, who blame colonial powers for preventing any one Arab state from uniting a large population with great oil wealth—almost no Arab states combine all the aspects of potential national power.[16] Egypt is large and has a strong state, but it lacks oil and has steadily lost both economic stature and ideological appeal since the 1960s. Saudi Arabia is wealthy, but it has a relatively small population and weak military. Iraq combines oil wealth with a sizable population, but it has been wracked by internal sectarian struggles and is checked by powerful neighbors (Iran, Turkey, Saudi Arabia, and Syria) on most of its borders.

Military Capabilities

Realism begins by identifying the great powers of the system, defined primarily by military capabilities. The strong do what they can, as Thucydides told us millennia ago, while the weak suffer what they must. Great powers are those with the material resources necessary to bid for regional leadership. Less powerful states—such as Jordan, Lebanon, or Yemen—tend to be takers rather than makers of regional politics.

Realists traditionally focus on material capabilities when evaluating power. The great powers would be those with the size, population, economic base, and military power to compete for leadership or to force their interests to be taken into account. The distribution of power among leading states—not ideology or identity—dictates state behavior. The area of the Persian Gulf is dominated by the balance of power between Iran and Iraq because two powerful states in close proximity will necessarily compete for influence and will fear for their security.

Because of the ultimate possibility of war, the essential measure of power is always military. But do military capabilities exhaust the nature of power in the Middle East? How is it measured, used, and understood? What exactly can Middle Eastern states do to, and for, one another? And based on these criteria, who are the great powers in the region?

Military power is not necessarily correlated with size. Qatar and the UAE today are able to project considerable military power abroad despite their tiny populations because they have developed very well-equipped, technologically advanced militaries with highly trained elite forces. They are also able to use their wealth and media empires to support like-minded groups across the region, giving them considerably greater power projection capability than their small size would suggest.

It is often claimed that the Middle East is uniquely war prone (see Table 8.1). This is not exactly correct, particularly given its level of economic development. Until recently, most of the region's wars have clustered around two nodes: Israel and Iraq. Nevertheless, the Middle East remains heavily militarized. The expectation of the possibility of war—so central to realist theory, turning the permissive condition of anarchy to concrete patterns of alliances and conflict—looms large in the Middle East. The perceived threat of war and the ongoing, grinding Israeli and Iraqi war clusters have contributed to a deep structural effect on regional politics. Since 2011, the wars in Syria, Yemen, and Libya have profoundly impacted their neighbors. The threat of war also has had a deeply constitutive effect on states themselves, justifying and sustaining political cultures and governing institutions dominated by national security.[17] Regimes have shared an interest in perpetuating an atmosphere of conflict and war as a justification for massive security apparatuses and failures of development.

Economic Factors

Oil and the distinctive political economy of the region have always played an important role in the balance of power and in the nature of politics. The intense international interest in the region

TABLE 8.1 ■ Major Wars, Interventions, and Conflicts	
1948	Arab–Israeli War
1956	Suez War
1958	Jordan, Lebanon interventions; Iraqi revolution
1962	Yemen proxy war
1967	Arab–Israeli War
1970	Black September (Jordan vs. Palestine Liberation Organization)
1973	October War
1979	Iranian Revolution
1980	Iraq–Iran War
1982	Israeli invasion of Lebanon
1987	Palestinian intifada
1990	Iraqi invasion of Kuwait
1991	Persian Gulf War (Operation Desert Storm)
2000	Palestinian al-Aqsa intifada
2001	al-Qa'ida attack on the United States on September 11
2003	US invasion of Iraq
2006	Israeli attack on Lebanon
2008–2009	Israeli attack on Gaza
2011	NATO intervention in Libya
2011–	Syrian civil war
2015–	Saudi–UAE intervention in Yemen

is primarily driven by the importance of the regular flow of petroleum at reasonable prices to the functioning of the global economy. The region's political structures have been deeply shaped by what many call the "oil curse," in which the massive flow of revenues directly into state coffers fuels an outsized state security and patronage apparatus while crippling other sectors of the economy. The impact of oil has gone far beyond the oil-producing states. Large numbers of Arabs migrated from the poorer states to the Gulf starting in the 1960s to help build these new states by working as engineers and teachers and in all other sectors and sending their wages back as remittances.

Wealth matters in the calculation of power not only because it can be converted into military power (as in massive Gulf arms purchases during recent decades) but also because it can be used to buy influence or to shape the media and public discourse. Arab oil states have used their wealth to establish or influence a wide array of politicians, newspapers, and television stations—from Saudi ownership of multiple media outlets in the 1980s to Qatar's creation of al-Jazeera in the 1990s. The Middle East, and especially the Gulf, is one of the most lucrative markets in the world for arms sales.

This also translates into diplomatic weight. Saudi Arabia, using its vast wealth to make itself the center of regional diplomacy, has sought to monopolize Arab conflict resolution. Saudi Arabia has funded the establishment of hundreds of mosques and institutions to spread its version of Islam and contribute to a transformation of public culture from below. Qatar and the UAE have used their wealth to support clients and to influence peace negotiations in arenas from Palestine to Libya and Somalia. Wealth also strengthens the domestic resilience of Gulf states such as Saudi Arabia and Qatar; in 2011, they were able to deflect popular uprisings and destabilization efforts sponsored by their rivals in part through significant increases in public spending. They also used these resources to prop up friendly governments (such as Jordan and Morocco) and to support opposition movements against their rivals (such as Libya and Syria). Wealth also creates vulnerabilities, particularly when it is rooted in petroleum resources beneath territory that could be seized by force (as Iraq attempted to seize Kuwait in 1990). But to the extent that war is impossible or highly unlikely (whether because of international constraints, such as US military bases on a country's soil or because of an institutional or normative environment in which conquest would not pay politically), then other resources besides military become relevant.

Some posit that the Middle East is uniquely outside of Western economic globalization. Again, this is somewhat misplaced.[18] It is true that the region is largely irrelevant in global trade, and it produces few products that are competitive on global markets. At the same time, the region is deeply involved in global capital flows, with petrodollar recycling an overlooked but crucial part of the global economic system.[19] It has been deeply affected by the global information revolution, with rapidly growing Internet penetration and a powerful role for transnational satellite television. It has also been a major contributor to global migration flows, both inside the region (Arabs to the Gulf) and to the outside (from the Arab world to Europe, especially, and from South Asia to the Gulf).

Ideology and Identity

What the Middle East lacks in formal international institutions it more than makes up for with transnational identity and a wide array of informal rules and norms. The Arab order has some characteristics of what Hedley Bull once called an "anarchical society," in which the absence of central authority is buffered by shared norms and expectations, and relationships. Personal relationships and the shadow of the past matter in a system where states are governed almost exclusively by long-serving autocrats. With repeated interactions over decades—and every expectation of decades of interaction to come—Arab leaders tend to know and understand each other quite well (for better or for worse). This has changed over the last decade, however, as long-serving leaders such as Egypt's Hosni Mubarak, Yemen's Ali Abdallah Salih, Libya's Muammar al-Qadhafi, Sudan's Omar Bashir, and Algeria's Abdelaziz Bouteflika were driven from office, and new leaders have risen to power in Saudi Arabia and Qatar.

In this environment, ideology can be an important form of soft power, with states vying to mobilize public opinion to put pressure on other leaders. Constructivists argue that states compete in part by presenting themselves as the most effective defender of a shared cause, such as Palestine or the Syrian people. Realists counter that ideas often follow material power. Arab politics have been dominated by Egypt and Saudi Arabia—and not by Jordan and Oman, for instance—because Egypt had a large population and military and the other, Saudi Arabia, had a bottomless checkbook, not because of some intrinsic appeal of their ideas.

A common language and a politically salient identity bind the Arab world together, focusing political attention on core issues of shared concern such as Palestine. This has been reinforced in the past several decades by the rise of transnational satellite television stations such as al-Jazeera, which broadcast across the region and tend to focus on issues of presumed shared concern and to frame issues within an explicit pan-Arab identity.[20] This regionwide public sphere, bound by a common language, common media, and common political frames, puts even the European public sphere to shame. This unusually robust transnational public sphere creates a political space that transcends state borders and creates a zone of political contention beyond either state or anarchy. The robust regional political culture and shared identity—a mismatch between state and nation—at least throw into question some of the basic assumptions about the logic of anarchy. When Jordan's King Abdallah warned in 2004 of a "Shi'a Crescent" of Iranian-backed states and movements spanning Iraq, Syria, and Hezbollah, for example, he pointed to a conception of regional politics defined by identity rather than by traditional realist concerns.

Defining identity is therefore a form of power. Regional politics look very different if defined by sectarianism (Sunni-Shi'ite), by religion, or by Arab nationalism. Defining Iran, Israel, or Turkey as fundamentally outside the system because of their non-Arab identity limits their ability to participate in regional institutions or to bid for regional hegemony. Israel's long exclusion from the Arab order defined the limits of its diplomacy and shaped its demand for "normalization" in the peace process. Identity also has behavioral effects. The power of a shared Arab identity could be seen in the rapid and intense diffusion of protests from Tunisia and Egypt to the entire Arab world in early 2011, as citizens across the Arabic-speaking world identified with popular struggles against repression. Such power for identity poses a sharp challenge to realists: Systems, they believe, should be defined not by self-conception but by security calculations. By this measure, Israel, Iran, and Turkey would be in—but marginal Arab countries might not. That few other regions have such potent arguments about who belongs is suggestive of the strength of identity in the foundations of regional politics.

Identity and ideology have been potent weapons and sources of threat for Arab states. More than twenty years ago, Steven Walt argued that Arab states prioritize threat rather than abstract considerations of material power. For Walt, an avowed realist,

> A different form of balancing has occurred in inter-Arab relations. In the Arab world, the most important source of power has been the ability to manipulate one's image and the image of one's rivals in the minds of other Arab elites. Regimes have gained power and legitimacy if they have been seen as loyal to accepted Arab goals, and they have lost those assets if they have appeared to stray outside the Arab consensus.[21]

Michael Barnett, a constructivist, went further: "Arab states fought about the norms that should govern their relations; social processes, not social structures—defining norms of Arabism was an exercise of power and a mechanism of social control."[22] Gregory Gause argues that "words—if it is feared that they will find resonance among a state's citizens—were seen as more immediately threatening than guns."[23]

Those who see identity as highly determinative in shaping political behavior—for example, Samuel Huntington in his famous "clash of civilizations" thesis asserting the centrality to world politics of deep and immutable conflict between Islam and the West—assume that states that share a common identity will be likely to cooperate with one another and act as a coherent bloc in international politics. By this account, Iraq should become an Iranian proxy because its leadership predominantly shares a Shi'i religious identity, rather than balancing against Iranian power regardless of religious or ethnic identity, as realists would expect. The constructivist theorist Michael Barnett argues convincingly, however, that there is no reason to assume that a shared identity leads to more cooperative behavior. Certainly, the Middle East is full of examples of a common identity driving conflict rather than cooperation. Ba'thist Syria and Iraq were archenemies despite a shared ideology and identity, while the 1960s were dominated by intense conflict among Arab states. Barnett details how strategic framing processes are used to exercise power among a shared identity group, through mechanisms that he labels *symbolic sanctioning* (where actors try to make others pay a political cost for their positions that stand outside the consensus), *symbolic competition* (outbidding, where actors are forced to up the ante in the face of political challenges), and *symbolic entrapment* (where actors are forced to deliver on rhetoric that they never meant to be taken seriously).[24] Should Islamists come to executive power in multiple Arab countries through postuprising elections or political bargains in the coming years, this argument would predict intense competition between such Islamist-led states for leadership rather than the easy emergence of a unified "Green Bloc."

Identity matters in other ways as well. Israel, Iran, and Turkey punch well below their material weight inside Arab politics because of their identity and status. For all its military might, Israel has had very little influence within the Arab world and was ruled out as a possible alliance partner by virtue of the widely shared and deeply felt hostility to the Jewish state and Arab support for the Palestinian cause. Israel's long struggle for security involved not only establishing military deterrence or peace treaties but also seeking "normalization" with a region that fundamentally rejected its legitimacy and identity. Iran's Shi'i and Persian identity place it outside the predominantly Sunni Arab identity consensus—a consensus generated in large part by its adversaries' efforts to deny it political influence. The active nurturing of sectarianism by Gulf states helped solidify the Arab front against Iran in the 1980s and has fueled at least some of the moves by Arab regimes in the 2000s to contain Iran even when public opinion views Iran more favorably. At the same time, Shi'a identity has proven a potent mechanism for Iran's construction of a regional network of proxy forces and allies, from Lebanon's Hezbollah to the Popular Mobilization Forces in Iraq to Yemen's Houthi movement. Turkey was a marginal player in the Middle East for decades because of the memories of its imperial past and because of its decision to orient its foreign policy toward the North Atlantic Treaty Organization and its efforts to be admitted into the European Union. It has returned to the Middle East in recent years in part by vocally embracing the Palestinian cause and pursuing dialogue with Iran and Syria, while seeking to maintain its good relations with the United States and Israel.

Identity and ideology have long been potent sources of power in the Middle East, defining the stakes of political competition. Egyptian power in the 1950s could not be reduced to its military might—indeed, its military defeat in 1956 transformed into a political victory that galvanized Gamal Abdel Nasser's pan-Arab message, and its military challenge to Israel stood at the heart of its ideological appeal. Yasir Arafat's Palestine Liberation Organization (PLO) commanded great power for decades despite lacking a territorial state or even a stable base of operations. This is not to say that ideological appeal is completely independent of material capabilities. Arab states often built and demonstrated military might in order to build credibility for their ideas or used wealth to purchase support in the public realm more directly. They also used their ideas to mobilize support inside other states, to put pressure on their rivals from below, and in some cases, even to overthrow externally powerful rivals (the fall of the monarchy in Iraq in 1958, the voluntary decision by Syria to dissolve itself into a union with Egypt in 1958, and the near collapse of the monarchy in Jordan in the 1950s being the premier examples).

The new Arab media space that emerged in the late 1990s reshaped the nature and salience of identity politics.[25] The satellite television revolution, fueled by the Qatari station al-Jazeera, shattered the ability of states to monopolize the flow of information or opinion. Al-Jazeera and its competitors focused on issues of regionwide concern, rather than local affairs, with heavy coverage of Palestine, Iraq, and the need for social and political reform all framed within an overt Arab identity. Arab satellite TV fueled outrage over the second Palestinian intifada in 2000 and the Israeli occupation of the West Bank in 2002, as well as the US occupation of Iraq and the war on terror. This tipped the balance of forces more toward the populist edge of the mass public than had been the case since the 1960s—although regimes soon found ways to hit back against protestors and sought to recapture control over the political narrative. This transnational media, including both satellite television and the Internet, played a crucial role in the diffusion of protests across the region in 2011, as protestors from Sanaa to Tunis chanted identical slogans and issued identical demands against their rulers. But there were always limits to the power of this regional public opinion; it is telling that in 2003, at the height of al-Jazeera's influence and audience and at a time of virtually unprecedented popular mobilization and anger, most Arab regimes felt comfortable quietly cooperating with the US-led invasion of Iraq. In recent years, they have invested heavily in the tools of digital authoritarianism, using electronic surveillance and coordinated inauthentic behavior to manipulate and disrupt online spaces.

Finally, it is important to note that there are several competing identities at play in the Middle East. Arabist identity competes with the nationalist identities cultivated by many states, with a real tension often appearing between the self-interest and patriotic feelings of an individual state and the collective interests or identity of the Arab world. Sectarian identity has become increasingly important to regional politics, as a broad struggle between Iran and the Gulf states intersects with the domestic concerns of Sunni monarchs ruling over Shi'i populations. Thus, the Asad regime in Syria, which long claimed an identity as a defender of pan-Arab interests, has been tagged with a *Shi'a* label because of its alliance with Iran and the heterodox Alawi religious identity of the Asad family. Sectarian identities and religious networks typically span borders as well, offering alternatives to state identity and creating opportunities for the mobilization of nonstate actors. Iran's ability to build and support Hizbullah in Lebanon and Shi'i political movements in Iraq have become an essential dimension of its regional power. Saudi Arabia and Qatar's mobilization of competing Sunni Islamist movements, and the UAE's fierce hostility to all Islamist trends, has similarly become an important part of each state's regional power and influence. Sectarian identities became increasingly central to regional politics following the invasion of Iraq in 2003 and the Syrian civil war after 2011, each of which facilitated the expansion of Iranian power and spread violent images of sectarian warfare.

The salience of identities waxes and wanes. Islam has become an extremely potent identity in the Middle East during the past two decades, but in the 1950s and 1960s, it played virtually no role whatsoever in the great domestic and international political battles of the day. Finally, many countries in the region have intense internal identity conflicts that shape their international behavior: Jordan is divided between Palestinian- and Transjordan-origin (or West Bank and East Bank) citizens; Iraq is divided among Arab Sunnis, Shi'a, and Kurds; and Israel faces tension between ultra-Orthodox Jews and secularists, as well as competing conceptions of whether the West Bank should be part of the state of Israel. Indeed, Benjamin Miller views the mismatch between *state* and *nation* as the most important driving force behind the conflict and instability of the Middle East.[26]

State Strength and Regime Security

Domestic state strength should be seen not only as a concern of comparative politics but also as a crucial variable in the international politics of the region.[27] If outright war has been uncommon, various forms of intervention across borders have been endemic. Strong powers routinely fought proxy political battles in weaker counterparts, from Syria in the 1950s[28] to Yemen in the 1960s[29] to Syria, Libya, Yemen, and Iraq today. The utility of such interventions is shaped in part by the degree of ideological potency and in part by variation in the opportunity to intervene—that is, domestic state strength. Since 1970, there has been significant "hardening" of Arab states, which has dramatically reduced their ability to engage in such meddling—except in those states, such as Yemen and Iraq, that are said to have "failed." The Arab uprisings of 2011 have reopened some previously "hardened" states such as Tunisia, Libya, and Syria to such external meddling and proxy conflict, however. The direct military intervention in Yemen led by Saudi Arabia and the UAE in 2015 and the Turkish deployments to northern Syria in 2017 and Libya in 2019 mark a potentially significant shift from covert proxy interventions toward the direct deployment of hard power.

During the US invasion of Iraq in 2003, the great power of Arab authoritarian regimes, with their vast security services and societal control mechanisms, allowed them to largely ignore a vocally pro-Iraqi popular opinion. This contrasts sharply with the 1950s when shaky regimes risked overthrow if they bucked the tides of a galvanized public opinion. While realists tend to emphasize external threats, in the Middle East "states overwhelmingly identified ideological and political threats emanating from abroad to the domestic stability of their ruling regimes as more salient than threats based upon aggregate power, geographic proximity and offensive capabilities."[30] The focus on regime security offers a unified theory that points toward a specific mechanism driving state foreign policy behavior: Norms and ideology matter when they can mobilize threats to the regime's survival while rising powers threaten when they can mobilize domestic opposition against the regime.

This makes domestic state strength a key variable in calculating power balances. Syria, for instance, went from a weak state to a strong one between the 1950s and 1970s not because of dramatic changes in its size, wealth, or military capabilities but because of the consolidation of state power under Hafiz al-Asad. As Syrian state capacity grew, it no longer served as a battlefield on which others could wage their proxy battles. But with the appearance of a sustained uprising in Syria in the summer of 2011, the state lost that smothering control, and the country again became the object of regional power politics and competitive proxy interventions by Iran, Saudi Arabia, Qatar, Turkey, and others. Iraq today is a minor player in regional politics despite its large size and vast resources, in large part because of the weak state and sharply divided political system that were the outcomes of the US occupation after 2003. Whereas Iraq before 2003 was a major actor in regional politics, after 2003 it became an arena in which the strong states waged their proxy wars. For that to change will require not a larger Iraqi army but a more stable and competent Iraqi domestic state.

The focus on regime survival, rather than state interest, has far-ranging implications. It helps to explain Iraqi behavior in the 1990s, for instance, if Saddam Hussein valued his personal survival over an abstract Iraqi national interest. As Gause convincingly argues, Saddam Hussein launched wars in 1980 and 1990 because he believed foreign forces (Iran, Kuwait, the United States) were working to destabilize the Ba'th regime and that not attacking meant a greater chance of his regime falling. If Syrian rulers fear that peace with Israel could threaten their hold on power by removing the justification for repressive rule, this could explain their hesitation to conclude an agreement with Israel over the Golan Heights. The regime of Bashar al-Asad, famously, was willing to burn the country to protect his hold on power. Even Israeli foreign policy can be understood within this approach, to the extent that major foreign policy decisions are driven by coalition and electoral politics rather than by external threats.

This dynamic has been significantly increased by the 2011 Arab uprisings. The wave of popular mobilization that swept the region in 2011 greatly increased both the perceived domestic threats to regime survival and the opportunities for external involvement in either supporting or undermining regimes. Leaders in the region feel pressure to intervene where they perceive an existential threat to their own survival from protest movements that diffuse across borders, or when failing states present opportunities for their rivals to advance their interests. This period, therefore, witnessed a dramatic increase in interventionist behavior by the small, wealthy states of the Gulf, Iran, and Turkey. Regime security, therefore, offers a clear alternative to realist logic based on the international dimension of domestic politics and state strength.

THE POWER STRUCTURE OF REGIONAL POLITICS

Based on this conception of the multiple sources of power—military, economic, ideological, institutional, and domestic—in Middle Eastern regional politics, it is now possible to sketch out the relationships among the major powers of the region. Geography matters as well: Some states are destined to be peripheral players by virtue of their location, while others are fated to be central because of their proximity to major zones of conflict. Iraq's long borders with Iran, Saudi Arabia, Turkey, and Syria mean that its security situation will always be very different from that of, say, Egypt, which enjoys relative security along its borders. Israel and Iran may be bitter ideological rivals, but the vast distance between them could potentially mitigate the security dilemma (see map on inside front cover of this book).

Egypt

For much of the history of the modern Middle East, Egypt aspired to leadership of the Arab world—in the 1950s and 1960s as the avatar of pan-Arabism and in the 1980s and beyond as the would-be leader of the pro-US moderate "peace camp." Its leadership claims rested on a material base as by far the largest Arab state in terms of population and a large, capable, and well-armed military. Its long history of a centralized, relatively effective state with a strong national identity rendered it largely impervious to the attempted interventions of other states and political movements. Its central location and proximity to Israel made it geostrategically important in ways that marginal powers such as Iran or Algeria could not be.

Egypt's influence began to wane as did its material power, however. With the massive shift of wealth to the Gulf following the oil price shocks of the early 1970s, Egypt found itself relegated to the level of a poor state searching for budgetary assistance, instead of a powerful leader. Its shift to an alliance with the United States represented in part a search for another source of power, this one through harnessing the superpower in its own interest. But the decline in Egypt's economic power and its increasing loss of ideational power as a US ally and peace partner with Israel at a time when both were unpopular increasingly undermined Egyptian influence.[31] The overthrow of President Hosni Mubarak and a long, chaotic transition led to a period of paralysis in Egyptian foreign policy and unprecedented dependence upon Gulf states for financial and political support. Realism would suggest that once Egypt recovers from its domestic turbulence it will have the opportunity to reassert itself as a popular, independent force in regional affairs.

Saudi Arabia

Saudi Arabia has enjoyed fabulous economic power, especially during periods of high oil prices. It used this wealth not only to purchase a wide range of advanced weapons systems but also as a key instrument of diplomatic influence through direct and indirect subventions to a wide range of actors. It cultivated close relations with the United States. It also used its wealth to purchase a great deal of control over the Arab media, both through individual journalists and through ownership of newspapers and television stations. Finally, it sponsored the spread of its distinctive version of Islam through the Middle East and the world by extending financial support to mosques, Islamic evangelism, and the publication of religious materials.

For all its assets, Saudi Arabia also had distinct vulnerabilities. Its domestic political system rested on tight control over society, with great power devolved to the religious establishment. Its extensive system of patronage and cradle-to-grave social welfare to purchase loyalty required high oil prices, which left it vulnerable at home when prices slumped. It also found itself challenged ideologically, as its domestic and foreign policies clashed with the austere Islamic ideas propagated by its own religious establishment. The attractiveness of radical ideas to many in the kingdom proved a potent challenge in the 1950s (Nasser) through the present (al-Qa'ida). Finally, despite all its expenditures on military technology, it remained a military pygmy, as was painfully revealed by its need to call on the United States to protect it from Iraq after the 1990 invasion of Kuwait and its poor performance in Yemen after 2015.

During the Arab uprisings, Saudi Arabia rose to an unusually dominant position in regional politics, leading a counterrevolutionary coalition and intervening widely across multiple theaters. Its relative domestic stability and its deep pockets due to high oil prices, along with the temporary weakness and disarray of competitors such as Iraq, Syria, and Egypt, allowed it to take a lead role in attempting to contain and to shape the direction of the regional changes. Saudi Arabia helped to revitalize the Gulf Cooperation Council and the Arab League. It pushed for a successful NATO military intervention in Libya in 2011, supported rebel groups, and lobbied for intervention in Syria, and in 2015 led a large-scale military intervention in Yemen. It supported fellow monarchies in the Gulf and farther afield, including an invitation to Jordan and Morocco to join the GCC, but also divided the GCC by launching a campaign against Qatar. Its media sought to frame regional politics around sectarianism and the need to contain Iran rather than around popular revolution. Since the rise of Crown Prince Mohammad bin Salman, Saudi foreign policy has become more erratic and assertive.

Iraq

Iraq was traditionally defined by its role as a central Arab state that combined oil wealth with a sizable population and geographic centrality. It has generally commanded a powerful military machine and supported it with an economic base that included both sizable oil reserves and an educated, mercantile middle class. It regularly bid for Arab leadership, offering a distinctively martial form of Arab nationalism rooted in an ugly ethnic Ba'thism directed against its Persian Iranian rival. It commanded significant support from the Gulf states for its long 1980–1988 war with Iran. Overall, it has been far more likely to launch wars with its neighbors and to use military force against its own people than most other regional states.

Iraq's weaknesses were equally telling. Like Germany in the European balance-of-power system (to which it was often compared), Iraq suffered from its geography, with long borders with powerful competitors that were difficult to defend or to police. Its internal sectarian and ethnic divisions always represented a threat to the central government, which generally led to authoritarian rule from Baghdad. The Kurdish provinces in the north posed an endemic challenge to state integrity, which led in the late 1980s to a vicious campaign of ethnic cleansing, including the use of chemical weapons.[32] This meant that the impressive military machine was often turned inward, against Iraqi society, as much as outward. More than a decade of sanctions after 1991 hollowed out the economy and military, significantly weakening the state. After the toppling of Saddam Hussein in 2003, insurgency and the weakness of the state apparatus transformed Iraq from one of the strong to one of the weak, the battlefield on which others waged their battles rather than a powerful player in its own right. Iraq's future regional role will depend heavily on whether it is able to establish effective sovereignty over its own territory, a stable and legitimate political order, and relative independence from its Iranian neighbor.

Syria

Syria ranked as a strong second-tier power in material terms—not quite as big as Egypt or Iraq and nowhere nearly as wealthy as Saudi Arabia or the Gulf states. It maintained a relatively large military, but its reliance on Soviet arms left it weak in comparison with Israel or even other Arab competitors such as Jordan, and its domestic instability meant that many of its guns aimed inward. It presented itself as the "beating heart of Arabism," the standard-bearer of Arab opposition to Israel (especially after Camp David)—although it found little difficulty in being one of the only major Arab powers to align with Persian Iran against Arab Iraq. From 1990 to 2005, it used smothering domination of post–civil war Lebanon as a crucial extension of its power—keeping Israel's northern front "hot" through support for Hezbollah and putting down efforts by the proxies of other great powers to exert influence. When the "Cedar Revolution," combined with significant US pressure, drove Syrian forces from Lebanon in 2005, the result was much less about democracy than about curbing Syrian power.

Syria's ability to be a power player at all is a testament to the importance of domestic state capacity as a crucial variable. During the 1950s and 1960s, Syria's famously unstable, coup-ridden, and ideologically divided domestic system made it a primary target of the great powers of the era, as recounted in Patrick Seale's masterful *The Struggle for Syria*. Between 1958 and 1961, Syria formally dissolved itself into the short-lived United Arab Republic with Egypt. After Hafiz al-Asad seized power in 1970, however, this all changed as he created a repressive national security state that prioritized regime survival over all other considerations. The stability at home that this achieved allowed Syria to play a much more active role as a regional power in the following decades. This asset collapsed in dramatic fashion in 2011, as a brutal crackdown on peaceful protestors fueled a spiral into civil war, reducing Syria once again to an object of competitive regional power politics rather than a significant player in its own right. The war that has raged since 2011 has produced one of the greatest humanitarian tragedies in recent history, leaving the state divided between regime-held areas, a variety of rebel factions, and the nascent Islamic State.

Iran

The importance of identity is seen clearly in the case of Iran, which has by far the strongest combination of material power—military, size, economic resources—and state capacity of any state in the region (even without nuclear weapons), but which has largely failed to convert this power into influence. Instead, it has consistently been viewed as a foreign power by the Arabs and as a particularly potent threat to those Arab states with sizable Shi'i populations. This was the case both before and after the 1979 Islamic revolution. Before the revolution, the shah of Iran was a key US and Israeli ally, one of the pillars of US grand strategy, and Iran was the dominant military power in the Gulf. Its identification with the conservative forces in the Arab Cold War limited its ability to wield influence with much of the Arab world. After the revolution, what inspired much of the Arab population terrified Arab leaders who feared both Iran's Islamic fervor and the example of a successful revolution. In the 1980s, Iraq and its Gulf backers mobilized an anti-Persian (and anti-Shi'i) campaign against Iran, similar to the anti-Shi'i fervor whipped up in the mid-2000s in the face of rising Iranian power following the invasion of Iraq. Iran extended its power and presence in Iraq and Syria, and to a lesser extent Yemen, in part by building a sophisticated network of proxy militias and local allies. The 2015 nuclear deal opened the possibility for a significant change in Iran's role in regional order, but those largely failed to manifest and the conflict between Iran and its rivals has again become one of the primary cleavages defining regional order.

Israel

Like Iran, Israel has been unable to convert its dramatic military and economic advantages over its Arab neighbors into influence for primarily ideational reasons. Its military advantages are unquestioned, from technological sophistication to an undeclared but well-known nuclear weapons capability. Israel also has an advanced economy and close relations with the United States, which paradoxically makes the United States perhaps the greatest threat to Israeli interests because of Israel's dependence on US support. Israel has been consumed since its creation by the difficulty of gaining acceptance in the region as a legitimate entity, which has made a constructivist battle over identity and legitimacy central to Israel's place in regional politics. Israel's relations with the Arab world have aimed both at physical security and at what might be called ontological security, a demand for normalization or recognition as a normal state in the region.

The Gulf States

The small Gulf states have become increasingly prominent in the regional balance of power. Their vast wealth, highly capable and repressive states, media empires, and small but well-equipped and well-trained militaries make them especially well adapted to the post-2011 regional environment. Qatar, one of the tiny but extremely wealthy Gulf ministates, set itself off from the other GCC states by using its petroleum wealth to fuel an ambitious diplomacy and the astonishingly successful al-Jazeera television station. For a tiny state that hosted a major US military base and had long enjoyed good relations with Israel, Qatar emerged as a surprising avatar of a renewed Arab nationalism positioned against the old Arab order. With its hyperactive diplomacy, often aimed at contesting the Saudi role, it brokered important agreements in Lebanon and Sudan and took an increasingly active role in the Palestinian issue. The UAE has similarly taken on a more active and muscular regional political role since the uprisings, taking a lead role in supporting Egypt's 2013 military coup and the 2015 military intervention in Yemen.

Turkey

Turkey, which for decades had shunned the Middle East and focused on its bid to join Europe, began to refocus on the Arab world after the election of the mildly Islamist Adalet ve Kalkınma Partisi (Justice and Development Party) and the diminished prospects for EU membership. After forming a close military alliance with Israel during the 1990s, during the second half of the first decade of the 21st century, Turkey distanced itself from Israel and began to form good working relationships across the region, including with Iraq and Iran. This earned it considerable popularity with Arab public opinion and considerable suspicion from the Arab states. It overplayed its hand in the Syrian civil war, however, as it pushed unsuccessfully for the overthrow of Bashar al-Asad. Its domestic turbulence, Syrian quagmire, and cross-border conflict with Kurds have sharply challenged its regional influence.

HISTORICAL PERIODS

The various theories described in the previous sections may apply differently in different historical contexts. Many argue that the power of identity and ideology waned in the 1970s after the ignominious Arab defeat in the June 1967 War, giving way to an era of more realpolitik behavior. Others point to the "hardening" of the Arab state in the same period, reducing regime security concerns and perhaps facilitating more realist maneuvering. In this section, I briefly describe a number of commonly identified periods in Middle Eastern regional politics and trace the evolution of Arab–Israeli relations, Iran's role, and the inter-Arab struggle for leadership.

Arab Cold War

During the so-called Arab Cold War of the 1950s and 1960s, the role of ideology and identity was exceptionally high while internal state strength was unusually low in a number of key Arab states. As the international structure shifted from multipolarity to bipolarity, with the crystallization of the post–World War II environment into the Cold War between the United States and the Soviet Union, the Middle East emerged as a key battlefield. The key lines of conflict were between the Arabist states such as Egypt and the conservative, pro-Western states, as well as between the Western- and the Soviet-backed camps. Those two lines only sometimes overlapped, and often, the local actors worked to harness a superpower to their cause by alleging that their enemies harbored allegiances to a superpower's enemy.

Wars were often key moments in either shaping or revealing the deep changes in the region's politics. The Arab failure in the 1948 Arab-Israeli war that created the state of Israel had deep effects across the region—revealing the hollowness of Arab cooperation and the weakness of Arab states. Transjordan, with a British-led Arab Legion that outperformed all other Arab armies, expanded to incorporate the West Bank as part of the new Hashemite Kingdom of Jordan. The poor performance of Egyptian troops badly delegitimized the monarchy, spreading the discontent that grew into the 1952 Free Officers coup.

The coup that brought Gamal Abdel Nasser to power in Egypt had the most obvious effects on the region's international politics. Nasser reoriented Egyptian foreign policy around a commitment to Arab unity. The broadcasts of the Voice of the Arabs radio station proved a potent weapon, galvanizing the passions of Arabs across the Middle East and elevating Egypt to a position of leadership. In 1956, Israel collaborated with France and Britain in part in an effort to limit Nasser's rising power after he nationalized the Suez Canal, but their venture failed when the United States under the Eisenhower administration objected for fear of driving the Arab world into Soviet arms. Nasser's political fortunes skyrocketed in the aftermath, despite his military defeat.

Although Israel was forced to pull back from Suez, it pursued a policy vis-à-vis its neighbors of massive retaliation intended to compel its neighbors to rein in Palestinian infiltration to avoid Israeli collective reprisals. These attacks did succeed in compelling the regimes to control their borders. They also militarized the environment and generated great suspicion, outrage, and anger that hardened Arab views of the new Jewish state. The cycle of reprisals and attacks contributed to the justification of both internal repression and rhetorically aggressive foreign policies. Israel's policy did establish deterrence, while it also generated a self-fulfilling prophecy of hatred and hostility that has yet to be overcome.

The period was defined by an ideological struggle over the definition and practice of Arabism. In general, this struggle was waged in the realm of ideological warfare and subversion, with fierce media battles driving domestic turbulence. Egypt used its pan-Arab ideology to bid for regional leadership as it sought to establish regional norms and dominate Arab collective action. Saudi Arabia's efforts at the regional level were driven at least in part by its own domestic insecurity as parts of the public and even of the royal family clearly preferred the Arabist model.

The combination of domestic instability, intense ideological polarization, and fierce competition for regional leadership shaped the turbulent dynamics of the Arab Cold War. Nasserist mobilization kept small states like Jordan and Lebanon in perpetual crisis for much of the 1950s, drawing Western military interventions in both countries in 1958. Syria became a central battlefield between the camps, with a series of military coups serving as the vehicle for regional power struggles. Syria's decisions to dissolve itself into the United Arab Republic with Egypt in 1958 and then to leave the union in 1961 were key moments in the ups and downs of the regional cold war. The Syrian decision to voluntarily merge with Egypt is, in fact, one of the more remarkable moments in contemporary international history—a major regional power surrendering its sovereignty, even temporarily, to another competing regional power out of ideological conviction rather than military threat. Iraq, another potentially powerful state, changed sides after the bloody 1958 revolution ripped one of the most powerful of conservative states into the ranks of the radicals. And from 1962 to 1967, Egyptian and Saudi forces clashed directly in a proxy war in the isolated mountains of Yemen.

This period in Arab politics culminated in the Arab disaster of the June 1967 War. That war was driven in no small part by the forces described here. Intense ideological competition between Egypt and a radical regime in Syria drove each to take ever-more radical positions toward Israel—including the demand to remove United Nations forces from the Sinai Peninsula—which in turn fueled Israeli fears of encirclement and attack. Egypt found itself in a high-stakes game of chicken with Israel at a time when much of its military was tied down in Yemen and its own economic and political problems at home argued against military adventurism. Because of the enormous popularity of radical positions toward Israel and the continuing instability of Arab regimes, few Arab governments could risk standing on the sidelines, at least rhetorically. When Israel caught Egypt by surprise and destroyed most of its air force on the ground, it rapidly defeated Arab forces and captured a vast swath of Arab lands—the Gaza Strip and the Sinai Peninsula from Egypt, the West Bank and Jerusalem from Jordan, and the Golan Heights from Syria.

PHOTO 8.1 Nasser cheered by supporters after nationalizing the Suez Canal, 1956.

Keystone/Hulton Archive/Getty Images

After 1967 to the End of the Cold War

The aftermath of the June 1967 War set in motion fundamental changes in regional politics. Israel went overnight from being perceived as a small, threatened, and likely transient part of the region to a military powerhouse that occupied vast swaths of Arab land. Much of the region's diplomacy and wars since have been focused on dealing with the aftermath of those occupations. The disastrous performance of the Arab militaries discredited the promises of Nasser's pan-Arabism, taking the air out of the ideological wars of the preceding decades and crippling Egyptian soft power. It also led to the emergence of the PLO as the bearer of Palestinian nationalism (see Chapter 2).

Israel's occupation of Arab territories and recognition as the predominant military power in the Mashriq transformed the security balance in the region. Its occupation of the Sinai, Golan Heights, and West Bank gave it a territorial strategic buffer, as well as something over which to negotiate with its neighbors other than its existence. Despite the *Three No*s of the 1967 Khartoum Arab Summit (no peace with Israel, no recognition, no negotiation), the diplomatic focus inexorably shifted toward those Arab states determined to reclaim their lost territories. Israeli military superiority also generated overconfidence, however, and Israel failed to take sufficiently seriously the warnings of a coming Egyptian and Syrian attack in October 1973. Even that war primarily aimed at improving the bargaining position of those states, however—and, in the Egyptian case, triggered a realignment away from the Soviet Union toward the United States.

The Israeli occupation of the West Bank and Gaza also transformed the politics of the Palestinian issue. The PLO emerged as the claimant of Palestinian identity and Palestinian sovereignty on the back of the *fedayeen* attacks against Israel (see Chapter 21). Israeli reprisals against the hosting states and the growing power of the PLO put Jordan, especially, in an impossible position. This came to a head in the wrenching 1970 civil war of Black September, when the Jordanian armed forces moved against the PLO and its supporters. The Arab world stood by helplessly as the Palestinians were crushed by an Arab army; a threatened Syrian intervention did not materialize, while Gamal Abdel Nasser's desperate mediation ended with his collapse from exhaustion and death. Nasserist pan-Arabism quite literally died with Black September.

The early 1970s also saw the beginnings of a dramatic shift in the balance of power away from Egypt and toward the oil-producing states of the Gulf. It was not only Egypt's pan-Arab ideas that faded after 1967; it was also its economic and military position. The enormous influx of wealth into Saudi coffers transformed Saudi Arabia's ability to shape inter-Arab politics and ideas, while Egypt shifted from a deal maker to a taker in its desperate efforts to open its ailing economy. Egypt's decision to negotiate a peace treaty with Israel in 1978 and 1979 confirmed its reorientation away from pan-Arabism toward the pro-US conservative camp. The subsequent Arab boycott of Egypt, including its expulsion from the Arab League, temporarily removed the most traditionally powerful player from the Arab equation. Egypt would not fully return to the inter-Arab game until the late 1980s.

With Egypt out of the military equation, Israel rapidly turned to the north and in 1982 launched a war against Lebanon in hopes of crushing the PLO. After initial easy military success, the Israeli military laid siege to Beirut and the PLO leadership. But then things began to go wrong, as international attention focused on horrors such as the massacre of Palestinians at the refugee camps of Sabra and Shatila by Lebanese forces in an area under Israeli control and the sufferings of Lebanese civilians in Beirut. Finally, the PLO leadership was allowed safe passage from Lebanon, and Israeli forces retreated to a buffer zone in southern Lebanon. Hezbollah, the Shi'i movement backed by Iran, emerged to wage a determined insurgency against this Israeli occupation—a campaign that included the devastating 1983 bombing of the US embassy in Beirut—which continued until Israel finally unilaterally withdrew in 2000. After the Israeli withdrawal, Lebanon collapsed into a horrific civil war that lasted until an Arab accord finally agreed in 1990 to establish Syrian military hegemony in order to oversee a fragile truce in a broken country.

The combination of the end of pan-Arabism and the rise of Saudi oil wealth contributed to the dramatic growth in the repressive capacity of most Arab states. In general, whatever regimes happened to be in power in 1970 benefited from the transformation, and with few exceptions, they remain in power to the present day. Oil wealth, along with strategic rents extracted from superpower patrons, allowed most Arab states to construct massive, overwhelming national security institutions designed primarily to ensure regime survival. Suffocating control of the political realm, the media, and even the economy became the norm as the Arab system hardened against the kind of cross-border mobilization that had characterized the previous era.

Then came the Iranian revolution of 1979. No single event—not even the 1967 war debacle or the horror of Black September—so shook the Arab status quo. Arab regimes designed for little more than remaining in power were confronted with their worst nightmare as a militarily strong, modernizing, wealthy Middle Eastern power closely allied with the United States crumbled in the face of a massive popular mobilization. The Arab response took several forms. Virtually the entire Arab world rallied to the side of Iraq when Saddam Hussein invaded Iran in 1980 out of fear for his own regime's survival in the face of a galvanized Shi'i population and out of hope that the Iranian revolutionary regime might be temporarily vulnerable during the transitional chaos of revolution. When that war degenerated into a bloody eight-year standoff, Arab states contributed both financial support and ideological backing to Saddam's campaign—with only Ba'thist Syria opting to side with Iran against its hated Iraqi rivals. The Arab states of the Gulf formed the GCC to coordinate their response to revolutionary Iran. The other face of the Arab response was to intensify the process of hardening national security states, crushing domestic opposition, and exercising suffocating control over any signs of independent political organization or independent critical public speech.

The Soviet invasion of Afghanistan also shaped regional politics in the 1980s as Saudi Arabia led a transnational campaign to support the Afghan mujahidin against Soviet occupation. While the details of that campaign are beyond the scope of this chapter, it is worth noting the extent to which the regionwide campaign to mobilize support for the Afghan jihad shaped and established the transnational Islamist networks that would later become so crucial to the evolution of al-Qa'ida. Islamist movements and nominally apolitical mosques alike, with the tacit or explicit approval of governments, raised money and support for the mujahidin. These efforts laid the foundations for the Islamist transformation of regional political culture to come.

In sum, the 1970s and 1980s saw the emergence of recognizably realist international politics in the Middle East. The appeal of transnational ideologies faded, although new Islamist trends were growing beneath the surface, while state institutions hardened against both external subversion and domestic dissent. Wars were waged over the narrow self-interest of states (the October 1973 War) and peace agreements negotiated based on the balance of power (Camp David). Power shifted from Egypt and the Levant toward Israel and the Gulf, and the Iranian revolution dramatically unsettled the region.

After the Cold War

The end of the Cold War between East and West was felt immediately in regional international relations, with the August 1990 Iraqi invasion of Kuwait. Although it took several years to be fully felt, the collapse of the Soviet Union led to a fundamentally new logic of unipolarity in the region and a much deeper, more direct US role in every facet of the region's politics. In the post-1990s Middle East, all roads led through Washington. By the mid-2000s, virtually every regime in the region was either allied with the United States or seeking some accommodation (for example, Libya and Syria). US military bases and troop deployments from Iraq to the ministates of the Gulf created a fundamentally new military and security situation. Across almost the entire region, Israel faced Arab competitors that shared the same superpower patron (the United States, which could presumably shape and to a large extent control their decisions about war) and increasingly conceived of their own interests much as the United States and Israel did—even as Arab public opinion turned in sharply different directions.

The Iraqi invasion of Kuwait took place in the eye of the storm caused by the end of the Cold War. Although he was motivated primarily by regime security concerns, frustration over Kuwaiti intransigence, and a bid for regional hegemony, Saddam Hussein also saw the closing of a window to act while the United States was distracted with the reunification of Germany and the reordering of Europe. The decision to invade Kuwait shockingly violated Arab norms (which tolerated competition and subversion but not cross-border invasion) and shocked Arab leaders who had been personally assured by Saddam that force would not be used—violations of norms that help explain why the Arab leaders were willing to undertake unprecedented open military cooperation with the United States.

Operation Desert Storm caused the United States to move much more deeply into the region in several ways. First, the basing of approximately five hundred thousand troops in Saudi Arabia proved a shock to the system that galvanized domestic criticism of the Saudi ruling family. Even when those forces dispersed to bases strung along the Gulf periphery (Bahrain, Qatar, Kuwait), the momentum of direct US military presence in the Gulf proved irreversible. The Clinton administration's policy of dual containment, which sought to maintain a balance of power (including sanctions and no-fly zones) against both Iraq and Iran (the traditional powers in the Gulf), required this massive US presence.

The war with Iraq also prompted a much more direct and intense US role in attempting to broker Arab-Israeli peace. The Madrid peace conference and the effort to implement the surprising Oslo accords between Israel and the PLO brought the United States in as a direct broker of negotiations at the most intimate possible levels.

Even as the regimes of the region adapted to this global international structure, public opinion went in quite a different direction. The forces of globalization came together around the focal point of the al-Jazeera satellite television station, which galvanized Arab identity with news coverage and popular debate programs focused on issues of shared, core Arab concern such as Palestine, Iraq, and general dissatisfaction with the political and economic status quo.[33] Arab anger with both the United States and their own governments peaked in the face of the official order's impotence during the second Palestinian intifada, the ongoing sanctions against Iraq, and then the 2003 invasion of Iraq. Meanwhile, Islamist movements across the region were transforming the political culture from below.

The terrorist attacks against the United States on September 11, 2001, built on the trends of the 1990s far more than has generally been realized. The George W. Bush administration's aggressive unilateralism, including the invasion and occupation of Iraq, only accelerated trends evident in the second half of the Clinton administration. The US imperium in the region had been developing for more than a decade, as had the trends in Arab and Muslim public opinion. The global war on terror that defined the Bush administration's engagement with the region combined close cooperation with security-minded Arab regimes with a vastly intensified engagement with all aspects of Arab politics.

The invasion and occupation of Iraq by the United States had a massive impact on regional international relations, even if the long-range verdict remains unclear. The removal of Iraq as a major power and then its reformulation as a democracy dominated by pro-Iranian Shi'i politicians tipped the balance of power in the Gulf decisively toward Iran even without the latter acquiring nuclear weapons. The spread of concern about the "Shi'i crescent" in the region was driven at least as much by regime fears of rising Iranian power as by genuine religious or sectarian rage (even if many Arab Sunnis were genuinely outraged by the demonstrations of violent sectarianism in Iraq). Many hope that Iraq will transition into a democratic, pro-Western state, but it is far too early to know—and it is important to recall that, for those subscribing to the theory of realism in international relations, such domestic considerations will not likely matter much as the new Iraq formulates its national interests in response to an intensely competitive international environment. For now, the most important effect has been Iraq's weakness, changing it from a powerful actor to an arena in which other powers fight their proxy wars. Whether Iraq reemerges in the near to midrange future as a fully sovereign and territorially unified state playing an active role in regional politics—and whether that role is in alignment with or against Iran—will be decisive in judging the long-term effects of the invasion.

The Arab Uprisings

The popular protests that swept the Arab world in 2010 and 2011 ushered in a distinctive new period in regional politics. The early period of the so-called Arab Spring witnessed an exceptionally intense integration of the Arab political space. Thanks to satellite television and the Internet, and the long cultivation of a shared Arab identity, protest ideas and forms rapidly spread across the region. The powerful regional demonstration effects meant that individual countries could not be meaningfully analyzed in isolation: The Egyptian revolution almost certainly would not have happened without the Tunisian example; and the Syrian uprising would have taken a very different form without the Libyan precedent. The rise of popular mobilization significantly increased the salience of regime security concerns and identity politics but did not sweep away the legacies of realist dynamics or the importance of material power and economic wealth.

If the first days of the Arab uprisings highlighted popular demonstration effects and challenges to regime survival, later developments demonstrated the resilience and power of authoritarian regimes. Saudi Arabia and the UAE, in particular, took the lead in crafting a renewed "official" Arab response to the uprisings that many dismayed activists decried as "counterrevolutionary." Saudi Arabia intervened directly in Bahrain, where it sent in its military forces to assist the al-Khalifa monarchy in repressing popular protests, and in Yemen, where it brokered a political transition removing President Ali Abdallah Salih while preserving the core of the regime. It offered financial support to other Gulf states, as well as to fellow monarchies such as Jordan and Morocco. And it led the official Arab push for intervention in Libya and Syria, which introduced a new form of military interventionism into the calculus of previously indigenous political struggles. Qatar, for its part, increasingly used al-Jazeera as a political instrument for promoting its own political agenda, most clearly in its unabashed support for the uprisings in Libya and Syria.

The years following the uprisings were shaped by several devastating civil wars and state failures, dramatically expanded proxy warfare, and escalating sectarianism and Islamist extremism. Syria's civil war was the epicenter of regional devastation. Years of war left hundreds of thousands dead and many millions displaced internally or abroad, while power in the areas outside regime control devolved to a dizzying array of rebel factions, including the Islamic State. The Asad regime has to this point survived and arguably defeated the rebels, with the support of Russia and Iran, while a US-led campaign has largely destroyed the Islamic State within both Iraq and Syria; Turkey has established control over parts of northern Syria. Libya's transition collapsed into an intense struggle between competing governments. Saudi Arabia and its allies launched a major but inconclusive military intervention in Yemen after the failure of its transitional government and the seizure of Sanaa and Aden by Houthi rebels. The nuclear agreement reached in 2015 between Iran and the international community held out the possibility for a fundamental restructuring of regional order, but instead, it led to even sharper conflict. Israel has formed ever-closer relations with key Arab states despite the failure to resolve the Palestinian issue. In 2017, Saudi Arabia and the UAE ripped apart the GCC by launching a blockade of Qatar, quietly ending the boycott in 2020 after accomplishing little.

CONCLUSION: POTENTIAL TRANSFORMATIVE FORCES

Are the international relations of the Middle East exceptional? Is there anything unique about the region that requires a theoretical lens different from that employed in the wider literature on international relations theory? The distinctive ideological preoccupations of the region and the transnationalism of its identities and political movements point to the region's singularity. Some theorists point to the unique, deeply embedded, and unchanging culture or religion[34]; the common language; and the weak national identities. Others point to the distorting effects of oil, including the rentier phenomenon that directed huge financial flows directly into the hands of the state.[35] Still others point to the absence of a single great power, the legacy of colonialism, and historical development.[36] Others point to the distinct persistence of Arab authoritarianism, the distinctively transnational media, the continuing payoffs to war and conquest, the level of international involvement, terrorism, Islamist movements, and Israel.

But such analyses may confuse the surface for the substance. Much of the behavior of Arab states appears to be grounded in a regime security variant of realism beneath the rhetoric, while many of the region's pathologies appear more typical of the third world than distinctive to Arab or Islamic culture. The resurgence of Sunni–Shi'i tension in late 2005 appeared to many observers as the eruption of timeless sectarian hostilities and the expression of the formative essentialism of religious identity.[37] To others, no such resort to essentialism or even to distinctive religious culture was required. The demonization of Shi'a in the Sunni-majority Arab countries was clearly led by states, promoted in their official media and in government-monitored mosques, and fairly clearly followed those regimes' concerns about rising Iranian power and influence in the region. A top-down mobilization of domestic hostility against a rising foreign power is not difficult for an international relations theorist to understand even without deep knowledge of the Middle East or its allegedly unique political culture.

What about the role of Islam and of transnational Islamist actors? During the past thirty years, Islamist movements such as the Muslim Brotherhood may not have taken power in Arab countries, but they have played important roles in the democratic process and have contributed to a dramatic transformation of the public culture across the region. Saudi Arabia has a deeply Islamist state that shapes its domestic politics and that seeks to export Islam across the region and the world. Extremist Islamists have waged insurgencies in several key Arab countries, including Egypt and Algeria in the 1990s and Iraq after the fall of Saddam Hussein. Al-Qaʻida and the Islamic State represent a new kind of transnational violent Islamist challenge to the official Arab order. Although all of these have clearly mattered in important ways, it is important to recall, despite the unique Iranian revolution, how rarely Islamist movements have succeeded in taking control of a Middle Eastern state—in Sudan, a military coup searching for an identity brought in Islamist ideologues, and in Turkey, a moderately Islamist party won elections and continues to govern today. The Arab uprisings have given new opportunities for Islamist parties to play a leading role in governments, from Tunisia and Egypt to Libya, but it is impossible to know at this point whether their ideology will drive significant changes in foreign policy or the demands of international politics will force them into pragmatic, realist policies. The most dramatic of these new Islamist actors has been the self-declared Islamic State, which seized control over a large swath of territory spanning Iraq and Syria and has established local franchises in areas such as Egypt and Libya but was militarily crushed within a few years.

The seemingly unique resistance of the Arab Middle East to political democracy, the deep focus on regime survival, and the oil-fueled overdeveloped state do seem distinctive to the region.[38] As discussed in Chapter 4, political systems in the region have rarely approximated Western notions of democracy, and the region largely resisted the various waves of democratization that swept other regions in the 1980s and after. The persistence of authoritarianism in the region could arguably have effects at the level of international—not only domestic—politics. International relations theorists have identified a wide range of effects of democracy, well beyond the oft-referenced "democratic peace thesis" that democracies do not go to war against each other. Theorists have argued that democratic systems differ systematically from nondemocracies by increasing the transparency of politics and introducing multiple veto points in the policy formation process and, also, by increasing the points of access for outside actors to engage in efforts to influence political outcomes.[39] The political transitions in key Arab countries since 2011, however partial at this point, will pose a challenging test of this hypothesis.

The history of the regional politics of the Middle East suggests a complex mix of enduring patterns and significant changes. The deep substructure remains relatively unchanged: regimes that primarily value their own survival and guarantee it through undemocratic means, the structuring effects of vast oil revenues, publics who value Arab identity, the Palestinian issue and the seemingly unresolvable Arab–Israeli struggle, and the enduring imbalances of power destabilizing the Gulf. Significant changes have occurred, though: The United States is much more directly present in the region than ever before. Arab states have become far more open to coordination—or even cooperation—with Israel despite the lack of progress on resolving the Palestinian conflict. Political Islam has risen from irrelevance in the 1950s to a dominant political-cultural position. Iraq has been invaded, occupied, and transformed by the United States. And Iran has gone from an Islamic revolution to what many think is the brink of a counterrevolution while getting ever closer to nuclear weapons capability. What kinds of change are possible in the future in the regional dynamics described in this chapter? What would represent genuine, fundamental change?

For realist theorists, the most likely source of enduring change would be a significant change in the balance of power at either the global or the regional level. The shift from the Cold War's bipolarity to the post–Cold War unipolar US imperium in the early 1990s led to profound change in the logic and patterns of regional politics. A comparable global change from unipolarity back to multipolarity would presumably have similar effects. Such trends are already clearly visible. The global financial crisis that devastated the United States and Western economies in 2008 and the vast US expenditures on the occupations of Iraq and Afghanistan have dramatically impacted US capabilities and willingness to intervene abroad. The dramatic shift of global wealth toward the East, especially India and China, and those countries' ravenous energy needs suggest a very high likelihood of the restructuring of the global order that will draw those powers into the Middle East. Three successive US presidents have declared their desire to scale back the American presence in the region and avoid new wars. Should that happen, Arab states would be faced with a plausible choice of great-power patrons for the first time since the 1980s, and many of the restraining effects of the US imperium could fade. This structural change could explain the increasingly independent and even erratic behavior of longtime US allies such as Saudi Arabia and the "hedging" behavior of those allies as they cultivate relationships and arms deals with Russia.

The balance of power could also change within the region. The occupation of Iraq created one such massive, unprecedented change in the distribution of power. This is likely to prove temporary, as Iraq reemerges as a centralized state with a competent military and continuing economic power. Should it not, however—whether through a partition that produces several smaller states (Kurdistan and some form of rump Iraq) or a perpetual condition of US or Iranian occupation or control that denies Iraq freedom of political action—then the balance of power in the region would fundamentally change.

Iran succeeding in obtaining nuclear weapons is often suggested as another game changer in terms of regional power dynamics. This is less obvious. Nuclear weapons have limited utility for conventional political influence; and although they might increase Iran's status, they could also increase its political isolation, at least in the short to medium term. Arab states threatened by increased Iranian destructive power would be more likely to solidify their anti-Iranian alliance choices than to climb on a bandwagon with a feared, rising competitor. Neither Indian nor Pakistani nuclear weapons have fundamentally changed the status or political dynamics in South Asia, and Iranian nuclear weapons might have a similarly limited impact. An Iranian nuclear deterrent could limit the US freedom of maneuver in the region as well as its ability to threaten Iranian interests—which could prove stabilizing, even as it frustrates US policymakers. Israel would also find its nuclear primacy challenged for the first time, which could lead either to a stable condition of mutual deterrence or to an unstable, tense, ongoing brinkmanship or even preventive war.

The entry of new actors into the political arena could also change the patterns if not the underlying structure of the political system. In Qatar, a more dynamic foreign policy fueled by massive oil and natural gas wealth, al-Jazeera's soft power, and an energetic young leadership have already challenged Saudi aspirations to monopolize conflict resolution and media discourse. Turkey's turn to the Middle East, driven by frustration with the European Union, significant economic and security interests, and domestic political trends, puts a powerful new player with great material power and considerable popular attractiveness into the equation.

What about the end of the Arab–Israeli conflict? A negotiated, two-state solution to the Palestinian–Israeli conflict and a Syrian–Israeli peace agreement would at least partially close the door on the most enduring conflict in the region. If this commanded popular support, it could help to fundamentally transform the political culture of the region as well as the strategic balance. Israel could become a legitimate security partner while a major source of destabilization and popular anger would be removed. This would not in and of itself change the power balance in the Gulf or any of the other trends, but it would almost certainly have a major impact across the region. In contrast, the failure of the peace process—the end of negotiations and return to some form of armed conflict—would likely reinforce existing patterns of regime security focus and competition.

Finally, would even successful democratization across the region (however unlikely that currently appears) change the fundamental patterns of politics? It would certainly change the nature of the regime security concerns that seem to be so central to the foreign policy decision-making of leaders in the region. Some, citing evidence of the rarity of democracies fighting wars with each other, argue that this would facilitate cooperation and moderation. This may be too optimistic, however. Arab leaders tend to be far more pragmatic, pro-US, and pro-Israeli than their disenfranchised populations are. More democratic states could increase opportunities for cross-border ideological mobilization as in the 1950s and complicate the well-established routines of international cooperation.

Regional politics in the Middle East have witnessed significant changes during the last half century, even as enduring patterns continue to play out in predictable ways. The shift to a unipolar world in the early 1990s brought the United States into the region in far more intense ways than in the past, a change that profoundly shaped all levels of politics. The steady shift of economic power to the Gulf beginning in the 1970s drove Egypt's decline and Saudi ascendance in shaping Arab political outcomes. Powerful forces of globalization—especially the information revolution—empowered democratic activists and popular protest, but security-obsessed authoritarian Arab regimes sought ways to retain their power. The Arab–Israeli conflict defied efforts at resolution, and popular mobilization around the Palestinian issue escalated dramatically in the 2000s, but the official Arab taboo against cooperation with Israel nevertheless faded. Iraq's removal from the equation created a vacuum at the heart of the Gulf that other, would-be powers struggled to fill—sparking regionwide conflict between Arab states and Iran. The rise of Islamist movements transformed public culture and sparked a new round of insurgencies and the global war on terror in response. Faced with the blizzard of developments and trends, it is essential to keep a careful eye on the underlying balance of power and the enduring imperative of regime security as states compete for power, security, and influence in a shifting and turbulent environment.

SUGGESTED READINGS

Ajami, Fouad. *The Arab Predicament*. New York, NY: Cambridge University Press, 1991.

Barnett, Michael. *Dialogues in Arab Politics: Negotiations in Regional Order*. New York, NY: Columbia University Press, 1998.

Gause, F. Gregory III. *The International Relations of the Persian Gulf*, New York, NY: Cambridge University Press, 2010.

Halliday, Fred. *The Middle East in International Relations: Power, Politics, and Ideology*. New York, NY: Cambridge University Press, 2005.

Kerr, Malcolm H. *The Arab Cold War*. New York, NY: Oxford University Press, 1971.

Lynch, Marc. *The Arab Uprising: The Unfinished Revolutions in the Middle East*. New York, NY: Public Affairs, 2012.

Lynch, Marc. *Voices of the New Arab Public: Iraq, Al-Jazeera, and Middle East Politics Today*. New York, NY: Columbia University Press, 2006.

Ryan, Curtis. *Inter-Arab Alliances*. Gainesville, FL: University of Florida Press, 2008.

Seale, Patrick. *The Struggle for Syria*. New Haven, CT: Yale University Press, 1986.

Walt, Stephen. *The Origin of Alliances*. Ithaca, NY: Cornell University Press, 1987.

PROFILES

9 ALGERIA

Lahouari Addi

A French colony from 1830 to 1962, Algeria is a vast country of close to forty-two million inhabitants WHO speak Arabic in the cities and the plains and Berber in the mountains. There is no official figures, but we can say that some 20–25 percent of the population speak the Berber language called Amazigh. The upper and middle classes also speak French, and the government is unofficially bilingual in Arabic and French. Under colonization, the natives suffered discrimination and were awarded full French citizenship only in the late 1950s. The economy rested essentially on wine and citrus fruits, which were exported to France, and on iron ore and phosphate mining. In 1956, at the height of the War of Independence (1954–1962), oil was discovered in the Sahara Desert, which covers 2,000,000 sq km of Algeria's territory of 2,380,000 sq km.

After the country won independence from France in 1962, following a bloody war that killed hundreds of thousands and lasted seven-and-a-half years,[1] Algeria embarked on a socialist path, with one-party rule and a state-controlled economy. Like many other countries governed by a single-party regime, it tried with difficulty to convert to democracy and economic liberalism after the fall of the Berlin Wall. The transition from single-party system led to political violence and a "dirty war" that has claimed approximately 200,000 lives since the annulment of the Islamists' electoral victory of December 1991. Algeria underwent what is called "the bloody decade" (1992–2002) that ended by a settlement of peace between the military and the insurgents. The majority of the Islamists accepted the amnesty offered by the government in the legal framework of the National Reconciliation Charter.

HISTORY OF STATE FORMATION

The Algerian regime is rooted in a populist ideology forged by a nationalist movement whose ultimate goal was not only independence but also equality and the fair distribution of wealth. The leader who most embodied this program was Colonel Houari Boumédiène, the former chief of staff of the clandestine army that fought for independence. He took power in June 1965 after overthrowing the president Ahmed Ben Bella, who had been elected in 1963. He was a charismatic leader, gaining the support of the masses with speeches that promised to meet the needs of the population and to improve the living conditions of the most impoverished. His regime was considered a model of authoritarian modernization. However, although the institutions were consistent with the one-party system, the regime did not rest on the ruling National Liberation Front (FLN) party, as in the Soviet experience, but rather the army. The political opponents in Algeria and abroad were hunted down by a political police (called Military Security) responsible to the minister of defense.[2]

PHOTO 9.1 President Ahmed Ben Bella (left) and Colonel Houari Boumediene (right)

echoroukonline.com, Public domain, via Wikimedia Commons

Boumédiène sought to implement economic and social development under the political supervision of the army. He proclaimed that his mission was to carry out the program of the nationalist movement—to catch up with the West while defending a culture that France, the former colonial power, had denied the people for more than a century. Attracted by the charismatic Egyptian president Gamal Abdel Nasser, Boumédiène also borrowed the political rhetoric of radical Arab nationalism. As the defender of national independence against France, he never spoke in French in public and never officially visited France, which he criticized vociferously. His project was a synthesis of nostalgia of traditional past, revolutionary utopia, exclusive nationalism, and socialist discourse. He tried to implement cultural, industrial, and agrarian revolutions to shape "the new man" with native authenticity and mastery of modern technology.

KEY FACTS ON ALGERIA

AREA 919,595 square miles (2,381,741 square kilometers)

CAPITAL Algiers

POPULATION 43,576,691 (2020 est.)

PERCENTAGE OF POPULATION UNDER 25 43.51

RELIGIOUS GROUPS (PERCENTAGE) Sunni Muslim (state religion), 99; Christian and Jewish, 1

ETHNIC GROUPS (PERCENTAGE) Arab-Berber, 99; European, less than 1

OFFICIAL LANGUAGE Arabic, Berber, and Tamazight; French also widely spoken

TYPE OF GOVERNMENT Presidential Republic

DATE OF INDEPENDENCE July 5, 1962

GDP (PPP) $495.56 billion; $11,511 per capita (2019 est.)

GDP (NOMINAL) $169.91 billion (2019 est.)

PERCENTAGE OF GDP BY SECTOR Agriculture, 13.3; industry, 39.3; services, 47.4 (2017 est.)

TOTAL RENTS (PERCENTAGE OF GDP) FROM NATURAL RESOURCES 30

FERTILITY RATE 2.55 children born/woman (2021 est.)

Sources: CIA. "The World Factbook." August 4, 2022, https://www.cia.gov/the-world-factbook/
World Bank. "International Comparison Program (ICP)." Accessed August 10, 2022, https://databank.
worldbank.org/source/icp-2017

Boumédiène's hostility toward the capitalist West pushed him to nationalize economic sectors held by foreigners and build an industrial base under the control of the state. He created large, nationwide corporations to deal with production and commercialization of goods and services and limited the private sector. In 1971, he nationalized 51 percent of French hydrocarbon companies. That same year, he launched the agrarian revolution to limit land property and benefit of landless peasants, who were encouraged to form cooperatives. In 1973, state finances were tripled following an increase in oil prices after the Arab–Israeli War in October. Boumédiène decided on an ambitious plan of public education, state-funded health care, and heavy, Soviet-style, industrialization, which created hundreds of thousands of jobs.

In 1976, Boumédiène sought to mobilize popular support by submitting to public discussion an ideological text—called the National Charter—that reaffirmed socialism and the choice of the one single-party system. After two months of debate in which all levels of society took part, the project of the National Charter was adopted by referendum in 1976. The same year, a National Assembly was elected with candidates only from the ruling party, the FLN. The following year, Houari Boumédiène was elected president of the republic, promising to carry out the program of the FLN contained in the National Charter. Thus, the regime gave itself the institutional legitimacy it had been lacking.

After Boumédiène's death in December 1978, the military establishment chose Colonel Chadli Bendjedid, from among the high-ranking officers, to lead the country. However, Bendjedid lacked charisma and authority. The regime faced growing social unrest, with riots in Tizi-Ouzou (1980), Oran (1982), La Casbah (Algiers, 1985), Sétif (1986), Constantine (1986), and nationwide in 1988. Moreover, due to a reduction in oil revenues starting in 1985, the state did not create as many jobs as it had in previous years. The decrease in oil revenues, the heavy external debt, and a chronic deficit of the public sector put the state's finances to a hard test. Algeria no longer had the means to import food, and this led in October 1988 to widespread riots. The army reestablished order by killing five hundred people and wounding more than a thousand. After a week of chaos, on October 10, the president announced important political reforms, including the end of the one-party rule and the state's monopoly over the economy. But the reforms were not genuine; they aimed for change *in* the regime, not a change *of* the regime.

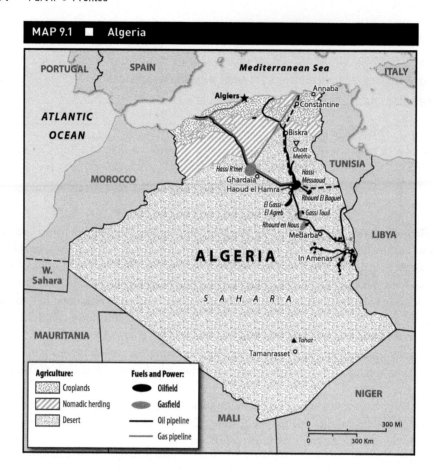

MAP 9.1 ■ Algeria

The military were not (and are not) ready to accept a political legitimacy stemming from the ballots and to give up economy as a political resource.

The riots of October 1988 marked a turning point in the history of the country. The constitution, modified accordingly in February 1989, legalized approximately sixty parties.[3] The soft-liners reformers believed that they could save the regime by liberalizing the economy and democratizing political life. Between 1989 and 1992, the country knew a political openness without precedent for an Arab country. On television and radio, debates were held in which opponents of the regime took part. Private newspapers were authorized, which freed speech more than anywhere else in the Arab world. The political openness empowered grassroots organizations. Although reticent, military leaders accepted the reforms, hoping that they would ameliorate the economic situation and reinforce the regime. Following the pressures of the International Monetary Fund (IMF) on the government, they accepted the multiparty system and privatization, which led to economic liberalization.

In June 1990, to the surprise of many, the Islamic Salvation Front (FIS), an Islamist party, won municipal elections with 80 percent of the vote.[4] The former ruling party (FLN) was the

PHOTO 9.2 High State Council President Mohamed Boudiaf (center) greets General Abdelmalek Guenaizia (left), the army chief of staff, in Algiers airport on January 16, 1992, upon his return to Algeria from Morocco after twenty-seven years of self-imposed exile. Boudiaf was assassinated in June 1992, allegedly by those who put him in office.

Abdelhak Senna/AFP/Getty Images

only party that resisted the Islamist landslide (the FFS, well established in Kabylia,[5] boycotted the elections). Strengthened by electoral support, the Islamists sought a confrontation with the government by calling for a presidential election before the legislative election scheduled for June 1991. They called for a general strike in May 1991, in which few participated, and they occupied the main public squares in downtown Algiers. In order to put an end to a quasi-insurrection, the army demanded the resignation of Prime Minister Mouloud Hamrouche and arrested hundreds of Islamists, including the two leaders of the FIS, Abbassi Madani and Ali Benhadj. The new leadership of the FIS proved to be more accommodating, renouncing the demand for an early presidential election and agreeing to participate in legislative elections postponed until December 1991.

In the first round of the elections held in December, the FIS won 180 seats (the FFS obtained 25 and the FLN, 15). Scheduled for January 1992, the second round would have given the FIS the absolute majority in the National Assembly. Chadli Bendjedid was ready to govern with an Islamist majority in the National Assembly, but the military forced him to resign. The potential loss of control of the state frightened the high-ranking military officers who decided to cancel the second round of elections. Many elected Islamists were arrested, and Algeria subsequently floundered in violence that has spared neither civilians nor members of the military and security services.[6] The cancellation of the election in January 1992 and the dismissal of the president Chadli Bendjedid reflected the army's key role in the state as the source of power.

CHANGING SOCIETY

Algerian society changed significantly between 1830, the year of the French conquest, and 1962, when the country won independence from France. In the 19th century, 80 percent of the population lived in rural areas, practicing agropastoralist activities, while the remainder consisted of craftspeople and traders who lived in cities. The tribal communities in rural areas were relatively self-sufficient and produced their own sustenance, essentially cereals and mutton. This self-sufficient economy was extensive and required collective vast pastoral lands (*arch*) for flocks of sheep. The colonial authorities declared this tribal property "ownerless," confiscated it, and distributed it to European settlers. On one million hectares, settlers would practice intensive modern agriculture exporting toward Europe. After several successive revolts, the largest of which was that of Shaykh Mokrani in 1871, the tribes were eventually defeated militarily.

In 1930, after a century of French domination, there were seven million inhabitants, of whom seven hundred thousand were Europeans living primarily in the four largest cities of the country (Algiers, Oran, Constantine, and Annaba). Eighty percent of the natives, who were denied civic rights, lived in the countryside as landowning families or permanent, seasonal, or daily agricultural workers in farms owned by European settlers. The other 20 percent were urban, coming from impoverished former urban families and, above all, from the rural exodus. Some Algerians worked in factories, ports, and railways and formed the nucleus of the urban proletariat. Others worked in small commerce and in informal sectors. Many unemployed or underemployed Algerians immigrated to France to find jobs. With the exception of a few hundred individuals, there were no teachers, doctors, or liberal professionals among the natives.

It was in this sociological context that modern Algerian nationalism was born in the 1920s. Its social basis was the poor peasantry, and its leadership came from the cities and Algerian immigrants in France. Some Algerian workers, who became activists asking for independence, learned in France concepts related to civic rights such as freedom of speech under the influence of French unions and their political culture.

In 1962, independence provoked a massive exodus from the countryside to cities where rural families occupied the urban housing abandoned by the Europeans known as *pieds-noirs*. The large migration of extended families to the cities gave birth to a new society, whose members had to live in buildings with neighbors who were unrelated to them and get accustomed to apartments built for nuclear families. In twenty years, the population of the cities grew from 20 percent to 65 percent. The urbanization was also pushed by the government's economic development policies. The rapid growth of the urban population caused a severe housing crisis that led to shantytowns, despite the efforts of the government to build social housing.

The public policies were focused on establishing industry and assuring education for all children six years and older. A new middle class of teachers, doctors, engineers, lawyers, and civil servants grew in a rather short period following the spread of public education and creation of several universities. In 1962, there were six hundred students; in 1972, there were one hundred thousand. Today, in 2021, there are more than two million students. Yet the growth of the number of students has not solved problems of underdevelopment. This has had significant socioeconomic consequences, including what is called "the graduate jobless."

However, the free education did profit women, who outnumbered the male students in universities. Their status improved, with women now working in education, administration, and hospitals. Close to 25 percent of urban women work, lowering the birth rate. Official statistics show that the median age of marriage for women rose from eighteen to twenty-eight between 1962 and 1980. That said, however, the family law still does not ensure equality between women and men; according to the family code of 1984, women are inferior in matters of marriage, divorce, and inheritance. Similarly, many women wear the *hijab* (veil) for social and religious acceptance. This is telling of the contradictions of Algerian society, which on the one hand aspires to modernity and on the other clings to the past.

INSTITUTIONS AND GOVERNANCE

Algeria shifted from single-party rule to the multiparty system based on electoral competition in 1989, with a constitutional reform. Formally, Algeria has a democratic régime with freedom of speech and free electoral competition. Any citizen, on the basis of criteria stated by the constitution, can run for office in presidential, legislative, and municipal contests. However, the reality is quite different. The political system rests on two legitimacies: the first one, hidden, is inherited from the Liberation War and embodied by the Army, while the second is formal, pertaining to the elections that are prepared upstream and downstream by the intelligence service dependent on the army (DRS, Direction Renseignement et Sécurité). The DRS is a vital institution for the regime. It shapes the political field so that neither the elections nor the opposition parties can threaten it. The army views its mission as choosing—through rigged elections—civilians who unfailingly respect the unwritten rule of the Algerian political system: the army is the only source of power. The source of power is not the electorate but the army, and state power is split between an unaccountable military leadership and an administration that takes its legitimacy from this same military leadership.[7] The high-ranking officers are reluctant to establish a military dictatorship because they emerged from an antimilitarist and antifascist liberation movement. They are convinced, however, that the civil elites must be supervised and controlled because they may betray the nation.

Thus, while Algeria formally abandoned the one-party system, it established only a superficial multiparty system. Indeed, the Algerian experience highlights the fact that elections are not a sufficient indicator of democracy. The Algerian regime promulgates the right of parties to compete, according to the constitution; however, it denies the sovereignty of the electorate by stuffing ballot boxes to favor parties of the administration and to distort electoral majorities. In this regard, the reforms came at the expense of the regime's ideological–political coherence. On the one hand, the regime changed too much because it moved away from the coherence of the one-party system; on the other hand, it changed too little because the army was unwilling to renounce its historical legitimacy and role as source of power. The lack of electoral accountability makes the population feel incapable of influencing the social and economic policies of the government. Many people do not vote, including young people who riot, upset about unemployment, corruption, and harsh conditions of everyday life.

The army's sovereign power is not institutional; it is not inscribed in the constitution, in which the army is presented as under the authority of the head of the state, himself elected by popular vote. Moreover, the constitution grants the president with the prerogative to appoint the high-ranking officers. Yet, the reality is far different, insofar as the military leadership chooses the candidate to be elected. Once elected, the president follows the instructions from the ministry of defense regarding crucial ideological orientations and political issues, including foreign policy. The presidency is in fact an annex of the minister of defense. It is the institution by which the army controls the state and draws the line for the government to follow.

Algeria's history clearly demonstrates the army's political role. In 1962, as soon as the liberation war ended, the military overthrew the civilian leadership embodied by the GPRA (Provisional Government of the Algerian Republic), imposing Ahmed Ben Bella as head of state. In 1965, Colonel Houari Boumédiène took over and put in jail the president Ahmed Bella who had been elected in 1963. Boumédiène ruled the country as head of state while retaining the functions of minister of defense and chief of staff of the army. After his death in 1978, the military (and not the party, as stated in the constitution) designated his successor, Colonel Chadli Bendjedid who had to resign in January 1992. The military replaced him with Mohamed Boudiaf, a founding member of the FLN in 1954, who had lived in exile since 1963. Assassinated five months after he was appointed president, he was poised to replace

PHOTO 9.3 President Abdelaziz Bouteflika in a wheelchair on May 4, 2017.

Zohra Bensemra/Reuters/Alamy Stock Photo

high-ranking officers by a new generation more faithful to him. In 1995, after an interim period led by Colonel Ali Kafi, the army appointed General Liamine Zéroual to run for office in elections he won without surprise. He tried to reach a political agreement with the Islamists to put an end to the insurgency, but as the military prevented him from doing so, he had to resign. He was replaced by Abdelaziz Bouteflika who was reelected in 2004, 2009, and 2014, although in 2005 he was sick, appearing publicly in a wheelchair.

The army not only controls the government, but it also controls the political field by infiltrating all grassroots organizations, political parties, unions, associations, the media, the universities, and so on. The DRS, the intelligence service, plays the role of a political police. During the bloody decade (1992–2002), this service gained so much influence that it challenged the military command. Its leader, General Tewfik Mediene, known as "the God of Algiers," became the most powerful high-ranking officer, threatening the power of his peers. In 2015, the military command dismissed him after Islamists allegedly attacked the installations of oil wells in the area of In Amenas (Sahara). The Islamists took hostages, among them many foreigners. Refusing to negotiate with the Islamists, the military command launched a bloody attack, killing thirty-three hostages. The military command reproached the DRS for its inability to secure such strategic places on which the economy of Algeria depends. Rumors say that the attack was planned by "fake" Islamists that the DRS had recruited without informing the military command. Since then, many high-ranking officers of the intelligence service have been pushed to retire, including General Tewfik Mediene. His deputy, General Hassan, was sentenced to jail for many years by a military court.

Thanks to the rise of oil prices that start in 2000, the Algerian political system seemed to be resilient. In 2011, Algeria did not experience the uprising of the "Arab Spring." The military were satisfied with president Abdelaziz Bouteflika who, despite his illness, was poised to run for a fifth term in 2019 at the age of eighty. Many Algerians were offended seeing their long-time president sitting speechless in a wheelchair, and in February 2019 the announcement that he would run for a fifth term sparked massive demonstrations across the country, from big cities to small villages. The scale of the nationwide protest surprised the military. The first weeks, the military leadership threatened the demonstrators, accusing them of participating in a foreign plot to undermine Algeria's stability. But over the weeks, the number of demonstrators grew. The protracted weekly protest led the military leadership to conclude that cracking down on such large crowds would be ineffective. General Gaid Salah, the chief of staff of the army, publicly stated that the army would be on the side of the people. In an attempt to appease the street, on March 26th, he officially asked the Constitutional Council to declare the president unfit to rule for health reasons, based on Article 102 of the Constitution. Bouteflika resigned one week later, and the speaker of the Senate, Ahmed Bensalah, was appointed as acting president according to the Constitution. The military leadership stated that the army was open to the idea of a transition, but that an elected president would monitor change and it would be implemented in the respect of the constitution.

Despite the ongoing weekly demonstrations, a presidential election was held on December 12, 2019. Five candidates, from small and almost unknown parties, ran for office in an electoral campaign bereft of supporters rallies. A former minister, Abelmadjid Tebboune, 74, was elected with 58.5 percent of the vote. The turnout was 39,93 percent according to the official figures. The military leadership feared the rise of an Algerian Erdogan who would call into question its supremacy. Abdelmadjid Tebboune was an ideal candidate. He served for many years as governor (wali) and minister, and although he was a minister in Bouteflika's government, he criticized the legacy of his predecessor who had become a scapegoat. From the vantage point of the generals, he was not a threat since he lacks charisma and is thus dependent on the army. In the aftermath of his election, he stated that he heard the demands of the hirak movement, asked them to stop demonstrations, and supported the prosecution and sentencing of former officials for mismanagement, including two former prime ministers. All of this suggested a change in the government but not change of the régime.

The parliament elections held in 2021 reflect the same lack of fundamental change. According to the official figures, the turnout was 23 percent. 5.6 million citizens participated to the vote out of 24 million constituents. A new National Assembly elected on June 12th 2021 was filled with the same political parties that took part in the previous elections. Notably, leaders of the two ruling parties, Ahmed Ouyahya for the Democratic National Rally (RND) and Djamel Ould Abbes for the FLN, were in jail, but members of their parties run again for office. The elected body was similar to the previous National Assemblies,[8] with the exception of the number of independent candidates. Neither the FFS nor the RCD, opposition parties, took part to the elections. Thus, there is no formal opposition in the new National Assembly dominated by the parties supporting the regime.

PHOTO 9.4 President Abdelmadjid Tebboune in an official Ceremony of Signature.

Murat Kula/Anadolu Agency via Getty Images

ACTORS, OPINIONS, AND PARTICIPATION

As in any political system, there are in Algeria actors, opinions, and a kind of political participation. However, the authoritarian nature of the regime does not accept autonomous actors. The intelligence service shapes the political field by infiltrating the parties, the unions, the NGOs, and the press, forcing them to submit to the unwritten rule of the system: that the army is the sole source of power. It decides the number of seats granted to the parties in the elected bodies. Out of almost 400 representatives in the National Assembly, only 50 seats are allotted to the formal opposition, a gesture intended to show that Algeria is a democratic state in which the government is freely criticized by political parties. The result is that the opposition is not inside the legal framework of the institutions. The different segments of the public opinion are not conveyed by legal grassroots organizations taking part in politics.

A closer look at the parties and electoral politics demonstrates the constraints on political participation. There are two ruling parties—the FLN and the RND—that perpetuate the style of the one-party system. They are faithful to the state administration, which provides them with the finances they need. There are some Islamist parties in competition with one another to obtain seats in the elected assemblies and cabinets in the government. They adjust their demands by insisting not on shaping the political system but on the symbol of Islam in the state and in society. These parties criticize the formal power but never the real power, implicitly accepting the structural bipolarity of the state power and expect the army to allow them to run the administration. They are faithful to the regime and play the role of the opposition, giving up the hope to have the majority of the parliament or to gain the presidential election.

An analysis of electoral results is telling. Fluctuating success of the parties (the RND dropped from 155 to 48 representatives in 2002; the MSP, from 69 to 34; the FLN went from 64 to 199; and Nahda, from 43 to 3 in 2007) indicate a quota system based on the parties' relationships with the administration. The elections are not an index of the popularity of the parties; rather, they are a way for the administration to award docile parties and punish unfaithful ones. The Algerian experience shows that elections are not sufficient to establish democracy insofar as democracy requires that, first, parties must be strong enough to defend their electoral results, and second, the judiciary system must be autonomous and able to try those accused of fraud.

If political life in democratic countries is defined by the freedom of choosing the rulers, we can say that in Algeria democratic political life is at a very low level. Elections are rigged, and the people who hold elected offices do not speak on behalf of the constituents. The result is a lack of accountability and a spread of corruption. The elected bodies are not the transmission belt between the people and the state administration because the parties are empty shells whose members are only in search of privileges. The salary of a representative at the National Assembly is twenty times the minimum wage.

There are also no negotiation channels between the different social groups and the administration. The official union of workers (UGTA, General Union of Algerian Workers) is dependent on the state, and unions find it difficult to have legal activities. They resort to illegal strikes with the consequences of arrest and crackdown. Moreover, the judiciary is not independent from the executive branch of the government, so any public protest could be repressed as crime or felony.

As for the press, it appears that the journalists have the freedom of speech. There are dozens of private newspapers in Arabic and French in which different opinions are expressed. Some articles are hostile to the policy of the government, giving the impression that journalists enjoy freedom of speech. Indeed, the press is free to report on corruption and many cases of embezzlement involving high-ranking civil servants or even the entourage of the president. The journalists, however, cannot write about corruption involving high-ranking officers or elaborate on the political power of the army. Any newspaper that would dare to do so will be deprived of advertisement. Censorship is not exercised through police arrest but through the threat of bankruptcy, a form of advertisement blackmail. This leads to a distrust of the press that tries to compensate in criticizing a scapegoat: the formal power, including the president and his ministers. The press thus tells a story that the president is an authoritarian ruler and his entourage corrupt. The military would have no responsibility in the mismanagement of the state. Any newspaper that does not endorse this narrative will not have the advertisement from ANEP (National Agency for Edition and Publicity).

RELIGION AND POLITICS

In Algeria, as in many Muslim countries, religion is linked to politics for two reasons. First, society is not (yet) secularized.[9] Second of all, the nationalist movement that fought for independence used Islam as a vector of popular mobilization against the colonial power. This strengthens the conservatives who oppose secularization of society. The conservatives imposed Article 2 of the constitution, declaring that the religion of the state is Islam, and in another article, it is stated that any candidate running for office has to be Muslim. The religious law still has influence with regard to family law: Polygamy is legal, and women inherit only half of what their brothers do.

Since there is no one interpretation of Islam, the sacred is used to vindicate vested interests at the detriment of fairness at all levels of society. Islam is used to defend self-interests and not the sacred—individualism replaced the old spirituality of past ages. A majority of young women, for instance, embraced the Islamist discourse to free themselves from the weight of traditional customs. They use Islam to enjoy freedom to study, to go out with their female friends, and even to have their word in the choice of the future husband. This is new in comparison with traditional society which is fading away.

The Algerian regime is symbolically respectful of religion, but the leaders do not claim religious legitimacy as leaders do in monarchies such as Morocco, Saudi Arabia, and Jordan. For the leaders, there is no conflict between Islam and the ideology of the régime. They state that when Islam "is better understood," it enhances the nationalist spirit. For them, there is a bad interpretation of Islam and a good one. The good one would be the religious doctrine taught in the public school. It has been elaborated by the reformist trend led by Cheikh Abdelhamid Ben Badis (1890–1940), who championed puritan Islam and opposed sainthood linked to popular Islam. After independence, the new state encouraged the puritan conception of A. Ben Badis at the detriment of popular Islam of the rural areas. Two decades after independence, the religious teaching radicalized, giving birth to Islamism that is the dialectical by-product of nationalism and puritanism.[10] After the Iranian revolution in 1979, Islamism became a popular political ideology expressing the utopia to achieve justice by implementing God's rules. For two decades (1980–2000), the Islamist movements in Arab countries were on the verge to taking over the states by street violence.

However, Islamism lost its momentum after 2001. Violence of the most extremist branches frightened the majority of the population. The emergence of DAESH ("l-Dawla al-Islamiya fil Iraq wa al-Sham" or the "Islamic State in Iraq and Syria") during the "Arab Spring" harmed the image of Islam in Western countries. The majority of Muslims disapproved of the attacks and assassinations of innocent people. This evolution made the Islamists to moderate their discourse, claiming that democracy and tolerance are Muslim values.

The commitment to condemn violence as a political means to take over the state gave birth to what is called post-Islamism. Islamists call for gradual and peaceful steps toward an Islamic state. They participate in elections and accept the political role of the army. Radical Islam still persists, but it does not have popular support as in the 1980s and 1990s. After the bloody decade (1992–2002) that took the lives of more than two hundred thousand people, the military have defeated the insurgents and allowed those who surrender to benefit from amnesty. In 1999, the army reached a secret settlement with the military branch of the Islamist party FIS. A referendum was organized in 2002 to approve a text called "National Reconciliation," and the majority of the population voted in favor of peace.

Since then, the military conflict largely ended. Algeria witnessed some terrorist attacks of radicalized Islamists who made allegiance to AQIM (Al Qaida of Islamic Maghreb), but the radical Islamists were largely silenced. The victory over the Islamists is a victory over the most popular and dangerous adversary of the regime. If the Islamists could not overthrow the regime, there will be no political force that can threaten it. Taking advantage of the increase in the oil income that started in 2000, some Islamists got involved in businesses, giving rise to what is called "Islamo-business."

PROTEST AND SOCIAL CONFLICT

The limited channels for participation, discussed above, lead to recurrent riots, strikes, and uprisings. The riot is an expression of grievances and of popular resentment. It is a constitutive element of Algerian polity to the extent that every week the security services report many local riots or violent protests about unemployment, shortage of running water, electric outage, housing crisis, and other issues.

Once the bloody decade (1992–2002) ended, the social demands surfaced again, putting pressure on the government. Workers and civil servants went on strikes asking for the rise of their salaries. The government met these demands, but it faced the anger of the unemployed young people, particularly in the southern part of the country. Numerous demonstrations took place in Ouargla, Ghardaia, Laghouat, and other cities of the Sahara. Thousands of young unemployed expressed their anger, shouting, "We are born in the Sahara, and we don't benefit from the oil of the Sahara." The government made some vague promises as the police cracked down on the protesters and jailed many activists. The protest amplified with opposition to the exploitation of shale oil. Huge demonstrations took place in all the cities of the Sahara, with people shouting, "You took our oil, leave our water clean." President Bouteflika answered the protest by saying that the shale oil is a gift of God and we shouldn't refuse it.

Beside the social protest about social issues, there is protest denouncing human rights abuses. The police, in general, and the intelligence community, in particular, often violate human rights of scholars, journalists, activists, and the like. Since the government does not like to appear in foreign newspapers as human rights abusers, the activists are often liberated under domestic and international pressure. In the aftermath of "the bloody decade," some families of people who disappeared during this period held regular protests, holding portraits of their beloved and asking to retrieve the bodies of their loved ones in order to bury them decently. The majority of these families accepted money under the condition they stop asking about those who disappeared, but some families joined the grassroots organization "SOS Disparus," asking for the truth and demanding the government to tell them the fate of those arrested by security services. The police regularly harass these families, despite support from nongovernmental organizations such as Amnesty International and Human Rights Watch. Many of these cases have been brought to the UN Commission for Human Rights in Geneva.

Algerians have also taken to the streets to call for ethnic recognition. The uprising in Kabylia, a mountainous area populated by Berberophones, located at 100 miles from Algiers, started in April 2001 after the assassination of a young student in a barrack of gendarmerie (the equivalent of the National Guard). The event triggered a large protest that became "a civic insurrection" against arbitrary violence and what Algerian people call "hogra" (contempt). During two years, the region experienced a deep social unrest that led to violent confrontations with the security services. More than one hundred people were killed.

The protest gave birth to village committees called "arouch" whose leaders wrote a text called "Platform of El Kseur" in which they formulated many demands, including a democratic management of the state and the official recognition of the Berber language. After many months of negotiations and hedging, the government took advantage of the population's desire to go back to normal everyday life. The government also managed to cut off the protest from the rest of the country by arguing that the activists would like to *replace* the Arab language by the Berber language. The identity issue prevented the movement to have a nationwide dimension.

Algeria was notably quiet during the "Arab Spring" in 2011, a fact that surprised many journalists and academics.[11] There were three reasons why Algerians did not revolt at that time. The first is that Algeria had just emerged from a traumatic period of ten years of bloody conflict (1992–2002) that claimed more than two hundred thousand lives. A majority of Algerians were scared to experience such a period again. The second reason is that the Western intervention in Libya also frightened Algerians. A young man in Oran said, "I hate Bouteflika but I do not want to give Sarkozy, the French president, the opportunity to bomb Algiers." The third reason is that the government responded as soon as 2011 by creating an organization called ANSEJ (*Agence Nationale de Soutien à l'Emploi des Jeunes*) to distribute free loans to any young person who wanted to create their own business.[12] This was possible in part because the state enjoyed a budget surplus of $200 billion, thanks to rising oil prices. Many of these businesses succeeded as

PHOTO 9.5 Algerian protesters remove a portrait of former President Abdelaziz Bouteflika on February 22, 2019 (AFP)

Ryad Kramdi/AFP via Getty Images

public transportations, cyber cafes, dry cleaners, and such, creating thousands of jobs, but others went bankrupt and were not able to reimburse the loans to the banks.

Rather, Algeria's protracted protest, or Hirak Movement, began in February 2019, in a small city, Kherrata, located in the eastern part of the country. A mob, refusing that President Bouteflika run for (and likely win) a fifth term, pulled down and trampled on a giant portrait of Bouteflika. The images of the event went viral on social media.

The next Friday, on February 22nd, all the cities followed Kherrata, demanding that the ailing president, in bad health since 2013, does not run for a fifth term. His long-time illness prevented him from attending meetings and rallies, where only his portrait in a giant frame was displayed. This photo was the laughingstock among young people who said that Algeria is ruled by a photo in a frame. The official announcement in February 2019 of his candidacy for a fifth term was the last straw for the population. Many people felt that being asked to elect a mummy was an insult to their national pride. On March 8th, International Women's Day, the number of demonstrators, including women, grew even more.

The Hirak Movement was born. It surprised the rulers who were not expecting such massive demonstrations, eventually lasting more than two years. The most striking feature of the uprising was that the gigantic rallies taking place were peaceful and socially mixed, with men and women, old and young, holding up signs deriding the rulers. It was the first time that Algeria experienced a peaceful uprising full of humor, giving the image of a festive national

PHOTO 9.6 Algiers, demonstration on March 8, 2019

Louiza Ammi/Abaca Press / Alamy Stock Photo

rally. Although they were peaceful, the hundreds of thousands of demonstrators were adamant to challenge the political legitimacy on which state institutions rested for decades. They spared the army as institution but accused the generals of taking advantage of their positions to enrich themselves and their families.

The strength of the Hirak Movement changed the balance of power in state affairs. It led the regime to knock down a part of its civilian façade. The demonstrators wanted more, hoping to end the military control over the state. Every Friday, they were chanting "the generals at the garbage" and "civilian state, not military state." Thus, the arrest of former Prime ministers, ministers, and other corrupt officials did not put an end to the Hirak Movement.

However, the movement lost its momentum. At the beginning, the demonstrators were hundreds of thousands, and over time, fewer arrived. Hundreds of people were arrested and sentenced to jail; in May 2021, the weekly demonstrations ended under the pressure of a severe crackdown. According to activists, the regime was looking for a violent confrontation with the demonstrators that could have led to the Libyan or Syrian scenario. The Hirak Movement preferred to recede.

For the military leadership, the uprising was the expression of a social unrest provoked by corruption of the civil elite that ruled the country. Since a big number of civilians accused of corruption have been arrested, for them the Hirak had no reason to continue. From this vantage point, they considered that the demands of the Hirak Movement were met. Two former Prime Ministers (Ahmed Ouyahya and Abdelmalek Sellal) were sentenced to more than ten years in prison. Many of the members of previous cabinets were arrested under the accusation of corruption and embezzlement. A group of businessmen who accumulated huge fortunes linked to corruption also were sentenced to jail. And last but not least, twenty generals went to jail or sought refuge in foreign countries.

To understand this unprecedented protest movement, one must be aware that the regime fuelled increasing social unrest by failing to reform the country's economy, mired as it is in the practices of corruption and by its obstinacy in continuing to hold fraudulent elections. The contradictions of the rentier economy and a refusal to allow meaningful political participation were the main factors behind the rupture between the population and the regime.

POLITICAL ECONOMY

Soon after Algeria's independence, the military instituted an economic policy that was consistent with a socialist-oriented, single-party regime. During three years (1962–1965), the farms and factories, abandoned by their European owners who left the country, were automanaged by the workers, but the state administration soon restricted the workers' autonomy. The administration imposed a centralized economic management, giving the state a bigger role aimed at fostering import-substitution industrialization. In 1971, the nationalization of the oil industry provided the state with financial surplus which it invested in a bold economic program. Between 1972 and 1979, almost 30 percent of the GDP was devoted to the creation of an industrial basis that would develop the economy.

However, the returns of these investments were not what was expected. The new industrial units were not profitable, despite heavy subsidies from the state. The failure of this industrialization made Algeria more dependent on oil prices of the international market. Following the sharp decrease of oil prices in the 1980s (from $40 to $10), the state lost its capacity to meet the social needs of the population. Shortages in consumption goods led to a deep social unrest. The riots of October 1988 erupted because the state could no longer afford to import goods of wide consumption such as cereals, coffee, sugar, cooking oil, and drugs.

The riots led the government to introduce a multiparty system and economic liberalization. The liberalization put an end to the state monopoly over foreign trade, hoping that the free market would create more wealth. The IMF welcomed the shift in the economic doctrine and granted loans with the condition of a deeper structural adjustment program. The IMF also encouraged the government to devalue the local currency in order to attract foreign investors. The argument was that a weak dinar, the local currency, would make the salaries competitive.

However, the IMF's reasoning was flawed, and the reforms had negative consequences. The devaluation of the currency created difficulties for a number of small- and medium-sized enterprises in the private sector because of the excessive cost of imported inputs. In 1995, one dollar was worth 8.96 dinars; In 2000, it jumped to 47.66 dinars. The local manufacturers suffered also from the competition of foreign products imported from Asian countries. Liberalization of foreign trade had opened the domestic market to Southeast Asian products, such as clothing and shoes, destroying domestic production. The reform did not help the economy become less dependent on oil prices. The private sector was thriving in trade, services, and speculative activities, but it was absent in the production of material goods that Algeria was importing from abroad.

At the end of the 1990s and the beginning of the 2000s, the oil prices started to increase. Between 1998 and 2014, the oil prices went from $18 to $107 per barrel. The financial surplus relieved the Algerian government of pressure from international monetary institutions. The increase of oil prices gave huge financial means to the state that allowed vast programs of construction and importation of commodities from abroad. More than $100 billion was invested during 2000–2014 to implement what was called the program of the president: one million apartment units, hundreds of freeway kilometers, tramways in big cities, hydraulic infrastructure for agriculture, and the like. Moreover, during the period 2000–2014, the state not only was able to pay off its external debt but also to accumulate financial reserves of nearly $200 billion. As the program got underway, the growth rate rose to 6.8 percent in 2003. The financial bonanza was an opportunity to sign massive contracts with foreign firms engaged in the exploration of oil and gas and also construction of infrastructure and housing.

The period from the beginning of the 2000s up to 2014 was one of financial euphoria. The middle class reclaimed part of its purchasing power, which had degraded during the preceding years. Private fortunes were built through import firms, a hectic estate market and widespread corruption.[13] The state implemented a generous welfare policy, allowing the increase of salaries of the civil servants, including the teachers and the law enforcement personnel. Even the poor benefited, gaining access to new housing and subsidized goods, which lowered both social discontent and potential threats to social peace. The effects of this public expenditure irrigated redistribution, which although inequitable, nonetheless benefited the population as a whole. The services sector created the most jobs (albeit most of them informal), relieving the pressure caused by unemployment. According to the Algerian Office National des Statistiques, the unemployment rate was 27.3 percent in 2001. By 2005, it decreased to 15.3 percent, and from 2015 to 2018 unemployment hovered between 10 and 12 percent.[14]

Despite this, youth unemployment remained disproportionately high; 29.1 percent of the population ages sixteen to twenty-five were out of work in the third quarter of 2018, specifically among urban centers, which explains the *harraga phenomenon*—young people trying to reach Spain and Italy in small boats that they make themselves. The government established an agency called ANSEJ, which made bank loans to hundreds of thousands of unemployed youths, thus allowing them to create their own opportunities across a number of sectors ranging from transport to construction firms to services.

The boom did not stimulate local production. Foreign companies, better equipped and more efficient than the national enterprises, were awarded contracts to carry out projects. The government did not reinforce the productive capacity of national enterprises—public or private—to implement projects submitted to international competition. Instead of enhancing the local enterprises and manufacturers, the government resorted to foreign companies, letting the domestic economy depend on oil income. The international market also tapped the expanding national demand, with foreign companies primarily dealing with infrastructure and housing. It is as if the régime could not or did not want to escape the contradictions of the rentier state. As far as the foreign companies are concerned, they are not present in the industrial production. They are

TABLE 9.1 ■ Oil Price per Barrel 2014–2020 (USD)						
2014	2015	2016	2017	2018	2019	2020
93.17	48.56	43.29	50.80	65.23	56.99	39.68

Source: US Energy Information Administration.

discouraged by a bureaucratic maze hostile to business climate. Algeria does not attract the foreign investment.

The state's financial capacity began to fall in 2014, when the price of oil started sinking. Indeed, between 2014 and 2015, the price of oil fell by nearly half, thus saddling the state budget with deficits that could only be paid with foreign currency reserve. During the following three years, reserves shrank by $60 billion, according to official data. And, oil prices, and associate revenues, failed to recover through the end of 2020 (see Table 9.1).

Having initially hoped for the price of oil to rise again, the government needed to find alternative sources of funding. It raised taxes, both direct and indirect, on all products with the exception of those already subsidized. In doing so, the government jeopardized the balance of redistribution that had upheld social peace for a decade. Recurrent riots reveal this structure, illustrating the political weakness of Algeria's economic system. In effect, the government was caught in a pincer by two intertwined constraints over which it has no control: the price of oil and pressure from the street.

The lesson to be drawn from the Algerian experience is that economic reform would succeed only if there is a political willingness to put an end to the rentier nature of economy. Embedded in politics, the Algerian economy reflects political rationality. As long as the economy is a political resource used to secure the régime, Algeria will go on depending on the oil prices. The huge private fortunes that emerged in the aftermath of the liberal reforms did not add wealth to the country; they are just a share of the oil income. The state budget did not benefit from the private sector as much as the latter profited from the state expenditures. In this case, the new bourgeoisie cannot ask for political change since, first, it benefits from the authoritarian rule and, second, it is politically weak insofar as its wealth depends on contracts with the state administration. It explains the hostility of the new bourgeoisie to democracy that could harm its immediate interests.

INTERNATIONAL AND REGIONAL POLITICS

During the 1960s and 1970s, Algeria symbolized the fight against imperialism and the right of people to self-determination. In 1973, Algiers hosted the summit of the nonaligned nations, which gave president Boumédiène an international status. Algiers was the mecca of the national liberation movements of Africa, Asia, and Latin America. They found there financial and diplomatic support. Even the American Black Panthers found an audience and hospitality in Algiers at the end of the 1960s. Before being imprisoned, Nelson Mandela went to Algeria several times to seek support against apartheid. In his speeches, Boumédiène referred to the struggles of South Africans and Palestinians—victims, in his view, of racism and Zionism. His bold position placed the Algerian regime in the anti-Western camp, which led it to increase its economic and military cooperation with the Soviet Union and strengthen its ties with the socialist countries of Europe and China. Relations with the United States and Western Europe were limited to the commercial sector.

After the death of Boumédiène in 1978, the antiimperialist rhetoric sharply decreased, then ceased completely after the collapse of the Soviet Union. The United States and Europe became respectable partners that invested in the hydrocarbons sector. The United States is second to Europe in exporting hydrocarbons and in foreign investment, but relations with the United States cooled in 1992 after the US State Department condemned annulment of the elections won by the Islamists. American officials irritated Algiers when they cited the human rights violations reported by the US State Department and Human Rights Watch. Disputing the security services' versions of events, Amnesty International and Human Rights Watch called for an inquiry into the murders of thousands of civilians. Their suspicions greatly weakened diplomatically the Algerian regime, put under pressure to settle an account in order to put an end to violence.[15]

After September 11, 2001, the US attitude changed radically, and numerous officials passing through Algiers affirmed their desire to learn from the Algerian government's experience in combating "Islamist terrorism." Since then, the CIA has worked in concert with the DRS in order to track the *Groupe Salafiste pour la Prédication et le Combat* (GSPC), an organization that lent its allegiance in 2003 to Osama bin Laden and from then on called itself *al-Qaʿida in the Islamic Maghreb* (AQIM). American authorities fear that Bin Laden's networks, undone in Iraq and weakened in Afghanistan, will spread into the African Sahel, from Mauritania to Chad. In order to counter this potentiality, the Americans asked Algiers if they could place the United States Africa Command (AFRICOM) in Tamanrasset, a city in southern Algeria. After hesitating for several months, the Algerian government refused under the pressure of the nationalist wing of the military. The Western countries needed Algeria's support to curb the Islamist in the vast Sahel region. However, the antiterrorist strategy in the area suffered from the conflict between Algeria and Morocco, which began after Morocco annexed in 1975 the Western Sahara, a former Spanish colony. To Algeria, the Saharan population must be allowed to choose between integration into Morocco or independence. The Organization of African Unity, the Arab League, and the United Nations got involved unsuccessfully to resolve the conflict, which prevents the two neighbors from normalizing relations and cooperating economically.

Weakened by the Islamist insurgency and discredited by the numerous violations of human rights, the Algerian regime is not heard anymore at the international or regional level. Its diplomacy focuses more on the conflict with Morocco about the Western Sahara than any other conflict in the Arab world. During the 2011 Arab uprisings, Algiers did not have a consistent position about Syria, Libya, Saudi Arabia–Iran antagonism, or the enduring conflict in Yemen. The government chose not to side with one or the other in crucial crises that were unfolding in the world in general and in the Arab region in particular. Since the 1990s, the foreign policy of Algeria became silent, with the exception of the Western Sahara conflict opposing Morocco to the POLISARIO about the former Spanish colony. Many African countries endorse the Moroccan position while some years earlier, they were acknowledging the POLISARIO. The last blow came in December 2020 from President Trump who, before leaving office, recognized the sovereignty of Morocco on the disputed territory. Until then, the United States defended the resolutions of the United Nations calling for a vote of the natives to choose between becoming Moroccan citizens or an independent state.

CONCLUSION

At the independence in 1962, Algeria chose the single-party system and took a path toward a state-led economy aimed at alleviating poverty and inequality. It invested a large proportion of its GDP in the industry, having nationalized hydrocarbons owned by foreign companies. However, the investment effort, one of the highest in the world per capita, has not kept its promises. Industrial enterprises created with advanced technologies have become a burden for the state budget forced to finance their deficits. The October 1988 riots showed the failure of the populist model defended by a single-party authoritarian regime. These riots occurred twenty-three years before the Arab Spring of 2011. The attempted democratic transition that followed failed, leaving a decade of conflict that resulted in more than two hundred thousand people dead. In 2019, the national protest known as the Hirak Movement, which lasted two years, brought change in the regime but not change of the regime. The increase of oil prices in the international market following the war in Ukraine will give one or two decades of respite before the next large scale protest.

The question to ask is why the Algerian experience of economic development failed, despite heavy industrial investments and the presence of qualitative human resources. The answer is to be sought in the limits of the ideology of radical Arab nationalism that also failed in Egypt, Syria, Iraq, and Libya.

SUGGESTED READINGS

Addi, Lahouari. *Radical Arab Nationalism and Political Islam*. Washington, DC: Georgetown University Press, 2017.

Hill, Jonathan. *Democratization in the Maghreb*. Edinburgh: Edinburgh University Press, 2016.

Martinez, Luis, and Rasmus Alenius Boserup. *Algeria Modern: From Opacity to Complexity*. Oxford: Oxford University Press, 2016.

Parks, Robert. "Algeria and the Arab Uprisings." In *The Arab Spring*. Edited by C. M Henry and Hyang Ji. New York, NY: Palgrave Macmillan Series, 2012.

Willis, Michael. *Politics and Power in the Maghreb: Algeria, Tunisia and Morocco from Independence to the Arab Spring*. Oxford: Oxford University Press, 2014.

10 EGYPT

Tarek Masoud

"Egypt is the most important country in the world," Napoleon Bonaparte is reported to have said during his imprisonment on the South Atlantic isle of St. Helena.[1] It is a sentiment that has been echoed repeatedly throughout history, albeit in slightly more modest form and by slightly more modest individuals. King Farouk I, who ruled Egypt from 1936 until his ouster in 1952, did not go so far as to say that his country was the most important on the entire planet, but he did declare it "the keystone in the arch" of the Arab world.[2] Of course, Farouk, as Egypt's head of state, had reason to overstate his country's case, but concurring opinions can be heard from less obviously biased quarters. Arnold J. Toynbee, arguably one of the 20th century's greatest historians, declared, "There is a great Arabic-speaking world of which Egypt is the cultural centre."[3] More recently, *The New York Times* pundit Thomas Friedman dubbed Egypt the "center of gravity of the Arab world," Israeli prime minister Benjamin Netanyahu called Egypt the "most important Arab country," and a White House aide explained that former President Barack Obama chose Cairo for the venue of his 2009 address to the Muslim world because Egypt "represents the heart of the Arab world."[4]

These encomia to Egypt's centrality are not simply due to its size—although, with more than one hundred million inhabitants, it makes up almost a quarter of the Arab world's population. Instead, Egypt commands our attention because practically every social, intellectual, and political movement of note in the Arab world finds its roots there. Among Arab states, Egypt was first in war—battling Israel in 1948, 1956, 1967, and 1973—and first in peace, becoming in 1978 the first Arab country to recognize and be recognized by the Jewish state. Arab nationalism (or pan-Arabism)—the grand project of unifying the Arabic-speaking peoples under one polity spanning from the Maghreb to the Arabian Gulf—had its greatest exponent in Gamal Abdel Nasser, Egypt's leader from 1954 to 1970.[5] Moreover, pan-Arabism's sole-surviving institutional manifestation, the twenty-two-member Arab League, was founded in 1945 in Egypt's capital, Cairo; is headquartered there; and, except for a brief period during which Egypt was expelled for making peace with Israel, has always been headed by an Egyptian.[6]

Political Islam, too, has Egyptian roots. Of course, the desire to subordinate political and social life to the will of Allah is in some ways as old as the faith itself, but it was 20th-century Egyptians who gave it a defined program and plan of action. From Morocco to Malaysia, some of the most popular and electorally successful political parties emerged from the Muslim Brotherhood, a semisecret "Islamist" movement that aims to refashion the world in the image laid out by the Qur'an and the traditions of the Prophet Muhammad, and which was born in the Egyptian town of Ismailia in 1928. Egypt is also the birthplace of Sayyid Qutb, the fiery Muslim thinker whose writings are thought to have inspired the men behind al-Qa'ida—Osama bin Laden and Ayman al-Zawahiri (another Egyptian). Egypt is home to al-Azhar University, one of the most important seats of Islamic learning for the world's 1.5 billion Sunni Muslims, which draws students from around the globe, and which bills itself as a bulwark against radicalism and militancy. On top of all of this, Egypt produces the bulk of the Arab world's books and movies (movies that have, by many accounts, rendered the Egyptian dialect the most familiar and recognizable of Arab vernaculars).[7]

In fact, the only notable Arab development not to have originated in Egypt is the so-called Arab Spring. That season of protest and revolution began not in Egypt, but in nearby Tunisia with the dramatic popular overthrow of dictator Zine al-Abidine Ben Ali in January 2011. To date, Egyptians, Libyans, Syrians, Bahrainis, Yemenis, and others in the Arab world have attempted—with varying degrees of success—to follow Tunisia's lead, but it was Egypt's revolution that made the diffusion of the Arab Spring possible. As the gifted scholar of revolutions Valerie Bunce has noted, the unprecedented and historic overthrow of Tunisia's dictator might never have resonated with other Arabs had not Egyptians followed suit and overthrown their own dictator, Muhammad Hosni Mubarak, scarcely a month later.[8] According to Bunce, Egypt was central and familiar to Arabs in ways that tiny Tunisia, a Francophone North African country of ten million, could never be. As a former operative of the Central Intelligence Agency put it, "As goes Egypt, so goes the Middle East."[9]

Today, more than a decade after the onset of the Arab Spring, where Egypt seems to be going is somewhere quite different from the liberal, democratic order that many scholars, observers, and activists believed was possible in those early days of 2011. People disagree about *when* Egypt's democratic experiment went off the rails, but there is little disagreement over the fact that it *has*. For some, the problem began shortly after Mubarak's overthrow, when power was assumed not by representatives of the people but by an interim government of military generals. For others, Egypt's democratic experiment ran aground when parliamentary and presidential elections convened in 2011 and 2012 delivered power to a collection of illiberal, Islamist parties led by the Muslim Brotherhood. And for still others, the end of Egypt's democratic hopes came when, in July 2013, the army, ostensibly in response to massive popular discontent, overthrew Egypt's first democratically elected president—an engineering professor and Muslim Brotherhood member named Muhammad Morsi—threw him into prison, and began a systematic crackdown against his party and all those who resisted the new dispensation. That crackdown included the August 2013 killing of hundreds of Brotherhood protesters encamped near the Rab'a al-'Adawiyya mosque in the Nasr City suburb of Cairo, and in Midān al-Nahḍa near Cairo University in Giza.[10]

Regardless of *when* one thinks Egypt's democratic experiment came to grief, it is clear that today, Egypt is a not an open society. In the years since the military coup of 2013, the country's leadership has focused its efforts on ensuring that the burst of revolutionary enthusiasm that led to Mubarak's overthrow would never be repeated. Although the country continues to face rumblings of political dissent, these have become less frequent in recent years, as the state—and particularly the military—has tightened its grip on civic life. Indeed, the military's role in all facets of Egypt's contemporary existence—from its politics to its society to its economy—is perhaps the defining feature of that country's current era. Thus, although it is beyond the scope of this chapter to try to define where Egypt is headed, it is difficult to be optimistic about the prospects for the emergence of genuine liberal, participatory, democratic government. In fact, one must wonder if the early testimonials to Egypt's regional importance and political centrality with which we began this chapter will continue to be accurate descriptions of a country whose people's creative energies are sapped daily by a military-led system of social, political, and economic control.

HISTORY OF STATE FORMATION[11]

Unlike many of its fellow Arab countries, such as Jordan or Iraq or Syria or Lebanon, which were essentially willed into existence by colonial administrators at the end of the First World War,[12] Egypt as an "identifiable polity" has existed since the time of the pharaohs more than three thousand years before the birth of Jesus.[13] The world's first historical document is Egyptian—an engraved piece of granite called the Narmer Palette, which allegedly relates the unification of northern (Lower) and southern (Upper) Egypt by Narmer in the 31st century BCE.[14] Egypt is the only country mentioned in the Qur'an, a fact from which Egyptians draw considerable national pride (even if one of Egypt's appearances in Islam's holy book is as the home of one of the faith's greatest villains).[15] But as the great historian Afaf Lutfi al-Sayyid Marsot points out, this ancient sense of Egyptian identity is coupled with an equally long history of political subjugation.[16] For most of the latter half of Egypt's five-thousand-year history—from the Persian invasion in 525 BCE to the Arab conquest of 642 CE to Napoleon's relatively brief incursion in 1798 to the formal end of the British occupation in 1954—Egypt was dominated by foreign powers. In fact, by some accounts Gamal Abdel Nasser was the first native-born Egyptian to rule his country since the pharaoh Nectanebo II, in the 4th century BCE.[17]

Egypt's ancientness makes any attempt at offering a brief history of the country an almost impossible undertaking. Where should one begin? The 7th-century Arab conquest eventually gave Egyptians a new language (Arabic) and a new religion (Islam), and, in a sense, a new history—today's Muslim Egyptians are much more likely to identify with the founding narratives of the early Islamic community in Mecca and Medina than with that of their pharaonic ancestors.[18] But between the Arab arrival and the present day is a history so rich and fascinating as to be daunting for any student of modern Egypt. It is a history punctuated by multiple personalities and dynasties: from the Fatimids, a Shi'i dynasty that ruled Egypt from 909 to 1171 and that in the 10th century founded al-Azhar, now the world's second-oldest university; to the Ayubids (1171–1250), a fiercely Sunni dynasty founded by Saladin, the great and chivalrous rival of Richard the Lionheart during the Third Crusade; to the Mamelukes, a class of slave warlords whose often predatory rule of Egypt survived the Ottoman conquest in 1517 until their final extermination three hundred years later by a remarkable man named Muhammad Ali (about whom more will be said shortly).[19]

KEY FACTS ON EGYPT

AREA 386,660 square miles (1,001,450 square kilometers)

CAPITAL Cairo

POPULATION 99,848,720 (2020 est)

PERCENTAGE OF POPULATION UNDER 25 51.5 (2020 est)

RELIGIOUS GROUPS (PERCENTAGE) Muslim (mostly Sunni), 90; Coptic Christian, 9; other Christian, 1

ETHNIC GROUPS (PERCENTAGE) Egyptian, 99.7; other, 0.3

OFFICIAL LANGUAGE Arabic; English and French widely spoken by upper and middle classes

TYPE OF GOVERNMENT Presidential Republic

DATE OF INDEPENDENCE February 28, 1922 (from UK protectorate status; the revolution that began on July 23, 1952, led to a republic being declared on June 18, 1953, and all British troops withdrawn on June 18, 1956)

GDP (PPP) $1.2 trillion; $12,000 per capita (2020 est.)

PERCENTAGE OF GDP BY SECTOR Agriculture, 11.7; industry, 34.3; services, 54 (2017 est.)

TOTAL RENTS (PERCENTAGE OF GDP) FROM NATURAL RESOURCES 7.978 (2019 est.)

FERTILITY RATE 3.23 children born/woman (2021 est.)

Sources: CIA. "The World Factbook." August 4, 2022, https://www.cia.gov/the-world-factbook/
World Bank. "International Comparison Program (ICP)." Accessed August 10, 2022, https://databank.worldbank.org/source/icp-2017
Central Agency for Public Mobilization and Statistic, Arab Republic of Egypt. "Statistical Yearbook." Accessed August 10, 2022, https://www.capmas.gov.eg/Pages/StaticPages.aspx?page_id=5034

Given the complexity and sweep of this history, most narratives of modern Egyptian politics and society begin with Napoleon Bonaparte's invasion in 1798.[20] Of course, one may complain that this—or any—starting point for a history of the Egyptian state is arbitrary. But by all accounts, though the French were in Egypt for only about seven years (Napoleon himself left scarcely a year into the adventure), they left a discernible and lasting impact on the course of Egyptian state formation.[21] Not only did they bring with them the radical ideals of *liberté, egalité, fraternité* but also they cultivated an abiding interest in the ancient history of Egypt (which lives on today in the form of the academic discipline of Egyptology); catalogued the Nile valley's flora and fauna; and imported revolutionary technologies such as the printing press.[22] But the most important French contribution to Egyptian history, and the reason the Napoleonic invasion is so often identified as the beginning of Egypt's modern era is that the French landing

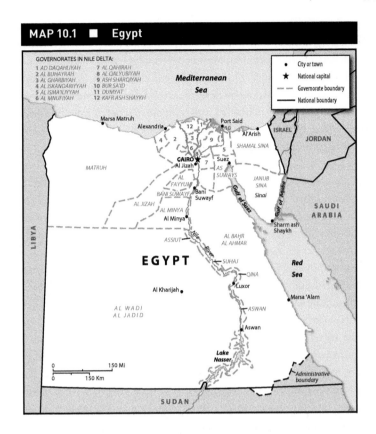

MAP 10.1 ■ Egypt

GOVERNORATES IN NILE DELTA:
1 AD DAQAHLIYAH 7 AL QAHIRAH
2 AL BUHAYRAH 8 AL QALYUBIYAH
3 AL GHARBIYAH 9 ASH SHARQIYAH
4 AL ISKANDARIYYAH 10 BUR SA'ID
5 AL ISMA'ILIYYAH 11 DUMYAT
6 AL MNUFIYAH 12 KAFR ASH SHAYKH

● City or town
★ National capital
--- Governorate boundary
— National boundary

set the stage for the appearance of the man who would grab Egypt by the scruff of its neck and shake it into a modern nation-state—the aforementioned Muhammad Ali.

Ali was an officer in an Albanian regiment dispatched by the Ottoman sultan in 1801 to recapture Egypt from the French forces (or what was left of them after Napoleon's exit). After all, Egypt was nominally a province of the Ottoman Empire, albeit, in Arthur Goldschmidt's words, a "poor, isolated, and neglected" one. And though the Ottoman Empire may have at that time already begun the steady downward march into the enervation and enfeeblement that would later earn it the unfortunate sobriquet "the sick man of Europe," it was not yet willing to accept the chipping away of its empire without a fight. Marsot tells us that the Ottomans were aided in their efforts to recapture Egypt by a British Empire eager to clip France's wings.[23]

Alas, though the Ottomans were successful in forcing the French out of Egypt, Ali would eventually do the same to his Turkish masters. By 1805, he had so ingratiated himself with Egyptian religious scholars and other notables that he was able to maneuver himself into the governorship of Egypt and again reduced the Ottomans to a negligible role in the country's governance.[24] Once safely ensconced in this position, he brutally eliminated all opponents and embarked upon the great task of harnessing Egypt's potential. It should be noted, however, that Muhammad Ali was not acting out of altruism, nor did he necessarily harbor a desire to better the lives of his subjects. Egypt for him was a grand plantation, and he was determined that it should turn a profit.

To that end, Ali imported European ideas and technology with an avidity approaching aban-don. And by all accounts, it worked. During his forty-five-year reign, he transformed the territory under his control: building canals and other transport systems, introducing cotton cultivation and textile manufacturing, fostering education, and bringing in scholars from Europe.[25] He also built a modern army and navy that were so effective that the Ottoman sultan relied on him to quell rebellions in the Hijaz (by radical Islamist forbearers of what is now Saudi Arabia) and in Greece.[26] But Ali's thirst for greatness was not easily slaked, and he soon turned his forces against his erst-while Ottoman masters, capturing the Levant (which, Marsot argues, he desired as a market for his cotton manufactures) in the early 1830s. By 1839, he was in a position to pose a challenge to the sultan himself. This the European powers would not countenance—not out of affection for the Ottomans, but from fear of the upending of the delicate balance of power that had been worked out between them. Intervening on behalf of the Turks, the European powers forced Ali to aban-don his imperial ambitions and, in the words of Lord Palmerston, the British secretary of state, to "retreat to his original shell of Egypt."[27] However, the adventure did enable Ali to achieve de facto independence from the Ottoman sultan and a guarantee of hereditary rule for his family, which reigned over Egypt (with varying degrees of competence) until 1952.

The historians tell us that Muhammad Ali's son, Ibrahim, who was one of the greatest military commanders in Egyptian history, died in 1848, a year before his father. It is possible that the course of Egyptian history, and of the dynasty of Muhammad Ali, would have been very different had the competent Ibrahim lived. Alas, however, when Ali himself passed away a year later, succession fell to his grandson, Abbas, who by all accounts reigned indifferently for five years and was succeeded by Ali's son (Abbas's uncle), Said.[28] It was the corpulent Said who granted the concession to the French entrepreneur Ferdinand de Lesseps for construction of the Suez Canal, which would link the Mediterranean and Red Seas, dramatically shortening the sea route from Europe to Asia.[29] The canal, dug with corvée labor at great cost to the Egyptian trea-sury, opened in 1869. The enterprise was profitable, and Said's successor, Khedive Ismail,[30] had, in the words of Max Rodenbeck, deluded himself into thinking "that he was rich enough to turn Egypt into France, Cairo into Paris, and his court into Versailles."[31] To fulfill his dreams, Rodenbeck tells us, Ismail embarked on an ambitious program of remaking Cairo in Paris's image. When his own funds proved insufficient, he borrowed from the many European banks that had "stampeded to offer credit."[32] When he was done, Ismail reportedly said to one of his creditors, "My country is no longer African, we now form part of Europe."[33]

As the gifted historian of modern Egypt Donald Reid has memorably written, Ismail's "wistful assertion that Egypt was now a part of Europe was to be realized in . . . a way that he had not intended."[34] Ismail had so indebted his country to the Europeans and had come to be seen as so financially incompetent that in 1879 they had him deposed. By 1882, the pros-pect of Egypt repaying its debts became so dim that Britain—eager to protect (and no doubt expand) its extensive financial holdings, including partial ownership (with France) of the Suez Canal Company—invaded the country outright. The British would remain in Egypt for almost seventy-five years.

Though Egypt was on paper a constitutional monarchy nominally run by the descendants of Muhammad Ali—who appointed and fired prime ministers and cabinets with regularity— there was little doubt that the British were in charge of the country's affairs. In 1914 at the outbreak of World War I, Britain declared Egypt a protectorate, ending the legal fiction that Ottoman sovereignty still prevailed. By the end of the war, a delegation (or *Wafd*) of leading Egyptian nationalists went to the Versailles peace conference to demand their country's independence from British domination, preferably in the form of a democratic republic. In 1922, Britain granted Egypt nominal independence, declaring it a monarchy and placing Fuad— the son of the deposed, spendthrift Ismail—on the throne. The delegation that had gone to Versailles soon became Egypt's premier political party, naming itself *Hizb al-Wafd* (the Party of the Delegation). A new constitution, with expanded powers for the elected legislature, was promulgated in 1923. A three-way struggle for power among the king, the Wafd, and the British characterized Egyptian politics for the next several decades.

In 1936, Fuad concluded a new agreement with Great Britain that, formally at least, led to the termination of the British military occupation. British troops remained along the Suez Canal, however, and London continued to exercise great influence over internal Egyptian affairs. During World War II, Egypt became a base of operations for Great Britain and its allies. Disputes between the British and the Egyptians continued, as did disagreements over the direction of the country between King Farouk (who had succeeded his father, Fuad, in 1936) and the Wafd. In 1942, Sir Miles Lampson, the British high commissioner for Egypt and the Sudan, fearful that the government of Egypt was tilting toward the Germans, demanded that King Farouk appoint a Wafdist prime minister. When the king refused, Lampson ordered British tanks to surround Abdin Palace. Fearful of being deposed, Farouk acquiesced to Lampson's demands. But this brazen violation of Egyptian sovereignty was to have a searing effect on the psychologies of many an Egyptian nationalist, including an army officer named Muhammad Naguib, who was so "disgusted" at the king's surrender to British bullying that he attempted to resign his commission. "Since the Army was given no opportunity to defend your Majesty," he wrote to the King, "I am ashamed to wear my uniform."[35] Farouk refused Naguib's resignation, an act he would have reason to regret a few years later.

Though under British tutelage, Egypt did attempt to assert some independence in foreign affairs. In 1945, Egypt joined other Arab states in establishing the Arab League, which became an important tool of Egyptian foreign policy. Three years later, King Farouk sent Egyptian troops to fight in the 1948 Arab–Israeli war (known by Israelis as the War of Independence and by Palestinians as the "Nakba" or "catastrophe," in light of its eventual outcome for them). The Arab armies were routed by the nascent Israeli state, which they imagined they would defeat within a matter of days. According to Marsot, during an Egyptian siege of an Israeli position in Gaza, one young Egyptian officer "often chatted across the lines with his Israeli counterparts and asked them how they had managed to get rid of the British presence in Palestine."[36] That officer, Marsot tells us, was a man named Gamal Abdel Nasser (of whom we will hear much more later). Egypt and the new state of Israel signed an armistice in February 1949, and Gaza—a small parcel of land along the Mediterranean coast—came under Egyptian administration.

Blame for the poor showing of the Egyptian army fell on the government, which was accused of corrupt military procurement and incompetent leadership. The Muslim Brotherhood, or *Ikhwan al-Muslimun*, a religious movement founded in 1928 in the town of Ismailia on the Suez Canal, was intent on ridding Egypt of the British presence and began intense protests both against the foreign occupier and the Egyptian government. The prime minister at the time, Mahmud Fahmi al-Nuqrashi, operating under British pressure, had the movement banned in 1948. When he was assassinated shortly thereafter, suspicion naturally centered on the Muslim Brotherhood. In February 1949, the movement's founder, Hassan al-Banna, was gunned down on the street (by many accounts, at the behest of the palace).[37]

The tense and volatile political atmosphere culminated in the breaking out of anti-Western rioting in Cairo in January 1952. In July of that year, the monarchy was overthrown by a group of military officers calling themselves the Free Officers, organized by Colonel Gamal Abdel Nasser (at one time a sympathizer of the Muslim Brotherhood) and headed by Major General Mohammed Naguib (the man whose resignation Farouk had refused to accept a decade earlier). Naguib served as president of Egypt for a short while but was cast aside by Nasser in 1954. The Muslim Brotherhood, which had been an ally of Nasser's, was repressed brutally (after allegedly attempting to assassinate the Egyptian leader in 1954).[38] Labor organizers, ostensibly representatives of the workers Nasser claimed to serve, were swiftly and cruelly brought under state control.[39] Once he had consolidated power, Nasser began a crash program of nationalization and industrialization; established "Arab socialism" as the hegemonic state ideology; and, in a way not seen since Muhammad Ali 150 years prior, put his stamp on modern Egyptian life. It is a legacy—of good and ill—with which Egyptians are still grappling.

INSTITUTIONS AND GOVERNANCE

Although Egypt has undergone three "revolutions" since 1952—the removal of Farouk in 1952, the popular overthrow of Mubarak in 2011, and the popularly backed military ouster of President Muhammad Morsi in 2013—the fundamental nature of Egyptian politics seems remarkably constant. Throughout the last seventy years, Egypt's political landscape has been marked by three interrelated phenomena—strong executive authority concentrated in the president (and before him, the king), the overweening role of the military in the country's politics and economics, and the endemic weakness of institutions charged with maintaining the rule of law.

Executive Supremacy

For most of the past sixty years, the configuration of Egyptian political institutions is one that is on the surface familiar to most Americans. Like the United States, Egypt has been a presidential republic. Unlike the United States, however—except for a brief period during the so-called Arab Spring—the Egyptian president has typically been all powerful and the legislature possessed of few resources to hold the president accountable. This tradition of executive dominance is deeply entrenched in Egyptian politics. Though Egypt has had some form of legislature ever since the French conquest in 1798, it has always been subordinate to the executive.[40] This includes the 156-member council established by Muhammad Ali, as well as the first *elected* assembly, established by Khedive Ismail in 1866.[41] It was not until the constitution of 1923 that a parliament with lawmaking authority was established, although even then the balance of power between the legislature and the monarchy always tilted toward the monarchy.[42] Thus, the super-presidencies of Nasser, Sadat, and Mubarak could be viewed as merely continuations of a long-standing pattern that began during Egypt's monarchic period.

Although one of the six guiding principles of the 1952 Free Officers' "revolution" was "establishing sound democratic life," this was just a slogan. Nasser may have fancied himself a man of the people, but he was not a democrat, and he had little faith in the formal institutions of representative democracy. He could be forgiven for this. During the colonial period, Egypt's parliament had come to be seen as an abode of corruption, factionalism, and instability (there were thirty cabinets in the thirty years between the promulgation of the 1923 constitution and the 1952 Free Officers' revolt). In a speech, Nasser declared that "democracy" was not to be found "in parliaments . . . but in the life of the people."[43] Thus, Nasser and the Free Officers moved quickly to dismantle the remnants of Egypt's admittedly dysfunctional democratic edifice. The constitution was abolished in 1952, and political parties were banned a year later. Political rivals—including members of the Muslim Brotherhood—were jailed, a tactic that persisted through Mubarak's time to today.

When a new constitution was enacted in 1956 (it was revised again in 1958 and 1964), it gave the president extraordinary powers, rendering the legislature a generally inconsequential cheering section for Nasser's policies. As Robert Springborg notes, Nasser's "commitment to political institutions was never wholehearted, and while on occasion he sought to mobilise support for his regime through its organisations, in the final analysis the magnet he relied on to attract support was not organisational but personal."[44] Nasser's strongman persona remains deeply popular among Egyptians, even as it brought with it a season of repression among the worst in Egyptian history.

When Nasser died in 1970, his successor, Anwar al-Sadat—who had been a member of the Free Officers' movement that overthrew the monarchy—sought to chart a different course from his charismatic predecessor and slowly set about liberalizing the country's economy and its politics. In part, Sadat was motivated by desire to shift Egypt out of the Russian orbit and into the American one, and he apparently thought that reforming domestic political institutions to make them more palatable to the West would aid in this effort.[45] Sadat also wanted to increase foreign investment in the country, and this too required a partial political overhaul in order to reassure investors wary of dumping their money into a fickle Middle-Eastern despotism. Sadat put a new, more liberal constitution in place in 1971 and strengthened judicial oversight of the government, particularly as it related to the violation of property rights.[46] The Arab Socialist Union—a totalitarian political party that was the sole legal political organization under Nasser—was slowly dismantled. In 1977, Sadat legalized the existence of political parties aside from the ruling organ, and in 1979, he held Egypt's first multiparty parliamentary elections since the end of the monarchy.

Sadat's changes had many of the desired effects. Egypt did become an American client, and foreign investment did increase. But the country's new democratic trappings masked the persistence of a deeper, authoritarian reality. The president remained almost all powerful. And when Sadat was faced with disagreement over his economic and foreign policies, he responded with the same heavy-handed tactics that Nasser had used. For example, a month prior to his October 6, 1981, assassination at the hands of Islamist extremists, Sadat had arrested more than a thousand of his political opponents from across the political spectrum.[47] The limits of Sadat's political liberalization had become painfully clear.

Sadat's successor, an air force general named Hosni Mubarak, also made an initial show of political liberalization early in his rule. He released political dissidents jailed by Sadat and declared war on corruption. *Newsweek* reported on December 21, 1981, that he commanded government ministers to turn down gifts and ordered the destruction of "523 luxury weekend bungalows owned by rich Egyptians (and a handful of Western embassies) near the Pyramids of Giza," including a "bungalow used by Sadat to entertain Jimmy Carter." This had the effect of winning over domestic opponents and reassuring foreign patrons. But Mubarak, too, eventually regressed to Egypt's long-standing dictatorial mean. The executive remained supreme. Though Mubarak had initially vowed to serve for only two terms, he reneged on the promise in 1993 and eventually served four complete terms before being ousted toward the end of his fifth. In 2005, he took the radical—and to many, promising—step of introducing multiparty elections for the country's presidency (previously, the president had been nominated by the parliament and voted up or down in a rigged national referendum). But that election proved no different from all of the others that had been held in Egypt over the previous decades. Mubarak's victory, with an improbable 88 percent of the vote, signified to all that the change was more cosmetic than real.

Most importantly, throughout Mubarak's term in office, the legislature remained the rubber stamp it had always been.[48] The president retained (and exercised) the power to dissolve parliament, block its laws, and bypass it completely with his own edicts and decrees. In addition, parliamentary elections—of which there were eventually six during Mubarak's thirty-year rule—were routinely rigged in order to guarantee that Mubarak's party maintained a comfortable legislative majority.[49] According to Springborg, this allowed the president's party "to terminate debate, pass legislation virtually without comment, reject opposition demands for investigation of alleged improprieties and illegal activities, and so on."[50]

After Mubarak's removal amid a national popular uprising in February 2011, there were great hopes that Egypt's political institutions would be reformed to trim executive power. However, this was not to occur. Although a parliament was democratically elected in January 2012, it was dissolved by court order a few months later, on the eve of Egypt's first democratic presidential elections. Thus, when that election brought the Muslim Brotherhood member Muhammad Morsi to power, the new president was unconstrained by any legislature.[51] A constitution passed during his administration in December 2012 introduced presidential term limits and enhanced legislative checks on presidential authority. However, Egyptians had no opportunity to observe whether these new constitutional provisions would have any effect: Elections to replace the dissolved parliament were never held, and Morsi was overthrown a little more than six months later. When new presidential elections were held after Morsi's ouster, the winner, with more than 95 percent of the vote, was the architect of the coup against Morsi, a former minister of defense and field marshall named Abd al-Fattah al-Sisi. Initially, Sisi ruled more or less by decre, and although parliamentary elections were completed in December 2015 and again in 2020, these were not observed by independent election observers, and in any case produced legislatures that did not meaningfully disrupt Egypt's lugubrious tradition of executive supremacy. Indeed, the scholar Robert Springborg has described Egypt's legislature as "politically supine."[52]

Military Dominance

Another fundamental and almost unchanging aspect of Egyptian politics has been the dominance of the country's military. Indeed, if the parliament is subordinate to the executive, both are subordinate to "deep state" comprised of the military and the assorted security and intelligence services.[53] It is worth remembering, after all, that until 2012 all of Egypt's presidents—Naguib (1952–1954), Nasser (1954–1970), Sadat (1970–1981), and Mubarak (1981–2011)—were military officers (as is Egypt's current president, Abdel Fattah al-Sisi). Muhammad Morsi was not just the first democratically elected president in Egypt's history, but he was also the first civilian one. Egypt's army has long been accustomed to what the scholar Steven Cook has called "ruling, but not governing"—which meant that the men with guns were the ultimate power behind the throne, even if they did not trouble themselves with the day-to-day business of making Egypt's trains run (it would be too much to say "on time").[54] Scholars have documented the military's control over large segments of the economy, including, as Springborg has noted, the production of everything from clothing to foodstuffs to pots and pans to kitchen appliances to automobiles.[55] They have also noted how local governments, the boards of major publicly owned companies, and the directorships of key government agencies are all studded with military men.[56] The overwhelming impression conveyed by these studies is of a military that sees itself as the natural ruler of Egypt and that is eager to maintain its political supremacy.[57]

The military's role in Egypt's governance since the overthrow of Mubarak in 2011 would seem to validate this perspective. When Mubarak resigned on February 11, 2011, he did not hand power to his vice president, Omar Suleiman (hastily appointed during Mubarak's last days) or to the speaker of the parliament (as the constitution required). Instead, he ceded authority to a twenty-one-member committee made up of the country's senior military leaders. This grandly named Supreme Council of the Armed Forces (SCAF), dissolved the parliament that had been elected under Mubarak and issued a declaration that would serve as the country's interim constitution. The document stipulated that, until elections could be held, the SCAF was both legislature and executive—with the power to make policy and pass and ratify laws at will.

If some feared that the SCAF was trying to establish direct military rule, the SCAF for its part made at least half-hearted attempts to demonstrate that this was not the case. Parliamentary elections were held from November 2011 to January 2012. And true to its promise, the SCAF relinquished its legislative authority once the new parliament was seated. But the SCAF retained its executive role, and it did not cede to the new legislature the right to appoint the prime minister or members of the cabinet. In June 2012 after the Supreme Constitutional Court ruled that the electoral law by which parliament had been elected was invalid, the SCAF dissolved the parliament and once again assumed legislative authority. In July 2012 after Muhammad Morsi's election to the presidency was certified, the SCAF officially ceded executive authority to the newly elected president but continued to claim to constitute the government's legislative branch.

In August 2012, Morsi came to a deal with the SCAF in which it relinquished its legislative powers to him, rendering him both president and parliament. However, although the military was now nominally excluded from policy-making, this state of affairs was to last less than a year. Amid calls for Morsi's resignation by political elites fearful of Islamists' consolidation of power and by ordinary Egyptians tired of the country's year-long flirtation with economic crisis, the minister of defense Abdel Fattah al-Sisi eventually stepped in and, with what appears to be by all accounts considerable popular support (as evidenced by mass protests), removed Morsi. Although the chief of the constitutional court was installed as interim president, many observers saw the July 3, 2013, intervention as a military coup intended to restore the armed forces to its place atop the Egyptian political pyramid.[58]

Evidence in support of this interpretation is provided by the provisions of the new constitution, passed in December 2013 after Morsi's overthrow by a body of mostly non-Islamist Egyptian elites. That document largely exempts the military's budget from parliamentary oversight, prohibits a civilian from serving as minister of defense, and places the regulation of military affairs in the hands of a council dominated by generals. It is worth noting, incidentally, that these provisions were largely held over from the 2012 constitution passed under Muhammad Morsi, suggesting that even Egypt's first democratically elected president had felt unable to seriously challenge the military's autonomy and political centrality. And of course, the elevation to the presidency of former minister of defense Abdel Fattah al-Sisi further reinforces the impression that Egypt's military is fully back in power.[59]

Weak Rule of Law

In addition to strong executive authority and an overweening military, Egyptian politics has long been characterized by poor, uneven, and erratic application of the rule of law. The two institutions that should serve as the pillars of any legal order—the police and the judiciary—have troubled histories.

The Egyptian police have long been accustomed to impunity, emboldened by a 1958 emergency law that expanded police powers and restricted political freedoms and which remained in more or less continuous application (with brief interruption between 2011 and 2013) from 1967 to 2021. Political activity—such as protests and demonstrations—was heavily regulated; any gathering of more than five people required a permit; opposition activists were routinely detained by the security services.[60] The police and the central security forces—and the Interior Ministry of which both are a part—were thus seen by the Egyptian people not as their protectors, but as their tormentors. The murder in the summer of 2010 of a young Alexandrian named Khalid Said by two policemen was merely one incident in a long history of police brutality. Habib al-Adly, the minister of the interior under Mubarak, was almost as much a focus of the Egyptian revolution as was Mubarak himself. It is therefore not an accident that protesters chose January 25—which is formally a national holiday to celebrate the police—to commence their demonstrations against the Mubarak regime.

However, if the police had been seen as too heavy-handed during Mubarak's time, they came to be seen as erring too much in the other direction after he was overthrown. Likely in response to popular anger at their abuses under Mubarak, the police reportedly took a hands off-approach to their duties during Morsi's tenure, resulting in a marked decay in daily order.[61] By many accounts, however, the police have recently resumed their old ways.[62] In fact, in June 2015, President Abdel Fattah al-Sisi took to the airwaves to ask for his countrymen's forgiveness for the police's infringement on their basic dignity, declaring, "I apologize to every Egyptian citizen who has been subjected to any abuse. I am responsible for anything that happens to an Egyptian citizen."[63]

Despite the president's sentiments, serious attempts at police reform remain elusive. In July 2015, the government released a draft "antiterrorism" law that would, according to press reports, expand police powers, muzzle journalists, and allow the government to circumvent judicial due process.[64] Thus, things seem to be moving in the wrong direction. As the scholar Yezid Sayegh has testified, until the government reforms the security sector, "the culture of police impunity will deepen and democratic transition will remain impossible in Egypt."[65] Although the emergency law was formally repealed in October 2021, many of its provisions found their way into other laws, with the result being that Egypt after the repeal of the emergency law is not appreciably freer than it was before.[66]

The judges, like the police, are important players in Egyptian politics and key to its future as a stable, prosperous society. Though the state legal apparatus that currently exists in Egypt is a holdover from the prerevolutionary era, the judiciary has traditionally been a highly legitimate institution in Egypt, benefiting from the respect of ordinary citizens.

This was not always the case. During Nasser's last years in power, he had attempted to emasculate the judiciary, and in 1969, he dismissed large numbers of judges and restructured the judiciary to bring it more firmly under executive control.[67] However, in an effort to increase foreign investment, Nasser's successor, Anwar al-Sadat, moved to strengthen the judiciary and the rule of law more generally.[68] Key to this effort was the establishment of a Supreme Constitutional Court with the power to review the constitutionality of government decisions.[69] The twenty-two-member court often decided against the regime; for example, in 2000 it ruled that all elections must be overseen by members of the judiciary.[70] And although the government could get around the Constitutional Court's rulings by amending the constitution itself—as it did in 2007 in order to remove grounds for judicial oversight of balloting—the fact is that the courts then and now represented the principal check on the executive's authority.

If the judiciary earned accolades during the Mubarak period for standing up to the regime, under Morsi it was often seen to be complicating Egypt's democratic transition. In June 2012, the Constitutional Court ruled that the Islamist-dominated parliament had been improperly elected, and it declared the body null and void. The ruling was decried as an attempt by Mubarak loyalists in the judiciary to thwart the will of the people. President Morsi tried to reconvene the parliament, but the SCAF backstopped the court's decision, and Morsi was forced to acquiesce.

The tussle over the parliament marked the opening scene in a year-long struggle between Egypt's first democratically elected president and the Supreme Constitutional Court. In November 2012, Morsi tried to sideline the judges entirely, issuing a dramatic amendment to

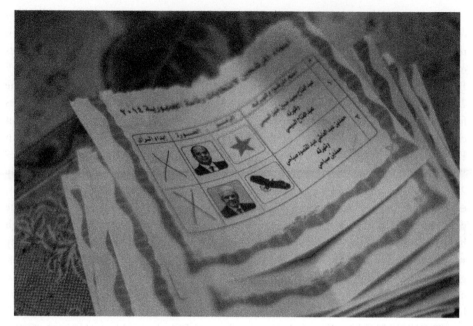

PHOTO 10.1 An invalidated ballot from the May 2014 presidential election. By drawing a large *X* next to each candidate's name, the voter has indicated his or her rejection of both Abdel Fattah al-Sisi (the eventual winner) and his opponent, Hamdin Sabahi.

Ibrahim Ramadan/Anadolu Agency/Getty Images

Egypt's interim constitution that rendered him beyond judicial oversight. Morsi's allies on the one-hundred-member committee then writing the country's constitution followed up this move by hurriedly finishing the draft constitution and putting it to a vote, which it passed. The episode caused many to view Morsi as a dictator-in-the-making who sought to loose himself of the shackles of the rule of law and did much to erode his already-fragile legitimacy.[71] But it also did much to erode the judiciary's legitimacy—casting it as a player in Egypt's polluted political game rather than as an honorable, impartial arbiter of the rules. Today, the Egyptian judiciary mainly receives international attention for passing dramatic, mass death sentences against supporters of the ousted president. For example, in 2014 a court sentenced more than 650 Egyptians to death for participating in a riot that resulted in the killing of a police officer.[72] This diminution of judicial legitimacy domestically and internationally cannot but constitute a major obstacle to the establishment of the rule of law in that troubled country.

PARTIES AND MOVEMENTS

Despite its relatively long history of elections and parliaments, Egypt today lacks the stable political parties and cleavages that mark more-established polities. Political parties had been banned under Nasser, and though allowed to reemerge under Sadat and Mubarak, none (aside from the ruling National Democratic Party) was a credible claimant for national power. To the extent that the political landscape did harbor a potential challenger to the ruling party, it was in the form of the Muslim Brotherhood, the Islamic pietist political movement established in Egypt in 1928 and banned by Nasser in 1954. Egypt under Mubarak did feature liberal, leftist, and secular political parties, but these were by all accounts weak—hemmed in by the authoritarian state and lacking the resources necessary to establish durable connections to voters.[73]

Given regime regulation of the political space, activists had to carve out opportunities for political participation wherever they could find them. Labor organization by textile workers, real estate tax collectors, and others constituted a major form of popular mobilization during the late Mubarak period.[74] Professional syndicates—akin to labor unions for doctors, lawyers, engineers, and journalists—became sites of considerable political debate and often provided opposition voices platforms for articulating grievances against the regime. Independently owned magazines and newspapers became increasingly bold in their criticisms of the regime, and the rise of satellite television and Internet-based social media generated a public sphere that the Egyptian government was nearly powerless to control.[75] Islamist political activists agitated against the regime and mobilized potential supporters through the country's myriad mosques and other religious institutions.[76] It is widely thought that these liminal spaces of political contestation eventually incubated the forces that compelled the military to overthrow Mubarak in 2011.

The political parties that emerged after Mubarak's overthrow were of three broad types.[77] The first were the Islamists. Chief among these was the Muslim Brotherhood's Freedom and Justice Party (FJP; *Ḥizb al-Ḥurriya wa al-ʿAdāla*), established in May 2011. In the parliamentary elections held from November 2011 to January 2012, the FJP captured 217 out of 498 elected seats.[78] In second place, with 107 seats, was the Party of Light (*Ḥizb al-Nūr*), also an Islamist party that grew out of a Salafi (or ultraorthodox) preaching society based in Alexandria.[79] The Salafi party was widely considered to be even more socially conservative than the Muslim Brotherhood, and its strong showing seemed to testify to a strong popular desire for Islamic law. In total, approximately 70 percent of the parliament elected after the revolution was made up of so-called Islamists.[80]

The second pillar of the political landscape was made up of so-called *secular* or *liberal* parties, although these terms must be used with caution. Chief among these was the Party of the Delegation (*Ḥizb al-Wafd*). Al-Wafd was founded in 1978 as the modern successor to the original al-Wafd Party of 1919, which had controlled the cabinet at several points between 1923 and 1952 and which in 1954 was banned by Nasser, along with all other Egyptian political parties. Though al-Wafd was the largest opposition party in parliament in 1984 and the second largest in 1987, by the end of the Mubarak period it had come to be seen as an almost inconsequential player in Egyptian politics. In 2005, the party controlled 5 seats out of 444, compared with the Muslim Brotherhood's 88. In the aftermath of that election, a leadership squabble in the Wafd resulted in the consumption by fire of a section of the party's headquarters, a multimillion dollar mansion in the once-affluent Cairo suburb of Dokki.[81] A new party leader, a media and pharmaceuticals tycoon named al-Sayyid al-Badawi Shahata, was elected in the summer of 2010 and promised to breathe new life into the party, but al-Wafd performed poorly in the 2010 elections later that year, winning only 6 seats (out of 508). However, after Mubarak's overthrow, the party's relatively high name recognition enabled it to capture a respectable 41 seats in the 2011 and 2012 parliamentary election.

Also in the secular camp was an electoral alliance of parties calling themselves the Egyptian Bloc (*al-Kutla al-Misriyya*). The Bloc captured 35 seats in the 2012 election. The major components of the Bloc were two new parties: The first, with 16 seats, was the left-leaning Social Democratic Party, and the second, with 15 seats, was the Free Egyptians Party (*Hizb al-Misriyin al-Ahrar*), founded by Naguib Sawiris, a billionaire industrialist and investor who was the scion of one of Egypt's most distinguished Christian families. Also part of the Bloc was the National Progressive Unionist Rally (usually called Tagammu, after its Arabic name, *al-Tajammu' al-Watani al-Taqadumi al-Wahdawi*), which was founded in 1978 by Khalid Muhyuddin, a legendary figure in Egyptian politics and a former member of the Free Officers. After the 2011 and 2012 parliamentary elections, however, the Bloc collapsed and failed to field a joint presidential candidate in the May 2012 presidential contest (see Figure 10.1).

Finally, there came the offshoots of the former ruling National Democratic Party. As several scholars have noted, the NDP was a "big-tent" party that coopted big businessmen, rural notables, and other community leaders by doling out the spoils of corruption. At its peak under Mubarak, the NDP claimed to have between two million and three million members. After the January 25, 2011, revolution, the party was dissolved by court order in April 2012 and its assets seized by the state. Predictably, a number of parties emerged to take up its mantle, scattering its already-diminished support base. Consequently, none of the NDP successor parties managed to earn more than a handful of seats in parliament. That said, it has been argued that the strong showing of former NDP member Ahmed Shafiq in the 2012 presidential election—who won approximately 48 percent of the vote in the second round of the June 2012 presidential election—was a testament to the residual strength of the now-defunct NDP's networks.

The weakness of non-Islamic political parties in post-Mubarak Egypt had far-reaching effects. It was not just that Egypt's first parliament was ideologically lopsided in favor of religious conservatives or that the country's first democratically legitimated constitution mandated what some considered an outsized role for religion. Instead, the major effect of the imbalance

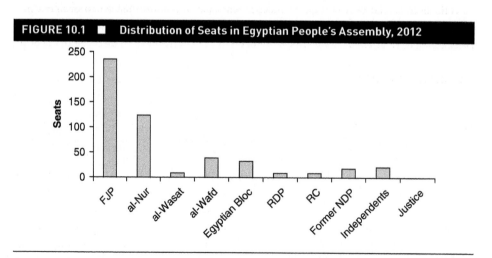

FIGURE 10.1 ■ Distribution of Seats in Egyptian People's Assembly, 2012

Source: Egyptian High Judicial Committee for Elections; *Al-Ahram* newspaper.

in Egypt's postrevolutionary partisan landscape was to convince non-Islamist politicians that electoral competition was not in their interests. Egypt's so-called secular, liberal politicians and parties came to believe that elections would always be won by the Islamists, who (in their view) played on popular religiosity. Thus, these liberals not only acquiesced in the military's seizure of power on July 3, 2013—they welcomed it, believing that a military coup was the only way to dislodge the Muslim Brotherhood from power.[82]

In 2015, Egypt conducted elections for a new, 596-seat parliament—after three years without legislature. However, far from ushering in a rebirth of political parties, it was clear almost from the outset that the opposite would happen. Several observers noted that electoral law by which the parliament would be elected was one that appeared designed to severely disadvantage political parties and privilege nonpartisan, "independent" members.[83] First, approximately 80 percent of the legislature's seats were elected according to a single-member district system in which individuals could run as independents, without being members of political parties. The remaining 20 percent of seats were divided among four districts (two with 15 seats, and two with 45 seats), in which political party lists would compete. However, unlike most party list systems in which seats are allocated to parties in proportion to the share of the vote they earn, this system was a winner-take-all affair in which the party that earned the majority of the vote would receive all of the seats in the district. The result of this system was a legislature dominated by independents with a smattering of partisan members. According to the official breakdown of members of parliament, 58.7 percent of members were independents (although by all accounts, these independents are largely regime supporters).[84]

Further evidence of the weakness of Egypt's political parties came during Egypt's 2018 presidential election, in which President al-Sisi won another four-year term of office. That election was notable for the fact that the only party that was able to muster a candidate to stand against al-Sisi was one that had actually formally endorsed the president's reelection (al-Sisi's "opponent" earned around 3 percent of the vote).

In 2020, Egyptians once again went to the polls, this time to elect a new parliament. This time, the bulk of seats were won not by independents, but by members of the "Nation's Future" party, which is shaping up to be the party of the president (even as the president is not formally a member of it) (Figure 10.2).

Domestic Conflict

It increasingly appears that the most consequential political conflict in Egypt will take place not at the ballot box, but on the battlefield. The five years since Morsi's overthrow have seen hundreds of Egyptians (including civilians, soldiers, and policemen) killed and thousands more jailed.[85] In September 2013, a group called *AnŠār Bayt al-Maqdis* (Supporters of the Sacred House, abbreviated ABM) attempted to assassinate Egypt's then–interior minister, Muhammad Ibrahim.[86] In May 2015, Islamist militants in the northern Sinai town of al-ʿArīsh massacred three judges, allegedly in retaliation for the death sentence handed down to former Egyptian president Muhammad Morsi.[87] The following month, in June 2015, Egypt's public prosecutor (akin to the US attorney general) was killed by a car bomb, allegedly planted by a group calling itself "Giza Popular Resistance."[88] Militants have especially targeted Egypt's Coptic Christians.

FIGURE 10.2 ■ **Results of Egypt's 2015 and 2020 Parliamentary Elections**

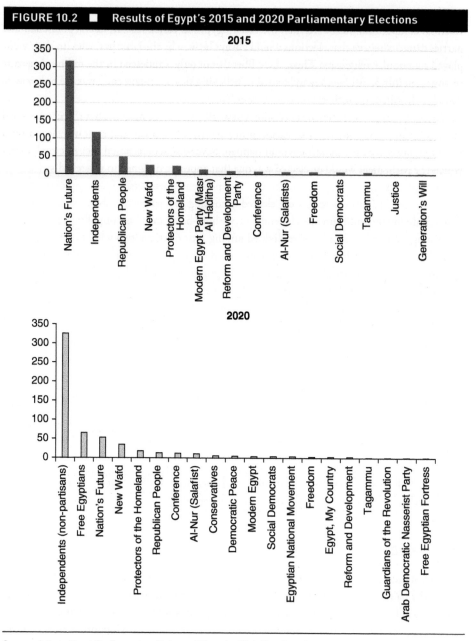

Sources: International Parliamentary Union and Egyptian High Elections Committee.

That long-beleaguered minority has seen several attacks against churches by Islamist militants, including bombings in April 2017 that killed almost fifty Egyptians and wounded scores more.[89] The deadliest attacks, however, have targeted Muslims. In November 2017, almost 250 worshippers at a mosque in the Sinai were killed by explosives and gunfire thought to be the work of the local affiliate of the so-called Islamic State in Iraq and the Levant.[90]

Much of the violence is related to the July 2013 military coup, but in this author's opinion, it would be a mistake to say that all of it is. For instance, attacks against military installations and personnel in the Sinai Peninsula, perpetrated by Islamic militants in the Sinai may, in this author's view, be more properly linked to long-standing grievances of the neglected inhabitants of the Sinai and to the regionwide emergence of affiliates of the Islamic State in Iraq and the Levant. Although by 2020, the most violent opponents of the Egyptian state in the Sinai seemed to have been largely brought to heel, long-term pacification of discontent in that region will therefore require not just the application of force against terrorists, but sustained attention to the issues of economic underdevelopment and underprovision of basic government services that render local populations supportive of the insurgents operating in their mid.

RELIGION AND POLITICS[91]

For any observer of Egypt's politics, it seems obvious that religion plays an important role in the life of the country. Egyptians have long been recognized to be a religious people. In fact, the electoral dominance of Islamists during Egypt's brief democratic interlude caused many so-called secular and liberal politicians and intellectuals to conclude that free and fair elections would only deliver Islamic theocracy. The Muslim Brotherhood, which is the country's major Islamic party, tried to allay these fears and repeatedly declared its commitment to democracy and pluralism, even putting some secular parties on its ticket in the parliamentary elections, but—as we now know—these efforts proved unsuccessful. More than twenty years ago, the American diplomat Edward P. Djerejian concluded that Islamist electoral victories in the Middle East would destroy democracy. In his view, this was because Islamists believed not in "one man, one vote," but in "one man, one vote, one time."[92] In other words—they would use elections to get into office, after which they would pull the democratic ladder up behind them. What Egypt's dismal post–2011 history reveals is that Djerejian was correct that Islamist victories would destroy democracy, but for the wrong reasons. It was not that Islamists were insufficiently committed to democratic procedures, but that their opponents were so fearful of continued Islamist dominance under democratic institutions that they decided to call upon the army to undo those institutions. Thus, understanding why Islamists dominated those elections in the first place can help us to understand why Egypt's democratic experiment was so brief.

At one level, the electoral dominance of Islamists in Egypt's postrevolutionary politics was not surprising. During the Mubarak era, the Muslim Brotherhood, though banned, was routinely able to win more seats in parliament than any other opposition party by running its candidates as independents. Scholars and journalists regularly predicted that the Muslim Brotherhood would win a parliamentary majority in Egypt if the country ever held a free and fair election. And when elections finally were held after Mubarak's overthrow, those predictions—as we have seen—came true.

For many scholars, the Islamists' capture of a supermajority in the 2011–2012 elections was evidence that Egyptians had a strong desire for Islamic law. For others, it was evidence of the superior organizational resources possessed by Islamists, who could mobilize voters through a variety of religious institutions such as mosques, Islamic charities, and religious schools.[93] The scholar Ellen Lust and her coauthors have argued that most Egyptian voters were actually concerned with bread-and-butter economic issues—an argument also advanced by the author of this chapter.[94] In the latter account, people are thought to have voted for Islamists not because they wanted to legislate 7th-century religious regulations, but because the disciplined, organized, and "locally embedded" Islamists did a better job than other parties of convincing voters that they would better their economic welfare.[95] The rapid diminution of popular support for Islamists over the course of 2011 to 2013 is evidence in support of the latter proposition. Recall that in the parliamentary elections of 2011 and 2012, Islamists captured a supermajority. A mere six months later, in the first round of the presidential election the main Islamist candidate, Muhammad Morsi, only managed to garner approximately 25 percent of the vote. And then, a year after his election millions of Egyptians (many of whom had voted for him) took to the streets to signify their discontent with him and his party, opening the way for the military's ouster of the president. These facts are inconsistent with a view of Egyptian voters as driven by fundamentally religious concerns. After all, if Egyptians really were seized by a desire to implement Islamic law, it is unlikely that they would have lost patience with the Muslim Brotherhood as rapidly as they did. That said, readers of this chapter should be aware that this is an active area of research for which settled answers remain elusive.

The Fate of Egypt's Christians

Though the question of how Islamists came to dominate Egyptian politics is obviously of great interest, almost no group had a greater stake in the answer than Egypt's Christians, who make up approximately 10 percent of the population. For this minority, long persecuted (although in ways more subtle than overt), the rise of the Muslim Brotherhood and the Salafis to power represented a genuine threat to the tolerance and pluralism that all Egyptians hoped for in the wake of Mubarak's overthrow. Though the Muslim Brotherhood during its time in power made attempts to reassure Christians that the group believed in equal rights for Egyptians of all faiths, its insistence on establishing the shari'a as the country's principal source of legislation, as well as the inflammatory statements of some of its militants and allies, rendered Christians doubtful of the sincerity of the Brotherhood's commitment to pluralism.

Christianity is not a recent import into Egypt—in fact, it was the religion of the majority of Egyptians on the eve of the Arab-Muslim conquests in the 7th century. Though Copts have been victims of official and nonofficial discrimination (and, at some times, communal violence), they are abundantly represented in the middle and professional classes. However, many live in villages in southern Egypt and are poor farmers. During Anwar al-Sadat's crackdown on dissidents shortly before his assassination in 1981, he banished Coptic pope Shenuda (1923–2012) from Cairo for allegedly inciting Coptic-Muslim strife and banned publications issued by Coptic associations. Only after Mubarak became president did hostilities between the government and the Copts begin to subside, and in 1985, the government allowed Pope Shenuda to return to Egypt. However, restrictions on the building of churches, in place for more than a hundred years, largely continued.

Violence against Copts continued throughout the 1980s and 1990s, including deliberate attacks by Islamists seeking to undermine the Mubarak government as well as episodes of tension between Muslims and Copts living in close proximity. In one particularly troubling incident, a dispute between two merchants provoked widespread violence in the village of al-Kushah in early January 2000, leading to the death of twenty-one Christians and one Muslim. A botched police investigation and perhaps a desire on the part of the government to avoid provoking Muslims could be the reasons why no one has ever been convicted of the killings. Though Mubarak made conciliatory gestures toward Christians—notably declaring Coptic Christmas (January 6) a national holiday in 2003—and Al-Azhar's Shaykh Tantawi (1928–2010) and Coptic Pope Shenuda frequently appeared together publicly to appeal for national unity, this did not put an end to tensions between the two communities. On January 1, 2011, an explosion at a Coptic church in Alexandria killed more than 20 worshippers and occasioned renewed critique of the Mubarak government—which would fall a little over a month later.

The postrevolutionary period saw an intensification of anti-Christian violence. On October 9, 2011, Christian demonstrators marched in Cairo to protest the destruction of a church in Upper Egypt by unknown elements (widely presumed to be Salafi jihadists). The then-ruling military junta cracked down on these peaceful protests by force, resulting in several deaths (among both the protesters and the soldiers sent to quell them). Less than a year later, during the presidency of Muhammad Morsi, a Coptic émigré in the United States produced a film denigrating the Prophet Muhammad, leading to massive protests in Cairo (in which some youths trespassed the grounds of the American embassy and took down the American flag). Though the protests were largely anti-American and not anti-Coptic in nature, the Muslim Brotherhood–controlled government commenced legal proceedings against several Copts living outside Egypt in a move that threatened to give the incident a communal cast.[96]

The Muslim Brotherhood's year in power gave Egyptian Christians plenty of reasons to fear for their status in Egyptian society. At best, the Muslim Brotherhood presented a schizophrenic face to their non-Muslim countrymen. Brotherhood literature is replete with references to the equality of Muslims and Christians (although they stop short of endorsing a Christian's right to serve as president). At the same time, however, Muslim Brotherhood supporters tended to frame their tussles with political opponents (most of whom were Muslim) in sectarian terms.[97] For instance, at a pro-Morsi rally in December 2012 Islamic preacher Safwat al-Higazi (currently imprisoned) delivered what he called "a message to the Egyptian Church and to all the symbols of the Church," warning Christian leaders, "Don't you dare ally with the remnants of the old regime against the legitimate elected representatives of the people."[98] Muhammad al-Biltāgī, the now-jailed secretary general of the Cairo branch of the Muslim Brotherhood's Freedom and Justice Party, said in a radio interview that 60 percent of the anti-Brotherhood protesters then encamped in front of the presidential palace were Christians angry at the ascent of Islam in Egypt.[99] During the first phase of voting in Egypt's December 2012 constitutional referendum, the Muslim Brotherhood published an article on its website claiming that Christians in the southern governorate of Sūhāg were being sent text messages from an anonymous source urging them to vote against the constitution. "Say no to an Islamic state," the text messages allegedly read. "We want a Coptic state."[100]

Incidents like this help to explain why the Coptic Church and most Egyptian Christians were supportive of the military's overthrow of Muhammad Morsi and the subsequent ban on the Muslim Brotherhood. In March 2014, the Coptic Pope Tawadros called on minister of defense Abd al-Fattah al-Sisi to run for president, saying that "Egyptians view him as a savior and the hero of the June 30 revolution."[101] The rule of Muhammad Morsi, he declared, "was not suitable under any circumstances for Egypt's civilization and history."[102] The wave of violence experienced by Egyptian Christians since Morsi's overthrow—ostensibly committed by supporters of the ousted president—highlights both the legitimacy of Coptic concerns over Islamist bigotry and the failure of the current regime to guarantee the safety of its citizens.

POLITICAL ECONOMY[103]

Egypt's largest economic challenge has long been generating jobs for a rapidly growing population, and its largest social challenge is educating that population to be qualified for the jobs being created. Unemployment for holders of university degrees exceeds 20 percent (see Figure 10.3). The problem of unemployment is particularly acute among the young, and this lack of opportunity for the country's youth was one of the main drivers of the revolutionary fervor that ended in Mubarak's removal and that continues to frustrate Egyptians today. As we have seen, since the mid-1970s the country has been in the process of a slow transformation from the statism embraced after the 1952 coup to a free-market economy, but many aspects of state control—extensive public subsidies, inefficient public industries, and a bloated government bureaucracy—remained in place because the country's leaders feared that dismantling them completely would generate social and political instability. The legacy of state socialism on

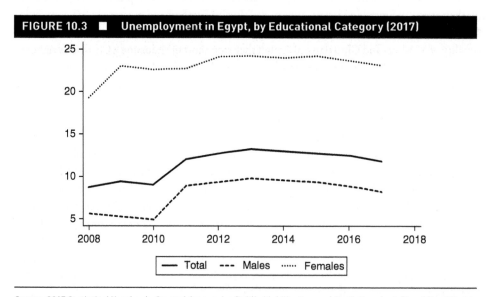

FIGURE 10.3 ■ Unemployment in Egypt, by Educational Category (2017)

Legend: — Total --- Males ····· Females

Source: 2017 Statistical Yearbook, Central Agency for Public Mobilization and Statistics, Arab Republic of Egypt.

Egyptian economic growth is hard to exaggerate. Consider that up until the mid-1960s the real gross domestic products (GDPs) per capita of Egypt and South Korea were roughly equivalent: In 1964, Egypt's per capita GDP was $1,620, while South Korea's was $1,983 (in 2005 constant prices). Since then, Egypt's income has increased 3.5-fold while South Korea's has increased 12-fold (see Figure 10.4).

Leading Egyptian exports include oil and petroleum (with bright prospects for increased natural gas exports), as well as steel, textiles, apparel, and cotton. The value of Egyptian exports has fluctuated in recent years, driven in part by the fluctuating price of fuel. Manufactured goods—the hallmark of an industrialized, advanced economy—as of 2007 made up only 19 percent of Egyptian exports (see Figure 10.5). Overall, exports have not risen appreciably as a share of the country's GDP (see Figure 10.6). Egypt's largest trading partner is the European Union, with the United States its largest single-country partner.

The service sector employs roughly half of the working population, with another third working in agriculture and the remainder in industry. The official unemployment rate is around 10 percent, but many observers suspect that the actual figure is more than double that; in addition, underemployment is rampant, particularly among the young and educated. Remittances from family members working abroad remain an important source of support to Egyptians. Most estimates of economic inequality in Egypt suggest that it is relatively low. However, this is likely due to Egypt's chronic underdevelopment (i.e., a large proportion of the population is poor) and due to shortcomings in the way that top-end incomes are measured. For a visual picture of Egypt's economic inequality, see Figure 10.7, which plots Egypt's GINI index (a measure of inequality) over the past three decades. (The United States' scores are included for comparison. Higher scores signify greater inequality.)[104]

Chronic budget deficits have perpetuated Egypt's dependence on foreign aid. US aid accounts for almost half of the economic assistance that Egypt receives from all foreign sources.

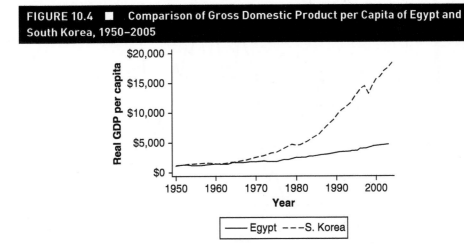

FIGURE 10.4 ■ Comparison of Gross Domestic Product per Capita of Egypt and South Korea, 1950–2005

Source: Alan Heston, Robert Summers, and Bettina Aten, Penn World Table Version 6.3, Center for International Comparisons of Production, Income, and Prices at the University of Pennsylvania (August 2009).

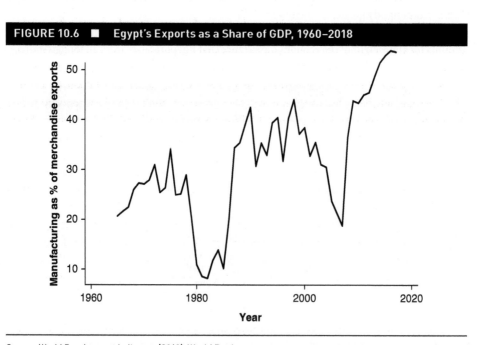

FIGURE 10.5 ■ Manufacturing as a Share of Egypt's Exports, 1965–2017

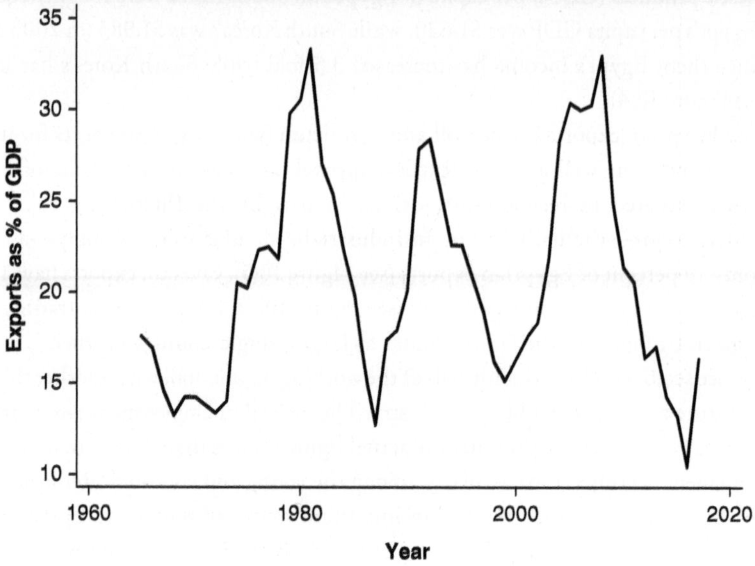

Source: World Development Indicators (2018), World Bank.

FIGURE 10.6 ■ Egypt's Exports as a Share of GDP, 1960–2018

Source: World Development Indicators (2018), World Bank.

FIGURE 10.7 ■ Inequality in Egypt and the United States Compared

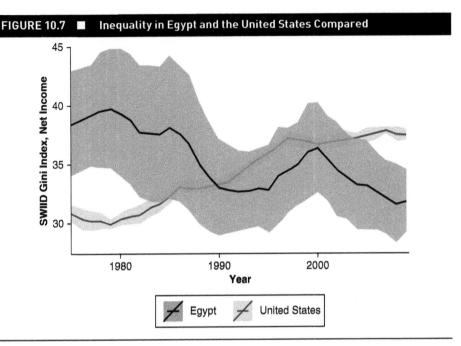

Source: Solt, Frederick. 2016. "The Standardized World Income Inequality Database." *Social Science Quarterly* 97. SWIID Version 7.1, August 2018.

Note: Solid lines indicate mean estimates; shaded regions indicate the associated 95 percent confidence intervals.

The rest comes chiefly from international lending institutions, such as the International Monetary Fund (IMF) and the World Bank, and the governments of Western Europe and Japan. Since the Camp David accords, Egypt has received about $64 billion in aid from Washington; only Israel has received more. That assistance, military and economic in various forms, for many years averaged about $3 billion a year for Israel and $2.2 billion for Egypt. By mutual agreement, economic assistance to both countries began declining gradually in the mid-2000s. In 2006, the United States gave $1.3 billion to Egypt in military assistance and $495 million in economic assistance (see Figure 10.8). Aid to Egypt is explicitly conditioned on its continued observance of the Camp David agreements and, as stipulated in the early 1990s, its pursuit of economic reforms.

Increasingly under pressure from the United States and the IMF to reform Egypt's economy, Mubarak gradually continued Sadat's conversion from a centrally controlled economy to a market economy more open to private enterprise and foreign investment. The IMF's demands included devaluing the Egyptian pound (effectively raising prices), eliminating state subsidies on consumer goods, reforming tax collection, and reducing imports. The dilemma for Mubarak's government was maintaining the delicate balance between the conflicting demands of foreign creditors and the masses of Egyptians living at or below the poverty line. These dilemmas have continued to bedevil Mubarak's successors.

FIGURE 10.8 ■ US Aid to Egypt and Israel, 1998–2008

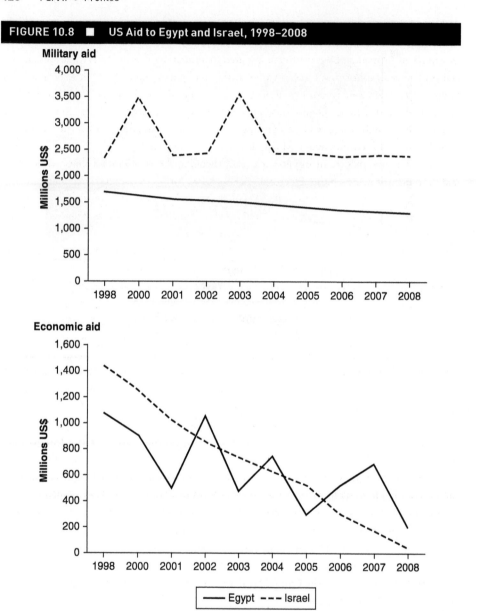

Source: US Overseas Loans and Grants (database), US Agency for International Development, http://gbk.eads. usaidallnet.gov/.

In 1991, Mubarak signed on to a comprehensive structural adjustment program under the aegis of the IMF and the World Bank. By 1998, Egyptian implementation of its IMF program had met with impressive results. Budget deficits, long a serious handicap to government economic activity, had been reduced to manageable levels. Foreign currency reserves had increased, and privatization had begun taking hold in the banking sector.

But after initial successes, the pace of reform stalled. In 2004, Mubarak appointed a cabinet of reformist technocrats, and the country embarked on a serious program of measures to encourage investment. The government initiated structural reforms in taxes, trade regulations, and the financial sector, and it resumed privatization of public industries.[105] It also floated the Egyptian pound in 2004, leading to a sharp drop in value and increase in inflation to approximately 18 percent. Real GDP growth hovered around 6 percent as of 2010, but unemployment and inflation remained major challenges and proved to be proximate causes of the widespread public protests that culminated in Mubarak's February 2011 ouster.

The economic picture in Egypt remains challenging. During Morsi's short tenure, limited progress was made on the structural reforms called for by international financial institutions. President Morsi's successor, Abdel Fatah al-Sisi, has been more aggressive in his pursuit of these reforms. Shortly after being elected in May 2014, President al-Sisi reduced subsidies on fuel, reportedly saving Egypt 50 billion EL (Egyptian pounds) per year.[106] His government has also attempted to reform the inefficient food subsidies regime, providing smart cards to indigent Egyptians enabling them to buy bread at any shop in the country, instead of the old system of paying selected bakers to produce cheap bread (which could be purchased by any Egyptian, rich or poor, willing to wait in line for it).[107] In 2016, the Central Bank announced that it would allow the Egyptian pound to float freely on international currency markets, resulting in a major devaluation (see Figure 10.9). These and other measures are estimated to shave billions of pounds off the Egyptian government budget, even as they result in short-term costs (in the form of price increases) for ordinary Egyptians. However, to the extent that the country has been able to stave off calamity, it is due to the largesse of its oil-rich neighbors across the Red Sea. According to a report produced by the Atlantic Council, a Washington-based think tank, Saudi Arabia, the United Arab Emirates, and Kuwait have together "given or pledged about $35 billion to Egypt in aid in the form of oil shipments, cash grants and central bank deposits since Morsi's removal."[108]

Perhaps in recognition of the fact that it cannot rely on the generosity of its oil-rich allies indefinitely, Egypt is trying to develop more independent sources of revenue. Shortly after his election in the summer of 2014, President al-Sisi announced that Egypt would undertake a project to enlarge a section of the Suez Canal, which would enable more ships to pass through the waterway and more than double the revenue earned from transit fees.[109] That project, whose likelihood of success was initially doubted by many observers (including the author of this chapter), has been completed, although recent statistics do not suggest a dramatic increase in revenue from the canal.[110] The 2015 discovery of the large Zohr gas field off Egypt's Mediterranean coast has resulted in a significant boost to Egyptian coffers—$2.5 billion annually, according to one estimate.[111] In March 2015, the government also held a large investment conference in the Red Sea resort town of Sharm al-Sheikh, which produced a reported $19 billion in promised foreign investments, as well as a $45 billion plan to construct a new capital east of Cairo, which was to be funded exclusively by foreign capital.[112] Negotiations between the Egyptian government and the United Arab Emirates–based firm that was to undertake the new capital's development failed, and the capital is now being built in part with investments from China.[113] The new capital, the development of which is led by the Egyptian military, was expected to begin operating in the end of 2021, with the transfer of several government agencies from their existing offices in Cairo.

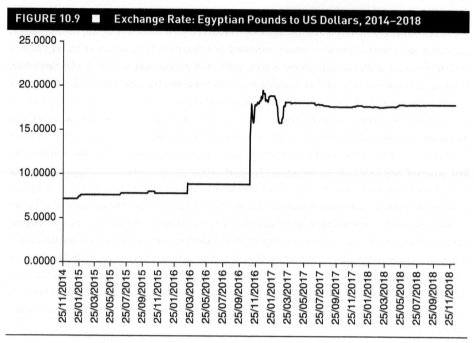

FIGURE 10.9 ■ Exchange Rate: Egyptian Pounds to US Dollars, 2014–2018

Source: Central Bank of Egypt.

REGIONAL AND INTERNATIONAL POLITICS[114]

As the Arab world's most populous country and the producer of much of its intellectual and cultural output, Egypt is one of the region's most important powers. In the years since Mubarak's overthrow, however, Egypt's regional position has been in considerable flux. The collapse of state authority in Libya, Iraq, Yemen, and Syria, the concomitant rise of the Islamic State (which also operates in the Sinai Peninsula), and an increasingly assertive Iran all have powerful implications for Egyptian foreign policy conduct in the coming period. In this section, we survey Egypt's international relations under Nasser, Sadat, and Mubarak before turning to the ways in which Egypt's foreign policies are being reshaped by the so-called Arab Spring and its unfolding aftermath.

Nasser Between the West and Eastern Bloc

For the past thirty years, one of the key features of Egypt's foreign policy was its close alignment with the United States. This relationship emerged after decades of near enmity between the two countries. When the Free Officers came to power in 1952, they articulated a policy of neutrality or "nonalignment" between the United States and its chief rival at the time, the Soviet Union. Nasser played a prominent role in the 1955 conference of nonaligned nations in Bandung, Indonesia, and shared the world stage with such leaders as Josip Broz Tito of Yugoslavia, Jawaharlal Nehru of India, and Zhou Enlai of China. But Egypt's neutrality was not to last for long. Western nations were reluctant to sell Egypt arms, and in 1955, Nasser agreed to purchase weapons from Czechoslovakia, which was at the time a member of the Soviet bloc. The US secretary of state, John Foster Dulles, viewed the purchase as a step by Egypt toward the communist world, despite Nasser's professed aversion to communism and his banning of the Egyptian Communist Party. On July 19, 1956, Dulles announced that the United States planned to withdraw financial support for the Aswan High Dam, the centerpiece of Nasser's economic planning. The Soviets were all too happy to step in.

The definitive break with the West came seven days after Dulles's announcement. Nasser seized the British- and French-owned Suez Canal Company and declared that he would apply the canal's revenues toward the dam project. Egypt promised to pay off the stockholders, but Britain and France were not of a mind to let Cairo control the waterway, Europe's lifeline to the petroleum of the Middle East. After months of secret negotiations among Britain, France, and Israel—whose ships were barred from the canal—Israeli forces launched an attack on Egypt across the Sinai Peninsula in October 1956. Britain and France, on the pretext of securing the safety of the canal, seized it by force. Under pressure from the United States, the Soviet Union, and the United Nations, they were forced to withdraw, as was Israel. President Dwight D. Eisenhower was furious that Britain and France, US allies, had acted without consulting him, and he denied them much-needed support. By March 1957, a peacekeeping force, the United Nations Emergency Force, was deployed on the Egyptian side of the 1948 Egyptian–Israeli armistice line.

Eisenhower's stand during the Suez crisis improved American relations with Nasser only slightly and only briefly. The crisis was a victory of sorts for Nasser. He had thumbed his nose at the West and gotten away with it. The outcome confirmed Egyptian control of the canal. In addition, when Nasser gained Soviet support for his Aswan High Dam project in 1958, he effectively sent the message to the West that he did not need to depend on it and that Western nations could not take the Arab states for granted. The Soviets soon assumed an important position in Egyptian foreign policy and became Egypt's major weapons supplier.

In 1958, Syrian rulers asked Nasser to head a union of Egypt and Syria. Nasser agreed, but only on the condition that the union be complete. Syrian political parties were abolished; Cairo became the capital of the new United Arab Republic (UAR); and a new political party, the National Union, was created. North Yemen later joined the republic in a federative manner with the UAR and Yemen and called it the United Arab States. The union fared badly, however, and was dissolved when Syrian antiunionists seized control of the Damascus government in 1961.

The dissolution of the UAR marked the beginning of a long string of policy failures for Nasser. In 1962, he sent troops to bolster officers in the North Yemeni army who had overthrown the ruling Hamid al-Din family. With as many as eighty thousand Egyptian soldiers engaged in the fighting, the Yemeni war became a drain on the Egyptian treasury. Nasser's efforts to control the Yemeni republicans and the brutal measures Egyptian forces used against royalist villages in Yemen tarnished Egypt's image.

Meanwhile, in November 1966, Israel had destroyed a village in the West Bank (controlled by Jordan) in retaliation for Palestinian guerrilla raids, and in April 1967, Israeli and Syrian air forces had skirmished. Nasser engaged in a series of threatening steps short of war, in part egged on by Arab leaders challenging his pan-Arab credentials. He asked the United Nations to remove some of its peacekeeping troops from the Sinai, closed the Strait of Tiran to Israeli shipping, and signed a mutual defense treaty with Jordan.

Israel launched a surprise attack on Egypt, Jordan, Syria, and Iraq on the morning of June 5, 1967. During the first hours of the attack, Israel virtually destroyed the air forces of the four Arab states as they sat on the ground. Without air support, the Arab armies were devastated, and by the time a cease-fire went into effect on June 11, the Israelis had taken the eastern sector of Jerusalem and all of the West Bank from Jordan; seized the Golan Heights from Syria; and pushed the Egyptians out of Gaza and the whole of the Sinai Peninsula, all the way to the Suez Canal.

The Egyptians were again humiliated, as in 1948. Nasser publicly blamed himself for the defeat, implicitly agreeing with the verdict of history that the war had resulted from his miscalculated brinkmanship. He had provoked Israel in the belief that the United States would prevent the Jewish state from going to war and that the Soviet Union would come to his rescue if war did ensue.

The effects of the defeat reverberated. Nasser resigned as president, but a massive outpouring of support persuaded him to remain in office. He then withdrew Egyptian troops from Yemen, purged the top echelons of the army, and reorganized the government. Perhaps most important, Nasser's foreign policy objectives shifted. The quarrel with Israel was no longer only a matter of securing Palestinian rights. The return of the Sinai—approximately one-seventh of Egypt's land area—became a top Egyptian priority. Toward this end and despite opposition from many Arabs, including the Syrian government and the Palestine Liberation Organization, Nasser accepted UN Security Council Resolution 242, which, among other things, recognizes the territorial rights of all states in the area (including Israel).

Nasser died in September 1970 of a massive heart attack. Following his death, tens of thousands of Egyptians took to the streets, passionately mourning the man who, more than any other single figure in modern Egyptian history, had confirmed Egypt's preeminent position in the Arab world. He had been an authoritarian leader, intolerant of dissent from any quarter. He had failed to provide any genuine institutions of political participation. He had presided over the most disastrous military defeat in modern regional history. His economic policies had not produced prosperity. Yet Gamal Abdel Nasser had changed the life of the average Egyptian, and to this day, he retains a large measure of respect and admiration, even as the political regime he established is widely recognized as having been undemocratic and responsible for significant human rights abuses.

Sadat Moves West

Disillusioned with the Soviets, Anwar al-Sadat had grown confident enough by mid-1972 to expel thousands of Soviet military advisers and civilian technicians—though without breaking diplomatic relations with Moscow—and to offer Washington an olive branch. According to Alfred Leroy Atherton Jr., ambassador to Cairo from 1979 to 1983, the Richard M. Nixon administration was preoccupied with its reelection campaign and the Vietnam War, so it did not respond promptly or fully to Sadat's overtures. Sadat, unable to draw upon US diplomatic clout to assist in the return of the Sinai Peninsula, decided on war.

Egyptian forces, better prepared than in 1967 and this time with surprise on their side, crossed the Suez Canal on October 6, 1973, and advanced deep into the Sinai while Syrian forces attacked in the east. By the time a UN-arranged cease-fire took effect on October 22, an Israeli counterattack had retaken most of the ground, and in one area, Israel held both sides of the canal. The final position of the armies, however, was less important than Israel's initial rout.

The war had a tremendous effect on Sadat's image in Egypt. Once viewed as an uncharismatic yes-man to the towering Nasser, Sadat became Hero of the Crossing (of the canal), a sobriquet he treasured. His standing in the world was further boosted by the display of Arab solidarity during the war—when the petroleum-producing Arab states, led by King Faisal of Saudi Arabia, implemented an oil embargo against Western nations that supported Israel.

After the 1973 war, Sadat finally had Washington's attention. Secretary of State Henry Kissinger began shuttling between Jerusalem and Cairo to work on a peace settlement (an effort that later earned the name *shuttle diplomacy*). His efforts led to the first of two disengagement agreements between Egypt and Israel on January 18, 1974, which went beyond the original cease-fire. That year, Egypt and the United States restored diplomatic relations, which Nasser had severed after the 1967 war. In addition, Nixon became the first president to visit Egypt since Franklin D. Roosevelt went there in November 1943 during World War II. US aid, cut during the Nasser years, resumed. The US Navy helped clear the Suez Canal of wartime wreckage, permitting its reopening in 1975.

Though Sadat had viewed the United States as the key to resolving the Arab–Israeli conflict, US-mediated negotiations with the Israelis bore no fruit. He then decided to go to Jerusalem to talk directly with the Israelis about settling their differences. His November 1977 trip to Jerusalem set in motion a chain of events that ultimately led to the Camp David accords. US president Jimmy Carter later prevailed upon Sadat and Israeli prime minister Menachem Begin to meet at Camp David, the presidential retreat in Maryland, for 12 days in September 1978. There they hammered out two documents—A Framework for Peace in the Middle East and A Framework for the Conclusion of a Peace Treaty between Israel and Egypt. On March 26, 1979, they returned to the United States to sign the treaty in a White House ceremony.

The peace with Israel cost Sadat and Egypt their standing in the Arab world. Most Arab leaders and peoples saw Sadat's agreement with Israel as a betrayal. Five days after the treaty signing, the Arab League expelled Egypt and instituted an economic boycott against it. Of the 21 remaining league members, all but Oman, Somalia, and Sudan severed relations. In May 1979, the forty-three-member Organization of the Islamic Conference also expelled Egypt. Similarly, it was cast from the Organization of Arab Petroleum Exporting Countries.

The Mubarak Era and Beyond

Hosni Mubarak, trying to steer a middle course in all matters, foreign and domestic, did not initially embrace the Egyptian "partnership" with the United States with the same fervor exhibited by his slain predecessor. He recognized the economic and military necessity of US assistance, however, and US officials generally gave him high marks for trying to minimize irritants in the relationship. By the end of Mubarak's time in office in 2011, then-US Vice President Joseph Biden illustrated the great value American officials had come to place on Mubarak as a partner and friend when he refused to call him a dictator even as protesters amassed against the Egyptian president in Tahrir Square.

During his time in office, Mubarak continued to promote the central tenet of Sadat's notion of peace with Israel—that the treaty meant the end of military hostilities and the establishment of a proper relationship—but its promotion often resulted in a cold peace beset by problems. Israel's unilateral annexation of the Golan Heights in 1981 and its invasion of Lebanon in June 1982, both of which Mubarak criticized, did not help build stronger relations. Egypt was still savoring the sweetest fruit of the treaty: On April 25, 1982, Israel had returned the remaining section of the Sinai that it had occupied since the 1967 war—except for Taba, a tiny strip of beach where the Israelis had built a resort hotel. After a seven-year dispute, Israel relinquished Taba on March 15, 1989.

The Egyptian–Israeli relationship continued to be bedeviled by regional and bilateral problems throughout the 1980s and 1990s, leading Egypt to withdraw its ambassador from Israel (and later return him) several times. Although both countries at times express disappointment—Israel that Egypt has not further normalized bilateral relations, and Egypt that no more progress has been made on resolving the Israeli-Palestinian dispute—the two continue to uphold the peace and cooperate on a range of political, economic, and security issues. In 2004, Egypt and Israel expanded their economic relations with encouragement from the United States, opening a series of "qualifying industrial zones" in which goods produced in Egypt with some Israeli inputs may be imported into the United States duty free. Fears that the Egyptian–Israeli relationship would be imperilled by the Islamist-dominated government that was elected after the Arab Spring proved unfounded, as Egypt continued its security cooperation with Israel during the Morsi presidency. Under the al-Sisi presidency, that relationship remains strong, with Israel reportedly providing clandestine military assistance to Egyptian efforts to pacify Islamist extremists in the Sinai Peninsula.[115]

Reconciliation With Arab Nations

A pivotal event on Egypt's road to reconciliation with its Arab neighbors took place in November 1987. At that time, 16 Arab League heads of state met in the Jordanian capital of Amman and issued a surprisingly strongly worded resolution attacking Iran for its "procrastination in accepting" a cease-fire proposal in what was then its seven-year war with Iraq. Jordan's King Hussein, the conference host, used the occasion to ask the participants—in the interest of Arab unity—to drop the league's ban on formal relations between its member countries and Egypt. The Arab states agreed, feeling they needed Egypt as a counterweight to Iran and the potentially subversive Islamic radicalism that it was attempting to export.

By the end of 1989, all Arab League members had reestablished relations with Egypt, which also was readmitted to the Arab League. On May 23, 1989, after a ten-year absence, Egypt took its seat at an Arab League summit in Casablanca, where Mubarak was accorded the honor of making the opening address. Only weeks before the meeting, the Organization of Arab Petroleum Exporting Countries had readmitted Egypt, which had already reentered the Organization of the Islamic Conference in 1984. To promote regional economic cooperation, Egypt, together with Iraq, Jordan, and Yemen, founded the Arab Cooperation Council in 1989.

In March 1991, the Arab League transferred its headquarters back to its original location in Cairo, finalizing Egypt's return to the Arab fold.

Mubarak, meanwhile, had become a leading supporter of the PLO and its chairman, Yasir Arafat, who became a frequent visitor to Cairo. After the first Palestinian uprising broke out in 1987 and the Palestine National Council held a historic meeting endorsing creation of a state alongside Israel, Mubarak implored Arafat to satisfy the US government's conditions for holding talks with the PLO, which Arafat did in December 1988. In November 1988, the Palestine National Council met in Algiers. It formally declared Palestinian independence and implicitly recognized Israel's right to exist, but US Secretary of State George P. Shultz demanded that Arafat explicitly renounce terrorism, accept UN Security Council Resolution 242, and recognize Israel's sovereignty.

After much prodding by Mubarak and a few false starts, Arafat on December 14, 1988, uttered the precise words that Shultz wanted to hear. Within hours, the secretary of state said US talks with the PLO could begin. According to diplomatic sources in Cairo, Mubarak was one of several Arab and Western European leaders who urged Shultz and President Ronald Reagan to accept Arafat's words as genuine.

Throughout the 1990s, Egypt acted as a leading participant in the peace process, serving as a mediator and interlocutor between the PLO and Israel in the wake of the Oslo accords of 1993 and an active participant in multilateral talks between Israel and its Arab neighbors. This relationship became increasingly complex after the acrimony generated toward Arafat by the United States and Israel following the breakdown of the Camp David talks in July 2000 and Israel's employment of overwhelming military might during the second Palestinian uprising that began in September 2000.

In 2004, Egypt reengaged in efforts to bring Palestinians and Israelis back to the negotiating table and eventually agreed to support Israel's unilateral withdrawal from Gaza. After the death of PLO chairman Arafat, the Egyptian government openly supported the efforts of his successor, Mahmud Abbas, to resume peace talks and served as a mediator between Abbas's Fatah Party and the Islamic Resistance Movement, or Hamas, which won a majority of seats in the Palestine National Council in January 2006 and now controls the Gaza Strip. To halt arms smuggling into Gaza, the Egyptian government began in 2009 to construct a steel wall along the Egypt–Gaza border. The wall, which extends more than 30 feet below ground, is intended to block the myriad tunnels that groups have used to smuggle arms, supplies, and people in and out of Gaza. The barrier has occasioned vehement protest from Egyptian opposition groups such as the Muslim Brotherhood, which complain that it prevents needed humanitarian supplies from reaching Gaza and renders Egypt complicit in what they view as Israel's isolation of that territory. After Mubarak's overthrow, there was a slight easing in the restrictions on traffic between Egypt and Gaza. However, in August 2012 an attack by Islamist militants from Gaza against Egyptian soldiers in the Sinai Peninsula prompted the government of Muhammad Morsi to initiate a sweeping military campaign in the area, which included shutting down all of the tunnels to and from Gaza. Under President Sisi, Egypt continues to try to contain a perceived threat of terrorism and smuggling from Gaza, while also seeking to ease the humanitarian crisis there.

The Gulf and Iraq Wars

The Iraqi invasion and occupation of Kuwait in August 1990 created a dilemma for Mubarak and Egypt: Opposing Iraq would put Egypt on one side of an intra-Arab conflict, but failing to oppose the invasion could potentially invite further aggression by Iraqi president Saddam Hussein, poison relations with the wealthy Arab states in the Gulf, and weaken Egypt's crucial ties to the United States. Under these circumstances, Mubarak chose to lead the Arab military and diplomatic effort against the invasion.

On August 10, eight days after the invasion, Mubarak hosted a meeting of the Arab League in Cairo, out of which came a decision by the league to oppose Saddam Hussein and send troops to help defend Saudi Arabia against any possible Iraqi attack. The first Egyptian troops began to land in Saudi Arabia the next day. Egypt ultimately sent four hundred tanks and thirty thousand troops to Saudi Arabia, the largest contingent of any Arab nation.

The opposition of some Egyptian Islamists to Egypt's participation in the anti-Iraq coalition was largely drowned out by a government campaign to win popular support by highlighting the brutality of the Iraqi occupation. Egyptian–Iraqi ties had already been strained by widespread reports of sometimes violent discrimination against Egyptians working in Iraq.

Mubarak's anti-Iraq position during the 1990–1991 Persian Gulf crisis and war and his success in persuading other Arab countries to participate in the multinational force earned him the gratitude of the United States and the Gulf countries. The participation of Egypt and other Arab nations undercut Saddam Hussein's claims that his invasion of Kuwait was a blow against US imperialism and advanced the Palestinian cause. Mubarak also held Egypt solidly in the coalition when it appeared that Israel might enter the war against Iraq. US leaders worried that if Israel retaliated against Iraqi missile attacks, Arab nations would withdraw from the coalition rather than fight on the same side as their old enemy. In the end, the United States prevailed on Israel not to attack. The United States rewarded Egypt by increasing military cooperation, forgiving a debt of $7 billion for arms purchased in the 1970s, and rescheduling its remaining debts. Saudi Arabia wrote off outstanding Egyptian debts of $4 billion.

In March 1991, the Damascus Declaration was signed, providing that Egypt and Syria join Gulf Cooperation Council (GCC) countries in a new Gulf security arrangement—GCC plus Two. Saudi Arabia's reluctance to station a non-Gulf Arab force in the area on an open-ended basis and its preference instead to rely on Western forces resulted in Mubarak's withdrawing Egyptian troops from the Gulf after the war. At the same time, the GCC countries, suffering from their own financial difficulties, cut back on their aid commitments to Egypt. Egyptian expectations for increased contracts, assistance, and cooperative ventures from the Gulf states for its efforts went largely unfulfilled. The Damascus Declaration essentially had become a dead letter.

After the failure in 2000 of the Arab–Israeli peace process pursued throughout the 1990s and the al-Qa'ida attacks of September 11, 2001, the transformation in US policy toward the Middle East put Egypt in an awkward position. As the United States shifted toward a confrontation with Iraq and began to advocate greater human rights and democratization throughout the Arab world, the long-standing but always somewhat-fragile relations between Cairo and Washington deteriorated.

During the Iraq War initiated by the United States in March 2003, Egypt distanced itself from US policy, in contrast with its open support of the coalition forces in 1991. Mubarak openly criticized the war on a number of occasions but quietly provided military cooperation, such as overflight permission and Suez Canal transits for coalition military forces. Egypt was the first Arab state to send an ambassador to Iraq after the 2003 invasion, but Ambassador Ihab al-Sharif was assassinated in July 2005. In 2006, Egypt and the United States inaugurated an annual strategic dialogue to discuss a wide array of controversial regional and domestic issues.

Politics of the Nile Basin

No analysis of Egypt's international and regional position would be complete without a discussion of the politics of water. Egypt is synonymous with the River Nile, which is practically its sole source of water. In fact, practically all of Egypt's population lives in a narrow strip of land along the banks of the Nile—the rest of the country is desert. But Egypt's claim on the four-thousand-mile-long river is precarious. The river is fed by three major tributaries: the White Nile, which originates in Lake Victoria, and the Blue Nile and Atabara, which both originate in Ethiopia and together account for 85 percent of the Nile's waters.[116] For much of Egypt's recorded history, the lands upstream did not make much use of the river, which meant that Egyptians had a virtual monopoly over it. But in recent years, some of the other so-called riparian countries—Burundi, Democratic Republic of the Congo, Eritrea, Ethiopia, Kenya, Rwanda, Sudan, Tanzania, and Uganda—have begun to assert their claims to the Nile, which has occasioned much tension with Cairo.

The usage of the Nile is governed by two international treaties, neither of which recognizes the rights of upstream states (with the exception of Sudan). The 1929 treaty of the Nile Basin, which was signed by Egypt and Britain (the latter acting on behalf of the Sudan), allocated the majority of the Nile's waters to Egypt (approximately 48 billion cubic meters, with a mere 4 billion to Sudan). The treaty gave Egypt the right to inspect and veto any proposed upstream usages of the Nile's waters. In 1959, Egypt and a newly independent Sudan came to a new agreement. By this time, the flow of the Nile was estimated at approximately 84 billion cubic meters. After allowing for the loss of 10 billion cubic meters due to evaporation, Egypt was allocated 55.5 billion cubic meters and Sudan 18.5 billion. Once again, the upstream riparian states were granted nothing.[117] Sudan also promised to build, with Egypt's help, a canal in the south of Sudan that would allow the Nile to bypass the region's marshes, thus stanching a considerable source of water loss (but at the cost of destroying the way of life of the tribes that depended on the marshes for their sustenance). The project actually commenced in 1980 with World Bank funding, but fighting in southern Sudan between that country's Arab Muslim central government and Christian separatists brought the project to a halt just short of completion.[118]

For much of the 20th century, the political instability that has plagued the upstream riparian states meant that they were unable to press claims to a share of the Nile's waters or even credibly threaten to violate international treaties and erect dams or irrigation schemes that would diminish the flow of water to Egypt. But that is changing. Drought-stricken Ethiopia, for example, has repeatedly pressed claims to use more of the Nile. A multinational Council of Nile Basin Ministers, established in 1998 to negotiate a framework for the sharing of the Nile waters, has so far failed to generate results as upstream countries accuse Egypt and Sudan of holding stubbornly to their claims over the river.[119] Egypt argues that since the upstream countries receive significant rainfall and Egypt receives none, its claim to the Nile is a matter of life and death. Upstream countries respond that Egypt wastes a great deal of the Nile's waters—for example, in 1997 it initiated the Toshka project to irrigate a portion of Egypt's southern desert (at great cost in terms of both money and water).[120]

In June 2013, reports that Ethiopia was planning to construct a grandly named "Grand Renaissance Dam" along the Blue Nile generated considerable alarm in Cairo, and then-president Muhammad Morsi convened a televised meeting of Egyptian political leaders to discuss how to deal with the potential threat to Egypt's water supply.[121] In May 2015, Morsi's successor, Abd al-Fattah al-Sisi, inked a framework agreement with the governments of Ethiopia and other riparian states that committed all states of the Nile Valley not to harm the interests of downstream states, but the details of a final agreement have yet to be worked out.[122] While the final dispensation of the Nile is in considerable doubt, what is not in doubt is that this issue will only increase in importance as all of the states along the Nile Basin seek to cope with growing populations and the imperatives of development.[123]

The Post-Mubarak Period

The period since Mubarak's overthrow has seen a reconfiguration of many of Egypt's key relationships. Foremost among these is Egypt's alliance with the United States. When the Muslim Brotherhood's Morsi came to power in July 2012, there was considerable fear in Western capitals that this traditionally anti-American leader of a traditionally anti-American organization would strike a defiant pose toward Egypt's erstwhile patron.[124] The irony, however, is that the Brotherhood came to be seen as generally cooperative with the United States. For instance, Morsi earned plaudits for his role in helping the United States to bring about a cease-fire between Israel and the Palestinian militant group Hamas in November 2012.[125] The true rupture in Egyptian–American relations has come since the Brotherhood's overthrow, as many Brotherhood opponents believe—albeit with little evidence—that the United States was supportive of the Islamists and conspired to keep them in power. On July 22, 2013, shortly after Morsi's removal, the front page of Egypt's principal state-owned newspaper, *al-Ahrām*, declared that it had "the details of the American conspiracy against Egypt and the final hours of Brotherhood rule," and alleged that the American ambassador had made a deal with the Muslim Brotherhood's deputy leader to help Morsi establish a parallel government that would be run from one of Cairo's mosques.[126]

For its part, the US administration has tried to maintain its close relationship with Egypt's leadership, ignoring calls to suspend aid to that country. However, it increasingly appears that the United States has been displaced as Egypt's principal patron by the Gulf countries, which, as we have seen, have collectively pledged more than $30 billion to Egypt since 2013. For comparison's sake, the US aid package to Egypt clocks in at around $2 billion per year. Egypt has also joined with Saudi Arabia and the United Arab Emirates in a blockade of the Arabian Gulf emirate of Qatar (on the grounds that Qatar supports Islamic extremists) and participates in a Saudi-led antiterrorism coalition that seems aimed at combatting groups such as al-Qaeda and the Islamic State while also targeting Muslim Brotherhood–affiliated groups and individuals (including Egyptian politicians who oppose the current military-backed regime). In 2017, Egypt opened a military base in the northwest part of the country that is intended to serve as a staging ground for troops from Egypt and the United Arab Emirates and their allies as they combat Islamist militias in neighboring Libya.

Although Egypt and its Gulf patrons currently experience an alignment of interests—particularly as they relate to quelling Islamist movements and militants in the region—there are likely limits to the current alliance. For instance, many domestic critics of President al-Sisi have criticized him for seeming to subordinate Egypt to foreign interests. For these critics, the most dramatic illustration of this subordination came in April 2016, when President al-Sisi ceded sovereignty over two Red Sea islands—Tiran and Sanafir—to Saudi Arabia.[127] There have also been clear and growing divergences in Egyptian and Saudi Arabian foreign policies.[128] Saudi Arabia has wanted greater Egyptian cooperation in confronting Iranian proxies in Yemen and Syria, whereas Egypt's approach to both countries has been to emphasize stability. Thus, where the Saudis wished to see Syria President Bashar al-Asad (an Iranian ally) overthrown, the Egyptians have not hidden their unease with any attempts to disrupt the Syrian state. It's worth noting that the Emirati position toward Syria has lately come to resemble the Egyptian one, as the UAE has initiated a thaw in relations with the Assad regime, and it is possible that Saudi Arabia will follow suit. But the current divergence between Saudi and Egyptian policy on the Syria issue should serve as a potent reminder of the contingent nature of Egypt's alliances with Saudi Arabia and all of its Gulf partnerships.

CONCLUSION

For much of the last decade, writing about Egypt has been like trying to hit a moving target. Especially in 2011 and in the two or three years following Mubarak's overthrow, potentially momentous changes occurred on a daily basis, and while one waited for the dust to settle on one set of developments, a new set of dramatic events would invariably throw everything into yet another disequilibrium. This was not the Egypt that many Egypt-watchers grew up studying and writing about. During the Mubarak era, the country's politics were so stable as to be called stagnant. After Mubarak's ouster, Egypt was suddenly vibrant and dynamic, with all of the attendant frustrations for social scientists. Today, however, with a military ruler back at the helm, the old stagnation of the Mubarak period seems to be returning—although with a much greater quotient of violence and danger.

It is hazardous to try to predict Egypt's future, but one can identify developments to watch. The first is the potential emergence of a movement for more democracy and freedom. Although there is clearly limited scope for political activism in today's Egypt, it is undoubtedly the case that large numbers of Egyptians chafe under the current highly restrictive system. Although periodic calls for protest have not yielded much in the way of popular action, the past need not be prologue. The scholar Mona El-Ghobashy, writing shortly after Mubarak's overthrow in 2011, has testified to the ways that citizens can suddenly come together to reshape the balance of power between regime and society.[129] For decades—she and others have pointed out—analysts ignored the Egyptian people's potential for dissent and focused instead on how regimes seemed to have gained complete control over their populations. Today, we risk making the same mistake—seeing only regime dominance and ignoring the potential for change that bubbles below the surface. After all, if the now-thwarted revolution of 2011 taught us anything, it is that the Egyptian people can make their voices heard when one least expects it.

The second development to watch for is the potential eruption of splits within the coalition undergirding the current regime. We tend to treat Egypt's military and security apparatus as a unified actor with a single set of interests, but there are reasons to believe that this analytic convenience is mistaken. We have already seen, for example, how Egypt's president has expressed unease with the conduct of the police toward protesters—suggesting that the army and the Interior Ministry may have different views over how to manage dissent. Moreover, if the experience of other countries is any guide, we should remain attuned to the potential for splits within the military itself, as different branches of the armed forces perceive themselves to have different interests. Most importantly, if the current president seems as unable to solve Egypt's economic problems as his predecessors, it is possible that at least some segment of the military will withdraw support from him in precisely the same way that it did with Mubarak and Morsi if faced with mass protest.

Finally, Egypt's evolving relations with the rest of the world, and particularly with its American ally, demand close attention. Will the country remain in the US orbit, continuing to receive almost $2 billion in military and economic assistance, as well as other diplomatic and security support? How will the dwindling largesse of the Gulf countries alter Egypt's foreign policy behavior? Will it start to chart a more independent course vis-à-vis its patrons on the Arabian peninsula? Finally, will Egypt deepen its relationship with Russia, which shares Egypt's preference for regional stability? And if so, does an increasingly aggressive and unstable Russia have the wherewithal to serve as the kind of patron that both the United States and the Gulf have been, and that Egypt so clearly needs?

This chapter began with a number of old and new testimonials to Egypt's regional centrality. As I noted at the outset of this essay, one out of every four Arabs is an Egyptian, so it seems beyond safe to say that this largest of Arab countries cannot help but continue to be an important player in a troubled region. But it is unclear exactly what role Egypt will play. For instance, one of the region's most momentous political changes—the signing of the Abraham Accords, which saw the United Arab Emirates, Bahrain, Morocco, and Sudan normalize their relations with the State of Israel—were notable in part for Egypt's complete absence, despite the latter country's nearly 50 years of peace with the Jewish state. Increasingly, it appears that Egypt's primary role in the Arab world is that of cautionary tale—an example of what can go wrong when people rise up to overthrow settled orders. It is difficult to imagine a more depressing outcome to the protests that so captured imaginations around the world in 2011. And yet, when one takes into view the entire span of Egypt's recent history, with its ups and downs, and its moments of political ferment that invariably followed its spells of quiescence, it is hard not to wonder whether Egypt's current season of political dormancy is maybe, just maybe, temporary.

SUGGESTED READINGS

Abu-Lughod, Lila. *Dramas of Nationhood: The Politics of Television in Egypt.* Chicago, IL: University of Chicago Press, 2004.

Bishara, Dina. *Contesting Authoritarianism: Labor Challenges to the State in Egypt.* Cambridge: Cambridge University Press, 2018.

Brooke, Stephen. *Winning Hearts and Votes: Social Services and the Islamist Political Advantage.* Ithaca, NY: Cornell University Press, 2019.

Brown, Nathan. *When Victory Is Not an Option.* Ithaca, NY: Cornell University Press, 2012.

Brownlee, Jason. *Democracy Prevention.* Cambridge: Cambridge University Press, 2012.

El-Ghobashy, Mona. *Bread and Freedom: Egypt's Revolutionary Situation.* Stanford, CA: Stanford University Press, 2021.

Goldberg, Ellis. *Tinker, Tailor, and Textile Worker: Class and Politics in Egypt, 1930–1952.* Berkeley, CA: University of California Press, 1986.

Ketchley, Neil. *Egypt in a Time of Revolution: Contentious Politics and the Arab Spring.* Cambridge: Cambridge University Press, 2017.

Mitchell, Timothy. *Rule of Experts: Egypt, Techno-Politics, Modernity.* Berkeley, CA: University of California Press, 2002.

Moustafa, Tamir. *The Struggle for Constitutional Power: Law, Politics, and Economic Development in Egypt.* New York, NY: Cambridge University Press, 2007.

Rutherford, Bruce. *Egypt After Mubarak: Liberalism, Islam, and Democracy in the Arab World.* Princeton, NJ: Princeton University Press, 2008.

Shehata, Samer Said. *Shop Floor Culture and Politics in Egypt.* Albany, NY: State University of New York Press, 2009.

Springborg, Robert. *Egypt.* John Wiley & Sons, 2017.

Stacher, Joshua. *Watermelon Democracy: Egypt's Turbulent Transition.* Syracuse, NY: Syracuse University Press, 2022.

Wickham, Carrie Rosefsky. *The Muslim Brotherhood: Evolution of an Islamist Movement.* Princeton, NJ: Princeton University Press, 2013.

11 | IRAN

Mehrzad Boroujerdi

On November 4, 1979, less than nine months after the victory of the Iranian Revolution, a group of Islamic militants took over the US embassy in Tehran and held fifty-two US diplomats hostage. The "Iranian hostage crisis" contributed mightily to the electoral defeat of the incumbent US president, Jimmy Carter, who saw the hostages released on January 20, 1981, just as he was handing over power to the newly elected president, Ronald Reagan. The hostage crisis echoed again when President George W. Bush, in a State of the Union address in 2002, referred to Iran as a rogue state and a member of an "axis of evil." There is no doubt that the 1979 revolution has given Iran a uniquely strained and precarious relationship with its former ally, the United States.[1]

The 1979 revolution was a watershed event that heralded the return of religious revolution to the annals of modern history. The rapid collapse of a strong autocratic regime, the use of religion as the primary instrument of political mobilization, the tremendous level of animosity displayed against the West, and the establishment of a "theocracy"[2] in the later decades of the 20th century offered serious and difficult questions for students of politics. And the revolution helped inaugurate a wave of religious political activism in the Muslim world that has been referred to as Islamic fundamentalism, Islamic militancy, or Islamic radicalism.

Iran also provides us with a rather novel, ingenious experiment in political statecraft. Its government is unique among contemporary political systems, as a theocracy infused with democratic elements. As the world's only theocratic republic, Iran's political system is organized around the principle that Shi'i clergy have a divine right to govern because they are the qualified interpreters of God's will. The country is led by a chief cleric who has the title of "Supreme Leader" and enjoys rather extensive powers.

Iran's political system also has strong democratic elements, as the constitution recognizes the principles of popular sovereignty and separation of powers; makes frequent reference to individual rights; and grants the electorate the right to elect the president, members of parliament, and members of the Assembly of Experts, as well as municipal councils.[3] This blending of theocratic and democratic features in the constitution has led to tension. The Islamic Republic's legitimacy rests in part on popular sovereignty and in part on its conformity to a revealed body of religious law. The people elect most policy-makers, but they are overseen by clerics who are not accountable to anything except their own religious conscience and one another. The Islamic Republic, thus, has a split in its bases of legitimation.

HISTORY OF STATE FORMATION AND POLITICAL CHANGE

Iran, a country with a history spanning more than three millennia, has one of the richest artistic, literary, and scholarly lineages of the Middle East. This tradition is due to the accumulated contributions of Persia's gifted craftsmen, gnostic and hedonist poets, and learned scholars in philosophy, science, and religion. Iran's rather complex political culture and self-identity are heavily influenced by a pre-Islamic notion of Iranian identity centered on nationalism, intellectual loans acquired in the course of encounters with Western modernity, and attachment to the minority branch of Islam known as Shi'ism. Each of these currents has served as a breeding ground for the formation of different types of political sentiments ranging from anti-Arab nationalism to secular humanism and finally to radical Shi'ism.

KEY FACTS ON IRAN

AREA 636,372 square miles (1,648,195 square kilometers)

CAPITAL Tehran

POPULATION 85,888,910 (2021 estimate)

PERCENTAGE OF POPULATION UNDER 25 37.47 (2020)

RELIGIOUS GROUPS (PERCENTAGE) Shi'i Muslim, 90; Sunni Muslim, 9; and Jews, Bahá'ís, Zoroastrians, and Christians, 0.3

ETHNIC GROUPS (PERCENTAGE) Persian, 61; Azeri, 16; Kurd, 10; Lur, 6; Baluch, 2; Arab, 2; Turkmen and Turkic tribes, 2; other, 1

OFFICIAL LANGUAGE Persian Farsi, 53 percent; Azeri Turkic and Turkic dialects, 18 percent; Kurdish, 10 percent; Gilaki and Mazandarani, 7 percent; Luri, 6 percent; Baluchi, 2 percent; Arabic, 2 percent; and other, 2 percent

TYPE OF GOVERNMENT Theocratic republic

DATE OF INDEPENDENCE April 1, 1979 (Islamic Republic of Iran proclaimed); December 12, 1925 (modern Iran established under the Pahlavi Dynasty)

GDP (PPP) $1.0 trillion; $12,389 per capita (2019)

GDP (NOMINAL) $510,000 billion (2017)

PERCENTAGE OF GDP BY SECTOR Agriculture, 9.6; industry and mining, 35.3; and services, 55 (2016)

TOTAL RENTS (PERCENTAGE OF GDP) FROM OIL 13.5

FERTILITY RATE 1.93 children born/woman

Sources: CIA. "The World Factbook." August 4, 2022, https://www.cia.gov/the-world-factbook/.
World Bank. "International Comparison Program (ICP)." Accessed August 10, 2022, https://databank.worldbank.org/source/icp-2017.
Statistical Center of Iran. Accessed August 10, 2022, https://www.amar.org.ir/english/.

In the 6th century BCE, Cyrus the Great established the first Persian empire. His grandson Darius then extended it to the Nile Valley and almost to Asia Minor through his conquest of Babylon and Egypt. The empire gradually shrank because of Greek and Roman conquests and internal decay. By the 7th century CE, it was beset by Arab invaders, who brought with them Islam and foreign rule.

The Safavid dynasty declared Shi'ism as the state religion. During the period of their reign (1501–1736), the Safavids managed to create the first modern Iranian nation-state. They were finally overthrown in 1722 by a group of Afghan tribes. The 18th century witnessed the rise and fall of a number of other dynasties in Persia before the Qajar dynasty was established in 1794. The reign of this latter dynasty, which lasted until 1925, was marked by a feebleness of the state at a time when colonialism was at its height. Several ill-advised conflicts with neighboring states such as Russia led to embarrassing territorial concessions for Persia.

The Pahlavis

It was against this background that in 1921 a military officer named Reza Khan seized power and four years later abolished the Qajar dynasty and declared himself the king (or shah) of a new Pahlavi dynasty. Reza Shah managed to create a centralized bureaucratic state by modernizing the economy and secularizing political life. He modeled his reforms after Ataturk in Turkey, and in 1935, changed the name of the country from Persia to Iran. He was forced to abdicate his throne in 1941, however, because of his pro-German sympathies during World War II. The Allied forces recognized his son Mohammad Reza Shah Pahlavi as the new monarch when he was only twenty-two years old.

Mohammad Reza Shah continued his father's policy of authoritarian modernization while being extremely pro-Western in his foreign policy. Disagreement with his prime minister, Mohammad Mossadeq, who was attempting to nationalize Iran's oil industry, forced the shah to leave the country in 1953. A few months later, the shah, with the help of British and US intelligence services, overthrew Mossadeq and returned to power.[4] The 1953 coup, by putting an end to legal organized political opposition (most importantly the Communist Tudeh Party), inadvertently transferred the locus of opposition from factories to educational centers and mosques. This development was only natural since the government could outlaw political parties and threaten striking workers with termination of employment but not storm the mosques, outlaw prayers, or close the universities indefinitely.

The shah's government saw its revenue from oil increase from $555 million in 1963–1964 to more than $20 billion in 1975–1976.[5] Oil revenue as a percentage of total government revenue jumped from 11 percent in 1948 to 84 percent in 1975. By this time, oil revenue made up 45 percent of Iran's gross domestic product (GDP) and 89 percent of its foreign export receipts. Furthermore, thanks to accumulating oil revenue, Iran's gross national product (GNP) grew at an annual rate of 8 percent from 1962 to 1970, 14 percent from 1972 to 1973, and 30 percent from 1973 to 1974. Between 1972 and 1978, Iran's GNP grew from $17 billion to an estimated $54 billion, giving it one of the highest GNP growth rates in the developing world (see Figure 11.1).

The income from oil made Iran into the textbook example of a rentier state, a state that derives a substantial portion of its revenue on a regular basis from payments by foreign concerns

MAP 11.1 ■ Iran

FIGURE 11.1 ■ Gross Domestic Product of Iran, 1965–1979 (Billion Iranian Rials, 1997 Prices)

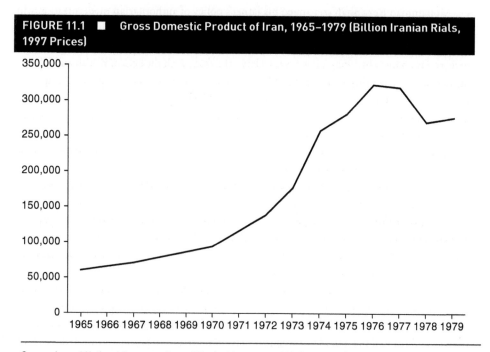

Source: Annual National Accounts, Central Bank of Iran, www.cbi.ir/simplelist/5796.aspx.

in the form of rent. Thanks to the massive infusion of new wealth, the state no longer had to rely on agricultural surplus for capital accumulation. It embarked instead on a fast-paced modernization process, the result of which was the transformation of the economy from one based on agriculture and commerce to a one-product economy, based on oil.

While the shah and his lieutenants embarked on rapid modernization of Iran's socioeconomic infrastructure, there was a half-hearted attempt to create an open political system. The shah founded the Rastakhiz (Resurgence) Party in 1975 as an inclusive party, and he encouraged all Iranians to join. In fact, all legal channels of participation were actually closed to the opposition, and the shah's call to participation was, in fact, only rhetorical. He failed to realize that, even among the rising moneyed class, rapid modernization could foster a sense of deprivation in terms of political participation, collective decision-making, and national independence. And more important for the lower classes, concerns about wealth distribution, conspicuous consumption, and moral decadence would prove to generate strong antistate emotions.

Hence, Iran's rentier economy and the shah's actual policies caused the gradual erosion of the bonds linking the state and civil society. Although the shah's state was viewed by most Iranian and Western observers as modernizing, secular, and stable, its claims of legitimacy proved tenuous and its hold on power fragile.

The 1979 Revolution

The 1979 revolution was a peculiar revolution on at least three counts: It was the first revolution in which the dominant ideology, forms of organization, and leadership cadres were religious in form and aspiration; the first contemporary revolution that has led to the establishment of a theocracy; and the only modern social revolution in which peasants and rural guerrillas played a marginal role.

The Iranian Revolution was second only to the Chinese Revolution in the number of participants mobilized. The revolution came out of conditions created by the shah post 1953. Determined to make Iran into a Middle-Eastern version of Japan, the shah embarked on a massive program of modernization. The so-called White Revolution (1963–1978) was made up of a dozen administrative, economic, and social reform initiatives, including the enfranchisement of women. The centerpiece of the reform package, however, was a land reform that dealt with some peasant grievances but also transferred capital and the regime's support base from rural landowners to the urban bourgeoisie. A modern economic sector emerged alongside more traditional ways of life. Aiming to undercut the public importance of Islam, the shah cultivated both a Western image that many conservative Iranians found offensive and pre-Islamic versions of Iranian identity that centered on nationalism rather than religion. By intervening in all significant decisions and demanding absolute loyalty, he managed to establish a patron–client relationship with the citizenry courtesy of huge oil revenues. All these measures deepened the economic and cultural chasm in the country.

Two factors contributed to the emergence of a revolutionary crisis. First, a 10-percent decline in oil prices in the late 1970s plus a 20-percent rise in consumer prices dented previously strong rates of economic growth, leading to widespread discontent. This cause invokes the *J*-curve theory of revolutions, in which a crisis occurs when a period of improvement and rising expectations suddenly gives way to disappointment. Second, the Carter administration's new emphasis on human rights, coupled with criticism from Western media and human rights organizations, led to US pressure on the shah to lift restraints on political opposition.

A broad revolutionary coalition began to crystallize. It consisted of the urban poor, the moderate-middle classes concerned with political freedoms, the leftist opposition, the bazaar (traditional) merchants, and the clergy. Compared with the other groups, the clergy had a set of advantages: a solid centralized internal structure, strong communication networks, capable orators, wide mobilizing networks, populist slogans, and financial independence from the state.

Demonstrations and strikes snowballed through late 1978 and into early 1979. The shah was finished when his conscript-based armed forces declared that they were now "neutral" and would not defend the regime. The first government, headed by Prime Minister Mehdi Bazargan (1907–1995), was overwhelmingly made up of lay liberal-minded Muslim nationalists. Then, as occurred in the French Revolution, the broad moderate coalition of the early stages gave way to progressively more ideological and radical factions. The lack of ideological consensus among the revolutionaries forced Bazargan's provisional government to resign in November 1979, fewer than nine months after it came to office. Through a series of maneuvers over the course of two years, the liberal-minded bloc was forced out by the clergy who set up a state with theocratic forms.

INSTITUTIONS AND GOVERNANCE

In addition to the institutions inherited from the *ancien régime*, the Islamic Republic created a plethora of assemblies, committees, councils, courts, and foundations to exert its control. In many cases, the new leaders chose to create parallel revolutionary organizations because they could not entirely trust the institutions they had inherited. For example, the Islamic Revolutionary Guards Corps (IRGC) was formed in addition to the regular army. Over time, as these organizations became arenas for factional infighting, overlapping responsibilities, and conflicting policies, the government decided to consolidate several of them into more established bureaucratic agencies. In other cases, the ideology of the new ruling elites compelled them to establish completely new institutions. The Guardian Council, Expediency Assembly, Assembly of Experts, and Special Court for Clergy are just a few examples. The appropriation of the inherited institutions and the invented new organs made the state even more byzantine and muscular.

Iran has a large and inefficient public sector. In the early years of its rule, the state ensured effective control over the civil service by purging, denying employment, and forcing into early retirement those whom it viewed as undesirables. Thereafter, a group of lay technocrats who have been culturally orthodox and have maintained close ties with the clergy have staffed the higher echelons of the bureaucracy. These individuals, who gained education and upward mobility under the Islamic Republic, come mainly from humble backgrounds.

Iran's ruling clergy after the revolution could be classified as an ideological elite who subjugated politics and public policy to religious convictions and made practical material issues take a backseat to a comprehensive vision of society. Generally, the promarket forces favoring a rapprochement with the outside world are connected with more modern business interests. The upper clergy have close, personal ties to conservative bazaar merchants. The base of the radical clergy is predominantly in the lower-middle class.

Policymaking at present involves the elected legislature, the clerical overseers, and the bureaucracy. The latter plays a crucial mediating role between the clergy and the public. Concerted reforms are difficult because of the fragmentation of power. Views on economic and cultural changes are cross-cutting. The liberal-technocratic camp on economic issues does not necessarily favor political liberalization. The intense factionalism has more often than not caused gridlock in policy-making.

Branches of Government

Many features of the Iranian political system are similar to other modern polities and, thus, are unremarkable. There is a president and a unicameral legislature, both elected directly by voters. Before 1989, the system was loosely parliamentary, with a prime minister and a weak president. A number of constitutional changes took place in 1989: One constitutional amendment led to the abolition of the office of prime minister and strengthened the office of the presidency to take its place. Iran's president is elected under universal suffrage, and election requires an absolute majority of votes. The term of office is four years and subject to a term limit of no more than eight consecutive years. The president chooses cabinet members, presents legislation to the parliament, and is entrusted to uphold the constitution and coordinate government decisions; however, the president is not strong enough to dominate thoroughly both the government and the legislature due to the executive power being divided between the president and the supreme leader (see Figure 11.2).

Iran is a semipresidential system in which the legislative branch is much less powerful than the executive branch, and executive power is bifurcated between the president and the supreme leader. The supreme leader is the country's most powerful political figure. In the name of upholding the Islamic state, he has the authority to overrule or dismiss the president, appoint the head of the judiciary and half of the members of the Guardian Council, and appoint the top echelons of the military. Initially, the supreme leader was required to be one of the highest-ranking Shi'i clerics and would be elected and periodically reconfirmed by the Assembly of Experts. While Ayatollah Ruhollah Khomeini (1902–1989) was alive, he was the undisputed supreme leader.[6] Upon Khomeini's death in 1989, another key amendment was introduced. In a triumph of political convenience over doctrinal coherence, the qualification for the supreme leader was downgraded from needing to be the highest-ranking cleric to being an established member of the clergy with a solid political-revolutionary pedigree. As such, the Assembly of Experts chose Ali Khamenei, a long-time lieutenant of Ayatollah Khomeini, as the new supreme leader. This smooth transition of power had none of the hallmarks of the succession crises besetting other revolutionary states.

Over the course of the last thirty some years, Khamenei has amassed a disproportionate amount of power through bureaucratic aggrandizement and use of informal politics. Thanks to "institutional assets" and "informal leverage" at his disposal, he has been able to bypass democratic rules enshrined in the constitution; emasculate such bodies as the Assembly of Experts,

FIGURE 11.2 ■ Structure of Power in Iran

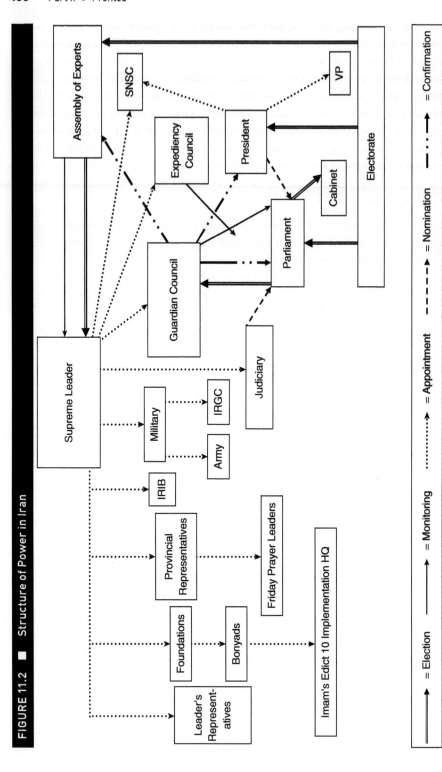

Source: Mehrzad Boroujerdi and Kourosh Rahimkhani, *Postrevolutionary Iran: A Political Handbook* (Syracuse, NY: Syracuse University Press, 2018), 37. Reprinted with permission.

the Guardian Council, and the parliament; and subdue the religious seminaries. These institutions have not demonstrated any serious proclivity to be independent from the supreme leader. Today, neither the press nor the proper governmental bodies can in reality investigate any of the organs under the supreme leader, nor can anyone overrule him.

The Guardian Council is a twelve-member council that, jointly with the supreme leader, has veto power over any legislation passed by the parliament that is deemed to be at odds with the basic tenets of Islam. In a sense, the Guardian Council operates like the upper house of parliament. Another important power granted to this council is the right to determine who can run in presidential, parliamentary, and Assembly of Experts elections. The council is made up of six clerical members who are appointed by the supreme leader and six lay members (lawyers) who are recommended by the head of the judiciary, subject to the approval of the parliament. While the six lawyers vote mainly on the question of the constitutionality of legislation, the clerical members consider the conformity of legislation to Islamic principles. The members of the Guardian Council are supposed to serve six-year terms. However, halfway through their term, three clerical members and three lay legal jurists will change, based on a lottery system to create staggered terms.

The Assembly of Experts is an eighty-eight-member assembly charged with evaluating the performance of the supreme leader. The Assembly is itself popularly elected, but it consists almost entirely of clerics because candidates must pass an examination on religious knowledge to be eligible.

The parliament is made up of 290 deputies who are elected by direct and secret ballot for four-year terms. The Iranian parliament is not a rubber-stamp institution. Thanks to the constant state of factional infighting among the elite, the parliament has been a rather boisterous arena where acrimonious debates (even fistfights) take place. The government is often obliged to lobby strongly to move legislation through the chamber. The regularity of elections has helped to institutionalize the place of parliament in political life, and the parliamentary elections can serve as a barometer of electoral sentiment. This barometer seems to show that anticlericalism is on the rise, as demonstrated by the fact that the percentage of clerics in the parliament has dropped 41 percent between 1980 and 2021.

Faced with frequent and serious policy disputes between the Guardian Council and the parliament, the ruling elite decided in 1988 to create yet another council, the Expediency Assembly (formally known as the Expediency Discernment Assembly of the State). Composed of about three dozen leading political personalities, this body is entrusted with the task of resolving any policy disputes in a way that serves the interest of the entire system. It also advises national leaders on matters of grave national importance. The council is made up of juristic members (clerical jurists of the Guardian Council, heads of the three branches of government, and cabinet ministers and parliament committee chairs) and natural members specifically named by the supreme leader. The current term is five years.

The judiciary, along with the supreme leader and the Guardian Council, is the third pillar of clerical political power. It is the most controversial of the three branches of government due to the fact that the supreme leader appoints the head of the judiciary who, by definition, must be a cleric.[7] According to the constitution (Article 156), the court system is supposedly independent, but its political role in practice reflects the ideological composition of judges who are quite uniformly conservative clerics either wholly opposed to or, rather, suspicious of allowing legal reform. They fear that removing brakes on dissent and personal behavior will allow liberal opponents to hijack the public sphere and eventually the state. The Supreme Court can prosecute the president but not the supreme leader. In a clear violation of their parliamentary immunity, the judiciary has on occasion summoned MPs regarding statements they made during parliamentary debates. The Revolutionary Courts are broadly responsible for judging certain offenses such as crimes against national security; insulting the founder of the Islamic Republic or the supreme leader; terrorism, espionage, conspiracy, or armed rebellion against the state; and trafficking in narcotic drugs.

Meanwhile, the constitution gives the parliament the right to investigate complaints concerning the work of the executive and judicial branches. The judiciary is constrained by such factors as an excessive volume of legal and penal cases, a shortage of judges, budgetary constraints, a burgeoning prison population, a rampant drug culture, and the large number of crime categories (1,500–1,600 categories of crimes, of which 70 percent to 80 percent warrant a prison sentence). The judiciary has been criticized by a wide variety of international human rights organizations for right abuses, and some of its high-profile judges are on US or European Union sanctions lists. Furthermore, according to Amnesty International, Iran executes more people (including juvenile offenders) than any other country besides China. The court system also enforces censorship laws to curtail public debates.

Constitution

After the 1979 revolution, shari'a, supplemented by laws to address modern conditions, was restored as the core of the legal system. A constitution ratified in December 1979 regarded "Islamic law" as "state law," and it became the foundation of Iran's social order, but the constitution is full of latent and manifest contradictions. Thanks to its ideological character, the constitution was riddled with oddities and paradoxes, as it simultaneously affirmed both religious and secular principles, democratic and antidemocratic tendencies, and populist and elitist predilections. The antiquity and the private character of shari'a law made it rather ill-equipped to deal with the legal and public needs of a modern, stratified polity. To deal with the anachronisms, complications, and inconsistencies resulting from the gap between text and practice, leaders increasingly resorted to the exigency of the state argument to circumvent the letter, as well as the spirit of shari'a.

Hence, while the constitution helped to establish a theocracy, the eclectic qualities of the society were such that secular agents, aspirations, ideas, institutions, language, and motifs continued to survive and—more importantly—manifested their significance in private and public space. These paradoxes gave rise to numerous debates concerning the politics of legal arrangements. For example, according to the constitution, the president has to be from the Shi'i sect and be a "well-known political personality." The sectarian qualification automatically disenfranchises Sunni Muslims, Christians, Jews, Zoroastrians, Bahá'ís, and other religious minorities. Furthermore, the vaguely worded "well-known political personality" clause has so far been interpreted to mean that it applies only to men, thereby allowing the Guardian Council to bar those women who wish to stand for election as president. Critics complain of many other inequities in how shari'a handles women's rights and family law. Although some controversial practices are due more to traditional and patriarchal social conditions than to shari'a, still there are rigidities in shari'a that cannot adequately be overcome through revisions, given the understanding of its sources.

In the age-old tradition of political tokenism, the constitution mandates that small "recognized" religious minorities—Christians, Jews, and Zoroastrians—have a total of five seats reserved to them in the parliament. This qualification also means that unrecognized religious minorities like the Bahá'ís cannot be represented in parliament.

Military Forces

The military establishment is made up of the regular army and the IRGC. The relationship between the IRGC and the clerical establishment during the past four decades has been both fluid and multifaceted. During the first decade of the revolution (1979–1989), the IRGC was a political factor but not a major political player independent of the clerical establishment. This was to a large extent due to two main factors: Ayatollah Khomeini's formal stricture forbidding military personnel from becoming involved in partisan politics and the preoccupation of the military with the Iran–Iraq War (Box 11.1). Mindful of the crucial role the IRGC was playing in the war, the clerical leadership allowed a short-lived (1982–1989) ministerial post for the IRGC. In 1989, with the conclusion of the Iran–Iraq War and the death of Ayatollah Khomeini, the civilian leadership tried to emasculate the IRGC by taking away its ministerial post and attempting to unite the IRGC and the regular army into a unified command structure. The latter effort failed, and each was allowed to keep a separate organizational structure and ground, air, and naval forces. This convoluted arrangement was made even more byzantine by the fact that the IRGC has two other forces as well: the Quds Force and the Basij Resistance Force. The Quds Force (Jerusalem Brigade) serves as the IRGC's overseas fighting force and advises foreign allied forces; the paramilitary Basij Resistance Force played an important role in the war against Iraq and was later used for internal security roles.

When President Akbar Hashemi-Rafsanjani (1934–2017) came to office in 1989, he embarked on a project to reconstruct the war-torn economy. The IRGC became involved in numerous economic activities, thanks to its political ties, its technological know-how, and the government's desire to provide the IRGC with financial autonomy in return for the services the corps had rendered in the course of the eight-year war. The IRGC set up numerous financial and economic enterprises that would then receive no-bid contracts. The IRGC also set up front organizations and quasi-state firms that were able to secure lucrative oil and gas contracts. Despite President Hashemi-Rafsanjani's willingness to strengthen the private sector, certain factors forced him and his successors to grant large projects to the engineering subsidiary of the IRGC. These factors included work in sensitive areas; security considerations in restive provinces; the need to meet quick deadlines; and requirements for a readily available workforce that could undertake large-scale projects like constructing tunnels, ports, dams, bridges, and oil and gas pipelines.

BOX 11.1

THE IRAN–IRAQ WAR, 1980–1988

In the early 1970s, Iran's relations with its neighbor Iraq were often strained. The ruling Ba'th Party in Iraq was secular and Sunni, while the majority of Iraqis are Shi'a with established links in Iran. Senior clerics from both countries studied together in the 1950s and 1960s at the religious centers in Najaf, Iraq, and Qom, Iran. Not only did this often promote a common ideology, but it also encouraged the migration of clerics from one country to the other. In 1969, Tehran was implicated in an attempted coup against the newly established Ba'thist government in Baghdad. The following years were tense, but good relations returned when both countries signed the Algiers Agreement in 1975, with Iran agreeing to stop supporting the Kurdish rebellion in return for territorial concessions from Iraq. After the Islamic revolution, however, Iraq again viewed Iran with suspicion, fearing another Shi'i revolt against the Ba'thist government in Baghdad. Border confrontations ensued, and Iraq retaliated with a bombing campaign in September 1980, beginning a long and bloody eight-year war.

The war against Iraq prolonged the revolutionary spirit in Iran, providing the backdrop for the government to further institutionalize the more radical elements of the Islamic Republic. Hundreds of thousands were mobilized by ideology and volunteered their own lives to challenge the military superiority of the Iraqis. In the end, thousands of young men were killed. Portraits of martyrs were painted on signs and buildings throughout cities, and streets were also renamed after the fallen. Various foundations were set up to take care of the families of the war wounded and martyred, creating new social networks of privilege. Both sides experienced dramatic losses during the course of the war, with official Iranian reports putting the number of those killed at 159,000 and many more thousands wounded. The war ended in 1988 with a United Nations–brokered cease-fire.

The prevalence of regional conflicts (including the Iran–Iraq War, the Arab–Israeli dispute, Afghanistan, Iraq, and Syria) combined with the tapestry of real and perceived domestic and international insecurities of the state has paved the way for the IRGC to enter the inner sanctums of power. Commensurate with its increasing economic power, the IRGC began to flex its muscles in the political domain as well. In July 1999, twenty-four high-level IRGC commanders published a threatening letter of ultimatum to reformist President Mohammad Khatami (b. 1943) about dealing with student protests. Meanwhile, numerous other IRGC members have exchanged their military uniforms for civilian careers as cabinet ministers, members of parliament, provincial governors, ambassadors, cultural attachés, journalists and newspaper editors, university administrators, directors of think tanks and foundations, business leaders, and chiefs of industrial companies. They have also become candidates in successive presidential elections.

The IRGC is entrusted with maintaining internal security while the army safeguards the borders. Unlike many other countries in the region with long histories of military coups, Iran's military has so far not played an open interventionist role in the country's politics, and the top brass has remained extremely loyal to the supreme leader. So far, the military has respected the orderly transfer of power. The veterans of the IRGC (and the Iran–Iraq War) have increasingly permeated the bureaucracy, economy, and government and will retain influence for the foreseeable future. Being in charge of the hydra-headed military-security institutions and championing the initial élan of the revolution, this constituency by and large shares the security outlook of the current supreme leader and has augmented its agenda-setting power. Yet it does not have the requisite cultural capital or street credibility to appeal to the broad urban public as political actors.

ELITES, PUBLIC OPINION, PARTIES, AND ELECTIONS

The intellectual rifts within the ranks of the officialdom have led to an ongoing tug-of-war between reformers and conservatives. This has produced not only a contentious domestic scene but also a fundamental change in the political culture and discourse of the country. Over the last four decades, the public has been involved in an internal conversation regarding the merits (or lack thereof) of the political systems of theocracy, democracy infused with religious sensibilities, and the nature of relations with the West. Opposition to today's regime has a range of content. Most people in what we might call the "loyal opposition" aim to reform the system but retain the basic principle of an Islamic state. Some see changing the Islamic Republic as a part of a larger effort to revitalize Islam for modern conditions. An influential group of critics, including the remnants of the pre-1979 upper and middle classes, seek a more radical break with clerical rule and a return to secularism. The political opposition across all of these differences remains fragmented and thus weak. Neither has any branch of the opposition, loyal Islamic or radical secular, made many inroads into crucial groups such as the clergy and the military. Against this background, the divisions within the state and across political subcultures continue to deepen in a country that has come to experience an "integrative revolution" (i.e., an explosion of political mobilization and participation).

While the establishment of a theocratic state improved the social standing and economic well-being of a good number of clerics, it also came to hurt many others. The corruption and unseemly luxurious lifestyle of those clergymen who could skim off revenue from state and semiofficial foundations called clerical legitimacy into question. As religion became tainted with the impurities and utilitarian compromises of politics and as clerics became civil servants, many citizens began to view them as overly traditionalist, ill-informed, corrupt, power-hungry, and opportunistic. Iranians managed to undermine or at least dilute the severity of the clergy's pronouncements by resorting to adroit humor, conspiracy theories, cynicism, dissimulation, symbolic discourse, and outright dissent.

One of the ironies of Iranian politics is the fact that citizens have not so far benefited from the presence of recognized, legitimate, or effective political parties. The most important political party, the Islamic Republic Party (established in February 1979), was dissolved in June 1987 on the order of Ayatollah Khomeini because of factional infighting in its ranks. For the next decade, there was a ban on any party formation. Political parties were finally legalized again in 1998, but they are still at an early stage of development and policy formation, and party discipline remains embryonic. Today, there are more than 240 registered "parties," but a great majority of them resemble professional groupings interested in policy issues. The largest party representing the reformist camp, the Islamic Iran Participation Front, was officially formed in December 1998 and banned in August 2010. Other established political entities also function more or less as political parties representing the reformists or the conservatives.

The Islamic Republic of Iran has managed to institutionalize elections. During its first four decades years in power, the Islamic Republic has had a remarkable number (38 as of 2021) of parliamentary, presidential, Assembly of Experts, and municipal council elections. Because of Iran's record of almost one election per year, one can say that electoral politics is now an ingrained part of the polity. Elections reflect the influence of various power centers, and they have also become a way of integrating various social groups into the political system. These functions should be understood against the background of the country's dramatic demographic transformation. Thanks to a population boom, the total number of eligible voters has increased threefold from 20 million people in 1979 to more than 59 million in 2021.

Until recently, elections were generally competitive, usually with high voter turnout (despite the high frequency of elections), and showed a candidate-to-seat ratio of better than 10 to 1. Both the contestation and participation dimensions of democracy are present, unlike in nearly all of the Arab Middle East. Yet elections are not synonymous with democratic governance. Not unlike elections under communist rule, voters have to choose from a set of hand-picked candidates. Candidates for office must be approved by the Guardian Council, an approval based on their familiarity with Islamic doctrine, revolutionary credentials, and broad acceptance of the principles of the revolution and theocratic state. This leads to prior disqualification of many presidential and legislative candidates in each election without the need for the Guardian Council to even provide an explanation for its actions.

Civil Society

As the new regime consolidated its authority, it showed no restraint in its willingness to encroach on individual and civil rights or dismantle civil initiatives and institutions all in the name of "safeguarding the welfare of the community." Yet the civil society managed to wage a tenacious fight. Many factors explain the logic behind this resistance. Chief among them is the demographic transformation as the citizenry becomes increasingly urbanized and educated. Moreover, the growing distance from the experience of the shah's rule and the revolution has made many youths reject as moribund the values promoted by the Islamic regime. Westernized sectors of the population retain interests in modern entertainment and global liberal ideology. The clergy's efforts to restrict what it believes to be contamination influences of satellite television and the Internet have proved fruitless.[8] In their "home territory," many Iranians treat Western popular culture as an invisible guest. In other words, modern cultural traditions and icons may have been driven underground, but their presence can still be felt.

Another paradox is the fact that the citizenry has come to enjoy an era of intellectual prosperity while living under a politically repressive state. The past four decades have seen an explosion of publications, a booming translation industry, and a thriving world-class cinema. These forums have ensured that Iran has a fairly lively public sphere. The boundaries of press freedom are clear on certain issues and blurred on others: There can be no criticism of Islamic doctrine or its revered personalities. No criticisms of Ayatollah Khomeini and Ayatollah Khamenei and their cult of personalities are permitted. Discussing sensitive issues of national security is also frowned upon by the state.

Notwithstanding this war against intellectual dissent and the pernicious brands of state and self-imposed censorship, Iranians enjoy an interesting print media. In addition to the government-owned and opposition newspapers, there are several hundred general and professional journals dealing with sports, economics, cinema, linguistics, health care, technology, the fine arts, and other subjects. Many of these journals manage to articulate a nonpolitical yet subtle criticism of the regime in their respective areas of expertise. In the region, the Iranian press is relatively free to criticize the government's domestic and foreign policies. Exposing the country's social ills or the government's managerial ineptitude, economic blunders, and foreign policy flip-flops is considered a legitimate journalistic practice.

Political Socialization

Political socialization in Iran during the second half of the 20th century and the first two decades of the 21st century can best be described as fragmented. Huge gaps existed between the values of different social groups. Western influence under the shah extended through members of the upper and middle classes who embraced liberal and technocratic values and showed some willingness to repress opponents for the sake of orderly modernization. Much Western influence came through Iranians who studied abroad (51,000 were studying in the United States in 1979). The postrevolutionary state has had to deal with the candid calls by a critical mass of prosecular technocrats, professionals, and industrialists for the liberalization of the educational system, relaxation of artistic and cultural restraints, abandonment of cultural xenophobia toward the West, and legal moderation.

Millions participated in the demonstrations that brought down the shah's government, and millions more have taken part in more than three dozen postrevolutionary elections. In this environment, students and youth in general have gained enormous political weight as elementary and secondary, and (as of 2020) university students have come to make up 31 percent of Iran's total population. A number of restrictions on individuals drew criticism. Many feminists object to the regulations on women's rights, including attire derived from an Islamic framework. Many people object to the regulated flow of information in the old and new media, as the state blocks millions of Internet sites to keep out "cultural pollution." Finally, the orthodox Islamic character of the state politically marginalizes religious minorities.

SOCIAL CHANGES AND CHALLENGES

In the decades before the revolution, Iran's population was rapidly urbanizing. Although the country began the 20th century as an agricultural society, by 1979 there were more Iranians living in cities than in rural areas. Crowded cities created new social pressures. Today, there are more than a dozen different ethnic minorities, including Turkic-speaking Azeris in the northwest, Gilakis and Mazandaranis in the north, Kurds in the northwest, Baluchis in the southeast, and Arabs along the southwest coast. In this patchwork of identities, the cleavages of ethnicity, language, and religion often cut across one another rather than overlap.

Each of the country's social classes has fared differently. The peasantry and urban, lower-middle class, the strong bases of religious orthodoxy, benefited somewhat from the patronage of revolutionary organizations and the state bureaucracy that provided them with some amenities like electricity and paved roads or outright subsidies. They have their own discontents, however, because of the overall poor performance of the country's economy and water scarcity.

Resistance to clerical rule by fiat has been most evident among Iran's stoic, and predominantly secular, middle class. As the middle class's economic capital has drastically shrunk, they hang on more than ever to their most precious badge of honor: cultural capital—the general cultural background, knowledge, disposition, and skills that are passed from one generation to the next. The middle class is irreconcilably lukewarm toward the clergy. Along with the upper, they are the strongest source of opposition to the regime. Other important social groups that have been politically relevant are women and youth.

In the decades before 1979, the shah's regime changed a number of legal and social practices in an effort to align gender relations with a modern, secular model. Family and divorce laws were changed, for example, and Western attire and mixed gatherings in public became normal custom for the upper and middle classes. Since the revolution, the Islamic Republic has sought to address women's concerns within the framework of Islamic law and gender complementarity—"equality-with-difference." Many of the shah's reforms were nullified. Divorce and custody laws now follow Islamic standards, and many see the restrictions on women's attire as repressive. It should be appreciated, of course, that these new regulations were mainly a restoration of traditional practices that the more conservative lower and middle classes had never fully abandoned. There are legal restrictions on women's ability to leave the country without the consent of male relatives. Women face numerous challenges in initiating divorce or gaining custody of their children under Islamic law. The legal system enforces sexual restraint in principle. The number of runaway girls has increased, and prostitution is reportedly widespread.

In a society where women's rights have been trampled, women continue to make important strides into the educational, cultural, and employment domains, thereby increasing awareness of women's rights and issues at the social level. Women's participation in public life has also increased. As the size of the nuclear family has decreased, women's demands for greater educational and employment opportunities, as well as social participation, have risen. School enrollment rates for boys and girls are now close to parity. Women's opportunities for education and professional advancement have expanded in many ways. Almost half of college students are now female. These factors can contribute to the further democratization of family life and institutionalization of political democracy.

Yet gender disparity still exists. According to Statistical Center of Iran, women labor force participation in 2020 was 14.1 percent, which is slightly higher than it was at the end of the Shah's regime in 1976 (13.8 percent). Furthermore, on average, women make up 3.8 percent of the national legislature, and over the last four decades, there was only one female government minister, who served as health minister for 39 months. The limits on political participation remain blurry, however, because some debate lingers over whether a woman can constitutionally be elected president. Tensions remain unresolved between women who sub-scribe to the Islamic and the secular versions of feminism.

Young people also present a major social challenge for Iran's leaders. Because 49 percent of today's population is younger than thirty, the majority of Iranians are too young to remember the revolution. Furthermore, a sagging, nonoil economy has produced high levels of youth unemployment (23.7 percent for 15–24-year-olds as of 2020), even though the majority of this population is well educated.

RELIGION AND POLITICS

Although Islam was introduced into Iran in the 7th century, Shi'ism was not officially recognized as the state religion until the beginning of the 16th century. Ironically enough, this took place around the time when Martin Luther's movement led to the emergence of a schism in Christianity that eventually led to the secularization of political life in Europe. Soon after coming to power in 1501, the Safavid dynasty declared Shi'ism as the state religion as a way of distinguishing themselves from the rulers of the Sunni-dominated, neighboring Ottoman Empire who considered themselves the sole Islamic caliphs. The clerical class came to enjoy the patronage of the Safavid kings.

The clerical polity in today's Iran differ in important ways with Islamist movements elsewhere. Most of the differences relate in some way to its Shi'i character, as opposed to the Sunni movements that predominate elsewhere. The greater importance of the clergy in Shi'i Islam is reflected in the semitheocratic form of the state. Islamist movements in other locations rest on a pious but lay stratum of intellectuals and lower-middle-class activists. Given the collaboration of much of the Sunni clergy with secular authoritarian states, such resistance has often been quite suspicious of clerics. Sunni Islam has tended to be quite austere and rigidly defined by a vision of shari'a law. The Shi'i clergy, both historically and in its current political role, has shown itself more disposed to innovate. Although the Shi'i clerical leadership has claimed to protect tradition, it has had to amend and break numerous age-old religious protocols for the sake of state expediency. The esoteric tradition, in which the Shi'i clergy saw itself as having access to sophisticated hidden meanings within Islam, undoubtedly has something to do with this flexibility. Also important are the highly unstructured nature of clerical oligarchy and the permissive character of Shi'i theological reasoning.

The central theoretical principle of the Islamic Republic of Iran is the theory of *velayat-e faqih* (jurist's guardianship) developed by Ayatollah Ruhollah Khomeini. During his fifteen years of exile in Iraq, he articulated an innovative system of political thought, which was a minority position among the highest-ranking Shi'i theologians. Breaking from the pattern of withdrawal from politics as a realm of injustice, Khomeini argued that the clergy must take a leading role in a modern Islamic state. Shi'i clergy who are familiar with Islamic theology and law should oversee such a state. Khomeini's thinking was influenced by Plato's ideal of the philosopher-kings, specially educated elite who would rule justly within a hierarchical social order. His charisma, imbued with all sorts of revolutionary credentials and religious mythology, led to the formation of a personality cult that has outlived him.

The state embraced and then attempted to disseminate Khomeini's views on Iran's identity, public affairs, and political socialization. This caused a number of major disagreements within the polity. One bone of contention between the clerically dominated state and its secular opponents was the question of nationalism and pre-Islamic Iranian identity. The Islamic regime initially had a troublesome relationship with ancient Persian lineage, customs, traditions, artifacts, and festivals. In their attempt to properly "Islamicize" the cultural reference point of citizens, they felt that they had to simultaneously fight Western cultural influences while deprogramming Iranians from any attachment to their notions of pre-Islamic values. They reluctantly realized that diluting the richness of Iranian culture was not an easy task and that they had no choice but to coexist with pre-Islamic Iranian culture, symbols, practices, and identity since the people were not going to abandon them. The clerics also had to digest a speedy ideological rapprochement with Iranian nationalism as the war with Iraq broke out in 1980. Those who had lamented nationalism as an insidious ideology for Muslims now had to wrap themselves in its mantle, embrace its iconography, and partake of its passionate discourse. While the war with Iraq enabled the members of the clergy to consolidate their power and subdue their opponents, the hostilities also bolstered Iranians' sense of self-confidence and national pride.

Khomeini's theocratic vision for Iran did not just alienate the secular nationalists, religious minorities, and those Shi'i Muslims who were not fastidiously religious; even some of the lay religious intellectuals found themselves objecting to the ideas and ideals of Khomeini and his lieutenants. Some objected to the use of state power to administer religious principles, while others rejected the clerics' claim that they have the conclusive grasp of Islam. For example, the philosopher Abdolkarim Sorush argued that the Shi'i clergy as a class is intellectually stagnant. He charged that instead of being contemporaneous, the clerics are mired in the past, and as such, their ideas and actions are incompatible with the complicated reality of the modern world. Furthermore, he maintained that part of the Iranian Shi'i establishment has become afflicted with the same type of disease as their Sunni counterparts—that is, they have become dependent on state handouts. Sorush argued that mixing religion and state power is not in the interest of religion because it will force the religious seminaries to speak the language of power and not that of logic, and it turns clerics into ideologues (Box 11.2).

BOX 11.2
UNDERSTANDING SHI'ISM

The Shi'i–Sunni split occurred during the mid-7th century over the question of who was eligible to succeed Prophet Muhammad (d. 632) as the new caliph (loosely analogous to the Catholic papacy). Sunni Muslims held that succession should flow to the ablest leader of the Islamic community, whereas Shi'a (today, some 15 percent of Muslims worldwide) maintained that legitimate rulership of the entire Islamic community could descend only through the heirs of the Prophet Muhammad. Shi'a accordingly consider Ali, a cousin of Muhammad who also married Muhammad's daughter, to have been the Prophet's rightful successor. In

661 CE, rivals assassinated Ali. His supporters, calling themselves Shi'at Ali, or the partisans of Ali, revolted against the Sunnis but were defeated in 680 at Karbala in present-day Iraq. Their leader, Hussein, Ali's youngest son, was killed. Large numbers of Shi'a fled to Persia.

Of the several Shi'i sects that were eventually formed, Twelve Shi'ism dominates in Iran. Their principal belief is that spiritual and temporal leadership of the Muslim community, in the person of the imam,[9] passed from the Prophet Muhammad to Ali, the first imam, and continued on to eleven of his direct male descendants. The twelfth and final imam is believed to have gone into hiding in the year 874 because of Sunni persecution and will reappear as the Mahdi, or messiah, on the day of divine judgment. Since then, Shi'a have held on to the messianic belief that the "hidden Imam" will return at the end of time and restore a just order. Shi'i political thinkers historically have held, based on these doctrines, that in the interim all secular authority is ultimately illegitimate.

Hence, compared with Sunni Islam, Shi'ism has remained more critical of monarchs and less fully reconciled with the political order. At best, the *Shi'i ulema* (religious authorities) would extend a provisional legitimacy to rulers who let Islamic institutions flourish unmolested. The *ulema* itself came to stand in collectively for the hidden Imam in his absence.[10] Over the centuries, they functioned as the conscience of the Shi'i community and thus occupied a role similar to that of the Christian priesthood in premodern Europe or the Confucian mandarins in premodern China.

Certain distinct features of religion–state relations bear noting, however. Compared with the Confucian mandarins, the Shi'i *ulema* were far more hostile to power holders and enjoyed more independence. Their religious functions were separate from the state and were usually unaffected by it. They also enjoyed a strong institutional base. They were self-organized in informal hierarchies that rested only on the esteem in which religious scholars held one another. They also had secure income from the voluntary religious taxes paid by the believers, as well as by mosques and charitable endowments inviolable under Islamic law.

Compared with the Christian priests, Shi'i *ulema* often refused to make peace with secular authorities based on the customary dividing line between church and state. Islamic doctrine has held that religion and politics flow into one another, as aspects of a comprehensive Islamic society. Rule by monarchs other than the hidden Imam was always viewed, therefore, as an unnatural condition—even if inevitable at the time. The Shi'i *ulema*'s withdrawal from political life before modern times reflected a desire to be untainted by the prevailing injustice, not a sense that some spheres of life lay outside the scope of religion. Hence, the religion–state relationship has always been problematic.

POLITICAL ECONOMY

When the clergy consolidated its political power in the early 1980s, it found itself in a predicament. It was a religious elite that had expanded its role horizontally, so to speak, to become a political elite as well. Yet it lacked any practical experience with the demands of governing. During its long history of eschewing involvement with secular authority, the Shi'i clergy had never held pure political power. It thus had few resources on which to draw when fulfilling the largely economic responsibilities of a modern state. Added to this inexperience were several pressures that worsened Iran's economic situation in the early 1980s: the nationalization of many large firms, massive emigration of skilled professionals, a decline in foreign investment, a drop in oil prices on the international market, and restructuring for the war effort and the burdens of the eight-year war with Iraq. All were complex pressures that cut across the domestic and international spheres.

Coupled with these circumstances was an intense ideological debate among factions of the clergy. The economic implications and agenda of the revolution had not been defined at the outset. Hence different factions could claim to speak for the revolution while upholding different views and agendas. The three major currents are usually identified as pragmatists, radicals, and conservatives. Pragmatists saw economic recovery as Iran's highest priority. They favored liberal economic policies such as restoration of foreign trade, removal of state controls, facilitation of foreign direct investment, and privatization of state-owned companies and banks. Radicals, with their base among younger and more militant clerics, called for measures to enhance social justice through traditional state intervention, price controls, and wealth redistribution. In the radicals' eyes, the revolution belonged to Iran's poorer strata. Land redistribution and assertion of national economic independence—with the accompanying suspicion of economic ties to the West—figured among their demands.

The higher-ranking conservative clerics, many of whom had personal ties to the bazaaris and rural landowners, reacted strongly against the radicals' vision. They affirmed sanctity of private property under Islamic law. Tensions among these factions persisted after the revolution, driven by the intersection between ideology and social base. This debate over economic priorities and justice is a good case of the "social question" that comes to the fore in any revolution.

A Rentier State

The 1979 revolution somewhat diminished Iran's status as a rentier state, as oil (including crude oil, gas, and petrochemicals) came to account for 67 percent of Iran's export commodities and 35 percent of government revenue. The country's economic woes have included disruption caused by the revolution; the devastation caused by the eight-year war with Iraq; legal ambiguities in the meting out of revolutionary justice; political and ideological infighting among the ruling elite; low labor productivity; shortages of investment capital, raw materials, and spare parts; a brain drain and flight of capital; peasant migration to the cities; and fluctuations in the global price of oil. Iran's most formidable economic problems, however, have been unemployment and deleterious effects of sanctions. Iran suffers from high unemployment (officially put at 9.8 percent but according to the research arm of the parliament, the real rate may be closer to 24 percent) because of the youth bulge, and the country has a high and unstable rate of inflation (officially put at 45 percent in 2021). The cumulative impact of these economic ills has been a dramatic rise in the number of unhappy and unemployed people, falling incomes, rising debts, and unrelenting job insecurity.

President Hashemi-Rafsanjani's era (1989–1997) saw a shift toward market-oriented pragmatism. Large numbers of technocrats—less concerned with ideology than with economic performance—were appointed to policy-making posts. Foreign trade expanded, especially with a range of developed countries in Europe and East Asia. Yet the economy remained under severe pressure throughout the 1990s, and a rising foreign debt required frequent rescheduling. Its finances squeezed by plunging oil prices; the government had to adopt an austerity budget while meeting its high external debt-repayment obligations.

Thanks to the cushion provided by the constant flow of petrodollars, there have been no economic catastrophes, but the government needs to undertake a Herculean effort to invigorate its economy. To revitalize the economy, the government needs to lower inflation, increase foreign exchange reserves, improve domestic productivity, create job opportunities, expand foreign and domestic investment, boost nonoil exports, strengthen the national currency, increase people's purchasing power, streamline the bureaucracy, and reduce government expenditures. Accomplishing even a few of these goals is a tall order, particularly in light of such impediments, as the relegation of the private sector to small-scale economic activities, the agricultural sector's dwindling significance, the operation of inefficient firms and foundations, subsidies for various essential commodities, sanctions, and the nonnegligible costs of foreign aid and military expenditures in such countries as Iraq, Lebanon, and Syria. Rising oil prices generates moderate growth, but reliance on one primary export creates long-term vulnerabilities. When oil prices plunge, the government faces severe cash shortages, fluctuations in social spending, and other financial shortfalls. Many economic experts recommend cultivating warmer ties with foreign investors. This debate reflects a broader contest between economic agendas. The radical social justice faction that prevailed in the early years of the revolution and reemerged under President Mahmoud Ahmadinejad's reign (2005–2013) advocated economic self-sufficiency as a goal. When Hasan Rouhani assumed the presidency in 2013, he decided to resolve the nuclear issue and the lifting of sanctions as a prelude to attract foreign trade and uplift Iran's economy. His administration was convinced that Iran was attractive to foreign investors, thanks to its massive oil and gas reserves, impressive human capital, technology infrastructure, and being the Middle East's largest potential market. President Trump's withdrawal from the nuclear deal put an end to such optimism.

Iran clearly has a state-dominated and highly politicized economic system where power is concentrated in the hands of the public sector. The informal economy is no less politicized. The bazaar merchants have been historically central to the economy and society as they have constituted the backbone of economic flows throughout the country. Faced by the challenge posed by the more modern sectors of the economy under the shah and the fact that they did not enjoy political representation equal to their economic weight, the bazaar merchants allied themselves with the clergy against the shah and financed many of the revolutionary activities. After the revolution, they came to enjoy a great deal of political and economic power. However, their fortunes have also been negatively impacted over the course of the past four decades, owing to economic regulations, sanctions, and the broader restructuring of trade patterns that have taken on a more modern and impersonal coloring. The cumulative effect of these changes has been to loosen the bazaaris' networks and mutual trust and reduce their political mobilizing capacity.

Any discussion of Iran's informal economy should make mention of the role of the myriad quasi-private foundations and religious endowments called *bonyads* that manage state-owned enterprises. These large conglomerates have a substantial grip on Iran's economy through their monopolistic and rent-seeking transactions. Vast amounts of property expropriated from the shah's family and other members of the old elite passed to state-run foundations and *bonyads*. These foundations became a key patronage mechanism, locking in the clergy's leverage over large sectors of the economy.

Public Policy

Social welfare in Iran, as elsewhere in the Islamic world, was traditionally a matter of private charity and funding from *waqf* endowments. The 1979 revolution affected indexes of social well-being in a number of ways. The Islamic Republic made social welfare a high priority, viewing it as a precondition for spiritual well-being.[11] The social justice legacy of the revolution has been manifested especially in four decades of massive effort in education and health. According to the United Nations Development Programme, "between 1990 and 2019, Iran's life expectancy at birth increased by 12.8 years, [and] mean years of schooling increased by 6.1 years. Iran's Gross national Income per capita rose about 43.5 percent between 1990 and 2019."[12] Educational opportunities, including for women, have greatly expanded. Although many female doctors have received training, the plan to create two parallel health systems segregated by gender, in accordance with Islamic principles, has not advanced (except in the case of the fields of obstetrics and gynecology). Yet despite the improvements, in 2000, Iran's health care system was still ranked 93 out of 190 by the World Health Organization. The country faces major problems, including a large subculture of drug users (estimated at more than two million). According to the UNAIDS, in 2021, there were also fifty-nine thousand cases of AIDS. Iranian authorities badly handled the COVID-19 pandemic. They were late in acknowledging the reality of the pandemic and could not afford to tell the citizenry to quarantine due to their empty coffers, and most importantly the supreme leader unwisely banned the importation of US- and UK-made vaccines in January 2021. By the last quarter of 2021, the official number of confirmed cases stood at 5.3 million and that of confirmed deaths was 115,000. Most analysts, however, believe the actual numbers are much higher than the official statistics.

One area of public policy where the government has been impressively successful has been in bringing down the birthrate. Births surged in a pronatalist campaign in the early 1980s. Eventually, however, this policy caused demographic pressure from a youth bulge. Faced with the challenges of high unemployment (3–4 million) and the political discontent of a sizable workforce (more than 27.3 million in 2018), the clergy approved policies to lower the birthrate and reduce long-term burdens from overpopulation. By 1986, the population growth rate, which was 2.7 percent in 1976, had risen to 3.9 percent. The government decided to reverse course and discouraged having large families. Thanks to a series of initiatives and social trends, such as mandatory sex education classes for couples getting married, a rise in the marriage age, and the greater educational and professional opportunities open to women, the government managed to bring the population growth rate down to 1.03 percent by 2021.

Less progress has been made with regard to the environment. Environmental protection efforts during the latter years of the Pahlavi regime focused on conservation, including wildlife preservation and the founding of national parks. The Islamic Republic has paid lip service to ecological

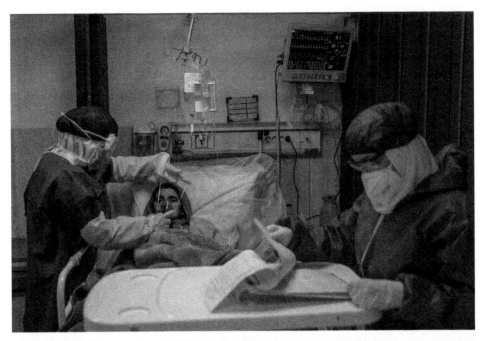

PHOTO 11.1 The Iranian government's handling of the COVID-19 pandemic was widely criticized

Majid Saeedi/Getty Images

concerns, but they were pushed to the margins by the 1980s war and prolonged economic hardship. The country suffers from deforestation, desertification, and water scarcity. Especially serious is the drying up of river basins. Given Iran's abundance of oil and gas resources, the state subsidizes many kinds of energy consumption and thus gives little incentive to increase efficiency or develop renewable energy sources. Iran did not sign the Kyoto Treaty, although it has received some international aid for environmental purposes through the World Bank.

Finally, Iran has been both the source and recipient of international migrants. The 1979 revolution caused a wave of emigration by large parts of Iran's professional class who were either linked to the shah's regime or apprehensive of the new religious climate. This was the continuation of a trend started in the 1960s and 1970s when many skilled professionals left Iran to study abroad, creating one of the largest educated diasporas in the world. Estimates by the government put the number of expatriate Iranians in 2018 between five and six million (equivalent to 7 percent of the country's total population).[13] Cognizant of the fact that their know-how, capital, and foreign networks can influence domestic politics, the government has attempted to court them, but so far, it has been largely unsuccessful. The diaspora Iranians make demands like general political amnesty, greater personal freedoms, and relaxation of rules of contact with the West, which the government does not seem to be able to provide at this time, given its ongoing ideological rifts and factionalism. At the same time, thanks to the 1979 Soviet invasion of Afghanistan and the subsequent tragedies besetting Afghan population over the last four decades, Iran plays host to over two million refugees from Afghanistan.

CONFLICT

Postrevolutionary Iran has had its fair share of conflict and violence. The jockeying for power by various political actors gave rise to numerous conflicts. Some of the most serious early conflicts were instigated by ethnic grievances, considering that 40 percent of the population is composed of minorities. In a multiethnic polity like Iran, the historically dominant definition of what constitutes a nation has been ethnolinguistic. Ironically, even though Persian emerged as the language of the political and literary elite, it never completely supplanted the local languages. The campaign to define *Persian* as the pillar of Iranian nationalism did not sit well with Arabs, Azeris, Baluchis, and Kurds. These minorities predominately live in some of the least-developed provinces of Iran, marked by lower rates of urbanization and literacy and higher rates of unemployment and poverty.

In March and April 1979, simultaneous ethnic uprisings began. The bloodiest conflict started when the Kurds, led by the Kurdistan Democratic Party, started demanding autonomy. The Turkmen and the Arab population also started similar ethnic, civil-based uprisings. In all these instances, the government managed to put down the uprisings by resorting to force.

Meanwhile, the takeover of the American Embassy in November 1979 led to the resignation of the Prime Minister, Mehdi Bazargan and his cabinet. Any liberal politician not sufficiently supportive of the crackdown on ethnic movements or the taking of US hostages was denounced or sidelined. By April 1980, as part of their campaign to consolidate their hold on power and instill orthodoxy into public life, the clergy turned their attention to university campuses that had become the main centers of opposition to the ruling clerics and launched a campaign of "cultural revolution." The universities were closed for thirty-two months, and liberal and leftist professors and staff were purged and eventually replaced with those more loyal to the new regime. The education system at all levels was revamped to impress the values of the Islamic state on students.

June 20, 1981, marked a turning point in the relationship between the regime and its main opposition. The People's Mojahedin Organization of Iran (PMOI) declared a campaign of armed struggle against the state. A week later, a powerful bomb in the headquarters of the conservative Islamic Republic Party killed more than seventy of its members. Among those killed was Ayatollah Seyyed Mohammad Beheshti, considered the second-most influential cleric after Khomeini and the chief rival to the French-educated President Bani Sadr. A month after the bomb attack, fearful of their lives, Bani Sadr and the leader of the PMOI, Mas'ud Rajavi, fled together and received political asylum in France. On August 30, Mohammad-Ali Raja'i, who had replaced Bani Sadr as president only four weeks earlier, was killed (along with his prime minister) in yet another bomb explosion attributed to the PMOI. The government's response to these attacks was swift. Not only PMOI sympathizers but also those affiliated with other militant opposition groups were rounded up and many of them executed. Iran's human rights record was particularly appalling during the 1980s as the regime used the pretext of the war with Iraq to put down any internal dissent from ethnic, leftist, and monarchist forces. In the summer of 1988, PMOI fighters attacked Iran from their basis in neighboring Iraq and were crushed. Ayatollah Khomeini, however, decided to punish those political prisoners loyal to opposition groups languishing in jails. Some 2,800–5,000 of them were executed that summer. The executions became so egregious that Ayatollah Hoseyn-Ali Montazeri, deputy supreme leader, publicly denounced them and was subsequently dismissed as heir apparent by Ayatollah Khomeini in March 1989. Moreover, Iranian agents carried out assassinations of more than one hundred opposition figures living in exile. To this day, there are still numerous and continued human rights violations, including the use of the death penalty, the use of torture in prisons, and a culture of impunity for vigilantes who commit abuses against state opponents and ordinary citizens who do not conform to strict Islamic codes of conduct.

In 1999, 2009, 2017, 2019, and 2022, Iran witnessed five more periods of political upheaval. In all instances, the regime dispatched its security forces and ruffians to crush demonstrators who were objecting to censorship, vote rigging, economic conditions and police brutality. While the regime's political capital suffered both domestically and internationally, it managed to survive these protests. Nowadays, the state does not seem to face any ethnic uprising or robust internal opposition that poses a grave threat to political stability. Yet while the omnipotence of the state has forced Iran's civil society into retreat, it has not caused it to entirely wither away.

Meanwhile, the state's regional power has been boosted, thanks to the wars in Afghanistan and Iraq that eliminated two of Iran's long-standing enemies (the Taliban and Saddam Hussein). Yet Iran has also suffered setbacks in its regional policy. In addition to its antagonistic relations with Israel, Iran has also found itself in an intense war of words with Saudi Arabia over the course of events in Bahrain, Iraq, Lebanon, Syria, and Yemen. Furthermore, the forces of the Islamic State (ISIS) attacked the Iranian Parliament and the mausoleum of Ayatollah Khomeini in June 2017 and seriously challenged the security of two of Iran's closest allies (post-Saddam Iraq and Syria) before being subdued. Once the Syrian civil war intensified, Hamas severed its ties with the Asad regime while Hizbullah and Iran had to intensify their support for him. The Taliban's return to power in 2021 may still pose fresh challenges to Iran.

INTERNATIONAL RELATIONS

After 1979, Iran adopted a worldview of Islamic internationalism and was motivated by ideological vision. It extended aid to Shi'i movements in Lebanon and elsewhere, through its overambitiously named Office of Global Revolution. Other factors, such as Iranians' sense of national pride, historic sense of grievance, and desire to remain the dominant power in the Persian Gulf, led them to embrace a basically revisionist view of the world order that wished to transform rather than preserve international power dynamics. Still, the new state faced an inherent tension in its foreign policy. On the one hand, its ideology suggested a pan-Islamic universalism, and on the other hand, the clerical regime had to work within the confine of the nation-state system.

The war with Iraq, while partly over territorial matters, also had an ideological coloring: the Islamic Republic versus the secular authoritarianism of the Ba'th Party. Over the long term, however, the logic of national interest has tended to win out over ideological fervor. After Khomeini's death, the government took a more pragmatic turn due to the pressures of the nation-state system, geopolitics, and economics. Today, Iran maintains strong alliances with Syria as well as with Iraq since the 2003 US-led invasion that deposed Saddam Hussein. It also has robust ties to Hizbullah in Lebanon, Hamas in the Gaza Strip, and the Houthis in Yemen. However, Iran's relations with Bahrain, Egypt, Israel, Saudi Arabia, and the United Arab Emirates remain problematical. The deterioration of relations with Saudi Arabia is particularly concerning, as it has deepened the Sunni–Shi'i cleavage in the region. While the Iranians point to Saudi's complicity in putting down the Bahraini opposition, their invasion of Yemen and the hostile policies toward Iran adopted by Crown Prince Mohammad bin Salman, the Saudis accuse Iran of having caused much mischief in Bahrain, Iraq, Lebanon, Syria, and Yemen.

After Iraq, the civil war in Syria, which began in 2011, posed the most serious challenge to Iran's regional policy. Iranian leadership decided to do everything it could to keep Bashar al-Asad in power. In addition to sending military personnel to fight alongside Asad's forces, Iran also collaborated closely with Russia to defeat ISIS forces. Naturally, Iran's intervention in Syria did not sit well with all those in the Arab world who detested Asad.

More importantly, Iran's nuclear policy caused it its most formidable dispute, as it endured twelve years (2003–2015) of sanctions over its nuclear program. Upon coming to power in 2013, President Rouhani's administration engaged in marathon negotiations with six world powers and the European Union, which finally led to the signing of the Joint Comprehensive Plan of Action (JCPOA) in July 2015. The deal revolved around Iran curbing its uranium enriching in return for sanctions relief. President Donald Trump, however, jeopardized the JCPOA as he announced in May 2018 that the United States was withdrawing from the deal since the agreement did not address Iran's missile technology and regional activities. Subsequently, Iranian currency reached record-breaking lows against the dollar in 2022. In an act of defiance, Iran also started to amass uranium enriched to higher levels, installed more advanced centrifuges, and limited the access of the International Atomic Energy Organization to its nuclear sites.

CONCLUSION

The term *competitive authoritarianism* refers to a category of governmental systems that combine democratic rules with authoritarian governance and have carved a space between full democracies and full authoritarian regimes. Iran can be characterized as such a state because it has many of the accoutrements: an ideologically divided elite, parallel institutions, public criticism of government policies, incessant squabbling between factions that have viable organizational assets at their disposal, and limited yet fierce electoral competition. The literature on transition to democracy suggests that competitive authoritarian regimes are more likely to metamorphose than hegemonic single-party authoritarian regimes. However, there is no guarantee that they will always transform into pluralistic systems. Iran seems to be vacillating between these two poles, as represented recently by the era of political liberalization under President Khatami (1997–2005), then the administration of hardliners under President Ahmadinejad (2005–2013), later the moderate administration of President Rouhani (2013–2021), followed by the hardline administration of President Raisi (2021–present).

Iran poses other theoretical puzzles. Scholars of authoritarianism often categorize these states into three types: personal, single-party, and military. The Iranian state borrows certain features from each type of state, but it does not fit in nicely with any of them. While the reign of the charismatic Ayatollah Khomeini (1979–1989) corresponded to the personal type of statecraft, the same cannot be said about his successor. Neither can the political system be captured with the sole explanation of clerical rule because the clerics constitute less than 30 percent of the pool of ruling elites. Furthermore, this is a regime that officially recognizes 240 political parties and associations and yet does not have a single, designated ruling party that can mobilize popular support for the governing autocrats or serve as a patronage machine. Nor can the Iranian system be characterized as military authoritarianism. The military (both the regular army and the Revolutionary Guards) has been under a clear civilian leadership so far. And it is remarkable that, despite bearing the brunt of a bloody eight-year war with Iraq and the absence of an external patron that could constrain the behavior of the military, there have been no major coup attempts since the revolution.

Thus, forty some years after the revolution that drove the shah from his throne, the Islamic Republic continues to survive, defying predictions that its government would collapse under domestic and foreign pressures. The state still faces the enormous task of reinvigorating its struggling economy and overcoming its lingering international isolation. As one looks into Iran's political future, the continuity scenario where the supreme leader maintains the status quo, controls factional infighting, and keeps in check the power of any potential rival looks the most probable. After all, serious alteration to the existing institutional arrangement is very costly due to path dependency, bureaucratic inertia, and the opposition of frontline bureaucrats. In this scenario, the possibility of domestic political reconciliation or accommodation between competing political blocs becomes less likely, and the power of nonelected institutions will be further boosted.

The balance sheet of the postrevolutionary period is interestingly bewildering—unprecedented progress juxtaposed with regressive change. The negative traits of this era include human rights abuses, extremism, economic hardship, and political violence, while the more positive developments include the development of a diversified economy with a large consumer base, greater self-sufficiencies, and the emergence of a self-defining, vibrant, and critical public discourse. The intellectual effervescence in postrevolutionary Iran cannot be contested.

As described in this chapter, a set of rather complex undercurrents is changing the political scene. Iranians are now being prevented by their theocratic rulers from trying to establish democratic rule. Indeed, the major challenge facing the country is whether it is possible to reconcile a theocracy with a democracy, as the citizenry makes louder demands for accountability, civil rights, democracy, a limited state, social justice, and tolerance and questions such long-standing features of Iranian political life as authoritarianism, censorship, cult of personality, statism, influence peddling, and violence.

In the economic domain, the greatest pressures were caused, respectively, by the demography and sanctions. Population growth of the 1980s has put a burden on public services and has created a large pool of surplus labor. Meanwhile, human rights, state sponsorship of terrorism, and nuclear-related sanctions imposed on Iran over the last four decades have worsened the economic situation in the country by causing the plummeting of the currency, eroding the industrial base, and forcing the economy to contract. The torturous relationship between Iran and the Western world has and will continue to leave its indelible mark on Iran's economy.

SUGGESTED READINGS AND WEBSITES

Abrahamian, Ervand. *A History of Modern Iran*. Cambridge: Cambridge University Press, 2008.

Amanat, Abbas. *Iran: A Modern History*. New Haven, CT: Yale University Press, 2017.

Boroujerdi, Mehrzad, and Rahimkhani Kourosh. *Postrevolutionary Iran: A Political Handbook*. Syracuse, NY: Syracuse University Press, 2018.

Ghazvinian, John. *America and Iran: A History, 1720 to the Present*. New York, NY: Knopf, 2021.

Kurzman, Charles. *The Unthinkable Revolution in Iran*. Cambridge, MA: Harvard University Press, 2004.

Schirazi, Asghar. *The Constitution of Iran: Politics and the State in the Islamic Republic*. Translated by Trans. John O'Kane. London: I. B. Tauris, 1997.

http://irandataportal.syr.edu

http://iranprimer.usip.org/

https://iranian-studies.stanford.edu/iran-2040-project/home

12 IRAQ

Julia Choucair-Vizoso

Iraq's modern history has been tumultuous. Since formal independence in 1932, Iraqis have been ruled by two foreign occupying powers and every type of domestic nondemocratic regime: monarchic, militaristic, and civilian. Iraq holds the infamous distinction of hosting the first coup d'état in the Arab world (in 1936), and many of its leaders have come to power through unconstitutional means. Since 1974, many Iraqis have lived almost continuously in a state of war, of different kinds: an insurgency by Kurdish nationalists in the north, a conventional inter-state war with Iran (1980–1988), US bombing campaigns during the First Gulf War (1991), a wave of popular violent uprisings (1991), the Second Gulf War (2003), an Anglo-American military occupation (2003–2011), multifaceted domestic armed conflict, and a transnational insurgency (2014–2018). Iraq has also served as the site of destructive international experiments, including the longest and harshest sanctions ever enforced on a state (the UN sanctions regime, 1990–2003) and one of the most controversial foreign military interventions in recent history.

A powerful narrative about this trajectory is that Iraq was doomed from the start by a diverse social fabric hemmed in by purported artificial borders—producing an "artificial state" that has inevitably fluctuated between repressive order or disorder. But studying Iraq in historical-comparative perspective challenges this narrative, guards against seeing political outcomes as inevitable, and turns our gaze elsewhere: to the historically contingent methods of power contestation and social control that have characterized the contemporary state.

HISTORY OF STATE-BUILDING: THE MAKING OF THE CONTEMPORARY STATE

The founding moment of the modern Iraqi state is often associated with an image common to other postcolonial origin stories: that of Europeans delineating arbitrary lines on a map. Yet in reality, the making of the Iraqi state was contentious, violent, and carried out in stages, with different borders demarcated at different times.[1] Moreover, although Britain and France played a central role, so too did local elites—those who controlled the economic, coercive, and symbolic resources in their societies. As they witnessed the demise of the Ottoman Empire—the system that had ordered the life of so many for centuries—they too sought to be protagonists in the nascent order.

To become successful modern state-builders, elites would need to map the terrains and populations living within new administrative boundaries in ways that facilitated the basic functions of a state, including taxation, conscription, and prevention of rebellion.[2] Crucially, they would have to pool their resources to create strong central institutions that could undertake these functions on a mass scale. Based on what we know from successful state-building experiments elsewhere, elites would have to follow one of two paths: either they could cooperate, or alternatively, some would expropriate or eliminate others' resources. Iraq did not follow either of these paths. In the shadow of colonial rule, elites had disparate preferences, lacked strong incentives to cooperate, and possessed sufficient independent resources to resist forceful incorporation.

The first ruler of the Iraqi state, King Faisal—installed by Britain through a rigged plebiscite in 1921—articulated two main state-building aspirations: to establish a conscript army and centralize taxation. Many local elites were skeptical of Faisal's agenda and resented how he had arrived at his position. Faisal was the son of the Grand Sharif of Mecca Hussein ibn Ali, custodian of the holy shrines in Mecca and Medina and patriarch of the Hashemis (who traced their lineage to the Prophet). Sharif Hussein had long yearned to break free from under the Ottomans and found his opportunity when Turkey made the fateful decision to ally with Germany against the Allied Forces. After trying to procure Britain's and France's support for an independent Arab state, Hussein and other Arab elites proclaimed the independence of Iraq and Syria (including Lebanon, Palestine, and Transjordan) as constitutional monarchies under Sharif Hussein's sons, Abdallah and Faisal, respectively.

This decision, reached during a meeting in Damascus in March 1920, reflected a historical understanding in the Arabic-speaking world of Iraq and Syria as geographical areas loosely centered on Baghdad and Damascus. Since at least the 8th century, Arab geographers had used the term *al-Iraq* to refer to the land between the Tigris and Euphrates (known in Europe as Mesopotamia). Ottoman maps from the turn of the 19th century also referred to *al-'Iraq al-'Arabi* (Arab Iraq) to designate an area that corresponded roughly to the Ottoman provinces of Basra and Baghdad (although this denomination was never used for administrative purposes). The Iraq articulated in the Damascus proclamation encompassed a much larger area than these earlier renditions—one significantly larger than the three Ottoman provinces that would end up in contemporary Iraq: Baghdad, Basra, and Mosul.[3] In response, Britain and France hastily convened a conference for European powers a month later in San Remo, Italy, where they accorded that Iraq, Palestine, and Transjordan would become British mandates, while Syria and Lebanon went to the French. Borders would be discussed later. French troops in Damascus ended Faisal's brief reign, and Britain offered him the throne of Iraq in the hope he would legitimize their mandate while preserving their core interests.[4]

Urban nationalists in the new Iraq resented monarchic rule on principle—especially one installed by a colonial power. Tribal leaders, accustomed to a degree of autonomy, worried that Faisal's centralizing institutions would undermine their power. Ethnic minority leaders opposed the Arab identity of the new state, and some demanded an independent state of their own. Leading Shi'i clerics had initially called for a son of Sharif Husayn to govern Iraq, but when the original conditions of their support—the withdrawal of British troops and a sovereign Iraqi state governed by a representative constitutional monarchy—were not fulfilled, they turned against Faisal.[5]

Disparate elite preferences do not foreclose successful state-building; other cases around the world have shown that certain conditions can compel elites to cooperate or to be coerced into the project. But Iraq's early political landscape lacked these conditions. For one, elites did not perceive the mass-based threats to their benefits, such as class conflict or widespread communal conflict, that could have cowed them into working together to preserve their dominance.[6] When elites in the new state did cooperate, it was to demand independence not to respond to threats from below.[7] Even then, demands to the British were articulated independently and not by all, as some viewed Britain as protector. A second condition that has been tied to successful state-building was missing: the necessity of waging external war. According to a popular argument, "war makes the state" because waging it necessitates the centralization of resources.[8] Although the delineation of the new state's borders with its neighbors was conflictive, even the fiercest disputes were settled by Britain's unrivaled airpower, which rendered obsolete the need to build strong Iraqi institutions.[9] Third, those elites who opposed centralization had the capacity to resist it. Some had military capabilities, such as the Assyrian leaders whom Britain had organized into exclusively Assyrian forces linked to its Royal Air Force (known as the *Assyrian levies*) and who demanded autonomy because of their Ottoman *millet* status. Others had the benefit of a geography conducive to evasion. Yazidis, who had neither previous *millet* status nor significant military resources, could avoid conscription by hiding in the Sinjar Mountains on the northwestern border with Syria or by crossing the border.[10] Many could count on protection from the British, who opposed universal conscription, gave tribal leaders tax exemptions and legal autonomy from Baghdad, and controlled what could have been a valuable weapon in Faisal's state-building arsenal—oil revenue.[11]

MAP 12.1 ■ Iraq

As a result of the environment surrounding elite power struggles in this period, Iraq's first state institutions included only a small segment of the array of political forces in the territory. The army was first established in 1921 out of six hundred former Istanbul-trained Ottoman officers of Iraqi origin, drawn almost exclusively from lower-middle-class Sunni Arab families. By the time conscription passed in 1934, these exclusionary origins were consolidated.[12] Many of these early conditions would change. Yet as we know from cases of state formation across the world, origins, timing, and sequencing shape long-term trajectories. Foundational periods are crucial, and Iraq's was not propitious for elites cooperating toward, or being coerced into, a strong state.

SOCIAL CHANGE

Ethnic and Religious Cleavages

In 1920, Iraq was home to 2,849,000 people, belonging to diverse and overlapping social categories: linguistic origin, religious denomination, occupation, social class, and regional and tribal affiliation. An estimated 75 percent spoke Arabic and most of the rest Kurdish, although there were also speakers of Armenian, Assyrian (referred to as Syriac in the constitution), South Azeri (referred to as Turkmen), and others. Linguistic minorities lived primarily in the rugged mountain terrain in the north and east (and the foothills that adjoin it), as well as in the cities of Baghdad and Basra. They had linguistic and cultural ties to residents of Syria, Turkey, and Iran. By religion, an estimated 92 percent were Muslim, 3 percent Christian, 2.5 percent Jewish, and the rest Yazidi and Sabean/Mandean. Aside from Yazidis, who were concentrated in the north, non-Muslim populations were mostly urban. No Iraqi census has ever recorded intra-Muslim distinctions; a 1932 British census put the number of Shi'a at 56 percent and Sunnis at 36 percent.[13]

KEY FACTS ON IRAQ

AREA 169,235 square miles (438,317 square kilometers)

CAPITAL Baghdad

POPULATION 39,650,145 (2021 est.)

PERCENTAGE OF POPULATION UNDER 25 58.43

RELIGIOUS GROUPS (PERCENTAGE) Muslim, 95–98 (Shi'i 64–69, Sunni 29–34); Christian, 1 (includes Catholic, Orthodox, Protestant, Assyrian Church of the East); and other, 1–4 (2015 est.)

ETHNIC GROUPS (PERCENTAGE) Arab, 75–80; Kurdish, 15–20; and Turkmen, Assyrian, or other, 5 (1987 government est.)

OFFICIAL LANGUAGE Arabic, Kurdish (official in Kurdish regions); Syriac and Turkmen are recognized in the constitution as "regional languages"

TYPE OF GOVERNMENT Federal Parliamentary Republic

DATE OF INDEPENDENCE October 3, 1932 (from League of Nations mandate under British administration)

GDP $372.3 billion; $9,300 per capita (2020 est.; NB—data are in 2017 dollars)

PERCENTAGE OF GDP BY SECTOR Agriculture 3.3; industry, 51; and services, 45.8

TOTAL RENTS (PERCENTAGE OF GDP) FROM NATURAL RESOURCES 39.8 (2019 est.)

FERTILITY RATE 3.32 children born/woman (2021 est.)

Sources: CIA. "The World Factbook." August 4, 2022, https://www.cia.gov/the-world-factbook/. World Bank. "International Comparison Program (ICP)." Accessed August 10, 2022, https://databank.worldbank.org/source/icp-2017.

Religious and ethnic (linguistic) identities in Iraq are crosscutting. Most Kurds are Sunni, but there is a sizable Shi'i minority that was based in central Iraq (known as Faili Kurds). Turkmen are more evenly divided between sects. According to the British census, 5 percent of Shi'a in the territory were of Persian origin. Ethnic and religious identities also cut across social class.

Iraq's linguistic diversity has been the source of one of its most persistent political divisions. Despite the diversity of the territory, British officials and King Faisal's supporters regularly referred to Iraq as an "Arab state."[14] Moreover, Iraq's first constitution (1925) stipulated that Arabic would be the sole official language, and the first school textbooks advocated the unification of Arab states (an ideology known as pan-Arabism). The interaction between the Arabic–Kurdish linguistic cleavage and the exclusionary foundation of the state has been a contributing factor to armed conflict throughout Iraq's history (see Domestic Armed Conflict section) and is still the source of great tension today (see Political Regimes and Governance section). One of the most heated debates during the drafting of the current constitution in 2005 involved the state's descriptor, with some insisting on including the "Arab state." The final document describes Iraq as a country of many nationalities, religions, and sects but includes compromise wording about its commitment to the Arab League. It lists Arabic and Kurdish as the two official languages and guarantees "the right of Iraqis to educate their children in their mother tongue."[15]

Religious identities at independence did not endow individuals with a sense of community, except for non-Muslims who had enjoyed a degree of self-rule and special status as religious minorities under the Ottoman *millet* system. Even then, however, multiple communities existed within each minority category, organized by geography. Shi'ism and Sunnism were not strongly instituted collective identities, and mass conversions between them were occurring as late as the turn of the 20th century. It was then when Shi'ism became a majority religion in Iraq, as a result of the rapidly declining nomadic economy.[16] As Sunni nomadic populations began to settle in southern cities, Shi'i clergy in the recently emergent strongholds of Shi'ism, Najaf, and Karbala worked to convert new arrivals.[17] The nonuniform patterns of migration and conversion meant that many tribes came to include Shi'i and Sunni members—a crosscutting cleavage that persists.

As in all Arab states, religious identities in Iraq are the basis for laws governing "personal status" matters: birth, marriage, divorce, inheritance, and death. Non-Muslims have always adjudicated these matters in religious courts independent from the regular court system. Since 1959, Muslims have adjudicated them in the secular court system, where judges rule based on codified law (based on Islamic law) that applies uniformly to Sunnis and Shi'a, rather than on their interpretation of religious sources.[18] Issued by decree by a left-leaning revolutionary government, the code of 1959 generally selected interpretations of Islamic law most favorable to women and is still considered a symbol of Iraq's progressivism on women's rights. Reform of this law was a very controversial issue in the drafting of the current constitution.[19]

Iraq is less diverse today than it was at independence. Economic and forced migrations have altered the demographic distribution. The population of non-Muslims has decreased from 8 percent to 1 percent. Multiple insurgencies and practices of collective targeting along ethnic and religious identity have also segmented the country, with millions of Iraqis being displaced internally to areas where their sectarian and ethnic identity would put them in the majority.[20] The 2006–2007 wave of killings throughout Baghdad forced families to flee neighborhoods, in which their religious identity was not in the majority, thereby drastically changing the demography and geography of the capital city.

Class Cleavages

Iraq's class structure has been defined by four main, interconnected processes: sedentarization, land reform, urbanization, and war. At the turn of the 20th century, Iraq still had a sizable nomadic population, but it was decreasing precipitously with the reduced demand for overland trade (due to developments in international transport and communication). Between 1867 and 1930, it decreased from 35 percent to 7 percent (from 50 percent to 8 percent in the south). As Iraq's inhabitants became almost exclusively sedentary, large-scale land privatization elevated tribal leaders to a new class of landlords. By the republican coup of 1958, Iraq had some of the largest private estates in the Middle East; about 1 percent of all landowners owned over 55 percent of all land.[21] Simultaneously, the failed feudal land tenure system was driving large numbers of impoverished peasants to cities.[22] This migration intensified despite the best intentions of the new republican leaders and their laws to dismantle large estates and reform the agrarian system.[23] By 1963, Iraq had become a food-importing country. By 1979, the state reverted course to reprivatizing agriculture.[24] By 1985, Iraq's urban population had doubled since 1950; many settled into the ever-expanding Baghdad public housing to absorb rural migrants.

The scale of rural-to-urban migration undermined existing social structures and created new class distinctions as rural Shi'i migrants settled in public housing such as the famous Madinat al-Thawra (Revolution City), later renamed Madinat Saddam, and currently named Madinat al-Sadr. The partial integration of migrants into urban life created new, sharp class distinctions between Baghdadi urbanites and new Shi'i migrants and between those who migrated and those who stayed behind. These distinctions would become violently salient in post-2003 Iraq, emblematized by the rise of the militant Mahdi Army, a militia organized by the son of the late Ayatollah Sadiq al-Sadr, Muqtada al-Sadr, who repurposed his father's welfare distribution networks in Madinat al-Sadr to challenge traditional Shi'i leadership in the south—eventually rising to the top of Iraqi politics as the leader of the largest coalition in the 2018 and 2021 elections. The Mahdi Army also played a central role in the intense Baghdad violence of 2006–2007, which some analysts refer to as "class struggle" in addition to its more common descriptor "sectarian strife."

Another salient change in Iraq's social structure over time has been the rise and fall of the professional middle class. Aided by increasing oil revenue beginning in the late 1950s, but especially in the 1970s, governments invested in public institutions to support an educated, professional, urban middle class. The sanctions regime and the violence since 2003 gutted this class, along with many sectors, especially healthcare and education. It is estimated that Iraq has seen the largest flight of doctors and other medical personnel from one single country in recent history.[25] The number of physicians per one thousand inhabitants was 0.85 in 2014 (the last year of available data), which is low in comparison to other countries in the Middle East and North Africa region (MENA; e.g., 3.4 in Jordan, 2.38 in Lebanon, 1.55 in Syria).[26] Since 2014, around 50 percent of specialized health care staff have left Anbar, Diyala, Ninawa, and Salahaddin.[27] In some ways, the flight of the middle class reflects a common migration pattern in conflict zones: the poorest and hardest hit are unable to leave, whereas those with some resources can fund their travel and try to pass restrictive entry tests in neighboring states. But another tragic dynamic has been at play in Iraq: Since 2003, schoolteachers, university professors, scientists, and physicians have been targeted for assassination and kidnappings precisely because of their profession.

POLITICAL REGIMES AND GOVERNANCE

Iraqis have been ruled by various regimes: a colonial power (1921–1932), monarchs (1921–1958), military officers (1958–1968), a ruling party (1968–1979), a personalist dictator (1979–2003), a foreign military occupation (2003–2004), and, currently, by an elected parliament that does not safeguard political, civil, or economic rights. These apparent ruptures in Iraq's political history raise two questions: Why have participatory and accountable forms of governance proved elusive? And how do we explain the origins and consequences of different nondemocratic regimes in Iraq?

On the first question, based on what we know about the determinants of democracy, its absence in Iraq, while not inevitable, is not puzzling. In terms of social-structural foundations, there was no strong middle class, the peasantry had not been destroyed, and agrarian elites were entrenched within the state apparatus.[28] Economic conditions—low levels of development, low income equality, low capital mobility, and reliance on oil—also did not bode well for democratization.[29]

On the second question, Iraq's variation across nondemocratic regime type over time illustrates that rulers select different governing structures in response to elite conflict, with consequential effects on their ability to survive in power. To balance discordant elite interests, King Faisal's parliamentary monarchy was characterized by very limited powers for parliament and low elite turnover. Parliament could bring down a cabinet, but the king had the right to confirm all laws, call for general elections, and prorogue the assembly. Political disagreements often led to cabinet portfolio reshuffles but very low membership turnover; the same 59 men rotated seats.[30] This exclusionary bargain was very restive; urban protests and tribal revolts were common, and the army was frequently called upon to suppress them.

Frustrated by the political elite's inability to control the country, army officers led a coup in 1936 to force a new arrangement, one that preserved the monarchy but transferred de facto power to the military. This split arrangement was very unstable, and eventually some officers lost confidence the monarchy would ever be able to settle conflict.[31] They particularly resented the monarchy's unwillingness to directly challenge the economic interests of the large landowning class to guide successful economic development. Inspired by Egypt's 1952 Free Officer Revolution, a group of fifteen top officers overthrew the monarchy in 1958. The murder of the royal family eliminated any possibility of a Hashemi restoration.

The new military rulers chose to fully merge military and government. Officers held the posts of president, prime minister, minister of defense, director general of security, and director of military intelligence, as well as various ministerial posts.[32] As in most military regimes, officers-turned-presidents were primarily concerned with preventing coups. Former coconspirators turned their gaze on each other, as struggles for power intermingled with emerging ideological differences over the central regional question of the time: pan-Arab unity. The 1958–1968 decade was marred by unstable military rule under three different leaders, all of whom ascended to power through coups.

Ultimately, these internecine battles resulted in the rise of a new regime in 1968, led by members of the Ba'th ("revival") party, which had been founded in Syria in the 1940s by middle-class intellectuals of diverse religious backgrounds who espoused pan-Arab nationalism.[33] Although they too were unsuccessful in stabilizing elite or mass politics, Ba'thists were able to survive in power by reducing the power of military officers. Ahmad Hasan al-Bakr, the army general who assumed the presidency, and his younger kinsman Saddam Hussein, whom he appointed vice chairman of the ruling Revolutionary Command Council (RCC, the highest legislative and executive body), purged military officers and established alternative security institutions, a network of intelligence agencies, a large bureaucracy, and an expansive ruling party. They were aided by unprecedented access to revenue after they nationalized the oil industry in 1972.[34]

Saddam Hussein used the security establishment to gradually concentrate power in his own hands. In July 1979, he pushed President al-Bakr aside and assumed personal control over the legislative, executive, and judicial branches of government. Although real discussion and consultation took place within the RCC, members did not oppose Hussein's initiatives. The regime also progressively narrowed membership in security institutions to regional and family networks, and it increasingly came to rely on four clans from in and around Hussein's hometown of Tikrit, which created tensions with other members of the regime. Although often mislabeled as a "Sunni regime," a more accurate characterization of Hussein's rule is that positions of coercive power had a narrow regional and familial basis. Multiple failed coup attempts from within the

Republican Guard and other security institutions rocked the regime in the 1990s—all of which were organized by Sunnis.

The concentration of decision-making power in Hussein's hands and his cult of personality can risk fostering the illusion that the regime was omnipotent. The reality was more akin to that of large bureaucracies worldwide, which always allow for ambiguities and autonomous spaces.[35] Hussein's power was undoubtedly unrivaled; he had placed himself at the top of each of the state's pillars as the broker of relations between them, and all channels of information passed through the Office of the President. Yet firewalls between organizations often backfired, causing inefficiencies in intelligence gathering.[36] Despite its pretensions to hegemony, the regime was never able to preempt either elite or mass dissent, which varied in magnitude across space and time, reflecting the lumpiness in the regime's intelligence gathering.[37] When the US invasion began in March 2003, the regime rapidly collapsed, armed forces deserted, and many bureaucrats looted their own workplace.

The US invasion launched a period of institutional engineering characterized by confusion, opaque decision-making, and severe human rights abuses.[38] What was at first supposed to be a short-lived occupation—focused on locating weapons of mass destruction, keeping the bureaucracy in place, and organizing elections as soon as possible—abruptly changed to an extended occupation in which Iraqi forces would regain control over security when the US military deemed them "ready," and a US administrator of the Coalition Provisional Authority (CPA) would have full executive, legislative, and judicial authority, as well as the power to dispose of all Iraqi state assets and direct all Iraqi government officials.[39] This surprising shift in policy left those Iraqis cooperating with the United States feeling deceived.[40] Moreover, the CPA's mandate did not clarify how Iraqi leaders or the CPA itself would engage with the 98 percent of American personnel who were not under CPA command. The surfacing of systematic abuse and torture of Iraqi prisoners by US military units in the notorious Abu Ghraib prison as well as the unlawful detention of over ten thousand Iraqis in US-run prisons undermined remaining trust in the process.[41]

Forged amid a violent and chaotic occupation, Iraq's current political regime is characterized by four related features. First, ethnosectarian identity is institutionalized as the basis of political representation; since 2004, political offices have been reserved for specific ethnosectarian communities based on their assumed demographic weight.[42] This was determined early on by the United States and its Iraqi allies, formerly exiled politicians who had organized their opposition in exile along ethnosectarian lines to the exclusion of other categories such as region or class.[43] Many Iraqis blame this quota system—which they call *muhasasa*—for the spread of party-based patronage and corruption networks throughout the public sector and for the absence of autonomous institutions.

Second, current governance reflects fierce disagreement over foundational questions: the parameters of federalism, the relationship between local and central government, the distribution of oil revenues, and the future of "disputed territories"—mixed-population areas between the Kurdish region and the rest of Iraq (the most famous of which is oil-rich Kirkuk). A full fifty-three articles of the new constitution were left to be resolved at some point in the future.[44] The Kurdistan Regional Government (KRG) and federal government in Baghdad have repeatedly clashed over their conflicting interpretations (see Domestic Armed Conflict section), culminating in the KRG unilaterally holding a referendum on Kurdish independence in September 2017.[45] To a lesser extent, southern politicians have also made efforts to form an autonomous region in the far south.

Third, Iraqi governance is framed by a vast and ever-growing security architecture outside the official state apparatus. The US decision to disband the Iraqi army in May 2003 created a security vacuum that was quickly filled by paramilitary units, armed militias, and private guards, whose influence has only grown in the past fifteen years as central security institutions have struggled to stem severe threats to territorial integrity. In addition to becoming formidable autonomous security forces that recruit widely among the youth, they also enjoy broad popularity among segments of the population and have capitalized on their battle victories to run successful electoral bids. Some have even established their own service provision institutions in direct competition with political parties.[46]

Finally, Iraq's current system is minimally democratic. Although there are regular elections, there are no checks and balances among different powers, and purportedly independent institutions and oversight agencies—including the theoretically independent electoral commission—are beholden to political parties. Increasingly, the electoral commission is perceived as beholden to partisan interests; campaign rules, including party finance rules, are lax and rarely applied, and individuals convicted of corruption have been allowed to participate in elections. Judicial independence is guaranteed by the constitution, but judges come under extraordinary pressure and have been unable to pursue cases involving organized crime, corruption, and militia activity. Citizens perceive official law enforcement as corrupt or ineffective, and they routinely turn to actors outside the judicial system to arbitrate disputes. Arbitrary arrest and detention are common in security-related cases, and there are credible reports of torture—both in Baghdad and in Iraqi Kurdistan.[47]

POLITICAL PARTICIPATION

For most of Iraq's history, citizens have had to express their demands outside formal institutional channels such as political parties and elections.

Political Parties

Political parties have played very different roles among themselves and over time—proving that what institutions do is more important than what they are called.

In the monarchic era, most political parties were collectives of urban notables rather than mass-based institutions. The exception was the Iraqi Communist Party, which formed in 1934 around a platform of social justice and antisectarian politics that quickly gained popular support among citizens of diverse religious and sectarian affiliations. Given that elections were rigged, opposition parties focused on street protest and labor mobilization. The government did not hesitate to suppress any opposition by declaring martial law. It was particularly harsh with the Communist Party, which still managed to become the largest and best-organized party in the country by 1958, with structures among peasants in the south as well as in the northern Kurdish region.

Under Iraq's military regimes, political parties made a fateful decision that undermined the development of political participation: Instead of insisting that military regimes preserve and develop parliamentary procedures and electoral politics, they chose to invest in extralegal alliances with rival military factions as a path to political ambition. Military rulers, in turn, did not hesitate to suppress independent party activity.

The Ba'th introduced unprecedented levels of physical coercion against all independent political participation. The Communist Party was targeted for a systematic campaign of arrests and torture. Any non-Ba'thist political activity by members of the armed forces (i.e., most of the adult male population, given universal conscription) was made a capital offense. The Ba'th party itself meanwhile became a formidable organization of political and social control. As with most nondemocratic ruling parties, the Ba'th was not a decision-making or power-sharing institution, but rather an instrument of selective cooptation and repression at both the elite and mass levels.[48] On the elite side, the party's hierarchical apparatus differentially allocated benefits and services based on the membership level, thus incentivizing its members to buy into the structure early on in return for increasing benefits.[49] On the mass level, the party was involved in almost every aspect of an individual's life. It determined who would be included and excluded from access to state benefits (including public employment, educational opportunities, and welfare), its structure ran parallel to all state institutions, and it gathered its own intelligence on the citizenry, often in parallel with security organizations. The system of positive and negative selective benefits extended the actions of citizens to their families, which encouraged intrafamily self-policing.

The fall of the regime in 2003 marked a turning point for political party life, as a plethora of parties formed or regrouped to contest competitive elections. Seven major parties dominated Iraqi politics after 2003: the Kurdistan Democratic Party, the Patriotic Union of Kurdistan, the Iraqi National Council, the Iraqi National Accord, the Supreme Council for Islamic Revolution in Iraq, the Dawa Islamic Party, and the Iraqi Islamic Party—all of whom had signed off on *muhasasa* as a governing principle before the US invasion.[50]

The most salient feature of Iraqi party politics today is the extent to which political parties are thoroughly embedded in state bureaucracy, giving them the economic and social capital needed to continue to dominate the political field.[51] Party bosses have the de facto power to appoint bureaucrats, and awarding of senior civil service jobs is part of the government formation negotiations.[52] As a result, access to government employment is only guaranteed by pledging allegiance to one of the dominant political parties. Parties also syphon public funds into their own operating budgets.[53] As a result of this behavior, in recent years, protesters have made political parties the target of their ire with slogans such as "No, no to political parties."

A second prominent feature of party politics is the influence of individual leaders, as opposed to collective decision-making bodies, internal governing procedures, or coherent ideologies and policies. For the most part, political parties operate as loose coalitions of convenience coalesced around prominent individuals who derive their authority from familial history or religious credentials. As a result, parties grow or fragment in election cycles, their "members" often do not act in unison in legislative politics, and election cycles feature new and surprising alliances.

Given this landscape, the nature of political divisions between parties is ever-changing. Nevertheless, we can identify some broad contours that persist across electoral cycles. One is the division between "exiles"—prominent figures who had fled Iraq when their parties were decimated by the Ba'th regime—and "insiders"—those still residing in Iraq on the eve of the US invasion. Until the 2018 parliamentary elections, exiles dominated executive and legislative politics.[54] Critics believe exiles' disproportionate role is a direct result of the US-led process of institutional engineering and particularly of the CPA's highly controversial de-Ba'thification Law (later replaced by the Justice and Accountability Law), which allowed for members of the Ba'th to be disqualified from running in elections based on the flawed assumption that all members of the top four ranks of the party were ideologically committed to Ba'thism or had committed acts that violated international human rights standards.[55] This law has been used repeatedly to disqualify candidates, often without the disclosure of the specific rationale, leading many to believe it has been thoroughly politicized by its implementers with an eye to securing electoral victories.[56] Critics also believe the United States explicitly favored exiles as partners in the transitional process; many did in fact work with US officials in the lead-up to the invasion, and five main political groups received support under the 1998 US Iraq Liberation Act.

A second way to interpret the party landscape is through the interplay between intra- and interethnosectarian divisions. Given the institutionalization of ethnosectarian quotas since 2004, the categories Kurdish, Arab Sunni, and Shi'i serve as the lens through which many politicians perceive their constituencies. At the same time, the fragmentation within each category and the existence of cross-sectarian parties demonstrate the limits of these identities as cohesive, mobilizing platforms. To give some examples, the largest parties have emerged within the framework of Shi'i Islamism, the most prominent of which are the Islamic Supreme Council of Iraq (ISCI), the Muqtada al-Sadr movement, and the Da'wa party, which are divided among other things by their disagreements over Iran's role in Iraqi politics. One of the peculiar expressions of this fragmentation is that all prime ministers have come from the weakest of these three, Da'wa, as a compromise between the stronger two. In the KRG, two main Kurdish nationalist parties have dominated for decades, the Kurdish Democratic Party (KDP) and the Popular Union of Kurdistan (PUK)—both of which are organized around prominent families and currently act as coruling parties. Their dominance is increasingly challenged by smaller opposition parties.

Elections

Elections occupied a peripheral space in Iraq until 2005. The monarchy held ten elections for the lower house of parliament between 1925 and 1958 but manipulated results and did not extend the suffrage to women.[57] No general elections were held between 1954 and 1980; that year, the Ba'th established a National Assembly that had no legislative powers.

Since 2005, parliamentary elections have been held every four years under a unicameral proportional representation system and, in the latest election in 2021, under a single nontransferable system (a first-past-the-post system conducted within multiseat constituencies). The initial choice of a proportional representation electoral system rendered Iraq, like other countries with this system, prone to deadlock over government formation as rival blocs try to organize coalitional majorities. In 2010, Iraq joined Belgium and Cambodia in the top three list of countries that have gone the longest between holding a parliamentary election and forming a government (289 days).

Elections have become progressively less free and fair—the most recent in 2021 and 2018 were marred by widespread allegations of fraud—and less participatory, with turnout dropping by half, from 77 percent in December 2005 to 36 percent in 2021.

The nature of coalitional politics and electoral results have varied widely across elections, with high MP (member of parliament) turnover. Yet a general trend has been the fragmentation of competition with every electoral cycle, as competition between political parties shifts further from inter- to intrasectarian and intraethnic.[58] In January 2005, the vote was dominated by three ethnosectarian coalitions—Arab Sunni, Shi'a, Kurdish—who between them secured more than 87 percent of the vote. Campaigning and voting patterns further entrenched the logic of electoral politics as an identity referendum. The 2010 election results were vastly different. This time, the Iraqiyya list, the only political alliance to attract both Shi'i and Sunni voters and to campaign on an expressly nonsectarian platform, drew the largest vote share (26 percent compared to 8 percent in December 2005).[59] By 2018, the top nine lists shared 80 percent of the vote, with the top performer attaining only 14 percent.

A second trend has been the rise of Muqtada al-Sadr's movement. In 2018, campaigning on a platform calling for institutional reform, condemning corruption, and opposing foreign intervention, the *Sa'irun* ("On the Move") coalition brought together Muqtada al-Sadr's movement with the Communist Party of Iraq and other leftist and secular parties and won the largest overall number of seats (54 of 329).[60] Almost 65 percent of the elected MPs were new to parliamentary politics. Notably, this marked the first time that Iraqi leaders who are not former exiles had won an election.[61] Al-Sadr's movement significantly increased its seat share in the 2021 elections, obtaining 70 of 329 parliamentary seats.

Tribe

The institution of *tribe* has also meant very different things over time with consequential effects on the parameters of participation. Before the Ottoman Tanzimat reforms (1839–1876), tribes operated as sociopolitical institutions of collective protection against threats to property and as interest groups to secure fertile lands and trade routes. Their internal social and economic organization varied, making it difficult to speak of a homogenous category of tribe beyond that of an institution of protection.[62] Their members defined themselves by their common patrilineal descent, more often fictive than biological. The authority of a tribal leader (*shaykh*, plural *shuyukh*) derived from two sources: professed lineage to historically prestigious pre-Islamic tribes or to the Prophet and his ability to "serve the community's interests by upholding the tribe's reputation through rituals of honor, generosity, and (in some cases) combat, while mitigating disputes and violence through negotiation skills and marital strategies."[63]

Beginning with the Tanzimat's Land Law, which introduced private property in agricultural land, tribes were gradually transformed into patronage institutions. Shuyukh became landlords who increasingly looked to the center to empower them vis-à-vis their constituents, exchanging acquiescence for tax exemptions, land rights, and autonomy to govern in their areas. They thus no longer derived authority from their conflict resolution skills, but rather from their wealth and translocal political alliances.[64] Many joined parliamentary politics, becoming urbanized elite and absentee landlords—but later lost significant power with the 1958 revolutionary land reform and the closure of parliamentary life.

Saddam Hussein altered traditional lines of authority even further by creating a directorate of tribal affairs that appointed shuyukh directly from the state, selecting less popular power-hungry individuals (whom Iraqis derogatorily refer to as "Shuyukh made in Taiwan").[65] When American troops arrived in Iraq, they were "confused by the proliferation of self-proclaimed shuyukh volunteering their services, each one of them boasting 'hundreds of thousands' of supporters."[66] Today, the institution of *tribe* is fully incorporated into the political system as a main form of clientelistic politics. The Iraqi parliament has a tribal affairs committee through which candidates dole out benefits in exchange for support in their security-related and electoral undertakings.

Associations

Associational activity has ebbed and flowed since 1920. In monarchic Iraq, there was a rise in associational activity as urban Iraqis formed professional associations (lawyers, physicians, engineers, and teachers), organizations for women and students, and labor unions. The development of oil and increased trade brought many strikes for better wages and working conditions, especially in the port city of Basra. Associational life was increasingly incorporated into the state—first through Qasim who made sure to try to control their activities and later (and much more comprehensively) through Ba'thist rule. Following the 2003 US invasion, it is estimated that somewhere between eight thousand and twelve thousand civil society organizations were registered with the state. The majority are social welfare organizations linked either to political parties or religious institutions and target narrow constituencies. Many professional associations are factionalized by political party affiliations.[67] Trade unions, however, have been very successful at mobilizing public opinion and creating political coalitions—most notably against the Oil and Gas Law (2006–2009) that would have disempowered parliament in relation to decisions around oil contracts.

Citizenship Rights

Iraqis not only had very limited institutional channels for *voice* before 2003, but they also often could not exercise the choice to *exit*.[68] Freedom of movement was severely curtailed in the 1980s. Citizens were unable to leave the country of their own free will; legal exit was viewed as a privilege to be granted by the government rather than a right to be exercised.[69] Following the Gulf War, the regime generally refused to issue passports to women under forty-five unless they would be traveling with a male guardian (in an effort to gain support among tribes).

For many Iraqis, however, exit was enforced upon them through the ultimate act of disenfranchisement—revocation of citizenship. This was meted out not as punishment for noncompliance, but through indiscriminate targeting based on religious identity. As in other countries, forcible removal of categories of populations was a by-product of international relations.[70] In the 1940s and 1950s, thousands of Iraqi Jews were stripped of their citizenship and property and forced to leave the country as political parties exploited Israel's founding and the ensuing Arab defeat in the Arab–Israeli war of 1948–1949 in their political tug-of-war.[71] Almost no one was left from Iraq's long-established Jewish community, which was around 117,000 (2.6 percent of the population) in 1947.

On the eve of the Iran–Iraq war in 1980, as underground Shi'i Islamist movements were emboldened in their dissent, the regime waged a campaign to expel Iraqis of "Iranian origins" (*taba'iyya iraniyya)*, or Shi'i Arabs and Kurds whose family line held Persian nationality under the Ottomans. Their properties were confiscated and auctioned off to other Shi'a in an attempt to make these complicit in the dispossession and thereby undermine potential coreligionist solidarity. In 1981, the regime provided financial incentives for men to divorce their "Iranian wives" (those connected to families who had been expelled or were marked for expulsion).[72] By some estimates, two hundred thousand people were expelled during the eight-year war.[73]

Protest

Under the Ba'thist regime, given the restrictions on participation through institutional channels, many Iraqis resorted to alternative forms of noncompliance, ranging from direct confrontation to subversive, hidden action: street demonstrations, participation in violent activity (insurgency, targeting of civilians), defection from the army, not joining the ruling party, spreading rumors about the regime, and other "everyday forms of resistance."[74] Formulating a full picture of these activities to explain why citizens partook in them is difficult, given the opaqueness of information in nondemocratic and violent settings and the fact that most of Iraq's archives remain in the possession of the US government, with a few exceptions. The evidence we have thus far suggests an interaction between the type of noncompliance citizens engaged in and the selectivity with which the regime doled out repression.[75]

Since 2005, Iraq has seen progressively larger waves of demonstrations that have transformed in scope, intensity, and character, culminating in the 2019 protests Tishreen (October) uprising, when mass demonstrations unseated the government and forced parliament to adopt a new electoral law. The 2019 uprisings were unprecedented in scale, spread, composition, and type of demands voiced. At some point, more than two million protestors were in the capital alone, a quarter of the city's population. Protesters stormed and burned state and party offices and buildings, including political party headquarters, local government offices, and offices belonging to militias. Protesters in Basra were able to close the port and shut down the border crossing with Kuwait.

The socioeconomic and gender diversity were particularly unprecedented features. As was the call for revolution, with protesters calling for the wholesale rejection of the political system and chanting "We want a homeland," or "We want a country." The uprisings also featured modes of creative action and expression that went beyond previous protest movements.

PHOTO 12.1 A protester carrying an Iraqi flag walks next to burning tires during ongoing antigovernment protests in Basra in November 2019.

Reuters/Essam al-Sudani/Alamy

In Baghdad, public space was transformed into what protesters wanted to present as inclusive spaces ruled and managed by the population—a miniature model for the kind of state they dreamed of, free of factional and sectarian politics and with public services. The presence of young women from different social classes was consciously emphasized by protesters as a new mode of sociability that transgresses social norms.[76]

The 2019 protests were also unprecedented in the levels of violence meted out by state and paramilitary forces, which left about 600 protesters dead and over 20,000 injured in the first six months.[77] The government also imposed media, Internet, and telecommunication blackouts, as well as curfews. Many protesters and activists were threatened, intimidated, arrested, beaten up, kidnapped, and even assassinated by security forces in the months that followed.

REGIONAL AND INTERNATIONAL RELATIONS

Iraq's relations with other states have tracked its rise and fall as one of the region's major powers. This trajectory has encompassed five stages.

Pan-Arabism (1930s–1960s)

Iraq's first leaders sought alliances across borders to get the upper hand in domestic struggles. In many cases, these alliances entailed ceding sovereignty through "unity projects," or voluntary agreements to unify with other Arab states. King Faisal never gave up aspirations to one day recreate the pan-Arab state his family had fought for against the Ottomans. Military rulers also sought regional allies against their own domestic opponents. In this, they were no different from many Arab leaders in the 1950s and 1960s—a period famously dubbed "the Arab cold war."[78] These projects were not an automatic expression of pan-Arab sentiment; their intermittent nature and their timing suggests that leaders chose to tap into these sentiments primarily as a policy instrument to deal with domestic power struggles.[79]

Militarization (1970s)

Flush with revenue from the 1972 nationalization of oil, Iraq became one of the world's leading arms importers (mainly from the United States and the Soviet Union). It was a central participant in the Persian Gulf's arms race; between 1975 and 1979, Iraq, Iran, and Saudi Arabia accounted for almost one-quarter of all global arms purchases.[80] By the decade's end, two transformative regional events would offer Iraq the opportunity to employ its military investments in a play for regional leadership. In 1979, Egypt, the most populous Arab state, lost its undisputed leadership status after its peace agreement with Israel. That same year in Iraq's eastern neighbor, Iran, a mass-based revolution brought to power Shi'i clerics intent on establishing an "Islamic republic."

Belligerence (1980s–1991)

From the Iraqi government's perspective, the transitional moment in Iran was a chance to force territorial concessions on long-standing territorial disputes. Moreover, Iran's new Islamist regime explicitly challenged the Ba'th's secular brand of antiimperialism, and its new leader Ayatollah Khomeini appealed to Iraqi Shi'a to topple their government. Assassination attempts of top Iraqi state officials in 1979 and 1980 gave credence to Saddam Hussein's accusations of Iranian interference in Iraqi affairs, and he ordered the invasion of Iran in September 1980. Confident in a speedy victory, Hussein had not prepared for the war that ensued: an eight-year trench war that became one of the deadliest interstate wars of the century, killing between 250,000 and 500,000 Iraqis and one million Iranians. One year before the war ended, 1.7 million Iraqi men were in arms, or 65 percent of all men aged eighteen to forty-five.[81] By the UN cease-fire resolution on July 18, 1988, Iraq had gained no new territory.

Far from consolidating Iraq's regional leadership, the Iran war devastated the economy, making it dependent on foreign aid, particularly from Kuwait and Saudi Arabia. When they refused Iraq's appeal to forgive its debts and restrict oil production quotas to raise prices, Hussein interpreted their rejection as an attempt to undermine his regime. Believing he was under threat and that the international community would see the invasion as his attempt to hasten a negotiated settlement, he ordered the invasion of Kuwait on August 2, 1990, and declared Kuwait Iraq's nineteenth province.[82] Like the Iran war, this invasion stemmed from Hussein's belief that military victory would assuage his regime's vulnerability and that the target was weak and isolated.[83] Once again, he miscalculated. International condemnation was immediate; UN

Security Council resolutions called for Iraq's unconditional withdrawal, imposed an embargo, and authorized war against Iraq. Beginning on January 16, 1991, a US-led coalition of twenty-eight countries waged a forty-two-day land and air invasion that dwarfed anything Iraqis had experienced in the Iran war.[84]

Pariah (1991–2003)

The 1991 Gulf War tracked a shift in US strategy in the Middle East. Although its interests were unchanged with the end of the Cold War—preventing any country from dominating oil flow and pricing—the United States was increasingly willing to use military means to protect energy resources. In the Persian Gulf, this entailed a strategic shift from "offshore balancing" to "dual containment." Before 1990, it balanced Iraq and Iran against one another. It supported the shah's regime in Iran but sold weapons to both states, then switched support to Iraq after Iran's revolution. During the Iran–Iraq war, the United States first supplied weapons, funding, and intelligence to both sides; later, it became an active participant against Iran, taking and inflicting casualties.[85] Iraq's invasion of Kuwait, however, had disrupted the status quo and threatened US relations with its regional clients. The aim would now be to isolate both countries economically, encourage regime change in Iraq, and support Saudi Arabia and the smaller Gulf monarchies. Such a strategy necessarily entailed a much more direct, unilateral role for the United States.

From the United States' perspective, the biggest threat to its energy interests stemmed from Iraq acquiring nuclear weapons. Such a scenario would effectively eliminate its vulnerability to US military action. UN Resolution 687, passed in April 1991, made Iraq's economic recovery dependent on the control of its military capabilities. Under its terms, international inspectors were to be allowed unlimited access to facilities housing weapons, including offices of the security services and presidential palaces. For the rest of the decade, Saddam Hussein resisted full transparency about Iraq's weapons' programs; in retrospect, it seems his strategic ambiguity was geared not toward the United States but toward those the regime saw as its primary enemies: Iran and its Iraqi allies.[86] In March 2003, in opposition to the United Nations Security Council, an Anglo-American invasion began.[87] Two months later, the Security Council formally recognized but did not endorse the United States and the United Kingdom as occupying powers.[88]

The full logic of the US decision to invade is still debated. Some argue it was a case of rational preventive war. Given that it could not confirm Saddam Hussein's plans, the United States opted for militarily engaging a nonnuclear Iraq now rather than risking a nuclear Iraq later. Even though preventive war was unnecessary in retrospect—Iraq did not have weapons of mass destruction—and the costs of war were much higher than expected, this line of reasoning holds that war was still a rational decision because the United States could not know these things ahead of time. In terms of the timing, this view cites US decision-makers' increased discomfort with uncertainty after the attacks of September 11, 2001.[89] An alternative argument is that war was driven not by a strategic rationale but by the Bush administration's irrational belief that Saddam Hussein was immune to deterrence by other means.[90] Seen in this light, the war would not have happened under a US administration with a different perception of Saddam Hussein.[91] It would have also been avoided by an administration with a different perception of the costs of war.[92] Others argue it was the logical conclusion of US oil policy and the militarization of the region.[93]

Battleground (2003–Present)

The 2003 invasion transformed Iraq from one of the region's major players to its battleground. The full dismantling of the Iraqi state altered the balance of power in the Middle East, pitting the two remaining hegemons in the Persian Gulf, Iran, and Saudi Arabia, against one another. The weakening of many Arab states since the 2011 uprisings has launched a dynamic reminiscent of the 1950s through the 1960s era: a contest for influence that plays out not through direct military confrontation, but in the domestic political systems of weak states.[94] This conflict has an identity component—hegemons and domestic allies often match on sect— but is not driven by it.

Iran and Saudi Arabia have sponsored a set of armed and nonarmed actors in Iraq, but Iran has been overwhelmingly more successful. Saudi Arabia's support of the secular Iraqiyya party in the 2005 and 2010 elections did not pay off, as the party was unable to form a winning coalition after its electoral triumph. Iran is undoubtedly the most influential player in Iraqi politics: It has close relations with governments, sponsors a number of Shi'i militias, and cooperates with the Kurdish Regional Government. Many of the political parties winning elections had established themselves in Iran for more than twenty years and maintain personal, financial, and ideological ties. Opposition against Iran's intervention, however, has increased in recent years and was one of the campaign slogans of the coalition that won the most seats in 2018.

DOMESTIC ARMED CONFLICT

Armed conflict and counterinsurgency have been central to Iraq's history. Symbolically, the event that convinced (some) Iraqi elites to institute universal conscription was a domestic, not foreign, threat.[95] Why has domestic political conflict taken the form of armed combat so often in Iraq's history? And why has it varied in the duration and intensity of violence?

A popular answer is that violent conflict reflects society's "master cleavages," which in Iraq are most often conceptualized as ethnicity (Arab vs. Kurd) and sect (Shi'i vs. Sunni). Yet the dynamics of Iraq's military confrontations reveal the limits of this "ethnic war" framework. First, violent conflict is never simply the outcome of long-standing intractable cleavages. Even though it can be tempting to use salient, visible categories to make sense of violence—especially given the poor quality of information about perpetrators and victims—many different incentives are usually involved.[96] Second, violence itself often unleashes new fault lines.

A better way to conceptualize violent conflict is through its "technologies of rebellion," or the joint military technologies of the parties engaged in armed conflict. Scholars of civil war distinguish between three technologies:

> Conventional civil war takes place when the military technologies of states and rebels are matched at a high level; irregular civil war emerges when the military technologies of the rebels lag vis-á-vis those of the state; and SNC [symmetric non-conventional] war is observed when the military technologies of states and rebels are matched at a low level.[97]

Each type has a different implication for the way violence is organized and sustained.

Iraqis have waged two types of war against each other—all but conventional war, which has been used instead in wars against other states. The persistent conflict between Kurdish nationalists and successive Iraqi regimes before 2003 was the archetype of irregular war. Kurdish nationalists had advocated for autonomy since before Iraq's independence and by 1960 had coalesced into one main organization: the Kurdish Democratic Party (KDP), founded by Mullah Mustafa Barzani in the 1940s after he was exiled by the monarchy to Iran. The Ba'th took an early seemingly conciliatory approach, signing an agreement with the KDP in 1970 that allowed Kurds the use of their language in schools and government institutions, some form of representation in national politics, limited autonomy, and the appointment of Kurdish administrators in Kurdish-majority areas. In those areas where majorities were in question, a census would determine whether they fell under Kurdish rule. Instead of planning a census, the Ba'th embarked on changing the demographic balance of contested areas, particularly that of oil-rich Kirkuk. By 1974, the KDP had launched an insurgency.

Kurdish rebels had the military capabilities to harass and challenge the central state, but they could not confront it in a direct and frontal way. Their ability to sustain the conflict stemmed from northern Iraq's rugged terrain and the material and logistical support from Iran, Israel, and the United States. As a neighboring state, Iran's support—and its willingness to keep open borders—was particularly crucial. When Iran's shah withdrew his support and closed the borders with Kurdish regions (in exchange for Iraqi concessions in the 1975 Algiers Agreement), the insurgency quickly collapsed. That year, the KDP also lost its monopoly on representation; young cadres, led by Jalal Talabani, challenged Barzani's leadership and established the Popular Union of Kurdistan (PUK). The split had generational, demographic, and linguistic roots.

The Ba'th was never able to establish as extensive an apparatus in the Kurdish areas as in the rest of the country. The regime had serious problems finding members who wanted to work in those areas and who could speak Kurdish, even though it offered additional "hardship" incentives. It was able to cobble together local militias (usually organized around Kurdish tribes), which helped policing the lowlands but were less effective in mountainous terrains. It employed policies of population redistribution and demographic engineering, destroying thousands of villages and forcibly moving their inhabitants (mostly Kurds and Turkmen).[98]

The Iran war launched a new, much more violent phase in the conflict. After 1982, Iranian troops increasingly drew support from Kurdish and other opposition parties of the North and were starting to push into Iraqi territory.[99] For the Ba'th, the conflict now became about controlling insurgent territories in the mid of a war they feared losing.[100] The regime decided to "alter the physical and human landscape of Iraqi Kurdistan" to eliminate any topographic and human barriers to state control.[101] In essence, this entailed the introduction of a policy of ethnic cleansing that included the use of chemical weapons, an economic siege, and a scorched earth policy.[102] In 1987, Saddam Hussein appointed his cousin, Ali Hassan al-Majid, giving him broad powers to deploy the security apparatus. Within three weeks of his appointment, al-Majid ordered the use of poison gas (which earned him the moniker "Chemical Ali") and began razing Kurdish villages that the Peshmerga relied on for food and shelter. Villages that could not be razed due to inaccessibility were attacked by air almost daily. During six months in 1988, tens of thousands of Kurds, the vast majority civilians, died during the operation codenamed *Anfal*. Human Rights Watch, which has carried out the only comprehensive investigation, estimates casualties to have been between fifty thousand and one hundred thousand.[103]

In 1991, in the wake of uprisings in Iraq's southern cities and the army's chaotic retreat from Kuwait under the international coalition's bombs, militants from a coalition of Kurdish parties took over the major cities, including Kirkuk. The international coalition chose not to intervene militarily at the behest of Turkey, which had always worried about the prospect of an independent Iraqi Kurdistan. The regime quickly reestablished its hold over the rebellious areas. However, as Kurdish refugees continued to pour into Turkey, the allied forces imposed a no-fly zone over the thirty-sixth parallel. This cease-fire line roughly matched the boundaries discussed in the 1974 KDP-Ba'th agreement, thereby creating a de facto autonomous Kurdish zone in Iraq's three northern provinces. By 1993, the KDP and PUK were engaged in violent conflict over territorial jurisdiction, the distribution of international economic aid, and the revenues of oil smuggling across the Iranian and Turkish borders. The KDP requested military assistance from Baghdad, greatly boosting Saddam Hussein's prestige, and demonstrating how quickly new fault lines could smooth out old ones. The factions eventually reconciled and formed an autonomous Kurdistan Regional Government (KRG).

Seeing this conflict as an example of irregular warfare accounts for crucial dynamics that do not conform to the logic of "ethnic war," such as the collaboration between Kurdish tribes and the Ba'th, the PUK-KDP infighting, and the KDP-Ba'th reconciliation.

The dynamics of the 1991 uprisings in the south are also better captured by the irregular warfare framework than the often-used sectarian lens. The *Intifada*, as the Iraqis call the uprising, began as a series of spontaneous revolts in southern cities instigated by bedraggled Iraqi soldiers returning from Kuwait. In three days, the rebellion spread to all the provinces south of Baghdad (and later to the Kurdish north).[104] Although the Damascus-based Iraqi opposition insisted the uprising was not sectarian, both the regime and Shi'i Islamist parties presented it in sectarian terms. Yet archival records of reports from party cadres in the provinces paint a more complex picture: Rebels' slogans and identities varied by locality; participants included returning prisoners of war, army deserters, former communists, and members of opposition parties who had been residing in Iran.[105] Moreover, the revolt spread to Sunni-majority cities such as Zubair, south of Basra, and did not uniformly spread to majority-Shi'i governorates (such as Wasit). Wary of an Iranian-style regime in Iraq, the United States and Saudi Arabia did not intervene when the Iraqi regime, and in particular the Republican Guard, launched a brutal counterinsurgency campaign, retaking the southern cities in fewer than ten days. As in the north, the regime tried to reengineer the physical landscape of terrains it deemed to be strategic liabilities, in this case the southern marshlands. It killed and forcibly removed the *Ma'dan* population, or so-called Marsh Arabs, from their ancestral homeland, reducing the area's population from 250,000 in 1991 to 20,000 in 2003.[106] The state also used hydrological infrastructure to divert water from the wetlands, permanently draining them, and causing an environmental disaster.[107] The only official casualties' figure of the 1991 uprisings is the 714 party members whom the regime honored as "martyrs," but most scholars and human rights observers believe that tens of thousands of unarmed civilians were killed by indiscriminate fire and summary executions.[108] Together, the counterinsurgency campaigns in the north and south resulted in the disappearance of between 250,000 and 290,000 people.[109]

Since 2003, most of Iraq's multiple armed conflicts have also been irregular. The post-2003 landscape was an aggregation of multiple, highly fragmented conflicts, often occurring simultaneously. We can categorize these into at least seven fault lines over time: (1) an insurgency against US forces in the western (mostly Sunni Arab) provinces; (2) strife between Shiʻi and Sunni militias centered primarily in and around Baghdad; (3) conflict among rival Shiʻi militias in the south; (4) a local (mostly Sunni) insurrection against al-Qaʻida in the western provinces; (5) territorial conflict between Arabs and Kurds in northern Iraq; (6) clashes among criminal mafias and smuggling networks; and (7) a transnational revolutionary insurgency (organized by the Islamic State of Iraq and the Levant) that sought to govern in the areas it captured.

These multiple conflicts reveal the shortcomings of the ethnosectarian, master-cleavage framework. For one, many actions were driven by economic incentives. For example, attacks against individuals and facilities employed in the oil industry were first interpreted by US policy-makers as Sunni grievances against the occupation. Yet these attacks had specific economic incentives: The rehabilitation of pipelines threatened a large alternative economy that had developed around the transportation of oil by tanker trucks during the 1990s embargo.[110] Moreover, the violent dissolution of the Iraqi state unleashed new fault lines. Emblematic of this was the rise of the Mahdi Army, an organization of young Shiʻi urban militants with a power base in the shantytowns and slums of a previous generation's rural–urban migration. They faced off not only against US troops but also against conservative coalitions comprising the Shiʻi traditional clergy, its tribal following, formerly exiled Islamist parties, and the urbanized elite.

Armed conflict was also driven by crucial intrasect splits. In 2007, US forces began to vet and fund armed nonstate actors to encourage resistance to insurgents from local communities in western Iraq that were increasingly opposed to the insurgents' disruption of the local economy, social mores, and political hierarchies. By the end of 2007, an estimated 75,000–85,000 men, largely Sunnis, had joined what was dubbed the Sons of Iraq militia, expanding from Anbar to Babil, Nineveh, Salah al-Din, Tamim, Diyala, and Baghdad. Within eight months, al-Qaʻida had been largely eliminated in al-Anbar province.

A new phase of the conflict began in 2014, through the dramatic ascent of the Islamic State of Iraq and the Levant (ISIS), which originated as a splinter faction from al-Qaʻida in Mesopotamia and rapidly captured much of northern Iraq—and aimed for Baghdad. Like previous coalitions of militants in the western provinces, ISIS included networks of former Baʻthist security personnel, Sunni Islamist militants, and foreign fighters. Yet its goal of revolutionary political and social change was novel. ISIS proclaimed itself a caliphate, a form of government associated with early Islam and with the successive Islamic empires that dominated the Muslim world until the early 1920s. While other Islamist groups view the caliphate as an ideal form of government that ought to be reinstated, they have not tried to establish it in the modern international system. More importantly, ISIS also sought to *govern* the territories under its military control, asserting control over the flow of water and oil resources, extracting taxes on goods and services, and taking charge of education and culture.

ISIS's territorial conquests followed the pattern of a symmetric nonconventional war: ISIS could engage the Iraqi army, Shi'i paramilitaries, and Kurdish Peshmerga directly, but given the absence of US troops (withdrawn from Iraq in 2011), all military technologies were matched at a low level. Moreover, unlike previous irregular conflict, this new phase displayed clear, if changing, frontlines. The army and police's disintegration in the face of a few thousand ISIS militants in the summer of 2014 revealed the corruption of security forces. According to the new prime minister appointed in the wake of the crisis, the army's payroll included fifty thousand "ghost soldiers" who received salaries without working. The United States resumed operations in Iraq in June 2014 because of the inability of Iraqi security forces to contain the movement. By 2017, Iraqi state security forces accompanied by Shi'i militias and aided by US air raids had recaptured the areas.

An estimated 183,000–206,000 civilians were killed between March 2003 and 2019.[111] Around 270,000 Iraqis were registered as refugees with the UN High Commissioner for Refugees (UNHCR) as of December 2020, but the total number of refugees is believed to be much higher.[112] The most recent wave of displacement began in early 2014, with more than 5.4 million Iraqis forcibly displaced between 2014 and 2017. In 2021, 1.2 million Iraqis continue to be internally displaced according to the UNHCR.[113]

RELIGION AND POLITICS

Religion and politics intersect in Iraq in multiple and fluid ways. Leaders have used different elements of religion as sources of claim making to legitimize their authority—sometimes articulating platforms grounded in different interpretations of religious *text*, other times highlighting their personal abidance by religious *practice*, and often injecting political symbolism into religious *ritual*. Even Ba'thists, who some see as the paragon of secular nationalism, promoted an idiosyncratic, Arab nationalist interpretation of Islam and used religious symbolism to undermine opposition movements, from the (Sunni) Muslim Brotherhood to Shi'i Islamist mobilization in the south.[114] Religion, as a *collective identity,* has also served as a source for bottom-up community building to demand collective rights—first, through religiously based social movements, militias, and diaspora groups and, since 2003, through political parties involved in electoral politics.

Scholars disagree on whether religion has unique effects on politics. While some argue its effects are no different from other forms of collective identification—such as class, ethnicity, language, or tribe—others posit religion is inherently unique due to doctrinal differences derived from sacred texts and the sheer magnitude of the stakes (i.e., eternal reward and punishment).[115] Iraq's experience suggests a third alternative: Religion can indeed play a unique role, but one that is rooted in the processes of state-building and breakdown rather than in doctrinal divisions.[116]

This dynamic is most apparent in Iraq's experience with the main division within Islam—that between Sunni and Shi'i Muslims.[117] As the site of the holiest shrines in Shi'i Islam and of prestigious religious seminaries in and around the shrine city of Najaf—known collectively as the "scientific place of learning" (*al-hawza al-'ilmiyya*)—Iraq holds unrivaled symbolism for Shi'a worldwide.[118] This unique place in transnational Shi'ism has endowed the Iraqi Shi'i clerical establishment with an independent source of power from Baghdad, encouraging it to make forays into politics that have challenged every central government. Clerics have not always enjoyed success in mobilizing large numbers of Iraqi Shi'a for political ends. Between the 1930s and 1970s, many urban middle, lower-middle, and working-class Shi'a, particularly in southern cities, actively supported the Iraqi Communist Party. The Ba'th's Arab nationalism also attracted many middle-class Shi'a in the 1960s, who joined the ranks at every level in the party hierarchy. The tide began to turn in favor of Shi'i Islamism in the late 1970s because of a confluence of factors: the Ba'th's violent crackdown on the communists (and its banning of all parties); the increasingly narrow regional base of the Ba'th's higher echelons (networks in north-central Iraq); and a regional trend of Islamist parties challenging secular movements' failures to deliver on socioeconomic development and political liberation. In sum, the appeal of Shi'i Islamism increased with the closure of alternative avenues for Shi'a to participate in the opposition or in the regime.

Iraq also occupies a second unique position with respect to Sunni–Shi'i identities in the Middle East. As the eastern frontier between the Ottoman Empire and its archenemy Persia and later between the Arab world and Iran, Iraq navigates religious identities through geopolitical channels. The Ottomans excluded Shi'a from military and bureaucratic positions because they feared them to be a potential Persian fifth column and enacted a law prohibiting marriage between Ottoman and Iranian citizens.[119] The consequences of this conflation between "Shi'i" and "Persian" would take more violent forms in modern Iraq, when the new state's demographic distribution injected an additional source of tension: Iraqi Shi'a have outnumbered Sunnis since 1920 (56–65 percent versus 32–37 percent).

The Iranian Revolution in 1979 marked a turning point. Not only did it bring to power Shi'i Islamists who proclaimed they would export their revolution—an event that shook the entire region—but it did so right next door. Before 1979, regimes' attempts to erode Shi'i clergy's independent power were those applied to all clergy: tight control of seminaries, rituals, processions; the appointment of government-approved clerics; and the sponsorship of those who were willing to disavow politics. To discourage its citizens from identifying with Iran, the regime launched a discursive campaign to distinguish "Arab Shi'ism" from "Persian Shi'ism." After 1979, the regime dealt harshly with Shi'i clergy who called for the establishment of an Islamic government, sentencing prominent clerics to death.[120] During the Iran–Iraq war, although most Iraqi Shi'a were fighting as conscripts in the Iraqi army, some Shi'i Islamist opposition parties fought alongside the Iranian army.

The post-2003 political process fundamentally changed how Sunni and Shi'i identities interact with politics. It is hard to overstate the role that Shi'i diasporic returnees have had on the politicization of sectarian identity in Iraq. Along with Kurdish parties, Shi'i exiles portrayed their suffering under dictatorship almost exclusively as one of communal victimhood and enacted an ethnosectarian power-sharing system that was meant to right past injustices. From this perspective, the Ba'th had solely victimized Kurds and Shi'a, and by extension, all Sunni Arabs were either complicit or had suffered less and thus were less deserving of a voice.

This narrative treated Sunni Arabs as a uniform, homogenous community, even though they are spread over provinces that encompass several confessional and ethnic groups (except for Anbar) and exhibit urban–rural divides. Although Arab Sunnis were overrepresented in state institutions since the Ottoman era, they did not see themselves as a differentiated group. Instead, Sunni identity was the "taken-for granted underpinning of an Islamic identity and in some cases the assumed marker of national identity . . . it required neither representation nor validation."[121] In response to the post-2003 feeling of disenfranchisement, multiple agendas emerged among Sunni Arabs, one of which took an extreme form of Islamism. Salafism has proved to be a useful mobilizing ideology: It attracts foreign fighters and financial assistance through global networks, and it combines very different foreign and domestic enemies (the United States, Iran, Shi'i parties, former exiles) into a single enemy category of "infidels."[122]

Aided by the country's demographic breakdown, the new ethnosectarian system, and their dominant narrative of victimhood, parties and movements that mobilize explicitly around a Shi'i Islamist identity are today the primary power brokers in Iraq. Yet they are deeply divided along religious and political lines: between following the religious authority (*marja'iyya*) of Iraqi Grand Ayatollah Ali al-Sistani or that of Iranian Grand Ayatollah Ali Hosseini Khamenei; between supporting the political process to date (e.g., Islamic Supreme Council of Iraq) or engaging in antiestablishment politics (e.g., Sadrist movement); and between advocating for Iran's interventionism in Iraqi politics or seeking to reduce Iranian influence.

POLITICAL ECONOMY OF DEVELOPMENT

Iraq's economic development has tracked three main dynamics over time: the production and transportation of oil, domestic and international armed conflict, and political corruption.

Oil

Iraq's economic development is inextricably linked with oil production; the country possesses the world's fifth-largest crude oil reserves.[123] Crude oil accounts for forty percent of GDP,[124] 85 percent of government revenue, and 80 percent of foreign exchange earnings.[125] The effects of natural resource abundance on political-economic outcomes are disputed. Resource curse theory claims that oil causes economic stagnation through the decline in other sectors' competitiveness and the volatility to state revenues. It also holds that oil increases the likelihood of authoritarianism by reducing accountability to citizens, facilitating repression, or increasing the costs of leaving office. Rentier state theory claims that oil causes weak and predatory state institutions. Yet cross-national empirical evidence challenges these theories; oil has no effect when other variables associated with these outcomes are considered and may, at best, have a conditional effect.

Iraq's experience corroborates these findings. For one, although it has not developed other economic sectors sufficiently—the contribution of nonoil sectors is relatively small both in GDP and in exports—it is unclear that oil is the cause. Governments repeatedly tried to increase agricultural productivity—before and after the boom in fuel rents per capita—and

FIGURE 12.1 ■ **Iraq's Petroleum and Other Liquids Production and Consumption (1990–2017), Million Barrels per Day**

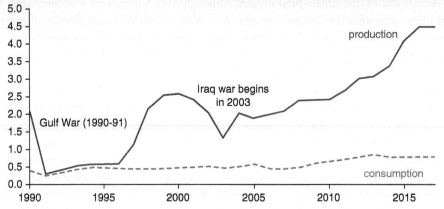

Source: U.S. Energy Information Administration, https://www.eia.gov/todayinenergy/detail.php?id = 37973

their failures were rooted in weak institutions (see next section). Second, authoritarianism and weak institutions preceded the oil boom, and there are no indications that the country was on a path to democracy. Third, rising oil revenues between 1952 and 1980 were invested in the development of impressive health care, education, and infrastructure systems, rendering the economy one of the strongest in the Middle East.[126] In the decade of the 1970s, per capita income rose from $306 to $3,734. Finally, although oil revenue has indeed faced dramatic volatility, the culprit was fluctuations in oil production and exports, not in prices as the resource curse theory expects. Oil production, in turn, has been shaped above all by war (see Figure 12.1).

Economies of War

Iraq's economic development was reversed by a series of wars beginning in 1980: the war with Iran, the war with Kuwait, the First Gulf War, the sanctions regime (dubbed the "invisible war"[127]), the Second Gulf War, and post-2003 conflicts. The economic costs were direct and indirect.

The war with Iran (1980–1988) radically transformed Iraq's economy from one dependent on oil into one dependent on foreign aid. Iranian attacks heavily damaged Iraqi oil-export facilities and Syria closed Iraq's pipeline to the Mediterranean. Iraq borrowed to cushion the immediate revenue loss, emerging from the war with a foreign debt of $50 billion to $82 billion, the bulk of it owed to Kuwait and Saudi Arabia. Military expenditures constituted about 70 percent of Iraq's GDP. Most of the population suffered a precipitous fall in their standard of living. Per capita GDP fell from $4,200 in 1979 to $1,756 in 1988. The war also drained human and financial resources away from manufacturing and agriculture. More than 20 percent of the labor force was employed in the armed forces; the vast labor shortages led to the recruitment of 1.5 million Arab (mostly Egyptian) workers to run the agricultural, industrial, and service sectors.

The 1990–1991 Gulf War dealt a further blow to the economy, both through the destruction of infrastructure and, more persistently, through the postconflict sanctions regime. According to the terms of the sanctions, Iraq owed Kuwait reparations and would have to comply with provisions concerning the dismantling of its weapons systems. Failure to conform would extend the comprehensive international embargo that precluded Iraq from oil exports. By 1997, GDP was at one-half to two-thirds of its prewar level. Government salaries lost almost all their value as the Iraqi dinar effectively became a worthless currency. In 1996, the UN Oil-for-Food Programme allowed the government to sell a portion of its oil, but all revenues had to be spent with UN approval. By 2000, Iraq had become one of the poorest countries in the region, with high malnutrition and child mortality rates.

Infrastructure—electric, water, health, and education systems—was further damaged by the widespread looting that followed the US invasion. When US forces entered Baghdad in March 2003, they only secured the Ministry of Defense, located in Hussein's Republican Palace, and the Ministry of Oil, allowing massive looting to occur in all other ministries. These initial three weeks of violence and theft severely damaged the state's administrative capacity: Seventeen of Baghdad's twenty-three ministry buildings were completely gutted. The estimated cost of the lootings is as much as $12 billion, equal to a third of Iraq's annual GDP.[128] One of the most deleterious effects of the preinvasion bombing and the subsequent looting was the damage to Iraq's electrical grid and transmission towers. Nationwide, the average electricity supply dropped from sixteen hours to twenty-four hours per day before the invasion to four hours to eight hours per day in May 2003.[129]

Another effect of the sanctions' regime was the rise in smuggling networks as Iraq's borders became increasingly porous. Some networks were run by the state or affiliated "contractor bourgeoisie" who linked between the state and neighboring traders. Others involved small-time operators trying to make a living (which also involved cross-border connections, though these were based on kinship, not access to power). The economic structures developed by these networks have been resistant to reform, and their beneficiaries have resisted violently. The CPA's tenure witnessed systematic attacks on the electricity grid (essential for the oil industry), over seventy attacks on oil-related infrastructure, and attacks on people working for the Ministry of Oil.[130] The attacks had clear economic incentives: to force the government to give up on transporting oil through pipelines and return to the pre-2003 tanker truck networks developed in the 1990s.[131]

Public Service Provision and Political Corruption

As rulers of a middle-income country, Iraq's leaders are severely underperforming in reconstructing core physical infrastructure and delivering basic services to the country's 39 million inhabitants. Two public sectors are the source of mounting public frustration: electricity and health. Although electricity provision has been increasing, most Iraqis continue to lack a reliable source of power—a brutal situation given that temperatures can rise above 120 degrees Fahrenheit in the summer. Multiple electricity ministers have been suspended from their posts

PHOTO 12.2 Protesters carry national flags and a fan in Baghdad's iconic Tahrir Square on August 7, 2015, amid a brutal heatwave with frequent power cuts

AP Photo/Karim Kadim, File

for allegations of corruption. According to the country's top finance and oil officials, $300 billion was paid to contractors for projects that were never completed.[132] The most senior government figure responsible for pursuing corruption from 2008 to 2011 identified the government's contracting process as "the father of all corruption issues in Iraq."[133]

The country's health care sector cannot accommodate citizens' needs; every year, tens of thousands of Iraqis travel abroad for medical care (primarily to India, Iran, Turkey, Jordan, and Lebanon). To fund international treatment, Iraqis sell belongings or are assisted by family, friends, political parties, and tribes.[134] Despite many promises to rebuild the health system, the last public hospital to be built in the country was in 1986. The failed response to the COVID-19 pandemic has been seen as emblematic of Iraq's failing health system and, by extension, the state.[135] In April 2021, in a tragically symbolic event, at least 82 people were killed and 110 injured when an oxygen tank exploded at a hospital treating COVID-19 patients on the outskirts of Baghdad, which lacked safety systems, fire extinguishers, or sprinklers.

The inadequate delivery of public services has its source in political corruption. About one-third of total government spending goes to public wages and compensation and nearly 40 percent to the Ministries of Interior and Defense. Underlying these figures is an increasingly generous wage scale and sharp growth in public sector numbers, which are believed to include ghost employees and double dipping.[136] Ministers have used their positions as power bases for appropriating resources and developing clientelistic networks.

CONCLUSION

Eighteen years after the fall of the Ba'thist regime, Iraqis cannot depend on elites to provide security, political and civil rights, and basic standards of living. The apportionment of the central state into personal fiefdoms and the absence of an independent judiciary to arbitrate has paralyzed the provision of essential services. Mass protests by Iraqi citizens against political corruption are greeted with promises for reform, but subsequent proposed changes seek to only insulate against dissent. In this environment, a revamped rebel organization was able to take over large parts of Iraq's territory, aided by previous governance experience, the state's weak security organizations, and local yearning for social order. Although the government was able to recapture territory by 2017 (heavily aided by international intervention), the underlying conditions that facilitated the rapid rise of the Islamic State persist.

The unprecedented scope and intensity of popular protests in recent years, coupled with a trajectory of fewer Iraqis voting in each election indicate that many Iraqis are alienated from the ruling establishment and have concluded that change will not come through elections or dysfunctional institutions. The prominent role of Iraqis under the age of 30 in protest movements, coupled with the fact that they overwhelmingly stayed home on Election Day 2018 and 2021, reveal an emerging generational divide between older generations and Iraqi youth who have only known a post-Ba'th Iraq.[137]

SUGGESTED READINGS

Al-Ali, Zaid. The *Struggle for Iraq's Future: How Corruption, Incompetence, and Sectarianism Have Undermined Democracy.* New Haven, CT: Yale University Press, 2014.

Blaydes, Lisa. *State of Repression: Iraq under Saddam Hussein.* Princeton, NJ: Princeton University Press, 2018.

Faust, Aaron M. *The Ba'thification of Iraq: Saddam Hussein's Totalitarianism.* Austin, TX: University of Texas Press, 2015.

Franzén, Johan. *Pride and Power: A Modern History of Iraq.* London: Hurst & Co, 2020.

"Middle East Learn and Teach Series: Iraq. "March 19, 2021. https://www.jadaliyya.com/Details/42523.

Khoury, Dina Rizk. *Iraq in Wartime: Soldiering, Martyrdom, and Remembrance.* New York, NY: Cambridge University Press, 2013.

Pursley, Sara. *Familiar Futures: Time, Selfhood, and Sovereignty in Iraq.* Stanford, CA: Stanford University Press, 2019.

Saleh, Zainab. *Return to Ruin: Iraqi Narratives of Exile and Nostalgia.* Stanford, CA: Stanford University Press, 2021.

Tripp, Charles. *A History of Iraq.* 3rd ed. Cambridge: Cambridge University Press, 2007.

13 ISRAEL

Lihi Ben Shitrit

A political system must be understood in terms of the people who live under it, their values and ideals, the resources at their disposal, the challenges that face the system, and the institutions developed to meet these challenges. Israel is a fascinating example of a complex system that has developed in a relatively short amount of time (since the 1880s) into a dynamic country undertaking colossal military, economic, and social commitments. The country has undergone tremendous domestic changes over the decades: the continued ingathering of Jews from around the world, parliamentary democracy characterized by the continuing reconstitution of coalition governments, major constitutional changes, and economic transformation. On the international scene, there have been waves of accommodation with its Arab neighbors, alongside continuing tension with Lebanon and Syria and struggles with the Palestinians over land and political rights.

HISTORY OF STATE-BUILDING

As discussed by Mark Tessler (Chapter 2), Israel emerged from interaction with the British mandate, the contact with the local Arabs, the reality of war in Europe, and Jews' collective memory of being a dispersed people seeking a homeland. At the time of establishment in May 1948, the new state faced many problems. The task of adapting the prestate institutions into national institutions in the fields of government, economics, welfare, internal security, and military took place in the shadow of war, economic crisis, and the challenges presented by absorbing vast numbers of new immigrants for which existing infrastructure was far from adequate.

The dominant Labor Party, Mapai, headed by David Ben-Gurion, was best positioned to take the lead during and after the 1948 war of independence as it dominated most of the prestate institutions. Two weeks into the war, the provisional government under Ben-Gurion transformed the Haganah, the main Jewish militia force in the prestate period, into the Israel Defense Forces (IDF) and banned independent militias. Other militias such as Palmach, Irgun, and Lehi, affiliated with rival political parties, were integrated into the IDF as separate units. These units were later disbanded, and their fighters were incorporated into the regular army units. The disbanding of the militias did not happen without casualties. In June 1948, the IDF sank the ship *Altalena*, which was carrying weapons purchased in France for the Irgun fighters. Several Irgun members were killed in the incident. Although the event left many Irgun supporters disaffected, it successfully established a state monopoly over the legitimate means of violence.

Elections were held in January 1949. Ben-Gurion's Mapai won the largest number of seats in the Knesset (46 seats out of 120; the *Knesset* is the name for Israel's legislature) and headed the coalition government. The first government worked to consolidate various institutions affiliated with the prestate political parties into a centralized state system dominated by Mapai. By promoting centralization and holding most of the important cabinet portfolios such as foreign affairs, treasury, education, and defense as well as controlling the labor union, Mapai achieved dominance to the extent that the party and the state became almost indistinguishable.

This close association had its benefits for Israel's workers and new immigrants. The Mapai-affiliated labor union, Histadrut, became a powerful actor in the Israeli economy. The Histadrut was committed to the protection and expansion of workers' rights and benefits and to the promotion of progressive labor legislation. The Histadrut was not only the largest labor union, it was also a workers' cooperative and, in that capacity, the largest public employer in Israel. It provided an array of services for workers, including health care, educational, and cultural services. The socialist ideology shared by the ruling Mapai and by the Histadrut and the identity between the leading personalities in the two bodies enabled the passage of the 1950s progressive labor laws that were the foundation of the Israeli welfare state. The association between the Histadrut and Mapai benefited the party as well. To find employment and receive benefits such as health care, workers often had to join the Histadrut. Joining the Histadrut inevitably meant an affiliation with Mapai.

State encouragement of Jewish immigration was another cornerstone of state-building in the years after independence. Through the Jewish Agency organization, the state facilitated a renewed immigration flow of Jews from Asia, the Middle East, Central Europe, and other parts of the world. The absorption and integration of these diverse immigrants and refugees became one of the state's main tasks, but the existing economy and infrastructure were inadequate for the population boom. Many of the new immigrants were settled in deserted Arab homes, in tent camps, and in hastily constructed "transition camps" (*maabarot*). In 1951, there were 127 such camps that were home to more than 200,000 immigrants by 1952. Camp residents suffered from poor living conditions and unemployment. Another challenge was the mental difficulty of adjusting to camp life, which entailed the breakup of traditional social structures and intimate interaction with people of diverse cultural backgrounds.

The state responded to the challenge of population expansion by focusing its effort on the establishment of agricultural settlements in the Israeli periphery. This effort came to answer several of the challenges facing the new state. It would alleviate the plight of the unemployed new immigrants in the camps by providing them agricultural work and permanent housing. It would also strengthen Israel's hold on the territories acquired as a result of the 1948 war and prevent Arab return into those areas. Finally, the expansion of the agricultural sector fulfilled the ideological and economic need for self-sufficiency. A great number of kibbutzim (socialist agricultural collectives) and moshavim (farm collectives with private ownership) were established. Nonagricultural "development towns" were also built to house the new population and to populate the Israeli periphery.

Another of Mapai's state-building projects was the construction of a unifying ethos that would provide a coherent Israeli identity to the diverse immigrant groups that made up the country's population. The state promoted seminal historical events of heroism, biblical stories, and the ideals of Zionism and pioneering as exemplifying the Israeli ethos while it devalued the periods of Jewish Diaspora. One vehicle for the creation of a unifying ethos was the education system. In the prestate years and in the first years of the state, independent school systems affiliated with various political parties took charge of the education of the nation. In 1949, the Knesset passed a law establishing mandatory education but did not end the independent school systems. Very early, Ben-Gurion began to push for a standardized state education system to replace the separate political streams. In 1953, the government terminated the political education streams and introduced a standardized state education system made up of two branches: religious and nonreligious.

Indeed, the question of religion in Israel has accompanied the period of state-building and remains a controversial one to this day. The Declaration of Independence of May 14, 1948, announced the establishment of a "Jewish state," but the specifics of what constituted the state as a Jewish one remained to be debated. To get the ultra-Orthodox Jewish community on board with the Zionist state project, in 1947 Ben-Gurion sent what became known as the "status quo letter" to its leaders, in which he outlined the relationship between state and religion in the nascent state. The letter made several concessions to the ultra-Orthodox community: It guaranteed that the Sabbath would be nationally observed as the holy rest day; that personal status matters would not be divided into religious and secular codes, thus ensuring the monopoly of religious law over such matters; and that the autonomy of the ultra-Orthodox education system from state control would remain intact. As a result of these guarantees, Agudat Israel, the leading ultra-Orthodox party, joined Ben-Gurion's coalition government after independence.

The years between 1948 and 1967 were the period of independence and state-building. The June 1967 War, in which Israel gained control over the West Bank and the Gaza Strip, and with them the large Palestinian population residing in these territories, marked the start of a new era of Israel's political history. Mapai dominated the first period of state consolidation and had been impressively successful in meeting the economic, security, and social challenges facing the new state. The second period has been consumed by the dilemmas attendant on the struggle to extricate the country from the fruits of the 1967 victory, including seeking accommodation with the Palestinians. This period saw a decline in Mapai dominance and the rise of the right-wing Likud Party. It also heralded the end of the melting-pot ideology that characterized the nation-building years and the dismantling of the highly centralized welfare state.

KEY FACTS ON ISRAEL

AREA 8,470 square miles (21,937 square kilometers)

CAPITAL Israel declares Jerusalem its capital, but this designation is not recognized internationally. Tel Aviv is the diplomatic capital.

POPULATION 9,140,500 (includes populations of the Golan Heights and East Jerusalem, annexed by Israel after 1967); approximately 22,000 Israeli settlers live in the Golan Heights; approximately 201,000 Israeli settlers live in East Jerusalem (2019 est)

DATE OF INDEPENDENCE May 14, 1948 (from League of Nations Mandate under British Administration)

RELIGION/ETHNIC GROUPS (PERCENTAGE) Jewish, 74.3; Muslim, 17.8; Christian, 1.9; Druze, 1.6; other, 4.4 (2018 est)

OFFICIAL LANGUAGE Hebrew; Arabic used officially for Arab minority; English widely spoken

TYPE OF GOVERNMENT Parliamentary democracy

GDP (PPP) $363.4 billion, $41,953 per capita (2020 est)

GDP (NOMINAL) $394.9 billion (2019 est)

PERCENTAGE OF GDP BY SECTOR Agriculture, 2.4; industry, 26.5; services, 69.5

PERCENTAGE OF POPULATION UNDER 25 43.04

RENTS (PERCENTAGE OF GDP) FROM NATURAL RESOURCES 0.093 (2019 est)

FERTILITY RATE 3.0 children born/woman

Sources: Central Bureau of Statistics. "Statistical Abstract of Israel 2021 – No.72.", July 4, 2021, https://www.cbs.gov.il/en/publications/Pages/2021/Statistical-Abstract-of-Israel-2021-No-72.aspx. CIA. "The World Factbook." August 4, 2022, https://www.cia.gov/the-world-factbook/.

Social Transformation and Challenges

Israel today is a contemporary society populated largely by immigrants attracted by the idea of a Jewish state. In 1948, fewer than 6 percent of the world's Jews lived in Israel, and by 2018, 45 percent did. Modern Israel is largely the result of Jewish immigration in the late nineteenth and early to mid-twentieth centuries. Mass immigration of Jews to Israel continues to enjoy wide support on an abstract level from Jews in Israel and abroad, although the fact is that most Jews of the world do not live in Israel.

Even though Israel has always encouraged Jewish immigration, this does not mean that conditions are equivalent for all of its Jewish residents. Most importantly, earlier waves of immigrants are advantaged compared with those who came later. Jewish immigration waves in the prestate years (described in detail in Chapter 2) raised their share of conflict between members of new and older waves over religion, ideology, and leadership. It also set off conflict between the newcomers and the local Arab population. From the beginning of the first wave of Jewish immigration (Aliya) in 1882 to the end of the fifth Aliya in 1939, the number of Jews had grown from 4 percent of the population to 30 percent through immigration. The new immigrants came mainly from Russia and eastern Europe and later from central Europe. Each Aliya had its specific demographic and ideological character with nationalism, socialism, economic opportunism, and the fear of persecution in Europe and Russia animating different waves. The demographic transformation, competing Zionist and Palestinian national claims, and economic difficulties sparked resistance among the Arab population, which reacted violently with demonstrations, strikes, and attacks in the 1920s and 1930s.

MAP 13.1 ■ Israel

With Israel's Declaration of Independence in May 1948, the Arabs again protested, this time through force of arms, with neighboring Arab states attacking the new state in an attempt to abort its birth. Many local Arabs left—some forced out by the Jewish fighting forces and some of their own initiative, thinking that this was but a temporary exodus until the fighting halted. Instead, these local Arabs became permanently displaced, and they currently form the crux of the Palestinian refugee problem that remains unresolved.

In 1948, the remnants of the European Jewish society who survived the Holocaust immigrated to Israel, but soon, communities of Jews born in Asia and Africa made up the bulk of the new immigrants. The large number of these immigrants doubled the Jewish population of the country within these years and heightened the already difficult economic conditions faced by the new country. Between 1948 and 1951, 700,000 immigrants were added to the 650,000 Jews already in Israel.

Waves of immigration came at a fast and furious pace. Jews came from Algeria, Bulgaria, Egypt, India, Libya, Morocco, Poland, Romania, Turkey, Yemen, and Yugoslavia and from as far away as Argentina. Nearly all of Yemen's 55,000 Jews left for Israel. The highest monthly immigration rate was recorded during the first seven months of 1951, when some 20,000 immigrants arrived in the country each month. After reaching a low annual figure of 18,000 immigrants between 1952 and 1954, the figure reached 7000 in 1957, and immigration between 1961 and 1965 reached 230,000, coming largely from Morocco and Romania. The government was hard-pressed to feed and house the new immigrants.

The Israeli economy was unprepared for the absorption of such a large number of immigrants. Israel experienced a severe balance of payment crisis, and austerity measures were introduced to curb the threat of inflation. Food and clothing were rationed, leading to long lines and shortages and creating a vibrant black market. The austerity measures also fostered rising resentment among the country's population. However, by 1953 the economy was starting to stabilize. Later, the inflow of funds from West Germany as part of its 1953 Holocaust reparation agreement with Israel as well as aid from the US government and the Jewish Diaspora slowly brought a recovery to the Israeli economy and contributed to rising living standards. Nevertheless, the absorption of this immigration wave of predominantly Middle Eastern (Mizrahi) Jews by a struggling Israeli economy, inadequate infrastructure, and a host society of largely European descent (Ashkenazi) spelled great difficulties to the newcomers. Loss of social and economic status as well as cultural marginalization of the new immigrants led to frustrations that would reach their height in the 1970s with mass protests and put an end to Mapai's political dominance.

Another demographic challenge presented itself in the aftermath of the June 1967 War. The conquest of the West Bank and the Gaza Strip brought the entire Palestinian population of these territories under Israeli control. The military rule Israel had imposed in the territories meant that Israel was now to a large extent responsible for the well-being of the Palestinian community. It also entailed the entrance of many Palestinian laborers into the Israeli workforce, effectively replacing Jewish laborers in low-income jobs in some fields such as agriculture and construction. Cheap Palestinian labor meant that Mizrahi Jews could no longer compete for low-paying agricultural and construction employment; but the consequence of the June 1967 War led to a boom in the Israeli economy, and many Mizrahi Jews were able to become employers, often as contractors to mainly Palestinian laborers.

By 1967, the sources of potential Jewish immigration had changed: The eastern European and North African reservoirs were largely dried up, leaving Western countries and the Soviet Union as places where large numbers of Jews lived. Of the 250,000 Jews given exit visas from the Soviet Union in the 1970s, however, only 160,000 came to Israel. The end of the Soviet Union in 1989 saw a resurgence of Jewish immigration to Israel. Between 1989 and 2007, 1.2 million Jews came to Israel. In 1990, 184,300 Jews arrived from the former Soviet Union and in 1991, an additional 146,700. The great bulk of the Ethiopian Jewish community came as a result of an airlift, Operation Solomon, in 1991; the operation involved 14,200 immigrants.

Most of the 609,900 immigrants from the former Soviet Union between 1989 and 1995 were well educated, secular, and steeped in Western and Russian culture. They came because the Soviet Union was crumbling, the political and economic future was uncertain, and they were concerned about anti-Semitism. Most of them discovered Zionism and Judaism in Israel, not in the Soviet Union. Many had brothers, sisters, and cousins who went to the United States and other Western countries during the same period, and many of these immigrants would have joined their relatives there if they could have. The major feature of this Soviet immigrant group was their high level of education; 60 percent were professionals, compared with 28 percent for the Jewish population already in the country.

These immigrants had to adjust to the multicultural and, in their view, significantly Levantine society in Israel. They also experienced a decline in social status as appropriate jobs meeting their qualifications were not readily available. Housing was another major challenge because of the large number of immigrants. The state had to reformulate its immigrants' absorption method from the practice of housing new immigrants in temporary "absorption centers" to providing each immigrant an "absorption package" that included financial assistance for renting an apartment and for subsistence. The cheap cost of living in the highly subsidized Jewish settlements in the occupied West Bank led to the settlement of a substantial number of the immigrants in these territories. To the chagrin of the Palestinians, this trend contributed to the growth of the Jewish population in the settlements.

Ethiopian immigrants, who had been literally picked out of their developing African homeland overnight, faced even greater difficulties. They came to a country that was very different from the one they had left and one that had very few former immigrants like them. Tracing their Judaism back to King Solomon and Queen of Sheba, the Ethiopians brought traditions that had developed separately from the rest of the Jewish world. Accordingly, in

PHOTO 13.1 Crowds at the Damascus Gate in Jerusalem reflect Israel's social diversity

Ahmad Gharabli/AFP/Getty Images

addition to their economic status and cultural difference, many were seen as lacking in a religious sense as well. They were required to undergo Orthodox conversion and to send their children to religious schools. Their social and economic integration faced serious challenges.

Ethnic Divisions: Intra-Jewish Cleavages

Intra-Jewish ethnic divisions have been a prominent feature of Israeli politics. The subject is a complex one, but the major distinction among Jews is between Ashkenazim, who came to Israel from Europe and America, and Mizrahim (also referred to as Sephardim), who immigrated from Middle Eastern countries. The terms *Ashkenazim* and *Sephardim* have their origins in the medieval period of the various communities' sojourning in the Diaspora following different expulsions throughout history. More appropriately, three divisions should be recognized: a Mizrahi (meaning Oriental or Eastern, in Hebrew) community of Jews who never left the Middle East; the Sephardim, whose language (Ladino) and ethnic culture originated in Spain before the expulsion of 1492; and the Ashkenazim (referring to Germany), whose hybrid language was Yiddish. It is the Ashkenazi-Mizrahi division that constitutes the main ethnic cleavage among Jews in Israel. Most of the world's Jews are Ashkenazim, but only about one-quarter of them live in Israel, compared with about two-thirds of the Mizrahim. Israel's Jewish population is roughly half Mizrahi and half Ashkenazi, but as the children of mixed marriages—between Mizrahi and Ashkenazi, now approximately 20 percent of total marriages—come of age, these distinctions become difficult to maintain.[1]

The Mizrahi-Ashkenazi nomenclature first emerged as a major theme in Israeli politics in the late 1950s. The integration of Jews from Middle Eastern countries in the 1950s and 1960s into the new Israeli state was replete with difficulties and discrimination. Many of these immigrants had to leave most of their possessions in their countries of origin and had to adjust to a lower socioeconomic status in Israel. They were sent to live in poor, peripheral "development towns" and were employed as blue-collar laborers and in agriculture although most were traders and craftsmen by profession. Many were less educated than their Ashkenazi counterparts, a factor that greatly affected their income levels compared with Ashkenazim.

In 1959, the dissatisfaction of Mizrahi immigrants over this state of affairs exploded in semispontaneous violent demonstrations and clashes with police. Known as the Wadi Salib incident, the protest began in a neighborhood of Haifa by that name and soon spread to Mizrahi towns across the country. The police successfully contained the protest, but in its aftermath, the government took some steps to alleviate the poor living conditions of the Wadi Salib residents by providing them new housing outside of the neighborhood. The government also increased budgets for addressing the economic hardships of *maabarot* residents.

Nevertheless, socioeconomic inequalities as well as discrimination and cultural marginalization continued. Although the conditions of second-generation Mizrahi Jews born in Israel improved in comparison with the conditions of their parents, they still achieved lower educational and income levels than second-generation Ashkenazim. While these gaps have been closing slowly, disparities have not yet disappeared. The cultural hegemony of Ashkenazi Jews has also deemed Mizrahi culture as "lower class" compared with the "upper class" or sophisticated European culture of the Ashkenazim.

It was in the 1970s when the Mizrahi-Ashkenazi cleavage reached its height in Israeli politics. In 1971, a group of young, second-generation Mizrahi residents of Jerusalem formed the Black Panthers movement, borrowing the name from its US counterpart. The group organized a series of mass demonstrations protesting the discrimination and marginalization of the Mizrahim. Golda Meir, Israeli prime minister at the time, refused to recognize the validity of the group's claims; her response was simply to state dismissively that the young Mizrahi organizers were "not nice." Although somewhat popular, the group failed to translate the momentum it had created into political power, and it disintegrated because of internal conflicts.

The Black Panthers protest, although unsuccessful, made the Mizrahi-Ashkenazi cleavage a central feature of Israeli politics. In 1977, the majority of Mizrahi Jews voted for the right-wing opposition Likud Party, a move that helped bring an end to the dominance of Mapai (later called Labor). Mizrahi Jews identified Mapai, the ruling party since Israel's establishment, as responsible for their discrimination. Menachem Begin, the Likud leader who was himself Ashkenazi, employed ethnic-grievance rhetoric as a way to attract Mizrahi voters. Aside from its rhetoric, however, the Likud government did little to improve the socioeconomic conditions of Mizrahi Jews, and it focused its efforts on the settlements in the Palestinian territories occupied in 1967. This inattention led to a new pattern of Mizrahi political organizing in the 1980s and 1990s—the rise of sectarian Mizrahi parties.

The first such party, Tami, was established in 1981. Its leaders broke away from the National Religious Party to form an explicitly Mizrahi one. The party won 3 seats in the 1981 elections, but it failed to widen its appeal, and by 1988 it no longer existed. The next and far more successful stage of Mizrahi organizing began with the establishment of the Shas Party in 1984. Shas branded itself as an ultra-Orthodox Sephardi party with an explicit agenda of improving the socioeconomic conditions of the Mizrahi population and reclaiming the lost pride of Mizrahi traditional religious culture. Shas was not simply a political party; it was also a social movement for religious and cultural Mizrahi revival, with its own separate education system that included religious schools, kindergartens, yeshivas, and synagogues. During the 1990s, the party's influence grew with each election. In the 1992 elections, the party won 6 seats in the Knesset. In 1996, its presence grew to 10 seats, and in 1999, it reached 17 seats. In the three 21st-century elections, the party won 11 or 12 seats each time, but in the 2015 election, its seats decreased to 7.

Although Shas has been the most successful ethnic party, its ultra-Orthodox religious orientation and its inability to deliver on economic promises to lower-income families have limited its appeal. Secular, leftist, and other segments of the Mizrahi population still divide their votes among the mainstream parties (generally Labor and Likud). In addition, as socioeconomic and cultural divisions between Ashkenazi and Mizrahi Jews become increasingly blurred, the political appeal of sectarian Mizrahi organizing is diminishing. Culturally, however, Israel has experienced a flourishing of Mizrahi cultural activism in the last decade, with activists working on mainstreaming Mizrahi music, art, literature, and heritage. Both the Left and the Right have tried to capitalize on this trend, claiming to be more "inclusive" of Mizrahis, a testament to the success and influence of this activism.

Another party that enjoyed ethnic appeal in recent years was the Russian-immigrant-affiliated Yisrael Beiteinu Party (Israel Our Home). By the mid-1990s, Russian Jews constituted

10 percent of Israel's population and began to vote increasingly along ethnic lines. In 1996, the Russian-immigrant-affiliated Yisrael Bealiya (the word *Aliya* means immigration of Jews to Israel) Party won 7 seats in the Knesset, but later dropped to 6 in 1999 and 2 in 2003. Yisrael Beiteinu, a far-right Russian-led party, won 11 seats in 2006 and 15 in 2009, as it attracted high numbers of Russian voters as well as non-Russian, right-wing voters and became the third-largest party in the Knesset in 2009. In the 2013 election, it merged with the governing Likud, but split from it in the 2015 election. A series of corruption scandals led to its poor performance in 2015, in which it won only 6 seats.

Palestinian Citizens of Israel

Before the establishment of the state of Israel, Palestinian Arabs were a large majority in mandatory Palestine: 96 percent in 1882 and 83.4 percent in 1939. With statehood in 1948, their relative weight fell to 18 percent because the new state boundaries did not include the West Bank and Gaza, and many refugees departed from areas that came under Israeli control. Jewish immigration after Israel's establishment further diminished the relative share of Arabs in the population, which reached a low of 11 percent in 1966. In 1967, following the June war, Israel's annexation of East Jerusalem increased their share to 14 percent. As of 2018, Arabs made up 20.9 percent of Israel's population, numbering 1.85 million. Of the Israeli Arabs, most are Muslim: approximately 1.56 million in 2017, comprising 17.8 percent of the population (see Figure 13.1). In addition, in 2017 there were 170,000 Christians (both Arab and non-Arab) and 141,000 Druze. Muslim children, however, made up approximately one-quarter of those under age fifteen in the country. The annual rate of growth of the Muslim population in Israel in 2017 was 2.5 percent, compared with 1.7 percent in the Jewish population.[2]

It is imperative to make a distinction between Palestinian Arabs who are citizens of Israel (called Arab citizens in this chapter) and those who live under the jurisdiction of the Palestinian Authority (PA) in the West Bank and the Gaza Strip (discussed in Chapter 20). Arab citizens of Israel are those who remained after the 1948 war; they are full citizens of the country. They can organize politically, vote, and be elected to the Knesset. Both Arabic and Hebrew are official languages of the state of Israel. This, however, has not always been the case. In the aftermath of the 1948 war, Israel viewed its Arab citizens with suspicion. They were subjected to a military rule that limited many of their democratic liberties until 1966, when Israel ended its military rule. Furthermore, in the early years of statehood, Arabs faced land confiscation by the state for security purposes, a practice that continued well into the 1970s.

Arabs are full citizens and no longer face the egregious violations of the early years, but their relationship with the state and its Jewish population remains tense. They live in a Jewish country whose symbols, flag, and national anthem are Zionist and give little expression to their Palestinian identity and heritage. They are not called to serve in the army—one of the important rites of passage for Israeli youth and a key to upward social mobility. They comprise some 20 percent of the population but account for half of those below the poverty line. Their towns and communities receive treatment by the authorities that is inferior to what is given to comparable Jewish ones.

FIGURE 13.1   ■   Population of Israel (in Thousands) According to Religious Affiliation, 1950–2020

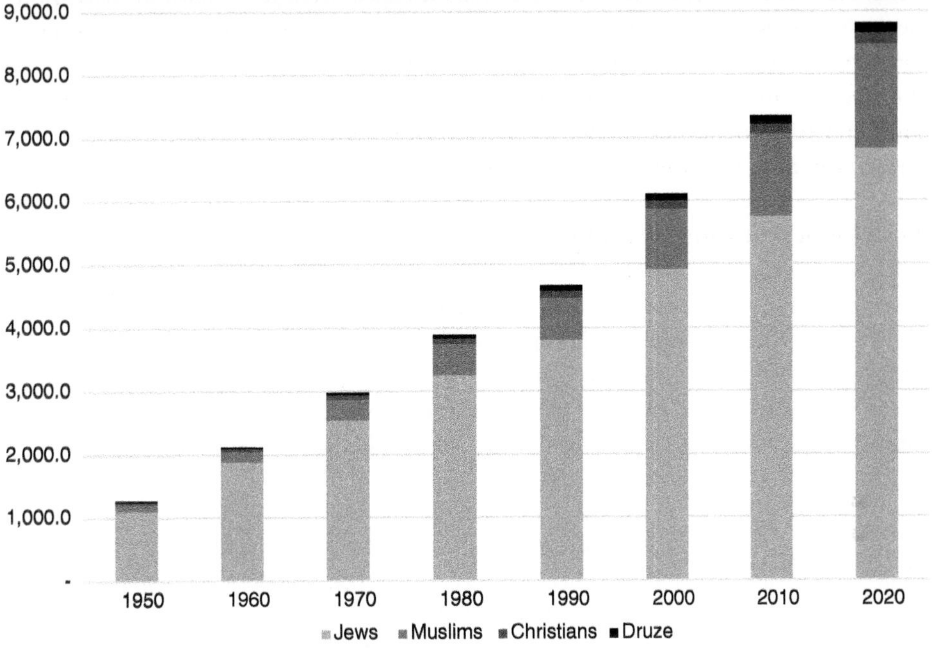

Source: Data compiled by author from the Israeli Statistic Bureau.

Arab citizens have mixed feelings about the state and their place in it, and they are cross-pressured by their ethnic and national ties to Palestinians in the West Bank and Gaza and by the Israeli government. Most identify with their Arab background, with their Palestinian roots, and with their refugee cousins, but many also identify themselves as Israelis. Relations between Israel and its Arab citizens faced a very serious challenge with the killing in October 2000 of thirteen Arabs by the Israeli police during demonstrations in support of the Palestinian struggle against Israel, days after the onset of the al-Aqsa intifada in the territories.

Following the incident, a national investigation committee was appointed. Among its recommendations was the call to address the discrimination of the Arab minority and the material inequalities between Jews and Arab citizens of Israel.[3] In reaction to the October events, most Arabs boycotted the 2001 elections and contributed to the electoral loss by the incumbent Labor Party and the rise of Ariel Sharon's right-wing Likud Party.

Relations between Arab and Jewish citizens have been deteriorating further since 2000. Arabs are increasingly vocal in their opposition to Israel's Jewish character. In 2006, the High Monitoring Committee of the Arab Citizens of Israel, a coordinating committee of the various Arab political, administrative, and social bodies, together with the Association of Arab Municipalities, published its *Future Vision for Palestinian Arabs in Israel.*[4] The document called for full equality between Arabs and Jews and for abolishing Israel's designation as a Jewish state.

For many Jewish Israelis, Arab citizens' identification with Palestinian nationalism and their opposition to a Jewish state branded them as disloyal to the state. Since 2009, under the leadership of Prime Minister Benjamin Netanyahu, incitement from government officials against the Arab population has reached unprecedented levels. The most overt incident occurred in the 2015 election in which the prime minister issued a public video warning against "hordes of Arabs swarming to the polling booths" and calling on his voters to turn out in high numbers to protect his right-wing government. Under Netanyahu, right-wing lawmakers have been competing among themselves in proposing laws that disenfranchise Arab citizens in different ways. The most egregious of these is the "Basic Law: Israel as the Nation State of the Jewish People," which the Knesset passed in July 2018. The aim of the law was to establish Jewish collective supremacy in Israel by various means. Among other things, it states, "The right to exercise national self-determination in the State of Israel is unique to the Jewish people," thus denying any national collective rights to Arabs. It also established Hebrew as the only official language of the state and determined that the "state views the development of Jewish settlement as a national value and will act to encourage and promote its establishment and consolidation." The law opens up new legal ways by which Arab citizens in the country could be discriminated against.

Arab citizens have been organizing in the past decades via civil society associations as well as through formal politics. Several small Arab parties in the Knesset have represented the Arab minority, most prominent among them the socialist Hadash (*al-Jabha*), the nationalist Balad (*tajamu‘*), and the Islamic Movement's United Arab List. A move to raise the minimum threshold for winning seats in the Knesset, introduced before the 2015 election in order to limit the representation of the Arab parties, had the unintended consequence of pushing all three Arab parties to unite. Running as the Joint List in the election, this coalition won 13 seats and became the third-largest party in the Knesset. The list split and united in following election cycles. Before the 2021 election, the Islamist branch of the list (*raam*) left it and in an unprecedented historic move joined the government coalition.

RELIGION AND POLITICS

Israelis often say that once the conflict with the Palestinians is resolved, the secular-religious schism is bound to take center stage. Indeed, the most significant internal cleavage among Jewish Israelis is the one between the religious and secular. The relation between religion and state in Israel is a complex one, requiring significant balancing acts and careful negotiations. The Israeli Declaration of Independence states that Israel shall be a Jewish *and* democratic state, but understandings of what is meant by "Jewish" vary. Two prominent interpretations exist. The first, which is shared by most secular Israelis, is the notion that Israel is "Jewish" in the sense that it is the national expression of the self-determination of the Jewish people. Judaism is both a religion and an ethnic identity, and the majority of nonreligious Israelis believe Israel's Judaism should be limited to the ethnic-national aspect of the term. On the other hand, the various strands of Orthodox religious groups in Israel, including religious Zionists and some ultra-Orthodox groups, advocate a greater role for religion in public life. As a Jewish state, they believe Israel should be ruled according to the *halacha*, or Jewish law.

The pioneer Zionists who established the state and controlled most of its institutions were secular socialists who subscribed to the ethno-national view. For them, Israel's Judaism was to be expressed in national symbols, such as the flag and anthem that draw on a Jewish symbolic vocabulary and in national holidays that correspond to the holy days of the Jewish calendar. In addition, the 1950 Law of Return and the 1952 Law of Citizenship, which granted any Jew in the Diaspora as well as their relatives the right to immigrate to Israel and become a citizen, were instated to ensure that Israel would continue to be a safe haven for Jews everywhere. The secular leadership, however, had to contend with religious Jewish groups present in the prestate years, as well as with their growing power over the years of statehood. Ben-Gurion and the ruling secular elite established a "status quo" arrangement that was meant to preserve the prestate accommodation of religion after independence. This arrangement included a monopoly of the religious courts (rabbinical courts) over matters of marriage and divorce, the observance of the Sabbath as the national day of rest, and the autonomy of the religious education system.

Since independence, the three major religious parties—the ultra-Orthodox (haredi) Agudat Israel, the Orthodox National Religious Party (NRP), and later Shas—have joined ruling government coalitions and have sought to strengthen the religious character of the state. These parties represent the main divisions within the religious camp in Israel. Agudat Israel is a non-Zionist, ultra-Orthodox party whose voters are concerned with preserving the cultural autonomy of the haredi community and the place of religion in the public sphere. The NRP combines religion with Zionism and sees the establishment of the state of Israel as a part of the process of religious redemption. It generally seeks to accommodate the secular Zionist sector and considers it a partner in the redemptive process. Finally, Shas has been mainly concerned with securing budgets for its extensive network of religious and educational institutions, spreading religiosity among Israelis and strengthening the religious character of the state. Both the NRP and Shas have sought control over the Ministry of Religious Affairs and the Interior Ministry while in government coalitions. The first allowed them to control budgets and appointments for religious services and institutions, and the latter cemented their hold over matters of personal status. The religious parties' insistence on the exclusion of the conservative and reform streams of Judaism, which are more progressive on many issues, from conducting marriages or conversions, has caused tensions with Jewish communities in the Diaspora, especially in the United States, where these streams are dominant.

Because religious parties can often make or break a ruling coalition, their influence extends far beyond their moderate electoral success. Major social transformations also contribute to their power. The immigration waves of Jews from the Middle East in the 1950s raised the number of observant Jews in Israel. In addition, the higher birthrates of the ultra-Orthodox have made this community the fastest growing in Israel. The influence of the religious parties caused a backlash from the secular Ashkenazi elites. In 2003, the party Shinui, which ran on a solely antireligious platform, won 15 Knesset seats and became the third-largest party. Shinui reflected the resentment felt by secular, middle-class, mainly Ashkenazi Israelis toward what they perceived as the privileges of the religious sector. The exemption of yeshiva students from military service, the extensive social welfare benefits enjoyed by poor haredi families, and the religious monopoly over marriage and divorce were among the issues Shinui sought to address. Its success, however, was short lived, and in the following election, the party disintegrated.

In the 1990s, the influx of immigrants from the former Soviet Union—the vast majority of them secular and about a third non-Jewish—seemed to have tipped the balance toward the secular camp. However, by 2009 the effect of the Russian immigrants was diluted by high birthrates in the haredi sector and an increase in religiosity. In a poll conducted by the Israel Democracy Institute in 1999, 52 percent of Israelis described themselves as secular, while 49 percent described themselves as haredi, Orthodox, or "traditional." By the end of 2016, the Israeli Central Bureau of Statistics (CBS) found that only 45 percent Israelis identified as secular, while the rest identified as "traditional" (25 percent), religious (16 percent), or ultra-Orthodox (14 percent).[5] Due to the high birth rates of the ultra-Orthodox community, demographic predictions by the CBS estimate their share among Israeli Jews to grow to 20 percent in 2040 and a staggering 40 percent in 2065.[6]

Disagreements over the place of religion in the public sphere continue to fuel conflict among Israelis. In recent years, protests by both the secular and religious communities have erupted. Sex-segregated public buses in religious neighborhoods and attempts to exclude women from public forums, as well as many other points of contention, have brought secular Israelis to the

PHOTO 13.2 Divisions between orthodox, progressive, and secular Jews over religion and the public sphere are a main cleavage in Israeli politics. In the picture: Clashes between ultra-orthodox and progressive Jews over prayer at the Western Wall

Lihi Ben Shitrit

streets in the last few years. Attempts by secular institutions like the Supreme Court to interfere with practices of the ultra-Orthodox community have caused mass protests on the haredi streets.

The future trajectory of religious–secular relations in Israel is unclear, as different trends are pulling in different directions. The fast-paced growth of the religious sector, and in particular of the ultra-Orthodox community, means that the democratic weight of religious parties is bound to increase. However, there is evidence that haredi groups are beginning to open up to modern Israeli society and that they will seek greater accommodation with the secular sector than before. The religious nationalist camp has since the 1970s focused its efforts on the settlement project in the occupied Palestinian territories and has been more ready to compromise on matters of religion and state. A resolution to the Israeli–Palestinian conflict, which will entail the dismantling of settlements, might cause religious nationalists to redirect their efforts toward making the state more religious. In the absence of a resolution to the conflict, however, it is likely that the historical "status quo" arrangement will persist.

INSTITUTIONS AND GOVERNANCE

Israel does not have a written constitution, mostly because of the debate between secular and religious Jews. Secularists have insisted that Israel must have a constitution like other modern, Western, liberal states, while religious leaders claim that the Torah and its rabbinical commentaries make up the written constitution of Israel. Because it was impossible to reach agreement on a complete document, the two sides decided to put the constitution together step by step; this legislation would, taken together, form Israel's constitution. Using this rationale, basic laws were legislated covering a variety of topics. Yet on the most challenging—such as the judicial system and a bill of rights—consensus has not been reached, even more than seventy years later. What exist today are compendiums of regulations such as the Basic Law: the Knesset and the Basic Law: the Government, while others are more declarative, such as the Basic Law: Jerusalem.

Government, Knesset, and Elections

Formally, the legislature generates and controls the government, but the primary fact of Israeli political life is that the government (formed by the prime minister)—not the Knesset—is the focus of the country's political power. The Knesset is the legislature that is elected by the people. The president of the state, who is elected by the Knesset every seven years, appoints a Knesset member as prime minister, usually the leader of the party that won the most Knesset seats in the election. After the government is formed, the Knesset must approve it.

Because no political party has ever won a majority of the vote in Israel's elections, coalition government is inevitable. Cabinet ministers are generally leaders of the political parties in the coalition. Occasionally, ministers are appointed who are not Knesset members, but as a rule, ministers are appointed because they lead parties that have decided to join the ruling coalition and not because of their expertise in the fields controlled by their ministries. As ministers, they have the political power, prestige, patronage, and budget that are related to their ministries.

Formal and informal powers rest with the government and its ministers. The government cabinet declares war and ratifies treaties. The prime minister and those close to the prime minister are at the top of the heap. Despite the prime minister's dominance, the Israeli governing system is based on the principle of collective responsibility. The essence of collective responsibility is that cabinet members may object to or vote against a decision in discussions in the cabinet, but once a decision is taken, they must support the decision unless specifically released from that obligation. Ministers are also held responsible for the voting behavior of their party members in the Knesset, and the prime minister, after notifying the Knesset, can remove them from office. This norm, while vocally praised, is applied with great flexibility, and there have been many instances of ministers voting against the government in which they served, especially on controversial issues such as the 1978 Camp David Accords and the 1993 Oslo agreements.

The Knesset, which selects and supports the prime minister and the ruling coalition, has 120 seats and is elected by a proportional representation list system in which very few procedural or technical obstacles face a group choosing to compete; in the recent past, some thirty-five party lists have competed. The Central Elections Committee, made up of representatives of the various parties in proportion to their strength in the outgoing Knesset and headed by a Supreme Court justice, is responsible for conducting the election, including the approval of lists. The law states that a list may not take part in elections for the Knesset if its goals or actions include one of the following: negation of the right of the state of Israel to exist as the state of the Jewish people, negation of the state's democratic nature, or incitement to racism.

Elections are to be "general, national, direct, equal, secret and proportional," which is expressed in Israel's single-district, proportional representational system.[7] Before the 2006 election, the minimum threshold for election was raised to two percent of the vote, and before the 2015 election, it was raised again to 3.25 percent. The Knesset's term is four years unless earlier elections are called.

Supreme Court

Israel's Supreme Court has acquired, by tradition and by the abdication of other institutions, the task of major guardian of justice and civil rights in Israel. The court was initially reticent about interfering in political issues, but since the mid-1980s, it has developed into a dynamic actor in the governmental system. Judges are selected on the recommendation of a nine-member appointments committee that consists of the president of the Supreme Court and two other justices of that court, the minister of justice, one other cabinet minister chosen by the cabinet, two members of the Knesset elected by secret ballot by majority vote, and two practicing lawyers who are members of the Israel Bar Association and approved by the minister of justice. The justice minister serves as chairperson of the appointments committee. Judges serve until the age of seventy.

Beginning in the early 1980s, the judicial activism of the court intensified. In the political sphere, the court overturned the ban by the Central Elections Committee on two parties before the 1984 election, and it did the same thing in 2003 and 2009. Citing the public's right to know, the court required political parties to make public the details of coalition agreements, which became a provision in the revised Basic Law: Government. Apprehension about the court's possible decision caused the Labor Party and the Shas Party to remove a clause in a draft coalition agreement stipulating that the government would introduce legislation circumventing any Supreme Court decision that impinged on the religious status quo. In other cases, the court virtually eliminated censorship in theater productions, reduced censorship for movies, and decided that the army censor could not block publication of an article that included criticism of the head of the Mossad, Israel's national intelligence agency, unless there was a "near certainty" that the content of the article posed a danger to national security. It also backed the right of newspaper reporters not to reveal their sources.

In the religious sphere, the court ordered the registration as a Jew and the granting of new immigrant status to a woman from the United States who had undergone a Reform conversion; forced a political leader who also served as a judge in the High Rabbinical Court to relinquish his judicial position; ordered the inclusion of women in religious councils and in the electoral groups that selected candidates for religious councils; and ordered El Al, the national airline, to provide a homosexual employee's partner the same benefits it provided other married workers. The Supreme Court's reputation for liberal decisions is diminished by its restraint on security issues. It upheld the expulsion of 418 members of the Palestinian Islamic resistance movement Hamas without a prior hearing, it approved demolishing the homes of terrorists, and it did not overturn the practice of using "moderate physical force" in interrogations of Islamic fundamentalists.

A leading figure for much of the court's activity, and for the attendant blame or praise, was Aharon Barak, who was appointed in 1978 and who served as president of the court between 1995 and 2006. Barak was directly involved in the constitutional revolution that took place in the country, expanding judicial review and the right of citizens to petition the Supreme Court. Barak led in applying the test of "reasonableness," under which the court can annul a cabinet or Knesset decision if it is deemed unreasonable in the extreme. The reasonableness doctrine signifies the court's changed perception of its role in the political system as one that goes beyond adjudication to the application of substantive criteria in its review of laws and policies. The use of the doctrine of reasonableness to invalidate legislation or administrative action, known as substantive due process in the United States, was accelerated in the 1980s when the Supreme Court overturned the government's appointment of a former Shin Bet agent as director general of the Housing Ministry; the court determined that he was not fit for public office because he had perjured himself during two security service scandals. Although the appointee had never been convicted, the High Court struck down the nomination on the ground that such an appointment was so unreasonable that it was illegal and, therefore, invalid.

Activist courts have raised opposition from both the public and the Knesset, and the level of trust in the Court reflected in opinion polls has decreased over the years. Calls have increased for limiting the scope of the court's jurisdiction, for changing the manner of appointing justices, for making provisions for a more varied group of justices, and for limiting or preventing judicial review of legislative actions. Political opponents, especially those from religious circles and from the right of the political spectrum, accused the Supreme Court of pursuing its own liberal political agenda. Debate over the nature of the Supreme Court has intensified in the 21st century but has not led to changes in the court's activism.

Military and Security

Defense is the policy area that commands the most attention, the largest concentration of budget, and years of active service of most Israelis. This policy area has overshadowed all others in Israel, and it often recruits top-level individuals to serve its demands and rewards, many of whom have reached the top of its hierarchies with prominent second careers in politics, business, and administration. Placing a priority on defense has become part of the Israeli way of life; an overwhelming proportion of the population sees it as the central issue facing the nation. The defense issue penetrates the value system of the country, as symbols of military strength, self-sacrifice, and heroism are given positive recognition in the culture. In recent years—since the Lebanon war in 1982, a war that many Israelis considered avoidable—some Israelis have criticized the military and questioned its security symbols. The crisis of military effectiveness in dealing with the intifada, the wars in Lebanon and Gaza, the years of occupation, and the use of the military to remove Jewish settlers from the Gaza Strip continue to undermine the status of the military in both leftist and rightist circles.

The impact of the defense issue is seen clearly in the arrangements that have been worked out regarding national service, which provides many an important form of identification with the country; for other Israelis—the Arab citizens—it signifies rejection of or exclusion from the mainstream of Israeli life. The defense issue segregates the Jewish from the Arab population by requiring army service from Israeli Jews while exempting Israeli Arabs. Military service is still an important requisite for many positions of power and importance in Israeli life; it is also the main vehicle for upward social mobility. Non-Jews are therefore severely disadvantaged.

Most Jewish Israeli men and about half of the women complete their compulsory army service. Men often serve in reserve units into their forties; women are exempted from service after they have a child. The pervasive structure of the military enterprise ensures that most Jewish families have a connection with the army. This universality ensures a high level of salience for military matters and tends to lend implicit public support to Israel's defense policies.

Two Jewish groups are exempted from army service for political reasons. The conscription of most yeshiva students is formally deferred—in effect, they are exempted—while they are studying. This arrangement began in the early days of statehood, when Ben-Gurion agreed to the demands of the ultra-Orthodox that some 400 of the 7000 yeshiva students be exempted from army service; technically, they were granted extensions of their call-up dates. The number of those receiving exemptions ballooned, increasing more than a hundredfold to more than 50,000. Religiously observant women may also avoid active service. Both groups are regularly attacked for shirking their duty. While alternative forms of national service are often suggested for religious women and Arabs, these exist only as voluntary options.

No area of Israeli public life is immune from the impact of defense. Major economic decisions in varied fields such as industrial infrastructure, natural resource development, privatization, and urban planning take defense considerations into account. Defense also affects cultural matters ranging from religious law to the development of an army slang that makes the army one of the most fertile areas for development of the Hebrew language. The structure of the education system is also influenced by the demands of defense. The curricula of vocational high schools are affected; Israeli university students tend to begin their studies after a number of years of army service and remain likely to be called up for reserve service, along with many of their teachers, during their years of study.

Every Israeli leader has reaffirmed the intention to maintain Israel's strategic nuclear deterrent capability, even in peacetime, and Israel boasts sophisticated and wide-ranging strategic deterrents founded upon the reach and power of its air force and its arsenal of undeclared nuclear weapons. The Dimona nuclear plant has reportedly been manufacturing plutonium for more than four decades; the quantity, deployment, and type of Israel's nuclear weapons and the doctrine regulating their use remain some of the state's deepest secrets. Israel's conventional and nuclear deterrent capabilities have convinced most of its Arab neighbors of the necessity of ending their military confrontation with the Jewish state. These capabilities, in Israel's view, permit it an unprecedented degree of flexibility in recasting its territorial engagements, and they form the foundation of a strategic partnership with the United States.

Although formally subordinate to the political leadership, the defense institutions have in fact become partners in the political process. No strong autonomous civilian ministry has been set up to oversee the functioning of the military since Ben-Gurion was the civilian in charge of the IDF, and his oversight was deemed sufficient. The Ministry of Defense has become a civilian aide for the army, with all major functions of budgeting, procurement, and military strategy situated in the army itself or duplicated in the Defense Ministry. The position of the military leadership at times plays an important part in the civilian leaders' political calculus. As a result of this power balance, civil–military relations in Israel are problematic, and frequently, the sides blur.

Even in a constitutional sense, civilian control over the military is blurred. We know who the chief of staff is, but it is more difficult to determine who the commander in chief is. Collective responsibility lies with the government, and many ministers often speak out on military matters to the discomfort of the minister of defense and the prime minister. The Basic Law: Israel Defense Forces, passed in 1976 in response to the evidence of a lack of clear lines of authority during the October 1973 War, formalized the constitutional decision-making hierarchy. The army is under the authority of the government, and the defense minister acts through the government's authority in defense matters. The highest decision-making level within the army is the chief of staff, who is appointed by the government on the recommendation of the minister of defense. The chief of staff is under the authority of the prime minister and the defense minister.

POLITICAL PARTICIPATION: THE LEFT–RIGHT SPECTRUM, POLITICAL PARTIES, AND CIVIL SOCIETY

Much of political discourse, and the ideologies and parties associated with it, is based on the assumption that political groupings can be ordered on a continuum from Left to Right. But the Left and Right (or liberal and conservative, in US parlance) are multifaceted at best, elusive at worst, and divergent over time and across polities. There are a number of reasons why *left* and *right* are terms too simplistic to capture the complexity of Israeli politics. Broadly, the Left represents the socialist values of equality, social justice, and international cooperation; the Right has historically been associated with capitalist values such as freedom of opportunity, competition, restricted government activity, and nationalism.

In certain senses, this description fits Israel, but in other important senses, it is incomplete. For many years and certainly since the June 1967 War, the major Zionist parties have competed for the nationalist mantle, placing the highest value on security and on the survival of Israel as a Jewish state. The Right tends to argue that these goals can be achieved using a firm, nonconciliatory policy, while the Left favors more flexibility and concessions. Nevertheless, it was the Left-leaning Alignment coalition that began the policy of settling the Palestinian territories, the Right-leaning Likud that ceded the Sinai to the Egyptians, and the Likud's (later, the Kadima Party's) Ariel Sharon, who accepted the principle of the unilateral withdrawal from Gaza. None of these government actions could have been anticipated via the Left–Right continuum alone.

In addition, in Israel the meaning of *left* and *right* may well change over time as party positions change, making the ranking provided by today's continuum somewhat different from that of earlier years. Another difficulty is that parties often employ general rhetoric in their election campaigns, which are unspecific on particular policy debates and are therefore hard to categorize as left or right. A final problem relates to how the continuum is perceived and understood by the electorate. For most people, politics is a matter of leaders and parties, whose images are no less important than ideological issues of left and right. Alternatively, some think of politics in terms of specific questions facing the polity or in terms of the ability of a party to satisfy group demands. The Left–Right continuum in Israel often fills a political function more than an ideological one. It is thus a simple but useful shorthand for the initiated to use to understand and order the political scene. A more in-depth look at political parties is provided in the next section.

Political Parties and Elections

The basic division of the Israeli party system has been between Likud and Labor, and it is useful to conceive of them as the major building blocks of the system. Until 2021, every Israeli prime minister has come from one of these parties, and one of these parties has been in every government coalition formed in Israel. Thus far, there have been three major periods in Israeli politics: dominance by Labor until 1977, a period of competitiveness between 1981 and 1999, and flux and dealignment since. In 1999, the combined size of the two parties in the Knesset was unprecedently low; between them, they controlled slightly more than one-third of the Knesset. Sectarian politics and fractionalization coincided with the introduction of the direct election of the prime minister, which was used for the elections between 1996 and 2001. After the repeal of the direct election of the prime minister, the Knesset elections again became crucial.

Parties of the Left won some 50–60 of the 120 seats in the Knesset since independence to 1977. In the early years of statehood, Mapai (now the Labor Party) was especially successful among those who identified with the dominant values of that epoch—independence, immigration, socialism, building the land, and security. After the founding of the state, these undertakings were continued, sometimes within different organizational settings and institutional arrangements but with much of the same symbolism and ideological justification. As the values of the party and movement permeated the society, the distinction between party and state was often blurred; achievements of state accrued to the benefit of the party. Jews who immigrated to Israel before independence and immediately thereafter continued to support Labor heavily, but the rate of support fell off among those who immigrated after 1955 and among Israeli-born voters.

The Likud saw the problems of the country from a different ideological perspective and consequently found its support among different groups, particularly the native-born and Mizrahim. These groups tended to have lower education and income levels as well as hawkish opinions on foreign and defense policy. In opposition until 1977, Likud gave the appearance of being broadly based in its electoral support because it blended the preferences of its two major components: the right-wing, nationalistic Herut movement and the bourgeois Liberal Party. Herut appealed disproportionately to lower-class and lower-middle-class workers and to Israelis born in Middle Eastern countries, although obviously many Ashkenazim also supported it. By contrast, the middle-class and upper-middle-class merchants and businesspeople, often more educated, were drawn to the Liberals. In the 1977 elections, the Likud campaign focused on socioeconomic and ethnic grievances for which it blamed Labor and on the catastrophic failure of the incumbent leadership in the October 1973 War. It succeeded in ousting Labor for the first time since independence.

The religious parties generally received about 15 percent of the vote—although in 1996 and 2006 their total shot up to some 20 percent—and they were regular coalition partners in the majority of governments, whether headed by Labor or Likud (or Kadima in 2006). The main religious parties were the National Religious Party (NRP), which pursued a right-wing nationalist, religious Orthodox agenda; the ultra-Orthodox parties, such as Agudat Israel, which were mainly concerned with budgets for the ultra-Orthodox community and its institutions as well as with the Jewish character of the state; and Shas, which has developed since the 1980s and into the 21st century as a major religious party. A Mizrahi ultra-Orthodox party, Shas carried out a campaign focused on socioeconomic and Mizrahi ethnic grievances and a return to religion. It won its major support from traditionalists with lower incomes, lower levels of education, and Middle Eastern backgrounds. The NRP lost votes in 1988 to the Likud for ideological reasons and to Shas for ethnic ones. It rebounded in 1996, but by 2006 was suffering from major setbacks while ultra-Orthodox parties were in ascendance. In 2013, now under the name The Jewish Home, it secured 12 seats in the Knesset, a number that fell to 8 and fewer since 2015.

Occasionally, small centrist parties have emerged, but generally these have been short lived. Among these, the Kadima Party has been the first successful centrist party in Israeli history. The party was formed by Ariel Sharon and was headed by Ehud Olmert in the 2006 elections. Kadima's leadership was made up mostly of former Likud Party ministers, and it positioned itself between the right-wing Likud and the left-wing Labor, promoting "disengagement"—a unilateral, partial Israeli withdrawal from Palestinian territories—as its alternative to the deadlock in Israeli–Palestinian negotiations. In 2009, Kadima, headed by Tzipi Livni, was the biggest vote-getter, with 28 seats, but the coalition was formed by Likud's Benjamin Netanyahu, who capitalized on the strength of religious and right-wing parties. This election saw the two big parties fade in popularity. Likud won only 27 of the 120 seats in the Knesset, although Netanyahu, its leader, was able to form the government; Labor won 13 seats. Labor was only the fourth-biggest party in 2009, smaller than Avigdor Lieberman's right-wing Israel Beiteinu, which won 15 seats. After the election, the Labor Party entered Netanyahu's coalition, a move that severely weakened the opposition bloc in the Knesset. Labor has scarcely recovered since, and by 2021 stood at only 7 seats.

As Figure 13.2 shows. The 21st century saw the strengthening (as well as radicalization) of the Right and the shrinking of the Left. The assassination of Labor Prime Minister Yitzhak Rabin in 1995 by a far-right Jewish militant and the outbreak of the Al-Aqsa Intifada in 2000 made many abandon the hope for peace that the Left had promised. Voters shifted to the Center and Center-Right, which scooped up many disaffected Labor voters and some moderate Likud voters.

In 2019 Israel entered an unprecedent electoral crisis. Benjamin Netanyahu of Likud, who ruled for a decade, faced a corruption indictment. Against this backdrop, two centrist parties—Yesh Atid and Kachol Lavan—repeatedly won enough seats to challenge Likud. But as neither Likud nor the Center could form a coalition, Israel underwent 4 election cycles in three years. Only in 2021 and by a tiny margin, the Centrist parties formed an unlikely coalition with the far-right, Labor, the leftist Meretz, and the Islamic Movement's party, and unseated Netanyhau.

Historically elections in Israel boasted high turnout rates, with average voting between 1949 and 2009 at about 78 percent. The highest rate of participation was in the first Knesset elections in 1949, in which 86.9 percent of the eligible population voted. In 2001, however, the rate fell to 62.3 percent (in an election only for prime minister); in 2006, it was only 63.5 percent—the lowest ever for Knesset elections. By 2009, it rose again to 65 percent. The steep declines in the start of twenty-first century reflected lower rates of participation among both Jewish and Arab voters. In 2001 (the special direct election of the prime minister), 68 percent of

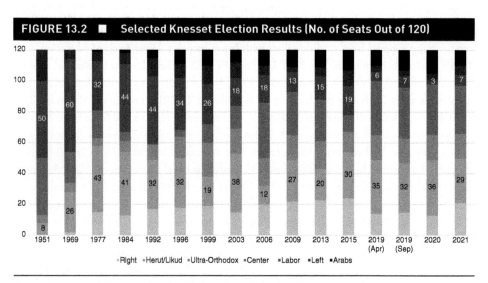

FIGURE 13.2 ■ **Selected Knesset Election Results (No. of Seats Out of 120)**

Source: Data compiled by author (number labels show seats held by Likud and Labor).

Jews voted, compared with only 19 percent of Arabs, bringing the overall turnout rate to 62.3 percent. The 2001 election was held shortly after the eruption of the al-Aqsa intifada and the October 2000 disturbances within Israel in which thirteen Palestinians, twelve of them Israeli citizens, were killed by the police. Arab voters blamed the government, and the disaffection of many Arab citizens was greater than ever. Arab political parties as well as civic organizations campaigned vigorously for a boycott of the 2001 elections. In 2003, the Jewish turnout level was approximately the same as in 2001 at 69 percent, but the Arab turnout rebounded in 2003 to 62 percent, raising the overall turnout rate to 68.9 percent. The 2015 election marked a significant change, with an overall turnout rate of 71.8 percent and about 65 percent turnout rate among the Arab population. The average overall turnout rate in the latest rounds of elections (2019–2021) was close to 70 percent.

Civil Society

In the first two decades of Israel's existence, the state together with the political parties dominated all areas of civic life. Each party had its own newspaper, health insurance and health care services, women's organization, and even sports association. Citizens tended to identify significantly with their political party, with which they interacted in almost all aspects of their lives. Very little political or social organizing took place outside the realm of the state and the political parties.

After the June 1967 War, changes began to appear. Most notably, independent social movements became increasingly visible and influential in the 1970s. The settlers' movement was successful in affecting government policies of settlement building in the West Bank and Gaza through action on the ground and lobbying. The Peace Now movement gained popular momentum with demonstrations and actions aimed at the relinquishing of the occupied Palestinian territories. The Black Panthers movement demanding equality for Mizrahi Jews and the women's movement also appeared on the scene. These social movements had a tremendous impact on Israeli politics, making independent civil society organizing an effective means of influencing government policies.

The 1980s, and even more substantially the 1990s, were marked by policies of decentralization, the dismantling of the Israeli welfare state, and the privatization of public services. As a result, Israeli civil society experienced a tremendous boom in its scale and responsibilities as nongovernmental and nonprofit organizations began to provide numerous services previously offered by the state. In addition, the diminishing size and importance of the political parties opened a space for unaffiliated civil society associations and clubs. The surge in civil society activity came to address the many economic, social, and cultural problems within Israeli society; however, most of the activities and organizations focused on service provision and cultural activity rather than on political advocacy. Currently, only a small fraction of civil society organizations are political advocacy groups.

By the start of the 21st century, the role of social movements and their popularity seemed to have diminished as Israelis increasingly turned away from politics, many becoming disaffected with the political system and focusing on nonpolitical community work. Nevertheless, to the surprise of most observers of Israeli civil society, in the summer of 2011 mass demonstrations spread throughout the country in protest of the high cost of living. Led by youth activists and the national student union and inspired by the Arab Spring, hundreds of thousands of Israelis took to the streets chanting, "The people demand social justice!" in what became the largest mass protest ever to take place in Israel. Ahead of the Knesset election scheduled for January 2013, several of the protest leaders joined the Labor Party in an attempt to translate the movement's mass appeal into political influence. However, an outbreak of violence between Israel and Hamas in November 2012 overshadowed the protest leaders' new discourse on social justice and placed, once again, the question of security and the Israeli–Palestinian conflict as the dominant issue for the 2013 and later the 2015 election campaigns. In recent years, the right-wing-dominated government has taken actions aimed at limiting the freedoms of political civil society organizations. Ministers have increasingly accused human rights and antioccupation organizations of working for the interests of foreign countries, and they have attempted to enact laws that would limit their funding or require special tags and identifications marking them as foreign agents. The most egregious interference, however, has been the outlawing of the northern branch of the Islamic Movement in November 2015. Considered the most popular social movement among Arab citizens, this move led to the forcible shutting of numerous religious, educational, and charitable associations and organizations affiliated with the movement.

POLITICAL ECONOMY

Israel has an advanced industrial economy, and its citizens enjoy a high standard of living on a par with western European nations: Its current gross domestic product (GDP) per capita is $38,277 (2017), and the unemployment rate is 3.9 percent. Its economy is also unique, shaped greatly by isolation from the markets of neighboring countries, a lack of natural resources, extraordinary expenditures on defense, and large quantities of international aid.

The Israeli economy began experiencing a profound transformation in the early 1990s. Buoyed by political rapprochement with Jordan and Egypt, the beginning of an agreement with the Palestinians, and the substantial increase in population from the former Soviet Union, the Israeli economy averaged annual growth rates of six percent to seven percent in the first half of the decade. Israel's economic managers have found success in reorienting the economy away from the traditional low-tech and heavy-industry sectors and toward services and the production of products for high-tech industries. Gross foreign direct investment rose from 0.7 percent of GDP in 1990 to 3.33 percent of GDP in 2003, increasing to 4.3 percent of GDP in 2005 and 9.3 percent in 2006. By 2009, the numbers dropped to only 2 percent, but they later rose to 4.1 percent by 2013.[8] In addition, the US-Israel Free Trade Agreement contributed greatly to an expansion of bilateral trade, which jumped from $18 billion in 2002 to $26.6 billion in 2005. In 2013, US goods and services trade with Israel stood at $46 billion.[9] Israel has concluded free-trade-area agreements with four other countries, the European Free Trade Association, and the European Union (EU).

Overall, Israel's economic success is derived greatly from aid from abroad. Israel receives an annual grant of approximately $2.4 billion from the United States—making it the single largest recipient of US foreign aid—and approximately $500 million in grants from the world Jewish community.

Israel has invested a large portion of its national wealth in creating an arms industry, primarily to ensure a reliable supply. The expertise gained in the maintenance and expansion of a defense industry producing top-of-the-line weapons systems for the IDF has allowed Israel to join the international competition for foreign arms sales, and Israel is one of the world's leading arms exporters. Its military-industrial complex and diamond-cutting sector now dominate industrial production and export sales, a significant change from the era when citrus and agricultural products were the country's most significant earners of foreign currency and its most popular international symbols.

As rapprochement with the Arab world stalled in the mid-1990s, so too did Israel's prospects for the coming economic integration that was supposed to boost regional demand for Israeli products and services. Economic growth slowed substantially beginning in the latter part of the 1990s, and the outbreak of the al-Aqsa intifada in September 2000 and the failure of efforts to reach a final status agreement with the Palestinians and Syria severely depressed economic prospects in the early 2000s. That said, Israel remains well positioned to compete in the knowledge-intensive industries of the 21st century, and its economy has the potential to continue to grow at a rate of approximately four to five percent per year, better than the OECD average (see Figure 13.3).[10] The proportion of scientists, engineers, and other skilled personnel in the Israeli labor force is high by international standards, and Israeli companies are

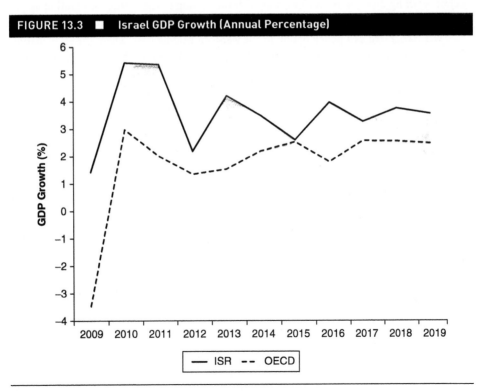

FIGURE 13.3 ■ Israel GDP Growth (Annual Percentage)

Source: OECD (2019), *Real GDP Forecast (Indicator)*, doi:10.1787/1f84150b-en.

rapidly developing experience in transforming technology into marketable products and services. Furthermore, the ongoing structural transformation of the economy, especially the shift from traditional to higher-value goods and services, should add to Israel's growth potential in the near future.

Two of the main challenges facing the Israeli economy are income inequality and poverty rates, which are higher than the OECD average. This is due largely to low levels of workforce participation by the ultra-Orthodox and Arab citizens, given discrimination and other barriers to entry they still face. For both of these groups, poverty rates stand at around 50 percent, in comparison to 13 percent for other Israelis. Today, haredis and Arabs make up about 30 percent of the population, but they are projected to constitute over 50 percent by 2059. Integrating them fully into the workforce is therefore a pressing matter if Israel's economic health is to persist.[11]

ISRAEL'S REGIONAL AND INTERNATIONAL RELATIONS

Israeli–Palestinian Conflict

Several peace treaties have been signed since 1979 between Israel and other nations, including Egypt, the Palestine Liberation Organization (PLO), and Jordan. A peace treaty has been in effect with Egypt since 1979, but it was with the signing of the mutual recognition agreements (also called the Oslo Accords) between Israel and the PLO in Washington in 1993 that peace was recognized as a policy option in the war-torn Middle East. Then, the assassination of Israel's prime minister by an Israeli radical in November 1995 stalled progress. Negotiations were not successful, with both Israeli and Palestinian political leadership reneging on commitments and the vision of coexistence; this resulted in a second intifada in 2000. A period of violence and political stalemate ensued, lasting until the end of the intifada in 2005. While the Fatah-dominated PLO had since largely abandoned an armed struggle in favor of diplomatic efforts, episodes of intense violence between Israel and Hamas, Fatah's Islamist challenger, took place in 2008, 2012, 2014 and 2021. These involved devastating attacks on the Gaza Strip by Israel and a barrage of rockets from Gaza onto Israeli cities.

The origins of the conflict are covered in Chapter 2 of this textbook. This section covers more specifically the Israeli policy toward the Palestinians in the more recent past and up to the present. Israeli authorities have historically conceived of the conflict in the region as being between nation-states. Once Israel was established, the questions were if, when, and on what terms Arab states would recognize Israel. Israelis have historically rejected the notion of a Palestinian state; some, such as Golda Meir in the 1970s and Benjamin Netanyahu in the 1990s, have argued that there is no such thing as a Palestinian nation. Others on the Israeli right added that the Arabs already had twenty-plus states and that an additional one was not needed for the relatively small Palestinian population—Jordan could become the Palestinian state.

Between the 1967 War and the 1993 Oslo Accords, the policy of Israeli governments was to avoid changing the legal status of the territories, except for Jerusalem and the Golan Heights, while supporting Jewish settlements in the territories. The entire city of Jerusalem and much of the countryside around it were annexed by Israel soon after the 1967 War, and Israeli law was applied to the Golan Heights (which had belonged to Syria) in 1982. The prospect of returning some portion of the occupied territories in order to make peace was consistently promoted as the platform of the Labor Party, and it became the policy of the government of Israel after 1993. The Likud Party did not accept this principle, however, and the dilemma of Netanyahu's government was to remain loyal to the traditional hard-line Likud platform while conforming to international agreements based on the land-for-peace principle that previous Israeli governments had approved.

Palestinians felt a prevalent sense of creeping annexation because of the persistent policy of all Israeli governments to expropriate land in the territories for Jewish settlements. This expropriated land, added to land taken over by the Israeli authorities after the retreat of the Jordanian army in 1967 and the properties purchased by Israelis from Arab owners, brought Israel's total holding to approximately one-third of the land on the West Bank.

The Labor government headed by Levi Eshkol proceeded with a settlement campaign soon after the 1967 war, especially along the Jordan River and around Jerusalem. This policy sought to change the demographic reality on the ground by installing a Jewish population on Palestinian lands. Initial Jewish settlement in territories with a large Arab population also began under Labor in 1974 when Yitzhak Rabin and Shimon Peres, both of Labor, were prime minister and defense minister, respectively. The big leap in settlement activity came during the Likud years between 1977 and 1992. In 1976, there were a little more than 3000 Jewish settlers in the West Bank (referred to as Judea and Samaria by Israeli nationalists). By 1988, the number had increased more than twentyfold, to about 70,000 Jews living there. In May 1977, there were thirty-four settlements in the West Bank; by 1984, the number had climbed to 114. During the periods of the national unity governments, the pace of settlement represented a compromise between the desires of the Likud Party to go faster and the wishes of the Labor Party to proceed more cautiously, although neither of the big parties opposed continued settling. The 1984 national unity government agreement limited new settlements to five or six new settlements annually, and the agreement that established the 1988 national unity government set eight settlements a year as its target, assuming that funds were available.

The 1990–1992 Likud government made settlements a high priority. The government of Prime Minister Yitzhak Shamir refused to halt their development in 1992 in order to receive $10 billion in loan guarantees from the United States to absorb immigrants from the former Soviet Union. This rift with the George H. W. Bush administration (along with the Likud's other problems) led to the 1992–1996 Labor government, which froze new settlements. While the pace of settlements continued to vary over the years, by 2009 approximately 500,000 Israelis resided in the settlement communities established since 1967 in the West Bank, East Jerusalem, and the Golan Heights. Not all of the settlers were ideologues. Residing in the territories became a popular alternative for young Israeli-born Jews seeking reasonably priced housing in the suburbs of Jerusalem and Tel Aviv and for new immigrants of limited means.

Although Israel takes pride in itself as a democracy, the Palestinian populations in the occupied territories were deprived of political and civil rights, and they experienced the frustrations, humiliations, and violence of living under military occupation. Under these conditions, the PLO, generally considered to represent the Palestinians, was established in 1964, with the ultimate goal of achieving national independence for the Palestinians. The Palestinian inhabitants of the territories achieved high levels of national solidarity with the advent of the PLO, even though they were cut off from the leadership of the organization, who resided outside of the country.

The Palestinian refusal to accept the status of Israeli occupation erupted in the intifada, an uprising of the Arabs in the territories, which began in December 1987. Palestinian civilians and Israeli soldiers engaged in skirmishes, with casualties mounting on both sides, although Palestinians incurred greater losses. A year later, in 1988, when the US government agreed to enter into discussions with the PLO, the organization's legitimacy reached a high point. Israeli opinion split over negotiations, although the portion of Israelis who were prepared to enter into negotiations with the PLO grew gradually, despite the fact that both major parties, Likud and Labor, rejected the notion. Some Israelis feared that the Palestinian position meant that they ultimately wanted to dismantle the state of Israel; therefore, tough policies were a matter of continued survival. Others felt that a solution could be reached only by political, and not by military, means. Either way, Israeli policy remained unchanged and the Palestinian uprising continued. The situation would change five years later.

In September 1993 in Washington, a handshake between Israeli prime minister Yitzhak Rabin and PLO leader Yasir Arafat marked the signing of the Oslo I agreement (formally known as the Declaration of Principles on Interim Self-Government Arrangements) between Israel and the PLO. The agreement included provisions for Palestinian self-rule in Gaza and Jericho and the transfer of specific government functions in the West Bank to the Palestinians. Two years later, in September 1995, the Oslo II agreement was signed. It provided for Palestinian rule in areas of the territories, led by the new PA, while it created three zones on the West Bank: Area A, to be controlled solely by the Palestinians, which included the cities of Bethlehem, Jenin, Nablus, Qalqilya, Ramallah, Tulkarem, and parts of Hebron; Area B, including many towns and villages in which activities of the PA would be coordinated and confirmed with Israel; and Area C, consisting mainly of unpopulated areas of strategic importance to Israel and Jewish settlements, to remain under sole Israeli control. In addition to its other provisions, Oslo II included a timetable for the redeployment of the IDF, elections to the Palestine National Council, and provisions for the beginning of negotiations regarding the permanent status. Theoretically, this meant self-rule for the Palestinians. Practically, however, it resulted in a further division of the West Bank and full diplomatic recognition of Israeli interests in the West Bank. The subjects of Jerusalem, refugees, and final borders were saved for a later date.

This agreement, however groundbreaking, meant little as neither side scaled back its political agenda. Israeli settlements were not removed, and all further reconciliatory policies were stunted in 1995 with the assassination of Yitzhak Rabin by a Jewish extremist. In addition, Palestinian attacks on Israeli territory, most notably embodied by suicide attacks by the Islamist group Hamas, continued. In 2000, shortly before leaving office, President Bill Clinton attempted to rekindle negotiations, summoning Israeli Prime Minister Ehud Barak and Yasir Arafat to Camp David for another round of talks. These proved unsuccessful, however, as the

Palestinian side deemed the proposed agreement unbalanced because no provision was made to ensure the creation of a viable, sovereign Palestinian state.

Shortly thereafter, another Palestinian uprising—called the al-Aqsa intifada—began. This renewed violence between the two sides led to substantial increases in the Israeli military occupation of the West Bank. Whereas previously the Israeli policy in the West Bank had been dominated by settlement, now a full infrastructure developed. This included Israel's military presence in all sectors of Palestinian society, a complex web of checkpoints and physical obstacles to Palestinian movement, and the full segregation of Israeli settler populations from Palestinians through a labyrinthine network of bypass roads.

This military conflict resulted in heated political discussion on both sides. In Israel, support for reconciliation with the Palestinians shortly gave way to the assumption that negotiations were impossible and that Israeli security would only be protected via full separation between Jews and Arabs. Labor's Amram Mitzna ran on a platform of unilateral separation in 2003 and was defeated in a landslide by the hard-line prime minister, Ariel Sharon. By 2004, however, unilateral separation had become Sharon's own policy preference, supported by a majority of the population. This precipitated the building of an actual physical security barrier around Jewish settlements in the West Bank. At issue for Israel was not whether the barrier should be built, but where to put it: Should it be placed on the 1967 borders, or should it protect settlements far inside the territories established since 1967? The international response was critical, as this move clearly violated international law as well as international norms of conduct. Indeed, many in the West likened the separation barrier to the Berlin Wall.

In 2004, Prime Minister Sharon made the unprecedented decision to end Israel's military and civilian occupation of the Gaza Strip and to dismantle four West Bank settlements. The plan's central strategic objective was intended to remove Gaza's 1.3 million Palestinians from the sphere of Israel's internationally recognized responsibility by ending the military occupation of Gaza that began in June 1967. At the same time, Israel would continue to exercise control over the entry and exit of people and goods—thus preserving the aspects of occupation most beneficial to Israeli security. Approximately 8000 settlers were removed in stages from twenty-one settlements in Gaza and four settlements in the northern West Bank. The disengagement met no significant Palestinian armed resistance, but it met substantial nonviolent settler resistance, especially from religious ideologues who felt betrayed by the state. This division in Israeli politics continues to simmer.

In 2006, elections were held for the Palestinian Legislative Council (PLC), with the Islamist group Hamas under leader Ismail Haniyah winning the elections. Following immediate US and Israeli pressure, international financial supporters cut funds to the PA. Soon thereafter, US and Israeli officials sought to build up Fatah, Hamas's primary competition for rule and heir to PLO leadership under Yasir Arafat. The internal division between Fatah and Hamas soon led to a violent schism in the Palestinian territories, with Fatah taking control of the West Bank and Hamas seizing Gaza.

During this period, despite putatively pulling out of Gaza and being committed to separation between the two populations, Israel continued to settle the West Bank. By the end of 2006, Israel's Interior Ministry reported a civilian population of 268,400 in the West Bank in approximately 125 settlement areas; in East Jerusalem, approximately 190,000 Israelis were in residence; and on the Golan, 18,000 settlers resided in thirty-two settlements. Indeed, despite the removal of more than 8000 settlers from Gaza, the total settler population increased in 2005. In addition to the more officially recognized settlements, there are more than one hundred settlement outposts throughout the West Bank, where construction is ongoing.

That summer a war raged between Israel and its northern neighbor, Lebanon, with skirmishes and rocket exchanges with the Islamist group Hizbullah. This led to massive, disproportionate devastation of Lebanon by Israeli forces in a manner not witnessed since the Lebanese civil war. The growing regional insecurity precipitated another attempt at conflict resolution, pushed this time by President George W. Bush. In November 2007, the Annapolis Conference called as many as forty additional countries into attendance. This convention marked the first time a two-state solution was articulated as the mutually agreed-upon outline for addressing the Israeli–Palestinian conflict. The objective was to produce a document on resolving the Israeli–Palestinian conflict along the lines of President Bush's Road Map for Peace.

Diplomatic headway was made, but resolution once again proved elusive. Much like the fissure that occurred within the Palestinian side after Camp David, the Israeli side fell apart at Annapolis. Prime Minister Ehud Olmert indicated that he would be willing to give parts of East Jerusalem to the Palestinians as part of a broader peace settlement at Annapolis, and this drew considerable criticism from right-wing Israeli and foreign Jewish organizations and Christian Zionists. The ultra-Orthodox Shas Party left the government coalition, thereby ending the coalition's majority in the Knesset. That development coincided with Olmert's resignation as head of Kadima because of pending charges of bribery and influence peddling. Olmert's problems aside, the ability of any Israeli prime minister to make concessions regarding Jerusalem remains in question.

Both sides were now at a diplomatic impasse, and the United States and Israel continued their attempts to undo the effects of the 2006 elections and eliminate Hamas's rule in the West Bank. By December 2008, the Israeli army returned to the Gaza Strip, in an operation code-named Operation Cast Lead, with the stated aim of stopping Hamas rocket attacks on southern Israel and arms smuggling into Gaza. Frequent Hamas rocket and mortar attacks on Israeli cities led to the targeting of Hamas bases, police training camps, and police headquarters and stations. Civilian infrastructure, including mosques, houses, medical facilities, and schools, were also attacked, with Israel stating that they were used by combatants and as storage spaces for weapons and rockets. Hamas intensified its rocket and mortar attacks against civilian targets in Israel throughout the conflict, hitting previously untargeted cities such as Beersheba and Ashdod; Israel countered with a ground invasion. Some 1,300 Palestinians and thirteen Israelis died in the conflict.

Since 2009, the Likud under the leadership of Benjamin Netanyahu formed increasingly hawkish government coalitions highly wedded to an agenda of settlement entrenchment and opposition to territorial withdrawals. On their part, the split Palestinian political landscape ties the Palestinian leadership's hands in moving forward on peace negotiations. Yet even in the event of internal Palestinian reconciliation, the prospects for a peace agreement are bleak. The Israeli government has declared that it would not negotiate with the PA in the case of a unity government with Hamas, which it considers a terrorist organization. The latest rounds of violence between Israel and Hamas in November 2012, July 2014, and May 2021, which devastated infrastructure in Gaza and witnessed rockets launched from Gaza at Tel Aviv and Jerusalem, have further set back the prospect of reconciliation. Gaza has effectively been under siege by Israel since 2007. This has created an economic and humanitarian catastrophe in the Strip. By 2017, the unemployment rate stood at 44 percent. Eighty percent of the population relies on assistance from humanitarian organizations, and 96.2 percent of local water is polluted and undrinkable. Electricity shortages make everyday life extremely difficult and limit hospitals, workplaces, and water treatment facilities from operating sufficiently.[12] The situation has put Hamas's government under increased strain and alongside its international isolation has weakened its bargaining position with Israel.

PHOTO 13.3 Jerusalem remains a main point of contention in the conflict, with sites holy to Jews, Muslims, and Christians concentrated in close proximity in the Old City

Lihi Ben Shitrit

Demonstrations by frustrated Gazans, with the encouragement of Hamas beginning in March 2018, which were met by Israeli sniper fire and led to over 200 dead and thousands injured, have led to renewed indirect negotiations between the sides, with the objective of easing some aspects of the suffocating siege. A lifeline to Hamas, however, serves Israel's interest in the continuation of the split between the West Bank and Gaza. Finding the path to fruitful negotiations between the Israelis and the Palestinians has eluded all who have attempted to bridge the seemingly unbridgeable gaps. The great mutual distrust and historical grievances, Israel's government continuing to drift toward the far-right, and the seemingly never-ending Fatah–Hamas split make the task of reaching a peaceful resolution to the conflict daunting.

Foreign Relations

The two central forces shaping Israel's foreign relations for much of its history have been the dynamics of the cold war in the region and Israel's fraught relations with its Arab neighbors. As a small and vulnerable state at its establishment in 1948, Israel searched for allies to secure its existence in a hostile Arab region. At first, Israel pursued a policy of nonidentification, hoping to maintain channels to both Eastern and Western blocs. However, the 1950s saw a deterioration in Israel's relations with the Soviet Union as the latter moved closer to the new leftist nationalist regimes in the Arab world. In 1953, the relationship hit a low point, with temporary severance of ties between the Soviet Union and Israel.

At this time, Israel began to move closer to Europe and the United States. France had been by far Israel's greatest ally since independence and its largest weapons supplier. In 1953, following the Holocaust reparations agreement between Israel and West Germany, diplomatic relations were slowly established with Germany, culminating in full diplomatic relations in 1965. In the 1950s, Israel also established contacts with a number of recently decolonized African nations and with Asian countries, providing many with development consulting and training based on its own successful experience, mainly in agriculture, irrigation, and rural development.

This state of affairs proved to be short lived. As relations with the Soviet Union worsened in the aftermath of the June 1967 War and the October 1973 War with Egypt, Israel's relations with many African and Asian countries in which Soviet influence was strong suffered. Israel's new status as an occupying power further diminished its esteem among the decolonized nations. Relations with France also cooled in the 1960s, owing to France's new rapprochement with the Muslim world following the end of its occupation of Algeria. As a result of these developments, Israel began to look mainly to the United States.

The United States, while providing some financial assistance to the new state in the 1950s, was invested in developing its ties with the Arab world in an attempt to contain Soviet influence in the region. After the demise of the Baghdad Pact with the regime change in Iraq, however, strategic relations of the United States with Israel picked up significantly. The United States came to Israel's aid in the 1973 war with Egypt, sending an airlift that saved the country from a devastating defeat. In the following years, the United States played a central role in pushing for Israeli–Arab reconciliation, again in hopes of containing Soviet influence in the Middle East. The US facilitation of the peace between Israel and Egypt in 1979 brought about the beginning of the country's unprecedented heavy military and financial support for Israel, which continues today.

Although 1979 was a year of peace between Israel and Egypt, 1979 also heralded the breakdown of ties between Israel and its most significant Middle Eastern friend at the time—Iran. The Iranian Revolution of 1979 ended the strong military and economic relations of the two countries.

In the 1980s, Israeli–Soviet relations improved, although full diplomatic ties were not renewed. With the breakup of the Soviet Union in 1989, the Gulf War in 1991, and the start of the Madrid talks between Israel and its Arab neighbors, Israeli foreign relations experienced a diplomatic blossoming. Ties between Israel and many African and Asian countries, significantly China and India, expanded. Israel's relations with Turkey improved, and the countries developed an increasingly strong diplomatic and military alliance. As for the United States, its strategic interest in Israel was transformed as the Cold War ended, and a new world order was introduced. The United States now focused more insistently on fostering peace between Israel and the Arab states in order to protect US interests in a stable Middle East. The 1993 Oslo Accords between Israel and the Palestinians enabled a transformation in the relations between Israel and some Arab and Muslim states: It led to a peace agreement with Jordan, and it also led to the opening of Israeli diplomatic representation in Tunisia, Morocco, Oman, and Qatar.

The failure of the 2000 Camp David and Taba efforts to resolve the Israeli–Palestinian conflict and the outbreak of the al-Aqsa intifada brought another round of deterioration in Israel's relations with the Arab world. Many Arab states suspended their ties with Israel, a violent conflict with Lebanon emerged, and tensions with Syria seemed to be escalating. The strong alliance between Israel and Turkey experienced some strains over Israel's conflict with the Palestinians. Relations with the countries of the European Union have also been affected by the Israeli–Palestinian conflict. While Europe sees itself as a natural mediator between the two sides, Israel prefers US facilitation, which it sees as more attuned to Israeli concerns.

The eruption of the Arab Spring brought with it at first some degree of uncertainty for Israel. The ousting of Hosni Mubarak in Egypt raised fears about the stability of Israel's peace treaty with its southern neighbor. The undermining of the Assad regime in Syria raised similar concerns. Though a staunch rival of Israel and a supporter of Hizbullah and Hamas, Syria has generally been a stable neighbor, abiding by the cease-fire agreement of 1974 and keeping the Israeli–Syrian border quiet.

Increasingly, Iran came to represent a growing threat in Israel's view, owing to Iran's pursuit of nuclear capabilities, its Supreme Leader's threats against Israel, and Iran's influence on Israel's neighbors in Syria and Lebanon. As prime minister, Likud's Benjamin Netanyahu has voiced his determination to prevent a nuclear Iran by any means, even at the cost of a unilateral Israeli strike against Iran, and his successor since 2021, Naftali Bennet, employs similar rhetoric. However, Israel does not possess the capability to carry out such a strike without military support from the United States. Furthermore, leaders from Israel's intelligence and military communities have expressed their opposition to military action and their support for the Joint Comprehensive Plan of Action, popularly known as the Iran Nuclear Deal, signed in 2015 between Iran and the P5+1 countries (see Chapter 11). In addition, the Israeli public does not view a strike favorably.

Yet Iran's growing influence in the region has also led to thawing in Israel's relations with the Arab world. Saudi Arabia and other Gulf states, who see Iran as their main rival, have been moving closer to Israel on security matters. Egypt and Saudi Arabia, close allies of the United States and opponents of both Iran and Muslim Brotherhood–style Islamists, find common threats with Israel, a fact that is reconfiguring alliances throughout the Middle East. Cementing these relations further was US President Donald Trump's antagonism toward Iran and Sunni Islamist movements. Standing unabashedly on the side of counterrevolutionary authoritarian regimes in the region and on the side of Israel, Trump abandoned US (nominal) commitments to democracy and human rights. He attempted to broker the "deal of the century" between Israelis and Palestinians, but his proposal reflected a far-right agenda that was unfeasable and unacceptable to Palestinian and ultimately had no positive impact. However, during the Trump administration several Arab countries—the UAE, Bahrain, and Morocco formalized their previously unofficial relations with Israel.

CONCLUSION

What stands out to the student of Israeli politics who is considering its decades of independence is the stable nature of the system alongside the perception of fragility and eminent crisis; in other words, we notice the familiarity and persistence of the parties, leaders, and issues, together with the long list of intractable issues that could tear the system apart. Inevitably in politics, each new crisis is also a resource for those in search of power. Thus, a crisis with the United States can be portrayed as proof positive that one version of the future is true: that the world is against Israel so Israelis might as well stand even taller and go it alone if needed or that without support of the world powers and cooperation with their leaders, the country is doomed. Thus, even though the pills are bitter (say both sides), Israelis have no choice but to swallow those pills if cherished goals are to be achieved. There can be debate on the prioritization of these goals (a Jewish state, a democratic state, peace, retaining the whole of Eretz Yisrael), but these topics consistently focus the political debate and structure electoral competition.

In the first decades of the state, a single party or political group (Mapai, Labor, the Left) gained dominance over the levers of power and over political discourse. What developed was a form of social democracy, a tough but conciliatory approach to issues of foreign policy, and containment of the religious issue by judicious negotiation. If it is fair to characterize those decades as dominated by the Left, the years since the Likud victory in 1977 look more and more like the introduction of decades of dominance by the Right. Social welfare rights were moderated, a tougher foreign policy position emerged, and a greater willingness to acquiesce to the demands of the religious parties was evident. While the details differed dramatically, the core structure of politics of the two periods remained; they were perhaps poorly made, but they were made of iron.

SUGGESTED READINGS

Arian, Asher. *Politics in Israel: The Second Republic*. 2nd ed. Washington, DC: CQ Press, 2004.

Ben-Porat, Guy. *Between State and Synagogue: The Secularization of Contemporary Israel*. Cambridge: Cambridge University Press, 2013. 42

Berda, Yael. *Living Emergency: Israel's Permit Regime in the Occupied West Bank*. Stanford, CA: Stanford University Press, 2017.

Burg, Avraham. *The Holocaust is Over; We Must Rise From its Ashes*. St. Martin's Griffin, 2016.

Cohen, Hillel. *Good Arabs: The Israeli Security Agencies and the Israeli Arabs, 1948–1967*. Translated by Haim Watzman. Berkeley, CA: University of California Press, 2010.

Dalsheim, Joyce. *Israel has a Jewish problem: self-determination as self-elimination*. Charlotte, NC: Oxford University Press, 2019.

Dowty, Alan. *Critical Issues in Israeli Society*. New York, NY: Praeger, 2004.

Goldscheider, Calvin. *Israeli Society in the Twenty-first Century: Immigration, Inequality, and Religious Conflict*. Waltham, MA: Brandeis University Press, 2015.

Hirsch-Hoefler, Sivan, and Cas Mudde. *The Israeli Settler Movement: Assessing and Explaining Social Movement Success*. Cambridge: Cambridge University Press, 2020.

Louer, Laurence. *To Be an Arab in Israel*. New York, NY: Columbia University Press, 2007.

Mustafa, Mohanad, and Ghanem As'ad. *Palestinians in Israel: The politics of Faith After Oslo*. Cambridge: Cambridge University Press, 2018.

Pedahzur, Ami. *The Triumph of Israel's Radical Right*. Oxford: Oxford University Press, 2012.

Rabinovich, Itamar. *Waging Peace*. Princeton, NJ: Princeton University Press, 2008.

Remennick, Larissa. *Russian Jews on Three Continents: Identity, Integration, and Conflict*. New Brunswick, NJ: Transaction, 2007.

Rozin, Orit. *A Home for All Jews: Citizenship, Rights, and National Identity in the New Israeli State*. Waltham, MA: Brandeis University Press, 2016.

Sachar, Howard M. *A History of Israel: From the Rise of Zionism to Our Time*. 3rd ed. New York, NY: Knopf, 2007.

Sasley, Brent E, and Harold M. Waller. *Politics in Israel: Governing a Complex Society*. Oxford: Oxford University Press, 2017.

Shafir, Gershon, and Yoav Peled. *Being Israeli: The Dynamics of Multiple Citizenship*. New York, NY: Cambridge University Press, 2002.

Shenhav, Yehouda. *The Arab Jews: A Postcolonial Reading of Nationalism, Religion, and Ethnicity*. Stanford, CA: Stanford University Press, 2006.

14 JORDAN

Laurie A. Brand

THE MAKING OF THE CONTEMPORARY STATE

During World War I, British troops ousted Ottoman forces from Palestine and Transjordan with the assistance of an army of Arab tribesmen raised by the Sharif Hussein of Mecca, the great-great-grandfather of the current king of Jordan, Abdallah II. In exchange, the sharif had been promised an Arab kingdom, a realm he expected would stretch from Palestine to Mesopotamia. London instead created thrones for two of his sons: Faisal, who, chased from an erstwhile kingdom in Syria by the French, was crowned monarch of Iraq, and Abdallah, who was named amir of the new entity of Transjordan.

From the amirate's inception, London provided a subsidy that constituted the majority of the annual budget. A civil service was also established, trained by the British, and, as was characteristic of Britain's involvement in Iraq and Egypt, all matters of foreign affairs, finance, and defense were part of the colonial purview. The British also established police and reserve forces, which were soon replaced by what was called the Arab Legion, troops drawn primarily from southern Bedouin tribes but commanded by British officers.

In the meantime, initial skepticism regarding the amir's value gradually evolved into confidence. Consequently, although the British continued to control the army and hold key advisory positions, Transjordan was granted formal independence on May 22, 1946. Abdallah was proclaimed king, the name of the country was changed to the Kingdom of Transjordan, and a new constitution was issued in 1947.

More important for subsequent developments was the crisis and then war in Palestine. On May 15, 1948, Transjordan's Arab Legion joined the battle, and by the time of the 1949 armistice, it controlled central and eastern Palestine, as well as East Jerusalem. Abdallah then initiated an annexation to the kingdom of these territories, which became known as the West Bank. The name of his realm was changed to the Hashemite Kingdom of Jordan, and by April 1950, the annexation was complete.

Abdallah's role in the Palestine debacle ultimately proved his undoing, as in July 1951 he was assassinated by a Palestinian. The reign of his successor, his son Talal, was brief (September 1951–August 1952), cut short by mental illness that forced his abdication. A regency was then established for Talal's eldest son, Hussein, who ruled until his death in 1999. King Hussein navigated the country through a series of regional wars and domestic challenges. Some derived from the country's involvement in the Arab–Israeli conflict; others were the result of the kingdom's lack of natural resources and the continuing search for economic stability.

SOCIETAL CHANGES AND CHALLENGES

When it was founded in 1921, Transjordan was a sparsely populated amirate whose perhaps 300,000 inhabitants could be divided between the Bedouin (both nomads and seminomads) and rural or small-town inhabitants. In the preindependence period, regime consolidation was intertwined with British efforts to coopt the indigenous Bedouin tribes through recruitment into the security and military forces. During the early 1920s the amir Abdallah developed a special relationship with the tribes which his grandson Hussein later institutionalized into a pillar of regime support.

As for the rest of the population, among the town dwellers were two minorities from the Caucasus region, the Circassians and Chechens, whom the Ottomans had given refuge from Czarist Russia. While relatively few in number, they have long had a close relationship with the Hashemites, enjoying designated seats in parliament and representation in government cabinets. The amir also recruited Syrians, Iraqis, and Palestinians to serve in the civil administration and the military. Many of these bureaucrats made Transjordan their home, and several rose in prominence to become the country's most powerful political figures. However, this importation of political elites also triggered resentment among the indigenous population and played a role in the emergence of a protonationalism among Transjordanians.

KEY FACTS ON JORDAN

AREA 34,495 square miles (89,342 square kilometers)

CAPITAL Amman

POPULATION 10,909,567 (July 2021 est.), including Syrian refugees

PERCENTAGE OF POPULATION UNDER 25 52.82

RELIGIOUS GROUPS (PERCENTAGE) Sunni Muslim, 97.2; Christian, 2.2; others, 0.6

ETHNIC GROUPS (PERCENTAGE) Arab, 98; Circassian, 1; Armenian, 1

DATE OF INDEPENDENCE May 25, 1946 (from the League of Nations mandate under British administration)

OFFICIAL LANGUAGE Arabic; English widely spoken

TYPE OF GOVERNMENT Monarchy

GDP (PPP) $ 101.738 billion (2019 est.), per capita $10,071 (2019 est.)

GDP (NOMINAL) $44,568 billion (2019 est.)

PERCENTAGE OF GDP BY SECTOR Agriculture, 4.5; industry, 28.8; services, 66.6 (2017 est.)

TOTAL RENTS (PERCENTAGE OF GDP) FROM NATURAL RESOURCES 1.29 (2016)

FERTILITY RATE 3 children born/woman

Sources: CIA. "The World Factbook." August 4, 2022, https://www.cia.gov/the-world-factbook/. World Bank. "International Comparison Program (ICP)." Accessed August 10, 2022, https://databank.worldbank.org/source/icp-2017.

Demographic Changes: Refugees and Migration

Jordan's history has been profoundly shaped by episodes of migration and waves of refugees. The first massive influx was triggered by the 1948 Arab–Israeli War: More than 700,000 Palestinians were expelled or fled from the part of Palestine that became the state of Israel. Some 70,000 went directly to the East Bank. Another 280,000 took refuge in the part of Palestine that subsequently came to be called the West Bank. Its population of approximately 720,000 (both refugee and indigenous inhabitants) was then annexed to the East Bank, and its Palestinian residents were subsequently granted Jordanian citizenship.

Some of the Palestinians who arrived in Jordan as refugees prospered economically; however, many others were left destitute by the war and came to reside in one of the refugee camps administered by the United Nations Relief and Works Agency for Palestine Refugees in the Middle East (UNRWA). The 1967 War then brought additional strains. Not only was the West Bank occupied by Israel, but some 265,000 of its inhabitants, many of them originally displaced in 1948, were forced across the Jordan River to the East Bank. The arrival of more than 250,000 destitute refugees further strained the resource-poor country. The UNRWA provided basic food rations as well as educational and health facilities to most of these refugees, but the impact on the kingdom was severe.

Subsequent refugee waves have also markedly affected the kingdom. Saddam Hussein's August 1990 invasion of Kuwait led to the return of about 200,000 Jordanian

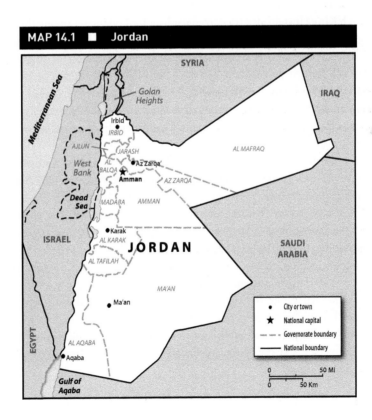

MAP 14.1 ■   Jordan

citizens. The kingdom struggled under the weight of these returnees, as its pleas to the international community for aid went largely ignored because King Hussein had refused to participate in the anti-Saddam international coalition. The launching of the war in January 1991 triggered another influx, this time of Iraqis, which continued over the following months.

The March 2003 US invasion of Iraq triggered yet another round of forced Iraqi immigration into Jordan, with estimates ranging between 400,000 and 500,000. This wave strained existing housing stock and significantly drove up prices just as the kingdom was reducing subsidies on many basic commodities. Most recently, beginning in mid-2011, the Asad regime's brutal repression of the Syrian uprising triggered new refugee flows. While total numbers may well have reached one million, as of June 2021 the number of Syrians formally registered with the United Nations High Commission on Refugees (UNHCR) in the kingdom was just under 670,000.

The Intercommunal Divide: Palestinian and East-Banker

King Abdallah's long-standing desire for a kingdom larger than Transjordan led him to oppose the emergence of a separate Palestinian state following the 1947 UN partition plan, as he hoped to add Palestinian territory to his own realm. To be successful, however, the Hashemites needed not only the territory but also the population. Through the 1954 Nationality Law, all of these Palestinians were accorded Jordanian citizenship.

Although King Hussein also tried to engender a Jordanianness among these Palestinians, the struggle over the national identity of Jordan's population of Palestinian origin has marked many aspects of the country's development. The incorporation of population through annexation is a fraught process, and for the Palestinians, the trauma of 1948 was intensified by rumors of Hashemite collusion with the Zionist leadership in Palestine. Not surprisingly, then, as the appeal of Arab nationalism grew in the 1950s, with its target not only Israel but also Western powers, Palestinians were generally eager partisans, as were many Transjordanians.

However, by the mid-1960s, a renewed Palestinian nationalism had emerged with the Palestine Liberation Organization (PLO) as its representative. After the 1967 Arab defeat, as the various Palestinian resistance (*fedayeen*) organizations grew in strength, a showdown between them and the Jordanian state became inevitable. It finally came in 1970 in a twelve-day assault by the Jordanian army: Black September, as it was called, destroyed much of the resistance and pushed the rest into the northwest of the country, from which it was expelled in mid-1971.

In this confrontation, there were Palestinians who fought with the Jordanian army, just as there were Transjordanians who belonged to various Palestinian guerrilla organizations. Nonetheless, the civil war led the regime and much of the Transjordanian population to regard Jordanians of Palestinian origin as potential traitors. The most immediate result was the initiation of an "East Banker first" policy aimed at preferential recruitment of Transjordanians into the bureaucracy and the virtual exclusion of Palestinians from high-level military or security-related positions.

In the meantime, the struggle to prevent the PLO from securing the loyalty of Jordan's Palestinians continued, along with Hussein's desire to restore Hashemite sovereignty over the West Bank. The competition for this loyalty affected the king's participation in the Arab–Israeli peace process as well as his involvement in inter-Arab politics. Finally, however, a combination of domestic and regional factors led to the king's July 1988 decision to disengage administratively and legally from the territory.

While this move settled many questions that had long vexed the relationship between the Hashemites and the Palestinians, it failed to address that of the identity of the remaining Jordanians of Palestinian origin, who now made up perhaps 50 percent of the population. Tensions have continued between the two groups: over Jordan's peace treaty with Israel, the Palestinian right of return, the threat of arbitrary withdrawal of citizenship from Jordanians of Palestinian origin, the continuing economic and political privileges that Transjordanians enjoy, and any developments in the "peace process" that suggest a definitive settlement of Palestinian refugees in Jordan.

RELIGION

The role of Islam in Jordan has been shaped in part by the ruling Hashemite family's lineage to the Prophet Muhammad. Its service under the Ottomans as guardians of Mecca and Medina has also accorded it a legitimacy that no other leaders in the Eastern Arab world can claim. Just as important, the close intertwining of the family's Muslim and Arab identities has been central to the broader historical narrative of the regime.

From the time of the amirate, the overwhelming majority of the population has been Muslim, and successive constitutions have enshrined Islam as the state religion. However, Jordanians are equal before the law with respect to rights and obligations "regardless of origin, language or religion," and freedom of belief and worship has been guaranteed, as has the right of religious congregations to establish their own schools, subject to government oversight.

In the critical realm of national education, Islamic history figures centrally in the curriculum. In addition, Muslim students take classes in Islam and Islamic upbringing, while Christians are offered their own lessons. Muslim holidays are part of the government school calendar; Christian schools may also have Sundays and their own holidays off. Successive educational laws have also stressed the importance of religion in building the citizenry.

State control over religion has long been viewed as critical, and has in part been secured through government administration of shariʻa courts in the case of Muslims and the Council of Religious Communities for non-Muslims. Shariʻa courts are appointed by royal decree, and matters of personal status (e.g., marriage, divorce, inheritance) fall within their exclusive jurisdiction when the parties are Muslim. The state has also long exercised control over mosques through appointing and dismissing imams and in guiding the content of Friday sermons.

In the realm of civil society, the most important group that historically has had a religious message at its core has been the Muslim Brotherhood (Ikhwan). While other parties and associations have experienced varying degrees of repression, the Muslim Brotherhood (MB) long operated openly, often with government support, as its conservative program reinforced the pro-Western orientation of the regime.

Throughout the 1970s and 1980s, religious activism grew with no objection from the state. Even after a crackdown in 1985 on the MB related to its ties with Syria, the relationship was not irreparably strained. Indeed, when economic riots shook the kingdom in April 1989, the MB aimed its criticism at the government, not the king, and worked to defuse tensions. Not until the signing of the peace treaty with Israel in 1994 did a real rupture occur. The relationship between the regime and the MB continued to be fraught, and further deteriorated following the Arab uprisings. Direct and indirect state and regional pressures finally led the group to split in 2015, with the progovernment faction taking the name the Muslim Brotherhood Society. In July 2020, the kingdom's highest court officially dissolved the original MB, although it continues to command considerable influence across the country.

Outside the realm of politics, the Hashemites have engaged in a number of high-profile endeavors to emphasize the family's responsibility to the broader Muslim community. In Jerusalem, King Hussein initiated restorations on the Muslim holy sites from 1952 to 1964 and again in 1969 (after a fire seriously damaged the al-Aqsa mosque), as Jordan continued its responsibility for their administration even under the Israeli occupation. From 1992 to 1994, the king spent more than US$8 million of his personal wealth to finance another restoration of the Dome of the Rock.

Promoting a moderate reading of Islam has also long been a hallmark of Jordanian policy. The first major initiative in this area was the Royal Aal al-Bayt Institute for Islamic Thought, established in 1980 by King Hussein. Another institution that has reinforced the Hashemite narrative of a tolerant Islam is the Royal Institute for Inter-Faith Studies (RIIFS). Established in 1994, it has supported the interdisciplinary study of religion, with particular reference to Christianity in Arab and Islamic society. Both of these institutions have high profiles, giving Jordan—but especially the royal family—a notable voice in the Islamic world and in the international community of interfaith organizations.

Such initiatives took on even greater importance after September 2001 and the growing focus on extremist groups such as al-Qa'ida. Most notable was the November 2004 Amman Message. Its call for tolerance and unity in the Muslim world has been regularly referenced by the regime, including in the context of the direct threat posed by the rise of the self-proclaimed Islamic State (ISIS/Da'esh) in Syria and Iraq. Official statements and policies have continued to denounce and suppress jihadist activity, while asserting an alternative model of Islamic tradition and practice promoted by the kingdom.

INSTITUTIONS AND GOVERNANCE

After Hussein's 1953 accession to the throne, he replaced his grandfather's governing style with one geared toward an increasingly complex modern state. The political system has continued to be a hereditary monarchy, in which the monarch both reigns and rules. The government comprises an executive consisting of the king, the royal court, and the cabinet (Council of Ministers); a legislature, composed of the popularly elected lower house (Council of Deputies) and the Senate (Council of Notables), whose members are appointed by the king; and a judicial branch, to which a nine-member Constitutional court was added in fall 2012. The constitution provides for a separation of powers between branches, but in practice, the monarch remains the ultimate arbiter.

In 2013, Abdallah officially gave the parliament a say in the selection of the prime minister, but in practice, it is still he who, in addition to having authority over foreign and defense policy, designates the head of government. Ministerial posts are assigned according to considerations driven by both external political challenges and internal power balancing and patronage distribution: Every cabinet has had to have representation from both the North and the South of the country, it must also have a couple of Christians and Circassians or Chechens, and there is the expectation of a predominance of Jordanians of East Bank rather than Palestinian origin. Among these calculations are those related to rotating portfolios among important tribes. Hence, professional qualifications for heading a particular ministry are often of secondary importance.

The early 1960s did witness moves to professionalize the domestic civil service, the diplomatic corps, and the judiciary, as well as to implement an economic strategy intended to reduce

PHOTO 14.1 The Hashemite Monarchs (left to right): King Abdallah I, King Hussein, King Abdallah II, King Talal, and Sharif Hussein

Courtesy of Laurie A. Brand

Jordan's dependence on external sources of revenue. Whether such attempts would ultimately have set Jordan on a more self-reliant course is impossible to know because the 1967 War intervened to drastically change the course of the kingdom's development.

The loss of the West Bank rendered problematic the holding of elections and the functioning of the parliament. In 1974, after the Arab League designated the PLO the sole, legitimate representative of the Palestinians, Hussein suspended parliament to ensure that there was no formal institution in which political conflicts, especially between Palestinians and East-Bankers, would surface. Not until 1978 was an alternative body established, the National Consultative Council, but its members were appointed by the king, and it had no legislative power. It was finally dissolved in 1984 when the king recalled parliament as part of a strategy to strengthen his hand with what was by then a weakened PLO. Nevertheless, only four years later a combination of domestic and regional pressures led to the king's decision to disengage from the West Bank (see The Intercommunal Divide: Palestinian and East Banker section).

Less than a year after the disengagement, economic riots rocked the kingdom. In response, Hussein announced that parliamentary elections, the first since prior to the 1967 War, would be held for a new National Assembly. This move was part of a political opening that followed, characterized by greater freedom of expression and a retreat of the security apparatus. Elections in November 1989 for the new 80-seat parliament were the freest since 1956.

The king further demonstrated his commitment to increased political liberalization in his April 1990 appointment of a sixty-member royal commission charged with drafting a national charter intended to reformulate the bases of the state–society relationship. Perhaps most significant, the charter legalized political parties in exchange for a societal statement of allegiance to the monarchy.

However, subsequent events demonstrated the weak regime commitment to political liberalization, for as opposition to a peace treaty with Israel grew, so did regime intolerance of opposition. To curtail the impact of dissent, the electoral law was changed in 1993 to favor tribal over ideological (in particular, Islamist) candidates; new laws curbed press freedom; municipal councils were restructured and filled with government appointees; and the *mukhabarat* (domestic intelligence services) was given freer rein to suppress civil society.

Toward the end of the 1990s, Hussein's health overshadowed political developments. Diagnosed in June 1998 with lymphatic cancer, he underwent six months of treatment in the United States. The king returned on February 4, 1999, changed the succession from his brother to his eldest son, Abdallah, and died three days later. The new king, Abdallah II, had not been groomed to rule; nevertheless, he quickly consolidated his position by ushering out several old-guard figures and recruiting a new generation of advisers.

In the summer of 2001, with the second intifada raging in the occupied West Bank and Gaza Strip, the king dissolved parliament, citing as justification the tense political situation between Israel and the Palestinian Authority. He proceeded to govern by royal decree over the next two years, issuing some 250 temporary laws, many of which further limited political freedoms. The post–September 11 "war on terror" facilitated this trend as the regime used it to justify its clampdown on Islamists.

Political freedoms suffered another blow when, in August 2002, the king again postponed elections, citing the impact of regional instability. When elections were held in June 2003, proregime candidates scored a major victory. The same was true of elections in 2007, which were marred by gross state interference. Nevertheless, Abdallah dissolved this parliament after only two years for failing to "address the people's needs." A new round of elections was held in 2010, with Islamists boycotting as they had in 2007 and progovernment candidates again taking a majority of seats.

Since the early 2000s, the king has periodically raised the issue of political reform, and a number of plans have been proposed, but few concrete changes have been introduced. However, when antiregime demonstrations broke out across the region in early 2011, small groups of activists from across the political spectrum organized protests focused specifically on the need for reform.

In response to popular demands, the government opened investigations into a range of corruption cases, although the parliament ultimately refused to proceed against any of those charged. A new electoral law, one that sorely disappointed those calling for reform, was approved in June 2012. Dissension over it, in the context of broader demands for change, led parliamentary elections, initially slated for the fall of 2012, to be postponed. When the polling was finally held in January 2013, a large number of tribal leaders and proregime loyalists once again won a majority of seats. The next round of parliamentary elections held in 2016 largely preserved the status quo, although the MB's Islamic Action Front (IAF) participated, ending a near ten-year boycott of elections.

A more interesting development came on August 15, 2017, when, as part of a broader program of decentralization, Jordan held its first-ever local elections for twelve new governorates and one hundred municipal and local councils, as well as for mayoralties. Over six thousand candidates competed for the 1,833 seats. The government strongly promoted participation in these polls, which were hailed as a reform marking a new era of greater citizen participation. In the end, however, the turnout was only 37 percent, ironically leading to successes by candidates affiliated with the MB.

The next round of elections, held in 2020 amid the COVID-19 pandemic, were widely criticized as marred by state interference and the lowest voter turnout (29 percent) in years. They produced a parliament in which the IAF lost five seats and in which representatives of the business community and powerful tribes maintained a majority. Popular dissatisfaction with parliament combined with growing economic woes exacerbated by the pandemic led the king in June 2021 to call upon former prime minister Samir al-Rifa'i to convene a 92-member committee tasked with proposing reforms to modernize the political system, primary among them the existing electoral and political parties laws. The committee's recommendations were expected in October 2021.

ACTORS, OPINION, AND PARTICIPATION

Associational life and political participation in Jordan have been marked by the many crises that have punctuated the kingdom's history. While the East Bank was not without civil society activity during the amirate period, the incorporation of the West Bank and its Palestinian population introduced institutions born during the pre-1948 struggle against Zionism. Organizations of women and workers, doctors, lawyers, and engineers all engaged in work related to charitable, social, or professional issues, but the ongoing conflict with Israel was never far removed from their concerns.

The same was true of political parties, which began to grow in importance with the surge of Arab nationalism in the mid-1950s. The parliamentary elections of 1956 marked a high point of political freedom in the country. Shortly thereafter, however, political instability triggered the imposition of martial law. Political parties were banned and political publications were closed. The MB, which opposed communism and other secular oppositional ideologies, then drew closer to the regime, thus laying the groundwork for what would be a near-forty-year symbiosis.

With political parties outlawed, elections in the 1960s produced little of the excitement that had characterized the process in 1956. However, the June 1967 War was a turning point because in its wake, with the West Bank occupied, elections for parliament—in which half of the seats were allocated to the territory—could not be held. In the absence of both legal political parties and parliamentary elections, professional associations began to play an outsized political role. Their leadership elections came to serve as a gauge of the strength of political currents in the country, and they became the only organized voices of opposition in the context of a martial law regime.

Not until the political liberalization of 1989 were political parties once again allowed to operate openly. However, after years of harassment and suppression by the regime, Arab nationalist and Leftist political parties were at pains to elicit much electoral support. Instead, it was the MB and associated Islamists who, through their networks of social welfare institutions operating at the grassroots level, took more than a third of the seats.

Still, political exiles started returning home, the media engaged a wider range of issues, and new publications began to appear. The Political Parties Law was finally passed in September 1992, allowing for the legal registration of parties, but of the twenty parties that registered in the first wave, the only one of any significance was the IAF, the political party extension of the MB. Since then, the country has seen the emergence and disappearance of myriad parties; with the exception of the IAF, most have had quite limited membership and staying power.

This post-1989 process of political liberalization might have continued had Jordan's move toward peace with Israel not intervened. Concern over popular opposition to a peace treaty led the regime to insist upon changes to the electoral law to cut the power of the Islamists and produce a more pliant parliament. As opposition continued, the regime resumed many of the practices that had characterized the martial law period. The new Press and Publications Law, enacted during the negotiations with Israel in 1994 and amended in 1997, was one key indicator of the state's retreat from previously granted political liberties.

Had peace on the Israeli–Palestinian front been secured, resistance to the kingdom's own peace treaty might have dissipated. However, the stalling of the Oslo Accords increased the legitimacy of the antinormalization front, a network of members of professional associations as well as of the MB and the IAF, which called for severing relations with Israel and abrogating the 1994 treaty. The outbreak of the second Palestinian intifada in 2000 only increased popular anger toward Israel and, by extension, the regime.

With peace in Israel/Palestine nowhere in sight and with Jordan supportive in various ways of the US military involvement in both Iraq and Afghanistan, the Islamists continued to constitute the most significant domestic opposition. Parliamentary elections in November 2007, the second under a 2001 law that increased the number of seats overall to 110 and allocated a quota of 6 seats to women, reduced the number of Islamist MPs from 17 (elected in 2003) to 6. Meanwhile, attempts to crack down on domestic support for Hamas, the Palestinian branch of the MB, and to shore up the sagging popularity of Fatah, the main Palestinian political faction in the West Bank, appeared only to backfire as Abdallah II's positions on a range of foreign policy issues were out of step with those of a majority of his subjects.

Yet it was not primarily these issues that produced near-weekly demonstrations as the regional contagion of antiregime protests arrived in Jordan in early 2011. Instead, it was the deterioration of the standard of living against a backdrop of economic corruption that brought not only groups of leftists and Islamists but also tribal groupings traditionally assumed to be strong backers of the regime to the streets.

Still, the regime was not seriously threatened, and the king promised the release of those protestors who had been arrested. Parliamentary elections were then finally held in January 2013. Although European Union (EU) observers praised the process, the decision by the MB and other opposition parties to boycott because of concerns over lack of progress on reforms and outcome-rigging led to a mediocre 56.5 percent participation level. By this time, however, the attention of Jordanians was increasingly focused on the threats posed by the instability in Iraq and the civil war in Syria. The security forces concentrated on the growing appeal of jihadist groups based in neighboring countries whose programs attracted supporters from salafist and socioeconomically disgruntled sectors of Jordanian society.

Encouraged by the Egyptian military's ouster of MB President Muhammad Morsi and by Saudi and Emirati support for a clampdown on Brotherhood branches elsewhere in the region, the Jordanian regime moved to further weaken its primary opponent. While it did not go as far as Cairo, which labeled the MB a terrorist organization, it jailed the deputy head of the MB for criticizing the UAE (United Arab Emirates), and then in spring 2015 colluded in a process aimed at splitting the MB: ousting the hard-liners and recognizing only the more dovish Muslim Brotherhood Society as legitimate.

Late spring 2018 brought a controversial income tax law to the Jordanian parliament as part of the ongoing implementation of economic reforms. The leadership against it came not from the MB, but from the professional associations, one of which—the large and powerful Engineer's Union—had just held elections in which the MB had lost its leadership position for the first time in 26 years. What ensued was an outpouring of popular anger, culminating in thirty-three unions and professional associations calling for a general strike against the proposed law on May 30. Such a dramatic wave of protest forced the king in June 2018 to dismiss the government and designate a new prime minister, Omar al-Razzaz, a former World Bank official who had been serving as minister of education and was respected as a reformer.

The greatest test of al-Razzaz's commitment to reform came from this very sector as in September 2019, the Teachers Union, the establishment of which in 2011 was one of the few concrete fruits of the Arab spring in Jordan, went on strike, demanding the 50 percent pay raise its members had been promised in 2014. This 100,000-strong union is not only the largest in the kingdom: its power also derives from a membership that cuts across all socioeconomic, regional, and communal divides. Widely supported across the country, the strike lasted four weeks, ending with government concessions on a scaled pay increase. However, tensions resurfaced in April 2020 after the pandemic led the state to freeze all public sector raises until the end of that year. The resultant threats to renew its protests proved too menacing to the regime: in late July 2020, police raided and closed its headquarters and branches across the country for an announced two years, and detained its leadership. The repression continued in August, with the arrest of another 1000 teachers. In December 2020, a preliminary court ruling was issued to dissolve the Union, but as of August 2021, the final disposition of the case remained to be decided.

POLITICAL ECONOMY

Jordan is an example of a rentier economy—that is, one that relies heavily on external sources of income and support rather than a robust domestic productive base for sustenance and growth. The external income or rent that Jordan has received over the years has taken different forms: general budgetary support, aid for the military and security services, grants or concessionary loans for development projects, payments from the UNRWA and UNHCR, royalties for oil pipeline passage, payment for overland transport, and remittances from Jordanians working abroad.

The roots of such an economic system can be traced to the beginnings of the amirate, as British subsidies constituted more than 50 percent of state expenditures. At the time, the country had a very small population, limited agricultural land, and few natural resources (phosphates and potash). The annual subsidy was particularly important in developing the various security forces that were critical to maintaining stability and which provided employment to influential tribes whose already often-precarious economic situation had deteriorated with the ending of tribal raiding and state attempts to forcibly settle them. Offsetting poverty was key to establishing the symbiotic relationship between the state and the tribes that became so central to the Jordanian political system.

World War II brought a boom to Jordan, but it was followed by the 1948 Palestine war, which introduced several hundred thousand largely destitute refugees who strained the state's limited capabilities. Still, British subsidies continued, and the UNRWA, established in 1950, took charge of the displaced Palestinians, ultimately helping to provide housing, education, basic food needs, and health care. In addition, the influx of Palestinians, combined with the subsequent annexation of the West Bank, increased the population by 200 percent and added territory, much of it productive agricultural land, to the kingdom's economic base.

Britain terminated its annual subsidies in 1956 in response to Hussein's dismissal of the British commander of the Arab Legion. However, the day that martial law was imposed following a purported coup attempt in 1957, the United States granted Jordan $10 million. Annual aid of $60 million continued uninterrupted until 1967, when Amman accused Washington of backing Israel in the June War.

With the Israeli occupation of the West Bank, Jordan lost 25 percent of its arable land and half of its industrial capacity, as well as its major tourist attractions and pilgrimage sites, most notably in East Jerusalem. GDP dropped by 40 percent, and a new wave of refugees was pushed onto the East Bank. The Arab states then stepped in to provide annual financial support to aid in postwar rebuilding. However, in the wake of the September 1970 battles with the PLO, Kuwait and Libya suspended their aid, and Syria closed its border, thus severely obstructing trade.

After a few difficult years, the growing oil boom and the payments Jordan received from Arab states following Hussein's acceptance of the PLO's 1974 designation as the sole, legitimate representative of the Palestinian people helped to speed recovery. Indeed, the combination of Arab support, a decrease in domestic unemployment owing to migration to the Gulf oil states, and the resultant remittances sent to the kingdom led to a marked rise in the standard of living and the emergence of a middle class. State sector employment also grew, although it disproportionately benefitted Transjordanians, who were preferentially recruited following Black September of 1970.

At the Arab League summit in Baghdad convened in the wake of Egypt's March 1979 signing of a peace treaty with Israel, the oil-producing states renewed their financial commitments to the remaining confrontation states—Jordan and Syria—and the PLO. Yet this marked the end of an era. The 1980s brought regional recession due to changes in the international oil market and the impact of the Iran–Iraq War. In response, the oil states gradually reduced or reneged entirely on their Baghdad promises. Moreover, many expatriates working in the Gulf failed to have their contracts renewed, as Gulf state budget cuts and forced them to return home.

The one market that showed promise was that of Iraq, into whose economic orbit Jordan was gradually drawn. Special lines of credit were opened to promote trade, and Aqaba became Iraq's primary sea access after its own port, Basra, was badly damaged early in the war. Overland trade also played a major role in sparing Jordan the worst effects of the regional recession. Nevertheless, fiscal mismanagement gradually continued to increase the kingdom's debt. So, too, did Hussein's renunciation of Hashemite claims to the West Bank in July 1988. This disenfranchisement of West Bankers, and the anxiety it triggered among even East Bank–resident Palestinians, led many to transfer their resources out of the kingdom. The resultant capital flight weakened an already frail system. The dinar lost half its value, and by January 1989 the kingdom was forced to go to the IMF to reschedule its debt.

The implementation of IMF-stipulated reductions in fuel subsidies in April 1989 triggered the most severe rioting the kingdom had witnessed since 1956. The unrest spread throughout the country (although it did not touch the capital) and led Hussein to call for new parliamentary elections as part of what would become an "Amman spring." While political liberalization did follow, so did the implementation of painful austerity measures that took a terrible toll on the poor and the middle class.

Then, suddenly, a new crisis compounded Jordan's woes. Iraq's invasion of Kuwait on August 2, 1990 led to the imposition of sanctions on Jordan's most important trading partner. Just as serious was the dramatic inflow of refugees (returning Jordanians and others). The sudden influx of some 200,000 expatriate workers from Iraq and Kuwait increased the size of Jordan's resident population by almost eight percent, driving up unemployment and leading to a loss in remittances, which had amounted to $623 million in 1989. Lost, too, was the economic aid that Jordan had received from Saudi Arabia and the other oil-rich states, which were furious with the king's stance on the crisis. Some estimates placed Jordan's economic losses from the Gulf crisis as high as $2 billion (even higher when the loss was projected over subsequent years).

Despite the obvious dangers of such heavy dependence on a single trading partner, Jordan reprised its role of Iraq's lifeline to the outside under sanctions following the 1991 war. Because of both Iraq's indebtedness to Jordan and Jordan's importance to regional security, Iraqi oil was allowed to continue to flow into the kingdom as an exception to the sanctions. The open border with Jordan was of particular importance to Iraq in the early 1990s, but even after Iraq accepted the oil-for-food regime in 1996, the close relationship continued.

In the meantime, the conditions of the IMF agreement continued to sting, with reduced state spending on food and energy subsidies, increased taxes, and cuts in domestic and foreign borrowing. The impact could have been worse had Jordan not been viewed by the IMF's Western backers as a key to regional stability and to the Arab–Israeli peace process. Its participation in the October 1991 Madrid peace conference helped repair relations with the United States and, as a consequence, increased the levels of US aid. Following the signing of its peace treaty with Israel, in 1994 and 1995 the United States offered some $700 million in debt relief to the kingdom. In 1997, the US Congress increased economic aid to Jordan to $150 million (up from $112 million in the previous year and only just over $36 million the year before) and military aid to $75 million (more than double that of the previous year).

Between 1998 and 2002, annual US economic aid to Jordan stood at approximately $150 million, with annual military aid around $75 million. Abdallah's subsequent willingness to work with the Bush administration in its "war on terror" and then with the 2003 US invasion of Iraq helped further raise the levels of assistance. Beginning in 2003, the total assistance package averaged more than $762 million per year; by 2014 it had reached $1 billion, thanks in part to annual supplemental appropriations to reimburse Jordan for its support of US military operations in the region. Of these funds, around $250 million was for Economic Support Funds, used both as cash transfers to service Jordan's foreign debt and to support US Agency for International Development (USAID) programs. In addition, approximately $200 million was allocated annually for the military. Although the Trump administration sidelined Jordan to a large extent in its regional policies, in 2018 the United States nonetheless pledged $6.3 billion in assistance over a five-year period to enable Jordan to implement development programs and to mitigate the impact of the cost of hosting over a million Syrian refugees.

The increased economic and military aid from the United States combined with the US aid program's focus on development of the private sector meshed well with Abdallah's announced intention to focus attention on the economy. One of his first initiatives was to diversify Jordan's trading partners, followed by his promotion of a range of reforms aimed at further integrating Jordan into the world economy. An Association Agreement with the EU came into force in 1999; Jordan gained entry to the World Trade Organization (WTO) in January 2000; the Special Economic Zone at the port of Aqaba was established in January 2001; and a Free Trade Agreement (FTA), which provided for gradual dismantling of tariffs and other trade barriers over a ten-year period, was signed with the United States in 2002. Jordan also established US-promoted Qualified Industrial Zones (QIZs), intended to encourage the establishment of Israeli–Jordanian joint ventures, in an effort to cement the peace while creating employment.

Jordan has also continued to rely to varying degrees on Gulf state financial support. In December 2011 the Gulf Cooperation Council offered $2.5 billion in aid to enable it to address the unrest of the Arab uprisings. This aid package expired in December 2016, but it was renewed for another five years in June 2018 following the economic protests that brought down the government of Prime Minister Hani al-Mulki.

The serious challenges that the country's economy has faced were further exacerbated by the impact of COVID-19. GDP growth (see Figure 14.1) in 2020 was –1.6 percent, down from 1.9 percent in 2018 and 2 percent in 2019.[1] Official unemployment levels, which have been rising steadily since 2014, climbed to 24.7 percent by the end of 2020, and youth unemployment reached an unprecedented 50 percent.[2] And those living in poverty, measured in 2018 at 15.7 percent of the population—although unofficial estimates put the numbers at more than one-third of all Jordanians—has also increased with the multifarious impact of the pandemic.

One somewhat offsetting element has been foreign aid (see Table 14.1) which, including concessional loans and grants to address the Syrian refugee crisis, was $3.15 billion in 2016 and $3.65 billion in 2017, although it then dropped to $2.526 billion in 2018 and $2.797 billion in 2019.[3] Nonetheless, in 2020 Jordan's foreign debt had surpassed $33 billion, having nearly doubled since 2010.[4] To alleviate the strains on the budget, the state gradually reduced a range of subsidies, most notably on oil and then electricity. However, February 2018 saw a reduction in the politically sensitive bread subsidy, which was replaced with direct transfers to the poor and to state employees. This move triggered protests in the streets and an MB-promoted

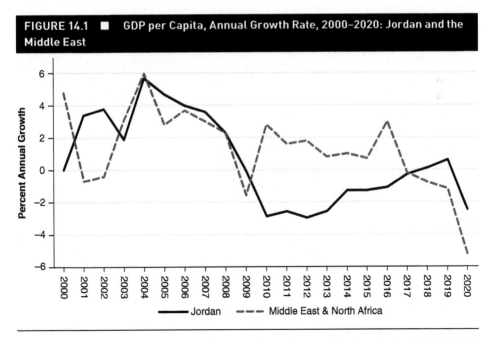

FIGURE 14.1 ■ GDP per Capita, Annual Growth Rate, 2000–2020: Jordan and the Middle East

Source: World Bank, "GDP per Capita Growth (annual %)," http://data.worldbank.org/indicator/NY.GDP.PCAP.KD.ZG/countries/1W-JO-ZQ?display=graph

TABLE 14.1 ■ Foreign Aid to Jordan	2005	2010	2015	2019
Net aid per capita (current US$)	$123	$131	$231	$277
Aid as percentage of GNI	5.5	3.5	5.6	6.3
Aid as percentage of central government expenditure	15.8	13.4	21.6	24

Source: Data from World Bank, http://data.worldbank.org/?display=default

no-confidence vote in the Parliament (which failed). The government did introduce a new law to raise tax rates and curb evasion, but the discontent continued, finally leading the king to dismiss Prime Minister Hani al-Mulki as a means of sapping popular anger. Unfortunately, the kingdom's financial problems remain deeply structural, and the impact of COVID-19 is only the most recent, stability-threatening challenge to the economy.

REGIONAL AND INTERNATIONAL RELATIONS

Jordan's relative economic and political weakness and the ongoing conflict over Israel/Palestine have been critical in shaping the alignments and alliances into which it has entered. Given Jordan's own limited resources, its kings have relied heavily on external support—military, financial, and political—to maintain the throne against threats both domestic and external.

Abdallah I's assassination and the 1952 overthrow of the monarchy in Egypt gradually introduced a new dynamic into regional relations. Egypt's President Gamal Abdel Nasser sought to bring Egypt's policies in line with what he called "positive neutrality." As ruler of a country in which British officers commanded the army, Hussein was a natural target of Egyptian propaganda, and the assaults launched over the Egyptian airwaves intensified as in 1955 Hussein announced his intention to join the US-sponsored Baghdad pact. Ultimately, however, popular anger that was manifested in street demonstrations led him to renounce Jordan's mutual defense pact with Britain and to dismiss the Arab Legion's British commander, General John Glubb.

Only months later, at the end of October 1956, Israel, followed by Britain and France, attacked Egypt after the government in Cairo nationalized the Suez Canal Company in response to the decision by the United States not to support Nasser's request for a World Bank loan to build a high dam near Aswan. Although Nasser lost the military battle, his willingness to stand up to Western states and Israel electrified the Arab world. Now regarded as the champion of Arab nationalism, the ascendant ideology in the Arab world, Nasser emerged as a formidable opponent to the Western-allied conservative regimes. Hussein managed to remain in power, thanks to the continued backing of his army, support from Saudi Arabia, and renewed Western assistance from the United States and the United Kingdom.

The next major external challenge to Amman came in the form of Egyptian sponsorship of the establishment of the PLO in May 1964. Lone among Arab leaders, Hussein saw his realm potentially threatened by the PLO: Its pool of potential recruits included the large number of Jordanians of Palestinian origin, and its desire to liberate Palestine could have been construed to include the West Bank. Hussein acquiesced only when PLO chairman Ahmad Shuqayri assured him that the land to be liberated did not include the West Bank nor would he recruit among the king's subjects.

Nevertheless, small Palestinian guerrilla groups began to emerge independent of Arab state control. The most important of these, Fatah, began launching its operations (largely acts of sabotage) against Israel in 1965. Guerrillas crossed into Israel via Jordan, leading to high-profile Israeli attacks, such as that on the West Bank town of al-Samu' in November 1966. With regional tensions rising and sensing that failure to align with Egypt could have serious implications for his throne if conflict broke out, Hussein flew to Cairo and signed a mutual defense pact just days before Israel launched the war on June 5, 1967. During the first few hours of the war, Israeli warplanes destroyed virtually the entire air forces of Egypt, Jordan, and Syria, leaving Jordan's ground forces vulnerable to air attack. Commanded by an Egyptian officer, Jordanian units desperately sought to defend Jerusalem but were ultimately forced to withdraw completely from the West Bank, with significant human and material losses.

Civil War

The 1967 War discredited the armies and leaderships of the so-called frontline states of Egypt, Syria, and Jordan, and the guerrillas of the Palestinian resistance movement seemed to offer a viable alternative. Recruitment soared after a combined force of Palestinian guerrillas and Jordanian army units repelled an Israeli incursion into the East Bank near the town of Karameh in March 1968. In a relatively short period of time, a semiautonomous set of guerrilla organizations emerged, operating in and launching attacks on Israeli targets from Jordan. Following the devastating 1967 defeat, the regime, its military, and its security apparatus were in disarray, and civilian support—tacit or overt—for regime methods was soundly shaken. With the regime's legitimacy compromised, Hussein had little choice but to allow the resistance organizations a freer rein.

Nonetheless, the contradiction between the prerogatives of a sovereign state and the needs of a liberation movement could not be suppressed forever. Clashes between the resistance and the Jordanian army became more and more frequent, ultimately leading to the 1970 Black September battles. Foreign ministers of surrounding Arab states then met in Cairo on September 22, 1970, to try to resolve the conflict. Nasser brokered a cease-fire agreement between Hussein and PLO Chairman Yasir Arafat and died the following day. Much of the resistance's infrastructure in and around Amman had been destroyed, but it still held bases in the northwest of the country. The regime continued to pursue the remnants of the Palestinian groups until July 1971, when the Jordanian army crushed the last PLO positions, leading to the arrest or flight of those fighters who remained.

The Road to Camp David

During the next few years, Hussein's regional preoccupations concerned the loss of the West Bank and how to maintain his claim to the territory in the face of the Israeli occupation and the reemerging Palestinian resistance. In order to repair relations with his Palestinian subjects and the Arab states in the wake of Black September, in March 1972 Hussein proposed a United Arab Kingdom plan. Such a new political entity required peace with Israel and its withdrawal from the West Bank. Based on a federal structure centered in Amman, it would have given greater autonomy to each of the two banks than in the past.

Unfortunately for the king, realities on the ground had already overtaken such a proposal. Black September had been a serious setback, but the PLO subsequently moved its center of gravity to Lebanon, where by the mid-1970s it had developed a parastatal apparatus that far surpassed what it had previously had in Jordan. Over the objections of King Hussein, at the October 1974 Arab League in Rabat, Morocco, Arab leaders officially recognized the PLO as the sole, legitimate representative of the Palestinian people.

In the meantime, after the PLO was drawn into what became the Lebanese civil war beginning in spring 1975, it made tentative attempts to reconcile with Jordan until Egyptian President al-Sadat's unexpected visit to Jerusalem in November 1977 changed the regional calculus. With US involvement and "land for peace" as a basis, al-Sadat's initiative was not unlike a formula Hussein had hoped would return the West Bank to Jordan. The Camp David Accords, signed a year later, prescribed a resolution to the Palestinian problem and presumed a Jordanian role in the final negotiations. Still, opposition in the Arab world to what was viewed as an Egyptian separate peace, was significant, particularly at the popular level. Given the large population of Palestinian origin on the East Bank, Hussein preferred to temporize. In the end, he opted not to join in the process because the West Bank territory offered was too little and did not include Jerusalem.

Instability in the Gulf

Jordan's refusal to join in the Camp David process led to a cooling of its relations with the United States, which had expected the kingdom to follow Egypt's lead. Relations might have continued to deteriorate had two other regional events not intervened. The first was the 1979 Iranian Revolution, which, in overthrowing the shah, deprived the United States of its reliable policeman in the oil-wealthy Persian Gulf region. The second was the September 1980 Iraqi attack on Iran.

As a Western-oriented monarch, Hussein viewed the advance of revolutionary movements anywhere in the region as a threat. The leaders of the Arab Gulf states also feared the call from Iran's new leader, the Ayatollah Khomeini, to export the Islamic revolution. It was this fear that led these states, including Jordan, to support Saddam Hussein's attack on Iran in an effort to overthrow the revolutionary regime. The Iranian threat from the East forced Jordan to decide between its then-strong relationship with Damascus, which was feuding with Baghdad, and Saddam. King Hussein chose the wealthier and more powerful Iraq, thus initiating a political, military, and economic relationship that would shape Jordan profoundly over the next two decades.

Competition with the PLO

In the meantime, developments on the Palestinian front had led to several shifts in relations between the PLO and King Hussein. The Israeli invasion of Lebanon in June 1982 destroyed much of what had become an extensive Palestinian political, military, economic, social, and cultural presence in the country. While the Syrians worried that a weakened PLO would be an easy target for outside pressures forcing a peace agreement with Israel, King Hussein viewed the organization's weakened position as an opportunity once again to assert Hashemite prerogatives in the relationship.

The new efforts to effect a rapprochement came against the backdrop of the Reagan plan, a blueprint for a future regional peace which was announced by the US administration in September 1982. Although it included the land-for-peace formula and spoke of the "legitimate rights" of the Palestinians, it had no provision for a Palestinian state; nor was the issue of Jerusalem directly addressed. Instead, it envisaged Palestinian self-government on the West Bank in association with Jordan. To Hussein's dismay, the PLO rejected the Reagan plan; however, PLO Chairman Yasir Arafat's weakness led him to reengage with Jordan. Relations warmed to the point that the Palestine National Council convened in Amman in 1984, and in February 1985, the two agreed to coordinate on the peace process.

Like other episodes of Jordanian-PLO coordination, however, this one was short lived, and the following February, the king announced its end. In the meantime, unsuccessful in his negotiations with Arafat and stung by the refusal of the US Congress in 1985 to sell Jordan mobile air defense missiles, F-16s, and Stinger missiles because of his rejection of the Reagan plan, Hussein turned his primary attention to inter-Arab relations. Although Egypt's membership in the Arab League had been frozen as a result of its separate peace with Israel in 1979, Jordan had never completely cut ties. Indeed, it was thanks to both these continuing ties and Jordan's geographic location that a line of material and human support for Iraq's war effort developed, beginning in Egypt and crossing Jordan.

The 1987 Arab League summit, held in Amman, constituted the high point of Hussein's diplomatic efforts in the Arab world. First, despite Damascus's support for Iran during the Iran–Iraq War, Hussein secured Syrian support for a resolution condemning Iran for holding Iraqi territory and for failing to accept a UN-sponsored cease-fire. Second, Asad agreed to a resolution explicitly permitting Arab League states to restore diplomatic relations with Cairo.

Yet Hussein's diplomatic triumph was soon eclipsed by the central arena of conflict. By this time, the Israeli occupation of the West Bank and Gaza was twenty years old, and Israeli land confiscation and settlement construction had intensified following the Likud electoral victory in 1977. In April 1987, Hussein, who had maintained secret channels of communication with Israeli leaders over the years, conferred with Labor Party leader Shimon Peres in London and reached an agreement to work toward a five-power international peace conference. The attempt at advancing negotiations foundered, however, when Peres failed to secure the Israeli cabinet's support. The pressures born of an increasingly oppressive occupation finally produced an explosion in December 1987.

The Palestinian uprising, or intifada, quickly spread and intensified, taking the Arab states as well as the Israelis by surprise. For Jordan, however, the unrest was more than a foreign policy issue. Given that perhaps half of his East Bank population was of Palestinian origin, Hussein's most immediate concern was that the violence might spill over the Jordan River, as the intifada was led by a new generation of Palestinian activists who were clearly nationalist, not Hashemite, in their orientation.

The United States, which at the time was still constrained by a 1970s memorandum promising not to talk directly to the PLO until it had renounced violence and accepted Israel's right to exist, continued, along with its Israeli partner, to insist on a central role for Jordan in the peace process. In response to the continuing uprising, an extraordinary Arab summit was held in June 1988 in Algiers. Two of its decisions were of particular importance to Jordan. The first was that the oil-producing states declined to renew their financial support for the kingdom. Had this not been sufficiently galling for Hussein, the second stipulated that funds from these states for the PLO, which had been channeled through a joint Jordanian–Palestinian committee, were now to go directly to the PLO, bypassing Jordan. The king's response took all observers by surprise.

Renunciation of West Bank Claims

On July 31, Hussein renounced all Jordanian legal and administrative ties to the West Bank and called on the PLO to take responsibility for the Palestinians in the Israeli-occupied territory. He dissolved the Jordanian parliament, half of whose members represented West Bank districts, and ordered Jordanian passports held by West Bank Palestinians to be changed to two-year travel documents. He thereby deprived of Jordanian citizenship and rendered stateless all those whose normal place of residence was the West Bank.

Initially shocked by the king's move, many criticized him for violating the norms of Arab unity. The PLO itself, only recently recovered from its 1982 expulsion from Lebanon, was caught off guard. Palestinians, both those West Bankers who suddenly found themselves stateless as well as those resident on the East Bank who wondered what their future held, initiated massive financial transfers from Jordanian banks, thus putting increasing pressures on an economy that was already reeling from the regional recession.

Ultimately, however, the PLO realized the opportunity the disengagement represented: Hussein's move opened up the West Bank as land that, in the event of an Israeli withdrawal, could form the basis of a Palestinian state. The Palestine National Council, in a historic meeting the following November, proclaimed Palestinian independence (which Hussein recognized immediately), accepted UN Security Council Resolution 242, recognized the existence of Israel in a formula finally deemed acceptable by the United States, and began a formal dialogue with Washington. The "Jordanian option" so dear to the United States and the Israeli Labor Party leaders—a solution to the Palestinian problem that avoided the creation of an independent Palestinian state—appeared to be dead.

The Persian Gulf Crisis

During the Iran–Iraq War, Iraq and Jordan had become heavily economically interdependent. Strong ties of cooperation had also developed between their two militaries, while Saddam

Hussein courted journalists with lavish gifts and the average citizen with a range of contributions, including the building of mosques. Whether King Hussein believed the press's rhetoric about Iraq's constituting Jordan's strategic depth is unclear; what is certain is that he had a strong personal relationship with the Iraqi leader.

At the same time, Jordan had close ties with Egypt, Saudi Arabia, the smaller Arab Gulf states, and the principal Western powers that quickly coalesced to oppose the invasion of Kuwait. The king's position was that, while he opposed the Iraqi move, the matter needed to be resolved diplomatically on an inter-Arab level. The Jordanian stance was, therefore, one of neutrality, but in a context in which neutrality had been effectively excluded as an option. Perhaps it was because of the strong pro-Iraqi reaction among the Jordanian population—both Palestinians and Transjordanians—that his policy was viewed abroad as tantamount to supporting Saddam Hussein. In any event, as a result, Jordan experienced near-complete international isolation. Yet despite the economic hardships that flowed from general adherence to the economic embargo, the loss of aid from members of the anti-Iraq coalition, and a large influx of refugees from Iraq and Kuwait, the king's popularity at home rose to new heights.

The Peace Process and the Israeli–Jordanian Treaty

Jordan's relations with Kuwait and Saudi Arabia (and, to a lesser extent, the other Gulf states) remained strained for years following the 1991 War, but its ties with the United States and other Western countries improved rapidly. Central to Jordan's rehabilitation by the Western states was the fact that the George H. W. Bush administration's decision to move ahead on an Arab–Israeli peace initiative following the war required a Jordanian role. Israel still refused to deal directly with a Palestinian negotiating team; hence, the participation of Jordan was critical. By July 1991, the United States had restored $35 million in economic aid, and following Jordan's participation in the first round of Arab–Israeli talks held in Madrid in October 1991, the United States extended an additional $22 million in military assistance.

The Madrid conference appeared to be a success, but as time passed, the bilateral and multilateral talks it spawned—including, ultimately, direct Israeli–Palestinian discussions—stalled. Then, in June 1992 the Labor Party, headed by Yitzhak Rabin, returned to lead the Israeli government. Soon thereafter, Israel opened a secret, direct dialogue with the PLO under Norwegian auspices, which culminated in mutual recognition and in the signing of the Declaration of Principles in Washington on September 13, 1993.

The Israeli–PLO agreement took King Hussein by surprise, and he was outraged that he had been excluded. He responded by authorizing the signing and publication of the Jordanian–Israeli peace settlement agenda that had been worked out in the Madrid-initiated bilateral negotiations. As a result, however, the strong domestic support the king had enjoyed since 1990 fractured. Leftist and Islamist members of the Jordanian parliament denounced both the Israeli–PLO agreement and the Israeli–Jordanian agenda. Just as important, those Transjordanians who worried that these agreements might "solve" the Palestinian refugee problem at the expense of Jordan—that is, through massive permanent settlement of Palestinians on the East Bank—also voiced concern.

Still, with the PLO heavily engaged with Israel in a peace process, Jordan had substantial political cover to pursue its own agreement. On October 26, 1994, the two sides signed a treaty providing for an exchange of ambassadors and broad cooperation in trade, tourism, water allocation, transportation, communications, environmental protection, and border arrangements. Both governments pledged not to allow third parties to use their territory for attacks against the other, and Israel recognized Jordan's role as a guardian of the Islamic holy places in Jerusalem. Hussein's hope was that the new relationship would translate into economic benefits that would strengthen the domestic constituency supportive of a peace agreement.

Ultimately, the anticipated "peace dividend" did not materialize to the degree anticipated, despite debt forgiveness and financial support from Western donors and some growth in the tourism sector. The Jordanian public, skeptical from the start, became increasingly frustrated with the failure of the Palestinian–Israeli agreement to provide a basis for a real peace and with the degree to which Jordan's accord reinforced Israel's power in its dealings with the Palestinians. Israeli settlement activity in the West Bank and Gaza proceeded apace, and the establishment of an independent Palestinian state seemed as distant as ever.

Abdallah's Succession

The challenges Abdallah II faced upon assuming the reins of power in February 1999 ranged from a tense regional situation, including a moribund peace process, to a distressed national economy and his own lack of political experience. On the foreign policy front, the young king first moved to repair Jordan's relations with the powerful oil producers that had been so strained by his father's neutrality in 1990. In April 1999, he chose Saudi Arabia as the destination for his first foreign visit. He also secured rapprochements with the smaller Gulf states, including Kuwait, aiming not only to rebuild trade ties but also to convince them once again to recruit Jordanian workers.

Strained relations with Syria, where the young Bashar al-Asad had succeeded his father in June 2000, also entered a new era. A shared interest in increased cooperation led to a far-reaching bilateral trade agreement in 2001 and to the initiation of the long-postponed joint al-Wahdah Dam project on the Yarmuk River. Abdallah concluded similar bilateral and multilateral agreements with Egypt, Morocco, Tunisia, and Yemen. Amman's relations with the region's non-Arab states—Iran and Turkey—also improved. The young king further moved to deepen Jordan's relations with the EU (above all, France, Germany, and Great Britain), Japan, and the United States.

Israeli–Palestinian Escalation

Only with the outbreak of the al-Aqsa, or second, intifada in September 2000 did the Palestinian issue return to the king's agenda. Like his father, King Abdallah II tried to serve as a mediator between Israel and the Palestinian Authority. As the violence continued, Jordan strongly supported the so-called Road Map, the three-step peace plan put forth in April 2003 by the Quartet—the EU, Russia, the United Nations, and the United States.

However, against the backdrop of Israel's "targeted assassinations" of Palestinians, the continued growth of Israeli settlements, the erection of a separation wall/barrier in and around the West Bank, Palestinian suicide bombings against Israelis, and the growing "militarization" of the Palestinian territories, the gap between the Hashemite regime's foreign policy and the Jordanian public's stance toward the Israeli–Palestinian conflict continued to grow. Nowhere was it more obvious than in Jordan's relationship with Hamas, the main Palestinian Islamist organization. Hamas's unexpected victory against the more secular Fatah in Palestinian parliamentary elections in January 2006 was as popular with Jordanians as it was problematic for a regime closely aligned with the United States, which refused to deal with the Islamic resistance movement. The regime even went so far as to assist the United States in arming Fatah in hopes it would militarily defeat Hamas as a low-level Palestinian civil war broke out in 2007. Worse, from the point of view of much of the Jordanian public, Jordan's position on the late-2008 Israeli war on Gaza, like that of Egypt and Saudi Arabia, was largely one of watching from the sidelines, hoping for the defeat of Hamas while Gazans were killed by the hundreds. Israel's even more brutal fifty-day war against Gaza in summer 2014, in which more than 2,200 Palestinians were killed and entire neighborhoods were leveled, only further underlined the fact that as long as Hamas was in control of the territory, Arab-state interest in ending the violence would remain weak.

New Regional Order: Continuous War

In the meantime, during the summer of 2002, Abdallah had tried to persuade the Bush administration not to attack Iraq, arguing that such a war would seriously threaten the regional balance of power. When it became clear, however, that the US government was set upon ousting Saddam Hussein, the king, unlike his father, discarded neutrality. He allowed the United States to use two air bases in the kingdom's eastern desert and station hundreds of soldiers on its territory. The two states also participated in joint military maneuvers in August and October 2002. In turn, the kingdom received $1.1 billion in US aid, which was officially designated as compensation for its war-related losses. Nevertheless, uneasy about the possible backlash from the Jordanian population, Abdallah and his government officially denied supporting the war.

To minimize the detrimental effects of the invasion and war on the kingdom and his throne, Abdallah straddled often-contradictory positions. On the one hand, he supported the US policy of maintaining its military presence in Iraq while gradually transferring political responsibilities to elected Iraqis. On the other, he spoke out fervently against the exclusion of Sunni Arabs when the Shi'i-Kurdish coalition gained an absolute majority in the January 2005 elections for the transitional legislature and in the December 2005 parliamentary polls. However, Jordan also trained several thousand Iraqi regular police with the aim of fighting the growing Sunni insurgency, and in June 2006, Jordan's *mukhabarat* cooperated with US agencies in tracking down and killing Abu Mus'ab al-Zarqawi, the Jordanian leader of al-Qa'ida in Iraq.

In the context of the growing power of Iran and of the Shi'a in Iraq, Abdallah made controversial statements regarding what he called the threat of a Shi'i crescent emerging in the region. His initial stance during the Israel–Lebanon war in the summer of 2006 was therefore not surprising: He condemned Hezbollah leader Hassan Nasrallah for the fighting, siding with the United

States and its regional allies—Egypt, Saudi Arabia, and Israel. Yet when it became clear that the Jordanian public overwhelmingly supported Hezbollah, he backtracked. He condemned the massive Israeli assault and called for an immediate and peaceful resolution of the conflict.

The continuing Israeli and US occupations and wars in the region led to a new set of regional alignments, with US-allied countries like Israel and the leadership in Jordan, Egypt, and Saudi Arabia on one side and most Arab populations, Hamas, Syria, and Hezbollah (and Iran) on the other. However, the outbreak of antiregime uprisings beginning in the spring of 2011 began to reconfigure these patterns as well. Mubarak's overthrow rendered Egypt a much less reliable member of the US-dominated axis, while increasing sanctions on Iran, combined with Hezbollah's continuing support of Asad's brutal regime and Hamas's abandonment of Damascus, weakened the anti-West axis. Jordan's position as part of the pro-Western group certainly had its domestic opponents, but it was not problematic for the leadership until the violence in Syria between pro- and antiregime forces heated up in late 2011. In this fraught context, Jordan sought a middle ground. It could not afford to alienate the Arab Gulf states and risk the termination of their largess by vocally opposing them, but it also worried about the potential domestic impact, not only politically and economically but also militarily, of Saudi and Qatari support for arming the Syrian opposition.

The increasing militarization of the Syrian uprising had a much greater and more immediate potential to undermine the kingdom's stability than did a purported Iranian threat or any other product of the Arab uprisings. Control of its northern border to limit the flow of Syrian refugees, prevent the smuggling of fighters, and keep the armed conflict at bay was of critical concern as extremist groups took control of large swaths of Syrian territory. Then, the brutal murder of a downed Jordanian pilot captured by ISIS opened the floodgates of Jordanian vengeance against the extremists to the north in early 2015. The government executed several convicted terrorists and unleashed an intensive, if short-lived, air campaign targeting ISIS encampments. In spring 2015, Jordan began to allow the United States to use one of its military bases to train Syrian rebels. But as the security forces occasionally pursued Islamist militants internally (most notably in Irbid in March 2016), the US presence also became the target of limited attacks by Jordanians (in November 2015 and 2016), leaving several soldiers and trainers dead. The northern part of the kingdom also periodically experienced attempts at infiltration, as well as damage from stray mortar shelling or, as in June 2016, the explosion of a car bomb. The kingdom finally closed its borders with both Syria and Iraq in June 2016. The main crossing from Iraq was not reopened until the end of August 2017, following the defeat of ISIS in both its Mosul, Iraq, and Raqqa, Syria, strongholds.

Resetting Jordanian–US Relations: From Trump to Biden

In the meantime, in June 2017, simmering Gulf Arab tensions erupted with the imposition by an emerging Saudi–UAE–Bahraini–Egyptian alliance of a siege on Qatar, which they charged with, among other things, support for terrorism. Concomitantly, Saudi Arabia's young Crown Prince Muhammad bin Salman's (MBS) and UAE Crown Prince Muhammed bin Zayid's (MBZ) open embrace of Israel, driven largely by a shared antipathy toward Iran, was further rescripting traditional regional roles. Under Donald Trump the center of US administration interest in this region shifted heavily in the MBS-MBZ direction, largely excluding Jordan. In this fraught context, Amman rejected and then awaited with trepidation the announcement of Trump advisor Jared Kushner's promised "deal of the century"—a plan that included the unacceptable call for Jordan to cede custodianship of the Muslim holy sites in Jerusalem—just as it had to deal with the theretofore unthinkable US decision to move the American embassy in Tel Aviv to Jerusalem. This break with long-standing US policy based in UN resolutions on the conflict came despite the pleading of the Jordanian leadership with the Trump administration, and it was met with outrage in the kingdom.

Some comfort could be taken from the fact that ISIS had been defeated in Syria and Iraq, that Syrian civil war was waning, even if there was no swift return of Syrian refugees to their homeland on the horizon, and that Kushner's "deal of the century" was dead on arrival at its announcement in June 2019. However, the Trump–Kushner brokering of the so-called Abraham Accords, a set of normalization agreements between Israel, on the one hand, and the UAE, Bahrain, Morocco, and Sudan on the other, just before the US elections was another set of developments that threatened the kind of solution to the Israeli–Palestinian conflict preferred by Abdallah II.

Understandably, then, Jordan welcomed the defeat of Donald Trump and the arrival of Joe Biden to the White House. Abdallah II was the first Arab leader to congratulate Biden on his victory and the first to visit Washington, in July 2021. However, well before he arrived in the US capital, not only was the Saudi–UAE siege on Qatar lifted, thereby opening the way for the king to reinvigorate his inter-Arab ties, but the Biden administration also moved swiftly to underline its commitment to Jordan and its regional role. The new administration wasted no time in reinstating the US aid for the Palestinians that had been cut under Trump, and it was quick to announce its support for the king and his government when a coup plot, involving one of Abdallah's half-brothers, Prince Hamzeh, a former palace advisor who had worked for MBS, Bassem 'Awadallah, and a distant Hashemite relative, was made public and its authors arrested in early April 2021. Yet, perhaps most indicative of the future of US–Jordanian relations was the announcement in early July 2021 that the United States planned to relocate to Jordan military material from three bases it was closing in Qatar, and that discussions of a larger base and US military presence in Jordan were underway. The regional security as well as the significant economic implications of such a development suggested this was more than just a reset of the bilateral relationship.

SUGGESTED READINGS AND WEBSITES

Anderson, Betty S. *Nationalist Voices in Jordan: The Street and the State.* Austin, TX: University of Texas Press, 2005.

Brand, Laurie A. *Citizens Abroad: States and Emigration in the Middle East and North Africa*, New York, NY: Cambridge University Press, 2006.

Brand, Laurie A. *Jordan's Inter-Arab Relations: The Political Economy of Alliance Making.* New York, NY: Columbia University Press, 1994.

Brand, Laurie A. *Palestinians in the Arab World: Institution Building and the Search for State.* New York, NY: Columbia University Press, 1988.

Clark, Janine A. *Local Politics in Jordan and Morocco: Strategies of Centralization and Decentralization.* New York, NY: Columbia University Press, 2018.

Ryan, Curtis. *Jordan and the Arab Uprisings: Regime Survival and Politics Beyond the State.* New York, NY: Columbia University Press, 2018.

Schuetze, Benjamin. *Promoting Democracy, Reinforcing Authoritarianism: US and European Policy in Jordan.* New York, NY: Cambridge University Press, 2019.

Schwedler, Jillian. *Faith in Moderation: Islamist Parties in Jordan and Yemen.* New York, NY: Cambridge University Press, 2007.

Schwedler, Jillian. *Protesting Jordan: Geographies of Power and Dissent.* Stanford, CA: Stanford University Press, 2022.

Tell, Tariq Moraiwed. *The Social and Economic Origins of Monarchy in Jordan.* New York, NY: Palgrave Macmillan, 2013.

Yom, Sean. *From Resilience to Revolution: How Foreign Interventions Destabilize the Middle East.* New York, NY: Columbia University Press, 2015.

www.jordantimes.com

http://en.ammonnews.net/

http://ar.ammannet.net/news/category/english

15 KUWAIT

Hesham Al-Awadi

Kuwait is known today for the prominent place it assumed in global politics during its 1990 and 1991 occupation by Iraq and its tremendous oil wealth. It is a small amirate located strategically on the northern end of the Persian Gulf, wedged between Iraq and Saudi Arabia. With its extensive history of trade and political agreements with foreign powers, Kuwait has long been a nation marked by diverse foreign influences with relative vulnerability to larger neighbors. And although a visitor is much likelier to find modern Kuwaitis poring over investment portfolios than manning the old dhow fishing vessels that characterized Kuwait's pre-oil era, it is a nation that is still largely defined by its ancient tribal and Islamic heritage.

The relatively quick transition from a society of fishermen and nomadic Bedouin to an oil-powered city-state has often been dramatic, and Kuwait is still sorting through massive social and institutional changes. A generous welfare system provides guaranteed schooling, housing, labor, health care, and monthly family allowances to its citizens. Meanwhile, the relative size of Kuwait's citizenry continues to shrink as foreign workers flood in from the Pacific, South Asia, and the West; non-Kuwaitis make up 85 percent of the country's workforce.

Kuwait's emerging democracy has also lately been rocked by change; in 2005, women were given the right to vote and stand for election to political office, and in 2013, two women were elected to serve in the fifty-member National Assembly. This marked a radical shift not only in popular political choices but also in social sensibilities and cultural persuasions. Today, the voice and presence of women in political life is becoming normal and is expected to expand in the coming years, adding to their already visible role in the nation's economic life, where they constitute 30 percent of the workforce.

Kuwait continues to face major challenges, however. Efforts to reduce the country's economic dependence on oil have been largely ineffective, as have attempts to slow the growth of Kuwait's massive bureaucracies and stimulate the private sector. Politically, the continuous tension between the government and parliament, leading to the periodic dissolution of both, has resulted in political paralysis and stalled development projects. Relations between the royal Al Sabah family and the wider opposition also remain tense, and the lack of charismatic young leaders among the Al Sabah, combined with the rising assertiveness of Kuwait's growing youth movements, leave the political future of this semidemocratic amirate very much up in the air.

HISTORY AND STATE-BUILDING

Tribalism, Islam, and foreign influence have largely shaped Kuwait's history and are just as relevant to its contemporary social and political dynamics. Tribalism and tribal politics were particularly evident in the founding of the original town in the seventeenth century and the rise of the Al Sabah to power in the eighteenth century. Islam continues to be the main religious faith of Kuwait's inhabitants and determines not only their daily lives but also their social and political behavior (as discussed in the following sections). Foreign interest and, more recently, external cultural influences have long characterized Kuwait's historical development. Even prior to the discovery of oil, Kuwait was of strategic interest to powers like the Portuguese in the 16th century and, since the 18th century, the Russians, the Germans, and the British. The discovery of oil in the 1930s confirmed Kuwait's global significance and gradually, foreign influence in the country shifted from Europe to the United States.

The Founding of Kuwait

Kuwait was founded in the 17th century by the Banu Khalid, an Arab tribe that emerged from Najd in central Arabia. By the middle of the seventeenth century, the Banu Khalid dominated

KEY FACTS ON KUWAIT

AREA 6,880 square miles (17,818 square kilometers)

CAPITAL Kuwait City

POPULATION 3 million (2021)

PERCENTAGE OF POPULATION UNDER 25 40.53

RELIGIOUS GROUPS (PERCENTAGE) Muslim, 85; Christian, Hindu, Parsi, and other, 15

ETHNIC GROUPS (PERCENTAGE) Kuwaiti, 45; other Arab, 35; South Asian, 9; Iranian, 4; Other, 7

OFFICIAL LANGUAGE Arabic; English widely spoken

TYPE OF GOVERNMENT Constitutional amirate

DATE OF INDEPENDENCE June 19, 1961 (from the United Kingdom)

GDP $126.93 billion; $71,000 per capita (2021)

PERCENTAGE OF GDP BY SECTOR Agriculture, 0.3; industry, 49.4; service, 50.2

TOTAL RENTS (PERCENTAGE OF GDP) FROM NATURAL RESOURCES 59.08

FERTILITY RATE 2.48 children born/woman

Sources: CIA. "The World Factbook." August 4, 2022, https://www.cia.gov/the-world-factbook/. Indexmundi. "Total Natural Resources Rents (% of GDP)." Last updated December 28, 2019. https://www.indexmundi.com/facts/indicators/NY.GDP.TOTL.RT.ZS.

northeastern Arabia, from Basra to Qatar. The Banu Khalid used Kuwait as a summer resort and storage place for their weapons and hunting tools. The original name of Kuwait was al-Qurain (Arabic for "high hill"), and the future country was no more than a small coastal fishing village. But around the 1670s, the Banu Khalid built a small fort, or *kut*, to protect their possessions from tribal raiding. Not only did the fort protect the flourishing village, but it also gave it a more defined existence. Kuwait, the current name of the country, is simply the diminutive of *kut*.

In addition to building the fort, the Banu Khalid were eager to maintain a degree of security in the territories under their control. Security from raids in the desert and piracy in the seaways was a crucial precondition for regular flow of revenue and the supremacy of the tribe. Their success in maintaining overall security eventually attracted more tribes to settle in the region; the Anaiza, from which the Al Sabah comes, was one of the settled tribes.

The Banu Khalid's supremacy over northeastern Arabia did not last long. It was challenged by internal strife and the emergence of regional contenders for power. In 1745, Najd saw the rise of Wahhabism, a religious movement named after its founder, Shaykh Muhammad ibn Abdul Wahhab. The Wahhabis aimed to spread their notion of Islam through territorial expansion and in the process became the bitter enemies of the Banu Khalid. But prior to the rise of the Wahhabis, the tribe was already going through an internal struggle for power. Both of the aforementioned factors caused the central authority of the tribe to weaken, thus paving the way for the rise of localized powers in the towns the Banu Khalid had once dominated. In Kuwait, power was subsequently shared locally by the leading subdivisions of the Anaiza tribe until the Al Sabah family finally dominated it.[1]

The Rise of the Ruling Family

The Anaiza tribe migrated from Najd in the second half of the 17th century in search of better living conditions. Because they were on good terms with the Banu Khalid, the Anaiza were permitted to travel eastward. They first reached Qatar, and by the early 18th century, they decided to settle in Kuwait.

The Anaiza's leading families in Kuwait soon filled the power vacuum created by the demise of the Banu Khalid. In addition to the Al Sabah, the Anaiza also included the Al Khalifa and the Al Jalahima, all of which had their share in managing the town's affairs. The Al Sabah became responsible for political and military affairs, while the Al Khalifa and Al Jalahima administered the town's land and sea trade. Sabah bin Jaber, or Sabah I, as he is commonly known, became the first local ruler of Kuwait.

Sabah I (1752–1762) was succeeded by his son, Abdallah I (1762–1814). During Abdallah's reign, a dispute erupted between the Al Khalifa and the Al Sabah, possibly over politics because the Al Khalifa had equal ambitions to rule, or over money because they also wished to become wealthier from pearling and trade. In any case, the disagreement was never resolved, and in 1766, the Al Khalifa, and later some of the Al Jalahima, decided to leave Kuwait for Qatar and then Bahrain. Despite the disruption this may have initially caused in the town's economy, it certainly consolidated the political power of the Al Sabah. Since that time, the Al Sabah has been the uncontested political family.

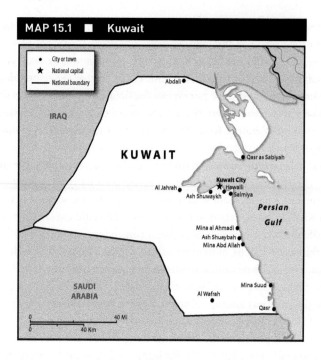

MAP 15.1 ■ Kuwait

Much of Kuwait's history and politics continue to be shaped by tribal identities and politics, but tribalism is not an exclusive factor in the politics of the Arabian Peninsula. Rather, it is also expressed occasionally in combination with other elements, most fundamentally religion. In the history of Kuwait, religion often constituted a force behind its relations with the Ottoman Empire.

Relations With the Ottomans

The Ottomans claimed Arabia in the mid-16th century, when Istanbul conquered Baghdad in 1534 and expanded southward to eastern Arabia in 1550. The Ottoman expansion was driven by a desire to resist the Portuguese incursion in the Gulf, and once the Ottomans achieved supremacy, their control waned. The empire's hegemony in the region ended in 1670 and was replaced in practical terms by that of the Banu Khalid.[2] But with the demise of the Banu Khalid, and given the Ottoman desire to centralize administration and maximize state revenues, the Turkish Empire's interest in the peninsula was resurrected. In the late 19th century, this interest marked a new phase of closer Ottoman–Kuwaiti relations.

During that period, the Al Sabah was eager to maintain Kuwait's autonomy from its powerful neighbors, especially the Wahhabis. Shaykh Abdallah II (1866–1892) was also prepared to recognize the Ottomans' moral leadership of the Sunni Muslim world. In 1871, Abdallah accepted the Ottoman title *qaimmaqam* (provincial governor), which meant, technically speaking, that he was responsible to the Ottoman governor of Basra for the administration of Kuwait. The title was no more than a formality, and Kuwaitis continued in practice to retain their autonomy over their daily affairs. However, Abdallah could not have imagined that his decision to accept the Ottoman title would later be manipulated by modern-day Iraqi leaders to justify the annexation of the tiny country of Kuwait.

The religious factors binding Kuwait to the Ottoman Empire should not be overstated. Kuwait had pragmatic reasons to forge closer relations with Istanbul. First, Kuwait, in addition to its own local wells, depended heavily on drinking water transported by boat from the Shatt al-Arab River in Ottoman-controlled Iraq. Second, the Al Sabah held large estates in Faw, which also fell under Ottoman control. Third, the Al Sabah and the Ottomans regarded the Wahhabis as their enemy.

Kuwait shed itself of Ottoman dominance only after the rise of Mubarak the Great, who is considered the founder of modern Kuwait. Mubarak, who ruled from 1896 to 1915, came to power after he murdered his brothers Muhammad and Jarrah, who ruled Kuwait in partnership from 1892 to 1896. The unprecedented murder paved the way for Mubarak to remove Kuwait from Ottoman dominance and placed it under British control, which lasted until the country became independent in 1961. Thus, foreign influence became a fundamental factor in shaping the country's modern history in addition to tribalism and religion.

Relations With the British

Kuwait's first recorded contact with the British dates to 1775, when the Persians occupied Basra and the British needed an alternative route for their mail and trade caravans from the Gulf to Aleppo, Syria. Kuwait, with its excellent harbor, seemed to offer a great advantage to the British sending goods from Bombay to the eastern Mediterranean and, eventually, to Western European markets. British caravans brought lucrative benefits to the elite of Kuwait and local commercial interests, but neither the British nor the Kuwaitis desired to take their friendly relations to a more formal level, primarily in order not to provoke the Ottomans. This situation changed when Mubarak came to power.

Mubarak's alliance with the British promised protection from the increasing Ottoman intervention in Kuwait's affairs. Turning to Britain guaranteed Mubarak greater freedom in how the town was managed under his authority. Initially, Britain refused Mubarak's overtures but later responded favorably as a reaction to the growing German and Russian interest in the region. In 1899, Britain signed with Mubarak a secret agreement that placed Kuwait under its protection. The agreement, which lasted until 1961, assured Mubarak the "good offices of the British Government" toward him, his heirs, and successors. It stipulated that Mubarak would not receive the representative of a foreign state or alienate any of his territory without the consent of Her Majesty's Government.[3]

British interest in Kuwait was part of Britain's broader interests in the Gulf. Before the invention of the telegraph and the opening of the Suez Canal, the Gulf provided Britain with the shortest and fastest route for trade and communications from Bombay to London. It also provided British manufacturers in India with access to lucrative markets in Persia and the Ottoman Empire. Such interests, however, changed with the discovery of oil during the first decades of the twentieth century. Since then, foreign intervention, oil, and local politics have become more than just intertwined.

Independence

After independence, Kuwait faced not only the task of nation-building (as did most Arab states when they obtained independence) but also the challenge of maintaining the integrity of the state in the face of Iraqi claims to the territory. Less than a week after British withdrawal on June 19, 1961, Iraq's prime minister, Abdul Karim Qasim, declared Kuwait part of Iraq and moved his troops to the border, threatening to annex the country. Kuwait's ruler, Shaykh Abdallah al-Salim (1950–1965), immediately called for British support. On July 1, British troops were deployed on the border until they were replaced by Arab forces from Egypt, Saudi Arabia, and Syria. The Iraqi threat ended with Qasim's execution in 1963 but resumed in 1973 when the new Ba'th regime in Iraq penetrated three kilometers into Kuwait's territory. Iraqi forces eventually withdrew under pressure from the Soviet Union, Iran, and Saudi Arabia. By that time, it became obvious to the Kuwaitis that while in the past the threat came from the Wahhabis, it now emerged from the radical secular regimes in Iraq.

External threats notwithstanding, the 1960s and 1970s saw the expansion of Kuwait's bureaucracy and welfare state. The 1962 constitution guaranteed Kuwaitis free education from primary school through university, and after graduation, a job in the public or private sector. It also guaranteed public housing, rent subsidies, subsidies for water and electricity, and a monthly family allowance. The generous allocation of social services was crucial in strengthening loyalty to the ruling elite and reinforcing patriotism in the recently independent country.

Kuwait's oil production peaked in the early 1970s, and that enabled the small state to play a role in regional and international politics. It supported the Palestinian cause by supplying money to Palestinian fighters, especially to the Palestinian Liberation Organization (PLO). The PLO chairman, Yasir Arafat, lived in Kuwait from 1958 to 1964, when he founded the Fatah movement. Kuwait was home to more than three hundred thousand Palestinians by the 1980s, and it increased oil prices to pressure the United States and other countries that provided military assistance to Israel during the 1973 war.

Iran–Iraq War and Domestic Tensions

The 1970s ended with the Iranian Revolution in 1979. The Revolution and the Iran–Iraq War, commencing in 1980, made the 1980s the most turbulent decade in Kuwaiti history. Ayatollah Khomeini was critical of the monarchical Gulf regimes and spoke about exporting the ideals of the Iranian Revolution to the region. He also disapproved of Kuwait's support of Saddam Hussein in his war against the Islamic Republic of Iran.

The Iranians began to target Kuwaiti oil tankers, which Iran argued was in retaliation against unfriendly regimes. In response, Kuwait requested help from the United States, Britain, and the Soviet Union. The United States and the Soviet Union began to reflag the Kuwaiti fleets with their respective flags as a form of protection. In 1987, the US Navy also began to provide military escorts for Kuwaiti and Saudi tankers sailing in and out of the Persian Gulf.

Khomeini's discourse and policies against the Gulf monarchies radicalized some Kuwaiti Shi'a. From 1983 to 1988, groups of Shi'i Muslims carried out a series of terrorist operations, which included bombing US and European interests in the country, sabotaging oil installations, hijacking Kuwaiti aircraft, and, most seriously, attempting to assassinate the ruler of Kuwait in 1985. Although the majority of the Shi'a condemned the terrorist acts, an air of distrust and suspicion dominated the state's view toward all Shi'a. Security became a serious concern and massive deportations of expatriates ensued, many of whom were Iranians.

The Iraqi Occupation and Liberation

Kuwait survived the Iran–Iraq War only to encounter the Iraqi threat once again in the 1990s. On August 2, 1990, approximately 120,000 Iraqi troops, supported by two thousand tanks and armored vehicles, invaded Kuwait. But unlike 1973, when the Iraqi forces occupied only three kilometers of Kuwait, in 1990 the Iraqis annexed the entire country, reaching the capital in less than three hours. The occupation lasted for seven months but had a dramatic, lasting impact on the Kuwaiti psyche.

Saddam Hussein proclaimed several reasons for his decision to occupy Kuwait: (1) Kuwait was historically part of Iraq; (2) Kuwait was stealing $2.4 billion worth of oil from Iraq by "slant drilling"—that is, by deliberately building oil wells that angled down across the Iraqi–Kuwaiti border in order to pump oil from Iraqi territory; (3) Kuwait was overproducing oil in violation of OPEC's mandate to lower oil prices and was, therefore, hurting the Iraqi economy; and (4) Kuwait refused to waive the repayment of funds given to Iraq to pay for its war with Iran (about $13 billion), which Iraq argued was fought to protect Kuwait from Iran. Saddam Hussein accused Kuwait of refusing repayment as part of a wide international conspiracy against Baghdad.

The occupation and atrocities that ensued signaled the failure of Kuwait's domestic as well as foreign policies. The government failed to take the Iraqi threat seriously, despite local and foreign intelligence sources confirming its imminence. The regime avoided arming and deploying its forces, speculating that doing so would only aggravate the situation. The result was that at least three-fourths of the armed forces were on leave or away from their posts, and those who remained lacked training, plans for defense, and ammunition.

On the other hand, Kuwait's diplomatic efforts since independence did yield some advantages. A military coalition of thirty countries, led by the United States, eventually came to liberate Kuwait in 1991. On January 17, a total of six hundred thousand multinational troops, including the United States, Britain, France, Kuwait, and Saudi Arabia, launched a massive air strike on Iraqi targets in what became known as Operation Desert Storm. The ground offensive to recapture Kuwait was launched on February 24, and two days later, it ended the Iraqi occupation. February 27, when Kuwait was fully liberated, marks a national holiday for Kuwaitis. The ruler, who resided in Saudi Arabia during the occupation, returned on March 14, 1991, to resume his power.

DEMOGRAPHIC AND SOCIAL TRANSFORMATION

Oil, tribalism, Islam, and foreign influence have also shaped Kuwait's social sphere. Kuwaiti nationals comprise one-third of the population of the small state (at roughly 6,800 square miles, it is smaller in size than New Jersey or Wales). Most Kuwaitis are descendants of tribes that migrated from the Arabian Peninsula in the early 18th century. Those who settled within the city constitute the urban sector of society, or the *hadar*, while those whose ancestors wandered the desert constitute the nomadic Bedouin, or the *bedu*. Although almost all Bedouin are now urbanized, the *hadar–bedu* division remains one of the important cultural distinctions in Kuwaiti society. Given Kuwait's small size and shortage of inhabitable land, most of the population is concentrated in and around the capital city.

Prior to oil, Kuwaiti society was simply divided into a ruling family, merchants, and pearl divers. After oil, and following the state's distributive policies, Kuwaiti society expanded and became divided along new lines of class, sect, and culture. Today, the royal family plays an important, distinct role, while expatriate–national, citizen–bidoon, and Shi'i–Sunni divisions are fundamental dividing lines in society.

The Ruling Family

Prior to oil, the ruling family did not exist as an institution. Instead, the ruler from the Al Sabah relied more on the merchants and intermarriage with leading Sunni families to augment his personal authority. But the discovery of oil liberated the ruler from his past allies and pushed him to rely more on his own relatives. This crystallized the ruling family as a socioeconomic and political institution, even more so after Kuwait's independence in 1961. Since then, members of the ruling family have been publicly recognized by the title *Shaykh* (*Shaykha* for a woman). All receive monthly stipends, and many are given prestigious posts in the expanding state bureaucracy.

Public discussions of the family's internal affairs were socially and politically taboo until the succession crisis in 2006. Internal rivalries broke boundaries and encouraged society to speak about competing wings within the family. Deputies and the press began to publicly criticize family members by name. One reason for this new trend was related to a generational change within the ruling family. A number of experienced and charismatic figures of the Al Sabah have passed away in recent years, leaving the scene to younger leaders who are ambitious yet impatient and lack their predecessors' personal appeal. Some of them are openly maneuvering against one another and are forming alliances with journalists and the opposition. In 2013, Shaykh Ahmad Al-Fahad, nephew of the amir, accused Shaykh Nasser al-Mohammad, another prominent member of the ruling family, of plotting a coup against the regime. Although Al-Fahad later apologized, admitting his false accusations, the scandal showed the degree of internal rivalries within the ruling family.

Expatriates

Since 1965, Kuwaitis have become a minority in their own country, outnumbered by the expatriates, who constitute the majority. The percentage of foreigners grew from 53 percent in 1965 to 60 percent in 1985 and 70 percent in 2018. Oil spurred job growth and demand for manual and skilled labor that could not be filled locally. Also, Kuwait's political neutrality during the Cold War made it a favored destination for Palestinians, Iraqis, Syrians, and other Arabs, as well as Indians who had been left behind when British protection ceased.

The government's immigration policy, although inconsistent, tended to restrict immigration and promote "Kuwaitization" in the public and private sectors to balance nationals with foreigners. During the occupation, an estimated 1.3 million, almost 60 percent of the total population, left the country, including some 250,000 Palestinians and Jordanians. Thousands of Palestinians were also expelled soon after the liberation in response to perceived collaboration with the Iraqis. Their departure radically reduced the size of the immigrant population. But in response to a growing demand for labor to assist in the postwar reconstruction and economic expansion, there was an influx of new labor, particularly from Asia, from 1992 onward.[4] Thus, between 2015 and 2021, Kuwait's population increased from 3.8 million to 4.3 million; of the 0.5 million increase, 68 percent were non-Kuwaitis. The COVID-19 pandemic, again, brought the debate on the need to reduce the number of expatriates, but no serious measures were taken.

Bedouin

Historically, Bedouin were desert nomads found outside the walled city. They began to migrate to and settle in Kuwait City in the 1950s as a result of oil discovery and in search of employment. The city expanded, and the wall was finally destroyed in 1957. The majority of Bedouin who settled in Kuwait came from the deserts of Saudi Arabia; the remainder came from Iraq and Syria. Important Bedouin tribes in Kuwait include the Ajman, the Awazim, and the Mutair, most of whom are represented in the cabinet and the assembly.

Most Bedouin were at first recruited into the military and oil fields as unskilled laborers, but with the spread of education, they were absorbed in other parts of the public sector. Despite urbanization, Bedouin continue to retain many of their tribal values and customs, particularly strong tribal loyalty, which is manifest during assembly elections when tribal members hold primaries prior to election day to elect the candidate who will represent them in parliament. Primaries, or tribal elections, are outlawed in Kuwait yet are regularly organized.[5]

Bedouin have been traditionally perceived as allies of the government. From 1960 through the 1980s, the state encouraged large numbers of tribal families to settle by granting them citizenship and welfare benefits (e.g. housing, schooling, and social services) in return for their support against the opposition in the assembly. Since their parents settled in the 1950s, however, Kuwaiti Bedouin have become increasingly politicized, and a number of outspoken critics of government policies come from tribal backgrounds. Reasons for the increased politicization include the rise of a politically ambitious young and educated generation that opposes a divided ruling elite and eroding state services.

Shi'a

Shi'a are a Muslim sect and a significant minority in Kuwait; they constitute about 25 percent to 30 percent of the population. Despite their collective name, the Shi'a in Kuwait are a heterogeneous community. Demographically, they are divided into Arabs with roots in Saudi Arabia and Bahrain and non-Arabs who originally migrated from Iran. Economically, they are subtly divided into the affluent old settlers who lived within the walled city and the less affluent latecomers, who were attracted by job opportunities in the oil sector. Politically, Shi'a, like any other community, are divided into secularists with either leftist or liberal leanings and Islamists. But adherence to Islam does not necessarily translate into political activism and may just be a matter of personal piety.

Like the Bedouin, Shi'a were historically viewed as allies of the ruling elite. They were never part of the early movement for political reform in the 1930s, and in the 1960s, they stood by the government against the threat of Arab nationalism. But relations between the Shi'a and the government deteriorated in the 1980s with the outbreak of the Iranian Revolution and the Iran–Iraq War. These events mobilized the Shi'a in Kuwait, particularly those who strongly opposed government support for Saddam Hussein, against Iran. Some even resorted to violence to express their rejection.

The turbulent period ended in the 1990s with Iraq's invasion of Kuwait and the Shi'a's impressive resistance against the occupation. The shared ordeal of Kuwaitis, irrespective of sectarian divisions, created a feeling of national solidarity. The restoration of the constitution returned three Shi'i deputies to the assembly in 1992, five in 1996, six in 2016, including one woman (Shi'a comprise around 17 percent of the electorate), and none in 2020. Despite the large measure of rights and recognition, Shi'a continue to have reservations about their minority status.[6]

Bidoon

Kuwait also has between 88,000 and 106,000 *bidoon* (without nationality), or residents who are stateless or without citizenship. Many are descendants of Bedouin tribes that moved across the deserts of Kuwait, Saudi Arabia, Syria, and Iraq before modern borders were drawn. Due to their transitory nature, many never retained formal documents to prove their belonging in the country and, hence, were classified as stateless. Until the 1980s, they were recruited into the army and police, but after the occupation were perceived as a security threat. The government argued that some *bidoon* collaborated with the Iraqis, while others were not genuinely *bidoon* and held other nationalities. Despite their increase in number and the government's granting of citizenship to four thousand since 2000, the ultimate fate of the *bidoon* in Kuwait has not yet been determined and continues to be a matter of public debate. In 2012 and 2014, inspired by the Tunisians and Egyptians, a few hundred *bidoon* took to the streets demanding citizenship, but they were harshly dispersed by the police using tear gas and rubber bullets.[7]

Other Social Sectors

The ruling elite, foreigners, Bedouin, and Shi'a are not exclusively separate social strata but, rather, interact and, on occasion, overlap. For example, many prominent Bedouin or tribal families are related to the Al Sabah through marriage. Moreover, other important sectors play an important role in Kuwaiti society, including merchants and women.

The merchants formed the backbone of pre-oil Kuwaiti society because trade revenue formed the basis of the city's income. They made up the core of the opposition to the ruling family. Oil undermined the merchants' political role but certainly not their economic status. During the 1960s and 1970s, a new group of small-business entrepreneurs began to emerge in the economic sector and have since competed with the traditional merchant families. But old merchant families continue to dominate major financial firms, including banks, investment houses, and the powerful Kuwaiti Chamber of Commerce, which was established in 1958. In addition, old merchants are gradually resuming their political influence, albeit in new ways, as the country privatizes.

Women also play an important part in Kuwaiti society and politics. Kuwait made political history when four women won seats in the May 2009 elections. Their suffrage came after a long campaign fought since the 1970s. The first proposal went to the assembly in 1971 but subsequently failed for religious and social reasons. It was not until the end of the 1990s that the ruler issued a decree conferring full political rights on women "in recognition of their vital roles in building Kuwaiti society and in return for the sacrifices they made during the various challenges the country faced."[8] The decree was issued in 1999 but required the assembly's approval. After heated debates and amendments to the decree—namely, that women should adhere to the dictates of Islamic law—the bill was finally passed on May 16, 2005. In the same year, the government appointed its first woman minister, but society had to wait until 2009 to elect four women representatives to the legislature.

It is important to note that not all Kuwaiti women are eligible to vote. Voting rights are only conferred on women whose ancestors resided in Kuwait prior to 1920 and maintained residence until 1959. Women whose ancestors settled after 1920 are naturalized Kuwaitis and are not eligible to vote until they have been citizens for ten years.

Naturalized or not, women continue to be discriminated against in law and in society. For example, women are not entitled to some of the welfare benefits that go to men (e.g., housing and child benefits). Unlike Kuwaiti men who marry non-Kuwaitis, Kuwaiti women who marry foreigners are legally and socially ostracized. Not only are their children non-Kuwaitis, but like their fathers, they are denied the political, economic, and social privileges to which Kuwaitis are entitled.[9]

RELIGION AND POLITICS

Religion is an important element in Kuwait's society and influences much of its everyday politics. The vast majority of Kuwaitis are Muslims, although there are about 400 Christian Kuwaitis who came from Lebanon, Palestine, and Iraq. Sunnis constitute the majority of Muslims in Kuwait; Shi'a are about 25 percent of the population. The Sunni–Shi'i divide is subtly manifested in residential areas and is more pronounced during election campaigns.

Shari'a is a key source of legislation, but not the only one. Unlike in the United Arab Emirates and Bahrain, alcohol is illegal in Kuwait (banned since 1965); yet unlike in Saudi Arabia, there are no religious police in the streets. Moreover, since 1980, Kuwait law has prohibited the naturalization of non-Muslims, but there are sizable Hindu and Buddhist and

Christian communities that enjoy freedom of worship under the constitution. (There are seven officially recognized Christian churches serving about 450,000 Christians, mostly expatriates.)

During the seven months of Iraq's occupation of Kuwait in 1990, hundreds of Kuwaitis fled to Saudi Arabia, the heart of Wahhabism, and some were subsequently influenced by it and other conservative interpretations of Islam. The result was clearly manifested in the first National Assembly after the liberation in 1992, which had a significant number of Islamist members. The rise of Islamism in Kuwait was also a response to increased waves of Westernization, if not Americanization, since the liberation of the country. There have been several attempts by Islamist deputies to make the shari'a public law, but many Kuwaitis, including successive ruling amirs, rejected any moves in this direction.

Islamists gained wide-scale popularity in the 1990s for their impressive role during the occupation, but their real rise to prominence began in the 1980s when the government turned to them as political allies instead of the Bedouin.[10] In the elections of 1999, Islamists became the biggest forces in parliament, controlling 36 percent of the seats. Islamists might be united on certain issues but are practically divided on priorities and tactics. Shi'i Islamists seek to end legal and social discrimination based on sectarian divisions, while the more conservative Sunnis (Salafis) tend to focus on ethical issues and matters of belief. The Muslim Brotherhood focuses more on wider issues of social and political reform.[11]

The real threat to Kuwait's society and regime has come from the so-called Islamic State (ISIS). In June 2015, the terrorist group claimed the attack on a Shi'i mosque that killed twenty-six and wounded hundreds. The government soon uncovered a local ISIS terror cell with at least five Kuwaitis, some of whom fought with the terrorist organization in Syria and Iraq.

INSTITUTIONS AND GOVERNANCE

Westerners generally tend to identify Kuwait more with oil and money, but events, such as the succession crisis in 2006 and first-time victory of women in parliamentary elections in 2009, reflect the great complexity of Kuwaiti politics. The ruler's succession and women's ascension to parliament are essentially manifestations of Kuwait's dominant political institutions—namely, the ruling family and the National Assembly, which do not operate alone but are governed by a constitution and a cabinet.

The Ruling Family

Prior to oil, the ruling Al Sabah governed in consultation with the merchants, the most powerful and dominant social force at that time. Merchants provided the Al Sabah with income in the form of customs duties (estimated at about $40,000 in 1938) and voluntary contributions in return for administration and security. Political power rested more on the ruler than on his family, and he was selected for his personal qualities.[12] Furthermore, religion and tribal customs were the basis of much of the Al Sabah's enforcement of law and order.

The discovery of oil in the 1930s consolidated the power of the ruling family over the merchant class, whose financial contributions were no longer needed. Much of the customs tariffs were eventually abolished, but that did not entirely dismantle the power of the merchants, who continued to dominate much of Kuwait's business. Nor did the ruling family enjoy absolute political power thereafter. The mobilization of a rising middle class since the 1950s and a liberal constitution enacted in 1962 have limited the power of the Al Sabah. Kuwait, a hereditary amirate, therefore, lies between a constitutional monarchy and an absolute monarchy.

In reality the ruler, or *amir*, is the most dominant force in Kuwaiti politics. According to the constitution, his person is "immune and inviolable." He shares control of legislative power with the National Assembly, control of judicial power with the courts, and control of executive power with the cabinet. In addition, he is the supreme commander of the armed forces, with the authority to declare a defensive war without the prior approval of the assembly. He can also independently conclude treaties that do not affect Kuwait's security or economy and can declare martial law in a state of emergency.

Since the early 20th century, the ruling family has developed an informal yet disciplined succession pattern by which leadership alternates between the descendants of Jabir and Salim, the sons of Mubarak the Great (see Figure 15.1). This alternation was violated once in 1965, when Abdallah al-Salim (1950–1965) was succeeded by his brother Sabah al-Salim (1965–1977), but resumed when Jabir al-Ahmad succeeded Sabah al-Salim in 1977 and named a member of the Salim line, Saad al-Abdallah al-Salim Al Sabah, as his crown prince. The crown prince also has traditionally served as the prime minister—again, an informal pattern since the 1960s.

With the ailing health of Shaykh Jabir and Crown Prince Shaykh Saad, both patterns were seriously disturbed. In 2003, the post of prime minister was separated from that of the crown prince and given to the long-time foreign minister, Shaykh Sabah al-Ahmad. Shaykh Saad continued to retain the title of crown prince. With the death of Shaykh Jabir in 2006 and the inability of Shaykh Saad to assume the expected duties of amir, the ruling family encountered its first serious succession crisis.

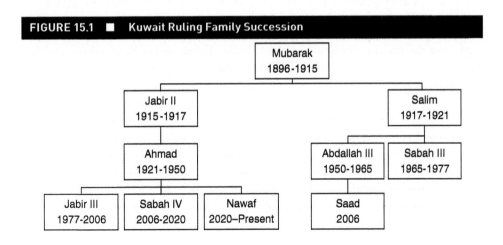

FIGURE 15.1 ■ Kuwait Ruling Family Succession

Shaykh Saad, who ruled for a mere nine days, abdicated and was replaced by Shaykh Sabah al-Ahmad, the current ruler of Kuwait. Shaykh Sabah immediately named his brother, Nawaf al-Ahmad, as crown prince and his nephew, Nasir al-Muhammad, as prime minister. Shaykh Sabah had consolidated the separation of the crown prince and the premiership and, in the process, denied the Salim clan both jobs. The crown prince and prime minister are members of the Jabir clan of the Al Sabah dynasty. Shaykh Nawaf, the current amir, since the death of Shaykh Sabah in 2020, named his brother Shaykh Mishal Al-Ahmad, as crown prince; thus consolidating the rule in the Ahmad clan.

The National Assembly

Kuwait's political system enjoys a degree of popular participation. The idea of a national assembly that shares legislative power with the ruler is stipulated in the constitution of 1962, yet it has actually existed in practice since the 1930s. Fearing a loss of status in the post-oil era, a group of merchants organized into a political movement and demanded a legislative council. Although the council was dissolved only months after it was founded in 1938, its fourteen elected members managed to significantly reform the economy, administration, and education. Henceforth, Kuwait survived without a national assembly until independence in 1961.

In 1962, Shaykh Abdallah al-Salim called for a general election to elect a constituent assembly to draft a constitution. At that time, Kuwait was confronting several crises, mainly Iraq's threat to annex the country. Shaykh Abdallah was under growing pressure to shift from a traditional to a modern system of governance, without totally dismantling the power of the monarch. The constitution has not been amended since its ratification in 1962 and continues to underpin Kuwaiti politics.

It was written during the peak of Arab nationalism and, thus, contained the obligatory mention that Kuwait is "part of the Arab nation" and a sovereign country in its own right. It also defined Kuwait as a hereditary amirate and confined succession to the throne to the descendants of Mubarak the Great. While the constitution recognized the civil rights of individuals and groups, it discouraged the formation of political parties. Political parties are technically banned in Kuwait, but political groupings do exist in the form of newspapers, clubs, and organizations.

The elections for the first National Assembly were held in 1963, and subsequent elections were held at the end of an assembly's four-year term in 1967, 1971, and 1975. Initially, the rulers envisioned that the assembly would be used to build alliances against the merchants and Arab nationalists. Allies were usually drawn from the politically quiescent Shi'a, conservative Sunnis, and Bedouin, all of whom soon became politicized and critical of their patrons' policies.

While the merchants were very influential in the early assemblies in 1963 and 1967, their power began to recede in 1971. In 1981 and 1985, the assembly was dominated by the rising middle class, which included Islamists, nationalists, and tribalists. The assembly increasingly became a political nuisance and, since the 1970s, has been at odds with the government regarding its oil and foreign policies. Amid mounting tension between the assembly and the government, the ruler dissolved the assembly and relegated its powers to the ruler and the cabinet.

The assembly remained illegally suspended from 1976 to 1981 and then from 1985 to 1992. According to the constitution, the ruler may dissolve the National Assembly for a period not to exceed two months from the date of dissolution. Beyond this period, any suspension is regarded as unconstitutional. The suspension in 1985 triggered a political coalition comprised of liberals, merchants, Islamists, and former assembly members who demanded restoration of the parliament. The coalition continued to be politically active in *diwaniyah*s (informal social gatherings of men) until the Iraqi occupation in 1990.

A year after the country was liberated from occupation, the ruling family decided to restore the constitution and called for parliamentary elections in 1992. Government failure to deal with the crisis, the proactive role of Kuwaitis inside and outside Kuwait during the period of the occupation, and Western pressure to expand democratic rights have contributed to the Kuwaiti push toward further democratization. One telling outcome of this trend was granting women full political rights in 2005, as discussed earlier. In that same year, the government appointed its first female minister.

The Government

The government is positioned between the ruler and the National Assembly. The ruler appoints the prime minister and other ministers; until 2006, he also named the crown prince. Once the cabinet has been formed, normally at the commencement of the legislative term, ministers are expected to submit their program to the assembly. According to the constitution, the members of the cabinet should not exceed one-third of the assembly's fifty members. Although cabinet ministers are not allowed to sit on assembly committees, they are allowed to participate in the assembly's general debates and are entitled to vote on bills.

The first cabinet was formed in 1962, and eleven out of its fifteen ministers were from the ruling family. They headed the key ministries of foreign affairs, interior, defense, information, finance, and oil. Over time, the Al Sabah's dominance waned as more cabinet ministers were drawn from the National Assembly, business sector, and professions. Recruitment to the cabinet has long been based on patrimony, family background, origins, and sectarian affiliations, among other factors, more than on merit. The regime has maintained the practice of appointing Shi'i and women ministers since 1975 and 2005, respectively. In the 2021 government, there are two—one woman and one Shi'i—but cabinet ministers have continued to be exclusively Muslim and predominantly middle-age, urban Sunni males.[13]

Much of Kuwaiti politics had been a struggle for control between the government and the assembly. Prior to the elections of 1981, the government pushed for an amendment to the electoral law in the hope that it would generate a more docile parliament. Since 1962, the law had divided Kuwait into ten constituencies, with five deputies representing each. The new amendment divided Kuwait into twenty-five constituencies, with two deputies representing each. Although redistricting was supposed to please government loyalists (usually tribal factions living on the outskirts of the city), the 1985 assembly proved to be one of the most vocal and critical of government policies. The assembly accused the justice minister, a member of the ruling family, of improper use of government funds during Kuwait's controversial stock market crash in 1982.

The parliament has limited power. During the illegal suspension of the assembly from 1976 to 1981, the government was free to issue a series of decrees that restricted political activities, curtailed freedom of expression, and, in general, empowered bureaucratic institutions to control opposing political ideas and practices. The justifications for the cabinet's repressive measures had much to do with Arab politics of the 1970s. The Lebanese Civil War (1975–1990) and the subsequent Syrian military intervention in Lebanon was blamed on press freedom. Many Kuwaitis feared that a misguided freedom of expression would lead to a repeat of the Lebanese experience, causing societal fragmentation and political anarchy. Arab tensions were coupled with outside pressures on Kuwait from conservative neighbors—namely, Saudi Arabia—to adopt a more authoritarian style of governing.[14]

The 1980s were troubling for Kuwait's security and politics. The Iranian Revolution in 1979 and the Iran–Iraq War from 1980 to 1988 added to the tension between the government and the assembly. History repeated itself when the ruler announced the assembly's second dissolution in 1986 and implied that some deputies had conspired to destabilize the country. Strict press censorship was introduced at that time. In 1989, deputies of the dissolved assembly began to press for its reinstitution. The government announced that it would not restore the assembly but would establish a national advisory council. The opposition boycotted the elections, and the council was interrupted by the Iraqi invasion.

The Iraqi occupation lasted for seven months and marked a turning point in Kuwaiti politics. Despite Saddam Hussein's unjustified aggression, there was equally a sense among Kuwaitis that government policies were responsible for the invasion. Critics argued that Kuwait's overproduction of oil since 1989 was a deliberate attempt to damage Iraq's economy. The government was also accused of censoring information about the seriousness of the Iraqi threat against which it had failed to prepare. Had the government taken Iraq's threat seriously or even negotiated with its representatives in good faith, perhaps the invasion could have been avoided.

Regime failure and the impressive role of Kuwaitis within the country and in exile during the occupation bolstered the push for democracy. The George H. W. Bush administration also pressed the amir to reestablish the parliament as soon as the country was liberated.[15] In 1992, seventeen junior members of the ruling family sent a petition to the amir in which they demanded democratization. In October of the same year, the amir called for parliamentary elections, free of irregularities or interventions. The National Assembly has never been illegally suspended since.

Yet the steps toward democracy did not end the tensions between the assembly and the cabinet; instead, it deepened them. The separation of the posts of crown prince and prime minister has added to the opposition's confidence in criticizing the government. In 2006, two deputies put forth a motion to prosecute Shaykh Nasser al-Mohammad, the prime minister and a prominent member of the ruling family, over the government's handling of electoral reform. It is a deputy's constitutional right to indict government officials, and they have done so in the past, but never had they tried a prime minister, who traditionally was also crown prince and therefore immune from parliamentary questioning. Such motions to impeach the prime minister have been systematically obstructed through either the resignation of the cabinet or the dissolution of the assembly. In 2011, hundreds of protestors stormed the parliament, chanting, "The people want to bring down the head [of government]!" recalling the cries of thousands of Egyptian demonstrators demanding Hosni Mubarak's ouster in 2011. In an unprecedented move, the prime minister indeed resigned in 2011, following serious corruption allegations—related to government bribes to parliamentarians—and the amir appointed a new member from the Al-Sabah (Shaykh Jabir al-Mubarak) in the same year. This, however, did not end public grievances; rather, it escalated the demands for further political reforms. In 2012, the amir dissolved a popular parliament with a majority of opposition and unilaterally changed the electoral law to give one vote, instead of four votes, to each eligible voter. Although the constitutional court later ruled the amir's action as being constitutionally sound, the leading opposition faction boycotted the 2013 elections, which resulted in a progovernment assembly.

DOMESTIC CONFLICT

Although Kuwaitis' demands for reform predated the Arab Spring, the revolutions in Tunisia and Egypt added a fresh impetus to a popular movement. The amir's dissolution of parliament in 2012 and change of electoral law to constrain the power opposition only added to the domestic tensions. The infuriated opposition took to the streets to voice their strong demands for radical reforms, including demands for an elected popular government. The opposition—comprised of Islamists, liberals, the youth, and major civil society organizations—failed to mobilize the masses, as did their counterparts in Egypt.

The government was successfully able to clamp down on members of the opposition, some of whom were stripped of their Kuwaiti citizenship. This, however, didn't end the political stalemate in the country. The parliamentary elections in 2020 yielded a stronger opposition, some of which wanted to start the session with a motion to grill the prime minister. The amir suspended the parliament for a month, a step aimed to defuse the tension. Not much changed, however. The government continued to push to diversify its economy and promote foreign investment. The desire to rely less on oil was exacerbated by the coronavirus pandemic and international calls for shifts to renewable energy.

More importantly, the government required the parliament to vote on legislation that would let it cover its budget deficit by borrowing from international markets—a step the opposition rejected. The parliament argued that the government should better manage its finances and fight corruption before resorting to debt. Instead, the parliament pushed for political reform, including the amnesty of exiled opposition figures such as Musallam al-Barrak, a former vocal assembly member and figurehead of political dissent. In an unprecedented step to end the stalemate, the amir called in 2021 for a national dialogue between the government and parliament to solve all pending problems.

POLITICAL ECONOMY

Kuwait's economy is largely based on oil production. Oil was first discovered in Kuwait in the 1930s, but commercial shipment to international markets did not begin until after World War II in 1946. By the 2019–2020 fiscal year, oil and petroleum accounted for about 43.9 percent of the gross domestic product (GDP) and 90 percent of Kuwait's annual revenue. With total oil production capacity of almost three million barrels per day and 10 percent of the world's crude oil reserves, Kuwait plans to make available four million barrels per day by 2020. The United States, Europe, and Japan are the main consumers of the country's oil. Thus, oil has an undeniable impact on the political economy of Kuwait. To understand the extent of this impact requires a brief discussion of Kuwait's economy prior to oil.

Pre-Oil Economy

As discussed earlier, Kuwait had always enjoyed a fine natural harbor—and, therefore, many of its pre-oil economic activities centered on the sea. In the 19th century, Kuwaiti sailors benefited from thriving trade routes and networks in the Indian Ocean, stretching from India to East Africa. The trading season commenced in September and continued for ten months. Sailors began their journey with dates brought from Basra and traded down the Gulf Coast to East Africa or to India across the Indian Ocean. Dates were traded for cash or goods, such as rice and spices from India, coffee from Yemen, tobacco and dried fruit from Persia, and wood for ship-building from East Africa. Kuwaiti merchants traveled widely and resided abroad for months at a time. As a result, they developed extensive regional networks, based on commerce, kinship, and marriage. This network helped develop an organized and powerful merchant class that came to shape much of Kuwait's politics until the discovery of oil in the 1930s.

In addition to trade, other pre-oil activities included fishing and pearling. Unlike fishing, which was largely for local consumption, pearling was a lucrative export trade in Kuwait. Just before World War I when the industry was at its peak, Kuwait had a large fleet of pearling boats from which about fifteen thousand men—a significant part of the population at that time—dove. The prosperous industry survived for centuries but was finally destroyed in the mid-20th century by the Great

PHOTO 15.1 Annual pearl-diving trips, held under the Amir's patronage, keep traditions alive

Yasser Al-Zayyat/AFP/Getty Images

Depression, the emergence of Japanese cultured pearls, the outbreak of World War II and, of course, the discovery of oil.[16]

Pre-oil activities were not only economic ventures but also affected how society was divided and organized. Divisions did not disappear totally with the discovery of oil; they simply took a different shape. Pre-oil Kuwaiti society was broadly divided into ship owners, ship captains, and crews, which included the divers who collected the oysters. Owners and captains, who were sometimes one and the same, amassed wealth from trade and pearling for their powerful families. They were usually the urban, Sunni families who claimed descent from the early Najdi settlers. The divers, at the bottom of the economic pyramid, were nomads from the desert, Shiʿa from Persia, and slaves from Africa.

Oil Economy

Kuwait's oil was discovered in 1938 by Kuwait Oil Company (KOC), originally a joint holding of the Anglo-Persian Oil Company, later British Petroleum (BP), and American Gulf Oil. By 1953, Kuwait had become the largest producer of oil in the Persian Gulf and in 1956, the largest in the Middle East. The government bought KOC in 1976, thereby becoming the first Arab oil-producing state to achieve full control of its output.

The state's full ownership of oil enabled it to develop an all-embracing welfare system that does not charge income tax and provides citizens with housing, generous retirement pensions, free health and education services, and comprehensive support for orphans, the elderly, and the handicapped. The welfare system is a reflection of the interrelated social responsibilities of the pre-oil era and is in keeping with local Bedouin traditions of paternalism. In addition, the state's ownership of oil provides the ruling coalition with a modern base of legitimacy to support its traditional one.[17]

Social and economic stratification in the post-oil era continued under a different guise. Pre-oil nomads, fishermen, and divers now turned into bureaucrats and technocrats in the developing state sectors, while ship owners and ship captains turned into businessmen. The government promised merchants new state contracts for development work, so when contracts were given to foreign firms, the government stipulated they take Kuwaiti partners. These and other policies maintained the merchants' pre-oil status in the new oil economy.

Oil has had a significant impact on the provision of state services and the population. In 2018, for instance, the literacy rate among Kuwaitis was more than 96.1 percent, which is on par with Western Europe. This is largely due to the government's increase in oil revenues and subsequent provision of free education to its nationals (those attending the local university receive a monthly stipend of about $870, and those who attend college overseas are also generously funded). As a result, the educational status of nationals has shown steady improvement. In the 1970s, for example, only 22 percent of technical staff in the government sector was Kuwaiti; by 2015, this figure exceeded 70 percent. With the rising level of education, traditional attitudes toward women's education and employment have changed. Kuwaiti women outnumber men in Kuwait University and constitute a significant labor force in the public sector (ministries, other public authorities, and state-owned oil companies).

Non-Oil Economy

Higher oil revenues enabled Kuwait to embark on an ambitious program of further diversifying its economy away from oil. The government became increasingly aware that oil was a nonrenewable resource and started to take serious steps to make its future economy less reliant on it. Many of Kuwait's efforts to diversify its income began in the 1960s with plans to industrialize. In 1964, the Shuaibah Industrial Zone was built to include distilling plants and electrical production facilities to support manufacturing. Factories to produce cement, asphalt, and other industrial chemicals, such as chlorine, were also constructed. Despite these efforts, industrial development has never reached the levels found in other Gulf countries, such as Saudi Arabia. Like industry, agriculture was never a success story in Kuwait, partially because of the country's difficult weather conditions. In 2019, agricultural products accounted for as little as 0.38 percent of the GDP.

A significant source of income comes from investment projects abroad. In 1976, Kuwait founded the Reserve Fund for Future Generations, in which 10 percent of oil revenues is deposited and invested. Initially, most of the investments—about $7 billion in the late 1970s—were concentrated in the United States and Europe. In the 1980s, investments were also made in Japan. With its carefully chosen and successful ventures, by the mid-1980s Kuwait was earning more from its overseas investments than it was from direct sales of oil: Foreign assets in 1987 reached $6.3 billion, and its oil revenues totaled $5.4 billion. Following the Iraqi invasion in 1990, these assets became the only source of funding for the Gulf War expenses and reconstruction. By 2020, assets in the Reserve Fund were worth more than $600 billion.

In addition to its overseas investment, Kuwait is relentlessly developing its private sector. To encourage private non-oil industry, the government began establishing joint ventures with private capital in the early 1960s and again in the 1980s, when it had to buy up shares to support prices on the local stock exchange. Kuwait's private sector, however, suffers from a narrow base and a lack of advanced technology. To improve and widen the role of the private sector, the government began in 1994 a privatization program, which has not been remarkably successful. Fewer than 5 percent of Kuwaitis were employed in the private sector in 2017. Nonetheless, the government relies more on the private sector to carry out public projects and is privatizing the production of some public goods and services. In 2000, Kuwait for the first time permitted foreigners to own shares in Kuwaiti companies, a change that turned Kuwait's local stock exchange into one of the most active in the Arab world. There are general fears, however, that privatization will result in higher unemployment among young Kuwaitis, most of whom prefer working in state sectors.

In an attempt to turn the country into a regional trading center, a free-trade zone allowing full foreign ownership was established in 1998, and a second one was approved for the northern area of the country. After a hiatus of thirteen years, trade with Iraq is wide open again; the effort to rebuild Iraq is creating massive opportunities for the transport and construction industries. Kuwait, with its developed ports and transport facilities, expects to be the import route of choice for the reconstruction of Iraq and to become a regional trading hub in the long run.[18]

FOREIGN POLICY

Following independence in 1961, Kuwait attempted to assert its political autonomy and achieve international recognition. It became a member of the Arab League in 1961, and in 1963, a member of the United Nations and some UN-related agencies, such as the World Bank and General Agreement on Tariffs and Trade (GATT). Regionally, Kuwait began to expand its relations with Saudi Arabia, Egypt, and Syria to thwart growing threats from Iraq. Indeed, during most of the 1960s and 1970s, the major regional threat to Kuwait's security and sovereignty came from Iraq, which continued to instigate minor border conflicts. In 1961, days after Kuwait's independence, Iraq threatened to annex the amirate, and in 1973, it mobilized troops along the border before finally standing down under pressure from other Arab countries.

To garner Arab support, Kuwait established the Kuwait Fund for Arab Economic Development in 1961, with the primary task of offering grants and low-interest loans to Arab states to develop their economies. Its capital dramatically increased from $150 million in 1961 to approximately $6.75 billion in the 1980s.[19] In 1984, Kuwait allocated 3.81 percent of its gross national product (GNP) to development assistance and has consistently been ranked among the top ten donor countries to Arab states such as Yemen, Tunisia, Sudan, and Jordan, and to the PLO.

Because of their generosity through the fund, the support that the PLO and the governments of Jordan, Yemen, and Sudan gave Saddam Hussein during the 1990 invasion shocked Kuwaitis, and they were hard pressed to formulate more pragmatic diplomacy. Prior to the Gulf War in 1991, Palestinians constituted the largest expatriate community in Kuwait (about 30 percent of the population). After liberation, thousands of Palestinians were forcibly expelled, reducing their number in 2006 from 350,000 to 4,000. Palestinians today make up less than 3 percent of the population, with little chance that their number (about seven thousand) will dramatically increase in the near future.

Kuwait has acted within the Gulf Cooperation Council (GCC) against the uprisings in the Middle East that began in 2011. It sent a naval force to Bahrain's coast in support of the GCC's military intervention to assist Bahrain's government against its Shi'i uprising in 2011. It also cooperated with the GCC to bring about the peaceful transition of power in Yemen. Kuwait is eager to maintain its relations with Egypt, even after the downfall of its ex-president and close ally, Hosni Mubarak, and the rise of the Muslim Brotherhood. Because Syria is aligned with Iran, Kuwait is hoping that the downfall of Bashar al-Asad in Syria would weaken Iran's position in the region.

Relations With Iran

In 1979, the Iranian Revolution radically changed the political scene in the region. The most serious threat to Kuwait during much of the 1980s came from Iran. During the Iran–Iraq War, Kuwait supported Saddam Hussein against Ayatollah Khomeini and sought international protection of its oil tankers from the Soviet Union and the United States. Until the end of the Cold War, however, Kuwait made serious diplomatic efforts to appear neutral in its relations with both superpowers. Although the British withdrew from the Gulf in 1971, the United States did not become Kuwait's key international ally until the Iraqi invasion of Kuwait in 1990.

Revolutionary fervor in Iran has abated since the death of Ayatollah Khomeini in 1989 and the presidency of Hashemi Rafsanjani from 1989 to 1997. Rafsanjani, pragmatic compared to revolutionary Khomeini, sought to improve relations with other Gulf countries, especially Saudi Arabia and Kuwait. Rafsanjani condemned the Iraqi invasion in 1990 and gave thousands of Kuwaiti refugees shelter in Iran. Relations between Kuwait and Iran have improved significantly since then. This is partially reflected in increased trade relations and Kuwait's recognition of a more active Iranian role in Gulf security.

Despite improved relations, Kuwait continues to harbor concerns over Iran's regional ambitions and influence, particularly on the Shi'a in Kuwait and Iraq. If Iran fosters sectarian violence inside Iraq, Kuwait fears it will spill over the borders. In 2015, Kuwait charged one Iranian and twenty-five Kuwaiti Shi'a with contacts with Iran and the Lebanese Hizbullah group in order to plot attacks inside the country. The authorities seized arms and explosives allegedly smuggled in from Iran.

Kuwait also worried that Iran's nuclear deal with the United States in 2015 will embolden Tehran to increase its backing for its allies in Syria and Yemen—at odds with Gulf Arab countries—and increase its interference in the internal politics of majority Shi'a Bahrain. Such concerns were diminished, at least somewhat, as the United States under the Trump administration distanced itself from this deal.

Relations With the EU

Kuwait's relationship with the member states of the European Union (EU) has been largely based on economic development rather than military cooperation. Kuwait's imports from Europe in 1994, for example, constituted 36.3 percent of its total world imports, and in 1995, Kuwait ranked number one in the consumption of European goods among the Gulf Cooperation Council (GCC) countries of Saudi Arabia, Kuwait, Bahrain, Qatar, the United Arab Emirates, and Oman.[20] Increased trade has also marked Kuwait's relations with individual European countries. In 2011, Kuwaiti imports from Britain rose by nearly 20 percent, and Kuwaiti exports to Britain reached €1.6 billion. In 2012, German exports to Kuwait came to €1.02 billion, and the country was the fourth-biggest exporter to the Gulf nation.

Economic cooperation has been the pattern governing GCC–EU relations, especially since they signed a formal cooperation agreement in 1988.[21] The EU, a major, diversified trading bloc, relies heavily on the export of manufactured goods and is, therefore, highly interested in continued access to lucrative markets in the Gulf states, including Kuwait. In 1992, the EU accounted for nearly 40 percent of the GCC's imports, in contrast to the United States, which accounted for less than 20 percent.

Although the EU plays a junior role compared to the United States in political and security matters of the Gulf, Kuwait and the rest of the GCC welcome greater European political involvement in the region. Kuwait, for instance, supports the European policy of engaging Iran through dialogue, in contrast to the punitive measures and coercive diplomacy of the United States. Furthermore, Kuwait anticipates a European role in the Arab–Israeli peace process that is more effective than the US role.

Relations With the United States

Kuwaiti–US relations date to the 1940s, when a US oil firm owned 50 percent of Kuwait Oil Company. The relationship changed from a commercial to a political one as Britain's influence waned in the 1960s. In 1971, the United States named its first ambassador to Kuwait, and in 1972, the US Department of Defense conducted an important survey of Kuwait's national defense requirements, paving the way for future arms sales.

Ties between the two countries began to strengthen in the 1980s, when Kuwait sought US protection from Iranian aggression during the Iran–Iraq War. In 1987, the US Navy escorted Kuwaiti tankers under the US flag to thwart attacks from Iran. At the end of the Iran–Iraq War in 1988, Kuwait loosened its ties with the States because it did not want to be seen as openly aligning with the West.[22]

Kuwaiti reluctance to pursue warmer relations with the United States changed in 1991. In that year, Kuwait declared the United States its strategic partner and signed a ten-year defense pact (renewed in 2001), which provided for stockpiling US military equipment in Kuwait, US access to Kuwaiti ports and airports, and joint training exercises and equipment purchases.

Before the George W. Bush administration (2001–2009), the main goal of US policy in the Gulf was to preserve a pro-US regional balance of power and prevent any hostile state from asserting its dominance. But in the wake of the September 11 terrorist attacks, the Bush administration decided to change the power configuration of the Middle East and the domestic politics of regional states. It invaded Iraq, defeated Saddam Hussein, and established a new government in Baghdad. The costs of this new policy were enormous for the United States, and the regional repercussions were largely negative.

While the United States may have ended the Iraqi threat forever in 2003, its military presence in the region is forging new enemies. In 2002, two Kuwaitis fired on US Marines conducting military exercises on Failaka Island, killing one and injuring another. Kuwaiti authorities were later informed that one of the gunmen had sworn allegiance to Osama bin Laden. There was another shooting involving American troops a week later. In 2003, another gunman shot dead an American civilian and wounded a second near Camp Doha, one of the main US military bases in Kuwait.

The presence of al-Qa'ida elements in Kuwait was confirmed in 2005 when Kuwaiti security forces rounded up a group of militants, among them Kuwaiti military personnel. Calling themselves the Lions of the Peninsula, they had plans to attack US bases and interests. Thirty-seven militants were charged; of them, thirty-four faced the death penalty. In August 2009, Kuwaiti authorities arrested six alleged al-Qa'ida militants who were planning to attack Camp Arifjan, the second-largest US military base, which houses fifteen thousand American soldiers.

Relations with the United States have fluctuated with different administrations. Under President Barack Obama, US policy was more moderate than under George W. Bush. The Obama administration took a balance-of-power approach to the Gulf, tried to maintain the United States' preeminent role, and worked to prevent hostile powers from dominating the region. The relationship between the United States and Kuwait is seen to be a strategic one, and whether during the Trump or Biden administration, it would remain strong, without pressure from the United States to normalize relations with Israel.

FUTURE PROSPECTS

Kuwait has survived serious challenges, including the Iraqi invasion in 1990. Current and future challenges, however, are no less daunting.

Domestically, the government and parliament have been at odds, more so since 2012, when the late Amir Sheikh Sabah Al Ahmed Al Sabah issued an Amiri decree to change the electoral system from a four-voting system to a single nontransferable vote, a move that led to a large election boycott movement and increased demand for electoral reform. The damaging impact of the COVID-19 pandemic on global economy, including low oil prices, has hampered the government's ability to continue to play the state welfare role it has played since 1961. This created even more conflict, between the government wanting to empower national and international private sectors so that it plays a bigger role in the national economy, and parliament that wants to please its popular constituencies and maintain the citizens' traditional privileges. The opposition in parliament criticizes the government's rhetoric, arguing that before it resorts to international loans and austerity measures, such as taxation and increased service charges, it must first seriously combat the corruption within its top ministers and officials.

Regionally, Kuwait is troubled by the discord in the Gulf Cooperation Council, most notably between Saudi Arabia and Qatar and the normalization of relations between Israel and the United Arab Emirates. Although, Kuwait congratulated Iran on its recent presidential elections and the victory of the conservative Ebrahim Raisi in 2021, it is certainly worried about the prospect of a nuclear Iran, let alone a military conflict in the Gulf. Following the US military withdrawal from Afghanistan in 2021, Kuwait is equally concerned about the future of its security arrangement, especially vis-à-vis Iraq. With an ailing, 84-year-old amir, a troubled region, and rapidly changing world, the future prospects of Kuwait is more uncertain than ever.

SUGGESTED READINGS

Abu Hakima, Ahmed. *History of Kuwait 1750–1965*. London: Luzac & Company Press, 1983.

Almdarires, Falah. *Islamic Extremism in Kuwait: From the Muslim Brotherhood to Al-Qaeda and Other Islamist Political Groups*. London: Routledge, 2010.

Anscombe, Frederick. *The Ottoman Gulf: The Creation of Kuwait, Saudi Arabia and Qatar*. New York, NY: Columbia University Press, 1997.

Casey, Michael. *The History of Kuwait*. Westport, CT: Greenwood Press, 2007.

Clements, Frank. *Kuwait*. Oxford: Clio Press, 1985.

Crystal, Jill. *Kuwait: The Transformation of an Oil State*. Boulder, CO: Westview Press, 1992.

Crystal, Jill. *Oil and Politics in the Gulf: Rulers and Merchants in Kuwait and Qatar*. New York, NY: Cambridge University Press, 1990.

Ismael, Jacqueline. *Kuwait: Social Change in Historical Perspective*. Syracuse, NY: Syracuse University Press, 1982.

Khouja, M. W., and P. G. Sadler. *The Economy of Kuwait: Development and Role in International Finance*. London: Macmillan, 1979.

Smith, Simon. *Kuwait 1950–1965, Britain, the Al Sabah and Oil*. Oxford: Oxford University Press, 1999.

16 LEBANON

Paul Salem

Since the founding of the modern state of Lebanon a century ago in 1920, the country has been a puzzling contradiction. On the one hand, it has repeatedly recovered from internal conflict to find a tentative path toward political and economic normality; on the other hand, it is a country that has remained deeply dysfunctional and divided along communal lines. It is the longest-standing constitutional democracy in the Arab world, dating back to 1926, yet its political system is one of the most archaic, characterized by confessionalism, clientelism, oligarchy, and corruption. It is a unique example of civilizational coexistence and cooperative Christian-Muslim government in a world bedeviled by rising civilizational clashes but is also a festering swamp of communal tensions and confessional narrow-mindedness. It has been a haven of free speech, free association, and civility; yet it is a highly stressed society, where freedoms are subtly or not so subtly curtailed, where communal tensions lurk dangerously below a civil surface, where weapons are readily available, and where armed organizations operate beyond the control of the state. It appears to be an open, secular society; however, it is a federation of inward-looking, conservative religious communities, each with its own religious hierarchy and fundamentalisms. It is a brazen little Arab country, the only to force an Israeli withdrawal from its territory; yet it is a precarious republic, limping along with myriad ailments, weaknesses, and stresses.[1] Its economic recovery after the 1975–1990 civil war seemed to exhibit an economic and fiscal resilience and ingenuity, but the deafening socio-economic collapse that started in 2019 has wiped out all postwar gains and driven the population to poverty and despair.

Today, a century after its establishment, the nation-state of Lebanon is in a condition of profound failure. Hizbullah—an armed sectarian group financed by Iran—is not just a state within the State, but a state that dominates the State, eliminating Lebanon's sovereignty over its own borders and territory. The political class that ruled the country for the past thirty years is mired in corruption and sectarianism, and the majority in Parliament is now held by Hizbullah and its allies. The fiscal, banking, and monetary policies that were pursued for the past three decades led to an extended economic bubble and—according to the World Bank—one of the worst economic collapses anywhere in the world since the mid-19th century. A recently middle-income country has been catapulted into mass poverty, with basic goods and services—such as electricity, fuel, medical care, and medicines—disappearing. Now, hundreds of thousands scramble to feed themselves and their families while anyone who is able flees the country.

As I write these lines in August 2022, the country faces a grim and uncertain future. The parliamentary elections of May 2022 brought many of the same faces and blocs to parliament, although Hezbollah and its allies lost their previous majority. More interestingly, a fresh group of 13 MPs, stemming from the civil society movement that erupted in October 2019, did break through. The group is too small to make a significant difference, but it might indicate the possibility of more socio-political change to be expressed in the next parliamentary elections of 2026. The country faces the challenge of electing a new president to replace Michel Aoun, whose terms ends in late October. Parliament might fail to agree on a new candidate, leading to an extended vacancy in the presidency and more governance drift. If parliament does manage to elect a new president, much will depend on who the next president is and what their political alignments will be. The beginning of a new president's term is significant because it brings with it other political changes, including the designation of a new prime minister and formation of a new government, the selection of a new head of the army, and potentially the appointment of a new head of the central bank. Given Lebanon's dire straits, the presidential election and what follows it is a make-or-break watershed: either a new president, prime minister, and governing team are put in place that can tackle domestic reform issues, engage with the IMF and international community, and turn around the collapsing economy, or the country will enter another extended period of poor governance, deterioration, and drift.

MAKING OF THE CONTEMPORARY STATE

Understanding Lebanon's institutions, political culture, and social environment is virtually impossible without a broader understanding of the historical processes that created them.

From Emirate to Special Province

In the 16th century, Mount Lebanon was an informally autonomous region within the Ottoman Empire. Its politics were based on negotiation, competition, and cooperation among prominent semifeudal families, topped by a local amir, who had been granted tax farming authority by the Ottoman Porte. For several centuries, the Druze community had been the dominant political and economic force in Mount Lebanon, but during the 18th and 19th centuries, the demographic and politico-economic balance began to shift to the Christian Maronite Catholics.[2]

This, as well as other regional political factors, led to a breakdown of the semifeudal order in 1840. Two decades of political troubles ensued, pitting Maronites and Druze against each other. An attempt during this period to set up two provinces—one Christian and one Druze—in order to reduce tension only made matters worse, as minorities in both provinces felt increasingly threatened. In 1861, after formal talks between the Ottoman state and the European Great Powers, a formal constitutional document, known as the Reglement Organique, was proclaimed. In it, the idea of a united Mount Lebanon was revived, but this time not as a semifeudal emirate but rather as a legally defined, special Ottoman province. The governor would be a nonlocal Ottoman Christian (from the Greek or Armenian Ottoman communities) appointed in consultation with the European Great Powers, some of whom regarded themselves as guardians of Lebanon's Christians. He would govern in consultation with an elected administrative council whose seats were apportioned to the main religious communities in the province (mainly Maronites and Druze, but also some Greek Orthodox, Greek Catholics, Sunnis, and Shi'a).[3]

KEY FACTS ON LEBANON

AREA 4,015 square miles (10,400 square kilometers)

CAPITAL Beirut

POPULATION 5,261,372 million total (2021 est.)

PERCENTAGE OF POPULATION UNDER 25 35.73 (2020 est.)

RELIGIOUS GROUPS (PERCENTAGE) Estimates: Muslim, 61.1 (30.6 Sunni, 30.5 Shia, smaller percentages Alawites, and Ismailis); Christian, 33.7; Druze, 5.2 (2018 est.).

ETHNIC GROUPS (PERCENTAGE) Arab, 95; Armenian, 4; other, 1

OFFICIAL LANGUAGE Arabic; French, English, and Armenian widely spoken

TYPE OF GOVERNMENT Parliamentary Republic

DATE OF INDEPENDENCE November 22, 1943 (from League of Nations mandate under French administration)

GDP (nominal, in US) $55 billion in 2019; $33 billion in 2020. GDP per capita (nominal) $4,800.

PERCENTAGE OF GDP BY SECTOR Agriculture, 3.9; industry, 13.1; services, 83 (2017 est.)

TOTAL RENTS (PERCENTAGE OF GDP) FROM NATURAL RESOURCES 0.001

FERTILITY RATE 1.72 children born/woman

Sources: CIA. "The World Factbook." August 4, 2022, https://www.cia.gov/the-world-factbook/. World Bank. "International Comparison Program (ICP)." Accessed August 10, 2022, https://databank. worldbank.org/source/icp-2017.

Note: No reliable statistics are available for the overall demographics of Lebanon. The most recent census was conducted in 1932. The current voter rolls are public and accurate, but they give information only about citizens above the age of twenty-one and do not indicate who resides inside or outside the country.

This period is important because it established several patterns still seen in modern Lebanese politics: political identities based largely on religious community, confessional competition and conflict, foreign intervention and influence, power-sharing based on confessional representation, and a habit of intercommunal negotiation and cooperation within an elected council.

Greater Lebanon: A Troubled Beginning

Greater Lebanon was established by the French in 1920 as the amalgamation of the special Ottoman province of Mount Lebanon and districts of the Syrian Ottoman provinces of Beirut (including Tripoli, Sidon, and Tyre) and Damascus (including the districts of Baalbek, Rashaya, Hasbaya, and Moallaka). The creation of Greater Lebanon—later, simply Lebanon—was a point of contention between Christians and Muslims throughout the interwar period, with many Muslims, particularly Sunnis, demanding unification with Syria. An agreement, known as the National Pact, in which the Sunnis accepted the creation of Lebanon in its present borders and renounced unification with Syria, was struck on the eve of independence in 1943. This was in exchange for the Maronites

MAP 16.1 ■ Lebanon

renouncing French protection or suzerainty and accepting that Lebanon would be an Arab country. The National Pact also specified that the president of the republic would be a Maronite, the prime minister would be a Sunni, and the distribution of seats in parliament and high offices of the state would be at a fixed six-to-five ratio between Christians and Muslims. This ratio reflected the Christian majority among the population that still existed at the time and was based on the census figures of 1932 to 1934. This balance would shift in favor of the Muslims in the 1950s and 1960s and would become a major bone of contention in Lebanese politics.[4]

The French, with local consultation, had promulgated a constitution for Lebanon in 1926 that was modeled after the French Third Republic. It has largely remained in force, until the present day. It was significantly amended twice: first, in 1943 to eliminate the authority of the French high commissioner, and again in 1990 to institute reforms agreed upon in the Taif Accord of 1989, which ended the Lebanese Civil War (1975–1990). The constitution stipulated that Lebanon was a parliamentary democracy. Legislative authority was vested in a chamber of deputies directly elected by the people (males over twenty-one years of age; women got the vote in 1956). Executive authority was vested in the president of the republic, who was elected to a nonrenewable six-year term by parliament. The president appointed a Council of Ministers and a prime minister, all of whom required an official vote of confidence from parliament.

From Independence to Civil War: 1943–1975

With independence from France in 1943 and the abrogation of the high commissioner post, the constitutional powers of the president became paramount. He enjoyed supreme executive authority, a secure six-year term, the power to appoint and dismiss prime ministers and councils of ministers, and could greatly influence elections to parliament, or dismiss it altogether. In practice, however, he had to share much of this power with the Sunni prime minister. Independence had been won under the banner of the National Pact and on the basis of a national alliance between Bishara Khoury, a leading Maronite, and Riad al-Solh, a leading Sunni. Their alliance symbolized the national coalition between Christians and Muslims, and the ethos of politics in post-independence Lebanon which always returned to the principle of power-sharing, particularly between the president and the prime minister.[5]

Khoury's first term in office set precedents for the future of Lebanese politics including close cooperation between a Maronite president and a Sunni prime minister; rotation and co-optation of other political elites through frequent changes of government; managing parliamentary elections to favor allies and clients; and managing elite politics through the patronage of jobs and services offered by the state.[6] During Camille Chamoun's presidency (1952–1958), Lebanon became dangerously embroiled in regional and Cold War politics. The United States was trying to align Middle Eastern allies against Soviet influence, while Egyptian leader Gamal Abdel Nasser was trying to align Arab countries under his Soviet-sympathetic, regional leadership. The tensions led to armed clashes and a brief civil war in 1958, which ended only after US Marines landed on the shores of Beirut and a deal was brokered, with Nasser's cooperation, to elect the centrist head of the army, Fuad Chehab, as president in place of Chamoun.

During his presidency (1958–1964), Chehab recognized that many of the country's problems were due to weak state institutions and socioeconomic inequalities. He strengthened the army and internal security forces, committed the state to provide public education and health services, and set up civil service training and control institutions.

In the period that followed, Lebanon was thrust into a web of regional conflict. After the Egyptian, Syrian, and Jordanian armies were summarily defeated in the June 1967 War, Palestinian refugees in Lebanon began to arm themselves, with support from Syria and other Arab states, as Lebanon became an arena for direct conflict between armed Palestinians and the Israeli army. A similar situation in Jordan led to a strong crackdown by the Jordanian state. However, in Lebanon, the state was unable to control these developments. In fact, after a series of incidents, in 1969, Lebanon and the Palestine Liberation Organization (PLO)—under Nasser's patronage—signed the Cairo Agreement in which the Lebanese state effectively ceded part of its territory to the PLO for cross-border operations against Israel. This loss of sovereignty that began in 1969 continues today—although, in 1969, it was to the PLO, and today it is to Hizbullah.

Tensions over the Palestinian armed presence and the Arab-Israeli conflict exacerbated internal political tensions among Christian and Muslim politicians and between rightist and leftist parties. Christian and right-wing parties began to arm themselves against the Palestinian presence, while Muslim and leftist parties moved into an alliance with the PLO to press the Maronite-dominated state for communal and socioeconomic concessions. With the political elites unable to resolve the crisis or agree on reforms, the situation escalated into months of strikes and demonstrations. Finally, in April 1975 one incident in a neighborhood of Beirut brought armed gangs into the streets and unleashed a wave of armed unrest. The state could have used the army to try and restore order, but disagreement among politicians and fears that the army itself might splinter along confessional lines caused the state to stand by as the country sank into full civil war.[7]

THE CIVIL WAR: 1975–1990

The period extending between 1975 and 1990 witnessed a plethora of events, conflicts, wars, and interventions that are hard to place under one label. In Lebanon, this period is variously described as "the war years," "the events," "the civil war," or "the war of others on Lebanese soil." The inability to agree on a name hints at the multiple perspectives, players, and forces that were involved during this period.[8]

The first phase is often referred to as "the two-year war," extending from the outbreak of fighting in April 1975 to the summer of 1976. It saw the rapid collapse of central authority and the outbreak of widespread fighting between two camps of rival militias: a group of mainly Christian right-wing militias on one side, and an alliance of leftist, Palestinian, and Muslim militias on the other. The fighting split the capital into West and East Beirut, and demolished most of the city's center. Alarm bells rang in Damascus, which feared that a PLO-dominated Lebanon could create a radical and uncontrollable neighbor. Syrian troops entered Lebanon beginning in January 1976, but then more forcefully in June. They stopped the advance of the leftist-Palestinian-Muslim coalition and put an effective end to this phase of the war. The United States indirectly brokered a "red-line agreement" in which Israel would tolerate the Syrian incursion into Lebanon on the condition that Syrian troops not deploy south of the Awwali River.

This phase ended with the election of a new president, Elias Sarkis, and an Arab agreement, brokered with Saudi Arabia and Egypt, to create an Arab deterrent force of which Syrian troops would be the main component. Syrian troops would stay in Lebanon for the next twenty-nine years.

The precarious calm was shattered in early 1977 by the assassination of the Druze leader, Kamal Jumblatt, near a Syrian checkpoint. Jumblatt had been the political leader of the leftist-Palestinian-Muslim alliance and had been on bad terms with the Syrians since their intervention in mid-1976. The assassination—the first in a string of political assassinations that would extend on and off through 2007—led to revenge killings of large numbers of Christians in the ethnically diverse southern Mount Lebanon region. These communal tensions would erupt again in 1983 into an all-out war between Christian and Druze militias.

Clashes were also escalating at this time between Palestinians and Israelis in southern Lebanon. In 1978, Israel launched an invasion and established a self-proclaimed "security zone," which it controlled and which was manned by a local Lebanese militia. The Israeli occupation would extend for twenty-two years.

Relations had also deteriorated between Christian and Syrian forces, leading to fierce fighting and the withdrawal of Syrian troops from East Beirut. The killings in the mountains in 1977 and the clashes with the Syrians in 1978 led some Christian leaders, guided by the young Bashir Gemayel, to build an alliance with Israel, which had now become a player in the country. Gemayel hoped to use Israeli power to defeat both the Palestinians and Syrians and to rebuild a Maronite-dominated Lebanese state. He figured that if the Israelis and Americans had helped King Hussein in Jordan to retain his state against Palestinian and Syrian power in 1970, they would do the same for him in Lebanon.[9]

The alliance led to the second Israeli invasion of Lebanon in 1982, which devastated the entire south of the country and reached all the way to Beirut.[10] The PLO and allied militias put up stiff resistance but were overwhelmed, and Syrian forces retreated after suffering losses. The war led to a prolonged siege of Beirut and the negotiated withdrawal of PLO leaders and fighters from Lebanon under the auspices of a US-led multinational force. The withdrawal of the PLO effectively ended almost fifteen years of strong Palestinian armed presence in Lebanon.[11]

Under Israeli guns, parliament met and elected Bashir Gemayel to the presidency. The grand plan to remake Lebanon with a restored Maronite domination and an alliance with Israel unraveled when Gemayel was assassinated a few days later by a member of the Syrian Social Nationalist Party. Christian militias retaliated with revenge massacres in Sabra and Shatila Palestinian refugee camps, and the US president, Ronald Reagan, ordered US peacekeeping troops to reenter Beirut after having just left. To fill the constitutional vacuum, parliament met again to elect Gemayel's more centrist brother, Amine, to the presidency.

Israel wanted Lebanon to sign a peace treaty that would increase Israeli influence, while the new Lebanese administration wanted to negotiate the withdrawal of Israeli forces and lean on US and Arab support to maintain its independence. The US-brokered withdrawal talks between both sides resulted in what became known as the May 17 (1983) agreement.[12] Although the Lebanese parliament overwhelmingly approved the agreement, it was never implemented. Israel sent a private side letter to the United States stating that it would not withdraw before Syrian troops did, and Syria rejected the agreement and urged various groups in Lebanon to oppose it.

With the stillbirth of the withdrawal agreement, the situation again began to unravel. Israel, giving up on peace with Lebanon, unilaterally began to implement a withdrawal from Beirut, the mountains, and points north of the Litani River to settle back into its southern 1978 security zone. Tensions in Beirut between the state and an ascendant Amal movement led to open clashes between both groups in August 1983 and again in February 1984. Tensions between Druze and Christian militias in the mountains after the Israeli withdrawal led to massive clashes, known as the "war of the mountain," that ended in a Druze victory and the displacement of dozens of Christians. This period also saw the birth of Hizbullah in Lebanon; it was organized with strong support from the new Islamic Republic of Iran and fed on popular opposition to the Israeli occupation.

Operatives linked to Hizbullah blew up the US embassy and Marine barracks in Lebanon, and opposition groups allied to Syria led a revolt against the authority of the Gemayel-led state in February 1984, taking over West Beirut. President Reagan ordered US troops out of

Lebanon, and Gemayel formed a new government led by a member of the Syrian-allied opposition, Rashid Karami, that renounced the May 17 agreement.

After the removal of the strong Palestinian presence in Lebanon, talks intensified among Lebanese groups to reach an agreement that would institute reforms and bring an end to the war. A first agreement, known as the Tripartite Agreement, between the main Christian, Druze, and Shi'i militias was brokered in Damascus in December 1985, but it collapsed after the leader of the Christian Lebanese Forces militia was unseated in an internal coup. A second round of talks made progress but came to a halt when the prime minister, Rashid Karami, was assassinated in 1987, apparently by Christian militia operatives.

This situation of stalemate continued through the end of Amin Gemayel's term in 1988. Parliament failed to meet and elect a new president, and as the minutes of his term ticked away, Gemayel appointed the head of the army, General Michel Aoun, to the post of prime minister, as the holder of the prime ministership could constitutionally exercise the powers of the vacant presidency. The appointment was contested by the incumbent prime minister, Salim al-Hoss, who refused to resign his post. Lebanon thus drifted into a situation of two governments, one with authority in mainly Christian East Beirut and surrounding areas and one with authority in West Beirut and allied areas.

Aoun proved an explosive leader. He first declared war on the country's militias and tried to close down their illegal ports; he then declared a "war of liberation" on Syria and vowed to drive it out of Lebanon. These moves plunged the country into various rounds of fighting that were among the fiercest since 1975.

The crisis galvanized Arab and international attention and led to a new wave of diplomacy to try to end the long Lebanese civil war. The efforts culminated in a round of meetings among Lebanese members of parliament in Taif, Saudi Arabia, in 1989. The meetings were sponsored by Saudi Arabia and the Arab League, and were supported by the United States and other international players. They resulted in the approval of the National Reconciliation Document that outlined key constitutional reforms to end the civil war and restore state authority. The document is commonly referred to as the Taif Agreement.

Michel Aoun rejected the accord and mobilized opposition to it, while the deputies elected a president, Elias Hrawi. The standoff between Aoun and Hrawi ended a year later, in October 1990, when Syrian-backed troops loyal to Hrawi's administration overran Aoun's positions in the eastern enclave. Aoun went into exile in France, and the postwar period began in earnest under strong Syrian dominance and within the framework of the Taif Agreement.

THE TAIF AGREEMENT

In terms of political reform, the agreement shifted power from the president to the Council of Ministers, which, as a collegial body, was vested with supreme executive authority.[13] While the president no longer enjoys hegemony within the executive branch, the office retains some procedural and symbolic powers. Whereas the pre-Taif system was dominated by the president, the post-Taif system introduces a wider distribution of power, primarily among the three "presidents" of the system: the president, the prime minister, and the speaker of parliament. Taif also mandated an equal representation of Muslims and Christians in parliament; this replaced the six-to-five ratio in favor of Christians. Article 24, which stipulates this parity, also dictates that this is a temporary requirement until such time as a parliament on a nonconfessional basis can be elected.

The document also dealt with issues related to the civil war, Israeli occupation, and relations with Syria, and contained provisions about the disarming of all nongovernmental militias and the extension of state authority throughout the country. Regarding the Israeli occupation of south Lebanon, the agreement urged "taking all necessary measures to liberate all Lebanese territory from Israeli occupation; extending the state's authority over its entire territory; deploying the Lebanese army to the internationally-recognized border area; and endeavoring to reinforce the presence of the UN Interim Force in Lebanon" (Article III.3.C). This clause exempted Hizbullah from the provision to disarm all nongovernment armed groups, as one of the "necessary measures to liberate all Lebanese territory," and was redefined more specifically as an anti-occupation resistance force. Palestinian militias in the various refugee camps in the country were also not disarmed. In other words, Lebanese state sovereignty was not fully reestablished after Taif.

With regard to international relations, Taif resolved that Lebanon would have "special" relations with Syria and that the two countries would coordinate policy in security, defense, foreign affairs, and other key areas.

THE POSTWAR PERIOD: 1990–2005

This period was marked by overwhelming Syrian influence. The end of the Cold War and the politics surrounding the first Gulf War largely explain this. When the Cold War ended, the United States no longer saw the expansion of Syrian power in Lebanon as a loss on the global chessboard. Additionally, the United States saw Syria as a desired partner in their efforts to push Saddam Hussein's forces out of Kuwait after the invasion of August 1990. Meanwhile, Michel Aoun had strayed from US favor by striking an alliance with Saddam's Iraq to counter Syrian power in Lebanon. Both the United States and Israel looked the other way as Syrian air and ground forces launched their attack on Aoun's strongholds in the Christian enclaves of Beirut in October 1990. Syria thus gained control of the main areas of the country, excluding the Israeli-occupied southern strip.

Syrian-Lebanese relations were institutionalized through a Treaty of Brotherhood, Cooperation and Coordination, a Supreme Council (including the presidents and prime ministers of both countries), and various other pacts and agreements, but represented a loose confederation at best. The reality was that Syria effectively controlled most of Lebanon and could dictate major policy decisions. The control was maintained by the presence of tens of thousands of Syrian troops, intelligence officials, and government offices working openly throughout the country.

The first steps after the war ended were the formation of a new government and the integration of most Taif Accord clauses into an amended constitution. Progress was also made in disarming and dissolving militias. Key militia leaders were co-opted by being awarded ministerial posts. Some fighters were integrated into the army or internal security forces; others receded into private life. Hizbullah and the remaining armed Palestinian groups were exempted from the dissolution order.

While attention was focused on security, a financial crisis led to the collapse of the national currency and the prioritization of economic issues. Within this context, Rafik al-Hariri, a Lebanese-Saudi billionaire, emerged as a postwar leader who could lead an economic recovery. After parliamentary elections were held in 1992, Hariri was named prime minister. He would become a dominant figure in Lebanese government and politics until his assassination in 2005.

Hariri served as prime minister for ten of the next thirteen years. He was given leeway by the Syrians in economic matters, while they and the Iranians worked with Hizbullah to maintain pressure on Israel. Hariri focused on rebuilding basic state institutions and the utilities infrastructure, and rebuilding the destroyed downtown of Beirut, hoping to transform it into a hub of banking, tourism, and other services. He started his tenure in 1992 around the time of the Madrid peace process, and he made his plans with the optimistic expectation that Lebanon would soon be part of a peaceful and prosperous region. When large-scale reconstruction funding was unavailable—most Western funding was focused on rebuilding central and eastern Europe—he did not hesitate to borrow, figuring that deficit financing would soon be alleviated by regional peace and rapid domestic economic growth. In 1995, when Yitzhak Rabin was killed, the peace process ground to a halt. Lebanon's boom fizzled, and the country found itself in a debt trap. By 1998, the national debt was already above 100 percent of the country's GDP.

The Syrians had always kept Hariri at arm's length. They were happy to have him focus on domestic economic issues while they attended to security and regional politics, and his premiership was part of their bargain with Hariri's ally, Saudi Arabia. By 1998, the relationship had soured. Hariri had gone well beyond his businessman profile, emerging as the most influential political leader in Lebanon. Syria's Alawite-dominated regime, which ruled over a Sunni majority, preferred to keep Sunni leaders cut down to size. In 1998, therefore, Syria engineered the election of Hariri's archrival Emile Lahoud, head of the army, to the presidency. Hariri was pushed out of the premiership, and between 1998 and 2000, Salim al-Hoss, a centrist former prime minister, filled the post.

Now in opposition, Hariri assembled a formidable coalition and returned in force by winning the parliamentary elections of 2000 and barreling back into the premiership. Hariri's second tenure, from 2000 to 2004, was troubled. His relationships with President Lahoud and the Syrians were bad, and his policy outlook was pessimistic, based on devising emergency rescue packages for an economy in massive debt and crisis. Hizbullah had also become a dominant force in the country and disagreed with Hariri's vision for the country.

Hizbullah had scored a signal success in 2000 by forcing an Israeli withdrawal from Lebanon after a twenty-two-year occupation. Indeed, this was the only time an Arab country had ended an Israeli occupation by force, and it was indeed trumpeted as such. However, liberation did not lead to the army being dispatched to the south or the end of Hizbullah's armed resistance. Instead, Syria pressed Lebanese decision-makers not to send the army, and Hizbullah insisted that there were still some areas of Lebanon—mainly the Shabaa farms, whose ownership between Lebanon and Syria was disputed—that were occupied, justifying the continuation of armed resistance. Eventually, Hizbullah would move farther beyond this logic, arguing that it had to remain armed indefinitely as a "deterrent" against potential Israeli aggression.

In general, this 1990–2005 postwar period, despite its many crises, managed to bring back much stability to the country after sixteen years of civil war. It saw the significant rebuilding of many state and economic institutions and a general return to normalcy. Three parliamentary elections were held during this period—albeit with terribly gerrymandered election laws—and local elections were held in 1998 and again in 2004. The Syrians provided much of the stability during this period, but they were also the main obstacle to acquiring full sovereignty or sustainable political and economic development.[14]

FROM THE SYRIAN WITHDRAWAL TO THE ARAB UPRISINGS: 2005–2011

The postwar status quo began to break down in 2003 when Syria and the United States parted ways over the US invasion of Iraq. Although Syria had cooperated with the United States vigorously after the September 11, 2001 attacks and had shared key intelligence, Syria vehemently opposed the US occupation of Iraq. Like Iran, Syria could welcome the fall of Saddam Hussein, but it was concerned about having US troops on its borders. The George W. Bush administration considered Syria an enemy and moved to push back its power. In Lebanon, that meant that the United States was no longer willing to go along with Syrian control of the country, which had been the case since 1990. The United States joined France in September 2004 in sponsoring UN Security Council Resolution (UNSCR) 1559 (aimed at Syria), which called for the withdrawal of all "remaining foreign forces" from Lebanon and the disbanding and disarming of all Lebanese (meaning Hizbullah) and non-Lebanese (meaning Palestinian) militias.

Syria interpreted the resolution as a direct threat and suspected Hariri of being partially behind it, given his close friendship with French President Jacques Chirac. Syria mobilized its allies in Lebanon and forced the extension of President Lahoud's expiring mandate for a further three years, while Hariri built an essentially anti-Syrian alliance, bringing together key Christian leaders as well as Druze leader Walid Jumblatt. The focus was on winning the upcoming parliamentary elections in the spring of 2005. Politicians in Lebanon, many of whom had cooperated with the Syrians in the 1990s, began to sense the winds of change under the Bush administration and believed that perhaps the Syrian regime's days were numbered.

Tensions escalated with the attempted assassination of Jumblatt's close associate, Marwan Hamadeh, in October 2004. But the situation erupted in February 2005 when a car bomb killed Rafik al-Hariri and a number of associates, aides, and guards. Mourners turned into demonstrators and openly accused Syria of killing Hariri. The demonstrations turned into what looked and felt like a people's revolution on March 14, when more than one million people congregated in Beirut's Martyrs' Square to call for a Syrian withdrawal. The size of the demonstration reflected the accumulated frustration with the long Syrian presence; the shock caused by Hariri's assassination; and the opposition to a demonstration organized a few days earlier, on March 8, by Hizbullah and allied groups who expressed their continued support for Syria and its presence in Lebanon.

Under intense international pressure and facing massive demonstrations in Lebanon, Syria abruptly withdrew its military and (visible) intelligence forces from Lebanon in April. This ended a twenty-nine-year era of direct Syrian presence and dominance in Lebanon.

The sudden withdrawal was hailed as a historic victory for what had now become known as the "March 14 coalition." Then, the coalition faltered. First, one of its main Christian members, General Michel Aoun, left it after apparent disagreements over his role. Second, the coalition agreed to hold the upcoming parliamentary elections on the basis of an old Syrian-gerrymandered law. General Aoun joined the pro-Syrian coalition, now dubbed the "March 8 coalition," which included Hizbullah, the Amal Movement, and the Marada party of Suleiman Franjieh. In the elections held in May and June of that year, the March 14 coalition won a 72-seat majority in the 128-seat parliament.

The new government worked with the United Nations to set up a special international tribunal to adjudicate the case of Hariri's assassination and moved to try to fill the vacuum left by the Syrian withdrawal. The government was stymied, however, by the continued opposition of President Lahoud and by the reluctance of Hizbullah and other opposition parties to support the March 14 agenda.

The situation was overtaken by the events of July 2006 when a border raid by Hizbullah on an Israeli patrol led to Israeli retaliation and an all-out Israeli attempt to cripple Hizbullah. The war lasted for thirty-three days and devastated much of south Lebanon and the southern suburbs of Beirut. Hizbullah, however, fought Israeli forces to a standstill in many areas and continuously fired rockets into northern Israel. The United States had encouraged Israel to escalate and prolong the attack, seeing it as an opportunity to deal a knockout blow to what some US officials considered "the A-team" of terrorism. The Lebanese government tried from the beginning to convince the UN Security Council to call for a cease-fire, but the United States delayed the move, hoping to give Israel enough time to achieve its goals. As devastation mounted and world public opinion rallied, and as it became clear that Israel was failing to achieve its objectives, the United States relented, and a cease-fire was negotiated. The terms were announced in UNSCR 1701 issued on August 11. The resolution called for the cessation of hostilities, the deployment of Lebanese army troops to the South, the expansion of the United Nations Interim Force in Lebanon (UNIFIL), the disarming of nonstate armed groups, and the stopping of cross-border arms smuggling. Hizbullah described the war as a "divine victory," but it resulted in a new buffer zone in the South, manned by a ten-thousand-strong multinational force and even more Lebanese army troops. Although Hizbullah is present (covertly) in this zone, the buffer has helped to maintain calm on the border until the present day.

Internal tensions in Lebanon escalated again after the war. Hizbullah had accused March 14 leaders of siding with the United States, and March 14 leaders accused Hizbullah of triggering the devastating war by their ill-timed cross-border raid of July 12. Tensions especially mounted over the issue of the special tribunal to investigate the Hariri killing. Shi'i ministers withdrew from the government in November 2006 over the way in which the tribunal issue was presented to the government, and this ushered in an open-ended stalemate. This tense situation continued into May 2008. On May 6, the government issued two decisions: one, to remove the head of security at Beirut International Airport, who was close to Hizbullah; and the other, to investigate Hizbullah's private communications network. Hizbullah interpreted this as a direct threat. Two days later, its fighters overran the capital in a matter of hours and besieged the March 14-led government.

Various mediation efforts led to meetings in Qatar, and the negotiation of the Doha Agreement. The agreement called for a cessation of hostilities; the election of a new president, army chief Michel Suleiman; the formation of a thirty-member National Unity government; the holding of parliamentary elections; and the resumption of "national dialogue" talks to discuss the relationship between the state and the armed resistance. The events of May underlined Hizbullah's military dominance in the country, and the Doha Agreement enshrined a new precedent: that if any of the main sectarian communities resigned from the government, then that government would be considered unconstitutional. This would further weaken central authority and strengthen the veto power of major sectarian parties over any government decision-making.

Suleiman was elected president in May 2008, a National Unity government was formed, and parliamentary elections were held in June 2009. In a closely fought contest, the March 14 coalition managed to secure a 71-seat majority. Saad Hariri, son of the late Rafik al-Hariri and leader of the coalition, was designated premier, and another National Unity government was formed in which power was shared between the two rival coalitions and the president.

In his first days in office, Saad Hariri made a historic visit to Damascus—this, after having repeatedly and publicly held Syria directly responsible for his father's assassination. The visit came after Saudi King Abdallah's visit to Syria and after Europe and the United States had started rebuilding their relations with Syria. Hariri's erstwhile ally, Walid Jumblatt, who had accused the Syrians of killing his own father, Kamal Jumblatt, had also made amends with the Syrians earlier that year.

The Hariri government did not last long. Differences between Hariri and Hizbullah over the Special Tribunal for Lebanon (STL) and other issues soured the relationship, and as Syria and Hizbullah felt on the ascendant, they used their influence to topple Hariri's government on January 12, 2011, and replace it with one more to their liking. Najib Mikati, formerly aligned with Hariri, broke away and accepted the prime ministerial nomination, this one with a March 8 majority and no participation from March 14 members. The coalitional spirit of the Doha agreement had crumbled.

The uprising in Tunisia had begun weeks prior to Hariri's removal from office, but few recognized that this was the beginning of a general Arab awakening that would spread throughout the region and soon take root in Syria. Initially, Lebanon avoided the shock waves of the Arab Spring. Arab protestors were generally militating to bring down a dictator and establish freedom and constitutional democracy. Lebanon had no dictatorship to bring down, and it already had a wide margin of political freedom and a constitutional democratic system—despite its many faults. In another interpretation, Lebanon had already had its Arab Spring in 2005, when a vast cross-section of the Lebanese public had flooded the streets to demand, and achieve, the withdrawal of Syrian forces.

A small civil society protest movement did emerge in early 2001, picking up the themes of the Arab Spring and demanding an end to the confessional political system. The movement persisted for several months but failed to spark wider national sympathies.

SURVIVING THE SYRIAN CIVIL WAR: 2011–2018

The Syrian civil war put enormous strain on Lebanon. On the political track, Lebanon witnessed continued government instability. When protests began and then spread in Syria, PM Mikati announced an official government policy of "dissociation" from the conflict; despite his coalition partner—Hizbullah—funneling support and troops to the Assad side in Syria. By the end of 2011, it was clear that the situation in Syria had morphed into the beginnings of an armed civil war, dividing the country along sectarian lines and drawing in regional and international proxy supporters. Rising casualties in Syria were exacerbating tension between Sunnis and Shi'a in Lebanon, and this was taking its toll on Mikati's own government. In May of 2013, Hizbullah leader Nasrallah publicly declared that Hizbullah was offering full support to Assad in Syria. This and other tensions led Mikati to submit his government's resignation in late May 2013.

A somewhat independent figure from the March 14 camp, Tammam Salam, was named to form a new government. After ten months of negotiations, Salam finally announced the formation of a national coalition government in February 2014 that included members from both March 8 and March 14, who now realized that the conflict next door would take much longer than initially expected. March 8 did not want sectarian tensions in Lebanon to erupt and distract them from the war in Syria, so they wanted March 14 leaders back in the fold. March 14 leaders, realizing that the Syrian crisis would be a long one, did not want to be out of power. They also did not want to see the sectarian fighting next door lead to an armed clash with Shi'a in Lebanon or to allow radical Sunnis to gain ground in Lebanon's Sunni areas. Indeed, the head of the March 14 movement, Saad Hariri, returned to Lebanon in August 2014 to shore up moderate support among the Sunni community and launch a political dialogue with Hizbullah.

In the meantime, however, the political system continued to decay. Parliamentary elections scheduled for June 2013 were postponed for a year and then again to 2017. The presidency subsequently fell vacant with the end of Michel Suleiman's term in May 2014. But after twenty-nine months of political deadlock, the various parties settled on electing Michel Aoun in October 2016. Saad Hariri was named back to the Prime Ministry and formed another national unity government with the March 14 and March 8 coalitions and Hizbullah.

But after the election of President Donald Trump in the United States and the rise of Crown Prince Muhammad bin Salman in Saudi Arabia, Hizbullah's coexistence within Lebanon came under external pressure. In a bizarre development, Prime Minister Hariri was summoned to Saudi Arabia in November 2017 and forced to read a letter of resignation, denouncing Hizbullah and Iran. The episode caused an uproar among both supporters and opponents of Hariri in Lebanon as blatant interference in Lebanese affairs and was also denounced by the United States, France, and Egypt. The Saudis backed down, and Hariri returned to Lebanon to a wounded hero's welcome.

After nine years, parliamentary elections were finally held in May 2018, under a new election law that featured proportional representation. Hariri's broad Future Movement was arguably the biggest electoral loser, and the Hizbullah-dominated March 8 coalition came out with a majority. Since that time, Hezbollah has used this parliamentary majority to dominate all branches of government. Despite his electoral losses, a chastened Hariri was once again designated to form a government, a process that took eight months to conclude and resulted in Hizbullah's continuingly strong political influence.

CRISIS AND COLLAPSE: 2019–PRESENT

The economic Ponzi scheme that started rapidly unraveling in 2019 was long in the making. Beginning in the early 1990s, Lebanon's leading postwar Prime Minister, Rafik Hariri, had—perhaps correctly—decided that Lebanon's postwar reconstruction and revival would require some measure of deficit financing and debt accumulation. With almost no previous debt and the expectation that postwar economic growth and the return of expat money to the country could carry and then pay down this debt, his policy was not unreasonable. But a major and sustained postwar boom never materialized, as Hezbollah and its Iranian and Syrian backers maintained an on-again off-again conflict with Israel that precluded the conditions for a major boom, such as that of Dubai in recent decades, or Beirut in the 1950s and 1960s.

The habits of deficit spending and debt accumulation proved hard to break long after the economic rationale for them had disappeared. Politicians were growing fat and building their patronage networks through the liberal spend-and-borrow approach; and no prime minister or government wanted to take the tough and unpopular decisions to curb spending, trim the public sector, and lift fuel subsidies in order to bring the budget and debt under control. The large private banking sector, and much of the moneyed upper classes and wealthy diaspora that held big deposits there, went along on the reckless joyride, reaping high interest rates year after year, ignoring the precipice that was drawing closer.

As the debt to GDP ratio became the third highest in the world, consuming 50 percent of government spending; and as the real economy struggled under the multiple burdens of gross corruption and mismanagement, the Syrian civil war, and targeted sanctions from the United States; the bubble burst. Between 2019 and 2021 the currency lost 90 percent of its value, the economy ground to a near halt, and banks effectively denied most depositors access to their money except in small amounts, wiping out years of savings for most. Poverty rates, once around 12 percent in Lebanon, surpassed 75 percent; unemployment skyrocketed; and electricity, fuel, and medicines or medical care have become in very short supply. The country is suffering a massive brain drain and population exodus, and even if put on the path of recovery, will take at least a decade or two to recover lost ground.

The economic unraveling triggered political movements. In October of 2019, the country erupted in the largest mass protests since 2005, demanding not only the resignation of the government but also holding all of the oligarchy responsible, chanting slogans such as "Everyone means everyone," and demanding an overall change to the political system. The Hariri government promptly resigned, and the pro-Hizbullah majority in parliament settled on a pliant political outsider, Hassan Diab, to form a supposedly 'technocratic' government to pull the country out of its economic spiral. But the Diab government simply reflected the will of the ruling majority, no part of which wanted to engage seriously with the International Monetary Fund (IMF), institute effective reforms, or put the country on a new governance trajectory.

Rather, the Diab government presided over the continued unraveling of the currency, the banking sector, the economy, and the social fabric.

On August 4, 2020, the biggest peacetime explosion of recent times detonated in a warehouse in Beirut Port, killing hundreds, wounding thousands, and devastating almost a third of the capital. The blast was caused by the storage of dangerously volatile ammonium nitrate, with the knowledge and probable complicity of Hizbullah and numerous government agencies. The explosion led to another wave of mass protest, and denunciations from around the world. The Diab government itself promptly submitted its resignation on August 10. It took 13 months and three designated prime ministers to finally form a new government. This new government, headed by two-time former prime minister Najib Mikati, was forged in September of 2021. It faces the urgent priorities of stopping the socio-economic collapse, negotiating with the IMF, and putting the country on the road to recovery.

PHOTO 16.1 Beirut, Lebanon, after the port blast on August 4, 2020.

iStockphoto.com/Hussein Kassir

SOCIETAL CHANGES AND CHALLENGES

The previous societal reality has been overtaken and transformed by the recent collapse of the economy. Lebanon, once a middle-income country, has been catapulted into poverty. And as of this writing, the country is in continuing decline, without clarity as to when a bottom will be reached. No clear data is available to measure month-to-month changes, but the World Bank estimates that a full 85 percent of the resident population might be in need of food assistance. It also reported that the severity of the Lebanese economic crisis is among the worst globally since the mid-1800s. Electricity, fuel, and medicine are in short supply, and medical services are barely functional. The once-large middle class lives in poverty, scrounging for scarce fuel, paying exorbitant private generator costs to maintain intermittent electricity, and deciding which costs to cut between schooling, housing, and food, as they seek to leave the country. Most of the previously low-income class has been pushed into abject poverty, not able to make basic ends meet, and driven to desperation and despair. Many members of the upper class have maintained access to hard currency through their own means, but even they contemplate leaving the country as basic goods and services are no longer reliably available, even to those with means. For several months, generous international and world bank cash transfer programs, which would alleviate much of this suffering, were held up due to political bickering, red tape, and the lack of a formed government. As of this writing, this relief is finally beginning to flow.

Due to this economic turmoil, transformations to social structure and dynamics are volatile and incalculable. The country is suffering a massive brain drain and an urgent exodus of anybody who can find a way out. For those stuck behind, the situation is unpredictable. Already, lawlessness and petty crime are rising dramatically and sporadic episodes of violence threaten to trigger sectarian conflict and/or the rise of armed gangs and militias throughout the country again.

The Lebanese Army and internal security forces already struggle to maintain a modicum of social stability. As the economic crisis worsens, soldiers and police officers find it more difficult to make ends meet and feed their families on the equivalent of $40 or $50 a month. The United States and the international community are channeling assistance to the army to preserve the only institution that stands between precarious stability and complete, chaotic, state collapse.

Society will take years, perhaps decades, to recover from the devastation of the Lebanese Great Collapse of 2019–2021, and the signs are not promising. Hizbullah is as strong as ever, backed by a resilient if not resurgent Iran. It has no plans of disarming and will continue to violate Lebanese sovereignty, undermine Lebanese stability, and prevent the conditions for good governance and robust economic recovery. The corrupt political class is also well-entrenched. Even while a majority of the population largely blames them for the current collapse, as people grow poorer they also grow more dependent on politicians that can provide social assistance.

It is hard to say what societal challenges Lebanon will face in 2022. It could fall into complete state failure and militia rule, in which refugee outflows and ensuring basic humanitarian support to an embattled population will be the main concerns. Or it could inch forward with a government that implements necessary initial reforms; this would enable some international aid to come into the country, and 2022 might see a slow economic recovery from record depths. For this to occur, strong support for parliamentary elections in the spring, the formation of a post-election government, and the pursuit of further economic and governance reforms would be the main priority. This would enable more rapid and robust recovery, bring unemployment and poverty levels down, and gradually transition Lebanon's dependence on international humanitarian aid to more sustainable economic growth.

Regarding other societal issues, the sectarian balance in the country remains a delicate and potentially explosive issue. The Taif Agreement settled on a 50–50 representation in parliament and government between Christians and Muslims. However, the demographic balance in the country is closer to 30–70 or 25–75. This has not translated into direct political eruption because the "Muslim majority" is actually deeply divided between Sunni and Shii communities in addition to Druze and Alawite minorities. Hezbollah and Amal politicians speak increasingly of a three-way balance between the Christian, Sunni, and Shia communities. In the wake of the Taif regime (1990–present), these individuals call for a new national pact with a 1/3-1/3-1/3 powersharing formula that would replace the previous 50–50 compromise. This new formula is known in Arabic as *muthalatha*.

Lebanon's refugee burden, the largest per capita of any country in the world, greatly adds to its challenges. The Palestinian refugees were for a long time the main refugee population, but their numbers are now dwarfed by the massive Syrian refugee population. Estimates of the Palestinian refugee population have dwindled to about 200,000; they live in squalid refugee camps, enjoy no rights to work or own property, and are outside of Lebanese government or security control. Cuts to UNRWA during the Trump administration made conditions worse for these refugees, but the agency's finances have improved in the last months. There are over one million registered Syrian refugees in the country and an estimated additional half a million that are unregistered migrants or residents. This 1.5 million burden in a country of originally only five million puts enormous strain on Lebanon's physical, energy, educational, and health infrastructure. So far, this population has not been politically mobilized, radicalized, or armed, but since they live outside of the Lebanese political system, there is always a risk that outside players might choose to mobilize them in various ways. Prospects of their return home to Syria are dim as conditions in Syria remain grim, and the Assad regime is not eager to see them come home.

The COVID crisis has exacerbated all of Lebanon's recent misfortunes. According to the World Health Organization, 13 percent of the population contracted the virus since the start of

PHOTO 16.2 The St. George Church and Al-Ameen Mosque in Downtown Beirut reflect Lebanon's religious diversity.

AP Photo/Nasser Nasser

the pandemic, over 8,000 have died, and almost half are vaccinated. When the pandemic hit, the health sector was already suffering under the weight of the economic collapse, medicines and equipment were in short supply, and the state was in a condition of near paralysis. But for many Lebanese, the pandemic—terrible as it was—was overshadowed by the collapse of their income, savings, jobs, and socio-economic prospects.

INSTITUTIONS AND GOVERNANCE

As described above, the institutions of governance are defined by the constitution of 1926 and the Taif Accord of 1989. Lebanon is a parliamentary democracy with a hybrid executive, as executive power is shared among the president, the prime minister, and the Council of Ministers as a collegial body. The further peculiarity of the system is that it fixes confessional quotas: 50/50 Christian-Muslim representation in parliament and government; equally specific subquotas for Sunnis, Shi'a, Druze, Alawites, Maronites, Greek Orthodox, Greek Catholics, Armenians, Protestants, and other minorities; and reservation of the presidency for a Maronite Christian, the prime ministership for a Sunni Muslim, and the speakership of parliament for a Shi'i Muslim. No other country in the world uses communal quotas as extensively as Lebanon does. Confessionalism is identified by many in the country as one of the main weaknesses of the system as it politicizes sectarian identities and keeps the country dangerously divided; indeed, the Taif Agreement stipulates that moving beyond political confessionalism is a national goal, and calls for the establishment of a national commission to devise a plan to do so. Taif suggests that an initial step would be to limit confessional quotas for a new Senate, who would have authority to decide only on major systemic issues (e.g., war and peace, change of constitution, or change of educational system). However such a body has not yet been established. Others defend this power-sharing system, arguing that it has sustained the most participatory system in the Arab world and provided the widest margins of political and individual freedom.

The system is dominated by a handful of sectarian political bosses. Recent parliaments have effectively been dominated by seven men: Saad Hariri, Hassan Nasrallah, Nabih Berri, Walid Jumblatt, Michel Aoun, Samir Geagea, and Suleiman Franjieh. The Lebanese system thus essentially functions as an oligarchy. When the oligarchs are in agreement, decision-making proceeds smoothly; when they are not, the government is paralyzed and disagreements translate into communal tensions or even violence.

Unlike most Arab countries, the military and the intelligence services, while influential, do not have a dominant role in government. Although several presidents have formerly been heads of the army, the armed services remain under the influence of government officials and, for better or for worse, political oligarchs.

Despite promises in the Taif agreement to strengthen the judicial branch, it remains more an arm of the executive than an independent third branch of government. The executive branch still controls appointments, promotions, and salaries within the judiciary and thus dominates it.

There are more than 1,100 municipalities in Lebanon, but the government remains highly centralized. Municipal elections are significant and free affairs that bring over 10,000 people into an elected office every six years, but municipalities have meager resources, and most of their decisions require approval from representatives of the central authority. Although the Taif Accord called for extensive administrative decentralization, this never happened. Currently, there is a draft administrative decentralization law but it is not likely to make it into parliament anytime soon as elites of the central government remain reluctant to cede resources and power to regionally elected bodies.

ACTORS, OPINION, AND PARTICIPATION

Parliamentary elections in Lebanon have been generally free and fair, but expensive: Hundreds of millions of dollars are spent in election campaigns to influence and buy votes. The election law changed in 2018 from a majoritarian block-vote system to a proportional system. The earlier system allowed powerful blocks to sweep all seats in their districts. The new law creates more varied outcomes. Nevertheless, the main oligarchic powerbrokers in the country still dominate the new parliament, and minor parties or new civil society groups score few breakthroughs.

Since the uprising of October 2019, a new political force has emerged. It is comprised of hundreds of small civil society groups and nascent political parties that are competing to mobilize and represent the hundreds of thousands of Lebanese who are opposed to the political status quo. Some of these groups have coalesced into broad coalitions and have recognized that making a strong showing in the 2022 parliamentary elections— if they indeed go ahead—requires a consolidation of effort and a pooling of potential voters. This nascent movement represents the potential for some measure of long-term political change in the country. Much will depend on its ability to further coalesce, present a coherent and convincing message, and put forward credible leaders both for parliamentary elections and national leadership.

Nevertheless, the main political actors in the country remain the principal sectarian parties. Among the Shi'a, Hizbullah is the dominant party, led by Hassan Nasrallah, followed by the allied Amal movement, led by parliament speaker Nabih Berri. A "third way" among the Shi'a, led by a coalition of leftist, secular, and old-family leaders, had a significant presence in the 1990s but since then has largely faded away.[15] Since 2019, there has been a small but growing set of voices and activists within the Shiite community that oppose Hezbollah and Amal's corrupt monopoly on Shiite voice and representation. In the Sunni community, the Future Movement established by Rafik al-Hariri and now led by his son, Saad, still holds the primary position although there are also significant rival politicians. In the Druze community, Walid Jumblatt and his Progressive Socialist Party enjoy a permanent majority based on old, semifeudal family loyalties. The Arslan wing, led by Talal Arslan, enjoys a permanent minority. In the Christian (mainly Maronite) community, leadership is more divided. Michel Aoun's Free Patriotic Movement is the largest single group, but its strength has receded since 2019. It competes for power with the Lebanese Forces led by Samir Geagea and the Kataib Party currently led by Sami Gemayel. They also share power in the North with Suleiman Franjieh, who has his own power base. The Syrian Social Nationalist Party is one of the few older parties—along with the Lebanese Communist Party—that does not have a sectarian basis. It has enjoyed support from the Syrian regime and has frequently had representatives in parliament and government.

It should be noted that almost all the post-2019 civil society and political groups are established on a non-sectarian—indeed often anti-sectarian—basis.

Today, Hizbullah is the most powerful political player. It is stronger than the Lebanese army, and since the election of its ally Michel Aoun to the presidency in 2017, and its coalition's success in the 2018 parliamentary elections, it has gained overall dominance over the Lebanese state. Its allies or clients have controlled the presidency, the office of speaker of parliament, and dominate the selection and tenure of any prime minister. But with power comes blame: as the socio-economic system collapsed and a large cross-section of the population rose up in 2019, many directly blamed Hezbollah for the collapse of the country while Hezbollah's leader, Hassan Nasrallah—once enjoying a taboo against criticism—was vilifed.

Civil society has been vibrant and continuous in Lebanon. The country has a liberal law of association, and several thousand nongovernmental organizations (NGOs). Some of these are service providers, receiving funds from the government or international sources to provide needed social or humanitarian services; others are communally based NGOs organizing activities and providing services with funding and guidance from local or religious authorities. The number of NGOs increased dramatically after the uprising in 2019, taking on a political orientation. The port blast of August 2020 further spurred civil society growth, especially in humanitarian relief and reconstruction.

Although new media presents new challenges, Lebanon has among the oldest and freest presses in the Arab world. It also has a plethora of private television and radio stations most of which are aligned with one party or another. Since the Syrians left, official censorship is virtually nonexistent, and one can find almost any opinion expressed somewhere. However, the media sector is heavily influenced by Lebanon's sectarian power structure. Television is the most powerful medium of opinion formation, but most stations belong to a particular confessional party or leadership and express those particular political points of view. Newspapers have declined dramatically in influence with the rise of satellite television and social media, and even there, some of the main newspapers belong to particular political parties or bosses. In recent years, the Internet, social networking sites, Twitter, and the like, have taken off, becoming public spaces where people—especially young people—communicate and interact. It is on these new media platforms that the uprising of October 2019, and the mobilization and activism by the new civic opposition took place.

RELIGION AND POLITICS

Lebanese writer and philosopher Khalil Gibran wrote, "Pity the nation that has many sects but is devoid of religion." Religion has all, and nothing, to do with politics in Lebanon. The political system is set up mainly along the contours of religious communities, but religion is largely a marker of political identity, not a core part of politics. The politics of the country still resemble the nature of politics in most other societies: a scramble for who gets what, when, and how. The majority of parties and leaders over the past century, from all communities, have run on various secular programs: nationalist, leftist, rightist, or even sectarian. Almost none have had overtly religious program agendas.

The exception has been a minority of Islamist parties in the Sunni community, and Hizbullah, but the latter is an exception of a different type. It has merged an overtly religious program with a political and military one. Whether religion is merely being used to serve a political and strategic objective or whether religion is at the core of its mission, I will leave for discussions elsewhere, but from its name (the Party of God) to its allegiance to the Velayat-e Faqih, the supreme leader of the Islamic Republic of Iran, Hizbullah has introduced a new form of religious politics into Lebanon and the Levant in general.

POLITICAL ECONOMY

As discussed earlier, the historic, multilayer collapse of the Lebanese economy since 2019 has been, by global standards, one of the worst seen anywhere in the past century and a half. Over two years, almost 40 percent of GDP along with the deposits and savings of several generations has largely been lost. The economy has ground to a halt, and the ranks of the poor, hungry, and unemployed have swelled dramatically.

Prior to the current collapse, Lebanon was a middle-income country with a GDP equivalent to $51.8 billion.[16] Services of various types (including banking, insurance, advertising, and trade) accounted for more than 70 percent of GDP, with industry and agriculture accounting for approximately 21 percent and 6 percent, respectively; imports exceeded exports by a margin of seven to one. The economy's main burden was the national debt, which stood at around $81 billion, or 157.3 percent of GDP.

It is hard to predict what the shape of the post-collapse economy will look like. On the one hand, the low pricing of labor and the inability to import at past levels should encourage investment back into the country and should also encourage some sectors like agriculture and manufacturing to make up for lost imports. On the other hand, the governance, transport, and energy sectors remain so poor that serious investment and growth will remain deeply hampered.

Lebanon's first steps toward stopping its backward slide and beginning to pivot toward recovery depend on engaging in talks with the IMF, implementing a serious economic reform program, and consequently unleashing billions of dollars of aid from the international community, as well as private investor money, which can then begin to see opportunity in a post-collapse recovery.

REGIONAL AND INTERNATIONAL RELATIONS

Over the past half-century, particularly since the civil war of 1975, leading parties of different communities in Lebanon have generally pursued different foreign policies. The Sunnis have traditionally had a special relationship with Saudi Arabia, although that has evaporated in recent years. The Christians have leaned toward close relations with France and the West. In the Shiite community, Hizbullah is fully aligned with Iran, and the Amal movement has had to remain close to the Iranian and Syrian orbits. The Druze leader Walid Junblatt has been the most mercurial, swinging between pro- and anti-Syrian positions, and using his small bloc in parliament to sway decisions in one direction or the other.

Differences over foreign policy were a major bone of contention in the 1930s and again in the 1950s, 1970s, and beyond. The National Pact of 1943 included an agreement over foreign policy in which the Christians would relinquish French protection in exchange for the Muslims relinquishing demands for unity with Syria or a larger Arab state. In the 1950s, differences between the pro-US Chamoun government and the pro-Nasser opposition led to a brief civil war. In the 1970s, disagreements over the Palestinian movement split the country again. During the civil war, the sides were divided over the roles of Syria, Israel, the United States, and others. The Taif Accord sought to settle the issue by declaring that Lebanon would coordinate with Syria on foreign policy. However, when relations with Syria soured after Hariri's assassination, tensions resumed. The March 14 coalition had strong relations with Saudi Arabia and the United States, and the March 8 alliance collaborated with Syria and Iran. During the height of the George W. Bush years, the regional confrontation among these states dramatically escalated tensions in Lebanon. Disagreements over foreign policy threatened to escalate tensions again during the Syrian civil war. The government tried to maintain an official policy of "dissociation." But as the Assad-Iran-Russia axis has gained the upper hand in Syria, Lebanon has fallen once again under stronger Syrian-Iranian sway.

Internal Conflict

In a way, Lebanon's political system is predicated on the enduring risk of internal conflict. The Taif Agreement was written to end a long civil war and prevent another one from erupting. The Syrians who dominated Lebanon from 1990 to 2005 exploited internal divisions to consolidate their rule. Sectarian elites today justify their monopolization of power—both within their communities and the central government—as a bulwark against the threat of sectarian violence or a return to civil war. Yet Lebanon managed almost three decades of relative post-1990 internal peace, even as countries next door disintegrated into sectarian and ethnic civil war. But as the economy has cratered since 2019, the despair and desperation of a large cross cross-section of the population is threatening this social stability and could lead to violence and chaos.

Lebanon has been affected by spillovers of the Syrian conflict. The main breach was in the northeastern Bekaa border area of Arsal. ISIS and Jubhat al-Nusra fighters set up an armed enclave there until the Lebanese army—which received support from the British and Americans—drove them out in August 2017. The army has been instrumental in preventing full state failure, but as its soldiers' pay dwindles into insignificance, many have deserted, and the army's capacity to hold the line is being tested.

The Lebanese armed forces have certainly not been able to curb Hizbullah. When Hizbullah fighters took over the capital in May 2018, armed forces stood idly by; as Hizbullah streamed fighters across the Lebanese-Syrian border to wage war in Syria, against the express policy of the government, the armed forces also did nothing. The hard reality is that if they tried, the army would likely split along sectarian lines, and the country would be driven back into civil war.

CONCLUSION

After a troubled century since its founding, the Lebanese Republic is at an existential low point. The state lacks sovereignty over its borders or territory. Hizbollah, which owes allegiance to Iran, dominates the security and political landscape. A corrupt political class has thrived within this arrangement enriching itself and building its sectarian networks, and the economy—which had survived external wars, civil wars, and previous global recessions—has fully collapsed.

The country's immediate future is deeply uncertain. It might fall into full state failure and militia proliferation like Libya, Somalia, parts of Syria, or 1975–1990 Lebanon, and not recover for decades. Or, the oligarchy could manage to keep it away from the brink, introducing just enough minimal changes and reforms to bring back a trickle of aid and recovery. A positive scenario would be for the new opposition that has arisen since 2019 to do well in the upcoming parliamentary elections and introduce a much-needed reform. But in all cases, the country's immediate future is grim. Hizbullah will remain heavily armed and beholden to Iran, the country's immediate neighborhood—between Syria and Israel—will remain volatile, the economic infrastructure will take years to rebuild, and the emergence of a new political culture, new political parties, and new leadership will require a slow, sustained, and focused effort.

SUGGESTED READINGS

Blanford, Nicholas. *Warriors of God: Inside Hezbollah's Thirty-Year Struggle Against Israel.* New York, NY: Random House, 2011.

El Khazen, Farid. *The Breakdown of the State in Lebanon, 1967–1976.* Cambridge, MA: Harvard University Press, 2001.

Hanf, Theodor, and Salam Nawaf, eds. *Lebanon in Limbo: Postwar Society and State in an Uncertain Regional Environment.* Baden-Baden, Germany: Nomos Verlagsgesellschaft, 2003.

Hirst, David. *Beware of Small States: Lebanon, Battleground of the Middle East.* London: Faber & Faber, 2010.

Hudson, Michael C. *The Precarious Republic: Political Modernization in Lebanon.* New York, NY: Random House, 1968.

Khalaf, Samir. *Lebanon's Predicament.* New York, NY: Columbia University Press, 1987.

Khalidi, Walid. *Conflict and Violence in Lebanon: Confrontation in the Middle East.* Cambridge, MA: Harvard Center for International Affairs, 1979.

Salibi, Kamal S. *A House of Many Mansions: The History of Lebanon Reconsidered.* London: I. B. Tauris, 1988.

Traboulsi, Fawwaz. *A History of Modern Lebanon.* London: Pluto Press, 2007.

17 LIBYA

Jacob Mundy

A decade after the upheavals of the Arab Spring, Libya's transition to a new political order continued to be undermined by various domestic and international forces. Following the violent revolution of 2011, Libya's weak and divided transitional leadership—despite holding several elections at the local and national level—failed to consolidate political power under a universally recognized central authority. In this context, the country's countless militias, who steadfastly refused to disarm after having plundered the state's vast armories in 2011, helped drive the country back into civil war in 2014. This new conflict played out against a backdrop of economic crisis: World oil prices had collapsed that year as well, depriving Libya's authorities of the means to quell an increasingly anxious population through public-sector salaries and mass subsidies on imported goods. As Libya's civil war dragged on, myriad factions vied for control over key urban spaces, pivotal economic resources, vital infrastructures, social allegiances, and sources of foreign support, both financial and military. Amid the chaos of this conflict, militants claiming allegiance to the Islamic State (*al-dawlah al-islamiyyah*)—a powerful transnational Islamist insurgency that grew out of the Syrian civil war and extended its territorial control to Iraq—managed to seize control of the coastal city of Sirte, halfway between the capital, Tripoli, and the country's second city, Benghazi, further east. Meanwhile, hundreds of refugees and migrants, facilitated by the boom in human trafficking and other illicit economic activities, attempted to cross the Mediterranean to European shores. In this context of fractured and incapacitated state institutions, no single individual, group, movement, body, military force, or ideology was able to achieve hegemony within Libya's multipolar political landscape.

For over forty years, Libyans lived under one of the Middle East's most durable regimes, that of Colonel Muammar al-Qadhafi, who came to power in a military coup in 1969. Since that regime's demise in 2011, it has been impossible to restore central authority. For decades, the political system in Libya seemed to be one of the most indelibly "personalist" yet consistently opaque to the outside world. Now, Libya's countless factions seem to be tearing the country apart, albeit with assistance from outside interests in the Middle East and further afield. How then to explain this discrepancy? How could a country that seemed so politically static and centralized for so long instantly become one of the world's most disconcertingly conflictual and fragmented in recent years? Had NATO and the Arab League, through their military intervention on the side of the rebels in 2011, unleashed implacable sociopolitical forces and an untamable war economy? At one level, the answer lies in the failed transitional period (2012–2014); at another, it is the legacies of the various social, political, and economic mechanisms of rule the al-Qadhafi regime used to maintain order. Finally, any account of Libya's current disarray also has to contend with the historically impoverished foundations of the state dating back to the periods of Ottoman and Italian rule, as well as the period after independence in 1951 under King Idris of the Sanusi order, a monarch installed by Libya's British and American patrons who had occupied the country during World War II.

HISTORY OF STATE-BUILDING

The history of modern efforts to assert or construct state power in Libya can be roughly divided into five periods: Ottoman (1551–1911), including periods of Karamanli rule in the West and the Sanusi rule in the East; Italian (1911–1943), immediately followed by an international protectorate (1945–1951); independent state-building under the Sanusi Monarchy (1951–1969); the al-Qadhafi regime (1969–2011); and the post-Qadhafi transition from 2011 to now. Throughout this chapter, we will examine the relationship between the first four periods of state-making and the latest phase of state-*unmaking*.

Several sociogeographical features of Libya, as well as the disruptive violence of foreign rule, have historically impeded the country's development. Whereas neighboring Tunisia enjoyed a smaller landmass, ample terrain for cultivation, and a history of centralized state-building, Libya has had the opposite conditions working against it. Ottoman and

MAP 17.1 ■ Libya

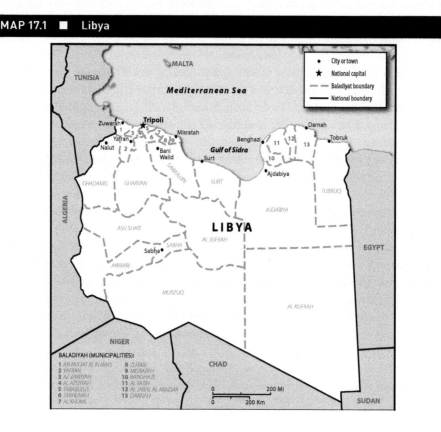

European imperialism had the opposite effect on Libya as well: Whereas Turkish (1574–1881) and French (1881–1956) rule helped to reinforce Tunisian political institutions, foreign dominion tended to preempt or disrupt what nascent state-building projects existed in Libya prior to 1951.

The territory that would become Libya is roughly equal in size to Iran and Sudan, yet it has never boasted a commensurate population. In terms of agriculture, water, and other resources (excluding oil), Libya's natural endowments were meager. The country's three main regions correspond with major population centers where simple agricultural livelihoods were historically eked out: the coast and hills of Cyrenaica in the East, the plains and mountains of Tripolitania in the West, and the Saharan oases of Fezzan in the Southwest. What might be considered Libya's fourth region, Kufra in the Southeast, was as historically associated with the populations in the unforgiving deserts of Sudan and Egypt as it was with the people of Cyrenaica.

KEY FACTS ON LIBYA

AREA 679,359 square miles (1,759,540 square kilometers)

CAPITAL Tripoli

POPULATION 7,017,224; includes 842,070 nonnationals (2019 est.)

PERCENTAGE OF POPULATION UNDER 25 48.86

RELIGIOUS GROUPS (PERCENTAGE) Sunni Muslim, 97; other, 3 (includes Christian, Buddhist, Hindu, Jewish, folk religion, unaffiliated, and other)

ETHNIC GROUPS (PERCENTAGE) Berber and Libyan Arab, 97; other, 3 (includes Greek, Maltese, Italian, Egyptian, Pakistani, Turkish, Indian, Tunisian)

OFFICIAL LANGUAGE Arabic; English is commonly spoken in major cities as a preferred second language; Berber is the native language to populations in the Nafusa Mountains and among Tuaregs of the Sahara.

TYPE OF GOVERNMENT Republic governed by UN-recognized, interim transitional authority established in the 2015 Libyan Political Agreement

DATE OF INDEPENDENCE December 24, 1951 (from UN trusteeship)

GDP $102.84 billion (2019); $15,174 per capita (2019)

PERCENTAGE OF GDP BY SECTOR Agriculture, 1.3; industry, 52.3; services, 46.4

TOTAL RENTS (PERCENTAGE OF GDP) FROM NATURAL RESOURCES 44.64

FERTILITY RATE 3.13 children born/woman (2021 est.)

Sources: CIA. "The World Factbook." August 4, 2022, https://www.cia.gov/the-world-factbook/. World Bank. "International Comparison Program (ICP)." Accessed August 10, 2022, https://databank. worldbank.org/source/icp-2017.

Under Ottoman rule, Libya—mainly Tripolitania and Fezzan—only experienced brief periods of stable, centralized, and coordinated governmental authority. Istanbul's dominion over Libya was also marked by efforts to dismantle domestic networks of social power. The growing machinery of modern governance (e.g., coercive taxation and land regulation) was either monopolized by foreign elites or hoarded by comprador classes (i.e., Libyans who acted on the behalf of foreigners to facilitate the country's political subjugation and economic exploitation). What periods of governmental stability Ottoman Libya experienced were frequently interrupted by global conflict, local revolutions, and other cataclysmic events that left new rulers essentially starting from scratch amid struggles to define the country's true political and geographical center(s) of power.

Italy entered the great imperial game in North Africa decades later than its competitors to the east (Britain in Egypt) and west (France in Algeria and Tunisia). Regardless of the meager recognition Italy had initially afforded indigenous Libyan leaders to win their support against the Ottomans, Rome's conquest of Tripolitania from 1911 onward gradually treated Libya as a blank slate, imposing its own political, social, and economic systems. Direct administration and territorial annexation of *Libia Italiana* also went hand-in-hand with settler colonialism so as to accelerate the territory's total incorporation into the Italian mainland from 1921 onward. These trends required mass dispossession of Libyan-held lands, resulting in significant violent conflict that reached genocidal levels of ethnic cleansing. The modern territory of Libya also began to take shape as French and British concessions in the Fezzan and Kufra, respectively, demarcated the country's current borders. A controversial concession to Italy was the Aouzou Strip along the Libya–Chad border, which was then retaken by the French after World War II and given to Chad at independence, thus planting the irredentist seeds of the Libyan–Chad war of the 1970–1980s.

After World War II and the collapse of Italian fascism, there was almost no state for King Idris to inherit. Qualified technocrats were rare, and the country's limited physical infrastructure was in a dismal state after the war. Even the most basic prerequisites for strong state rule—such as taxation and monopoly of violence—were lacking. With little means to incentivize cooperation or to make credible threats of force, King Idris faced steep challenges. As a dynastic order based largely in Cyrenaica, the Sanusi monarchy did not enjoy support from all Libyans, notably in Tripolitania. As the regime grew increasingly suspicious of its opponents and more dependent on the Anglo-American presence, it actively refused to build certain elements of a functioning state for fear of creating competent opponents in either the bureaucracy, the military, or civil society. This trend—regime-building at the expense of state-building—was amplified by the growing oil wealth in the 1960s. As petrodollars poured into the country, corruption became rampant and effectively routinized under the Sanusi regime's systems of public and private patronage.

Independent Libya's first constitution ostensibly created a federal monarchy with an elected bicameral parliament. The national government was given basic state functions: defense, diplomacy, currency, and resolving interregional disputes via a supreme court. The three regions otherwise enjoyed significant autonomy. Though federalism in the United Kingdom of Libya had aimed to counter the demographic and developmental advantages held by a rapidly urbanizing

Tripolitania, this trifurcated state inevitably reinforced regional tensions while impeding the efforts of the Sanusi regime to consolidate power through control over the country's burgeoning oil wealth. With little popular opposition, King Idris declared the end of the "United Kingdom" of Libya in 1963, nullifying each region's legislative and judicial systems. The country's territory was reassigned into ten districts (*al-muqata'at*) with royally appointed administrators overseen by the Central Interior Ministry. This redistricting conveniently helped expedite oil concessions that would have otherwise been disputed between the three regions.[1]

Meanwhile, the extended royal household (*Diwan*) of the Sanusis became the real center of power. As a neo-patrimonial network penetrating the government, the bureaucracy, the military, markets, and the polity, the agents of the *Diwan* worked to enhance the uncontested supremacy of the monarchy within the political system. This was facilitated by the regime's tendency to disperse national oil revenues on an increasingly *ad hoc* basis to appease clients, allies, and other constituents irrespective of previous national development plans. Even in the realm of security, tribal militias were more central to the security of the Sanusi monarchy than the actual police and army. At the time of the 1969 coup, the national army numbered 6,500 men, whereas the royal guards—fighters donated from loyal Cyrenaican allies—were the most competent security force in the country, second perhaps only to the monarchy's 1,600 British military advisors.[2]

Growing public discontent with Sanusi rule easily paved the way for the September 1969 coup. The years that followed under Al-Qadhafi can be divided into four periods of state development: quasi-constitutional rule under a single party (1969–1977); the early years of the *Jamahiriyyah* (1977–1988); the decay of the *Jamahiriyyah* system from 1988 onward; and then the failed transition to neoliberal authoritarianism in the first decade of the 2000s.

Similar to other revolutionary republics across the Middle East and North Africa (MENA), the leaders of the 1969 military coup, the Revolutionary Command Council (RCC), envisioned Libya under a kind of single-party state. This party, the Arab Socialist Union (ASU), was heavily modeled after the kind of centralized, authoritarian rule instituted in Nasser's in Egypt. Political debate, social grievance, and economic expectations would be channeled through the *internal* politics of the party rather than through multiple rival parties. And as in Iraq and Algeria, control over plentiful oil revenues provided the wherewithal in Libya to resist civil challenges and meet constituent demands. An important task for the RCC was first to invent the ideological legitimacy and the popular basis of its domestic and international initiatives, a task that would largely fall on the shoulders of the charismatic leader of the coup, al-Qadhafi.

In order to reengineer state–society relations, redistricting was one of the first major policies of the RCC, one that targeted the social basis of Sanusi rule by fracturing the political geography of the unitary Kingdom. Though these changes seemed to constitute one of the first assaults of the RCC on "tribalism" and the Sanusi politics of personal and familial rule, they ostensibly paved the way for the creation of a modern and impersonal bureaucracy. In reality, the revolutionary state was instead being purged of experienced administrators so as to be replaced by those who demonstrated the most enthusiasm for the revolution.

Yet not even the ASU—nor many of al-Qadhafi's colleagues in the RCC—would survive the thoroughgoing nature of the revolution outlined in al-Qadhafi's *The Green Book*, published in the mid-1970s. In this new phase of the revolution, governmental decision-making, administration, the economy, and ultimately sovereignty would be devolved to Basic Popular Congresses (*mu'tamar sha'bi 'asasi*) across the country. This new state, the *Jamahiriyyah* (often translated as "state of the masses"), was formally declared in 1977, a year after the first General People's Congress (*mu'tamar al-sha'bi al-'am*), the annual meeting where the will of all the congresses was supposedly brought to the national stage. From this point onward, Libya operated without a constitution. "The revolution" was the polity's new compass, to be guided by the Revolutionary Committees, the RCC, and particular revolutionary personalities, al-Qadhafi chief among them, as a revolutionary "guide" (*murshid*). Given the absence of a constitution, administrative codes, and written laws (even some of the core institutions of the *Jamahiriyyah* were not mentioned in *The Green Book*), Libyan lawyers and judges were often forced to look to Ottoman, Italian, and UN documents to find precedents or a textual basis for legal opinions and rulings.

On paper, the foundation of government and administration were the Basic Popular Congresses (over four hundred of them), convened every four months at the level of the municipality (*al-baladiyyah*) to discuss local affairs and national debates. All adult Libyans belonged to the Congress in addition to local worker associations. Local administration, drawn from the base congresses, was the purview of People's Committees (*al-lajnah al-sha'biyyah*). In 1988, twenty-six provincial-level districts (*al-sha'biyyah*) were added to this system to handle more regional-level issues, though these operated in the same way as the municipal-level congresses. The General People's Congress was the forum where the will of the base congresses was brought to a national level, and its executive, the General Popular Committee (*al-lajnah al-sha'biyyah al-'ammah*), functioned as a kind of ministerial council. That the *Jamahiriyyah* actually represented a real example of direct democracy was belied by poor participation rate, reportedly never surpassing 25 percent. The real state, as most Libyans knew quite well, was the parallel—and far more powerful—institutions of the Revolutionary Committees, the RCC, and ultimately al-Qadhafi and those close to him.[3]

Libya's once-feeble security sector initially benefited the most from the 1969 revolution, as the country went on an arms buying spree in the 1970s. Other sectors of the bureaucracy also ballooned as the government quickly became the dominant employer. The regime was nonetheless always careful to prevent the emergence of effective opposition from within the government or the military. In coordination with the widespread revolutionary bodies of the *Jamahiriyyah*, the intelligence services ran an extensive network of informants (*mukhabarat*) inside the country. Public executions and imprisonment for dissent (real and alleged) became commonplace from the 1970s onward. Though such overt signs of repression diminished during the final decade of the al-Qadhafi regime, it was also true that Libya's once-powerful military—after being shamed on the battlefields of Chad in the 1980s and starved by international sanctions in the 1990s—had been reduced to a mere shadow of its former Cold War glory of the 1970s. The most effective security forces in the years leading up to the 2011 Arab Spring were the elite guard units and intelligence services that catered exclusively to the al-Qadhafi family's interests and protection. Though the regime pursued efforts to address the bloated state bureaucracy, the derelict institutions of the *Jamahiriyyah*, inefficient markets, and its own human rights failings, these piecemeal and superficial reforms only convinced many Libyans that they had no choice but to revolt against the regime in 2011.

THE POLITICAL ECONOMY OF DEVELOPMENT

The challenges of state-building and economic development in Libya have always had to confront the country's austere geography, which has historically only been able to support a relatively small population. Libya was in fact one of the world's poorest countries in 1951, and its prospects for development were abysmal. As Libya's population grew rapidly in the wake of independence and the 1960s oil boom, the country became more and more dependent on imports, particularly food, to sustain its growth. According to the World Bank, Libya is only able to support farming on less than 9 percent of the land. By contrast, its North African neighbors—Morocco (68 percent), Sudan (47 percent), Tunisia (64 percent), and Algeria (17 percent)—boast a much stronger agricultural base. Though Egypt supports a population of over eighty million with less than 4 percent of its land being agriculturally viable, the key difference is the Nile. In Libya, there are no perennial rivers, and rainfall patterns have become increasingly unpredictable over the previous century.

The extension of Ottoman control over Libya from the mid-16th century onward not only facilitated the Empire's projection of military power in the southern and western Mediterranean but it was also motivated by the economic benefits to be gained from taxing shipping and trans-Saharan trade, particularly its major downstream terminal like Tripoli. The burdens of rule—taxation, appeasing clients, suppressing revolts—were largely outsourced to local deputies, while the metropole enjoyed all the benefits. At the height of the trans-Saharan trade, largely propelled by slavery and gold, there were three major trade routes through the Sahara to the Libyan coast: two western routes through Fezzan to Tripoli (originating in the central and western Sahara) and an eastern route to Benghazi via Kufra, connecting Lake Chad and the eastern Sahel to the Mediterranean. Yet the latter half of the 1800s then saw the end of the international slave trade and the emergence of European colonial possessions in sub-Saharan Africa, which further undermined the need for trans-Saharan caravans.[4] The decimation of the trans-Saharan trade devastated Ottoman Libya. The traditional merchant classes of the coastal cities and Saharan way stations were particularly undermined by the decline, as were populations all along the established routes. By the end of that century, the Ottoman presence was criticized domestically and internationally for its economic mismanagement, if not outright neglect.

Rome's economic interest in Libya had almost nothing to do with providing Libyans with a better life. Instead, Libya was a place to send Italy's growing population, which would keep them in the Italian national market and thus provide a beneficial alternative to migration to North America. Though the new Italian rulers of Libya were quick to highlight the alleged benefits of their governance, colonialism entailed the wholesale destruction of communities and their traditional modes of economic survival. Yet Libya was never as important to the Italian economy as Algeria was to the French or Egypt to the British. Apart from Libya's symbolic geo-political value, which ostensibly signaled Italy's standing as a major European power, the Italian government was pouring far more resources into Libya than it was getting out of it by the 1930s. Massive outlays were required to subsidize the settler population, the colony's infrastructural requirements, and to maintain a secure order in a territory nearly six times the size of Italy. By the end of the 1930s, there were some 40,000 Italian troops in Libya as the storm clouds of global war loomed. Indeed, one of the largest "development" projects was the great *Litoranea*, a highway connecting Tunisia and Egypt via Tripoli and Benghazi. Finished just in time for World War II, some decried the project as Hitler's highway to the Suez Canal.[5]

Upon Libya's independence, international financial institutions, along with Britain and France, frequently questioned the newly formed state's viability. The World Bank and the International Monetary Fund were keen to help jump-start the Libyan economy in the 1950s, but domestic expertise and institutions—both public and private—were sorely lacking. Libya's major export in the early 1950s was scrap metal from the battlefields of World War II.[6] Italian-run plantations remained a cornerstone of the Tripolitanian economy, by far the wealthiest and most developed of Libya's three regions. The bloody insurgency of the 1920s and the battles of World War II had done much to set Cyrenaica even further behind. The lack of significant industrial production in Libya or migrant Libyan industrial labor in Italy inhibited the growth of indigenous economic classes beyond agriculture, merchants, rentiers, and the bureaucracy. Meanwhile, French and British aid to their Cyrenaican and Fezzani clients indirectly undermined progress by fueling corruption and the traditionalist patron–client networks that had historically ordered social, political, and economic life in Libya.

Further inhibiting coordinated development was the autonomy of the three regions; their individual development plans often trumped national ones. Regional governments would also operate on deficit spending and then look to the central government—the coffers of the Sanusi monarchy, enriched by foreign aid and, later, oil—to cover their shortfalls. Local government soon became the largest formal employer in Libya in the 1950s, yet this only accounted for less than 10 percent of the potential workforce. What little mineral and other natural resources had been explored in Libya by the 1950s were often considered economically unviable for a number of simple reasons: the distances between deposits and ports; the lack of basic infrastructure like roads, electricity, and telecommunications; and prevailing global market prices.

For these and other reasons, the Sanusi monarchy was obliged to live off the patronage of the British and, increasingly, the United States, both of which maintained military bases in Libya. In the mid-1950s, this aid was estimated to be US$26 million per year (the equivalent of over $200 billion in today's dollars). As the regime had done very little to develop Libya's potential since independence, it was fast becoming indebted to finance basic governmental activities. This dependency on foreign aid actually became worse as the oil economy developed from the late 1950s onward. By 1963, oil accounted for over 98 percent of the country's exports, most of that being processed by British and US firms. The Sanusi regime was thus not only dependent upon London and Washington for direct economic and political support but also their oil firms' technological support as well. Though oil was a major source of industrial jobs in Libya (albeit indirectly more than directly), Libya's middle and professional classes were still minuscule. Oil did not result in a radical transformation of state–society relations as much as an amplification of political and economic arrangements already in place.

Just before the 1969 coup, a World Bank economist suggested that the rapid growth experienced in Libya in the 1960s would have been unbelievable if it were presented as a hypothetical or abstract case of national development. Per capita gross national product, for example, went from nearly $40 at independence to $1,018 in 1967; between 1960 and 1969, per capita income went from $50 to $2,000. Libya's exports in 1960 (dominated by agriculture) totaled $11 million; in seven years, oil would push this figure to $1.16 billion, placing Libya among the top-ten petroleum exporters worldwide. As a consequence of this rapid growth, the skyrocketing cost of living challenged average Libyans who had yet to benefit from increased general employment or a functional welfare state. Libya went from being one of the world's poorest countries to the host of the ninth-most expensive city in the world—Tripoli—in less than two decades. In light of this crippling inflation and rising inequality, Libya was viewed as a situation of economic growth without economic development.[7]

The context of the Cold War also helps to explain Libya's rapid economic transformation. The nationalization of oil production in Iran (1951) and the Suez Canal crisis (1956) prompted North Atlantic interest in hydrocarbon resources that were closer to Europe and easier to control, places like Algeria (before independence in 1962) and Libya under the Sanusis. Washington was likewise keen to secure a stable energy base to sustain the reconstruction of Europe and the postwar economic boom. As an impoverished country, Libya could seemingly afford to sell its oil cheaply to nearby European markets and to offer acreage to international oil corporations (IOCs) at bargain prices. Of an exceptionally "light" and "sweet" quality, Libyan oil was also easy for refineries to process into high-demand transportation and heating fuels. Following the 1967 Arab–Israeli war and the closure of the Suez Canal until 1975, Libya's distance from the Levant made its oil all the more attractive.[8] The al-Qadhafi coup of 1969, however, would soon upend these efforts to find a stable source of oil and natural gas amid the growing chaos of the Cold War.

Oil transformed Libya by allowing the state and the society the ability to overcome its basic geographical and demographic challenges. The oil boom naturally saw an explosion in construction, which allowed for growth in personal and public transportation options, as well as rapid electrification. These trends drove the rapid urbanization of Tripoli and Benghazi; each saw 60 percent increases in their populations in the decade prior to 1964. In the countryside, agriculture stagnated as the government prioritized imports over domestic production, a strategy that only encouraged even more urbanization. In the early days of oil, Libya initially faced a labor shortage of highly skilled workers for most positions in oil, manufacturing, and other industries. Later, Libya faced a shortage of unskilled labor, which resulted in a significant influx of workers from neighboring countries in the Maghrib and Africa. At the same time, Libya suffered a kind of internal "brain drain" as competent, bureaucratic elites found better positions in the private sector, draining the government of important talent.[9]

The 1969 coup attempted to address the ills of Libya's oil-based economy, particularly the inequalities and corruption that had developed under the Sanusis. Recuperating lost revenues followed by outright nationalization of oil production was just the first step in the process of bringing Libya's immense natural resource wealth to heel. Al-Qadhafi's *The Green Book* not only put forward a radical image of unmediated democracy, but also imagined the end of economic relations based on markets, wages, and private property. Putting this philosophy into action first required a massive expansion of the welfare state to provide basic goods such as food and housing in the early 1970s. In the latter half of the decade, this economic program became even more radical, as "the masses" (i.e., the regime) seized assets and redistributed agricultural lands; workers were compelled into associations; Libyans were tricked into depositing all their cash and savings into the national bank in 1979, only to have their cash seized in 1981; and all imports and exports were controlled by the state in the name of a planned economy, one in which goods and services would be allocated by central authorities. In this new financial and commercial environment, informal and illegal markets began to compensate for the economy's obvious shortcomings.

If Libyans accepted these contradictions and the haphazard nature of the new regime being erected around them, this acceptance was eased by the fact that soon 75 percent of Libyans were employed by the state. Libya's oil economy quickly outgrew the size of Libya's population in the 1970s. Foreigners soon constituted 40 percent of the workforce, from simple laborers (60 percent) to skilled workers (30 percent) to professionals and the managerial class (over 50 percent). Bringing these classes into conflict was the fact that the economy eventually had a difficult time absorbing all the highly educated graduates the new school and university system was producing, resulting in an expulsion of foreign laborers in 1985 as oil prices began to fall. Though these decisions and their effects were ostensibly rooted in al-Qadhafi's ideology, they also helped to displace or dislocate traditional classes—merchants, landowners, agricultural laborers, and the like—who had been central to Ottoman, Italian, and Sanusi rule.[10]

The sustainability of this economic order was called into doubt by several developments in the 1980s: the 1985 to 1986 collapse in oil prices; military confrontations with the North Atlantic powers; a disastrous intervention in Chad; growing international isolation, especially following the Pan Am 103 and UTA 772 bombings; and the sheer absurdity of the *Jamahiriyyah* economy, such as its chronically empty state-run supermarkets. All of these developments and many more forced the regime to reconsider its approach and initiate a new period of economic "*infitah*" (opening). Direct control over trade, commerce, and production was eased in many sectors (except oil and large industry), as were some of the political mechanisms that seemed to exert an overbearing influence on the society (e.g., the Revolutionary Committees and Courts). These reforms helped the regime survive the 1990s, a decade in which there were UN sanctions, attempted coups, an Islamist insurgency, and other efforts to organize opposition to the regime domestically and abroad. That said, the regime continued to find the wherewithal to lavish its international allies with funding (for both development and conflict), to continue massive public works projects (e.g., the Great Manmade River), and to fund senseless white-elephant projects like the attempted transformation of Sirte—al-Qadhafi's home city—into a kind of Libyan Brasilia.

The slow end of international isolation following the 1999 rendering of the Lockerbie suspects and the 2003 acquiescence to other international demands helped the al-Qadhafi regime promote Libya's economic potential in the age of globalization. What the world found in Libya was a country entirely dependent on oil to subsidize a population largely employed, or otherwise supported, by the state. For the quarter of the population not employed by the government (mainly youths), options outside of informal labor and illegal markets were limited. The only advantage of the Libyan economy was the relatively low rates of poverty when compared to its African and Middle Eastern neighbors. Renewed efforts to liberalize the economy and privatize the oil sector were launched amid top-level changes in government that saw technocratic managers like Shukri Ghanem ascend. Foreign direct investment continued to gravitate entirely toward hydrocarbons as global prices picked up in the 2000s. This environment of rejuvenation was led by Libya's heir apparent, Saif Al-Islam, the British-educated eldest son of al-Qadhafi who easily spoke the international *lingua franca* of human rights, open markets, and democratic governance. The Arab Spring protests of February 2011 nonetheless revealed that the failures of the al-Qadhafi regime had been as much economic as they had been political. Even with significant cash reserves, the regime could not contain the economic shock of the late 2010 global food price spike, a shock that exploded polities across MENA.

SOCIAL CHANGE

To understand the social basis of the current crisis facing Libya, as well as the patterns of rule and resistance that narrate its history, one must understand the various constituent elements that have come to make up the complex Libyan social mosaic. Though generally characterized as an Arab state, Libya is a multiethnic polity including large numbers of Imazighen (Amazigh people, or "Berbers"), notably communities in the Nafusa mountains and western coastal plain along with the Tuaregs of the southwestern Sahara regions. Additionally, there is a sizable population of Tebu (or Toubou) on the Chadian and Sudanese border in Libya's south-central and south-eastern regions. While the Imazighen and Tebu are often described as Libya's indigenous populations given the distinct nature of their languages, the waves of Arab conquests from the 7th century onward, which brought Islam and the Arabic language to North Africa, were perhaps more cultural than demographic in nature, as recent genetic studies have suggested. Moreover, Libya has been historically embedded in civilizational struggles across the Mediterranean and the Sahara for millennia: Phoenicians, Greeks, Romans, Vandals, Byzantines, Persians, Normans, Andalucíans, Jews, Ottomans, and others have all left their marks on Libya and the Libyans, as did the Islamic empires of North and Sahelian Africa. Libya is also home to one of the great pre-Islamic civilizations of the Sahara Desert, Garamantes (ca. 3000–1300 BP), of the Fezzan region.

Though Libya is overwhelmingly a Sunni Muslim country at one level, there are notable religious differences at other levels (Sufis, Ibadis, and Ashraf families). The Turkish influence is particularly noticeable in the presence of the *Kulughli* or *Cologhli* population of Ottoman descent. The descendants of former slaves and mixed households, *shwashna*, are also present, as well as the lasting imprint of European, Christian (notably Coptic), and Jewish populations. Although the al-Qadhafi regime attempted to foster an environment of vicious anti-Semitism, there are those Libyans who recognize the profound ways in which Jewish populations contributed to Libyan history before the Arab–Israeli wars and the al-Qadhafi regime made their presence untenable.

The al-Qadhafi regime was likewise antagonistic toward the Amazigh identity, even going so far as to deny the existence of such ethnic or linguistic differences among the populations in the North. With the growth of Arab nationalism in the 20th century as a response to European imperialism, regimes across Northern Africa often downplayed or suppressed the Amazigh identity in an effort to create a homogenous political community. The Italian colonizers had, after all, attempted to exploit the various divisions within Libya, from the religious (Muslims and Jews) to the ethnic (Arabs and Imazighen), just as the French did in Morocco and Algeria.[11] The 2011 "Arab" Spring nonetheless revealed a strong Amazigh community in northern Libya, one that had helped lead the revolution against the old regime. Since then, Amazigh communities have struggled to force Libya's interim authorities to recognize their cultural rights.

Tuareg communities, by contrast, have suffered since 2011 due to their long association with al-Qadhafi, who had been a strong "supporter" of Tuareg Imazighen of the central Sahara, though this often meant his constant meddling in their affairs, across the states of Algeria, Niger, and Mali. Similarly, the al-Qadhafi regime had ambivalent relations with Libya's "black" populations, whether indigenous (e.g., Tawerghans) or migratory. Though thousands of sub-Saharan Africans found work in Libya in the 1970s and 1980s during the oil boom, many were forced to leave when Libya's economic and geopolitical fortunes turned for the worse. When the 2011 uprising erupted in February, al-Qadhafi claimed he would raise an army of African mercenaries to defeat the rebellion. Though he was unable to do so, Libya has been marked by a vicious racial politics since then, which has taken the form of an ongoing "citizenship" debate (i.e., who will benefit from the state's wealth), as well as the ethnic cleansing of 40,000 Tawerghans from their home city in 2011 and rampant human trafficking in the context of the Mediterranean migration crisis of recent years.

Though race and racism are often overlooked elements of contemporary societies in the MENA region, the question of tribes and tribalism is not. Accounts of Libya's politics, or lack thereof, often focus on its putatively tribal nature in order to understand the durability (or lack thereof) of any given sociopolitical order. A nuanced understanding of the social basis of rule in Libya must first acknowledge the fact that functional governmental institutions have often been sorely lacking throughout the modern and postcolonial history of Libya. Libya's oil wealth tended to exacerbate this problem, allowing the Sanusi and al-Qadhafi regimes to rule through informal mechanisms rather than through continuous, robust, transparent, and accountable institutions. The absence of coherent national-level governance in Libya tends to be the primary argument for the allegedly tribal nature of the society. Yet the absence of one does not necessarily prove the existence of the other. The discourse of Libyan tribalism is, moreover, confused and contradictory and often orientalist in its assumptions. It is difficult to disentangle the ostensibly fixed basis of the tribe (rooted in notions of blood and land) with the tribe's changing function across the regimes of the Ottomans, Italians, the United Nations, Sanusis, al-Qadhafi, the 2011 revolution, and the failed transition. What is important to recognize, however, is that social relations *of various kinds*, including extended kinship networks (tribes), have been reinforced by the historical and contemporary absence of meaningful central authority.

Regionalism is also presented as one of the defining aspects of Libyan society. Historically, Libya's three main regions were largely independent from each other and socially and economically oriented toward other centers of culture, power, and trade: Tripolitania toward Tunis, Cyrenaica toward Cairo, and Fezzan toward Lake Chad and the Niger River. Modern regionalism in Libya was also the result of the Ottoman state's noticeable presence in Tripolitania and the *de facto* autonomy Cyrenaica and Fezzan enjoyed. Cyrenaican identity not only grows out of a sense of an independent destiny and the traditions of the *Sanusiyyah*, but also the extensive brutality of the Italian pacification campaign of the 1920s. Both the Ottomans and Italians engaged in massive population transfer schemes and resettlement efforts that variously undermined and reinforced regionalism depending on the context of the relocation. The Sanusi monarchy, with its historical base of power in the East and the Sahara, tended to promote Cyrenaican interests (e.g., by promoting Benghazi as a co-equal capital), a trend that the al-Qadhafi regime somewhat reversed, though Tripolitania's demographic hegemony and Cyrenaican demands were balanced by al-Qadhafi's efforts to promote the region around Sirte as a new center of power. In contemporary Libya, Cyrenaican identity tends to be the most pronounced of these three regional identities, which can be witnessed in regional movements for autonomy, a return of the federalist system, and support for a restoration of the monarchy. Subregional identity groups are also important, such as the Arab and Amazigh communities of the Nafusa or the marginalized communities of the central oases whose lands sit between historical Tripolitania and Cyrenaica.

Undoubtedly, the most significant change the Libyan society has experienced during the modern period regards its size. In the early 1800s, Libya's urban population was minuscule. Cities like Tripoli and Misrata housed populations of no more than 12,000; smaller towns such as Murzuq, Benghazi, and Derna boasted little more than 5,000 residents each. By contrast, Tunis and Cairo would have claimed populations an order of magnitude larger than Tripoli or Benghazi. Under direct Ottoman control from the 1830s onward, Tripoli's population merely doubled, as did the other key population centers, by the time of the Italian conquest in 1911. In other places, Libya's population declined with the slow end of the trans-Saharan slave trade. Fezzan was particularly hard hit, going from 75,000 residents in 1789 to roughly 30,000 in 1919. Cities like Ghadamis and Murzuq saw their populations respectively dwindle to a quarter (3,000) and a fifth (1,000) of their early 1800s peak. The Italians did little to change this; in fact, their occupation and colonization was, in effect, genocide. Libya's native population halved in the face of land expropriations for settler plantations and a counterinsurgency campaign premised on ethnic cleansing.

Libya's rapid growth, urbanization, and education after independence and the 1969 coup were matched by a steady rise in per capita incomes and wealth. During the early years of oil, the effects of the burgeoning welfare state were already manifesting in terms of illiteracy (dropping from 81 percent in 1954 to 56 percent in 1964) as school enrollment jumped from 45,000 in 1951 to 300,000 in 1968. These social gains continued during the al-Qadhafi years, despite the increasing political repression, economic mismanagement, and international isolation. Looking at the 2010 United Nations *Human Development Report* on the eve of the Arab Spring, Libya ranked fifty-third globally, well ahead of its neighbors Algeria (84th), Chad (163rd), Egypt (101st), Niger (167th), and Tunisia (81st), as well as the other states of the Maghrib—Mauritania

(136th), Morocco (114th), and Sudan (154th). Based on a number of indicators (including life expectancy, schooling, and income per capita), the United Nations judged Libya's development in 2010 to be ahead of countries like Saudi Arabia, Mexico, Russia, Iran, Brazil, and Turkey in the *high human development* range. On average, Libya's 6.2 million citizens and residents lived in relative comfort despite the regime's other shortcomings. When gender was factored into these results (health, labor, education, and participation in government), Libya continued to perform well above its neighbors and Arab peers.[12] Though Libya's development index ranked as *high* in the years after the 2011 uprising, the social welfare systems began showing obvious signs of stress as the country headed into a new civil war in 2014 and global oil prices collapsed in early 2015.

Research on women in Libya is sadly lacking. This is often attributed to the austere and modest nature of the society, its long international isolation, and the socially conservative tendencies exhibited in both the Sanusi monarchy and al-Qadhafi regime. The country's first constitution even formalized this discrimination at the most basic level by not allowing women to vote. The al-Qadhafi regime, despite its progressive veneer (from promoting women's education to al-Qadhafi's personal squad of female bodyguards), nonetheless directly supported and unwittingly abetted social policies that saw gender norms become increasingly regressive as the *Jamahiriyyah* system failed to revolutionize the society. Moreover, women's participation in the consultative structures of the government never passed 11 percent.[13] According to some observers, this widespread and increasing embrace of Islamic "tradition" (notably in the high percentage of Libyan women who wear the *hijab*) was rooted in basic survival strategies. Social conservatism not only allowed average citizens to pass modestly and unnoticed by the expansive surveillance state, but it was a part of alternative modes of economic and social organization, religious networks in particular, that compensated for the failures of the *Jamahiriyyah*. Ironically, the poor performance of radical and reformist Islamist parties in Libya's first elections in 2012 was often attributed to the fact that the society had long ago adopted the major social practices that Islamists tend to advocate in other countries, especially those concerning gender and sexuality.

POLITICAL INSTITUTIONS AND PARTICIPATION

It was only in the aftermath of the 2011 uprising, six decades after independence, that Libyans finally began to enjoy the freedom to form an independent civil society and to voice their political will in national elections and referenda. Where the Sanusi monarchy eventually abolished all parties, al-Qadhafi's *Jamahiriyyah* ostensibly implemented a form of direct democracy that negated the need for contested elections, nongovernmental organizations, and other checks on state power like an independent press. Despite its populist veneer, the *Jamahiriyyah* failed to engage Libyans who understood that power truly rested in the state's "revolutionary" organs and personalities. The explosion of dissent in 2011 nonetheless revealed a polity that was both yearning for significant change and quite capable of organizing, though not in ways that were always conducive to civil concord. Though there appeared to be a national consensus in late 2011 and early 2012, this soon dissipated as the business of leading the transition and writing a constitution became increasingly conflictual, eventually leading to a low-intensity civil war in 2014 and the birth of two rival governments.

The modern elements of political participation and civil society in Libya can be traced back to the failed efforts of the Ottomans to establish more local forms of governance in Tripolitania and Cyrenaica in the late 1800s. The proliferation of antiimperialist ideologies across the Middle East and North Africa, whether taking the form of Arab nationalism or Islamic reform movements, began to take root among Tripolitanian elites as well. By contrast, Cyrenaica had a longer and different experience of associative life under the *Sanusiyyah*, a Sufi religious brotherhood that eventually transformed into a political dynasty. Unfortunately, the Libyan political forces that were amalgamated by the international community to govern the country from 1951 onward, notably the Sanusi monarchy, were often detached from the public at large and had little experience navigating the distinct political traditions used in Tripolitania, Cyrenaica, and Fezzan.

The struggle to determine the postcolonial fate of Libya catalyzed the creation of a number of political parties representing the various regional and political tendencies. One of the few manifestations of "national unity" during this period was Tripolitania's opposition to a return of Italian rule after World War II, which was visible in several large protests. The major political forces in Tripolitania, having declared the first independent Arab republic in the world in 1919, wanted self-determination and unification of the three regions, but only as much as that meant the definitive end of Italian rule. In Fezzan, the political elites had benefited from French protection and thus worried about their status in an independent Libya dominated by Tripoli or the Sanusis. Though Cyrenaica was only home to a quarter of Libya's one million inhabitants, there was a palpable desire to pursue independent statehood without Fezzan or Tripolitania. "Libya," for many Cyrenaicans, was a figment of the Italians' colonial imagination.[14] Making matters worse, Libya's putative leaders during the post–World War II administration were not in complete control of the ten-member council charged with helping the United Nations formulate the first independent Libyan state once self-determination was mandated in 1949.

Libya's first constitution, finalized in November 1950, proposed a federalist monarchy overseeing an elected bicameral government with annually alternating capitals (Tripoli and Benghazi). Sebha, the most populous city in southern Libya, would serve as the regional capital of Fezzan. The upper house balanced the three regions with eight representatives each, four of those being royally appointed and the other four being elected by provincial assemblies. The lower house allowed Tripolitania thirty-five deputies to flex its demographic advantage over Cyrenaica (fifteen) and Fezzan (five). A major concern for the Sanusis after independence was the possibility of a united Tripolitanian bloc using their majority to rewrite the constitution so as to dilute or end the federal system. Tripolitania was also well known for hosting the most vocal proponents of a republican order. This did not come to pass in Libya's first elections in February 1951, which saw an urban–rural split divide the vote in Tripolitania. However, the national electorate at the time—all male, of course—was only one-seventh of the total population.

The opportunity for King Idris to institute a more absolutist monarchy presented itself in the form of protests by the Tripolitanian National Congress Party of Bashir Bey Al-Sadawi. This created the pretext for a crackdown that not only led to Sadawi's exile and the banning of his party but indeed a total ban on all political parties that effectively lasted until the 2011 revolution. Despite regular elections, the parliament effectively became a mechanism for the automatic legitimation of the monarchy's policies. Soon, all major government postings were royal appointees, as foreign aid (military base leases) and oil became the government's primary source of funding. Even in a context of rapid development following the discovery of oil, popular dissatisfaction had gotten to the point in the late 1960s that the military coup was accepted with little protest.

To describe the events of September 1, 1969, as a "revolution" would be accurate in the sense that one regime forcibly replaced another. Though the 1969 coup was well received, it was not built upon a popular movement for a republic nor did it bring together a front of clandestine revolutionary organizations. The 1969 revolution was popular in the sense that it was largely uncontested. Two years would pass, however, before the RCC created a proper institution, the ASU, for the society at large to engage in the political system. Participation in this one-party state was facilitated through local cells, which would later transform into the early structures of the *Jamahiriyyah* in 1973 (the "people's revolution") and the formalization of the new system in 1977 (the era of "people's power"). All along, the institutions of the revolution (the RCC, Revolutionary Committees, and particular individuals) continued to act as the real power and source of law in Libya and would continue to do so alongside the "direct democracy" of the *Jamahiriyyah*'s congresses, committees, and associations.

Participation in the *Jamahiriyyah*'s basic consultative structures was never very strong and declined throughout the career of the institutions. The demands of these institutions (frequent meetings and travel) were often considered too onerous for the facade of democratic input they promised. More often than not, these structures became opportunities for particular groups to advance their own personal, familial, political, or economic agendas. Disenchantment with the *Jamahiriyyah* was also rooted in the overbearing power of the revolutionary organs, which provided new institutional structures for sycophants and self-promoters to engineer their way into the corrupt patron–client networks of the al-Qadhafi regime. For most Libyans—the three-fourths who never participated—daily survival, particularly as the command economy faltered in the 1980s, was more important.[15] That said, the *Jamahiriyyah* and, more importantly, its revolutionary structures would not have survived for so many years had they not somehow cultivated forms of support and even devotion among enough constituencies to weather four turbulent decades.

The explosion of civil society following 2011 revealed a Libyan civil society that was already well organized, despite having had to maintain a subterranean existence for years, if not decades. Despite years of repression, the Muslim Brotherhood and other Islamist groups were some of the first to make a strong impression of organizational coherence in the lead-up to the July 2012 elections for the new parliament that would form a democratically elected transitional government. That said, the Libyan electorate, which turned out in strong numbers, showed a clear preference for technocratic expertise, ideological moderation, and political independence. Unfortunately, the leadership that emerged to govern the transition, headed by Ali Zeidan, proved incapable of coordinating and implementing effective national policies. Above all was the need to disarm, demobilize, and reintegrate the thousands of heavily armed militia fighters who had ousted the al-Qadhafi regime in 2011, which Libya's transitional authorities have so far failed to do. Elections in May 2014 to reconstitute a new interim legislature not only failed to turn out a fifth of the electorate, but the contested results split the country between rival parliaments, governments, and military coalitions. In the years since, local-level governance, mainly at the municipal level, has been the only effective and responsive form of leadership in the country.

RELIGION AND POLITICS

Though Libya has never been under the rule of an explicitly Islamist regime or political party, all of its modern rulers, with the obvious exception of the Italians, have viewed Islam as central to governmental authority and the cohesion of the polity. The Sanusi monarchy began in the 19th century as a Sufi brotherhood. Their approach to Sufi thought and practice stressed the role of learned interpretation (*al-ijtihad*) of Islamic law and practice (*al-shari'ah*) over scriptural literalism and other orthodoxies found in the established schools of Sunni thought.

The *Sanusiyyah* effloresced within the particular cultural milieu of eastern Libya by articulating their religious ideas and practices with a popular tradition, one found all across North Africa, of venerating local religious figures and community leaders who seemed particularly endowed by Allah with *al-barakah* (blessing). This could include spiritual intuition, natural leadership skills, healing abilities, and, most importantly, the demonstrated favor of Allah during trying times. Using these cultural traditions, the founder of the *Sanusiyyah*, Sidi Muhammad Al-Sanusi (1787–1859), who was from Algeria (though he studied in Arabia), used his alleged lineage to the family of the Prophet Muhammad to obtain a saint-like status during his lifetime, thus becoming the eponymous founder of one of the greatest movements of northern Africa.

Contrary to the Western image of Sufis as individualistic and pacifist mystics who seek to transcend the baseness of social and political life through quiet meditation, chanting, music, or repetitive physical exertion, Al-Sanusi denounced asceticism and solipsism within Sufi thought and practice. He instead stressed the need to accept the plurality of ways in which Muslims practiced Islam and the need to engage socially, as these were all paths to understanding Allah. The author of more than forty books, Al-Sanusi criticized the main Sunni schools of thought as overly divisive. He instead advocated for a firm grounding in the Qur'an as opposed to its subsequent exegesis in the copious volumes that comprise the Hadith.

Though ostensibly living under Ottoman sovereignty, the *Sanusiyyah* went on to create quasi-governmental institutions that served the socioreligious, economic, and security needs of populations in Cyrenaica, as well as parts of Fezzan, northern Chad, western Egypt, and other areas where the Brotherhood was strong. These functions included courts, education, trade regulation, and law enforcement. The physical manifestation of *Sanusiyyah* commitment to social engagement was the *zawiyyah* (lodge), which functioned as a hub for spiritual practice, religious learning, and worship for adults and children, as well as the center of the community, a refuge for travelers, the residence of the *shaykh* and his family, the offices of his assistants who functioned as Sanusi administrators, and as the local armory. The location of *zawiyyahs* was not only determined by community need and enthusiasm but was often chosen in relation to the movement's commercial interests (mainly trans-Saharan trade), the need to unify particular social groups and the *Sanusiyyah*'s subtle political competition with the Ottomans. That Al-Sanusi had created much more than a personality cult was demonstrated in the continuing proliferation of Sanusi *zawiyyahs* after his death. From around fifty in 1859, the *Sanusiyyah* went on to add over ninety more by 1920. A third of these were located in Cyrenaica, and another fifth were in western Egypt; the remainders were primarily in Tripolitania, Fezzan, Kufra, and the central Sahel, with a small number in the Hijaz.[16] The Sanusi's limited penetration of the urban core of Tripolitania had much to do with the fact that the new urban elites of Ottoman Tripoli often followed reformist (*al-islah*) and orthodox (*al-salafiyyah*) currents in turn-of-the-century cosmopolitan Islam, while the religious establishment (*al-'ulama*) in Tripolitania was already a central player in the Ottoman state's educational, judicial, and religious administration. In the Nafusa mountains, meanwhile, adherents of Islam's third major branch, *Ibadiyyah* (Ibadis), were to be found among the Amazigh population. Nonetheless, most Libyans would come to see Umar Mukhtar (1861–1931), who led the Sanusi resistance to Italian occupation in Cyrenaica, as one of the country's most important national heroes.

After World War II, the traditions and institutions of the Sanusiyyah were allowed to come back to Libya during the international mandate period, though these were a shadow of their former glory. The robust political, social, and economic networks that had underwritten *Sanusiyyah* power had been greatly eroded by the long demise of trans-Saharan trade (the movement's main source of financing) and even more extensively damaged by the violent Italian pacification in the 1920s. For most of its ostensible reign over Libya, the Sanusi monarchy lived in exile under British protection. Upon his return, King Idris relied as much on Anglo-American patronage as the decayed networks of the *Sanusiyyah*. The political and religious elites of Tripolitania begrudgingly accepted Sanusi rule as the least-worst option for political leadership. Under the Sanusi monarchy, the *ulama* was politically coopted although its religious autonomy was respected.

The regime established after the 1969 coup made almost no room for either traditional religious elites or new Islamic movements. Al-Qadhafi's ideology was revolutionary but certainly not secular.[17] The regime regularly used its coercive, coordinating, and ideational capacities to devolve religious authority to the masses by disabling traditional networks of religious power and by preventing the coalescence of underground Islamist movements. Al-Qadhafi, as the guide of the revolution, thus functioned as the country's leading religious authority as well, instituting rules ranging from the strange (instituting a new Islamic calendar with a different Year Zero) to the stringent (total prohibition on alcohol sales and consumption). The seizure of lands and properties held by the *'ulama* was one of the first such initiatives. When these initiatives were met with resistance, al-Qadhafi encouraged mobs to occupy them in the name of the *Jamahiriyyah*. Dissident Imams were also imprisoned.

When it came to new Islamic movements, the al-Qadhafi regime seemed to view the Muslim Brotherhood as a particularly dangerous source of opposition. While the Sanusi monarchy had sheltered members of the Egyptian Muslim Brotherhood fleeing Nasser's repression, the Brotherhood also made important inroads into Libyan society as Egyptian migrant laborers poured into the country to meet the needs of the booming economy in the 1960s and 1970s. Controlling the ideational territory of religion was not an easy task for the al-Qadhafi regime, particularly as standards of living increased and more Libyans traveled abroad for employment and education. But as repression escalated in al-Qadhafi's Libya, the most dominant voices of organized Libyan Islamism were largely coming from exile. A noted figure to come out of the Libyan Brotherhood and associated dissident student movements was Muhammad Al-Magariaf, who helped found the National Front for the Salvation of Libya (NFSL) in 1981 with the help of other dissidents, the CIA, and the Chadian dictator Hissène Habré. Though the NFSL wanted to present itself as a nonpartisan "big tent" front organization of al-Qadhafi opponents, its membership was heavily influenced by the Libyan Brotherhood.

Inside Libya, the Brotherhood was able to develop clandestine structures and leadership uniting Cyrenaican and Tripolitanian members despite the oppressive environment of the *Jamahiriyyah*. Popular sympathy for the Brotherhood, if not Islamist politics in general, grew as al-Qadhafi's massive sociopolitical experiment began to falter due to the international pressure of isolation and the collapse of oil prices in 1985. Yet so total was the regime's control over the polity through intense surveillance and violent coercion that the Libyan Brotherhood could not even engage in the kinds of social welfare and charity programs that had generated mass support for Islamists in places like Egypt, Algeria, and the Gaza Strip.[18]

A more militant strain of Islamic resistance began to take shape in the 1990s, as Libyan veterans of the 1980s *jihad* against the Soviet Union, many of them affiliated with the early al-Qa'ida network, returned to fight the al-Qadhafi regime in the 1990s. Similar organizations in Algeria were waging widespread rural and urban guerrilla warfare by 1993; unlike these, however, the Libyan Islamic Fighting Group (LIFG) had to be much more circumspect about its activities, just to establish cells inside Libya. Only in 1995 did the LIFG make itself known through its efforts to organize an insurgency that never amounted to anything more than several brief skirmishes with the security forces and a botched attempt on al-Qadhafi's life. Even under UN sanctions and facing extreme international isolation, the al-Qadhafi regime proved quite capable and resilient in the face of this armed challenge, which was effectively stamped out by 1998. Following the events of 9/11, the al-Qadhafi regime then willingly offered its intelligence services to Washington and London, which included torturing suspected al-Qa'ida members for information.

As Libya slowly began to emerge from international isolation in the early 2000s, the regime set about trying to organize a reconciliation effort with its radical and moderate Islamist opponents, initiatives led by Saif Al-Islam. However, when the 2011 revolution erupted, Islamists were often split between those who had reconciled with the regime and those who remained in opposition, especially abroad. Large swaths of Libyan society were moreover skeptical about the new Islamist movements and parties that began to populate the postrevolutionary landscape, as some of these Islamists had seemed too willing to reconcile with the regime only years beforehand. The Libyan Islamist movement itself was split between moderate and radical elements, with former members of LIFG, including Abdelhakim Belhadj and conservative clerics like Ali Sellabi, coalesced under the banner of the *Hizb Al-Watan* (Homeland or National Party) for the July 2012 elections, as a Turkish- or Moroccan-style moderate Islamist party. Meanwhile, the more implacable Libyan elements of the transnational Islamist movement found outlets for their convictions in the battlefields of Afghanistan, Pakistan, Iraq, and the Sahara-Sahel region. The 2011 uprising and the 2014 civil war also provided openings for Libyan *jihadis* to return to their homeland under the banner of al-Qaʿida and, later, the Islamic State (see Domestic Conflict and Rebel Governance section).

DOMESTIC CONFLICT AND REBEL GOVERNANCE

When Libyan activists decided to join the regional wave of protests that had already toppled the regimes in Tunis and Cairo in the early weeks of 2011, the date of February 17 was chosen to mark the fifth anniversary of protests in Benghazi that had been brutally crushed in 2006. The tricolor Libyan flag of the Sanusi monarchy, not seen since 1969, rapidly became the symbol of this revolt, as Cyrenaica rid itself of the most nefarious structures and agents of the late *Jamahiriyyah*. Communities in the West, however, had a more difficult time shaking off the old state; protesters in Tripoli were relentlessly persecuted through killings and detention. The National Transitional Council (NTC) soon formed to represent the rebellion and was led by a number of prominent domestic and diasporic dissidents, as well as ex-regime figures like its chair, Mustafa Abul Jalil, and its top military commander, Abdul Fatah Younis. In addition to courting international support from governments in the North Atlantic and the Middle East, the NTC drafted an interim constitution that plotted a course to an open parliamentary system. In the weeks that followed, proregime and revolutionary forces waged pitched battles in the eastern oil crescent, around the city of Misrata, and in the Nafusa mountains. With air support from NATO and the Arab League, the tide began to turn during the long summer of 2011, and the rebels took control of Tripoli in September.

Though the summary execution of al-Qadhafi outside of Sirte in October should have formally brought the armed uprising to its end, the issue that would haunt the Libyan polity in the years to come was the revolutionary militias (*thuwar*). Countless heavily armed groups refused to lay down their weapons in the aftermath of the 2011 revolution, often going about seizing key state assets—from hydrocarbon infrastructures to luxury hotels—in order to use them as bargaining chips. The NTC quickly proved incapable of taming the militias and governing across Libya's multiplying political cleavages. Though often depicted as a growing split between Islamists and secularists, the most important divide was between those seeking some accommodation with former members of the ousted regime and those seeking a total revolution to extirpate all persons tied to al-Qadhafi's rule. Among the latter, prominent voices in the new Libya were suggesting that the revolution had called for a clean-slate approach, with prominent Islamist parties and organizations, notably the Muslim Brotherhood, backing such demands. In the absence of security and effective central governance from 2011 onward, thousands of Libyans with ties to the old regime fled to Egypt and Tunisia out of fear. Meanwhile, militias detained thousands of suspected collaborators in their privately run prisons all across the country. Loyalist strongholds like Bani Walid were subjected to siege-like conditions while the city of Sirte was effectively placed under occupation by revolutionary militias.

Militias and political factions also began to enjoy support from foreign sponsors. Unified by the collective suffering of the brutal siege it suffered in 2011, the city of Misrata, for example,

PHOTO 17.1 Revolutionary graffiti in Tripoli mocking deposed leader Muammar al-Qadhafi in which he says "Forward!" while mounted backward on a donkey.

Courtesy of Jacob Mundy

parlayed a number of advantages—a city with deep historical ties to Turkish trade and industry, as well as a large and functional shipping port—into a dominant position within the postrevolutionary situation. The unified way in which Misratan militias and political leaders navigated the growing tensions of the transitional years of 2012 and 2013, notably in their alliance with the Muslim Brotherhood, stood in sharp contrast with the lack of unity in major cities like Tripoli and Benghazi, where highly localized neighborhood militias often clashed with rival groups or rival towns. Libya's moderate Islamists, including members of the LIFG insurgency in the 1990s, found some support among the population but were often viewed suspiciously because of their sponsorship by states like Turkey and Qatar. Indeed, Libya's first elections in July 2012, which replaced the NTC with an elected (yet still interim) legislature, the General National Congress (GNC), saw overtly Islamist political parties perform poorly despite early and glitzy advertising campaigns.

With a strong turnout of two-thirds of the registered electorate, the most dominant party in the 2012 elections was the centrist National Forces Alliance led by Mahmoud Jibril El Warfally, a Western-trained technocrat who had only served in the al-Qadhafi regime during its final years. Jibril's party, with nearly half of the popular vote, won 39 seats out of the 80 reserved for parties. A moderate Islamist grouping associated with the Muslim Brotherhood, the Justice and

Construction Party, came in second place, securing just 10 percent of the vote (17 seats). All other parties failed to secure more than 3 seats each. The GNC, however, was dominated by the 120 seats held by individuals, which tended to represent provincial interests rather than coherent national party agendas. As former al-Qadhafi officials were not allowed to hold leadership positions, a human rights lawyer who had lived in exile for many years, Ali Zeidan, served as the country's first prime minister.

There were a number of major national issues facing the GNC during its limited tenure: security sector reform (integrating the militias into formal military and police structures), rebuilding neglected or destroyed infrastructure, resettling displaced communities, recovering Libya's significant financial assets held abroad, transitional justice (prosecuting former regime elites, processing the thousands of loyalist prisoners, and reconciling pro- and anti-al-Qadhafi communities), and the questions of citizenship and native Libyan status. That Libya remained an essentially lawless country with weak central institutions and powerful local actors was vividly demonstrated when a US diplomatic compound was raided on September 11, 2012, killing several people, including the US Ambassador.

As the power of the militias grew, the ability of Libya's elected government to operate independently of them shrank. Moreover, the NTC and GNC had adopted laws that not only immunized all militias from prosecution for crimes committed in 2011, other initiatives—compensation and salaries for militia members who joined "state" forces—effectively incentivized more young men to join the armed groups, though the GNC had almost no power to compel the militias to cooperate with the transition. The militias thus regularly exercised their power as spoilers to undermine the transition through terrorism or economic sabotage. For example, a militia led by Cyrenaican federalists, having seized control of Libya's most important oil export facilities in the East of the country, regularly deprived the central government of vital revenues in order to have their demands met. Confronting these issues head-on in the city of Benghazi, Khalifa Haftar, a former officer in al-Qadhafi's army before seeking exile in the late 1980s, launched a campaign in early 2014 to rid the city of militias, particularly the more violent Islamists. Haftar's so-called Libyan National Army (LNA) and its Operation Dignity increased tensions in the country between the revolutionary Islamists and moderate accommodationists, tensions that revealed themselves in the dismissal of Prime Minister Zeidan, who soon fled the country, fearing for his life.

In an effort to reconstitute a legitimate central authority, elections were held in June 2014 for a new House of Representatives. The vote, however, was widely boycotted and saw a dismal turnout of less than 20 percent. Contesting the result, various militias that had been occupying Tripoli went to war with each other, resulting in the newly elected House decamping to the far eastern city of Tobruk, where it fell under the protection of Haftar's LNA (later rebranded the Libyan Arab Armed Forces or LAAF). In the ensuing chaos, most foreign embassies closed, and the UN mission moved to Tunisia. What was left of the GNC attempted to press ahead with backing from the city of Misrata and allied Islamist militias, though the international community recognized the House as Libya's legitimate government. Though there were very few Libyan voices calling for the complete restoration of the al-Qadhafi system, the House and Operation Dignity more or less represented those Libyans who felt that one, former regime officials were being unfairly marginalized in the postrevolutionary order and, two, the country could no longer afford to turn a blind eye to the violent excesses of the radical Islamist militias. Some argued that the passage of the Political Isolation Law by the GNC in 2013, which barred former regime officials from holding office, had set the country on a course toward civil war between prorevolution and proaccommodation camps.

Taking advantage of the new civil war that erupted in 2014, various *jihadi* militias in Libya—some claiming affiliation with the Islamic State movement that had developed out of the civil wars in Iraq and Syria—eventually took over the city of Sirte in May 2015. Meanwhile, an explosion of human trafficking in Libya saw hundreds of African and Asian migrants leave Libya's shores in an attempt to reach Europe. Unwilling to let the situation deteriorate any further, the United Nations and the North Atlantic powers pressed for a peace agreement that would reconcile Libya's two governments. A new arrangement emerged in late 2015 when the Government of National Accord (GNA) combined the House and the GNC into a new body headed by a Presidential Council. This proved hardly more effective, although its international legitimacy allowed Libya's new head of state, Fayez Serraj, to authorize foreign interventions against the Islamic State and other terrorist groups. Working with the US Marine Corps, Misratan militias finally drove the Islamic State from Sirte by late 2016.

In the years that followed, the LNA, with backing from Egypt, the UAE, Saudi Arabia, France, and Russia, gradually extended its sphere of influence beyond Cyrenaica. With the "liberation" of Benghazi in 2017, Haftar then seized Libya's key eastern oil facilities and pressed into the Fezzan. Though local-level governments in Libya were often quite competent and democratically chosen throughout the civil war, Serraj's administration—beholden to the militias controlling Tripoli—was never able to complete Libya's transition to constitutional governance while the LNA slowly encircled Tripolitania. Yet Haftar's final assault on the capital, launched in the spring of 2019, proved to be a strategic blunder. A decisive intervention by the Turkish military in early 2020, requested by Serraj, helped beat back the LNA offensive. The LNA's retreat also created the diplomatic space necessary for a UN political dialogue process to move ahead. In early 2021, Libya's interim authorities were reconstituted as a new Government of National Unity, headed by Prime Minister Abdul Hamid Dbeibeh, with the ambitious goal— amid the global coronavirus pandemic—of holding elections that December for a permanent, constitutionally based government that would finally end Libya's prolonged transition and unify its state institutions, including the armed forces.

REGIONAL AND INTERNATIONAL RELATIONS

The majority of Libya's modern history over the last several centuries has been defined by its existence as a dominion, colony, or protectorate of greater powers. Prior to the exploitation of oil in the mid-20th century, Libya likewise lived in the economic shadow of its regional neighbors, Cairo and Tunis. As one European traveler wrote in 1897, the land along the Mediterranean that would become Libya represented nothing more than "a buffer state of sand" nestled between Tunisia and Egypt (i.e., France and Britain).[19] For the very same reasons that the Ottomans continued to prize Libya until the end of their empire (i.e., that Libya proved the Ottomans still had an empire), the Italians likewise coveted Libya (i.e., as a means to enhance Rome's imperial credentials and holdings in Africa). Inside Libya, native political forces were often finding common cause with the emergence of Arab nationalism and modern Islamic political thought across MENA in the late 1800s and early 1900s. These networks would see Arab and Muslim volunteers come to Libya—from as far as Chad and India—in the name of fighting European colonialism and defending Islam when the Italians arrived.[20] Fezzan, as with most of the Libyan Sahara, continued to enjoy a kind of de facto independence from the intrigue of the North, though France's much more aggressive imperialism in the Sahel region began to affect populations in Libya's vast hinterland as well.

When it came to power in 1951, the Sanusi monarchy was highly indebted to its British and American patrons for liberating the country in World War II and helping establish independence under its rule. Yet the overbearing presence of Britain and the United States in Libya challenged the Sanusi monarchy when it came to some of the region's most pressing international conflicts: the Arab–Israeli wars; the occupation of the Suez by France, Israel, and England; the Algerian insurgency; and the Palestine question. Though King Idris backed the Arab armies in the 1967 war and provided logistical support, his conservative attitude toward pan-Arabism was one of the major motivations driving the organizers of the 1969 coup that removed the Sanusis from power.

Ironically, it was al-Qadhafi's unmoderated enthusiasm for pan-Arabism, the Palestinian cause, and Third Worldism that not only helped to propel him to power, but it would also eventually alienate many of his early Arab and African allies. This revolutionary zeal likewise set his regime on the path of international pariah states. When not being accused of engaging in international terror directly, al-Qadhafi was more often than not being accused of supporting it through financing, arms, training, and bases.

Though the al-Qadhafi regime lavished billions of dollars of aid on the poorer nations of sub-Saharan Africa, many governments across the continent felt ambivalent. Al-Qadhafi's fingerprints were to be found on a number of African conflicts, including Uganda, Western Sahara, Congo, South Africa, Tuareg revolts, Sierra Leone, and Liberia. But it was the war in Chad that became a major preoccupation for the regime in the late 1970s and 1980s. Libya's involvement in Chad's civil war (and its later occupation of the North) was initially rooted in a territorial dispute over the Aouzou Strip, mistrust of French intentions in the region, and Libyan support for a rebel group, the National Liberation Front of Chad. This support dated back to the years of King Idris and was facilitated by the fact that the Saharan populations of the region, mainly Tuaregs and Tebu, had been divided by artificial colonial boundaries. To many, however, it became clear that al-Qadhafi's occupation of Aouzou in the 1970s was becoming a platform for larger territorial ambitions as joint Chadian and Libyan forces descended farther south. International opponents of al-Qadhafi like Saudi Arabia and the United States helped unite and support the anti–al-Qadhafi forces in Chad so as to roll back the Libyan intervention.

Libya's defeat in Chad in the mid-1980s came at a time of growing international isolation, even in the community of North African states. In the late 1980s, Mauritania, Morocco, Algeria, Tunisia, and Libya formed the Arab Maghrib Union (UMA) to enhance regional economic and political cooperation. While several summits were held to advance the union, it faltered for several reasons, though mainly because of the ongoing Moroccan occupation of Western Sahara, the Islamist insurgency in 1990s Algeria (with fears of a spillover into Morocco), and finally the unpredictable foreign policies of the al-Qadhafi regime. Though Moroccan–Algerian antagonisms over Western Sahara were frequently cited as the main reason for the UMA's failure, it was often suspected that this became a convenient excuse when the other states wanted to prevent al-Qadhafi from chairing the organization.

On the global stage, it was Libya's direct confrontations with the North Atlantic powers that drew the most attention, culminating in the 1986 US raid on Libya (a failed attempt at regime change) and the Libyan bombing of a US-bound flight over Lockerbie, Scotland, in 1988, that killed hundreds. Very early in its existence, al-Qadhafi's regime had taken issue with Western policies and was eager to see the closing of foreign bases on Libyan soil. A more important investment in Libya, from the perspective of London and Washington, was the oil infrastructure British and US firms had helped build and maintain. Nationalization of the hydrocarbon industry in Libya was a particular affront to Anglo-American interests because it established a precedent of "weaponized oil" that paved the way for the 1973 Arab oil embargo. Libya then used the massive windfall of profits during the 1970 oil boom to purchase large quantities of arms, much of it from the Soviet Union as al-Qadhafi's relations with the West faltered.

The bombing of Pan Am 103 and the French UTA flight 772 over Niger in 1989 allowed Washington to confront the Libyan regime's international terrorism activities through UN sanctions. Though nowhere near as devastating as the sanctions placed on Iraq in the 1990s, Libya's international isolation was painful enough to the regime that it soon began seeking ways to appease the West. The two key Lockerbie suspects, Abdelbaset Megrahi and Lamine Fhima, both believed to be Libyan secret agents, were finally handed over to international authorities in 1999. Negotiating the protocols for the Megrahi-Fhima trial had been arduous, resulting in a conviction (Megrahi) and an acquittal (Fhima), an outcome that seemed to satisfy no one given the mysteries that continued to haunt the bombing and the trial.[21] In the years that followed, al-Qadhafi nonetheless began to enjoy a kind of international renaissance in the 2000s; publicly condemning terrorism in the wake of 9/11 and dismantling Libya's nuclear and chemical arms programs recast al-Qadhafi as a progressive reformer in the eyes of British and American politicians.

Having been marginalized in MENA, the al-Qadhafi regime used its oil wealth to have more of a presence in the Organization of African Unity (OAU) and the African Union (AU). Libya not only hosted an important meeting in Sirte that saw the transition of the OAU to the AU in 1999, but as chair of the AU in 2009, al-Qadhafi again championed the cause of bringing the states of Africa into a closer confederation like the European Union, if not a United States of Africa. Though such was viewed as a dream from a bygone era, parts of the continent remained the last bastion of support for al-Qadhafi in his final years. During the 2011 crisis, al-Qadhafi's last friends in Africa were some of the few voices calling for a negotiated settlement to the spiraling violence.

In the years before the Arab Spring, foreign investment, particularly in the oil sector, began to flood into Libya as the new face of the regime, Saif Al-Islam, seemed to balance his father's eccentricities with promises of economic and political reform. Further indications of Libya's rehabilitation came in 2008, when it joined the UN Security Council and, in the following year, became the president of the UN General Assembly. It thus came as a surprise to many that Saif Al-Islam did not respond pragmatically to the eruption of protests in February 2011 but instead used the same uncompromising and intimidating rhetoric his father was spouting. If there had been any hope that the regime could reform itself under Saif Al-Islam, it became utterly clear in the context of the early Arab Spring that those hopes had been disastrously misplaced.

Libya's 2011 revolution was eventually successful because of the significant military intervention NATO and the Arab League mounted to support the rebellion. At the same time, it could be argued that the failure of Libya's transition in 2012 and 2013, along with its collapse into civil war from 2014 to the present, could be attributed to the power vacuum that was created when the international community (i.e., the UN Security Council) refused to play a more robust peacekeeping role in post-Qadhafi Libya. While this is an important consideration, foreign powers have often helped to exacerbate Libya's manifold conflicts since then by supporting one faction or another. For example, Turkey and Qatar have been widely accused of supporting political and military factions allied to the Libyan Muslim Brotherhood, whereas the United Arab Emirates and Saudi Arabia have been accused of supporting opposing religious factions, with Egypt and Russia having been the main sponsors of Haftar's ambitions. Meanwhile, the North Atlantic powers have been accused of prioritizing counterterrorism over political stability by collaborating with all sides in the ongoing civil war in Libya so as to contain the threats of transnational jihadism, the Islamic State, and illegal migration that have proliferated in Libya since 2014. The violent instability and political disarray Libya has experienced for a decade have thus put the country at the mercy of others' agendas while successive interim governments have failed to define a coherent Libyan foreign policy that is not beholden to one set of foreign patrons or another. The one apparent area of consensus among the various factions in Libya today is the necessity to maintain oil exports to keep the country from descending into a far-worse state of affairs. With the country's weakened social welfare and health care systems straining after a decade of conflict, the global coronavirus pandemic in 2020 and 2021 only added more urgency to the need for reliable state revenues.

CONCLUSION

For several decades, the lack of democracy and other basic freedoms in Libya has often been theorized in relation to the country's vast oil wealth. Those revenues allowed two regimes—Sanussi and al-Qadhafi—to rule without popular consultation by creating a robust welfare state to appease social and economic demands. Such "rentier states" are not only said to be corrosive to democracy, but they are also allegedly antithetical to the growth of civil society. The 2011 uprising in Libya, however, revealed the extent to which an already-existing democratic civil society had been hiding beneath the surface of the decayed *Jamahiriyyah*. The most visible forms of organization witnessed during the 2011 conflict were the armies of the regime and the militias of the rebellion, but throughout the country, local communities quickly organized councils, associations, and other kinds of networks for survival and support. In many locations, these networks had existed to provide goods and services otherwise unobtainable through the formal political and economic channels of the *Jamahiriyyah*. This efflorescence of democratic organization and civil society action demonstrated the extent to which it had long existed in an informal capacity but was invisible to the theories of the rentier state.

The predicament that Libya faces today—*how to organize a legitimate central government, one that has a monopoly over the use of force*—is tragic in the way it was produced by the failures of the *Jamahiriyyah*. At the same time, the *Jamahiriyyah* oddly succeeded in devolving state power to small communities by failing to deliver the most basic functions of a state, thereby forcing localities to organize on their own. With the outbreak of a revolutionary uprising in 2011, these modes of survival transformed into armed resistance, which was supported by an array of other networks. Today, many Libyan communities, rightfully weary of the excesses of centralized authority, maintain their local monopolies of violence in the best spirit of the *Jamahiriyyah*— the ideal of the sovereign masses. This was the ideal that al-Qadhafi was seemingly willing to die for but was never capable of turning into reality. In Libya today, there is a deep irony in all of the fierce competition over the future of the state. The major actors who now view themselves as the guardians of the 2011 revolution have helped make the state of the masses al-Qadhafi never could.

SUGGESTED READINGS

Anderson, Lisa. *The State and the Social Transformation in Tunisia and Libya (1830–1980)*. Princeton, NJ: Princeton University Press, 1986.

Baldinetti, Anna. *The Origins of the Libyan Nation: Colonial Legacy, Exile, and the Emergence of a New Nation-State*. New York, NY: Routledge, 2010.

Cole, Peter, and McQuinn Brian, eds. *The Libyan Revolution and Its Aftermath*. New York, NY: Oxford University Press, 2015.

Lacher, Wolfram. *Libya's Fragmentation: Structure and Process in Violent Conflict*. London: I.B. Tauris, 2020.

Mundy, Jacob. *Libya*. New York, NY: Polity, 2018.

Pack, Jason, Smith Rhiannon, and Mezran Karim. *The Origins and Evolution of ISIS in Libya*. Washington, DC: Atlantic Council, 2017.

Vandewalle, Dirk, ed. *Libya Since 1969: Qadhafi's Revolution Revisited*. New York, NY: Palgrave Macmillan, 2008.

18 THE LOWER GULF STATES

Michael Herb

The four countries of the lower Gulf share much in common. They are all monarchies in a world where ruling monarchies are rare. They are rich in oil. Their citizen populations are largely Arab in origin. Alongside these similarities, we also find some important differences. The United Arab Emirates (UAE) has partly diversified its economy away from oil, making itself into a center for trade and tourism. Along with this has come a spectacular demographic imbalance: Emiratis (that is, citizens of the UAE) are only 11.5 percent of the total population of the country. Qatar is one of the world's richest countries and the improbable host of the 2022 World Cup: Its efforts at diversification have clearly been influenced by the UAE, and it has a similar demographic imbalance (the largest national groups in Qatar are Indians, then Nepalis, then Qataris). Oman is somewhat more conventional than the others: it is not quite so rich in oil, and citizens are a majority of the population. It has regular elections, but to a representative assembly with few powers. Finally, Bahrain has the most serious internal political problems of the four, suffering from chronic strife between the Sunni regime and the Shi'i citizen majority. In this chapter, I begin by discussing the factors that the four lower Gulf states share in common. I then examine each country individually, in order of total population size.

COMMON THEMES

History of State Formation

Before oil, the agricultural economy of the lower Gulf consisted mostly of date plantations, fishing, and livestock husbandry. The land was not particularly fertile because the lower Gulf states are among the world's driest countries. The economy also depended on trade and pearling. These activities did not support a large population or complex state structures, and most local states were little more than towns along the shores of the Gulf, some of which occasionally grew into somewhat larger states built on trading routes.[1]

The British brought the lower Gulf states under loose British control from the early 19th century, starting with the principalities of what is now the UAE.[2] The Gulf rulers, for the most part, did not oppose British influence, which made their rule more secure. The British supported the local rulers as long as they maintained the peace and avoided dealings with foreign powers. The British imposed their hegemony in the Gulf by means of a small group of warships

MAP 18.1 ■ Lower Gulf States

and did not seek to rule the hinterlands. Britain based its warships at a naval base in Bushire (Bushehr, now part of Iran) and from 1935 in Bahrain. The base now houses the Fifth Fleet of the US Navy.

The lower Gulf states achieved their independence relatively late, in 1971, and reluctantly. The ruler of Abu Dhabi famously volunteered to pay the costs of a continued British presence if the British would agree to stay on.[3] His offer was not accepted.

At independence, the British initially wanted all of the lower Gulf states, except Oman, to form a single independent state (along the lines of what happened in India and Malaysia at independence). Qatar and Bahrain demurred, preferring independence over union with their neighbors. Abu Dhabi and Dubai went under one flag, bringing with them the five poorer emirates. Thus, Bahrain, Qatar, the UAE, and Oman each became an independent sovereign state, complete with a seat in the United Nations and all of the trappings of sovereignty. This owes much to oil, which allowed the rulers to convince the world their realms could be independent sovereign states.

Institutions and Governance

Ruling Families

Except in Oman, the four Gulf states are family regimes, though in recent years some Gulf rulers have increasingly broken away from the tradition of family rule. The chief characteristic of family rule—or dynastic monarchy—is that the leading posts in the state are held by members of the ruling family.[4] These almost always include the post of prime minister (where it exists) and the heads of the ministries of defense and interior. Usually, though not always, the minister of foreign affairs is also a member of the ruling family, and other members of the ruling family are found in various roles in the states, as head of the national guard, ambassador, head of the central bank, minister of oil, and so forth. The monopoly of the ministries of defense and interior (responsible, respectively, for the military and the police) is not accidental: These are the core coercive arms of the state, crucial to maintaining the family's control over political power (see Table 18.1). These family regimes have proven to be very resilient; while monarchies have fallen elsewhere in the Middle East (in Iran, Libya, Egypt, Yemen, and Iraq), all of the Gulf family monarchies have remained in power through the salad days of Arab nationalism in the 1960s and 1970s, the Islamist challenge in the following decades, and since 2011, the Arab Spring.

TABLE 18.1 ■ Ruling Families and the State in the Lower Gulf Monarchies[5]				
	Bahrain	**Oman**	**Qatar**	**UAE**
Ruling family	Al Khalifa	Al Said	Al Thani	Abu Dhabi: Al Nahyan Dubai: Al Maktoum Sharjah & Ras Al Khaimah: Al Qasimi Ajman: Al-Nuaimi Umm Al Quwain: Al Mu'alla Fujairah: Al Sharqi
Ruler	Hamad bin Isa	Haitham bin Tariq	Tamim bin Hamad	Mohamed bin Zayed
Cabinet posts held by the ruler		Prime minister	Defense	
Major cabinet posts held by other members of the ruling family	Prime minister Deputy prime minister (4) Finance Interior Justice & Islamic affairs Oil	Deputy prime minister for defense Deputy prime minister for international relations Culture, sports & youth	Prime minister Culture Trade & industry Foreign affairs Interior	Prime minister (Al Maktoum) Defense (Al Maktoum) Finance (Al Maktoum) Foreign affairs (Al Nahyan) Interior (Al Nahyan) Tolerance & Coexistence (Al Nahyan)

Source: CIA, 'Chiefs of State and Cabinet Members of Foreign Governments'. Available at https://www.cia.gov/library/publications/world-leaders-1/index.html.

In recent years, the family nature of these regimes has begun to erode, with individual rulers rising above their families and threatening the basic character of family rule. This is most obvious in Saudi Arabia where the current crown prince has brutally repressed any dissent from members of his family. The Saudi example is likely to be influential in the rest of the Gulf, providing a road map for monarchs to use their constitutional powers—which have few formal limits—to circumscribe the role of their families.

Representative Assemblies

The Gulf-ruling families have not completely ignored demands for more modern forms of political representation. Two of the four states—Bahrain and Oman—hold regular elections to a national-level representative assembly. Qatar held its first elections to its national representative assembly in 2021, while the UAE has a representative assembly whose members are elected by a limited electorate composed of citizens selected by the rulers. In all four countries, the representative assembly has limited powers, and these assemblies cannot challenge the monopoly of political authority by the ruling families. Progress toward greater democracy in these countries requires more than just elections. These countries need to take four steps to achieve full democracy:

- First, the countries that do not hold elections need to do so.

- Second, the elections need to be free and fair, and candidates must be able to campaign on the issues.

- Third, elected parliaments need to have some actual authority over the executive branch; full democracy requires that elected deputies in the parliament appoint the prime minister and, through the prime minister, the rest of the ministers in the cabinet.

- Finally, authority must be lodged in the cabinet, not the ruler's palace.

None of the monarchies of the lower Gulf have moved very far on the third and fourth points, and there is little prospect that most will do so any time soon, or perhaps ever. But it is useful to keep this yardstick in mind when measuring the actual impact of the reforms championed by Gulf rulers.

Political Economy

The economies of the lower Gulf states depend on the export of oil and natural gas, though in some, economic diversification away from oil has occurred, especially in the UAE and Bahrain. Two of the lower Gulf states—Qatar and the UAE—have among the very highest per capita levels of oil income of any countries in the world. Oman and Bahrain have less hydrocarbon wealth per capita, though their economies still mostly depend on oil.

The first of the lower Gulf countries to discover oil was Bahrain, which started exports in 1934; Qatar followed in 1949, then the UAE in 1962, and Oman in 1967. The ruling families spent generously building modern state institutions. The states built schools, from the primary level to university level, and hired teachers from other Arab countries to staff the schools (in more recent years, citizens have replaced many expatriates as teachers). The states set up modern healthcare systems and built the physical infrastructure of first-world countries, including electricity, roads, airports, desalination plants for water, and the like. The regimes also spent a good deal of money on the police and the military and have extended the state's monopoly of coercion throughout their national territories.

Labor Markets

From the very beginning of the oil age, Gulf states began hiring citizens into jobs in the state.[6]

The regimes employed citizens, in part at least, as a way of distributing the oil wealth. Foreign workers also came to the Gulf to take up jobs, especially in the private sector. Over time, this led to the emergence of two separate labor markets, one for citizens and the other for foreigners. We see this most clearly today in the two richer lower Gulf states. Qatar and the UAE receive enough oil wealth to provide a job, at a good wage, to virtually all citizen graduates. The wage rates for citizens in these public-sector jobs are higher than the equivalent salaries for noncitizens—a political logic drives hiring and wage decisions, not a market logic. The working hours at these jobs are not onerous, nor are the working conditions. As a result, citizens strongly prefer to work in the public sector.

A market logic prevails, however, in the private sector. Foreigners typically come from much less wealthy countries and are willing to work for much lower wages in more difficult conditions and for longer hours than are citizens. Sometimes states force private businesses to hire citizens, and occasionally, citizens have skills that expatriates lack. But as a rule, businesses in Qatar and the UAE hire foreign labor when they can. Figure 18.1 shows the relative number of employees in each sector, by citizenship, in Qatar and Bahrain.

Bahrain and Oman are not as rich and cannot offer all graduates a public-sector job. This, however, does not much change the private-sector preference for foreign labor, especially for less-skilled positions. The lack of public-sector jobs has led citizens to push foreigners out of the public sector (see Figure 18.2). The other result is unemployment, especially among less-skilled citizen labor.

The Dubai Model

In recent years, Dubai has led the way in the Gulf toward diversifying its economy, with a focus on tourism, logistics, trade, and air travel. This diversification, however, is built on inexpensive foreign labor. This makes it very economically disruptive, and costly, for the UAE to wean itself from foreign labor. Indeed, Dubai's success raises the possibility that, in the long run, citizens could become a caste of state employees living off the taxes generated by noncitizens.

The Dubai model, as it has come to be known, has had a wide influence on the rest of the Gulf.[7] Qatar has built a national airline, seeks out tourists, and has a demographic imbalance that is almost as severe as that in the UAE. Dubai's economy relies on a vast pool of inexpensive labor, something that is possible because citizens can seek refuge in employment in the state. Qatar can be similarly generous with state jobs for citizens. Oman and Bahrain, however, are not so rich. The influence of the Dubai model in these countries thus gives rise to political and economic challenges as citizens compete directly with low-cost foreign labor for private-sector jobs.

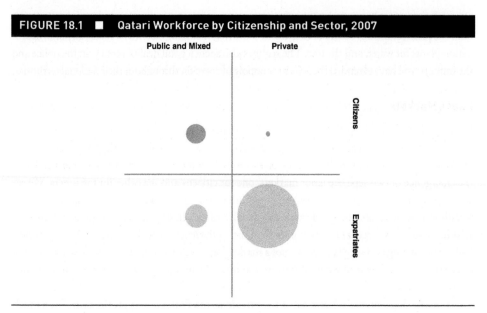

FIGURE 18.1 ■ Qatari Workforce by Citizenship and Sector, 2007

Source: Michael Herb, *The Wages of Oil: Parliaments and Economic Development in Kuwait and the UAE* (Ithaca, NY: Cornell University Press, 2014), 32.

Note: Circle size is proportional to the number of workers.

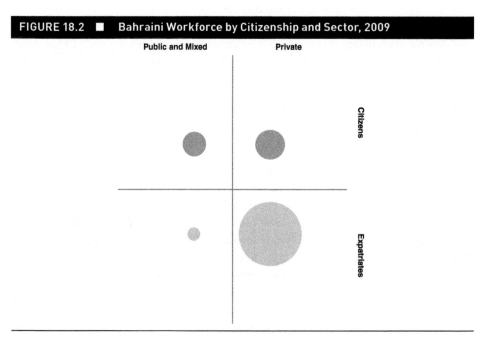

FIGURE 18.2 ■ Bahraini Workforce by Citizenship and Sector, 2009

Source: Michael Herb, *The Wages of Oil: Parliaments and Economic Development in Kuwait and the UAE* (Ithaca, NY: Cornell University Press, 2014), 31.

Note: Circle size is proportional to the number of workers.

Social Structure

KEY FACTS ON LOWER GULF STATES

	Bahrain	Oman	Qatar	UAE
AREA	293 square miles (760 square kilometers)	119,499 square miles (309,500 square kilometers)	4,473 square miles (11,586 square kilometers)	32,278 square miles (83,600 square kilometers)
CAPITAL	Manama	Muscat	Doha	Abu Dhabi
POPULATION	1,526,929 (2021 est.); includes 687,118 nonnationals (2019)	3,694,755 (2021 est.); includes 1,823,787 nonnationals (2019)	2,479,995 (2021 est.); includes 2,192,315 nonnationals (2015)	9,856,612 (2021 est.); includes 8,588,709 nonnationals (2019)
RELIGIOUS GROUPS	Shi'a, 55; Sunni 45; Christian 9.3; Other 16.9 (2019)	Muslim (roughly half Ibadi, half Sunni, with a small Shia minority) 85.9; Christian 6.5; Hindu 5.5; Other; 2 (2019)	Citizens are mostly Sunni, with a Shi'i minority. Overall population: Muslim 65.2; Christian 13.7; Hindu 15.9; Buddhist 3.8; Other 1.4 (2020)	Citizens are mostly Sunni with a Shi'i minority, especially in Dubai. Overall population: Muslim (official) 76; Christian 9%; other (incl. Hindu, Buddhist, Sikh, Ahmadi, Parsi) 15
ETHNIC GROUPS	Sunni Bahrainis, and most Shi'i Bahrainis, are Arab. A minority of the Shi'i population is of Persian origin.	The Omani interior is very largely Arab. Citizens on the coast speak Arabic and come from a variety of backgrounds, including Arab, Baluch, and others, reflecting the orientation of the coast to the sea. Non-citizens are largely South Asian and African.	Qatari citizens are Arabs; some members of the Shi'i minority are Persian in origin.	UAE citizens are Arabs; some members of the Shi'i minority are Persian in origin. Non-citizens are primarily South Asian, Egyptian, and Filipino (2015).

(Continued)

(Continued)

	Bahrain	Oman	Qatar	UAE
OFFICIAL LANGUAGE	Arabic; English is widely spoken, along with Farsi, Urdu, Hindi, and other languages.	Arabic; English, Baluchi, Urdu, and other South Asian languages are widely spoken.	Arabic; English is widely spoken, along with Farsi, Urdu, Nepali, Hindi, and other languages.	Arabic; English is widely spoken, along with Farsi, Urdu, Hindi, and many other languages.
TYPE OF GOVERNMENT	Constitutional Monarchy	Absolute Monarchy	Absolute Monarchy	Federation of seven monarchies
DATE OF INDEPENDENCE	August 15, 1971 (from the United Kingdom)	1650 (expulsion of the Portuguese); effectively independent from the United Kingdom in 1971	September 3, 1971 (from the United Kingdom)	December 2, 1971 (from the United Kingdom)
GDP (PPP)	$69.95 billion; $40,900 per capita (2020)	$135.79 billion; $27,300 per capita (2019)	$245.66 billion (2021); $85,300 per capita (2020)	$655.79 billion (2021); $67,100 per capita (2019)
GDP (NOMINAL)	$38.47 billion (2019)	$76.88 billion (2019)	$191.29 billion (2018)	$721.08 billion (2019)
PERCENTAGE OF GDP BY SECTOR	Agriculture, 0.3; industry, 39.3; services, 60.4 (2017 est.)	Agriculture, 1.8; industry, 46.4; service, 51.8 (2017 est.)	Agriculture, 0.2; industry, 50.3; service, 49.5 (2017 est.)	Agriculture, 0.9; industry, 49.8; service, 49.2 (2017 est.)
TOTAL RENTS (PERCENTAGE OF GDP) FROM NATURAL RESOURCES	3.8 (2019 est.)	26.7 (2019 est.)	20.7 (2019 est.)	16.76 (2019 est.)
FERTILITY RATE	1.768 children born per woman (2021 est.)	2.7 children born per woman (2019 est.)	1.9 children born per woman (2019 est.)	1.65 children born per woman (2021 est.)

Sources: CIA. "Chiefs of State and Cabinet Members of Foreign Governments." Accessed August 10, 2022, https://web.archive.org/web/20201128063511/https://www.cia.gov/library/publications/world-leaders-1/. Gengler, Justin. *Group Conflict and Political Mobilization in Bahrain and the Arab Gulf: Rethinking the Rentier State.* Bloomington, Indiana University Press, 2015.

Gulf Labour Markets and Migration. "Total Population and Percentage and of Nationals and Non-Nationals in GCC Countries (National Statistics, 2017-2018) (With Numbers)." Accessed August 10, 2022, https://gulfmigration.grc.net/gcc-total-population-and-percentage-of-nationals-and-non-nationals-in-gcc-countries-national-statistics-2017-2018-with-numbers/.

Priya DSouza Communications. "Population of Qatar by Nationality—2019 Report." August 15, 2019, http://priyadsouza.com/population-of-qatar-by-nationality-in-2017/.

Sultanate of Oman, National Centre for Statistics & Information. "Data Portal." Accessed August 10, 2022, https://data.gov.om/.

By far the most important social cleavage in the lower Gulf societies is that between citizens and noncitizens. This distinction is important in employment, education, treatment by the police, and in many other aspects of life. The distinction is clearly visible: Citizens often wear a distinctive national dress specific to their own country (and when they do not, it can be difficult to distinguish citizens from foreigners). Female dress styles are somewhat less nationally distinctive, though it is usually not difficult to distinguish female citizens from female expatriates. In the Gulf, the term *national* is widely used instead of *citizen*. In this chapter, I prefer the term *citizen* because it keeps the focus on the crucial legal difference between nationals and nonnationals, which is the possession of citizenship by nationals. Residents who lack citizenship are typically called *expatriates*, especially those with an education or those from the West.

Citizens

The demography of the citizen population of the Gulf today owes much to its trading past. The small trading cities and towns of the pre-oil Gulf were diverse and cosmopolitan. They were ruled by families descended from the inland Najdi tribes. Residents were Arab (from Najd and elsewhere) and of Persian, Baloch, Iraqi, African, Indian, and other origins. Those who arrived before oil, by and large, became citizens when the states decided, after oil, to formally designate who was a citizen and who was not.

The lower Gulf states do not release public figures on the ethnic or sectarian composition of their citizen or expatriate populations. It appears that in Bahrain, the Shi'a compose between 55 and 60 percent of the citizen population, and in Oman, the Ibadis are around half of the citizen population.[8] Qatar and the UAE have Sunni majorities.

All four lower Gulf states have citizen populations with large Arab majorities. Many are descended from the Arab tribes of the Arabian Peninsula, including most of the ruling families. Some Arabs are of nontribal origin. The most important non-Arab citizen group in the lower Gulf states is of Persian descent; they are also typically Shi'i. Persians are important in Dubai especially. Other non-Arab citizen groups include Balochis, from what is now Pakistan and Iran, along with a variety of migrants from all around the Indian Ocean and the Middle East. Many Omanis trace their origins to the African parts of Oman's empire, including a sizable number who migrated back to Oman after the revolution in the former Omani possession of Zanzibar. Slavery was common in the Gulf before the oil boom, especially in Omani date farming and Gulf pearling, and many citizens are of African origin.[9] In modern times, many Gulf men have married foreigners, increasing the diversity of the citizen population. When citizen women marry foreigners however, their children usually do not receive the citizenship of their mothers.

Expatriates/Noncitizens

Gulf regimes rarely grant citizenship to the many foreigners who work in the Gulf. This is the result of a straightforward economic fact. Citizens, by virtue of being citizens, receive jobs, educations, health care, and many other benefits from the state. These benefits are paid out of their country's finite oil wealth, not out of tax revenue. In a developed nonoil economy, new citizens pay taxes that—on average—cover the government services that they receive. In the Gulf, by contrast, the size of the pie (viz, oil revenues) is fixed, and each new citizen makes the share of existing citizens smaller.

Gulf states do not publish data on the national origins of expatriates in the Gulf, though it is clear that most hail from South Asia, and especially India, Pakistan, Nepal, and Bangladesh. Many others come from non-GCC Arab countries, including Yemen, Egypt, Syria, Lebanon, and elsewhere. There are many Filipinos in the Gulf and expatriate communities from elsewhere in Asia, Africa, and other parts of the world.

Foreign workers, especially those with little education from poor countries, are vulnerable to mistreatment. A foreigner who wants to work in the Gulf states typically needs a sponsor, or *kafeel* (thus, the *kafala* system, as it is known). In the classic *kafala* system, still more or less in effect across much of the Gulf, the *kafeel* secures the visa, and once in the country, the worker's permission to work is dependent upon the sponsor (though the person who provides the visa, the legal sponsor, and the eventual employer may not be the same). In many cases—though certainly not all—those who want to work in the Gulf pay a fee to labor recruiters to secure a visa. Thus, when they arrive in one of the Gulf states, many are already in debt. Workers often find it difficult to move to a different employer, and sometimes cannot leave the country without their employer's permission. The overall effect of the system is to make the immigrant worker dependent upon their sponsor and employer.[10] This dependence opens the door for abuse. Health and safety regulations are not always followed closely, and workers frequently die on the job in the lower Gulf states. Employers sometimes withhold wages. Women who work and live in their employers' houses as household servants are vulnerable to abuse.

The governments of the lower Gulf states, and especially Qatar and the UAE, are increasingly sensitive to criticism about their treatment of foreign workers and have taken some steps to try to improve the lives of foreign workers. States have sometimes punished employers who withhold wages. Regulations—not always enforced—limit outside work in the middle of the day in the summer. Qatar, in particular, put in place reforms that responded to criticism of its treatment of foreign labor in preparations for the World Cup in 2022. While the reforms have helped, the vast imbalance in power between citizens and noncitizens leaves abundant room for abuse.

While the negative aspects of foreign labor in the Gulf deserve abundant attention, the positive aspects must also be kept in mind. Millions of people from poor countries come to the Gulf to work, sending home vast sums of money used to educate children, build businesses, fund retirements, and improve the lives of people who often have few good choices in their lives.

Gulf citizens are not the only rich people who benefit from cheap labor. So too do the citizens of the United States, Europe, and other rich countries, who import vast amounts of clothing, toys, electronics, and other goods manufactured by people earning very low wages and often working in poor conditions. What makes the Gulf countries different is that they import not just goods but also labor. By doing so, they make unmistakably visible the vast gulf between rich and poor in the modern world economy. The juxtaposition of enormous wealth and deep poverty is unsettling to the visitor to the Gulf who is accustomed to a society that profits from the labor of poor foreigners only at a distance.

Actors, Opinion, and Participation

None of the lower Gulf regimes are democracies. Before the Arab Spring, their repression of dissent tended to be muted by regional standards (except in Bahrain); after the Arab Spring, the regimes have become much more repressive. The severity and triggers of repression still vary across the region, but the overall trend has been very much in the wrong direction. Political parties are not allowed in any of the four lower Gulf states, though in Bahrain, political societies act as political parties. In Qatar, the UAE, and Oman, those who are elected to representative assemblies are elected as independents and do not have party affiliation. In most cases, in practice, they do not have an affiliation with a formal interest group of any sort. Instead, most of those elected, in practice, represent their family, clan, or tribe. This tends to exacerbate the division of society by tribal or clan group and inhibits the formation of non-clan-based interest groups and political associations.

Although the constitutions provide for freedom of association, in practice the governments impose serious limits on civil society groups. Thus, formal human rights organizations in the lower Gulf states are linked to the governments and are not independent NGOs (nongovernmental organizations). Informal, nonpolitical charitable organizations are often dealt with more tolerantly by the regimes, and ascriptive organizations—such as tribes—are usually encouraged. Generally, the capacity of formal civil society actors to contribute to the political discourse in the lower Gulf states—not to speak of participation in decision-making—is minimal.

All four lower Gulf states severely restrict press freedoms. Two satellite television stations, Al Jazeera, based in Qatar, and Al Arabiya, based in Dubai, influence Arab public opinion, and Al Jazeera helped lead the Arab Spring revolutions. These stations, however, do not criticize their own regimes. On occasion, they will criticize the politics of other Gulf monarchies, and this contributed to the rift between Qatar and its neighbors.

Bahrain has long-run prisons that torture and abuse political prisoners, especially from among the country's Shi'i majority. In recent years the UAE too has imprisoned political prisoners—especially those affiliated or thought to be affiliated with the Muslim Brotherhood—in abusive conditions. Across the lower Gulf, and especially in Bahrain and the UAE, it is increasingly costly to express political opinions that the ruling regimes do not like.

Avoiding Demands for Participation

How have the regimes avoided pressure for greater political participation? In Bahrain, there is a lot of plain repression. In the other three lower Gulf countries, however, rulers have maintained what appears to be a substantial reservoir of support from their people.

One explanation for how rulers maintain public support is that they consult a great deal with their citizens or, at least, give the impression that they do. The traditional form of this consultation is the *majlis*, an open meeting in which citizens can meet the ruler and ask for help. Yet the traditional majlis imposes no institutional constraints of the sort that a parliament might on the ruler; it is a forum for asking for the ruler's favor. Actual consultation typically is reserved mostly for the elite. That said, many Gulf rulers have managed to sell the idea to their citizens that they are connected to their societies and pay attention to citizen opinion.

Oil wealth helps the Gulf rulers stay in the good graces of their citizens, though its ability to make rulers popular should not be overstated.[11] Not so long ago, Qatar, the UAE, and Oman were abjectly poor. Today, they are well off or rich. While the ruling families are not primarily responsible for this, the ruling families nonetheless benefit from the general sense of good fortune. But oil wealth alone is not responsible for political quiescence in the lower Gulf. The citizens of Kuwait, a country as rich as the UAE or Qatar, have a long tradition of protest (though there is little support for actually deposing the ruling family). Nor does it quite make sense that rulers can simply buy the support of their citizens; most citizens think it is their money in the first place, and buying off opposition tends to create more of it.

The Gulf rulers benefit from comparisons with neighboring states, the condition of which allows the monarchs to argue that their citizens could have it a lot worse.[12] Former monarchies in the Middle East include Libya, Iraq, Egypt, Yemen, and Iran. That is not a list that inspires Gulf citizens to go to the barricades. The aftermath of the civil war in Syria is also not an argument for the benefits of rebellion against an autocratic regime. To be sure, not all citizens think along these lines, but many do, and this creates a constituency for stability and order.

The rulers also use nationalism to their advantage, as do most authoritarian rulers. In Qatar, the threat from the Quartet (see the Regional and International Relations section) boosted the amir's popularity, while the rulers of the UAE have used the country's foreign adventures to build support. This, of course, is a strategy that can backfire if foreign adventures go wrong in a way that reflects badly on the rulers.

Finally, in Qatar and the UAE especially, citizens are a small and very privileged minority. The status quo provides many benefits to this minority, and the regimes protect citizen prerogatives. The privileged citizen minority has much to lose from genuine political participation by the noncitizen majority, while expatriates lack any of the resources necessary to demand real political change from the regimes.

Religion and Politics

The lower Gulf regimes and most citizens view the protection and promotion of religion as an appropriate use of state power. Political leaders refer to Islam frequently in their public pronouncements and make public shows of their piety. Each state formally acknowledges in its constitution or similar document that Islam is the religion of the state—though none specify a specific school of Islamic law.

The dynasties that rule the lower Gulf states (with the partial exception of Oman) did not rely on their religious establishments in their rise to power, and as a result, the religious establishments are not as politically influential as in Saudi Arabia. The firm grip of the ruling families on political power has also limited the influence of political Islamist groups such as the Muslim Brotherhood. Perhaps the most important political role of religion in the lower Gulf states is as a source of political identity. The central cleavage in Bahraini politics, for example, is between Sunnis and Shi'a—and the political tension between the two communities is all about the division of power and wealth, not about the theological points that divide the two sects.

Domestic Conflict and Rebel Governance

None of the Gulf regimes has suffered a regional rebellion since the 1970s in Oman (in the southern region of Dhofar). Like much else in the Gulf, this is a consequence of the combination of oil revenues and monarchism. Oil revenues provide the revenues necessary to build and maintain an effective state apparatus that effectively governs the national territory. Monarchism—and especially the Gulf variant of dynastic monarchy—provides political stability at the top of the regime and inspires loyalty among more traditional-minded citizens.

The Arab Spring largely skipped over Qatar and the UAE. In Oman, citizens protested in some cities, but the protests were relatively mild. In Bahrain, however, Shiʻi citizens took to the streets to demand the fall of the regime, an episode that has much to do with sectarian tensions and is discussed in the section on Bahrain.

Regional and International Relations

Command outside Doha at the Al Udeid Air Base, and Jebel Ali in Dubai is often said to be the port most visited by the US Navy outside the United States itself. The Americans have kept a large military presence in Kuwait since liberation in 1991.

While the United States maintains a robust military presence in the Gulf, its political influence has been on the decline since its high point following the liberation of Kuwait in 1991. George W. Bush invaded Iraq in 2003 against the advice of the Gulf monarchs, who feared an expansion of Iranian influence. The Obama administration angered the Gulf monarchs by negotiating an agreement normalizing relations with Iran. The Trump administration's lack of policy coherence further weakened the US position in the Gulf. And the Biden administration's chaotic withdrawal from Afghanistan did little to reassure regional allies.

The relative decline of American influence can be most clearly seen in the more assertive foreign policies of the Gulf states. In recent years, rather than following the lead of the United States, they have pursued their own regional ambitions, sometimes dragging the United States along with them, other times operating independently of the United States.

American decline, however, should not be exaggerated. At its peak, following the Gulf war of 1990–1991, the United States enjoyed an extraordinary influence, and decline from that point is not too surprising. America has not been pushed to the side. No other country has the ambition or the ability to replace the United States in the region. And the foreign policies of the Gulf monarchies, while more independent than in the past, are still pursued with one eye firmly on Washington.

Relations among the Gulf States

One would think that small, oil-rich Sunni monarchies in the Gulf, facing threats from all sides and resembling each other in so many ways, would keep their disagreements with each other in check. One would be right for most of the modern era in the Gulf, from the 1960s through the Arab Spring or so. In 1981, the monarchies formed the Gulf Cooperation Council (GCC) in response to the outbreak of the war between Iraq and Iran; the idea was to eventually create a union capable of defending the monarchies from the neighbors. It never turned into that, but there were some useful efforts to coordinate regulations and promote the movement of goods and people among the six monarchies. There even developed something of a sense of common identity among GCC citizens, one that does not compete with (much stronger) national identities, but which does serve to distinguish Gulf Arabs not only from non-Arabs and the many expatriates in their own societies but also to some degree from the citizens of other Arab states.

The sense of common identity provided by the GCC, the shared circumstances of the citizens of the oil-rich monarchies, and their common vulnerability, have not, however, prevented serious internecine disputes between the ruling families. The most serious of these disputes emerged after the Arab Spring, and especially during the Trump administration, when Saudi Arabia, the UAE, Bahrain and Egypt imposed a siege on Qatar in which Qatar's neighbors appear to have seriously considered invading it.

During the Arab Spring, the amir of Qatar had fancied himself the leader of a regional power—albeit one thin on people but with plenty of cash. This deeply annoyed his neighbors. In 2014, the Saudi Arabia and the UAE, along with Bahrain, pulled their ambassadors from Doha shortly after Amir Hamad, who had led Qatar's international activism, resigned in favor of his son Tamim. The new amir cut back Qatar's foreign-policy adventurism, and for a time, it appeared that Qatar had mended fences with its neighbor. Tensions reemerged in 2017. One trigger may have been a massive ransom Qatar paid to groups—some linked to Iran—to secure the release of a hunting party kidnapped in Iraq that included members of the Al Thani ruling family. A second trigger may have been the new administration in Washington. Donald Trump made his first international visit to Saudi Arabia (rather than the traditional choices, Canada or Mexico), and the Saudis captivated him with pomp and circumstance. Before Trump had even left the region, the UAE kicked off a series of events that resulted in the imposition of a blockade by the Quartet two weeks later.

Shortly after imposing the blockade, a group of states dubbed the Quartet (led by Saudi Arabia and the UAE, with Bahrain and Egypt) issued a set of thirteen demands to Qatar that sums up, more or less, its problems with Qatar.[13] The Quartet did not like Qatar's links with Iran and Turkey, its patronage of the Muslim Brotherhood, and its provision of refuge to opponents of neighboring regimes. And it did not like Al-Jazeera, which gave a platform to the Muslim Brotherhood and to opponents of other Arab regimes.[14] Unsaid, but lurking behind all of this, was a sense that the Qatari ruling family needed to be cut down to size—a size that should be smaller than that of especially the ruling family of Saudi Arabia.

The US defense establishment and the state department tried to contain the rift between traditional US allies in the Gulf on the grounds that it threatened long-term US interests in the region. The US air base in Qatar, after all, has been integral to US war efforts in Afghanistan and Iraq. This might explain why Trump himself is said to have discouraged the Saudis from actually invading Qatar when they considered the idea early in the crisis.

In the end, the blockade was a resounding failure: the Quartet failed to achieve virtually any of its political goals. Qatar rejected the demands of the Quartet, and its wealth allowed it to absorb the economic shock. Qatar's ruler, Amir Tamim, benefited from a wave of public support as he stood up for Qatar's sovereignty. The Qataris launched a successful attempt to gain influence with Trump's inner circle,[15] lessening the pressure from Washington. The dispute wound down in the later part of the Trump administration, and on January 4, 2021— as the Biden administration was preparing to take office—the Quartet formally threw in the towel and resumed diplomatic relations with Qatar, having accomplished nothing of note. The costs of the blockade, however, were real and substantial: the myriad economic ties between the nations were largely severed. Families were divided and careers disrupted as Gulf citizens and expatriates were forced to choose sides.

The timing of the resolution of the conflict suggested that events in Washington still have a profound influence on the Gulf. So too did another prominent Gulf development during the Trump administration, the UAE decision to normalize relations with Israel, followed by a similar decision by Bahrain (these are the Abraham Accords). The Accords strengthened relations between the UAE and the United States, and were in part aimed to counter Iran, a country seen as a paramount threat by both Israel and the UAE.

THE UNITED ARAB EMIRATES

The United Arab Emirates is a federation of seven emirates, each with its own territory, ruling family, and eponymous seaside city. Six of the emirates are along the Gulf shore: from the south, Abu Dhabi, Dubai, Sharjah, Ajman, Umm Al Quwain, and Ras Al Khaimah. The seventh emirate, Fujairah, faces the Gulf of Oman, which opens to the Indian Ocean.

History of State Formation—the UAE

The history of state formation in the coastal shaykhdoms revolves around control of trade in the Gulf. The British, as part of their effort to reduce "piracy" and thus to control trade, in 1819, destroyed the fleet of the Qasami state based at Ras Al Khaimah and induced rulers of the area's shaykhdoms to sign a treaty prohibiting piracy. Additional treaties followed, and as a group, the principalities came to be known as the Trucial States, or the Trucial Coast, until independence in 1971. The British brought together the emirates in a common institutional framework when it set up the Trucial States Council in 1952. At independence in 1971, the poorer emirates of the UAE had little option but to join with Abu Dhabi, which possesses the vast majority of the UAE's oil wealth. Ras Al Khaimah held out until 1972, when it became clear that oil would not be found in commercial quantities on its territory. Dubai's more oil reserves and its preindependence commercial success allowed it to enter the federation as a partner of Abu Dhabi.

Institutions and Governance—the UAE

The leading political institution in the UAE is the Supreme Council, composed of the seven rulers of the constituent emirates of the UAE. The Supreme Council must approve all legislation, the appointment of the prime minister, all treaties, the annual budget, and any changes to the constitution. Decisions require a supermajority of five of the seven members. Abu Dhabi and Dubai, alone, each have a veto. The Supreme Council elects the president of the UAE for a five-year term. The rulers have always elected the ruler of Abu Dhabi to fill the post.[16]

The president appoints the prime minister, who has always been a member of the Al Maktoum ruling family of Dubai. The cabinet includes members of the ruling families of Abu

Dhabi and Dubai, members of some other ruling families, and Emiratis from outside the ruling families. The government initiates legislation that then goes to the Supreme Council for approval. Its powers are thus both executive and legislative.

The Federal National Council (FNC) is what passes for a representative assembly at the national level in the UAE. It has forty members, eight each from Abu Dhabi and Dubai, six each from Sharjah and Ras Al Khaimah, and four for the rest. The FNC has few formal powers; it cannot remove ministers from office, and it cannot prevent the passage of legislation or force legislation through against the opposition of the Supreme Council. Half of its members are appointed, and the other half are elected. The electorate, however, is itself appointed by the rulers of each of the seven emirates. For the first elections in 2006, the electorate was a mere 6,689 (drawn from a citizen population above twenty years of age of around 400,000). In subsequent elections, the regime expanded the electorate to 130,000, in 2011 after the Arab Spring, to 224,000 in 2015 and to 338,000 in 2019. While elections now occur on a regular four year schedule, turnout remains low at 35 percent in 2019. The government trumpeted a 48.6 percent increase in votes cast compared to 2015, but the size of the electorate increased 50.6 percent. The low turnout suggests citizens who did not think much of the exercise.

Each of the seven emirates controls its own oil wealth, and Abu Dhabi has the vast majority of the oil. As a result, the federal government depends on the willingness of Abu Dhabi to fund its operations. The 2018 VAT (value-added tax), collected by a federal tax authority with 30 percent of the proceeds going to the federal government, gives the federal government an independent source of revenue. This is unlikely, however, to diminish the outsized voice of Abu Dhabi in the politics of the UAE. The Defense Ministry, for example, is nominally headed up by a member of the Al Maktoum but is headquartered in Abu Dhabi, paid for by Abu Dhabi, and is understood to be wholly under the control of the ruling family of Abu Dhabi.[17] The foreign policy of the UAE, similarly, is set by Abu Dhabi.

In the past, Dubai has been jealous of its independence within the UAE. This led to a long-running constitutional crisis in the 1970s when Abu Dhabi sought to strengthen the federation (with itself in the lead) at the expense of the other emirates. Dubai resisted, in part to retain the freedom to pursue its economic growth policies, which were not (and are not) that popular among Emiratis in general. Dubai won the battle over the constitution in the 1970s but was reined in by the economic crisis that started in 2008 and that led to the insolvency, for a period, of the Emirate's government. Abu Dhabi bailed out Dubai; the symbolic price was the abrupt renaming of the world's-tallest building, which had been known as Burj Dubai, after the ruler of Abu Dhabi: It is now Burj Khalifa. More substantively, it is widely understood that the bailout reduced Dubai's independent voice in the federation. The bailout, however, has not led to an appreciable change in the economic growth policies pursued by Dubai, likely because these policies now have the support of the ruling family of Abu Dhabi.

Political Economy—the UAE

In per capita terms, the UAE is one of the world's richest oil exporters. Yet defying the predictions of many scholars who study oil exporters, the UAE has partially diversified its economy away from oil, led by the emirate of Dubai. The rulers of Dubai, with limited oil wealth, sought to avoid falling into irrelevance by making Dubai into a major entrepôt, tourist destination, logistics hub, and business center. In 2019, before COVID travel disruptions, Dubai's airport was the fourth busiest passenger airport in the world. The container port is the 11th busiest in the world. The explosive economic growth of the early 2000s, however, has leveled off in recent years following the successive shocks of the 2008 economic crisis, the decline of oil prices in 2014–2015, and most recently disruptions from the global pandemic, which led to an unusual population decline in 2020.

Dubai's rulers run the emirate like a private business (which is why it is sometimes called Dubai, Inc.). The boundaries between the finances of the emirate of Dubai and the ruler himself are not particularly clear. In many ways, the ruler can be understood as a real estate developer. He owns a great deal of real estate and controls undeveloped land. He and the Dubai government both profit from economic and population growth in Dubai. The massive land reclamation projects (namely, the creation of the "palms" that project from the coastline into the Gulf and which are so prominent when flying into Dubai and on satellite images) are controlled, ultimately, by the ruler, and companies associated with the ruler and the emirate's government profit from them. The ruler himself personally owns one of the largest real estate companies in the emirate, Dubai Holding, and this company receives free grants of land from the emirate. The ruler and companies partly or wholly owned by the emirate government

PHOTO 18.1 The Palm Jumeirah Project in Dubai.

NASA/Commander Leroy Chiao

control a dizzying array of businesses, including Emirates Airways, hotels, port operators, and the like.

Dubai's insolvency in 2009 resembles, more than a little, the sort of bankruptcies suffered by real estate developers. The emirate borrowed heavily to fund growth, and market enthusiasm led to a real estate bubble. When the bubble burst, the emirate's government and its associated companies were overextended and could not make payments on their debt. Abu Dhabi provided the loans necessary to keep Dubai, Inc. solvent.

Social Structure—the UAE

While the government of the UAE does not release data on the nationalities of expatriates in the UAE, it is widely thought that there are roughly twice as many Indian citizens in the UAE as there are Emirati citizens. Pakistanis also outnumber UAE citizens. Emiratis themselves are the third largest national group, followed by Bangladeshis. Many expatriates live in the UAE for a few years only and then go back home. A significant number, however, are longer-term residents. Statistics on births illustrate the permanence of the foreign community: Noncitizen births outnumber citizen births by almost two to one.

Abu Dhabi has more citizens than any other emirate; Dubai and Sharjah are probably next in population size (exact figures are not available). The federal government distributes a good deal of Abu Dhabi's oil wealth to the citizens of poorer emirates (via the federal government), but the citizens of Abu Dhabi are nonetheless notably better off than those of the poorer emirates. This is, in part, because of the distribution of real estate to Abu Dhabi citizens by the emirate government. Those from the poorer emirates often must find work in government offices in Abu Dhabi or Dubai, and this can require long commutes. Passports distinguish among the citizens of different emirates, and an Abu Dhabi "family book" confers extra benefits on the citizens of the emirate.[18] Despite this, over four decades of independence has produced a strong sense of national identity among UAE citizens, a sense of identity reinforced by the presence of so many foreigners in the UAE.

Actors, Opinion, and Participation—the UAE

Citizens of the UAE have expressed relatively little political dissent over the past several decades. In the 1970s, disputes between Abu Dhabi and Dubai opened up a space for the expression of more political opinions by Emirati citizens, and there were demands for a stronger federation, more political participation, the distribution of Abu Dhabi's oil wealth more equitably throughout the federation, and for limits on Dubai's growth—including the influx of foreigners associated with that growth. The leaders of the two emirates, however, resolved their differences, and citizen demands for political change faded.

Emiratis remained largely quiet during the Arab Spring; the main expression of dissent took the form of a petition signed by 133 Emirati intellectuals, activists, and others. The regime responded with repression focused on the Emirati branch of the Muslim Brotherhood. In subsequent years, the regime has, if anything, grown even less tolerant of internal dissent. As Kristin Diwan has pointed out, the regime has also embraced a sometimes-pugilistic nationalism of a sort that is new in the Gulf, and which mobilizes citizens to support political leaders as an expression of nationalist enthusiasm. Thus some Emirati nationalists on Twitter aggressively supported the decision by the regime to normalize relations with Israel, adopting the narrative that it advanced the UAE's specific national interests.

Religion and Politics—the UAE

The UAE population as a whole (that is, including noncitizens) is religiously diverse, and the government tolerates the free practice of a wide variety of religions. While the regime is tolerant of religious diversity, it abhors political Islam, and the Muslim Brotherhood specifically. Most Emirati citizens are Sunni Muslims, as are the rulers of all seven emirates. A substantial Shi'i minority is found in the northern emirates, especially Dubai and Sharjah. The state funds most Sunni mosques, pays the imams, and maintains close control over sermons. Control over Shi'i mosques is less stringent, though the state apparently does provide some financial support to Shi'i religious institutions. The curriculum in public schools (where citizens are educated) is Sunni. The governments of the emirates regularly provide grants of land for the construction of non-Muslim houses of worship. There are Coptic Orthodox churches in the UAE, along with Hindu temples, a Sikh temple, a worship center for the Church of Latter Day Saints (Mormons), and others.

Regional and International Relations—the UAE

Over the past decade and more, the UAE has emerged as a potent military power in the region, dubbed by the American military a "little Sparta."[19] In the past decade, the UAE has adopted a vigorously expansive foreign policy, intervening in the civil war in Yemen (with Saudi Arabia) and engaging in a struggle for influence in the Horn of Africa, with military bases in Eritria and Somaliland and investments in ports in the region. This grows from an effort to participate in the burgeoning economies of especially Ethiopia, which is landlocked, and competition with Turkey. Because Qatar is allied with Turkey and is more sympathetic to political Islam, the complex competition in the Horn of Africa (which includes Egypt and China also) reflects the intra-Gulf divide between Qatar and the UAE, and between those opposed to political Islam in the region and those who generally favor it.[20] More recently, however, the UAE has retrenched, at least in part. The UAE by and large left Yemen, retaining a presence on strategic Yemeni islands. Elsewhere in the Horn of Africa, the UAE reduced its presence in Eritrea, and more generally, the UAE has dialed back, but by no means abandoned, its regional ambitions.

OMAN

Oman has a larger land area and citizen population than the other lower Gulf states. It is one of two GCC countries (with Saudi Arabia) in which citizens outnumber noncitizens. A well-populated coastal plain, Al-Batinah, runs from the UAE border almost to Muscat, the capital and historical center of the Omani trading empire. The Hajar mountain range runs inland behind the coast; Nizwa, the former capital of inner Oman, lies on the other side of the mountains behind Muscat. The city of Salalah is found much farther south, toward Yemen, in the Dhofar region.

History of State Formation—Oman

Oman's rulers adhere to the Ibadi sect of Islam, which is practiced almost exclusively in Oman and is distinct from both Sunni and Shi'i Islam. The distinctive political doctrine of Ibadism is the requirement that the ruler—called the imam—gains office through a sort of election by notables and religious scholars. In practice, however, a series of hereditary dynasties have ruled Oman over the past centuries.[21] The current ruling family came to power in the mid-18th century; its rulers dropped the title of imam in favor of sultan and focused on building a maritime trading empire that ruled territories from what is now Pakistan to Zanzibar. In 1861, the empire split, with a sultan in Muscat and another in Zanzibar. The Muscat sultanate went into economic decline and also lost control over the Omani interior, where a contending Ibadi imam emerged. A war in the 1950s united the country under the Muscat sultanate.

The modern period in Oman started abruptly in 1970 when the founder of modern Oman, Qaboos bin Said, overthrew his father, Said bin Taimur, who famously spent little of Oman's new oil revenues on development. Qaboos's father viewed modern education in particular as a threat to his rule. In 1970, Oman had no secondary schools, one real hospital, and six miles of paved road.[22] The palace coup that brought Sultan Qaboos to power ushered in an era of development, as Qaboos invested Oman's oil resources in education, health, and public infrastructure. By the end of his reign, in 2020, Oman was transformed— but rarely has a country's entry into the modern world been associated so completely with one ruler.

Institutions and Governance—Oman

The Monarchy

Sultan Qaboos was widely known to have been ailing in the final years of his rule. He had no children of his own, and refused to publicly appoint a successor. Instead, he said that his family would meet after his death to pick a successor. If they could not agree, he placed a name in a sealed envelope. The absence of a named successor, and the uncertainty surrounding the unusual succession mechanism, raised concerns about instability after the death of Qaboos. In the event, the succession proceeded smoothly. On the day Qaboos's death was announced, his family simply opened the envelope, which contained the name of Qaboos's cousin Haitham bin Tariq. Haitham took the oath of office the same day.

Sultan Qaboos, in contrast to the practice in the rest of the Gulf, reserved many of the top posts for himself: He was the prime minister, the minister of defense, the minister of finance, the minister of foreign affairs, and the governor of the Central Bank of Oman. Haitham bin Tariq, after coming to power, has relied to a greater degree on members of his family. His full brother is deputy prime minister for defense, a post equivalent to minister of defense. His half-brother is deputy prime minister for foreign affairs, a nephew was named to be head of the board of governors of the central bank, and other relatives hold key posts in the state. This brings Oman more closely in line with the monarchical regime type of its neighbors. A year after coming to power, the new sultan—in sharp contrast with his predecessor—named a crown prince, his eldest son, and amended the basic law to set in place a system of primogeniture in which the eldest son of the sultan takes power on his death.

Majlis Oman

Oman's Basic Law, issued by the sultan in 1996 and revised in 2021, makes official what was already clear: Oman is an absolute monarchy with no real constraints on the power of the monarch. The law calls for elections to the lower chamber of a bicameral parliament, the Consultative Council or *majlis al-shura*. The upper chamber is the State Council (*majlis al-dawla*); the sultan appoints its members by decree. The appointed chamber cannot have more members than the elected.

Oman holds higher-quality elections than any Gulf monarchy except Kuwait. Earlier elections had a very limited suffrage, but the five elections held every four years from 2003 to 2019 were thought to be technically fair, in the sense that the government did not stuff the ballot boxes. However, political parties are illegal. Candidates have had little freedom to adopt clear policy positions, and as a consequence, the elections are mostly about tribe and clan loyalties.[23] In a sign of some progress, three deputies who participated in Oman's Arab Spring protests were elected to the Council in 2011, and the 2019 elections featured more robust debates than had been the case in previous elections.

The Consultative Council has only very modest powers. Majlis Oman must pass laws before they come into effect, but if the two houses disagree, the differences are resolved in a joint session by majority vote, which dilutes the weight of elected deputies. The Council cannot remove confidence in ministers, a key power enjoyed by the Kuwaiti National Assembly. Some ministers—those leading "service" ministries, such as the Ministry of Health—can be questioned by the Majlis. Further democratization in Oman requires not so much better elections but instead a more powerful elected assembly.

Social Structure—Oman

Although the Omani government publishes no data on the sectarian affiliations of Omani citizens, Marc Valeri estimates that Ibadis make up 48 to 53 percent of the citizen population, Shi'a 3 to 4 percent, and Sunnis the balance (that is, just under half). The ruling family is Ibadi. Interior Oman is more Arab and Ibadi, while the coast—the Batinah and Muscat—is more oriented to the sea and more varied in origin. Slave labor was common in the Batinah date plantations, which flourished in the 19th century and first decades of the 20th century, and this has influenced the demography of coastal areas.[24]

In recent years, sectarian conflicts have torn apart several Arab countries. In Oman, by contrast, we find little sectarian strife. It helps that Ibadis are found almost only in Oman, so that there are no larger regional dimensions to the sectarian difference. And it helps more that Ibadis and Sunnis have little history of directly sectarian clashes over political power, economic resources, and the like. The war between interior Oman and the coastal sultanate of the 1950s was fought between two Ibadi rulers.

Omanis are divided by region as well as by sect. Dhofaris rebelled in the 1960s and 1970s, and there remains a sense of Dhofari regional distinctiveness that may reassert itself. There has always been a divide between the more ethnically diverse coast (the Batinah and greater Muscat) and inner Oman. Observers of Omani politics will closely watch to see if, and how, these regional and sectarian divisions become more visible in the post-Qaboos era.

Actors, Opinion, and Participation—Oman

Unlike Qatar and the UAE, Oman experienced street protests during the Arab Spring. These started with protests in Muscat then spread to the industrial town of Sohar in the North, where protests took on a more working-class nature. Demonstrators did not call for the fall of the regime but instead professed their loyalty to the sultan. They complained about competition from foreign laborers, corruption in the government, unemployment, and the like.[25]

In the decade and more since the Arab Spring, a tradition of periodic street protests has emerged in Oman, focused on demands for employment. This has continued into the reign of the new sultan Haitham bin Tariq. The regime has typically responded with a mix of concessions and repression, with the emphasis mostly on concessions that take the form of promises of new jobs in the state and in private industry. But the repression has also been very real. As the Arab Spring turned to regime-led counterrevolution around the Arab world, Oman's rulers tightened down on civil liberties and jailed several dissenters—including a member of the Consultative Council elected in 2011.

Religion and Politics—Oman

The Omani state promotes a "generic" Islam that elides the doctrinal differences between Sunni Islam and Ibadi Islam. Nonetheless, in official appointments, observers find a tendency to favor the ruler's Ibadi sect: ministers of Justice and Religious Affairs have been Ibadi, as have been the sultanate's muftis. This Ibadi favoritism is tempered by the fact that historically the Al Said dynasty has been a dynasty of the (predominantly Sunni) coast and Muscat more than the Ibadi interior, so the dynasty has succeeded in avoiding the perception of siding entirely with one religious community or the other.

Islamist political groups, like other political organizations, have little public presence in Oman. The Muslim Brotherhood was blamed for organizing a coup conspiracy in 1994, and the Brotherhood was said to have had a role in the protests in Sohar in 2011.[26] Should the political system open up, we might see a more public presence of Salafi and Brotherhood groups among Oman's Sunni population. Omani history also suggests that there is the potential for dissent among the sultanate's Ibadis—in 2005, the security forces arrested a group of Ibadis accused of conspiring to reestablish the Ibadi imamate.

Political Economy—Oman

Oman has only a fraction of the oil of its neighbors (5.3 billion barrels of proven reserves, compared to 98 billion for the UAE) and has a larger citizen population. Oman needs to build a nonoil economy that productively employs citizen labor but, unfortunately, has made only modest progress in this direction. In recent years, following the Arab Spring, the regime hired even more Omanis into government jobs, and today, most Omanis who are employed for a wage work for the state. The private sector hires only a few Omanis. Sooner rather than later, Oman will need to build a productive, job-generating, nonoil economy with citizen labor. There are some grounds for optimism. The neighboring UAE is a rich market for Omani goods and services. Oman is politically stable—at least thus far. Even in the best scenario, however, a fall in per capita incomes in the sultanate is likely as oil revenues eventually decline. In recent years, dissent in the sultanate has focused on economic demands, and some of the responses by the regime—adding yet more employees to the government payroll—have not addressed Oman's long- term economic challenges.

Regional and International Relations—Oman

Oman has long pursued an independent foreign policy, which in practice means something akin to neutrality. In the spring of 2015, Oman declined to support Saudi Arabia and the other members of the GCC in their military campaign against the Houthis in Yemen. Earlier, in March of 2011, Oman declined to send forces to Bahrain to support the Sunni ruling family against Shi'i protesters. And Oman did not join Saudi Arabia and the UAE in their campaign against Qatar. This careful foreign policy has arguably served Oman's national interests well, as it has solid relationships with a variety of regional and world powers. This foreign policy was the creation of the late sultan Qaboos; his successor, sultan Haitham, appears to be continuing the policy of his predecessor, at least in the first year or two of his reign.

QATAR

History of State Formation—Qatar

Until oil, Qatar was at the periphery of the periphery, a scarcely populated peninsula jutting into the gulf and ruled by the Al Thani clan. In 1872, the Al Thani came under Ottoman suzerainty, a situation that lasted until the Ottoman withdrawal, after which Al Thani dynasty entered into direct treaty relations with Britain in 1916. Oil was exported from 1949, and in the subsequent decades, oil revenues brought prosperity, rapid immigration, and social change.

Institutions and Governance—Qatar

Qatari amirs have a tradition of abdication, which is not common elsewhere in the Gulf—three of the last four amirs abdicated, and the fourth was deposed by his son (in 1995). The current amir, Tamim, came to power when his father abruptly stepped down in 2013. Despite this turnover at the top, Qatar remains very much a family regime, with the family firmly in control of state institutions.

Although Qatar works actively on promoting its international image as a forward-thinking and liberal state, until very recently Qatar lacked any sort of elected national representative assembly beyond the municipality (which, given Qatar's small size, encompasses the entire country). Since 1999, Qatar has held six elections to its municipal council, the most recent in 2019. The municipal council, however, has little authority.

The 2005 constitution calls for elections to two-thirds of the seats in Qatar's Consultative Assembly. The elections were delayed many years and finally held in the fall of 2021. The election law excluded most naturalized Qataris from voting or running in the elections, and this led to more public dissent that is usual in Qatar (which is, to be sure, very little): the law excluded many members of a sizable tribe that has been crosswise with the regime for some time. Those were allowed to vote were divided into districts based on the "place of residence of their tribe or family, as the case may be." This magnified the influence of tribe and clan in the voting. When the elections were held, turnout was reported to be 64 percent of, presumably, registered voters.

The remaining one-third of the seats in the Consultative Assembly are appointed by the emir. While the constitution gives the Assembly powers that, at first glance, seem comparable to those of Kuwait's National Assembly, a close read of the constitution makes it clear that the Assembly has no real ability to hold the regime institutionally accountable.

Political Economy—Qatar

Qatar has the third-largest natural gas reserves in the world, after only Russia and Iran. Qatar's hydrocarbon revenue comes mostly from natural gas, not oil, and its natural gas resources will last for at least one hundred years.

What has Qatar done with its wealth? Like other rich Gulf states, much has been invested in a sovereign wealth fund—that is to say, it has been invested (mostly abroad) for the future. At home, Qatar has adopted elements of the Dubai model, at least in the sense of building an internationally known brand (Gulf countries are self-conscious about branding) and developing an entrepôt and a tourist economy. Al Jazeera is one of the leading Arabic-language satellite channels; Qatar Airways competes with other Gulf airlines and attracts millions of visitors yearly to Doha's airport. World-famous architects (including I. M. Pei) have designed museums in Doha. Education City features branch campuses of six US universities (along with one French and one British university). And Qatar won (or, by some accounts, purchased) the right to host the World Cup in 2022. This pell-mell development has resulted in a demographic imbalance in Qatar that rivals that in the UAE. Unlike the UAE, however, it is not clear that the Qatari economy has made much progress in diversifying its economy substantially beyond hydrocarbons.

Social Structure—Qatar

Many Qatari citizens are members of Sunni tribes that resided in Qatar and the Arabian Peninsula before oil. The country also has a fairly sizable Shi'i minority of Persian descent, though specific numbers are not available. At the height of the pearling boom earlier in the 20th century, many African slaves were brought to Qatar to work in the pearling industry, and their descendants are Qatari citizens. Remarkably, the government has built a museum of slavery in Doha.

The Qatari government does not release figures for the total number of citizens in the country (which gives a sense of just how sensitive the subject is), but it appears that citizens numbered around 330,000 in 2019, at the time around 10.5 percent of the total population: the pandemic led to a dip in the number of noncitizens in Qatar, as in the other Gulf monarchies. The Qatari government also does not release information on the national origin of expatriates, though it appears that the most populous national groups in Qatar are from India, Bangladesh, Nepal, and Qatar itself—in that order.[27]

Actors, Opinion, and Participation—Qatar

There are no organized opposition groups in Qatar and hardly any organized political groups of any sort whatsoever. The Muslim Brotherhood, which Qatar has supported internationally and which is associated with the Al Jazeera satellite station, had a branch in Qatar but disbanded in 1999 because its former leader later said the state was carrying out its Islamic responsibilities.

One small expression of dissent surfaced in 2012 when a Qatari citizen, Ali Khalifa Al Kuwari, published an edited book with the title *The People Want Reform . . . in Qatar, Too.*[28] Despite the lack of opportunities for political participation and the regime's thoroughgoing authoritarianism, Qataris expressed less dissent during the Arab Spring than the citizens of any other Arab nation.[29] And the Quartet's blockade seems to have boosted Amir Tamim's popularity via a rally-round-the-flag effect.

Religion and Politics—Qatar

Qatar's ruling family adheres to the Wahhabi school of Islamic jurisprudence, as do the Al Saud of Saudi Arabia. The Al Thani's interpretation of Wahhabism, however, is not nearly as strict as that of the Al Saud: Women in Qatar can drive (as they can in all of the lower Gulf states), alcohol is sold legally, and social norms, while not as free as Dubai, are much freer than in Saudi Arabia. Occasionally, however, the regime does emphasize its Wahhabism, at least in symbolic ways—the new national mosque is named after Muhammad Ibn Abdul Wahhab, the founder of the Wahhabi movement. Mehran Kamrava, in his book on Qatar, attributes this to the balancing strategy of the Al Thani: While the ruling family embraces globalization, the ruler makes occasional gestures to the beliefs of Qatar's more conservative citizens.

Regional and International Relations—Qatar

Until very recently Qatar has been at the center of a major political dispute with its neighbors. The account of that dispute in the earlier section of this chapter—on common themes in the lower Gulf states—covers the crucial aspects of Qatar's foreign relations.

BAHRAIN

History of State Formation—Bahrain

Bahrain is a tiny island nation that lies in the Gulf between Qatar and Saudi Arabia's Eastern Province; since 1986, a causeway has linked it to Saudi Arabia. It is ruled by the Al Khalifa, a Sunni ruling family that conquered the island in 1783, subjugating the island's Shi'i Arab population, the Baharna.[30] This history of conquest colors the relations between the ruling family and Bahraini citizens to this day.

Despite its small size, Bahrain was a major trading port in the Gulf before oil, rivaling Kuwait and more important than Dubai. Great Britain moved its main Gulf naval base to Bahrain in 1935, and from 1946, the chief British political figure in the Gulf was based in Bahrain. Before independence in 1971, the shah of Iran revived Iran's claim to Bahrain. A United Nations team visited Bahrain and concluded that independence had overwhelming support among Bahrainis. The shah dropped his claim, and Bahrain won its independence in 1971.

Institutions and Governance—Bahrain

Following independence in 1971, Bahrain adopted a constitution modeled on Kuwait's, the most liberal in the Gulf. Elections were held in 1973, but the amir dissolved the chamber in 1975. The Al Khalifa ruled for the next several decades without an elected parliament of any sort.

The current king, Hamad bin Isa, initiated a political opening after coming to power in 1999. He invited political exiles to return to Bahrain and held a national referendum on the need for a new constitution that would introduce a new upper house of parliament (he also promoted Bahrain from an emirate to a kingdom, and himself from amir to king). Yet the new constitution, drafted after the referendum, disappointed the opposition.[31] It gave the elected deputies much less authority than did the 1973 constitution. The elected lower house, under the new 2002 constitution, requires a majority of two-thirds of its members to withdraw confidence in a minister, a very high hurdle. Legislation must pass both the elected Council of Representatives and the appointed upper house; if there is a disagreement between the two, they meet as a single body to vote—and both houses have an equal number of members.

Social Structure—Bahrain

The Shi'a composed around 58 percent of the citizen population of Bahrain in 2009. Most Bahraini Shi'a are Arab and come from a group known as the Baharna; they share much in common with the Arab Shi'a of Saudi Arabia's Eastern Province.[32] Other Shi'a are of Persian descent. Some Bahraini Sunnis come from the Persian side of the Gulf but are of Arab descent, while others, including the ruling family, are tribal and come from the Arabian Peninsula.

A majority of Bahrain's citizens are Shi'i, but the ruling family is Sunni. One wing of the ruling family views the Shi'a as a security threat that should be ruthlessly repressed, while the crown prince (and current prime minister) is more moderate. Overall, the Bahraini political system is built around the oppression of Shi'i citizens. The Shi'a are almost entirely excluded from positions in the security services or the military.[33] The electoral law, through gerrymandering and malapportionment, ensures that the Shi'i deputies win fewer than half the seats in the Council of Representatives. The regime banned Al-Wefaq, the main Shi'i opposition group, in 2018 and sentenced its leader to life in prison. While educated Shi'a receive state jobs at a rate similar to that of educated Sunnis, less-educated Sunnis are far more likely to hold positions in the public sector than are less-educated Shi'a, many of whom are unemployed. The state tends to neglect infrastructure in the Shi'i villages.

Bahrain's regime has given citizenship to many foreigners in recent years, almost all of them Sunnis. The goal appears to be to change the sectarian balance in the population. Many have been employed in the security services; they receive state jobs while native Bahraini Shi'a must make do in the private sector. Noncitizens make up a majority of the population, at a bit over 50 percent. This is a less severe population imbalance than is found in Qatar or the UAE, but Bahrain also has much less oil wealth per capita. Many Bahraini citizens, especially less-educated Shi'a, cannot find jobs in the public sector and are often unemployed.

Actors, Opinion, and Participation—Bahrain

The Arab Spring brought many Bahrainis, mostly Shi'a, out onto the streets in massive demonstrations. While the main Shi'i opposition group, Al-Wefaq, demanded reform rather than the overthrow of the ruling family, calls for revolution became more prominent as the protests continued.[34] The crown prince, with American support, sought to negotiate a settlement with the Shi'i opposition, while hardliners in the ruling family argued for repression. The hardliners won when Saudi, Emirati, and Qatari troops crossed the causeway in support of the Sunni regime. This brought Bahrain to a political dead end. There is a strong tendency among Sunnis in the ruling family and among Bahrain's citizens to view the political struggle with the Bahraini Shi'a as a zero-sum game: The Sunni win everything, or the Shi'a win everything. This view often dominates Bahraini politics and provides a justification for the relentless repression of the Shi'a as the only alternative to a Shi'i regime that would turn Bahrain into an Iranian satellite state with no place for Sunni citizens.

This view is belied by the moderate positions taken by Al-Wefaq, which has been the main political organization among the Bahraini Shi'a and which has long sought a middle ground with the regime. Nonetheless in the summer of 2015, the regime sentenced Ali Salman, the head of Al-Wefaq, to a four-year prison sentence. In 2018, the regime sentenced him to life in prison and outlawed Al-Wefaq. Having blocked political participation by the country's Shi'i population, the regime invites radicalization. It then uses this radicalization to justify further repression. The regime cannot be removed, given its iron control over the security forces, which are completely Sunni, and its support from Saudi Arabia. The result is a bitter, endless stalemate.

Religion and Politics—Bahrain

The main fault line in Bahraini politics is sectarian, between the country's Sunni and Shi'i citizens. Following the constitutional changes of 2002 Bahrain, unlike the other lower Gulf states, allowed the formation of political societies that function much like political parties. Almost all of the electorally successful societies are organized on sectarian grounds. The main Shiʻi political group, Al-Wefaq, participated in the 2006 and 2010 elections but boycotted those of 2002 and 2014: when it did compete, Al-Wefaq won most of the parliamentary seats held by Bahraini Shiʻa. Its jailed leader, Ali Salman, is a cleric. Among the Sunnis, the most prominent political societies have been those of the Muslim Brotherhood and the Salafis, though in the 2014 elections, all political societies fared poorly. In 2018, the Muslim Brotherhood won no seats in the parliament, likely due to anti-Islamist pressure from Bahrain's allies Saudi Arabia and the UAE.

Political Economy—Bahrain

Bahrain has the smallest oil reserves in the GCC, and most of its revenues come from the Abu Safa oil field. This field lies in an area in the Gulf under Saudi sovereignty, but Bahrain receives half the revenues of the field as a result of a 1958 border agreement. In periods of low revenues, Saudi Arabia has given Bahrain all of the revenues from the field. Saudi Arabia also sends crude oil to Bahrain for refining, supporting a key industry. And the causeway to Saudi Arabia feeds the Bahraini tourism industry, also crucial to its economy. In short, the Bahraini economy relies heavily on Saudi Arabia, creating an economic dependence not seen elsewhere in the Gulf.

Bahrain's economy is somewhat diversified, with a large banking sector and some heavy industry. Yet Bahrain, unlike Qatar and the UAE, does not have enough oil wealth to offer a job in the public sector to all citizen graduates. As a result of the sectarian divide, the government focuses less than it otherwise might on employing Bahrainis who are unable to secure public-sector jobs—these citizens are mostly Shiʼi Baharna. Business owners, many of them Sunni, have hobbled labor market reforms that would have favored citizen labor.

Regional and International Relations—Bahrain

Bahrain's regional and international relations are driven by its dependence on Saudi Arabia and its fear of Iranian influence over its own population. The moderate Shiʼi opposition in Bahrain understands the dangers of being associated with Iranian influence in the Gulf and has declared that it does not seek to overthrow the ruling family. The ruling family, however, blames domestic dissent in Bahrain on Iranian influence, despite abundant evidence that the opposition of the Bahraini Shiʻa has vastly more to do with a long history of Al Khalifa repression than Iranian instigation. The Bahraini ruling family misses few opportunities to claim that Iran wants to make Bahrain into a satellite state, and it portrays itself as the defender of Sunni Arabs against Iranian Shiʼa. The GCC Sunni ruling families—and especially the Al Saud—deeply fear a Shiʼi revolution in Bahrain that would create an Iranian satellite state on the southern shores of the Gulf, next to the oil-rich Eastern Province of Saudi Arabia. Bahrain's foreign policy in the region reflects its dependence on Saudi Arabia: Its policies on Yemen, Qatar, and Iran hew closely to those of Saudi Arabia.

CONCLUSION

The four lower Gulf states, for all that they share in common, face very different challenges in the future. Bahrain's dilemma is easy to diagnose, though very difficult to overcome: Sunni and Shi'i Bahrainis must learn to share political power in a way that preserves the security and dignity of both communities. Of the four, Oman is the one with the best prospects for democracy—which is not to say that those prospects are particularly good but that the prospects in the other three lower Gulf states are not good at all. In Oman, elections are held regularly and honestly. Oman's economic task is straightforward, though difficult: It needs to start transitioning away from oil by building a diversified economy that puts citizen labor to productive use in the private sector.

The UAE has diversified its economy, but only through the use of inexpensive foreign labor. Qatar appears to be following in that same path. There is much that is positive about the economic growth in these countries: this growth creates wealth and gives many expatriates a chance at a better life. But these are also countries in which citizens are becoming a small, if privileged, caste of government employees living off oil revenues and, perhaps someday, tax revenues, while the bulk of the population—and virtually everyone working in the private sector—lacks citizenship. These systems are stable, but nonetheless have created a model of economic and political development that is found nowhere else in the modern world, and one not in tune with modern sensibilities concerning democracy. The long-term future of these states will be all about the clash between their economic success, political authoritarianism, and denial of citizenship to their residents.

SUGGESTED READINGS

Crystal, Jill. *Oil and Politics in the Gulf: Rulers and Merchants in Kuwait and Qatar.* Cambridge: Cambridge University Press, 1990.

Davidson, Christopher M. *After the Sheikhs: The Coming Collapse of the Gulf Monarchies.* London: Hurst & Co, 2012.

Fromherz, Allen J. *Qatar: A Modern History.* Washington, DC: Georgetown University Press, 2012.

Gause, F. Gregory. *The International Relations of the Persian Gulf.* Cambridge: Cambridge University Press, 2010.

Gengler, Justin. *Group Conflict and Political Mobilization in Bahrain and the Arab Gulf: Rethinking the Rentier State.* Bloomington, IA: Indiana University Press, 2015.

Heard-Bey, Frauke. *From Trucial States to United Arab Emirates: A Society in Transition.* Dubai: Motivate, 2004.

Herb, Michael. *All in the Family: Absolutism, Revolution, and Democracy in the Middle Eastern Monarchies.* Albany, NY: State University of New York Press, 1999.

Herb, Michael. *The Wages of Oil: Parliaments and Economic Development in Kuwait and the UAE.* Ithaca, NY: Cornell University Press, 2014.

Kamrava, Mehran. *Qatar: Small State, Big Politics.* Ithaca, NY: Cornell University Press.

Onley, James. *The Arabian Frontier of the British Raj: Merchants, Rulers, and the British in the Nineteenth-Century Gulf.* New York, NY: Oxford University Press, 2007.

Valeri, Marc. *Oman: Politics and Society in the Qaboos State.* New York, NY: Columbia University Press, 2009.

19 MOROCCO

Saloua Zerhouni and Driss Maghraoui

Morocco is very often viewed as a state that has historically combined both traditional and modern concepts into a general synthesis of social and political organization. The religion of Islam remains an important source of political legitimization, while new values and institutions associated with the modern secular state have been introduced. Morocco's monarchy, which is the main component of the political system, bases its legitimacy on Islam and, at the same time, proclaims its attachment to democracy and modernization. The late king, Hassan II, accumulated the roles of *amir al-muminin* (commander of the faithful) and the supreme representative of the nation. Since the early phases of independence, he was able to create a regime resonant with Islamic traditions and colored with democratic and secular values. The Moroccan regime has over the years played a crucial role in the ideological construction of this political hybrid.

The globalization process as well as the internationalization of the discourse of democracy and human rights have pushed the monarchy to look for ways to adapt to this new era of rapid economic, technological, political, social, and cultural changes. The constellation of these forces has combined not only to shape in positive ways the political landscape of Morocco but also to flush out the inherent inconsistencies of the political system. In many ways, the weight of the Moroccan past comes back to haunt the present, while concerns for political survival impose new strategies of adaptation for the future. It is this relationship among the past, the present, and the future that this chapter seeks to address when dealing with the ambiguities and contradictions of the Moroccan political regime.

Indeed, while a number of countries in the Middle East were going through a series of revolutions and social upheavals in the year 2011, the Moroccan regime, through well-planned constitutional reforms and the election of an Islamist party to government, was able to avoid in a very astute way some of the violent outcomes that framed the reactions of other authoritarian regimes in the region. An important component of achieving this goal was ultimately the role that the Islamist Party of Justice and Development (PJD) was allowed to play by the regime in order to achieve what some Moroccan analysts called the "second *alternance*."[1] What made this scenario possible were not only the astute political maneuverings of the monarchy and its state machinery, as well as its well-established strategies of segmentation and various forms of cooptation, but also the presence of the PJD as an alternative to other predominantly discredited Moroccan parties. From 2012 to 2021, the PJD was at the forefront of formal politics of government institutions. After 10 years in government, however, the PJD lost its credibility.

The party was not able to go ahead with the kinds of reforms that it had promised its electorate because the real power resides within the inner informal circles of the monarchy. The monarchy is consistently able to manipulate the partisan scene and to bring in political parties such as the Independents and the Party of Authenticity and Modernity (PAM). These parties were presented in a well-orchestrated campaign by official media as potential actors to deal with the post-COVID-19 socioeconomic effects and to improve the social conditions of the marginalized classes. The dominant discourse in 2021 is about the need for a technocratic elite that has the necessary skills to manage the current crisis. The 2021 elections were yet another moment for the performance of a democratic façade where the political scene is well under control of the regime and parties are clearly deprived of agency and accept to play along.

Considering the nature of political authority of the Alawite dynasty in Morocco, we are very often confronted with two competing paradigms. On the one hand, cultural interpretations insist on the charismatic role of the Moroccan sultans and their ability to accumulate religious symbols of authority (*baraka*) based on sharifism or the claim of descent from the Prophet Muhammad.[2] The *bay'a*, or the oath of allegiance to the ruler, was very significant because it sustained a sense of political belonging and facilitated a communal and territorial entity of the medieval Moroccan state.[3] From this angle, the *bay'a* to the Moroccan king by different dignitaries of the state has continued to play an important performative role as a symbol of the monarch's dominance and as an act of obedience to him. Therefore, legitimacy in postcolonial Morocco has revolved around the ways in which the monarchy has been able to draw upon an enduring cultural heritage of authority and a rich field of symbolic language of politics in order to maintain and reinvent its political power.[4] To this end, the Moroccan king as the center of power can be viewed as being politically very potent.[5]

On the other hand, some analysts of the Moroccan political scene have tried to bring attention to the political strategy and historically coercive, if not violent, nature of the *makhzen*. The *makhzen*, which literally means "storage," was historically used to mean the sultan's court, the regional and provincial administration, the army, and all individuals connected with these institutions. One of the most important functions of the *makhzen* was the collection of taxes. When different social groups refused to pay, the *makhzen* often resorted to coercive measures.[6] From this angle, the strength of the monarchy is therefore interpreted as part of the ability of the *makhzen* to rule through the control of the modern coercive apparatus of the state.[7] The monarchy makes use of a cultural mechanism of power, but it has historically relied on a combination of administrative control and, most important, armed forces to sustain its hold over political power.

In this line of interpretation, the purely cultural facets of power in Morocco cannot be fully grasped if they are not examined with other factors such as force and fear.[8] Under Hassan II, more specifically, the monarchy was able to establish its power by making use of the civilian and military elite who had proven themselves to be easily amenable and ready to be coopted. With a few exceptions, the army has been proroyalist and very loyal, and it has in return benefited from the financial opportunities and social privileges that are associated with a well-entrenched system of patron–client relationships that has so strongly characterized the Moroccan regime. Under King Mohammed VI, repression has been part of the tactics used by the state to silence

MAP 19.1 ■ Morocco

Western Sahara is under Moroccan control but is being contested.

peaceful protest movements such as the February 20 Movement or Hirak al-Rif, a movement that emerged in a marginalized mountainous region in northwestern Morocco. But the protests can also provide the Moroccan regime with an opportunity to deal in a more dynamic way with the society and respond to some of its socioeconomic needs by undertaking changes and putting forward new policy transformations that are meant to reinvent its legitimacy.[9]

KEY FACTS ON MOROCCO

AREA 172,413 square miles (446,550 square kilometers)

CAPITAL Rabat

POPULATION 36,561,813 (2021 est.)

PERCENTAGE OF POPULATION UNDER 25 43.59 (2020 est.)

RELIGIOUS GROUPS (PERCENTAGE) Muslim, 99; other, 1

ETHNIC GROUPS (PERCENTAGE) Arab-Berber, 99; other, 1

OFFICIAL LANGUAGE Arabic (official); Amazigh since 2011; French often the language of business, government, and diplomacy

TYPE OF GOVERNMENT Parliamentary Constitutional monarchy

DATE OF INDEPENDENCE March 2, 1956

GDP (PPP) $264.29 billion; $6,900 per capita (2020 est.)

GDP (Nominal) $118.858 billion (2019 est.)

PERCENTAGE OF GDP BY SECTOR Agriculture, 14; industry, 29.5; services, 56.5 (2017 est.)

TOTAL RENTS (PERCENTAGE OF GDP) FROM NATURAL RESOURCES 0.3

FERTILITY RATE 2.29 children born/woman

Source: CIA. "The World Factbook." August 4, 2022, https://www.cia.gov/the-world-factbook/.
World Bank. "International Comparison Program (ICP)." Accessed August 10, 2022, https://databank.
worldbank.org/source/icp-2017.

HISTORICAL OVERVIEW

Moroccan state formation dates back to the medieval period, when it was associated with a politicoreligious movement under the leadership of Idris ibn Abdallah. The first major Islamic state emerged in the 8th century. The rise of what became known as the Idrissid state (788–959) created a pattern of political organization that made political power dependent on a combination of religious legitimacy, coercive authority with the effective support of religious and tribal leaders, and, eventually, control over regional trade networks. This historical pattern of political development characterized much of the history of medieval Morocco and has continued to be relevant in different forms, even in the modern era.

Coming to power in 1666, the current Alawite monarchy is one of the oldest regimes in the world. The centrality of the monarch in the political landscape is constant and a feature that makes the Moroccan case unique. Neither Algeria nor Tunisia nor Libya has a political system and a reigning monarchy that dates back to the 7th century, and no Middle-Eastern state has similar structures. Compared with Algeria, for example, the monarchy in Morocco was able to use the army and simultaneously mobilize the language and symbols of nationalism that the powerful nationalist Independence Party (Istiqlal) had initially monopolized in its own struggle against colonialism.

However, the Moroccan state and the nature of its political system are not static. There have been changes that have constantly pushed the monarchy to adapt itself to a changing historical environment with new challenges. Political authority in Morocco is the result of a combination of precolonial forms of political structures and of the colonial administrative and military apparatus that was created under the French. At the same time, Morocco has also been able to develop a well-established party system with more or less regular elections. Since independence, therefore, the regime has always claimed some form of democratic legitimacy.

Morocco's claim to being a democratic state started with the first constitution of 1962, which stipulates that Morocco is a "democratic, social and constitutional monarchy." This constitution established a multiparty system and guaranteed the citizens a number of individual liberties. The constitutional initiative was largely the work of Hassan II, who designed the first constitution and those that followed in 1970, 1972, 1992, and 1996.[10] The different stages of the constitutional dynamic took into account the modernization of the traditional institutions, but it constantly aspired to give the impression of liberalization of political life. Conscious of the importance of the democratic legitimacy for the continuity and the stability of his family's reign, Hassan II after 1972 accumulated the status of "supreme representative."[11] Over the years, the monarchy surrounded itself with a number of institutions that could not claim a "sovereign legitimacy" because their credibility, existence, and continuity depend on another authority that is superior to them. The monarchy deployed this strategy in order to retain its position as the only vital institution for the functioning of a political system in which the persona of the king constantly remains at the center.

By establishing himself as an arbiter, the king determined to a large extent not only his relationship with other political actors but also the relationships among them. The king also used repressive measures in response to the opposition's demands for power sharing. Over the years, Hassan II succeeded in perpetuating elite *immobilisme* and creating a clientelist network in which economic self-interest became part of the elite's shared values.[12]

In the 1990s, the search for democratic legitimacy became even more pressing for the regime, which needed to constantly reinvent itself. The 1990s symbolized a new era in the political history of Morocco as the monarchy started to engage in a process of political liberalization. Different measures were taken in order to consolidate the rule of law. Following the 1992 constitutional revision, administrative tribunals were established as well as a council responsible for the control of the constitutionality of laws (1994). The local and legislative elections of 1993 and 1997 were held under relatively transparent conditions, and opposition newspapers and a number of nongovernmental organizations (NGOs) and political parties flourished. Various measures were taken in order to improve the country's human rights record.[13]

In addition, the king was involved in negotiations with the opposition parties in order to form a new government. After an unsuccessful attempt in 1994,[14] Hassan II succeeded in convincing Abderrahmane Youssoufi, the leader of the Socialist Union of Popular Forces (USFP), to build a government of *alternance*.[15] Formed in 1998, this government was largely drawn from opposition parties (the USFP and the Independence Party), which were excluded from power during a long period of Hassan's reign.

The regime also tolerated the participation of moderate Islamists in political life. The inclusion of moderate Islamists, notably the Justice and Development Party (PJD), and the socialists was part of a strategy to contain potential challengers to the regime. As it functions in the Moroccan system, cooptation is mainly about absorption. The opposition in Morocco is often coopted by the political system and eventually absorbed by it. Once integrated into the *makhzen* system, any potential challenger becomes a de facto supporter of that same system. Once common interests are developed between the central power and opposition groups and once opposition groups have access to privileges, the prospect of challenging the system becomes very limited. In the last ten years of his rule, Hassan II was portrayed as a protector of human rights and a promoter of reforms, thus providing the right conditions for a smooth succession.

With the ascendance to power of King Mohammed VI in July 1999, there was continuity in the discourse of "constitutional monarchy."[16] Mohammed VI initiated genuine reforms in various fields. To improve women's rights, he appointed a royal committee to reform the *moudawana* (the legal code and the set of laws relating to families and family issues). This initiative culminated in the adoption of a family code that is one of the most progressive in the region.[17] He established a Moroccan commission for truth and justice in 1999 in order to compensate the victims of the "years of lead," a reference to the years of human rights abuses and illegal detentions and imprisonment of opposition leaders.[18] The press witnessed more freedom than it had under Hassan's rule. Mohammed VI called for a fight against poverty and established the National Initiative for Human Development. In the educational field, a National Charter for Education and Training was initiated.

Despite the positive changes and the more liberal style of Mohammed VI, no constitutional reforms have been aimed at establishing a balance of power among different political institutions. The system of *alternance* was reversed with the appointment of a technocrat as prime minister in 2003. The monarchy has continued to monopolize and decide upon the process and pace of reforms in Morocco, and the king and his closest *makhzen* entourage have designed most of the reforms. Priority is given to social and economic reforms, while the debate on political reforms has been marginalized.

Even after the 2011 constitutional reform, there is an executive monarchy with a shadow government of advisers and royal committees asserting control over key strategic issues.[19] The monarchy has reinforced its power, a fact that became more apparent in the formation of the new government following the 2021 general elections. The new government is composed mainly of parties that are seen as close allies to the palace (RNI, PAM, and the Istiqlal). The government included also technocrats that were given a "political color" and parachuted into these parties at the last moment. This was a clear sign that the monarchy has further reinforced its monopoly control over the executive power in a context where parties are mainly passive observers if not domesticated participants. Meanwhile, the key "ministries of sovereignty," such as the Ministry of the Interior, Foreign Affairs, Islamic Affairs, and the General Secretariat of the Government and the Defense Ministry, remained in the hands of people under palace umbrella. In addition, four members of a Royal Committee in charge of the new model of economic development were appointed ministers. The 2021 composition of the government has shown that the palace, through a government of technocrats and a dramatically reduced representation of political parties, continues to exert a major control over the political scene.

SOCIAL TRANSFORMATION AND CHALLENGES

Historically, colonialism and the gradual integration of Morocco into the world economy were the most important forces behind major social transformations. To a large extent, the liberalization of the economy and the structural adjustment programs from the 1980s until the present day are a different version of the same historical phenomena that in the early 20th century set in motion the forces of capitalism and modernity, with their complex and drastic social and cultural transformations throughout the developing world. As in other countries in the Middle East, there have been different facets to the social transformations that affected Moroccan society. Probably the most important transformations manifested themselves through the increasing waves of immigration, the rural–urban divide, change in labor formation, and education. All of these social changes were interrelated.

Since independence, Morocco's economic policy has concentrated on growth. The country was able to improve the standard of living of small segments of Moroccan society in the 1960s, but the social condition of the majority did not necessarily change. From a geographical point of view, the immediate postcolonial period perpetuated the colonial distinction that existed between *al-maghrib annafi'i* (useful Morocco) and *al-maghrib gayr annafi'i* (useless Morocco), as economic growth was limited to the northwestern and central areas, while the southern parts, the Rif area, and some parts of the Atlas remained unaffected, if not marginalized. More significant concern for social development started to emerge in the 1970s, especially with the 1973–1977 development plan that involved more spending in the social field and in the educational sector. Between 1970 and 1975, public spending on education went from 3.5 percent to 5 percent of the country's gross domestic product (GDP). From the 1980s to 2000, spending on education remained relatively constant, at an average of 5.7 percent of GDP. Income per capita in Morocco remained one of the lowest in the Middle East and North Africa (MENA) region. In 1975, it was estimated at $2,186, while in the mid-1980s, it reached $2,805. Between 1990 and 2001, it went from $3,096 to $3,374.

Adult literacy has remained relatively low, even though it has improved over the years. There has been a steady increase in the literacy rate, from 19.8 percent in 1970 to 28.6 percent in 1980, and from 43.9 percent in 1995 to 49.8 percent in 2001. Women were comparatively less affected by this improvement, as we see positive but slower changes taking place. In 1970, the female adult literacy rate was 8.2 percent, and it reached 20 percent in 1985. Between 1990 and 2001, the literacy rate for women went from 24.9 percent to 37.2 percent. But social and educational problems were too deep, and overall, the condition of large segments of Moroccan society did not improve. Organized very often under the umbrella of trade unions and leftist parties, social movements intensified and were therefore a permanent feature of the 1970s and 1980s. While social unrest remained part of the Moroccan landscape, it became less consolidated and more spread out and dispersed in the 1990s and in the first decade of the 21st century.

Statistics about internal migration reveal the kind of social transformations that over the years have affected Moroccan society. Between 1907 and 1955, Casablanca, for example, went from having a Muslim population of 20,000 to having one of 400,000. During the same period, Fez doubled its population from 8,000 to 16,000.[20] By the mid-1980s, the old medina of Fez had a population of 250,000, far exceeding the 100,000 people it was supposed to sustain. In some areas, the density was as high as 10,000 people per hectare.[21] The concentration of the population in old cities like Fez has contributed to some alarming health conditions and a deteriorating infrastructural urban environment. Overall, urban dwellers in Morocco made up 27.7 percent of the country's population in 1955 and 31.9 percent in 1965. Throughout the 1970s and 1980s, the urban population grew steadily, moving from 34.6 percent in 1970 to 48.8 percent in 1990. By 2021, 64.06 percent of Morocco's population lived in urban areas.

One of the immediate effects of the massive waves of immigration that started to take place in different cities was not simply the metamorphosis of the architectural and urban landscape but also the social transformations that resulted. Cities in Morocco became attractive destinations for poor peasants who were territorially displaced from their tribal context and gradually integrated into a kind of lumpen proletariat associated with a growing, market-oriented economy. In the 1950s and 1960s, between 5 percent and 10 percent of the landholding families owned more than 60 percent of the land in Morocco, 50 percent to 55 percent owned less than 40 percent of the land, and about 40 percent owned no land at all.[22] This created a situation whereby the lure of economic opportunities became the main factor driving landless peasants to migrate to cities. It was not by coincidence that the majority of migrants came from areas with the most meager resources, areas such as the Sous, Draa, Tafilalet, and Figuig in the southern part of Morocco. The mountainous areas of the Anti-Atlas, High Atlas, and Rif were also major sources of rural migration.[23]

One of the immediate gender effects of structural adjustment programs is the transformation of the workforce. Morocco's industrial labor force increased from 223,000 to more than one million between 1975 and 1990; and garment manufacturing, which started to employ women, has been most important. Women by 1993 made up 25 percent of the 95,000 Moroccans who were working in the manufacturing labor force. The rapid growth of the garment industry contributed not only to the transformation of the Moroccan economy but also to the country's social and cultural fabric.[24]

The fact that Morocco began to increase its exports of manufactured products in such sectors as garments and canned fruit and vegetables facilitated the conditions for opening up the industrial labor force for women. The focus on labor-intensive manufacturing for export had as a consequence the large-scale incorporation of women into the Moroccan workforce. Following the 1980s and the economic readjustment programs that removed taxes and favored exports, we see a major expansion of the Moroccan garment industry. Almost all who work in garment factories are now female.[25] This has been a drastic change in a generally patriarchal society where women in the 1960s and 1970s were not supposed to participate in public enterprises or be incorporated in industry. Before the 1980s, private garment industries employed mainly men or limited women to low-paying and unskilled labor. The Moroccan garment industry has been a major factor contributing to the transformation of the labor force.

In the long run, however, women workers have started to feel occupational instability and insecurity as the garment factories, in the face of the recent economic downturn, started to shut down. The competitive aspect of the garment industry and the economic crisis of 2008–2010 have created for these women constantly unstable economic conditions. For Moroccan workers in general and women more specifically, employment has turned out to be increasingly insecure and short-lived. Workers are confronted by new situations in which they might be hired for only a short period of time before they are laid off. As Moroccan workers have moved into the 21st century, they are suddenly finding themselves confronted with the difficult realities of a consumer society, the elusive nature of labor legislation, and the economic ups and downs of an economy that is increasingly market-oriented. More and more workers, including women, are employed in industries and factories without basic labor rights and without protective regulations concerning minimum wages, working hours, or benefits. While liberalization in Morocco is providing jobs for some, it is simultaneously widening the gap between the rich and the working poor and contributing to the creation of a feeling of alienation not only among the workers but in the middle class as well.[26] According to the 2022 World Bank report, poverty will affect 7.4 percent of the population by the end of 2022.

POLITICAL INSTITUTIONS

Morocco is one of the first countries in the MENA region to have established modern political institutions. However, this system came hand in hand with the elaboration of a constitutional arsenal that was designed to limit the establishment of democratic institutions and guarantee the political supremacy of the monarch. The first political parties were created before or soon after independence. The Party of Independence (PI; 1944) gained its strength and legitimacy during the colonial period. The fragmentation of the PI gave rise in 1959 to the left-wing National Union of Popular Forces (UNFP), which was itself later displaced by the emergence of the USFP (1974). The bifurcation of political parties has gradually led to the creation of an assortment of proroyalist political parties of various ideological stripes, such as the National Rally of Independents (RNI, 1978) or the Constitutional Union (UC, 1983). This started to pave the way for the establishment of a fragmented partisan scene largely manipulated by and under the control of King Hassan II.

Over the years, the main political parties have gradually lost their credibility and have been subject to further fragmentation. In the 1990s, new political parties were created as a result of a split from existing political parties, such as the Front of Democratic Forces (FFD), whose leading figures were members of the Party of Progress and Socialism (PPS). Other parties were created as a result of the integration of or fusion with existing political parties; such is the case for the PJD (1998). Since the ascendance to power of King Mohammed VI, there has been a growing tendency to create small political parties organized around issues related to environment, liberalism, and Islamism. During the past twenty years, twenty-three political parties were created.

Despite the 2006 party bill, Morocco continues to have a growing number of small political parties that are not necessarily based on competing "societal projects" but are rather the outcome of "personal projects" of an opportunistic elite aiming at taking advantage of their position as leaders of political parties to approach the inner circle of power (Maghraoui and Zerhouni, 2014).[27]

The fragmentation of the party system in Morocco was exacerbated by a whole range of trade unions. This contributed to additional segmentation of the political scene and subsequently to the reinforcement of the centrality of the monarchy.[28] In the more recent past, unions have gone further in terms of deepening their internal divisions. As has been the case for political parties, most of the trade unions have lost their power and ability to mobilize significant numbers of people.

As for the parliament, despite its establishment since 1963 and the reinforcement of its prerogatives from one constitution to the other, it remains weak and subordinate to the monarchy. Its primary role, as its history shows, is to serve as an institutional framework that contributes to the stability and continuity of the political system. Between 1963 and 2021, Morocco had ten legislatures. The parliament has continued to exist on a permanent basis except for a short period during which it was dissolved.[29] From one legislature to another, the constitutional powers of the parliament have been reinforced but without giving it the necessary tools to have an impact on political outcomes.

With the 2011 constitution, more powers were given to the parliament in the fields of lawmaking and government oversight. The domain of the law was enlarged to cover different sectors of political, economic, and social life (Article 71). The power to initiate laws concurrently belongs to the head of government and to members of the parliament (MPs; Article 78).[30] In the field of government oversight, the current parliament reserves one meeting per year to evaluate public policies (Articles 70, 101). One meeting per month is reserved for the head of government to respond to general policy questions (Article 100) and for a report on the government's activity (Article 101). The new constitution makes it easier to create fact-finding committees; one-third is required instead of the majority of the members of one Chamber (Article 67). Another important change in the 2011 constitution is its condemnation of parliamentary transhumance.

Despite the relative strengthening of the parliament's constitutional powers and the change in its composition, the legislative body still confronts limitations imposed by the constitutional provisions. The parliament remains relatively inaccessible to civil society organizations; the constitutionalization of the secrecy of committee meetings (Article 68) contradicts the principle of access to information and transparency of parliamentary work. The parliament remains subordinated to the government. In terms of parliamentary oversight powers, the control of the budget is still limited by the constitutional rule to maintain macroeconomic balance (Article 77). The head of government can dissolve the Chamber of Representatives (Article 104). This is a new provision that gives the government more control over parliament. Some sectors, such as the security services, escape parliamentary control altogether.[31]

The monarchy maintains its predominance over the parliament, which allows it to orient and influence the parliament's work. The king addresses messages to the parliament when presiding over the opening sessions of the legislative year. These messages, which cannot be the object of any debate, set the political and parliamentary agenda for the year and serve as a reference for MPs in their debates. The king can demand that the two chambers proceed to a new reading of any draft or proposed bill, and the parliament cannot refuse (Article 95). The king maintains the power to dissolve one or both chambers (Article 96). Finally, the king signs and ratifies treaties. Parliament does not have the power to approve treaties that have a political or military dimension or those that can result in a law being either abrogated or modified.[32]

Besides constitutional limitations, the Moroccan Parliament is constantly confronted with the challenge of translating its new constitutional powers into practice. Ten years after the promulgation of the 2011 constitution, the process of implementing some provisions has been very slow. In terms of adopting the nineteen organic laws stipulated in the 2011 constitution, only five were adopted by mid-2014. Some important organic laws such as the one on introducing the Amazigh language were adopted in 2019.

Moreover, the parliament suffers from its tarnished image[33] and a crisis of representativeness: The right to vote is not granted to all Moroccans, including those who live outside the country. The new constitution recognizes their right to vote; however, the organic law of the Chamber of Representatives introduced the procedure of proxy voting. There is also a tendency among Moroccans to vote less, which is very much indicative of the crisis of the political offer. Since the 2007 legislative elections, abstention rates were higher compared with previous elections (37 percent in 2007, 45 percent in 2011, and 43 percent in 2016). The electoral system and districting (gerrymandering) do not favor the emergence of a strong parliamentary majority. During the first two legislative elections organized following the 2011 constitutional reform, even though the PJD won a majority seats, the party leader had to negotiate with ideologically different political parties to be able to build a majority.

In Morocco, political parties, unions, the parliament, and the elections remain under the effective control of the central power. Since 2013, the PJD has been instrumentalized to adopt very critical social policies and laws. With the COVID-19 pandemic, the PJD-led government was criticized for its poor management of the crisis and its weak achievements in developing key sectors such as health and education. At the same time, the monarchy was portrayed by official media as the sole political institution capable of managing the health crisis. Indeed, most of the decisions aimed at alleviating the social and economic effects of the pandemic were associated with the monarchy. The fact that parties such as the RNI and the PAM were perceived as allies of the palace could have played a role in their electoral success. In parallel with what appears to be a well-orchestrated strategy of controlling the outcome of the electoral process, discrediting

PHOTO 19.1 A supporter of the Islamist Justice and Development Party shouts slogans during a campaign rally ahead of the communal and regional elections in the City of Tinghir in Southeastern Morocco on August 31, 2015. The local elections were the first since King Mohammed put forward a new constitution

Reuters/Youssef Boudlal/Alamy Stock Photo

the PJD led to its electoral failure both at the national level (from 125 seats in the Chamber of Representatives in 2016 to 13 seats in 2021), the regional level (from 174 in 2015 to 18 seats in 2021), and the local level (from 5021 seats in 2015 to 777 seats in 2021).

POLITICAL ECONOMY

When Hassan II came to power in 1961, he was able to acquire large amounts of land that were previously under the control of the colonial settlers. Granting positions in the 1970s to senior administrators in the public and private sectors became part of what provided the monarchy with powerful leverage for constantly rotating its elite, segmenting and subsequently controlling them. Hassan II was able to concoct different political and economic strategies to maintain a permanent factionalism of the elite.[34] The use of economic power for political maneuvering and the use of politics for economic gains were possible through the control of key sectors such as banking, industry, and agriculture.

In its modern structure, and with more sophisticated means, the *makhzen* has been able to have a stronger hold over the economy.[35] With the economic policies of structural adjustment programs since the 1980s and an overall shift toward a more market-oriented economy, the *makhzen*'s use of economic power, which started under Hassan II, has in fact been much further elaborated and more accentuated under the current king, Mohammed VI. It has become part of what has been termed an *economization* of the strategies of legitimization.[36]

The most frequently cited example of the monarchy's hold on economic power is Omnium Nord African, commonly known among Moroccans as ONA, an industrial conglomerate that has gross revenues that exceed five percent of Morocco's GDP. Thanks to a close circle of elites who are well trained as technocrats and financiers, ONA was able to diversify its investment in order to include such varied sectors as commercial banking, supermarkets, telecommunications, real estate, and agro-industry. Overall, the policies of economic liberalization have resulted in a greater concentration of wealth and have therefore accentuated the historical power of the monarchy's well-entrenched patronage system. For the past twenty years, Morocco has experienced a "technocratic turn" under the auspices of the palace and more entrepreneurs gained seats in both chambers of the Parliament. The government that was formed following the 2021 general elections was led by Aziz Akhanouch, one of the richest men in Africa. While the dominant political discourse has evolved in ways privilege neoliberal economic policies, there is simultaneously a consistent pattern of the growing relationship between business and politics.

The systematic push for structural adjustment programs during the past three decades has encouraged a free-market economy, foreign investment, private education, employment in the private rather than public sector, and more flexible labor policies. Service sector industries like marketing, finance, education, tourism, and the media have been promoted. With these reforms, the rate of urban employment among the young and educated rose significantly by 2000, to reach close to 30 percent of the active urban labor force. Wealthy businesspeople have been able to adapt themselves to structural adjustment. Morocco's most famous professional organization, the Confédération Générale Economique Marocaine (CGEM), has often worked in harmony with palace politics and since the 2011 constitutional reform, the CGEM has secured representation in the House of Councils, Morocco's upper house. The monarchy is therefore immune to any form of pressure from business leaders.[37] The elite social classes that have been able to integrate the different networks of this new economic environment are able to benefit from it. The children of these elite have access to capital and to power to help them find jobs, facilitate business deals, and accumulate more wealth.

From a macroeconomic perspective, the programs of structural adjustment gradually weakened the traditional role of the state to generate jobs, provide services for the people, and satisfy their various demands. This situation has led to increased poverty in major cities and in the countryside. Neighborhoods such as Darb al-Sultan, Hay al-Mohamadi, Sidi Maʻarouf, and Sidi Othman in Casablanca; Taqadoum and Douar al-Doum in Rabat; and similar areas in other cities have some of the highest levels of poverty and unemployment in the country. According to reports by the World Bank, one Moroccan in five currently lives below the poverty level. Morocco is now known for what are commonly called *les barques de la mort* (the death boats), which illegally carry young people in search of a better future across the Mediterranean Sea to Europe; many die during the journey. Economic changes have also brought about more social problems, job insecurity, social melancholy, alienation, and a general sense of disconnection and detachment from social and political practices.[38]

Whether it is expressed by the young people who are crossing the Strait of Gibraltar in the death boats, members of the Moroccan association of the unemployed, factory workers in Casablanca, contractual high school teachers or small farmers in the Souss and the Atlas, there is in Morocco a growing social dissatisfaction with the state and its inability to deal with pressing social issues. Hence, the traditional social role of the state has started to be gradually replaced by the rise of an active Moroccan civil society, supported most often by international NGOs. Representatives from Moroccan human rights associations, women's solidarity groups, and many local civil society groups are trying to capture the attention of a growing number of marginalized youth who are easily attracted by Islamist discourse or by radical religious ideologies.

The Islamists of the PJD and the Monarchy

In March 2011, the king of Morocco announced the reform of the constitution. The PJD was at the forefront of the supporters of the constitutional reforms orchestrated by the palace. The PJD clearly found the new regional and national context to constitute an ideal opportunity to finally convince the regime that it could be trusted and relied upon. They called upon Moroccans to vote yes on the project of the constitution that was submitted to referendum on July 1, 2011. The PJD's secretary general, Abdelilah Benkirane, declared repeatedly that he supports a monarchy that reigns and governs. For him, a monarchy following the Spanish or British model is not a convenient alternative for Morocco because of the role of the monarch as arbiter and as *amir al mouminin*.

On November 25, 2011, the PJD was able to win a historical election, obtaining 107 out of 395 seats in the Chamber of Representatives, a position that gave the Islamists the right to lead the Moroccan government (Article 47 of the 2011 constitution). The success of the PJD in these elections was, in a way, good news for both the party and the *makhzen*. For the PJD, this was what they had been looking for since their integration into the political system. The PJD was able to progressively move from winning nine seats in 1997 to 42 seats in the 2002 election. While in 2007 they were able to win 47 seats, in 2011 they scored a significant victory with 107 seats. From the official state's perspective, the voter turnout was 45.4 percent, which was an increase in comparison to the 37 percent from the 2007 parliamentary elections. It is important to mention that eligible voters numbered more than twenty million, and only thirteen million of them were registered for the polls. Only six million voters actually cast their ballots, among which 22.3 percent cast invalid ballots.

Regardless, the Moroccan state capitalized on the success of the PJD. A positive outcome for the regime was that the elections could be seen as a continuation of the strategy of adaptation and the ability to defuse the more recent social and political tensions that had started with the reform of the constitution. These had naturally resulted with the election of a new parliament and the establishment of a new government drawn largely from the PJD and three other parties, including the communists. Meanwhile, political life seemed to have been resuscitated in the sense that elections are regularly held under a veneer of democratic procedures under the effective control of the monarchy. It is clear that the Moroccan political scene continues to provide us with a peculiar context whereby democratic practices and the techniques and procedures associated with democracy help sustain an undemocratic system of rule.

During the 2011 election campaign, the PJD had announced that it would create about 240,000 jobs, cut poverty in half, and raise the minimum wage by 50 percent. On December 3, 2011, ten PJD members became ministers as a result of a coalition government that included the conservative party of the Istiqlal as well as the Popular Party and a left-wing party known as the Party of Progress and Socialism. The PJD managed to have its members be the heads of key ministries such as the Ministry of Justice and the Foreign Ministry. The establishment of the PJD government was, however, confronted with a major crisis when five of the Istiqlal ministers resigned from the coalition government in July 2013, a situation that threatened to dissolve the government. However, in the long term this political move of the Istiqlal party proved to be more damaging to the Istiqlal than to the PJD, as members of the Independent Party, who were in the opposition, decided to join the coalition government of the PJD. In a matter of months, the Moroccan people were confronted with a situation whereby the political party which was in the opposition became part of the government and an Istiqlal party that was in the government became part of the opposition.

This kind of political behavior is clearly revealing not only of the incoherence of political parties in Morocco but also of the fact that regardless of the changing and illogical composition of the government, power resides not in the government but in the "deep state" of the *makhzen*. Ministers of governments in this political context act out as managers and implementers, and they can be replaced regardless of their programs or ideological backgrounds. The fact is that the PJD head of government was limited in terms of initiatives and freedom of action because most of the ministers are not responsive to him but to the "deep state." The ambivalence of this became political reality during the election of the head of the second chamber of parliament, with the members of the Independent Party voting against their PJD allies in the government.

The PJD managed to implement some reforms in the field of justice. It also managed to deal with thorny economic issues and put forward more liberal economic policies that cut government subsidies for basic goods in order to reduce budget deficits. The government attempted to reform the retirement plan and raise the age of retirement to sixty-three, a move that confronted a strong opposition from labor unions. The long-term success of the PJD Islamists in the Moroccan political scene depended, however, on their ability to make things change for Moroccans as far as social and economic realities are concerned. It also depended on their ability to carve out an independent political space vis-à-vis palace politics and the *makhzen*. This was unlikely to happen, as the PJD was strongly attached to its strategy to normalize its presence in the Moroccan political scene and be further blessed by the monarchy. In the long term, the PJD lost credibility, as has been the case of the USFP.

By the end of 2015, it was evident that the palace did not want Abdelilah Benkirane to remain the head of government. It was also time to think of new strategies to curb the popularity of the PJD leader in gradual ways without necessarily removing Benkirane's Islamist party from the government. The signs of this strategy started to appear during the election campaign, which incited Moroccans against Benkirane and his party. This included a well-orchestrated but obscurely organized rally against the so-called "Islamization of the state." However, the results of the 2016 parliamentary elections showed that the PJD continued to be an important winner in the electoral battle. Indeed, the PJD increased its number of seats in parliament from 107 to 125, while the PAM succeeded in reaching only 102 seats. Benkirane's charisma was an important factor for the party's win in the October 2016 elections.

As Benkirane was lacking a comfortable majority, he had to look for partners to form a coalition government. Behind the scenes, political maneuvering and the instrumentalization of other political parties were sufficient to block the formation of coalition government headed by Benkirane. Winning the battle of the election did not mean that the PJD and more specifically Benkirane would win in the process of forming the government. The potential coalition parties were clearly more attuned to palace politics rather than the electorate. Following six months of this deadlock, Benkirane was displaced and replaced by El Othmani, who was finally appointed by the king to form a new coalition government. Since his appointment, El Othmani was a weak head of government, and the PJD witnessed internal divisions and subsequent setbacks which culminated in the 2021 elections. The election results showed a devastating defeat for the PJD, which went from holding 125 seats to just 12. Its defeat in the elections is not only a sign that the regime wanted to engage in a new recycling of the political elite but also that the PJD's concern for normalizing its place in the political scene proved to be a miscalculation. The political pragmatism of the PJD did not necessarily play favorably in terms of guaranteeing the blessing of the monarchy nor did it serve its popularity vis-à-vis the people, who negatively viewed the party's support for different socioeconomic measures such as lifting subsidies for fuel or raising the retirement age.

Women's Movement

One of the characteristics of the women's movement in Morocco is that it goes beyond gender issues in order to push for political, legal, and educational reforms. Hence, the women's movement became intertwined with other pressing issues, such as human rights, social and economic equality, parliamentary politics, and religious and educational reforms. The movement brought together women who were activists in the women's sections of political parties and in associations. Their experience within political parties made them aware of their marginalization within what they often perceived as men's clubs. For many years, political parties used the pretext of religious and cultural constraints in order to keep women's issues outside of their political agenda and to limit women's visibility and their impact in public life. Many women started to organize themselves into separate associations within which they could easily express their points of view, be heard, and defend their common interests. Women's associations started to emerge in the mid-1980s with the aim of developing a gender-based agenda and engaging in actions that defended their specific interests.

The culmination of the success of the Moroccan women's movement was the passing of the new family law in 2004. Known commonly as the *moudawana*, this family code resulted in new reforms meant to improve the roles and relationships between men and women within the family. Between the late 1950s and 2004, when the new family law was passed, there was not much change in the status of women under civil law. Under the laws of the 1950s, women were legally considered minors, and their access to divorce was limited. Under the new civil law, women are considered equal to men, but under the *moudawana*, they were required to have the consent of their fathers and husbands to open a business or obtain a passport. Women also had only limited property and inheritance rights. The reform of the family code was therefore a major achievement after a long struggle by various associations of women.

Since the early 1990s, reform of the legal system has become the most important issue for the women's movement. One of the main groups promoting women's rights, the Union de l'Action Féminine, organized a campaign to collect one million signatures in order to urge King Hassan II to reform the *moudawana*, the family code. The women's associations had very specific goals: first, to raise to eighteen the minimum age for women to marry; second, to require a judge's authorization for polygamy; third, to have the right to divorce their husbands; fourth, to have new rights to assets acquired during marriage; and finally, to reinforce children's rights. King Hassan II agreed to hear the women's concerns, and he called on a council of religious leaders to look into the matter. By 1993, the women had gained some success in the reform of the *moudawana*,[39] but it was very limited. The most important effect of the reforms was the fact that the *moudawana* was opened for the first time to change and, hence, began to be perceived as something less than a sacred legal text.

Under Mohammed VI, the women's movement gained more ground, and the demands for reform of the *moudawana* became more pressing. Women activists were able to make the reforms part of a national debate. The fact that some of the dispositions in the reform plan touched upon the shari'a (Islamic law) raised the eyebrows of different segments of Moroccan society. More specifically, the Islamists of the PJD, in collaboration with other factions such as Abdessalam Yassine's Al-adl wal-Ihsan (Justice and Spirituality Movement), organized mass rallies against the proposed plan of action. On March 13, 2000, the Islamists launched a large rally in Casablanca, which brought together approximately 300,000 demonstrators.[40] Simultaneously, some of the more liberal women's NGOs organized a demonstration in Rabat, but it was less successful, at least in terms of the number of people who participated. Their rally drew an estimated 100,000 demonstrators.

In October 2003, in a speech before the nation, the king announced important reforms aimed at improving the situation of women and elevating their subservient status in marital laws. The new family code dealt with some of the grievances that had been formulated by the women's movement since the beginning of the 1990s. It gave women equal rights over the custody and welfare of their children and restricted the practice of polygamy. The legal age of marriage was raised from fifteen to eighteen, and the new code stated that the family is legally under the responsibility of both husband and wife. Wives now could also seek divorce in the same way as husbands, and divorce could be obtained only by mutual consent, which was a change from the former practice of repudiation that did not require the involvement of the court. *Wilaya* in marriage—tutelage, a practice that considered an unmarried woman to be a minor under the law regardless of her age—was abolished. In the new legal text, women can make decisions based on their own free will, choice, and consent.

Although feminists in Morocco and abroad applauded the reforms of the family code, the women's movement is still very actively addressing obstacles to implementation and advocating more legal changes.[41] The Association Démocratique des Femmes du Maroc is working hard through different campaigns, such as the Equality without Reservation campaign, to press the government and legal institutions to respect the rights of women and to call for equal status in social and economic fields. The women's movement brought the reform of the family code into the public debate while it succeeded in politicizing women's issues and creating more space for their political participation. Women in Morocco have been able to achieve much in comparison with other Middle-Eastern and developing countries.

In the local and legislative elections, there have been some signs of improvement as more women are being included. In 1976, no women were elected in the local elections, but by 1983, women comprised 43 out of 15,000 locally elected candidates. The numbers of elected women in 1992 and 1997 were, respectively, 77 and 83. Women representation at the local level has increased substantially under the rule of King Mohammed VI (from 3.406 seats in local councils in 2009 to 6.673 seats in 2015). Following the 2021 general election, their representation at the regional level has increased substantially (38%). Women increased their presence in leadership positions with the election of three women as mayors of three big cities in Morocco (Casablanca, Marrakech, and Rabat) and one women as president of one region. In legislative elections, women had no representation in parliament between 1977 and 1984. They made their entry to the lower house in 1993 with only two women. Despite advances in education, women remained underrepresented in the 1997 legislature (four women out of 595 members of parliament). In 2002, the adoption of a quota system played an important role in increasing women representation from 4 seats to 95 seats in 2021. This increase remains below the expectations of women's movement in Morocco and does not translate the constitutional provision concerning the establishment of parity.

The debates over the status of women and their gradual involvement in political participation in the public sphere should be viewed in the broader context of the efforts by the Moroccan state to move ahead with some forms of liberalization and also to contain the social and political forces unleashed by the rise of political Islam. More recent debates about rape, sexual harassment, and equal rights for inheritance have surged in the public sphere, and it is more likely to be on the agenda of women's rights for the years to come. In 2016, the parliament adopted a law on violence against women. Despite its limits, it provides a legal framework to protect women's rights, especially when it comes to domestic violence.

Amazigh Movement

The rise of the Amazigh movement within the past two decades can be considered one of the most important forms of cultural discourse and will likely reshape the cultural map and politics in Morocco. Amazigh refers to the cultural identity of the original inhabitants of Morocco, and *Imazighen* means literally "free people" or "noble people." The Amazigh label came to replace Berber, which is believed to be pejorative and part of a colonial construct.[42] Since independence, the social movement for Amazigh identity has been more often marginalized, if not repressed. The gradual emergence of civil society in the 1990s has, however, given new life to the movement as a significant expression of identity. Amazigh associations have proliferated in Morocco and today total more than one hundred, with varying degrees of influence.[43] Although these associations have different foci and political agendas, they all agree on the necessity to safeguard Amazigh culture and defend the linguistic and cultural rights of the Amazigh people.

To avoid the setbacks of the Amazigh problem as it was manifested in Algeria, the Moroccan monarchy reacted to identity politics in a gradual and calculated way. The initial reaction to the emerging influence of the Amazigh issue came from Hassan II. In his speech on August 20, 1994, the late king insisted on the necessity for preserving Amazigh culture and for introducing the Tamazight language into schools. Four days after the speech, national television started to broadcast the news in Tamazight three times a day. King Mohammed VI has continued the same kind of policy. The monarchy has sought to appropriate the Amazigh cause and make it part of its own field of politics.[44] On October 17, 2001, Mohammed VI created the Institut Royal de la Culture Amazighe (IRCAM). In addition to promoting Amazigh culture and art, one of the main goals of the institute is the introduction of the Tamazight language into the Moroccan educational system. In March 2010, a special Amazigh television channel was launched. In the 2011 constitution, the Amazigh language was recognized and became official in different state institutions

Like the Islamist movement, the Amazigh movement is by no means homogeneous. The fragmented nature of the movement was revealed in a more pronounced way around the issue of introducing the Amazigh language into the educational system. The various Amazigh associations had different views concerning the choice of the linguistic character and transcripts of Amazigh writing. Three systems of transcription were suggested: the Arabic alphabet, the Latin alphabet, and the Tifinagh alphabet. Those who advocated the use of Arabic argued that the Amazigh language has always been written in Arabic and identified with Islam. Composed mainly of Islamist associations, the proponents of Arabic transcripts rejected the use of Latin characters. Latin was considered an expression of Western hegemonic values that would ultimately be threatening to the preservation of Amazigh identity.

In contrast, the promoters of the Latin alphabet argued that since most of the scholarly work related to the Amazigh language (e.g., dictionaries and grammars) had been done in the Latin alphabet, it would make more sense to retain the Latin alphabet, as it is familiar to a much wider audience. In their view, this would contribute to spreading the language. This group generally emphasizes the fact that there are large numbers of publications, including reviews, literature, and books, that will facilitate the task of preserving the culture.

Finally, those who support the Tifinagh alphabet argue that it is the original Amazigh script, which dates back more than 3,000 years. It is important to note that the royal institute, IRCAM, recommended the use of Tifinagh, and King Mohammed VI approved its use. Thus, in February 2003 a communiqué of the Royal Cabinet announced the adoption of the Tifinagh script because it was believed to be meeting the requirements of upholding the integrity of the Amazigh language in its historical and cultural aspects.

As the decision reflects the king's will, most of the political actors did not attempt to criticize it. Protest came more from some Amazigh associations, which considered the king's decision as part of the "domestication of the Amazigh cause." For instance, the TADA association (whose name means "body" in the Amazigh language) strongly denounced the hypocrisy of the Moroccan monarchy in dealing with the demands of the Amazigh movement. For TADA, by introducing the Amazigh language into schools the monarchy is only trying to "appropriate, be in control and weaken the cause by emptying it from within."[45] For the members of this confederation, the government was not providing the necessary means for the introduction of the Amazigh language, which had already officially started in some schools in September 2003.

The Amazigh cultural awakening has been a significant challenge to Moroccan political and cultural life. Although the introduction and officialization of the Amazigh language is seen by some as a positive sign of cultural diversity within Moroccan society, others do not appreciate the utility or pragmatic function of introducing a language that is not widely spoken in the international and global economic context. At the national level, the Amazigh awakening is going to continue to significantly affect the Moroccan political scene. The movement is more likely to strengthen its position in the future as more associative networks beyond borders organize themselves to defend their cultural rights (the Réseau Amazigh pour la Citoyenneté, 2004).

Protest Movements

During the past fifteen years, more and more Moroccans have gone to the street to ask for their rights. It is in the context of weak labor unions and highly discredited and politically impotent Moroccan political parties that the February 20 Movement was able to lead the calls for nationwide protests that demanded economic equality as well as major political changes, including the reform of the constitution. It was referred to as the February 20 Movement because on that date in 2011, approximately 150,000–200,000 Moroccans in fifty-three cities across Morocco went to the streets and called for major democratic reforms, chanting the popular Arabic phrase of *al-sha'b uridu dusturan jadid* ["the people want a new constitution"]. The February 20 Movement was undoubtedly inspired by the revolutions in Tunisia and Egypt and used similar kinds of internet and communication means such as Facebook, which made it possible for thousands of young Moroccans to join the movement and subsequently become active in the protests. But it would be misleading to perceive the February 20 Movement simply in terms of its relation with what has happened as a result of the Arab Spring. For a while, the Moroccan context had started to witness a dynamic civil society that became gradually more active in the recent past.[46] What is important to note is that the Arab Spring has clearly given more momentum to the movement, which itself has energized a Moroccan political field that over the years had become depoliticized.[47]

The February 20 Movement was not mainly the result of economic problems and the critical unemployment situation, nor was it a continuation of the famous "bread riots"[48] of the 1980s. While the youth called for more social and economic equality and better social welfare services in the fields of health, education, and housing, their demands were more specially focused on political issues. What united the movement was a set of grievances that addressed very clearly the major structural problems that historically characterized the Moroccan political system. Some of the main demands related the principle of establishing a more democratic constitution with the principle of popular sovereignty as the basis of rule in Morocco. The protestors called for an independent judiciary and the separation of powers.[49] The people in the streets called for the freedom of the press and an independent media. Prominent in the demands of the February 20 Movement was an end to despotism, the system of corruption, and the trial of key officials who were believed to be involved in the mismanagement of public funds. One of the main slogans in the marches was *"achaab yurid iskat al istibdad, achaab yurid iskat al fassad"* ["the people want the fall of tyranny; the people want the end of corruption"].

Like the different political forces that played themselves out in the context of the 2011 dynamic of revolts in the region, the February 20 Movement was a combination of different ideologies and politically varied social groups united mainly by their opposition to *makhzenian* rule in all its different manifestations. Many young people would typically not want to associate themselves with any political party or association, and the members of the February 20 Movement did not want to claim any form of ideology. From its inception, the movement did not have any formal leadership. In many cities, there was the so-called *tansikiyat*, which were a kind of coordination committees assembling representatives of some left-wing political parties such as the Unified Socialist Party and the Democratic Way (Annahj Demmocrati), human rights associations such as the Moroccan Association of Human Rights (AMDH), and representatives of Al-Adl wal-Ihssan. These *tansikiyat* were involved, to a certain extent, in giving advice to the youth and coordinating political actions and protests. In many ways, the movement was the initiative of the youth, but it gradually was able to attract all sorts of people and ages.

The regime combined different strategies in its reactions to the demands of the protestors. Reform, cooptation, repression, and intimidation were all used at different moments of the first months of the life of the February 20 Movement to weaken it and discredit it in the eyes of the Moroccans. The regime was able to maintain its reign in the face of popular protests by appropriating the main demands of reform. In March 2011, the king announced the constitutional reform and its willingness to establish a parliamentary monarchy. It has organized early legislative elections in November of the same year. In addition, the regime has successfully bought off opposition by bringing in figures from the former opposition PJD to lead the government. Since May 2011, some of the marches of the movement have been violently repressed by the police. The regime tried to coopt some of the leaders of the movement, such as Oussama Lakhlifi. The latest became a member of the PAM. Besides that, most mainstream political parties established a distance vis-à-vis the movement in order to keep their cozy political positions with the Moroccan regime. While they have appropriated the demands of reform to mobilize during legislative elections, they did not ally themselves with the movement.

With hindsight, the weakening of the movement has been the result of the regime's reactions vis-à-vis the demands of the protestors. It has also to do with internal and regional factors. In terms of internal factors, the movement was not very well organized and ideologically scattered. With the withdrawal of the movement of Al-Adl wal-Ihssan in December 2011, its capacity to mobilize large numbers of protestors has been reduced. In terms of regional factors, the instability and violence that characterized most of the countries in the region, such as Libya and Syria, influenced the capacity of the movement to mobilize around its demands. Moroccans were in a position of "wait and see" and did not want to go to the streets because there was the fear of losing stability.

More importantly, the regime was successful in weakening the movement; however, it was not able to address major issues that mobilized Moroccans in 2011, such as fighting corruption, establishing social justice, and dealing with youth unemployment. Thus, since 2011, protest and discontent have continued. Besides this, most of the youth of the movement keep their activism in the virtual sphere or by reinvesting the public space through informal initiatives that aim at sensitizing Moroccans to their rights and exerting more pressure on the regime for more openness and more political reform.[50]

Up to 2018, the movement of protests continued in different regions and forms. The most important protest, known as *al hirak* in Morocco, took place in 2017 as the people in the Rif region, known for its symbolic capital of resistance, went to the streets to claim social and economic rights. The Rif is one of the areas that have been historically marginalized by the monarchy. The demands of the *Hirak* protests were mainly associated with economic hardship and the lack of infrastructures such as a university and a hospital. These social demands were expressed in peaceful ways and became part of new contentious politics that started to take place in other peripheral regions, such as Jerada in the northeastern part of Morocco. The Moroccan state has reacted with an iron fist to these demands, as many of the protestors were arrested and received prison sentences. The leader of the movement, Nasser Zefzafi, was sentenced to twenty years in prison. These recurrent protests suggest that Morocco is in the long term very likely to face major social upheavals that could contribute to more political instability.

In 2018, Moroccans started to engage in new forms of action associated with economic boycott through the use of social media. A major "people's campaign" took place to denounce the high prices of milk, mineral water, and fuel. The campaign represented a new form of social movement "from below" against the rising costs of living. Using Twitter and Facebook and establishing pages to raise awareness, different individuals managed to create a momentum of an unprecedented social solidarity that started to have a major economic effect. The Moroccan government initially downplayed the impact of the boycott, but it became more serious as the boycott started to bring to the public sphere debates about social inequality, the predatory behavior of the private sector, the relationship between business and political power, major socioeconomic problems, and the inability of the state to deal with these social issues. While the boycott campaign managed to reduce the prices of a number of products, such as dairy, mineral water, and fuel, it has also exacerbated the lack of confidence that Moroccans have about their political institutions.

REGIONAL AND INTERNATIONAL RELATIONS

Morocco's external policy mirrors its internal policy; its functioning reflects the institutional hierarchy characterized by the predominance of the monarchical institution. The influence of the government, the parliament, and civil society organizations has been limited. These actors fulfill a complementary role by carrying out the royal directives concerning specific issues. Geographical factors, strategic interests, and the personality of the late king, as well as his vision of Morocco's role in the MENA region, have played crucial roles in defining the country's regional and international policies.

Morocco has often succeeded in striking a balance in the conception of its foreign policy. Before 1990, Morocco played the "East" card in order to put the West under pressure whenever its interests were not taken into consideration. Since the fall of the Berlin Wall, Morocco has used its relationship with the United States as a way of defending its interests in the Euro-Mediterranean basin. Indeed, Hassan II was skilled at establishing good diplomatic relationships even with opposing sides. In the Middle East conflict, he was a trusted mediator while having a relatively good relationship with the state of Israel.[51] In terms of his relationship with the West, he was courting simultaneously both the United States and Europe.

Under King Mohammed VI's rule, Africa was placed at the center of Morocco's foreign policy. Morocco strengthened both its diplomatic and economic presence in the continent. In 2017, the Kingdom rejoined the African Union after thirty-three years of absence. Another characteristic of Morocco's foreign policy during the past 20 years is the diversification of its relations through partnerships with key international actors such as China, Russia, India, and Brazil among others. The diversification of its external relations provides Morocco with more options to defend its interests when the latter are compromised by traditional allies such as the European Union (EU) and the United States.

Actors in Morocco's Foreign Policy

The conception of foreign policy is part of the king's *domaine reservé*. The king's supremacy has been enshrined by different constitutions, which granted him substantial prerogatives in the field of foreign affairs.[52] Besides the king's constitutional powers, the elaboration of foreign policy in Morocco is dependent on

> Subjective parameters relative to the king who evaluates, strictly according to his personal convictions, the pace and tactics of any diplomatic enterprise involving Morocco, defines the criteria guiding the designation of national diplomatic operators, determines the scope and limits of alliances, and translates priorities.[53]

Hassan II's charismatic personality and the close relations he entertained with several heads of state accounted for the success of the foreign policy of the kingdom during his reign. Since Mohammed VI has been in power, there have been no changes in the constitutional powers of the monarchical institution, but the new king differentiated himself by consulting a number of political actors and prompting them to formulate suggestions on certain strategic matters such as territorial integrity.[54]

The Ministry of Foreign Affairs, one of the so-called *ministères de souveraineté* (ministries of sovereignty),[55] plays a key role in providing the king with technical facts concerning specific foreign policy issues and in coordinating the activities in this field. The ministry also negotiates international treaties and supervises the work of Morocco's diplomatic missions abroad. The governmental structure mandates that several other departments are also indirectly involved in foreign policy, notably the prime minister, the minister of interior, the minister of finance, and other ministries that are regularly called on for specific missions depending on their competencies and domains.[56] Depending on the politicodiplomatic situation, the king may designate the actors to be in charge of a specific issue. For instance, under the late King's rule, the handling of the Western Sahara conflict was monopolized by the palace and the interior minister. Under Mohammed VI's rule, political parties and civil society representatives have been more involved in defending Morocco's position.[57]

Despite the fact that the parliament has little room for maneuver in the field of foreign affairs, since the 1980s, there has been an increasing role for parliamentary diplomacy.[58] The parliament has established friendship associations with several countries and has regularly received diplomatic delegations. These friendship groups cooperate in different areas of activity such as the promotion of investments, cultural dialogue, peace, human rights, and democracy. The parliament's diplomatic activity has been instrumental to achieving at least three different goals: (1) promoting the image of Morocco on the international stage, mainly through international forums and conferences; (2) campaigning for the legitimacy of Morocco's position concerning the Western Sahara conflict[59]; and (3) reinforcing regional cooperation, particularly in the Mediterranean basin.[60] The increasing role of parliamentary diplomacy is, however, still disregarded by the text of the constitution, which acknowledges only the parliament's classical functions—namely, legislation and control of the government. So far, parliament's diplomatic function has been regulated by the internal rule of the Chamber of Representatives in 2017.

Other actors whose role has become increasingly more visible in foreign affairs are the civil society organizations. Their involvement in Morocco's foreign policy ties in with a broader vision of Morocco's diplomatic actors. This new vision of diplomacy is grounded in the diversity of foreign policy issues, the scope of international cooperation, and globalization. This fact is best captured by the words of King Mohammed VI: "The involvement in diplomatic activities of new actors such as the parliamentary assemblies, local communes, non-governmental organizations, companies and even individuals like performers, intellectuals, artists, [and] sports champions" is essential for the success of diplomatic activities.[61]

This new concept of diplomacy also complies with the EU's declared aim of encouraging Mediterranean civil society actors to multiply initiatives and exchanges in order to build mutual understanding among the peoples of the region. Their active involvement has the potential to contribute to a revival, if not reinvention, of the Euro-Mediterranean project. The Moroccan case is significant in this respect. The active involvement of NGOs in the Mediterranean basin and their participation at different forums play a crucial role in reinforcing Morocco's position and its relations with the EU country members. Although Moroccan NGOs are not directly involved in the conception of foreign policies, they contribute to their implementation. Civil society actors are the necessary partners of international NGOs. Projects supporting the reforms undertaken by Morocco (human rights and rights of women, immigration, local development, and the fight against poverty or youth radicalization) are implemented through partnerships with local associations.

Determinants of Morocco's International Relations

Morocco's regional and international relations have been determined by at least three inter-related factors: its history and geographic position, its strategic and economic interests, and the Western Sahara conflict. The geography and history of Morocco have made it a bridge between the countries of the MENA region and the West. Its borders with southern African states have also made it a bridge between Arab Africa and sub-Saharan Africa. As Hassan II stated in one of his speeches in 1976, "Morocco is like a tree whose nutrient roots reach deep into the African soil and whose leaves breathe in the winds of Europe." It is not by coincidence that Morocco's geostrategic position has determined to a large extent its politics at the regional and international levels. It has played a considerable role in the development of a number of constant characteristics related to the conception and implementation of Moroccan foreign policy.

Geographically, Morocco is part of five nonhierarchical concentric circles: the Euro-Mediterranean circle, the Maghreb circle, the Arab circle, the Muslim circle, and the African circle. Which circles are given priority in Moroccan foreign policy varies according to the interests of the regime. It depends also on whether one refers to these circles as circles of cooperation or circles of identity.

Historically, governmental actors have prioritized the first two circles. Relations between Morocco and the EU are crucial for the kingdom's economic interests. Thus, the Euro-Mediterranean space constitutes Morocco's first circle of cooperation, predominated by bilateral relations with France, Spain, and Italy. In the 1980s, priority was also given to the Maghreb, whose unity is of political and economic importance. Solving the Western Sahara issue is both a determinant factor and an objective of Morocco's foreign policy in its relations with its immediate neighbors on the southern and northern coasts of the Mediterranean. During the past decade, there has been increasing tensions between Morocco and Algeria leading to cutting diplomatic ties in August 2021.

As for the last three circles, it is clear that Morocco's foreign policy also relies on keeping its ties of solidarity with the Arab and Islamic world. Hassan II was keen to play a major role in the Israeli–Palestinian conflict.[62] But the most recent move of Moroccan foreign policy is its more open normalization with the state of Israel. As part of a negotiated deal the Trump administration recognized Morocco's sovereignty in the Western Sahara in return for the normalization of relationships with Israel. The move toward this policy of normalization was part of a form of realism that has characterized Morocco's foreign policy that has historically promoted its diplomatic and security interests. The more concrete outcomes and benefits of this move toward normalization with Israel is yet to be more concretely shown. Morocco's African relationships have also been important for the monarchical institution. With the ascendance of Mohammed VI to power, more interest has been given to cooperation and investment in sub-Saharan Africa. Various agreements have been signed in the fields of commerce, investment, transportation, and telecommunications. The metaphor of the tree is significant. Morocco is first and foremost an African country; its alliance with Europe has strategic purposes, but the kingdom does not neglect its ties with the Maghreb, the Arab region, and the Islamic world.

Morocco's opening to the West is certainly a strategic choice. Starting with simple agreements on trade cooperation in 1969, Morocco has progressed considerably in its relations with its northern Mediterranean neighbors. Whether during the reign of Hassan II or Mohammed VI, Morocco has always searched for a status that exceeds mere association with Europe. Despite their considerable scope, the past agreements between Morocco and the EU do not meet Morocco's ambitions to gain a higher status.

The economic situation of Morocco has also been a determining factor for conducting its foreign policy. Following the comprehensive economic liberalization undertaken in the past twenty years, Morocco's strategic focus lies in multiple alliances with economic actors on the African, Asian, and American continents. Taieb Fassi Fihri, then minister delegate of foreign affairs, stated that the free-trade agreement signed with the United States ties in with royal directives for a liberal and preferential policy capable of "mobilizing all opportunities for diversifying our partnership, serving the interests of our country and reinforcing the position of the kingdom on the regional level in order to create a platform for attracting investments." Several theses have been advanced to explain Morocco's motives for a free-trade agreement with the United States. Some saw it as a strategy to put pressure on the EU in view of obtaining "advanced status," something that Morocco managed to achieve. Others considered the agreement as a part of Morocco's European vocation.

Strategic Role of the Euro-Mediterranean Policy in Morocco's International Relations

Morocco's Euro-Mediterranean policy has been crucial in its overall regional and international relations. It is the only state among the southern Mediterranean countries to have succeeded in constructing a Mediterranean policy that openly aims at membership in the EU. Since the 1960s, Morocco has continuously cooperated with the northern Mediterranean countries in different fields.[63] The policy aiming at a special status with the EU was first expressed in 1984 with a solemn demand by King Hassan II for accession to the European Economic Community (EEC), an initiative that proved Morocco's interest in a new relationship with Europe in the form of a political and strategic alliance. Moreover, it was a clear demand for differential or preferential treatment of the Moroccan case over the EEC's other partners with regard to economic, financial, and commercial cooperation. Apart from its objective to extend cooperation on the basis of a special status, the request for membership was clearly connected to the problems concerning the possibilities of modernizing Morocco.

Morocco's accession to the Barcelona Process in 1995 confirmed Morocco's wish to join the EU. The conclusion of the Association Agreement in 1996 (which became effective in March 2000) was another step forward in the cooperation between Morocco and the EU. In addition, the kingdom was the first beneficiary of the MEDA I (1996–1999)[64] and MEDA II (2000–2004)[65] programs that deployed financial aid to countries that encouraged reforms in various domains.[66] Through that process, cooperation was extended to include not only sectors relevant to the country's economic and social development but also further cooperation at the political and security levels.

With King Mohammed VI's succession to the throne in 1999, the state reinforced its ambition for lasting cooperation with the EU, centering on the economic aspect.[67] Like his father, the king has stressed the importance of the European agenda for Morocco and has expressed interest in "a partnership that would be more—and better—than a revised and improved association. . . but not a full membership."[68] During his visits to several European countries, notably France, Italy, and Spain, Mohammed VI pleaded for a strong and well-balanced partnership. To ensure Morocco's standing on the international scene and to assume an active role, the new king has called for an "offensive strategy" as part of "an integrated and coherent plan based on the enlargement already initiated in three concentric circles, namely good neighbourhood, active solidarity and strategic partnership."[69]

Despite the general criticism regarding the European Neighbourhood Policy, there was overall support for Morocco's wish for obtaining advanced status and being offered greater economic integration as well as establishing intense cultural and political relations.[70] The free-trade agreements concluded with the EU are capable of boosting economic development, but they are also a means to reduce migratory movements and consolidate the European presence in the southern Mediterranean. The declaration of Romano Prodi, president of the European Commission in 2002, that "we have to be ready to propose more than a partnership and less than a membership," and his concept, formulated later, of "sharing everything but the institutions," correspond with Morocco's current political objective of reinforcing its partnership with the EU. The implementation in 2003 of a think tank concerning Morocco's advanced status met the ambitions of the kingdom. It is part of the country's diplomatic strategy of pushing for the maximum and justifying its demands with the political, economic, and social progress achieved by the reforms of the past two decades.

CONCLUSION

Morocco is an interesting case for analyzing the kinds of political syntheses that have historically resulted from attempts at combining traditional forms of political authority with modern forms of institutions. In its quest for some form of political modernity and democratic legitimacy to face the challenges of the 21st century, Morocco remains at this time essentially incapable of detaching itself from the weight of its own authoritarian past. In 2021, the prospects of democracy seem to be bleak, especially as the freedom of speech is even more threatened. Through various strategies, newspapers in Morocco can no longer report critically about the state as associated with the *makhzen*. In the 2021 World Press Freedom Index compiled by Reporters Without Borders, Morocco ranks today 136th.[71]

In more recent years, there is an increasing absence of a public sphere for meaningful political debate. Practically all independent newspapers have ceased to exist either as a result of economic sanctions or by targeting and jailing journalists. The Moroccan judicial system is instrumentalized to control and ultimately jail courageous journalists who take risks to confront the state. It is the centrality of the monarchy that has remained a constant factor in the political landscape of the country. In a political context that has been largely monopolized by the king, the ideological discourse about democracy has never yet been absent. It is clear that the language of democracy and the shallow institutional ramifications that come out of it have so far served mainly the interests of the monarchy very well.

To more optimistic observers, the fact that Morocco had a strong monarchy in parallel with a multiparty system and a parliament makes the country very well equipped politically to embark on the road to democracy. On the more pessimistic side, the omnipotent *makhzen*, its archaic political culture, and the overall clientelist structures of the state represent major stumbling blocks to any real democratization in the country. In the absence of a real democratic constitution and popular sovereignty, the PJD—like the Istiqlal, the USFP, or the Independent Party before it—is more likely to remain an instrument in the hands of an authoritarian *makhzen* in constant search for adapting itself and guaranteeing its survival.

Whatever position one takes, it is clear that the prospects of democratization in Morocco will be determined by a number of concrete political factors. Probably the most important is the political will on the part of the monarchy to give up some of its powers and to move toward another political logic for the establishment of a more democratic constitution that takes more into consideration some of the basic components of a democratic system such as the separation of powers and accountability of the decision-makers. Another factor is the ability of different political actors, including the monarchy, the business elite, the army, political parties, and the Islamists, to go beyond the short-term visions of survival and realize the long-term value of democracy as a stable form of political system. An equally important factor is to limit the number of parties and to strengthen their position vis-à-vis the monarchy in order to be able to present a more viable democratic political project. Independent and constitutional, more powerful political institutions such as the parliament and the government are essential to the long-term democratic vision. It is only in such conditions that Moroccans can regain confidence in their political parties and that political parties can regain legitimacy by being more courageous and proposing realistic but democratic political alternatives instead of supporting the status quo.

SUGGESTED READINGS

Charrad, Mounira M. *States and Women's Rights: The Making of Postcolonial Tunisia, Algeria, and Morocco*. Berkeley, CA: University of California Press, 2001.

Hammoudi, Abdellah. *Master and Disciple: The Cultural Foundations of Moroccan Authoritarianism*. Chicago, IL: University of Chicago Press, 1997.

Sater, James N. *Morocco: Challenges to Tradition and Modernity*. London: Taylor & Francis, 2010.

Storm, Lise. *Democratization in Morocco: The Political Elite and Struggles for Power in the Post-Independence State*. London: Taylor & Francis, 2009.

Waterbury, John. *The Commander of the Faithful: The Moroccan Political Elite—A Study in Segmented Politics*. London: Weidenfeld & Nicolson, 1970.

20 PALESTINE

Alaa Tartir and Benoît Challand

Where and what is Palestine? This is a question that elicits emotional debates, largely due to the importance of Jerusalem for the three revealed religions. Historically, it is the area between the Mediterranean Sea and the Jordan River, bounded on the north by Lebanon and on the south by Gulf of Aqaba. This is called "historic Palestine." Following the establishment of the State of Israel in 1948 and the Israeli occupation of the West Bank and Gaza Strip in 1967, "Palestine" became a reduced version of historic Palestine. Today, Palestine refers to the Occupied Palestinian Territory (oPt), including the West Bank and Gaza Strip, comprising 22 percent of historic Palestine. The Palestine Liberation Organization (PLO) informally accepted this reduction of Palestine in 1974 and formally adopted it in 1988.[1] In 1993, the PLO signed the Oslo Peace Accords with Israel, which stipulated the emergence of the Palestinian Authority (PA) as the Palestinian governing body in the West Bank and Gaza Strip. According to the Oslo Accords, a Palestinian state—next to Israel—was meant to be established at the end of the decade on the 1967 borders/Green Line through gradual negotiations with Israel.[2]

However, an independent and sovereign Palestinian state never materialized. After two decades of a failed peace process, the PA approached the United Nations (UN) in 2011, requesting the recognition of Palestine as an independent state. In 2012, the UN offered Palestine the status of a nonmember observer state. But, this state only exists on paper. The recognized State of Palestine lacks the main pillars of statehood: control over borders and sovereignty, including the ability to exert independent policies and management of the population and finances.

This state also does not include or represent more than half of the Palestinian people who live as refugees in exile. Not only is "Palestine" reduced, but also the Palestinian people have been reduced to only those who live in the occupied West Bank and Gaza Strip. The recognized governing body of Palestine, represented by the PA, partially governs the 5.23 million Palestinians living in the West Bank (including East Jerusalem) and Gaza Strip. But many more Palestinians (another 8.57 million, of which 1.95 million are living as "second-class" citizens of Israel [see Israel, Chapter 13]) are scattered around the region, not under the PA's control.[3] Technically, they rely on the PLO, an umbrella organization that federates the majority of nationalist Palestinian parties and that has been internationally recognized as the sole legitimate representative of the Palestinian people. However, today the PLO institutions are largely absent, coopted by the PA or simply ineffective, and the PLO suffers from a deep legitimacy crisis, as it does not include the Islamic Resistance

Movement (Hamas), which was the dominant political party in the last legislative elections of 2006. Furthermore, since the intra-Palestinian divide in 2007, the PA does not control the Gaza Strip. Despite the nominal claim by the Fatah-led governments in the West Bank since 2014 (particularly the 17th and 18th Ramallah-based governments), the Gaza Strip remains governed internally by Hamas and its de-facto governing institutions within an Israeli–Egyptian blockade.

This chapter examines how the lack of a sovereign Palestinian state and the continued Israeli military occupation, which is illegal according to international law, have profoundly affected the social transformation, institutional development, political economy, and politics of Palestine. This chapter also outlines the ongoing struggle between the two main Palestinian parties, Hamas and Fatah, and explores how the ambiguity of the relations between the quasi-state institutions of the PA and the officially prominent role of the PLO affect Palestinian politics. Finally, it highlights more recent developments such as the growing impact of the Palestinian-led Boycott, Divestment, and Sanction (BDS) movement, the accession to the International Criminal Court (ICC), the consequences of the wars on Gaza in 2008, 2014, and 2021, the wave of protests in the Gaza Strip called "The Great March of Return," and the impact of the US Trump and Biden administrations.

KEY FACTS ON THE WEST BANK AND GAZA STRIP[4]

AREA 2,325 square miles (6,020 square kilometers); West Bank (including East Jerusalem), 2,184 square miles (5,655 square kilometers); Gaza, 141 square miles (365 square kilometers)[5]

SEAT OF GOVERNMENT Ramallah and Gaza City; intended capital: East Jerusalem

POPULATION West Bank, 3,120,448 (plus 688,262 Israeli settlers in the occupied West Bank and East Jerusalem 2019); Gaza, 2,106,745 (2021)[6]

PERCENTAGE OF POPULATION UNDER 25 West Bank, 55.7; Gaza, 60.5 (2020)[7]

RELIGIOUS GROUPS (PERCENTAGE) Muslims (Sunni Islam), 97; Christians, 3 (Note: In the West Bank, Christians live mainly in Jerusalem, Beit Jala, Beit Sahur, Bethlehem, and Ramallah; the main Christian denomination is Greek Orthodox.)[8]

LANGUAGE Arabic; Hebrew spoken by many Palestinians; English widely understood

TYPE OF GOVERNMENT Some Palestinian self-government; Israel retains ultimate authority as the occupying power[9]

GDP (NOMINAL) West Bank and Gaza, $14,843 million; $3,018 per capita (2021, baseline scenario)[10]

PERCENTAGE OF GDP BY SECTOR Agriculture, forestry, and fishing: 7.4, Industry 11.6, Construction 5.5; Service and other 59.8% (baseline 2021 scenario)[11]

TOTAL RENTS (PERCENTAGE OF GDP) FROM NATURAL RESOURCES West Bank and Gaza: Figures not available

FERTILITY RATE West Bank: 3.8 children born/woman; Gaza: 3.9 children born/woman (2017–2019)

KEY POLITICAL FIGURES President: Mahmoud Abbas (also known as Abu Mazen); Prime Minister: Mohammad Shtayyeh (Fatah, West Bank)

Sources: Palestinian Central Bureau of Statistics. "Preliminary Results of the Population, Housing and Establishments Census, 2017." February, 2018, https://www.sesric.org/imgs/news/1945-Preliminary-Results-Report-EN.pdf.
Palestinian Central Bureau of Statistics. "Palestine Statistical Yearbook." 2021, https://arabdevelopmentportal.com/publication/palestine-statistical-yearbook.
Palestinian Central Bureau of Statistics. "National Accounts (GDP)." Accessed August 10, 2022, https://www.pcbs.gov.ps/site/lang__en/741/default.aspx.[12]

HISTORY OF STATE-BUILDING: THE CREATION OF A QUASI STATE

The famous picture taken on the White House lawn on September 13, 1993, portraying the US President Bill Clinton inviting Israeli Prime Minister Yitzhak Rabin and the PLO Chairman Yasir Arafat to shake hands, was taken during the signing of the Declaration of Principles. The Declaration aimed "to put an end to decades of confrontation and conflict, recognize their mutual legitimate and political rights, and strive to live in peaceful coexistence." It marked the mutual recognition of the PLO and Israel and set the two parties on a path toward a two-state solution.

The handshake marked what many hoped to be the end of a decades-long conflict. For Palestinians, the establishment of Israel in 1948 was a *Nakba*, the Arabic word for catastrophe. Palestinians lost 70 percent of the territories of historic Palestine, and more than seven hundred thousand either fled or were expelled by Israeli troops from their homeland. It began the Palestinians' long quest for their own independent leadership to be able to enter into full negotiations with Israel. Only when new facts on the ground changed the international calculus in the early 1990s that a bilateral peace process transformed into negotiations over nascent state structures.[13]

One new reality that forced Israelis and Palestinians to start negotiating was the new world order created in the wake of the 1991 Persian Gulf War. The collapse of the Soviet Union and the success of the US-led coalition against Saddam Hussein during Operation Desert Storm in 1991 toppled the international balance on which the PLO had based its strategy. Arafat feared that, unconstrained by Soviet vetoes, Washington would impose a settlement of the conflict favorable to Israel but short of the "international legitimacy" enshrined by the UN Security Council Resolutions (UNSCRs) 242 and 338. The exclusion of the PLO as the representative of the Palestinians at the October 1991 Madrid Conference compounded his apprehension.

Second, by 1993, the PLO was broke. Arafat's decision to support Saddam Hussein in 1990 had estranged the PLO from its Gulf supporters, losing the organization an estimated $10 billion in assets from Gulf states' support and the remittances that some four hundred thousand Palestinians from the region would have handed over to the PLO. Even as Arafat was approving the principle of secret direct negotiations between the PLO and Israel in the Norwegian capital of Oslo in August 1993, his organization was laying off thousands of functionaries. The emergence of a high-profile Palestinian delegation from the oPt at the 1991 Madrid Conference aggravated Arafat's fear that the PLO stood at the point of eclipse. A new leadership from the oPt could take the lead, or so it appeared to Arafat.

Third, the multilateral negotiating process born of the Madrid Conference was going nowhere. For ten rounds, the Palestinian delegation insisted that Israel accept the applicability of UNSCR 242 to the oPt as a precondition for negotiations. Meanwhile, the Israelis preferred to discuss the minutiae of Palestinian self-government. In addition, Israel launched an expansion of Jewish settlements in the oPt, fueled in part by the immigration of four hundred thousand Jews and others from the former Soviet Union. A new and enduring Israeli strategy emerged: procrastinating during negotiations in order to change the facts on the ground. In 1992, former prime minister Yitzhak Shamir said that his aim at Madrid had been to keep the talks going for ten years, by which time Israel's annexation of the West Bank "would be an accomplished fact," a statement echoing that of a close aide of Prime Minister Ariel Sharon in 2004, who said that Israel's decision to disengage from the Gaza Strip—a move that was completed in August 2005—was only meant as "the freezing of the political process.... The disengagement is actually formaldehyde. It supplies the amount of formaldehyde that's necessary so that there will not be a political process with the Palestinians."[14] Time and again, serving Israeli prime ministers declared their deep objection to a recognition of a Palestinian state, a tendency that was again endorsed by the US administration under President Trump.[15]

The Declaration of Principles, also known as the Oslo I agreement, and the Oslo II agreement, which paved the way for the creation of the PA in July 1994, rescued the flagging fortunes of Arafat and the PLO, but they did not establish a lasting peace. Arafat was facing the challenge of an independent leadership from the oPt and the prospect of increasingly popular Islamist movements that grew stronger with the first intifada (1987–1993),[16] and the Oslo Accords gave the PLO recognition as a quasi-state actor and new financial leverage, as international donors promised hundreds of millions of dollars of aid to build a new Palestinian state. For Israel, the Accords only committed it to a gradual negotiation with the Palestinians. It could always pull the plug on the negotiations and continue changing facts on the ground that enhanced its bargaining position.

The first euphoric moments of the Oslo years temporarily hid the problematic asymmetric architecture of the Oslo Accords. By renouncing the PLO's "use of terrorism and other acts of violence" and vowing to discipline "violators," Arafat conceded that the basis of the peace process would be Israel's security and not, as the Palestinian delegation had insisted at Madrid, international law. By annulling in 1996 all articles of the covenant of the Palestinian National Council (the PLO legislative body) inconsistent with Israel's right to exist, Arafat was, for many Palestinians, affording legitimacy to the Jewish state prior to any reciprocal recognition of the legitimacy of a Palestinian state in the territories occupied by Israel in the June 1967 War. As many observers noted, with Oslo, Israel had ceded *representative* legitimacy to the PLO but had not given the Palestinians right to self-determination. Instead of peace for land, the logic of Oslo was an outsourcing of Israeli security concerns,[17] a task that the nascent PA took seriously, especially when it came to cracking down on groups opposed to Oslo and, in particular, Islamist groups. This is the logic that made it possible for Israeli governments to realize a strategy of asymmetric containment.[18]

SOCIAL TRANSFORMATION: DISPLACED ELITES AND FRAGMENTATION

Palestinians are fragmented based on territorial, social, political, and economic divisions. The *Nakba* and the displacement of more than seven hundred thousand Palestinians dealt heavy blows to Palestinian society: Most of the previous landowning or commercial elites left the region in 1948 and 1949, leaving the remaining Palestinian people without clear political and economic leaders, and dependent on external powers. Rashid Khalidi suggests that there was already a Palestinian identity in the second half of the 19th century, most notably among urban elites.[19] Yet given the massive dislocation of 1948, the incapacity of Palestinians to keep the PLO free from external Arab influences, and the fact that Egypt and Jordan administered the Gaza Strip and the West Bank, respectively, from 1948 to 1967 meant that Palestinians had neither the power nor the institutions to reinforce their sense of national cohesion. Moreover, the dispersion of Palestinians across the globe, as well as very different experiences for those living under rule of Israeli, Egyptian and Jordanian rule (in the Gaza Strip and West Bank, respectively, until 1967), led to fragmentation and diverse social conditions for the Palestinian people. Even those remaining within historial Palestine are fragmented. To some extent, Israel has fostered these divisions in an attempt to sustain its occupation and matrix of control. The UN Development Program's (UNDP) Human Development Report 2010 argued that "the State of Israel has systematically segregated Palestinians communities into a series of fragmented archipelagos (referred to variously as isolated islands, enclaves, cantons, and Bantustans) under a system that has been deemed 'one of the most intensively territorialized control systems ever created.'"[20]

Thus, for instance, there are great differences within the Palestinian community with regard to birthrates. It is often heard that Palestinians' high fertility rate represents a challenge to Israel, if not a threat. However, many studies suggest that once Palestinians reach a higher standard of living, birthrates drop significantly. Thus, most of the Palestinians living inside Israel match, in terms of fertility rate, the level of advanced capitalist societies (i.e., one or two children per family).[21] For Palestinian refugees living outside Palestine, particularly under legal regimes in Lebanon and Syria that prevent or hinder them from practicing their professions as doctors or lawyers or from carrying out entrepreneurial activities, Palestinian refugees are confined to the fringes of those societies. All of these factors have led to forms of social division and growing resentment that foster escalating violence from the population.

Thus, in 1987, with no end to the occupation in sight and no direct contacts with the PLO leadership in Tunis possible, Palestinians in the oPt took their fate into their own hands. They revolted against the creeping violence of occupation and land expropriation, beginning the first *intifada* (in Arabic, literally, to "shake off") in December 1987. Within weeks of the intifada's beginning, a new political faction emerged: *Hamas.* "HAMAS" is an acronym standing for Movement of the Islamic Resistance, and a word that means zeal or ardor in Arabic. Hamas rapidly became a thorn in the flesh of both the PLO and Israel.[22] For the PLO, Hamas became a serious contender for popular support among the Palestinian population; for Israel, the Islamist movement quickly became uncontrollable. The first intifada, unlike the second, remained at a low level of violence, but Israel did not manage to quell what was a truly popular revolt at least until 1991 when the international environment ushered in the new reality of negotiations, first in Madrid and then in Oslo. With Oslo, new hopes blossomed for more political participation of the Palestinians at large, but these remained wishful thinking. The so-called PLO returnees who came back from Tunis in 1994 with the advent of the PA and monopolized key positions as a reward for their past activism contrasted with the insiders (i.e., the local residents who were born inside the oPt), who very often felt excluded in terms of jobs and a voice inside Fatah. Class formation, people with access to a job and resources from the PA, coincided in part with the formation of a new PA bureaucracy, but whose legitimacy depended on the ability to mobilize aid from influential international donors. Many Palestinians remained outside of these network creating a social rift.[23]

Outside of the sphere of Fatah's political influence, it is worth underlining the relevance of the formation of popular committees. In these new, self-managed structures, people would function locally on a voluntary basis to provide missing services such as health, education, or agriculture, or to organize women's committees. In reality, these committees were replicated all over the oPt, but along the lines of small numbers of political groupings, thus reflecting a form of political obedience to one or another of the main Palestinian political factions that Israel had officially forbidden.[24] At that time, these popular committees were almost exclusively secular and linked to one of the following factions, which, by 1990, were all members of the PLO: the Communist Party (PCP, later to become the Palestinian People's Party); two Marxist formations, the Popular Front for the Liberation of Palestine (PFLP) and the Democratic Front for the Liberation of Palestine (DFLP); not to mention Fatah's own popular committees. Many of these committees became NGOs during the Oslo years, providing another locus for social ascension.[25]

Instrumental for the development of more active and powerful popular committees were access to higher education and the growing role of women. Universities and professional colleges were created in the oPt beginning in the early 1970s, with new universities created in Bir Zeit, Bethlehem, Gaza, Nablus, and Hebron; and many more Palestinians obtained degrees abroad, a large share in the former Soviet bloc for those Palestinians of Leftist political leanings. This was also a period in which women were dedicated proponents of national liberation, and many of these committees paved the way for the active political participation of women. Palestinians also managed, once again, to mobilize new resources in reaction to negative outside influences. In this case, the challenges were Israel's policies of de-development, or what Roy (2007:4) defines as "the deliberate, systematic and progressive dismemberment of an indigenous economy by a dominant one, where economic—and by extension, societal—potential is not only distorted but denied."[26] This form of social revolution turned out to be incomplete, however,[27] because of the faulty Oslo agreements and the creation of a gradually more corrupt and autocratic PA. Such an out-of-touch elite also explains the popular discontent, especially of Palestinian youths, during the "days of rage" similar to the ones organized in Tunis or Cairo in the first months of 2011. As in other countries, police crushed the spirit of revolt, but it still simmers under the ashes. Since 2011, sporadic protests have erupted in the oPt; however, the PA and its security forces severely beat up these protests, and by doing so, these forces moved in the direction of establishing a police state through visible authoritarian transformations and trends and increasing repression.[28]

RELIGION AND POLITICS: EVOLVING RELATIONS

As pointed out in Chapter 5, one has to be careful in assuming the politicization of social groups invoking Islam is based solely on religion. In the Palestinian context, one has to understand the emergence of the main Islamist faction, Hamas, in the light of a protracted conflict with Israel and gradual dissatisfaction of the population with an increasingly isolated and corrupt PA leadership and with a moribund PLO. Hamas arose in the context of the outbreak of the first intifada and the demise of the Palestinian Left after the collapse of the Soviet Union.

A number of factors led to the increasing strength and popularity of Hamas over time. First, the religious imbalance has grown further toward an overwhelming Muslim majority. Christian Palestinians have always been a minority inside Palestine, but they comprised close to one-third of all Palestinians at the beginning of the 20th century. This figure now amounts to a meager three percent, due to the massive Christian exile, first in 1948 and later in 1967.[29]

Second, Hamas benefited from the spaces that Israel granted historically to Islamic institutions. In an attempt to undermine the political influence of the PLO, from the late 1970s onward, Israel allowed Islamic groupings to increase their influence in the territories. This strategy was consistent with other steps that Israel repeatedly took to undermine the possibilities of a united Palestinian population and leadership. Turning a blind eye to Islamist charities proved to be a tragic mistake for Israel, however. Islamists were also nationalist organizations, committed to the same means of armed struggle, even if a decade later than other Palestinian parties.

Third, Hamas adapted its strategy, in particular the use or renunciation of violence, to the environment. During the two intifadas, Hamas borrowed from and imitated secular organizations in their strategy of active armed resistance. But in other moments, Hamas took a backseat and let author Palestinian actors take the lead. As the news of Oslo became public, it quickly denounced this agreement as a sell-out of the original goal to establish a Palestinian state in all of historic Palestine.[30] It stayed out of the 1996 legislative contest because its leadership believed that participating would legitimize the logic of Oslo, and focused instead on Islamization of Palestinian society from below.

Fourth, Hamas excels in riding the wave of popular discontent against the PA leadership. With the Oslo years and the massive pouring of foreign aid, two social groups were able to get in better economic positions. People connected to the PA bureaucracy and the ruling party, Fatah, (in particular a very large security sector) and those evolving in the fields of development, NGOs, and empowerment. Hamas has worked hard to represent the vast majority of Palestinians left out of these networks. Thus, Hamas is more than an Islamist organization. Many Christian Palestinians voted for Hamas in the 2006 elections, which suggests that

Hamas benefited from disaffection of Fatah and corrupt practices. With the 2007 Palestinian divide between Gaza Strip and the West Bank (see below), Hamas has retained most of its legitimacy in the much poorer Gaza Strip. The entrenchment of Hamas's rule in Gaza is remarkable considering the limited financial resources it has: Although the PA's governments headed by Prime Ministers Rami Al-Hamdallah and Mohammad Shtayyeh are supposed to be the sole legitimate governments since 2014, Hamas has an effective "shadow" government that runs the Gaza Strip.

On the issue of violence, Hamas, like other resistance groups, believes it is legitimate to target Israelis inside the oPt as an occupying force. Often it is specific events that have made Hamas use of suicide attacks in the 1990s and 2000s or the use of rockets since 2010. For example, the series of bombing of Israeli buses in 1994 occurred after a spiral of violence, in which a Jewish extremist, Baruch Goldstein, killed twenty-nine Palestinians praying in the main Ibrahimi mosque in Hebron, that Hamas retaliated with suicide attacks inside Israel in the spring of 1994 (Table 20.1). The same dynamic occurred again in April and May 2021 when

TABLE 20.1 ■ Palestine: A Chronology	
1920–1948	Mandatory Palestine under British control
1948	Israel established; Palestinian Nakba; the West Bank under Jordanian administration and the Gaza Strip under Egyptian administration
1958	Fatah founded
1964	Palestine Liberation Organization (PLO) founded in Egypt
1967	June 1967 War; Israel occupies the West Bank and Gaza Strip
1968	Yasir Arafat becomes new PLO chairman
1970	Black September; PLO is expelled from Jordan
1974	PLO recognized by Arab League
1982	PLO expelled from Lebanon
1987–1993	First intifada
1988	Declaration of independence made by PLO in Algiers
1991	Multilateral peace negotiations launched at Madrid Conference (PLO excluded)
1993	Declaration of Principles/Oslo Accords
1994	Creation of the Palestinian Authority (PA)
1995	Oslo II

(Continued)

TABLE 20.1 ■ Palestine: A Chronology (*Continued*)	
1996	Presidential and legislative elections
2000	July: Camp David fails to reach final agreement; September: second intifada breaks out
2004	President Yasir Arafat dies
2005	Mahmoud Abbas elected president for four years
2006	Hamas wins majority at legislative elections (PLC). No stable governments formed
2007	June: Hamas's takeover of Gaza; division of a de facto government under Hamas in Gaza and a Fatah-led PA in the West Bank
2008– 2009	Israeli Operation Cast Lead in Gaza
2012	Israeli Operation Pillar of Defense in Gaza; recognition of Palestine as a nonmember observer state by the UN General Assembly
2013	June: Prime Minister Salam Fayyad resigns and is replaced by Rami Al-Hamdallah (West Bank)
2014	July: Israeli Operation Protective Edge in Gaza
2015	April: Palestine joins the International Criminal Court (ICC)
2017	Hamas elects new leadership and amends charter/political document
2018	After twenty-two years of waiting, PLO's Palestinian National Council convened in Ramallah and chose a new leadership; Trump administration recognizes Jerusalem as the capital of Israel and moves US Embassy to Jerusalem; The Great March of Return erupts in Gaza
2019	April: Mohammad Shtayyeh replaces Rami Al-Hamdallah as Prime Minister and formed the 18th Palestinian government
2020	US-led Abraham Accords signed and declared between Israel, United Arab Emirates (UAE), and Bahrain; Normalization deals between Israel, Sudan, and Morocco were announced.
2021	30 April: Presidential and legislative elections postponed/canceled; 6–21 May: War on Gaza/ Israeli Operation Guardian of the Walls; April/May escalation across Palestine/Israel; Major protests against the PA across the West Bank

an increasingly marginalized Israeli Prime Minister Netanyahu sent heavy-handed police and support ultranationalist Jewish settlers to crush legitimate Palestinian protests in Sheikh Jarrah and Haram al-Sharif, which pushed Hamas to launch rockets on Israel in a new round of war on Gaza. Hamas's supporters also come from different constituencies. Some embrace the gradualist path toward Islamization of Palestine in the mode advocated by the Muslim Brotherhood. Others support a more active, at times violent, path toward the reestablishment of Palestinian control over historical Palestine.

DEVELOPMENT OF PA INSTITUTIONS

The PA was developed over the Oslo years (1993–2000). As noted previously, when a Palestinian state was declared, the PA was a mere collection of formal political institutions without the contours of a proper state. It lacked two basic elements of a modern state: clear borders and sovereignty over its territory. Borders were part of the final status agreement package, and Israel continued to exert external sovereignty, confirming the validity of the thesis that Oslo was based on a logic of asymmetric containment in favor of Israel.

The PA was a constituent body—aimed at both governing Palestinians living in the occupied territories and delineating the arrangement of a future Palestinian state to be established through a final agreement with Israel. For example, a basic law (the equivalent of a constitution) was drafted in this interim period by the legislative body (the Palestinian Legislative Council [PLC]), and different institutions were created in the spirit of classical checks-and-balances functions, with the creation of a separate judicial system, the nomination of an ombudsman for human rights issues (the Independent Commission for Human Rights), and civil-society watchdog associations. Executive power was granted to an elected Palestinian president (Yasir Arafat in 1996), who then would appoint a cabinet made up of about twenty ministries and in direct charge of security bodies. In a nutshell, the PA was a republican presidential regime, based on majority voting for the presidential elections (with a 4-year mandate) and a unicameral legislative body (members of the PLC were originally elected for four years on a proportional basis). Palestinian political parties were finally free to form and take part in this electoral process. However, it was mainly Fatah that participated in this election, as many other political parties boycotted the elections because they rejected the Oslo Accords framework. Therefore, there was hardly any political competition. Moreover, Arafat, and the PLO's, clientelistic and neopatrimonial governance undermined the effectiveness of the PLC and prospects for democracy.

Three elements further limited this system. First, the international community pressured the Palestinian factions to make the Oslo peace process its absolute priority. Political conditionality was the main tool for pressuring Palestinians to accept the Oslo Accords, and political actors that refused to play the Oslo tune were sidelined. Without external funding (which has been massive, as Figure 20.1 demonstrates) and given their boycott of the PLC elections, many of the Leftist factions that opposed Oslo lost political support, funding, and visibility. International pressure also undermined the rule of law: To respect the logic of the peace process (and therefore guarantee Israeli security), the PA often had to crack down on Palestinian groups violently opposing Oslo, even if it was through State Security Courts' expedited judgments leading to capital punishment. Patterns of torture by Palestinian police forces against their own population, documented both in the West Bank and in the Gaza Strip, contributed to limited freedom of expression in the oPt.

The second limitation came from Israel. Israel often lamented that the PA was not a democratic and accountable government, but if some of the PA institutions did not exert their power, it was also because of Israel's role. Israel demanded security but could delegate the dirty job of implementation to the PA. Israel also controlled sovereignty over the borders of the oPt, forbade the running of a proper foreign ministry, and arrested Palestinian legislators on many

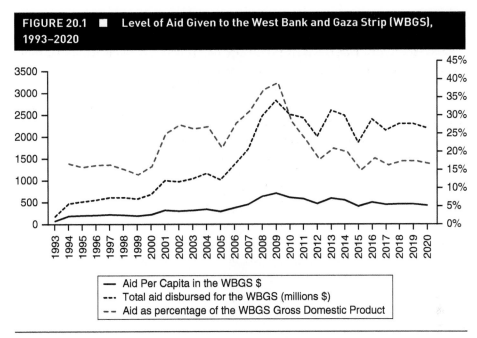

FIGURE 20.1 ■ Level of Aid Given to the West Bank and Gaza Strip (WBGS), 1993–2020

— Aid Per Capita in the WBGS $
--- Total aid disbursed for the WBGS (millions $)
-- Aid as percentage of the WBGS Gross Domestic Product

Source: As compiled by the authors based on OECD-DAC Aid Database and main statistics from Palestinian Central Bureau of Statistics (PCBS).

occasions, preventing the second PLC from reaching the legal quorum to make any decisions. Furthermore, Israel controlled the land and the circulation of goods and people. To enter into the PA-ruled zone, one needed to pass through Israel, meaning that the PA had no sovereign control over its territory and Palestinians enjoyed only extremely limited freedom of movement, in particular those living in Gaza (see Map 20.2). This had to do with the system of territorial fragmentation inherent in the logic of Oslo.

When the PA came into existence in July 1994, the PA controlled only parts of the Gaza Strip and the West Bank town of Jericho. Later in 1995, eight other cities of the West Bank came under PA rule. In the West Bank, the PA only had control over so-called Area A, a zone that includes the Palestinian cities and that increased from 2 percent of the oPt in 1995 to 17 percent after the Sharm al-Shaykh summit in 1999. Israel and the PA shared control over Area B, which is roughly 25 percent of the oPt—that is, the rural zones, meaning that security is in Israeli hands and civil administration under PA control. The majority of the occupied West Bank, called Area C—namely, all that does not fall in Area A or Area B, 72 percent in 1995 and 59 percent at the end of the 1990s—remains under full Israeli control. A simple glance at a map of the different areas (see Map 20.1) shows that the PA only had limited authority over a series of disconnected administrative units.[31]

The third main source of problems for the PA was the personalization of power. Presidents Yasir Arafat and Mahmoud Abbas took over different key functions, such as chairman of the PLO, president of the PA, head of Fatah, and highest military leader, and limited democratic competition in the oPt. The concentration of power in the hands of Arafat and later of Abbas

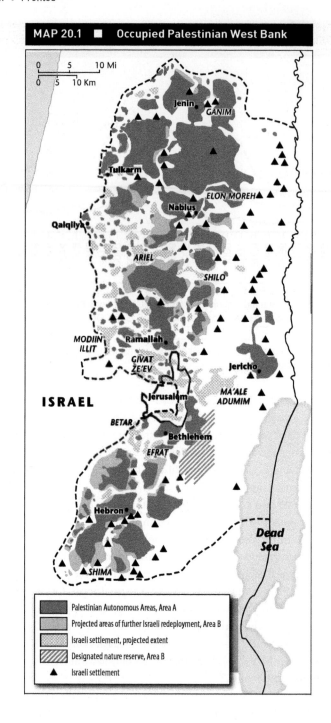

MAP 20.1 ■ Occupied Palestinian West Bank

Palestinian Autonomous Areas, Area A

Projected areas of further Israeli redeployment, Area B

Israeli settlement, projected extent

Designated nature reserve, Area B

▲ Israeli settlement

MAP 20.2 ■ Gaza Strip

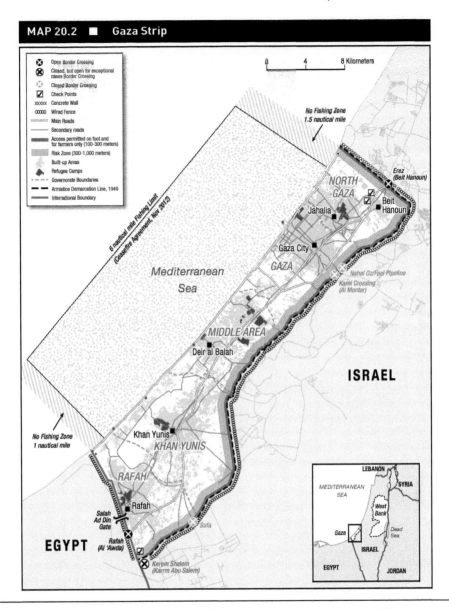

Source: OCHA 2016. https://www.ochaopt.org/content/gaza-strip-access-and-movement-august-2016

can best be understood if one takes a look at the policing of the oPt. Arafat created up to twelve different police units, which he used as channels for clientelism, leading to systematic neopatrimonial practices inside the PA. Until his death, Arafat was also acting minister of interior in the different governments that administered the oPt, and thus controlled the key decision centers of the PA (Table 20.2). The Interior Ministry is in charge not only of straightforward security issues but also of questions of intelligence, and it deals with the matter of freedom of association.

	PLO	As the sole legitimate representative of the Palestinian people, superior to the PA and its term of reference ⟶	PA
TABLE 20.2 ■ The Palestine Liberation Organization Versus the Palestinian Authority, 2021[32]			
Establishment	Established in 1964; recognized as sole legitimate representative of the Palestinian people at the Arab Rabat Summit and by the UN in 1974, by Israel in 1993		Established on the basis of the Palestinian–Israeli *Declaration of Principles of Interim Self-Government Authority (DoP)*, Washington DC, September 13, 1993, and the subsequent Oslo I and II Accords
Head	**Chairman** Head of the Executive Committee elected by the PNC Currently: Mahmoud Abbas		**President** Ex-officio member of the PLC elected by the Palestinian people in the West Bank, Gaza Strip, and East Jerusalem Currently: Mahmoud Abbas
Executive	**Executive Committee (EC)** Elected by the PNC—18 members **Central Council (CC)** Intermediary between PNC and EC—143 members		**Cabinet** Appointed by the president (including the prime minister)

(Continued)

TABLE 20.2 ■ The Palestine Liberation Organization Versus the Palestinian Authority, 2021[32] (*Continued*)					
	PLO	As the sole legitimate representative of the Palestinian people, superior to the PA and its term of reference ⟹			**PA**
Legislative	**Palestinian National Council (PNC)** Parliament in exile; members are mostly appointed by the Executive Committee	Headed by a president Currently: Salim Zanoun	Headed by a speaker Currently: Aziz Dweik		**Palestinian Legislative Council (PLC)** Parliament—132 members (88 in the first 1996 election) Elected by the Palestinian people in the West Bank, Gaza Strip, and East Jerusalem
	Represents trade unions, professional organizations, and so forth, and most factions, *excluding Hamas and Islamic Jihad* The PNC is said to comprise 747 members (other estimates suggest that the current number of members is 794) from Palestine and the diaspora.	Members			Does not represent Palestinians in the Diaspora; members are independents or affiliated with Fatah, Fida, PFLP, PPP, DFLP, Al-Mubadara, Third Way, or Hamas
	Ultimate decision-making body and legislative authority; formulates policies; sets guidelines for the EC Declared Palestinian independence on November 15, 1988				Powers limited by the Palestinian– Israeli agreements; legislation excludes issues left for the final status negotiations No involvement in the 2012 bid of statehood at the UN

(*Continued*)

TABLE 20.2 ■ The Palestine Liberation Organization Versus the Palestinian Authority, 2021[32] (Continued)

	PLO	As the sole legitimate representative of the Palestinian people, superior to the PA and its term of reference ⟶	PA
Armed Forces	Palestinian Liberation Army (PLA) Outside the occupied Palestinian Territories		Palestinian Security and Police Forces West Bank Gaza Strip
Foreign Relations	Conducts foreign relations and related activities (e.g., negotiations)		Has no *formal* foreign relations powers
Finances	Palestinian National Fund Chair elected by PNC		PA Finance Ministry/ Palestinian Monetary Authority

Source: Adapted with permission from PASSIA, "PLO vs PA," September 2014. For the original source see http://www.passia.org/media/filer_public/8a/e7/8ae7c030-ac1d-4688-b3f4-606fbd50cd41/pa-plo2.pdf

All NGOs and other civil society organizations had to register with the powerful Ministry of Interior rather than with the more neutral Ministry of Justice, and many interpreted this as a sort of intimidation on dissenting voices inside the oPt.

Despite these weaknesses, the leadership that emerged in this crippled PA setting comforted its base and gradually extended its power. This led to what could be termed a *system à la Arafat* (and later, in 2005, *à la Abbas*), in which neopatrimonialism was the basis of action and Fatah was the main vehicle for the redistribution of resources, be they economic (rent, control over a monopoly) or prestige-based advantages (VIP vehicles, freedom of movement). Arafat offered a number of Palestinian capitalists monopolies over basic services and goods, while Abbas secured privileged economic niches to his two sons. The links between those capitalists and the political leadership were fraught with corruption and mutual benefit.[33] Arafat died in 2004, but his successors have fallen in the same tendency of not sharing power and benefits associated with top political positions.

A new president, Abbas, was elected in 2005, but the 2006 legislative elections precipitated a violent split of power, with Fatah controlling the West Bank and Hamas the Gaza Strip. There, Hamas created its own government and security forces and tapped into its own resources, as it was perceived as a "terrorist entity" by most Western government. Hamas dependency on the tunnel economy was critical for its survival, and also to alleviate some of the political and economic pressure it—and the people in Gaza—were, and continue to be, under. The actors who dominated the "tunnels scene" also dominated the governance realm. And although Gaza's tunnel complex (controlled by Hamas) was a short-lived phenomenon, it brought lasting impacts in terms of governance structures, emergence of new Hamas' private sector, businessmen class, and financial institutions, rise of new taxation regime, and above all an empowered security establishment that is able to rule with an iron fist.[34] In the West Bank, under the premiership of Western darling Salam Fayyad (2007–2013), the PA with the support of the donor community pursued state-building through the four pillars of reform of the security sector and the enforcement of the rule of law; the building of accountable PA institutions; the provision of effective public service delivery; and economic growth led by the private sector in an open- and free-market economy. The idea was to build effective institutions to acquire statehood. However, this state-building paradigm has not changed the trend of a massive portion of the Palestinian population detained or incarcerated by Israeli occupying forces.[35] It has also polarized opinions. Some celebrate the PA's reforms and argue that the improved performance of the PA has contributed to peace, state-building, and the enhancement of Palestinian lives; others argue that it has sustained the occupation, reengineered Palestinian society, and revised historical national goals of the Palestinian people. Despite the glowing rhetoric of the PA's state-building project, the life of the Palestinians in the last 15 years remained characterized by further fragmentation, entrenched internal division, and higher levels of inequality and frustration. In sum, the PA's state-building project not only entrenched neoliberalism in the oPt, but it also failed to generate a state or even make Palestinians closer to statehood. On repeated occasions, when Gaza was pounded by Israeli bombs (2008, 2014, 2021), the PA leadership and President hardly criticized the disproportionate use of violence by Israel.

POLITICAL PARTICIPATION

In this section, we look at the most significant features of political participation and see how political contention is not only limited to both internal Palestinian struggles (as is most obvious in the Fatah–Hamas standoff) and external factors—especially Israeli politics. Indeed, the second intifada (2000–2005) is often considered only as a struggle between Israel and Palestine, but it is also an internal Palestinian revolt.

Participation from below has always been very rich and creative. This has been the case in different moments. In the 1970s, invigorated by the emergence of this new robust PLO leadership in exile, a new generation of Palestinian nationalist leaders emerged in the oPt and confronted Israeli occupation. As a rule of thumb, one could say that every time such a new nationalist leadership emerged, Israel tried in one way or another to coopt alternative and docile groups of local leaders willing to acquiesce in order to gain economic or social benefits. Thus, in the 1970s when a new professional middle class emerged to fight against the occupation of the Palestinian territories, Israel decided to run municipal elections in 1976, pushing for its own set of accommodationist candidates. The population refused to play along these lines, and the Israeli move backfired by galvanizing these new nationalist leaders.[36] Israel tried again to promote collaborators in official positions with the Village Leagues in the 1980s, but all that managed to do was to incite additional Palestinians to embrace the nationalist stance and practice the politics of *sumud* (steadfastness) or resilience in the face of the de-developing policies of Israel.[37] One famous example of such nonviolent resistance to enduring occupation was in Beit Sahour (a town a few miles from Bethlehem), where the population refused to pay taxes to Israeli authorities for many months because they thought this was simply subsidizing the occupation, and where the Israeli army looks after eighteen cows in Beit Sahour to undermine the self-reliance and resilience of the community (*The Wanted 18* is a 2015 film that illustrates these dynamics powerfully).

On what was originally a rather informal level of mobilization, Palestinians of the oPt tried to react to Israel's ban on nationalist parties. We have seen how popular committees were continuing to become more active on sectoral issues and how they allowed political parties to operate indirectly. Islamist groups, influenced by the mobilization model of the Muslim Brotherhood, active in Palestine since the 1940s, started their own network of charities, in part based on the blueprint of the secular popular committees in the late 1970s. Israel originally saw these Islamist organizations in a good light, as it considered them potential allies against the spread of Palestinian nationalism and a way to tackle Fatah's popularity in the oPt in the 1970s and 1980s.

Another important segment of political activism worth analyzing is the transformation of the secular Left. Very strong from the 1960s until the collapse of the Soviet Union, Palestinian Left-wing parties shrank during the Oslo years. Many in the Leftist camp were active in the past in popular committees. With the first intifada, these committees began a process of professionalization, and with the showering of aid concomitant with the peace process from 1993 onward, one witnessed a mushrooming of NGOs throughout the West Bank and Gaza.[38] Within civil society organizations, Leftist activists predominated. The problem with this aid was that it moved the focus of these NGO leaders away from local-population priorities and gradually cut many NGOs off from their local bases.[39] In synthesis, while Fatah was concentrating on the negotiation process and on running the PA's always-bigger apparatus (around 165,000 public servants in 2021), Leftist movements became more accountable to international donors than to the local population because of the necessity of scrambling for funding to keep their NGOs alive.

In this context of a disaffected Left and a radicalized Hamas whose heels were dug deep into the rejection of Oslo, the failure of President Arafat and Prime Minister Ehud Barak to reach a final deal at Camp David during the summer of 2000 brought ominous tensions to the peace process. The peace process then became a topic of almost uniquely domestic contention. The surge of opposition groups such as Hamas is the best evidence of this fact in Palestine. In Israel, also, one can observe this phenomenon. When Ariel Sharon, then the opposition leader in the Knesset, decided to pay a visit to the Temple Mount or *Al-Haram ash-Sharif* in September 2000, he did it mostly to boost his credentials within his party, Likud, because Benjamin Netanyahu, former prime minister and ex-leader of the Likud, was on the brink of a political comeback after his resignation one year earlier due to corruption charges (Fast forward to May 2021, while still facing corruption charges, Netanyahu aimed to achieve similar political gains through the escalation around Al-Aqsa Mosque.) With Sharon's provocative visit to the Al-Aqsa mosque (he was protected by dozens of armed police), the Palestinian streets erupted into intense battles with Israeli police, first in Jerusalem, then in the rest of the oPt, and eventually also inside Israel (Similar trends occurred in April/May 2021, resulting in the rise of the Unity Intifada.) The second intifada had started, casting the darkest shadows ever seen in the region, and the oPt gradually descended into months of military violence. A year and a half later, most of the West Bank was again, de facto, under complete (rather than indirect) military control of the Israeli troops.

Barrels of ink have been poured into trying to make the case of whether or not the Palestinian leadership had planned and organized this uprising. Surely, the fact that Palestinian police were entitled to have small arms in their ranks led to further escalation and militarization of the clashes. But the vast majority of protests were spontaneous and driven by the population's discontent with the ongoing occupation, not by policies coming from above. As an occupied, fragmented, dispossessed, and resilient nation, Palestinians could be seen as a social-movement society.[40]

With the death of Arafat, the ruling party, Fatah, took on water from all sides, and the entire political system seemed to sway with it. Arafat was the only person with the necessary charisma and historical legitimacy to hold the different factions of Fatah in one single movement. With his death, the riddle of the formal relations between the PA and PLO resurfaced, with PLO leaders who had opposed Oslo but kept silent during Arafat's rule suddenly reappearing in internal debates.[41] Some even suggested that the PA be dissolved and the PLO resume negotiations with Israel. With the presidential elections of January 2005, Mahmoud Abbas, second to Arafat in the PLO and in Fatah's structures, won an easy four-year mandate (although Marwan Barghouti, at the time in jail in Israel for alleged terrorist activities, was a threatening alternative to Abbas in opinion polls). With Abbas aging, the question of succession within Fatah and the PLO resurfaces regularly, in particular in 2018 with the PNC meeting that took place in Ramallah after twenty-two years of waiting, and in the aftermath of 2021 protests against the PA and its security establishment across the West Bank. However, the outcome of the 2018 PLO meeting highlighted a key message: The existing PA/PLO leadership is neither interested in nor willing to grant space to a new generation of leaders.[42] General elections were announced by President Abbas for the summer 2021—a long overdue election to renew the PLC whose official mandate had expired in 2010 due to be renewed on May 22, followed by presidential elections on July 31 (whose mandate has expired in 2009) and the PNC formation on August 31. But invoking the Israeli refusal to allow the elections in East Jerusalem and to a lesser extent COVID-19 difficulties, Abbas suspended the entire process on April 30, 2021.[43] It is worth highlighting that the real reasons were related to the multiple intra-Fatah division and fragmentation, and the fear of the PA leadership that Hamas or "non-Abbas Fatah" factions will win the elections.

Even if the left and other secular movements have run out of breath in the 2000s, there have been vigorous campaigns of political participation. University students have used campus for mobilization and for criticizing the stalled reconciliation between Fatah and Hamas since 2007. In 2011, in the wake of the "Arab Spring," protesters occupy urban centers, organized strikes, and called on the end of internal divisions. Closer to us in 2018 and 2019, the Great March of Return in Gaza unified political factions in weekly protests that revitalized demand for confronting the Israeli siege, but also infused domestic demands for more political particiatpion to the West Bank and Gaza governments. The 2021 Unity Intifada is the latest episode that illustrated the ability of the Palestinian people to mobilize and act across all Palestine and across the co-called Green Line, despite the multiple forms of oppression and repression they live under.

DOMESTIC CONFLICT: FATAH–HAMAS DIVIDE

These questions of stalled unity and entrenched divisions between Gaza Strip and the West Bank go back to 2006. Although Fatah used various political expedients to boost its chances of winning by augmenting the number of seats to 132 and introducing a two-track voting system, it went to the elections with cracks in all parts of its structure. The result was predictable and epochal: Fatah lost, Hamas won.[44]

However, no one expected such a clear victory for Hamas, maybe not even Hamas itself. Many old PLO companions of Arafat suffered from abysmal electoral results. In Hebron, again, Jibril Rajoub, former head of the Preventive Security Forces in the West Bank and an essential piece of the neopatrimonial network built by Arafat in the 1990s, ran on a Fatah ticket but got only 38,367 votes—that is, twenty thousand short of the top performer in Hebron, who happened to be his brother, Nayyef Rajoub, a top local adherent of the Islamist party, Hamas. It was the first time Fatah had been beaten in a significant national election. If anything, Fatah emerged from defeat even more divided, especially in its stance toward the new Hamas government that ran the oPt on its own for one year. Such intra-Fatah divisions continue until the present day as illustrated in 2021. As part of the preparations for the legislative elections, other Fatah-affiliated electoral lists were created by Mohammed Dahlan (Fatah—Democratic Reform Bloc) and Nasser Kidwa with the support of Marwan Barghouti (National Democratic Assembly).

In June 2006, Fatah and Hamas prisoners in Israeli jails agreed to the so-called National Reconciliation document. It set forth the goal of national struggle for a Palestinian state on the territories occupied in 1967, sought to confine resistance to these areas, and designated the PLO as the only body responsible for negotiations with Israel. It also asserted that all Palestinian parties should accept a final settlement on the basis of "international and Arab legitimacy," code words for UNSCRs 242, 338, and 194 and the 2002 Saudi-led Arab Peace Initiative, suggesting an exchange of the formal recognition of Israel by all Arab states for a permanent settlement of the Israeli–Palestinian conflict, according to the pre-1967 situation. The National Reconciliation document would eventually form the doctrinal spine of the national unity government agreed to by Hamas and Fatah in Mecca in February 2007.

Yet while one wing of Fatah preached unity, another practiced subversion. They feared that Hamas's rise would weaken their hold on the PA and its resources. This faction spurned unity for opposition, hoping that the Israeli and international embargoes would weaken the Hamas government after the 2006 elections. Its members were not averse to sowing a little disorder to hasten a collapse. Abbas appeared to have a foot in each stream. On the one hand, he welcomed the National Reconciliation document although he knew it fell short of Israel's and the international community's conditions for lifting sanctions against the PA. On the other hand, Abbas stripped Hamas's government of any authority over the security forces, a move that had the backing of Israel and the United States but stood in violation of the PA constitution. Hamas, in turn, welcomed the National Reconciliation document, but were skeptical about the intention of Fatah to abandon or share power, while at the same time Hamas was keen on ruling the Palestinian political domain and system.

The result was a year during which negotiations for a unity government were punctuated by violent clashes between Fatah and Hamas, mostly in Gaza. Militias, PA institutions, and security forces split along factional lines and fought to the death for an authority that was bankrupt and largely nominal. The point of no return came in December 2006, when Abbas declared that the unity talks were "dead" and new elections necessary. During the next two months, ninety Palestinians were killed in Gaza. It took the intervention of Saudi Arabia to bring the leaders to Mecca and agree on a document that had been waiting to be signed for seven months.

All direct foreign aid to the PA ceased in March 2006 when Hamas formed a government on its own after Fatah turned down offers to join a broad coalition government, in part over the issue of who controlled the police forces; in addition, Israel refused to transfer an estimated $500 million in tax rebates that legally belonged to the Palestinian people. Donors have instead bypassed the Hamas-led PA, funneling an average of $1.5 billion of aid (mostly given by the European Union (EU), followed by the United States) through the presidential office since 2006, leading to a skyrocketing level of aid, as seen in Figure 20.1. This mechanism has made the Palestinians even more dependent on the world for their own welfare and increased political factionalism inside Palestinian society.[45] It can therefore be sustained that conflict over access to external economic rents, be it from international donors or from Israel, exacerbates or helps maintain internal divisions.

With these emerging dynamics, Fatah hawks (with the blessing and active support of the United States and Israel), preferring to confront Hamas directly, prepared for a coup to oust Hamas from its stronghold in Gaza during the spring of 2007. Hamas found out about this and preemptively organized its own coup against the military forces of Fatah and the PA in the Gaza Strip in June 2007.

Since then, Gaza has been run by Hamas on its own while the West Bank has remained under the control of Fatah, and both persist under the ultimate Israeli control and occupation. From the end of 2007 until 2021, both factions engaged in rounds of failed reconciliations, the latest was in the lead to the postponed/canceled May 2021 elections. No agreement could be reached, although immediately after the end of the Israeli Operation Cast Lead (December 2008/January 2009), the two factions committed to resume talks, a promise restated in the wake of the Arab revolts in May 2011 and June 2012. The wave of Arab uprisings forced the two factions to resume reconciliation talks both because of the pressure exerted regionally on Hamas's leadership and by the local population, and due to internal political, leadership, and financial crises within the two parties. However, neither the 2014 al-Shati' refugee camp reconciliation agreement between both factions, nor the numerous rounds of meetings and declarations in 2020/21, bridged the divide between the Gaza Strip and the West Bank; instead, the division remains intact and increasingly entrenched.

POLITICAL ECONOMY

As a result of the international community's attempt to buttress a tormented peace process, Palestinians have received over US$43 billion of aid since 1993, which made them one of the highest per capita recipients of nonmilitary aid in the world. Of the US$43 billion, around US$30 billion (75 percent of the total aid) was allocated between 2007 and 2019, according to the Organisation for Economic Cooperation and Development (OECD) aid database. On average, over the past decade, US$2.2 billion of aid funds were poured annually into the Palestinian economy, representing around 20 percent of the WBGS's Gross Domestic Product (GDP) and around US$520 per capita aid per year in a low-income economy.[46] A glance at the figures of Figure 20.1 and the high level of foreign aid illustrates the fact that the Palestinian economy is a very political one.[47] As with political participation, there are strong links of dependency and containment between the Palestinian and the Israeli economies. For the political economy, we have underlined the question of asymmetric containment that Israel managed to introduce in the framework of Oslo, in particular, with the economic rents linked to the management of security forces that had the blessing of and control by the Israeli military leadership. This led to a paradoxical situation where the economy seemed to be booming when there was conflict because development and economic dividends are intrinsically tied to the apparatus of occupation, often controlled by key military-industrial actors.[48]

Between 1967 and 1990, the Palestinian territories became a captive market for Israel, which could employ cheap Palestinian labor for its construction and agriculture industries. The result of Israeli policies has been effective de-development of Palestine and an increase in the dependence of Palestinians on external aid. With the Oslo process, the Palestinian economy ran into new difficulties. The system of three different areas—A, B, and C—impeded freedom of movement for both individuals and goods. The key words here are *territorial fragmentation*. Area A appeared as an archipelago of small islands with no contiguity (see Map 20.1). It was therefore easy for Israel to cut each into bits and pieces, for a total of more than two hundred different enclaves, and to prevent Palestinian freedom of movement in case of security threats. Israel applied the lessons learned during the first intifada when it started its policy of closure of the Gaza Strip as a whole, and Israel expanded this mode of internal closure to the West Bank. At the time of the 1991 Gulf War, 180,000 Palestinians worked in Israel; this represented nearly 33 percent of the total labor force in the oPt and included thirty thousand who moved back and forth every day between Gaza and Israel. In 1993, Israel started limiting access from the Gaza Strip, and through the Oslo agreements, Israel did the same with the West Bank workers. The number of Palestinians still working inside Israel decreased to 145,000 by 2000 (a figure that also includes the Palestinians working in settlements, including Palestinian children who are

MAP 20.3 ■ West Bank Barrier Route, June 2020

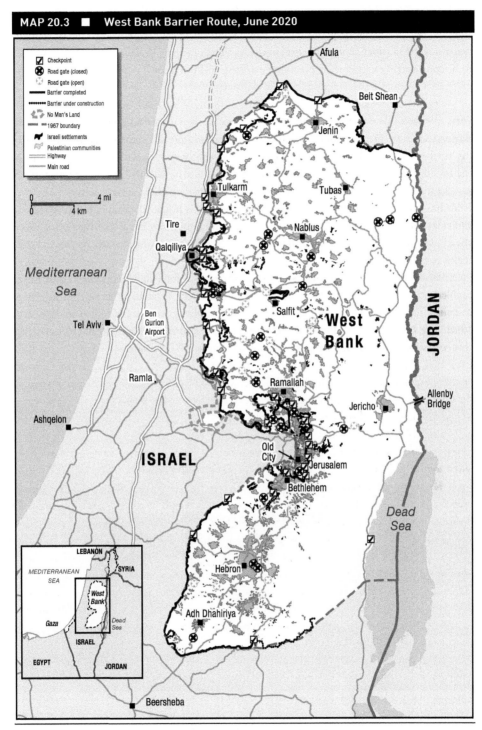

Source: Adapted from United Nations Office for the Coordination of Humanitarian Affairs, occupied Palestinian Territory (OCHA oPt), July 2011, http://www.ochaopt.org/documents/ocha_opt_west_bank_barrier_route_update_july_2011.pdf

facing continuous denial and violations of their rights as documented by a Human Rights Watch report).[49] In 2019, the number of Palestinian workers in Israel and Israeli settlements was around 133,000 (22,900 workers in the settlements and 110,400 in Israel), but is likely to be considerably higher if Palestinians working without permits or with merchant or special needs permits were included in these estimates.[50]

With the construction of the separation wall in the West Bank beginning in the middle years of the 2000s (see Map 20.3), this trend has further increased and has been increased during the COVID-19 pandemic, with Palestinians left out of vaccination schemes, justifying further an asphyxia of the oPt economy. The wall permits fewer Palestinians access to the Israeli job market. Israel's argument is that this "security barrier" is a way to stop suicide attacks inside Israel. An international ruling on the legality of the wall asserted that even if Israel has the right to self-defense, the route of the wall is not acceptable in terms of international law because it does not follow the 1967 border but allows Israel to annex other bits of the oPt and at times go deep into the newly annexed areas in order to protect Israeli settlements (see Photo 20.1).

Limited freedom of movement and loss of daily bread for Palestinians ushered in a third problem: that of underperforming economic development. The PLO leadership also bears responsibility for this situation because of the economic agreements it signed in 1994 with Israel. The Paris Economic Protocol (PEP) of April 1994 formalized a de facto customs union that had existed between the two economies after Israel's 1967 conquest.

PHOTO 20.1 Separation Wall in Bethlehem

Courtesy of Andrea Merli

The logic behind such lopsidedness was simple: Palestinian negotiators were prepared to defer economic sovereignty in return for integration into the Israeli economy. This corresponds with the notion of economic peace, where economic solutions are proposed to solve political problems. For Palestinian critics of the PEP, skewed economic relations meant increasing Israeli asymmetric containment of the Palestinian economy, especially if "peace" would once again become war. The opposition's fears proved to be prescient.

This model of economic cooperation relates to a further defect of a crippled PA: poor redistribution of rents. There emerged a ruling elite able to absorb this rent and turn it, internally, into a carrot-and-stick scenario to create political support. Far from being a transparent authority, the PA turned into an opaque and corrupt governing body redistributing economic advantages to only a happy few; and most of these actions were taken with Israeli blessings.[51]

These dynamics solidified over the past decade—especially with the unprecedented levels of aid to the PA to support its state-building and security sector reform project—and were accompanied with increased levels of authoritarian trends in both the West Bank and Gaza Strip. These authoritarian trends, in turn, were complemented by a neoliberal economic package in the West Bank, and a distorted economic model in Gaza Strip. In the West Bank, easy and facilitated access to credit, nourished culture of consumerism, sky-rocketing levels of public debt, shallow nominal service-sector-based economic growth, and astonishing levels of vertical and horizontal inequalities were key features of the West Bank economy that became further contained by the Israeli economy and further dependent on the increased donor aid funds. On the other hand, the political economy of Gaza continued to be shaped by the dynamics of blockade, the magnitude of international humanitarian aid, the political conditionality of the regional financial flow, the relationship between Hamas as a governing body and the traditional as well as the new Hamas-created private sector actors, not to mention the increased levels of poverty, food insecurity, and unemployment. Nearly three decades after the creation of the Oslo Accords economic and aid frameworks, neither a viable Palestinian economy is any closer, nor any meaningful development process.

With the advent of the Trump administration in 2017, drastic cuts in aid to Palestine occurred, in particular to the United Nations Relief and Works Agency for Palestine Refugees in the Near East (UNRWA). The US administration took various measures that indicate even more open support of Israel—for example, the move of the US Embassy to East Jerusalem (on stolen, private Palestinian land) in May 2018. It also threatened to cut aid to UN bodies and international organizations that deliver aid to Palestinians. Other European countries also seem on the verge of altering their long-standing policy of supporting Palestinian NGOs and UNRWA, policies that mirror the shift to alt-right xenophobic and antirefugee attitudes in much of Europe. The Abraham Accord, touted by President Trump as a major diplomatic success at the end of his mandate, was actually very thin in substance. The UAE, Bahrain, and later Morocco and Sudan normalized diplomatic relations with Israel, but this was done with no consultation whatsoever with the PA and in full disrespect of international law, United

Nations Security Council (UNSC) resolutions and international humanitarian law. From a critical Palestinian perspective, the so-called Abraham Accords are neither peace agreements nor historic breakthroughs. Instead, they are rather a prime example of the distortion of the very meaning of peace.[52]

REGIONAL AND INTERNATIONAL RELATIONS: WARS ON GAZA INSTEAD OF PEACE NEGOTIATIONS

Cycles of violence seem to take a regular pattern in Gaza, obscuring the possibility of genuine peace negotiations. As in 2008, the Gaza Strip was under heavy Israeli fire in November 2012, again during the summer months of 2014, and in May 2021 with identical motives for escalations. Israel used disproportionate force, and despite the heavy casualties among Palestinians on all occasions (in 2008, approximately 1,300 dead, compared with thirteen Israeli casualties; 2014 attacks led to the killings of more than 2,100 Palestinians and about seventy-five Israelis; while the 2021 war led to nearly 300 deaths in Palestine and thirteen Israeli fatalities[53]), Hamas did not disappear from the political map. Public opinion polls suggest that Hamas even gained further popularity, at least in the short run. Following the May 2021 war on Gaza, a poll conducted in June by the Palestinian Center for Policy and Survey Research (PSR) in the West Bank and the Gaza Strip found that support for Hamas, and willingness to vote for it, increases dramatically while support for Fatah drops significantly. The poll found that a majority of the Palestinians think that "Hamas is more deserving of representing and leading the Palestinian people while a small percentage thinks Fatah under Abbas' leadership is the one who deserves to do that."[54] Israel's military objectives have never been clear, but if the aim of Operation Cast Lead—and the subsequent operations—was to oust Hamas from power, then it was a failure. If, however, the objective was to divide the Palestinian factions even more, it might have been a success, but only a partial one. If the aim of the Israeli government was to regain the confidence of the Israeli public in the Israel Defense Forces (IDF)—confidence that had been lost after the 2006 Lebanon war and was now regained through an operation in which Israel suffered hardly any casualties—then the objectives were met. In addition, this would also explain the IDF's use of disproportionate force and heavy artillery. The 2014 and 2021 war rehearsed this dynamic of an all-out retaliation from Israel but on such a disproportionate basis that the international community could only disapprove of the violence unleashed by Israel.

When President Abbas initially placed the blame for the Israeli operations in 2008 on Hamas, it seemed as though this was the final blow to any hope of bringing the two main Palestinian factions back together. Indeed, it turned out that the vast majority of the Palestinian population sided with the civilian victims and their sisters and brothers in Gaza. People could not understand Abbas's position, which was seen as indirectly justifying the official Israeli argument of self-defense. Abbas's positions and decisions toward Gaza and its people continue to be controversial and problematic, especially when accompanied by punitive policies such as withholding public servants' salaries. The 2018 Great March of Return in Gaza, with regular clashes every Friday between Gazan civilians marching toward the buffer zone built around Gaza and Israeli troops, is not only an expression of revolt against the Israeli-imposed blockade but is also a revolt against the failure of the Palestinian polity in both the West Bank and Gaza Strip to address the plight and suffering of the besieged Palestinians in Gaza.

CONCLUSION

As of 2021, lack of unity has been the main characteristic of Palestinian politics. Both factions, Hamas and Fatah, have only paid lip service to internal Palestinian reconciliation. The biggest hurdles for the end of the split remain the formation of a national consensus government and the pending reform of security forces. Another strong divergence has to do with the crucial question of the PLO reform, which should allow Hamas to contest Fatah's domination inside the PLO. It is enough to take a look at how Fatah elites have been opposing the profound rejuvenation of their leadership by constantly postponing Fatah's sixth general congress during the last twenty years. This sixth congress was eventually held in August 2009 in Bethlehem without its grassroots supporters from Gaza. It produced stormy debates between the old and young guards of Fatah, and the more senior attendees tried in various ways to use cosmetic changes to create the appearance of reform. A similar pattern followed in 2018 when the Fatah-dominated PLO's National Council convened its meeting in Ramallah and "elected" Abbas, by clapping instead of voting, as the chairman of the PLO. Abbas in turn effectively appointed and chose the members of the PLO's Executive Committee in an ultimate expression of his personalized style of governance and one-man rule. Palestinian democracy was once again denied by the Palestinian leadership and their narrow factional politics.

This does not mean that politics in Palestine has not or will not evolve in the coming years. The Palestinian question remains more than a conflict between two nations fighting for control of the same land. Its deep emotional and symbolic dimensions confer international and regional resonance.

To conclude, we will look at recent international dynamics that might affect the prospect or course for future negotiations between Israel and Palestine.

First, the 2012 UN bid led to a renewed awareness among the international community. By 2015, more than 130 states recognized Palestine on a diplomatic level. Even European countries, such as Sweden, have given formal recognition, while other European parliaments have asked their government to do so. As of 2021, however, these forms of recognition seem to be largely symbolic and ineffective, as they are unable to change the Israeli-imposed facts on the ground. International efforts to resume peace negotiations, such as the 2015 French Initiative and the Trump's promise for "the deal of the century," led nowhere. The UN remains effectively absent, and the EU remains occupied with its internal troubles. The rise of Trump and his "deal of the century" was an episode that aimed to impose a kind of solution with no substance to the Palestinian–Israeli conflict. Yet what Trump, his administration, and his advisers were promising is anything but peace, as they are only asking Israeli leaders how they envision a peace deal, rather than shuttling between the two countries' leaders to find constructive solutions to land and resource sharing as well as demographic flows. The Biden Administration will return to the old normal. Biden will neither be a savior for the Palestinians, nor for peace, but likely he will be a savior for the peace process (with the emphasis on the process). However, a return to the old normal will make the prospects for real, meaningful, and true peace even grimmer.

Second, BDS, an international campaign led by Palestinian activists and calling for the boycott of Israel, has gathered important momentum over the last decade. In 2005, inspired by the South-African experience and the apartheid nature of the Israeli state, Palestinian civil society issued a call for a global campaign of boycotts, divestment, and sanctions (BDS against Israel until it complies with international law by

> ending its occupation and colonization of all Arab lands occupied in June 1967 and dismantling the Wall; recognizing the fundamental rights of the Arab-Palestinian citizens of Israel to full equality; and respecting, protecting, and promoting the rights of Palestinian refugees to return to their homes and properties as stipulated in UN Resolution 194.[55]

The BDS campaign became the main source of hope for Palestinians inside and outside the oPt. It achieved numerous successes over the last few years, exposed those companies that are benefiting from the occupation, and practiced global pressure on many others to stop their operations in Israel and its settlements, deemed illegal under international law, and divest from Israel. BDS is gaining more momentum over time and proves to be an effective tool to expose Israel, its occupation, and the complicity of international actors, and it holds Israel and the international actors accountable, to the extent that Israel considers the BDS movement as an existential and strategic threat and equates it with the Iranian threat. As a transnational movement, BDS provided the space and tools to the people all over the world to play an effective role in the Palestinian quest for justice and self-determination. And fundamentally, BDS is a prime example of a peaceful approach to and form of resistance that constitutes another instrument to change the balance of power between the occupied and the occupier.[56]

As an additional attempt to internationalize the Palestinian–Israeli conflict and hold Israel accountable to international law, the State of Palestine signed the Rome Status and joined the ICC in April 2015.[57] While the investigation of the ICC might take a long time to materialize or reach conclusions, coupled with the very complex technical and legal matters, this additional tool to realize Palestinian rights might yield positive consequences that contribute to a long-term solution to the Palestinian–Israeli conflict.

Despite his problems of alleged corruption, Netanyahu's reelection and the forming of a new Right-wing nationalist coalition in 2015, and in various temporary forms after four rounds of elections between April 2019 and March 2021, solidified the basis of an expansive Zionism paying no attention to the situation of Palestinians. In July 2018, Israel changed its Basic Law (constitution) as its government and parliament passed the "Israel as the Nation State of the Jewish People" law. The new Basic Law defines "the state of Israel" as the national home of the Jewish people, and adds the right to exercise national self-determination in the state of Israel is unique to the Jewish people.

This law further entrenches the character of Israel as a colonial and apartheid state, observers argue.[58] In addition, under President Trump, US policies have taken a more passive turn on "managing" a dormant peace process and ended their term with the declaration of the so-called Abraham Accords to normalize relations between Israel and some Arab states.

Debates about the (missing) democratic and statist credentials of Palestine or its degree and extent of formal recognition as a state are probably only excuses not to tackle the roots of this nearly hundred-year-long conflict and try to resolve it on the basis of international law (i.e., the right to self-determination and respect for the UN resolution calling for Israel to withdraw to the 1967 borders) that could lead to a two-state solution.

SUGGESTED READINGS

Baconi, Tareq. *Hamas Contained: The Rise and Pacification of Palestinian Resistance*. Stanford: Stanford University Press, 2018.

Benoît, Challand. *Palestinian Civil Society: Foreign Donors and the Power to Promote and Exclude*. London: Routledge, 2009.

Khalidi, Rashid. *Palestinian Identity: The Construction of Modern National Consciousness*. New York, NY: Columbia University Press, 1997.

Khan, Mushtaq Husain, George Giacaman, and Inge Amundsen, eds. *State Formation in Palestine: Viability and Governance during a Social Transformation*. London: RoutledgeCurzon, 2004.

Le More, Anne. *International Assistance to the Palestinians after Oslo: Political Guilt, Wasted Money*, London: Routledge, 2008.

Roy, Sara M. *The Gaza Strip: The Political Economy of De-Development*. 2nd ed. Washington, DC: Institute for Palestinian Studies, 2001.

Sayigh, Yezid. *Armed Struggle and the Search for State: The Palestinian National Movement 1949–1993*. New York, NY: Oxford University Press, 1997.

Tartir, Alaa, Tariq Dana, and Timothy Seidel eds. *Political Economy of Palestine. Critical, Interdisciplinary, and Decolonial Perspectives*. London: Palgrave MacMillan, 2021.

Thrall, Nathan. *The Only Language They Understand: Forcing Compromise in Israel and Palestine*. New York, NY: Metropolitan Books, 2017.

Turner, Mandy, ed. *From the River to the Sea: Palestine and Israel in the Shadow of "Peace"*. Lanham, MD: Lexington Books, 2019.

21 THE KINGDOM OF SAUDI ARABIA

Dina Al Sowayel

The Kingdom of Saudi Arabia is best known as the birthplace of Islam and for its abundant oil reserves. The Kingdom, however, is much more than this. Located at the crossroads of Asia, Africa and the Mediterranean Basin, it plays a vital economic and political role regionally and globally. Saudi Arabia's strategic location, the presence on its soil of the two holiest sanctuaries of Islam—the Grand Mosque of Mecca and the Prophet's Mosque in Medina—its formidable oil production, and its renewed focus on the sciences and arts accounts for the country's regional and global relevance. A lot has changed in the Kingdom in the last ten years. The current King, Salman bin 'Abdelaziz (Salman), and the Crown Prince, Mohammed bin Salman (MBS), reign at a pivotal time in the country's history. They continue the well-established rule of the al-Sauds, the founding family of Saudi Arabia, but also have made key political and social changes in the last few years. The al-Sauds have reigned over various parts of the Arabian Peninsula for nearly 280 years, since the creation of the first Saudi State in 1744. The first state was short-lived (ended in 1818), but it was followed by a second Saudi State (1824–1891) and then third Saudi State established in 1902 by 'Abdelaziz ibn Saud. The third state endures today, with 'Abdelaziz's son, King Salman, at its helm. The state's history, political economy, and present challenges and opportunities for the Saudi government are the subject of this chapter.

The chapter proceeds as follows. First, this chapter examines the key historical and political features that have shaped the Kingdom. We begin with state formation as that established the institutions upon which the al-Saud's legitimacy rests. Next, we consider the key role that oil has played in determining the Kingdom's current position. Finally, we explore the contemporary political conditions of the Kingdom, with an eye toward the dynamic relationship among salient economic, social, and political variables.

KEY FACTS ON SAUDI ARABIA

AREA 0756,981 square miles (2,149,690 square kilometers)

CAPITAL Riyadh

POPULATION 34.78 million (2021 est.), 38.3% of whom are nonnationals (2019 est.)

PERCENT POPULATION UNDER 25 39% (2019 est.)

RELIGION The country counts a majority of Sunnis at 85–90%, minority of Shi'a at 10–15%, and Christian, Hindu, Buddhist, and atheist communities, notably among the foreign residents (statistics not available)

OFFICIAL LANGUAGE Arabic

TYPE OF GOVERNMENT Authoritarian Monarchy with Basic System of Government and nascent-local elections

DATE OF UNIFICATION September 23, 1932

GDP (PPP) $1.609 billion (2021 est.)

NOMINAL GDP $792.85 billion; $46,962 per capita (2019 est.)

PERCENT GDP BY SECTOR Agriculture, 2.6; industry, 44.2, services, 53.2 (2017 est.)

TOTAL RENTS (% GDP) FROM NATURAL RESOURCES 24.81 (2019 est.)

FERTILITY RATE 1.95 children born/woman

LITERACY Male 97%, Female 91.1%

Sources: CIA. "The World Factbook." August 4, 2022, https://www.cia.gov/the-world-factbook/.
General Authority for Statistics, Kingdom of Saudi Arabia. "Statistics." Accessed August 10, 2022, https://www.stats.gov.sa/en/statistics-overview.
World Bank. "International Comparison Program (ICP)." Accessed August 10, 2022, https://databank.worldbank.org/source/icp-2017.

MAP 21.1 ■ Saudi Arabia

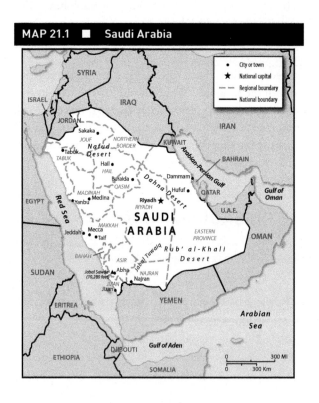

STATE FORMATION: A MAN FOR A KINGDOM
AND A KINGDOM FOR A MAN

On September 16, 1932, the Kingdoms of Saudi Arabia (al-Mamlaka al-Arabiya al-Suudiya) was established. The founder, 'Abdelaziz ibn Saud (1876–1953), was a young al-Saud prince who restored his family's power over Najd (central Arabia) between 1902 and 1912. During a daring nighttime raid on January 15 in 1902 'Abdelaziz ibn Saud, on a camel and with only a sword, led a band of followers to reclaim his ancestral home in Diriya, on the outskirts of Riyadh.[1] He and his followers went on to conquer Najd, Hejaz, and the Eastern Coast and to unify these lands into the Kingdom of Saudi Arabia in September of 1932. In so doing, 'Abdelaziz ibn Saud became the founder of the third Saudi State. Consequently, 'Abdelaziz holds a mythic place in Saudi tradition.

'Abdelaziz's successful conquest of the Nejd in part reflected his personal skills. Charismatic, pious, and inspiring he is admired and the source of great pride among most Saudis. The restoration of the Saudi rulers in Riyadh in the first half of the 20th century also reflects 'Abdelaziz's political acumen. Stories describing his wit and wisdom are common, especially in Riyadh, the capital.[2] Two tales reflect his purported skills. In one battle during unification, 'Abdelaziz was carried off the field severely wounded. Rumors of his impending death led the more fickle members of his force to consider leaving. They quickly changed their minds when they learned he asked for the hand of a young woman from a nearby village. "Needless to say, the crowd went wild—what a guy! Shot in the stomach and still a stallion." Even more strategic is the story of his response to a British request to move troops through Saudi Arabia during World War II (WWII). "'Abdelaziz assembled his advisors and asked how he should respond. All agreed that under no circumstance should the British be allowed to enter the country. When they had finished the king asked, 'If the British Army decides to march across Saudi Arabia, just how are we going to stop them?' He suggested it would be much wiser to welcome them, help them get on their way, and get their implicit agreement that the route they proposed to take was part of Saudi Arabia."[3] This strategy would later serve the king well, having garnered good will with the British when he entered negotiations about the Saudi border. Moreover, as Rundell notes in relating these stories, "Whether true or exaggerated, they are widely believed and often intentionally focus on the old king's role in creating and preserving the nation."[4]

'Abdelaziz also enjoyed political legitimacy, given his connection to the preceding Saudi States and his role as a unifier. In the mid-1700s, Muhamammad bin Sa'ud (d. 1795) and Muhammad bin 'Abd al-Wahhab (d. 1793), a Muslim revivalist, joined to create a formidable duo. That politico-religious partnership went on to consolidate the first Saudi State, the Emirate of Diriyah, in 1744. The first Saudi State led the many states of the Arabian Peninsula to unify and freed them from Ottoman expansion. Muhammad bin Sa'ud's control expanded quickly from the vicinity of Riyadh to a territory roughly comparable to what is now Saudi Arabia, with some incursions as far north as Karbala and Damascus, and as far south as Sanaa. The 1802 annexation of the holy cities of Mecca and Medina put an end to almost three centuries of Ottoman custodianship of the two sanctuaries and of the annual pilgrimage (*al-Hajj*). Instructed by the Ottoman Empire to repress what Europeans feared was a "revolution" trying to restore the "caliphate of the Umayyads," Muhammad 'Ali Pasha, Ottoman ruler of Egypt

(1769–1849), sent a military expedition to Arabia under the command of his son Tusun Pasha (1794–1816). The first Saudi polity was defeated by the Ottoman envoy in 1818.

Between 1824 and 1891, a second Saudi State, emerged. The Emirate of Nejd ended due to internecine strife within the ruling Al Saud clan and the ascendance of the rival Al Rashids, allies of the Ottomans in central Arabia. The Al Rashid eventually took over the city of Riyadh and forced the Al Saud into exile. They eventually settled in Kuwait until Abdelaziz's triumphant return to Riyadh in 1902. Indigenous roots, a mythic founding story, piety and courage aided 'Abdelaziz in his effort to unite the Kingdom and supported his legitimacy to be its ruler. But there is more.

Created in 1913, the Bedouin army of the *Ikhwan* (the Brethren) also provided considerable military support for 'Abdelaziz bid for power. United by the Sunni revivalist creed inspired by Muhammad bin 'Abd al-Wahhab and settled in agricultural colonies, the Ikhwan were the spearhead of 'Abdelaziz's conquest of Arabia. In the late 1920s, some members of the Ikhwan disagreed with the al-Saud mission and instigated a rebellion. That rebellion was quashed by forces loyal to al-Saud by January 1930. This was the precursor, however, to the next serious challenge to al-Saud legitimacy which would come in 1979, by a group who would also call themselves "Ikhwan."[5]

Prudent and tactical marriages also helped unify the Kingdom. There is no consensus on the number of wives (some say dozens) that 'Abdelaziz had, although it is generally agreed he did not have more than the Islamically permissible four at any one time. Political salience, however, led him to make numerous unions and guided 'Abdelaziz's choice of wives. It also produced countless descendants: 'Abdelaziz had forty-three sons, with perhaps an equal number of daughters. Consequently, today these descendants, numbering in the thousands, constitute the Saudi Royal Family. The Royal Family is thus not a small group removed from the reality of everyday life, like the Windsors of England or the Pahlavis of Iran. The Royal Family members are at least "one half of one percent of the entire population."[6] This has both benefits and disadvantages for the Saudi State, more fully assessed below.

'Abdelaziz ruled for fifty-one years. During his rule he unified the Kingdom, solidified al-Saud rule by creating a pattern of succession and saw the coming of oil. When 'Abdelaziz died in 1953, the crown passed to his son, Saud. This established the mode of succession and, therefore, who would lead the Kingdom. Since 1953 the Saudi throne has passed from one son of 'Abdelaziz to the other. Six sons have ruled since the passing of 'Abdelaziz (see Tables 21.1 and 21.2).

The current king, Salman bin 'Abdelaziz (born 1935), acceded to the throne in 2015, when his older half-brother King 'Abdullah bin 'Abdelaziz passed away. It appears, however, that de facto decision-making power rests in the hands of his son, Mohammed bin Salman (born 1985), appointed Crown Prince in 2017. As governor of the Riyadh province for almost fifty years, between 1963 and 2011, Salman engineered the transformation of the capital into a bustling metropolis of more nearly eight million inhabitants. Known for his intimate knowledge of the networks that crisscross society and for his blend of charm and ruthlessness, King Salman has handled family disputes and commercial rivalries in a similar resolute manner; he is considered an anchor for the family.

TABLE 21.1 ■ Saudi Arabia: A Demographic Snapshot 2020	
Total Population	**35.34 Million**
Expatriate population	13.49
Population annual growth rate	1.50%
Fertility rate children/woman	2.27
Population under 15	25%
Urban population	84.1%

Sources: United Nations data cited in globalmediainsight.2021

TABLE 21.2 ■ The Kings of Saudi Arabia	
The Kings of Saudi Arabia	**Date of Rule**
'Abd al-'Aziz bin 'Abd al-Rahman Al Sa'ud	1932–1953
Sa'ud bin 'Abd al-'Aziz Al Sa'ud	1953–1964
Faisal bin 'Abd al-'Aziz Al Sa'ud	1964–1975
Khalid bin 'Abd al-'Aziz Al Sa'ud	1975–1982
Fahd bin 'Abd al-'Aziz Al Sa'ud	1982–2005
'Abd Allah bin 'Abd al-'Aziz Al Sa'ud	2005–2015
Salman bin 'Abd al-'Aziz Al Sa'ud	2015–present

King Salman's decisiveness helped him solve the ever-recurring question of the succession to the throne. A few months after ascending the throne, King Salman named his nephew Muhammad bin Nayif (b. 1959) Crown Prince and his son Muhammad bin Salman (b. 1985) Deputy Crown Prince, thus ending the succession of the aging sons of 'Abd al-'Aziz to the throne in favor of the next generation of princes. Then in June 2017, King Salman went a step further in anchoring his rule when he removed his nephew and appointed his son, Muhammad bin Salman (MBS, born in 1985), to replace him as Crown Prince. Today it appears that de facto decision-making power rests in the hands of MBS.

Succession has not always been smooth. The al-Sauds witnessed a period of internal tension as a fierce battle erupted between King Saud and his brother Faisal, who insisted on defining government organization and responsibilities. In 1964, King Saud, who had lost the favor of Aramco (the national oil company), faced a financial crisis and a devalued Saudi Riyal. With the support of the ulema, senior princes, and cabinet members he was deposed by Faisal. Another challenge to succession occurred in 1975 when King Faisal was assassinated by a nephew. The motivation for the murder remains unclear, with explanations ranging from mental imbalance to old family issues.[7] Whatever the motivation, this test of the Saudi political system passed, as succession was achieved smoothly and without dispute. Crown Prince Khalid, another son of Abdelaziz was declared King within hours of Faisal's death by the Council of Senior Princes.[8] Established by King Faisal, the Council of Senior Princes advises and supervises succession.

The historical establishment of the Saudi State has important implications today. First, Saudi Arabia continues to reflect the union of the Wahhabis and al-Sauds, with Wahhabis providing a religiously based foundation for the political legitimacy of the government. Second, Saudi Arabia has a proud history of independence, which shapes its regional and international engagement. Unlike the al-Ali Dynasty in neighboring Egypt and the Hashemites of Iraq and Jordan, 'Abdelaziz was not given his country in the service of British colonial interests. Also unlike most of its neighbors, Saudi Arabia was never colonized or mandated (Sykes–Picot). Finally, the country continues to draw on 'Abdelaziz's legacy for guidance. Chief among these is the inspiration he provides for the current king, Salman, an ardent student of his father's method of governing.[9] MBS, the Crown Prince, also looks to his grandfather 'Abdelaziz for inspiration and "refers to continuing King 'Abdelaziz's legacy. Websites showing the face of 'Abdelaziz morphing into that of MBS echo the point."[10]

OIL! THE POLITICAL ECONOMY OF SAUDI ARABIA

At its formation in 1932, the economic survival of the Kingdom depended on pilgrimage (al-Hajj) revenue, loans from the merchant class, and British subsidies. When the Saudi Arabian state was cemented in 1932, it was first and foremost the expression of the alliance between 'Abdelaziz ibn Saud, the powerful Bedouin tribes and the Hejazi (western province) merchant class that provided al-Saud with loans and social recognition. For example, 'Abd Allah Sulayman, the first Saudi finance minister, who was in charge of the British subsidy, nicknamed "the uncrowned king of Arabia,"[11] became a successful businessman along the way.

A few months after the creation of Saudi Arabia, on May 29, 1933, the newly established King approved a concession agreement with Standard Oil of California (SoCal). This agreement would forever change the Kingdom and its international geopolitical relevance. The agreement with SoCal provided for the exploration of oil in the Eastern Province of the Kingdom. After five years of intense exploration and six wells that proved unsatisfactory, Dammam 7 gushed oil.[12] In March of 1938, after 10 months of digging at a depth of 1440 meters Dammam 7 produced commercial quantities of crude oil.[13] Number 7 produced 32 million barrels in its nearly 50 years of working life before it was retired in 1982.

The huge size of the Saudi finds required a new partnership in response. A joint venture, named Aramco (Arabian American Company), was formed in 1944. This partnership brought together the Saudi Arabian Government, Standard Oil of California (Chevron), the Texas Oil Company (Texaco), Standard Oil of New Jersey (Exxon), and Socony-Vacuum (Mobil). In 1950 Aramco agreed to share oil profits with King 'Abdelaziz on a 50/50 basis. By 1988 Aramco was fully nationalized and named "Saudi Aramco." Aramco became essential in creating a class of technocrats as it provided a "key building block in the shaping of Saudi society for decades to come" based on article 23 of the original concession agreement that read: "shall employ Saudi nationals as far as practicable, and in so far as the company can find suitable Saudi employees it will not employ other nationals." By 2016 the expatriate workforce was down to 15 percent of the total.[14] Today, almost all of Saudi Aramco's senior management and 80 percent of its 75,000 employees are Saudis, with women as 20 percent of its new hires.[15]

Today, Saudi Aramco owns and operates the largest oil fields in the world. Both in Saudi Arabia, Ghawar (on-shore) and Safaniya (off-shore) have been producing for decades and have considerable reserves.[16] Saudi Aramco is the world's largest and most profitable oil company.[17] Set up by Americans from Standard Oil, Texaco, and Mobil in partnership with the Saudi Government, it has been historically well managed, financially competent, and independent from the government.

Two significant features are characteristic of Aramco's political history. First, unlike the violent seizure of national resources in countries like Mexico, Iraq, and Iran, the nationalization of Aramco was relatively smooth.[18] The takeover was achieved via commercial negotiations and the purchase of the company from Chevron and Exxon Mobil[19] and completed in 1980. Second, by providing education, employment, roads, health care, and business opportunities outside of its gates, for the Saudi community, Aramco became well regarded and respected in the Kingdom.

POLITICAL IMPLICATIONS OF OIL

The 1933 concession agreement between 'Abdelaziz and SoCal marked the beginning of a new era characterized by greater economic certainty, entrenchment in the global economy, and increased global significance of the Saudi Arabia. Huge oil finds coupled with increased worldwide demand along with the fall of Iran's Pahlavi Dynasty and the rise in the price of oil subsequent to the 1973 embargo, thrust Saudi Arabia prominently onto the world stage. The embargo's duration was short, but its political and economic significance endures. After the embargo the price of a barrel of crude oil skyrocketed, it went from $1.38 in 1969 to $12.38 in 1973.[20] In the decades after WWII oil revenues experienced spectacular increases. Oil revenue which was $10 million in 1946 rose to $104 billion in 1980.[21] A number of opportunities and challenges resulted from the windfall.

Among the results of the oil embargo was a shift in the balance of power to the oil producers (office of historians) as the perceived scarcity of oil made them key political actors. Saudi Arabia was a vital player among the producers because of its enormous proven reserves. In 1964, H.E. Ibrahim al-Sowayel, a trusted advisor, was sent by King Faisal as his ambassador to Washington and was later to oversee the effects of the oil embargo placed on the United States and others perceived to support Israel during the 1973 Arab–Israeli war.

Three of the many consequences of the oil boom are especially noteworthy. These must be considered in terms of the Kingdom's efforts to balance modernization (as defined in the post WWII era) with traditional notions prevailing in the Kingdom. King Faisal (who reigned from 1964 to 1975) presided over the first coordinated economic development plans. King Faisal understood that the stability of the Kingdom depended on satisfying dual and competing obligations: modernize while maintaining tradition. Consequently, King Faisal and his successors embraced modernization within an Islamic framework. Economic progress would proceed while maintaining traditional values. As he said:

> Our religion… requires us to progress and advance and to bear the burden of the highest tradition and best manners. What is called progressiveness in the world today, and what reformers are calling for, be it social, human, or economic progress, is all embodied in Islamic religion and laws.[22]

This is a striking departure from the forced Westernization implemented by Ataturk in Turkey and the Pahlavis in Iran. It is also an example of arguing for progress using the logic of the traditionalists, a method the Saudi leadership would use often.[23] Given that Saudi Arabia is the birthplace of Islam and the site of its holiest cities, this makes sense. Moreover, it addresses traditionalist concerns about the direction and pace of change. Rather than sidelining or silencing conservative forces, the Saudi leadership appears to coopt their arguments and use them to advance development goals. This approach, used by King Faisal and his successors, is one way to address political threats to stability potentially coming from the religious establishment and other conservative voices.

After the 1973 oil boom, the revenues of the state increased tenfold in a short period of time, jumping from $4.3 to $43.3 billion between 1973 and 1977.[24] This sudden increase in liquidities had a sweeping effect on state-building. The first consequence of increased revenue was the rapid infrastructural development of the Kingdom. Before oil, there were no roads to speak of. The first five-year plan covered the period from 1970 to 1975. Oil allowed the financing of highways, schools, hospitals, and other necessities basic to a fully functioning polity. "Before oil, King 'Abdelaziz had no money for basic infrastructure."[25] Furthermore, Saudi Arabia's ecology and environment limited physical development, these limitations were greatly reduced by oil revenue.[26] The first five year plan saw a boom in the construction sector.[27] In large part this was due to the phenomenal growth in urbanization and massive importation of foreign labor needed to fulfill the infrastructural development goals.[28] Saudis also flocked to the major cities to profit from growing opportunities.

Second, more revenue meant a more sophisticated economy, which required an institutionalized system of government to deliver growing services. The Saudi political economy became increasingly linked with private and public international institutions, including the World Bank; the Bechtel Corporation; AT&T; the French, British, and American armies; Harvard and Stanford experts and the Ford Foundation. These international organizations were among the first consulted in the creation of the economic development plans. For example, the Ford Foundation worked with the Saudi Central Planning Organization in the early 1960s to author one of the first comprehensive planning documents.[29] While King 'Abdelaziz had designated a successor, at the time of his death in 1953, there were no substantive governing institutions.[30] Apart from the Council of Ministers, or cabinet, created by 'Abdelaziz in his last decree in 1953,[31] there was little governmental institutionalization. Since then, the government's structure has grown more complex to serve domestic and international needs. The growth of the state came, at times, at the cost of the growth of the private sector.

Third, and perhaps most significant, is the development of human capital, creating a healthy well-educated citizenry that can contribute to national growth. Here the post-oil change is striking. Life expectancy in 1950 was 39, by 2019 it was 75.[32] "By 1960 the majority of Saudis still lived at no more than subsistence level, their nutrition was poor even by developing world standards. Safe drinking water was unavailable…. cholera, malaria and bilharzia were common."[33] Today, these diseases are mostly just a memory. Healthcare services are provided for free to the general public through the Ministry of Health and military hospitals among others.[34] As far as education is concerned, prior to the 1930s there was no public school system. Six universities opened under Kings Saud, Faisal, and Khalid between 1960 and 1980; university enrollment in 1969 was 6900 and by early 1980s it rose to 65,500.[35] Today, Saudi Arabia has 29 public and 14 private universities, these exist alongside the numerous community and junior colleges.[36] Thirty-six universities allow women to enroll, and a smaller subset of universities are exclusively for women. The first university for women, the Princess Nourah bint 'Abdulrahman University, opened in 2010, and today it is the largest all women campus in the world with an enrollment capacity of 60,000 students.[37] High school education has seen similar development; in 2018 alone, 719 new schools were built. This is an important feature of the educational system when we consider that 50 percent of the population is under 25. Education, like health care, is free today.

It is important to observe that much of the development's implementation was managed by a group known as the "technocrats," members of the technically skilled elite. As such, they are among the stakeholders in the Kingdom's political arena, though not as powerful as some others. Often Western-trained, these Saudis are the managers of change at the ministerial and subministerial levels. In charge of ministries such as education and transport, they oversaw the infrastructural development of the Kingdom, transforming oil wealth into social benefits for the Kingdom's citizens. Oil has created many tangible benefits for Saudi society, but also significant social, economic, and political challenges.

CHANGES AND CHALLENGES IN SOCIETY

While some core characteristics have remained consistent, there has also been tremendous change. Since formation and particularly since the discovery of oil, the country has witnessed a significant demographic transformation.

One of the most important changes in Saudi Arabia since the 1970s is the incredibly rapid urbanization of the country. The kingdom was once Bedouin; in 1974, nomadic Bedouin represented slightly more than one-fourth of the population. Today, fewer than two out of 35 million live nomadic lives.[38] In 1970, the majority of the population lived in the countryside; this was reversed by 1980. In 2013, the urbanization rate was 82.7 percent, making Saudi Arabia one of the most urbanized countries in the Middle East, on par with Western Europe. Today, more than 80 percent of the population is concentrated in urban centers. The great majority live along the Jeddah–Dammam axis in the cities of Jeddah, Mecca, Riyadh, and Dammam-Khobar-Dhahran.

Saudi society is also very young. The fertility rate, which was about seven children per woman from the 1950s through the 1980s, has plummeted to three children per woman in

2019, or 16/1000.[39] Nevertheless, today 29 percent of the population is below the age of fifteen, and 66 percent are under 30.[40] The country is accomplishing this transition, however, in large part because MBS speaks to this demographic. While committed to consolidating and strengthening al-Saud rule, MBS thought that the ulema, technocrats, and tribes had gained too much authority.[41] Furthermore, he sympathized with the youthful Arab Spring protestors who rejected the corrupt elite.[42] All of this resonates with the sizeable younger demographic.

Indeed, under the reign of King Salman and Crown Prince MBS, the pace of social change has quickened dramatically. This is most evident regarding the status of women, for whom many previous restrictions were lifted. Guardianship, except for marriage, is no longer required. Women are free to travel, live alone, and represent themselves in court. The abaya is no longer required, nor can the religious police chastise women for going without it. Public facilities are no longer segregated by sex, including gyms, restaurants, and government offices. Employment opportunities for women are more available than ever before in both the public and private sectors; many women have been promoted to ministerial and deputy ministerial positions and also employed by the courts. In the Shura Council, women were active initiators of significant bills submitted for government approval.

Recall that in 1990, forty-seven women drove their cars in downtown Riyadh to protest the ban on women's driving; They were briefly detained, lost their jobs temporarily, and were restricted from travel. Just thirty years later, the government is issuing driver licenses to women. These changes are momentous, and even more staggering is the ease with which these changes are accepted. This, too, reflects the desires of a younger, more worldly population.

Extended families have also declined, and nuclear families tend to be more numerous. All over the Kingdom, young men and women are moving across the country in search of better opportunities. New housing caters to this growing migration. In the 2000s, endogamy was still high among less-educated women (58 percent of illiterate women and 50 percent of women holding elementary degrees) and decreased with the level of education (36 percent among women with university degrees).

The country has an important migrant community (approximately one-third of the population). Because of the long absence of a unified immigration policy, the proportion of immigrants has increased steadily since the 1980s. The availability of foreign labor allowed the business community to maintain low wages and poor management standards, thus excluding many Saudis from the job market. In 2013, Indians, Pakistanis, Bangladeshis, and Indonesians formed the most important foreign communities, closely followed by Egyptians, Syrians, Yemenis, Sudanese, Filipinos, Sri Lankans, Afghans, Nepalese, and Palestinians.[43] Saudi Arabia is not a country of immigrants, however. The state views immigrants as "guest workers" who eventually will return to their home countries.

However, many communities seek to permanently settle and acquire Saudi citizenship. The shift to Asian migrant workers was intended to break a regional imbalance between labor-exporting countries (Yemen, Egypt, and Syria) and the currency-exporting, oil-rich countries of the Gulf. But the emergence of a second generation of Arabic-speaking Asian immigrants, born and raised in the country and disconnected from their homelands, prompted the state to take a harder line on immigration in 2004 and toughen the naturalization law. Despite this severity, the absolute and relative numbers of migrants have continued to increase over the last decade.[44]

INSTITUTIONS AND GOVERNANCE

Saudi Arabia's principal governing institutions have developed since unification in the 1930s. These include the Monarchy, the Council of Ministers, The Basic Law of Governance, The Consultative Council, the Ruling Princes and the Royal family. Formally speaking, Saudi Arabia is an authoritarian, dynastic monarchy with a summary Basic Law of Governance (*al-nizham al-asasi li-l-hukm*, 1992). According to the letter of the Basic Law of Governance, the principle of power resides in the sons and grandsons of 'Abdelaziz al-Saud, and its reality lies in the hands of the king, who is "the source" of the "powers of the state," that is, "the judicial power, the executive power, the legislative power" (Article 44). According to one long-time American diplomat in Saudi Arabia, in "2020, the monarchy remains the principal institution holding Saudi Arabia together."[45]

Since the death of 'Abdelaziz, his six sons have managed the monarchy successfully, developing and defining the position while maintaining stability. Although not politically challenged by any part of the state apparatus, the king's authority is technically limited by various political stakeholders (these are identified below). Indeed, since unification, each of the seven kings has balanced and negotiated with competing interests. The next candidates for the monarchy will most likely come from the third generation of princes, the grandsons of 'Abdelaziz. This transition was cemented by the current King, Salman, when he appointed his nephew, Prince Mohammed bin Naif to be the deputy crown prince on the day that King Abdullah, King Salman's predecessor died. It was a historic move.[46] The third generation's succession to the throne presents an interesting but as yet undetermined dimension to the monarchy.

Created in 1953, the Council of Ministers (Majlis al-Wuzera') is one of the main governing institutions of the state. The King, the supreme decision-maker, heads it, and its members are appointed by Royal Decree. According to a Royal Decree issued in 1958, the Council of Ministers are:

> …responsible for drawing up internal and external policies, including financial, economic, educational and defense policies and supervising their implementation. It shall have executive authority and be the final authority in financial and administrative affairs of all ministries and government agencies.[47]

Put differently, the Council of Ministers is the cabinet. This body advises the king and makes policy. When it was created in the 1950s, it brought together all the ministers in a single body and was considered to be a first step in the transition from personal rule to the more institutionalized rule of the founder's sons.[48] Today princes hold less than 15 percent of cabinet posts, with nonroyal technocrats holding the rest.[49]

The Basic Law of Governance provides guidelines for how the government is to be run. The Basic Law of Governance was established by Royal Decree in January of 1992 under the reign of King Fahd. It is not a constitution, but it does set forth the rights and responsibilities of citizens. Article One states that the constitution of Saudi Arabia is "the Holy Qur'an and the Sunna of the prophet Muhammed".[50] And, according to the Basic Law, the shariah is the only source of law in the Kingdom.[51] Furthermore, the Basic Law confirmed that the monarchy was the form of Saudi Government and that succession passes through the sons of Abdelaziz and their male descendants.[52] At the time it was decreed, the Basic Law was not innovative, but rather formalized the existing political patterns.[53]

The Consultative Council (Majlis al-Shura) was initially created in 1926 in the Hejaz, held in abeyance since the 1950s, and only reopened in 1993 by King Fahd (1921–2005), as a response to the 1991–1992 opposition movement (see stakeholders and political participation). It is a legislative body of 150 members appointed by the king. Each member serves a four-year renewable term. Since its 1993 inception, the Council has grown in political significance, and since 2003 it can initiate legislation. In fact, in 2013 thirty women were appointed to this body. The Council does not, however, have budgetary authority and very limited oversight authority.[54] According to one scholar of the Saudi monarchy, the renewal and expansion of the Consultative Council "can be viewed as an exercise in royal co-optation designed to broaden the political base of the monarchy."[55]

The core positions in the state are held by members of the royal family. The number of al-Saud princes is unknown but estimated anywhere between a few thousand and a few dozen thousand. When all the branches of family are combined, the Royal family may well number over 100,000.[56] The politically important princes are, however, not more than a few dozen. They are in charge of the core functions of the state, form the backbone of the country's civil administration, fill positions of power in the sovereignty ministries (e.g., interior, defense, and until recently foreign affairs), and serve as assistants or advisers in some technical ministries (e.g., information, petroleum). They also fill crucial positions in the local administrations and the army and patronize the main youth institutions.[57] In addition, continuing the strategy employed by 'Abdelaziz, many major and minor princes marry into the main tribes, further solidifying those relationships. The ruling subset of princes manage the important day-to-day questions, policies, and concerns. However, almost all princes, regardless of their official position, act as mediators between the general public and the ruling elite.[58]

One observer of the family describes the process by which a prince can become a part of the ruling elite in the following manner:

> the Al Saud operate something like baseball's farm team system, in which ambitious young princes start off with relatively minor league positions and, if they are talented and fortunate, advance to more senior league posts.[59]

STAKEHOLDERS, THEIR POLITICS, AND HOW THESE WORK IN THE KINGDOM

The Religious Establishment (Ulema and Others)

One look at the Saudi flag confirms the centrality of Islam to the politics of the Kingdom. Against the green background, in striking calligraphy, is the Shahada asking the adherent to profess, "there is no god but God, and Mohammad is his messenger." Reciting the shahada is one of the five duties of a Muslim, and by placing it on the flag, the Saudi State emphasizes the centrality of religion. So too, the first article of the 1992 Basic Law of Governance states that "its constitution is the Qur'an and the Sunna" (the actions and words of the Prophet Muhammad), even though the king is described by the same text as the ultimate source (*marja'*) of power.[60]

Indeed, the relationship between the monarchy and the religious establishment is one of the most important relationships in the Kingdom. It is a mutually beneficial one whose contours were established under the rule of 'Abdelaziz, Saudi Arabia's first king. Since 1932, the official *ulema* (legal scholars), regrouped in 1971 in the council of senior scholars, have in general been deferential to political authority and have not voiced any strong opposition to the al-Saud. With some exceptions, their concerns have been limited to moral and narrowly religious matters. They have overall "contributed to the consolidation of a state that is politically secular and socially religious."[61] The religious establishment provides a legitimating anchor to the rule of the al-Saud's. The monarchs rule in the name of defending Islamic beliefs and values, and that association with Islam (and the religious establishment) strengthens the al-Saud claim to the rule.

Recall that the religious establishment has been a significant political player since the Kingdom's inception.[62] First, the prominent role of religion can be attributed to the formidable alliance between Mohammad 'Abdelwahhab and Mohammed ibn Saud in the 18th century. The former equipped with considerable religious credentials and the latter a powerful political force.[63] Their union was the basis of the First Saudi State. Moreover, as Saudi Arabia was never colonized, the religious establishment was never sidelined by a Western presence that prioritized secularization. Some leaders in the region believed that modernization could not occur without secularization and Westernization. Where Ataturk (Turkey) or the Pahlavis (Iran) policies of forced Westernization marginalizing the role of religion, that has never been the case in Saudi Arabia.[64] Consequently, Saudi Arabia has not had significant backlash as evidenced by the rise of Islamists in Turkey and the 1979 revolution in Iran.

Thus, since the rule of 'Abdelaziz, the relationship between the religious establishment and the rulers has been one of respect. The monarch respects the religious establishment in return for the establishment's support of the government's policies and development plans.[65] That respect, however, was tempered by royal authority. For example, when oil wealth in the 1970s provided the resources for social development, King Faisal pursued unprecedented social development policies such as bringing television stations (1963) and public education for girls (1960) to the Kingdom.[66] These were met with strong opposition by the religious establishment, which believing that these would alter the fabric of Saudi life. Faisal went ahead and brought them anyway, but made concessions. TV would broadcast a lot of sermons, in addition to other programming, and the ulema (Muslim scholars) could oversee programming. Similarly the religious establishment would supervise the educational curriculum.[67] Thus, the general policy was put forth by the royal leadership, but the religious establishment retained significant authority.[68] In 2020 this continues to be the case as the state continues to rely on religion as a form of legitimization.[69] King Salman and MBS seem to be following the method of negotiation established by the founder and cemented by King Faisal.[70]

Support for the al-Saud is found in the 1979 seizure of the Grand Mosque in Mecca. In the early morning hours of November 20, 1979, while more than 50,000 Muslims gathered to pray, 200 men led by Juhayman al-Utaybi, snuck in weapons and took control of the holiest site in Islam, The Grand Mosque in Mecca.[71] They pushed the prayer leader aside and, within one hour accomplished the unthinkable: the complete control of the sanctuary. There are a number of significant observations regarding this event. First, the use of force is Quranically prohibited in Mecca.[72] Therefore a fatwa had to be issued for Saudi security forces to enter and restrain the insurgents. The main religious scholars complied when they acceded to King Khalid's request for religious validation. Second, this was a particularly tumultuous period in the region: that same month 52 American diplomatic personnel were held hostage at the American embassy in Iran, while Iran's revolution was in progress; The Soviet Union invaded Afghanistan; and Saddam Hussein came to power in Iraq. Third, al-Utaybi attacked the religious legitimacy of the al-Saud, which is tantamount to attacking their political legitimacy. He condemned the degeneration of social and religious values in the Kingdom. Like the original Ikhwan movement, al-Utaybi criticized the Saudi government for using religion to further their own interests.[73] Most likely these criticisms reflect the inevitable tension brought by rapid change owing to oil revenue and the urge to cling to what is familiar. With oil money the fabric of Saudi life appeared to be altering beyond recognition. Fourth, the seizure led to reforms in the kingdom which established Majlis al-Shura and the Basic Laws of Governance. Finally, the seizure fed Islamic revivalism domestically and regionally.[74] Some believe that this event is among those that inspired Osama bin Laden to launch al-Qaeda.[75]

It has been more than 40 years since these events, but the implications of that unexpected rebellion continue. In the Kingdom, the rebellion resulted in stricter enforcement of conservative Islam.[76] This is why, perhaps, MBS said, before 1979, "We were living a normal life like the rest of the Gulf countries, women were driving cars, there were movie theatres in Saudi Arabia."[77] We were normal people developing like any other country in the world before events of 1979.[78] And, it is that normal that he seeks to re-establish with the recent reforms.

The Tribes (Qaba'il)

In January of 2018, twelve camels were disqualified from Saudi Arabia's annual camel beauty pageant.[79] They were eliminated for the illegal use of Botox, intended to enhance their beauty. Their owners lost the chance to win millions of dollars in prize money; nearly 32 million dollars are allocated to the beauty pageant. The pageant is part of a month-long festival celebrating the camel, upon which tribal bedu life used to depend. The festival, which also includes races, attracts more than 30,000 visitors. The camel festival, like the falcon races, is supported by the government in a show of respect to the tribes and what they value.[80] The King and Crown Prince are frequent guests at these events.

The importance of the tribes derives from their centuries-old existence on the Arabian Peninsula and from the services that they provide to their members. As one scholar put it, "Saudi Arabia is a young country with an old history and culture."[81] Much of that history and culture is represented by the tribe. Before unification in the 1930s, the tribe was the dominant form of social organization.[82] Membership in a tribe is determined by ancestry, derived from the male patriarch and transferred by the father.[83] The leader of the tribe is called by the honorific, "sheikh." The harsh desert environment meant that reliance on the collective was required for survival, the tribe provided safety and sustenance, this was especially true before oil.[84] While tribal significance waxes and wanes, it has not disappeared. Indeed, tribal affiliations can still determine social and political alliances as well as the distribution of resources.[85]

Tribal importance to the social and political fabric of Saudi life rests on a number of foundations. First, outside of the Hejaz, most Saudis claim a tribal affiliation; there are more than 20 major tribes in Saudi Arabia.[86] That means that a large majority of Saudis define their identity by bloodlines.[87] Second, aspects of tribal attributes were woven into the national narrative of state-building.[88] Tribal independence was diminished at unification, but the state coopted and maintained much of that structure. For example, Saudis often look to their political leaders in the same way they relied on the head of the tribe: to be generous and enthusiastic in helping to navigating life's hardships.[89] It is considered their duty. The tribe once provided everything from physical security to community support much like a government. Today, those needs are met by the central government.

Nevertheless, tribal affiliations remain a source of identity, social status and pride. As one scholar relates from discussion with a Saudi. "My family has been Saudi for 90 years, we have been Muslim for 1400 years. We have been Shammar (a tribe) for 3000 years."[90] Bedu tribalism used to determine occupation, but today it is shown in patterns of behavior. Among the strongest are the rules around marriage, "you don't marry your daughters to strangers."[91] For the tribal, the nontribal are strangers, irrespective of citizenship.

The political importance of the tribe is evident in several arenas. There are no political parties in Saudi Arabia; tribes, however, are organized and can mobilize politically and easily. Often, a person's last name is the name of the tribe to which that person belongs, Shammar, Qhatan, Ghamdi are examples. The municipal elections offer a good example: in the 2015 campaigns, tribal mobilization led to their members' election to offices in the rural areas. Second, it might seem that tribalism is anathema to a centralized government system and that there is a tension between the urge for tribal independence and the al-Saud government's wish to centralize. Wisely, when 'Abdelaziz unified the Kingdom, he gave no preference for one tribe over another, instead he enlisted a coalition of tribes to support his mission[92]. This move assured that no one group dominated another, a problem that has caused civil unrest in Iraq and Syria, where one group is perceived to be favored at the cost of others. Furthermore, the al-Sauds have been careful to respect and honor tribal ways. Not only do they celebrate tribal culture, they also heed many tribal preferences and work closely with regional sheikhs. Finally, the Saudi National Guard (SANG) provides an institutional example of the relationship between tribe and government. Founded in the 1950s, it is distinct from the Saudi army as it is constituted of tribal elements loyal to the al-Saud. It is well equipped and well funded. SANG provides training, jobs, and healthcare, at times to the extended family of the guard.[93] The al-Saud effort to maintain the tribes' status has resulted in loyalty to the central government. In this regard, the central government's strategy is much like the one employed with the religious establishment. This could be attributed to Saudi Arabia's lack of colonial history which meant that the indigenous traditions captured by religion and tribe were not forsaken in favor of rapid Westernization.

RELIGION AND POLITICS

Saudis are in great majority Sunnis, yet Saudi Arabia is more religiously diverse than often believed. The official doctrine of the state stresses the pure Sunni nature of the kingdom but accepts the religious diversity of a country that hosts almost every branch of Islam and various other faiths. Located mainly in the Eastern Province, in the cities of Najran and Medina, there is a Shi'i minority which still protests against discrimination. Most Saudi Shi'a are "Twelvers," that is, they believe in a lineage of twelve imams after the Prophet; the Shi'a of Najran, in the south, are Ismailis, who believe in a more metaphorical interpretation of sacred texts. In the Hejaz and Najd, Sufi communities flourished amid Najdi revivalist Islam (sometimes mistakenly called Wahhabism). The nonnational population of the country (although no statistics on religion are available) comprises Muslims, Christians (among whom are over a million Catholics, notably Indians and Filipinos), Jews, Buddhists, Hindus, animists, and atheists.

An exclusive focus on state-sanctioned Sunni revivalism obscures the complex links between religion and politics, and the fact that many, mostly religious, transnational networks crisscross the country. It is often forgotten that Arabia has not only exported, but also imported, religious ideas and practices. The two holy mosques of Mecca and Medina have attracted pilgrims, students, and travelers since the beginning of Islam. The urban Hejaz is traditionally linked to all corners of the Islamic world through education and worship, which the state has tried, with uneven success, to institutionalize and control since 1932. The state intended the Sharia College of Mecca (1949) and the Islamic University of Medina (1961) to provide a structure for scholars and students attracted to the holy cities. The holy cities and the nascent Saudi State captured the imagination of numerous scholars from all over the Islamic world, and many intellectuals and adventurers flocked to Saudi Arabia, especially the Hejaz. The most famous were the Egyptians Muhammad Qutb (b. 1919) and Muhammad al-Ghazali (1917–1996), the Syrian Muhammad Nasir al-Din al-Albani (1914–1999), the Palestinian 'Abd Allah Azzam (1941–1989), and the Moroccan Muhammad Taqi al-Din al-Hilali (1894–1987). Saudi Arabia became a haven particularly for the Muslim Brothers, who were subjected to violent repression in Egypt, Syria, and Iraq during the 1950s and 1960s. Although they were officially prevented from creating a Saudi branch of their movement, the Muslim Brothers could direct their Egyptian, Iraqi, Syrian, and Palestinian branches from Saudi Arabia. They also participated in the creation of the Muslim World League (1962), the Organization of the Islamic Conference (1969), and the World Assembly of Muslim Youth (1972), all international institutions that fostered Saudi influence in the Islamic world. They have been both an instrument of Saudi influence and an autonomous player in the region.

The oil-rich Eastern Province is home to a Shi'i minority, which is closely connected to Shi'i communities in Bahrain, Kuwait, Iraq, and Iran. The community faces discrimination from the state, Aramco, and the religious establishment. Indeed, King Faisal's policies led Shi'a to revive historic sectarian relationships across national borders. "The success of the Iranian Revolution in 1979 turned several Shi'i activists into 'Muslim rebels.'"[94] Iranian influence has, however, never been as obvious as the Saudi State claims. During the 1970s and 1980s, Saudi Shi'a were linked to Iraq and Kuwait through Muhammad al-Shirazi (1926–2001), a cleric from Karbala, Iraq, who settled in Kuwait in 1971 and was actually an intellectual rival of Ayatollah Ruhollah Khomeini.[95] In 1991, the Organization for the Islamic Revolution in the Arabian Peninsula, created in 1979 and headed by Sheikh Hassan al-Saffar (b. 1958), renamed itself the Reform Movement and abandoned its radical objectives. In 1993, it settled an agreement with the Saudi government that allowed its exiled leaders to return to Saudi Arabia.[96] Since the fall of Baghdad in 2003, Shi'a have revived their Gulf networks. Yet the Al Sa'ud still see Saudi Shi'a as an Iranian fifth column, and they escalated the confrontation between the state and the religious minority.

Because of its central position in the political economy of the Middle East, Saudi Arabia has been a launching pad for activists who threaten the existing regional order. Osama bin Laden was the main leader of this trend and al-Qa'ida its main label. His and other militant networks are truly international, however, and are not traceable to one particular country: "It is the cross-fertilization of religious thought in the Hejaz that produced Bin Laden, who cannot be anchored in one locality of intellectual tradition."[97] In Saudi Arabia, Afghanistan, Chechnya, Bosnia, Yemen, Sudan, Somalia, Iraq, Egypt, Algeria, Morocco, and the Gulf states, violent activism benefited from numerous regional crises. Defined as *al-fi'a al-dhallah* (those who have gone astray) by the Saudi State, these groups attacked the US presence in the region and the prolonged dependence of Middle Eastern regimes on the United States. Besides Osama bin Laden, Abu Muhammad al-Maqdisi (b. 1959), Yusuf al-'Ayyiri (1974–2003), and the anonymous Internet writer "Lewis 'Atiyat Allah"[98] are the main organizers or promoters of these networks. The creation of ISIS in Iraq in 2006, its extension to Syria in 2013, and its subsequent expansion at once epitomize the failure of the US interventions in the region and reveal the fragility of the postcolonial Arab state system. The violence of the Syrian and Egyptian regimes within their borders, the violence of ISIS in Iraq and Syria, the Yemeni quagmire, and the continued Israeli violence in Palestine all point to considerable challenges for the Saudi State.

INTERNATIONAL AND REGIONAL POLITICS

Once a neglected imperial frontier, Saudi Arabia has become one of the most important countries for the world's economy and security. Its vast oil resources and its strategic location account for this spectacular transformation. The national oil company, Aramco, was instrumental in bringing the country to the forefront of the United States' new interest in the Middle East. When WWII began, oil became a commodity of crucial strategic importance, and US experts estimated that the center of oil extraction was shifting from the Americas to the Arabian Gulf. Meanwhile, Britain was strengthening its economic influence over the Saudi State, which prompted US oil companies to react and champion a long-lasting US–Saudi alliance. On February 18, 1943, responding to the advice of Standard Oil, President Franklin D. Roosevelt added Saudi Arabia to the list of beneficiaries of the 1941 lend–lease program. Saudi oil production increased dramatically during the last years of WWII and supported the Allies' victory over the Axis powers. Construction of a US military base began in 1944 in Dhahran, near the oil fields and the Aramco compounds. The famous meeting between President Roosevelt and King

'Abd al-'Aziz on board the USS *Quincy* in the Suez Canal in 1945 clearly signified that Britain's influence in the Middle East was on the wane. Saudi Arabia was officially the first Middle Eastern country to enter the sphere of US interests; many other countries in the region followed it, and the Middle East became "the most penetrated international relations sub-system in today's world"[99].

The Saudi role in US international politics became even more vital with the beginning of the Cold War. Strategically located between the three continents over which the United States and the Soviet Union competed, less affected by European colonialism and less populated than its neighbors, Saudi Arabia was an ideal ally in times of global tension. Its oil fueled the postwar reconstruction of Western Europe and Japan and supported the dominance of US oil companies over the global oil market. The "Saudi connection"[100] or "neotriangular trade"[101] established by US presidents Roosevelt and Truman among the United States, Saudi Arabia, Western Europe, and Japan provided cheap and abundant oil and air force bases to the Western world. It also made Islam an important weapon in the US Cold War ideological arsenal. King Sa'ud bin 'Abd al-'Aziz (1902–1969), who succeeded his father in 1953, adhered in 1957 to the Eisenhower doctrine, and Saudi Arabia became a powerful anti-Communist instrument in the Middle East, providing help and services in what has been called the "Arab cold war,"[102] notably against Nasserite Egypt, republican North Yemen, and communist South Yemen. Under the Nixon doctrine (1969), Saudi Arabia became, along with Israel and the Pahlavi Shah's Iran, one of the pillars of US dominance in the Middle East.

Meanwhile, the creation by Faisal bin 'Abd al-'Aziz (1903–1975) of the World Muslim League (Rabita al-'Alam al-Islami, 1962) and of the Organization of the Islamic Conference (Munazhzhama al-Mu'tamar al-Islami, 1969) produced pan-Islamic bodies in which Arab nationalist regimes were marginalized. This policy aimed at destroying Soviet influence in the Arab world. After the Soviet invasion of Afghanistan in 1979, Saudi Arabia again mobilized its finances and its Islamic networks—exiled Muslim Brothers from neighboring Arab countries and Saudi Muslim Brothers—in support of the Afghan resistance to the Red Army, contributing to the eventual defeat of the Soviet Union in Central Asia.

US–Saudi relations were partly overshadowed by the recurrent question of Palestine. During his 1945 meeting with President Roosevelt, King 'Abd al-'Aziz asked him, "What injury have Arabs done to the Jews of Europe?" Over a year later, President Truman infamously answered by telling American diplomats, "I have to answer to hundreds of thousands who are anxious for the success of Zionism; I do not have hundreds of thousands of Arabs among my constituents."[103] Pan-Islamism, although used against the Soviets' ambitions in the Arab world, was also an attempt to transcend the Arab nationalist position on the issue of Palestine. At the request of King Faisal, the Organization of the Islamic Conference created a fund for the holy war against Israel during its second meeting in 1972.

The 1973 oil embargo was triggered by the October war between Egypt and Israel. On October 17, 1973, the ten Arab oil-exporting states reduced their production by at least five percent every month until the end of the Arab–Israeli conflict. A few days later, they suspended the oil supply to the United States. Within six months, the Saudi oil revenue increased fivefold. In January 1974, after the end of hostilities, oil production resumed. In March 1974, Saudi

Arabia insisted on ending the embargo on oil exports to the United States. This mild use of the oil weapon had not managed to influence the US policy toward Israel. Yet the embargo allowed Saudi Arabia to replace Egypt as the leader of the Arab world. Despite the US threat to invade the Saudi oil fields in order to restore production and export, the embargo paradoxically strengthened the US–Saudi relationship. In the aftermath of the Iranian Islamic revolution of 1979, Saudi Arabia became, alongside Israel, the paramount US ally in the Middle East.

Since the end of the Cold War, Saudi Arabia's leading position in the Middle East has been strengthened by the unilateral politics of the United States. The high revenues of the Saudi State have exposed it to continuous US and British pressures to sign extremely costly military agreements. Since 1973, the country has spent roughly one-third of its budget and approximately 25 percent of its GDP on the military. Still, Saudi Arabia has had to rely on foreign aid whenever threatened, as it did in 1979 or, more recently, during the 1990–1991 Gulf war. The financial and military link to the United States, along with Saudi Arabia's performance as an oil producer, explains why the political alliance has remained so strong.

Because of its wealth and close relationship with the United States, Saudi Arabia has become an important economic and political crossroads. Its cultural influence is perceptible through its religious networks and its control over many print media and television channels across the Middle East.[104] Most pan-Arab media are controlled by the Saudi royal family. The exceptions are, among others, the Qatari, US, and Iranian satellite TV channels al-Jazeera, al Hurra, and al Alam, and the Palestinian daily *al-Quds al-'Arabi*. The satellite channel al-Arabiya and the dailies *al-Hayat* and *al-Sharq al-Awsat* are the main media outlets of Riyadh.

This regional vocation also expresses itself in many other ways, from diplomatic mediation to direct intervention. Saudi Arabia has offered to arbitrate many conflicts: with Saudi help, the Lebanese civil war ended with the Taif agreement of 1989, the Lebanese National Pact was renegotiated, and French-imposed sectarianism in Lebanon was destined for abolition. More recently, the Hamas–Fatah agreement, signed in Mecca in February 2007, was an attempt to resolve intra-Palestinian tensions. In the Arabian Peninsula, Saudi Arabia has exerted a very strong influence on its neighbors through its economic importance, its "immigration diplomacy" (toward Yemen),[105] and the formation in 1981 of the Gulf Cooperation Council (GCC)—first and foremost a Saudi club—which includes Kuwait, Bahrain, Qatar, the United Arab Emirates, and Oman. In recent decades, it has also exerted direct influence over Yemen by funding many political forces, tribal forces, and Islamic and communist groups.

The 2015 war on Yemen, waged by Saudi Arabia leading the coalition formed by Kuwait, Bahrain, Qatar, the United Arab Emirates, Jordan, Morocco, Egypt, Sudan, and Senegal, is a perplexing escalation. Officially started to restore the Yemeni government of president 'Abd Rabbo Mansur Hadi against the rebellion led in the north of Yemen by the al-Houthi family, the war soon turned into a humanitarian disaster, and Yemen, nicknamed in the 19th century "the graveyard of the Ottomans" for its staunch resistance to the Turks, is now becoming "Saudi Arabia's Vietnam."[106]

After serving as a Cold War ally of the United States, Saudi Arabia now seeks autonomous leadership, notably through its 2002 Israeli–Palestinian peace plan, which is at the forefront of the Arab peace effort. This dynamic political environment witnessed Saudi Arabia taking a leadership role in diffusing tensions and countering Iranian aspirations. Saudi Arabia is now involved in several new positions. At first backing the Syrian opposition jointly with the CIA and Saudi Intelligence until it was infiltrated by extremists and complicated by Russian intervention, waging war against the Houthi rebels in Yemen, and supporting the Egyptian military regime of field marshal 'Abd al-Fattah al-Sisi. Outside of its borders Saudi Arabia is investing in regional alliances, political and economic. This means a strengthening of ties with Egypt. Efforts to offset Iranian and Turkish bids for hegemony include overtures to Iraq to solidify relationships and moves toward cooperation with Oman. The latter includes plans for a land bridge connecting the two countries. Relations with Qatar have been mended and cooperation has resumed.

POLITICS AND DOMESTIC CONFLICT

Saudi Arabia's economic, political, and social activism has intensified with King Salman's accession to the throne in 2015. Domestically the activism has taken a social bent with the attention-grabbing reforms initiated by MBS. These include the expansion of women's rights (discussed above) and opening of movie theaters. They also extended to a controversial crackdown on corruption, made famous by the detention of princes, senior officials, and businessmen at the Ritz Hotel in Riyadh during the fall of 2017. Citizens also speak of an app where infractions maybe reported and rewarded monetarily.

These social and political measures are viewed as steps towards fulfilling of Vision 2030, and toward increasing citizens' trust in the government. Announced by MBS in 2016, Vision 2030, is an ambitious plan to diversify and develop the traditionally oil reliant economy. Unfortunately, the coronavirus pandemic slowed progress toward the Vision 2030. In part, this was due to global economic disruptions (such as lower oil prices, market instability and tourism freezes). It was also due to proactive measures. After the first case was detected in March 2020, Saudi Arabia suspended flights and monitored all entry points to Mecca and Medina (important points for the Hajj), subjected mosques were subject to daily disinfection, requested adherents to pray at home, pivoted schools and universities pivoted to remote learning, and instituted other measures to counter the pandemic.

Vision 2030 was developed by Council of Economic Development Affairs, which is chaired by Deputy Crown Prince Mohammed bin Salman. It includes a number of goals and reform strategies for the Kingdom's long-term economic success. See Saudi embassy.net

CONCLUSION

Inside Saudi Arabia, the main challenge remains the balancing of pressing needs. These are made that much more difficult with lower oil prices and the consequences of COVID. As in so many places, COVID has forced the closure of many businesses, reduced tourism, and generally slowed economic growth. Second, Vision 2030, the ambitious diversification plan articulated by MBS, has also experienced a diminished energy. The development of nonoil sectors, a priority of Vision 2030, remains one of Saudi Arabia's main concerns. Third, a mostly young population, age 30 and below, poses unchartered territory for the kingdom. Their engagement, employment, and participation are the focus of much of King Salman and Crown Prince MBS' policies. The next few years hold much opportunity for the Kingdom. How it engages with this will determine the future.

SUGGESTED READINGS

Al-Enazy, Askar. *The Creation of Saudi Arabia: Ibn Saud and British Imperial Policy, 1914–1927*. London: Routledge, 2010.

Al-Rasheed, Madawi. *Contesting the Saudi State: Islamic Voices from a New Generation*. New York, NY: Cambridge University Press, 2007.

———. *A History of Saudi Arabia*. New York, NY: Cambridge University Press, 2010.

———, ed. *Kingdom without Borders: Saudi Arabia's Political, Religious and Media Frontiers*. London: Hurst, 2008.

Alshamsi, Mansoor. *Islam and Political Reform in Saudi Arabia: The Quest for Political Change and Reform*. London: Routledge, 2011.

Citino, Nathan. *From Arab Nationalism to OPEC: Eisenhower, King Sa'ud, and the Making of U.S.-Saudi Relations*. Bloomington, IN: Indiana University Press, 2002.

Commins, David. *The Wahhabi Mission and Saudi Arabia*. London: I. B. Tauris, 2006.

Jones, Toby Craig. *Desert Kingdom: How Oil and Water Forged Modern Saudi Arabia*. Cambridge, MA: Harvard University Press, 2010.

Le Renard, Amélie. *A Society of Young Women. Opportunities of Place, Power, and Reform in Saudi Arabia*, Stanford, CA: Stanford University Press, 2014.

Menoret, Pascal. *The Saudi Enigma: A History*. London: Zed Books, 2005.

———. *Joyriding in Riyadh: Oil, Urbanism, and Road Revolt*. Cambridge: Cambridge University Press, 2014.

Munif, Adelrahman. *Cities of Salt*. New York, NY: Vintage, 1989.

———. *The Trench*. New York, NY: Vintage, 1993.

———. *Variations on Night and Day*. New York, NY: Vintage, 1994.

Vassiliev, Alexei. *The History of Saudi Arabia*. London: Saqi Books, 2000.

Vitalis, Robert. *America's Kingdom: Mythmaking on the Saudi Oil Frontier*. New York, NY: Verso, 2009.

22 SYRIA

Raymond Hinnebusch

The Syrian state, founded under the French (1920–1946), was ruled by a liberal landed oligarchy until military officers associated with the Arab Ba'ath Socialist Party launched a socialist "revolution from above" (1963–1970). After years of instability, President Hafiz al-Asad (1970–2000) consolidated an "authoritarian-populist" regime; Hafiz then passed power to his son, Bashar al-Asad (2000–), whose attempted transition to a semimarket economy helped prepare the way for the Syrian Uprising beginning in March 2011. A decade of violent conflict resulted in a partially failed state.

This chapter outlines the process of state formation, postindependence social change; the rise of the Ba'ath regime, its structures and processes; key political struggles (over political Islam and democratization); political economy under the Ba'ath; the Syrian Uprising; and Syria's foreign policy and international relations.

STATE FORMATION: HISTORY AND SOCIAL COMPOSITION

Syria's geography and history shaped its current statehood. Historically, Syria was a trading civilization, with its largest cities, particularly Aleppo and Damascus, living off the East-West trade routes. A substantial grain-growing agricultural sector existed, albeit vulnerable to periodic drought, and pastoralists raised animals on the steppes. Cohesion was fragile owing to large urban–rural gaps, localism fostered by geographic complexity—a land of plain, desert, oasis, and mountain—and Syria historically lacked a centralizing state, making it a prize fought over by more cohesive neighboring river valley empires. This, combined with Syria's ethnic and religious diversity (discussed below), made for a fragmented society with strong loyalties to substate communal groups, cities, and regions. Indirect rule of religious identity groups (*millets*) through religious leaders and notables during the Ottoman Empire (1500–1918) strengthened substate identities. Ethnic minorities include Kurds (7 percent), Armenians, and small numbers of Assyrians, Circassians, and Turkmen; while some urban Kurds were Arabized, some one hundred thousand settled under the French mandate were disaffected, having been denied citizenship. Religious minorities include Greek Orthodox Christians (8 percent), various smaller Christian sects, and several Islamic minority sects—the most important being the Alawites (12 percent), the Druze (3 percent), and the Ismailis (1.5 percent). Countering this fragmentation, a vast majority of Syrians are Arabic speakers and ninety percent are Muslim.

The imposed creation by Western imperialism of the modern Syrian state, following the collapse of the Ottoman Empire during World War I (see Chapter 1), left a permanent sense of national frustration. Britain and France agreed to divide up historic Syria, *bilad ash-sham*. Lebanon was detached from western Syria, Jordan from its south, Iskandarun (Alexandretta) was ceded to Turkey, and Palestine was turned over to the Zionist movement. French rule in Syria was imposed through the repression of several uprisings in the early 1920s and a policy of divide and rule that played off minorities against the Sunni Muslim majority.[1]

The colonial experience generated enduring irredentist and antiimperialist sentiments. The truncated Syrian state, seen as an artificial creation, did not enjoy the strong loyalty of its citizens, who were mostly attached either to substate communities or to suprastate ideologies, pan-Syrianism, pan-Islam, or pan-Arabism. The most successful political elites and movements championed Syria as part of a wider Arab nation even if they accepted its (possibly temporary) separate statehood. Seeing itself as the "beating heart of Arabism," Syria gave birth to Ba'athism, a movement that sought to unify the Arab states. Decades of conflict with Israel generated a particular Syro-centric form of Arabism in which Syria claimed to be the most steadfast defender of the Arab causes, notably Palestine. After a half-century of separate statehood, a Syrian Arab identity gradually emerged with the boundaries of the contemporary state largely accepted. But since most Syrians still saw Syrian identity as Arab, the idea of a Syrian nation-state distinct from the Arab world did not achieve hegemony, and sub- and supra-Syrian identities retained credibility. In the post-2011 uprising, insecurity from civil war led many Syrians to fall back on sectarian and ethnic identities and protection at the expense of common national identification. Syrian identity remains contested today, but Arabism has been eclipsed as its dominant content, squeezed between a stronger Syrian state (civic) identity and a variety of Islamic identities.

KEY FACTS ON SYRIA

AREA 71,498 square miles, including about 500 square miles occupied by Israel (185,180 square kilometers)

CAPITAL Damascus

POPULATION 18,028,549 (2017); includes 20,500 people living in the Israeli-occupied Golan Heights (2014)

PERCENTAGE OF POPULATION UNDER 25 51.2

RELIGIOUS GROUPS (PERCENTAGE) Sunni Muslim, 74; Alawite, Druze, and other Muslim sects, 16; Christian, 10; tiny Jewish communities in Aleppo, Damascus, and al-Qamishli

ETHNIC GROUPS (PERCENTAGE) Arab, 90.3; Kurds, Armenians, and others, 9.7

OFFICIAL LANGUAGE Arabic; Kurdish, Armenian, Aramaic, French, Circassian, and English also spoken

TYPE OF GOVERNMENT Nominal republic, but in reality, authoritarian with domination by the Ba'ath Party

DATE OF INDEPENDENCE April 17, 1946 (from League of Nations mandate under French administration)

GDP (PPP) $50.28 billion; $2,900 per capita (2015)

GDP (NOMINAL) $24.6 billion; per capita not available

PERCENTAGE OF GDP BY SECTOR Agriculture, 20; industry, 19.6; services, 60.4 (2017)

TOTAL RENTS (PERCENTAGE OF GDP) FROM NATURAL RESOURCES Not available (20.7 in 2007)

FERTILITY RATE 2.5 children born/woman (2017)

Sources: CIA. "The World Factbook." August 4, 2022, https://www.cia.gov/the-world-factbook/.
UNHCR. "Situations – Syria." Last updated July 31, 2022, https://data.unhcr.org/en/situations/syria.

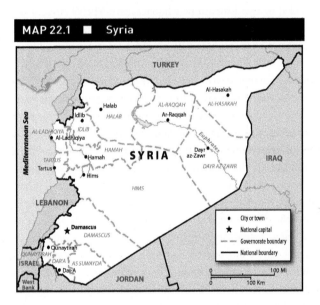

MAP 22.1 ■ Syria

POST-INDEPENDENCE SOCIAL AND POLITICAL CHANGE

The first quarter century of Syria's independence was a continuation of the politics of Ottoman notables. Landlord, tribal, and merchant families overwhelmingly dominated parliament and cabinets.[2] Half the land was concentrated in great landed estates, while more than two-thirds of the peasants were landless sharecroppers. An indigenous agrarian and industrial capitalist class emerged after independence, investing in grain and cotton cultivation and new agricultural industries. This new wealth fed the growth of the state apparatus and enlarged the salaried and professional middle class. An important stratum of this new class was drawn from the rural towns and the peasantry—many of them of minority background—forming a partly urbanized, rural intelligentsia. Of pivotal importance, the army officer corps, which was rapidly expanded to deal with separatist threats and border conflicts with Israel, became a channel of upward mobility (via free admittance to the military academy) for peasant- and lower-middle-class youth, while the scions of the upper classes eschewed military careers.[3]

A smouldering landlord–peasant struggle was ignited when landlords started replacing traditional sharecropping with mechanization and wage labor, disrupting whole villages and generating a mobile agrarian proletariat.[4] By the mid-1950s, Syria's laissez-faire capitalism stalled as an unskilled workforce and a limited market constrained further growth. Many Syrians believed a major role of the state in the economy and land reform was required to drive development and social justice, but the ruling oligarchy resisted and began to disinvest as it lost confidence that it could control political events.[5]

As a result, several radical middle-class parties emerged to contest the power of the oligarchy; of these, the Ba'ath Party eventually became the main political vehicle that overthrew the old regime. The party was founded by two Damascene schoolteachers: Michel Aflaq, a Christian, and Salah ad-Din Bitar, a Sunni Muslim. On an eventually merging parallel track were Alawites Zaki Arsuzi, a teacher and refugee from Iskandarun, and Wahib al-Ghanim, a medical doctor from Latakia. The Ba'ath later also merged with Akram al-Hawrani's Arab Socialist Party, which had organized educated youth and peasant tenants to challenge Hama's great feudal magnates. The social base of the Ba'ath was lower-middle class and rural, as its early followers were peasant youth who came to the city for education. Many of them were from minority communities, notably Alawites, attracted by a secular, nationalist message that accepted minorities as equals. The party acquired special strength in the two professions that were most open to people of modest backgrounds—the army and teaching[6]—and which were also keys to the command of force and the shaping of opinion.

Ba'ath ideology was a mixture of nationalism and social reformism. It held that imperialism had artificially divided the Arab nation into many states to keep it weak. The mission of the party was to awaken the slumbering Arab nation and lead its unification. It mixed pan-Arabism with a call to overthrow "feudalism," a major role for the state in national development, social welfare services, labor rights, and agrarian reform. The ideology's appeal was instrumental in making the Ba'ath Party the most important and ultimately successful of the radical movements that arose in postindependence Syria. The Ba'ath slogan, *wahdah, hurriyah, ishtirakiyah* [Unity, Freedom, Socialism], became the trinity of Arab nationalist politics throughout the Arab world.

Syria's fragile liberal institutions, though initially oligarchic-dominated, might have been democratized by the inclusion of wider class strata. Indeed, in the 1954 election radical middle-class parties, including the Ba'ath, won a minority but high-profile bloc of seats in parliament. At the same time, however, as the officer corps, dominated by the middle class and former peasants, was politicized and radicalized, it turned against the oligarchy. A duality of power emerged between the parliament, still led by landowners, and the army—a stalemate that prevented major reform and fostered instability.

In parallel, Syrians were deeply divided over foreign policy between supporters of pro-Western Iraq, which advocated security through membership in the Western-sponsored Baghdad Pact, and followers of Egypt's Gamal Abdel Nasser, who opposed the pact in the name of nonalignment. Because the fate of the Pact was believed to turn on Syria's choice, a regional and international "struggle for Syria"[7] took place (1954–1958). Nasser's rising stature as a pan-Arab hero, especially after the Suez War, strengthened those aligned with Cairo—above all, the Ba'ath and led Syria into a merger with Egypt in the United Arab Republic (1958–1961); although the union failed, the oligarchy could not thereafter be restored. In sum, the postindependence rise of middle-class radical nationalism, combined with peasant land hunger, destabilized the semiliberal old regime and paved the way for the Ba'ath coup of 1963.

INSTITUTIONS AND GOVERNANCE

Formation of the Ba'ath Regime

The coup that brought the Ba'ath Party to power in 1963 initially ushered in an era of instability. Although the coup leaders called it a revolution, the new regime was the product of a conspiracy by a handful of "ex-peasant" military officers, not of mass mobilization from below, and it faced the combined opposition of the old oligarchs, the Muslim Brotherhood, and Nasserist agitation over its failure to reunite Syria and Egypt. Key to its survival was its launching of a "revolution from above" in which nationalization of big business and land reform demolished the class power of the old oligarchy, gave the Ba'ath control of the levers of the economy, and allowed it to mobilize a mass constituency. This was accompanied by intense class struggle between regime and opposition (Table 22.1).

TABLE 22.1 ■ The Rise of the Ba'ath Party: A Chronology	
1943	Michel Aflaq and Salah ad-Din Bitar call their followings the "Ba'ath movement"
1947	Founding conference of the Ba'ath Party
1953	Merger of Ba'ath and Arab Socialist parties
1954	Ba'ath Party wins parliamentary presence
March 8, 1963	Ba'ath military and allies seize power in Syria
October 1963	Sixth National Congress of Ba'ath Party radicalizes party ideology
February 1966	Radical coup led by Salah Jadid ousts Aflaq and Bitar
November 1970	Hafiz al-Asad seizes power, ousts radical Ba'ath faction
2000	Hafiz al-Asad dies; his son, Bashar, accedes to the presidency
2005	Ba'ath Party congress consolidates Bashar's power, retires "Old Guard," and approves transition to a "social-market economy"; Syria forced to withdraw from Lebanon
2011	Beginning of the Syrian uprising against Ba'athist rule
2012	New constitution removes clause designating Ba'ath as the leading party

Adding to the instability, the regime soon internally split between party patriarch Michel Aflaq, who prioritized pan-Arab union, and younger radicals of minority rural origin who prioritized social revolution. In intraregime struggles, ideological and personal rivalries overlapped with sectarian divisions between Sunnis and the minorities who had long been disproportionately represented in the party and army. Because Alawites increasingly won out, thereby disaffecting Syria's Sunni majority, the regime was pressured to prove its Arab-nationalist credentials. A radical faction under Salah Jadid seized power in a 1966 intraparty coup.[8] Driven by ideological militancy and a search for legitimation, the radicals supported Palestinian fedayeen raids into Israel, in spite of the unfavorable Syrian–Israeli balance of power, thereby provoking the 1967 defeat and Israeli occupation of Syria's Golan Heights. The recklessness of the radical faction discredited it, allowing the 1970 rise of a newly pragmatic wing of the party under General Hafiz al-Asad.[9]

Hafiz al-Asad's coup ushered in the consolidation of the Ba'ath regime. He established a "presidential monarchy" that concentrated power in his own hands; used his control of the army to free himself of Ba'ath ideological constraints; and placed a core of personal and sectarian followers in the security apparatus to give him autonomy from the army. Secure in control of the party and army, he appeased the private bourgeoisie through limited economic liberalization through which elements of the Damascene Sunni bourgeoisie were brought into tacit business alliances with Alawite military elites, while at the base, the party and its auxiliaries incorporated a popular following from both Sunni and non-Sunni villages. Thus, Asad built a cross-sectarian coalition, whose effectiveness proved itself in defeating the major Islamic fundamentalist uprising of 1978–1982. To build his regime, he also depended on external resources—that is, Soviet arms with which he built up the army and Arab oil money with which he expanded the bureaucracy and coopted the bourgeoisie. Only as the state was stabilized and the regime attained relative internal cohesion was Asad able to confront Israel and make Syria a player, rather than a victim of regional conflicts. The legitimacy of Asad's regime was largely based on its relative success in doing this, beginning with the 1973 Arab–Israeli war.[10]

Regime Power Structures and Intra-Elite Politics

The president was the main source of policy innovation and had numerous powers of command, appointment, and patronage. When Bashar al-Asad succeeded his father as president, he initially had to share power with the old guard, his father's lieutenants; but he used his appointment powers to replace them with his own loyalists and establish himself as the prime decision-maker.

The presidency rested on three overlapping pillars of power—the party apparatus, the military-police establishment, and the state bureaucracy. Intraelite politics was played out largely in the relationship between the presidency, party, and security barons, and informal networks of actors linking these power centers operated behind the scenes of formal institutions,[11] which were arenas for their rivalry and instruments of policy implementation.

The security services made up under Hafiz al-Asad of his trusted network of military and intelligence officers—a majority of them Alawites—were second only to the president in influence; charged with surveillance of threats to the regime, they were also instruments through which the president controlled the other regime power centers. Their role in vetting all candidates for office and keeping files on everyone's peccadilloes and loyalty, along with the extralegal powers acquired in fights with the regime's many enemies, allowed top security barons to become powerful political brokers whose support ambitious politicians and prominent businessmen sought.

Next in importance was the Ba'ath Party's Regional Command (*al-qiyadah al-qutriyah*), the top collegial leadership body, roughly divided between senior military commanders, the most powerful cabinet ministers, and provincial governors, and top party apparatchiks. A periodically assembled party congress of some 1,200 delegates was a main arena in which ideological and later bureaucratic intraelite conflicts were compromised, elite turnover engineered, and a stamp of approval given to major new policies. In the early Ba'athist state (1963–1970), ideological conflicts were settled at party congresses and by intraparty military coups. Once Hafiz al-Asad consolidated the regime, the articulation of material interests was funneled through the party and corporatist institutions (unions and associations). This often took the form of contestation over economic policy, which politicos, technocrats, and business representatives incrementally adjusted to deal with chronic economic difficulties.

The Regional Command controlled the party apparatus, a main pillar of power; in 2000, party membership of nearly two million incorporated teachers, students, state employees, peasants, and workers and the apparatus controlled the worker, peasant, and professional unions. Party institutions gave the regime roots in society and helped bridge sectarian and urban–rural gaps.

The army was another pillar of power. It was differentiated into elite units, primarily charged with regime defense and staffed on the basis of political loyalty and (Alawite) sectarian affiliation; and the wider professional army charged with defending the state's borders. The last pillar was the state bureaucracy headed by the Council of Ministers (cabinet) and charged with policy implementation. It was responsible to the *Majlis ash-Shab* or people's council (parliament), in which two-thirds of seats were reserved for candidates of the National Progressive Front (NPF), the alliance of the Ba'ath Party with small leftist and nationalist parties. In order to coopt elements outside the regime's state- and rural-centered power base, independent candidates, mostly from the urban bourgeoisie, were allowed to contest the remaining one-third of parliamentary seats. The judiciary was politicized through party control of appointments and failed to guarantee rule of law or civil liberties; hence, redress of grievances often depended on informal clientele connections.

These structures proved very enduring, even under the extreme pressure of the Syrian Uprising. Although both party and government penetration of the countryside contracted, with half of Syrian territory falling out of regime control, the bureaucracy persisted and the party was increasingly "militiaized" to defend proregime areas (as is detailed in the section on Domestic Conflict and Rebel Governance).

POLITICAL STRUGGLES: ACTORS AND ISSUES

Religion and Politics: The Struggle Between Ba'athism and Political Islam

Despite the avowedly "secular" character of the Syrian state, religion became inseparable from politics in Ba'athist Syria because of a certain overlap between sectarian identity and political forces. The Alawite minority had become overrepresented in the armed forces and the Ba'ath Party, the two institutions that together came to rule Syria after 1963.[12] The Sunni Muslim majority, the religiously minded of whom regard the Alawites as heretical,[13] inevitably resented their disproportionate political power. As such, the Ba'ath regime generated its antithesis—political Islam—which reflected the interests and values of the roughly half of Syrian society excluded from the Ba'athist state. Political Islam was historically concentrated in traditional urban quarters, where the mosque and the *suq* (market) came together. From this milieu, politi-cized *ulema* (religious scholars) and the Muslim Brotherhood (*al-ikhwan al-muslimun*), whose members were typically recruited from urban-merchant families, mounted the main opposition to the regime. Beginning in the 1960s, as the state takeover of foreign trade and restrictions on imports deprived merchants of business, the Brotherhood denounced Ba'ath socialism as Marxist and atheist. As the youth of traditional neighborhoods went to university, a growing proportion of Islamist activists came to be drawn from the university educated.[14]

From 1977 to 1982, the Muslim Brotherhood instigated a violent insurrection against the regime. Corruption, sectarian favoritism, Hafiz al-Asad's 1976 confrontation with the Palestinians in Lebanon, and Sunni resentment of minority domination generated fertile conditions for Islamist revolt. The Ikhwan attacked the Alawites as unbelievers and, reflect-ing the urban-centric and antistatist worldview of the *suq*, denounced the regime's land reform and called for an Islamic economy based on free enterprise. Financed by the aggrieved nota-bility of Hama and Aleppo, the foot soldiers of the insurgency were recruited from the *suq* and sharia students, primarily from northern cities and towns. Hama was a historic center of Islamic piety, and the Hamawi notables resented the presence of Ba'ath provincial officials and the favor shown surrounding villages they once dominated. By contrast, the Damascene Sunni bourgeoisie, enriched by the disproportionate share of public money expended in the capital, remained quiet during the uprising. The Islamist revolt failed owing to its fragmented and largely unknown leadership and the urban and northern bias of its social base. The regime, backed by its rural base, remained cohesive, and the security apparatus mounted a repressive campaign of unusual ruthlessness, marked by the 1982 sack of Hama in which fifteen thousand to thirty thousand people were killed.

With the Ikhwan's leaders exiled,[15] Islamist revolution had failed, but a less politicized, less oppositional Islamization from below was thereafter tolerated by the regime as it sought to tame political Islam through an alliance with moderate Sufi Islam, expressed in the appointment of Ahmad Kaftaro as Grand Mufti. Muhammad Sa'id al-Buti preached a moderate Islam in the media. Bashar al-Asad continued the strategy of fostering moderate Islam as a counter to both radical Islamists and the secular opposition, resulting in the spread of Islamic schools and chari-ties, conservative attire, and mosque attendance. Islamist intellectuals and businessmen were coopted into parliament, and recognition was given to the Qubaysi movement that preached Islam among upper-class Damascene women. This largely nonpolitical Islam, concentrating on personal piety, rejecting violence, and mobilizing around issues such as opposition to liberal reform of Syrian family law, seemed less threatening to the regime.[16] While the outlook of the *ulema*, recruited from the *suq* merchant class, was sharply at odds with Ba'athist socialism, it was convergent with Bashar's increasingly neoliberal tangent. Bashar al-Asad also built alliances with the interlocked business and religious elite of formerly oppositionist Aleppo. Islamists were not, however, politically incorporated and instead the regime continued efforts to control them by appointing the senior *ulema*, such as muftis and imams of the big mosques; exploiting differences between Sufi orders and their Salafi critics as well as between conservative imams and modernists; and according those who sought accommodation with the regime the freedom and resources to spread their networks.[17] The government's coming to terms with political Islam initially enhanced stability, but the consequent erosion of secularism carried real dangers that manifested themselves in the Islamic color of much of the uprising starting in 2011.

In the environment of extreme conflict after 2011, Islamic ideology and discourse mutated and deepened: The previously dominant peaceful Sufi strand of Islam, which had accommodated itself to the regime, suffered contraction, while political Islam, salafism and jihadism, became the main mobilizing ideologies of the insurgency. Increasingly, sectarian discourse (Sunni Islam vs. Shi'a and Christians) was used to mobilize support and demonize opponents. Governance in rebel-controlled areas came to be based on various forms of supposedly "Islamic" practice, such as "Islamic courts."

Stalled Democratization and Authoritarian Upgrading

When Bashar al-Asad assumed power in Syria in July 2000, his project, according to Volker Perthes,[18] was to "modernize authoritarianism" in Syria. This required limited political liberalization and more rule of law, but not democratization. The regime's initial tolerance of the Damascus Spring of 2000–2001 suggested that a coalition was taking form between regime modernizers and the loyal opposition,[19] behind a gradual peaceful political liberalization. But when hard-line opposition figures attacked the legacy of Hafiz and spotlighted the corruption of regime barons, Bashar shut down his political liberalization experiment.[20] Western democracy, he declared, could not just be imported and had to follow social and economic modernization, not precede it.

There were, in fact, several structural obstacles to any "democratization from above." The minority Alawite elite feared sectarian voting (as in Iraq) would allow the Sunni majority to drive it from power. Bashar's neoliberal economic policies (see ahead under Political Economy) could be blocked if the masses were empowered by the vote. Demand for democratization was concentrated in a limited number of middle-class intellectuals and a minority of the private bourgeoisie who were deeply divided. Additionally, the fear that democratization would spread the "Iraqi disease"—sectarian conflict—to Syria briefly generated for the regime what might be called legitimacy because of a worse alternative.

As a substitute for democratization, Asad embarked on a process of "authoritarian upgrading"—the fostering of alternative constituencies to substitute for the alliance with workers and peasants the regime was abandoning. The regime coopted an alliance of reforming technocrats and the business class, that, dependent as it was on the state for opportunities (contracts, licenses), had no interest in democratization. To appease the urban middle class, Asad allowed a certain political decompression, which enabled new government-sponsored civil society organizations for the well-off, such as junior chambers of commerce. Critics of the regime were treated more leniently, albeit within boundaries highlighted by episodic instances of selective repression. Similarly, the introduction of the Internet and mobile telephones was seen by Asad as an essential tool of economic modernization, which the regime also used to mobilize supporters and legitimize itself. But these moves also gave political activists the ability to build networks, overcome atomization, and publicize abuses[21]; they paved the way for the 2011 uprising, as will be detailed in the section on Domestic Conflict.[22]

POLITICAL ECONOMY

Ba'ath Populist Statism (1963–2000)

The Ba'ath regime was founded amidst "revolution from above" that effected a significant redistribution of economic assets through land reform and the nationalization of industry, banks, and other big businesses; opened education and public employment to the lower strata; and established welfare entitlements, including labor rights and food subsidies. Formerly rigid class lines were broken, unleashing substantial social mobility.[23] There was a major transformation of the countryside through land redistribution, irrigation, and land reclamation; the spread of education, health care, and electrification; and the subsidization of agriculture, which increased incomes and opportunities for rural residents. This considerably mitigated the historic urban–rural gap, although rural poverty remained a fact of life.[24]

The economy significantly expanded in the 1970s, as the state channeled investment and substantial foreign aid from the East bloc and Arab oil producers into factories, railways, dams, and irrigation projects in an effort at statist import-substitute industrialization (ISI). By the mid-1980s, however, the exhaustion of Ba'ath statism was apparent in balance-of-payment and foreign exchange crises and a chronic savings investment gap, reflective of the failure of the public sector to accumulate capital. This was because of systemic corruption, massive military spending, inefficiencies in public-sector management, and the general subordination of economic rationality to political imperatives. Meanwhile, the private sector, confined after the nationalization of big business to small-scale enterprises, failed to invest, and the rich exported their capital. The economy became excessively dependent on foreign aid, petroleum revenues, and transfers from Syrians abroad.[25]

The regime responded to the weaknesses of statism with three waves of liberalization—in the early 1970s, late 1980s, and early 1990s, resulting in an ever-greater role for the private sector, whose share of investment and GDP exceeded that of the public sector in the 1990s. Economic liberalization generated a new "military-merchant complex" at the heart of the regime as senior regime stalwarts, notably Alawite military and security officers, went into business with Sunni private-sector partners, often rent seekers exploiting their connections with the state. In time, as the sons of the elite went into business, their intermarriage and business partnerships with the private business class generated a new upper class, which partly bridged old sectarian divides. Parallel to emergence of this new rich, mounting inflation threatened the livelihoods of the publicly employed middle class, and class distinctions sharpened.[26]

There was, however, resistance to a full transition to a market economy. Populism was institutionalized in the ruling party and the "social contract" under which citizens surrendered political rights in return for economic entitlements. The ability of the regime to buy loyalty through patronage would have been risked by full withdrawal of the state from the economy. Sustained economic liberalization required reconstruction of an entrepreneurial bourgeoisie, which, willing to invest, could provide a viable alternative to the public sector as a source of jobs and taxes; but the old bourgeoisie was politically opposed to the regime; newer elements were largely commercial and rent seeking; all evaded taxes; and capital was exported in the absence of investor confidence, which required greater rule of law, policies favoring investors over labor, and ending regional conflicts. Rent windfalls—oil revenues and Arab aid—and bursts of investment following liberalization initiatives temporarily relieved pressure for deeper economic liberalization. Rent and relative lack of debt to the West buffered the regime from International Monetary Fund–imposed structural adjustment.

Postpopulist "Reform" Under Bashar al-Asad (2000–)

Bashar al-Asad's economic reform project was driven by several imperatives: Since the 1980s, GDP per capita had stagnated, as economic growth barely kept up with population growth, resulting in burgeoning youth unemployment. Revenues from petroleum exports, which had funded half the state budget, were declining. With the global failure of the socialist alternative to capitalism, private capital investment appeared to be the only solution to the exhaustion of Syria's statist economy. Ba'ath Party ideologues and apparatchiks gradually lost power to new, liberalizing technocrats. To stimulate growth through private investment meant prioritizing the needs of investors[27]: thus a multitude of new laws was designed to create the legal framework for a more market-oriented economy, reinforce property rights, and restrict political interference in economic administration. Private banks and insurance companies opened, and trade and foreign exchange were liberalized. Private companies were permitted in virtually all fields, although they still required nontransparent official approval. Foreign capital could now be repatriated; foreign banks could wholly finance projects; and labor laws were relaxed. Syria jumped from 145th out of 157 countries on the Index of Economic Freedom in 2006 to 91st in 2008.

Many reforms, however, went wholly or partially unimplemented, owing to the underqualified, poorly motivated, sometimes-hostile bureaucracy charged with carrying out reform or due to the resistance of vested corrupt interests. Moreover, the regime aimed to survive a transition from a statist to a market economy by creating its own fraction of the emerging capitalist class; indeed, the new class of "crony capitalists"—the rent-seeking alliances of political brokers led by Bashar's mother's family—acquired a stranglehold on the economy that deterred investment by more productive entrepreneurs. The role of the state in the economy remained substantial: Its investment was the main economic stimulator; the public industrial sector was not privatized, although contracting its management to private firms might have been a privatization by stealth. Because the public sector also supplied contracts and intermediate goods at low cost to the private sector, their relationship was symbiotic.

Under the new political economy, average GNP growth was only 3 percent between 2000 and 2006, barely above population growth. After 2004, a spurt of investment due to excess liquidity in the Gulf from rising oil prices and Syria's improved business climate drove a private-sector boom in trade, housing, banking, construction, and tourism. But the failure to invest in significant job-creating enterprises severely limited the trickle-down effects. Socioeconomic inequality steadily increased. While the new bourgeoisie was enriched, the failure of official salaries to keep up with inflation since the 1980s impoverished the salaried middle class, and public-sector workers normally had to work multiple jobs. A 2005 United Nations Development Program (UNDP) study found 30 percent of Syrians lived near the official poverty line, and unemployment was estimated at close to 18 percent. At the same time, the government started reducing subsidies on basic consumption commodities that had provided a sort of social safety net for ordinary people, especially on fuel products (that had encouraged smuggling to neighboring countries at the expense of the treasury). Public health and education services deteriorated under austerity budgets. Syria's scores on the Human Development Index (HDI), which improved from 0.580 in 1980 to 0.691 in 2000, with life expectancy about seventy years and the literacy rate at 76 percent, reflected momentum from earlier social investments. The country still ranked 108 out of 173 countries on the HDI, with an official per capita annual income of approximately $4,800, although this figure did not adequately capture the large informal economy.

All of Syria's developmental gains were dissipated in the civil war that broke out after 2011: Four years after the civil war started, GDP had been at least halved; unemployment stood at 57 percent; 7.9 million fell into poverty and, of these, 4.4 million into extreme poverty.[28] Eleven million Syrians were displaced, and massive numbers left the country to become refugees in neighboring countries. With the ruin of the normal economy, the market shrank to local household production, or else people survived by human, arms, and drug trafficking; looting; or else enlisting as fighters, with the Gulf-funded Islamist groups the best able to recruit and pay them. Syrian capital fled the country, and exiled businessmen became major investors in Turkey. War profiteers connected with the regime enriched themselves on scarcities, smuggling, and monopolies, and regime stalwarts exported their funds and families to Dubai.

DOMESTIC CONFLICT AND REBEL GOVERNANCE

The Syrian Uprising

By mid-2011, mass peaceful mobilization demanding the fall of the Bashar al-Asad regime had swept large parts of Syria, putting the regime on the defensive. The seeds of the uprising can be seen in the "authoritarian upgrading" by which Bashar al-Asad sought to fix the vulnerabilities of the regime he inherited from his father, notably the exhaustion of statist development. This strategy drove regime tax cuts and currency and trade liberalization, designed to attract expatriate capital and surplus liquidity from the Gulf and Turkey. The priority on investment sidelined the preexisting populist "social contract" ensuring a minimum of fair income distribution. This was especially dangerous since rapid population growth generated legions of unemployed youth whose access to economic opportunities contracted. The removal of subsidies on agricultural inputs and decline of farm support prices, combined with the terrible drought of 2007–2009, led to agricultural decline. Poor neighborhoods around the cities burgeoned with the influx of drought victims and Iraqi refugees. The conspicuous consumption of the new urban rich alienated those in the surrounding deprived suburbs.[29] Importantly, as opportunities declined for most people, regime favoritism toward Alawites became ever more resented, helping to delegitimize the regime.

In parallel, to advance his postpopulist reforms, Asad concentrated power in the presidency in an extended struggle with the Ba'athist old guard. Uprooting Sunni old-guardists destroyed the clientele networks that had incorporated key segments of Sunni society into the regime. This made the president overdependent on the presidential family, Alawi security barons, and technocrats lacking bases of support. Also, seeing the party apparatus and the worker and peasant unions as obstacles to economic reform, Asad debilitated them. This weakening of the regime's organized connection to its rural and Sunni constituency contracted its social base, making it more minoritarian and more upper class. Parallel to this, authoritarian upgrading did foster alternative constituencies, mostly in the big cities.

While mounting grievances and narrowing regime support made the regime vulnerable to the Arab uprising, it was the overreaction by the security forces, starting in Dara where protests were met with violence, that precipitated revolt in Syria. The protests initially demanded democratic reforms, not revolution, and Asad might therefore have reacted with democratic concessions; however, given the minority core of the regime and the debilitation of its former cross-sectarian base, this would have risked conceding the advantage to Sunni oppositionists. He chose to stand with the hard-liners in the security forces and to demonize the protestors as Islamist terrorists to justify their repression; however, the regime's use of violence only spread the protests to further areas and precipitated maximalist demands—fall of the regime—from the burgeoning opposition. This was encouraged by the regional Arab Uprisings, which spread the idea that popular protests could succeed in overthrowing authoritarian rulers and broke the "fear barrier" in Syria. Internet technology was used to generate opposition networks and deliver their revolutionary message, while local committees sprang up to coordinate protests.[30]

Despite the mobilization of mass protest sweeping large parts of Syria, no regime overthrow took place. This was partly because the uprising, geographically dispersed away from the capital, never acquired momentum at the center of power. Rather, beginning in the rural peripheries, it then spread to small towns, suburbs, and medium-sized cities, such as Homs and Hama, where its foot soldiers were unemployed youth, refugees from drought, and medium- and small-sized traders and manufacturers, victimized by trade liberalization and also resentful of the expansion of the Alawis into business sectors. The regime, moreover, had its own support base—it relied on those who had benefited from its policies or felt threatened by the uprising, notably the crony capitalists and the minorities, especially Alawis. It had support in neighborhoods of Damascus and Aleppo, where the investment boom and the new consumption were concentrated. The middle class of the two main cities feared instability and loss of their secular modern lifestyle if traditional rural insurgents took power. Exiled businessmen who had lost out to regime-connected operators were big funders of the insurgency; but much of the in-country business class saw no alternative to the regime. In summary, there were enough grievances to fuel an uprising in Syria but only among a plurality of the population, with a significant minority adhering to the regime as a better alternative than civil war and a near majority on the sidelines.[31]

All efforts to find a political solution to the crisis failed. Even though the regime ostensibly conceded some reforms, they were considered inadequate and insincere. Besides the moral outrage at the killings perpetuated by the government, opposition activists believed that they could only be safe from its retribution if the regime was removed. The opposition strategy depended on a level and scale of protests such that the security services would be stretched thin and exhausted, perhaps so provoked they would increase violence that would lead to such disaffection in the army that it would become an unreliable instrument of repression. Indeed, the streets of scores of towns and small cities were swamped with protestors, putting regime control of public space at risk. However, the military, organized around its Alawi core and closely linked to the presidential clan, but also long invested in the regime through the military branches of the Ba'ath party, remained largely cohesive and loyal for a long time. It did not turn against its superiors, and Alawi-dominated units, such as the Fourth Division headed by Maher al-Asad and the Republican Guard, were most involved in repression. Alawis (and others) were also mobilized in militias (the *shabiha*), later organized into a formal national guard; with much to lose if the regime fell, they remained its most reliable shock troops.

A major escalation of the conflict was the battle for cities in which the opposition sought to escape from confinement in the peripheries. It realized it could not win without breaking the alignment between the regime, on the one hand, and parts of the bourgeoisie and middle class, on the other hand, in the two main cities, Damascus and Aleppo. It was initially thought that the turmoil and Western sanctions would paralyze the economy, cause the business elites to desert the regime, and sap the regime's revenue base, hence its ability to pay salaries and sustain the loyalties of the state administration. However, an economic collapse did not take place, and the regime proved capable of perpetuating itself financially. Ultimately, therefore, to turn the main cities against the regime, parts of the opposition sought to show, through bombings and armed infiltrations into urban neighborhoods and suburbs, that the regime could not guarantee stability; the regime, in turn, used heavy weapons against suburban neighborhoods harboring the insurgents to send the message to populations that such armed groups should not be tolerated in their midst. Homs, which slipped almost entirely under opposition control, became a particular victim of this dynamic in which regime violence against urban neighborhoods was particularly bloody.

The regime sought to rally its base, by sectarianizing the conflict—accusing the opposition of Islamic terrorism—to win the support of minorities who could expect retribution if the regime fell. The opposition initially sought to win over the minorities with a rhetoric of civic inclusion; however, as democracy activists either exited Syria or fell back on religious zeal in a time of high insecurity, the balance shifted to Islamist hard-liners, empowered by money and guns from the Gulf. For the opposition, framing the conflict in sectarian terms potentially allowed it to mobilize the Sunni majority. In fact, however, while Asad's increasing use of lethal force against nonviolent protestors alienated wide swaths of the public, because society rapidly became polarized along *both* sectarian and class lines, no bandwagoning against the regime similar to that in Egypt happened. As the conflict morphed into semi-sectarian civil war, whole communities became entrapped in the "security dilemma," seeing the "other" as enemies. Mass flows of refugees emptied the country of those caught in between and also of many of the secular, middle-class peaceful protestors, leaving the field to the radical Islamists.

This was paralleled by militarization of the conflict. Although the mass protests had been nonviolent, the regime's violence generated a desire for revenge and legitimized the notion of armed self-defense among the opposition. Army defectors, the core of armed resistance to the government, formed the Free Syrian Army (FSA), while many of the protestors joined armed Islamist groups, which could soon deploy tens of thousands of fighters, bolstered by foreign jihadists. Strategic areas, such as the Ghouta—rural suburbs of Damascus—eastern Aleppo city, Raqqa, and Idlib fell under the control of armed Islamist groups. The armed opposition's capacity to deny the regime control in many areas and the army's lack of sufficient reliable manpower to repress what became widespread, armed insurgency, led the regime to withdraw into its strategic southern and western heartlands; this left much of rural northern and eastern Syria out of government control.

Partially Failed State: Governance Amid Civil War

As the civil war deepened, the regime was subtly transformed to fight the opposition. The Ba'ath party militarized and was supplemented by militias, and local self-defense forces, some originating in the pro-regime thugs (*shebiha*) that have repressed protestors; while the regime made an effort to institutionalize and reassert central control over these groups by incorporating them into "National Defense Forces," local groups dependent on raising their own resources and defending their own communities inevitably acquired considerable autonomy, thereby decentralizing power. Shi'i militias, particularly Hezbollah but also Iraqi militants recruited by Iran, established a semiautonomous presence in certain areas as well and formed the shock troops of government offensives. In parallel, the regime attempted to sustain a monopoly of state services, to the point of continuing to pay officials' salaries even in opposition-controlled zones, while also seeking to preempt efforts by the opposition to establish a counteradministration in key urban areas such as western Aleppo and Douma, through sieges and bombings. This, combined with the failure of the opposition to provide services and security in their zones, precipitated population movements into government-controlled areas. As regime resources became scarcer, however, it increasingly tied access to state services to loyalty to the regime.

Meanwhile, the militarization of the conflict and the relative withdrawal of state-delivered welfare and security from opposition-controlled areas left a vacuum of order that rival groups sought to fill. Local councils, initially set up by young protest leaders and civil society groups, attempted to provide public services and humanitarian aid, but as this first-generation leadership was detained, killed, or fled the country, civil society groups were marginalized. Amid growing insecurity, citizens looked to informal traditional institutions such as clan, tribal, and sectarian/ethnic groups for protection and support. Autonomous armed groups proliferated as the Free Syrian Army gradually morphed into warlord bands and jihadist movements. Jihadist groups tended over time to prevail at the expense of secular civil society and over the FSA because they combined superior financial resources and the best motivated and armed fighters. Endless permutations of salafist armed groups merged into umbrella coalitions (e.g., Islamic Front, Syrian Islamic Liberation Front) and splintered over time (being in competition with each other as well as fighting the regime); the most powerful and enduring were the al-Qaʿida avatars, such as *Jabhat al-Nusra* and the Salafist *Ahrar al-Sham*. Sharia courts (or authorities) were established to manage conflicts between armed groups and were often recruited from them; when run by jihadist groups, they imposed radical interpretations of Islam on populations. Even initially secular groups promoting inclusive citizenship over time mirrored the Islamic discourse pervading the opposition-controlled areas. Still, even in towns controlled by jihadists, civil society groups occasionally mobilized demonstrations against their arbitrary treatment of citizens.

A war economy emerged, and conflict came to be driven by competition over resources, giving warlords and jihadi groups a stake in its continuance. Among the most important resources were oil fields, gas, electricity, and water, in addition to profits from border fees and checkpoints and from looting of banks and factories. Jihadists looted billions from the bank in Al-Raqqa and seized flour mills and oil fields and pipelines. Economic deals crossed political divides: In Aleppo, a "water-for-electricity" deal was agreed between government and opposition, and in Deir ez-Zor, the regime and Al-Nusra shared oil profits. A three-way struggle for power emerged among the regime, "moderate" opposition, and jihadists, themselves split, with the balance of power different in each area. In Raqqa, civil society groups had elected a council after the regime withdrew, but jihadists soon took over and then themselves came to blows. In Aleppo, rural Islamist militias infiltrated and seized the poorer eastern section of the city; the regime's barrel bombs, however, led to increasing population flight from the opposition-controlled half of the city. Deir ez-Zor also remained contested between regime and rival opposition forces.

The interventions of rival outside forces further fragmented authority. The disparate exiled groups in Turkey were grouped in the National Coalition of the Syrian Revolution and Opposition Forces (NC). It used international funding to build patronage connections to the nongovernment-controlled areas but was perceived as detached from grassroots interests and was divided between the clients of Saudi Arabia and Qatar, whose funding of rival groups also fragmented the armed opposition on the ground. Western governments, via subcontracted private agencies backing different groups, also contributed to fragmentation in the opposition areas.[32]

The subsequent evolution of the conflict was basically shaped by the military balance of power between regime and opposition, as well as their external backers and their capacity to intervene. A major 2014 development that radically altered the balance was the rise of the extreme jihadist Islamic State (IS) which established control over wide areas of western Iraq and eastern Syria, for a period expanding at the expense of all other contenders through its combination of extreme brutality, motivated militants, bureaucratic capacity to deliver a modicum of welfare and security and coopt tribes and activists, and the ideological appeal of the restoration of the "Caliphate." In early 2015 after the fall of Palmyra to IS and after the formerly divided Islamist clients of Qatar and Saudi Arabia came together to seize Idlib, the regime looked to be in a precarious position. The Russian military intervention, a reaction to these advances by the militant Islamists, combined with intervention of the US–Western coalition against IS in the eastern part of the country, particularly Raqqa, again substantially shifted the internal power balance but back toward the regime. It began a series of seemingly inexorable advances, retaking the northern cities, including Eastern Aleppo, Palmyra, and eastern areas from IS, then completing the defeat of the opposition in the Ghouta, Dara, and the South in 2018. Regime advances were backed by Shia militias and Russian airpower, but were also facilitated by deals to relocate opposition fighters to Idlib, which became an island of opposition militants. Meanwhile in the East, many IS-held regions fell to the US-backed, Kurdish-led Syrian Democratic Forces. In the North, Turkish incursions in support of its own client FSA forces captured al-Bab from IS and contested the Kurdish PYD control of the border areas, notably taking Afrin from the PYD in 2018. By mid-2018, the division of the country has been stabilized: the regime commanded the country's heartland, biggest cities, and 73 percent of the population; but grain- and natural-resource-rich northeastern areas, and especially Kurdish-majority regions, remained under control of the SDF (with 10 percent of the population) while the Turkish-controlled northern belt contained 17 percent of the population. The active civil war appeared to be winding down, but as will be seen in a subsequent section, it was moving not toward a military or political resolution but toward a frozen conflict.

REGIONAL AND INTERNATIONAL POLITICS

Syria's foreign policy is shaped by historical grievances and geographic vulnerability. It has had a limited manpower base, few natural boundaries, little strategic depth, and exposure on three sides to stronger countries: Iraq had designs on Syria, and Turkey has, at times, pressured Damascus by troop movements or control of the water of the Euphrates River, which runs through both countries. Grievances originating in the dismemberment of historic Syria produced an Arab nationalism that brought conflict with a militarily stronger Israel, with which Syria fought several major wars (1948, 1967, 1973, and 1982).

Syrian Foreign Policy Under Hafiz al-Asad (1970–2000)

The struggle with Israel was at the center of Syrian foreign policy, particularly after the 1967 Arab–Israeli war in which Israel occupied the Syrian Golan Heights. But only under Hafiz al-Asad did Syria become a credible actor in this contest. He prioritized recovery of the Arab lands occupied by Israel in 1967 above all the Golan Heights. But he combined this with an insistence on achieving Palestinian statehood in the West Bank and Gaza under a comprehensive peace and eschewed for a quarter century a potential separate settlement with Israel over the Golan at the expense of the Palestinians. In parallel, Asad significantly upgraded Syria's capabilities. Convinced that Israel would never withdraw from the occupied territories unless military action upset the post-1967 status quo, his main aim after coming to power in 1970 was preparation for a conventional war to retake the Golan. Syria's alliance with the Soviet Union and with Arab oil states enabled the rebuilding and expansion of the armed forces. Alliance with Sadat's Egypt, the most militarily powerful Arab state, which shared Syria's interest in regaining the occupied territories, was necessary to take on a more-powerful Israel.[33] Egypt and Syria went to war with Israel in 1973 to recover their occupied territories. Syria failed to recover the Golan Heights militarily, but Asad sought to use the political leverage from the Arabs' credible challenge to Israel and the simultaneous Arab oil embargo to get international pressure on

Israel to withdraw from the occupied territories. Henry Kissinger's mediation resulted in a 1974 disengagement agreement on the Golan expected to be the first step in total Israeli withdrawal. However, Sadat's subsequent separate deals with Israel undermined Syria's diplomatic leverage in bargaining for recovery of the remainder of the Golan and put a comprehensive Arab–Israeli settlement off the agenda. Thereafter, for Damascus, the threat of an Israel emboldened by the neutralization of its southern front had to be contained, and the resumption of peace negotiations depended on restoration of the Arab–Israeli power balance.

Syria's 1976 intervention in Lebanon's civil war was part of Asad's attempt to construct a Syrian sphere of influence to substitute for the collapsing alliance with Sadat's Egypt; it also enabled Asad to station his army in the Bekaa Valley against the threat of an Israeli drive threatening to Syria's soft Western flank. Asad also sought, via the intervention, to control the Lebanon-based PLO, hence the "Palestine card": Syria's diplomatic bargaining leverage would be enhanced if it could veto any settlement of the Palestinian problem that left Syria out and overcome rejectionist Palestinian resistance to an acceptable settlement. Asad also conducted a low-level conflict on Israel's Lebanese border, using proxies such as Palestinian and later Hezbollah guerrillas, designed to show Israel it could not have peace without a settlement with Syria. He simultaneously worked to obstruct schemes to draw other Arab parties into partial, separate settlements with Israel that circumvented Syria. Thus, he took great risks to obstruct the 1983 Lebanese–Israeli accord in defiance of US and Israeli power.[34]

Just as Egypt withdrew from the Arab–Israeli power balance, the 1979 Islamic revolution transformed Iran from a friend of Israel into a fiercely anti-Zionist state and potential Syrian ally. When Iraq attacked Iran, Asad condemned the invasion as diverting the Arabs from the Israeli menace. His stand with Iran was vindicated after the 1982 Israeli invasion of Lebanon when the dramatic effectiveness of the Iranian-sponsored Islamist resistance to Israel—out of which Hezbollah was born—helped foil a mortal threat to Syria. Asad's support for the Western-led war coalition in the Gulf War following Iraq's 1990 invasion of Kuwait was driven by the desire to contain the hostile Iraqi regime, but also by the perceived opportunity to trade membership in the anti-Iraq US coalition—whose credibility Syria's Arab nationalist credentials arguably enhanced—for US promises to broker an acceptable Arab–Israeli settlement after the war.[35] Hafiz entered the US-brokered Madrid peace process in the early 1990s and later, bilateral negotiations with Israel. The two sides came very close to a settlement, but Israel's demands to keep its surveillance station on Mount Hermon, 5 percent of the Golan, and control of the Sea of Galilee led to collapse of the negotiations in 2000 (Table 22.2).[36]

Foreign Policy Under Bashar al-Asad (2000–)

Bashar al-Asad inherited a deteriorating strategic situation: end of the peace negotiations with Israel, a new Turkish–Israeli alliance, and opposition to Syrian forces remaining in Lebanon following Israel's withdrawal from southern Lebanon in 2000. With the collapse of Syria's Soviet arms supplier, he could not sustain the conventional military balance with Israel. Asad affirmed that Syria was willing to resume peace negotiations if Israel accepted a full withdrawal to the June 4, 1967, borders on the Golan; but also supported Hizbullah operations against Israeli forces in southern Lebanon, as a way of pressuring Israel, and relied for deterrence on

TABLE 22.2 ■	The Conflict Between Syria and Israel: A Chronology
1948–1949	War in Palestine; Syrian irregulars and, later, regular forces participate
1955	Israeli attack on Syrian border positions inflames Syria's Arab nationalism
1965–1966	Jordan River waters dispute with Israel; Syrian-backed Palestinian guerrillas raid Israel
June 1967	Third Arab–Israeli war; Israel occupies Syrian Golan Heights
October 1973	Fourth Arab–Israeli war: Syria fails to recover Golan
May 1974	Henry Kissinger brokers Syrian–Israeli disengagement on the Golan
1981	Israel "annexes" Golan
1982	Israeli invasion of Lebanon; major clashes with Syrian troops
1984	Syria foils Israeli–Lebanese peace accord
July 1991	Syria enters Madrid peace negotiations with Israel
May 1996	Likud election victory in Israel dims Syrian–Israeli peace prospects
1999	The Election of Ehud Barak in Israel revives Syrian–Israeli peace prospects
2000	Asad–Clinton meeting marks breakdown of Israeli–Syrian peace negotiations
2006	Syria backs Hezbollah during the Hezbollah–Israeli war in Lebanon
2008	Turkish-brokered indirect peace talks between Syria and Israel fail
2011+	Israeli airstrikes against Hezbollah and Iranian forces in Syria punctuate the period of the Syrian uprising

Hezbollah's asymmetric warfare capability. He also sought to construct or strengthen compensating alliances, with Iran/Hezbollah but also former foes such as Saddam Hussein's Iraq.

This was all the more urgent as Syria's relations with the United States sharply deteriorated under George W Bush. After 9/11 Washington announced that all states not with the United States in its "war on terror" were foes; Syria, regarding groups on the US terrorism list—Palestinian militants and Hezbollah—as national liberation movements and "cards" in its struggle with Israel, evaded US demands that it cease support of them. Syrian–US relations further worsened as Syria reopened the closed oil pipeline with Iraq, allowing Saddam to circumvent sanctions, thereby gaining the Syrian treasury a badly needed windfall of a billion dollars yearly in oil revenues. At the UN and in the Arab League, Syrian diplomats attempted to delegitimize the looming 2003 US invasion of Iraq and following it, allowed resistance fighters to transit Syria's border into Iraq. After triumphing over Saddam Hussein, the United States upped the pressure on Syria which did end overt support for the resistance in Iraq. One cost of Syrian defiance of the United States was economic sanctions that obstructed aspects of the regime's economic liberalization by discouraging Western banks and companies from doing business in Syria. Another was the United States and French promoted an international tribunal to investigate Syria's alleged role in the assassination of former Lebanese Prime Minister Rafiq al-Hariri and their engineering of UNSC Resolution 1559 calling on Syria to withdraw its military forces from Lebanon, to which Syria reluctantly submitted. However, after Syrian withdrawal, Hezbollah effectively protected Syrian interests in Lebanon. As Syria faced isolation in the West, its links with similarly isolated Iran strengthened. Also, to compensate, Syria moved into close alignment with formerly hostile Turkey, ending the long dispute over Euphrates river water and Syrian sanctuary for the Kurdish PKK and joining a brief 2008 effort by Ankara to broker a peace with Israel.

A major consequence of Syria's stands in the Iraq and Lebanon conflicts was a shift in its regional alignments. Two axes emerged—a "moderate" one led by the United States including Saudi Arabia, Egypt, and Jordan, with Israel an unofficial partner, and a "resistance front" led by Iran and Syria, aligned with Hezbollah and Hamas and enjoying wide support in Arab public opinion, with Iraq, Lebanon, and Palestine the main battlegrounds.

The International Politics of the Uprising: From Proxy War to de Facto Partition

However, the 2011 uprising reshuffled the cards and unleashed a "New Struggle for Syria." Weakened by the uprising, Syria was turned from a pivotal actor in the regional power struggle into an arena for the struggle of external forces, largely via proxy wars that would end in the division of the country into the spheres of influence of external powers.

At stake in this struggle for Syria was the balance between the pro-Western "moderate" (and Sunni) axis and the Iran-led "Resistance Front." While the Syrian uprising was essentially indigenous, external forces sought from the beginning to use it to their advantage. Qatar used Al-Jazeera to amplify antiregime protests, while the Saudis funneled money and arms to antiregime tribes. An anti-Asad coalition, led by the United States, France, Saudi Arabia, Qatar, and Turkey, began financing, training, arming, and infiltrating insurgents into the country. As Syria became a partly failed state, it became a magnet for jihadis and al-Qa'ida militants, some funded or armed from the Gulf and assisted by Turkey. The Asad regime's only chance of slipping out of this tightening stranglehold was its links to "Shi'i" partners, Hezbollah in the West and, in the East, to Iraq and Iran. Meanwhile, Russia and China, antagonized by the West's use of a UN humanitarian resolution to promote regime change in Libya, protected Syria from a similar scenario.

In parallel, a diplomatic struggle over Syria took place, initially within the framework for settlement set by the Geneva Declaration of 2012 that prescribed a political transition involving power sharing, while remaining silent on the role of the incumbent president. The opposition's insistence on his departure and the regime's unwillingness to accept power sharing, the backing for their uncompromising positions by their respective regional patrons, and the unwillingness of their great powers patrons—the United States and Russia—to apply pressure on their clients to compromise led to paralysis of the Geneva process and diplomatic stalemate.

This only ended when the military stalemate on the ground was broken after the 2015 Russian intervention. Turkey, preoccupied with the threat of Syrian Kurdish presence on its borders, abandoned its anti-Asad stance, while Gulf states' support for the opposition gradually declined as they became preoccupied with other arenas (Yemen) and were divided by deepening Saudi–Qatar rivalry. The United States, and the West as a whole, had in parallel shifted their concern to the defeat of IS at the expense of removing Asad. This provided the conditions for Russia to back Asad's drive to subjugate opposition areas through siege and bombardment that forced them into various forms of truce involving de facto power sharing or the evacuation of militants unwilling to accept such "reconciliation" to Idlib, which became a militant redoubt outside Damascus's military control. Russia also brought Turkey and Iran into diplomatic efforts at Astana and then Sochi to reach a political settlement that would leave Asad in power and entail limited power sharing with the "acceptable" wing of the opposition.

Nevertheless, it soon became apparent that, far from the regime and its backers triumphing, enduring battlelines were hardening as several competing powers carved out spheres of geopolitical influence in the country. The first battleline in the northwest pitted regime forces against Islamist pro-Turkish forces buttressed by the Turkish army in a battle over Idlib and control of strategic highways adjacent to it. Idlib had become home to a dense concentration of militants intensely opposed to the regime and the Russians, many of them having been relocated from other conflict zones after regime sieges forced their surrender. There were 60–70,000 armed combatants, including 20,000 jihadists of al-Qaida offshoot, Hayat Tahrir al-Sham. Under a 2017 agreement at the Astana talks between Russia, Turkey, and Iran Idlib was designated a "deconfliction zone" for which Turkey would take responsibility; this enabled Turkey to establish a "protectorate" over the area which it used to settle Syrian refugees, establish its claim on Syria's future trajectory, and contain what it saw as a Kurdish threat on its borders. This was contested by a Syrian government offensive from December 2019 to mid-January 2020 in which Damascus regained some territory in the northwest until blocked by a Turkish counteroffensive, after which Russia brokered a cease-fire that left the status quo largely intact.

The second battleline was an Israeli–Iranian proxy war concentrated in the south but spilling as far northeast as Deir ez-Zor. Israel, fearing the delivery of upgraded Iranian missiles to Hezbollah, waged a campaign of hundreds of air strikes against targets in Syria. While Israel (and the United States) demanded Iran's full withdrawal from Syria, for Iran, its presence in Syria and Hezbollah's capabilities represented strategic depth in the regional power struggle and a deterrent against Israel. Russia tried to broker a compromise under which pro-Iranian forces would pull back from the borderlands near Israel, but this failed. Inspite of regular Israeli air attacks on Iranian-aligned forces which neither Iran, the regime nor Russia seemed able to deter, Iran remained dug into positions across regime-controlled Syria.

The third battleline was in the northeast where the war against IS drew the competing powers into a race to fill the vacuum as the territory controlled by IS contracted. With US air support, Kurdish-led "Syrian Democratic Forces" (SDF) irregulars pushed IS out of Raqqa and Hassakeh province and set out to govern these vast Arab-populated eastern provinces. In parallel, Asad regime forces with Iranian backing moved toward Deir ez-Zor, strategic for its oil fields and border crossing at Abu Kamal, in competition with the SDF; US attacks on progovernment forces when they advanced toward SDF positions and toward the country's eastern borders signaled Washingtons determination to prevent the Syrian government from reestablishing sovereignty over its eastern provinces; it and its Iranian-aligned allies had to be content with parts of the Deir ez-Zor province while the oil reserves fell into US and SDF hands.

Meanwhile, Turkey was outraged that the United States had employed Kurdish-led forces to retake Sunni Arab areas from IS, which, it believed, inflated Kurdish ambitions to establish a Kurdish state along its southern border. Turkey invaded and took over the Kurdish-run town of Afrin on the western extremity of Kurdish populated regions and Erdogan vowed to create a "security zone" inside Syrian territory along the whole border at the expense of the Kurds. The United States pulled its forces back from the Turkish border, allowing the Turkish army and its Syrian proxies (FSA units) to take control of a 20-mile-deep buffer zone between Tell Abyad and Ras al-Ain. This did not include border areas further East where the United States pull-back allowed Russian and Syrian government troops to be deployed, at Kurdish invitation, to prevent a full Turkish takeover of Syria's northern borderlands.

At the same time, the United States relocated its forces to bases further south in Deir ez-Zor and Hasakah provinces, enabling it to keep control of most of Syria's oil fields, to obstruct Iranian supply lines to Syria, and to prevent the Asad regime from reasserting control over its territory and the oil resources it needed for postwar rehabilitation of the country.

In parallel, Washington also moved to block international reconstruction funding for regime-controlled areas and agreed with the EU that they would provide no reconstruction funding without a political transition as specified in UNSC resolution 2254 of 2015. The Asad regime, having survived the military threat from the opposition, was not about to concede an effective regime change through political agreement and Russia seemed unprepared to pressure it into major concessions. The United States, therefore, upped the ante, using its dominance of the world financial system, to deploy secondary sanctions that punished any state or firm that invested in or did business with Syria. The effect was catastrophic for the Syrian economy, not only obstructing any reconstruction but also causing a sharp decline in the value of the Syrian currency and a dramatic worsening of living conditions for all Syrians (except regime insiders who were well positioned to evade and profit from sanctions).

The COVID pandemic hit Syria at a time when its healthcare system had been decimated by years of civil war. COVID mitigation measures contributed to economic decline, poverty, and food insecurity. It was also a factor in winding down the military dimensions of the conflict. While official statistics greatly undercounted infections (30,000) and deaths (3000), actual infections might have been 100,000 in Damascus alone, while the northeast was also badly hit. The pandemic exacerbated the misery of ordinary Syrians.

Thus, the struggle for Syria changed from a military contest into a battle over economic rehabilitation and reconstruction in which the United States sought to keep Syria a failed state that would make it a resource-draining burden for Russia and Iran, rather than an asset. This risked keeping Syria a black hole of instability damaging to its Middle Eastern and European neighbors, notably by preventing a return of refugees and generating further flows as the millions of Syrians living in the regime-controlled areas were deprived of all hope.

CONCLUSION

Hafiz al-Asad constructed a robust authoritarian regime that translated into enhanced Syrian statehood. Bashar al-Asad's effort to adapt this state to the post–Cold War age of globalization and his mismanagement of peaceful protests for political reform led to a civil war that cost Syria much of its previous achievements. After a decade of protest and then civil war, the balance of military power shifted to the Asad regime; but with a political settlement out of reach, the conflict froze into de facto territorial division and economic collapse that spelled failed statehood.

SUGGESTED READINGS

Abboud, Samer. *Syria*. London: Polity Press, 2015.

Drysdale, Alasdair. "Ethnicity in the Syrian Officer Corps: A Conceptualization." *Civilisations* (1979): 359–73. 29, no. 3/4

Haddad, Bassam. *Business Networks in Syria: The Political Economy of Authoritarian Resilience*. Stanford, CA: Stanford University Press, 2012.

Hinnebusch, Raymond. *Syria: Revolution from Above*. London: Routledge, 2001.

Hinnebusch, Raymond, and Imady Omar, eds. *The Syrian Uprising: Domestic Origins and Early Trajectory*. London: Routledge, 2018.

Hinnebusch, Raymond, and Zintl Tina, eds. *Syria from Reform to Revolt: Political Economy and International Relations*. Syracuse, NY: Syracuse University Press, 2015.

Kerr, Michael, and Larkin Craig, eds. *The Alawis of Syria: War, Faith and Politics in the Levant*. London: Hurst, 2015.

Perthes, Volker. *The Political Economy of Syria under Asad*. London: I. B. Taurus, 1995.

Phillips, Christopher. *The Battle for Syria: International Rivalry in the New Middle East*. New Haven and London: Yale University Press, 2016.

Pierret, Thomas. *Religion and State in Syria: The Syrian Ulama from Coup to Revolution*. Cambridge: Cambridge University Press, 2013.

Rabinovich, Itamar. *Syria Under the Ba'th, 1963–1966: The Army-Party Symbiosis*. New York, NY: Halstead Press, 1972.

Seale, Patrick. *Asad: The Struggle for the Middle East*. Berkeley, CA: University of California Press, 1988.

Seale, Patrick. *The Struggle for Syria*. New York, NY: Oxford University Press, 1965.

23 SUDAN

Liv Tønnessen

Sudan, officially the Republic of the Sudan, has had a complex and conflictual political history. Sudan has seen multiple armed conflicts. These have been between the North and South (which culminated in South Sudan's independence in 2011), but also within the North, as political and economic marginalization of some regions led to armed rebellion. Indeed, competition for economic resources (both oil and land) as well as ethnic, cultural, and religious divisions are basic ingredients of Sudan's conflictual history.

This chapter provides an overview of how Sudan's political economy has shaped, and been shaped by, these conflicts. It outlines Sudan's historical development, highlighting how Sudan fluctuated between military dictatorships and "democratic" or civil multiparty rule before the Islamist-Military regime of Omar al-Bashir, which ruled the country with suppressive measures for three decades from 1989 until 2019. It explores Sudanese resistance. Unlike many of its neighbors in the Middle East and North African region, Sudan has a rich history of nonviolent popular uprisings. These included the October Revolution in 1964, the April uprisings in 1985, and the uprisings in 2019 that brought an end to the al-Bashir regime. Finally, it considers the current governance and challenges facing Sudan. Until general elections in 2024, Sudan is set to have a hybrid transitional government, led by Prime Minister Abdallah Hamdok and with the Sovereign Council, made up of both civilian and military actors, including some of Bashir's old supporters from the military, as the official head of state. Economic crisis, counterrevolutionary movements, the COVID-19 pandemic, deep wounds from decades of armed conflict, and the strong political and economic position of military actors make transition to democracy demanding.

HISTORY OF STATE-BUILDING/FORMATION

Sudan's history of state formation is the story of two interrelated struggles. The first is the attempt to create a unified nation from socially diverse, distinct communities. The second, and related, has been the attempt to extend state control over vast territory.

Forging a National Identity

Before independence in 1956, Sudanese territory was home to a series of small political communities, some of which developed into sultanates and kingdoms. The country's early history is intertwined with the history of ancient Egypt. Ottoman-Egyptian rule was established through conquest in 1820–1821, following a pattern of economic marginalization and exploitation until 1824.[1] During that time, the South was subject to slave raids on the command of the Khedive of Egypt, Muhammed Ali who needed slaves for his army to conquer new territory.[2] Sudanese resisted: In 1885, a Sudanese Islamic revolutionary army led by Muhammad Ahmad Ibn Abd Allah, known as the Mahdi, entered Khartoum and beheaded British officer General Charles Gordon. In 1899, however, Egyptian rule in Sudan was restored but as part of the Anglo-Egyptian condominium. Darfur was only included into the Anglo-Egyptian condominium in 1916 as it remained a sultanate under the Madhi.[3]

The central state has had limited capacity to dominate the Sudan's vast territory. Thus, patron–client relationships as a means of state-building have been a dominant feature from the onset of British rule. Sudan was ruled as two Sudans during the Anglo-Egyptian condominium.[4] The British created an indirect rule which is known as Native Administration, where they governed through village sheikhs and tribal paramount chiefs.[5] This separation has been seen as an important root of recurring civil wars between the North and the South.[6]

The British recognized the importance of Sudanese involvement in government during the decolonization process through the Advisory Council for the Northern Sudan (ACNS). The ACNS consisted exclusively of Northern Sudanese elites and was made up mainly of representatives from two main Islamic sects in Sudan, the Khatmiya and the Ansar, which would later become the bases for the two largest political parties in independent Sudan, namely the Democratic Unionist Party (DUP) and the Umma Party (UP). The ACNS participated in the Sudan Administration Conference, which defined the steps toward national independence and self-government and resulted in the creation of a legislative assembly in 1948. Agreements signed in 1952–1953 defined the process that would bring Anglo-Egyptian rule to an end. Britain granted Sudan independence in 1956, and handed over political power to northern elites.[7]

From independence in 1956 until 2019, a small northern political elite dominated the state. This elite has been made up of mainly three Muslim Arab ethnic groups concentrated in the north along the Nile River; the Shayqiyya, Ja'aliin, and Danagla.[8] (Prime Minister Abdalla Hamdok, in office 2019-October 2021, a member of the Kenani from North Kordofan, is the first Sudanese leader from outside these ethnic groups.) Other ethnic groups, in the West of Darfur, East, and in the Nuba mountains have been as politically, economically, and culturally marginalized as the ethnic groups in South Sudan.[9] Thus, armed opposition to Khartoum has been a national issue and not fighting between the North and South. Two civil wars between the North and the South have taken place; the first from 1955 to 1972 and the second from 1983 until 2005. However, armed conflict also erupted in Darfur in 2003 and in the East from 1994 to 2006. All armed groups in Sudan have framed their struggles as a result of pervasive marginalization.[10]

Post-independence governments have sought to create a Sudanese national identity on the basis of Arab culture and Islam.[11] This nation-building was based on the wrongful assumption that Arab culture and language in combination with the Islamic religion were in tune with local interest and demands.[12] Since independence, the state thus used education to propagate an Arab-Islamic identity,[13] and during Sudan's longest authoritarian regime, Omar al-Bashir (1989–2019) implemented the "Civilization Project." This was a violent, ideological venture aimed at top-down Arabization and Islamization of the country. Imposing a conservative understanding of Islam on state and society, the al-Bashir regime centralized political authority at the expense of Sudan's marginalized regions, dominated the economy and state bureaucracy through nepotism, and created security and military organizations to suppress political opposition to the regime.[14] These Arabization policies accompanied the emergence of an ideology which dictated Arab racial supremacy, which manifested itself most clearly in the Darfur conflict.[15] Hassan al-Turabi, who is regarded as the main ideologue of the Islamist movement and mastermind behind the 1989 coup d'etat, was frozen out of the regime in 1999. The policies became less ideologically founded and more pragmatic in its orientation, especially with regards to its economic policies and with regards to negotiating peace.[16] In general, however, these attempts failed to build a sense of nationalism among the diverse ethnic, cultural, and regional groups.[17]

Territorial Control, Civil Wars, and Countless Peace Agreements

Sudan's state-building history has also been characterized by complex armed conflict, or "interlocking civil wars."[18] The causes are multiple and often interlinked. They range from being resource-based (oil, gold, land), to religion, ethnicity, and culture. Regional actors as well as the international dimension also play a role.[19]

Already on the eve of its independence from Britain, Sudan was plunged into prolonged violent conflict that is still raging. The British deprived South Sudan of its share of power, which led to the first civil war, named "Anyanya."[20] Underdevelopment and political, economic, and cultural marginalization of the South sparked a demand for regional autonomy among southern rebel groups. The Addis Ababa peace agreement was signed in 1973 and ended the first civil war and, furthermore, granted South Sudan regional autonomy.

Sudan's second civil war erupted when Jafaar Nimeiri abrogated the Addis Ababa Agreement in 1983, declaring that revenues from oil recently discovered in the South were to accrue to the central government, rather than to the South. Nimeiri had come to power in 1969 as a socialist, but later recast himself as an Islamist. Thus, in 1983, Nimeiri also imposed sharia law, further marginalizing Sudanese in the South. In response, southerners launched their own state-building project, opposing the central government's Islamization and Arabization policies. Southern grievances resulted in the establishment of the Sudan People's Liberation Army and the related Sudan People's Liberation Movement (SPLM/A), a rebel group led by Dr. John Garang until his death in 2005. Repeated peace initiatives during the 1990s were gridlocked over the relationship between religion and the state. During these years, Islamic terminology such as *jihad* and martyrdom became essential features of the government's official discourse on the war against the South.[21]

But the East also witnessed war, often termed the forgotten conflict of Sudan. In 1993, the Beja Congress (BC), which had formed in 1958, joined the National Democratic Alliance (NDA) based in Asmara, Ethiopia. This was an umbrella organization that brought together parties committed to ending the hegemony of Arab, Muslim, and Northern elites in Khartoum. They rallied around the slogan of a "New Sudan," which would bring an end to decades of marginalization. In 1994, it began an armed rebellion against Bashir. In 2005, the BC joined the Rashaida Free Lions and together they established what is known as the Eastern Front.[22] This conflict, similar to Sudan's civil wars, was the result of a political and economic marginalization (described in more detail below). Political tensions between Sudan and Eritrea also played a role.[23]

In 2005, the Bashir regime and SPLM/A signed the Comprehensive Peace Agreement (CPA). Peace talks had started in the early 2000s under the auspice of the Intergovernmental Authority on Development under Kenyan leadership, supported by a "Troika" of the United States, United Kingdom, and Norway.[24] The CPA established a one-state, two-system rule, in which the North imposed sharia law while the South remained secular, and it eventually led to South Sudan's independence in 2011. A year later, the Eastern Sudan Peace Agreement (ESPA) was signed. Although the peace agreement ended the armed violence, it did not successfully bring an end to the historical marginalization of the East.

Although in the short term, the CPA resolved the war between the North and the South, and the ESPA the conflict in the East, but these were not comprehensive solutions.[25] The piecemeal approach to peacemaking failed to address the fundamental issue of the center's marginalization of the periphery.[26] Framing the CPA as between a unified North and a unified South excluded the voices of other marginalized peripheries which eventually drove some of them towards armed rebellion. For example, these frustrations contributed to the outbreak of war in Darfur in 2003 between the government and the two rebel groups, the Sudan Liberation Army/ Movement and the Justice and Equality Movement.

The Darfuri armed groups rebelled against what they regarded as the Sudanese government's continuous marginalization of the region and its non-Arab population. They published the *Black Book: Imbalance of Power and Wealth in Sudan*.[27] The book provides statistical evidence of how the riverine elite centered in Greater Khartoum had divided the North along racial lines. The book provided an explanation and rationale for political conflict both within Darfur and against the central government. Nationally, the roots of this conflict, as in the case of the long conflict between North and South, lie in the domination of a small Muslim Arab and northern political elite who have concentrated resources in Khartoum, at the expense of the country's peripheral and marginalized areas. The government used the Arab militia called Janjaweed, which has later been institutionalized under the Sudanese Army as the RSF, to target civilians in notorious operations of ethnic cleansing, including widespread and systematic rape against women of African descent to make "Arab" babies. A Darfur Peace Agreement was signed in 2006.[28] In 2009, the International Criminal Court (ICC) charged several individuals, including ex-president Bashir, for war crimes, crimes against humanity, and genocide in Darfur. Another attempt at peace was made with the Doha Agreement in 2011, but it was ultimately unsuccessful.

After South Sudan's secession in 2011, Africa's youngest nation-state descended into a civil war of its own. Although the North acknowledged South Sudan as an independent nation, unresolved issues concerning the border where oil resources are located led to the outbreak of violence almost immediately after the split in 2012. The loss of oil revenues combined with the large spending on military and police to sustain repression and armed conflicts in many parts of Sudan eventually led to economic crisis. The popular uprising, sparked by rising prices of basic commodities, led to the downfall of the Islamist arm of the regime in April 2019. However, the military is still in position of power in Sudan's transitional government (2019–24). A major concern of the transitional government has been to secure peace. In 2020, it negotiated peace with

10 rebel groups known as the Juba Peace Agreement. This included a roadmap to end the armed conflict in Darfur and to cooperation with the ICC.[29] The five geographic regions or "tracks" are Northern, Eastern, Darfur, Central, and Two Areas which refer to two border areas between Sudan and South Sudan.[30] However, there are major rebel groups which have refused to sign the peace deal. There have also been protests, especially in east Sudan, that the agreement fails to address the root causes of marginalization and conflict.

KEY FACTS ABOUT SUDAN

AREA: 718,723 sq mi; 1,861,484 sq km

CAPITAL: Khartoum

POPULATION: 46,751,152 (2021 est.)

PERCENTAGE OF POPULATION UNDER 25: 62.95% (2020 est.)

RELIGIOUS GROUPS: Sunni Muslim, small Christian minority

ETHNIC GROUPS (PERCENTAGE): Unspecified Sudanese Arab, approx. 70%; other, 30% (including Fur, Beja, Nuba, Fallata)

OFFICIAL LANGUAGE: Arabic and English

TYPE OF GOVERNMENT: Presidential republic[32]

DATE OF UNIFICATION: January 1, 1956 (from the Anglo-Egyptian condominium)

GDP (PPP): $176.63 Billion (2017 est.)

GDP (NOMINAL): $40.53 Billion (2017 est.)

GDP (PER CAPITA): $3,958 (2019 est.)

PERCENTAGE OF GDP BY SECTOR: Agriculture: 39.6% (2017 est.), industry: 2.6% (2017 est.), services: 57.8% (2017 est.)

TOTAL RENTS (PERCENTAGE OF GDP) FROM NATURAL RESOURCES: 5.842% (2019 est. World Bank)

FERTILITY RATE: 4.66 children per woman (2021 est.)

Sources: CIA. "The World Factbook." August 4, 2022, https://www.cia.gov/the-world-factbook/. World Bank. "International Comparison Program (ICP)." Accessed August 10, 2022, https://databank. worldbank.org/source/icp-2017.

POLITICAL ECONOMY

Sudan's political economy is based on agriculture and oil. Historically, agriculture is the main source of income and employment; it currently provides for more than 60 percent of the population. Oil is Sudan's main export, and represents around 90 percent of Sudan's total exports from 2004 to 2008.[31] Oil wealth in Sudan has neither been used to invest into other sectors of the economy such as agriculture nor been invested wisely to develop the country, however.[32] Rather, it has been a driver of armed conflict, nurtured patronage networks and corruption, and economically empowered elites with close ties to the Military-Islamist dictatorship of Bashir.

OIL, CONFLICT, AND SECESSION OF SOUTH SUDAN

Oil has been intricately connected to the conflict in Sudan. First oil has shaped the conflict. The oil fields are located primarily in South Sudan, and during the civil war, armed groups targeted oil pipelines, since they helped keep the regime in power. Oil has fed into practices of militarization under the Bashir regime.[33] Government spending kept increasing during "the oil decade" between 1999 and 2011, but defense, security, and the police received the bulk of the budget.

Oil also has motivated the regime to genuinely engage in peace negotiations in the hope of reaping economic benefits.[34] Sudan's oil adventure started with the American oil company Chevron soon after the first civil war between the North and the South that ended with the Addis Ababa peace accord in 1972. This was during the regime of Jafaar Nimeri (1969–85) who welcomed stronger diplomatic relations with the United States. However, Chevron pulled out when the civil war resumed in 1983. With worsening diplomatic relations after the Islamist coup d'état in 1989 and American economic sanctions since the 1990s, Sudan was forced to look elsewhere for partners in oil production. When new peace talks between the North and the South were initiated, China emerged as a significant partner. Economic sanctions on Sudan did little to deter Chinese companies hoping to benefit from Sudanese oil.[35]

Peace agreements have also had a direct impact on oil. Oil has been connected to the North–South conflict, and thus the CPA between the SPLM/A and the Government of Sudan in 2005 included an agreement on wealth sharing that had ramifications for the country's oil revenues. The South's separation from the North in 2011 had an even greater impact on oil. The secession meant

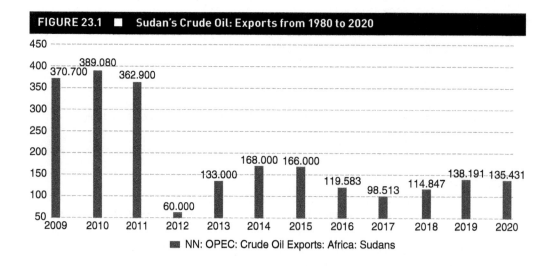

FIGURE 23.1 ■ Sudan's Crude Oil: Exports from 1980 to 2020

NN: OPEC: Crude Oil Exports: Africa: Sudans

that Sudan immediately lost 75 percent of its oil revenues, initiating a dramatic economic decline. As a result, Sudan saw depreciation of the Sudanese pound and the need to resort to the lifting on subsidies on basic commodities. These, in turn, sparked antiregime protests in 2012 and 2013.

With South Sudan in control of most of the oil production but Sudan in control of essential export routes and processing facilities, the two countries have strong economic reasons to collaborate. Although in 2012 renewed conflict between the two countries broke out based on the fair division of oil revenues,[36] an agreement was negotiated between the two countries. At the time, oil prices were high, granting Sudan a set price for exporting oil through its pipelines at 25 USD per oil barrel. Since then, oil prices fell internationally, and at the time of this writing, South Sudan is receiving the lowest price ever for its oil. Oil production has further fallen due to the outbreak of a civil war in South Sudan in 2013. All of this has had negative impacts on the economies of both Sudan and South Sudan.[37]

KHARTOUM'S OVEREXPLOITATION OF SUDAN'S REGIONS

Although the Sudanese economy was booming in the years before South Sudan's secession in 2011, it failed to convert oil revenues into robust investment in public education, health, and infrastructure. Indeed, Sudan's 2019 Human Development Index (HDI) is below the average for countries in the low human development group. Yet, there is also great variation in development across regions.

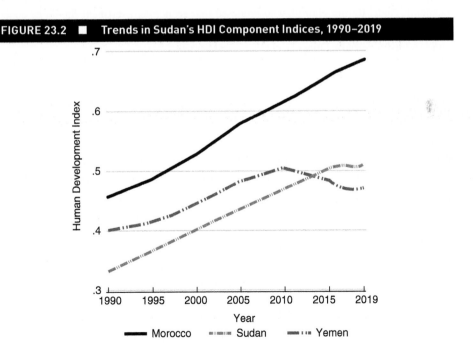

FIGURE 23.2   ■   Trends in Sudan's HDI Component Indices, 1990–2019

The states along the Nile, including the capital of Khartoum, rank considerably higher on key indicators of human development compared to the marginalized conflict prone areas of Darfur, Eastern Sudan, and Southern Sudan before secession which rank among the lowest globally.[38] Major parts of the country are marginalized, impoverished, and suffer repeated emergencies including famines. An estimated 7.3 million people in Sudan are food insecure,[39] with levels of children malnourishment in Sudan among the highest in the world. International aid has contributed to the postcolonial state's exclusionary development processes as it has continued to provide food to Sudan's impoverished regions. Meanwhile, the state has done nothing to get Sudan onto a new path and redistribute its resources so that food security becomes a reality.[40]

The overexploitation of Sudan's regions is not new to the Bashir regime. In fact, it has a long trajectory and can be traced back to Sudan's colonial economy.[41] British colonists initiated projects in and around Khartoum, including setting up the Gezeira irrigation scheme, the world's largest at the time, to cultivate cotton for export. Little was done elsewhere, resulting in gross economic disparities between Sudan's regions.

Not much changed during the postcolonial period. State's policies have exploited and displaced people. For example, the Unregistered Land Act of 1970 abolished customary land use and ownership, by stipulating that land slots which are not privately owned would automatically be the property of the state. This practice has been continuously used by political rulers in their mission to modernize agriculture. This led to land dispossession, impoverishment, and displacement of large populations that in turn gave rise to conflict in several parts of the country.[42] The disparities in economic development accelerated during the regime of Bashir.[43] This was illustrated by the emergence of the Hamdi triangle. Named after a minister of Finance and Economic Abdel Rahim Hamdi, who proposed that economic investment should be concentrated in places within a day's drive of the capital, it refers to the development within the triangular region bordered by Dongola, el Obeid, and Sennar.

NEPOTISM, CORRUPTION, AND THE ECONOMIC POSITION OF THE SECURITY AND MILITARY

The Islamists initiated a comprehensive *tamkeen policy*, Arabic for "consolidation of power," which entailed the penetration of the military, civil service, and the economy. This entailed mass dismissals of civil servants following the appointment of Islamist loyalists, as well as the president's family members and ethnic group, to positions of power.[44] It also led to a downgrading of skills in the civil service whereby regime loyalists were put in place regardless of their skills, qualifications, and experience, and those with skills, edged out of their positions, emigrated, primarily to the Gulf. A largely merit-based civil service was thereby replaced with regime loyalists and also other government institutions were affected by nepotism. With an increasingly educated youth, about 65 percent of the total population, there was growing dissatisfaction with a regime in which loyalty triumphed merit.[45]

The economic *tamkeen* policy basically entailed a process of privatizing state-owned companies to regime loyalists and their kin at bargain prices. Islamist businesses enjoyed privileges such as exemptions from taxes. Instead of distributing state contracts through public

MAP 23.1 ■ Map of Sudan

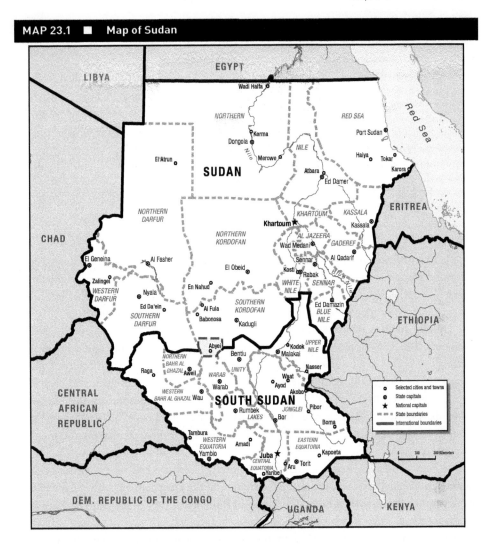

procurement, regime loyalists were prioritized. This negatively affected the market economy. Companies owned by the regime and its loyalists controlled the economy and used the wealth to buy political support. This included a systematic and increasing involvement of both Sudan Armed Forces (SAF) and National Intelligence and Security Services (NISS) in economic and business activities.[46]

Paramilitary forces also gained important economic power during the Bashir era. In 2012, large gold reserves were discovered in Darfur, but 90% of the gold was located in conflict areas largely controlled by the paramilitary group Janjaweed. After the loss of oil revenues alongside South Sudan's secession, it became Sudan's primary source of hard currency. It constitutes 40 percent of the country's exports. The Janjaweed militia were instrumental in the Darfur genocide, and then formally incorporated into the Sudanese army in 2013 under the name Rapid Support Forces (RSF).[47]

TABLE 23.1 ■ Transparency International's 2019 Corruption Perceptions Index		
Highest Scores	Seychelles	66/100
	Botswana	61/100
	Cabo Verde	58/100
Lowest Scores	Sudan	16/100
	South Sudan	12/100
	Somalia	9/100

Source: Data from Transparency International.

Note: 49 African countries were assessed and the average regional score was a 32/100.

As a consequence of three decades of nepotism and kleptocracy, Sudan is considered one of the world's most corrupt countries.[48] Sudan ranks 173 out of 180 in Transparency International's 2019 Corruption Perceptions Index (Table 23.1). After Bashir's removal from office, he was prosecuted for corruption and sentenced to two years in a social reform facility.[49]

Despite Bashir's removal from office, the military and security still control Sudan's economy. The RSF has monopolized the gold mining industry, and they and other military actors have stakes in a number of businesses involved in the export and import of a number of goods such as oil, gold, gum arabic, sesame, weapons, fuel, wheat, and cars. They are also involved in a range of other businesses, such as telecommunications, banking, water distribution, and real estate. The security sector even controls the firm that produces Sudan's banknotes. There is little public information about these companies and their corrupt practices.[50]

Moreover, they are firmly entrenched in power. Currently half of the members of the Sovereign Council acting as the head of state during the transition are from SAF and RSF, with commander in-chief of SAF Abdelfattah El Burhan and RSF Mohamed Hamdan Daglo at the forefront. Their strong economic position, and the entanglement of economic interests, state nepotism, and corrupt practices, means they have vested interests in maintaining political power. What is described as the deep state may pose serious obstacles to Sudan's transition to civilian rule.

CHANGES AND CHALLENGES IN SOCIETY

Demographic Changes

Sudan's society is ethnically, linguistically, and religiously diverse. The census of 1955, conducted when Sudan was the largest African country,[51] representing more than eight percent of the African continent, showed that Sudan was home to at least 570 ethnic groups. In broad terms, these ethnic groups could be regrouped into six categories: those of Arab descent (40 percent); southerners (30 percent); westerners, including mainly non-Arab parts of Darfur and South Kordofan (13 percent), Nubaians from the Nuba mountains in Southern Kordofan (six percent); the Beja of eastern Sudan (six percent), and Nubians of northern Sudan (three percent).[52] In terms of regional concentration, the Arabs formed the majority in central and northern parts of Sudan, while other groups were concentrated in the marginalized, impoverished, and conflict-prone regions.[53] The overwhelming majority of Sudanese are Muslim, but non-Muslim southerners still reside in the North and some have assumed citizenship. In addition, there are Coptic Orthodox and Greek Orthodox Christians, albeit small, in Khartoum, El Obeid in North Kordofan, River Nile, Gezira, and parts of eastern Sudan.

The political elites who dominated postindependence Sudan have never considered this ethnic diversity to be a strength. As discussed above, the largely Arab Muslim elites institutionalized racial hierarchies, where those of African descent were placed at the very bottom. Racial slurs have been commonplace, including the word slave for southerners and other ethnic groups of African descent. There is a strong societal preference for light skin rather than dark skin because dark skin is associated with the legacy of slavery and Africaness. (Skin bleaching is a common practice in the country.) Thus, due to these forms of marginalization, diversity has led to conflict and strife.

Sudan's population has been growing steadily despite reoccurring wars in different parts of the country. The population is growing fastest in urban centers, and Sudan is globally among one of the fastest urbanizing countries. Urbanization has been driven by collapse of rural economy coupled with conflict and natural disasters like floods and famines. Sudan is among the countries notorious for having the largest number of internally displaced persons (IDPs). However, internal displacement has decreased, especially after the secession of South Sudan.[54] At one point, however, Sudan hosted largest number of internally displaced persons (IDPs) in the world. In 2009, the country hosted almost five million IDPs.[55] (Currently, there are about 2.5 million IDPs in Sudan.)

Khartoum is growing the most. At independence the population in Khartoum was estimated at 250,000 to an estimated 2,831,000 in 1993 to between 4.5 million to 7 by 2005, depending on whether you rely on official or unofficial estimates. Historically, migration to Khartoum was seasonal, something which meant that migrants often returned to their areas of origin. But the reasons for migration have changed and now it is mainly a response to war, natural disasters, and economic despair. Just as economic resources are increasingly concentrated at the center (at the expense of the regions of course), people move to Khartoum with a hope of a better life.

INSTITUTIONS AND GOVERNANCE

Sudan has witnessed alternation between civilian and military regimes. The country saw multiparty parliamentary rule (1953–1958, 1964–1969, and 1985–1989) and military dictatorships (1958–1964, 1969–1985, and 1989–2019),[56] and is currently in a military–civilian transitional government after the 2019 popular uprising which ousted the military dictator Omar al-Bashir.[57] To date, however, neither the civilian nor military regimes are able to resolve the fundamental problems of political stability

Given its democratic periods, Sudan has held many elections since independence, and the right to vote for women was introduced in 1965. However, these elections had serious short-comings. In particular, they excluded large parts of the Southern Sudanese population.[58] Until 2008, a plurality voting system was utilized whereby candidates were elected in single-member districts, on the first-past-the-post basis. After that a new electoral law introduced elements of proportional representation and a reserved seats quota for women. Against the backdrop of per-petual armed conflict , it comes as no surprise that the establishment of democratic institutions has met obstacles.[59]

The common element across the regimes, and obstacle to governance in Sudan, has been that both parliamentary and military regimes have been based on a minority of urban-based elites in Khartoum.[60] This rivalry among Khartoum's Northern, Muslim, and Arab elites has been described as a game of musical chairs in competing for state office.[61] Weak political institutions combined with sectarian politics dominated the postindependence era until the military coup d'état in 1969. For most of Sudan's history, military dictatorships have ruled the country: first under Nimeiri and later under Bashir. A common feature between them was the attempt to destroy the traditional sectarian political parties and their support base and instead impose socialism and Islamism as ideologies through which Sudan will build a united nation and state. [62]

The first era of civilian rule began in 1953 through a parliamentary election. However, at this point in time the political parties can be described as loose alliances based in the religious sects and its leaders were motivated largely by personal interests. At that time Sudan was mov-ing toward independence which was later proclaimed by the parliament in 1956. From the 1953 elections until July 1956, Ismail al-Azhari became Sudan's first prime minister and was, thus, instrumental in achieving Sudan's independence. The National Unionist Party (later renamed into the DUP) of which al-Azhari was the secretary general, won the elections with the sup-port base in the Khatmiyya sect. From July 1956 until November 1958 a new government was headed by Abdallah Khalil, secretary general of the UP, enjoying the support of the Ansar sect.

Late in 1958, a bloodless military coup d'état by General Ibrahim Abbud dissolved major political institutions. The first period of military rule lasted from 1958 to 1964. At first, General Abbud seemed to bring needed stability to Sudan. However, he became increasingly dictato-rial as his policies. Abbud attempted to bring an end to the civil war by military victory and only escalated the conflict.

In 1964, a popular uprising led to the fall of the Abboud regime and the restoration of a civilian parliamentary system. The outcome of the elections was a foregone conclusion. Of the 173 seats in parliament, the UP gained 76 and the DUP 54; thus, neither could rule without the other's support. At the same time, none of the so-called ideological parties—the communists or the Muslim Brothers, who gained eleven and five seats, respectively—were strong enough to have a meaningful effect on policy. The UP and DUP were no more effective than they had been in the 1950s in finding solutions to Sudan's social or economic problems, or in bringing an end to the civil war. As before, parliamentary government was characterized by factional disputes. As a result, another group of soldiers promised to end the chaos created by the politicians and took over the government in May 1969.

The new military regime was led by Jaafar Nimeiri, who remained in power until 1985. At various times during the second era of military rule, the old patterns seemed to have been broken. In 1972, Nimeiri was able to negotiate peace by recognizing special autonomy for the South. In the mid-1970s, there was much discussion that Sudan might become the "breadbasket of the Arab world," and large amounts of capital began to flow into economic development. Nimeiri was committed to a relatively radical program, defined in terms of Arab socialism. Through the Sudanese Socialist Union (SSU), he attempted to create a new style of political organization that would replace the traditional sectarian parties, and he hoped that the new ideology of Socialism would provide the basis for a national identity. However, at the beginning of the 1980s, Nimeiri reignited the civil war when he began a program of Islamization referred to as the "September Laws." Active opposition was organized in the South by SPLM/A, and it subsequently grew in the North as the growing costs of the civil war created a major economic crisis.

Mass civil demonstrations undermined the military regime, as they had in 1964. Military autocracy and the inability to resolve the basic issues of national unity and the economy opened the way for another restoration of parliamentary rule. The transition to parliamentary rule was handled by a Transitional Military Council (TMC) led by General Abdul Rahman Siwar Dhahab. The TMC was a group of high-ranking officers that overthrew Nimeiri in April 1985, promising elections and the restoration of civilian rule in a year. The pledge was kept, and elections in the spring of 1986 returned the old political parties to control of Sudan. The SPLM did not participate in the transition, charging that the new government was only continuing Nimeiri's policies in a new format.[63]

However, the restored parliamentary government was more a repetition of the 1960s than a continuation of Nimeiri's regime. The major parties, and even many of the leaders, were those who had been active in the earlier era. The Prime Minister was Sadiq Mahdi, the leader of the UP. Unfortunately, the new government was ineffective and unable to reform the economy. A continually shifting coalition of parties provided little political stability.[64] Some negotiations had taken place with the SPLM/A, but the civil war continued. In this context, a group of officers again declared that Sudan had to be saved from the politicians, and on June 30, 1989, Sudan returned to military rule. This regime built on an Islamist ideology and stayed in power for 30 years until a new popular uprising started in December 2018.[65]

The uprising led to the fall of Bashir and the declaration of a new order. The 2019 constitutional charter presents a roadmap for Sudan's transition to democracy. According to this roadmap, the military-civilian transitional government is to be replaced by an elected government in 2024. Although hopes are high for a successful transition to democracy, Sudan continues to be one of the world's most fragile states.[66]

Political Parties

Political parties in Sudan are closely related to sectarian bases. Most Sudanese Muslims had traditionally belonged to one of the major Sufi sects in the country. The two largest are the

Ansar sect which was led by the al-Mahdi family and the Khatmiyya sect led by the al-Mirghani family. Historically, the Ansar has had its constituencies in the West and the Khatmiyya in the East. It was upon this Islamic sectarian basis that state–society relations took shape and political parties are built.[67] The Ansar and the Khatmiyya founded the two most dominant parties, the Umma Party (UP) and the National Union Party (which later became the Democratic Union Party, DUP). Each of the parties had and still has a strong Islamic sectarian base.

The UP was established in 1945, more than a decade before independence. The party is currently led by Miraim al-Sadiq al-Mahdi, the daughter of the long-term leader of the party and imam of the Ansar Sadiq al-Mahdi, who had served as prime minister from 1966 to 1967 and again from 1986 to 1989. Although the Ansar were found throughout Sudan, the group's main support base was found in western Darfur and Kordofan.[68] Since Sudan's independence, the UP has experienced political success during the short periods of civilian rule and political persecution during the periods of military reign. The political party is not secular: it has a support basis in the Ansar and roots going back to Muhammad Ahmad al-Mahdi, known as the Mahdi, who is the great-grandfather of Sadiq al-Mahdi. Under the banner of Sharia, the Mahdi led a successful revolution against Turco-Egyptian rule in Sudan from 1881 to 1885. Muhammad Ahmad Abdullah proclaimed himself to be the Mahdi, or leader, sent by God to establish justice and God's will on earth.[69]

The DUP, the other major political party, has a similar tie to a religious organization, the Khatmiyyah Order. A Muslim organization led by the Mirghani family, the Khatmiyyah Order had roots in popular Muslim devotional revivalism in the early 19th century. It has never been so directly political as its rival, the Mahdist movement, but when party politics began during the Anglo-Egyptian condiminium, the Mirghanis gave their support to a nationalist party that advocated unity with Egypt.

The UP and the DUP are northern Sudanese political parties that have dominated civilian politics. However, their mass support is not directly related to the performance of these parties; rather, it depends on the prior loyalty of Islamic sect. As a result, civilian politics after long periods of military rule has typically resulted in the recreation of sectarian politics. However, the 2010 general elections showed that the DUP—like UP—suffered both from internal factionalism and from an erosion of its traditional base.[70]

Deep sectarian rivalry between the Ansar and the Khatmiyya has historically characterized Islam in Sudan's political process, but the emergence of communism and Islamism at the political scene challenged the sectarian nature of Muslim politics in Sudan. These include, most notably, the Sudanese Communist Party and the Muslim Brotherhood. Both, however, are dominated by riverine elites based in Khartoum, particularly at the University of Khartoum.[71]

The Sudanese Communist party (SCP) was established in 1946. It built important ties to the developing trade union movement and had significant support among educated Sudanese. During the 1960s, the SCP was the largest communist party in Africa, although it never became a mass party. Adhering to Marxist ideology, the party did not reject a role played by religion.[72] Women members of the communist party organized the League of Sudanese Women in 1946, the same year the SCP was established and made women's emancipation part of its main goals. The SCP became Sudan's first political party to allow women members, doing so in 1946 before its traditional sectarian counterparts even considered it.[73] The gender ideology of the party did not address women's subordination and issues like violence against women and equality within family law, however.[74] Communists played an important role in the early years of the Nimeiri regime, but the party was harshly suppressed after a group of leftist officers with communist connections attempted to overthrow Nimeiri in the summer of 1971. The SCP joined the other civilian parties in opposition and was then active in the parliamentary politics of the 1980s. However, during the regime of Bashir the SCP was severely suppressed, and many of its cadres went into exile.

The Muslim Brotherhood (MB) became another "non-sectarian" political force in Sudanese politics. Like the SCP, the MB emerged as a political grouping of educated Sudanese in Khartoum, but advocated a program of strict adherence to Islam and the implementation of the sharia in Sudan. The Sudanese MB was founded in the end of the 1940s as an independent student organization at the University of Khartoum. In 1964, Hasan al-Turabi who emerged as the main ideologue and mastermind behind the coup d'état in 1989, was pivotal in establishing the first Islamist political party in Sudan. The Islamic Charter Front (ICF) was founded in October 1964 with Turabi as secretary general. The most important item on the agenda for the ICF was comprehensive Islamization of Sudan's laws and lobbying for an Islamic constitutions guided by sharia.[75] The fiercest competitor in advocating a viable alternative to the status quo was the SCP, and thus, Turabi increasingly emphasized women's rights, partly in an effort to compete with the communists.[76] In the process of developing into a political party, the Islamists spearheaded by Turabi gradually became stronger as they interacted with the political system.[77]

The May 1969 coup d'état of Nimeiri began as a left-oriented affair, but his regime ended up veering in the opposite direction and adopting sharia. After a process of national reconciliation, Turabi and the Isamists were included into the government, and the Islamization of the legal system in Sudan was initiated in 1983 with the September Laws.[78] The ICF was renamed the National Islamic Front (NIF) and, under the leadership of Turabi, cooperated with the Nimeiri dictatorship from 1977 to 1985 and afterwards with the civilian government until the Islamists seized power through a military coup d'état (against a government in which they themselves participated) in 1989.

This coup marked a radical ideological shift. The initial goal of the MB during the 1940s and 1950s had been to Islamize from below; now, the strategy was one of Islamization from above through the capture of state power. From 1999, the NCP was established and became the ruling party, meanwhile the Popular National Congress joined the opposition. The Bashir regime's response to the 2013 protests, internal calls for reform coupled with Bashir's decision to run for election in 2015, further fragmented Islamists. A group of core Islamists led by Gazi Salaheldin deserted the ruling party and formed the Reform Now Party.[79] The NCP has been banned by the transitional government and other Islamist forces isolated. The Islamist political parties that were in opposition to Bashir are likely to be allowed to run for elections again in 2024.

SPLM emerged as the only political party with an explicit secular agenda and with leadership and member base outside of the Arab and Muslim constituencies. Southern political groups have emerged in the context of civil war. The SPLM, under the leadership of the late John

Garang, was the strongest organization speaking for the formal recognition of the religious and ethnic diversity of the peoples of Sudan. Officially, the SPLM has called for the establishment of a secular democratic state and the end of what it sees as Arab and Muslim hegemony.[80] After the secession of South Sudan in 2011, SPLM under the leadership of Salwa Kiir became the ruling political party and the SPLA transformed into the country's armed forces. The Sudan branch of the movement established itself as SPLM-North and was based in the states bordering the new Southern neighbor, still working for a secular Sudan in which ethnic and religious diversity is recognized.[81]

During the transitional period (2019–24), several new political parties have emerged. Bashir was to a large extent successful in destroying the traditional political parties in Sudan, but added to that there is a new generation of youth who have been completely disillusioned with these old traditional political parties and demand a new vision for building Sudan as a nation going forward. The death of two major political figures, Hasan al-Turabi in 2016 and Sadiq al-Mahdi in 2020, might signal a new political era in Sudan. If Sudan goes back to politics as usual, then at least it will be without them.

ACTORS, OPINION, AND POLITICAL PARTICIPATION

As noted above, Sudanese are no strangers to political engagement. They have engaged in political parties and elections, but also have a long history of participation through civil society movements and uprisings.

Civil Society

The beginning of the civil society in Sudan can be traced back to groups that resisted British colonial rule. These included trade unions, which have been instrumental in Sudan's many successful popular uprisings. The Graduates' Congress, established in 1938, led the resistance against the colonial authorities until 1956 when Sudan became independent.[82] The Sudanese Women's Union (SWU) was established already in 1952 as one of the main civil society organizations of its time, calling for women's political empowerment. In 1965, it had branches throughout the country and considerable gains in women's rights had been gained in terms of women's rights to vote and stand for election, equal pay for equal work, and the right to maternity leave. In addition, its president, Fatima Ibrahim, was the first woman elected to parliament in Sudan and in the Arab world more generally.[83] Trade unions have also historically been influential in Sudan, beginning during the country's anticolonial struggle.[84] After independence, trade unions have been instrumental in overthrowing the military dictatorships of Ibrahim Abboud in 1964, Nimeiri in 1985, and Bashir in 2019. [85]

For the most part, northern civil society organizations and NGOs have operated in Khartoum, whereas their southern counterparts remained mostly Nairobi-based and affiliated with SPLM/A. Many civil society organizations emerged in the context drought, famine, and civil war. In addition, large numbers of international NGOs and relief agencies arrived, directing their efforts to serving the victims. [86]

Civil society organizations have also been subject to periods of repression. Following the 1989 coup, all trade unions and NGOs were dissolved. This disrupted and destroyed the vibrant civil society that was starting to emerge in Sudan from 1985 to 1989 and effectively silenced opposition to Bashir's rule, including the media.[87] With the peace process, civil society gradually re-emerged. In addition to the opportunities that the peace process presented to organize freely, receiving money from international donors made a huge difference.[88] However, Sudanese civil society was largely excluded from the peace process that led to the signing of the CPA, which was made into an internal affair between the Bashir regime and SPLM/A only.[89] The 2005 CPA allocated some political space to civil society, resulting in an explosion of NGOs, including human rights groups, and women's groups were particularly vocal in demanding legal reform of a series of discriminatory laws codified in the name of sharia by Bashir's regime.[90] Yet, while the CPA allocated some space for political opposition, a series of laws have been enacted to severely restricted civil society's room for maneuver. The Voluntary and Humanitarian Work Act of 2006 imposes severe restrictions on both international and national NGOs, and has resulted in the expulsion of several international organizations and the shutting down of national ones.. Moreover, after the ICC issued a warrant for the arrest of President Bashir, the regime viewed independent civil society as collaborators with the ICC.[91] In 2009, the regime expelled 13 international NGOs and revoked the registration of three national NGOs, including the Amal Centre for Rehabilitation of Victims of Violence; the Khartoum Centre for Human Rights and Environment Development; and the Sudan Social Development Organization.[92]

In spite of these restrictions, there was an emerging landscape of human rights and youth movements in the country during the Bashir era. A new generation of activists emerged with an appetite for change, and few believed in the old political party ideologies based on a narrow vision of the Sudanese nation-state as Arab and Muslim. One of these youth movements was a nonviolent resistance group, Girifna, which worked to topple the Bashir regime. Girifna, which means "we are fed up" in Arabic, was established in 2009 in preparation for the elections in 2010 and was quickly branded as a terrorist organization. Also several LGBT organizations were established (although not officially registered as NGOs) in a context where homosexuality is criminalized. Some organizations were shut down, and members were forced into exile or put under arrest, but many continued to operate in informal networks that pushed for regime change and fundamental human rights.

During the transitional period after the toppling of Omar al-Bashir and the dissolution of the NCP, several new civil society groups emerged. Counterrevolutionary actors are equally likely, however. Despite promises of a new era, the transitional government has repeated the Bashir regime's repressive tactics, albeit with less violent force. Sudan is still considered by freedom house as "not free" in terms of political rights and civil liberties.[93]

Popular Uprisings

Sudan has experienced three popular uprisings which have successfully taken down military dictatorships. As such it is unique in the MENA, a region in which nonviolence protest ousted authoritarian leaders for the first time in 2011.

The October Revolution in 1964 brought an end to Ibrahim Abbud's military regime. It all began with a symposium on the civil war at the University of Khartoum. The police clamped down on the symposium and killed the student Ahmad al-Qurashi. This resulted in a massive, yet nonviolent, protest. The funeral procession of the student activist was used to call for demonstrations throughout the capital. Three days into the popular uprising, several trade unions announced a general strike. As a consequence, the economy suffered greatly. In addition, the general strike made it more difficult for the government to wage war by disrupting communications networks and furthermore interrupting supply chains to the armed forces located in the war zones of the South.

The symposium on the civil war between the North and the South initially sparked the popular uprising, but it is seen as first and foremost representing the northern intelligentsia's fight for political freedom rather than a serious attempt at tackling the question of marginalization and exploitation of the South. The fact that no southerners were invited to the symposium speaks for itself. One of the great achievements of the revolution noted in Sudanese history books was the extensive participation of women in the protests, among other things demanding universal suffrage and the right to be elected to office; both granted by the new civilian government. The participation in the revolution was mainly limited to the capital and its leadership to the Khartoum based urban professionals (trade unions in particular) and political leaders of the main political parties. [94]

The April uprising or *intifada*, as it is labeled in Sudanese history books, led to the downfall of the military regime of Nimeiri in 1985. Growing economic problems, closer political alliances the United States, combined with Nimeiri's Islamist turn in 1983 and the reigniting of the North–South civil war the same year, were all factors contributing to the popular protests. Antigovernment demonstrations began in March 1985 demanding a return to liberal democracy, but was met with live ammunition. Doctors of Khartoum hospital organized a strike to showcase their strong objection against the shooting of protestors. Other professional groups joined and in April 1985 a general strike was announced in Khartoum and also other major cities. The strike was led by the National Alliance, which composed of a group of opposition parties and professional and student unions, and it effectively paralyzed economic life throughout the country. Meanwhile Nimeiri was on a visit to the United States.

The economic crisis played a major role in the outbreak of the protests, but Nimeiri had become increasingly unpopular because of his domestic and international political maneuvers, which had led some even describe him as mentally unstable.[95] Sudan had cut all ties with the United States in the wake of the Arab–Israeli war in 1967. But Nimeiri had reestablished these diplomatic ties with the Americans in 1972, despite widespread public resentment. Further, in 1983 Nimeri went from a socialist ideology to introduce sharia law in Sudan. In 1985 before protests erupted, one of Sudan's most liberal Islamic thinkers, Mahmoud Muhammed Taha, was executed.[96] Taha, a modernist Islamic thinker and the leader of the Republican Brothers, opposed the sharia laws of Nimeiri. He was prosecuted and executed for apostasy, opposing Islamic law, disturbing public order, and inciting antigovernment sentiments. Nimeiri's Islamist turn also reignited a return to civil war in the South.[97]

The next attempts at popular uprisings came in the aftermath of the Arab Spring, first in 2011 and later in 2012 and 2013. Demonstrators were unsuccessful in bringing down Omar al-Bashir's dictatorship, however. The regime suppressed protesters with gunfire, and thousands of protesters were arrested and tortured. As a response to national pressure and anti-regime demonstrations, Omar al-Bashir has strengthened his authoritarian grip. The NCP's grip of political power, therefore, was strengthened as South Sudan's independence entailed the end of a power sharing government where NCP had to share political power with the SPLM/A.

The 2019 revolution toppled Bashir. In doing so, it presents an historical trajectory opposite to elsewhere in the region, where the Arab Spring saw the toppling of secular authoritarian regimes and the emergence of Islamists into formal politics. In Sudan, the people ousted an Islamist authoritarian regime which had ruled for three decades. As such, it differs significantly from previous popular uprisings, which were mainly Khartoum-based and Khartoum-led.

The revolution began in mid-December 2018, when nonviolent protests broke out in towns in the Sudanese provinces (Damazin, Atbara, and Dongola) and rapidly spread throughout the country, including the capital. For the months that followed, millions of Sudanese took to the streets. In a country where 61 percent of the population is under the age of 25, this was a revolution of youth and especially young women. Women had participated in previous revolutions, but they were in majority in many locations in the 2019 revolution. Grass-roots groups, and in particular neighborhood resistance committees, also played a key role in the social movement and the revolution. The neighborhood resistance committees are mostly youth led and have been instrumental in the organization of demonstrations and have also played a vital role within local neighborhoods in political awareness. They emerged partly in protest to the mainstream political parties which have failed to attract the youth and largely has lost legitimacy and trust.[98]

Although the popular uprising was sparked by economic despair, protesters were quick to blame it on political mismanagement and corruption and demand the ousting of the Bashir regime. Demonstrations, strikes, and other forms of civil disobedience took place for months despite harsh repression, arrests, tortures, and killings by the security forces and other armed forces defending the regime. At the beginning of April 2019 succeeded in ousting Bashir and his Islamist cadres from power. But the protest continued after the TMC seized control of the state as the council was considered supporters of Bashir. A sit-in was formed outside the location of the Army Headquarters in Khartoum. The massacre by the security and military forces at the "sit-in" area on June 3, 2019, with more than a hundred deaths, injuries, rapes, and missing persons, represents the most tragic event in the popular uprising. Negotiations between the Forces for Freedom and Change coalition (FFC) and the Transitional Military Council culminated in the constitutional charter and the formation of a transitional government headed by the economist Abdallah Hamdok. It entailed the inclusion of military actors, including those responsible for the massacre, within the Sovereign Council, a transitional period of three years ending with free and fair elections and a transition to democracy.[99]

REGIONAL AND INTERNATIONAL POLITICS

Islamic Foreign Policy and State Sponsor of Terrorism

Arab nationalism has been an enduring theme, central to Sudanese governments' foreign policy. Islam became an important element after the Islamist-military takeover in 1989, whereas Africanism has remained distinctly secondary.[100] Islamization under Bashir entailed a pan-Islamic foreign policy, something which entailed alienation of Western powers and closer alliances with Islamic states like Iran. Sudan has also kept its doors wide open for Hamas.[101]

For such reasons, Sudan has been branded as harboring terrorists. US President Clinton added Sudan to the State Sponsor of Terrorism (SST) in 1993, after the first attack on the World Trade Center in New York the same year. Sudan was also notorious for hosting Islamist militant groups as well as al-Qaeda leader Osama bin Laden after Saudi Arabia revoked his citizenship. The SST listing, together with economic sanctions, made Sudan an international pariah. It has blocked Sudan's international financial relations by making the country ineligible for seeking debt relief by preventing the country from seeking much needed loans from the World Bank and the IMF.[102] Because of the SST and American economic sanctions, China emerged as the main partner in Sudan's oil adventure from 1995 onward,[103] although this relationship changed when South Sudan became an independent nation in 2011.

Sudan was removed from the SST list in December 2020, but only after it agreed with the Trump administration to pay economic dispensation to US victims of terror attacks after al-Qaeda's 1998 bombing of the US embassies in Kenya and Tanzania. Additionally, and as part of this deal, Sudan signed the "Abraham Accords" paving the way to normalizing diplomatic ties with Israel. This entailed repealing a 1958 law stipulating the boycott of Israel. The United Arab Emirates (UAE) was also a strong advocate for Sudan's move to normalize relations with Israel, and together with Saudi Arabia, the UAE has significantly contributed with aid to Sudan, especially after 2011. They also have vested economic interests. Sudan today exports a substantial amount of gold to the UAE; an industry controlled by military actors. These countries have backed the military actors within the transitional government.[104]

The Abraham Accords are necessary for economic reform, but they also have potential negative political implications for the transitional government of Hamdok. The Accords strengthen the position of military actors at the expense of the civilian component.[105] Abdel Fattah Al-Burhan, the head of the Sovereign Council, was key in paving the way for the Abraham Accords. Moreover, he independently met with Israel's Prime Minister without even consulting the Abdallah Hamdok and the FFC, which is the political incubator of the civilian component of the transitional government. This created rifts in the fragile ruling coalition. The UP and the SCP rejected any step toward normalization considering Sudan's historical position supporting Palestine, while others accepted because of Sudan's desperate economic situation.[106]

South Sudan's Secession and Sudan's Changing Regional Loyalties

South Sudan's secession had negative economic consequences for Sudan, and it made it difficult for Bashir to maintain his extensive and expensive patronage system. This increased his dependence on external patrons such as the oil-rich Gulf countries like Saudi Arabia and the

United Arab Emirates, China, and Russia in order to secure financial support, something which is essential for his own political survival.[107] In order to secure such support, Bashir had to give something back. Among other things this included the leasing of the RSF to the Saudi-led military campaign against Houthi rebels in Yemen.[108] Bashir also had to cut diplomatic ties with the Iranian regime.[109]

The 2017 diplomatic crisis within the Gulf Cooperation Council (GCC) also affected Sudan. With Egypt's support, Saudi Arabia, the UAE and Bahrain broke relations with and imposed a land, sea, and air blockade of Qatar. The GCC crisis added another layer of complexity to a regime under growing pressure. For a number of years, Qatar had provided much financial and political support to Sudan, including hosting Darfur peace negotiations in Doha. Sudan under Bashir tried hard, together with other Gulf countries, such as Kuwait and Oman, to adopt a neutral position during the GCC crisis. Ultimately, Sudan was forced to pick sides, favoring Saudi Arabia over the UAE.[110]

Relations between Sudan and South Sudan during the regime of Bashir were hostile, at best.[111] During the South Sudanese civil war, Bashir supported the rebellion against Salwa Kiir and the South Sudanese government. Thus, South Sudan wholeheartedly welcomed the fall of the Bashir regime. However, the two countries have yet to agree on the definite borders between Sudan and South Sudan.

Porous Borders and Increasing Migration Control

Sudan shares borders with Central African Republic, Chad, Egypt, Eritrea, Ethiopia, Libya, and South Sudan. Before secession of the South in 2011, it also shared borders with Congo, Kenya, and Uganda. All of these borders were arbitrarily created during colonialism and lack geographical logic. The Beja live both in Sudan and Eritrea, al-Zaghawa in Chad as well as Darfur, and the people of Nuba mountains have more in common in terms of culture and language with the South Sudan rather than Sudan. These ethnic groups, many of which are pastoralists and nomads, have historically converged peacefully across borders. However, the porosity of borders have made Sudan vulnerable to refugees when famine and war occur in neighboring countries. Sudan is both a destination and transit country for refugees and migrants from its neighbors. In some instances these refugees have used Sudan as a base to attack their homelands. For example, the Sudanese government aided Eritrean and Ethiopian militias (based in refugee camps in the east of the country) to overthrow the Ethiopian government in 1991.[112]

Sudan has a long history of generous refugee policy, especially towards Arabs.[113] A peaceful and humanitarian refugee policy, which abides by nonrefoulment, and pushes the goal of self-sustaining livelihoods for the refugees. However, with the Khartoum Process, Sudan took steps to control its borders, especially to stop illegal migration toward Europe. Moreover, although some European countries mirrored the US position toward Sudan under Bashir, this changed with the refugee crisis. In 2014, the European Union (EU) launched the Khartoum Process or EU-Horn of Africa Migration Route Initiative aimed at combatting illegal migration from the Horn of Africa region, including Sudan. EUR 160 million has been allocated to Sudan, including funds for antiimmigration patrols along Sudan's borders. This gave Bashir some legitimacy in Europe as well as much needed aid after the economy plummeted in 2011 with the loss of oil revenues. The EU completely ignored the fact that Sudan is not only a transit country for refugees, but because of its three decades of authoritarian politics under Bashir and multiple armed conflicts is also a major country of origin for refugees en route to Europe.[114]

Of course, much of the EU-funded training and equipment given to Bashir's regime has been used to control the borders, but also for surveillance of those opposing the regime and numerous human rights violations.[115] The RSF was tasked with patrolling Sudanese borders which it has strategically used for its economic benefit by engaging in human trafficking and smuggling of weapons.[116]

Water, Ports, and Geopolitics

The Nile River, which originates in Uganda (White Nile) and Ethiopia (Blue Nile) and passes through Sudan and Egypt to the Mediterranean sea, is an important resource. Egypt and Ethiopia have competing interests and Sudan has been trying to navigate meanwhile keeping good relations with both neighboring countries. For Egypt, the Nile is in fact the sole source of water and its access to it is secured through the 1959 Nile Water Agreement. However, the Grand Ethiopian Renaissance Dam (GERD), under construction since 2011, has become a major threat to Sudan's and Egypt's access to the Nile waters.[117] In 2012, however, Bashir announced that Sudan supported GERD as he feared being isolated from the Nile basin countries such as Ethiopia, Kenya, Rwanda, Tanzania, Uganda, and Burundi, which all rejected the 1959 Nile Water Agreement [118]. As such he seemed to have reasoned that Sudan benefited more from keeping good relations with Ethiopia rather than with Egypt.[119] Bashir started a process of reconciliation with Ethiopia after decades of turbulence between the two countries, which may have been Bashir's major foreign policy achievement.[120] As a consequence, the relationship with Egypt became even more strained. The relationship between the two states has been tense during the Bashir regime as Egypt under Mubarak feared the influence of Islamism.

GERD remains contested. As Sudan can easily get caught in a military or proxy conflict between Ethiopia and Egypt, the country has been active in promoting mediation from AU. Both Egypt and Ethiopia have put pressure on Sudan, something which has been a source of conflict between different fractions of the transitional government in Khartoum. In 2021, the UN Security Council held a session to discuss the dispute over GERD.

The Red Sea, including Sudan's port, has great geopolitical interest historically and contemporarily. The sea separates the coasts of Egypt, Sudan, and Eritrea to the west from those of Saudi Arabia and Yemen in the east. It links the Suez Canal to the Gulf of Aden, which makes it one of the most traveled waterways globally. A number of countries in Europe, North Africa, and Asia depend on access to Sudan's port. It is also a vital navigation route for military forces, including the United States, Turkey, and Russia. In March 2019, just before the ousting of Bashir from office, Sudan signed a draft military agreement with Russia that involved a fleet logistics center in the vicinity of Port Sudan. The UAE and Saudi Arabia have also established military bases in Sudan and take great interest in the port for their own national security concerns.[121] But it has also had military importance historically. The British took control over the Sudanese port city of Suakin in 1884 and 1885 in an effort to prevent French takeover. This seizing of all Egyptian ports in the Red Sea in the late 19th century was essential for the British Empire to secure sea lanes to support its colonial status as a superpower.[122]

Regional powers thus have vested interests but also major disagreements. This was as exemplified most recently by the Saudi Arabian-led armed intervention in Yemen (2015) in which Sudanese RSF soldiers have participated on behalf of the Saudi government. Central to the tension among Egypt, Ethiopia, and Sudan is also a wider regional conflict between several Arab countries against Turkey. The same year the Bashir regime gave Turkey, which backed Qatar in during the GCC crisis in 2017, the rights to restore Suakin, which is an old Ottoman port, and construct a dock for civilian and military vessels, something that escalated these tensions.[123]

RELIGION AND POLITICS

The majority of Sudan's Muslims are sufis. The Qadiriyyah is the oldest of the Sufi orders or the *tariqah*s in Arabic and it entered Sudan from the Middle East as early as the 16th century. This is probably the oldest of the Muslim mystic (Sufi) orders in the continent. Other major tariqahs formed important support bases for the traditional sectarian political parties. But whereas Islam had a latent presence through the sectarian political parties, throughout Sudan's postindependence history, the Islamists called for a comprehensive Islamization and an Islamic Constitution.

After the revolution for national salvation, as the Islamist-Military regime of Bashir called itself during the early 1990s, sharia became the guiding principle of state policy.[124] Shortly after the *coup d'etat*, a decree was announced and it stipulated that sharia should be the main source of law and reference of the Sudanese state.[125] This involved Islamization of the country's legal, political, and economic system from above by force and is unparalleled by any other attempts to introduce sharia in Sudan. However, the Islamization of the legal system started before the Islamists colluded with the military and took power in 1989. In September 1983, Nimeiri issued several decrees, known as the September Laws, which involved the enforcement of *hudud*. *Hudud*, which is plural of hadd and translates into limit, restriction, or prohibition, are regarded as crimes against God and they have fixed punishments which are derived from the Islamic sources. Turabi, the attorney-general at the time, headed a commission with the mandate to revise all of Sudan's laws in accordance with Islamic law.

Successive regimes since independence in 1956 have attempted to unite culturally, linguistically, and religiously disparate peoples and regions of the country around Islamic and Arab nation building projects.[126] A question that has haunted the country since 1956 is the role of Islam in the country's permanent constitution. The question of an Islamic constitution dominated the political debates.[127] As early as 1956, Sheikh Hassan Muddathir, the last Egyptian Grand Qadi appointed to Sudan, advocated (much in line with the Islamists) for Sudan to be guided by an Islamic constitution. In 1957, the UP and DUP issued a statement where they announced the call for Sudan to become an Islamic Parliamentary Republic with Islam as the main source of law, which makes clear the Islamic base of these political parties.[128] All Sudanese constitutions since independence have proclaimed Sharia as a main source of law. However, the 1998 Constitution featured the most Islamic elements. These included that state supremacy is to God, that Islam is the religion of the majority, and Arabic the official language, and that sharia remained unchallenged as source of legislation; the ultimate signal of an Islamic state.[129]

Sharia, Decolonialization, and Women's Rights

Sharia has been a source of law since before Sudan's independence. Sudanese sharia courts were mandated by the British to apply Hanafi doctrine in the 1916 Mohammedan Law Courts Procedures. Whether by ignorance or design, they did not recognize the Maliki traditions of most Sudanese. British rule also continued the Ottoman separation of the civil law and the sharia with the latter being confined to personal and family matters. The Islamists' call for Islamization was seen as decolonialization. In practical terms, it included among other things a 1985 merger of civil and sharia courts, thereby reversing the British system.[130]

The Islamist-Military state of Bashir initiated comprehensive Islamization of Sudan's legal system. This entailed Sudan's first codification of a Muslim family law in 1991. Until that point in time, family law (regulating marriage, divorce, maintenance, inheritance, and custody of children) were dealt with according to the sharia developed through judicial circulars throughout most of the 20th century.[131] For Sudanese Islamist, the codification symbolized a Sudanization of the gender arrangements under the law. By many women's rights activists historically and contemporarily, the 1991 law has been described as a backlash against women's rights because it legalized child marriage, stipulated male guardianship, called for a wife's obedience to her husband, and denied women the possibility of working outside of the home without the permission of male guardians.[132] As such, it is the most conservative Muslim family law in the region.[133]

Women's rights under sharia, including the family law, served as a symbolic political signifier of political projects in Sudan.[134] Civilian and military regimes in Sudan throughout the independent era have equally failed to guarantee gender equality and introduce policies to better women's condition.[135] However, the civilization project launched by Islamists in 1989 interpreted Islamic law in a particularly fundamentalist way, and political leaders introduced new sharia laws that significantly changed women's citizenship rights to the worse.[136] Islamization of law also segmented ethnic and class hierarchies in important ways.[137] For example, the Labor Act of 1997 restricts women's working hours but differentiates between women of different class positions. *Unskilled* women are not allowed to work during evenings and nights, but *skilled* women like doctors are allowed to do so.[138] The law which Bashir's regime became most renowned for was what popularly known as the public order laws. These laws severely restricted women's movement and dress in public spaces and have been resisted since its inception. By Islamists they were regarded as women's entry ticket into public spaces, including education, politics, and economy. In their view, it was a symbol of what they saw as modern Islam where women's public participation was coupled with piety and modesty. These laws formed an important backdrop to their wide participation in the 2019 revolution. One of the first acts of Abdallah Hamdok's cabinet was to abolish them.[139]

ISLAMISM AND THE EMERGENCE OF SALAFISM

Ansar al-Sunna is the main Salafi group in Sudan, and it can be traced back to Abd al-Rahman Hajr, who was an Algerian religious scholar residing in Sudan from 1870 to 1939. However, the Salafi ideology has radicalized over time. The first Salafis in the country fought for Sudan's independence alongside other Islamic groups, including both the Sufis and Muslim Brothers. This is a rather distinct feature of Sudanese Salafism focused on fostering peaceful relations with Sufi brotherhoods. However, this history of peaceful relations changed during the reign of Bashir.[140]

The Islamist-Military regime of Bashir delineated the boundaries of what it considered authentic and correct Islamic views and practices, distinguishing them both from what it viewed as "traditional" Islam (Sufism) or what they referred to as "backward" Islam (Salafism). The Islamists' political project aimed to homogenize Sudanese Islam under the auspices of political authority, calling for an end to differences and divisions between religious schools of law and sectarian affiliations in the country. This process of homogenizing Islam involved political suppression of both Sufism and Salafism, especially in the early 1990s, despite the fact that many of these movements did not have political ambition at the time. Ansar al-Sunna has primarily engaged in Islamic missionary and preaching activities and has never developed into a political party.[141]

However, this strategy widened the opposition to Bashir's rule to include Salafi Islamic clergy (*ulema*) in the country. The principal shaykhs of Ansar al-Sunna, Abu Zayd Muhammad Hamza, and Muhammad al-Hadiyya were detained after declaring the regime un-Islamic in 1994. The same year, five men killed 26 worshippers inside an Ansar al-Sunna mosque, orchestrated by the Bashir regime.[142] However, relations gradually became more friendly and some Ansar al-Sunna's members joined the government and decided to participate in elections, either under the National Congress Party umbrella or as independent candidates. The increasing political pragmatism of the Islamists after 1999 have continued to be the cause of relentless critique by Salafi movements, including its stance on women's public participation.[143] This marriage of convenience that Bashir offered allowed Salafi groups to preach freely without much interference from the state. The increasingly lenient policy toward Salafi groups, included militant Salafism, increasingly caused violent clashes with the dominant Sufi brotherhoods toward the end of Bashir's rule. This stands in deep contrast to the history of fostering peaceful cohabitation among opposing Islamic groups.[144]

CONCLUSION

Sudan is a country of perpetual conflict and violence. Instability and rivalry among Khartoum's riverine elites—combined with marginalization of the peripheries—have been constant features of Sudanese politics and perhaps the most important cause of political instability and armed rebellion. The gap between Sudan's linguistically, culturally, and religiously diverse population and the North's relentless attempts to build a national identity based on Islam and Arabism have been major obstacles to peace and democracy in the country.

Despite periods of civilian rule and three successful popular uprisings in 1964, 1985, and 2019, democracy remains a distant vision. During most of Sudan's independence, military dictatorships have been the rule. The regime of Omar al-Bashir has been the worst of the worst that Sudan has seen in terms of violating human rights, war crimes, corruption, and overexploitation of Sudan's regions. Yet, if Sudan follows its troubled historical trajectory, then the civil–military transitional government headed by Abdallah Hamdok will be replaced by an authoritarian military regime.

There are reasons to believe this will materialize. The military actors within the transitional coalition have an upper hand, especially considering its control of the economy. Added to that, there are strong regional actors that want to see Sudan under military rule. Sudan's strategic location, its natural resources, makes the country geopolitically important, but also vulnerable to outside interference. Even the EU, in its search for a partner in crime to stop mitigation to Europe, has benefited from these military actors, especially the RSF. The increasing rivalry within the civilian component of the transitional government are disturbingly familiar as it has a constant feature of Sudanese politics since before independence, and something that unfortunately strengthens the military. However, the Juba Peace Agreement gives a glimpse of hope for a new future for Sudan in which diversity might be respected, a reversal of a historical marginalization of Sudan's regions is put center stage and transitional justice. The delisting of Sudan as a state sponsor of terrorism in 2020 makes economic recovery more possible than ever before.

SUGGESTED READINGS

Berridge, Willow. *Civil Uprisings in Modern Sudan, the Khartoum springs of 1964 and 1985*, Bloomsbury Academic, 2015.

Sørbø, Gunnar, and Ghaffar M. Ahmed Abdel. *Sudan Divided: Continuing Conflict in a Contested State*, Palgrave, 2013.

Abdullahi, A Gallab. *The First Islamist Republic: Development and Disintegration of Islamism in the Sudan*, Routledge, 2008.

Aldan, Young. *Transforming Sudan: Decolonization, Economic Development and State Formation*, Cambridge University Press, 2017.

Samia, al-Nagar, and Liv Tønnessen. "Sudanese Women's Demands for Freedom, Peace, and Justice in the 2019 Revolution." In *Women and Peacebuilding in Africa*, edited by Affi Ladan, Liv Tønnessen and Marie Tripp Aili, James Currey, 2021.

Einas, Ahmed. "Militant Salafism in Sudan." *Islamic Africa.* 6, no. 1–2 (2015): 164–84.

Hanna, Ramy Lofty.*Transboundary water resources and the political economy of large-scale land investments in the Nile: Sudan, hydropolitics and Arab food security*, Routledge, 2016.

24 TUNISIA

Intissar Kherigi[1]

On December 17, 2010, the day that protests for economic dignity and antiregime calls began across Tunisia, the World Bank released a competitiveness and integration report on the Tunisian economy.[2] The report underscored the longtime portrayal of Tunisia as a *bon élève*, or good pupil, stressing the need to continue along the path of economic liberalization and reform:

> The global integration strategy has allowed it to gradually become a fairly diversified and open economy. . . . The development model that Tunisia pursued over the past two decades has served the country well, but it has shown to be increasingly inadequate to reduce unemployment and promote growth of high value–added sectors.

That same day, in the central town of Sidi Bouzid, a young produce vendor named Muhammad Bouazizi immolated himself after a local police officer confiscated his produce, cart, and scales. The dramatic act of suicide represented Bouazizi's frustration with the lack of possibilities for basic economic sustainability or advancement, symbolizing a broader anger at corruption in the country's powerful network of privileged families. Muhammad Bouazizi's tragic act represented the plight of millions of Tunisians excluded from economic advancement and denied political expression by the repressive policies of ex-President Zine al-Abidine Ben Ali and his small clan of powerful families.[3]

Within hours, Bouazizi's self-immolation unleashed waves of protest, first in Sidi Bouzid, then across Tunisia's interior, eventually culminating in a nationwide movement, which by early January was calling for freedoms, social justice, dignity, and the removal of the regime. January 14, 2011, marked the Tunisian Revolution, the immediate flight of President Ben Ali, and the end of his single-party regime.[4]

The rupture broke many of the mechanisms of a fifty-four-year-old authoritarian regime, but the dynamics of postrevolution politics and institution building also reflect a continuity of Tunisia's experience with state-building and social change, extant political institutions, modernization programs, resistance movements, and its position in the regional and global economy. This chapter begins with an overview of postrevolution politics, highlighting critical developments from January 14, 2011 to the present. Subsequent sections focus on state-building and social change, institutions and government, political actors and participation, Islam and politics, and underscore historical tensions around modernization and reform in the country.

OVERVIEW OF TUNISIA'S TRANSITION

Nature abhors a vacuum, and in the months following January 2011, Tunisia's government would go through several permutations. Ben Ali–appointed Prime Minister Mohammed Ghannouchi declared himself Interim President on January 15, 2011, only to be replaced the following day by then-Speaker of the Chamber of Deputies Fouad Mebazza, following a ruling of the Constitutional Council, which itself was dissolved in March 2011. Mebazza promptly named Ghannouchi his prime minister, who formed a national unity government and promised elections within six months. Deemed too tainted by the Ben Ali regime, Ghannouchi was replaced by Beji Caid Essebsi, a longtime minister of Habib Bourguiba—Tunisia's first president—on February 27.

KEY FACTS ON TUNISIA

AREA 101,663 square miles (163,610 square kilometers)

CAPITAL Tunis

POPULATION 11,811,335 (2021 est.)

PERCENTAGE OF POPULATION UNDER 25 38.18 (2020 est.)

RELIGIOUS GROUPS (PERCENTAGE) Muslim (Sunni), 99.1; other (includes Christian, Jewish, Shia Muslim, and Baha'i), 1

ETHNIC GROUPS (PERCENTAGE) Arab, 98; European, 1; Jewish and other, 1

OFFICIAL LANGUAGE Arabic; French and Berber also spoken

TYPE OF GOVERNMENT Republic

DATE OF INDEPENDENCE March 20, 1956 (from France)

GDP (PPP) $114.97 billion (2020 est.); $9,700 (2020 est.)

GDP (NOMINAL) $38.884 billion (2019 est.)

PERCENTAGE OF GDP BY SECTOR Agriculture, 10.1; industry, 26.2; services, 63.8 (2017 est.)

TOTAL RENTS (PERCENTAGE OF GDP) FROM NATURAL RESOURCES 2.17 (2019 est.)

FERTILITY RATE 2.03 children born/woman (2021 est.)

Sources: CIA. "The World Factbook." August 4, 2022, https://www.cia.gov/the-world-factbook/. World Bank. "International Comparison Program (ICP)." Accessed August 10, 2022, https://databank.worldbank.org/source/icp-2017.

In February 2011, in the face of calls for political reforms, Prime Minister Mohamed Ghannouchi nominated legal scholar Yadh Ben Achour to head the newly created National Commission for Political Reform, tasked with drafting a new constitution. But in the face of continued public demands for a popularly elected national constituent assembly that would draft a new constitution, interim President Fouad Mebazaa announced the holding of elections for a National Constituent Assembly (NCA) in July 2011. In the face of pressure from opposition forces for their inclusion in the transition, the National Commission for Political Reform was expanded into a High Authority for the Realization of the Objectives of the Revolution, Political Reform, and Democratic Transition (referred to as the *Ben Achour Commission*), including political and civil society representatives alongside legal experts. Less than a month after its creation, the Ben Achour Commission announced the procedures that would frame anticipated elections for the NCA.

On October 23, 2011, Tunisians voted for the 217-seat NCA, a body tasked with drafting a democratic Tunisian constitution, while monitoring the work of an interim government formed by the prime minister. With a 51.97 percent turnout,[5] the election results stunned many: The previously banned Islamist Ennahdha party, led by Rached Ghannouchi, and the Congress for the Republic (CPR), led by longtime Ben Ali opponent Moncef Marzouki,[6] came first and second in the polls. Ennahdha won a large plurality, with 37.04 percent of the vote, translating into 89 NCA seats. Marzouki's CPR won 29 seats, with 8.71 percent of the vote. They joined the fourth-ranked party (20 seats), Ettakatol, led by longtime reformist opposition leader Mustapha Ben Jaafar, to create a 130-seat parliamentary majority. The *Troika*, as the coalition would be called, supported the candidacy of Mustapha Ben Jaafar for speaker of parliament. In December, the Troika-dominated NCA adopted the "Law on the Interim Organization of Public Powers," which served as an interim "miniconstitution" while the NCA drafted a new constitution. That law defined the prerogatives and limitations on executive, government, and parliamentary authority. Two days after the law was passed, the NCA elected Moncef Marzouki as interim president, who in turn nominated Ennahdha executive-committee member Hamadi Jebali as prime minister, tasking him to form a government to run day-to-day affairs while the NCA drafted the constitution.

INTERIM TENSIONS

The interim government was immediately confronted with a range of socio-economic challenges. By the time the NCA began to draft the constitution, the economy had been in contraction for a year. According to the World Bank, 2011 GDP growth fell to 1.6 percent, while unemployment spiked to a national aggregate of 18.1 percent. Alarmingly, the International Labor Organization (ILO) reported unemployment at 42.3 percent for Tunisians between the ages of twenty-five and thirty-five years old. According to the World Bank, foreign direct investment (FDI) in manufacturing, agrobusiness, and tourism receipts plummeted as foreign investors and potential visitors shied from the aftershocks of revolution. FDI fell from US$1.3 billion in 2010 to just over $400 million in 2011,[7] and Tunisia received close to two million fewer tourists in 2011 than in 2010.[8]

Immediately touched by the economic context, workers demanded swift action to increase employment options and salaries. Worker movements also had been at the forefront of resistance to the Ben Ali regime, most notably during the 2008 Gafsa Mining Basin rebellion.[9] While the main union federation, the General Union of Tunisian Workers (Union Générale Tunisienne du Travail, UGTT), eventually joined the anti-Ben Ali protest movement calling for a general strike on January 13, 2011, it had lost control over much of its rank and file. According to one estimate, the number of strike movements increased by 122 percent between 2010 and 2011, involving 340 companies and over 140,000 workers.[10] This had a major effect on manufacturing and extractive industries, which saw a reduction of 40 percent of value added in mining, primarily due to labor unrest in the phosphate sector. Phosphate production, eight million tons in 2010, fell to 2.5 million tons in 2011.[11] Since 2011 and especially following 2014, strikes and protests in the mining regions have increased exponentially as a response to Tunisia's weak economy, but also because of poor working and social service conditions. In 2017, phosphate production was just over half of that produced in 2010—4.15 million tons.

While 2012, the first year of the NCA, was marked by a slight upturn in economic growth, none of Tunisia's economic sectors had rebounded to 2010 levels. In the context of prolonged economic contraction and the effervescence of revolutionary sentiment, social and political unrest continued. In addition to a sagging economy, the Troika government had to contend with a rise in radical social movements and political violence. Accredited immediately after the revolution, Ansar Al-Sharia and Hizb Tahrir are two distinct Salafi movements that created much hostility among the political class, especially among secular-leaning elites. Anti-Ennahda voices painted the rise of Salafism as part of Ennahdha's long-term strategy for the Islamization of the country, fears largely unfounded given the many Ennahdha public statements regarding the party's commitment to democracy and pluralism. Hizb Tahrir sought and eventually won accreditation as a political party in July 2012, whereas Ansar Al-Sharia rejected the democratic process and opposed Tunisian political institutions, including the NCA and future constitution. In September 2012, Ansar Al-Sharia received authorization to organize a protest in front of the US Embassy in Tunis in response to a homemade YouTube video that allegedly insulted the Prophet Mohamed. Turnout was larger than authorities expected and quickly turned violent as protesters stormed the embassy walls, setting fire to the structure and ransacking the nearby American School. Moncef Marzouki, then president, condemned the attacks and called them "unacceptable, considering its implication on our relations with Washington."[12]

The attacks on the US Embassy marked the beginning of a political crisis that would stall the constitution drafting process, incite political infighting, and block important political reform agendas around transitional justice and judicial reform. While the NCA and Troika worked diligently to keep Tunisia on its path to democracy, public criticism of the postrevolutionary environment was coopted by a rising political opposition force, *Nidaa Tounes* (Call for Tunisia), formed of secularists, leftists, labor representatives, industrialists, big-business interests, and former regime elements. Supporters of the Troika blamed the opposition for obstructing the work of the assembly for its own political gains. Some of the Troika's most ardent critics used this occasion for a public campaign to question a democratic future that could accommodate both religious beliefs and the rights paradigm of secularists under rule of law.

In February 2013, five months after the US Embassy attacks, Chokri Belaid, a leftist Tunisian politician and vocal critic of the Ben Ali regime and the Troika, was assassinated in front of his home in Tunis. The assassination spiraled the country into deeper crisis, underscoring existing political tensions. Tens of thousands of Tunisians turned out at the Belaid funeral, and the UGTT called for a national strike. In response, Prime Minister Hamadi Jebali proposed to form a temporary technocratic government and schedule elections to weather the deepening political crisis. Jebali's plan was rejected by Ennahdha. Faced by opposition within his own party, Jebali resigned, stating,

> I promised if my initiative did not succeed I would resign as head of the government, and this is what I am doing following my meeting with the President. Today there is a great disappointment among the people and we must regain their trust and this resignation is a first step.[13]

Deepening political tensions provided an opportunity for the rise of Nidaa Tounes (Nidaa), led by former Interim Prime Minister Beji Caid Essebsi. Building a platform that criticized the postrevolution period as one of insecurity and instability, Nidaa's popularity was amplified following the country's second postrevolution political assassination. In July 2013, Mohamed Brahmi was murdered in front of his family while leaving his home. Brahmi was a member of the same leftist coalition as Chokri Belaid, and his assassination sparked the *Rahil* (Departure) movement, which convened daily in front of the NCA. *Rahil* was supported nationwide in smaller protests calling for the dissolution of the NCA. The leftist coalition *Jabha Shaabia* (Popular Front), led by long-standing dissident Hamma Hammami, joined forces with Nidaa to form the National Salvation Front (NSF). Opposition parties represented in parliament joined the ranks of the NSF, and their deputies withdrew from parliament. Lawyers, judges, intellectuals, revolutionary activists, and civil society organizations joined the movement. The constitutional process was thus on the brink of collapse. *Rahil* expanded to include members of the UGTT and consisted of daily demonstrations calling for the dissolution of the NCA. Within two weeks, the protests were gathering tens of thousands of protesters, which the NSF claimed represented a "national consensus" stronger than the electoral legitimacy of the Troika.[14] Troika supporters called the NSF undemocratic and detrimental to Tunisia's political transition.

The culmination of the street-based *Rahil* protests and the NSF's widespread support pushed Ennahdha and the opposition to negotiate a political compromise. A national dialogue (*hiwar watani*) led by the quartet of the Tunisian General Labor Union (UGTT), the Tunisian Union of Industry, Trade, and Handicrafts (UTICA), the Lawyers' Union, and the Tunisian League for the Defense of Human Rights brought the Troika and its opponents to reach a consensus in October 2013: the NCA would complete the Constitution by early 2014; upon its adoption, the Troika would step down to be replaced by a technocratic government that would organize legislative and presidential elections within a reasonable time frame, to be organized by an independent election commission elected by the NCA, the Instance Supérieure Indépendante pour les Élections (Higher Independent Election Commission, ISIE). The national dialogue was hailed by many observers as a key moment that led Tunisia out of political deadlock, while laying the groundwork for Tunisia's first postauthoritarian parliamentary and presidential elections.

Despite continued protests, the NCA worked relentlessly to complete an acceptable draft of the Constitution, which was unanimously approved on January 26, 2014: Two hundred deputies voted for the Constitution, twelve against, and four abstained, constituting an overwhelming majority of 92 percent. Amid nationwide celebration on January 27, 2014, Interim President Moncef Marzouki, NCA Speaker Mustapha Ben Jaafar, and Prime Minister Ali Larayedh signed the document. Observers hailed the landmark Constitution as a successful result of a compromise between Ennahdha and the oppositional forces. The Constitution mandates power sharing along a dual executive (President and Prime Minister), gives significant powers to the legislature, and for the first time in the history of the Arab world, requires gender parity in all public elected bodies.

Two days after the signing of the Constitution, the Troika ceded power to a technocratic government led by former Minister of Industry Mehdi Jomaa. At the time, NCA President Ben Jaafar declared, "The peaceful transfer of power has occurred in an extraordinary way that history will not forget."[15] Ennahdha deputies and supporters defended their party's performance in light of fierce attacks by religious extremists as well as relentless protests by leftists and the secular-leaning anti-Ennahdha front. Deep-seated prejudices against the moderate Islamist party and open statements that all Islamists were terrorists continued into the October 2014 legislative elections and the December 2014 presidential polls. At the same time, the secular opposition was painted immediately as a resurgence of the Ben Ali regime, despite its great internal ideological diversity.

Nidaa swept the legislative vote, and Essebsi unseated Marzouki as president. Many journalists and international observers characterized the victory as the triumph of secularism over Islamism, but important scores by smaller parties indicated a shift of politics beyond the religion–secularism divide: In addition to Ennahdha, the Free Patriotic Union (UPL) led by Tunisian businessman and soccer club owner Slim Riahi (who became Secretary General of Nidaa in October 2018), the leftist *Jabha Shaabia* led by Hamma Hammami, and the liberal *Afek Tounes* constituted the runner-up parties. The surprise performance of the populist UPL underscored the continued salience of populism among the Tunisian electorate. To the surprise of many, Nidaa entered into a coalition government with Ennahdha, sparking the first internal crisis within Nidaa. Its secretary general, Mohsen Marzouk, split from the party with fourteen Nidaa deputies in March 2016, forming a new party, *Machrouu Tounes*. This move tilted the balance of seats within Parliament, and Ennahdha once again became the largest parliamentary bloc with 68 deputies. In May 2016 at its first party congress since 2012, Ennahdha surprised many by announcing it was no longer Islamist, but rather a party of Muslim Democrats.

After the 2014 elections, Tunisia's democratic transition was once again shaken by two devastating events: deadly terrorist attacks on tourists at the Bardo National Museum in Tunis on March 18, 2015 as well as a deadly terrorist attack at a tourist beach in Port El Kantaoui (Sousse) on June 26, 2015. President Essebsi declared a state of national emergency following the attacks, putting increased security services visible in public and tourist spaces, while human rights activists have criticized the government for reversing freedoms and derailing advances made toward democracy. The attacks created pressure to quickly adopt a new Anti-Terrorism Law, which was criticized for endangering human rights, as well as creating an environment in which security sector reform became even more challenging. The terrorist attacks also led to greater international support for Tunisian armed and security forces, which saw their budgets significantly expand, provoking concerns regarding the growth of the security sector, which had been associated with human rights abuses under the former regime.

For critics, the new security focus represented a dangerous formula reminiscent of the repressive Ben Ali years, when economic security was traded for the protection of human rights and social justice, what Béatrice Hibou calls the "security pact." Policies rooted in the security–economy nexus are dually perilous because expansive and vaguely defined national-security imperatives can be used to suppress democratic expression, while at the same time used to impose unpopular economic development projects. Indeed, Beji Caid Essebsi's July 4, 2015, declaration of a state of national security—renewed to the time of writing— gives security forces broad powers of arrest and prolonged detention, and can be used to target opposition. Similarly, policies to amnesty Ben Ali–era state cadres and businessmen with links to the Ben Ali regime have been viewed as attacks on the important Truth and Reconciliation process. Balancing security and human rights protections as well as addressing the past while building a stable future are key challenges for Tunisia's political future.

The 2016–2018 period also witnessed the further disintegration of Nidaa Tounes. Internal divisions soon emerged over control of the party and governmental appointments and policies. The determination by Essebsi to place his son, Hafedh, at the head of the party, also provoked deep opposition among party activists. In addition to the break-off party formed by former secretary general of Nidaa, Mohsen Marzouk, in March 2016, mass resignations took place in 2016–2018, as the party failed to hold its first party congress to elect governing structures. This led to open acrimony and even violence at party meetings, as well as legal disputes in the courts over control of the party.

These divisions had a direct impact on various reform processes, including the decentralization process launched under the 2014 constitution, which sought to transfer powers and resources from central government down to regional and local elected councils. Given its internal divisions, Nidaa Tounes was not keen to hold local elections and repeatedly delayed the election date. After multiple delays, on May 6, 2018, Tunisia held its first postrevolution municipal elections.[16] With a 33 percent voter turnout for 350 municipalities, independents received 32.2 percent of the vote, Ennahdha 28.6, and Nidaa Tounes 20.8 percent. During this period, Prime Minister Youssef Chahed (August 2016–February 2020) reshuffled his government three times, increasingly bringing in Ben Ali–era figures into prominent government positions.

The 2014–2019 period also saw a growing confrontation between the two heads of the executive, the president of the republic and the prime minister. The first prime minister after the 2014 elections, Habib Essid, was a veteran technocrat, having served as a high-ranking bureaucrat under Ben Ali. Although he was selected by President Beji Caid Essebsi and was a close ally, they soon began to clash as Essebsi sought to exert greater control over the government. Nidaa Tounes also accused the prime minister of not consulting the party enough on governmental decisions. By June 2016, President Essebsi was calling for the removal of Essid and the formation of a government of national unity headed by a new prime minister. When Essid refused to resign, Essebsi launched his own political dialogue with nine political parties, the UTICA and the UGTT, issuing the Carthage Pact containing a roadmap for a new government. A vote to withdraw confidence from the government was scheduled in the Assembly of People's

Representatives (ARP) on July 30, which Essid lost. Essebsi nominated Youssef Chahed, a close ally, to form a new government. Chahed's proposed government was approved by the ARP in August 2016.

However, this did not bring an end to tensions between the two heads of the executive. Youssef Chahed himself fell out of favor with President Essebsi after entering into conflict with Essebsi's son, Hafedh, the Executive Director of Nidaa Tounes. The conflict precipitated a national political crisis, as President Essebsi pushed the parties in Chahed's coalition government, particularly Ennahdha, by then the largest bloc in parliament, to withdraw confidence from Chahed. Ennahdha's refusal to do so prompted a serious breakdown in relations between President Essebsi and head of Ennahdha, Rached Ghannouchi. In January 2019, Chahed announced the formation of a breakaway party, Tahya Tounes, led by him.

The run-up to the 2019 legislative and presidential elections was thus characterized by a return to polarization. However, unlike the 2014 elections, there was no "big-tent" party to unite the secularist camp, due to Nidaa's scission into multiple competing parties. The frustrations with political in-fighting among elites, recurrent political crises and the fragmentation of the political landscape, as well as a stagnant economy unable to produce enough jobs and decent working opportunities, contributed to the rise of populist voices that came to dominate the 2019 elections—in particular, two parties from opposing sides of the political spectrum who sought to attract votes away from the two mainstream parties, Nidaa and Ennahdha, which had represented the Islamist and secularist camps in the 2014 elections. On the secularist side of the spectrum, the Free Destourian Party (*Partie Destourien libre*, PDL) emerged, led by Abir Moussi, the assistant secretary general for women's affairs of the former ruling RCD party under Ben Ali. With the downfall of Nidaa Tounes and divisions among former regime elites, the PDL emerged as a political force that galvanized former regime figures, openly criticizing the revolution, invoking nostalgia for the old regime, and calling for a return to strong-man rule. The party deployed a radical anti-Islamist discourse similar to Nidaa's discourse in 2013–2014 but its central promise was to do what Nidaa had not—form a government without Ennahdha. On the other side of the spectrum was Etilaf Al-Karama, a new electoral alliance of socially conservative, prorevolution independents led by lawyer Seifeddine Makhlouf. The alliance adopted a highly prorevolutionary discourse that critiqued the compromises made since 2011 by prodemocracy forces, particularly Ennahdha, and promised to introduce radical change and fulfill the demands of the revolution.

The results of both the 2019 legislative and presidential elections confirmed the rise of antisystem populists. The legislative elections saw both Etilaf Al-Karama and PDL perform well, coming in fourth and fifth, respectively. Ennahdha, the only governing party that had remained intact, came first with just under 20 percent of the vote. Qalb Tounes, a centrist economically liberal party led by businessman and media mogul Nabil Karoui, who had played a leading role in the creation of Nidaa Tounes, came second with 14.5 percent. At-Tayar Ad-Dimoqratti (the Democratic Current), the leftist party that had formed as an offshoot of CPR, led by former minister under the Troika Mohamed Abbou, came third, a significant improvement on its 2014 results. These parties were trailed by a long list of smaller parties, making the legislature highly fractured.

The presidential elections also saw a rise in populist discourse. The victory by Kais Saied, a constitutional law professor with no prior experience in politics, was a surprise for all observers, as he had led a small campaign, had no party of his own, and had presented no electoral program. His political outlook defies classification and has been described as combining Arab nationalism, Marxism, localism, and social conservatism. His election slogan, "*acha'ab yourid*" (The People Want) and his electoral campaign focused on calls to restore national sovereignty and achieve the "will of the people." Saied's image as an outsider to the political elite and his antisystem discourse appealed to prorevolutionary voters and young people, who felt marginalized by the postrevolution politics of consensus-building and pact-making among elites. Saied promised to overhaul the system of governance by amending the 2014 constitution and changing the existing system of representative democracy. His program focused on abolishing the directly elected parliament and replacing it with a "bottom-up" system of what he called "direct democracy," in which elections would be limited to local bodies, which would send members to regional councils and a national legislature.[17]

The fragmentation within the 2019 elected legislature produced difficulties in forming a cohesive government. After intensive negotiations, Ennahdha's candidate for prime minister, Habib Jemli, failed to secure the majority needed within parliament. In accordance with the constitution, President Kais Saied then nominated a candidate, Elyes Fakhfakh, a former minister from the social democrat Ettakattol Party, who won a vote of confidence in parliament in February 2020. The coalition government that backed Fakfakh was ideologically diverse, composed of the Islamist Ennahdha, the left-wing Attayar, the Arab Nationalist Harakat Al-Chaab, and the economically liberal center-right Tahya Tounes and Al Badil Attounsi. This coalition came to an end when revelations emerged that Fakhfakh was involved in a conflict of interests, as a company in which he owned shares had won contracts with the Tunisian state worth millions of dollars, which he had failed to disclose. After Fakhfakh's resignation in July 2020, President Saied's nominee, Hichem Mechichi, Saied's former legal advisor and former interior minister in the Fakhfakh government, formed a government which received legislative support from Ennahdha, Qalb Tounes, the National Reform Bloc, Tahya Tounes, and Al-Moustakbal Bloc.

In 2020–2021, tensions began to emerge once again between the two heads of the executive, and between President Saied and the legislature, headed by the newly elected Speaker of Parliament Rached Ghannouchi, head of Ennahdha Party. Tensions between President Saied and Prime Minister Mechichi soon appeared, turning into complete political deadlock after Mechichi's dismissal of Minister of Interior Taoufik Charfeddine, a Saied appointee.[18] After a government reshuffle by the Prime Minister in January 2021, President Saied refused to allow the incoming ministers to be sworn-in, although they had been approved by parliament. The following months witnessed an increasingly hostile exchange of words between President and Prime Minister, as each sought to assert his prerogatives. Control over the Ministry of Interior and security forces was a particularly central issue, and in April 2021, President Saied made a speech stating that the constitution granted the President of the Republic control over not only the armed forces but security forces as well. In the absence of a constitutional court, there were no legal mechanisms for resolving the conflict between the two heads of the executive by pronouncing on the scope of their powers.

On July 25, 2021, after months of political stalemate between the President of the Republic and the Prime Minister, President Saied invoked Article 80 of the constitution. The provision states that "The President of the Republic, in a state of imminent danger threatening the integrity of the country and the country's security and independence, is entitled to take the measures necessitated by this exceptional situation, after consulting the Prime Minister and the Speaker of the Cabinet." Saied justified his measures by reference to protests that took place on July 25 and the rising death toll due to the coronavirus pandemic and what was seen to be an inadequate government response to the crisis. President Saied dismissed the Prime Minister Hichem Mechichi and announced that he was taking over executive authority until the appointment of a new prime minister. He announced that he was "freezing" parliament and lifting the parliamentary immunity of all members of parliament. Parliamentarians headed to the parliament on the same night to find that army tanks had blocked all access to the parliament on the orders of the president in contravention of Article 80, which states that parliament must remain in permanent session throughout the application of the provision.

The July 25 measures were met with initial popular support due to the health and economic crisis, which aggravated years of economic stagnation, political in-fighting, and failure to tackle systemic corruption. Groups of protesters took to the streets after Saied's announcement to celebrate. However, popular support dwindled in the weeks and months following the announcement as President Saied failed to appoint a prime minister or announce any clear economic recovery plans, and as the financial and economic situation worsened.

The July 25 measures provoked mixed reactions among Tunisian political parties and social forces. The two largest parties in parliament, Ennahdha and Qalb Tounes, immediately categorically rejected the measures and stated that they constituted a "coup," as did Etilaf Al-Karama.[19] Meanwhile, the Arab nationalist Harakat Ach-Chaab supported the measures, while remaining parties abstained from declaring a clear position. However, the imposition of restrictions on media and travel bans and house arrests on a number of politicians, judges, businessmen, and outspoken critics of the president in the weeks following the coup provoked growing concerns, as did the prosecution in military courts of a number of parliamentarians. Most political parties declared their opposition to the measures and called for a return to the constitution and for a political dialogue involving political parties and civil society in order to set a roadmap to end the crisis.

Rather than entering into a political dialogue, President Saied instead expanded his takeover of executive and legislative powers. Two months after the introduction of the July 25 measures, President Saied issued Decree 117 of September 22, 2021, which purported to suspend much of the 2014 constitution. The Decree granted the president sole control over executive power, wide legislative powers, and greater control over the judiciary. Saied also announced plans to form a committee to draft a new constitution. The move was criticized by the vast majority of Tunisian political parties, as well as numerous civil society organizations[20] and international organizations.[21] In October 2021, Saied appointed a new prime minister, Najla Bouden, the Arab world's first woman prime minister. Bouden faces a challenging economic situation, with Tunisia seeking an International Monetary Fund (IMF) loan to plug a hole in its 2022 budget.

HISTORY OF STATE-BUILDING

In 1881, French troops crossed into northwest Tunisia from French-occupied Algeria, and in less than a month had forced the ruling Hussaynid ruler, Sadok Bey, to sign the Bardo Treaty. While the Bey continued to be the country's leader, the treaty ceded French control over defense and taxation policy, as well as control of many daily governance functions, while attempting to keep minimum costs to the French Republic.

The establishment of the French protectorate changed the political economy, accelerating formation of social classes and political strata. To bolster French claims, the Protectorate enticed French farmers, merchants, and administrators to immigrate. In 1892, the French mandated annual land transfers to a central commission set up to encourage colonization. By 1915, close to one-fifth of arable land had been transferred to French settlers and colonial agrobusiness. These transfers encouraged newly dispossessed peasants to migrate to Tunisia's major cities, where many integrated into the new colonial economy. French military conscription of Tunisian men, as elsewhere in colonial empires, served to politicize them. Similarly, Tunisian laborers developed a class and nationalist consciousness, working alongside French and Italian laborers who excluded them from their unions. French control of territorial administration extended to technical ministries responsible for public services, infrastructure, and industry in the 1890s. These independent bureaucracies excluded Tunisians. By 1939, only 5,500 of the 14,000 administrative posts were held by Tunisians. Public education only reached about 20 percent of citizens by 1955.

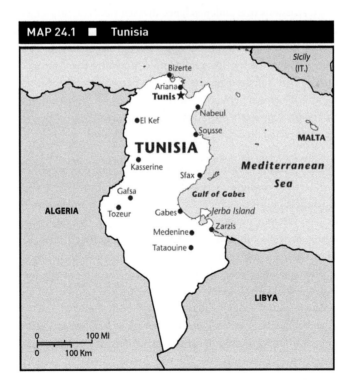

MAP 24.1 ■ Tunisia

The Rise of the National Movement: Toward Independence

While the Tunisian nationalist movement evolved in three stages, often with overlapping membership,[22] it organizationally coalesced in 1934 with the founding of the Neo-Destour party (NDP)—a schism from an earlier nationalist group. Founded by Habib Bourguiba, Bahri Guiga, Mahmoud Materi, Tahar Sfar, and Salah Ben Youssef, the NDP attracted young men who received their secondary education at the Sadiki College in Tunis and then went on to postgraduate studies in France. The NDP's founding leadership emerged from modest origins, predominantly from the Sahel region. They believed that only mass mobilization could ensure economic and social development in preparation for an independent Tunisia. In line with these progressive views, the NDP supported women's rights, modern education, and a secular state, enshrined in a liberal constitution.

The NDP successfully mobilized most segments of Tunisian society, actively working with Tunisia's nascent sectoral organizations, including the UGTT (ca. 1946); the UTICA(ca. 1947); the General Union of Tunisian Farmers (UGAT; ca. 1949); and the General Union of Tunisian Students (UGET; ca. 1952). Founded in 1946, the UGTT played a major role in mobilizing workers in support of the NDP and the independence movement. Independence sentiments promoted by the Neo-Destour, the UGTT, and other sectorial movements forged national unity among rich and poor, bourgeoisie and peasant alike during French occupation.

Radical Transformation and Mass Mobilization

In the mid-1950s, discussions over independence divided the NDP movement between followers of two of its historical leaders, Habib Bourguiba and Salah Ben Youssef, leading to intraparty violence in 1955. The crisis pitted supporters against opponents of France's limited autonomy proposal—supported by Bourguiba and opposed by Ben Youssef. As a founding member of the party, Ben Youssef had served as the party's second secretary general from 1948 to 1955 and forged his own popularity during this period by expanding the ranks of the party. Bourguiba and his supporters prevailed in late 1955; Ben Youssef fled the country, and many of his supporters were jailed. Ben Youssef was assassinated in Frankfurt, Germany, in 1961.

After independence, Bourguiba further strengthened his hold over the NDP and its control over the administration through a series of centralizing administrative and party reforms. Bourguiba justified these political changes by the need to rapidly modernize the country and resistance to the Neo-Destour he encountered along the way. Bourguiba faced opposition surrounding his progressive family code reforms. Shortly after independence, he enacted the 1957 Personal Status Code, which granted expanded rights to women. The new code abolished polygamy, provided equal rules for divorce, fixed a minimum age for marriage, and acknowledged a near equality of women in providing for the family. The new regime also sought to reduce the power of religious institutions in both the rural and urban milieu. In 1956 and 1957, the regime dissolved religious endowments (*habous*), which prevented up to a fifth of Tunisian land from being used in commercial transactions. More than just an attack on traditional property mechanisms, the reforms undermined the authority of religious leaders, who had managed this land in parallel to state social welfare institutions. Similarly, Bourguiba integrated the Zaytouna mosque—the Maghreb's premier site of Islamic learning—into the national education system. On July 25, 1957, Bourguiba deposed the Beylic and declared Tunisia a republic.

Forging National Unity Through Economic Centralization and Repression

A decade after independence, the state sought to reform the agriculture sector to boost economic production. The regime's new enthusiasm for state-led development was reflected in the party's name, which was changed to the Socialist Destourian Party (PSD) at the 1964 party congress. That year, the Tunisian state had recuperated all of the nearly one-fifth of arable land ceded to French interests during the protectorate. In 1965, former head of the UGTT and Minister of Agriculture Ahmed Ben Salah announced the integration of these and all other state-owned lands into modern cooperative production units (CPUs).[23] Despite complaints from workers and small farmers who had been forced to join the program, it continued to expand and, by 1968, integrated close to 1.8 million hectares of land. In March 1969, Ben Salah announced plans to incorporate all Tunisian land into the cooperative movement. Under pressure from peasants and his PSD allies, Bourguiba announced the end of forced collectivization, and Ben Salah, visionary of the state-led experiment, was arrested and charged with treason.[24]

In the 1970s, the government shifted its focus to private-sector development, promoting private investments in agriculture, agroindustry, light industry, and tourism. The new economic direction increasingly isolated the UGTT, which organized the 1978 general strike. The regime responded harshly to that act of defiance, which revealed both the degree to which the population did not embrace the new economic orientation and the new leadership's inability to capture the political hearts of an increasingly vocal population.

Calls for political reform had already begun in the 1970s. The failed cooperative movement revealed to many the limits of a single-party system. These tensions came to a head at the 1971 PSD party congress, when Minister of Interior Ahmed Mestiri and a group of political liberals, which included current President Essebsi, called for a political opening.[25] While that effort failed, the regime agreed in 1981 on a limited-political opening, allowing Mestiri's Socialist Democratic Movement (MDS) and the Tunisian Communist Party (PCT) to participate in elections. Neither party was allowed to play a significant role in politics, and both failed to win a seat during the 1981 legislative elections. During the same period, opposition groups had begun to coalesce on university campuses. That same year, Rached Ghannouchi[26] and Abdelfattah Mourou, (later to become speaker and deputy speaker of parliament, respectively, after the 2011 uprising) requested political accreditation for the Islamic Tendency Movement (*Harakat al-Ittijah al-Islami*, MTI), a movement that rejected Bourguiba's regime and many of his modernization policies, which they saw as an attack on Tunisia's Arab-Muslim culture. Its application was rejected, but over the next few years the MTI would exponentially grow into a major political force.

The political arena continued to contract following the 1984 bread riots, a violent response to an IMF demand that the government cut key subsidies. The PSD had lost much public support, while political intrigue blocked significant efforts to push for either greater economic or political reform. A sign of the degree of political fragility, in July 1986, Prime Minister Mohamed Mzali (1980–1986)[27] was replaced by rival Rachid Sfar, who proposed a political alliance with the UGTT in the November 1986 elections. Accredited only five years before, both the MDS and PCT chose to boycott the 1986 legislative elections. Sfar was himself replaced by Zine al-Abidine Ben Ali in October 1987.

In 1986, the government claimed that a radicalized MTI wing was responsible for a series of bombings in Sousse. In 1987, Bourguiba tried to reopen court cases against its leaders, seeking death penalties. Fearing that such actions would plunge Tunisia into civil war, Ben Ali had Bourguiba declared unfit for rule. On November 7, 1987, the bloodless coup d'état was met with surprise and hope for an end to autocracy.

Ben Ali came to power with promises to liberalize the political system, taking a number of steps to open dialogue with the *'ulama*, disaffected social groups, opposition parties, Islamists, labor, human rights organizations, and civil society groups. The result of these discussions was the much-touted November 1988 National Pact, which promised pluralism and inclusive state-society engagement. Ben Ali organized presidential and parliamentary elections in April 1989. Ben Ali, though, ran uncontested, winning 99.27 percent of the popular vote, while the Democratic Constitutional Rally (RCD)—the revamped PSD—obtained all 141 seats in the Chamber of Deputies with 80 percent of the vote. In 1991, the regime cracked down on Ennahdha, arresting thousands of its rank and file and leadership. Imprisoned, many were tortured, while key leaders were sentenced to long terms of solitary confinement. Others, like Ghannouchi, were forced into political exile and would not return to Tunisia until after the 2011 revolution.

In 1999, the regime apportioned a token percentage of parliamentary seats to the "losing" parties in the winner-take-all system: 20 percent in 1999 and 2004, and 25 percent in 2009. In the 2000s, Ben Ali changed the constitution to expand the political elite and RCD patronage to professional associations.[28] A 2002 amendment created a bicameral legislature with an upper house, the Chamber of Counselors supplementing the lower house, and the Chamber of Deputies. Ben Ali also amended constitutional limits on presidential terms and the maximum age of the president so that he could stand for the 2004 elections.

The 2009 Tunisian presidential and legislative elections were held in October, and Ben Ali sought yet a fifth presidential term, inciting an organized oppositional movement, the *18 Octobre Collectif.* Prior to elections, parliament passed a 2008 constitutional amendment that required presidential candidates to receive recommendations from thirty parliamentary members and to have served at least the past two years as party leader. The 2008 law derailed the candidacies of Mustafa Ben Jaafar (Ettakatol) and Nejib Chebbi of the Progressive Democratic Party (PDP). The 2009 presidential elections were the last failed elections prior to the revolution. The complete shutdown of the political arena left little room for formal and electoral contestation. However, the opposition grew through informal political spaces and extended to citizens disenfranchised with the Ben Ali regime. That opposition grew as the regime's policies produced widening inequalities and economic and political exclusion, resulting in the uprising of 2010-11.

SOCIAL CHANGE IN TUNISIA

Pays pilote, or model country, Tunisia has always been an early innovator in the Arab world, from the Beylical period (1705–1957) to the contemporary era. Founded in 1946, the UGTT was the Arab world's first independent labor union. The 1956 Family Code transferred personal status from religious to civilian courts—the first time ever in an Arab country. In 1861, Tunisia's precolonial government drafted the Arab world's first constitution.

1956 Personal Status Code

Tunisia's Family Code significantly altered the nation's social fabric. The Family Code is in reality a bundle of laws that transferred law pertaining to personal status from religious courts to positive law. These laws required marriage in civil courts, banned polygamy, gave women the right to divorce while protecting them from spousal abandonment, defined alimony requirements, and set out a reorganization of inheritance laws.

Subsequent laws economically and politically emancipated women, giving women the right to vote; to guaranteed access to primary, secondary, and higher education; to work; to open bank accounts; and to move without a tutor's authorization. Bourguiba tasked the National Union of Tunisian Women (UNFT) to educate women of their expanding rights. By 1960, the UNFT had 14,000 members and 115 branches across Tunisia—attesting to both the popularity of the reforms among women and the degree to which Bourguiba was willing to support his cause.[29] Women's rights throughout both the Bourguiba and Ben Ali regime were closely tied to the PSD and later the RCD party; by the late 1980s, the UNFT was instrumentalized to oppose Tunisia's nascent Islamist movement.[30]

Though not fitting squarely into the Personal Status Code, equally important reforms were a series of public health laws, especially the 1962 laws that gave women access to contraception and a 1965 law guaranteeing access to safe abortion.[31] The effects on fertility were profound. Adolescent fertility rates fell from 66 in 1,000 (ages 15–19) in 1960 to 7.6 in 1,000 in 2016.[32] Overall fertility rates also declined. Whereas in 1960, fertility rates averaged seven children per female, they dropped to 2.2 children per female in 2016.

In September 2017, President Essebsi annulled a decree banning the marriage of Muslim women to non-Muslims dating back to 1973. A second, more controversial proposal was announced in tandem with the release of the COLIBE (The Individual Freedoms and Equality Committee) report in June 2018, proposing equal inheritance for both men and women. The proposal generated a several-thousand-strong protest in August 2018. Opponents claimed that the law and some recommendations in the report contradicted Islam, while the project itself was Western-imposed.

Expanded Education Opportunities

Educating Tunisians was a priority for all of Bourguiba's modernization projects. While in 1971, net primary, secondary, and tertiary enrollment was 79 percent, 23 percent, and 2.5 percent, respectively, in 2013 primary enrollment was close to 100 percent, secondary enrollment 90 percent, and 33 percent of Tunisians were pursuing higher education. Gains for women have outpaced male enrollment, reflecting the effects of the Family Code across time. Net female primary school enrollment has jumped from 65 percent in 1971 to 98 percent in 2008, whereas female primary school completion has increased from 43 percent in 1973 to 98 percent in 2013. The degree to which Tunisia has promoted women since independence is most salient in higher-education enrollment. In 1971, just over 1 percent of Tunisian women were enrolled at university, compared to 4 percent of Tunisian men. In 2000, for the first time ever, women enrollment at universities surpassed men, and by 2013, 42 percent of Tunisian women are pursuing college educations or postgraduate studies compared to only 26 percent of Tunisian men.

While the Tunisian regime's commitment to output is uncontested, the quality of Tunisian education can be improved. A 2011 Trends in International Mathematics and Science Study survey on fourth- and eighth-grade student mathematics scores, for example, places Tunisia well below the international average, with only 30 percent and 2 percent of students reaching the intermediate or higher international benchmark, respectively.[33] In addition to ongoing reforms in K–12 education, the Tunisian Ministry of Higher Education has also embarked on an ambitious Tunisia 2020 reform project funded by international organizations and bilateral aid projects to link higher education to critical skills needed in the job market.

Women in Politics and the Workforce

Tunisia's proclaimed progressive policy of equity, enshrined in both the 1957 and 2014 Constitutions and through organic law, has had a major effect on the economic, political, and social rights of women in Tunisia, both inclusive and exclusive. Whereas women only gained the right to vote in 1957 and the right to run for office in 1958, women won close to 27 percent of seats in the NCA elections of 2011, increasing to 31 percent in the 2014–2019 parliament, thanks in part to a quota system in candidate lists. Despite the positive changes since the revolution, only 148 of the 1,500 competing lists in the 2014 legislative elections were headed by a woman, reflecting continued patriarchal biases in Tunisian national politics. Women candidates have fared better at the local level, due to the expansion of the quota system in the 2016 election law to include horizontal gender parity (50 percent of any party's electoral lists were required to be headed by women and 50 percent by men) as well as vertical parity on all electoral lists (alternating men and women on the same list). Because the electoral law required both vertical and horizontal parity, the 2018 elections saw women win 47 percent of the seats allotted in Tunisia's 350 municipalities; 27 percent of those elected officials were the heads of competing lists.

While access to education and politics has made Tunisia a model for developing (and many developed) nations, women continue to face discrimination. In 2020, the ILO estimated female unemployment at 22.7 percent, compared to 12.4 percent for men and a 16.7 percent national average. Though it is unclear that this necessarily reflects discriminatory hiring practices, the breakdown of the active workforce is more revealing. In 2019, the percentage of female labor force participation was only at 28 percent, compared to 68.9 percent for men.

Many have hailed Tunisia for its promotion of women's rights and expanding economic and educative opportunities to much of its population. However successful, the modernization program also excluded vast segments of the country's population. While in the past, authoritarianism and corruption limited both access to and quality of these services, democratization presents new opportunities for new visions of progressive social change through the empowerment of Tunisian citizens via the urn.

STATE INSTITUTIONS AND GOVERNANCE

The Tunisian state played an important transformative role during the years of Tunisia's two autocrats, Habib Bourguiba and Zine al-Abidine Ben Ali. The monopolization of power by a single ruling party came to an end with the 2011 Revolution, and Tunisia was governed by ten governments between 2011 and 2021—the transitional government headed by Beji Caid Essebi (March–October 2011); the Troika coalition (November 2011–January 2014, which involved two successive governments led by Hamadi Jebali then Ali Laarayedh); the Mehdi Jomaa technocratic government (January 2014–February 2015); the 2014-elected Nidaa Tounes–Ennahdha coalition (February 2015–July 2016 headed by Habib Essid, then two governments headed by Youssef Chahed in August 2016–February 2020); the 2019-elected coalition government (February–September 2020) led by Elyes Fakhfakh; a technocratic government (September 2020–July 2021) led by Hichem Mechichi; and a government appointed by President Kais Saied led by Najlaa Bouden (October 2021–present).

Constitution and Powers

Political Authority Prior to the Revolution

Prior to the revolution, authority was founded upon the constitution of 1959 Tunisia. That document established a republic, with Arabo-Islamic foundations (Article 1), vesting sovereignty in the people (Article 3). The constitution founded the republic upon the rule of law and political pluralism, yet it stipulated that state and society strive for "solidarity, mutual assistance and solidarity among individuals, social categories and generations" (Article 5). The 1959 constitution specified rights, liberties, and obligations and granted freedoms of the press, publication, association, assembly, and labor organization (Article 8). Article 8 as revised in 2002 also stipulated that parties be free of violence and hatred, without organization on exclusionary premises such as religion, race, sex, or region. Subsequent constitutional amendments introduced by Presidents Bourguiba and Ben Ali qualified or modified the articles, introducing ambiguity and de facto reductions in freedom. Rights of association were subject to contradictory amendments that stipulated that groups be approved by the state and elsewhere stipulated that all Tunisians respect public order, social progress, and national defense. The state did not apply articles fully, and it rested on a politicized judiciary to rule arbitrarily in its favor.

2014 Constitution

The 2014 constitution was the result of a consensual drafting process in the 2011 NCA. Adopted on January 26, 2014, the Tunisian Constitution is hailed as the Arab world's most progressive constitution. During the drafting process, special constitutional committees were created to debate some of the most controversial articles, while a special consensus committee of twenty-two deputies was established to mediate and reach agreements on contentious articles prior to voting and adaptation. The constitution establishes parity between men and women in elected assemblies (Article 45), and executive powers have been reduced as part of a contentious debate on the separation of powers throughout the process (Article 90). The document reflects an unprecedented consensus between Islamic, liberal, socialist-leftist, and nationalist voices represented in the NCA.

July 25 and Decree 117 of 2021

The organization of political authority took a radical turn away from the 2014 constitution after the July 25, 2021 measures introduced by President Kais Saied. Presidential Decree 117 of September 22, 2021 purported to suspend much of the 2014 constitution. The Decree states that only the preamble to the constitution and the first two chapters on rights and freedoms continue to apply. In addition, it states that in the case of a conflict between presidential decree-laws and the constitution, the former will prevail. President Saied also announced the formation of a committee to draft a new constitution and establish "a true democracy in which the people are truly sovereign." Article 22 of the Decree provides that the composition of the committee will be solely determined by the president.

Decree 117 significantly amends the distribution of powers between branches of government and establishes a constitutional regime in which the president holds almost all power.[34] President Saied stated that Decree 117 would be temporary but provided no indication of how long it would remain in force.

Legislative Authority

2014 Constitution

The 2014 constitution provides for an elected parliament that exercises important legislative and oversight powers. The Assembly of People's Representatives is the cornerstone of the new constitutional system, as it has the power to approve the government, through a vote of confidence, and to dismiss it, through a vote of no-confidence. Parliament also exercises important oversight powers over governmental work, including ratifying commercial and international treaties, approving external loans, and adopting the annual state budget. The constitution also provides important guarantees for the opposition, including chairing the Finance Committee, "adequate and effective representation in all bodies of the Assembly, as well as in its internal and external activities," and the right to establish and head a committee of inquiry annually (Article 60).

July 25 Measures and Decree 117 of 2021

Following the suspension of Parliament on July 25, 2021, Presidential decree 117 of September 22, 2021 promulgated by President Kais Saied transferred all legislative power to the president of the republic, while maintaining the suspension of parliament. The decree allows the president to issue "legislative texts" by decree and grants the president exclusive legislative authority, while placing presidential decrees above any judicial oversight. Decree 117 also strips members of parliament of their immunity from prosecution, contrary to Article 68 of the constitution.

Executive Authority

Prior to the revolution, power was concentrated in the executive, allowing former Presidents Bourguiba and Ben Ali to dominate the legislative and judicial branches of government. Prime ministers, ministers of government, ambassadors, judges, and often the heads of nongovernmental organizations were named by and beholden to the executive. During the NCA, the premiership directed government with a cabinet of forty-three members. Presidential power was limited to foreign policy and commander-in-chief of the armed forces. Under the 2014 constitution, the president is the symbol of national unity (Article 71) and represents the state, orienting national defense, security, and foreign relations, in consultation with the prime minister (Article 77). The president formalizes the composition of government, determined by the premiership, and can only call for two votes of confidence during a presidential term (Article 99). Disputes between the presidency and premiership can be referred to the Constitutional Court by either party (Article 101).

Decree 117 of 2021

Presidential decree 117 of September 22, 2021 promulgated by President Kais Saied transfers executive powers to the president of the republic. While the Tunisian constitution of 2014 states that the government, headed by a prime minister, is to be approved by Parliament and answerable before it, Decree 117 gives the president of the republic the exclusive authority to appoint and dismiss the prime minister, as well as individual ministers. According to Decree 117, the president is assisted by a government that acts at the president's discretion. The president chairs the Council of Ministers and has sole authority to determine government policy on all issues after "consulting" the cabinet.

The Judiciary

The judicial system has not been entirely overhauled since the revolution. Former President Ben Ali appointed the majority of judges currently in office. Under the former constitution, the judiciary was an extension of the presidency. Chapter 5, Section 2 of the 2014 constitution provides for the creation of a Supreme Judicial Council, which is responsible for organizing the sound functioning of the justice system and protecting its independence. The council, created in 2016, enjoyed financial and administrative independence, and oversaw professional matters and disciplinary measures within the judiciary. However, the council was dissolved by President Saied in February 2022 and replaced with a temporary judicial council appointed by him in March 2022.

Chapter 5 of the 2014 constitution mandated the creation of a new Constitutional Court to replace the Ben Ali–era court, dissolved in March 2011. Unlike the previous court, which functioned as a tool of the executive, the new Constitutional Court was given powers to review and determine the constitutionality of proposed laws, treaties, and laws referred to it by lower courts as the result of a legal claim, as well as the parliamentary rules of procedure. The court was to be composed of twelve members, appointed by the president, parliament, and Supreme Judicial Council in equal shares. Attempts were made by Parliament to elect four members in 2018 but only one court member was elected due to the failure to agree among key political parties. The legislature elected in 2019 also attempted to facilitate the election of a constitutional court by adopting a law reducing the majority required for electing the four members of the constitutional court chosen by parliament. However, the law was twice rejected by President Saied.

In the interim, awaiting the election of a constitutional court, a judicial body to monitor the constitutionality of laws was put in place from 2014 to 2021, tasked with reviewing the constitutionality of all draft bills referred to it by parliamentarians. However, Presidential decree 117 of September 22, 2021 promulgated by President Kais Saied dissolved the interim body. The decree provides that the president has exclusive authority to interpret the constitutional order.

The decree provides for no form of recourse to challenge presidential decrees, meaning that all such decrees are above any form of judicial oversight. The decree also grants the President full legislative authority over "the organization of justice and of the courts" (Article 5(2)). This effectively does away with Chapter 5 of the 2014 constitution on judicial independence.

Transitional Justice

Shortly after Ben Ali's ouster, the interim government organized two ad hoc commissions[35] to investigate police abuse and corruption. These commissions filed their final reports in December 2011 and May 2012, but despite more than 10,000 requests, 2,000 examinations, and 300 judicial case transfers, few have been brought to trial, and few assets have been returned to Tunisia. The Tunisian state did confiscate 1.4 billion dinars (around $450 million) from Ben Ali and from 113 other members of his elite circle. A number of senior officials were tried, including former President Ben Ali, who was found guilty by a military court of ordering the death of protesters and sentenced to multiple life sentences in absentia.

The first postrevolution institution of transitional justice was the new Ministry of Human Rights and Transitional Justice, led by former Ennahdha political prisoner Samir Dilou, himself a victim of arbitrary arrest under Ben Ali. On June 9, 2014, the government launched the Truth and Dignity Commission (IVD). Headed by human rights activists and oppositional journalist Sihem Ben Sedrine, the IVD investigated human rights violations committed by the Tunisian state against citizens since independence, providing compensation and rehabilitation for its victims. The IVD received sixty-five thousand files and organized thirteen public hearings by victims and perpetrators on prime-time television. However, the transitional justice process ran into difficulties in 2014 with the victory of Nidaa Tounes, a party containing former regime figures. In July 2015, the coalition government proposed an economic reconciliation law granting amnesties to senior government officials and business people for "economic crimes" or misuse of public funds in exchange for repaying unlawfully obtained proceeds. The proposal provoked a public outcry and widespread protests, and was criticized by the IVD and human rights groups for encouraging impunity. A watered-down version of the law that covered only civil servants was passed in 2017.

More broadly, the IVD faced various obstructions by executive institutions when seeking to investigate historical abuses under the former regime. President Essebsi refused to attend its public hearings and stated that Tunisia needs "to not talk about the past" in order to move forward. The difficulties faced by the transitional justice process illustrate wider conflicts between old regime figures and new political actors, and struggles over not only interests but also over defining Tunisia's past and future. In the spring of 2018, the IVD began transferring files to specialized chambers within the Court structure to hear human rights trials. While the IVD's mandate ended in December 2018, cases continued to be adjudicated in the special chambers, and a special fund for reparations has been set into place.

Military–Civilian Relations and Security

Prior to the revolution, the military and security apparatuses were concentrated in the hands of the presidency and were themselves divided into multiple institutions in order to maintain civilian authoritarian rule.

The Tunisian presidency has fewer powers over the military and security establishment than under the previous two regimes, but it nevertheless retains an important degree of power. According to the 2014 Constitution, the Tunisian president is commander in chief of the Tunisian Armed Forces (TAF), which includes the army, navy, and air force, and chairs the National Security Council (Article 77). While control of the military and security forces is assured by government via the minister of defense and interior (respectively), who themselves are appointed by the prime minister, the president appoints and dismisses individuals to senior military and police positions, in consultation with the head of government (Article 78). The president is required to preside over the Council of Ministers on all issues relating to defense, foreign policy, and national security (Article 93). Article 80, furthermore, mandates the president to take any measures to protect the stability of the republic and can approve a thirty-day state of emergency, in consultation with the prime minister and speaker of the assembly of representatives. This provision was invoked by President Kais Saied on July 25, 2021, who relied on the army to suspend the work of parliament and block access to it.

The TAF has historically been small. Domestic spending for the TAF in 2010 was 1.3 percent of GDP, compared to 3.5 percent for both Algeria and Morocco.[36] This figure has increased in the postrevolution period, especially as security threats multiplied along the Algerian border near Kasserine and along the Libyan border to the southeast. By 2018, the military was estimated at between 40,000 and 65,000 members and was reinforced and professionalized through cooperative agreements with Algeria, the United States, and most recently NATO.

Whereas the TAF was historically sidelined, the various apparatuses within the ministry of interior—including the National Guard, Judicial Police, Presidential Guard, Rapid Intervention Brigades, regular National Police, and General Directorate of Information—were actively used by Ben Ali to identify and punish political opponents through harassment, incarceration, and torture. Violence and deaths during the revolution were directly attributed to various elements of the Ben Ali police force. Following the revolution, there was much discussion on investment in security sector reform, which remained slow. While the exigencies of counterterrorism in the current period make security sector reform both a pressing need and risky endeavor, the July 2015 Anti-Terrorism Law, voted by the Assembly of the Representatives of the People, reinforces the government's ability to gather information on and detain suspected members of terrorist organizations.[37] While reinforcing counterterrorist measures, many view the law as a potential regression for human rights.[38]

Public Administration

Under the 2014 constitution, Tunisia's elected assembly drafts and passes laws, but implementation is incumbent on the state administration—the central nervous system of the polity. Adapted from the French model, the Tunisian bureaucracy is composed of state cadres from the various national and regional administrations, ministries, public-sector enterprises, and municipalities, with an estimated 785,000 employees (close to 7 percent of the population).[39]

The current administration is deconcentrated into twenty-four governorates and 264 delegations, each led by a high-ranking cadre from the ministry of interior. On May 6, 2018, Tunisia held its first postrevolution municipal elections. Currently, Tunisia's 350 municipalities are governed by elected mayors and municipal councils, a departure from the previous system of appointing mayors and members of municipal councils.[40] Souad Abderrahim became the first female mayor of Tunis, running as an independent on the 2018 Ennahdha list. The Local Authorities Law also provides for elected regional councils, which were due to be elected in 2022. However, following the July 25 measures and Decree 117, changes may be introduced to the local governance system.

ACTORS AND PARTICIPATION

The Tunisian Revolution successfully overturned a system of controlled contestation within the political arena that had persisted and matured since the early beginning of the Tunisian state. Since independence, Tunisian political space was effectively controlled by a one-party state, despite cosmetic efforts to introduce a multiparty system in 1981 and following Ben Ali's 1987 constitutional coup. Despite these changes, Tunisia continued to operate as a de facto single-party state until the January 14, 2011, revolution, as indicated in Table 24.1.

TABLE 24.1 ■ Political Parties in Tunisia

Main Registered Parties With Seats in Parliament

2014–2019 Coalition

1. Nidaa Tounes (ca. 2012). Secretary General Mohsen Marzouk. "Big Tent Party," economically liberal. (86 seats in 2014 legislature)

2. Ennahdha Party (ca. in 2011). President Rached Ghannouchi. Islamist, economically liberal. (69 seats in 2014 legislature)

3. Free Patriotic Union (ca. 2011). Chairperson Slim Riahi. Populist, economically liberal. Fused with Nidaa Tounes in October 2018. (16 seats in 2014 legislature)

4. Afek Tounes (ca. 2011). President Yacine Brahim. Centrist, economically liberal. (8 seats in 2014 legislature)

Parliamentary Opposition

1. Popular Front (ca. 2012). Secretary General Hamma Hammami. Socialist. (15 seats in 2014 legislature)

2. Congress for the Republic (ca. 2001). Secretary General Imed Daïmi. Nationalist, socialist. (4 seats in 2014 legislature)

3. Democratic Current (ca. 2013). President Mohamed Abbou. Nationalist, socialist. Schism from CPR. (3 seats in 2014 legislature)

4. People's Movement (ca. 2011). Secretary General Zouhair Maghzaoui. Nationalist, socialist. (3 seats in 2014 legislature)

5. National Destourian Initiative (ca. 2011). President Kamel Morjane (Minister of Defense and Minister of Foreign Affairs under Ben Ali). Centrist, economically liberal. (3 seats in 2014 legislature)

(Continued)

TABLE 24.1 ■ Political Parties in Tunisia (*Continued*)

Main Registered Parties With Seats in Parliament—2019 legislative elections

1. Ennahdha Party (ca. in 2011). President Rached Ghannouchi. Islamist, economically liberal. (52 seats in 2019 legislature)

2. Qalb Tounes (ca. 2019). President Nabil Karoui. Centrist, economically liberal. (38 seats in 2019 legislature)

3. At-Tayar Ad-Dimoqratti (Democratic Current) (ca. 2013). President Mohamed Abbou. Center-left, social democrat. (22 seats in 2019 legislature)

4. Etilaf Al-Karama (Dignity Coalition) (ca. 2019). Coalition of independents headed by Seifeddine Makhlouf. Populist, prorevolution, socially conservative. (21 seats in 2019 legislature)

5. Free Destourian Party (ca. 2013). President Abir Moussi (Secretary General of former ruling party under Ben Ali). Populist, centrist, proformer regime. (17 seats in 2019 legislature)

6. Harakat Ach-Chaab (ca. 2011). Secretary General Zouhair Maghzaoui. Arab nationalist, socialist. (15 seats in 2014 legislature)

7. Tahya Tounes (ca. 2018). President Youssef Chahed. Centrist, economically liberal (offshoot of Nidaa Tounes). (14 seats in 2019 legislature)

8. Machrouu Tounes (ca. 2016). Secretary General Mohsen Marzouk. Secularist, center-left (offshoot of Nidaa Tounes). (4 seats in 2019 legislature)

9. Errahma Party (ca. 2012). President Said Jaziri. Salafist. (4 seats in 2019 legislature)

10. Al Badil Ettounsi (ca. 2017). President Mehdi Jomaa. Centrist, economically liberal. (3 seats in 2019 legislature)

11. Nidaa Tounes (ca. 2012). Secretary General Ali Hafsi. "Big Tent Party," centrist, economically liberal. (3 seats in 2019 legislature)

12. Republican People's Union. (ca. 2011). President Lotfi Mraihi. Neo-Bourguibist. (3 seats in 2019 legislature)

13. Afek Tounes. (ca. 2011). President Yacine Brahim. Centrist, economically liberal. (2 seats in 2019 legislature)

14. Amal wa 'Aamal (ca. 2019). Political movement headed by Yassine Ayari. (2 seats in 2019 legislature)

15. Aich Tounsi. (ca. 2018). Political movement led by Olfa Terras. (1 seat in 2019 legislature)

16. Popular Front. (ca. 2012). Electoral alliance of nine left-wing parties. (1 seat in 2019 legislature)

17. Democratic and Social Union. Center-left electoral alliance composed of Al-Massar, Al-Jomhouri and Movement of Socialist Democrats. (1 seat in 2019 legislature)

18. Tayar Al-Mahabba. (ca. 2011). President Mohamed Hechmi Hamdi. Populist, socially conservative. (1 seat in 2019 legislature)

19. Socialist Destourian Party. (ca. 2016). President Chokri Balti. Neo-Bourguibist. (1 seat in 2019 legislature)

20. Farmers' Voice Party. (ca. 2014). President Faycal Tebbini. Agrarianist. (1 seat in 2019 legislature)

21. Independent lists. (11 seats in 2019 legislature)

Postreveolution Elections

2011 National Constituent Assembly Elections

One of the lynchpins to widening the political arena was the establishment of the independent Higher Independent Authority for Elections, which organized the 2011 NCA elections, the first free elections held in Tunisian history.

Of the 8.3 million eligible Tunisian voters at home and overseas, 4.3 million, or 51.7 percent, registered to vote. Representatives of seventeen parties, one coalition list, and thirty-two independent lists were elected. Of the total vote count, 68.2 percent of voters cast ballots for successful parties, revealing that 1.3 million voters cast ballots for small or local parties and lists. Most of the political parties that participated were either not registered or banned during the Ben Ali years. Ennahdha won the elections, capturing 89 of 217 seats, revealing the success of the network it kept alive under Ben Ali's repression. This, and the movements' perceived distance from the single-party state, garnered it popular legitimacy. The top secular parties—one social democratic (Ettakatol) and the other leftist-(Arab) nationalist (CPR), likewise performed well because of long-standing oppositional status. Parties along the liberal–secular lines, including clusters of fractured leftist fringe parties and well-established loyal oppositional parties, performed poorly, in part because of their staunch and ill-perceived anti-Islamist rhetoric.

2014 Assembly of the People's Representative Legislative Elections

In October 2014, Tunisia organized its first elections under the framework of the new constitution. The elections were viewed as a plebiscite on the Troika government's performance. Unlike the 2011 elections, where Ennahdha opponents were largely divided into a coterie of small, disorganized movements and newly accredited political parties, the 2014 elections were marked by recently founded Nidaa Tounes's campaign to "vote strategically." The slogan set out to remind voters of the futility of voting for small parties, while underscoring the party's own campaign promises to competently run government.

With a relatively high 66 percent turnout, the October 26 legislative elections reconfigured the political landscape in a number of ways—with both Tunisian and regionwide significance. First, the results showed that political Islam could be defeated at the polls. Nidaa Tounes, a big-tent, anti-Ennahdha party, carried the election, with close to 38 percent of the vote, translating into 86 seats. Though coming in second, Ennahdha received 10 percent fewer votes than its rival, with close to 28 percent of the ballots and 69 seats. Ennahdha's defeat marked the first time in the history of the Arab world that an Islamist political party lost power in a free and fair election. Following the presidential elections, Nidaa and Ennahdha formed a coalition government, which led to the initial leadership split within Nidaa and defections by deputies, resulting in Ennahdha becoming the largest bloc within Parliament. The Nidaa–Ennahdha coalition lasted until 2018, as the balance of power was significantly tilted when Ennahdha beat Nidaa at the polls during the May 2018 municipal elections.

Second, the 2014 election results revealed the continued salience of populism and workers' issues in postauthoritarian Tunisia. A populist party, the UPL, which ran on money and soccer, came in third, with 4 percent of the vote and 16 seats (mirroring the Popular Petition's 2011 results), closely followed by the Popular Front, a party that combined multiple schisms of the former PCT and which received close to 4 percent and 15 seats.

Finally, and linked to the first point, the incumbent Troika government was punished for transitional instability. Speaker of Parliament Mustapha Ben Jaafar's Ettakatol failed to win a single seat, while the CPR, of which President Marzouki was the founder, garnered just over 2 percent of the vote, securing only four seats.

2019 Assembly of the People's Representative Legislative Elections

In October 2019, Tunisia organized its second legislative elections under the 2014 constitution. These elections were characterized by a far higher level of fragmentation than the 2014 elections, due to the splintering of Nidaa Tounes into several smaller offshoots. In addition, the Popular Front electoral alliance had also splintered due to internal disagreements. As opposed to the 2014 elections, which had revolved around a dual polarization between Nidaa Tounes and Ennahdha, due to the emergence of Nidaa Tounes as a "big tent" secularist party, the 2019 elections saw the secularist camp highly divided among a large number of parties. The elections produced a fragmented legislature, with 20 parties and electoral lists and 11 independents entering the parliament. The voter turnout was also much lower than the 2014 legislative elections, falling to just under 42 percent.

Presidential Elections in the Post-2011 Period

A month after its first free legislative elections under the new constitution in October 2014, Tunisia organized its first postauthoritarian presidential elections. Though the presidency had been relegated to a largely symbolic post by the 2014 Constitution, the presidential elections nevertheless underscore the continuously dynamic Tunisian political landscape. A telling dynamic has been the strengthening of the presidency and executive by Beji Caid Essebsi, mirroring executive strength in the regimes of Bourguiba and Ben Ali. The post-2014 landscape has witnessed a struggle between presidents and prime ministers, beginning with the resignation of Prime Minister Habib Essid after he fell out of favor with President Essebsi, followed by Prime Minister Youssef Chahed. More recently, tensions between President Saied and Prime Minister Hichem Mechichi have led to a political stalemate that set the stage for the suspension of the constitution in what many have termed a 'coup'.

A number of noteworthy and telling observations can be drawn from the 2014 and 2019 polls. First, Tunisians did not shy away from voting for candidates with links to the authoritarian era. In the first round of the 2014 presidential elections, 39 percent of Tunisians voted for Beji Caid Essebsi, former minister of interior in the Bourguiba era and head of the Chamber of Deputies under Ben Ali. He enjoyed a six-point lead ahead of incumbent President Moncef Marzouki, who won 33 percent. The gap widened in the second round where Essebsi won close to 56 percent of the vote compared to Marzouki's 44 percent. In the 2019 elections, a party created by Nabil Karoui, a businessman who had been very close to Beji Caid Essebsi, came second, while the PDL led by former RCD Secretary General Abir Moussi came fifth. Former regime elites have thus continued to be active in political life through various parties and have garnered significant levels of support.

Second, the electoral system has significantly shaped political life and contributed to a highly fragmented, divided, and often turbulent political landscape. The election law first drafted in 2011 by the Ben Achour Commission adopted a closed-list proportional representation system using the Hare Quota with Largest Remainders (HQ-LR) formula, which remains in place till today. This system has had significant implications for coalition-building and the dispersal of power among political forces. The 2011 electoral law was designed for the purpose of constructing an inclusive constitution-drafting process that would reflect all political views. This was effective in preventing the emergency of a dominant majority in the NCA by increasing the number of parties gaining representation in the assembly. This encouraged negotiation and compromise between political forces, and prevented a monopoly on political decision-making. However, while suitable for an inclusive constitution-drafting process, the implications of this electoral system for effective governance have been questioned. The electoral law has contributed to the fragmentation of decision-making power among a large number of political parties, which undermines accountability to the electorate and obstructs the development of programmatic political parties, since parties are required to enter into governing coalitions that contradict their ideological frameworks and undermine internal party cohesion.

Third, Tunisia's successive elections and coalitions illustrate the difficulties of establishing a consensus among elites regarding new political and economic governance arrangements. The 2014–2019 Nidaa–Ennahdha coalition was justified by these parties on the grounds of the need to develop a new elite consensus on the "rules of the game." Ennahdha justified the pact to its own members on the basis that it was dragging Nidaa into an embrace of democracy, thus preventing a return to dictatorship. Nidaa justified it to its membership on the basis that it was dragging Ennahdha into an embrace of the modern civil state, thus protecting the gains of the postindependence Bourguibist state. This pact succeeded to some extent in these aims. Ennahdha distanced itself from political Islam by calling itself a Muslim Democratic party. Nidaa Tounes, meanwhile, renounced its exclusionary and polarizing discourse of the 2012–2014 period, reconciling itself with Ennahdha and its right to exist in the political scene. Both parties were forced, by their coalition, to give up on the more radical demands of its members.

The Nidaa–Nahdha pact can thus be seen as an elite pact or a situation of "bargained competition" similar to those seen in many other political transitions, under which actors agree not to harm each other or threaten each other's vital interests, thereby "moving the polity towards democracy by undemocratic means."[41] This pact has been seen by some as "the secret to keeping Tunisia on the rails of a fragile transition to democracy," helping it to overcome political conflicts that would otherwise have led to a return to one-party rule.[42] However, it has also been critiqued for neutralizing the revolution by taking deeper more structural reforms—of the economy, security sector, and transitional justice—off the table.[43]

Finally, Tunisia's postrevolution electoral politics demonstrate the difficulties of seeking to impose a "secular vs. Islamist" or "right vs left" interpretive framework on a complex political field. Around the 2011 elections, the political spectrum was widely divided along two broad dimensions: Islamist–secular and liberal–socialist. However, following the 2011 elections, the Troika was formed, a governing coalition between secular and Islamist parties that were brought together around their shared history of opposition to authoritarian rule and their support for the revolution. Meanwhile, the opposition to the Troika brought together political forces across the political spectrum that were highly unlikely bed fellows, such as the former regime-linked centrist, economically liberal Nidaa Tounes together with the communist-leaning Popular Front, which had a history of opposition to the former regime.

Coalitions following the 2019 elections also confound a simplistic Islamist vs secularist axis. Ennahdha allied with the secular economically liberal Qalb Tounes representing established economic elites, together with the populist prorevolutionary Etilaf Al-Karama. In addition, regional identities play a role, as the South and West tend to vote more strongly in favor of Ennahdha, while coastal regions have greater support for modernist parties. In sum, Tunisia's political spectrum has multiple dividing lines that combine to produce unexpected coalitions in a context of massive fragmentation and coalition-building.

Civil Society

Following independence, the Tunisian state shaped social organization rather than integrating independent societal interests. In the 1960s and 1970s, the state created institutions and policies that lent themselves to creating organizations and shaping associational interests. Two cases of state-sponsored development are most often cited and are not dissimilar from other postcolonial state-building projects in the Arab world: women's organizations following the Personal Status Code revisions at independence and the rise of a Tunisian business-entrepreneurial class that benefited from private-sector promotion policies since the 1970s. In both cases, demands for policies and institutions originated within the state and did not emanate from society. The NDP specifically dominated social organizations with overlapping leadership in both state positions and societal organizations. The state otherwise destroyed and resuscitated groups, such as the UGTT in the 1980s.

Under Ben Ali, civil society was largely state sponsored and coopted. Few associations enjoyed any distance or autonomy from the regime, and many became coopted over time at different political moments, exemplified in the relationship between the UGTT and the Tunisian state. The corporatist and repressive response of the state to associational life was marked by state security infiltration and surveillance to control criticism and contestation within Tunisia's civil society. Direct and indirect critiques of the Ben Ali regime led to harassment, arrest, detention, and torture. Independent civil society organizations were denied accreditation. Only state-sanctioned organizations qualified for state support. In this restricted space, an independent and multilayered civil society that could stand as a buffer between the state and society was highly limited.

The culture of opposition and independent associational life that developed in Tunisia despite heavy state repression has played an important role in mobilizing masses and orienting political discussion during and after the revolution.

Expanded Civil Society

Since the revolution, civil society has played a crucial role in shaping Tunisia's political environment. During the March 2011–October 2011 period preceding NCA elections, the number of civil society organizations increased exponentially, in part thanks to an enabling legal framework. Decree-Law 88, issued in September 2011, significantly opened up civic space and made it significantly easier to establish civil society organizations.

Ten years into the country's democratic transition, civil society had imposed itself as a significant force within the Tunisian public sphere.[44] Millions of democracy assistance dollars through bilateral and multilateral development streams as well as local, regional, and global foundations have assisted in the creation of a civil society that is autonomous from the Tunisian state. While the majority of funds are directed toward supporting the democratic transition, homegrown associations have been able to garner popular support and public prestige. Most notably, a set of transparency-focused organizations observing the work of government and the parliament have used creative and low-cost tools to monitor state institutions. Global organizations, including Amnesty International, the Carter Center, Human Rights Watch, the National Democratic Institute, International Republican Institute, and Transparency International, have established local networks of organizations and strengthened their work through training, education, and skill-building activities. Finally, newly established observatories or policy institutes on issues such as transitional justice, judicial reform, elections, economic and social development and justice, and election data collaborate with clusters of civil society organizations that have the technical know-how as well as the local expertise across issues and regions to strengthen the work of these policy initiatives.

Tunisia's civil society has also played a major role in navigating political crises that have threatened to derail democratization since the revolution. In 2011, the social movement Ekbes ["Get a move on"], for instance, was formed by a youth wing of Ennahdha and successfully pressured the interim government to fire former regime members via the "purge campaign." Following Mohamed Brahmi's assassination in the summer of 2013, long-standing civil society actors were crucial in negotiating the country out of its political crisis through a national dialogue (*al-hiwar al-watani*) in which the Bar Association, national human rights association, the UGTT, and the largest business association, UTICA, mediated between the Troika government and its opponents, resulting in a road map that led to adoption of the 2014 Constitution, the replacement of the Troika by a technocratic government, and the legislative and presidential elections in late 2014.

In summary, Tunisia's burgeoning civil society has been able to carve out an important public space to inform the work of government, policy institutions, and citizen programs as well as participate and navigate the country out of political crises. Despite criticisms by activists and civil society leaders of harassment and shutting down of some organizations, civil society was nonetheless able to reposition itself in Tunisia's political landscape at a scope that the country has never experienced before. However, this civic space appears to be at risk with the increasing monopolization of power since July 25, 2021. In January 2022, a draft decree was leaked that would replace Decree 88 and impose significant restrictions on the formation and activities of civil society organizations. In February 2022, President Saied vowed to amend the legal framework to prevent civil society receiving international funding, calling such organizations "extensions of foreign powers, which seek to control the Tunisian people through their money."

RELIGION, SOCIETY, AND POLITICS IN TUNISIA

Tunisia is 98 percent Sunni Muslim, with very small indigenous Jewish and Ibadi communities. Traditionally, Islamic jurisprudence was based on Maliki legal interpretation,[45] which is enshrined in Article 1 of the 2014 Tunisian Constitution. However, since the late 19th century, permutations of a reformist movement originating in Egypt, called *al-Nahda*, have marked Tunisian Islamic thought. Later, the intellectual thought of the Muslim Brotherhood inspired a new generation of activism, while more recently individual preachers and small groups called Salafis[46] have drawn from the Hanbali tradition of Islamic jurisprudence, which originated in the Arabian Peninsula (Table 24.2).

TABLE 24.2 ■ Political Mobilization of Civil Society Around Issues			
Women's Organizations[a]	**Transitional Justice and Judicial Reform**	**Labor and Social Justice**	**Popular Protest, Strikes, Social Movements**
National Union of Tunisian Women (semi-official)	Observatory for Transitional Justice	UGTT	Regional protest movements
ATFD (*Association Tunisienne des Femmes Démocrates*)	Al-Kawakabi	Tunisian Forum for Economic and Social Rights	Union of Unemployed Graduates (UDC)
Association des Femmes Tunisiennes pour la Recherche et le Développement	Observatory for Judicial Reform Bar Association		Thala and Kasserine and Siliana—popular protests: jobs, compensation of families of the victims of the revolution
Tounssiet	Association of Tunisian Judges Tunisian Union of Judges		Gafsa—protests and strikes in southern mining basin since December 2010 and in years following the revolution; many supported by rank-and-file UGTT
LED—*Ligue des electrices tunisiennes*	Network for Transitional Justice		2015 teacher and student strikes
Bayti (focus on assisting victims of domestic violence)	Truth and Dignity Commission (IVD)		Protests over regional disparities in development and job opportunities; absence of services and rights
			Winou El Petrol? Movement
			FEMEN
			Rahil Movement
			Tamarod

(Continued)

TABLE 24.2 ■ Political Mobilization of Civil Society Around Issues (*Continued*)			
Longstanding Human Rights Organizations	**Outlawed Violent Extremist Movements**	**Transparency Organizations**	**Business and Employers' Organizations**
Tunisian League of Human Rights (LTDH) National Council for Tunisian Liberties (CNLT) Tunisian chapter of Amnesty International	Ansar Al-Sharia: Salafist Islamic movement of scholars and jihadists advocating Islamic reform, shari'a law, and jihad; radical Islamists formerly imprisoned Okba Ibn Nafaa Brigade AQIM ISIS/ISIL	I-Watch (anticorruption, transparency, voter awareness) Al-Bawsala (transparency) Mourakiboun (election related) ATIDE Marsad Chahed Tunisian Election Data Le Labo' Democratique (The Democracy Lab) Management and disposition of regime's secret police files OpenGovTN: Transparency of the National Constituent Assembly (related issues) Youth Decides Nawaat (oppositional bloggers; exposing inaction on new constitution) Inkyfada (investigative journalism platform)	UTICA CONECT (*Confédération des Entreprises Citoyennes de Tunisie*) IACE (*Institut Arabes des Chefs d'Entreprises*) Regional Chambers of Commerce and Industry

[a]*Note:* This list is not exhaustive, but rather includes examples of the wide range of associations representing these four interests.

TABLE 24.3 ■ National Election Results, 1959–2019		
Election	**Winning Party/Candidate**	**Percentage of Popular Vote/Number of Seats**
Presidential 2019	Kais Saied	Turnout: 55 percent Kais Saied: 72.71 percent Nabil Karoui: 27.29 percent
Parliamentary 2019	Ennahdha	Turnout: 41.7 percent Ennahdha: 19.63 percent of votes, 52 of 217 seats Qalb Tounes: 14.55 percent, 38 seats At-Tayar: 6.42 percent, 22 seats Etilaf Al-Karama: 5.94 percent, 21 seats
Presidential 2014	Beji Caid Essebsi	Turnout (second round): 60.1 percent Beji Caid Essebsi: 55.7 percent Moncef Marzouki: 44.3 percent
Parliamentary 2014	Nidaa Tounes	Turnout: 66 percent Nidaa Tounes: 37.6 percent of votes, 86 of 217 seats Ennahdha: 27.8 percent of votes, 69 seats Free Patriotic Union: 4.1 percent of votes, 16 seats Popular Front: 3.6 percent of votes, 15 seats
Constituent assembly Prime minister 2011	Moncef Marzouki (CPR) (president chosen by the NCA) Hamadi Jebali (Ennahdha)	Turnout: 51.4 percent Ennahdha: 41 percent of votes, 89 of 217 seats Congress for the Republic (CPR): 29 seats Ettakatol: 20 seats Progressive Democratic Party (PDP): 16 seats
Presidential 2009 Parliamentary 2009 (bicameral)	Ben Ali (RCD) RCD	Turnout: 89.4 percent Ben Ali: 89.6 percent of votes RCD: 161 of 214 seats (75.2 percent) Independent opposition: 2 seats
Presidential 2004 Parliamentary 2004 (bicameral)	Ben Ali (RCD) RCD	Turnout: 91.5 percent Ben Ali: 94.5 percent of votes RCD: 87.6 percent of votes RCD: 152 of 189 seats (80.4 percent) Progressive Democratic Party (PDP) withdrew

(Continued)

TABLE 24.3 ■ National Election Results, 1959–2019 *(Continued)*		
Election	**Winning Party/Candidate**	**Percentage of Popular Vote/Number of Seats**
Presidential 1999 Parliamentary 1999	Ben Ali (RCD) RCD	Turnout: 92 percent Ben Ali: 99.2 percent of votes RCD: 148 of 182 seats (81.3 percent) Prime Minister: Mohammed Ghannouchi
Presidential 1994 Parliamentary 1994	Ben Ali (RCD) RCD	Turnout: 95.5 percent Ben Ali: 99 percent of votes RCD: 97.73 percent of votes RCD: 144 of 163 seats (88.3 percent)
Presidential 1989 Parliamentary 1989	Ben Ali (RCD) RCD	Turnout: 76.5 percent Ben Ali: 99.27 percent of votes RCD: 141 of 141 seats (100 percent) 40 percent abstentions/Islamists 15 percent–20 percent in independent vote
Parliamentary 1986	Patriotic Union (PSD, UGTT, the employers', farmers', and women's unions)	Turnout: 82.9 percent PSD: received near totality of votes 125 of 125 seats (100 percent) Opposition party boycott; independent candidates (15) withdrew prior to elections; Prime Minister: Rachid Sfar
Parliamentary 1981	National Front (PSD and UGTT; UGTT split on participation)	Turnout: 84.5 percent PSD/National Front: 94.8 percent of votes PSD/National Front: 136 of 136 seats (100 percent) No cabinet changes; Mzali remains prime minister
Parliamentary 1979	PSD	Turnout: 81.4 percent PSD: 121 of 121 seats (100 percent) Boycott by opposition groups; Mzali (1980) named prime minister
Presidential 1974 Parliamentary 1974	Bourguiba (PSD; later declared president for life)	Turnout: 96.8 percent PSD: 112 of 112 seats (100 percent) PSD unopposed; civil servants (60) over half of deputies

(Continued)

TABLE 24.3 ■ National Election Results, 1959–2019 (*Continued*)		
Election	**Winning Party/Candidate**	**Percentage of Popular Vote/Number of Seats**
Presidential 1969 Parliamentary 1969	Bourguiba (PSD) PSD	Turnouts: 94.7 percent legislative, 99.8 percent presidential 101 of 101 seats (100 percent) Bourguiba unopposed; PSD unopposed Bahi Lagham (1969); Hedi Nouira (1970) prime ministers
Presidential 1964 Parliamentary 1964	Bourguiba (PSD) PSD	Bourguiba: 96 percent of all votes PSD: 90 of 90 seats in parliament
Presidential 1959 Parliamentary 1959	Bourguiba (Neo-Destou) Neo-Destour/National Front (UGTT, unions of farmers; craftsmen and merchants)	(Unopposed) Neo-Destour/National Front: 90 of 90 seats (100 percent) Communist Party fielded list in Gafsa and Tunis; later banned in 1963

Source: Interparliamentary Union. Available at http://www.ipu.org/parline-e/reports/2321_arc.htm.

Religion and Politics in Contradiction, 1956–1981

Because the vast majority of Tunisians are Muslim, to some, distinguishing the interaction between religion and politics from the larger phenomenon of politics would seem strange. To others, the two are discreet: Islam is a religion, politics are politics, and the two should not overlap. For some, religion provides a road map for a more just society and way of ruling. These divergent perspectives on the place and role of religion in public life graft onto Tunisia's turbulent history of secularism and political Islam, which has swung from periods of contradiction to conflict, cooptation, repression, and most recently, agreement. Indeed, since 1956 the debate over the role of Islam in public life has shifted from total separation (*laïcité* in the French sense of the term) to inclusion (secularism in the American sense of the term).[47]

For Habib Bourguiba, religion and politics were a contradiction: Politics were politics, and religion was an individual set of beliefs to be excised from larger communal obligations. This perspective informed the new regime's modernizing policies, which included the transfer of personal code from shari'a to positive law, the corpus of laws known as the Family Code (1957), the liquidation of public (1956) and private (1957) religious foundations, the transfer of authority over mosques and imams to the Ministry of Religious Affairs (1958), and the dismantling of the Zaytouna mosque—the most important site of religious learning in the Maghreb—as an independent-leaning institution and transferring the teaching of theology to the Ministry of Religious Affairs (1958).

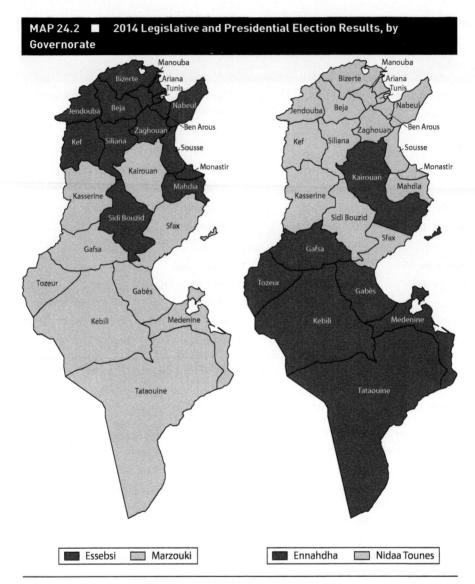

MAP 24.2 ■ 2014 Legislative and Presidential Election Results, by Governorate

Legend: Essebsi | Marzouki Ennahdha | Nidaa Tounes

Source: Maps derived from Wikimedia Commons. Available at https://commons.wikimedia.org/wiki/File:President_Tunisia_2014_2_round.svg and https://commons.wikimedia.org/wiki/File:2014-parliamentary-election-results.png.

While segments of Tunisian society and international observers celebrated Bourguiba's modernizing reforms, a distinct subset strongly resented what they believed to be an authoritarian denaturing of their society. Many, including Ennahdha founder Rached Ghannouchi, were later drawn to pan-Arabism's selective rejection of Westernization, but they increasingly gravitated to reformist Islamic thought and the more politicized arguments proposed by Saïd Qutb and Hassan al-Banna. Initially a group of small, like-minded, informal student groups on university campuses, they quickly coalesced.

Conflict: 1981–1987

In 1981, Rached Ghannouchi and Abdelfattah Mourou filed for Ministry of Interior accreditation for the MTI, a party built around a student movement called the Association for the Protection of the Quran.[48] Their request for accreditation was denied, and within a month, Ghannouchi, Mourou, and hundreds of supporters were arrested and sentenced to prison. Released in 1984, Ghannouchi was again arrested in 1987, and as the leader of a major social and political movement opposed to Bourguibism, he was sentenced to death. For Bourguiba, the MTI was an affront to the modernity and the state he had created: While Islam and politics were to be distinct, public religion remained the monopoly of the state. And the state was the monopoly of Bourguiba.

Confrontation and Repression: 1987–2011

While supporters of Zine al-Abidine Ben Ali's November 7, 1987, coup have argued that he acted from fear that Bourguiba's policies would lead to civil war, the new president's honeymoon with political Islam was short lived. The new regime refused to give the MTI party accreditation, which had changed its name to Ennahdha to avoid religious connotations in the party name. The party ran independent candidate lists in the 1989 legislative elections but failed to win a single seat. Ballot stuffing and the majoritarian electoral rules set in place precluded significant opposition gains. The 1990 Iraqi invasion of Kuwait and American build-up to intervention provided the MIT, along with other anti-Ben Ali groups, an opportunity to take to the streets and revealed, perhaps for the first time, the size and power of the movement.

   The crackdown was swift and violent. Leveraging fear of the rise of the Islamic Salvation Front in neighboring Algeria, in February 1991 the regime decapitated Ennahdha's leadership, arresting thousands of militants, many of whom were given harsh sentences by military tribunal. Repression against Ennahdha increased following the passage of the 2003 antiterrorism law, which effectively superimposed the term *terrorist* onto *political prisoner*, and permitted the regime to mete out harsher prison sentences on suspected opponents. Tolerated as a movement from 1987 to 1991, membership in the group would remain a serious crime until the revolution on January 14, 2011. Ben Ali attempted to perfect Bourguiba's monopoly over religion and religious thought; he systematically removed independent spheres of religious thought or symbolic practice, and when possible, incorporated it into the state apparatus through the Ministry of Religious Affairs as well as into the commercial sector through initiatives such as Banque Zaytouna and Radio Zaytouna.

Ferment: January 14, 2011–October 2014

The collapse of Ben Ali ended the state's monopoly on Islamic thought in the public sphere. Ennahdha quickly reemerged as a political force, symbolically highlighted by the euphoric crowds that met Rached Ghannouchi at Carthage International Airport on January 31, 2011, upon his return from exile. Ennahdha was the most popular political party in the immediate postrevolution phase. Having worked with the legal and illegal opposition during the Ben Ali years, Ennahdha played a major role in the transition from authoritarianism to the NCA elections in October 2011.

Ennahdha won the 2011 elections, forming a coalition government with two secular parties, attempting to reform key parts of the judiciary, security apparatus, and economy, while simultaneously drafting a constitution for a democratic Tunisia. The coalition government was unable to maintain its standing in popular opinion: Political, economic, and security instability were increasingly linked to the Troika. The assassination of two leftists in 2013 served as a catalyst that solidified a broad anti-Troika movement, culminating in the Bardo protests during the summer of 2013.

Following a protracted political crisis, the Troika government agreed to sit at the table with its harshest critics and negotiate a road map for the adoption of a new constitution, the handover of power to a technocratic government, and the setting of a new election schedule. While Ennahdha agreed to hand over power, the political battles that were waged during the 2011–2014 transitional period marked the political end of Bourguibism on a pure separation of religion and politics, as well as an end on the state monopoly over religion. In May 2017 during its second post-2011 party Congress, Ennahdha surprised with its announcement to separate religion from politics within the party and change its political label from Islamist to Muslim Democrats. This was both as a result of its unity government with Nidaa but also a clear effort to distance itself from other Islamist movements and create its own Tunisian brand of a conservative political party. One year later, Ennahdha beat Nidaa in Tunisia's first postrevolution municipal elections, once again reconfiguring its position in Tunisian politics by democratic means.

Muslim Democrats and Tunisian Politics in the Future

Though defeated at the polls in the October 2014 elections, that Ennahdha could still capture close to 30 percent of the popular vote revealed two important aspects of Tunisian politics. First, it underscored the vitality of Ennahdha as a political party, which was most evident in its success in the 2018 local elections. Its membership base and institutional structures effectively mobilized party turnout. Second, it confirmed political conservatism in Tunisia's political arena, alongside economic liberalism, socialism, and Arab nationalism. These factors, in addition to its legislative seats, allowed it to enter into a coalition government as a junior partner, following Nidaa Tounes's failed and heavily criticized first attempt to negotiate an Ennahdha-free coalition in January 2015. The coalition government has confused many Tunisians: Only a few months earlier, the two parties had led political campaigns based on seemingly mutually exclusive political platforms, best summed by a total war between secularism and Islamism.

The alliance has left many critics wondering whether the amplified secularist–Islamist divide of the 2011 and 2014 elections might not have hidden other equally important aspects of politics in the postrevolution period. Many Tunisians viewed the October 2018 Ennahdha and Nidaa Tounes split as a cynical reconfiguration in anticipation of the 2019 legislative and presidential elections. For some, including youth in Ben Guerdane, Gafsa, Kasserin, Redeyef, and Sidi Bouzid, demands for greater social justice and the redistribution of wealth via a new developmental pact have been occulted. Not surprisingly, demands for wealth redistribution as well as state performance around social service policy have only increased. Writing on the night of the 2014 legislative elections, Laryssa Chomiak reminded us of this:

> In Gafsa, the phosphate-rich epicenter of southwest Tunisia, and the neighboring mining town of Redeyef, lofty debates about religion and secularism mean very little to residents. Unemployment in the area soars, and disgruntled residents complain of no improvement since the 2011 toppling of Ben Ali, blaming Ennahdha's governance as much as the corrupt interests of the lingering old guard in Tunis.[49]

For others, like Nadia Marzouki, the 2014 current government was a "rotten compromise" and was the result of undue focus on debates over secularism and Islam during the constitution-drafting process and subsequent elections that turned focus away from three crucial goals of the revolution and democratic transition: legislative reform, transitional justice, and renewal of the political field.[50]

POLITICAL ECONOMY

While much has been written on the economic effects of the 2011 revolution, Tunisia's economy has been in flux for much longer. In 2008, for instance, a prolonged labor dispute in Gafsa virtually ground the mining of phosphates to a halt, while the manufacturing and tourism sectors of the economy suffered from the effects of global economic contraction. The country's economy was challenged again with the revolution.

According to a World Bank report, GDP growth fell to 1.6 percent in 2011. While it partially recovered, running at 4 percent in 2014, the 2015 terrorist attacks on the tourism sector contributed to another drop. In 2017, Tunisian GDP grew by 2 percent, whereas GDP per capita only grew by 0.8 percent. Unemployment continues to be high, though it has fallen to 15 percent from 18.1 percent in 2011. FDI continues to fluctuate and has yet to reach prerevolution levels. In 2017, the country attracted $809 million. As the economy continues to contract, labor unrest has spiked. This has had a major effect on both manufacturing and mining industries.

Given these overlapping challenges, it remains surprising that Tunisia's economy is not in worse shape and that more social unrest has not occurred. Tunisia has been able to navigate recent economic pressures, in part, due to good rainfall at home and poor olive harvests in Europe. More importantly, skilled economists and technocrats were appointed to key ministerial posts after the revolution, who were able to push through a 2013 $1.75 billion IMF Stand-By Arrangement (SBA).

Historical Overview: "A Good Pupil"

Tunisia's various postindependence governments have cautiously managed the Tunisian economy. And in doing so, Tunisia has historically been considered a "good pupil" of international financial institutions. In the 1950s and 1960s, Tunisia built infrastructure and attempted to rationalize its agriculture sector (then the largest employer to the economy). In the 1970s and

1980s, Tunisia developed its private sector, especially promoting industries in textiles and food processing as well as a nascent tourism sector. Since the late 1980s to present, Tunisia has engaged globalization and managerial rationalization, marked by limited structural reforms and deepened finance reform and regional and global market integration.

Postindependence Rationalization: 1956–1969

After independence, the government implemented economic policies that included the nationalization of foreign-held sectors and the establishment of Tunisia's economic institutions. The 1960 Social Security Law served as an economic road map, defining the relationship between the private-sector and labor interests. The law required the private sector to make contributions to the state for employees, while guaranteeing employee rights to social security and protection from employer abuse. Those policies, however, failed to draw capital from the real estate, small-business, and agriculture sectors into light and heavy industry, forcing the state to assume investment and management leadership in utilities, transportation, and mining. For its part, the UGTT called for more robust state-led development, even if it came at the expense of the private sector.

In 1961, President Bourguiba nominated former head of the UGTT (1954–1956), Ahmed Ben Salah, to be the minister of planning, finance, and economy. Ben Salah promoted the modernization of agriculture, the nationalization of heavy industry, and, ultimately, the forced state-led development of commerce. In 1961, the state nationalized foreign-owned land and the phosphates sector a year later. At the 1964 party congress, the Neo-Destour changed its name to the PSD to reflect a socialist outlook, and Ben Salah announced the forced collectivization of state land and surrounding tracts of private land. In 1966, the government nationalized rail services between Gafsa Mining Basin and industrial ports of Sfax and Gabes (1966). Between 1964 and 1969, the government expanded the collectivization to agriculture to include nearly all of Tunisian land and proposed a similar state-led collectivization plan for commerce. Following a critical 1969 Central Bank report on the underperformance of the cooperative movement, and in a climate of growing opposition to Ahmed Ben Salah, Bourguiba sacked his minister and in 1970 appointed the head of the Central Bank, Hedi Nouira, as prime minister.

State-Managed Private-Sector Development and Labor Unrest: 1970–1985

While Ben Salah's dismissal marked the end of Tunisia's socialist experiment, it did not end state-led development. Nouira dismantled the collective farms and embarked on an economic policy to promote private-sector investment in agroindustry and tourism, while encouraging its nascent textiles industry through FDI. In 1972, Bourguiba's government liberalized the foreign-investment code and provided a ten-year tax exemption to exporting firms. The state increased investments in phosphates, consolidating phosphate mining, transport, and processing into the Compagnie des Phosphates de Gafsa (CPG) in 1976. Phosphate production grew from 2.7 million to 4.0 million tons during the decade and would double Phosphates by 2007 (8.005 million tons). Tunisia's economy became outward oriented and mixed, encouraging private investment, while the state supplied infrastructure, utilities, heavy industry, and products linked to national food security.

Despite growth, primary-sector commodities provided unstable contributions to GDP; Tunisian manufacturing increased its share of GDP behind gains in textiles, food processing, and leather production. Small family firms with fewer than ten employees dominated manufacturing, comprising 90 percent of the sector. These firms were closed, inexperienced, and focused on producing those goods that, as merchants, they once sold. The export manufacturing sector preferred flexible labor, including young women who worked prior to marriage. Many manufacturers owed their start to agricultural rents and state loans.

Manufactures did not keep macroeconomic difficulties at bay: fluctuations in oil, phosphate, and wheat prices and rising international lending rates deteriorated Tunisia's fiscal budget and foreign debt. Inflation renewed labor militancy for cost-of-living increases. In 1977, the unions negotiated terms for inflation-adjusted wage setting, but a January 1978 general strike by the UGTT sparked widespread civil violence and vocal expression of dissatisfaction with autocratic rule. By 1982, the signs of state austerity planning were visible, and by 1983–1984, a deep recession in France coupled with an international liquidity crisis prevented Tunisia from securing the credit and exchange on private, international markets needed to float debt and repay loans. The economic crisis turned social on December 29, 1983, when the government increased the price of semolina, setting off protests in southern oases and in poor communities. Through January 3, rioting spread throughout secondary cities, reaching Sfax and Tunis. Rioters targeted government officials and property and directed anger toward the upper and middle classes. Two days of rioting left more than 150 people dead and thousands wounded, as the government rolled out military forces to quell it. On January 6, President Bourguiba annulled price hikes for bread, and calm returned.

Structural Reform and Globalization: 1985–Present

In 1985, Tunisia approached the IMF for an emergency loan and introduced a program to stabilize its current account and fiscal deficits. Foreign exchange and trade balances were corrected through monetary devaluation, making imports more expensive and exports more competitive abroad. Fiscal deficits were stabilized through reductions in subsidies and in government spending. Given the shallowness of the deficits, the World Bank program stressed structural adjustments in agriculture, industry, finance, public enterprise, and trade. The state pursued stabilization by privatizing state-owned assets; limiting public-sector employment; and raising subsidized prices for foodstuffs, utilities, and services. To cushion the immediate crisis, Tunisians turned to networks of family and social solidarities.

Economic liberalization increased under the Ben Ali presidency. In 1993, the government reformed its investment code to promote foreign investment in "offshore" export sectors, while it protected domestic Tunisian majority ownership in "onshore" markets.[51] In 1994, the Tunisian government enabled the convertibility of the dinar for current account operations. The government also established free-trade zones, where designated companies import raw or semifinished goods without customs duties or taxes for reexport. By 2008, FDI by 2,973 foreign firms and joint ventures accounted for one-third of all exports and one-fifth of employment (290,000 workers).

In 1995, Tunisia entered the Euro-Mediterranean Partnership (Barcelona Process), which progressively removed tariffs on industrial products (over a twelve-year period), with a progressive reduction in tariffs on agricultural, afro-food, and fisheries projects. A decade later in 2006, the government ratified the Agadir Agreement, setting into place the Euro-Mediterranean free-trade area, removing tariffs on trade between the EU, Tunisia, Egypt, Jordan, and Morocco.

Tunisia's Economy Today

While postrevolution governments have made efforts to kick-start the economy, IMF efforts to push investment deregulation and labor code reforms have been mired in debate between ruling parties, on the one hand, and with opposition and labor groups, on the other. As a result, postrevolution economic reform measures have been largely limited to dismantling the regime-supported private-sector oligopolies created by previous regimes. Unsurprisingly, then, while the 2018 World Bank Doing Business Report ranks Tunisia at 80th out of 190 countries on the *ease of doing business*, the Heritage Foundation classifies Tunisia's economy as mostly *unfree*, ranking it at 90th out of 180 countries.

While the estimated 50 percent of the population that constitutes the middle classes has eroded over the past decade, it nevertheless outperforms the Middle Income Country (MIC) average in GDP per capita. In 2019, national unemployment stood at 15.1 percent, youth unemployment hovered at around 35 percent, and regional unemployment in the disadvantaged regions of the South and West ranged from 20 percent to 40 percent. In 2000, the richest 20 percent of the population accounted for 47.3 percent of all expenditures, while the poorest 20 percent accounted for only 6 percent of expenditures. Disparities in wealth and opportunity remain significant. These have been aggravated by the effects of the COVID-19 crisis, with unemployment rising to 17.8 percent in 2021 and a significant rise in poverty and extreme poverty.

Tunisia's GDP per capita in 2019 (adjusted for purchasing power parity) stood at $11,096, which remains high in comparison with non–oil-exporting nations in the Middle-Eastern and North African (MENA) region and to MIC averages. Growth has been led by manufacturing, which first surpassed agriculture's contribution to total domestic product in the 1980–1990 period. Industry (22.7 percent) and services (61.7 percent) remain important economic contributors (see Table 24.3). However, GDP contracted by 8.8 percent in 2020 due to the effects of the COVID-19 health crisis.

Tunisia's trade regime is open. In 2019, imports plus exports comprised 107.9 percent of Tunisia's GDP, with a bias toward imports over exports. Benefits from remittances from Tunisians living abroad amount to $2.1 billion in 2020 (6 percent of GDP) and small exports of oil ease the current account deficit. Finally, Tunisia benefits from substantial FDI, which is concentrated in export sectors ($989 million in 2018). Prior to the revolution, FDI increased with liberalization of telecommunications, bank privatization, and investments in newly developing sectors. It began falling in 2006 and dropped significantly in 2009 following the 2008 global financial crisis. FDI dropped dramatically in 2011 and began to recover in 2012, though it has yet to attain pre-2011 levels.

TABLE 24.3 ■ Major Economic Indicators for Tunisia

Indicators[52]	Year	Current Data	Year	Comparative Data
Gross domestic product (US$ billion)	(2019)	39.196	(1980)	8.74
GDP growth (percentage)	(2019)	1.043	(1970–1980)[53]	7.5
Agriculture (percentage)	(2019)	10.2	(1965)	23.74
Industry (percentage)	(2019)	22.7	(1965)	21.94
Manufacturing (percentage)	(2019)	14.8	(1965)	9.24
Services (percentage)	(2019)	61.7	(1965)	54.32
Current account (US$ million)	(2019)	−3284	(1999)[54]	−442
Exports (US$ million)	(2019)	14,944	(2001)	6,606
Imports (US$ million)	(2019)	21,574	(1999)	9,521
FDI (US$ million)	(2019)	810	(2000)	752.18
FDI (percentage of GDP)	(2019)	2.07	(2000)	3.50

Source: Unless otherwise indicated, all figures are taken from the World Bank World Development Indicators Databank and the Central Intelligence Agency *World Fact Book.*

Sectoral Overview

Tunisian tourism, which accounts for anywhere between 7 and 10 percent of GDP, is underperforming and recovering from several crises. Already a sector earning less revenue per tourist than tourism sectors in Egypt, Morocco, and Turkey, the number of tourists and tourism receipts dropped following the revolution. Tunisia's 2014 tourism receipts came close to those of 2010, but recovery efforts were shattered following the March 2015 Bardo Museum attack and the June 2015 Sousse attack, in which nineteen and thirty-eight tourists were targeted and murdered, respectively. Following the June Sousse attack, the United Kingdom, which accounted for nearly half a million visitors to Tunisia in 2014, declared Tunisia off-limits. From 7.16 million arrivals in 2014, the number of tourists dropped to 5.36 million in 2015 and 5.72 million in 2016. Rallying in support of Tunisia, Algerian citizens created a "visit Tunisia" campaign, saving the industry from implosion. Numbers were up again in 2017, 2018, and 2019, rising to 9.42 million in 2019 (4.9 million of which were from the rest of the Maghreb), exceeding 2010 levels (Table 24.4).

The textiles sector, which constitutes approximately 17 percent of value-added in manufacturing, has fared slightly better. The 2005 expiration of the Multi-Fiber Arrangement slowed textile sector growth prior to the revolution, but Tunisia produces high-end textiles for European markets. As a result, it was not as hard hit by the 2008 economic crisis as the low-end package tourism sector. While the revolution itself did not directly affect the textile

TABLE 24.4 ■ Tunisia's Major Demographic Indicators				
Indicators[55]	Current Data		Comparative Historical Data	
	Year	Data	Year	Data
Population	2020	11.82 million	1975	5.61 million
Population growth (percentage)	2020	1.1	1980–1984	2.50
Age dependency ratio	2020	49.62	1960	84.56
Unemployment rate[56] (percentage)	2019	15.13	1980–1989	13.6
Primary school net enrollment rate (percentage)	2013	98.8	1995–2004	97
Secondary school net enrollment rate (percentage)	2016	92	1995–2004	72
GDP per capita (PPP, $)	2019	11,096	1999	5,581

Source: Unless otherwise indicated, all figures are taken from the World Bank World Development Indicators Databank.

sector, continued international pressures as well as an increase in strikes in postrevolution Tunisia have decreased productivity. Such structural and contextual pressures, moreover, have forced foreign investors to reassess their willingness to invest in the country, as indicated in declining FDI receipts—monies that are crucial to the continued modernization of that sector.

Export agriculture has advanced but faces competition in the southern Mediterranean. In the late 2000s, Tunisia produced on average 100,000 metric tons of olive oil per annum—close to 10 percent of Tunisia's exports—in a sector that employs nearly 300,000 people (20 percent of all agricultural labor and 10 percent of the total workforce) directly and more than one million people indirectly. Olive oil production reached a record-breaking 400,000 tons in 2019 after government campaigns to plant more than 100,000 hectares of trees. During the 2019–2020 harvest season, Tunisian cultivation of *Deglet Nour* dates in the Djerid oasis (Tozeur, Nefta) had a record 305,000 tons—up 7.8 percent on the previous season.

Reshaping the Economy

In 2013, the Tunisian transitional government signed an SBA with the IMF to offset the costs of political transition. The agreement committed Tunisia to reform its macroeconomic framework, restoring fiscal and external buffers, applying deregulation to support private-sector growth, and strengthening social-assistance mechanisms to reduce income disparities.

Discussed at length in the World Bank's groundbreaking *All in the Family* report[57]—which underscored the degree to which the Ben Ali clan of families and associated businesses used market regulation, expropriation, and cronyism to amass billions of dollars—Tunisia is in great need of financial sector and regulatory reform. Prior to the revolution, Tunisia's private sector was dominated by holding companies with close relations to political power and to financial institutions.[58] Of the more than 500 buildings, 300 companies, and 370 bank accounts that were seized following the revolution,[59] for example, 220 belonged to the Ben Ali family and alone appropriated 21 percent of all private-sector profits and accounted for 3 percent of private-sector output. In December 2012, for example, the government generated $10 million from the sales of a single Ben Ali estate.[60]

An overhaul of the banking sector is a critical component of laying the groundwork for a productive, postrevolution economy. Currently, close to 20 percent of public-sector bank loans are nonperforming, nearly double the private sector, or 14 percent of all bank assets.[61] To a significant degree, this public-sector portfolio is likely linked to loans given to the Ben Ali family or political allies. Additionally, public-sector banks are overexposed to the ailing tourism sector. The financial system's first priority is establishing and abiding by a more uniform regulatory environment that is aligned with international norms, while increasing both the financial and human resources dedicated to financial-sector management.

FOREIGN RELATIONS

A small country neighbored by Algeria, Libya, and Italy, Tunisia has always positioned itself at a crossroads—linking Africa, the Mediterranean, and the Middle East—and has enjoyed strong relations with its neighbors. Tunisia is a member in the Arab League, African Union, Maghreb Union, and Mediterranean Union, while also participating in larger international initiatives when they suit its immediate and long-term interests.

Inter-Arab Relations and the Arab League

Tunisia joined the Arab League in 1958, and in 1979, the Arab League moved its headquarters from Cairo to Tunis in reaction of Egypt's participation in the Camp David Accords, where it would remain until 1990. In 1982, Tunisia agreed to host the Palestinian Liberation Organization (PLO), which had been expelled from Lebanon. The PLO headquarters would remain in Tunis until 1994, when the PLO leader Yasser Arafat returned to Ramallah following the Oslo Accords.

Tunisia does not have formal relations with the State of Israel. Following the Oslo Accords in 1996, the two countries opened "interest sections." In 2000, however, Tunisia ended the relationship following then-Israeli Prime Minister Ariel Sharon's provocative visit to the Al-Aqsa Mosque in occupied Jerusalem.

Inter-Maghrebi Relations and the Maghreb Union

During colonial occupation, nationalists from Algeria, Morocco, and Tunisia considered their national struggle as a collective, regional cause. The collective struggle ended with national independence: Morocco and Tunisia gained independence in 1956, while Algeria won freedom after a brutal war of independence in 1962. While collective political positions were untenable in the postindependence era, cooperation between Algeria and Tunisia has generally been good, whereas an attempted political union with Libya in 1974 failed, creating tense relations that would last until the late 1980s, culminating in a Libyan-sponsored attempted revolution in Gafsa in 1980 and expulsion of 30,000 Tunisian workers in 1986.

In 1989, leaders from Algeria, Libya, Mauritania, Morocco, and Tunisia announced the formation of the Arab Maghreb Union (UMA). Ostensibly the institutional framework for eventual economic and possible political unity, the Maghreb Union has never come to fruition: Tensions between Algeria and Morocco over the Western Sahara effectively block integration of the region's two largest markets. Further economic or political cohesion has broken down altogether.

Despite these setbacks, Tunisia retains good relations with Algeria, and military cooperation is increasing along their shared borders, especially since 2011. In May 2014, Algeria agreed to a financial package worth $250 million—two loans for $100 million each, and a further $50 million in nonreimbursable aid money—to stabilize the economy, adding to the 2013 IMF loan. Relations with post–al-Qadhafi Libya were also initially very good. However, relations and trade between the two states were affected by Libya's political crisis pitting a UN-recognized government in Tripoli against a self-proclaimed government in eastern Libya. Currently, Tunisia is constructing a berm, or earthen wall, along the Libyan border, while Algeria is doing the same along the Tunisian border.

Relations With Europe and the European Union

Notwithstanding episodic crises, relations between France and Tunisia have been warm along economic trade and aid lines since independence. A 1957 preferential trade relationship between France and Tunisia has ensured that Tunisia's number-one trading partner remains France. France's leading role in the European Community has expanded this preferential relationship to EU countries. In 1969, Tunisia signed a bilateral agreement with the European Community that imposed quotas rather than tariffs on Tunisian-manufactured items, promoting investment in Tunisia's then-nascent textiles industry. The agreement also allowed for the importation of citrus and olives. The bilateral agreement was modified in 1976, with the European Community's Global Mediterranean Policy (GMP), which expanded economic exchange to trade in financial protocols.

Tunisia was the first country to sign a European–Mediterranean Association (EU–MEDA) agreement as an outcome of the 1995 Barcelona Accords that ended the Uruguay Round of the General Agreement on Tariffs and Trade. EU-MEDA provides European economic assistance to Tunisia (and other countries) to support building free trade with neighboring European countries. From 1996 through 2007, Tunisia and Europe agreed to progressively liberalize the trade of goods over the twelve-year period, with Brussels providing funds to support Tunisia's economic reforms. The European Neighborhood and Partnership Instrument (ENPI; 2007–2010), and its more recent corollary, the Union for the Mediterranean, continue to govern Tunisia–EU economic and political relations. The EU has supported the democratic transition through financial support for political and economic reforms. In October 2012, Tunisia was granted "Privileged Partner" status, which provided between €400 and €600 million over a period of five years. Since 2016, Tunisia and the EU have been in negotiations to sign a new free trade agreement on expanding mutual market access for goods, services, and investments.

In addition to economic cooperation, Tunisia has engaged the EU on security and immigration issues. In April 2011, Italy granted Tunisia €200 million to buttress its security in the wake of spiked illegal immigration following the flight of Ben Ali. This offer was matched by a €400 million grant to promote joint EU–Tunisian immigration measures. In September 2011, an EU–Tunisia joint task force met to determine the EU's contribution to supporting the 2012–2016 development plan, with EU pledges of €150 million for a €1 billion multidonor plan.

Relations With the United States

True to its position of Souverainism, the Tunisian government did not support the 1991 Gulf War, the 2003 invasion of Iraq, or the 2011 NATO strikes against Colonel Muammar al-Qadhafi's military apparatus.

However, the Tunisian government has maintained a close relationship with the United States following the September 11, 2001, attack and subsequent US-led War on Terror. Former President Ben Ali leveraged the US-led War on Terror to classify elements of opposition as domestic terrorists, as per the 2003 Tunisian antiterrorism law. Using the War on Terror, thousands of opponents to the Ben Ali regime were arbitrarily arrested, imprisoned, and often tortured, despite the fact that they did not belong to terrorist groups. The regime also strengthened the Ministry of Interior's monitoring of the country's political and civic elite, consolidating Tunisia into a police state. The regime also cooperated with the United States, relaying information on known terrorist networks, such as the Tunisian Combat Group.

In 2011, the United States pledged a $100 million cash transfer to alleviate the burden of debt payments. US–Tunisian relations symbolically frosted briefly following the September 2012 attack on the US Embassy in Tunis; however, the United States continued to assist Tunisia, especially through its democracy promotion program, and relations have once again strengthened since the 2014 and 2015 elections. Tunisian President Beji Caid Essebsi visited Washington, DC, in May 2015. The event was epitomized in *The Washington Post*'s joint op-ed by the two heads of state, US President Barack Obama and Essebsi. During the visit, President Obama pledged to support Tunisian democracy financially and militarily. Shortly after the visit, Tunisia was declared "a major non-NATO ally," which permits greater military cooperation between the two states. However, relations have been placed under pressure following President Saied's measures on July 25, 2021, which prompted the United States to express concerns and call for a return to the constitutional process and parliamentary democracy.

DOMESTIC CONFLICT

Tunisia's postrevolutionary institutional development—through the Ben Achour Commission, 2011 NCA elections, 2011–2014 constitution writing process, 2014 and 2019 legislative and presidential elections, and 2018 municipal elections—set up a framework that largely limited domestic conflict to political institutions. However, calls for greater economic redistribution have continued, voiced by social movements, and continued social contestation since 2011.

Politics Within Institutions

Street protests and demonstrations throughout the transition period have abetted, not hindered, the development of an institutionalized democratic political system, epitomized by the 2014 Constitution. During the period of the interim government, popular protests ensured that former autocrats were excluded from participating in the transitional process; contention during the NCA transitional government pushed staunch secularists and Islamists to negotiate with each other, initiating denser discussions and laying the groundwork for the 2015 Nidaa Tounes–Ennahdha coalition government, which unraveled in October 2018.

Protests over socioeconomic and social justice issues have been on the rise since 2015. Nationwide social movements, including *Manish M'Sameh* ["I will not forgive"] and *Fech Nestanew* ["What are we waiting for?"], have organized large-scale campaigns against a presidential proposal to amnesty corrupt Ben Ali-era businessmen and for increases in basic subsidies, respectively. Both movements are popular with Tunisia's young educated and unemployed population. Other campaigns, such as the Jemna oasis workers' self-management scheme, have challenged the legitimacy of state management over land and resources that have long belonged to local populations.

Outside of the loud claim-making seen in social movements, protests, and strikes, Tunisian politics are institutionalized. Domestic conflict was, until 2021, resolved through elections. However, the July 25 measures announced by President Saied have ushered in a period of significant uncertainty as to the future shape of the political system.

While largely excluded at the early stages of the revolution, members of the dissolved RCD party have been free to participate in new political parties. Indeed, Ben Ali's former minister of defense and foreign affairs, Kamel Morjane, was permitted to found a political party, the National Destourian Initiative, which participated in and won five seats in the October 2011 NCA elections. In the November 2018 government reshuffle, he was named Minister of Public Administration. The RCD's former Secretary General, Abir Moussi, is also at the helm of a political party that enjoys high levels of support according to opinion polls. Within the current political system, Ansar Al-Sharia is the only movement that is actively banned from politics. It was declared a terrorist organization in August 2013 by the Troika government in connection to the role it played in the 2012 attack on the US Embassy and for its alleged links to the 2013 assassinations of Chokri Belaid and Mohamed Brahmi.

Terrorism and Spillover Effects

A weakened postrevolution state has permitted the growth of armed groups who are currently fighting the state, though it is difficult to situate these groups outside of a larger regional context. Groups linked with terrorist organizations located in Algeria to the west and Libya to the east have expanded into Tunisia. In western Tunisia, along the Algerian border, the Okba Ibn Nafaa brigade has been attacking military convoys, police, and customs agents since 2012.

Linked to al-Qaida of the Islamic Maghrib (AQIM), based in eastern Algeria and led by an Algerian, the group's range is congruent to existing smuggling channels between Algeria and Tunisia. Cross-border movements have pushed the Algerian and Tunisian governments to militarily collaborate against the group, with some success.

While less-organized groups exist along the Libyan border, an Islamic State branch in Libya has claimed responsibility for Tunisia's most notorious violence since the revolution: The March 2015 attack at the Bardo Museum in Tunis and the June 2015 attack at a resort in Sousse collectively killed fifty-seven tourists. Young Tunisians who had trained with groups rallied to the Islamic State in Derna carried out both attacks. Tunisia's experience with terrorism has been horrific and its impact important to national politics, but terrorist groups are hardly expressions of deep-seated domestic conflict in the country and should be viewed within a regional context.

CONCLUSION: DEMOCRATIC CONSOLIDATION OR REVERSAL?

Tunisia's transition from dictatorship to democratizing polity over a period of 10 years is remarkable and clearly distinguishes the North-African nation from the rest of the Arab world. Tunisia nevertheless faces a series of highly placed hurdles, clearly manifested in 2021, with growing socioeconomic challenges, populist voices, and political wrangling. For many of Tunisia's citizens, democracy means jobs, social justice, and economic redistribution. For others, democracy is the right to free speech, political association, and elections. While these are not mutually exclusive demands, overfocusing on the claims of one group to the detriment of another in the transition process is fraught with risk. The July 25 measures introduced by Kais Saied have been variously interpreted as being a "correction of the democratic path" and a return to authoritarianism. At the time of writing, opposition to the measures is growing among political and civil society forces. Meanwhile, it appears the wider public are waiting to see whether Saied can tackle the socioeconomic challenges that have hobbled the democratic transition over the past decade.

The new government's most daunting challenges will be reviving the economy, containing the COVID-19 pandemic, and developing a dialogue with political forces, who have been entirely locked out of decision-making since July 25, and many of whom view the government as being illegitimate and unconstitutional. President Kais Saied's plans to amend the constitution are also likely to provoke a debate not only on the contents of such changes but also on whether constitutional reforms are really the appropriate response to urgent economic challenges. This tense relationship between political and economic reforms lies at the heart of Tunisia's transition, as successive governments have grappled with an economy that continues to be characterized by oligopolies, protected by influential actors and interests. The effects of the COVID-19 crisis have placed further pressure on an economic system unable to generate the growth and dignified jobs demanded by the protesters in 2010–2011 who overthrew the Ben Ali regime. It remains to be seen whether contention, debate, negotiation, and dialogue will continue to be the mechanisms used to resolve these issues, or whether pressing socioeconomic demands and growing opposition will be met with a restoration of authoritarian rule.

SUGGESTED READINGS

Ajl, Max. "The Social Origins of Development and Underdevelopment in Tunisia." *Maghrib in Past & Present* Podcasts. https://www.themaghribpodcast.com/2018/03/interview-with-max-ajl.html

Bellin, Eva. *Stalled Democracy: Capital, Labor, and the Paradox of State-Sponsored Development.* Ithaca, NY: Cornell University Press, 2002.

Ben Jaafar, Mustapha. *Un si long chemin vers la démocratie. Entretien avec Vincent Geisser.* Tunis: Nirvana, 2014.

Bettaïb, Viviane, ed. *Dégage: La Révolution Tunisienne [Édition du Patrimonie Tunisie].* Tunis: Patrimoine, 2011.

Boubekeur, Amel. "The Politics of Protest in Tunisia: Instrument in Parties' Competition vs. Tool for Participation." *SWP Comments* 13 (March 2015).

Caïd, Essebsi, and Beji. *Bourguiba: Le bon grain et l'ivraie*, Paris: Sud Éditions, 2009.

Camau, Michel, and Geisser Vincent. *Le syndrome autoritaire: Politique en Tunisie de Bourguiba à Ben Ali.* Paris: Presse de Sciences Politiques, 2003.

Cammett, Melani. *Globalization and, Business Politics in Arab North Africa: A Comparative Perspective.* Cambridge: Cambridge University Press, 2007.

Carnegie Endowment for International Peace. SADA Debates with Duncan, Pickard, Mullin Corinna, McCarthy Rory, and Cherif Youssef. "Will Security Challenges Endanger Tunisia's Transition?" May 1, 2015. http://carnegieendowment.org/2015/05/01/will-security-challenges-endanger-tunisia-s -transition/i81r

The Carter Center. "National Constituent Assembly Elections in Tunisia." *[Final report]* October 23, 2011. www.cartercenter.org/resources/pdfs/news/peace_publications/election_reports/ tunisia-final-Oct2011.pdf.

Chomiak, Laryssa. "The Revolution Continues." *Middle East Institute* September 2016. http://www.mei.edu/publications/revolution-tunisia-continues-0

Ghannouchi, Rached. "How Tunisia Will Succeed." *New York Times* (November 19, 2014).

Henry, Clement M, and Springborg Robert. "The Tunisian Army: Defending the Beachhead of Democracy in the Arab World." *Huffington Post.* January 26, 2011. www.huffingtonpost.com/ clement-m-henry/the-tunisian-army-defendi_b_814254.html.

Béatrice, Hibou. *The Force of Obedience: The Political Economy of Repression in Tunisia.* Cambridge: Polity Press, 2011.

Human, Rights Watch. "Flawed Accountability: Shortcomings of Tunisia's Trials for Killings during the Uprising." January 12, 2015. https://www.hrw.org/report/2015/01/12/flawed-accountability/ shortcomings-tunisias-trials-killings-during-uprising

Marzouki, Moncef. "The Arab Spring Still Blooms." *New York Times* (September 27, 2012).

Marzouki, Nadia. "Tunisia's Rotten Compromise." *Middle East Research and Information Project* (July 10, 2015).

McCarthy, Rory. *Inside Tunisia's al-Nahda: Between Politics and Preaching.* Cambridge: Cambridge University Press, 2018.

Moore, Clement H. *Tunisia Since Independence: The Dynamics of One-Party Rule.* Berkeley, CA: University of California Press, 1965.

Obama, Barack, and Béji Caïd Essebsi. "The U.S. Stands Ready to Help Tunisia Realize Its Democratic Promise." *Washington Post* (May 20, 2014).

Perkins, Kenneth. *A History of Modern Tunisia*. Cambridge: Cambridge University Press, 2008.

Pierre Piccinin da Prata. *Tunisie. Du triomphe au naufrage: Entretiens avec le Président Moncef Marzouki*, Paris: L'Harmattan, 2013.

Rijkers, Bob, Freund Caroline, and Nucifora Antonio. "All in the Family: State Capture in Tunisia." *World Bank Policy Research Working Paper. WPS* (Washington, DC: World Bank, 2014). http://elibrary. worldbank.org/doi/pdf/10.1596/1813-9450-6810. 6810

Stepan, Alfred. "Tunisia's Transition and the Twin Tolerations." *Journal of Democracy* 23, no. 2 (April 2012): 89–103.

Tamimi, Azzam S. *Rachid Ghannouchi: A Democrat within Islamism*. Oxford: Oxford University Press, 2001.

25 TURKEY

Mine Eder

Most scholars used to see Turkey as an exception in the Middle East. Save a brief occupation and the subsequent war of liberation in the 1920s, the country has never been colonized. Despite frequent interruptions from military coups, Turkey's democratic experience had been relatively persistent since its foundation as a unitary republic in 1923. On the global stage, Turkey's membership in the NATO, the Council of Europe, and the OECD cemented its place among Western democracies and within the globalist economy; the country's economic success in terms of diversification, export orientation, and private-sector development, along with its continuous efforts to combine democratization with economic growth, set the country apart from its Middle East counterparts. Yet the continuous democratic backsliding and growing economic fragility have dispelled all notions of Turkish exceptionalism.

Problems with state formation, democratization, and long-lasting patronage politics, as well as stop-go conflict cycles over the Kurdish issue (Turkey's major ethnic minority), plague Turkish politics. These troubles, coupled with the recent democratic breakdown and the institutionalization of authoritarian control, indicate that Turkey has taken a turn away from the West. Its economy is still diversified and globalized, but the country's economic problems such as poverty, informality, inequality, and financial instability—coupled with corruption and clientelism—further separate it from the other functioning democracies of the world.

HISTORY OF STATE FORMATION

Modern Turkey descended from the Ottoman Empire (1299–1922), a patrimonial monarchy based on the extensive power of the sultan. Starting as a small princedom, the empire expanded to unseat the Byzantine Empire and take over Constantinople (later Istanbul) in 1453. The Ottoman Empire collapsed in 1922, leaving two important legacies for the new Republic of Turkey in 1923: (1) the elaborate system of public administration, heavily centralized in Istanbul around the sultan's court and palace and (2) the multicultural nature of the empire based on the *millet* system.

The nature of the imperial court and the degree to which the Ottoman state was able to centralize its power and extend its control over society have come under particular scrutiny from those focusing on the rise and fall of absolutist states.[1] Lacking a European feudal legacy, the sultan had direct control of the land, with the ability to co-opt and cajole his subjects—both preventing a European-style peasant uprising—and managed to incorporate "potentially contentious forces."[2] Such early centralization of the state power, combined with the absence of much social resistance, shaped state–society relations in the subsequent Turkish republic.

The *madrasa*, an Islamic education system catering to developing cadres for the palace and the courts, and the *devşirme*, an annual conversion of some 3,000 Christian boys from the Balkans to serve in the sultan's court and royal army known as *janissaries*, further hampered the development of any social resistance. The combination of *ilmiye* (religious authorities), *seyfiye* (the army), and *kalemiye* (a primitive bureaucracy) all led by the palace entourage, constituted the heart of the Ottoman state.

The second legacy was the *millet* system. All monotheistic religious communities in the Ottoman Empire formed distinctive *millets* with their own laws, institutions, and religious leaders, be they Armenians, Greeks, or Muslims. The *millets* were established by retaining each area's individual religious laws, traditions, and language under the general protection of the sultan. Although this plurality was important for the longevity of the empire, each area was subject to the sultan's full authority. The attempt to create a common and equal citizenship based on a vague notion of Ottomanism in the latter half of the 19th century failed, perhaps worsening relations between Muslims and non-Muslims in the empire. Ironically, it was the attempts to centralize the power of the state in the midst of rising nationalism, as well as the attempt to create an Ottoman identity and a modern state first through the Tanzimat (reorganization) reforms from 1839 to 1876 and later with the 1908 Young Turk revolution and the political ascendance of the Committee of Union and Progress (1908–1919), that contributed to the decline of the empire (see Chapter 1 of this volume). The 1915 deportation of Armenians during World War I, which has led to intense debates over genocide, and the voluntary and involuntary departure of non-Muslims during the 1920s and 1930s substantially tainted the empire's image of benevolent multiculturalism. Immigrant policies that prioritized Turkic origins and Muslims also became heavily intertwined with the nation-building processes during the early years of the republic.[3]

KEY FACTS ON TURKEY

AREA 302,535 square miles (783,562 square kilometers)

CAPITAL Ankara

POPULATION 82,482,383 (July 2021 est.)

PERCENTAGE OF POPULATION UNDER 25 39.08 (2020 est.)

RELIGIOUS GROUPS (PERCENTAGE) Muslim, 99.8; other (Christian, Jewish), 0.2

ETHNIC GROUPS (PERCENTAGE) Turkish, 70–75; Kurdish, 18; other, 7–12

OFFICIAL LANGUAGE Turkish; Kurdish, other minority languages

TYPE OF GOVERNMENT Republican parliamentary democracy (Turkish-style presidentialism since 2018)

DATE OF INDEPENDENCE October 29, 1923 (successor state to the Ottoman Empire)

GDP (PPP) $2.394 trillion; $28,400 per capita (2020)

PERCENTAGE OF GDP BY SECTOR Agriculture, 6.8; industry, 32.3; services, 60.7 (2017 est.)

TOTAL RENTS (PERCENTAGE OF GDP) FROM NATURAL RESOURCES 0.315 (2019 est.)

FERTILITY RATE 1.94 children born/woman

Source: CIA. "The World Factbook." August 4, 2022, https://www.cia.gov/the-world-factbook/.

From the Ottoman Empire to the Turkish Republic

The causes for the decline and eventual collapse of the Ottoman Empire are myriad, including shifting trade routes, diffusion of French Revolutionary thought, and growing antipathy among increasingly secular institutions within the existing *millets*. Perhaps most important was the rise of nationalism. The devastating Balkan Wars of 1912–1913 and the loss of World War I finally made collapse inevitable.[4]

MAP 25.1 ■ Turkey

After their victory in World War I, the Allies—Britain, France, Italy, and Greece—negotiated a complex and at times vague partition to divide Anatolia among themselves, eventually formalized as the Treaty of Sèvres. The government of Sultan Vahdettin, who had succeeded Reshad in 1918, accepted the plan in August 1920, but a movement of national resistance led by Turkey's most distinguished general, Mustafa Kemal, decisively opposed the treaty. In April 1920, members of the last Ottoman parliament gathered in Ankara after escaping arrest by Allied forces in Istanbul. With newly elected deputies, they proclaimed their sovereignty "in the name of the nation" as the Grand National Assembly (GNA) of Turkey, in effect launching a rebellion against the sultan's government as well as the occupying powers.

In the resulting war of national resistance, the French and Italians decided that it would not be worth fighting another war for the sake of their territorial claims in Anatolia, and they withdrew their forces in 1921. To the east, the new Bolshevik regime in Russia reversed the policy of its czarist predecessors by establishing cooperative relations with Kemal's government, supplying it with arms and money. This left Greece as the only one of the wartime allies prepared to press its claims by force of arms. The Greeks overreached, however, occupying far more territory than they could defend or justifiably claim. By August 1921, they had advanced into Anatolia, fifty miles west of the Turkish nationalist base in Ankara. It was at this point that the Turks turned the tide in a massive battle, halting the Greeks in their tracks.

By October 1922, the Turks achieved military victory. Essentially within its present borders, Turkey was recognized as sovereign by the Lausanne peace treaty. The struggle in Anatolia from 1920 to 1922 had profound effects on Turkey's internal political structure and established Mustafa Kemal, who assumed the surname Atatürk (father-Turk) in 1936, in a position of virtually unchallengeable national authority. He used it to affect a sweeping reconstruction of the state and launch a determined campaign of cultural reorientation.

Atatürk's Cultural Revolution

Turkey was declared a republic on October 29, 1923, with Atatürk its president and Ankara its capital. With the abolition of the sultanate came the separation of the office of the caliph from the head of state; soon afterward, in a dramatic step toward secularism, an act of the GNA abolished the caliphate and closed the *madrasas*.[5]

A new constitution incorporating these momentous changes was proclaimed in April 1924. In addition, the wearing of the fez—at the time, the symbol of male Turks' attachment to Islam—was banned by law in 1925, and the sufi religious orders (*tarikats*) were officially closed. Although a reference to Islam as the state's religion remained in the constitution until 1928, the new order swept away the Islamic legal system in 1926 and replaced it with secular criminal, civil, and legal codes, copied with little alteration from Western Europe. Turkey also became the first Muslim country, well ahead of its Western counterparts, to accept virtually equal legal and voting rights for women.

In 1928, as a symbol of modernity and an aid to literacy, a version of the Latin alphabet replaced the Arabic script that had been used for writing Turkish. This change represented part of a sustained attempt to nationalize culture by promoting the principle that the Turks stood culturally and historically apart from the Muslim world. The campaign was not entirely successful among the rural population, but it significantly affected the educated elite and, as time passed, nonelite groups as well.

Atatürk's regime proved to be culturally progressive but politically authoritarian. A fundamental political debate in contemporary Turkey revolves around the interpretation of the Atatürk era. While revisionist historians emphasize its authoritarian and elitist aspects—what has been called an example of "modernization from above"—more staunch defenders of republicanism and secularism have emphasized the progressive aspects of Atatürk's reforms and cultural transformation.[6]

CHANGING SOCIETY: TURKEY'S TUMULTUOUS MODERNIZATION AND CONTESTATIONS

One of the major challenges in the transition from an empire to a modern republic was to create a secular, Turkish national identity. Nation-building has proven difficult due to four overlapping cleavages: center–periphery cleavages, economic cleavages, ethnic cleavages, and secular versus Islamist cleavages. This final cleavage has become particularly deep with the rise of the pro-Islamist Justice and Development Party (AKP) in 2002.

Center–Periphery Cleavage

Şerif Mardin argues that the primary social cleavage and confrontation that originated in the Ottoman Empire and has continued into the Turkish republic has been the center–periphery cleavage.[7] Largely understood as a critic of the state-led, top-down modernization of the country, Mardin argues that, unlike in Europe, the state and society linkages during the Ottoman Empire, relying heavily on religion, were not sufficiently institutionalized. The unique Ottoman "state tradition" and the patrimonial nature of the sultan's rule were largely to blame. In the secular republic, a bureaucratic class, coupled with an elitist intelligentsia, constituted the center of Turkish society; the masses occupied the periphery and are characterized by religious heterodoxy, localism, and regionalism. The more religion was ousted from the central cultural system, Mardin argued, the more removed the center became from its periphery.

Although criticized as orientalist and heavily influenced by the modernization theories of the 1970s, Mardin's center–periphery terminology has reemerged with the intensification of debates on political Islam and the rise of the pro-Islamist AKP in Turkey in 2002.[8] For some, the AKP's rise to power meant the periphery had finally become the center.[9] Others had long pointed out the failure of the secular republican state elite to establish institutionalized channels with the society and provide basic services such as education and health.[10] With a brief exception in June 2015 elections, the voters on the so-called periphery systematically vote for the AKP, while those in the center vote for the CHP (Republican People's Party).[11] Still others suggested that with the AKP, the periphery has become the modernizing, progressive force, while the "old" center has turned against liberalization and democratization, becoming the conservative antimodernists.[12] The AKP's authoritarian tendencies increased following the failed coup of 2016. The April 2017 constitutional referendum granted vast executive powers to the president and raised genuine concerns over how Turkey's "new" center is increasingly rolling back most of the initial liberalizing, antimilitarist, and democratizing trends, drifting instead into an autocratic regime especially following the transition to a Turkish style presidential system in 2018.

Poverty, Regional Disparity, Gender Gap, and Informality

An exclusive focus on the center–periphery, however, does not capture Turkey's regional and class divisions. Absolute poverty appears uncommon, thanks in large part to strong family ties and solidarity networks. Nevertheless, poverty ratios (calculated according to the 50 percent of median equalized household disposable income) have been systematically increasing since 2017, reaching 15 percent in 2020.[13] COVID-19 and financial instabilities have deepened poverty in the country. Regional inequalities between the East and West are also of grave concern. The top five provinces with the worst human development indicators and the thirteen provinces with second worst are all located in eastern and southeastern Anatolia.[14] In contrast, the western portion of Turkey is far more integrated into the world economy in terms of trade and tourism, enjoying higher levels of investment and infrastructure and accounting for 78 percent of the total gross domestic product (GDP). Significant regional differences in terms of access to quality education also signal that these social and economic differences are sticky.[15]

Added to these regional differences is a significant gender gap, forged in part by early marriages and cultural stigmas. Turkey has seen significant improvement since the 1990s, but there remain significant gaps in the education of girls at all levels, leading to higher illiteracy rates and lower participation in the labor force. The proportion of illiterate women has dropped from 33.9 percent to approximately 9.4 percent (still more than four million women), and the percentage of women with university education is still 11 percent.[16] Women are also marrying at a later age and mothering fewer children. One out of every five women aged between 18 and 45 got married at a child age, and one in every three women who got married at a child age also became a mother at a child age. Half of the women who were married before 18 experienced physical violence.[17]

Perhaps most striking, women's economic conditions remain poor. The 34 percent women's labor force participation as of 2019 is the lowest among OECD countries, where the average is 62 percent. Though a third of the working population, women produce only 10.4 percent of earned main-work income. Only 18.7 percent of salaried wage labor is female, producing only 15.1 percent of total main-work income. Of all the employers in the country, 97.2 percent are male, creating 98 percent of main-work income; on average, men earn four times what women earn.[18] The rate of women's wages in Turkey compared with those of men who work in similar jobs is 0.62. Overall, in 2021 the World Economic Forum's global gender gap report ranked Turkey as 133rd out of the 156 countries surveyed.[19] Political representation of women is no better. As of 2020, only 104 MPs out of 600 were women (lower than Saudi Arabia). A weak knowledge of political and electoral processes combined with a lack of resources to run effective campaigns are among the challenges stifling female political representation. Not surprisingly, in the Human Development Report of 2020, Turkey ranked sixty-eighth out of the 155 countries in terms of gender inequality index.[20]

Another major problem is the informal nature of Turkey's economy. Though declining, almost half of those working are doing so informally, without any coverage by social insurance. High-dependency ratios also indicate a strikingly low employment rate in the country. The wage gap between those employed formally and those in the informal sector has also widened considerably.

Finally, income distribution is a persistent problem in the country. As of 2020, national income share of the top decile in Turkey was 54.4 percent, while the bottom 50 percent accounted for 11.9 percent of national income.[21] Income disparity increased by 21 percent in Turkey between 2000 and 2014, making it the third-fastest country in terms of deterioration in income equality after Egypt and Hong Kong in that period. The country's lopsided tax system, which draws two-thirds of its revenue from indirect taxes while collecting only a small portion of income tax from wealthier people, is blamed for Turkey's social inequality. Limited trade and labor union rights and high unemployment remain major issues for Turkey.[22]

Debates Over Secularism, Religion, and Politics

Four revolutionary legal reforms between 1924 and 1926 were at the forefront of the new secularization agenda of the early republic: (1) the elimination of the caliphate and the closure of religious courts, sects, shrines, convents, and monasteries; (2) the replacement of the Ministry of Religious Law and Pious Foundation by the Directorate of Religious Affairs; (3) the unification of the education system; and (4) the reworking of the Turkish Civil Code.

Women were among the primary beneficiaries of the new republican agenda. Abolishing shari'a law, prohibiting polygamy, and ratifying a "new civil code (based on Swiss code) that gave women equal rights and equal opportunities of education and employment," Turkey set a new precedent for workforce gender equality in Muslim nations, and indeed many Western countries, by the 1930s.[23]

The most important consequence of this secularization program was the emergence of two wildly different groups: secularists and Islamists. In effect, these two contrasting groups that emerged *sui generis* are the same that color the Turkish political landscape today, albeit with very different political powers. The secularists, consisting of the educated, the business community, the mainstream press, the judiciary, and—most importantly—the army, were all committed to minimizing the role of Islam in public life. The other side, the Islamists, opposed these republican reforms and, marginalized on the bases of their religious and provincial backgrounds, were pushed out of political power.

The political rise of the AKP sparked a debate on the relationship between not only Islam and democracy, but also Islam and modernity. The transition to a more open-market economy along with the economic reforms of the then-prime minister, Turgut Özal, in the 1980s was already reshaping the economic landscape in the country. The rising socioeconomic profile of small Anatolian producers facilitated greater franchise for peripheral groups,[24] especially for Muslim conservatives and political Islamists. By increasing Islamists' participation in business, media, and education, economic liberalization reshuffled their interests from confronting the state to constructing a network of microtransformations operating within civil society.

These changes ushered in arguments that Islamism did not have to be revolutionary but could entail the gradual shift of norms and everyday practices.[25] Implicit in these arguments was a strong criticism of the secular state. Secularists, in contrast, have argued that a democracy without secularism, and the guarantee of universal and equal rights regardless of religious faith or identity, is simply impossible. They suggest that the language of political moderation from the AKP is simply a *takkiye*, hiding genuine intentions and beliefs. They suggest that, with the monopolization of power by the Islamists[26] and the Islamization of social practices, the fate of democracy is at stake.[27] The lifestyle concerns and mounting criticisms of too much "social engineering" (bans on alcohol consumption, admonishment of public kissing, incursions into family planning, etc.) also constituted one of the fundamental themes of the May 2013 Gezi

Park Protests. The annulment of Istanbul Convention (which aimed to end domestic violence and offer legal protection to women) amid major protests by a presidential overnight decree on March 2021, on false claims that the convention "normalizes" homosexuality, indicated the scope of this social engineering. Even today, after nearly twenty years of incumbent rule and executive aggrandizement, most of the political debates during the AKP government still revolve around recasting, redefining, and "defending" secularism in the country.[28]

Headscarf Controversy and Education "Reform"

The headscarf issue had been a source of tension long before the tenure of the AKP government. Since the 1960s, Turkish governments have sporadically implemented a headscarf ban in public office. The rise of Necmettin Erbakan's pro-Islamist Welfare Party and the coalition government formed together with the True Path Party in the aftermath of the December 1995 elections and increased the political tensions over secularism and the headscarf. In pressuring Erbakan to resign from his post in 1997, the sensibilities of the Turkish army and its self-acclaimed mission to guard the secularist foundations of the republic were underscored. It was then, too, that women were banned from wearing headscarves during state employment, in elected posts in the parliament, and, most importantly, while attending universities.

The attempt of a member of parliament (MP) to enter into the parliament with a headscarf caused much controversy in 1999. The Islamists framed the entire issue in terms of individual rights and liberties. The secularists voiced concerns that the presence of a woman wearing a headscarf in parliament posed both a symbolic and real threat to the secular foundations of the republic.

Although lifting the headscarf ban was one of the AKP's electoral promises before the 2002 elections, the party initially kept a low profile on the issue. The injustice of not having access to higher education on the basis of wearing a headscarf was voiced frequently, but the AKP government was careful not to take on the Higher Education Council directly, the council that was designed to coordinate (or, according to some, control) universities in Turkey, staunch defenders of secularism at the time.

In 2007, mainly because his wife wore a headscarf and he was an Islamist, the prospect of having Abdullah Gül, then minister of foreign affairs, as the new president became problematic. This was enough not only to mobilize millions of people into joining street demonstrations and protest rallies but also to trigger a so-called "e-coup." The Turkish army put a memorandum on the Internet on April 28, 2007, to "urge" the Constitutional Court to refuse Gül's presidential bid on the grounds of insufficient parliamentary votes. The decision of the court to declare the vote unconstitutional made choosing a president impossible, paving the way for new elections.

The 2007 elections were largely an attempt to respond to the military's efforts to block the election of Abdullah Gül. The subsequent 46.6 percent electoral victory gave the AKP a comfortable margin to elect Gül and remains a major victory against the tutelary powers of the military. Though considerably relaxed before then, the headscarf ban was officially lifted for all public officials (with exceptions of security personnel and judges) in 2013. Women MPs with headscarves started appearing in the parliament from 2013 onward. In 2015, the Supreme

Board of Judges and Prosecutors (HSYK) lifted the ban on female judges and prosecutors. In 2017, women were allowed to wear a headscarf as a part of their uniform both in the police and the army, in effect ending this controversy.

Another controversy on the nexus of religion and politics emerged over the issue of the educational reform package that was literally forced through the lower-parliamentary commission with fistfights and voted on in the national assembly in 2012. The reform package lowered the minimum age for starting primary school to five and changed the uninterrupted eight years of compulsory education (merging the primary and middle school) into an interrupted twelve-year (four + four + four) system, which the secularists saw as an attempt to bring back the religious middle schools (*imam hatips*), hence starting religious education for younger children. The eight years' uninterrupted education law was passed shortly after the February 28 e-coup in 1997 and was largely seen as an attempt to reduce the role of religious middle schools and to relegate the religious high schools to a "vocational" status. The move was thus seen as retaliation to an earlier law with the aim of mainstreaming the religious educational institutions. Since the implementation of the reforms, some of the "regular" high schools have been converted to *imam hatip* schools, sparking intense controversy.

AKP and the Gülen Movement: Turkey's "(Parallel) State" Controversy

One of the most influential claims of the AKP as the party rose to power has been that, despite their electoral wins, political parties never fully controlled the state in Turkey. The AKP insisted that it was controlled indirectly by the military, a secular judiciary, and bureaucracy, sometimes referred to as the "Kemalist establishment." The AKP government also claimed that the military and the higher courts were politicized and that there were concealed clandestine activities to remove nonsecular actors from the government, often referred to as the "deep (parallel) state."

Putting an end to this tutelary democracy and rooting out this Kemalist establishment was also the common goal that brought together the Gülenist Islamist movement and the AKP. The Gülen movement, led by Fetullah Gülen, a preacher and Muslim scholar in self-imposed exile in Pennsylvania, was built through long and extensive investment in education in Turkey and abroad; it offered a Turco-Islamic synthesis. The movement (known as *Hizmet* [Service]) claims to have founded more than five hundred educational institutions in ninety countries. The admirers of the Gülen movement saw it as a liberal, moderate Islamic network built on cooperation, democracy, and interfaith dialogue: a "civic movement" with no linkages to Islamic extremism and with no political aspirations. Critics, on the other hand, saw the movement as a nontransparent, chameleon brotherhood, whose supporters had begun to control Turkey's courts and police as well as its intelligence community.

It was clear that what started as a reactive movement against Kemalism and modernism has turned into a proactive social movement attacking the major actors of the ancient regime. The first attack on the military establishment began in 2008 through an investigation into this "deep state." This was followed by various waves of mass arrests that included some high-level retired and active-duty army officials, intellectuals, civil society leaders, and media figures and pundits, all of whom were charged with involvement in a secret network that came to be known as *Ergenekon*.

The Gülenists alleged that Ergenekon was responsible for, among other things, secret plots to bomb mosques, assassinate prominent figures, and start wars to stir chaos. Having taken control over the judicial system through political appointments to the court (all initially welcomed by the AKP), prominent journalists, activists, academics, and businesspeople, known for their views opposing the AKP, were arrested for having alleged linkages to Ergenekon. Islamists have hailed the Ergenekon trials as an effort to "clean out" the deep state, while secularists have claimed that Ergenekon is mostly manufactured to threaten and silence opposition and that the AKP has created its own deep state with the help of the Gülenists.

The year 2010 saw a new wave of arrests with the aim of revealing an alleged coup plot against the AKP government. The September 12, 2010, constitutional amendments, which empowered the civilian courts to prosecute and try military personnel, widened the scope and rank of arrests—culminating in legal charges against the architects of the 1980 coup and even the arrest of former army chief in January 2012. More than three hundred military staff at all levels, charged with plotting a coup, were arrested in 2010, and most were sentenced with the maximum penalty, ranging from twenty to thirty years.

The Islamists have argued that this is the final step in the democratization and demilitarization of Turkish society; secularists, on the other hand, have characterized these steps as a political strategy to intimidate the political opposition and completely eliminate the independence of the judiciary system. The fact that these cases were handled by specialized "heavy penal courts" with questionable "due process" and that these generals are known for their staunchly secular, anti-AKP views, they argued, proves that these trials were intensely political and revanchist.

The corruption scandal in 2013 over a recorded phone conversation of Erdoğan ordering his son to tuck away millions of dollars was when the long-standing alliance between the Gülen movement and the AKP utterly collapsed. The AKP government as well as Prime Minister Erdoğan saw the charges as a direct attack to overthrow the government and as part of an international (US and Israeli) conspiracy. Erdoğan started a legal battle to remove or transfer all the prosecutors, judges, and the police officers involved in the graft investigation and accused the Gülenists and his sympathizers of forming a "parallel state."

The complete turnaround of the old battle between the secularists/military and the Islamists into a battle between the two major political actors within political Islam in Turkey had major legal and political consequences. As if going on a legal merry-go-round, 2014 saw Turkey's highest criminal court order the release and retrial of 230 military officers who were convicted by pro-Gülenist judges and prosecutors. Most of the sentences and court decisions made by Gülenist judges and prosecutors started to be overturned.

Gülenists were also widely acknowledged to have orchestrated the failed coup of July 2016 by infiltrating the upper echelons of the army—a charge Gülenists have repeatedly denied. The "state of exception" rule established right after the coup, which gave extensive powers to the government enabling them to rule by decree and by circumventing parliamentary scrutiny, ushered an era of massive purges against the Gülenists across civil service, education, journalism, judiciary, and military. Under this emergency rule, which was extended until July 2018, an estimated 160,000 judges, prosecutors, high- and low-level soldiers, police officials, teachers, academics, and civil servants were suspended or dismissed. Likewise, more than 77,000 people had been formally charged with various degrees of crimes, ranging from attempt to overthrow the government to terrorist propaganda. These waves of purges largely targeted (but were by no means limited to) the Gülenists, which were then categorized as a terrorist group.

Meanwhile, determined to root out the movement, the Turkish government continued to pressure various states to close international schools and universities opened and operated by the Gülenists. It also appointed trustees to more than five hundred high-profile, pro-Gülenist business corporations, confiscating their assets and transferring them to Savings Deposit Insurance Fund (estimated at around $US13 billion), and formally demanded the extradition of cleric Gülen himself from the United States.[29] The degree of infiltration of the Gülenists into a wide range of state apparatus (increasing revelations about secret communication channels, manipulations on entrance exams to enter into the army and civil services, and shady appointments based on mafia-like loyalties and paybacks), which was initially accepted and even welcomed by the AKP for harvesting the fruits of the joint victory over the Kemalist establishment, has now become a liability. Even six years after the coup, arrests of active army officers and others across various occupational groups continue. An estimated 20,000 Gülenist army officials have since been purged.[30] The large-scale cutbacks of business and financial privileges that the AKP itself had long provided to the Gülenists also suggest that the AKP is likely to continue to target Gülen supporters and replace them with party sycophants.

Ethnicity and the Kurdish Question

The Kurdish question has been closely connected with both the building of the nation and its identity based on civic Turkishness during the early years of the republic. Many scholars have argued that the Kurdish question and Kurdish identity have been inextricably intertwined with the very definition of *Turkishness*.[31] The trauma of the Sèvres Treaty, which included the prospect of establishing an independent Kurdish state, framed the discussion of the Kurdish question as a threat to national unity and the territorial integrity of the republic. According to the 1923 Lausanne Treaty, the only minorities that are officially recognized are non-Muslims, Armenians, Greeks, and Jews, in line with the earlier *millet* system of the Ottoman Empire. It was not until the 1990s that Turkish politicians actually came to terms with the Kurdish reality.

Today, an estimated fifteen million Kurds live in Turkey (up to 19 percent of the population), although Kurdish nationalists claim much higher numbers. Approximately half live in the Southeast, while the rest of the Kurdish population is spread about the eastern region and throughout major cities (these figures often include as Kurds the Zaza people, a similar yet ethnically and linguistically different group).[32] Obtaining reliable figures has proven difficult, as the Kurds were categorized as *mountain Turks* until the 1990s.

This nonrecognition, or "deliberate neglect," of the Kurdish identity, regional disparity, and economic deprivation in heavily Kurdish-populated regions of the Southeast, combined with the harsh treatment of the Kurds in the aftermath of the 1980 military coup, fueled an armed conflict led by the Kurdistan Workers' Party (PKK) against the Turkish state.[33]

Between 1984 and 1999, the PKK, led by Abdullah Öcalan, who combined leftist, Marxist rhetoric with Kurdish nationalism, launched a series of terrorist attacks in the region. The conflict led to greater military involvement, bringing a declared state of emergency within the region until 2002, forced displacement of populations, and human rights violations. Significant depopulation also occurred in the region, thanks to PKK atrocities against Kurdish clans they could not control, the poverty of the Southeast, and the Turkish state's military operations. It is estimated that more than 40,000 people have died since the beginning of this conflict. The PKK also shifted strategies during these years, targeting urban areas and accelerating its terrorist tactics.

Despite ongoing political tensions, the conflict subsided between 1999 and 2004, when Abdullah Öcalan, leader of the PKK, was captured and imprisoned for life. But the US invasion of Iraq and a souring relationship with the EU (and its declining anchor role) "conflated into a new anti-Western brand of Turkish nationalism."[34] Negotiations slowed, and the international community's ability to influence domestic reforms dwindled. The fighting between the Turkish army and PKK during the 2004 through 2012 period continued as a low-intensity conflict, with offenses and counterattacks and temporary unilateral ceasefires by PKK. The AKP's new Kurdish initiative (peace process) to open a dialogue raised new hopes and ushered in a new era. Yet cessation of conflicts proved difficult amid increasing arrests of Kurdish activists, journalists, and political leaders. Nevertheless, the Kurdish conflict subsided as the government launched negotiation rounds with Abdullah Öcalan in İmralı, the island where he is serving his life sentence, and the PKK.

However, the civil war in Syria rapidly pushed the internationalization of the Turkish–Kurdish conflict, as it created an opportunity for the PKK to develop alliances with the Kurdish movement in Syria (PYD) and the security wing of the party, the People's Protection Unit (YPG). In addition, the military aid received from the United States raised hopes for the sequestering of an autonomous region and eventually a state for the Kurds. The Turkish government became increasingly uneasy about this international support.

A concomitant push occurred on the political front, beginning with the first-time entry of the pro-Kurdish Party, the HDP (People's Democratic Party), into the parliament. The interim government accused HDP of not severing its ties with PKK, while PKK called off the cease-fire. The unprecedented speed of escalation of the conflict in between two elections, June 7 and November 1, 2015, revealed the fragility of the peace process.

While the HDP accused the government of security failures in the Southeast and directly blamed the AKP, the AKP launched a widespread campaign against "all terrorism," citing security threats from both ISIS (Islamic State of Iraq and Syria) and PKK bombings. The clashes between the army and the PKK took a particularly violent turn in urban sites during December 2015–April 2016 and marked not only a radicalization of both PKK strategies, moving from rural to urban sites, but also remilitarization of the conflict. According to the International Crisis Group, more than 4,000 casualties have been reported in the conflict since July 2015.[35] This remilitarization also led to Turkey's cross-border military operations into Syria. While on paper this was in response to the threat of ISIS, the prospect of preventing a Kurdish enclave across the border was not lost.

Remilitarization played a significant role in the major challenges pro-Kurdish parties have faced in the country. Every pro-Kurdish political party has been systematically closed by Constitutional Court decisions because of their alleged links to the PKK. The highly controversial 10 percent national threshold, which requires all the parties to have a minimum of 10 percent of the popular vote to have parliamentary representation, had also kept the Kurdish parties out of parliament. The pro-Kurdish parties had either to form a preelection coalition with existing parties or enter independent candidates from their respective districts, allowing the party to form a group within the GNA afterwards. Because the national threshold does not exist in local elections, a significant number of Kurdish local representatives were able to come to power, particularly in southeast Turkey.

The HDP, the most recent pro-Kurdish party, emerged in 2014 and started an initiative to launch the party as an all-inclusive party with the aim of democratizing the country. At the forefront was presidential candidate Selahattin Demirtaş, who called for a coalition against AKP, citing the authoritarian measures of Erdoğan. Following the coup attempt of July 2016 and the crackdown on pro-Kurdish political representatives, Selahattin Demirtas was jailed. In the June 2018 presidential elections, Demirtaş was a candidate again for HDP but had to run his campaign from jail. Meanwhile, 90 out of the 102 elected HDP majors in local municipalities were removed from office and replaced by "trustees" appointed directly by the government. Many pro-Kurdish journalists and activists were also detained and jailed; media outlets closed. Despite these political pressures, HDP managed to pass the national threshold in 2018 parliamentary elections and captured 67 seats. Systematic attempts, however, to delegitimize HDP, through removing the legal immunity of HDP MPs, three of whom lost MP status since 2018, as well as the 2021 "party closure" case brought to the Turkish constitutional court by state prosecutor, on grounds of "destroying the indivisibility of the nation and the state" and alleged ties to the PKK, coupled with complication of the issue with Syria and YPG, all suggest that political resolution of the Kurdish problem remains highly unlikely.

POLITICAL INSTITUTIONS, GOVERNANCE, AND TURKEY'S DEMOCRATIC BACKSLIDING

Turkey's democratic experience was interrupted several times. Four military interruptions and four transitions to democracy have occurred since the 1923–1945 single-party era. While concerns over Turkey's democracy were formerly centered on the military's influence on democracy, the attempted coup in 2016 and the ensuing purge of high-ranking officers has neutered the military's political role. Since the rise of AKP as the single-dominant party, winning consecutively six national elections (2002, 2007, 2011, June 2015, November 2015, and June 2018), the focus of concerns over Turkey's democracy have gradually shifted away from the military toward issues like freedom of expression (with jailing and silencing of journalists and political opponents), escalating police violence (as was evident in the case of Gezi Park Protests), and executive aggrandizement. Mirroring the rhetoric associated with the military threat, opposition parties have characterized the personalization of power by President Tayyip Erdoğan and the AKP's entrenchment as a "civil coup."

The failed coup of July 15, 2016 (which resulted in 248 people dead and 1,400 people injured, as civilians, upon a dramatic call from President Erdoğan to the public through FaceTime, took to the streets to fight against the coup-makers) can be seen as a turning point when all these democratic backsliding processes sped up significantly, resulting in an evident democratic breakdown and full-blown transition to autocracy. The coup attempt and the heightened security threat created a fertile ground for executive aggrandizement. The declaration of a state of exception and its extension for two years allowed the government to avoid all institutional checks and balances; the urgent need to address the problem of Gülenists also gave the government an opportunity to silence all the opposition, Kurdish party members, activists, journalists, and academics without any legal liability and often without due process.

In the aftermath of the coup attempt of July 2016, the two-year long "state of exception"—essentially characterized by the suspension of rule of law, massive public-sector purges, widespread rights abuses, and suppression of political opposition—set the stage for the transition into an executive presidency in 2017. The concentration of so much executive power in the office of the presidency has generated a growing consensus that Turkey, after decades of multiparty politics, is no longer a democracy. Freedom House registered the Turkish case as the largest one-year decline in freedom in the world in 2016 and the largest ten-year decline in 2017. Since 2018, Turkey's status is reported as *not free*. Largely thanks to reports of election fraud, especially during the April 2017 referendum on transition to presidentialism and the June 2018 national/presidential elections, the country failed to meet even the basic requirements of an electoral democracy.[36] Opposition victories in 2019 municipal elections also showed, however, that the president's power is not unlimited.

The coup also fostered rapprochement between the AKP and the Nationalist Action Party (MHP), which had started with the militarization of the Kurdish conflict and collapse of the Kurdish peace process in 2015. It was, in fact, the MHP that announced in October 2016 that they would support AKP's bid for a presidential system and initiated the parliamentary vote to take the issue to referendum. The rise of this Islamist–Nationalist power-sharing arrangement culminated in an electoral alliance known as *Cumhur İttifakı* (People's Alliance). In June 2018, joint presidential and national elections were held, in which the MHP supported the reelection of President Erdoğan and the two parties prepared a common MP list for the parliament. In short, the failed coup, the state of exception, and the MHP's decision to support Erdoğan's bid for a presidential system, combined with the criminalization and weakening of opposition parties, ensured Turkey's democratic breakdown.

Though different categorizations are used in describing Turkey's democratic decline (majoritarianism, illiberal democracy, competitive authoritarianism), the question as to why and how Turkey turned from a formal democracy (even upheld as a democratic model for the rest of the Middle East) to an autocratic regime remains a crucial question. Whether this was a result of slow process of executive aggrandizement or sudden breakdown at various crucial political moments (e.g., the Gezi protests or 2013 corruption scandals) remains highly contested.

Whether incremental or sudden, the emerging literature offers various explanations as to why Turkey has suffered such a democratic decline. Some argue that after twenty years of incumbent rule and political packing into the state institutions including the judicial system, the AKP and the state have effectively merged, allowing the party to use vast state resources to create and consolidate its own constituency. Others underscore how the AKP transformed Turkey's political economy, creating its own business elite through privatization, public procurements, and public transfer of private capital from AKP-dissident businesses to those defending the AKP. This capital was used for political gain, increasing cash transfers, and various social assistance programs in order to maintain the support of the urban poor.[37] Such a transformation (the growing dependence of business and urban poor on the discretion of the AKP) essentially raised the cost of replacing the AKP and, at the same time, reduced the costs of suppressing and silencing the opposition. Growing evidence of a personality cult surrounding Erdoğan and the entrenchment of clientelism, along with transition to a Turkish style presidential system in 2018 with unchecked powers, made Turkey a case for institutional decay.[38] In effect, this decline revealed the dark side of majoritarianism, where once a political party receives the majority of the votes, it can systematically legalize and normalize the politicization of all institutions, eliminate all checks and balances, and renounce pressures for transparency or accountability. Politicization of the judiciary, as AKP loyalists replaced the Gülenist judges and prosecutors, for instance, effectively criminalized all opposition voices, packaging them as potential terrorists conspiring against the government, severely curbing freedom of expression and undermining the rule of law.

Still, some academics argued that Islam is incompatible with democracy and how Islamists in Turkey were never democratic to begin with.[39] Others focused on how the severity of polarization, wherein opinions on even the most mundane issues were defined by political loyalties, might account for democratic decline.[40] The monopolization of all media outlets, either by the government or pro-AKP businesses, have also enhanced the ability of the government to "spin" all its policies, demonizing and silencing opposition. Such aggrandizement and abuse of executive power partially account for the weakening power of opposition parties and the disappearing civil society organizations that are critical of the government.

The last partial explanation for Turkey's democratic decline is linked to weakening ties to the West. Dimming prospects of EU membership and the crucial gatekeeping role Turkey plays with regard to the Syrian refugee crisis diluted Turkey–EU relations, meaning that the EU can no longer play a major political anchoring role. Meanwhile, suspicions of US involvement in the 2016 coup, the row over sanctions on Iran, and the US arming of Kurds in Syria have strained relations with the Americans. Turkey seems to be drifting to the "East," as evidenced by increasing coordination between Turkey, China, Iran, and Russia on the international stage (e.g., the Syrian cease-fire agreement in 2016), and by Turkey's decision to buy S400 Russian defense systems in 2020 amid protests from its NATO allies and sanctions/retaliations from the United States. Thus, the United States and the EU have clearly lost their leverage to promote democratization and liberal principles.

Constitution

The Turkish constitution, first ratified in 1921, has been revised (or rewritten) several times during its history: once in 1924, again in 1961 following the military coup of 1960, and in 1982 in the aftermath of the 1980 coup. The 1921 constitution ratified by the GNA, which acted as both a constitutional convention and a parliament, established the basic principles of the republic. Following the proclamation of the founding of the republic on October 29, 1923, the new 1924 constitution defined Turkey as a parliamentary democracy and established the separation of powers. In less than a year, however, the country adopted a single-party rule by the CHP, which lasted twenty years.

The transition to a multiparty system occurred in 1946 when CHP deputies Celal Bayar (Atatürk's prime minister, 1938–1939), Adnan Menderes, Fuat Köprülü, and Refik Koraltan left the party to form the Democrat Party (DP) and went on to win the 1950 elections in a landslide. The 1924 constitution remained in effect until 1961, but with two major amendments: one eliminated the sentence "The religion of state is Islam" from Article 2 of the constitution in 1928; the other occurred in 1934 and gave women the right to vote and be elected to office. In 1937, six founding principles of the CHP—republicanism, nationalism, populism, etatism, secularism, and reformism—also made their way into the constitution.

Though dovetailing with the May 27, 1960, coup, the 1961 constitution is ironically considered the most democratic and "liberal" in terms of its emphasis on individual rights. This particular constitution is also known for establishing an upper chamber—the Senate—as a way to counterbalance the political dominance of the majority parliamentary group in the GNA, a change largely seen as a response to the problems, power abuses, and intolerance of opposition observed during the majoritarian control of the GNA by the DP. A Constitutional Court designed to supervise the constitutionality of legislation passed by the GNA was also established. Finally, this was also the time the term *social state* first made its way into the constitution.

The last and current constitution was ratified in 1982, once again following a military coup. Approved by an overwhelming majority of the population in a national referendum, the 1982 constitution emphasized stability over liberties. It was largely a response to the political fragmentation, ideological polarization, instability, and ineffective coalition governments of the prior decade. The 1982 constitution abolished the Senate, returned to a unicameral GNA, kept the Constitutional Court and Higher Appeals Court but diminished their scope, and severely limited the autonomy of universities. The universities were targeted because they were considered polarized, divided along left–right ideological lines, and were sites for numerous legal, illegal, and paralegal youth activities before the coup. Political parties and associations were also put under strict regulation and control.

The 1982 constitution has been heavily criticized as undemocratic and restrictive. It has been changed a total of ten times, in effect changing one-third of the text. Most of these changes took place within the context of harmonization with the EU. One of the most important changes was the abolition of the death penalty in 2002. Other changes aimed at containing the political influence of the military and increasing the transparency of its budget, eliminating state security courts, and eliminating army representation in the higher education council. There were also changes that aimed to reinforce gender equality and freedom of expression, such as allowing for Kurdish broadcasting.

The 2007 constitutional reform followed the controversy over Abdullah Gül's presidential bid. The change was approved through a referendum and involved electoral reform: the president, formerly elected by a two-thirds majority within the GNA, will now be elected by popular vote. The presidential term will be reduced from seven years to five, with eligibility to run for a second term, and elections will be held every four years instead of five.

In May 2010, the government also passed a series of constitutional amendment proposals from the parliament, which involved amendments to twenty-three articles of the constitution. Though the amendments included some noncontroversial items such as extending collective bargaining rights to government employees, privacy of information, allowing civilian courts to judge military personnel charged with criminal activities, and repeal of constitutional protection for 1980 coup-makers, the most controversial amendments involved changes in the institutional structure of the Constitutional Court and the HSYK. Since the HSYK is the sole body overseeing the appointment of judges and prosecutors, under the new provisions the minister of justice and the permanent secretary became "natural members" of the board, paving the way for more political influence in judicial appointments and ultimately weakening the independence of the judiciary. Nevertheless, a referendum took place on the symbolic date of September 12, 2010 (the thirtieth anniversary of the 1980 coup), and resulted in a 58 percent yes and a 42 percent no vote.

But arguably the most significant constitutional change occurred through a referendum on April 16, 2017, in which the country's parliamentary regime was in effect replaced by a Turkish-style presidentialism known as "executive presidency." Though the political debates about a shift to presidentialism have long been around, mostly supported by Erdoğan (the new president had actively campaigned prior to June 2015 elections and appealed to the voters to bring a sufficient majority in the parliament to change the regime toward a presidential system), the AKP did not have the sufficient number of votes to pass it through the parliaments, where two-thirds majority is needed, or bring it to referendum. The debates mostly took place along partisan and highly ideological lines, where Erdoğan and AKP supporters claimed that a presidential system would ensure more effective and speedy governance, a process better for stability and economic development. The opposition saw this as creeping authoritarianism, with Erdoğan formalizing his de facto powers and the country disintegrating into a one-man's rule.

The referendum was on eighteen amendments that gave extensive powers directly to the president. With the referendum, the president started to serve both as head of state and as head of the executive; appoint the cabinet of ministers and a significant portion of high judiciary and senior public officials without any oversight from parliament; restructure all ministries and appoint top-level bureaucrats to public institutions (including even university rectors); issue presidential decrees (albeit with some restrictions); and dissolve parliament by calling new legislative and presidential elections. All these amendments were approved by a thin margin (51.41 percent for and 48.59 percent against) amid electoral fraud allegations as the Higher Election Council declared unstamped ballots as valid in the midst of vote counting. As such, there was a significant shift of governing authority from the parliament to the presidency, with the concentration of executive power in a single individual.

Legislative Branch

Until the 2018 national elections when the number of MPs increased from 550 to 600, the GNA was a unicameral parliamentary body comprising 550 deputies. The full term of the GNA was four years but increased to five years in 2018. The election of deputies is based on multimember districts where the parties entering the elections come up with the party list, and the voters vote for either independent candidates or party lists. Members who are at the top of the party list in a given district (who will have the highest chance of being elected) are often party insiders and in the leader's personal circles. Sometimes, local notables are so prominent that the parties promise them safe seats in order to get their constituent votes delivered. Powerful tribal leaders, religious brotherhood groups, or rich landed families, common in the East and Southeast of the country, can then deliver the votes for their respective parties. Such linkages reinforce patron–client relationships and political inequalities. The fact that the party leadership has almost unlimited power to draw up district party lists also means that party discipline is vital and constantly maintained. Internal party debates and pluralistic views within a party are very limited.[41]

Historically, the GNA's power has risen and declined depending on the political context. Not surprisingly, the parliament was a rubber-stamp institution during the single-party era. With the DP's rise to power in 1950, the parliament became the arena of intense political contestation. With the legacy of the single-party era intact and with a very comfortable majority in the parliament, the DP was not at all attentive to the opposition, causing the easy fusion of executive and legislative powers.

In effect, the 1961 constitutional reforms reflected concerns over what happens when a majority party in the parliament goes unchecked and unopposed. To that effect, the 1961 constitution established a second house, the Senate, and the Constitutional Court to supervise the constitutionality of the laws passed by both houses of parliament. Despite efforts to establish some degree of separation of powers, the 1961–1980 period is considered to have been a politically unstable period for the GNA, when the coalition governments and ideologically charged debates in parliament paralyzed the political system amid ongoing crises—the oil crisis in 1973, the Cyprus crisis in 1974, and the deepening economic crisis and escalating street violence—both foreign and domestic. In fact, it was the paralysis of the GNA and the inability of any of the parties to create sufficient consensus to get a president elected in the parliament that became the pretext for the military to intervene in September 1980. The 1982 constitution disbanded the Senate but retained the Constitutional Court with its supervisory powers.

Despite heated debates on the floor, the AKP's majority in the GNA since 2002 gave the party power to pass its legislative agenda, ultimately reducing the influence of the GNA. The AKP lost its majority briefly in June 2015, putting a temporary hold on the ultimate transition toward presidentialism; however, by November 2015 the AKP claimed a new majority with 49.5 percent of the votes. With 316 seats, the AKP was positioned just 14 seats short of calling a referendum for constitutional change.

But when the National Action Party shifted its position in support of presidentialism, following the coup attempt in 2016, all political calculations changed, allowing the AKP's proposal for a constitutional referendum to pass through the parliament with 348 votes. The win of the 2017 referendum and formal shift to executive presidency in 2018 significantly reduced the power of the parliament. The parliament can now be dissolved directly by the president; it can no longer be tasked with overseeing the council of ministers; it no longer has the power to draft the state budget; call for a vote of "no confidence," and it has very limited powers to amend the president's budget proposals.

The referendum also bridled the potency of any parliamentary checks and balances. The right to submit oral and written questions as a part of MPs' auditing process was also curtailed. Inquiries are only allowed via "written submission" to vice presidents and ministers, and none are allowed to be sent to the president, rendering the president, in effect, above legislative scrutiny—a major and dramatic break from past practice.

Another change is that the parliament needs an absolute majority of its entire membership (50 percent + 1) to repass a bill that the president sends back to the parliament for reconsideration, whereas the former constitution allowed the parliament to bypass the president's objections by a simple majority of the quorum. Last but not least, this shift also makes it very difficult to impeach the president. As long as the president's party enjoys a majority in parliament, which is the case with the AKP, holding the president wields both executive and legislative powers.

Executive Branch

Prior to the shift to executive presidency in 2018, the president still sat at the top of the executive branch and was the commander in chief with the power to appoint the prime minister and approve the cabinet. The 1982 constitution gave the president the power also to appoint members of the Constitutional Court, judges, rectors of universities, and all other political appointments. Presiding over the National Security Council (NSC) and the cabinet was also within the powers of the office, should the president see it as necessary. That is why at the time Ersin Kalaycıoğlu had argued, "Such aggrandizement of power by the president somewhat undermines the parliamentary character of the Turkish democratic regime. . . . Turkey can be characterized as a hybrid of parliamentarism, and semipresidentialism or a semiparliamentary regime."[42]

But prior to 2018, the office of prime minister and the ministries were still where most of the operational political power lay in Turkey. Particularly those prime ministers who enjoyed majorities in parliament had practically fused executive and legislative powers. The power of the prime minister and the effectiveness of the cabinet were contingent, however, upon the party holding a majority in parliament. During coalition governments in Turkey (1961–1965, 1973–1980, and 1991–2002), the power of the prime ministers dwindled owing to their governments' vulnerability to a vote of no confidence. Because of the majority of the AKP in the parliament, the power and the influence of the office of prime minister have increased considerably since 2002.

However, in 2014 the election of former PM Tayyip Erdoğan as the new, first-time popularly elected president of the country ushered in a new wave of debates on Turkey's transition toward a de facto presidential system. The opponents had already started to underscore that the elected president in 2014 had already stepped on the boundaries of the existing constitutions by frequently presiding over the cabinet, by giving indirect support to the AKP, and by issuing political statements rather than remaining neutral.

The 2017 referendum laid the framework for a new presidential system to begin after the following general elections. After the reelection of President Tayyip Erdoğan in June 2018 (winning in the first round with 52.6 percent) and his inaugural in July, the formal implementation of the eighteen amendments turned the de facto presidential rule into an enlarged, de jure one.

With the post of prime minister and the twenty-six-member cabinet under him in the previous system abolished, Erdoğan restructured the cabinet by presidential decrees, appointed a vice president, and established sixteen ministers who report only to him. As the top bureaucratic post of undersecretary was eliminated in all ministries, two or three deputy ministers helped with the task of implementing presidential directives. In addition, sixty-five existing boards, committees, and commissions were merged into nine presidential policy boards on science, technology and innovation, education, economy, security and foreign policy, law, arts and culture, health care, and local administration and social policies. They all have a vice chair and two other members and report directly to Erdoğan. The new Finance, Human Resources, Technology, and Investment Offices within the presidency also wield considerable influence in the coordination and implementation of Erdoğan's policies. At the same time, the restructuring of the key institutions of National Intelligence, Defense Industries Directorate, High Command of the Armed Forces, and the National Security Council under full presidential control have also strengthened Erdoğan's authority in security matters, giving unprecedented powers to the president and establishing one-man rule.

Judicial Branch

Since the 1924 constitution, the judiciary has been organized as an independent branch of government. The 1961 constitution established the Constitutional Court to oversee laws and resolutions of the GNA. The Supreme Administrative Court acts as the highest court on administrative, civil, commercial, and criminal matters in Turkey. The head of the Supreme Administrative Court is also considered the chief prosecutor in the country. Judges and public prosecutors are under the control of the Higher Board of Judges and Prosecutors, a five-member body of the higher-court judges.

Politically, particularly within the context of the 1982 constitution, the eleven-member Constitutional Court has had the power to shut down political parties for violating the principles of the constitution. Violating the principles of secularism in the constitution or threatening the "territorial integrity and national unity," in the case of pro-Kurdish parties, has been sufficient reasons. Party closures have drawn criticism both inside and outside of Turkey and clearly disrupted the political process. Most parties have simply regrouped and reorganized the same constituencies, albeit with a different name and party symbol. One of the September 12, 2010, constitutional amendments finally made it much more difficult for the courts to shut down political parties, requiring a majority consensus of parties in parliament. Legislators from banned parties would be able to keep their seats and re-form under a new name after three years.

Another odd legacy of the 1982 constitution was the state security courts (DGMs in Turkish) that were designed to try cases involving crimes against the security of the state and organized crime. The three-judge panel included a military judge, which raised eyebrows particularly in the European Court of Human Rights (ECtHR), a body that has handed down severe penalties on Turkey for human rights violations. In 1999, the military judge was removed, and in 2005, DGMs were closed, replaced by "special Heavy Penal Courts." Though civilian, these courts enjoyed special prosecuting powers and played a crucial role in the arrest of many political and military figures accused of crimes against the state and the government. Under heavy criticisms of lengthy arrest periods, scanty evidence, and legal and procedural mishaps, the government passed a legal reform act in 2012, shutting down these special courts after their existing cases are completed. But the HSYK was now in a position to bestow on any court it sees fit "prosecuting powers" in accordance with terrorism law in the country. So the principle of courts with special prosecuting powers has remained, though the existing special courts have been shut down.

The most important change in the judicial branch of the government came with the 2010 constitutional amendments. These amendments expanded the Constitutional Court by six, to seventeen members, and expanded the powerful HSYK to twenty-one members from the current seven. The president and parliament—both controlled by the AKP—received a significantly increased role in appointing members in judicial bodies, which raised serious questions over judicial independence.

Though the Constitutional Court manifests traces of judicial independence through processing individual complaints about rights violations, another 2010 amendment largely designed to curtail heavy penalties by the ECtHR, concerns over judicial neutrality heightened as the dispute between the Gülen movement and AKP government took a legal turn. Accusing the Gülen movement of forming a parallel state within the state in concert with police, prosecutors, and judges in the aftermath of the December 2013 corruption scandals, the AKP launched a counterattack, removing prosecutors and judges associated with Gülen. The purge drew out a series of revelations—relying on fabricated evidence, lack of due process, unwarranted arrests, jail sentences, and appeals, only to be followed by reversals, retrials, and acquittals—raising the level of mistrust in the legal system. Replicating the same Gülenist strategies of political packing, the judges and prosecutors accused of being Gülen supporters began to be systematically replaced by AKP loyalists, a process that escalated after July 2016, eliminating any semblance of judicial independence.

Another blow to an independent judicial system came with the transition to the executive presidency in which the president can directly appoint four of the thirteen members of the Council of Judges and Prosecutors (HSK; previously named as HSYK), the highest body responsible for appointing judges and prosecutors (the other seven are appointed by the parliament, also controlled by AKP). Finally, the justice minister and his undersecretary, themselves already appointed by the president, are automatic members. This new institutional design thus put HSK directly and indirectly under the control of Erdoğan and the AKP.

Last but not least, with executive presidency, the power of the Constitutional Court also got significantly curtailed. The Court already adopted a "hands-off" approach, declaring that all of the emergency decrees in the post-2016 coup period are outside the jurisdiction of the court. The Constitutional Court lost significant international prestige when it failed to implement the clear and final 2020 ECtHR ruling to end the pretrial detention of both Osman Kavala (a well-known philanthropist, held in prison since 2017) and Selahattin Demirtaş (the coleader of HDP, imprisoned since 2016). This signaled that the court can no longer serve as an effective check on the presidential system and that the political packing in the Constitutional Court is now complete.

Contested Role of the Military[43]

One of the most striking features of Turkey's political system has been the persistent and powerful role of the military, particularly after the 1960 coup. The Turkish army draws its legitimacy and power from the war for national independence, which led to the foundation of the republic in 1923.

The Turkish military did not indefinitely retain power after its interventions in government. Instead, it voluntarily returned power to civilians after short periods of time. During its interventions, the military also managed to maintain some degree of legitimacy. It intervened only during moments of genuine political anarchy and economic collapse, thus convincing the public that it was defending the general interests of the nation. On all three occasions, the public trust in civilian governments had waned considerably, and the GNA was unable to resolve political crises prior to the coups. This also explains why the military used to be the most trusted institution in the country.

On the negative side, the military regimes of 1970–1973 and 1980–1983 were responsible for serious human rights violations. The power of the military was also greatly expanded in these periods. As Samuel Valenzuela explains, such powers included "broad oversight of the government and its policy decisions while claiming to represent vaguely formulated fundamental and enduring interests of the nation-state."[44] Among the most visible institutions established with the 1961 constitution, and expanded by the 1982 constitution, was the NSC, placing the prime minister and the chief of the general staff under the leadership of the president of the republic. In line with the harmonization with European requirements, the powers of the NSC were significantly curbed in 2003.

The September 12, 2010, constitutional amendments empowered the civilian courts to prosecute and try military personnel. This widened the scope and rank of arrests culminating in legal charges against the architects of the 1980 coup. Armed with a newly politicized judiciary, the antimilitary and anti-Kemalist coalition between the Gülen movement and the AKP could now target the upper echelons of the army, charging them with the conspiracy to overthrow the government. The ensuing arrests of military personnel allowed the Gülenist to staff those positions with their own supporters. For some, these were successful signs of demilitarization. For others, this was a deliberate, political move to clean the "secular elements" within the army.

The status of the military in Turkey dramatically changed in the aftermath of the 2016 coup attempt. Convinced that the Gülenists who had infiltrated the army were behind the coup and feeling "deceived" by their Islamist brothers, Erdoğan and the AKP launched a major purge, dismissing and arresting more than half of the generals and high-level military personnel, closing all the military academies, reorganizing military hospitals, and placing the chief of the army firmly under the government's control. Though the political role of the military was effectively ended, the fact that a particular faction within the army could break the chain of command, fire upon civilians, and bomb major buildings (including the parliament building) all taking place while the commander in chief was detained in secret dealt a serious blow to the credibility of the military. What exactly happened on the night of the coup still remains a mystery along with questions on whether there are still Gülenists within the army as the arrests of active military personnel continues six years after the coup.

Even with this breakdown of institutional structure and the major overhaul, the Turkish army (NATO's second largest) continues to play an important role in the country's international entanglements. With the escalation of the Kurdish conflict and humanitarian and military operations across the borders—exacerbated by the instability and uncertainty in Iraq and Syria—this role is here to stay.

ACTORS, OPINION, AND POLITICAL PARTICIPATION

Despite these periodic interruptions of military coups and the seemingly patronage-based, clientelistic party system in the country, political participation in Turkey has been vibrant. Until the recent democratic breakdown, various actors, from nongovernmental organizations (NGOs) to political parties, had continuously expanded opportunities to influence and actively shape policymaking.[45]

Elections and Voting Behavior

Turkey has had seventeen multiparty national elections since 1945. Those in 1946, 1961, and 1983 took place under extraordinary circumstances, as they were the elections of democratic transition. The first multiparty election of 1946 took place under unfair electoral rules and has been the only election, until 2017, showing widespread electoral fraud. Elections in Turkey have been under the legal supervision of the Higher Electoral Board since 1950.

Turkey's electoral laws changed significantly over the years. From 1945 to 1960, a majoritarian, multimember district electoral system created landslide victories for the DP, producing single-party governments after the 1950, 1954, and 1957 elections. After years of persistent majoritarian authoritarianism, the electoral system was changed to allow proportional representation, specifically in multimember districts. After 1961, more minor, radical, and fringe parties could elect their representatives to parliament. The 1980 coup brought this parliamentary pluralism to an abrupt end.

The 1983 elections, this time concerned with political instability and fragmentation, introduced a national threshold requiring a minimum of 10 percent of the popular vote to achieve parliamentary representation. Voting also became mandatory, even though the participation ratio in elections had been systematically high—lowest in the 1969 elections at 64 percent and highest in the 1987 elections at 93 percent.

One of the most striking features of Turkey's political system has been the increasing volatility of electoral behavior, particularly in the 1990s,[46] suggesting that party identification is no longer a strong determinant for voting behavior. Instead, as shown in Yilmaz Esmer's study of the 1995 and 1999 elections, ideological self-placement in the left–right spectrum emerged as the primary predictor of voting.[47] Among the social cleavages, religiosity and ethnicity have the highest correlation with party preferences.[48] Although some pocketbook voting exists, confessional affiliations play a significantly larger role in determining and shaping political behavior.

Turkish voters have usually placed themselves on the Right.[49] The DP in the 1950s and its replacement, the Justice Party (AP), have been hugely popular among the electorate. The strongest showing for the center-left parties emerged in 1977 with a little more than 40 percent, but even then the center-right parties enjoyed a 60 percent presence.[50]

The ideological polarizations also became evident as voter profiles for the parties became sharply divided. Staunch secularists have systematically supported the CHP. The pro-Kurdish parties have enjoyed considerable support, particularly in the Southeast. The Kurdish parties have not, however, performed all that well outside the Southeast, probably owing to strategic voting and the less pressing nature of identity issues outside the region. In fact, most electoral studies have found that the voters in the Southeast diverge significantly from the national political preferences.[51] The MHP has consistently drawn voters among the Turkish nationalists who have adopted a hard-line strategy toward the Kurdish issue. Finally, those who identify themselves as Sunni Muslims and have high levels of religiosity have systematically voted for a variety of center-right parties and pro-Islamist parties, including today's AKP.

The 2016 failed coup remarkably changed the electoral landscape. Armed with emergency rule powers, the AKP started using its power to systematically silence opposing political parties, especially the pro-Kurdish politicians. After lifting the immunity of the MPs, the AKP initiated a wave of political arrests, curtailing and often criminalizing regular party activities. Both the April 2017 referendum and the June 2018 presidential and national elections took place under emergency rule, giving the AKP an unprecedented incumbent advantage. The AKP's growing control over the media, including the highly politicized National Public Television (TRT), also meant that the election campaigns were taking place under highly asymmetric conditions. Erdoğan was given 181 hours of coverage during the campaign by the state broadcaster TRT, while Muharrem İnce, CHP's candidate, was accorded fifteen hours. Demirtaş's campaign, coordinated from his jail cell, was given just thirty-two minutes.

Worse yet, there was growing evidence of electoral fraud, dating back to the 2017 referendum when the Higher Election Council, seen as above politics until then, changed the rules of validating ballots—unstamped votes would also be accepted as valid. An estimated 1.5 million to 2.5 million unstamped ballots were counted as valid votes, enough to change the results of the referendum. In the June 2018 elections, the decision to count the unstamped ballots as valid was left to the chairs of some 180,000 Ballot Box Committees who are all civil servants. But since civil servants, unlike their European counterparts, are also highly politicized in Turkey, this raised serious concerns about the safety and neutrality of voting and vote counting. Many irregularities were indeed reported, especially in the southeast pro-Kurdish party provinces. Despite record-breaking 87 percent electoral participation in the country, the legitimacy of electoral results from the last two electoral cycles was called into question. Ironically, after losing in two major cities (Ankara and Istanbul) in local elections in March 2019, it was the AKP that cried foul play and forced the Higher Election Council to schedule a new election for the Istanbul mayor in June. In the midst of all allegations, AKP suffered major losses during March 2019 municipal elections across major cities and lost Istanbul's majorship after 25 years by a wide (10 percent) margin in the rerun election.

Political Parties and Party Systems

The early years of the republic were based on the single-party rule of the CHP. The legacy of Atatürk and İsmet İnönü, the second president and the long-time leader of the party, sealed an image of the CHP as a state party. After the transition to a multiparty system, Turkey experienced a typical two-party system. For years, the main parties were the CHP and the DP. After the 1960 coup, the army banned the DP from the political scene for violating the constitution. The unnatural death of the DP and its leadership led to intense competition among parties seeking to claim the DP legacy.[52] In the 1965 and 1969 elections, Süleyman Demirel was able to establish the AP as the DP's legitimate heir, and the party won comfortable majorities in parliament. The elections in the 1970s again produced fragmented parliaments. The two leading parties, the AP and the CHP, found parliamentary competition in the National Salvation Party (MSP) and the Nationalist Action Party (MHP), two highly ideological parties, leading most political analysts to characterize the 1970s as a time of extreme and polarized multipartism.[53]

The ensuing turmoil helped legitimize the military coup of 1980, which closed down all political parties without exception. Furthermore, the military imposed a ten-year ban on party leaders and five-year bans on incumbents of the central party institutions. The 1983 election was a transitional election in which only three new parties were allowed to enter: the Nationalist Democracy Party (MDP), the Populist Party (HP), and the Motherland Party (ANAP). The ANAP received an absolute majority in parliament and went on to win the 1987 elections as well. From 1983 to 1991, Turkey was politically stable, led by a single-party government, the ANAP.

To the dismay of the military, the political ban on the pre-1980 political leaders was lifted after a 1986 referendum, which led to the emergence of new parties under old leadership. So by 1991, political fragmentation and polarization in the party system had made a comeback. The Kurdish parties and the Islamist parties during this period faced continuous constitutional bans, only to follow suit and regroup under different names. Following each of the AKP's five electoral victories, with the exception of the June 2015 to November 2015 period, the AKP garnered enough seats to remain in power as a single-party government. As such, the 2002–2018 period can be characterized as a single-dominant party system in which AKP enjoyed and exercised significant incumbent power. The only novelty has been the ability of the HDP to enter into the parliament, passing the national threshold in 2015 and 2018.

There are three main reasons why the Turkish party system has proved so volatile. One is the legacy of the military coups, rupturing the entire political process, and the decisions of the empowered Constitutional Court to close down several political parties. Second, until recently the political parties lacked the voters' trust because of their reputation as centers of patronage and clientelism and their inability to address economic and social difficulties.[54] Third and perhaps most important, as Ergun Özbudun points out, is the failure of political parties to develop links with civil society groups or nongovernmental institutions, although the AKP and HDP parties may be exceptions.

Overall, party membership remains very low and is often associated with being a mere party supporter. Local-party organizations often only become alive prior to elections and do not get involved in day-to-day political activities and indoctrination. However, the AKP, since its rise to power, has developed powerful party machinery at the local level. Nevertheless, internal party pluralism remains considerably low, a phenomenon common to most parties in Turkey.

Finally, although AKP is a splinter party from the pro-Islamist Welfare Party before coming to power in 2002, it is an exception to the rule, as forming a splinter party and developing a bottom-up party organization remain a major challenge. The most recent example is the formation of İyi Party (Good Party) in 2017, led by Meral Akşener, a former MHP MP who disagreed with MHP leadership in its support of presidentalism and Erdoğan. However, neither Akşener's presidential bid in 2018 nor the national election results turned out as expected despite the alliance called *Millet İttifakı* (Nation Alliance); the party struck with CHP to overcome the 10 percent national threshold. Notable among the new splinter parties which have emerged as a part of the Nation Alliance are the Democracy and Progress Party (DEVA) led by Erdoğan's former Economic Minister Ali Babacan and Future Party led by Ahmet Davutoğlu (former Prime Minister 2014–2016).

Civil Society Groups, NGOs, Social Movements, and Gezi Park Protests

Until the 1970s, Turkey's associational life could largely be seen as corporatist rather than pluralist, centering on major business associations and chambers and much less on powerful unions. The 1980 military coup severely dampened prospects of a pluralist associationalism. The 1980s witnessed a diversification and expansion of noneconomic-interest groups, which had increased their voice, only to be severely silenced since 2013.

Business Groups

Business interests at first were represented by the Turkish Union of Chambers of Commerce, Industry, Maritime Trade, and Commodity Exchanges (TOBB), which held a monopoly over the certification of every enterprise and could represent all businesses, big and small. Unhappy with the TOBB's representation, the Turkish Industrialists and Businessmen Association (TUSIAD) was founded in 1971 to represent a group of large, select businesses, including a significant segment of the manufacturing industry. TUSIAD's initial aim, along with the Turkish Confederation of Employer Associations (TISK), was to create a united front against the growing power of labor unions in the 1970s.

These associations tried to influence policymakers through press conferences and research reports, particularly on democratization and political and economic conditions in the country. TUSIAD usually avoided confrontation with the government. The only exception was its all-out campaign against Ecevit's government of 1979, which is largely believed to have contributed to the government's fall. Relations between the current AKP government and TUSIAD are also lukewarm, as TUSIAD has been outspokenly critical of some of the AKP's policies.

A newer group, the Independent Industrialists and Businessmen Association (MUSIAD), is closer to the AKP. Some have called MUSIAD the rising "Islamist bourgeoisie," representing small- and medium-sized enterprises (SMEs) and Anatolian small-town entrepreneurs with some connections to Islamic capital abroad.[55] In addition, the Confederation of Businessmen and Industrialists (TUSKON) was established in 2005 and is organized in all eighty-one provinces in the country. TUSKON, often associated with the Gülen movement, was initially close to the AKP government and represents a parallel or alternative organization to TUSIAD. Relations have soured since the fallout between Gülenists and the AKP, and

TUSKON has been shut down, as pro-Gülen businessmen who had initially accumulated significant wealth under AKP government faced a reversal of fortunes. Their assets were confiscated and placed under government-appointed trustees. With democratic backsliding in the country, even though the tensions between MUSIAD and TUSIAD continue, the business associations have all become increasingly weary of openly criticizing the government's economic policies.

Unions

Unions have always been weak in Turkey, both organizationally and politically. Strikes, lockouts, and collective bargaining only became legal in the liberal atmosphere of the 1960s. The 1960–1977 period can be seen as the apex of union activity in the country, although demonstrations on May 1, 1977, led to chaos and many deaths, ending the period on a bleak note. At the height of unionization in 1979, membership reached not quite 27 percent of workers, well below counterparts in Europe. The union membership ratio has since hovered around an estimated 10 percent of the working population. One explanation is a lesser degree of large-scale industrialization in Turkey. There are also serious limitations to union activities, such as strict restrictions on any form of political activism. Unions do not have the right to organize in workplaces with fewer than fifty workers, and they are also strictly under state tutelage.

There are three major trade union confederations in the country. First is the Confederation of Trade Unions of Turkey (TÜRK-İŞ). Founded in 1952, TÜRK-İŞ is seen as a cooperative umbrella confederation, focusing on wage issues rather than political concerns. The Confederation of Revolutionary Trade Unions (DİSK), formed in 1967 because of dissatisfaction with TÜRK-İŞ, has been more radical and politically active. DİSK was banned in the aftermath of the 1980 coup, and its leadership was arrested, only to regroup and reorganize in 1986. The Confederation of Real Trade Unions (HAK-İŞ) was established in 1976 and became quite active in the 1980s. The union has claimed Islamic brotherhood as the basis of its organization rather than conflict-ridden unionism. Not surprisingly, HAK-İŞ has been politically close to the AKP. Finally, the Confederation of Public Servants (KESK) became quite active and vocal in the 1990s.

After the 1980 coup, unions were saddled with additional limitations and supervision of their activities; for example, strikes were outlawed in some "crucial" sectors. More important has been the liberalization of the economy since the 1980s, which accelerated the search for cheap, nonunionized workers, leading to a subcontracting boom and informal employment that have challenged the unions.

The new labor law passed under the AKP in 2003 introduced short-term contracts, established temporary employment agencies, and significantly curtailed the collective rights of workers. This was designed to create more flexible labor markets. Under the emergency rule after the post-2016 coup attempt, most strikes were indefinitely postponed or banned in the name of national priorities. Excessive politicization of unions and lack of union leverage vis-à-vis the government, which often surface during minimum wage bargaining as well as lingering constraints on strikes and lockouts, remain fundamental challenges.

Other Social Movements: Islamism, Feminism, and the Alevis

Turkey's history of social movements is quite short and fragmented. Still, Islamism can be considered one of the oldest social movements in the country. There have been countless Islamic revolts against the central authority during both the Ottoman and the Republican periods. But it is after the 1980s that Islamism became much more widespread and organized, beginning to influence the political process. What started as slow, libertarian-right claims of women university students to wear headscarves have gradually progressed with increasing numbers of *imam hatip* (religious) schools in the 1980s, as well as a proliferation of religious presses, publications, and TV channels. Establishment of nonalcoholic cafés, a rise in Qur'an courses, and increased success in pro-Islamist local governments as well as a rise in Islamist charities all point to the success of the Islamist movements. These Islamist movements were crucial in the eventual political success of both the Welfare Party and the current AKP.[56]

Similar trends are visible in Turkey's feminist movement. The early Turkish feminist movement, called Kemalist feminism, in the 1930s tied the prospects for women's empowerment to secularization and modernization. Before organizing as autonomous "new" social movements in the 1980s, women were very active among leftist organizations, coupling women's issues to those of socialism and antiimperialism. But it was in the rather depoliticized atmosphere of the post-1980 coup that a diverse set of feminist groups and associations began to flourish, ranging from Kemalist feminists to liberal feminists to Marxist feminists to Islamist feminists. While the liberal and Islamist feminists have cooperated in protesting the ban on the headscarf, significant disagreement and very little communication between these groups exist, so much so that they have their separate journals and run different seminars and conference series. Though some significant progress has been made in women's rights, the rise in reported domestic violence, violence against women, sexual harassment, and rape cases suggests that patriarchal norms still remain.

Also forming among the new social movements in Turkey are the Alevis. A religious sect, the Alevis are a community whose beliefs combine elements of Shi'i Islam and pre-Islamic folk customs and who constitute 15 percent to 16 percent of the population in Turkey. Historically, Alevis—both Kurds and Turks—have embraced the secular ideology, particularly during periods of the rising influence of Sunni Islam, but they have mostly kept a low profile publicly until the 1980s. After the military coup of the 1980s, however—partly as a response to the military's implementation of a Turco-Islamist policy as a way to address the left–right political cleavages of the earlier decade, partly as resistance to the military's rather assimilationist approach toward the Alevi community (building mosques in Alevi villages, for instance)—the Alevi movement and identity became much more visible. Just like the Islamists, Alevis began forming their cultural and religious foundations and associations (e.g., Cem Vakfi) and setting up journals and TV stations. This Alevi revivalism has never managed to translate into political success, as Alevi-based political parties were either closed down or did not succeed at the ballot box. Nevertheless, since the Alevi movement has its origins in the leftist movement in the country, and largely because of its commitment to secularism, Alevis have predominantly voted for the CHP, and though never pronounced, CHP's leader since 2010, Kemal Kılıçdaroğlu, is an Alevi and a Kurd.[57]

Gezi Park Protests and the Decline of Civil Society

The Gezi Park Protests started on May 27, 2013, as a peaceful sit-in by less than one hundred environmental activists contesting the demolition of Gezi Park near Istanbul's Taksim Square and its conversion into a complex of shopping malls and residences. The protest spread nationwide in a matter of days, mainly with the outrage triggered by police violence. Contestations over the Taksim Square and Gezi Park lasted more than a month and managed to bring together a variety of voices of discontent, ranging from the simple demand for more parks and inclusive public spaces to resistance against residential gentrification, commercial upscaling, and violent urban transformation. But the movement was also significant as it was the first large-scale political protest against the government under the AKP rule. Turkish government and its policies, as well as the prime minister's authoritarian style, particularly interventions into the lifestyle of the citizens (alcohol, abortion, etc.), became the major themes of the protests. The disproportionate use of police violence, tear gas, and cannons, which led to ten deaths and left many wounded, and the dismissal of protestors as looters and losers and marauders (known as *çapulcu*, from which the protestors coined the term *chapulling* meaning "fighting for rights") by the government, widespread arrest of the protestors, and severe media censorship and disinformation during the protests raised serious concerns about the country's freedom of political participation and expression. Mass arrests of protestors with charges of overthrowing the government and prolonged trials in their aftermath also raised questions about judicial independence. But the Gezi Park Protests were still significant, as they were the first public unrest of this magnitude under the AKP rule, bringing together widely different political/apolitical, organized/unorganized, and young/old participants.

Although initially most of the legal charges against Gezi participants were dropped in the aftermath of the protests, the 2016 coup attempt and the subsequent emergency rule have again criminalized Gezi Park protestors, labeling them as either Gülenists or collaborators with international forces, aiming to overthrow the government. One particular case is that of Osman Kavala, a well-known philanthropist, held in prison since 2017, on charges, among others, of masterminding Gezi protests. In fact, criticism of Gezi Park Protests became a signal for widening the scope of criminalization in the country, where President Erdoğan and the AKP, in effect, equated journalists, academics, and pro-Kurdish groups (and anyone highly critical of the government's policies) as potential terrorists engaged in act of treason. Public protests and marches are regularly banned. The changes to the criminal law in 2018 vastly broaden the definition of *terrorism* and *antistate activities* and gave the governors vast powers, which in effect meant the emergency rule that was adopted as "a state of exception" has now become normalized and legalized and remains instrumental in this regard. One symbolic example is the criminalization of students and academics at Boğaziçi University who were peacefully protesting against the top-down appointment of their rector in defense of academic autonomy in 2021. The ease with which one can become criminalized (even for sending antigovernment or anti-Erdoğan tweets) also raises grave concerns over freedom of speech, human rights, and due process in Turkey.

Media

Media ownership remains concentrated in the hands of a few large, private holding companies that earn the majority of their revenue from nonmedia assets. These were Doğan Media Group, which used to own widely circulating mainstream newspapers and TV channels, Doğuş Media Group, Turkuvaz Media Group of Çalık Holding, Çukurova Media Group of Çukurova Holding (taken over in 2013), and Ciner Media Group. Because of dominant business interests of these media groups, governments have found various ways to pressure and control the media conglomerates. During AKP's rule, however, the centralization of public procurement decisions within the prime minister's office has led to increasing use of economic leverage against these holding companies to force them to toe the party line. The prime minister's office directly controls the Privatization High Council (OİB), the Housing Development Administration (TOKİ), and the Defense Industry Executive Committee, which together account for tens of billions of dollars in procurement contracts per year. Wiretap recordings leaked in December 2013, for instance, indicated that the government dictated which holding companies would purchase the Sabah-ATV media group in exchange for a multibillion-dollar contract to build Istanbul's third airport. The Savings Deposit and Insurance Fund (TMSF) has also been used to transfer media assets to supportive businessmen, as in November 2013 when Ethem Sancak, a Turkish businessman with close ties to Erdoğan, bought three media outlets previously owned by the Çukurova Group from TMSF. The most blatant takeover, however, occurred in 2018 when the pro-AKP Demirören Group bought the entire Doğan Media Group, the largest mainstream media conglomerate in the country, with credits extended by a major public bank, in effect allowing the AKP to monopolize almost all of the media outlets largely known as "pool media." Not surprisingly, strategies such as news deprivation, surveillance, and punishing critical content ensued. Website blocking, and social media bans were also too common.

Shifting from *partially free* to *not free* first in media freedom, then in internet freedom, Turkey ranked as 154th among 180 countries in press freedom according to 2021 *Reporters without Borders* report.[58] Hundreds of journalists have lost their jobs, most jailed on either charges of terrorism or charges of "insulting the president," a crime under the Turkish Penal Code (TCK), Article 299. In a law that passed in 2022, known as "disinformation act," government in effect legalized censorship and expanded the scope of criminalization through establishing various controls in the social media. In sum, as Freedom House reports indicate, intimidation, mass firings, bans, buying off or forcing out media moguls, wiretapping, and imprisonment have been widely used again in silencing the media in the country.[59]

TURKEY'S POLITICAL ECONOMY

In broadest terms, Turkey's economic transformation can be divided into five periods: etatism (1930–1950); rural modernization (1950–1959); the import substitution industrialization (ISI) regime (1960–1979); liberalization (1980–2013); and a shift toward patrimonial economy under the AKP (2013–present). Over these periods, Turkey transformed from a rural, agrarian economy to a largely urban economy, with significant increases in per capita income, life expectancy, and adult literacy.[60] Although it does not have petroleum to offer the world, its dynamic export sector and its customs union with the EU have integrated it into the global markets in terms of trade, production, and finance. Yet regional inequality, a fragile, highly-indebted economy, and a ranking on the Human Development Index well below countries with a similar per capita income, coupled with serious financial instability and fragility, result in a report card on Turkey's political economy that is mixed at best.

Etatism

Turkey's nation-building project, coupled with top-down modernization efforts in the 1930–1950 period, meant that bureaucratization and state-building occurred long before private-sector development and that the private sector remained largely "state dependent."[61] The early years of the republic focused on jump-starting the economy, with particular emphasis on agricultural recovery in war-ravaged Anatolia. In 1923, Turkey had an agrarian economy with very rudimentary industries and abundant, uncultivated land.

Rapid economic growth and recovery were important; they would legitimize the new republican project and help pay the Ottoman debt, extensively negotiated in the 1923 Lausanne Peace Conference and the Paris Conference of 1925. The large population exchange agreement between Greece and Turkey did not help the situation: 1.2 million Greeks left Anatolia, and 500,000 Muslims came from Greece and the Balkans to settle in Turkey. Losing a quarter of its population, including much of the merchant class, decreased Turkey's agricultural production by 50 percent and the GDP by 40 percent.[62] The absence of a Turkish bourgeoisie to replace this merchant class meant economic recovery would require heavy state involvement.

The period from 1923 to 1929 was a market-friendly interval of successful economic recovery. Yet Turkey's economy was badly hit by the Great Depression in the 1930s, and demand for Turkey's agricultural exports dropped dramatically.[63] Purchasing power also dropped significantly. In parallel with the trends in the developing world and largely as a response to the Great Depression, Turkey entered a period of etatism. During this time, a combination of strict import controls, a protectionist trade regime, and balance of payment controls were put in place. Public investment also shifted toward industry, education, and agriculture. State monopolies emerged in alcohol, sugar, tobacco, oil, and explosives. Despite its neutrality throughout World War II, Turkey maintained a fully mobilized army during the war years, which proved costly and led the CHP government to adopt draconian measures to cope with wartime economic crises.

Rural Modernization

Transition to a multiparty system in 1950 and the DP's rise to power was, in part, a response to the deterioration of the living standards of the peasantry. Thanks to the DP's influence, the redistribution of some state-owned land to landless peasants and the Marshall Plan following World War II nearly doubled agricultural production from 1947 to 1953.

But extensive state intervention in the economy through infrastructure investments and the expansion of state economic enterprises (SEEs) remained unchanged. The DP's economic liberalism proved short-lived. As agriculture prices collapsed, the huge price support program of the government triggered unsustainable inflation. Uncontrolled expansion and fiscal indiscipline made adjustment inevitable and highlighted the limits of state-financed agrarian development. Then, in 1958, Turkey faced its first currency crisis and encounter with the International Monetary Fund (IMF).

Import Substitution Industrialization Regime

The abrupt and dramatic end to the DP's populism came through the 1960 military coup and not the IMF programs, marking the bureaucratic elite's return with a vengeance. A new governing coalition comprising the military, the bureaucracy, and the increasingly powerful urban-middle class took over. On the economic front, the 1960–1979 period witnessed the return of full-fledged etatism. State-sponsored ISI, domestic-market-oriented production, and protectionism marked a significant, albeit slow, transformation of Turkey's economy from strictly agrarian to increasingly preindustrial. Urbanization and rapid industrialization (industry grew annually around nine percent throughout the 1960s) managed to meet domestic demands, although the common problems associated with ISI policies—entrenched business interests reluctant to shift to exports, problems of overvalued currencies, technology issues, and ultimately the foreign exchange crises—impeded the country's road to large-scale industrialism.

Turkey's Liberalization Experiment: What Went Wrong?

The authoritarian military regime from 1980 to 1983 reflects the aftermath of ISI exhaustion—that is, fiscal crisis and scarcity of foreign exchange. The government, with an economic team led by Turgut Özal (the deputy prime minister who, following the ANAP victory in 1983, became the country's prime minister and president), began implementing a typical IMF package, agreed upon in early 1980.[64] Elimination of price controls (including controls over interest rates), foreign exchange rate reforms, liberalization of trade and foreign direct investment (FDI), and the privatization of the SEEs were the main elements of this stabilization program. It was argued that etatism was finally dead.[65]

Despite periodic setbacks, the transformation of the Turkish economy from an ISI-based development model to an open, liberal economy has been remarkable. What had started during the Özal years as a major adjustment program continued throughout the major coalition governments of the 1990s. For better or worse, the Turkish adjustment has accomplished a major reorientation of the economy. The financial markets were opened internationally and developed in depth. The Turkish lira became convertible in 1989, and a new wave of trade liberalization also occurred, particularly in the aftermath of Turkey's entry into the customs union with the EU in 1996.

However, Turkish economic liberalization in the 1980s was unorthodox in many ways.[66] While there was considerable liberalization in foreign economic policy, Özal's agenda was also accompanied by the expansion and concentration of the state's economic power.[67] It is, therefore, not surprising that the fate of economic reforms was very much linked to who was in power. Patronage played an extensive role in disbursement provision and financial support.[68] Center-right coalitions of the Özal governments after 1987, as well as Demirel's and later Tansu

Çiller's coalitions with the Social Democrats, focused mainly on their constituencies. With side payments and inconsistent economic policies, it makes sense that, in the 1996 World Bank report on privatization, Turkey was among the worst three performers among privatizing countries. Between 1987 and 1997, total revenue from privatization did not exceed $3 billion.[69]

Turkey's problems with economic reform are first associated with the nature of state–society relations in Turkey and the absence of what Evans has called "embedded autonomy of the state."[70] The absence of institutionalized channels of information and negotiation between state and society (embeddedness), along with a certain degree of insulation of state bureaucracy (autonomy) to provide for policy coherence, led to continuous policy oscillations and inconsistencies throughout the 1990s. At times, the Turkish state suffered from too much rent-seeking, falling prey to interest groups, and incumbents' electoral desires. At other times, it was the vast autonomy of the Turkish state, or the lack of "embeddedness," that proved problematic.[71]

Second, and perhaps more importantly, populist pressures rose from the nature of distributional conflicts. Turkish liberalization created a number of losers. The agricultural sector, the urban workers, and the industrialists familiar with the import substitution policies were among those opposing the liberalization agenda. Various governments since the late 1980s and 1990s have tried to mediate these conflicts by distributing state rents to their respective constituencies. Regardless of what may have caused these populist strategies and the distribution of state rent by the political elite, increased state spending and growing public deficits had fully returned by the second half of the 1980s. Payoffs to constituents, particularly to the rural sector, and the financing of SEE deficits resulted in a relaxation of austerity measures and spiraling inflation, creating macroeconomic instabilities. The expected benefits of liberalization—increased capital flows, FDI, and exports—failed to materialize. That is why the 1990s are often described as the lost decade in terms of unstable coalition governments and boom-bust cycles. Investor confidence declined, launching a well-known vicious cycle of rising interest rates and spiraling public debt. This only undermined macroeconomic stability, leading to further loss of confidence, higher deficits, and higher interest rates.

The 2000–2001 Financial Crisis and AKP Period

Unable to cope with its skyrocketing domestic and international debt, the fragile coalition government led by Bülent Ecevit requested an IMF loan and signed a Stand-By Arrangement (SBA). This 1999–2002 IMF SBA was the seventeenth of its kind in the history of the republic and envisioned severe belt-tightening measures, fiscal discipline, and an ill-fated pegged currency system that fixed the value of the Turkish lira vis-à-vis the dollar. The inability of the government to implement the bitter pill of structural reform, the false consumption boom that emerged with the pegged currency system, and the crisis in the Turkish banking system that failed to adjust to the low-interest environment ushered in the worst economic crisis in the republic's history.

With a nine percent decline in GDP and more than one million jobs lost, it was no surprise that the political parties of the coalition were literally wiped out of the political scene in the 2002 elections. The AKP government came to power with the promise of economic stability. Fully implementing the IMF program, the AKP indeed brought down inflation to single digits, lowered the interest rates, and managed to achieve an average annual GDP growth of six percent during the 2002–2007 period before the global crisis hit the Turkish economy.

The most remarkable change occurred in external economic ties and the rising FDI, though mostly through the sales of SEEs and banks whose asset values more than halved after the 2000 and 2001 financial crisis, as well as in increases in international trade. More importantly, the government was able to implement some of the fundamental structural reforms envisioned in the IMF and the World Bank programs, such as elimination of product subsidies in the agricultural sector, closure or downsizing of the agricultural sales cooperatives, and liberalization of agricultural trade, which together ushered in an unprecedented and rapid decline in rural employment. The government also reformed the tax system to increase compliance and passed a social security reform package under guidelines provided by the World Bank.

The shortcomings of this rapid transition were the persistently high unemployment numbers, the rapid pace of debt accumulation that makes the country extremely fragile in periods of financial uncertainty, and the softening of fiscal discipline because of the global economic crisis as well as the election cycles in the country. Though the current account deficits are still a problem in the economy, Turkey weathered the 2008–2009 global financial crisis surprisingly well, with real GDP growth of 9.2 percent and 8.5 percent in 2010 and 2011. However, rising private debt, which reached 60 percent of the country's GDP; extreme reliance on external financial flows, which led the analysts to call Turkey "the most" vulnerable in case of a drop in capital inflows among the "five fragile emerging markets"; and the declining GDP growth hovering around three percent since 2012 raised significant concerns about the country's economic outlook. Led largely by the construction boom, fueled by mega projects such as Istanbul's Erdoğan airport (world's largest), and the third Bosphorus bridge, rising consumer debt, coupled with the absence of long-term structural reforms in education and technology, have also led to debates over whether the country can avoid a "middle-income trap." As Daron Acemoğlu and Murat Ucer sum up, Turkey's quality economic growth in the first half of the AKP's long tenure has been followed by an institutional slide leading to slower and low-quality growth.[72] The political uncertainty, the escalating Kurdish conflict, suicide bombings, terror attacks, the Syrian conflict, and the refugee crisis followed by a dramatic coup attempt in 2016 have all led to a severe decline in tourism income and FDI, raising questions on long-term macroeconomic stability.

Toward Crony Capitalism

The AKP has radically transformed Turkey's political economy during its twenty years of incumbent rule. The first half of AKP rule was guided by economically liberal international pressures imposed in the aftermath of the 2000 and 2001 financial crisis. Notwithstanding the well-known social side effects of the liberal reforms, the country was receiving FDI, improving its exports, revolving its debt, and experiencing, albeit unsustainable, overall economic growth. With economic slowdown, the shrinking global liquidity following the 2008 world financial crisis, and the termination of ties with the IMF, the AKP began to loosen its fiscal discipline in order to generate growth. It openly started using public resources for consolidating its own political and economic power—so much so that the public procurement laws that were designed to make bids for public projects transparent were modified more than a hundred times in ways that promote pro-AKP businesses. Presumably nonpartisan licensing and regulatory boards were politicized, issuing licenses for supporters, and pro-AKP business were "encouraged" to donate to the urban poor (a major constituency of the AKP) in return for favors from the government. The AKP has also kept its urban-poor constituency by expanding social assistance and cash transfer programs, consolidating its own power both from below and above.

Clearly, Turkey's private sector has long been state-dependent, and every government has since tried to create its own supporting business elite. But the AKP has coupled this common strategy of preferential treatment by slapping opposing businesses with tax code penalties and/ or regulatory harassments. With the escalation of the conflict with the Gülenists, the severe purges against pro-Gülenist businesses have pushed the AKP into this awkward position, having to eliminate the very foundations of the economic elite that it has helped flourish. The emergency rule following the 2016 coup attempt also raised serious concerns about the rule of law and due process in the country, scaring potential investors and lowering Turkey's scores by international rating agencies.

Last but not least, executive aggrandizement associated with the shift to executive presidency and concentration of enormous power in the hands of President Erdoğan also reinforced impressions of personalized, arbitrary, even sultanistic rule. The appointment of his own son-in-law, Berat Albayrak, as the economic czar in the 2018 which ended in a dismal performance in 2020, along with main ministerial and Central Bank appointments visibly based on absolute loyalty to the president rather than qualifications and merits, underscored the personalized nature of Erdoğan's governance. Turkey's debt, currency and inflation crisis which started with an initial 10 percent currency plunge in August 2018, continued with president's insistence on lower interest rates in 2021 which was in complete defiance of economic rationale. The result was an unprecedented 75 percent dive in the value of the currency and 78.6 percent increase in inflation in June 2021-2022 period , highest since 1998. The crisis, packaged again as a grand international conspiracy—a new economic war, as the president coined it—revealed the frailty of Turkey's economy. The worsening economic downturn, skyrocketing inflation volatility of the currency, and "gray-listing" of the country in 2021 for failing to head off money laundering and financing terrorism (which is likely to scare the investors even further), all underscore that the AKP's growth model based on cheap labor–based exports, the debt-financed construction sector, and consumption is no longer sustainable. To what extent Erdoğan and the AKP can maintain their tight coalition based on pro-AKP business and the urban poor in the midst of an economic slowdown remains to be seen. The changing political economy under the AKP is clearly a testimony to the fact that liberal reforms are, in fact, quite compatible with possible authoritarian turns and can certainly disappear altogether from the agenda once the democratic breakdown occurs.

REGIONAL AND INTERNATIONAL RELATIONS

Turkey's location has made it an important partner both regionally and internationally. Throughout the Cold War years, however, the overemphasis on the geostrategic importance of the country impeded a multidimensional foreign policy. After the Cold War and the collapse of the Soviet Union, as well as with the opening up of the former Soviet bloc countries, relative progress in the EU membership, and recent stronger ties with the Middle East and Africa, Turkey had clearly started to adopt a more multiregional foreign policy.

Turkey–EU Relations: A Tumultuous Partnership From the Ankara Agreement of 1963 to Accession

Turkey's prospects for converging with the EU will depend on the domestic political, economic, and social reforms the country is able to undertake. Turkey–EU ties have been problematic from the start. On the one hand, state–society interaction in EU-member states limits the EU's capacity to undertake commitments or impose sanctions with a view to anchor Turkey's convergence toward European standards. On the other hand, the type of state–society interaction in Turkey induces Turkish policymakers to engage in frequent deviations from the policy reform required for convergence. Thus, the EU's failure to act as an effective anchor increases the probability of policy reversals in Turkey—which, in turn, induces the EU to be even more reluctant about anchoring Turkey's convergence toward European standards.[73]

Turkey applied for an association agreement with what was then the European Economic Community (EEC) in 1959, only a few months after Greece. Long rounds of talks led to the Ankara Agreement in 1963, making Turkey an "associate member." In May 1967, based on the Ankara Agreement, Turkey asked to begin a transition to a customs union. But it was really with the Additional Protocol (AP) in 1970 and its aftermath that Turkey's populist tendencies became evident to the EU. The AP provided for a twenty-two-year transitional period that would end in a customs union, as specified in the association agreement. Then, the Turkish State Planning Organization began to argue that the AP was a barrier to ISI policies as well as to SEEs, which the Turkish political parties saw as crucial for dispensing state patronage to their respective constituencies.

Against this background of entrenched ISI interests, systematic demands for state patronage and particularistic privileges, and the vulnerability of the political parties to such pressures, the Turkish government first decided on the unilateral suspension of the AP in 1978 and also requested a five-year freeze of relations in 1979. These policy reversals created serious credibility problems in terms of Turkey's commitment to the EU, scarring Turkey–EU ties in subsequent years.[74]

The military coup in 1980 created yet another estrangement. Meanwhile, Greece gained full membership and subsequent veto power, creating yet another hurdle for Turkey. The association agreement was finally reactivated in 1986 and was followed in 1987 by Turgut Özal's application for full EU membership. The European Commission decided to defer the application, and it suggested a focus on the customs union and the association agreement. The acceptance and ratification of the customs union in 1996 was a watershed in Turkey–EU relations and became an integral part of Turkey's membership. But once again, within the context of the customs union, the typical problems of Turkish political economy held strong: circumventing institutions, lingering patronage politics, and hollowing out economics from the political and public debate. Not surprisingly, the results have been disappointing.

Relations hit rock bottom when the Luxembourg European Council in 1997 refused Turkey's candidacy while it threw the doors wide open to eastern European and central European candidates. Turkey thus broke off political dialogue with the EU. Finally, the Helsinki European Council reversed the Luxembourg decision by formally recognizing Turkey's candidacy in 1999, which meant Turkey would have to begin reform processes to meet the European criteria. After the EU Council formally accepted the Accession Partnership—essentially a road map for Turkey's accession—the Turkish government accelerated its reform processes considerably with a series of harmonization packages.

Three harmonization legal reform packages were passed in the GNA. Some of the major changes included abolishing the death penalty, easing restrictions on broadcasting and education in minority languages, short detention periods, and lifting the state of emergency in the Southeast. The AKP government passed six additional reform packages, including an overhaul of the penal code and one that addressed human rights concerns. The AKP government's significant shift over the Cyprus issue, in which the Turkish side agreed to accept the Kofi Annan plan to reunite Cyprus as a bizonal federal republic, also eliminated a technically invisible although very much present barrier to Turkey's accession. In referendums on both sides of the island in April 2004, Turkish Cypriots accepted the Annan plan, but the Greek Cypriots rejected it.

Although the AKP government signed the AP in 2005, it refused to submit it to the GNA for ratification. In October 2005, the EU formally began accession negotiations with Turkey, but with the proviso that the Turkish GNA ratify the AP by the end of 2006. When December 2006 arrived, no progress had been made. The European Council decided to suspend some of its negotiations with Turkey.

It was clear that Turkey's path toward EU membership would be strewn with obstacles. The political victories of Nicolas Sarkozy in France and Angela Merkel in Germany, neither of whom favored Turkey's full membership, meant that there was mistrust on both sides, especially since both Sarkozy and Merkel have suggested an alternative "privileged partnership" for Turkey. Moreover, the European support for Turkey's EU membership has systematically declined in recent years.

However, the Syrian war, which triggered massive refugee inflow to Europe in 2015, began to change the mutually reluctant partnership between Turkey and the EU in 2016. Major European states have sought Turkey's cooperation in managing the crisis and persuaded Turkey not to allow passage for the refugees in return for opening some chapters on accession negotiations; they also offered $3 billion in aid to help Turkey keep the refugees. To what extent this migration-based cooperation and coordination efforts can help revitalize Turkey's path toward Europe, however, remains to be seen.

Another major source of political tension was the 2017 referendum and shift to presidentialism that was heavily criticized by the European Council's Venice Commission, which saw it as a path toward a personal rule with prospects of eliminating checks and balances. Both the European Council and the parliament warned that with these constitutional amendments, Turkey would no longer be able to maintain its status as a prospective member of the EU as it fails to fulfill the main Copenhagen criteria of a "functioning democracy." The controversy over rulings of European Court of Human Rights (including the Kavala case), and European Council's insistence on compliance have also increased tensions. To those criticisms, Erdoğan has largely adopted an anti-European/anti-Western discourse and claimed national jurisdiction. Meanwhile, energy disputes over Turkey's drilling activities in Eastern Mediterranean, related tensions over Libya, the controversy over Turkey's withdrawal from Istanbul convention on violence against women seen largely as country's straying away from European values, have all strained Turkey–EU ties. As such, Turkey's likely accession into the EU largely remains an illusion.

Turkey–US Relations[75]

Turkey and the United States were important strategic partners throughout the Cold War years. Turkey was a significant part of the US containment policy toward the Soviet Union and was a beneficiary of both the Truman Doctrine and the Marshall Plan. The United States was also the major sponsor of Turkey's membership with the NATO when it joined in 1952. The partnership was based on Turkey providing military bases in return for extensive military and economic aid. Toward the end of the Cold War, Turkey emerged as the largest recipient of foreign aid in the region after Israel and Egypt.

The Turkey–US relationship was tested three times throughout the Cold War: during the Cuban missile crisis of 1962 when the United States removed its missiles in Turkey, raising doubts about the US commitment; the humiliating letter that then-prime minister, İsmet İnönü, received from the US president, Lyndon B. Johnson, that in effect banned the use of US weapons in Cyprus and threatened withdrawal of support against the Soviet threat; and the US arms embargo that followed the Turkish invasion of Cyprus in 1974.

Turkey–US relations recovered in 1980 with the signing of a defense and economic cooperation agreement in the aftermath of the fall of the shah of Iran and the Soviet invasion of Afghanistan. Relations between Turkey and the United States were particularly vibrant under the leadership of Turgut Özal, who envisioned a greater international role for Turkey through a closer partnership with the United States. But the end of the Cold War and the Gulf War in 1990 changed the security concerns of Turkey and changed the Turkey–US relationship in two major ways.

One change was that the source of threat shifted from the Soviet Union to issues related to Kurdish nationalism and the violence and instability in Iraq. During the first Gulf War, the Turkish government provided full support to the US military campaign with the expectation of developing a strategic partnership and increasing its chances of entering the EU via EU support. But Turkey paid an economic and political price for this support, as it lost pipeline fees and trading opportunities in the Southeast, which many believe exacerbated Kurdish separatism and enhanced the activities of the PKK.

But the real change in the relations came with the US decision in 2003 to invade Iraq. The Turkish government had to decide how to react to the proposal, first put forward in July 2002 by the US deputy secretary of defense, Paul Wolfowitz, that in the event of war in Iraq, Turkey should allow significant numbers of US forces to enter Turkish territory to open a northern front against Iraq. The vast majority of Turkish opinion, including that of the military and the government, opposed the invasion of Iraq in principle, primarily on the grounds that it might allow Iraqi Kurds to establish an independent state, exacerbating Turkey's internal Kurdish problem.

By February 2003, Turkey's government had reluctantly decided that because the George W. Bush administration was determined to attack Iraq, Turkey would be better off inside the US tent than outside it, with the condition that Turkish troops should also be allowed to enter northern Iraq, as a counter to Kurdish militia forces. A substantial bloc of the AKP parliamentarians opposed the US plan, however, and it was defeated by three votes in the GNA. This result caused shock and anger in Washington.

Although relations have since recovered, anti-American sentiment and the fear of a US-backed independent Kurdish state still run deep among the politicians and the public. Nevertheless, in 2003 more than 70 percent of the military cargo sent to Iraq was flown through İncirlik Air Base, and some 80 percent of Turkey's arms purchases and defense industrial activity is still with the United States. Despite Turkey's growing unease with the collaboration between the United States and the YPG in Syria, which the AKP government categorically sees as a terrorist organization with ties to PKK, the two countries had started working closely, given the conflict in Syria and the threat of ISIS. However, Turkey's acquisition of a Russian S-400 surface-to-air defense system in 2019, followed by Turkey's removal from the F-35 Joint Strike Fighter program (multibillion dollar consortium), and Trump Administration's sanctions on Turkey's defense procurement agency have seriously strained US–Turkey ties. Booming US–Greece defense ties with rising concerns over control and energy exploration of Eastern Mediterranean as well President Biden's recognition of the Armenian genocide in 2021 have also raised Turkey's concerns.

Turkey's Regional Role: From "Soft Power" Balancer to Conflictual Entanglements? Syria and Beyond

Since the 1990s, Turkey's foreign policy has clearly become multidimensional, and the country has begun to adopt a much more active foreign policy, particularly with its neighbors. There are also significant Turkish investment flows to the neighboring countries. As Turkey relaxed its visa requirements for countries like Greece, Russia, and successor states of the former Soviet Union, the total number of people traveling to, from, and through Turkey had begun to increase.[76] "The total number of third-country nationals entering Turkey increased from just over 1 million in 1980 to around 25.5 million in 2009."[77] Turkey has not had a visa requirement for Iranians since the early 1960s and lifted visas for Syrian nationals in 2009. In terms of mobility of goods and people, Turkey had clearly become a regional hub.

A major part of the shift toward multidimensional foreign policy has been the growing ties with Russia and successor states of the former Soviet Union. Turkey–Russia ties have improved dramatically since the 1990s, despite intense disagreements over conflicts such as Nagorno-Karabakh and the war in Chechnya. Energy has been an important driver in this relationship. Russia supplies 65 percent of Turkey's natural gas imports, which are expected to rise in the next decade, and 40 percent of its crude oil imports.[78] Another region that is of great interest to Turkey is Central Asia. Since the collapse of the Soviet Union, Turkey has envisioned for itself a bridging role in the region, particularly in the early 1990s for the Turkic republics, an initiative that was led by President Özal. Although Turkey's interest in these republics died down toward the end of the 1990s, the AKP government has aimed to revitalize them and has envisioned a much more active role.[79]

Another thorny issue in the region has been the Turkish–Armenian rapprochement, which is strongly supported by both the EU and the United States but is paralyzed, owing to intense and politically charged disagreements over how Turkey should address the events of 1915, which included a massive number of deaths and forced deportations of Armenians.

Finally, Turkey's revitalized ties with the Middle East also constituted an important dimension of its multiregional strategy. During the 1950s, Turkey's foreign policy and votes in international forums dismayed the Arab world, but these policies gave way to a more equidistant system in the 1960s and 1970s, when Turkey tried to remain neutral and outside the major conflicts in the region and favored the status quo. The eagerness of the republic to define itself as part of Europe rather than the Middle East, the emphasis on secularism, and the distancing of the country from its Ottoman past all contributed to this cautious and almost unengaged approach.

Turgut Özal started the transformation of Turkey's foreign policy toward the Middle East in the 1980s and early 1990s, emphasizing economic ties, trade, and relationships by playing a positive role in the return of Egypt to the OIC (Organization of Islamic Cooperation), in which Turkey became very active. Another major breakthrough occurred with the increased military and economic cooperation between Israel and Turkey. Trade and tourism between the two countries exploded in the 1990s, and the two countries signed a series of military and industrial agreements. Turkey became one of the few countries in the region that had close contacts with both Israel and the Arab world.

During the first half of the AKP government, Turkey has defined a much more active role for itself in the Middle East. This trend has also been supported by the United States, despite initial US reservations about close ties between Turkey and Syria and Iran. The active engagement of the AKP government included, first and foremost, the notion of going beyond the security questions and the Kurdish issue in the case of Iraq and developing close ties with the Iraqi government. Though Iraqi Kurdistan was initially perceived as a possible threat, Kurdish regional government has become Turkey's major economic ally in the region, while Shi'i southern Iraq is largely perceived as being under the influence of Iran. As of 2011, Iraq has become the second-largest export market for Turkey. Second, the AKP initially aspired to play the mediator in conflict resolution between both Israel and the Palestinian Authority and Israel and Syria. But strains in Turkey–Israeli relations during the AKP government—particularly in the aftermath of the Mavi Marmara flotilla affair in May 2010, where Israeli naval commandos killed nine aid workers heading to Israeli-blocked Gaza—have since dimmed such prospects. Erdoğan's outspoken criticism of Israeli operations and its pro-Palestinian stance initially increased Erdoğan's popularity in the Arab world but strained Turkey–Israeli relations.

The political changes in the aftermath of the Arab uprisings began to highlight both Turkey's rising influence as well as the enormous challenges it faces. Turkey has supported the moderate Islamists in Tunisia (developing strong ties with the En-Nahda movement) and

Egypt, where Turkey supported the Muslim Brotherhood. But in the cases of Libya and Syria, where Turkey had strong economic ties with the existing regimes, Turkey's position has been more dubious. Initially opposed to NATO's intervention in Libya, Turkey changed its position when it became clear that Colonel Muammar al-Qadhafi would be ousted.

A similar shift of policy occurred in Egypt as AKP-backed Egyptian President Mohamed Morsi was toppled in a military coup in 2013. Relations between the two countries strained sharply as Erdoğan became the staunchest critic of President Sisi and overall Western support offered to Egypt. An intense campaign started by Egypt and Saudi Arabia against Turkey made it lose its predicted easy victory of membership in the United Nations Security Council in 2014.

But the biggest policy reversal came with Syria, where Bashar al-Asad, once a close ally of the AKP government, failed to respond to Turkey's pressures for political opening. Asad's regime became a major enemy as Turkey actively began supporting anti-Asad forces in Syria. Escalating tensions with Syria left Ahmet Davutoğlu, the architect of Turkey's foreign policy toward the Middle East, who initially coined the phrase "zero problems with neighbors" (the foreign minister of the country [2009–2014] and prime minister since 2014), faced with two enormous challenges. One is that the outbreak of a bloody civil war in Syria has triggered the largest refugee influx into Turkey[80] since World War II. As of 2021, 3.7 million Syrian refugees have arrived and currently reside in Turkey under a so-called temporary protection. The precarious conditions of these refugees, their accommodation problems, insufficient support for education, exploitative labor relations, and child and sex trafficking, along with legal ambiguities, have pushed some of these migrants to take perilous boat journeys across Greek islands and across Europe in 2015. Aided by Turkey's open-door policy, which the EU urges Turkey to change, an estimated 750,000 migrants mostly from Syria, Iraq, and Afghanistan made this journey to Europe in 2015, with a death toll of more than 3,000 triggering a serious migration crisis for Europe as well.

The second major challenge the Turkish government faced has been the longevity of the Asad regime and the continued threat of ISIS. As fighting ISIS became a bigger priority than toppling the Asad regime, Turkey became increasingly intimidated by the protection of ethnically affiliated Turkmens and Yezidis, which the government sees as part of the moderately Islamist forces opposing Asad. The US decision to withdraw troops from Northeastern Syria in 2019 has refueled concerns over the empowerment of the Kurds which led to the Turkish government's decision to launch a cross-border offensive to create a "safe zone." Announcing resettlement plans for Syrian refugees to this safe zone drew international criticisms, further complicating the country's engagement with Syria as well as its regional partners. Lukewarm relations with Shi'i Iraqi's central government, an ambiguous relationship with ISIS that included a capture and release of Turkish diplomats in Mosul in 2014, uneasy relations with Iran further complicated by Iran–US rapprochement, the policy of "zero problems with neighbors" was clearly in shambles.

In short, the shifts in the US engagement with the Middle East (primarily in Syria, Libya, Afghanistan) as well as Russia's growing role have pushed Turkey toward a balancing act between the two. "Engaging in an intense competition with the Saudi Arabia–UAE axis throughout the region, Turkey's new Middle East policy is characterised by heightened threat perceptions, zero-sum competition with other regional powers, the increasing resort to the use of military force, risky behaviours and brinkmanship, and a preference for unilateral action."[81] Meanwhile, the purchase of S400s from Russia despite major disagreements over Afghanistan, Libya, and Syria, and economic rapprochement with China through Turkey's active engagement with China's global infrastructure project called "Belt and Road Initiative" program, despite significant disagreement over treatment of Uyghur Turks and other Muslim communities, spurred claims that Turkey is shifting its axis toward the East in its foreign policy.

This means that Turkey has also introduced a major policy dilemma both for Europe and the United States. While they need the cooperation and coordination of Turkey in dealing with a wide range of issues, most visibly crisis in Afghanistan, the refugee crisis, the threat of ISIS, and the future of Syria, and war in Ukraine, they have become increasingly wary of the declining quality of democracy and pluralism in the country and visible process of democratic decline.

CONCLUSION

After years of multiparty politics, Turkey's democratic backsliding and its eventual democratic breakdown raise a number of crucial questions: At what point in a given polity does the cost of losing power for the incumbent become too costly, while the cost of suppression of the opposition declines, in effect, opening the path toward autocracy where the autocrats become ready to do almost anything to stay in power? Is democratic backsliding a process of developing and "locking in" political and economic coalitions whose futures depend on the incumbent's continuous power? Or is it a story of institutional decline where parliaments, courts, and media can no longer constrain or countervail the use and abuse of executive power? In what ways do majoritarianism, frequent referendums, and elections all become instrumentalized for executive aggrandizement? Why and how does economic development not suffice to ensure democratic consolidation and might, in fact, be quite compatible with authoritarianism?

Indeed, Turkey has become a test case for exploring these questions. A set of major political and economic challenges in the country, such as extensive polarization between the Islamists and secularists, between Kurdish and Turkish nationalists, between Sunnis and Alevis, between those favoring ties with the EU and the West versus those with anti-Western sentiments, all combined with worsening income and regional inequalities, have clearly rendered "living differentially" and in harmony with the rule of law and democratic principles very difficult. Such cleavages and polarizations also offer a fertile ground for political instrumentalization and populist mobilizations. But it is precisely in such heterogeneous societies defined by deep cleavages and polarities where these democratic principles are most needed and can curtail such populist tendencies.

Can reconciliation, moderation, and peaceful resolution ever be possible without democratic principles—for instance, after years of militarized Kurdish conflict in southeastern Turkey? How does one address the perils of radical nationalism and curb it? What is the role of third-party players in ensuring peaceful coexistence? As the Kurdish conflict becomes increasingly intertwined with the Syrian conflict, is it ever possible to solve such ethnic conflicts when they are so entangled in regional and international strategies?

Meanwhile, as a typical developing country with a huge debt burden and vulnerability in global financial markets, whether Turkey can maintain economic stability in the midst of rising polarizations and conflicts also remains an open question. With its social state capacity stretched thin with rising inflation and currency crisis, how can the economic vulnerabilities and uncertainties emerging from both wars in the border, the refugee crisis, and globalization be addressed? The substantial transformation of Turkey's political economy from a relatively globally integrated, liberal, and market-driven economy during the early years of the AKP to an intensely more clientelistic, patrimonial economy after 2013 underscores, once again, that in the absence of fully functioning democratic institutions, liberal economic reforms are not likely to stick. A modern economy and liberalizing market cannot, in and of themselves, prevent or contain democratic breakdown.

As a country no longer pounding on the doors of the EU, Turkey also raises important questions on the identity and nature of the European project. Is the EU an economic and political project based on laws and agreements, or as Brexit experience has shown, are there other factors defining the borders of the EU? Faced with the biggest refugee crisis since World War II, can Europe live up to its democratic and humanitarian ideals? Or is the EU bound to become an exclusive club of privileged citizens?

Ultimately, Turkey was an experiment in democratization—an experiment that has largely failed. With military interventions and weak party organizations, a lack of accountability, and long-standing military tutelage, Turkey was always a flawed democracy. The AKP's initial steps toward a more inclusive politics and increasing demilitarization had raised hopes that the country was catching the wave of deepening democratization. However, increased corruption and excessive concentration of power in the executive branch—the shift to a Turkish-style presidential system under the unaccountable, personalized political style of Tayyip Erdoğan—have dimmed such hopes. More seriously, the rising authoritarian tendencies along with the erosion and suspension of the rule of law, civil liberties, politicized judiciary, and the silencing of the media and opposing voices, top-down economic decision-making, coupled with escalating police violence and intimidation as well as the remilitarization of the Kurdish conflict, all signal that Turkey's democratic experiment has come to a screeching halt.

SUGGESTED READINGS

Ayşe, Buğra, and Osman Savaşkan. *New Capitalism in Turkey: The Relationship between Politics, Religion and Business*. Cheltenham: Edward Elgar, 2014.

Çarkoğlu, Ali, and Ersin Kalaycıoğlu. *Fragile But Resilient?: Turkish Electoral Dynamics*, 2002–2015. Ann Harbor, MI: University of Michigan Press, 2021.

Hale, William. *Turkish Foreign Policy 1774–2000*. London: Frank Cass, 2002.

Mardin, Şerif. "Center-Periphery Relations: A Key to Turkish Politics?" *Daedalus* 102, no. 1 (Winter 1973): 169–90.

Özbudun, Ergun. *Party Politics and Social Cleavages in Turkey*. Boulder, CO: Lynne Rienner, 2013.

Pamuk, Şevket. *Uneven Centuries Economic Development of Turkey since 1820*. Princeton, NJ: Princeton University Press, 2018.

Sayarı, Sabri. *Müsil Pelin Ayan and Demirkol Özhan. Party Politics in Turkey: A Comparative Perspective*. Oxon and New York: Routledge, 2018.

Toprak, Binnaz. "Islam and Democracy in Turkey." *Turkish Studies* 6, no. 2 (June 2005): 167–86.

Yeşim, Arat. *Rethinking Islam and Liberal Democracy: Islamist Women in Turkish Politics*. Albany, NY: State University of New York Press, 2005.

Yeşim, Arat, and Pamuk Şevket. *Turkey Between Authoritarianism and Democracy*. Cambridge: Cambridge University Press, 2019.

Zürcher, Erik Jan. *Turkey: A Modern History*. 3rd ed. London: I. B. Tauris, 2004.

26 YEMEN

Sarah G. Phillips

The viability of Yemeni unity—and the ability of its citizens to simply survive—has never been so widely questioned as at the time of this writing. In September 2014, a political and military group called the Houthis (also sometimes known as Ansar Allah) overran the capital city of Sanaa, having already seized military control elsewhere in the north. They did so with the help of factions of the military (mostly the Republican Guard) that were still loyal to former President Ali Abdallah Salih, who had been ousted in late 2011 but was granted immunity from prosecution under an agreement brokered by the Gulf Cooperation Council (GCC)—the "GCC Initiative"—that provided a timeline for Yemen's political transition. Despite his resignation as president, Salih remained politically active as the head of the former ruling party (the General People's Congress, GPC), a position that he used to undermine his successor, President Abd Rabbuh Mansoor Hadi. In January 2015, Houthi militias surrounded the presidential palace and placed President Hadi and other senior government figures under house arrest. In an apparent attempt to call their bluff, President Hadi and his cabinet resigned, leaving the Houthis (and their erstwhile allies, Salih and the Republican Guard) militarily dominant but politically overstretched and increasingly unpopular.

President Hadi fled to the southern city of Aden, declaring it to be Yemen's new capital, and withdrew his resignation. On March 25, the Houthis, again drawing on parts of the military still loyal to the former president, captured the al-'Anad Air Base just north of Aden and took Hadi's defense minister hostage. Hadi fled to Saudi Arabia from where he called for the kingdom to lead a military campaign against the Houthis and former president Salih to restore his leadership. "Operation Decisive Storm"—a coalition of nine Arab states led by Saudi Arabia—began bombing targets in Yemen that night, transforming a civil conflict into one that is ever-more internationalized, complex, and catastrophic for the civilian population. The United States and the United Kingdom both openly—and controversially—supported the airstrikes (subsequently renamed to "Operation Renewal of Hope") against the Houthis, though they also devastated civilian infrastructure and caused an unknown number of casualties. The combination of violent conflict and the coalition's blockade on key ports of entry has caused levels of starvation bordering on famine, the world's-largest outbreak of cholera in fifty years, and has left some 22 million (of approximately 29 million) people in need of humanitarian assistance or protection. In 2018, the UN Secretary General referred to Yemen's situation as "the world's worst humanitarian crisis," and while this statement receives much coverage, some dispute that it accurately reflects the situation on the ground, particularly when compared to the devastation caused by war in places like Syria or South Sudan.

The number of parties to the Yemeni conflict is large and in flux. Domestically, they include the ousted government of President Hadi, which is ostensibly (if inconsistently) backed by members of the GCC coalition; the Houthis, a largely kinship based network that controls Sanaa and much of the North and who have waged incredibly violent assaults on the midlands city of Taizz, and on al-Baydha and Marib; factions of the military still loyal to former President Salih and his family; various movements calling for southern independence (most notably, the Southern Transitional Council, or STC); violent extremist groups like al-Qa'ida in the Arabian Peninsula (AQAP) and ISIS; some Salafi groups fighting the Houthis; and a plethora of local militias and residents defending their local areas against each of these groups, some of which also have international backing.

In addition to GCC states and their Western supporters referred to previously, Iran is the other key international player, supporting and arming the Houthis. Although their level of control over Houthi fighters remains debated, it has undoubtedly increased substantially since the conflict began. International parties to the conflict also include a number of proxy forces that are directly funded and trained by the United Arab Emirates (UAE), including the Hadhrami and Shabwani Elite Forces, the Security Belt Forces (*al-Hizaam al-Amni*), and the Giants' Brigade (*al-'Amlaqah*). There is a growing and underreported contestation between the members of the GCC coalition as well, particularly Saudi Arabia and the UAE.

As is often the case in war, alliances between these groups are fluid and combustible. One striking example of the latter came in late 2017, when Houthi fighters executed former President Salih as he fled Sanaa. Another was in 2019, when the UAE openly battled the Yemeni government forces that they were ostensibly engaged to support. This chapter must, therefore, apply the caveat that some of the issues it addresses are rapidly changing.

THE HISTORY OF STATE-BUILDING: DEVELOPMENT OF THE REPUBLIC OF YEMEN

Early History

The territory of Yemen, known to the ancient Arabs as al-Yaman (the South), was once divided into kingdoms and enclaves of various sizes. Strategically poised at the junction of major trading routes between Africa and India and endowed with an abundance of fertile land, Yemen's kingdoms grew prosperous and powerful. Its centers of civilization included the fabled Kingdom of Saba, purportedly ruled by the Queen of Sheba of biblical fame.

Around 1000 BCE, the Kingdom of Saba was a great trading state with a major agricultural base supported by a sophisticated system of irrigation at the heart of which stood the large Marib Dam. In the northern part of Yemen, the Kingdom of the Mineans arose, coexisting with Saba and maintaining trading colonies as far away as Syria. During the 5th century BCE, the Kingdom of Himyar was established, reaching its greatest extent and power in the 5th century CE. Christian and Jewish kings were among its leaders.

KEY FACTS ON YEMEN

AREA 203,850 square miles (527,968 square kilometers)

CAPITAL Sanaa

POPULATION 30,399,243 (2021 est.)

PERCENTAGE OF POPULATION UNDER 25 60.4 (2018 est.)

RELIGIOUS GROUPS Shafi'i (Sunni) Muslim, 65; Zaydi (Shi'a) Muslim, 34; Jews, Christians, and Hindus, 0.9 (2010 est.)

ETHNIC GROUPS Predominantly Arab; some Afro-Arabs, Europeans, and South Asians

OFFICIAL LANGUAGE Arabic

TYPE OF GOVERNMENT In Transition

DATE OF INDEPENDENCE May 22, 1990

GDP (PPP) $73.63 billion; $2,500 per capita (2017 est.)

GDP (NOMINAL) $54.36 billion (2018 est.)

PERCENTAGE OF GDP BY SECTOR Agriculture, 20.3; industry, 11.8; services, 67.9 (2017)

TOTAL RENTS (PERCENTAGE OF GDP) FROM NATURAL RESOURCES 5.44 (2019)

FERTILITY RATE 3.1 children born/woman

CIVILIAN CASUALTIES FROM CURRENT CONFLICT Unknown; the UN estimated around 10,000 casualties in the first year or so of the war. The Armed Conflict Location & Event Data Project (ACLED) recorded just over 60,000 conflict related casualties from January 2016–November 2018 but noted that the real figures were likely higher. Save the Children estimated that tens of thousands more have died from conflict-related causes like disease and starvation.

Sources: CIA. "The World Factbook." August 4, 2022, https://www.cia.gov/the-world-factbook/.
World Bank. "International Comparison Program (ICP)." Accessed August 10, 2022, https://databank.worldbank.org/source/icp-2017.
Note: Due to the Yemeni conflicts, the reliability of these figures is limited.

The growth of the Roman Empire primarily brought about the decline of pre-Islamic civilization in Yemen. New trade routes established by Europeans bypassed the old caravan trails, and the Yemeni frankincense trade died because Christian Romans did not use the resin in their funeral rituals as the pagans had. By the 6th century CE, the Marib Dam had collapsed, symbolizing the political disintegration in southern Arabia that helped pave the way for the followers of Islam to capture Yemen in around 630 CE, during the Prophet Muhammad's lifetime.

During the 8th and 9th centuries, after the Shi'a split from the mainstream Sunnis in what is today Iran and Iraq, large numbers of persecuted Shi'a fled to the highlands of northern Yemen. One of their leaders, Yahya bin Hussein bin Qasim al-Rassi, claimed descent from Muhammad

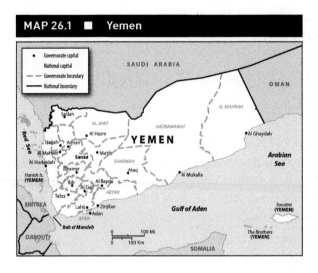

MAP 26.1 ■ Yemen

and proclaimed himself imam in 897 CE, establishing a Zaydi dynasty that existed in various manifestations until the overthrow of the 111th imam in the 1962 revolution.

In the 16th century, the Ottoman Turks captured the Yemeni plains and the port of Aden, but a young Zaydi imam led a successful resistance, forcing the Ottomans to conclude a truce and eventually leave Yemen in 1636. One of his successors unified the mountains and plains into a single entity extending to Aden, with the northern city of Sanaa as its capital, but war and upheaval soon returned to Yemen. In 1728, the sultan of the southern province of Lahej broke from the Zaydi regime, creating a division between North and South that prevailed until 1990.

The Ottoman sultan in Constantinople continued to claim suzerainty over all of Yemen, but Ottoman control was tenuous. Turkish administration of Yemen officially ended after the Ottomans' defeat in World War I. The Zaydi imam Yahya Hamid al-Din was left in control of the coastal areas of the North evacuated by the Turks. He subsequently tried to consolidate his control over all of northern Yemen, but the British, their local protégés in the South, and the Saudis in the North opposed his efforts. The 1934 Saudi-Yemeni Treaty of Taif temporarily settled one war between Yemen and Saudi Arabia. Although it represented a humiliating defeat for Imam Yahya, the Saudi king allowed him to maintain control of much of northern Yemen.

With the development of large steamships in the 19th century and the opening of the Suez Canal in 1869, the port of Aden gradually became a major international fueling and bunkering station between Europe, South Asia, and the Far East. In 1937, the British made Aden a crown colony and divided the hinterland sultanates in the South into the West and East Aden Protectorates; the Aden colony itself remained a separate entity. The British further developed the port facilities in Aden in the 1950s and built an oil refinery there. Aden, a densely populated urban area with a rapidly growing working class, consequently became the dominant economic center in southern Arabia.

Imam Yahya, whose isolationism and despotism had alienated a large number of Yemenis, was assassinated in a coup in 1948. He was succeeded by his son Ahmad. Growing nationalism among the Arab countries after World War II—exemplified by the rise of Egypt's Gamal Abdel

Nasser as a pan-Arab leader—as well as better communications and the emergence of Arab oil wealth forced Ahmad to abandon the isolationist policies of his father. In 1958, he joined Egypt and Syria's ill-fated United Arab Republic, which was then renamed the United Arab States, and sought aid from communist and capitalist nations alike.

The Yemeni Republics

After the disintegration of the United Arab States, Imam Ahmad and the Egyptian government increasingly exchanged rhetorical hostilities. As the popularity of Arab nationalism grew throughout the region, Cairo sensed strong anti-imam sentiment building throughout the country as a result of Ahmad's repressive domestic policies. Ahmad died in his sleep in September 1962 and was succeeded by his son Muhammad al-Badr. On September 26, 1962, just one week after Badr's ascension to power, a group of junior army officers mounted a coup and announced the establishment of the Yemen Arab Republic in the North, with Sanaa as its capital. The coup brought an end to the imamate, one of the oldest and most enduring in history. Within days, Egyptian soldiers arrived in Yemen to assist the fledgling republic, and Egypt remained one of the two major external players (the other was Saudi Arabia) in the country's ensuing civil war.[1]

In southern Yemen, still under British colonial rule, the coup became a source of inspiration to underground groups agitating for their own political independence. The rise in nationalism, combined with severe problems in congested Aden, furthered instability in the South. The British, hoping to withdraw gracefully from the area while protecting their interests, persuaded the sultans in the West and East Aden Protectorates to join Aden in 1963 in forming the Federation of South Arabia, which was to be the nucleus of a future independent state.

Arab opponents of the British plan mounted a campaign of sabotage, bombings, and armed resistance. Britain, failing to persuade the various factions to agree on a constitutional design for a new independent state, announced early in 1966 that it would withdraw its military forces from Aden and southern Arabia by the end of 1968 (London had signed a treaty in 1959 guaranteeing full independence to the region by 1968). Britain's announcement turned the anti-British campaign into one of interfactional competition. The National Front for the Liberation of South Yemen (or the National Liberation Front, NLF), backed by the British-trained South Arabian army, emerged as the victor among the various factions, and on November 30, 1967, Aden and southern Arabia became an independent state—the People's Republic of Southern Yemen, later changed to the People's Democratic Republic of Yemen.[2] Over the ensuing years, relations between Aden and Sanaa were soured by political and ideological differences, despite mutual advocacy of Yemeni unification.[3]

North Yemen

Civil war raged in North Yemen for eight years after the establishment of the Yemen Arab Republic (YAR) in 1962, drawing foreign intervention. The last imam, Muhammad al-Badr, Imam Ahmad's son who had held power for one week, fled Sanaa after the coup and mustered support among tribal royalists to wage war against the new republican government. Aid from Saudi Arabia and Jordan helped sustain his resistance movement. In response, the new president, Colonel Abdallah al-Sallal, turned to Egypt's Nasser, who sent a large military force to support the new republic.

Hostilities between Badr and the republic continued. Meanwhile, fighting broke out among the republican leaders themselves, primarily about the future role of Egypt in Yemen. President Sallal was removed from office in 1967 and succeeded by Abd al-Rahman al-Iryani. Moderate republicans, led by General Hassan al-Amri, seized power and pushed back a serious monarchist offensive against Sanaa. After the withdrawal of Egyptian forces in late 1967, Saudi Arabia began reducing its commitment to the royalists, and in 1970, it recognized the YAR after the monarchists agreed to drop their claims and cooperate with the republican regime.

In the early 1970s, stability increased somewhat under the government led by President Abd al-Rahman al-Iryani. During this period, Saudi Arabia became a major provider of foreign aid, perhaps to forestall greater Soviet aid to Sanaa and to counter the growing Marxist orientation of the PDRY to the south, but also to counter unwelcome political changes in its largest neighbor. Relations between the two Yemens deteriorated and flared into sporadic border fighting, pushing the YAR closer to Saudi Arabia.

In 1974, Colonel Ibrahim al-Hamdi ousted the civilian government of President Iryani and set out to heal old factional wounds. A popular leader, Hamdi was assassinated in 1977 in an act believed to have resulted partially from his attempt to diminish the political power of the tribes. It also remains widely believed within Yemen that Ali Abdallah Salih (who became president of North Yemen the following year) played an important role in Hamdi's assassination with the support of Saudi Arabia. Hamdi's successor, Ahmad al-Ghashmi, was assassinated just eight months later in 1978 by an envoy sent by PDRY President Salim Rubayyi' Ali. Lieutenant Colonel Abdallah Salih took over as president and remained in power until 2012. Under Salih's rule, the position of the northern tribes within the military and bureaucratic elite was greatly expanded, an issue decried among nontribal Yemenis and many in the former South who felt excluded. Salih's ability to accommodate, incorporate, and co-opt his rivals strengthened the regime and brought about a period of relative political stability. Under Salih, the army and the civil service were relatively modernized, and some outlying tribal regions were brought under a modicum of state authority.[4]

In March 1979, the YAR and PDRY announced plans to unify. Although the unification failed, Salih's government sought to reassure Saudi Arabia and the United States that its intention was not to abandon its traditional policy of nonalignment and that its proposed merger with the PDRY did not mean the emergence of a Soviet-oriented alliance.

Early on, the major threat to the Salih government came from the National Democratic Front (NDF), a coalition of opponents engaged in political and military action against the government and backed by the PDRY. Despite significant early NDF victories and occupation of much of the southern part of the YAR, Salih turned the situation around through military action and reached a political compromise with PDRY leader Ali Nasser Muhammad in May 1982. Muhammad agreed to halt support for the NDF in return for amnesty for and political incorporation of NDF elements. This agreement led to a gradual normalization of the situation in the YAR and strengthened Muhammad against his hard-line opponents in Aden who wanted to vigorously support NDF military operations.

With the increased central government control over workers' remittances in the 1980s and the discovery of oil later that decade, the Salih regime financed the building of schools, hospitals, and better roads and the creation of other jobs and services that increased his government's presence. The promotion of such infrastructure and the payments extended to a broad swath of tribal sheikhs helped to at least partially co-opt some once-autonomous tribes. This is not to say, however, that loyalties were necessarily diverted in whole, or in part, to the state in the tribe's stead.

In an attempt to institutionalize the prevailing political power structures, in 1982 Salih created the General People's Congress (GPC), which became the ruling party in the unified republic until the "transitional government" was instated in November 2011, whereupon it held 50 percent of cabinet positions. In 1988, Salih permitted elections to establish a long-promised People's Constituent Council. In the voting, 1.2 million Yemenis chose 1,200 delegates to the body, which had no authority to initiate legislation but could amend or critique laws enacted by the executive. The council merged with the Yemeni Socialist Party's People's Supreme Council upon unification in 1990 and formed a unified interim parliament.

South Yemen: The People's Democratic Republic of Yemen

At independence in 1967, the People's Republic of Southern Yemen had a strong socialist orientation. The ruling party, the National Front for the Liberation of South Yemen, preached "scientific socialism" with a Marxist flavor. Its first president, NLF leader Qahtan al-Sha'bi, sought closer ties with the Soviet Union and China, as well as with the more radical Arab regimes. Saudi Arabia joined the YAR in opposing the South's Marxist regime and backed opposition efforts there. The outward ideological schism endured until unification. Cleavages remained, however, and fueled increasing dissent in the South based on regional identities, the location of natural resources, and the perceived exclusion of southerners by the northern elite.

Sha'bi's orientation was not radical enough for some elements of the NLF. In 1969, a group led by Salim Rubayy'i Ali overthrew him, and in 1970, the new regime, which gained a reputation as an austere Marxist government, renamed the country the People's Democratic Republic of Yemen. The regime took extreme steps, including repression and exile, in an attempt to break traditional patterns of tribalism and religion and to eliminate vestiges of the bourgeoisie and familial elites, but these identities persisted under the surface regardless. Ideological clashes between northern conservatives and southern socialists persisted. Each side devoted considerable energy and resources to supporting opposition movements in the other. This mutual animosity developed into border wars in 1972 and 1979.

Ali had a powerful rival in Abd al-Fattah Ismail, secretary general of the NLF (renamed the National Front). Ali was considered a Maoist with pro-China sympathies, whereas Ismail was viewed as a pragmatic Marxist loyal to Moscow. He attempted to control society through tight police surveillance, but the factional violence among the leaders of the NLF severely undermined the regime's efforts to genuinely transform the PDRY. In June 1978, Ismail seized power and executed Ali. He reorganized the National Front into the Yemeni Socialist Party (YSP), became chairman of the Presidium of the People's Supreme Assembly, and named Ali Nasser

Muhammad as prime minister. In October 1979, Ismail signed a friendship and cooperation treaty with the Soviet Union.

Ismail, however, was unable to hold on to power. In April 1980, he relinquished his posts as presidium chairman and YSP secretary general. The party indicated that he had resigned because of poor health, but it appeared that Ismail had lost an internal power struggle, in part because of his foreign policy positions. The YSP Central Committee named Ali Nasser Muhammad to replace him. Ismail had intended to further cement ties with the Soviet Union and Eastern Europe, and on this point, he and Muhammad had been in agreement. The latter, however, also wanted to improve relations with Saudi Arabia and other Gulf countries to end the PDRY's isolation in the Arab world, secure new sources of foreign aid, and facilitate union between the two Yemens. Muhammad began his tenure with visits to the Soviet Union and to Saudi Arabia, the YAR, and other neighboring countries.

Overall, Muhammad's regime pursued a more conciliatory path than had Ismail's, cultivating economic ties with the West, achieving political reconciliation with the YAR and Oman, and moderating some tribal rivalries. In the fall of 1985, Ismail returned to the PDRY, and a vicious power struggle for party leadership ensued. Ismail was reappointed as one of the secretaries of the YSP, which increased pressure on Muhammad to relinquish power. Concerned about his position, Muhammad called a meeting of Ismail's advisers and staff in January 1986. Once those unfavorable to Muhammad had gathered, Muhammad's bodyguards entered and opened fire, killing a number of officials, including Ismail, and setting off a brief but vicious civil war that led to thousands of civilian deaths. Muhammad fled to the YAR.

Haidar Abu Bakr al-Attas, the prime minister in Muhammad's government, who happened to be out of the country during the conflict, returned to Aden on January 25 and was named provisional president. In October 1986, he was elected president for a full term. His government also followed a local brand of "pragmatic Marxism," pursued a close relationship with the Soviet Union, discussed unification with the YAR, and supported mainstream Arab causes. Aden restored diplomatic relations with Egypt in 1988 and considered reestablishing ties with the United States.

The period after the 1986 civil war was one of soul searching for the regime, and the YSP allowed more pluralism in an attempt to recover from the massive societal and political rifts caused by the conflict. By the time of unification, the press in Aden had more freedom than anywhere else on the Arabian Peninsula.[5]

Unification

The Republic of Yemen was formed in May 1990 when North Yemen (the Yemen Arab Republic, YAR) united with South Yemen (the People's Democratic Republic of Yemen, PDRY) in a move that took many observers at the time by surprise. The popular optimism that surrounded the union soon abated as the two sides were unable to find common ground over how they should share power. Each believed, probably correctly, that the other side was trying to outplay it, and by April 1994, the new state descended into a two-month civil war. The North was victorious, and the belief that it then benefited disproportionately from the natural resources in the South contributed to the growth of secessionist sentiments. These and other significant grievances eventually contributed to the emergence of *al-Harak* (below) in 2007.

The YAR and PDRY had pursued independent destinies in a climate of mutual suspicion throughout much of the 1980s. In the second half of the decade, however, fundamental changes in the global and regional geopolitical map set the stage for Yemeni unification. Most observers trace the beginning of the unification process to the spring of 1988, when presidents from both countries met to reduce tensions at their common border, create an economic buffer zone for joint investment, and revive discussions on unification. In 1989, the YAR initiated a series of talks with the PDRY aimed at fulfilling this goal.

The crumbling of the Soviet Union in the late 1980s undermined Moscow's capacity to provide economic and military aid and, coupled with regional instability in the wake of the Iran-Iraq War, led the PDRY to conclude that unification with the YAR was in its best interest. The PDRY's economy had sagged under the government's socialist principles. After independence in 1967, industrial production declined, the once-famous port of Aden lay in disrepair, and workers' remittances from the oil-rich Gulf states provided half of the government's annual budget. Due in part to substandard Soviet technology, the PDRY's oil sector, which had the potential to lift the country economically, sat in shambles. Only in 1989 did the PDRY begin exporting oil in significant quantities.

The YAR's leadership also had compelling reasons for considering unification. Salih saw a merger as a means of increasing the power and influence of his country as well as procuring his place in history as the broker of Yemeni unification. Furthermore, oil had been discovered along the border between the two states, and it became clear that any decision over exportation rights would be extremely tense. Finally, the prospect of unification was popular on both sides of the border. The northern and southern leaderships believed that achieving the long-held dream of Yemeni unification was a good way of bolstering their legitimacy.

Sanaa, the capital of the former YAR and the largest city, became the capital of the unified republic. Aden, the capital of the former PDRY and once one of the busiest and most significant ports in the world, was officially designated the economic and commercial capital of unified Yemen (Sanaa now dominates these sectors as well).

In their unification agreement, the two countries divided ministerial positions, although local bureaucracies in the North and South remained intact. Salih retained his position as head of state, and Ali Salem al-Baydh, leader of the YSP, became vice president. The militaries exchanged senior staff but left rank-and-file personnel unintegrated. In its early days, the new republic maintained two separate armed forces, a state of affairs that haunted the fledgling state when North and South fought a civil war in 1994.

Soon after unification in May 1990, Iraq's invasion of Kuwait in August compounded Yemen's domestic instability. At that time, Yemen held a temporary rotating seat on the UN Security Council. From this position, it condemned the involvement of Western forces, advocating instead an "Arab solution." By so doing, it angered its wealthy Gulf neighbors, upon whom it relied considerably for economic support. Saudi Arabia expelled nearly 1 million Yemeni workers, whose remittances were crucial to Yemen's economy. Unemployment and poverty rose significantly in 1991. Popular frustration and disillusionment with the new government, bloated and inefficient because of unification, mounted. A devalued currency and a rising cost of living resulted in protests throughout 1992. As tensions mounted and national elections loomed, high-level officials of various political persuasions became the object of harassment or assassination attempts, although southern officials undeniably bore the brunt.

On April 27, 1993, the Republic of Yemen held its first elections after a delay of several months. Thousands of candidates competed for 301 seats in the parliament. Before Election Day, members of the GPC-YSP interim ruling coalition traded accusations of vote buying, inflating the electoral register, and unfairly using the media. The government deployed more than 35,000 troops on the streets of Sanaa to keep order on Election Day. With a large and generally peaceful turnout, Salih's GPC won the most parliamentary seats but failed to win an absolute majority. A new northern-based Islamist party, the Yemeni Reform Gathering (Islah), narrowly beat the YSP, which had been expected to pick up considerable support in the North while maintaining its position in the South. Despite problems with the process, international observers declared the vote relatively free and fair. Several opposition parties picked up seats— a step toward multiparty democracy that was, at least on the surface, unprecedented in the Arab Gulf region and was widely heralded as Yemen's first tentative move toward genuine democracy.

Rivalries within the new three-party government were strong, however, and were largely based on the old North-South division. Al-Baydh refused to be inaugurated as the vice president in the new government, and in August 1993, he boycotted the five-person presidential council and returned to Aden, accusing Salih of refusing to integrate the military and of hiding oil revenues. Al-Baydh subsequently charged Salih and his followers with responsibility for the assassination of key YSP officials and supporters.

Tensions continued to build between the two sides, and political assassinations remained frequent. Sporadic skirmishes between northern and southern troops began in February 1994, and observers believed both sides to be mobilizing for war. International mediators attempted to settle the dispute, but on April 27, 1994—exactly one year after the country's first elections—full-scale fighting erupted. On May 5, northern troops began attacking the territory of the former South. Al-Baydh declared a separate government on May 21 and established a presidential council and a rump parliament to lead the so-called Democratic Republic of Yemen—a state recognized only by the unrecognized Republic of Somaliland. The larger northern army invaded the South and pushed toward Aden and the oil port of Mukalla, about three hundred miles to the east. The northern forces dealt a crushing blow to the southern army, capturing Aden and Mukalla in early July, as southern fighters abandoned the cities or melted into the populace. The civil war lasted just over two months, but it devastated Yemen's economy and caused at least $2 billion in damage; some estimates put this figure much higher.

Because most Yemenis supported unification, there was widespread relief when the fighting ended. President Salih emerged from the civil war in a stronger position, though the way the war was fought—particularly the sanctioned looting of southern land and property by northern elites, forces, and irregulars—created a level of acrimony that continued to simmer. (Indeed, after tensions reignited in the mid-2000s, southerners widely recalled the abuse.) Thousands of southerners returned to Yemen under a general amnesty, and some southern leaders engaged the Sanaa government in discussions on recovering from the war. The conflict decimated the southern Yemeni Socialist Party (YSP), and the northern General People's Congress (GPC) and Islah quickly formed a new coalition government. With the YSP no longer a major political obstacle, the new government amended the constitution in September 1994, considerably expanding the powers of the presidency and introducing shari'a, Islamic law, as the "sole basis" of legislation.

The 1994 civil war reversed the optimism that had surrounded the unification of North and South Yemen in 1990, and discontent slowly gathered momentum in the South. Southerners charged that northern elites built their survival on the extraction of the South's natural resources, while entrenching a system that excluded southerners from government employment and other benefits. Southerners argued that they were stripped of their once-robust system of law and order (*nizam*) and were subsumed by the chaotic and personalized rule (*fawda*) of the North.

In 2007, that discontent became more organized, and by 2008, some had begun to protest, openly calling for secession and raising the flag of the former southern state. The early protests were against a set of specific grievances, particularly the forced retirement and insufficient pensions of southern military officers, but they quickly spread into a much wider phenomenon, moving into the northern governorates of Taizz and Ibb, where they involved much broader issues of regime legitimacy.

The frequency and intensity of protests surged across the country following the removal of President Hosni Mubarak in Egypt in February 2011, culminating one year later in the formal replacement of President Ali Abdallah Salih after thirty-three years in office. The violent response by the regime against the protesters throughout 2011 prompted high-level defections within the regime from March 2011, although the rifts among its elites had also been apparent for some time.[6] In November 2011, an agreement was reached that mapped out a time frame for Yemen's political transition (the GCC Initiative). The GCC Initiative called for a hasty process of reform: elections for a new president within ninety days, a new transitional government of national unity to be comprised equally of ruling party and opposition members, amendments to the electoral system and constitution, an overhaul of the security apparatus, and the creation of a National Dialogue Conference. However, the Initiative was principally driven by external actors, particularly Saudi Arabia and the United States, and left many Yemenis unconvinced that it was really likely to deliver the systemic changes they had demanded throughout the year. The National Dialogue Conference began in March 2013, with 565 delegates tasked with negotiating a new political framework for the country. The initial catharsis of the Conference gave way to frustrations over the exclusion of many of those who drove the 2011 uprising in favor of elites more amenable to perpetuating the status quo. These tensions remain unsolved and underpin many of the more proximate causes of the current violence.

SOCIETAL CHALLENGES

Yemen's population is estimated to be nearly 29 million, according to 2018 figures, making it the second-most-populous country on the Arabian Peninsula, after Saudi Arabia, whose census data are widely thought to be inflated. Its population is growing rapidly at a rate of 2.3 percent annually, which is one of the highest rates in the world.

Yemen ranks lowest among Arab states on the Human Development Index. Before the war, figures from 2014 suggested that life expectancy in Yemen was about sixty-three years (61.8 for men and 64.5 for women). The average Yemeni woman gave birth to 4.1 children, compared with an average of 1.9 in the United States and 1.4 across Europe. The literacy rate was approximately 66 percent; roughly 50 percent of the women are illiterate. Each of these figures has likely changed since the violence, displacement, starvation, and disease increased from 2014, though there are no accurate figures about the degree to which they may have done so.

Malnutrition and poverty were rampant even before the current crisis, particularly in the hinterlands of the South and in the Tihama on the Red Sea. Then, Yemen's infant mortality rate previously stood at 5.47 percent (for children under twelve months old), compared with a world average of 4.2 percent, while the mortality rate for children under five years old was 7.3 percent. Approximately 45 percent of Yemenis were believed to live below the poverty line of two dollars a day in 2011, with the number of people considered by the UN World Food Programme (WFP) to be *severely food insecure* doubling between 2009 and 2011. The proportion of Yemenis considered to be *food secure* nationally was then only 56 percent. While there are again no reliable indicators of the new figures, conditions are deteriorating by the month. In 2018, United Nations Secretary General Antonio Guterres called Yemen "the world's worst humanitarian crisis" and stated that 18 million Yemenis were *food insecure* and that "a horrifying 8.4 million of these people do not know how they will obtain their next meal." Yemen has also reportedly experienced the worst cholera epidemic the world has seen in half a century, with over 1 million people thought to have contracted the disease since September 2016. While some dispute the veracity of these headline claims that Yemen is the worst humanitarian crisis or that it experienced 1 million cholera cases, there is no doubt that the crisis has had a catastrophic impact on the lives of Yemenis.

Education and employment have not kept pace with the rapidly growing population. Yemeni women complete an average of seven years of formal education; men complete an average of eleven. Education and health services are largely confined to urban centers and remain quite inadequate—and the current conflict has caused serious disruptions to even these services, with many schools being forced to close and hospitals lacking basic medical supplies and electricity. At least one-third of Yemenis were unemployed, according to the WFP in 2012, though this figure did not include underemployment, which is also high, and appears to have only worsened in recent years. Unfortunately, again estimates are difficult to verify, as figures since the start of the war are notoriously unreliable.

Arabic is spoken nearly everywhere, although some people in the extreme eastern part of the country (in the governorate of al-Mahra) and on the island of Socotra speak the local languages of al-Mahri and Socotri, respectively. In terms of ethnicity, Yemenis pride themselves on being primarily Qahtani, or southern Arabs, with the most ancient roots, as opposed to Adnani, or northern Arabs. The vast majority of the population is Muslim, and in the former North Yemen, Muslims fall into two principal groups of roughly equal size: the Zaydis, a Shi'i sect found predominantly in the northern mountain areas; and the Shafi'is, a Sunni sect located primarily in the southern region and along the coastal plain. The Zaydi-Shafi'i division has been a source of some tension throughout Yemen's history, but the larger obstacles to inclusive development have been regional, tribal, externally fueled, or economic rather than sectarian. Yemen was also formerly home to a significant Jewish minority that traced its roots to biblical times and was well integrated into Yemeni society. Most of Yemen's Jewish population eventually emigrated to Israel, and as a result, Yemeni Jewish culture has largely disappeared, although some small communities remain in the northern Sa'dah governorate and in al-Rawda, just north of Sanaa. Even these, however, have largely disappeared, with many taking up residence in Sanaa as a result of the ongoing al-Houthi insurgency in the Sa'dah governorate.

Yemen did not enjoy nearly the level of socioeconomic development in recent decades that its neighbors in the Arabian Peninsula did. In part, this is because it does not possess as much oil and has always a significantly larger population. Yemen's political leadership also failed to invest sufficiently in the country's human capital, and a significant portion of the country's oil wealth was squandered through corruption.

Even before the war, Yemen had one of the most heavily armed populations in the world; carrying a weapon to guard against external predation is a tradition. Although the often-heard claim that there are "60 million guns and 20 million people" is certainly overstated, the Small Arms Survey (the latest available with reliable data) estimated in 2003 that there were between 6 million and 9 million small arms and light weapons in Yemen.[7] The number of publicly owned firearms per capita in Yemen is second only to the United States. Again, definitive figures are not available, but the vast majority of Yemen's privately owned weapons are held by the tribes in the northern highland areas. Yemen is also known as one of the region's largest suppliers of illicit small arms.

Despite Yemen's large rural population, the World Bank estimates that rates of urbanization have fluctuated between 6 percent and 8 percent annually, which is at least twice the average annual rate for Middle Eastern and North African (MENA) countries. Greater urbanization has led to some increase in the opportunities for women in education and employment, but gender-based discrimination is still very widespread.

INSTITUTIONS AND GOVERNANCE

When Yemen unified in May 1990, it declared that the new state would be democratic. The political sphere, repressive on both sides of the old border, was rapidly and quite dramatically liberalized. Political parties were legalized, new laws allowing greater levels of free expression and free association were enacted, an interim parliament was established, and the first parliamentary elections were planned for 1992. New media outlets and civil society organizations quickly sprang up amid strong optimism that Yemen's unprecedented experiment with democracy would succeed.[8] There seemed to be a genuine belief that democracy, however vaguely defined, was the best means of unifying the two Yemens and their elites into one coherent political system.

Despite maintaining some of the formal aspects of a democratic system, including a reasonable level of political pluralism, the government remained authoritarian in practice. The system of decision-making was predominantly informal and exclusive of ordinary Yemenis, and its survival was largely dependent on state-sponsored political patronage. As oil revenues diminished, the regime found it increasingly difficult to contain dissent, the accumulation of which was certainly a factor behind the traction that the mass protests gained in 2011, and again in 2014, prior to the Houthi rebels occupying Sanaa.

Military and Security

Before the rupture of the formal state apparatus in 2014, Yemen spent approximately 7 percent of its GDP on its military—one of the highest percentages in the world. Due to Yemen's notoriously inaccurate statistics and its deliberate opacity on security matters, precise confirmation and analysis of this figure is difficult. The military is the most important state institution and, like all others, is controlled at least indirectly by the president—something that was on stark display as the protesters in 2011 challenged Salih and his family's right to wield such power.

Throughout Salih's presidency, members of President Salih's family held most key military positions. His son Ahmed Ali Abdallah Salih controlled the Republican Guard, a force of some 30,000 men. President Salih's half-brothers, cousins, and nephews also held important posts, such as Central Security Commander Mohammed Abdallah Salih, Air Force Commander Mohammed Salih al-Ahmar, National Security Agency Deputy Commander 'Ammar Mohammed Salih, Head of the First Armored Division Ali Muhsin al-Ahmar (who was the first major commander to publicly defect from the regime during the protests), and National Security Agency Commander Yahya Mohammed Abdallah Salih. The domestic intelligence apparatus, the Political Security Organization (PSO), also reported directly to President Salih.

Following Salih's resignation, President Hadi began to try to remove some of these figures from their positions, though some did not go without a fight. In June 2014, forces loyal to Hadi attacked the headquarters of a television channel that was affiliated with Salih, resulting in open conflict in central Sanaa. As noted at the beginning of this chapter, the Houthis captured the capital city of Sanaa in September 2014; and in 2015, Salih publicly declared what had been well known within Yemen since 2012: that he was in a military alliance with his former enemies, the Houthis, against President Hadi. In February 2015, the Houthis and Salih dissolved the parliament and declared instead the Supreme Revolutionary Council, a transitional body of 15 members that was to govern the territory under the coalition's control. A year and a half later, they established the Supreme Political Council and formed a new cabinet. The Houthi-Saleh alliance, always shaky, ended with Salih's death at the hands of Houthi fighters in December 2017, days after Salih publicly severed his link with them. Salih's nephew Tariq now commands the remnants of the family's military network, which is most active in and around the Red Sea port city of Hodeidah.

Yemeni government forces are scattered, with few personally loyal to President Hadi. They are supported by members of the GCC coalition to varying degrees, but it is the proxy forces that are directly funded and trained by the coalition (largely the UAE) that are most present on the ground and through which some of the tensions between the GCC coalition can be seen. These include both the Hadhrami and Shabwani Elite Forces, the Security Belt Forces (al-Hizaam al-Amni), and the Giants' Brigade (*al-'Amlaqah*). In addition to these forces there is a multitude of local militias and tribal groups engaged in more localized conflicts.

In the areas under Houthi control, regime security is maintained, in part, through a "supervisory" (*mushrifeen*) system. Supervisors are embedded into existing security and administrative structures on the basis of their loyalty to (and often membership of) the Houthi kindship network. These are not formal positions but act alongside the formal authorities and, in practice, often supersede them as they form a bridge between local authorities and the Houthi leadership.

Tribes

For many Yemenis—particularly those who live outside of urban centers—the tribes are extremely important social, political, and economic institutions, though their influence has waned in recent decades. The tribal system still offers an important means of local dispute resolution, with many seeing the state judicial institutions as ineffective or corrupt, and there is reason to believe that their relevance is increasing again as the conflict wears on.

Tribes remained far stronger in northern Yemen than they did in the southern area. The ruling party in the former PDRY saw tribes as an anachronism and attempted to dismantle them.

PHOTO 26.1 Houthi rebels seized the towns of Houth and Khamri, the seat of the Hashid tribal chief, in February 2014

Yemen-Strife/Reuters/Khaled Abdullah/Alamy Stock Photo

Even so, they endured and, with the collapse of the PDRY, reemerged as a significant political and social force in parts of the South. The tribal system often serves as a buffer against substantial poverty in Yemen's countryside, and communalism sometimes helps to mask the enormous gaps in the state's capacity or willingness to deliver services to the people.[9]

The impact of Yemen's tribal system on the country's political development remains a passionately debated issue among politically engaged Yemenis. Some argue that tribalism poses a serious obstacle to the establishment of formal state institutions, while others state that because of tribalism's egalitarian foundations, many of its norms constitute an indigenous form of democracy and is a means of holding authority accountable. Some tribes consider their territories states within the state, control the central government's entry, and desire at least a degree of autonomy from the central government. Their authority, including the use of physical force, has always posed obstacles to the state exercising full sovereignty throughout all Yemeni territory. Equally, however, the state under President Salih also imposed its own limitations for full territorial sovereignty by allowing—some argue benefiting from—some tribes to resist formal centralized authority.

The relationship between the state and the tribe is not always adversarial. The Yemeni regime has historically relied upon the tribes in a number of important ways to maintain its rule.[10] The central government absorbed most politically significant tribal leaders, increasing their wealth and power and the state's access to tribal areas. As a result of the state's co-optation of tribal leaders, some are no longer seen as advancing their communities' interests, and tribal traditions, such as group solidarity and egalitarianism, are widely believed undermined.[11]

ACTORS, OPINION, AND PARTICIPATION

The Yemeni constitution specifies a relatively high level of participation for its citizens. When the country unified in 1990, all adults over the age of eighteen were given the right to vote; political parties were legalized; and a new press law promised free expression, independent media, and access to information. Almost overnight, there was an explosion in the number of publications. The political atmosphere shifted considerably after the civil war in 1994, and the public space became increasingly limited. Some of Yemen's laws also seem to contradict the spirit of the constitution, and their application has been arbitrary, leading sometimes to strict controls.

Civil Society

The idea that civil society is the most important factor in transition to democracy has been widely questioned in the Middle East in recent years (see Chapter 5), and this debate has been reinvigorated since the ousting of several leaders with, as yet, uncertainties over the level of systemic change that has occurred as a result. Rapid growth in the number of civil society organizations (CSOs) throughout the region did not signal systemic political change in Yemen. The fact that the protests of 2011 began outside the auspices of any of Yemen's organized political parties or CSOs further underlined their lack of deep social penetration. After the movement gained momentum, organized groups became more visible, which became a source of tension on the streets between those who felt that they "started" the movement and those parties—particularly Islah—who many believed were attempting to co-opt it.

Political Parties

Yemen has had many different formal political parties since unification, though most of them were said to exist only during election time. There are three main political parties: the ruling GPC (General People's Congress), Islah, and the YSP (Yemeni Socialist Party), though all are in a major state of flux at the time of writing and are not the most significant actors.

The GPC

Once the ruling party of North Yemen and then of the unified Republic, the GPC's positions in cabinet were reduced to 50 percent when it was forced to enter into a transitional coalition government with the JMP (Joint Meeting Parties), a coalition of opposition parties, when President Salih was removed from office in late 2011. Members of the GPC come from diverse backgrounds, and most have historically been attracted to it because it was the country's ruling party, not necessarily because of ideological preferences.

Islah

Acknowledging the caveats that opened this chapter, Islah was the largest and best-organized opposition party in Yemen, though after the collapse of the government, found itself in violent conflict with its former (partial) allies, those loyal to Salih, the Houthis, and a number of UAE sponsored militias. Islah historically had considerable grassroots support and a strong record in charitable work, which helped the party penetrate society beyond the elite. An Islamist party, it had long offered the only ideological, if incoherent, alternative to the status quo. The party's membership exhibits a number of different schools of thought, which at times caused tension within the party, although its leaders were careful to publicly deny such schisms. The main schools of thought that exist within the party are those that are aligned with the Muslim Brotherhood and more conservative Salafis (that express various degrees of religious tolerance). The party has also served as a base for some tribal elites—particularly members of the influential al-Ahmar family and religious businessmen.

The YSP

Although it once ruled the former South and had a clearer ideology than the GPC, the YSP was a party in decline for the two decades that preceded the crisis. The party never recovered from its loss in the 1994 civil war and ongoing harassment from the GPC that followed the war. It won only 7 of 301 seats in the 2003 parliamentary elections. The unrest in the South, which erupted in 2007, exacerbated divisions within its leadership. While the party long claimed that it was playing a lead role within the "southern movement" (see The Southern Movement—Harak section), its leaders' ability to gain genuine grassroots traction within the movement was limited.

Elections

Even prior to the collapse of the central government in 2015, Yemen's electoral cycles had changed several times as a result of changes to the constitution and (extraconstitutional) decisions to postpone the elections in 1992 and 2009. Formally, there are 301 seats in the Yemeni parliament. The parliamentary term was initially four years but was extended to six years in 2001. The current parliament was elected in 2003 but due to a series of postponements continues to serve, albeit irregularly. Local councils also serve six years, and voters elect representatives to serve in 333 districts and twenty-one governorates. The presidential term was previously five years, but it was extended to seven years in 2000. When Abd Rabbuh Mansoor Hadi won the presidential election in 2012 (in which he was the only candidate) following Salih's resignation, he obtained the right to serve as a transitional president until full elections could be held in 2014. These elections were also postponed.

DOMESTIC CONFLICTS

As a mood of popular protest gripped the region in the wake of the events in Tunisia and Egypt in early 2011, Yemenis took to the streets in increasing numbers. Like other leaders in the region, President Salih initially experimented with various mechanisms of control in an attempt to contain the unrest but quickly resorted to high levels of violence. On March 18, 2011, snipers killed more than fifty unarmed civilians on the streets of central Sanaa, which provided the stage for the defection of the second-most-powerful man in the Salih regime—General Ali Muhsin. Muhsin's defection was not simply a response to the murder of the protesters, as he claimed, but was built on long-standing tensions within the regime's inner circle over the distribution of resources and the inheritance of power. The protests continued throughout the year and eventually forced President Salih to accept an offer of immunity in exchange for his resignation. Salih was replaced by Vice President Abd Rabbu Mansoor Hadi as acting president in late 2011, after which he was confirmed as president in a single-candidate election in February 2012. Hadi's presidency was initially greeted with enthusiasm, but his inability to stem the deteriorating political, economic, and security situation strengthened the hand of his opponents (particularly those affiliated with former President Salih) and built the sense that dramatic action was necessary to alter Yemen's course. That dramatic action came, first, when the Houthi-Salih militias took Sanaa in September 2014 and then again when they expelled President Hadi from the country in March 2015 after failing to agree to power-sharing arrangements. Underlying the whole crisis, one issue has remained constant: At one level, all actors are involved in a struggle over what constitutes a legitimate successor to Salih's leadership and the political order that he presided over.

The National Dialogue Conference

The Conference ran from March 2013 to January 2014 and was established out of the GCC Initiative (2011) that formalized President Salih's resignation. It was, at least theoretically, an attempt to resolve the multifaceted conflicts that the 2011 uprisings brought to the surface.

While initially cathartic, the process was undermined by a number of factors, particularly the determination of its external sponsors to preserve an ill-defined (and externally perceived) "stability" and ongoing dissatisfaction with the deal that granted Salih immunity from prosecution.

Prior to the youth-led uprising, there were two main social movements challenging the status quo, both of which gained ground dramatically after the seismic shifts of 2011: the al-Houthi movement, which fought a series of wars against the Salih regime in and around the northern governorate of Sa'dah between 2004 and 2010; and the southern secessionist movement. Both are now deeply implicated in the conflicts currently engulfing the country.

The Southern Movement—Harak and the Southern Transitional Council (STC)

The "southern movement" (*al-Harak*—the movement) emerged from a series of antigovernment protests that began in the South on the anniversary of unification (May 22) in 2007. While not all those affiliated with Harak consistently called for the full independence of the South, they ultimately united in this goal, though they disagreed about the best way to achieve it. The movement was plagued by a lack of clear internal domestic leadership but became more coherent and broad based as the threat from northern actors (particularly the Houthis and Salih loyalists) increased. Harak developed an armed "Southern Resistance" element that fought off the Houthi-Salih militias and "invaded" the South in 2015 in a conflict that was both bloody and underreported in the international media.

Even though President Hadi is from Abyan in the South, Harak saw him as a part of the northern-based system from which they wish to secede. This was partly due to Hadi's connection to historical rivalries within the South, and partly due to his legacy of fighting the South in the 1994 civil war. In April 2017, Hadi fired the Governor of Aden, Aidarus al-Zubaidi, for being loyal to al-Harak instead of to his internationally recognized government. Shortly afterward, al-Zubaidi announced the establishment of the Southern Transitional Council (STC), which seized control of the government's Aden offices in early 2018 with the support of the United Arab Emirates. Control over the South has been split between forces aligned with the STC and those aligned with Hadi despite the finalization of the Riyadh Agreement in November 2019 which was, theoretically, supposed to compel their integration under the auspices of Hadi and his supporters.

The Houthis

The Sa'dah-based insurgent group, Ansar Allah, is better known as the Houthis, named after the family that has led the movement since it began in the early 1990s. The group fought a series of civil wars against the central government (though, more specifically, against the First Armored Division, which was commanded by General Ali Muhsin) between 2004 and 2010 and surprised many with their resilience and ability to project influence beyond their traditional base. As a predominantly Zaydi Shi'a movement, it was long charged that the Houthis were fighting to further a sectarian-based ideology. In reality, the ideological dimension, while always present, also grew over time, gaining traction as Yemen's war became more violent and internationalized.

The Houthis have ties to Iran, though the duration and strategic depth of their association remains a matter of conjecture. Both Saudi Arabia and Iran have cause to overstate the level of coordination between Iran and the Houthis to their domestic audiences. Iran's ability to drive events in Yemen through the Houthis was historically limited but has undoubtedly increased considerably since Saudi Arabia and the UAE have become active participants in Yemen's war. The Houthis' initial success in Yemen was, however, largely a product of local political factors (including factional rivalries within the Salih regime), military capacity, and support. The Houthis steadily gained influence since the departure of Ali Abdullah Salih as president by articulating the widespread anger over the failures of Hadi's government, such as when it cut fuel subsidies in August 2014. The following month, Houthi militias overran the capital city of Sanaa with—somewhat ironically—the assistance of factions of the military loyal to Salih.

The Houthis have demonstrated a poor capacity for governance. While political allegiances are difficult to capture with any precision, it is fair to say that they are unpopular outside of their core support base as a result of their often-ruthless use of violence, mismanagement, and increasingly exclusive sectarian and ideological agenda, though this does not suggest that their opponents necessarily support the actions of the GCC coalition either. Enmity for one side in Yemen's war does not mechanically confer legitimacy upon the other—something that is often missed in Western media commentary about the conflict, which tends to presume a zero-sum game.

RELIGION, SOCIETY, AND POLITICS

The vast majority of Yemen's population is Muslim, with a majority of the population in Upper Yemen being Zaydi Shi'i Muslims (20 to 25 percent of the total population) and the vast majority of Lower Yemen and the former People's Democratic Republic of Yemen (PDRY) being Shafi'i Sunni Muslims. Zaydism is doctrinally closer to the Sunni sects than it is to other Shi'i sects, particularly the Ithna'asharis, and it is commonly referred to as the "fifth school" of Sunni Islam. There has not been significant religiously fueled animosity between the two communities historically, although some have noted a sometimes antagonistic "us-them" feeling between them based on cultural, social, and political grounds.[12]

Before aligning with the Houthis, Ali Abdallah Salih had charged that the movement called for the reestablishment of the Zaydi imamate that governed northern Yemen for more than 1000 years (with minor interruptions) until 1962. As a family of Sayyids—that is, those who claim descent from the Prophet Muhammad through his daughter Fatima and her husband Ali—members of the al-Houthi family would theoretically be eligible to claim the title of imam for themselves. Revival of the imamate is rejected by Yemen's Sunni majority and also by many Zaydis as well, and although the Houthis deny it, many Yemenis believe that this is indeed their aim.

The conflict between the Houthis and other factions (including the Southern Resistance, the Islah Party, al-Qa'ida in the Arabian Peninsula, and the Saudi-led coalition) is being increasingly framed in sectarian terms. However, its origins are predominantly political, and aspects of it are deeply rooted in the factional rivalries of the old Salih regime. It is clear that the more the conflict is framed in sectarian terms, and the more that both sides use sectarian language in their recruitment strategies, the more identities are being hardened around instrumental narratives of primordial hostility. Al-Qaʻida also seeks to exacerbate sectarianism for political gains, and the geopolitical tensions between Saudi Arabia and Iran find reflection in Yemen's domestic politics as well.

POLITICAL ECONOMY

Under President Salih, Yemen's political economy was largely based on the distribution of patronage at the elite level. In part because of the state's inability (some say unwillingness) to maintain a monopoly on the legitimate use of violence, the Salih regime complemented its coercive power with the ability to co-opt, divide, reward, and punish other elites through patronage and exclusion. President Hadi did not move significantly away from the logic employed by his predecessor when distributing resources and other benefits to his political allies, overlooking the corrupt practices of certain elites and offering major tax breaks for businessmen of political significance. In other words, systemic change within Yemen's political economy did not occur with the transition of power to President Hadi, and neither has it occurred under the Houthis, though the war itself has become the largest driver of the economy under their rule.

Other than through oil exports, Yemen has remained poorly integrated into the global economy, and even these have been seriously disrupted by the large-scale violence. When Saudi Arabia and Kuwait expelled Yemeni workers in 1990, labor was Yemen's most significant export. The country never fully recovered from reabsorbing so many unemployed workers at one time.[13] Prior to unification, the YAR and PDRY economies had relied on a combination of workers' remittances, coffee exports, the fishing industry, and foreign assistance. Shortly before unification, revenues from oil exports supplemented these sources in both states. During the oil booms of the 1970s and 1980s, the exodus of Yemeni workers to other parts of the Gulf had made it difficult for Yemen to develop its own agricultural and industrial bases. With unification, the Republic of Yemen agreed to assume the international obligations of the YAR and PDRY, saddling the unified nation with a combined official debt of approximately $7 billion.

The two-month civil war of 1994 had a disastrous effect on Yemen and prodded the government toward a course of economic restructuring.[14] In April 1995, worsening economic conditions prompted the government to adopt an aggressive economic recovery plan. The primary objectives were to secure control of the rapidly increasing budget deficit; reinforce the value of the riyal; initiate privatization of many state-run sectors; and encourage national, Arab, and foreign investment by providing better facilities for investors.

Under this plan, Yemen attracted hundreds of millions of dollars in foreign aid and investment from the International Monetary Fund and the World Bank, the European Union (EU), Japan, and the United States. It brought rampant inflation under control, decreasing it from more than 55 percent in 1995 to less than 6 percent in 1997, and stabilized its exchange rate. Despite this, Yemen experienced a sharp rise in its budget deficit, in part because of low oil prices and decreased demand in the late 1990s.

Agriculture occupies around one-third of the workforce, and in many remote areas, farming is the only viable livelihood. Yet agriculture accounts for only approximately 10 percent of the country's GDP. This means that Yemen is highly dependent on external sources for its food, which makes it highly sensitive to international price shocks—and vulnerable to the air and naval blockade that Saudi Arabia applied to its key ports of entry. A significant number of Yemen's remaining workers provide unskilled labor to the Arabian Peninsula's labor-poor, capital-rich countries. Their wages provide an unsteady but important source of funds to the country's economy.

Since unification, Yemen has relied on oil revenues for virtually all of its essential needs. Initial estimates of its total oil reserves were around four billion barrels, but this figure was drastically revised downward. Yemen's oil production peaked in 2003 at around 450,000 barrels a day and comprised about 75 percent of the government's revenue. It appears highly unlikely to reach this level again. Significantly higher oil prices between 2004 and 2008 had a positive impact on Yemen's revenues and budget deficit. By 2009, however, the country was only producing 280,000 barrels a day, which, combined with the dramatic drop in oil prices later that year, again put serious strain on Yemen's budget.[15] As the political crisis deepened in 2011, disruptions to production became both regular and severe, meaning that Yemen had to import (or receive donations of) oil from abroad. By early 2015, production was estimated to be only around 140,000 barrels a day, though again exports plummeted once the Saudi-led coalition began its bombing campaign and partial naval blockade led in March of that year. Yemen is grappling with the fact there is no other source of external revenue, other than foreign assistance, that looks capable of replacing oil in the short- or even medium-term future. Yemen has an estimated 17 trillion cubic feet of natural gas reserves, but these reserves are not anticipated to cover the loss of oil income.

Yemen has also historically relied on the largesse of its wealthy GCC neighbors, particularly Saudi Arabia. Saudi Arabia has funneled huge amounts of money annually (usually estimated in the billions) to both the central government and to various political, social, tribal, and religious actors in an effort to both project political and ideological influence and to prevent Yemen's troubles from breaching its own borders.[16] The GCC's war in Yemen has put all of these avenues of income into question, and it is impossible to know how it will affect these streams of revenue in the future.

In addition to natural resources and access to external funding, the widespread social practice of chewing qat is central to Yemen's political economy, though it has been long bemoaned (particularly by foreigners) as an economic scourge. Many men and women of all social classes chew the mildly narcotic leaves of the qat shrub daily. After several hours of providing mild stimulation, the plant induces lethargy. The qat bush is easy to grow, tolerates frequent cropping, and provides instant returns in cash. According to the World Bank in 2007, qat production directly employed around 14 percent of Yemenis, though this is almost certainly an underestimation. As a result of demand, some fields that previously grew edible and exportable crops have been converted into qat fields, contributing to the transformation of Yemen into an import-dependent country. Qat is a water-intensive crop—a serious concern for Yemen, which is one of the most water-poor countries in the world. However, it was international donors, particularly the IMF and World Bank, that pushed the Yemeni government to move from the subsistence agriculture that had sustained its population for centuries to a model that prioritized farming more water-intensive crops (including oranges and grapes) for export in exchange for international loans. The watering practices required to sustain these crops in the arid highlands region had an extremely deleterious impact on the water basin, for which qat was never solely responsible.[17]

INTERNATIONAL RELATIONS AND SECURITY

Whether regionally or internationally, Yemen's external relations have long been viewed predominantly through the lens of security concerns. For the West, the perceived threat is from the actions of terrorist groups. For regional actors, particularly Saudi Arabia, the concerns are broader and include mass migration and the political threat posed by Republicanism (and, presumably, representative government) on its border. The degree to which Iran's involvement in Yemen is driving Saudi concerns remains a matter of debate, but is stated by Saudi Arabia as the main reason for its current military intervention in Yemen. Saudi Arabia also has a long history of political influence in Yemen, the maintenance of which is widely believed to constitute a further layer to its actions.

Having maintained a low-level presence in the country since the end of the war against the USSR in Afghanistan, violent extremist groups have gained strength in Yemen since 2006, when twenty-three al-Qa'ida figures escaped from a prison in Sanaa under suspicious circumstances. Although some of the escapees were recaptured or killed reasonably quickly, some resurfaced to launch attacks against government infrastructure, foreign embassies, and civilians. In January 2009, a new Yemeni-Saudi organization—al-Qa'ida in the Arabian Peninsula (AQAP)—was announced by two of the 2006 fugitives, Nasser al-Wahayshi and Qasim al-Raymi, along with two Saudi militants, Sa'eed al-Shihri and Mohammed al-'Awfi. The very public establishment of this group, its subsequent attempts to hit high-profile foreign targets (particularly American and Saudi Arabian), its claimed responsibility for the attacks on the *Charlie Hebdo* office in France, and its ongoing deadly attacks and ability to gain territory within Yemen contributed to the widespread view that it is the most active operational franchise of al-Qa'ida. A group calling itself "Islamic State in Yemen" also began to claim responsibility for suicide bombings in Yemeni mosques in March 2015, suggesting that its aim was to distinguish itself from AQAP by being more viciously sectarian in its targeting practices than its competitor. AQAP has become reasonably operationally sophisticated and has pursued alliances with tribal groups for safe haven, gaining a degree of territorial control in some parts of the South, most recently in the port city of Mukalla (2015–2016). The Yemeni government's capacity to combat al-Qa'ida or Islamic State, already limited, was further weakened by a security vacuum in parts of the country where al-Qa'ida is active[18] but also by ongoing accusations that factions of the regime (particularly former president Salih and the current vice president General Ali Muhsin) or the Houthis have, at times, actively facilitated AQAP or Islamic State.[19]

Other than the now-internationalized war that is pitting GCC actors and their supporters against Iran and its supporters, another issue in Yemen's contemporary international relations and security is the American air campaign against AQAP targets. In August 2021, the Bureau of Investigative Journalism stated that there had been at least 336 drone strikes conducted in Yemen since 2002, killing between 1,020 and 1,389 people and injuring hundreds more.

OUTLOOK

With the violent conflicts between the Houthi militias, scattered government forces, Islahi militias, local militias, Southern Resistance fighters, Salih loyalists, and others, Yemen remains in an extremely dangerous period. People are suffering dreadfully with insecure access to basic humanitarian necessities like food, water, and medical supplies. Its problems are being exacerbated by external powers and interests vying for political, economic, or security gains. In the longer term, the best prospect for improvement may be in developing long-term sustainable industries that use Yemen's large labor sector, its unique historical, cultural, and agricultural assets, and that take advantage of its strategic geographic location. With the many problems outlined earlier and the unwillingness of most external actors to see Yemen as more than a security problem to be solved, it is unlikely that this will be realized in the near future.

SUGGESTED READINGS

Al-Dawsari, Nadwa. *Tribal Governance and Stability in Yemen*. Washington, DC: Carnegie Endowment for International Peace, 2012.

Bonnefoy, Laurent. *Yemen and the World: Beyond Insecurity*. Oxford: Oxford University Press, 2018.

Caton, Steven C. *Yemen Chronicle: An Anthropology of War and Mediation*. New York, NY: Hill and Wang, 2005.

Day, Stephen W, and Noel Brehony, eds. *Global, Regional, and Local Dynamics in the Yemen Crisis*. Cham: Palgrave Macmillan, 2020. (This volume contains useful contributions by Yemeni authors.)

Dresch, Paul. *Tribes, Government, and History in Yemen*. Oxford: Oxford University Press, 1989.

Lux, Abdullah. "Yemen's last Zaydī Imām: the *shabāb al-mu'min*, the *Malāzim*, and '*ḥizb allāh*' in the thought of Ḥusayn Badr al-Dīn al-Ḥūthī." *Contemporary Arab Affairs 2*, no. 3 (2009): 369–434.

Orkaby, Asher. *Beyond the Arab Cold War: The International History of the Yemen Civil War, 1962–1968*. Oxford: Oxford University Press, 2017.

Phillips, Sarah G. *Yemen and the Politics of Permanent Crisis*. London: Routledge, 2011.

Wedeen, Lisa. *Peripheral Visions: Publics, Power, and Performance in Yemen*. Chicago, IL: Chicago University Press, 2008.

Weir, Shelagh. *A Tribal Order: Politics and Law in the Mountains of Yemen*. London: British Museum Press, 2007.

NOTES

FRONT MATTER

1. According to the Pew Charitable Trust, only about 20 percent of the world's Muslims live in the Middle East and North Africa; see Pew Forum on Religion and Public Life, "Mapping the Global Muslim Population" (October 2009), http://pewforum.org/Muslim/Mapping-the-Global-Muslim-Population(2).aspx.

CHAPTER 1

1. See Nikki R. Keddie, "Is There a Middle East?" *International Journal of Middle East Studies* 4, no. 3 (July 1973): 255–71.

2. See Molly Greene, "The Ottoman Experience," *Daedalus* 134, no. 2 (Spring 2005): 88–99.

3. See Heather J. Sharkey, *A History of Muslims, Christians, and Jews in the Middle East* (New York: Cambridge University Press, 2017).

4. See Christine M. Philliou, *Biography of an Empire Governing Ottomans in an Age of Revolution* (Berkeley: University of California Press, 2010).

5. Non-Muslims for a variety of reasons used the shari'a or Islamic courts. See Najwa Al-Qattan, "Dhimmis in the Muslim Court: Legal Autonomy and Religious Discrimination," *International Journal of Middle East Studies* 31, no. 3 (1999): 429–44.

6. See Juan Ricardo Cole, "Feminism, Class, and Islam in Turn-of-the-Century Egypt," *International Journal of Middle East Studies* 13, no. 4 (November 1981): 387–407.

7. Cenghis Kirli, "Coffeehouses: Public Opinion in the Nineteenth Century Ottoman Empire," in *Public Islam and the Common Good*, eds. Armando Salvatore and Dale Eickelman (Leiden: Brill, 2004), 75–97.

8. For an account of the French occupation, see 'Abd al-Raḥmān Jabartī, Louis Antoine Fauvelet de Bourrienne, and Edward W. Said, *Napoleon in Egypt: Al-Jabartî's Chronicle of the First Seven Months of the French Occupation, 1798* (Princeton, NJ: M. Wiener, 1993).

9. See M. Şükrü Hanioğlu, *A Brief History of the Late Ottoman Empire* (Princeton, NJ: Princeton University Press, 2010).

10. For a concise description of this phenomenon, see James Gelvin, *The Modern Middle East: A History,* 5th ed. (New York: Oxford University Press, 2020), 70–89.

11. Enver Bey, a major figure in turn-of-the-century Ottoman governments, writing in 1908.

12. Albert Hourani, "Ottoman Reform and the Politics of Notables," in *The Emergence of the Modern Middle East* (Berkeley: University of California Press, 1981), 36–66.

13. See Saba Mahmood, *Religious Difference in a Secular Age: A Minority Report* (Princeton, NJ: Princeton University Press, 2016), 1–110.

14. See Mostafa Minawi, *The Ottoman Scramble for Africa: Empire and Diplomacy in the Sahara and the Hijaz* (Stanford, CA: Stanford University Press, 2016).

15. See Taner Akçam, *From Empire to Republic: Turkish Nationalism and the Armenian Genocide* (London: Zed Books, 2004); Taner Akçam, *A Shameful Act: The Armenian Genocide and the Question of Turkish Responsibility* (New York: Holt, 2007).

16. Joshua Schreier, *The Merchants of Oran: A Jewish Port at the Dawn of Empire* (Stanford, CA: Stanford University Press, 2017).

17. On this new print culture and the broader question of popular culture, see Ziad Fahmy, *Ordinary Egyptians: Creating the Modern Nation through Popular Culture* (Stanford, CA: Stanford University Press, 2011).

18. The definitive analysis of this debate remains Leila Ahmed's "The Discourse of the Veil" in her *Women and Gender in Islam* (New Haven, CT: Yale University Press, 1992), 144–68.

19. See Michelle Campos, *Ottoman Brothers: Muslims, Christians, and Jews in Early Twentieth-Century Palestine* (Stanford, CA: Stanford University Press, 2011).

20. On the development of Syrian nationalism, see Benjamin Thomas White, *The Emergence of Minorities in the Middle East: The Politics of Community in French Mandate Syria* (Edinburgh: Edinburgh University Press, 2011).

21. Priya Satia, "The Defense of Inhumanity: Air Control and the British Idea of Arabia," *The American Historical Review* 111, no. 1 (February 2006): 16–51.

22. Robert Vitalis, "Black Gold and White Crude: An Essay on American Exceptionalism, Hierarchy, and Hegemony in the Gulf," *Diplomatic History* 26, no. 2 (Spring 2002): 194.

23. See Avi Shlaim, "The Protocol of Sèvres, 1956: Anatomy of a War Plot," *International Affairs* 73, no. 3 (1997): 509–30.

24. See Malcolm Kerr, *The Arab Cold War: Gamal 'Abd Al-Nasir and His Rivals, 1958–1970* (Oxford: Oxford University Press, 1971).

25. See Shaul Mishal and Avraham Sela, *The Palestinian Hamas: Vision, Violence, and Coexistence* (New York: Columbia University Press, 2006).

26. See Yaroslav Trofimov, *The Siege of Mecca: The Forgotten Uprising in Islam's Holiest Shrine and the Birth of al-Qaeda* (New York: Doubleday, 2007).

27. See Saba Mahmood, *Politics of Piety: The Islamic Revival and the Feminist Subject* (Princeton, NJ: Princeton University Press, 2005).

28. On the origins of the Arab Spring see Omar S. Dahi, "Understanding the Political Economy of the Arab Revolts," *Middle East Report* 259 (Summer 2011).

CHAPTER 2

1. This chapter draws heavily on Mark Tessler, *A History of the Israeli-Palestinian Conflict,* 2nd ed. (Bloomington: Indiana University Press, 2009). Drawing upon nearly one thousand primary and secondary sources, representing virtually all relevant political perspectives, this volume provides a great deal of additional detail about the events covered in the present chapter.

2. Abraham Joshua Heschel, *Israel: An Echo of Eternity* (New York: Farrar, Straus and Giroux, 1967), 22–54.

3. Guenter Lewy, *Religion and Revolution* (New York: Oxford University Press, 1974), 91.

4. Samuel Katz, *Battleground: Fact and Fantasy in Palestine* (New York: Bantam Books, 1973), 84–86.

5. See Tessler, *A History of the Israeli-Palestinian Conflict*, 285.

6. Shlomo Avineri, *The Making of Modern Zionism: The Intellectual Origins of the Jewish State* (New York: Basic Books, 1981), 3–4.

7. Peter Mansfield, *The Arabs* (Middlesex: Penguin Book, 1978), 121.

8. David Vital, *The Origins of Zionism* (Oxford: Oxford University Press, 1975), 43.

9. Vital, *The Origins of Zionism*, 3.

10. Tessler, *A History of the Israeli-Palestinian Conflict*, 266–67.

11. Ann Mosley Lesch, *Arab Politics in Palestine, 1917–1939* (Ithaca, NY: Cornell University Press, 1979), 85–86.

12. Yehoshua Porath, *The Emergence of the Palestinian-Arab National Movement: 1918–1929* (London: Frank Cass, 1974), 81.

13. Tessler, *A History of the Israeli-Palestinian Conflict*, 158.

14. Paul L. Hanna, *British Policy in Palestine* (Washington, DC: American Council on Public Affairs, 1942), 73.

15. David Waines, "The Failure of the Nationalist Resistance," in *The Transformation of Palestine: Essays on the Origins and Development of the Arab-Israeli Conflict*, ed. Ibrahim Abu-Lughod (Evanston, IL: Northwestern University Press, 1971), 219.

16. See John Ruedy, "Dynamics of Land Alienation," in *The Transformation of Palestine: Essays on the Origins and Development of the Arab-Israeli Conflict*, ed. Ibrahim Abu-Lughod (Evanston, IL: Northwestern University Press, 1971), 129.

17. Barbara Kalkas, "The Revolt of 1936: A Chronicle of Events," in *The Transformation of Palestine: Essays on the Origins and Development of the Arab-Israeli Conflict*, ed. Ibrahim Abu-Lughod (Evanston, IL: Northwestern University Press, 1971), 248.

18. *Report of the Palestine Royal Commission* (London: United Kingdom Government, 1937), 110–11.

19. Christopher Sykes, *Crossroads to Israel, 1917–1948* (Bloomington: Indiana University Press, 1965), 174.

20. Simha Flapan, *The Birth of Israel: Myths and Realities* (New York: Pantheon Books, 1987), 42.

21. Tessler, *A History of the Israeli-Palestinian Conflict*, 291–307.

22. Yair Evron, *The Middle East: Nations, Superpowers and Wars* (New York: Praeger, 1973), 34; Itamar Rabinovich, *The Road Not Taken: Early Arab-Israeli Negotiations* (Oxford: Oxford University Press, 1991), 199–200; and Mahmoud Riad, *The Struggle for Peace in the Middle East* (London: Quartet Books, 1981), 7.

23. Riad, *The Struggle for Peace in the Middle East*, 10.

24. Fred J. Khouri, *The Arab-Israeli Dilemma* (Syracuse, NY: Syracuse University Press, 1976), 227.

25. Ernest Stock, *Israel on the Road to Sinai, 1949–1956* (Ithaca, NY: Cornell University Press, 1967), 221.

26. Richard Parker, *The Politics of Miscalculation in the Middle East* (Bloomington: Indiana University Press, 1992), chap. 1.

27. Randolph Churchill and Winston Churchill, *The Six Day War* (Boston, MA: Houghton Mifflin, 1967), 28.

28. Mansfield, *The Arabs*, 80.

29. Arthur S. Lall, *The UN and the Middle East Crisis, 1967* (New York: Columbia University Press, 1968), 263.

30. Saadia Touval, *The Peace Brokers* (Princeton, NJ: Princeton University Press, 1982), 145.

31. Laurie A. Brand, *Palestinians in the Arab World: Institution Building and the Search for State* (New York: Columbia University Press, 1988), 186–220.

32. Abdallah Laroui, "The Arab Revolution Between Awareness and Reality" [in Arabic], *Mawaqif* 10 (July/August): 138.

33. Fouad Ajami, *The Arab Predicament: Arab Political Thought and Practice since 1967* (New York: Cambridge University Press, 1981), 29.

34. Arthur Hertzberg, *The Zionist Idea* (New York: Atheneum, 1970), 203.

35. Jillian Becker, *The PLO: The Rise and Fall of the Palestine Liberation Organization* (New York: St. Martin's Press, 1984), 75.

36. Abdallah Frangi, *The PLO and Palestine* (London: Zed Books, 1983), 111.

37. Alain Gresch, *The PLO: The Struggle within, toward an Independent Palestinian State* (London: Zed Books, 1985), 206.

38. *The Israel Administration in Judea, Samaria and Gaza* (Tel Aviv: Ministry of Defense, 1968), 5.

39. Tessler, *A History of the Israeli-Palestinian Conflict*, 503–5.

40. Rael Jean Isaac, *Party and Politics in Israel: Three Visions of a Jewish State* (New York: Longman, 1981), 156–58.

41. *Jerusalem Post*, April 15–May 5, 1982.

42. *The Karp Report: An Israeli Government Inquiry into Settler Violence against Palestinians on the West Bank* [English translation; original in Hebrew] (Washington, DC: Institute for Palestine Studies, 1984), 42.

43. M. Thomas Davis, *40 Km into Lebanon: Israel's 1982 Invasion* (Washington, DC: National Defense University Press, 1987), 68.

44. Ze'ev Schiff and Ehud Ya'ari, *Israel's Lebanon War* (New York: Simon & Schuster, 1984), 204–5; Tessler, *A History of the Israeli-Palestinian Conflict*, 582–84.

45. Tessler, *A History of the Israeli-Palestinian Conflict*, 576–77.

46. *Karp Report*.

47. Khalil Shikaki, "The Intifada and the Transformation of Palestinian Politics," *Universities Field Staff International Reports*, no. 18 (1989–1990): 3.

48. Emile A. Nakhleh, "The West Bank and Gaza: Twenty Years Later," *Middle East Journal* 42 (Spring 1988): 210.

49. Hirsh Goodman, "When Extremism Eclipses Reason," *The Jerusalem Post* (International Edition), October 24, 1987.

50. Tessler, "The Palestinian Uprising and the Israeli Response: Human Rights, Political and Security Dimensions," *Wisconsin International Law Journal* 8 (Spring 1990): 309.

51. Asher Wallfish, "The Perils of Talking to the Troops," *Jerusalem Post*, January 23, 1988.

52. *New York Times*, December 5, 1989.

53. *Jerusalem Post*, September 11, 1988.

54. Neri Livneh, "Border of Fear" [in Hebrew], *Hadashot,* September 29, 1989.

55. Victor Cygielman, "The Impact of Two Years of the Intifada," *New Outlook,* December 1989, 5.

56. *New York Times,* April 2, 1989.

57. Schiff, *Security for Peace: Israel's Minimal Security Requirements in Negotiations with the Palestinians* (Washington, DC: Washington Institute for Near East Policy, 1989), 2.

58. Naseer Aruri, *Honest Broker: The U.S. Role in Israel and Palestine* (Cambridge, MA: South End Press, 2003), 90.

59. Caryle Murphy and Nora Boustany, "When Former Enemies Turn Business Partners," *International Herald Tribune,* May 24, 1994.

60. Rashid Khalidi, *The Iron Cage: The Story of the Palestinian Struggle for Statehood* (Boston, MA: Beacon Press, 2006), 143.

61. Mark Tessler and Jodi Nachtwey, "Palestinian Political Attitudes: An Analysis of Survey Data from the West Bank and Gaza," *Israel Studies* 4 (Spring 1999): 22–43.

62. Tessler, *A History of the Israeli-Palestinian Conflict,* 805–7; Shimon Shamir and Bruce Maddy-Weitzman, eds., *The Camp David Summit: What Went Wrong?* (Brighton: Sussex Academic Press, 2005).

63. Ehud Barak, "The Myths Spread about Camp David Are Baseless," in *The Camp David Summit: What Went Wrong?* eds. Shimon Shamir and Bruce Maddy-Weitzman, 122–23.

64. Robert Malley, "American Mistakes and Israeli Miscon ceptions," in *The Camp David Summit: What Went Wrong?* eds. Shimon Shamir and Bruce Maddy-Weitzman, 108.

65. Ibid., 111.

66. Zeev Maoz, *Defending the Holy Land: A Critical Analysis of Israel's Security and Foreign Policy* (Ann Arbor: University of Michigan Press, 2006), 470.

67. *New York Times,* March 14, 2007.

68. Yaacov Bar-Siman-Tov, Ephraim Lavie, Kobi Micahel, and Daniel Bar-Tal, *The Israeli-Palestinian Violent Confrontation, 2000–2004: From Conflict Resolution to Conflict Management* (Jerusalem: Jerusalem Institute for Israel Studies, Teddy Kollek Center for Jerusalem Studies, 2005), 25–26.

69. *Christian Science Monitor,* March 29, 2005.

70. For a detailed discussion, see Bernard Avishai, "A Plan for Peace That Still Could Be," *The New York Times Magazine,* February 7, 2011.

71. For an insightful account based on close to one hundred interviews with Israeli, Palestinian, and American officials, as well as others, see Ben Birnbaum and Amir Tibon, "The Explosive, Inside Story of How John Kerry Built an Israel-Palestine Peace Plan—and Watched It Crumble," *New Republic,* July 20, 2014.

72. For critical reflections on BDS, see Cary Nelson, *Dreams Deferred: A Concise Guide to the Israeli-Palestinian Conflict and the Movement to Boycott Israel* (Bloomington: Indiana University Press, 2016).

73. These and many other nationally representative surveys were carried out by the Ramallah-based Palestinian Center for Policy and Survey Research.

74. Khalil Shikaki, "Can Hamas, and Does It Want to, 'Lead' the Palestinian People?" *Critical Policy Brief,* Palestinian Center for Policy and Survey Research, Number 5, 2021.

75. Emma Green, "Israel's New Law Inflames the Core Tension in Its Identity." *The Atlantic,* July 21, 2018.

CHAPTER 3

1. The author gratefully acknowledges constructive feedback from Mehrzad Boroujerdi, Mine Eder, Calvert Jones, Matthew Longo, Stephen N. Ndegwa, Sarah Phillips, and reviewers of previous editions.

2. Max Weber, "Politics as a Vocation," in *From Max Weber: Essays in Sociology*, trans. and ed. and with an introduction by H. H. Gerth and C. Wright Mills (New York: Oxford University Press, 1946), 78.

3. For a more nuanced discussion of sources of legitimacy in the Arab world, see Michael C. Hudson, *Arab Politics: The Search for Legitimacy* (New Haven, CT: Yale University Press, 1977).

4. Charles Tilly, *Coercion, Capital and European States: A.D. 990–1992* (Malden, MA: Blackwell, 1992), 1.

5. Joel Migdal, *Strong Societies and Weak States: State-Society Relations and State Capabilities in the Third World* (Princeton, NJ: Princeton University Press, 1988); see also the earlier classic by Gunnar Myrdal, *Asian Drama: An Inquiry into the Poverty of Nations* (Harmondsworth: Penguin Press, 1968).

6. For the definition of *failed states* that is used in the Failed States Index, see "FAQ & Methodology: How the Failed States Index Is Made," *Foreign Policy*, www.foreignpolicy.com/articles/2009/06/22/2009_failed_states_index_faq_methodology.

7. Figures from the Fund for Peace, Fragile States Index, https://fragilestatesindex.org (accessed October 31, 2021).

8. Lust, 2015.

9. UNHCR, "Syrian Regional Refugee Response," https://data2.unhcr.org/en/situations/syria/location/36 (accessed October 31, 2021). It is important to note that this does not include unregistered refugees, and thus likely undercounts the numbers of refugees in these countries.

10. Joe Macaron, "What Will the Taliban Takeover Mean for the Middle East?" https://www.aljazeera.com/opinions/2021/8/19/what-will-the-taliban-victory-mean-for-the-middle-east (accessed October 31, 2021).

11. For a review of these pressures on neighboring countries, see Ellen Lust, "Syrian Spillover: National Tensions, Domestic Responses and International Options," *POMED Policy Report* (April, 2015).

12. Ahmed Abdelkareem Saif, "Yemen: State Weakness and Society Alienation," al-Bab, n.d., www.al-bab.com/yemen/pol/saifstate.htm; see also Shelagh Weir, *A Tribal Order: Politics and Law in the Mountains of Yemen* (Austin: University of Texas Press, 2007).

13. The UN Office for the Coordination of Humanitarian Affairs, "About OCHA Yemen," https://www.unocha.org/yemen/about-ocha-yemen (accessed October 31, 2021).

14. In 2011, Syria's rating was 85.9, in the low warning range. See http://www.fundforpeace.org/global/library/cr-11-14-fs-failedstatesindex2011-1106p.pdf, 33.

15. For more detail, see "Doctors in the Crosshairs: Four Years of Attacks on Health Care in Syria," *Physicians for Human Rights*, March 2015, https://s3.amazonaws.com/PHR_Reports/doctors-in-the-crosshairs.pdf.

16. See Khedar Khaddour, "The Assad Regime's Hold on the Syrian State," *Carnegie Middle East Center Report*, Beirut: July 2015, http://carnegieendowment.org/files/syrian_state1.pdf.

17. Droz-Vincent, P, "Fighting for a Monopoly on Governance: How the Asad State," *The Middle East Journal* 75, no. 1 (2021): 33–54.

18. Klaus Schwab, "The Global Competitiveness Report 2017–2018," *World Economic Forum*, 178, http://www3.we forum.org/docs/GCR2017-2018/05 Full Report/The Global Competiti veness Report 2017–2018.pdf.

19. Sami Nader, "Lebanon: Private Education Soars, Public Education Sinks," *Al-Monitor*, February 26, 2013, http://www.al-monitor.com/pulse/originals/2014/05/lebanon-education-reform-private-public.html#.

20. World Bank, Lebanon Economic Monitor: Lebanon Sinking (To the Top Three). Spring 2021, http s://documents1.worldbank.org/curated/en/394741622469174252/pdf/Lebanon-Economic-Monitor-Lebanon-Sinking-to-the-Top-3.pdf (accessed October 31, 2021).

21. David Leonhardt and Sanam Yar, "Lebanon's Crisis," *The New York Times,* October 15, 2021, https://www.nytimes.com/2021/10/14/briefing/lebanon-financial-crisis-lira. html (accessed October 31, 2021).

22. Sonja Grimm, Nicolas Lemay-Hébert, and Olivier Nay, "'Fragile States': Introducing a Political Concept," *Third World Quarterly* 35, no. 2 (2014): 198. See also Olivier Nay, "Fragile and Failed States: Critical Perspectives on Conceptual Hybrids," *International Political Science Review* (2013): 1–16.

23. For a prime example, see the World Bank, *World Development Report 2011: Conflict, Security and Development*, www.scribd.com/doc/56133164/World- Development-Report-2011.

24. Thomas Hobbes, *Leviathan* (Oxford: Oxford University Press, 1998 [reissue]); Robert Nozick, *Anarchy, State, and Utopia* (New York: Basic Books, 1974).

25. Charles Tilly, "War Making and State Making as Organized Crime," in *Bringing the State Back In*, eds. P. Evans, D. Rueschemeyer, and T. Skocpol (Cambridge: Cambridge University Press, 1985), 169–91; Tilly, *Coercion, Capital and European States*; Mancur Olson, "Dictatorship, Democracy and Development," *American Political Science Review* 87 (September 1993): 567–76.

26. Benedict Anderson, *Imagined Communities: Reflections on the Origin and Spread of Nationalism* (New York: Verso, 1991).

27. Note that precolonial states existed and have had a lasting impact on the development of modern states; see Iliya Harik, "The Origins of the Arab State System," in *The Arab State*, ed. Giacomo Luciani (London: Routledge, 1990), 8–28.

28. Great Britain recognized Saudi Arabia as an independent state in 1927, but others did not do so until 1932.

29. Because elections allow citizens to influence policy by their control over leaders, they should result in lower inequality (Allan H. Meltzer and Scott F. Richards, "A Rational Theory of the Size of Government," *Journal of Political Economy* 89, no. 5 (1981): 914–27; Adam Przeworski, *The State and the Economy Under Capitalism* [Harwood Academic, 1990]), better provision of public goods (*The Logic of Political Survival*, eds. Bruce Bueno de Mesquita et al. [Massachusetts Institute of Technology, 2003]; David A. Lake and Matthew A Baum, "The Invisible Hand of Democracy: Political Control and the Provision of Public Services," *Comparative Political Studies* 34, no. 6 [August 2001]: 587–621), greater involvement in trade agreements (Edward D. Mansfield and Jack Snyder, "Incomplete Democratization and the Outbreak of Military Disputes," *International Studies Quarterly* 46, no. 4 [December 2002]: 529–49), and the avoidance of catastrophes such as famine (Amartya Sen, "Work and Rights," *International Labour Review* 139, no. 2 [2000]: 119–28).

30. Tarek Amara and Angus Mcdowall, "Tunisian President Moves to Cement One-Man Rule," *Reuters*, September 23, 2021, https://www.reuters.com/world/africa/tunisia-president-takes-new-powers-says-will-reform-system-2021-09-22/(accessed October 31, 2021).

31. Lisa Anderson, "Absolutism and the Resilience of Monarchy in the Middle East," *Political Science Quarterly* 106, no. 1 (Spring 1991): 1–15.

32. See Mohamed Madani, Driss Maghraoui, and Saloua Zerhouni, "The 2011 Constitution: A Critical Analysis," Stockholm: International Institute for Democracy and Electoral Assistance (IDEA), 2012, http://www.constitutionnet.org/files/the_2011_moroccan_constitution_english.pdf, p. 24.

33. Articles 34 and 36 of Jordan's constitution state that the king may dissolve the Chamber of Deputies and the Senate or relieve any individual senator of membership. Article 96 of Morocco's revised constitution allows the king to dissolve the government or one or both of the houses of parliament by royal decree. Similarly, Article 107 in the Kuwaiti constitution allows the amir to dissolve the National Assembly.

34. For divergent versions of the importance of religious legitimacy in Morocco specifically, see M. E. Combs-Schilling, *Sacred Performances: Islam, Sexuality, and Sacrifice* (New York: Columbia University Press, 1989); Combs-Schilling, "Family and Friend in a Moroccan Boom Town: The Segmentary Debate Reconsidered," *American Ethnologist* 12, no. 4 (1985): 659–75; and Henry Munson, *Islam and Revolution in the Middle East* (New Haven, CT: Yale University Press, 1988).

35. On Kuwait's National Assembly, see Jill Crystal, *Kuwait: The Transformation of an Oil State* (Boulder, CO: Westview Press, 1992).

36. Michael Herb, *All in the Family: Absolutism, Revolution, and Democracy in the Middle Eastern Monarchies* (Albany: State University of New York Press, 1999).

37. See Iris Glosemeyer, "Checks, Balances and Transformation in the Saudi Political System," in *Saudi Arabia in the Balance: Political Economy, Society, Foreign Affairs*, eds. Paul Aarts and Gerd Nonneman (New York: NYU Press, 2005), 219; Herb, Chapter 18 in this volume.

38. Alan Richards and John Waterbury, *A Political Economy of the Middle East* (Boulder, CO: Westview Press, 1996), 297–98.

39. Laurie Brand, "Al-Muhajirin w-al-Ansar: Hashe-mite Strategies for Managing Communal Identity in Jordan," in *International Dimensions of Ethnic Conflict in the Middle East*, ed. Leonard Binder (Gainesville: University Press of Florida, 1999).

40. Rex Brynen, Bahgat Korany, and Paul Noble, "Conclusion: Liberalization, Democratization and Arab Experiences," in *Political Liberalization and Democratization in the Arab World*, vol. 2, *Comparative Experiences*, eds. Brynen, Korany, and Noble (Boulder, CO: Lynne Rienner, 1995). It is interesting to note that Brynen, Korany, and Noble question whether family- based leaders in the Gulf shaykhdoms would also play such a role and promote political divisions. In the logic of this argument, they should.

41. Beatriz Magaloni and Ruth Kricheli, "Political Order and One-Party Rule," *Annual Review of Political Science* 13 (May 2010): 132.

42. Samuel Huntington, *Political Order in Changing Societies* (New Haven, CT: Yale University Press, 1968), 425.

43. Magaloni and Kricheli, "Political Order and One-Party Rule."

44. In Egypt before 2011, the oath for members elected to the assembly, including the president, stated:

I swear by Almighty God to uphold the Republican system with loyalty to respect the Constitution and the Law, to look after the interests of the People in full, and to safeguard the independence and territorial integrity of the motherland.

In prerevolutionary Tunisia, according to Article 42, the president took an oath indicating the supremacy of law: I swear by God Almighty to safeguard the national independence and the integrity of the territory, to respect the Constitution and the law, and to watch meticulously over the interests of the Nation.

45. For instance, under Mubarak, Articles 109 to 114 in the Egyptian constitution gave both the president and deputies in the People's Assembly the right to propose laws. Unlike the king, the president also cannot pass a law by decree. Furthermore, although the president can veto a law passed in the People's Assembly, the legislature can override the veto with a two-thirds majority. Under Mubarak, Article 85 of the Egyptian constitution provided for impeachment of the president with the approval of a two-thirds majority of assembly members. The Tunisian case was quite similar. For instance, Article 28 in the Tunisian constitution gives both the president and the legislature the right to initiate legislation, although priority was given to legislation initiated by the president.

46. Samuel Huntington, *Political Order in Changing Societies;* Geddes, *Paradigms and Sand Castles: Theory Building and Research Design in Comparative Politics* (Ann Arbor: University of Michigan Press, 2003); Beatriz Magaloni, "Credible Power-Sharing and the Longevity of Authoritarian Rule," *Comparative Political Studies* 41, nos. 4–5 (2008): 715–41; and Jason Brownlee, *Authoritarianism in an Age of Democratization* (Cambridge: Cambridge University Press, 2007).

47. Anne Meng, "Ruling Parties in Authoritarian Regimes: Rethinking Institutional Strengt," *British Journal of Political Science* 51, no. 2 (2021): 526–40. doi:10.1017/S0007123419000115.

48. For a review of this literature, see Magaloni and Kricheli, "Political Order and One-Party Rule," 13; for discussion of the role of parties, legislatures, and elections in the MENA specifically, see Michele Penner Angrist, *Party Building in the Modern Middle East* (Seattle: University of Washington Press, 2006); Lisa Blaydes, "Competition without Democracy: Elections and Distributive Politics in Mubarak's Egypt" (dissertation, Stanford University, 2009); Jason Brownlee, "Harbinger of Democracy: Competitive Elections before the End of Authoritarianism," in *Democratization by Elections: A New Mode of Transition,* ed. Staffan I. Lindberg (Baltimore, MD: Johns Hopkins University Press, 2009), 128–47; Jennifer Gandhi and Ellen Lust-Okar, "Elections under Authoritarianism," *Annual Review of Political Science* 12 (June 2009): 403–22; Ellen Lust-Okar, *Structuring Conflict in the Arab World: Incumbents, Opponents and Institutions* (Cambridge: Cambridge University Press, 2005); Ellen Lust-Okar, "Elections under Authoritarianism: Preliminary Lessons from Jordan," *Democratization* 13, no. 3 (June 2006): 456–71; Ellen Lust-Okar, "Legislative Elections in Hegemonic Authoritarian Regimes: Competitive Clientelism and Resistance to Democratization," in *Democratization by Elections,* ed. Staffan I. Lindberg, 226–45; Tarek Masoud, *Counting Islam: Religion, Class, and Elections in Egypt* (Cambridge: Cambridge University Press, June 2014); Samer Shehata, "Inside Egyptian Parliamentary Campaigns," in *Political Participation in the Middle East,* eds. Ellen Lust-Okar and S. Zerhouni (Boulder, CO: Lynne Rienner, 2008), 95–120; Gunes Murat Tezcur, "Intra-Elite Struggles in Iranian Elections," in *Political Participation in the Middle East,* eds. Ellen Lust-Okar and Elias Zerhouni, 51–74; Elias Zerhouni, "The Moroccan Parliament," in *Political Participation in the Middle East,* 217–39; and Elias Zerhouni, "Looking Forward," in *Political Participation in the Middle East,* 259–66.

49. See Bernhard Michael, Edgell Amanda, and Lindberg Sara, "Institutionalising Electoral Uncertainty and Authoritarian Regime Survival," *European Journal of Political Research* 59 (2020): 465–87. https://doi.org/10.1111/1475-6765.12355.

50. Barbara Geddes, Erica Frantz, and Joseph G. Wright, "Military Rule," *Annual Review of Political Science* 17, no. 1 (2014): 147–62.

51. Beatriz Magaloni, "Credible Power-Sharing and the Longevity of Authoritarian Rule," *Comparative Political Studies* 41, no. 4–5 (2008): 715–41.

52. Barbara Geddes, "The Consequences of Military Rule: Juntas Versus Strongmen," in *Oxford Research Encyclopedia of Politics* (2020).

53. Kim Noel Kardashian and Kroeger Alex M, "Regime and Leader Instability under Two Forms of Military Rule," *Comparative Political Studies* 51, no. 1 (2018): 3–37. See also Barbara Geddes, Erica Frantz, and Joseph G. Wright, "Military Rule," *Annual Review of Political Science* 17, no. 1 (2014): 147–62; and Barbara Geddes, The Consequences of Military Rule: Juntas versus Strongmen.

54. Dankwart Rustow, "Transitions to Democracy: Towards a Dynamic Model," *Comparative Politics* 2 (1970): 337–63.

55. For further discussion, see Lust-Okar, *Structuring Conflict in the Arab World*.

56. Joel Barkan, "Legislatures on the Rise?" *Journal of Democracy* 19, no. 2 (2008): 124–37.

57. M. Steven Fish, "Stronger Legislatures, Stronger Democracies," *Journal of Democracy* 17, no. 1 (2006): 5.

58. For example, in Iran only 83 of 275 parliamentarians returned in 1992, and fewer than 60 of 290 parliamentarians returned in 2000 (the newspaper *Kayhan*, cited in G. M. Tezcur, "Intra-Elite Struggles and Iranian Elections," in *Political Participation in the Middle East*, eds. Ellen Lust-Okar and Elias Zerhouni) and in Jordan, only 19 of the 110 members elected in 2003 returned from the 1997 parliament, and only 20 of the deputies who won in 1997 elections were returning from the 1993 parliament (Hani Hourani and Ayman Yassin, *Who's Who in the Jordanian Parliament: 2003–2007*, ed. Terri Lore, trans. Lola Keilani and Lana Habash [Amman, Jordan: Sindbad, 2004], 204). See also Kristen Kao finds that the highest percentage of returning MPs in the Jordanian parliaments between 1993 and 2013 occurred in 2007, when the percentage reached 26 percent [Kristen Kao, "Elections as Reliable Method of Redistribution," unpublished manuscript, 3].

59. Hassan Shehata, "Inside Egyptian Parliamentary Campaigns," in *Political Participation in the Middle East*, eds. Ellen Lust-Okar and Elias Zerhouni, 100–101.

60. A 2006 survey found that fewer than 60 percent of Algerians would take a direct route to relevant agencies of government for resolution of disputes, with over three-quarters of those asked believing there are more effective means. These sentiments are mirrored in Jordan by surveys conducted in 2000 and 2005 and supported by anecdotal evidence from Egypt, Iraq, Lebanon, Morocco, the Palestinian Authority, and Syria.

61. Michael Johnston, ed., *Political Parties and Democracy in Theoretical and Practical Perspectives* (Washington, DC: National Democratic Institute for International Affairs, 2005).

62. Giovanni Sartori, *Parties and Party Systems: A Framework for Analysis*, vol. 1 (Cambridge: Cambridge University Press, 1976).

63. See Ellen Lust and David Waldner, "Parties in Transitional Democracies: Authoritarian Legacies and Post-Authoritarian Challenges in the Middle East and North Africa," in *Parties, Movements and Democracy in the Developing World*, eds. Nancy Bermeo and Deborah Yashar (Cambridge: Cambridge University Press, 2016).

64. Ellen Lust-Okar, "The Management of Opposition: Formal Structures of Contestation and Informal Political Manipulation in Egypt, Jordan and Morocco," in *Arab Authoritarianism: Dynamics and Durability*, ed. Oliver Schlumberger (Stanford, CA: Stanford University Press, 2007), 39–58.

65. Thomas Carothers, "The Rule of Law Revival," *Foreign Affairs* 77, no. 2 (March/April 1998): 95–106.

66. Ghada Shahbandar, leader of the Egyptian electoral monitoring group, cited in Michael Slackman, "Melee in Cairo Reveals Stress in Government," *New York Times,* April 28, 2006, www.nytimes.com/2006/04/28/world/middleeast/28egypt.html.

67. For indices, see Daniel Kaufmann, Aart Kraay, and Massimo Mastruzzi, *The Worldwide Governance Indicators, 2012. Update: Aggregate Indicators of Governance 1996–2011* and World Justice Project, "Rule of Law Index, 2017–2018," http://data.worldjustice project.org/#table (accessed December 13, 2018).

68. F. Shen-Bayh, "Strategies of Repression: Judicial and Extrajudicial Methods of Autocratic Survival," *World Politics* 70, no. 3 (2018): 321–57.

69. World Population Review, "United Arab Emirates 2018," http://worldpopulationreview.com/countries/united-arab-emirates-population/ (accessed December 13, 2018).

70. Tamir Moustafa, "Law versus the State: The Judicialization of Politics in Egypt," *Law and Social Inquiry* 28, no. 4 (Fall 2003): 883–930; Mona El-Ghobashy, "Constitutionalist Contention in Contemporary Egypt," *American Behavioral Scientist* 51, no. 11 (July 2008): 1592.

71. Tamir Moustafa, *The Struggle for Constitutional Power: Law, Politics, and Economic Development in Egypt* (Cambridge: Cambridge University Press, 2007).

72. Marc Lynch, *State Interests and Public Spheres: The International Politics of Jordan's Identity* (New York: Columbia University Press, 1999).

73. For details, see Ellen Lust and Jakob Wichmann, "Three Myths about the Arab Up Risings," *Yale-Global*, July 24, 2012, http: //yale global. yale. edu / content / three-myths-about-arab-up risings.

74. For discussions of the role of the media in uprisings, see contributions in Khatib and Lust, eds., *Taking to the Streets*.

75. See classical modernization arguments (Seymour Martin Lipset, "Some Social Requisites of Democracy: Economic Development and Political Legitimacy," *American Political Science Review* 53, no. 1 [March 1959]: 69–105] as well as more recent reformulations (Przeworski, Alvarez, Cheibub, and Limongi, *Democracy and Development*) and rebuttals (Carles Boix and Susan C. Stokes, "Endogenous Democratization," *World Politics* 55, no. 4 (2003): 517–49).

76. Stephan Haggard and Robert Kaufman, *The Political Economy of Democratic Transitions* (Princeton, NJ: Princeton University Press, 1995).

77. Michael L. Ross, "Does Oil Hinder Democracy," *World Politics* 53, no. 3 (2001): 325–61; Rex Brynen, Pete W. Moore, Bassel F. Salloukh, and Marie-Joëlle Zahar eds., *Beyond the Arab Spring: Authoritarianism and Democratization in the Arab World* (Boulder, CO: Lynne Rienner, 2012), 194–98; Jill Crystal, *Oil and Politics in the Gulf* (Cambridge: Cambridge University Press, 1990); Kiren Chaudhry, *The Price of Wealth* (Ithaca, NY: Cornell University Press, 1997); Hazem Beblawi and Luciani, *Nation, State and Integration in the Arab World,* vol. 2, *The Rentier State* (New York: Croom Helm, 1987); Dirk Vandewalle, *Libya since Independence: Oil and State-Building* (Ithaca, NY: Cornell University Press, 1998); and Ross, "Does Oil Hinder Democracy?" *World Politics* 53, no. 3 (April 2001): 325–61.

78. Jason Brownlee, Tarek Masoud, and Andrew Reynolds, "Why the Modest Harvest?" *Journal of Democracy* 24, no. 4 (October 2013): 29–44; Jason Brownlee, Tarek Masoud, and Andrew Reynolds, *The Arab Spring: Pathways of Repression and Reform* (Oxford: Oxford University Press, 2015).

79. Patrick Geddes, "The Effect of Regime Type on Authoritarian Breakdown: Empirical Test of a Game Theoretic Argument." Paper presented at the American Political Science Association Annual Meeting, 1999. See also Geddes, Wright, and Frantz, *How Dictatorships Work: Power, Personalization and Collapse* (Cambridge: Cambridge University Press, 2018).

80. Jason Brownlee, *Authoritarianism in an Age of Democratization* (New York: Cambridge University Press, 2007).

81. Jennifer Gandhi and Adam Przeworski, "Authoritarian Institutions and the Survival of Autocrats," *Comparative Political Studies* 40, no. 11 (2007): 1279–301; Jennifer Gandhi, *Political Institutions under Dictatorship* (New York: Cambridge University Press, 2008); and Milan Svolik, *The Politics of Authoritarian Rule* (New York: Cambridge University Press, 2012).

82. Levitsky and Way argue that the durability derives from the development of cohesive ruling parties, the destruction of independent power centers, partisan control over security, and powerful coercive apparatuses. It should be noted that most, but not all, of their revolutionary cases are one-party states. Iran, for example, is an exception. See Steven Levitsky and Lucan Ahmad Way, "The Durability of Revolutionary Regimes," *Journal of Democracy* 24, no. 3 (July 2013): 5–17.

83. For the most compelling argument that dynastic monarchies are durable, see Michael Herb, *All in the Family* (Albany: SUNY Press, 1999). Analysis by Lachapelle, Levitsky, and Way (2015) also find that monarchies are resilient. (See Jean Lachapelle, Steven Levitsky, and Lucan A. Way, "The Durability of Revolutionary Regimes since 1990." Paper presented at the American Political Science Association Annual Meeting, San Francisco, CA, September 3–6, 2015.) Similar findings are reported in Barbara Geddes, Joseph Wright, and Erica Frantz, "Autocratic Breakdown and Regime Transitions: A New Dataset," *Perspectives on Politics* 12, no. 2 (June 2014): 313–31.

84. Some scholars view the relationship between regime age and stability differently. For instance, in the classic work *Political Order in Changing Societies* (New Haven, CT: Yale University Press, 1968), Huntington argued that older, more institutionalized parties were more likely to promote regime stability. More recently, and focusing specifically on the age of leaders, Bueno de Mesquita, Smith, Siverson, and Morrow suggest that regimes become less likely to break down the longer rulers are in office since they have time to obtain greater knowledge over preferences and retain only loyal followers (see *The Logic of Political Survival* [Cambridge: MIT Press, 2003]). While tenure in office may have this effect in the absence of significant threats to the regime, it may also create a narrow, ossified coalition unable to withstand significant pressures. This appears to have been the case for long-standing rulers of one-party regimes in the MENA.

85. Larbi Sadiki, *Like Father, Like Son: Dynastic Republicanism in the Middle East* (Washington, DC: Carnegie Endowment for International Peace, 2009), www.carnegieendowment.org/files/dynastic_republicanism.pdf.

86. For a more detailed discussion, see Ellen Lust, "Elections," in *The Arab Uprisings Explained*, ed. Marc Lynch (New York: Columbia University Press, 2014).

87. There is evidence that the resilience of monarchies holds up over time. See Victor Menaldo, "The Middle East and North Africa's Resilient Monarchs," *Journal of Politics* 74, no. 3 (July 2012): 702–22.

88. Michael Herb, "Monarchies and the Arab Spring." Paper presented at Arab Spring Exploratory Conference, Princeton University, May 5–6, 2012. See André Bank', Thomas Richter, and Anna Sunik reminding us that not all monarchies have dynastic rule and point to the importance of dynastic rule in maintaining five of the eight monarchies (e.g., Bahrain, Kuwait, Qatar, Saudi Arabia, and the United Arab Emirates; Bank', Richter, and Sunik, "Durable yet Different: Monarchies in the Arab Spring," *Journal of Arabian Studies* 4, no. 2 [2014]: 163–79). Brownlee, Masoud, and Reynolds (2014) take a more expansive approach, seeing dynasticism not only in the oil monarchies but also in republics. They argue that the problem in Tunisia and Yemen was not too much dynasty, but too little dynastic success, and they point to Asad's Syria as an example where successful dynastic transfer of power strengthened the regime. For reasons presented previously, I take issue with this view. However, the case of Syria does remind us that elites in the inner circle of both dynastic and minority- based regimes, as that which exists in Syria, may have strong incentives to remain loyal to the ruler.

89. Adria Lawrence, "Kings in a Democratic Age: Collective Protest and the Institutional Promise of Monarchy." Paper presented at the Middle East Studies Association Annual Meeting, November 2014. Zoltan Barany, "After the Arab Spring: Revolt and Resilience in the Arab Kingdoms," *Parameters: The U.S. Army War College Quarterly* 43, no. 2 (Summer 2013): 89–101. For a full discussion, see Marc Lynch, ed., *The Arab Monarchy Debate* (Washington, DC: Project on Middle East Political Science, December 19, 2012).

90. Russell Lucas, "Monarchies and Protests in the Arab Uprisings: Path Dependencies or Political Opportunities?" *Journal of Arabian Studies* 4, no. 2 (2014): 195–213; Menaldo, "The Middle East and North Africa's Resilient Monarchs."

91. Sean Yom and Gregory Gause III, "Resilient Royals: How Arab Monarchies Hang On," *Journal of Democracy* 23, no. 4 (October 2012): 74–88.

92. Eva Bellin, "Reconsidering the Robustness of Authoritarianism in the Middle East: Lessons from the Arab Spring," *Comparative Politics* (January 2012): 127–49.

93. For detailed discussions of how such organizations contested authoritarian regimes in the lead-up to the 2011 uprisings, see Lina Khatib and Ellen Lust eds., *Taking to the Streets: Activism and the Arab Uprisings* (Baltimore, MD: Johns Hopkins University Press, 2014).

94. Madawi Al-Rasheed, *Contesting the Saudi State: Islamic Voices from a New Generation* (Cambridge: Cambridge University Press, 2006).

95. Guillermo O'Donnell, Philippe Schmitter, and Laurence Whitehead, eds., *Transitions from Authoritarian Rule: Comparative Perspectives* (Baltimore, MD: Johns Hopkins University Press, 1986); Juan Linz and Alfred Stepan, *Problems of Democratic Transition and Consolidation: Southern Europe, South America and Post-Communist Europe* (Baltimore, MD: Johns Hopkins University Press, 1996).

96. Doug McAdam, John D. McCarthy, and Mayer N. Zald, eds., *Comparative Perspectives on Social Movements: Political Opportunities, Mobilizing Structures, and Cultural Framings* (Cambridge: Cambridge University Press, 1996); Sidney Tarrow, *Power in Movement: Social Movements and Contentious Politics* (Cambridge: Cambridge University Press, 1998); Jillian Schwedler, "Islamic Identity: Myth, Menace, or Mobilizer?" *SAIS Review* 21, no. 2 (2001): 1–17; Quintan Wiktorowicz, ed., *Islamic Activism: A Social Movement Theory Approach* (Bloomington: Indiana University Press, 2004); and Schwedler, *Faith in Moderation: Islamist Parties in Jordan and Yemen* (Cambridge: Cambridge University Press, 2006).

97. Stephan Haggard and Robert Kaufman, "The Political Economy of Democratic Transitions," *Comparative Politics* 29, no. 3 (April 1997): 263–83; Noura Hamladj, "Do Political Dynamics Travel? Political Liberalization in the Arab World" (working paper, European University Institute, 2002).

98. The extent to which these regimes are aptly described as "secularist" is debatable, and it became even more questionable as the regimes sought to counter Islamist opposition by establishing their own religious legitimacy. Thus, even avowedly secularist, socialist regimes such as those in Egypt and Syria increasingly have used religious rhetoric and promoted conservative Islamic leaders who seek social, although not political, change. For more detail on this argument, see Michael Herb, "Islamist Movements and the Problem of Democracy in the Arab World". Paper presented at the American Political Science Association annual meeting, September 1–4, 2005; and Ellen Lust, "Missing the Third Wave: Islam, Institutions and Democracy in the Middle East," *Studies in Comparative International Development* 46, no. 2 (June 2011): 163–90.

99. Ellen Lust, "Why Now? Micro-Transitions and the Arab Uprisings," *Comparative Politics-Democratization Newsletter* (Fall 2011), www.ned.org/apsa-cd/APSA-CDOctober2011.pdf; Janine A. Clark, "The Conditions of Islamist Moderation: Unpacking Cross-Ideological Cooper-ation in Jordan," *International Journal of Middle East Studies* 38 (2006): 539–60; and, more generally, Hendrik Kraetzschmar, "Mapping Opposition Cooperation in the Arab World: From Single-Issue Coalitions to Transnational Protest Networks," *British Journal of Middle East Studies* 38, no. 3 (2011): 287–302; Eva Wegner and Miguel Pellicar, "Left-Islamist Opposition Cooperation in Morocco," *British Journal of Middle East Studies* 38, no. 3 (2011): 303–22.

100. Mahmoud Soueid and Shaykh Muhammad Hussayn Fadlallah, "Islamic Unity and Political Change: Interview with Shaykh Muhammad Hussayn Fadlallah," *Journal of Palestine Studies* 25, no. 1 (1995): 62.

101. Amaney Jamal, *Of Empires and Citizens: Pro-American Democracy or No Democracy at All?* (Princeton, NJ: Princeton University Press, 2012).

102. Sarah Sunn Bush, *The Taming of Democracy Assistance* (Cambridge: Cambridge University Press, 2015).

103. See David Patel and Valerie Bunce, "Turning Points and the Cross-National Diffusion of Popular Protest," in *Comparative Democratization Newsletter* (January 2012), www.ssrc.org/work space/images/crm/new_ publication_3/%7Ba116de05-8659-e111-b2a8-001cc477ec 84%7D.pdf; and Mark Beissinger, "Structure and Example in Modular Political Phenomena: The Diffusion of the Bulldozer/Rose/Orange/Tulip Revolutions," *Perspectives on Politics* 5, no. 2 (June 2007): 259–76.

104. For more detailed overviews of this literature, see Eva Bellin, "The Robustness of Authoritarianism in the Middle East: A Comparative Perspective," *Comparative Politics* 36, no. 2 (January 2004): 139–57; David Brumberg and M. Plattner Diamond, "Introduction," in *Islam and Democracy in the Middle East,* eds. M. Plattner Diamond and David Brumberg (Baltimore, MD: Johns Hopkins University Press, 2003), xiii; Marsha Pripstein Posusney, "The Middle East's Democracy Deficit in Comparative Perspective," in *Authoritarianism in the Middle East: Regimes and Resistance,* eds. Pripstein Posusney and Michele Penner Angrist (Boulder, CO: Lynne Rienner, 2005). Not all literature focused on stability, however, or saw it as inevitable. For a discussion of this literature in hindsight, and whether it shapes our current studies, see the debate in *Perspectives on Politics,* including Marc Morje Howard and Meir R. Walters, "Explaining the Unexpected: Political Science and the Surprise of 1989 and 2011," *Perspectives on Politics* 12, no. 2 (2014): 394–408; Eva Bellin, "Response to Howard and Walters," *Perspectives on Politics* 12, no. 3 (2014): 409–12; Ellen Lust, "Response to Howard and Walters," *Perspectives on Politics* 12, no. 3 (2014): 413–14; Marc Lynch, "Response to Howard and Walters," *Perspectives on Politics* 12, no. 3 (2014): 415–16; and Marc Morjé Howard and Meir R. Walters, "Response to Eva Bellin, Ellen Lust, and Marc Lynch" (with Meir R. Walters), *Perspectives on Politics* 12, no. 2 (2014): 417–19.

105. See note 81.

106. See, for instance, Adam Przeworski, Michael Alvarez, José Cheibub, and Fernando Limongi, *Democracy and Development: Political Institutions and Material Well-Being in the World* (Cambridge: Cambridge University Press, 2000) and compare with Carles Boix and Susan Stokes, "Endogenous Democratization," *World Politics* 55, no. 4 (2003): 517–49.

107. See, for example, Michael Ross, "Does Oil Hinder Democracy?" *World Politics* 53, no. 3 (April 2001): 325–61.

108. See http://www.reuters.com/article/2015/02/14/us-libya-security-idUSKBN0LI0KP20150 214. https://www.reuters.com/article/us-libya-security-oil-idUSKBN1JA23I.

109. Even Ross, in "Does Oil Hinder Democracy?" finds that when oil, Islam, and a dummy variable for the Middle East are included in the same analysis of democratization, the dummy variable for the Middle East remains highly significant. In contrast, using a more nuanced analysis of rents, Herb (in "No Representation without Taxation? Rents, Development and Democracy," *Comparative Politics* 37, no. 3 [2005]: 297–316) finds that oil rents do not "hinder democracy." The presence of oil does not fully explain the persistence of MENA authoritarianism. Furthermore, oil rents do not account for the persistence of authoritarianism in the oil-poor states in the MENA. Many of the nonrentier states are as wealthy as, or wealthier than, states in sub-Saharan Africa and parts of Asia that have seen much more significant liberalization. Finally, scholars increasingly argue that we need to examine oil factors such as the nature of sociopolitical relations and institutions, regional conflict and rents, and different types of rents to better understand authoritarian durability and rents. See Brynen et al., eds., *Beyond the Arab Spring*, 198–208.

110. Benjamin Smith and David Waldner, *Rethinking the Resource Curse* (Cambridge: Cambridge University Press, 2021).

111. Samuel Huntington, "Will More Countries Become Democratic?" *Political Science Quarterly* 99, no. 2 (Summer 1984): 208.

112. For a similar critique, see Robert W. Hefner, *Civil Islam: Muslims and Democratization in Indonesia* (Princeton, NJ: Princeton University Press, 2000), 7–10.

113. In his inaugural address, Abu Bakr is reported to have said, "Now, it is beyond doubt that I have been elected your Amir, although I am not better than you. Help me, if I am in the right; set me right if I am in the wrong. Truth is a trust; falsehood is a treason. The weak among you will be strong with me till, God willing, his rights have been vindicated; and the strong among you shall be weak with me till, if the Lord wills, I have taken what is due from him. Obey me as long as I obey Allah and His Prophet; when I disobey Him and His Prophet, then obey me not. And now rise for prayers; may God have mercy on you."

114. Mark Tessler concludes: "There is little evidence, at least at the individual level of analysis, to support the claims of those who assert that Islam and democracy are incompatible." Tessler, "Do Islamic Orientations Influence Attitudes toward Democracy in the Arab World? Evidence from Egypt, Jordan, Morocco, and Algeria," *International Journal of Comparative Sociology* 43, no. 3 (2002): 229–49; see also Tessler, "Religion, Religiosity and the Place of Islam in Political Life: Insights from the Arab Barometer Surveys," *Journal of Middle East Law and Governance* 2, no. 2 (August 2010): 1–32.

115. Alfred Stepan, "Tunisia's Transition and the Twin Tolerations," *Journal of Democracy* 23, no. 3 (April 2012): 89–103.

116. In Egypt after 2011, 44 percent preferred a civil democratic state, 46 percent preferred an Islamic democratic state, and 10 percent preferred a strong state, even if it was not democratic. Four surveys carried out by the Al-Ahram Center for Political and Strategic Studies from December 17–27, October 10–26, September 11–21, and August 5–17, with representative samples each between six hundred and one thousand respondents of Egyptian nationality above eighteen years of age. See also Lust and David Waldner, "Parties, Polarization and Democratic Development in the Middle East."

117. J. Doces and B. Nega, "Democracy in Sub-Saharan Africa: Is There a Neighborhood Effect?" *Perspectives on Global Development and Technology* 12, no. 5–6 (2013): 639–60, doi:10.1163/15691497-12341280.

118. Lisa Blaydes and Eric Chaney, "The Feudal Revolution and Europe's Rise: Political Divergence of the Christian West and the Muslim World Before 1500 CE," *American Political Science Review* 107, no. 1 (2013): 16–34.

119. Bo Rothstein and Rasmus Broms, "Governing Religion: The Long-Term Effects of Sacred Financing," *Journal of Institutional Economics 9*, no. 4 (2013): 469–90. See also Rasmus Broms and Bo Rothstein, "Religion and Institutional Quality: Long-term Effects of the Financial Systems in Protestantism and Islam," *Comparative Politics* 52, no. 3 (2020): 433–54.

120. Jacob Gerner Hariri, "A Contribution to the Understanding of Middle Eastern and Muslim exceptionalism," *Journal of Politics* 77, no. 2 (2015): 477–90.

CHAPTER 4

1. Most scholars avoid using the word *fundamentalist* to describe those we are calling Islamists who wish to use Islam for social and political purposes. Islamists do not necessarily adhere to more literal interpretations of the Qur'an; nor do they have a monopoly on the "fundamentals" of the religion.

2. Pew Research Center, "The Countries with the 10 Largest Christian Populations and the 10 Largest Muslim Populations," April 1, 2019

3. Pew Research Center, "*Global Religious Diversity*," April 13, 2014. 7

4. Pew Research Center, "*Mapping the Global Muslim Population: A Report on the Size and Distribution of the World's Muslim Population*," October 7, 2009, 8–11.

5. Department of State, International Religious Freedom Report, 2020.

6. World Population Review, 2021.

7. Department of State, International Religious Freedom Report, 2020.

8. Paul A. Marshall, *Religious Freedom in the World* (Lanham, MD: Rowman & Littlefield, 2007).

9. Pew Research Center, "Why Muslims Are the World's Fastest-Growing Religious Group," April 6, 2017.

10. See http://www.pewresearch.org/fact-tank/2014/05/19/middle-easts-christian-population-in-flux-as-pope-francis-visits-holy-land/.

11. The question and proposed responses seem confusing. To the question "How frequently do you perform the five prescribed prayers of Islam?" the proposed responses were "five times a day," "every day," or "one to two times a week," for example. One can imagine that some respondents thought that "every day" meant praying five times in a day. Those doing the survey probably hoped that such respondents would have replied "five times a day." An anonymous reviewer of this chapter points out that the question may not work well among Shi'a, who are permitted to combine prayers under certain circumstances.

12. World Values Survey, Four-Wave Aggregate of the Data Studies, variables F066 and F190 (Iran, 2000; Iraq, 2004; Turkey, 2001; United States, 1982, 1990, 1999), online analysis.

13. Look at Iranian figures for frequency of Muslim prayers.

14. Pew Research Center, "Israel's Religiously Divided Society," March 2016.

15. See Charles S. Liebman and Elihu Katz, eds., *The Jewishness of Israelis: Responses to the Guttman Report* (Albany: State University of New York Press, 1997). See also Robert D. Lee, *Religion and Politics in the Middle East* (Boulder, CO: Westview Press, 2009), chap. 4.

16. World Values Survey, collected data 1982–2002, online analysis.

17. Pew Research Center, "The World's Muslims: Religion, Politics, and Society," April 2013, 9, 12.

18. World Values Survey, collected data 2006–2008, online analysis.

19. World Values Survey, 1990–2004, online analysis. Percentage mentioning "people of another religion": Algeria, 32.1; Iran, 20.1; Iraq, 34.8; Jordan, 32.5; Morocco, 33.8; Saudi Arabia, 40.4; Turkey, 35.1.

20. Abu Dhabi Gallup Center, "Progress and Tradition in the Gulf Cooperation Council States," May 2011, 47.

21. Mark Tessler, *Islam and Politics in the Middle East: Explaining the Views of Ordinary Citizens* (Bloomington: Indiana University Press, 2015), 69–70.

22. Ibid., 111.

23. Jonathan Fox, *A World Survey of Religion and the State* (Cambridge: Cambridge University Press, 2008), 47.

24. See Fred M. Donner, *Muhammad and the Believers: At the Origins of Islam* (Cambridge, MA: Harvard University Press, 2010).

25. Mark Tessler, "Popular Views about Islam and Politics in the Arab World," *II Journal,* University of Michigan (Fall 2011), http://quod.lib.umich.edu/i/iij/11645653.0001.101/--popular-views-about-islam- and-politics-in-the-arab-world?rgn=main;view=fulltext. Survey data are based on interviews in eight Arab countries. See the Arab Barometer Project.

26. See Fariba Adelkhah and François Georgeon, eds., *Ramadan et politique* (Paris: CNRS Editions, 2000).

27. John L. Esposito, *Political Islam* (Syracuse, NY: Syracuse University Press, 1998), 138.

28. Janine A. Clark, *Islam, Charity, and Activism: Middle-Class Networks and Social Welfare in Egypt, Jordan, and Yemen* (Bloomington: Indiana University Press, 2003), 12.

29. Sara Roy, "Hamas and the Transformation(s) of Political Islam in Palestine," *Current History* (January 2003): 16.

30. Khaled Hroub, *Hamas: A Beginner's Guide* (New York: Pluto Press, 2010), 69.

31. Sara Roy, *Hamas and Civil Society in Gaza: Engaging the Islamist Social Sector* (Princeton, NJ: Princeton University Press, 2011).

32. Clark, *Islam, Charity, and Activism.*

33. See Pieternella Van Doorn-Harder, "Copts: Fully Egyptian, but for a Tattoo?" and Charles D. Smith, "The Egyptian Copts: Nationalism, Ethnicity, and Definition of Identity for a Religious Minority," in *Nationalism and Minority Identities in Islamic Societies,* ed. Maya Shatzmiller (Montreal, QC: McGill-Queen's University Press, 2005).

34. "Islamist Social Services," *POMEPS Studies* 9 (2014).

35. Charles Kurtzman and Ijlal Naqvi, "Do Muslims Vote Islamic?" *The Journal of Democracy* (April 2010): 50.

36. Vickie Langhor, "Of Islamists and Ballot Boxes: Rethinking the Relationship between Islamists and Electoral Politics," *International Journal of Middle East Studies* 33 (2001): 591.

37. Ellen Lust, "Missing the Third Wave: Islam, Institutions, and Democracy in the Middle East," *Studies in Comparative International Development* 46 (2011): 163–90.

38. For a review of the literature on Islamic moderation through participation, see Langhor, "Of Islamists and Ballot Boxes," and Jillian Schwedler, "Can Islamists Become Moderates? Rethinking the Inclusion-Moderation Hypothesis," *World Politics* 63, no. 2 (2011): 347–76.

39. Jillian Schwedler, "Democratization, Inclusion and the Moderation of Islamist Parties," *Development* 50, no. 1 (2007): 59.

40. Stacey Patrick Yadav, "Understanding What Islamists Want: Public Debate and Contestation in Lebanon and Yemen," *The Middle East Journal* 64, no. 2 (2010): 199–213.

41. Cary Rosefsky Wickham, "The Path to Moderation: Strategy and Learning in the Formation of Egypt's Wasat Party," *Comparative Politics* (2004): 205–28; and Janine Clark, "The Conditions of Islamist Moderation: Unpacking Cross-Ideological Cooperation in Jordan," *International Journal of Middle East Studies* 38, no. 4 (November 2006): 539–60.

42. Janine A. Clark and Jillian Schwedler, "Who Opened the Window? Women's Activism in Islamist Parties," *Comparative Politics* (2003): 293–312; Mona El-Ghobashy, "The Metamorphosis of the Egyptian Muslim Brothers," *International Journal of Middle East Studies* 37, no. 3 (2005): 373–95; and Anthony Shadid, *Legacy of the Prophet: Despots, Democrats, and the New Politics of Islam* (New York: Basic Books, 2002).

43. Berna Turam, *Between Islam and the State: The Politics of Engagement* (Stanford, CA: Stanford University Press, 2007); Jason Brownlee, "Unrequited Moderation: Credible Commitments and State Repression in Egypt," *Studies in Comparative International Development (SCID)* 45, no. 4 (2010): 468–89; and Eva Wegner and Miquel Pellicer, "Islamist Moderation without Democratization: The Coming of Age of the Moroccan Party of Justice and Development?" *Democratization* 16, no. 1 (2009): 157–75.

44. Gunes Murat Tezcür, "The Moderation Theory Revisited," *Party Politics* 16, no. 1 (2010): 69–88.

45. Lust, "Missing the Third Wave."

46. Kurtzman and Naqvi, "Do Muslims Vote Islamic?" 51.

47. Charles Kurtzman, "Votes versus Rights: The Debate That's Shaping the Outcome of the Arab Spring," *Foreign Policy* (February 10, 2012).

48. Ibid.

49. Gilles Kepel, *The Prophet and Pharaoh: Muslim Extremism in Egypt* (London: Al Saqi Books, 1985); Olivier Roy, *The Failure of Political Islam* (Cambridge, MA: Harvard University Press, 1996); and Sivan Mishal and A. Sela, *The Palestinian Hamas: Vision, Violence, and Coexistence* (New York: Columbia University Press, 2006).

50. Tarek Masoud, *Counting Islam: Religion, Class, and Elections in Egypt* (Cambridge: Cambridge University Press, 2014).

51. Janine A. Clark, *Islam, Charity, and Activism: Middle-Class Networks and Social Welfare in Egypt, Jordan, and Yemen* (Bloomington: Indiana University Press, 2003).

52. Lust, "Missing the Third Wave," 163–90.

53. Mohammed M. Hafez and Quintan Wiktorowicz, "Violence as Contention in the Egyptian Islamic Movement," in *Islamic Activism: A Social Movement Theory Approach*, ed. Quintan Wiktorowicz (Bloomington: Indiana University Press, 2003).

54. Ibid.

55. Omar Ashour, *The De-Radicalization of the Jihadists: Transforming Armed Islamist Movements* (New York: Routledge, 2009).

56. Mohammed M. Hafez, "From Marginalization to Massacres: A Political Process Explanation of GIA Violence in Algeria," in *Islamic Activism: A Social Movement Theory Approach*, ed. Quintan Wiktorowicz (Bloomington: Indiana University Press, 2003), 46.

57. Ibid.

58. Ashour, *The De-Radicalization of the Jihadists*.

59. Full text, www.pbs.org/newshour/terrorism/international/fatwa_1998.html.

60. Mohammed Ayoob, *The Many Faces of Political Islam: Religion and Politics in the Muslim World* (Ann Arbor: University of Michigan Press, 2008), 149.

61. "Al-Qaeda Disavows ISIS Militants in Syria," BBC (February 3, 2014), http://www.bbc.com/news/world-middle-east-26016318.

62. For recent literature on ISIS, see Michael Weiss and Hassan Hassan, *ISIS: Inside the Army of Terror*, Simon & Schuster, 2015; Jessica Stern and John M. Berger, *ISIS: The State of Terror*, HarperCollins, 2015.

63. See www.oic-oci.org.

64. For example, see Pippa Norris and Ronald Inglehart, *Sacred and Secular: Religion and Politics Worldwide* (Cambridge: Cambridge University Press, 2004).

CHAPTER 5

1. The author would like to thank Gibran Okar for his help in the researching and editing of this chapter. This chapter draws from the previous edition, authored by Janine A. Clark and Lina Al-Khatib.

2. Some countries, like Syria, continue to have a one-party system, while Saudi Arabia, Qatar, Kuwait, Oman, Bahrain, and the U.A.E. ban parties altogether.

3. Holger Albrecht and Oliver Schlumberger, "'Waiting for Godot': Regime Change without Democratization in the Middle East," *International Political Science Review* 25, no. 4 (2004): 371–92.

4. Jennifer Gandhi and Ellen Lust-Okar, "Elections under Authoritarianism," *Annual Review of Political Science* 12 (June 2009): 403–22. See also Lisa Blaydes, *Elections and Distributive Politics in Mubarak's Egypt* (Stanford, CA: Stanford University Press, 2011); and Marsha Pripstein Posusney, "The Middle East's Democracy Deficit in Comparative Perspective," in *Authoritarianism in the Middle East: Regimes and Resistance*, eds. Pripstein Posusney and Michele Penner Angrist (Boulder, CO: Lynne Rienner, 2005): 1–20.

5. Jillian Schwedler, *Faith in Moderation: Islamist Parties in Jordan and Yemen* (Cambridge: Cambridge University Press, 2006).

6. Ellen Lust-Okar and Amaney Jamal, "Rulers and Rules: Reassessing Electoral Laws and Political Liberalization in the Middle East," *Comparative Political Studies* 35, no. 3 (2002): 337–70; Ellen Lust-Okar, *Structuring Conflict in the MENA: Incumbents, Opponents and Institutions* (Cambridge: Cambridge University Press, 2005); and H. Albrecht, "How Can Opposition Support Authoritarianism? Lessons from Egypt," *Democratization* 12, no. 3 (2005): 378–97.

7. Ellen Lust-Okar, "Competitive Clientelism in the Middle East," *Journal of Democracy* 20, no. 3 (2009): 122–35. See also Ellen Lust-Okar, "The Decline of Jordanian Political Parties," *International Journal of Middle East Studies* 33, no. 4 (2001): 545–69.

8. Given that the AB Wave V (2018-19) asked respondents about voting in the last elections, data extracted from IDEA corresponds to the last parliamentary elections held before (2018-19) to allow for the comparison. Some countries had more recent parliamentary elections, for which the VAP turnout is shown in Table 5.1 below.

9. I. McAllister and S. Quinlan, "Vote over Reporting in National Election Surveys: A 55-nation Exploratory Study," *Acta Polit* (2021).

10. Ellen Lust and David Waldner, "Parties in Transitional Democracies: Authoritarian Legacies and Post-Authoritarian Challenges," in *Parties, Movements and Democracy in the Developing World*, eds. Nancy Bermeo and Deborah Yashar (New York: Cambridge University Press, 2016).

11. Survey questions from Arab Barometer Wave V: *"What is the most important challenge facing [Country] today?"*... AND *"If first challenge is mentioned, what is the second important challenge facing [Country] today?"*

12. For example, see: Ernest Geller, *Conditions of Liberty: Civil Society and Its Rivals* (New York: Penguin Books, 1996); Bernard Lewis, *What Went Wrong? The Clash Between Islam and Modernity in the Middle East* (New York: Harper Perennial, 2003); and Hisham Sharabi, *Neopatriarchy: A Theory of Distorted Change in Arab Society* (New York: Oxford University Press, 1988).

13. Samuel Freije-Rodriguez and Michael Woolcock, "Reversals of Fortune," *World Bank, Poverty and Shared Prosperity Report 2020* (2020).

14. Source: PovcalNet (http://iresearch.worldbank.org/PovcalNet/), World Bank.

15. Ibid.

16. Survey question from Arab Barometer Wave V (2018-19): *"A democratic system may have its problems, yet it is better than other* systems." % of respondents answering "I strongly agree" or "I agree," by country, in descending order: Jordan - 85.1%; Lebanon - 83.1%; Tunisia - 78.7%; Iraq - 75.8%; Palestine - 74.7%; Libya - 74.3%; Sudan - 70.5%; Egypt - 70%; Algeria - 69.3%; Morocco - 63.7%; Kuwait - 62.9%; Yemen - 51.8%. *Used with permission.*

17. Larry Diamond, "Toward Democratic Consolidation," in *The Global Resurgence of Democracy*, 2nd ed., eds. Larry Diamond and Marc Plattner (Baltimore, MD: Johns Hopkins University Press, 1996): 227–40.

18. Alexis de Tocqueville, *Democracy in America*, ed. and abr. by Richard D. Heffner (New York: New American Library, 1956): 200.

19. Robert Putnam with Robert Leonardi and Rafaella Y. Nanetti, *Making Democracy Work: Civic Traditions in Modern Italy* (Princeton, NJ: Princeton University Press, 1993): 176.

20. See Amaney Jamal, *Barriers to Democracy: The Other Side of Social Capital in Palestine and the MENA* (Princeton, NJ: Princeton University Press, 2007).

21. Robert Huckfeldt, Eric Plutzer, and Jon Sprague, "Alternative Contexts of Political Behavior: Churches, Neighborhoods, and Individuals," *Journal of Politics* 55, no. 2 (May 1993): 365–81; Steven J. Rosenstone and John Mark Hansen, *Mobilization, Participation, and Democracy in America* (New York: Macmillan, 1993); and Sidney Verba, Norman H. Nie, and Jae-on Kim, *Participation and Political Equality: A Seven-Nation Comparison* (New York: Cambridge University Press, 1978).

22. See, for example, Samuel Huntington, *The Third Wave: Democratization in the Late Twentieth Century* (Norman: University of Oklahoma Press, 1993); Adam Przeworski, *Democracy and the Market: Political and Economic Reforms in Eastern Europe and Latin America* (Cambridge: Cambridge University Press, 1991); and Peter Evans, "The Eclipse of the State? Reflections on Stateness in an Era of Globalization," *World Politics* 50, no. 1 (1997): 62–87.

23. Saad Eddin Ibrahim, "Liberalization and Democratization in the MENA: An Overview," in *Political Liberalization and Democratization in the MENA, Volume 1: Theoretical Perspectives*, eds. Rex Brynen, Bahgat Korany, and Paul Noble (Boulder, CO: Lynne Rienner, 1998): 29–60.

24. Janine Clark, *Islam Charity and Activism: Middle-Class Networks and Social Welfare in Egypt, Jordan, and Yemen* (Bloomington: Indiana University Press, 2004): 1-236; Maha M. Abdelrahman, *Civil Society Exposed: The Politics of NGOs in Egypt* (London: I.B. Tauris, New York: St. Martins/Macmillan: The American University in Cairo Press, 2004).

25. Alexandre Lamy, Halima El-Glaoui, and Xerxes Spencer, "Contributing to a Culture of Debate in Morocco," *Journal of Democracy* 10, no. 1 (January 1999): 157–65; Azzedine Layachi, *State, Society and Democracy in Morocco: The Limits of Associative Life* (Washington, DC: Center for Contemporary ARAB Studies, Georgetown University, 1998).

26. Melani Cammett and Pauline Jones Luong, "Is There an Islamist Political Advantage?" *Annual Review of Political Science* 17 (Palo Alto, CA: Annual Reviews, 2014): 187-206.

27. Rex Brynen, "The Politics of Monarchical Liberalism: Jordan," in *Political Liberalization and Democratization in the MENA* 2, eds. Rex Brynen, Bahgat Korany, and Paul Noble (Boulder, CO: Lynne Rienner, 1998): 71–100; Carrie Rosefsky Wickham, *Mobilizing Islam: Religion, Activism, and Political Change in Egypt* (New York: Columbia University Press, 2002).

28. Sidney Tarrow, "Social Movements in Contentious Politics: A Review Article," *The American Political Science Review* 90, no. 4 (December 1996): 874-883.

29. Ibid., 881.

30. Doug McAdam, Sidney G. Tarrow, and Charles Tilly, *Dynamics of Contention*, Cambridge Studies in Contentious Politics (Cambridge: Cambridge University Press, 2001).

31. Rabab El-Mahdi, "Enough!: Egypt's Quest for Democracy," *Comparative Political Studies* 42, no. 8 (August 2009): 1011–39.

32. Laryssa Chomiak, "The Making of a Revolution in Tunisia," *Middle East Law and Governance* 3, no. 1 (2011): 68–83.

33. Janine A. Clark and Lina Khatib, "Actors, Public Opinion, and Participation," in *The Middle East*, ed. Ellen Lust (Thousand Oaks, CA: SAGE/CQ Press, 2016): 273.

34. Seçkin Sertdemir Özdemir, "The Gezi Park Protests as a Pluralistic 'Anti-Violent' Movement," *The Pluralist* 10, no. 3 (Fall 2015): 247–60.

35. Carol McClurg Mueller, "Conflict Networks and the Origins of Women's Movements," in *New Social Movements*, eds. Enrique Larana, Hank Johnston, and Joseph R. Gusfield (Philadelphia, PA: Temple University Press, 1994): 234–63.

36. Repertoires of contention are the established ways in which pairs of actors make and receive claims bearing on each other's interests" in, Charles Tilly, "Contentious Repertoires in Great Britain, 1758-1834," in *Social Science History* 17, no. 2 (Cambridge: Cambridge University Press, Summer, 1993): 265.

37. On the use of symbolism in social movements, see Alberto Melucci, *Nomads of the Present: Social Movements and Individual Needs in Contemporary Society* (Philadelphia, PA: Temple University Press, 1989).

38. Donatella della Porta, *Where Did the Revolution Go?: Contentious Politics and the Quality of Democracy*, Cambridge Studies in Contentious Politics (Cambridge: Cambridge University Press, 2016).

39. Martha Crenshaw, "The Causes of Terrorism," *Comparative Politics* 13, no. 4 (July, 1981): 379–99.

40. Ibid.

41. See, for example: Randall Collins, *Violence: A Micro-sociological Theory* (Princeton, NJ: Princeton University Press, 2008); Stathis Kalyvas, "The Ontology of 'Political Violence': Action and Identity in Civil Wars," *Perspectives on Politics* 1, no. 3 (Cambridge: Cambridge University Press, 2003), 475–94; and Frances Stewart, "Root Causes of Violent Conflict in Developing Countries," *BMJ (Clinical research ed.)* 324, no. 7333 (2002): 342-45.

42. Lisa Wedeen, "The Politics of Deliberation: *Qāt* Chews as Public Spheres in Yemen," *Public Culture* 19, no. 1 (2007): 63–6.

43. Lisa Wedeen, "Concepts and Commitments in the Study of Democracy," in *Problems and Methods in the Study of Politics*, eds. Ian Shapiro, Rogers M. Smith, and Tarek E. Masoud (Cambridge: Cambridge University Press, 2004), 287; Wedeen, "Politics of Deliberation," 67.

44. Ibid., 296.

45. Abdullah Mohammad Alhajeri, "The Development of Political Interaction in Kuwait Through the 'Diwaniyas' from Their Beginnings Until the Year 1999," *Journal of Islamic Law and Culture* 12, no. 1 (2010): 24.

46. Mary Ann Tetreault, "Civil Society in Kuwait: Protected Spaces and Women's Rights," *Middle East Journal* 47, no. 2 (1993): 279.

47. Alhajeri, "The Development of Political Interaction," 37.

48. Ibid., 37–40.

49. Ibtisam Awadat, "King Lashes Out at 'Political Salons'," *The Star*, July 4, 2002.

50. "How Did the Ultras First Appear? And Where Have They Ended Up?" BBC Documentary, 2017, https://www.youtube.com/watch?v=0CzMw8pLN-8.

51. Connor T. Jerzak, "Ultras in Egypt: State, Revolution, and the Power of Public Space," *Interface: A Journal for and About Social Movements* 5 no. 2 (November 2013): 240-62.

52. Diane Singerman, *Avenues of Participation: Family, Politics, and Networks in Urban Quarters of Cairo* (Princeton, NJ: Princeton University Press, 1995), 14.

53. Asef Bayat, *Life as Politics: How Ordinary People Change the Middle East* (Stanford, CA: Stanford University Press, 2009); Bayat, "Politics in the City-Inside-Out," *City & Society* 24, no. 2 (2012): 110–28.

54. Ibid., 56.

55. Ibid., 60.

56. Clark, *Islam, Charity and Activism*, 153–54.

57. Janine Clark, "Islamist Women in Yemen: Informal Nodes of Activism," in *Islamic Activism: A Social Movement Theory Approach*, ed. Quintan Wiktorowicz (Bloomington: Indiana University Press, 2004): 164-84.

58. Gwenn Okruhlik, "Making Conversation Permissible: Islamism and Reform in Saudi Arabia," in *Islamic Activism*, ed. Quintan Wiktorowicz (2004): 250–69.

59. Ibid., 256.

60. Ibid., 263–64.

61. Al-Hayat, "Statement by 99 Syrian Intellectuals," Translated by Suha Mawlawi Kayal, in *Middle East Intelligence Bulletin* 2, no. 9 (5 October 2000), https://www.meforum.org/meib/articles/00 10_sdoc0927.htm.

62. Janine A. Clark and Lina Khatib, "Actors, Public Opinion, and Participation," in *The Middle East*, ed. Ellen Lust (Thousand Oaks, CA: SAGE/CQ Press, 2016): 283.

63. Marc Lynch, *Voices of the New ARAB Public: Iraq, Al-Jazeera, and Middle East Politics Today* (New York: Columbia University Press, 2006); Mohamed Zayani and Sofiane Zahraoui, *The Culture of Al Jazeera: Inside an ARAB Media Giant* (London: McFarland & Company, 2007).

64. Khatib, *Image Politics in the Middle East.*

65. Quoted in Deborah Wheeler, "Working around the State: Internet Use and Political Identity in the MENA," in *Routledge Handbook of Internet Politics*, eds. Andrew Chadwick and Philip N. Howard (New York: Routledge, 2009), 310.

66. Wheeler, "Working around the State," 307; Brian Whitaker, *What's Really Wrong with the Middle East* (San Francisco, CA: Saqi Books, 2009).

67. Halim Rane, Jacqui Ewart, and John Martinkus, *Media Framing of the Muslim World: Conflicts, Crises and Contexts* (London: Palgrave Macmillan, 2014); "YouTube interview: Robert Kyncl," Interview by Shane McGinley, *Arabian Business*, 29 October 2012, https://www.arabianbusines s.com/youtube-interview-robert-kyncl-477659.html.

68. Khatib, *Image Politics in the Middle East.*

69. Jan Rydzak, Moses Karanja, and Nicholas Opiyo, "Dissent Does Not Die in Darkness: Network Shutdowns and Collective Action in African Countries," *International Journal of Communication* 14 (2020): 4264–87.

70. Marc Lynch, "Reflections on the Arab Uprisings," *The Monkey Cage*, November 17 2014, http://www.washingtonpost.com/blogs/monkey-cage/wp/2014/11/17/reflections-on-the-arab-up risings/.

CHAPTER 6

1. The extent of "modernization" is captured in quantitative and qualitative information on socioeconomic/human development, political institutions, and cultural changes, including attitudes toward women and the family. The early version of the modernization thesis was simplistic and linear and suggested a form of Westernization. A more sophisticated version, found in World Values Survey scholarship, posits that economic prosperity is a catalyst for cultural development, leading to social values that favor liberalization and thus promotes effective democracy (see Ronald Inglehart and Christian Welzel, *Modernization, Cultural Change, and Democracy: The Human Development Sequence* [New York: Cambridge University Press, 2005]), although the attitudes among the population are also found to be highly correlated with the philosophical, political, and religious ideas that have been dominating in the country (see http://www.worldvaluessurvey.org/WVSContents.jsp). The modernization perspective has a superficial similarity with a certain Marxist notion of the base-superstructure correspondence but lacks the latter's emphasis on class and conflict.

2. Within the noncommunist world, Argentina first implemented a quota in 1991 to enhance women's political representation, and the subsequent parliamentary election brought women's presence to 36 percent. For details on the "quota revolution," see Pamela Paxton and Melanie Hughes, *Women, Politics, and Power: A Global Perspective* (Thousand Oaks, CA: SAGE, 2014).

3. Eva Bellin, "Reconsidering the Robustness of Authoritarianism in the Middle East: Lessons from the Arab Spring," *Comparative Politics* 44, no. 2 (2012): 27–49; Jason Brownlee, Tarek Masoud, and Andrew Reynolds, "Why the Modest Harvest?" *Journal of Democracy* 24, no. 4 (October 2013): 29–44; Paul Amar and V. J. Prashad, eds., *Dispatches from the Arab Spring: Understanding the New Middle East* (Minneapolis: University of Minnesota Press, 2013); John Foran, Global Affinities: The New Cultures of Resistance Behind the Arab Spring, in *Beyond the Arab Spring: The Evolving Ruling Bargain in the Middle East*, ed. M. Kamrava (New York: Oxford University Press, 2014), 47–72; Asef Bayat, *Revolution without Revolutionaries: Making Sense of the Arab Spring* (Redwood City, CA: Stanford University Press, 2017); and Mansour Moaddel, The Tenacity of the Arab Spring in People's Perceptions: Trends in Values among Egyptians, ERF Working Paper 1179 (April 2018).

4. On sociological theories of social change, see Daniel Chirot, *Social Change in the Modern Era* (San Diego, CA: Harcourt Brace Jovanovich, 1983). World polity theory is a variant of modernization theory that posits the global spread of similar institutions, standards, and organizational forms, sometimes claimed as "Western." See John Meyer, John Boli, George Thomas, and Francisco Ramirez, "World Society and the Nation-State," *American Journal of Sociology* 103, no. 1 (1997): 144–81; John Boli and George M. Thomas, "World Culture in the World Polity," *American Sociological Review* 62, no. 2 (April 1997): 171–90; and John Boli, "Contemporary Developments in World Culture," *International Journal of Contemporary Sociology* 46, nos. 5–6 (2005): 383–404. World-system theory grew out of dependency theory, continued the latter's critique of modernization (the theory and the practice), and posited a single capitalist world-system, driven by waves and cycles of accumulation and crisis, consisting of an unequal system of states and markets, led by a hegemon, across the economic zones of core, periphery, and semiperiphery, with outbreaks of antisystemic movements. See Christopher Chase-Dunn, *Global Formation: Structures of the World Economy*, 2nd ed. (Totowa, NJ: Rowman & Littlefield, 1998).

5. Raymond A. Hinnebusch, "Liberalization without Democratization in "Post-Populist" Authoritarian States," in *Citizenship and the State in the Middle East*, eds. Nils A. Butenschon, Uri Davis, and Manuel Hassassian (Syracuse, NY: Syracuse University Press, 2000): 123–45; Daniel Brumberg, "Democratization in the Arab World? The Trap of Liberalized Autocracy," *Journal of Democracy* 13, no. 4 (October 2002): 56–68.

6. Hisham Sharabi, *Neopatriarchy: A Theory of Distorted Change in the Arab World* (New York: Oxford University Press, 1988). This was a theory of a new version of patriarchy, found at macro, meso, and micro level structures and relations, which evolved in the context of dependent capitalist development.

7. The concept of state feminism was first applied to Nordic countries; see Helga Hernes, *Welfare State and Women Power: Essays in State Feminism* (Oslo, 1987). On its application in Egypt and especially Tunisia, see Mervat Hatem, "Economic and Political Liber[aliz]ation in Egypt and the Demise of State Feminism," *International Journal of Middle East Studies* 24, no. 2 (1992): 231–51; Mounira Charrad, *States and Women's Rights: The Making of Postcolonial Tunisia, Algeria, and Morocco* (Berkeley: University of California Press, 2001); and Jane Tchaicha and Khedija Arfaoui, *The Tunisian Women's Rights Movement: From Nascent Activism to Influential Power-Broking* (London: Routledge, 2017).

8. Ronald Inglehart and Pippa Norris, *Rising Tide: Gender Equality and Cultural Change around the World* (New York: Cambridge University Press, 2003).

9. Massoud Karshenas and Valentine M. Moghadam, "Female Labor Force Participation and Economic Adjustment in the MENA Region," in *The Economics of Women and Work in the Middle East and North Africa*, ed. Mine Cinar (New York: JAI Press, 2001), 51–74.

10. Valentine M. Moghadam, "A Political Economy of Women's Employment in the Middle East," in Women and Development in the Middle East, eds. Nabil Khoury and Moghadam (London: Zed Books, 1995); *Modernizing Women: Gender and Social Change in the Middle East*, 2nd ed. (Boulder, CO: Lynne Rienner, 2003), chap. 2; "Women's Economic Participation in the Middle East: What Difference Has the Neoliberal Policy Turn Made?" *Journal of Middle East Women's Studies* 1, no. 1 (Winter 2005): 110–46. See also Michael Ross, "Oil, Islam, and Women," *American Political Science Review* 102 (2008): 107–23.

11. Massoud Karshenas, "Macroeconomic Policy, Structural Change, and Employment in the Middle East and North Africa," in *Overcoming Unemployment*, eds. Azizur Rahman Khan and M. Muqtada (London: Macmillan, 1997), 320–96; Ece Kocabicak, "What Excludes Women from Landownership in Turkey? Implications for Feminist Strategies," *Women's Studies International Forum* 69 (2018): 115–25.

12. Valentine M. Moghadam, *Women, Work, and Economic Reform in the Middle East and North Africa* (Boulder, CO: Lynne Rienner Publishers, 1998), ch. 1.

13. Karshenas, "Macroeconomic Policy."

14. Quintan Wiktorowicz, *Islamic Activism: A Social Movement Theory Approach* (Bloomington: Indiana University Press, 1994); Jillian Schwedler, *Faith in Moderation: Islamist Parties in Jordan and Yemen* (New York: Cambridge University Press, 2006); and Valentine M. Moghadam, *Globalization and Social Movements: Islamism, Feminism, and the Global Justice Movement*, 2nd ed. (Lanham, MD: Rowman and Littlefield, 2013).

15. Scholars have identified economic, political, and cultural/ideological dimensions of globalization. See Leslie Sklair, *Globalization: Capitalism and Its Alternatives*, 3rd ed. (Oxford: Oxford University Press, 2002); Manfred Steger, *Globalization: A Very Short Introduction* (Oxford: Oxford University Press, 2003); Valentine M. Moghadam, *Globalizing Women: Transnational Feminist Networks* (Baltimore, MD: Johns Hopkins University Press, 2005), chap. 2. See also ESCWA, *Survey of Economic and Social Developments in the ESCWA Region 2007–2008* (Beirut: UN Economic and Social Commission for Western Asia, 2008).

16. Leslie Sklair, *The Transnational Capitalist Class* (Oxford: Blackwell, 2001); William I. Robinson, *A Theory of Global Capitalism* (Baltimore, MD: Johns Hopkins University Press, 2004).

17. Valentine M. Moghadam, "Women's Economic Participation in the Middle East: What Difference Has the Neoliberal Policy Turn Made?" *Journal of Middle East Women's Studies* 1, no. 1 (Winter 2005): 110–46; M. Riad el-Ghonemy, *Affluence and Poverty in the Middle East* (London: Routledge, 1998); Richard Adams, "Evaluating the Process of Development in Egypt, 1980–1997," *International Journal of Middle East Studies* 32 (2000): 255–75; and Valentine M. Moghadam, "The Feminization of Poverty in International Perspective," *Brown Journal of World Affairs* 5, no. 2 (1998): 225–48.

18. Philippe Fargues, "Demographic Islamization: Non-Muslims in Muslim Countries," *SAIS Review* 21, no. 2 (Summer–Fall 2001): 103–16.

19. Elizabeth Ferris and Kimberly Stoltz, "Minorities, Displacement, and Iraq's Future," Brookings Institution and University of Bern, Project on Internal Displacement (December 2008), www.brookings.edu/papers/2008/1223_minorities_ferris.aspx. See also United States Committee on International Religious Freedom, Annual Report 2010, www.uscirf.gov/images/annual%20report%202010.pdf.

20. Todd M. Johnson and Gina A. Zurlo, "Ongoing Exodus: Tracking the Emigration of Christians from the Middle East," *Harvard Journal of Middle Eastern Politics and Policy* 3 (2013–2014): 39–48.

21. Farzaneh Roudi, "Population Trends and Challenges in the Middle East and North Africa," Policy Brief (Washington, DC: Population Reference Bureau, October 2001).

22. On the "youth bulge," see Ragui Assaad and Farzaneh Roudi-Fahimi, *Youth in the Middle East and North Africa: Demographic Opportunity or Challenge?* (Washington, DC: Population Reference Bureau, 2007), http://prb.org/pdf077/YouthinMENA.pdf; Philippe Fargues, *Emerging Demographic Patterns across the Mediterranean and Their Implications for Migration through 2030* (Washington, DC: Migration Policy Institute, 2008), http://www.migration policyi nstitute.org/transatlantic.

23. "World Urbanization Prospects, 2014 Revision," United Nations. See also https://www.worlda tlas.com/articles/largest-cities-in-the-middle-east.html (accessed June 2021).

24. Syria's population in 2010 was 21 million but in 2017 was about 18.27 million. For details on Syria's population changes, see http://world population review.com/countries/syria-popu -lation/.

25. Abdel R. Omran and Farzaneh Roudi, "The Middle East Population Puzzle," *Population Bulletin* 48, no. 1 (July 1993): 21; Ragui Assaad, "Urbanization and Demographic Structure in the Middle East and North Africa with a Focus on Women and Children," Regional Papers, no. 40 (New York: Population Council, January 1995): 21.

26. Sulayman Khalaf, "The Evolution of the Gulf City Type, Oil, and Globalization," in *Globalization and the Gulf*, eds. John W. Fox, Nada Mourtada-Sabbah, and Mohammed al Mutawa (London: Routledge, 2004), 244–65. See also Syed Ali, *Dubai: Gilded Cage* (New Haven, CT: Yale University Press, 2010). The figures are from the Dubai Statistics Center, http://www.dsc.g ov.ae/En/Pages/Home.aspx; and census data, UAE, http://tedad.ae. See also K. G. Fenelon, *The United Arab Emirates: An Economic and Social Survey* (London: Longman, 1973), 126; Christopher Davidson, *Dubai: The Vulnerability of Success* (London: Hurst, 2008); and Jon Henley, "Agog on Planet Dubai," *The Guardian Weekly*, December 11, 2009, 25–27.

27. In April 2018, Egypt introduced stricter penalties up to 10,000 Egyptian pounds ($558) in a bid to deter any kind of harassment and pestering of tourists. See Shahira Amin, "Egyptian Outrages at Plans to Leave Best Beaches to Tourists," *Al-Monitor*, July 3, 2018, http://www. al-monitor.com/pulse/originals/2018/07/alexandria-to-launch-tourist-only-beaches.html#i xzz5KZmd6BON. On the planned underwater museum, see https://www.smithsonianmag.co m/innovation/underwater-museum-egypt-could-bring-thousands-sunken-relics-into-view- 180957645/

28. On the cutting of trees throughout Egypt, see http://www.al-monitor.com/pulse/originals/201 8/11/egypts-trees-chopped-down-for-roads-residences.html #ixzz5Wf7df1Zn.

29. See https://www.unescwa.org/prevalence-covid-19-arab-region (accessed 25 July 2020).

30. For details, see http://eraiturkey.com/2017/03/17/10-on going-mega-projects-of-turkey-in -2017/.

31. UN Development Program (UNDP), Human Development Report 2011, Table9,159.

32. See World Bank, *World Development Indicators* (Washington, DC: World Bank, 2000), 108, Table2.18; UNDP, *Arab Human Development Report 2009* (New York: UNDP, 2009); UNDP, *Human Development Report 2019* (New York: UNDP, 2019), Table 1.

33. Moghadam, *Modernizing Women*, chap. 6.

34. Maia Sieverding, Caroline Krafft and Nasma Berri, "How Are Families Changing in Jordan? New Evidence on Marriage and Fertility Rends among Jordanians and Syrian Refugees." *ERF Policy Brief* no. 35 (May 2018): 2, 4.

35. Farzaneh Roudi, *Iran Is Reversing Its Population Policy* (Washington, DC: Woodrow Wilson Center, Viewpoints 7 (August 2012)); Scott Peterson, "In Turkey, Cruel Tradition Trumps 'Picture Perfect' Gender Laws," *The Christian Science Monitor*, https://www.csmonitor.com/World/Middle-East/2018/0124/In-Turkey-cruel-tradition-trumps-picture-perfect-gender-laws. See also ESCWA, *A Review of Literature on the Changhing Role of the Family in Care Provision in Arab Countries* (Beirut: ESCWA, 22 January 2013), https://archive.unescwa.org/sites/www.unescwa.org/files/publications/files/e_escwa_sdd_13_wp-1_e.pdf (accessed June 2021).

36. Data from UNDP, Arab Human Development Report 2009, 36, 232, Table4.

37. See Henrik Urdal, *The Devil in the Demographics: The Effect of Youth Bulges on Domestic Armed Conflict, 1950-2000* (Washington, DC: The World Bank, Social Development Paper, Conflict Prevention & Reconstruction Paper No. 14, July 2004).

38. The Economist, citing UNHCR data, June 30, 2018, 41–42.

39. Ragui Assaad, Rana Hendy, Moundir Lassassi, and Shaimaa Yassin, "Explaining the MENA Paradox: Rising Educational Attainment, yet Stagnant Female Labor Force Participation," IZA DP no. 11385 (Berlin: Institute of Labor Economics, March 2018). See also Moghadam, *"Where Are Iran's Working Women?" Viewpoints: Special Issue on the Iranian Revolution at 30* (Middle East Institute, January 2009), www.mideasti.org/.

40. MENA consistently ranks lowest on indicators pertaining to women and work, including laws and policies. See, for example, the World Bank's report Women, Business, and the Law 2018, Fig.1.5: http://pubdocs.worldbank.org/en/999211524236982958/WBL-Key-Findings-Web-FINAL-2.pdf. Other sources on institutional barriers are the OECD's States, Institutions, Gender Index (SIGI) and the World Economic Forum's annual Global Gender Gap Report.

41. These are among the findings of the international research project, "Female Employment and Dynamics of Inequality in the Middle East, North Africa, and South Asia—2016–2018," housed at London University's School of Oriental and African Studies. For data and reports on female employment in Egypt, Jordan, and Tunisia, see Economic Research Forum for the Arab Countries, Iran, and Turkey (ERF). See also Niels Spierings, Jeroen Smits, and Mieke Verlook, "Micro- and Macrolevel Determinants of Women's Employment in Six Arab Countries," *Journal of Marriage and Family* 72, no. 5 (October 2010): 1391–407.

42. Massoud Karshenas and Valentine M. Moghadam, "Female Labor Force Participation and Women's Employment: Puzzles, Problems, and Research," in *The Routledge Handbook of Middle East Economics*, ed. Hassan Hakimian (London: Routledge, 2021); data from UNESCO Institute of Statistics, "Data for the Sustainable Development Goals," http://uis.unesco.org/en/home#tabs-0-uis_home_top_menus-3.

43. Moghadam, "Women's Economic Participation in the Middle East."

44. ESCWA, Survey of Economic and Social Developments in the ESCWA Region, 1994; Radwan A. Shaban, Ragui Assaad, and Sulayman S. al-Qudsi, "The Challenge of Unemployment in the Arab Region," *International Labor Review* 134, no. 1 (1995): 65–81; and International Labor Organization (ILO), *World Labor Report 1999* (Geneva: International Labor Organization, 1999).

45. Valentine M. Moghadam, "Gender Aspects of Employment and Unemployment in a Global Perspective," in *Global Employment: An International Investigation into the Future of Work*, eds. Mihaly Simai, Valentine M. Moghadam, and Arvo Kuddo (London: Zed Books and UNU Press, 1995), 111–39.

46. Christine Bose, "Patterns of Global Gender Inequalities and Regional Gender Regimes," *Gender & Society* 29, no. 6 (December 2015): 767–91.

47. OECD, "COVID-19 Crisis in the MENA Region: Impact on Gender Equality and Policy Responses, June 19, 2020, 7, https://www.oecd.org/coronavirus/policy-responses/covid-19-crisis-in-the-mena-region-impact-on-gender-equality-and-policy-responses-ee4cd4f4/.

48. May El Habachi, "Is COVID-19 Pushing Women in Egypt Out of Workforce?" *Al-Monitor*, August 28, 2020, https://www.al-monitor.com/originals/2020/08/egypt-workforce-women-children -education-coronavirus.html, citing http://dailynewsegypt.com/2020/08/17/covid-19-nudges -egypt-unemployment-up-to-9-6-in-q2-2020-capmas/.

49. Aseel Alayli, "COVID-19 Magnifies Pre-Existing Gender Inequalities in MENA," *Arab Barometer*, December 1, 2020, https://www.arabbarometer.org/2020/12/covid-19-magnifies-pre-existing-gender-inequalities-in-mena/.

50. UNDP, Human Development Indices and Indicators 2018, 3, http://hdr.undp.org/sites/default/files/2018_human_development_statistical_update.pdf.

51. For data on the 1990s, see World Bank, *Implementing the World Bank's Strategy to Reduce Poverty: Progress and Challenges* (Washington, DC: World Bank, 1993), 5; ESCWA, *A Conceptual and Methodological Framework for Poverty Alleviation in the ESCWA Region* (New York: United Nations, 1993), 6, 121; see also ESCWA, *Survey of Economic and Social Development in the ESCWA Region, 1994, and ESCWA, Survey 1997* (New York: United Nations); Middle East Times, November 3–9, 1996, 19.

52. Ali Emami and Nora Lustig, *Poverty Reduction Efforts in Iran: The Wrecking Force of Inflation* (Cairo: Economic Research Forum, June 12, 2018), https://theforum.erf.org.for example/2018/06/12/poverty- reduction-efforts-iran-wrecking-force-inflation.

53. Moghadam, "The Feminization of Poverty?" See also UNDP, Arab Human Development Report 2009, 229, Table3.

54. Cited in UN ESCWA, "Measuring Urban Poverty in the Arab Region: Localizing Global and National Strategies," *Social Development Bulletin* 6, no. 1 (2017): 3.

55. See Michael Todaro and Stephen P. Smith, *Economic Development*, 10th ed. (New York: Addison Wesley, 2008), chap. 3 on W. W. Rostow's notion of stages of economic growth study and chap. 5 on the Kuznets curve.

56. UNDP, *Human Development Report 2016: Human Development for Everyone* (New York: UNDP, 2016), 27; El-Ghonemy, *Affluence and Poverty in the Middle East*; Larbi Sadiki, "Popular Uprisings and Arab Democratization," *International Journal of Middle East Studies* 32 (2000): 71–95; *Arab Human Development Report 2002* (New York: UNDP, 2002); Massoud Karshenas, "Social Development, Income Distribution and Poverty under the Islamic Republic in a Comparative Perspective," *Iran Nameh* 30, no. 1 (Spring 2015): 70–82; and Facundo Alvaredo, Lydia Assouad, and Thomas Piketty, Inequality in the Middle East, Vox: CEPR Policy Portal, 2018, https://voxeu.org/article/inequality-middle-east.

57. ESCWA, *Wealth Inequality and Closing the Poverty Gap in Arab Countries: The Case for a Solidarity Wealth Tax* (Beirut: June 2020); Facundo Alvaredo, Lydia Assouad, and Thomas Piketty, "Inequality in the Middle East"; Vladimir Hlasny and Shireen Al Azzawi, Asset Inequality in Egypt, Ethiopia, Jordan and Tunisia, ERF Forum (July 24, 2018), https://theforum.erf.org.for example/2018/07/24/asset-inequality-for exampleypt-ethiopia-jordan-tunisia/.

58. CIA, *World Factbook 2009* (Washington, DC: Central Intelligence Agency, 2009).

59. World Bank, *World Development Indicators 2017*, 82–86.

60. Paul Collier, *The Bottom Billion: Why the Poorest Countries Are Failing and What Can Be Done about It* (New York: Oxford University Press, 2007); Gregory Hooks, "War and Development: Questions, Answers, and Prospects for the Twenty-First Century," in *Handbook of the Sociology of Development*, ed. Gregory Hooks (Berkeley: University of California Press, 2016), 440–62; Hamid E. Ali and James Galbraith, "Military Expenditures and Inequality: Empirical Evidence from Global Data," University of Texas at Austin, UTIP Working Paper No. 24 (October 10, 2003); and Unal Tongur and Adem Elveren, "Military Expenditures, Income Inequality, Welfare and Political Regimes: A Dynamic Panel Data Analysis," *Defense and Peace Economics* 26, no. 1 (Oct. 2015): 49–74.

61. Meyer et al., "World Society and the Nation-State"; Boli, "Contemporary Developments in World Culture."

62. Gawdat Bahgat, "Education in the Gulf Monarchies: Retrospect and Prospect," *International Review of Education* 45, no. 2 (1999): 127–36.

63. Monica M. Ringer, "Education in the Middle East: Introduction," *Comparative Studies of South Asia, Africa and the Middle East* 21, nos. 1–2 (2001): 3–4; Betty Anderson, "Writing the Nation: Textbooks of the Hashemite Kingdom of Jordan," *Comparative Studies of South Asia, Africa and the Middle East* 21, nos. 1–2 (2001): 5–14; and Bradley James Cook, "Egypt's National Education Debate," *Comparative Education* 36, no. 4 (2000): 477–90.

64. Michaela Prokop, "Saudi Arabia: The Politics of Education," *International Affairs* 79, no. 3 (2003): 77–89. See also Amélie Le Renard, *A Society of Young Women: Opportunities of Place, Power, and Reform in Saudi Arabia* (Stanford, CA: Stanford University Press, 2014).

65. Hicham Alaoui and Robert Springborg, "The Political Economy of Education in the Arab World," in *The Political Economy of Education in the Arab World*, eds. Alaoui and Springborg (Boulder, CO: Lynne Rienner Publishers, 2021), 5.

66. World Bank, *World Development Indicators, 2006–2009*.

67. World Bank, *The Road Not Traveled: Education Reform in the Middle East and North Africa, MENA Development Report* (Washington, DC: World Bank, 2008), 16, Table1.5; UNDP, Human Development Report 2019, Table1.

68. See UNESCO Institute of Statistics, http://uis.unesco.org/en/country/ir.

69. Hans Lueders and Ellen Lust, "We Don't Need No Education: Resource Endowments and the Demand for Social Service Provision" (unpublished MSS, July 2018). TIMSS test scores available through "Education Statistics (edstats)," World Bank, http://go.worldbank.org/47P 3PLE940. See also Stephen P. Heyneman, "The Quality of Education in the Middle East and North Africa (MENA)," *International Journal of Educational Development* 17, no. 4 (1997): 449–66; *Education in the Middle East and North Africa: A Strategy towards Learning for Development* (Washington, DC: World Bank, 1998); William A. Rugh, "Arab Education: Tradition, Growth and Reform," *Middle East Journal* 56, no. 3 (2002): 396–414; and ESCWA, *The Impact of Economic Variables on the Social Dimension of Development: Education and Health* (New York: United Nations, 2005).

70. This paragraph draws on Lueders and Lust, "We Don't Need," Figure 2, p. 21. See also Andre Elias Mazawi, "Wars, Geopolitics, and University Governance in the Arab States," *International Higher Education* (Summer 2004), https://www.bc.edu/content/dam/files/r esearch_sites/cihe/pdf/IHEpdfs/ihe36.pdf (last accessed June 2021); Ghada Barsoum, The Allure of "Easy: Reflections on the Learning Experience in Private Higher Education Institutions in Egypt," *Compare: A Journal of Comparative and International Education* (March 2016), 11; Mongi Boughzala, Samir Ghazouani, and Abdelwahab Ben Hafaiedh, *Aligning Incentives for Reforming Higher Education in Tunisia* (Cairo: ERF Working Paper No. 1031, July 2016); Hicham Araoui and Robert Springborg, Education in the Arab World: A Legacy of Coming Up short, Wilson Center Viewpoints (April 5, 2021), https:/ /www.wilsoncenter .org/article/education-arab-world-legacy-coming-short?utm_medium=email&utm_sou rce=article&utm_campaign=mep&emci=4078abc7-fa9e-eb11-85aa-0050f237abef&emdi= 7ae2ae25-0fa1-eb11-85aa-0050f237abef&ceid=228706 (accessed April 2021).

71. La Revue du CREDIF, no. 49 (December 2015): 63, 68–69; UNWomen, *Progress of the World's Women 2015–2016: Transforming Economies, Realizing Rights* (New York: UN, 2015), 263.

72. Michael J. Handel, Alexandria Valerio, and Maria Laura Sánchez Puerta, *Accounting for Mismatch in Low- and Middle-Income Countries: Measurement, Magnitudes, and Explanations* (Washington, DC: The World Bank, 2016), xv.

73. Golnar Mehran, "The Paradox of Tradition and Modernity in Female Education in the Islamic Republic of Iran," *Comparative Education Review* 47, no. 3 (2003): 269–86. On FGM in Egypt, see UNICEF, "Female Genital Mutilation in Egypt: Recent trends and projections" (February 2020), accessed June 2021.

74. On mobile usage: https://data.worldbank.org/indicator/IT.CEL.SETS.P2; on Internet penetration: https://internetworldstats.com/stats.htm (accessed June 2021); see also The Arab Social Media Report 1, no. 2 (May 2011): 12, Dubai School of Government.

75. Hoda Rashad, Magued Osman, and Farzaneh Roudi-Fahimi, *Marriage in the Arab World* (Washington, DC: Population Reference Bureau, 2005); for more recent data on early marriage, see https://www.icrw.org/wp-content/uploads/2018/04/Excutive-Summary-FINAL.p df, p. 5, citing data from the Demographic and Health Surveys and UNICEF (accessed June 2021).

76. Maia Sieverding, Caroline Krafft, and Nasma Berri, "How Are Families Changing in Jordan? New Evidence on Marriage and Fertility Trends among Jordanians and Syrian Refugees," *ERF Policy Brief*, no. 35 (May 2018): 1.

77. See World Bank, *World Development Indicators 2017*, 36–42; and for 2019 figures: https://dat abank.worldbank.org/source/world-development-indicators https://data.worldbank.org/in dicator/SP.ADO.TFRT. Iran lags behind Algeria and Tunisia in adolescent fertility. According to UNICEF data, 5 percent of Iranian women aged 20–24 gave birth before age eighteen, compared with Algeria's and Tunisia's 1 percent. See https://data.unicef.org/country/irn/ (accessed June 2021).

78. Navtej Dhillon, Paul Dyer, and Tarik Yousef, "Generation in Waiting: An Overview of School to Work and Family Formation Transitions," in *Generation in Waiting: The Unfulfilled Promise of Young People in the Middle East*, eds. Navtej Dhillon and Tarik Yousef (Washington, DC: Brookings Institution Press, 2009), 11–38.

79. Valentine M. Moghadam and Fatemeh Haghighatjoo, "Women and Political Leadership in an Authoritarian Context: A Case Study of the Sixth Parliament in the Islamic Republic of Iran," *Politics & Gender* 12 (2016): 168–97.

80. Najmeh Bozorgmehr, "Young Iranians Find Freedom in Wild Camping," *Financial Times*, 26 May 2021; Pardis Mahdavi, *Passionate Uprisings: Iran's Sexual Revolution* (Stanford, CA: Stanford University Press, 2008). See also Pardis Mahdavi, "'But What If Someone Sees Me?' Women, Risk, and the Aftershocks of Iran's Sexual Revolution," *Journal of Middle East Women's Studies* 5, no. 2 (Winter 2009): 1–22.

81. Bochra Bel Haj Hamida, Tunisian lawyer and Association Tunisienne des Femmes Démocrates activist, comments to the author, Helsinki, Finland, May 2003.

82. Fatima Mernissi, *Beyond the Veil: Male-Female Dynamics in Modern Muslim Society*, rev. 2nd ed. (Bloomington: Indiana University Press, 1987).

83. On Iran, see Azal Ahmadi, "Recreating Virginity in Iran: Hymenoplasty as a Form of Resistance," *Medical Anthropology Quarterly* 30, no. 2 (2016): 222–37. doi: 10.1111/maq.12202.

84. Leila Hessini, "Abortion and Islam: Policies and Practice in the Middle East and North Africa," *Reproductive Health Matters* 15, no. 29 (2007): 75–84. Tunisia first legalized abortion in 1965 for women with five children or more; in 1973, it extended that right to all women during the first trimester and without a spouse's approval.

85. Sylvia Walby, *Theorizing Patriarchy* (Oxford: Blackwell, 1990), and "The 'Declining Significance' or the 'Changing Forms' of Patriarchy?" in *Patriarchy and Development: Women's Positions at the End of the Twentieth Century*, ed. Valentine M. Moghadam (Oxford: Clarendon Press, 1996), 19–33; John Lie, "From Agrarian Patriarchy to Patriarchal Capitalism: Gendered Capitalist Industrialization in Korea," in *Patriarchy and Development*, ed. Valentine M. Moghadam, 34–55; Deniz Kandiyoti, "Bargaining with Patriarchy," *Gender & Society* 2, no. 3 (September 1988): 274–89; Germaine Tillion, *The Republic of Cousins: Women's Oppression in Mediterranean Society* (London: Al-Saqi Books, 1983); and Mounira Charrad, *States and Women's Rights: The Making of Postcolonial Tunisia, Algeria, and Morocco* (Berkeley: University of California Press, 2001); Moghadam, *Modernizing Women*.

86. Suad Joseph, "Gendering Citizenship in the Middle East," in *Gender and Citizenship in the Middle East*, ed. Suad Joseph (Syracuse, NY: Syracuse University Press, 2000), 1–31.

87. See Valentine M. Moghadam, "Maternalist Policies vs. Economic Citizenship? Gendered Social Policy in Iran," in *Gender and Social Policy in a Global Context: Uncovering the Gendered Structure of "The Social"*, eds. Shahra Razavi and Shireen Hassim (Basingstoke: Palgrave, 2006), 87–108.

88. Amira al-Azhary Sonbol, *Women of Jordan: Islam, Labor, and the Law* (Syracuse, NY: Syracuse University Press, 1993), 89–99.

89. Rania Maktabi, "Patriarchal Nationality Laws and Female Citizenship in the Middle East," in *Routledge Handbook of Citizenship in the Middle East and North Africa*, eds. Role Meijer, James Sater, and Zahra Babar (London: Routledge, 2020), 311–35.

90. Collectif Maghreb Egalité 95, Guide to Equality in the Family and in the Maghreb [authorized trans. of Dalil pour l'égalité dans la famille au Maghreb] (Bethesda, MD: Women's Learning Partnership for Rights, Development, and Peace, 2005). The principal authors are Alya Cherif Chamari, Nadia Ait Zai, Farida Bennani, and Sanaa Benachour.

91. Valentine M. Moghadam and Elham Gheytanchi, "Political Opportunities and Strategic Choices: Comparing Feminist Campaigns in Iran and Morocco," *Mobilization: An International Quarterly of Social Movement Research* 15, no. 3 (September 2010): 267–88.

92. Fatima Sadiqi, "Literature Review, Morocco," report prepared for the ESRC/GCRF project, "Female Employment and Dynamics of Inequality in the Middle East, North Africa, and South Asia" (SOAS, Univ. of London), February 2018.

93. UNDP, *Arab Human Development Report 2005* (New York: UNDP, 2006), 132.

94. Kathrin Thomas, "Women's Rights in the Middle East and North Africa" (August 2019), p. 10, www.arabbarometer.org

95. Marwa Shalaby and Laila Elimam, "Women in Legislative Committees in Arab Parliaments," *Journal of Comparative Politics* 51, no. 1: 139–67; Valentine M. Moghadam and Fatemeh Haghighatjoo, "Women and Political Leadership in an Authoritarian Context: A Case Study of the Sixth Parliament in the Islamic Republic of Iran," *Politics and Gender* 8, no. 12 (2016): 168–97; and Hanane Darhour and Drude Dahlerup, "Sustainable Representation of Women through Gender Quotas: A Decade's Experience in Morocco," *Women's Studies International Forum* 41, no. 2 (2013): 132–42. See also World Economic Forum, Global Gender Gap Report 2020, p. 13.

96. Valentine M. Moghadam and Fatima Sadiqi, "Introduction and Overview: Women and the Public Sphere in the Middle East and North Africa," *Journal of Middle East Women's Studies* 2, no. 2 (Spring 2006): 1–7.

97. Islah Jad, "The 'NGOisation' of the Arab Women's Movement," in *Repositioning Feminisms in Development*, eds. Andrea Cornwall, Elizabeth Harrison, and Ann Whitehead (Sussex, NJ: Sussex University Press, 2004); Amaney Jamal, *Barriers to Democracy: The Other Side of Social Capital in Palestine and the Arab World* (Princeton, NJ: Princeton University Press, 2007).

98. See V. M. Moghadam, "Gender Regimes in the Middle East and North Africa: The Power of Feminist Movements," *Social Politics: International Studies in Gender, State & Society* 27, no. 3 (Fall 2020): 467–85, https://doi.org/10.1093/sp/jxaa019.

99. See, for example, Lindsey Benstead, "Explaining Egalitarian Attitudes: The Role of Interests and Exposure," in *Empowering Women after the Arab Spring*, eds. Marwa Shalaby and Valentine M. Moghadam (London: Palgrave Macmillan, 2016), 119–46. She uses data from the World Values Survey 2006–2008 for Algeria, Lebanon, Jordan, Morocco, Palestine, and Yemen.

100. Saied Jafari, "Iranian Women's Movement Pushed for More Rights, at Its Own Pace," *Al-Monitor*, July 6, 2018.

101. Veronica Kostenko and Eduard Ponarin, "Attitudes toward Gender Equality in Arab Countries," *ERF Forum* (24 April 2018), https://theforum.erf.org.for example /2018/04/24/attitudes-towards-gender-equality- arab-countries/.

102. Mansour Moaddel, "The Tenacity of the Arab Spring in People's Perceptions: Trends in Values Among Egyptians," ERF Working Paper 1179 (April 2018).

103. Aseel Alayli, "COVID-19 Magnifies Pre-Existing Gender Inequalities in MENA," *Arab Barometer*, December 1, 2020, https://www.arabbarometer.org/2020/12/covid-19-magnifies-pre-existing-gender-inequalities-in-mena/; May El Habachi, "Is COVID-19 Pushing Women in Egypt out of workforce?" *Al-Monitor*, August 28, 2020, https://www.al-monitor.com/originals/2020/08/egypt-workforce-women-children-education-coronavirus.html, citing http://dailynewsegypt.com/2020/08/17/covid-19-nudges-egypt-unemployment-up-to-9-6-in-q2-2020-capmas/; Yahia Hatim, "NGOs Condemn Surge of Violence Against Women in Morocco," *Morocco World News*, June 19, 2020, https://www.moroccoworldnews.com/2020/06/306342/incidents-of-violence-against-women-in-morocco-prompt-reaction-from-ngos; and "Tunisia Lockdown Briings More Domestic Violence," *Asharq Al-Awsat*, March 30, 2020, https://english.aawsat.com/home/article/2206776/tunisia-lockdown-brings-rise-domestic-violence (Last accessed June 2021).

104. Nadir Mohammed, Djibrilla Issa, and Aminur Rahman, "Why the COVID-19 Impact on Firms in MENA Differ from Other Regions?" *World Bank*, https://www.worldbank.org/en/news/opi nion/2021/03/19/why-the-covid-19-impact-on-firms-in-mena-differ-from-other-regions. See also Caroline Krafft, Ragui Assaad, and Mohamed ali Marouani, "The Impact of COVID-19 on Middle Eastern and North African Labor Markets," *ERF Policy Brief* no. 55 (February 2021), Fig.1, https://erf.org.for example/app/uploads/2021/04/1618385045_704_1003556_pb55_fin al_2.pdf.

105. See Arab Barometer, "Bearing the Brunt: COVID's Impact on MENA Women at Home and at Work," *MaryClare Roche*, July 23, 2021, https://www.arabbarometer.org/2021/07/bearing-the -brunt-covids-impact-on-mena-women-at-home-and-at-work/.

106. Shamiran Mako and Valentine M. Moghadam, *After the Arab Uprisings: Progress and Stagnation in the Middle East and North Africa* (Cambridge and New York: Cambridge University Press, 2021).

107. Massoud Karshenas, Valentine M. Moghadam, and Randa Alami, "States and Social Rights: Social Policy after the Arab Spring," *World Development* 64 (September 2014): 726–39. On government responses to the pandemic, see www.menatracker.org.

F. Roudi, *Iran Is Reversing Its Population Policy* (Washington, DC: Woodrow Wilson Center for International Scholars, 2012). Viewpoints No. 7. Retrieved from, www.wilsoncenter.org/public ation/iran-reversing-its-population-policy.

CHAPTER 7

1. The chapter follow the classification in Cammett et al. 2015, as explained in Box 7.1. It focuses largely on the Gulf states (Bahrain, Kuwait, Oman, Qatar, Saudi Arabia, the United Arab Emirates, and Yemen), the countries of the Levant (Iraq, Jordan, Lebanon, Palestine, and Syria), the North African countries (Egypt, Algeria, Morocco, and Tunisia), Turkey, and Iran. Israel is excluded because its economic structure and unique history differs in many ways from the rest of the region.

2. In 2018, the World Bank defined *high income* as a GNI level of greater than $12,055 per capita, *upper-middle income* as $3,896–$12,055 per capita, *lower-middle income* as $1,996–$3,895 per capita, and *low income* as $995 per capita or less.

3. We prefer not using more recent figures in order to abstract from the negative economic effects of the COVID-19 crisis, which are expected to be largely transitory

4. It is worth noting that Libya defies easy classification. On the one hand, its per capita oil rents and income level place it in the HOC group. On the other hand, its per capita GDP is lower than all other HOC countries and its longtime ruler, Muammar al-Qadhafi, distributed oil rents far more unevenly among citizens than most other HOC countries (see Chapter 17).

5. Ishac Diwan and El Mouhoub Mouhoud, "Regional and Global Integration of Arab Countries," *Middle East Economies in Transition*, eds. Ishac Diwan and Ahmad Galal. International Economic Association Series (Palgrave, 2016).

6. Though average tariffs have reduced over time, they remain high, and importantly, non-tariff barriers (e.g. burdensome technical regulations, import authorisation procedures, cumbersome customs clearance and border controls) are obstacles to both regional and global integration. See OECD (2018).

7. Kandiyoti Deniz, "Rethinking Bargaining with Patriarchy," *Feminist Vision of Development: Gender, Analysis and Policy* (2005): 135–54. A. Alexander and C. Welzel, "Islam and Patriarchy: How Robust Is Muslim Support for Patriarchal Values? *World Values Research* 4, no. 2 (2011): 40–70. Ishac Diwan and Irina Vartanova, "The Effect of Patriarchal Culture on Women's Labor Force Participation," *Economic Research Forum Working Papers*. No. 1101. 2017.

8. ESCWA statistics. See also ESCWA: 2020:Arab Sustainable Development Report, 2020.

9. World Bank, *Iraq Household Socio-Economic Survey* (Washington, DC: World Bank, 2007).

10. Sara Roy, "De-Development Revisited: Palestinian Economy and Society since Oslo," *Journal of Palestine Studies* 28, no. 3 (1999): 65.

11. World Bank, *Palestinian Economic Prospects*, 10.

12. This section draws on Roger Owen and Şevket Pamuk, *A History of Middle East Economies in the Twentieth Century* (Cambridge, MA: Harvard University Press, 1998).

13. Roger Owen, *State, Power and Politics in the Making of the Modern Middle East* (London: Routledge), 117–18.

14. Alan Richards and John Waterbury, *A Political Economy of the Middle East*, 3rd ed. (Boulder, CO: Westview, 2008), chap. 7.

15. Marsha Pripstein Posusney and Michele Penner Angrist, eds. *Authoritarianism in the Middle East: Regimes and Resistance* (Boulder, CO: Lynne Rienner, 2005).

16. Cammett Melani and Ishac Diwan, "The Middle-oil Country Curse of the Middle East," in *New Perspective Son Middle East Politics: Economy, Society and International Relations*, ed. Robert Mason (Cairo: American University in Cairo Press, 2021).

17. Kiren Aziz Chaudhry, *The Price of Wealth: Economies and Institutions in the Middle East* (Ithaca, NY: Cornell University Press, 1997); Jill Crystal, *Oil and Politics in the Gulf: Rulers and Merchants in Kuwait and Qatar* (Cambridge: Cambridge University Press, 1995).

18. Richards and Waterbury, *A Political Economy of the Middle East*, 193–94.

19. Algeria, Iran, and Syria initiated their own economic reform programs.

20. Diwan Ishac, "Understanding Revolution in the Middle East: The Central Role of the Middle Class," *Middle East Development Journal* 5, no. 1 (2013): 1350004.

21. Heydemann, *Networks of Privilege in the Middle East*; Diwan, Malik and Atiyas, *Crony Capitalism in th Middle East*.

22. Cammett et al. (2015), Chapter 1.

23. Cammett et al. (2015), Chapter 8.

24. Kiren Aziz Chaudhry, "The Myths of the Market and the Common History of Late Developers," *Politics and Society* 21, no. 3 (September 1993); Karl Polanyi, *The Great Transformation*, 1944.

25. Marcus Noland and Howard Pack, *Arab Economies in a Changing World* (Washington, DC: Peterson Institute, 2007), 11.

26. Asef Bayat, "Transforming the Arab World: The Arab Human Development Report and the Politics of Change," *Development and Change* 36, no. 6 (2005): 1225–37.

27. See Max Weber, *The Protestant Ethic and the Spirit of Capitalism* (Mineola, NY: Dover, 2003 [1958]). For a critique of Weber's arguments vis-à-vis Islam and capitalism, see Maxime Rodinson, *Islam and Capitalism* (Austin: University of Texas Press, 1979); Bernard Lewis, *The Muslim Discovery of Europe* (New York: W. W. Norton, 1982); and Noland and Pack, *Arab Economies in a Changing World*, 10, 143–44.

28. Timur Kuran, "Why the Middle East Is Economically Underdeveloped: Historical Mechanisms of Institutional Stagnation," *Journal of Economic Perspectives* 18, no. 3 (Summer 2004): 71–90; Timur Kuran, *The Long Divergence: How Islamic Law Held Back the Middle East* (Princeton, NJ: Princeton University Press, 2010).

29. Murat Çizakça, "Review of Timur Kuran, *The Long Divergence: How Islamic Institutions Held Back the Middle East,*" in H-Net, June 2011, http://eh.net/book_reviews/long-divergence-how-islamic-law-held-back-middle-east; Jack Goldstone, "Review Essay: Is Islam Bad for Business?" *Perspectives on Politics* 10, no. 1 (March 2012): 97–102.

30. Giacomo Luciani, "Allocation v. Production States: An Analytical Framework," in *The Arab State*, ed. Giacomo Luciani (London: Routledge, 1990), 65–84.

31. Michael L. Ross, *The Oil Curse: How Petroleum Wealth Shapes the Development of Nations* (Princeton, NJ: Princeton University Press, 2012).

32. Peter Evans, *Embedded Autonomy: States and Industrial Transformation* (Princeton, NJ: Princeton University Press, 1995).

33. Cammett, Melani, Ishac Diwan, and Andrew Leber. "Is Oil Wealth Good for Private Sector Development?" *Economic Research Forum Working Papers*. No. 1299. 2019.

34. World Bank, *Unlocking the Employment Potential in the Middle East and North Africa: Toward a New Social Contract* (Washington, DC: World Bank, 2004), 2.

35. Henry and Springborg, *Globalization and the Politics of Development in the Middle East.*

36. Peter Evans, *Embedded Autonomy*; Atul Kohli, *State-Directed Development: Political Power and Industrialization in the Global Periphery* (Cambridge: Cambridge University Press, 2004).

37. Daron Acemoglu, Simon Johnson, and James A. Robinson, "Reversal of Fortune: Geography and Institutions in the Making of the Modern World Income Distribution," *Quarterly Journal of Economics* 117, no. 4 (2002): 1231–94; James Mahoney, *Colonialism and Postcolonial Development: Spanish America in Comparative Perspective* (Cambridge: Cambridge University Press, 2010).

38. Diwan Ishac, Nadim Houry, and Yezid Sayigh, *Egypt after the Coronavirus: Back to Square One.* Arab Reform Initiative, August 2020.

39. After the first full election of 2014, political pacification pushed for the formation of a national coalition government between the two largest parties, Nidaa Tounis and Ennahdha, later formalized in the 2016 Carthage Agreements.

40. Diwan Ishac, "Tunisia's Upcoming Challenge: Fixing the Economy before It's Too Late," *Arab Reform Initiative*, September 23, 2019.

41. Diwan Ishac, "Fiscal Sustainability, the Labor Market, and Growth in Saudi Arabia," in *When Can Oil Economies Be Deemed Sustainable?* eds. G. Luciani and T. Moerenhout (Palgrave Macmillan, 2020), 31–53.

42. This compares to employment rates of about 65 percent in the OECD.

43. Currently, Saudis working in the private sector earn about half as much as those who work in the private sector, and twice what expats earn in the private sector.

44. Ellen Lust-Okar, "Divided they Rule: The Management and Manipulation of Political Opposition," *Comparative Politics* (2004): 159–79.

CHAPTER 8

1. Stephen M. Walt, *The Origin of Alliances* (Ithaca, NY: Cornell University Press, 1987).

2. F. Gregory Gause III, *The International Relations of the Persian Gulf* (New York: Cambridge University Press, 2010); Curtis Ryan, *Inter-Arab Alliances* (Gainesville: University of Florida Press, 2008).

3. Fred Halliday, *The Middle East in International Relations: Power, Politics, and Ideology* (New York: Cambridge University Press, 2005); Laurie Brand, *Jordan's Inter-Arab Alliances* (New York: Columbia University Press, 1994); Lisa Anderson, "Peace and Democracy in the Middle East: The Constraints of Soft Budgets," *Journal of International Affairs* 49 (1995): 819–32.

4. Michael Barnett, *Dialogues in Arab Politics: Negotiations in Regional Order* (New York: Columbia University Press, 1998); Marc Lynch, *Voices of the New Arab Public: Iraq, Al-Jazeera, and Middle East Politics Today* (New York: Columbia University Press, 2006); and Ewan Stein, *The International Relations of the Middle East* (New York: Cambridge University Press, 2021).

5. L. Carl Brown, *International Politics and the Middle East: Old Rules, Dangerous Game* (Princeton, NJ: Princeton University Press, 1984).

6. Malcolm Kerr, *The Arab Cold War* (New York: Oxford University Press, 1971); Barnett, *Dialogues in Arab Politics*.

7. Raymond Hinnebusch, *The International Politics of the Middle East* (Manchester: Manchester University Press, 2015).

8. David A. Lake, *Hierarchy in International Relations* (Ithaca, NY: Cornell University Press, 2009).

9. Ibid.

10. Ryan, *Inter-Arab Alliances*.

11. Shibley Telhami, *Power and Leadership in International Bargaining: The Path to the Camp David Accords* (New York: Columbia University Press, 1990).

12. Stephen M. Walt, "Alliances in a Unipolar World," *World Politics* 61, no.1 (2009): 86–120.

13. Lake, *Hierarchy*; Peter J. Katzenstein, *A World of Regions: Asia and Europe in the American Imperium* (Ithaca, NY: Cornell University Press, 2005).

14. Kristina Kausch, "Competitive Multipolarity in the Middle East," *International Spectator* 50, no. 3 (2015): 1–15.

15. Marc Lynch and Curtis R. Ryan, "The Arab Uprisings and International Relations Theory," *PS: Political Science and Politics* 50, no.3 (2017): 643–46; Sean Yom, "US Foreign Policy in the Middle East: The Logic of Hegemonic Retreat," *Global Policy* 11, no. 1 (2020): 75–83.

16. Ian Lustick, "The Absence of Middle Eastern Great Powers: Political 'Backwardness' in Comparative Perspective," *International Organization* 51 (1997): 653–83.

17. Halliday, *The Middle East in International Relations*; Steven Heydemann, ed., *War, Institutions, and Social Change in the Middle East* (Berkeley: University of California Press, 2000).

18. Lynch, "Globalization and Arab Security," in *Globalization and National Security*, ed. Jonathan Kirshner (New York: Routledge, 2007).

19. Adam Hanieh, *Money, Markets and Monarchies: The Gulf Cooperation Council and the Political Economy of the Contemporary Middle East* (New York: Cambridge University Press, 2018).

20. Lynch, *Voices of the New Arab Public*.

21. Walt, *The Origin of Alliances*.

22. Barnett, *Dialogues in Arab Politics*.

23. Gregory Gause, "Balancing What? Threat Perception and Alliance Choice in the Gulf," *Security Studies* (2003/2004): 274.

24. Barnett, *Dialogues in Arab Politics*.

25. Lynch, *Voices of the New Arab Public*.

26. Benjamin Miller, "Balance of Power or the State-to- Nation Balance: Explaining Middle East War Propensity," *Security Studies* 15, no. 4 (2006): 658–705.

27. Gause, *The International Relations of the Persian Gulf*; Ryan, *Inter-Arab Alliances*.

28. Patrick Seale, *The Struggle for Syria* (New Haven, CT: Yale University Press, 1986).

29. Kerr, *The Arab Cold War*.

30. Gause, "Balancing What?"

31. Telhami, *Power and Leadership in International Bargaining*.

32. Joost Hiltermann, *A Poisonous Affair: America, Iraq, and the Gassing of Halabja* (New York: Cambridge University Press, 2007).

33. Lynch, *Voices of the New Arab Public*.

34. Fouad Ajami, *The Arab Predicament* (New York: Cambridge University Press, 1991).

35. Anderson, "Peace and Democracy in the Middle East."

36. Lustick, "The Absence of Middle Eastern Great Powers."

37. Vali Nasr, *The Shia Revival: How Conflicts within Islam Will Shape the Future* (New York: W. W. Norton, 2006).

38. Nazih Ayubi, *Over-Stating the Arab State* (New York: I. B. Tauris, 1996).

39. Bruce Bueno de Mesquita, Alistair Smith, Randolph M. Siverson, and James M. Morrow, *The Logic of Political Survival* (Cambridge: MIT Press, 2004).

CHAPTER 9

1. See Alistair Horne, *A Savage War of Peace: Algeria 1954–62* (New York: Penguin Books, 1987). See also *The Battle of Algiers*, directed by G. Pontecorvo.

2. Military security is an intelligence service under the minister of defense. It functions as a sort of political police, whose mission is not only the security of the state but also that of the regime. In the 1980s, it changed its name to Département de Renseignement et de Sécurité (DRS).

3. Certain groups already existed in secret, such as FFS (Front des Forces Socialistes), PAGS (Parti de l'Avant Garde Socialiste), and MDA (Mouvement pour la Démocratie en Algérie). Others grew, although with no popular foundation.

4. The FIS, Front Islamique du Salut (Islamic Salvation Front), was the most popular Islamist party in Algeria. See Lahouari Addi, "Islamicist Utopia and Democracy," in *The Annals of American Academy of Political and Social Science* (November 1992).

5. Kabylia is a mountainous area in eastern Algeria, which is inhabited by Berber speakers generally hostile to the government. It has been a stronghold of Algerian nationalism.

6. See Hugh Roberts, *The Battlefield: Algeria 1988–2002: Studies in Broken Polity* (London: Verso, 2003).

7. See Lahouari Addi, "The Algerian Army and the State," in *Political Armies: The Military and Nation Building in the Age of Democracy*, eds. Kees Koonings and Dirk Kruijt (London: Zed Books, 2002).

8. The FLN gained 105 seats, the MSP 64 seats, RND 57 seats, El Moustaqbal 48 seats; El Bina 40 seats; and seven other parties had between 3 and 1 seats. Independents held 78 seats.

9. See Lahouari Addi, *The Crisis of Religious Muslim Discourse. The Necessary Schift from Plato to Kant* (London: Routledge, 2021).

10. See Lahouari Addi, *Radical Arab Nationalism and Political Islam* (Washington, DC: Georgetown University Press, 2017).

11. See Gianni Del Panta, "Weathering the Storm: Why Was There No Arab Uprising in Algeria?" *Democratization* 24, no. 6 (2017): 1085–102; Frédéric Volpi, "Algeria versus the Arab Spring," *Journal of Democracy* 24, no.3 (2013): 104–15.

12. Since its foundation, the ANSEJ has at time of writing financed 367,980 projects for a total of $50 million, which has led to the creation of 900,000 jobs. According to data provided by the agency, 10% of projects go bankrupt, but debts are paid by the state.

    See « L'ANSEJ à l'heure des bilans », *El-Watan* 28th February 2017; « ANSEJ: les dettes épongées », *Liberté* 27th June 2017

13. Upon signing such contracts, some high-ranking officers and ministers receive significant commissions which were deposited in offshore bank accounts or transferred to accounts in tax -havens. The NGO Transparency International possesses numerous documents that provide accounts of these financial improprieties. See Djillali Hadjadj, "Algeria: A Future Hijacked by Corruption," *Mediterranean Politics* 12, no. 2 (2007): 263–77;

14. See the Office National des Statistiques official website (www.ons.dz) for the comprehensive employment reports with demographic and regional breakdowns.

15. From 1992 to 2002, there were two hundred thousand deaths in a "dirty war" in which Islamist guerrillas and counterguerrillas took the civilian population hostage. One of the stakes of this war was international public opinion, especially French, in order to discredit the adversary and gain support in the West. There were massacres of villagers, including women and children. In the absence of credible reporting, Human rights organizations, including Amnesty International, demanded an international commission of inquiry, which was never set up because of French support of the Algerian government. In 2000, the new president, Abdelaziz Bouteflika offered amnesty and money to those who left the ranks of the insurgents. Since then, violence has decreased, although some Islamists refused his offer.

CHAPTER 10

1. The quotation comes to us from John Holland Rose's *Life of Napoleon*, but it is used to open the Earl of Cromer's 1908 *Modern Egypt*. According to Rose, Napoleon made the statement "emphatically" in his first interview with the governor of St. Helena. The diminutive French conqueror was referring to Egypt's agricultural abundance and its location at the crossroads of Europe, Africa, and Western Asia.

2. L. Carl Brown, *Diplomacy in the Middle East: The International Relations of Regional and Outside Powers* (London: I. B. Tauris, 2004), 101.

3. Arnold J. Toynbee, "The Present Situation in Palestine," *International Affairs* 10, no. 1 (1931): 42.

4. Thomas L. Friedman, "The Land of Denial," *New York Times,* June 5, 2002; Egypt State Information Service, "Mubarak: Peace Is Made by Strong, Brave Leaders," May 11, 2009; Helene Cooper, "Obama to Speak from Egypt in Address to Muslim World," *New York Times,* May 8, 2009. One might reasonably ask, of course, why Obama would choose the heart of the Arab world for an address to the Muslim world, given that the former makes up only a small part of the latter.

5. We often read that Nasser ruled Egypt from 1952 to 1970, although this is technically incorrect. See, for example, Asad Abu Khalil, *The Battle for Saudi Arabia: Royalty, Fundamentalism, and Global Power* (New York: Seven Stories Press, 2004), 32–33; Ninette S. Fahmy, *The Politics of Egypt: State-Society Relationship* (New York: Routledge, 2002), 33; and Milton Viorst, *In the Shadow of the Prophet: The Struggle for the Soul of Islam* (New York: Anchor Books, 1998), 42. Though the coup that brought down Egypt's monarchy did occur in 1952, Nasser emerged as the undisputed leader of the so-called Revolutionary Command Council only in 1954, after a power struggle with Egypt's first president, Muhammad Naguib. Even then, his official title was "prime minister" until his appointment to the presidency in late 1955. The reason this matters is that extending Nasser's rule all the way back to 1952 obscures the fact that there was great uncertainty and debate in those early years about what kind of government Egypt would have. Though Nasser eventually won, his victory was by no means assured.

6. The Arab League has twenty-two members: Algeria, Bahrain, the Comoros, Djibouti, Egypt, Iraq, Jordan, Kuwait, Lebanon, Libya, Mauritania, Morocco, Oman, the Palestinian Authority, Qatar, Saudi Arabia, Somalia, Sudan, Syria, Tunisia, the United Arab Emirates, and Yemen. Of the Arab League's six secretaries general, only one was not Egyptian: From Egypt's expulsion in 1979 until 1990, the Arab League was headed by a Tunisian politician named Chedli Klibi.

7. Data on book and film production comes from UNESCO's Institute for Statistics, www.uis.unesco.org. The scholar Fouad Ajami (in "The Sorrows of Egypt," *Foreign Affairs* [1995]) noted that Egypt "produces a mere 375 books a year" and invited us to "contrast this with Israel's 4,000 titles." But according to UNESCO, Egypt in 1995 actually produced 2,215 titles. Israel, in contrast, was reported to have produced 1,969 books (although that figure is from 1998, the only year for which the Israeli data were available). Of course, Israel's much smaller population (five million to Egypt's eighty million) means that the Jewish state has a much higher ratio of books produced per person than does Egypt. On the question of the Egyptian dialect as the *lingua franca* of the Arab world, see Hussein Amin, *New Patterns in Global Television: Peripheral Vision* (London: Oxford University Press, 1999), 102.

8. David Patel, Valerie Bunce, and Sharon Wolchik, "Fizzles and Fireworks: A Comparative Perspective on the Diffusion of Popular Protests in the Middle East and North Africa," in *The Arab Uprisings in Comparative Perspective*, ed. Marc Marc Lynch (New York: Columbia University Press, 2014).

9. Robert Baer, *The Devil We Know: Dealing with the New Iranian Superpower* (New York: Random House, 2008), 151.

10. The precise number of dead in that incident is a matter of dispute. Human Rights Watch claims more than one thousand deaths (https://www.hrw.org/news/2014/08/12/egypt-raba-killings-likely-crimes-against-humanity). But Egyptian government sources claim a smaller number of casualties—see, for example, http://www.dailynewsegypt.com/2013/08/16/health-ministry-raises-death-toll-of-wednesdays-clashes-to-638/.

11. The architecture and many of the details of this section are drawn from two magisterial sources: Afaf Lutfi al-Sayyid Marsot, *A Short History of Modern Egypt* (Cambridge: Cambridge University Press, 1985); P. J. Vatikiotis, *The Modern History of Egypt* (London: Weidenfeld & Nicholson, 1969). It also draws, with permission, on material from the chapter on Egypt from the eleventh edition of this volume.

12. The historian Roger Owen has memorably referred to the "somewhat artificial appearance" of many Middle Eastern states, with their "dead-straight boundaries that were so obviously the work of a British or French colonial official using a ruler." See Roger Owen, *State Power and Politics in the Making of the Modern Middle East* (New York: Routledge, 2002).

13. J. Patrick Bannerman, *Islam in Perspective: A Guide to Islamic Society, Politics and Law* (New York: Routledge, 1988), 129.

14. See https://en.wikipedia.org/wiki/Narmer_Palette.

15. The Arabic name for Egypt, *misr,* appears seven times in the Qur'an: Chapter 10, Verse 87; Chapter 12, Verses 21, 43, 74, 94, and 99; and Chapter 43, Verse 51.

16. Afaf Lutfi al-Sayyid Marsot, *A Short History of Modern Egypt* (Cambridge: Cambridge University Press, 1985), 1.

17. Andrew McGregor, *A Military History of Modern Egypt: From the Ottoman Conquest to the Ramadan War* (Santa Barbara, CA: Greenwood, 2006), 10. It's possible to take this too far. The fact is that Egypt always had a knack for, in the words of one nineteenth-century writer, "conquering its conquerors" (Charles Dudley Warner, "Editor's Drawer," *Harper's Magazine* 82, no. 492 [1891]: 971–72). The descendants of Muhammad (Mehmet) Ali, for example, were largely Egyptianized by the time of their expulsion in 1952.

18. The erasure of the pre-Islamic histories of the "converted peoples" is explored, if in somewhat polemical fashion, in V. S. Naipaul, *Among the Believers: An Islamic Journey* (New York: Knopf, 1981); *Beyond Belief: Islamic Excursions Among the Converted Peoples* (New York: Random House, 1998).

19. Dates for the Fatimid, Ayubid, and Mameluke dynasties are from Heinz Halm, *The Fatimids and Their Traditions of Learning* (London: I. B. Tauris, 1997). A highly readable account of the rivalry of Saladin and Richard is James Reston Jr., *Warriors of God: Richard the Lionheart and Saladin in the Third Crusade* (New York: Doubleday, 2001).

20. See, for example, Arthur Goldschmidt Jr., *Modern Egypt: The Formation of a Nation-State,* 2nd ed. (Boulder, CO: Westview Press, 2004), 15.

21. For Napoleon's sojourn in Egypt, see Alan Schom, *Napoleon Bonaparte: A Life* (New York: Harper Collins, 1997), 107–87.

22. In addition to cataloging these impacts of the French expedition, Max Rodenbeck, *Cairo: The City Victorious* (London: Vintage, 2000), 121, reports another contribution made by the French to Egyptian society: "To this day," he writes, "peasant women of the Nile Delta wear dresses cut in the fashion of late eighteenth century France."

23. Marsot, *A Short History of Modern Egypt*, 51.

24. Ibid., 52.

25. For an account of Ali's attempts to make Egypt an economic and political power and a controversial explanation for why they ultimately failed, see David Landes, *The Wealth and Poverty of Nations: Why Some Are So Rich and Some So Poor* (New York: W. W. Norton, 1998), 392–421.

26. Ibid.

27. Ian S. Lustick, "The Absence of Middle Eastern Great Powers: 'Political Backwardness' in Historical Perspective," *International Organization* 51, no. 4 (2003): 653–58.

28. Marsot, *A Short History of Modern Egypt*, 66.

29. According to Marsot, Said and de Lesseps were old friends from de Lesseps's day as French consul. Said, she tells us, was always obese, and he chafed under his father's increasingly draconian weight-loss regimens. De Lesseps, she says, helped the young Said circumvent these restrictions by sneaking him plates of pasta—a favor Said would return years later by granting de Lesseps the Suez Canal concession on exceedingly favorable terms (Marsot, *A Short History of Modern Egypt*, 66).

30. In recognition of Egypt's special status, Ismail Pasha had secured from the Ottoman sultan the right to label himself a *khedive* (Persian for prince, ruler, or sovereign) instead of the traditional term, *vali*, which was used for Ottoman governors. In 1914, the title bestowed on Egypt's rulers changed when the country was declared a sultanate, and it changed yet again in 1922 when formal Egyptian independence from the British Empire rendered Egypt a kingdom. See Majid Khadduri, "The Anglo Egyptian Controversy," *Proceedings of the American Academy of Political Science* 24, no. 4 (1952): 82–100.

31. Rodenbeck, *Cairo: The City Victorious*, 131.

32. Ibid.

33. This statement is quoted in a variety of places. The earliest mention I could find of it is in Appleton's *Annual Cyclopaedia and Register of Important Events of the Year 1878: Embracing Political Civil, Military, and Social Affairs: Public Document; Biography, Statistics, Commerce, Finance, Literature, Science, Agriculture, and Mechanical Industry* (New York: D. Appleton & Company, 1890), 266. According to this source, Ismail made the statement to the British representative of his creditors. Though it is often hinted that Ismail's statement was an idle boast, it appears from the context of the remark that Ismail was speaking less about the grandeur of his architectural achievements than of the need to reform his country.

34. Donald M. Reid, "Egyptian History through Stamps," *The Muslim World* 62, no. 3 (1972): 213.

35. Mohammed Naguib, *Egypt's Destiny* (London: Gollancz, 1955), 80.

36. Marsot, *A Short History of Modern Egypt*, 102. According to a biography of Nasser penned by his daughter, his rank at this time was that of major. See http://nasser.bibalex.org/Common/pictures01-%20sira_en.htm#3

37. Richard P. Mitchell, *The Society of the Muslim Brothers* (New York: Oxford University Press, 1993), 71.

38. Donald M. Reid, "Political Assassination in Egypt, 1910–1954," *International Journal of African Historical Studies* 15, no. 4 (1982): 625–51.

39. Robert Bianchi, "The Corporatization of the Egyptian Labor Movement," *The Middle East Journal* 40, no. 3 (1986): 429–44.

40. Jacob M. Landau, *Parliaments and Parties in Egypt* (New York: Hyperion Press, 1979), 7.

41. Ibid. According to Landau, Muhammad Ali's legislative council included "33 high-ranking officials, 24 district officials and 99 of the notables of Egypt."

42. Fahmy, *The Politics of Egypt*, 44.

43. Don Peretz, "Democracy and Revolution in Egypt," *The Middle East Journal* 13, no. 1 (1959): 27. The revolution's six principles included ending feudalism, the British occupation, and the domination of capital; and establishing democracy, a strong national army, and social justice.

44. Robert Springborg, "Patrimonialism and Policy Making in Egypt," *Middle Eastern Studies* 15, no. 1 (January 1979): 49–69.

45. See Jason Brownlee, *Democracy Prevention: The Politics of the US-Egyptian Alliance* (Cambridge: Cambridge University Press, 2012).

46. Tamir Moustafa, *The Struggle for Constitutional Power: Law, Politics, and Economic Development in Egypt* (New York: Cambridge University Press, 2007).

47. Mona Makram-Ebeid, "Political Opposition in Egypt: Democratic Myth or Reality?" *The Middle East Journal* 43, no. 3 (1989): 423–36.

48. See Samer Shehata and Joshua Stacher, "The Brotherhood Goes to Parliament," *Middle East Report* 240 (2006); Brownlee, "The Decline of Pluralism in Mubarak's Egypt," *Journal of Democracy* 13, no. 4 (2002): 6–14.

49. For an in-depth exploration of the dynamics of parliamentary elections under Mubarak, see Lisa Blaydes, *Elections and Distributive Politics in Mubarak's Egypt* (Cambridge: Cambridge University Press, 2010).

50. Robert Springborg, *Mubarak's Egypt: Fragmentation of the Political Order* (Boulder, CO: Westview Press, 1989), 192.

51. Morsi attempted to reverse the court's dissolution of the Islamist-majority parliament but was blocked by the military. One wonders how Egyptian politics might have turned out had the legislature remained in place. Though the Muslim Brotherhood constituted a plurality of the parliament, it did not possess a majority, and its Salafist allies could not have been counted on to serve as a mere rubber stamp for Morsi's policies. There are thus reasons to believe that the dissolution of parliament was a grave setback for Egyptian pluralism, even as the court that undertook it likely believed it was doing the opposite.

52. Robert Springborg, *Egypt* (Hoboken, NJ: John Wiley & Sons, 2017).

53. Ibid.

54. Steven A. Cook, *Ruling but Not Governing: The Military and Political Development in Egypt, Algeria, and Turkey* (Baltimore, MD: Johns Hopkins University Press, 2007).

55. Alex Blumberg, "Why Egypt's Military Cares about Home Appliances," *NPR News*, February 4, 2011, http://www.npr.org/blogs/money/2011/02/10/133501837/why-egypts-military-cares-about-home-appliances. [February 4, 2011], http://www.npr.org/blogs/money/2011/02/10/133501837/why-egypts-military-cares-about-home-appliances.

56. See Robert Springborg, "Egypt's Future: Yet Another Turkish Model?" *The International Spectator* 49, no. 1 (2014): 1–6. See also Zeinab Abul-Magd, "The Egyptian Republic of Retired Generals," *Foreign Policy Middle East Channel* (May 28, 2012), http://foreignpolicy.com/2012/05/08/the-egyptian-republic-of-retired-generals/.

57. Peter Harling and Yasser El Shimy, "Egypt's Quest for Itself," *Orient XXI*, January 13, 2014, http://orientxxi.info/magazine/egypt-s-quest-for-itself,0474.

58. See Sharan Grewal, "Soldiers of Democracy: Military Legacies and Democratic Transitions in Egypt and Tunisia" (Doctoral dissertation, Department of Politics, Princeton University, 2018).

59. See Yasser M. El-Shimy, "Fumbled Democracy: Why Egypt's Transition Floundered." Paper presented at the *Midwest Political Science Association Annual Meeting* Midwest, Chicago, April 2015.

60. Mona El-Ghobashy, "Unsettling the Authorities: Constitutional Reform in Egypt," *Middle East Report* 226 (2003): 28–34.

61. See, for example, Patrick Kingsley, "Egyptian Police Go on Strike," *The Guardian*, March 10, 2013, http://www.theguardian.com/world/2013/mar/10/egypt-police-strike.

62. See Max Siegelbaum, "In Egypt, Police Are the Real Hooligans," *Foreign Policy*, February 10, 2015, http://foreignpolicy.com/2015/02/10/in-egypt-police-are-the-real-hooligans-deaths-cairo-soccer-stadium/.

63. "Egypt's al-Sisi Apologises for Police Brutality," *Al-Jazeera*, June 8, 2015, http://www.aljazeer a.com/news/2015/06/egypt-sisi-apologises-police-brutality-150607172031792.html.

64. Kristen McTighe, "Proposed Terror Law Provokes Outcry in Egypt," *Financial Times*, July 8, 2015,http://www.ft.com/intl/cms/s/0/e6abb6f8-256b-11e5-9c4e-a775d2b173ca.html#axzz3f WUzQ3QM.

65. Yezid Sayegh, "Missed Opportunity: The Politics of Police Reform in Egypt and Tunisia," *Carnegie Endowment for International Peace*, March 17, 2015, http://carnegie-mec.org/2015/03 /17/missed-opportunity-politics-of-police-reform-in-egypt-and-tunisia.

66. "Egypt: Emergency Provisions Made Permanent," *Human Rights Watch*, November 5, 2021, ht tps://www.hrw.org/news/2021/11/05/egypt-emergency-provisions-made-permanent# (Last accessed November 7, 2021).

67. Tamir Moustafa, "Law versus the State: The Judicialization of Politics in Egypt," *Law and Social Inquiry* 28, no. 4 (2003): 883–930.

68. Ibid.

69. Moustafa, "Law versus the State"; Moustafa, *The Struggle for Constitutional Power*.

70. Nathan J. Brown and Michele Dunne, *Egypt's Controversial Constitutional Amendments: A Textual Analysis* (Washington, DC: Carnegie Endowment for International Peace, 2007).

71. See, for example, Jason Brownlee, "Morsi Was No Role Model for Islamic Democrats," *Middle East Institute*, July 17, 2013, http://www.mei.edu/content/morsi-was-no-role-model-islamic-democrats.

72. Karl Vick, "Egypt's Courts Mock Justice with More Death Sentences," *Time*, April 28, 2014; appended, May 1, 2014.

73. On the weakness of opposition parties in Egypt and the Arab world more broadly, see Ellen Lust-Okar, *Structuring Conflict in the Arab World: Incumbents, Opponents, and Institutions* (Cambridge: Cambridge University Press, 2005).

74. See Dina Bishara, *Contesting Authoritarianism: Labor Challenges to the State in Egypt* (Cambridge: Cambridge University Press, 2018).

75. Marc Lynch, *Voices of the New Arab Public: Iraq, Al-Jazeera, and Middle East Politics Today* (New York: Columbia University Press, 2006).

76. See Carrie Rosefsky-Wickham, *Mobilizing Islam: Religion, Activism, and Political Change in Egypt* (New York: Columbia University Press, 2002).

77. Readers interested in learning more about the menagerie of Egyptian political parties in the immediate aftermath of the January 25, 2011, revolution are advised to consult the Egyptian Parties and Movements website composed by the online magazine *Jadaliyya* and the Egyptian newspaper *al-Ahram*, http://www.jadaliyya.com/pages/contributors/43055.

78. The Brotherhood's FJP actually ran in coalition with several smaller parties as part of a grandly named "Democratic Alliance." In addition to the Brotherhood's 217 seats, other alliance members won 11 seats.

79. The Party of Light ran in coalition with other Islamist parties, which together captured around 16 additional seats on top of the 107 captured by al-Nūr.

80. Allocation of seats by party in the new legislature is available at the website of the Egyptian Higher Elections Committee (http://parliament2011.elections.eg/) and can be viewed in English here: http://en.wikipedia.org/wiki/Egyptian_parliamentary_election,_2011.

81. "Ahdath damiyya fi hizb al wafd [Bloody Events in the Wafd Party]," *Al-Ahram*, April 2, 2006.

82. See Tarek Masoud, *Counting Islam: Religion, Class, and Elections in Egypt* (Cambridge: Cambridge University Press, 2014).

83. Details of the system, on which this account draws, are found in Mohamed Menshawy, "Egypt's New Parliamentary Election Law: Back to the Future," *Middle East Institute*, July 17, 2014, http://www.mei.edu/content/at/egypts-new-parliamentary- election-law-back-future.

84. According to the website of the Egyptian chamber of deputies, the current parliament is comprised of 348 independents and 244 party members. See http://www.parliament.gov.eg/HOM E/AdmissionMain.aspx.

85. An important, if tendentious, account of the violence that has wracked Egypt since 2013 is provided by Human Rights Watch at https://www.hrw.org/world-report/2014/country-chapters/ egypt.

86. See http://www.nytimes.com/2013/09/06/world/middleeast/egypts-interior-minister-survives - attack.html. For ABM's claim of responsibility for the attack, see http://www.longwarjournal.or g/archives/2013/10/ansar_jerusalem_rele.php.

87. See http://www.independent.co.uk/news/world/africa/three-egyptian-judges-shot-dead-in- sinai-hours-after-mohamed-morsi-sentenced-to-death-10255067.html.

88. See http://www.upi.com/Top_News/World-News/2015/06/29/Egyptian-prosecutor-Barakat -killed- in-car-bomb-assassination/2051435584537/.

89. Tamara Qiblawi and Bryony Jones, "Grief and Desperation in Egypt's Coptic Community after Palm Sunday Attacks," *CNN*, April 10, 2017, https://www.cnn.com/2017/04/10/middleeast/ egypt-coptic-community-grief-anger/index.html.

90. Ian Lee, Laura Smith-Spark, and Hamdi Alkhshali, "Egypt Hunts for Killers after Mosque Attack Leaves at Least 235 Dead," *CNN*, November 24, 2017, https://www.cnn.com/2017/11/24 /africa/egypt- sinai-mosque-attack/index.html.

91. This section draws, with permission, on material from the eleventh edition of this volume.

92. Edward P. Djerejian, "The U.S. and the Middle East in a Changing World," Address at Meridian House International (Washington, June 2, 1992).

93. This argument has been made most effectively by several scholars, including Quintan Wiktorowicz, Diane Singerman, and Carrie Rosefsky Wickham, among others. Masoud (2014) examines empirical evidence for this proposition.

94. Ellen Lust, Gamal Soltan, and Jakob Wichmann, "Egypt's Swinging Centre," *Al-Jazeera*, July 26, 2013, http://www.aljazeera.com/indepth/opinion/2013/07/201372612477541330.html. See also Masoud, *Counting Islam: Religion, Class, and Elections in Egypt*, especially Chapter 5.

95. Testimonials to the "local embeddedness" of Islamists—which I take to mean the organic, daily participation of Islamist activists in the social lives of their communities—can be found in Wickham (2002) and Janine Astrid Clark, *Islam, Charity and Activism: Middle Class Networks and Social Welfare in Egypt, Jordan and Yemen* (Bloomington: Indiana University Press, 2004). Melani Cammett and Pauline Jones-Luong, "Is There an Islamist Political Advantage?" *Annual Review of Political Science* 17 (2014): 187–206, among others. For an interesting comparison with Hindu fundamentalists in India, who appear to share some of these organizational and behavioral characteristics, see Tariq Thachil, *Elite Parties, Poor Voters: How Social Services Win Votes in India* (Cambridge: Cambridge University Press, 2014).

96. Ed Payne and Saad Abedine, "Egypt Charges Coptic Christians Linked to Infamous Video," *CNN*, September 18, 2012, http://www.cnn.com/2012/09/18/world/film-protests/.

97. This paragraph draws on material previously published in Tarek Masoud, "Losing Egypt," in *The Arab Revolutions and American Policy*, ed. Nicholas Burns (Washington, DC: Aspen Institute Press, 2013), 96.

98. See video at http://new.elfagr.org/Detail.aspx?nwsId=242959&secid=1&vid=2#.UNOF5o5Avd4.

99. Essam el-Ibaidi, "Christians Angry after Biltagi and Higazi Declare That Copts Are Fighting the Islamic Project," *Al-Wafd*, December 14, 2012.

100. Hussam Abd al-Raziq, "Christians Send SMS Messages to Voters in Suhag Instructing Them to Vote against the Constitution," *Ikhwanonline*, December 15, 2012, http://www.ikhwanonline.com/new/Article. aspx?ArtID=131916&SecID=230.

101. "Al-Bābā Tawāḍrūs muhājimān al-rabī' al-'arabī wa ḥukm Mursī: tarshīḥ al-Sīsī wājib waṭanī [Pope Tawadros Attacks the Arab Spring and Morsi's Rule: al-Sisi's Nomination Is a National Duty]," *CNN Arabic*, March 23, 2014, http://arabic.cnn.com/middleeast/2014/03/23/tawadrous- egypt-mursi-sisi.

102. Ibid.

103. This section is based on material from the eleventh edition of this volume, with permission.

104. The author thanks Diana Greenwald of the University of Michigan for pointing him to the source of this data.

105. Egypt's Ministry of Investment, which is responsible for overseeing Egypt's privatization program, reports that its portfolio of companies up for privatization includes 153 public sector companies as well as shares in 669 public-private joint ventures. See "Egypt Investment Observer, Third Quarter, January–March, Fiscal Year 2008–2009" (Cairo: Ministry of Investment, Arab Republic of Egypt, 2009).

106. See https://www.middleeastmonitor.com/articles/africa/12880-al-sisi-raises-prices-for-the-poor-to-subsidise-the-wealthy.

107. See http://www.reuters.com/article/2015/01/12/us-egypt-bread-idUSKBN0KL14520150112.

108. See http://www.atlanticcouncil.org/blogs/egyptsource/one-year-on-the-economy-under-sisi.

109. See http://www.telegraph.co.uk/news/worldnews/africaandindianocean/egypt/11014605/Egypts-president-announces-plans-for-new-Suez-Canal.html.

110. Readers may explore Suez Canal monthly revenues at https://www.ceicdata.com/en/egypt/maritime- transport-revenues/maritime-transport-suez-canal- revenues.

111. See http://www.egypttoday.com/Article/3/41562/Zohr-gas-field-in-numbers.

112. See http://english.ahram.org.eg/NewsContent/3/162/125127/Business/EEDC-/Live-updates-Gulf-leaders-pledge--bn-in-aid,-inves.aspx.

113. See http://www.thecairopost.com/news/157108/business/contract-negotiations-on-egypts-new- capital-city-in-progress-minister.

114. This section (sans updates added by the author) first appeared in the eleventh edition of this volume. The material is reused here with permission.

115. See https://www.washingtonpost.com/news/worldviews/wp/2018/02/05/israels-growing-ties-with-former-arab-foes/?noredirect=on&utm_term=.d4ed7596d606.

116. Ashok Swain, "Ethiopia, the Sudan, and Egypt: The Nile River Dispute," *Journal of Modern African Studies* 35, no. 4 (1997): 675–94.

117. Arthur Okoth-Owiro, "State Succession and International Treaty Commitments: A Case Study of the Nile Water Treaties," *Konrad Adenauer Stiftung Occassional Papers* (2004), 28.

118. The details in this paragraph draw from "Nile River Dispute," Inventory of Conflict and Environment Case Study, American University, http://www1.american.edu/ted/ice/bluenile.htm.

119. Mohamed Hafez, "Testing the Waters," *Ahram Weekly*, May 6–12, 2010, http://weekly.ahram.org.eg/2010/997/eg15.htm.

120. Mike Thomson, "Nile Restrictions Anger Ethiopia," *BBC News*, February 3, 2005, http://news.bbc.co.uk/2/hi/africa/4232107.stm.

121. See http://www.dailynewsegypt.com/2013/06/04/morsi-forms-committee-on-dam-meeting-mistakenly- televised/.

122. See http://www.aljazeera.com/news/2015/03/egypt- ethiopia-sudan-sign-accord-nile-dam-15032 3193458534.html.

123. John Waterbury, "Is the Status Quo in the Nile Basin Viable?" *Brown Journal of World Affairs* 4, no. 1 (1997): 287–99.

124. See, for example, Tarek Masoud, "Provocateur-in-Chief," *Slate*, July 2, 2012, http://www.slate.com/articles/news_and_politics/foreigners/2012/07/mohammed_morsi_may_be_unpredictable_new_factor_in_egypt_s_relations_with_the_united_states_and_israel_.html.

125. See http://www.nytimes.com/2012/11/22/world/middleeast/egypt-leader-and-obama-forge-link-in-gaza-deal.html?_r=0.

126. Front page, *al-Ahram*, July 22, 2015.

127. See https://www.nytimes.com/2016/04/11/world/middleeast/egypt-gives-saudi-arabia-2-islands-in-a-show-of-gratitude.html?module=inline.

128. See http://news.yahoo.com/saudi-arabia-egypt-show- discord-over-syria-193501210.html.

129. Mona El-Ghobashy, "The Praxis of the Egyptian Revolution," *MER258* 41, Spring 2011, http://www.merip.org/mer/mer258/praxis-egyptian-revolution#_6_.

CHAPTER 11

1. See James A. Bill, *The Eagle and the Lion: The Tragedy of American-Iranian Relations* (New Haven, CT: Yale University Press, 1989).

2. We should bear in mind that there are some important conceptual differences between a theocracy and a liberal democracy. Theocracy assumes that an objectively true belief system must be promoted in public life. Liberalism has a thinner view of public life as a space for individuals to coexist despite their diverse private beliefs. Liberal democracy presupposes that all citizens are eligible to hold all leadership positions, but a theocratic system holds that top officials must be drawn from a minority of people specially trained in religious doctrine.

3. See the full text of the constitution at https://bit.ly/2Ojtqr5.

4. See Mark Gasiorowski and Malcolm Byrne, eds. *Mohammad Mosaddeq and the 1953 Coup in Iran* (Syracuse, NY: Syracuse University Press, 2004).

5. Oil was first discovered in Iran in 1908, and its extraction began in 1911.

6. See Mehrzad Boroujerdi and Kourosh Rahimkhani, "The Office of the Supreme Leader: Epicenter of a Theocracy," in *Power and Change in Iran: Politics of Contention and Conciliation*, eds. Daniel Brumberg and Farideh Farhi (Bloomington: Indiana University Press, 2016), 135–65.

7. Because the supreme leader appoints the head of the judiciary and has a say in the allocation of many posts held by high-level judicial officials, the principle of separation of powers and the independence of the judiciary are severely undermined.

8. According to the World Bank, 70 percent of the Iranian public was using the Internet by 2018. See https://bit.ly/3kbBUCG. Furthermore, nearly 70% of Iran's population uses smartphones. Available at https://bit.ly/3Cdrdpq.

9. In addition to being a political leader, the imam must also be a spiritual leader who can interpret the Qur'an and shari'a (the canonical law of Islam).

10. The *ulema* have played a prominent role in the development of Shi'i scholarly and legal traditions. The highest religious authority is vested in *mujtahids*, scholars who, through their religious studies and virtuous lives, act as leaders of the Shi'i community and interpret the faith as it applies to daily life. Prominent Shi'i clerics are accorded the title of *ayatollah* which means "sign of God."

11. See Kevan Harris, *A Social Revolution: Politics and the Welfare State in Iran* (Berkeley: University of California Press, 2017).

12. UN Development Programme, "Human Development Report 2020 The Next Frontier: Human Development and the Anthropocene, Iran (Islamic Republic of)," https://bit.ly/2Lq3UD0.

13. See https://bbc.in/2mJAWPx.

CHAPTER 12

1. For a summary of how the delineation of borders unfolded over time, see Sara Pursley, "'Lines Drawn on an Empty Map': Iraq's Borders and the Legend of the Artificial State," parts 1 and 2, *Jadaliyya*, June 2, 2015, http://www.jadaliyya.com/Details/32153/%60Lines-Drawn-on-an-Empty-Map%60-Iraq%E2%80%99s-Borders-and-the-Legend-of-the-Artificial-State-Part-2.

2. James C. Scott, *Seeing Like a State: How Certain Schemes to Improve the Human Condition Have Failed* (New Haven, CT: Yale University Press, 1998), 2.

3. Iraqi nationalists at the 1920 Damascus meeting called for territory from the Persian Gulf to the bank of the Euphrates north of Dayr al-Zur in present-day Syria and to the Tigris near Diyarbakir in present-day Turkey. The Ottoman division of the territory into three provinces was relatively recent—about thirty years old—and had been preceded by multiple alternative sub-divisions. For a summary of these changes, see Reidar Visser, "Proto-Political Conceptions of 'Iraq' in Late Ottoman Times," *International Journal of Contemporary Iraqi Studies* 3, no. 2 (2009).

4. Britain sought to guarantee a strategic location on the route to the crown jewel of their empire, India, control Iraq's agricultural trade, and launch petroleum exploration by the Turkish Petroleum Company (after 1929, the Iraq Petroleum Company). Under the terms of the mandate, King Faisal, like his counterparts in Egypt and Transjordan, would heed Britain's advice in financial, international, security, and (some) judicial affairs, and British officials would serve as advisers and inspectors throughout the government.

5. See Sara Pursley, *Familiar Futures: Time, Selfhood, and Sovereignty in Iraq* (Stanford, CA: Stanford University Press, 2019), Chap. 1.

6. For the argument that the perception of endemic and unmanageable threat leads to elite collective action, see Dan Slater, *Ordering Power: Contentious Politics and Authoritarian Leviathans in Southeast Asia* (New York: Cambridge University Press, 2010).

7. The most notable was the 1920 revolt, in which Shi'i clerics, urban intellectuals, and tribal leaders across northwestern, central, and southern Iraq articulated nearly identical demands: a "completely independent" Iraqi state stretching from the Persian Gulf to somewhere north of Mosul, distinct from Syria, and with its capital in Baghdad. Britain suppressed the revolt through extensive aerial bombardment and arrested and exiled many of its leaders. An estimated six thousand Iraqis and five hundred British and Indian soldiers died in the revolt, which became part of the founding myth of Iraqi nationalism. [See Charles Tripp, *A History of Iraq*, 3rd ed. (Cambridge: Cambridge University Press, 2007), 44]. The British Royal Air Force put down disturbances an additional 130 times before independence in 1932, but these did not feature similar levels of elite coordination [Mohammad A. Tarbush, *The Role of the Military in Politics: A Case Study of Iraq to 1941* (London: Kegan Paul International, 1982), 17].

8. Charles Tilly, "Reflections on the History of European State-Making," in *The Formation of National States in Western Europe*, ed. Tilly (Princeton, NJ: Princeton University Press, 1975), 42.

9. The present-day border with Saudi Arabia was settled by officials negotiating a line connecting wells in the desert in December 1922 after a British air offensive halted the northward military expansion of Abdulaziz ibn Saud of Najd. The Syrian border remained mobile until independence, when it was finalized by a historically contingent decision (Eliezer Tauber, "The Struggle for Dayr Al-Zur: The Determination of Borders Between Syria and Iraq," *International Journal of Middle East Studies* 23, no. 3 (1991): 361–85). The Turkish border was the most contentious of this period, yet even there, Arab, Kurdish, and Turkish nationalist claims were settled in 1926 by British air power and oil interests (Britain awarded the Mosul province to Iraq—despite vehement Turkish and Kurdish separatist opposition— because it had secured oil concession from King Faisal in 1925. Turkey agreed to sign a border agreement in 1926. Oil was discovered in Kirkuk in 1927). The Kuwait and Iran borders remained undefined in this period—a legacy that would later precipitate two major interstate wars.

10. Nelida Fuccaro, "Ethnicity, State Formation, and Conscription in Postcolonial Iraq: The Case of the Yazidi Kurds of Jabal Sinjar," *International Journal of Middle East Studies* 29, no. 4 (November 1997): 559–80.

11. Ibrahim Al-Marashi and Sammy Salama, *Iraq's Armed Forces: An Analytical History* (New York: Routledge, 2008), 24–26.

12. Tripp, 47.

13. Religious Statistics for Iraq, 1 August 1932, FO 406/70.

14. Pursley.

15. For an English translation of the 2005 constitution, see https://www.constituteproject.org/constitution/Iraq_2005.pdf.

16. M. S. Hasan, "Growth and Structure of Iraq's Population, 1867–1947," *Bulletin of the Oxford University Institute of Economics and Statistics* 20, no. 4 (1958): 344.

17. Yitzhak Nakash, "The Conversion of Iraq's Tribes to Shi'ism," *International Journal of Middle East Studies* 26, no. 3 (1994): 443–63.

18. Nathan J. Brown, "Debating Islam in Post-Baathist Iraq," Carnegie Endowment for International Peace March 2005, http://carnegieendowment.org/files/PO13.Brown.FINAL2.pdf.

19. Shi'i religious parties claimed it violates religious freedom by not allowing Shi'a to practice their own law. Ultimately the constitution does not overturn the law but adds ambiguous language regarding individuals' freedom in matters of personal status according to their "religions, sects, beliefs, or choices." Nathan J. Brown, "The Final Draft of the Iraqi Constitution: Analysis and Commentary," Carnegie Endowment for International Peace (2005), https://carnegieendowment.org/2005/09/13/final-draft-of-iraqi-constitution-analysis-and-commentary-pub-17423.

20. International Organization for Migration, *Five Years of Post-Samarra Displacement*, February 2011, https://reliefweb.int/report/iraq/iom-iraq-report-5-years-post-samarra-displacement.

21. Marion Farouk-Sluglett and Peter Sluglett, "The Transformation of Land Tenure and Rural Social Structure in Central and Southern Iraq, 1870–1958," *International Journal of Middle East Studies* 15, no. 4 (1983): 491–505.

22. Between 1947 and 1957, the population of Iraq's three largest cities, Baghdad, Basra, and Mosul, increased by 54, 62, and 33 percent, respectively. Hanna Batatu, *The Old Social Classes and Revolutionary Movements of Iraq: A Study of Iraq's Old Landed and Commercial Classes and of its Communists, Ba'thists and Free Officers* (Princeton, NJ: Princeton University Press, 1978), 35.

23. The government was unable to replace landlords' functions, farmers were unenthusiastic about cooperatives, and smaller farms impeded extensive mechanization and economies of scale. Marion Farouk-Sluglett and Peter Sluglett, *Iraq since 1958: From Revolution to Dictatorship* (London: I. B. Tauris, 1987).

24. For a discussion of the privatization of the agricultural sector, see Robert Springborg, "Infitah, Agrarian Transformation, and Elite Consolidation in Contemporary Iraq," *Middle East Journal* 40, no. 1 (1986): 33–52.

25. Omar Dewachi, *Ungovernable Life: Mandatory Medicine and Statecraft in Iraq* (Stanford, CA: Stanford University Press, 2017), 14.

26. World Health Organization, "Density of Physicians: Latest Available Year," http://www.who.int/gho/health_workforce/physicians_density/en/.

27. World Bank, "Iraq Systematic Country Diagnostic," February 3, 2017, http://documents.worldbank.org/curated/en/542811487277729890/Iraq-Systematic-Country-Diagnostic.

28. As Barrington Moore famously put it, "no bourgeoisie, no democracy." He also argued that the destruction of the peasantry was critical to the formation of liberal democracies (*Social Origins of Dictatorship and Democracy: Lord and Peasant in the Making of the Modern World* [Boston, MA: Beacon Press, 1966]). David Waldner argues that democracy requires the autonomy of the state from the agrarian property system ("Democracy and Dictatorship in the Post-Colonial World," unpublished manuscript).

29. Evidence for the relationship between economic indicators and democracy is mixed. For the argument that economic development increases the likelihood of democratization, see Carles Boix and Susan C. Stokes, "Endogenous Democratization," *World Politics* 55, no. 4 (2003): 517–49. For the argument that it does not, see Adam Przeworksi, Michael Alvarez, Jose Antonio Cheibub, and Fernando Limongi, *Democracy and Development* (New York: Cambridge University Press, 2000). For the link between inequality and democratization, see Carles Boix, *Democracy and Redistribution* (New York: Cambridge University Press, 2003); Daron Acemoglu and James A. Robinson, *Economic Origins of Dictatorship and Democracy* (New York: Cambridge University Press, 2005). Boix also discusses capital mobility. See the Political Economy section for the literature on oil reliance.

30. Between 1920 and 1936, urban elites comprised 70 percent of the government (14 percent of which was military), while landowners and tribal leaders comprised 21 percent and 9 percent, respectively. In terms of religious breakdown, 71 percent of total posts were held by Sunni Arabs who made up only 36 percent of the population. Shi'i ministers had 24 percent of posts (compared to 56 percent of the population). Apart from Sunni and Shi'i ministers, two cabinet members were Christian, and one was Jewish. Between 1920 and 1936, cabinets had an average lifespan of eight months (Tarbush, 46–50).

31. General Bakr Sidqi, who led the 1936 coup, was assassinated less than a year later. Between 1937 and 1941, four colonels known collectively as the "Golden Square" held de facto power, with the king as figurehead until his suspicious death in a car accident in 1939 (which many Iraqis blame on Britain).

32. The leader of the coup, Brigadier 'Abd al-Karim Qasim, became prime minister, minister of defense, and supreme commander of the armed forces. His deputy, Colonel 'Abd al-Salam 'Aref, became deputy prime minister and minister of interior. In 1964, newly nationalized public sectors were also placed under the direction of military officers.

33. The party was founded in Syria by Michel 'Aflaq, an Orthodox Christian, and Salah al-Din al-Bitar, a Sunni Muslim. When it was established in Iraq in 1952, its first leadership was Shi'i Muslim, until it was deposed in 1961. The second leadership cadre that took control of the party was headed by a Faili Shi'i Kurd, Ali Salih al-Sadi, who led the first successful Ba'thist coup d'état in February 1963. See Chapter 22 on Syria for a discussion of the origins of the Ba'th.

34. The number of bureaucrats more than doubled between 1968 and 1978, to about 20 percent of the total labor force. Armed forces personnel increased from 100,000 in 1970 to 250,000 in 1980. A civilian militia, the Popular Army, created to serve as a counterweight to the regular armed forces, grew to 175,000 members. A further 260,000 Iraqis worked for the police by the end of decade.

35. Achim Rohde, *State Society Relations in Ba'thist Iraq: Facing Dictatorship* (London: Routledge, 2010), 119.

36. Aaron M. Faust, *The Ba'thification of Iraq: Saddam Hussein's Totalitarianism* (Austin: University of Texas Press, 2015).

37. Lisa Blaydes, *State of Repression: Iraq under Saddam Hussein* (Princeton, NJ: Princeton University Press, 2018).

38. The process began with the creation of a twenty-five-member Iraqi Governing Council (IGC) by the United States in consultation with its Iraqi allies. In June 2004, the IGC approved a provisional constitution (the Transitional Administrative Law, TAL), the Iraqi Interim Government was appointed, and the UN Security Council recognized Iraq's sovereignty. The process continued through the election of a provisional parliament (January 2005), the formation of an interim government, and the appointment of a constitution-drafting committee. A permanent constitution was finalized in August of that year and approved by popular referendum in October. The process ended with elections for a full-term parliament in December 2005.

39. There is still no consensus over when and by whom a decision was taken to mount such an extended occupation, although evidence points to Vice President Cheney's office (James P. Pfiffner, "US Blunders in Iraq: De-Baathification and Disbanding the Army," *Intelligence and National Security* 25, no. 1 (2010): 76–85).

40. James Dobbins, Seth G. Jones, Benjamin Runkle, and Siddharth Mohand, *Occupying Iraq: A History of the Coalition Provisional Authority* (Santa Monica, CA: RAND, 2009), xiv, https://www.rand.org/pubs/monographs/MG847.html.

41. Human Rights Watch, "The Road to Abu Ghraib," June 2004, https://www.hrw.org/report/2004/06/08/road-abu-ghraib.

42. There has been no post-2003 census reflecting Iraq's sectarian and ethnic composition; the United States based its policies on rough percentages, according to which Arab Shi'a were around 60 percent, Sunni Kurds around 17 percent, and Sunni Arabs around 20 percent. The exact source of such percentages is unclear (International Crisis Group, "Make or Break: Iraq's Sunnis and the State," *Middle East Report* 144, August 2013, https://www.crisisgroup.org/middle-east-north-africa/gulf-and-arabian-peninsula/iraq/make-or-break-iraq-s-sunnis-and-state).

43. Toby Dodge, "Muhasasa Ta'ifiya and Its Others," *POMEPS Studies* 35, October 2019, https://pomeps.org/muhasasa-taifiya-and-its-others-domination-and-contestation-in-iraqs-political-field.

44. David Waldner, "The Limits of Institutional Engineering: Lessons from Iraq," *United States Institute for Peace Special Report* 222, May 2009, https://www.usip.org/publications/2009/05/limits-institutional-engineering-lessons-iraq; Nathan Brown, "Is Political Consensus Possible in Iraq?" *Carnegie Endowment for International Peace*, Policy Outlook, November 2005, http://carnegieendowment.org/files/PO23.Brown.FINAL.pdf.

45. On September 25, 2017, the Kurdistan Regional Government (KRG) of Iraq staged a referendum in areas under its security forces' control (both inside and outside the region's boundaries) that asked voters to tick "yes" or "no" to a single question: Do you want the Kurdistan region and the Kurdistani areas outside the [Kurdistan] region to be an independent country? Preliminary results suggest that some 93 percent of voters affirmatively answered that question, with a participation rate among registered voters of 72 percent. For details, see International Crisis Group, Oil and Borders: How to Fix Iraq's Kurdish Crisis,*Briefing* 55, October 2017, https://www.crisisgroup.org/middle-east-north-africa/gulf-and-arabian-peninsula/iraq/55-settling-iraqi-kurdistans-boundaries-will-help-defuse-post-referendum-tensions.

46. International Crisis Group, "Iraq's Paramilitary Groups: The Challenge of Rebuilding a Functioning State," *Middle East Report* 188, July 2018, https://www.crisisgroup.org/middle-east-north-africa/gulf-and-arabian-peninsula/iraq/188-iraqs-paramilitary-groups-challenge-rebuilding-functioning-state.

47. See https://www.hrw.org/news/2014/02/06/iraq-security-forces-abusing-women-detention.

48. A phenomenon Iraqis called *tarhib wa targhib* (literally, "terror and enticement," but its English equivalent is "sticks and carrots").

49. To rise through the ranks, a person had to spend a specific amount of time and demonstrate a particular skill set before he could be promoted; the party's upper echelon was drawn from individuals with long party histories. Tracking exact membership numbers over time is difficult, but by September 2002, a few months before the Anglo-American occupation, party records listed almost four million affiliates (compared to a little over 1.5 million in 1986), of which 276,000 were involved in active party work. The Ba'th Party had ten membership levels, and the first four levels did not denote active party work: supporter, partisan, advanced partisan, nominee, member in training, active member, divisional member, section member, branch member, and secretary general. Almost all members of the party leadership in a particular area were local to that area, except in insurgent Kurdish zones in the north (these were considered hardship destinations). These party figures are from party records, cited in Joseph Sassoon, *Saddam Hussein's Ba'th Party: Inside an Authoritarian Regime* (New York: Cambridge University Press, 2012), 52, 286.

50. Dodge, 40.

51. Tareq Y. Ismael and Jacqueline S. Ismael, *Iraq in the Twenty-First Century: Regime Change and the Making of a Failed State* (Abingdon: Routledge, 2015), 116, 122.

52. This is a second component of the *muhasasa* system: *muhasasa hizbiyya* (party apportionment) as opposed to *muhasasa ta'ifiyya* (sectarian apportionment). See Fanar Haddad, "The Diminishing Relevance of the Sunni-Shi'a Divide," *POMEPS Studies 35*, October 2019.

53. Dodge, 40.

54. An estimated 38 percent of Iraq's leaders from 2003 to 2006 were exiles, 19 percent were inhabitants of Iraqi Kurdistan, and only 26.8 percent still lived under Ba'thist rule in 2003 (Phebe Marr, "Who Are Iraq's New Leaders? What Do They Want?" USIP Special Report [Washington, DC: United States Institute of Peace, 2006]).

55. A complete text of all CPA orders can be accessed at http://www.iraqcoalition.org/regulatio ns/#Orders. These decisions were discussed in the US Department of Defense and approved by the White House but had not been adequately considered by the rest of the national security establishment. CIA Director George Tenet said, "In fact, we knew nothing about it until de-Baathification was a fait accompli... Clearly, this was a critical policy decision, yet there was no NSC Principals meeting to debate the move." (George Tenet, *At the Center of the Storm* [Harper Perennial, 2008], 426).

56. Beth K. Dougherty, "De-Ba'thification in Iraq: How Not to Pursue Transitional Justice," *Middle East Institute*, January 30, 2014, https://www.mei.edu/publications/de-bathification-iraq-how -not-pursue-transitional-justice.

57. Relatively open elections for parliament were held only once (June 1954), and when reformist candidates were elected, the prime minister annulled the elections, changed the electoral laws, and guaranteed a more quiescent parliament.

58. Haddad, 50.

59. Its victory reflected three changes. First, Arab Sunni public opinion had shifted over the best way to ensure a voice; rather than mobilize around a "Sunni identity," the intention was to reject the ethnosectarian basis of the system and emphasize broad political participation. Second, many citizens were exhausted by the violence and believed the limited capacity of the state was a direct result of sectarian politics. Third, the Shi'i Islamist grand coalition was fragmenting. The 2014 election witnessed a return to ethnosectarian campaigning and voting.

60. For analysis of the leftist-Sadrist alliance, see Benedict Robin-D'Cruz, "Social Brokers and Leftist–Sadrist Cooperation in Iraq's Reform Protest Movement: Beyond Instrumental Action," *The International Journal of Middle Eastern Studies* 51, no. 2 (May 2019): 257–80.

61. Joost Hiltermann, "The Iraqi Elections: A Way Out of the Morass?" *International Crisis Group*, May 18, 2018, https://www.crisisgroup.org/middle-east-north-africa/gulf-and-arabian-peninsula/iraq/iraqi-elections-way-out-morass.

62. For an empirical demonstration of the variation in tribal structure in nineteenth-century Iraq, see Samira Haj, "The Problems of Tribalism: The Case of Nineteenth-Century Iraqi History," *Social History* 16, no. 1 (1991): 45–58.

63. Peter Harling, "Beyond Political Ruptures: Towards a Historiography of Social Continuity in Iraq," in *Writing the Modern History of Iraq*, eds. Jordi Tejel, Peter Sluglett, Riccardo Bocco, and Hamit Bozarslan (Singapore: World Scientific, 2012), 68.

64. Hosham Dawood, "The Stateization of the Tribe and the Tribalization of the State: The Case of Iraq," in *Tribes and Power: Nationalism and Ethnicity in the Middle East*, eds. Faleh A. Jabar and Hosham Dawood (London: Saqi, 2003).

65. David Baran, *Vivre la Tyrannie et lui Survivre: L'Irak en Transition* (Paris: Mille et Une Nuits, 2004).

66. Harling, 69.

67. NGO Coordination Committee for Iraq, "Iraq's Civil Society in Perspective," April 2011, http://reliefweb.int/sites/reliefweb.int/files/resources/Full_Report_476.pdf.

68. Albert O. Hirschman, *Exit, Voice, and Loyalty: Responses to Decline in Firms, Organizations, and States* (Cambridge, MA: Harvard University Press, 1970).

69. Alan Dowty, *Closed Borders: The Contemporary Assault on Freedom of Movement* (New Haven, CT: Yale University Press, 1987). Dowty finds that Iraq was among twenty-one states that imposed such restrictions. All were single-party states and, except for Iraq, Burma, and Somalia, were self-defined Marxist-Leninist regimes.

70. Harris Mylonas finds that such policies depend on whether communities are supported by other states and whether these other states are allies or enemies (Harris Mylonas, *The Politics of Nation-Building: Making Co-Nationals, Refugees, and Minorities* [Cambridge: Cambridge University Press, 2013]).

71. Pan-Arabists, who aspired to create a political union between Iraq and other Arab states, saw this as a moment to impugn the nationalist credentials of their adversaries in the Iraqi nationalist movement, which included Iraqi Jews. The narrative that Jewish members of the nationalist movement were disloyal Zionists was also convenient for the monarchy as a scapegoating strategy to deflect criticism of the army's poor showing in the war. Others, encouraged by both the government and Israeli authorities, took advantage of a 1950 law allowing them to renounce their citizenship.

72. Tripp, 230.

73. Khoury, 46.

74. James C. Scott, *Weapons of the Weak: Everyday Forms of Peasant Resistance* (New Haven, CT: Yale University Press, 1985).

75. Lisa Blaydes, *State of Repression: Iraq under Saddam Hussein* (Princeton, NJ: Princeton University Press, 2018).

76. Zahra Ali, "Iraqis Demand a Country," *MERIP* 292/3, Fall/Winter 2019, https://merip.org/2019/12/iraqis-demand-a-country/.

77. International Crisis Group, "Iraq's Tishreen Uprising: From Barricades to Ballot Box," Report 223, July 26, 2021, https://www.crisisgroup.org/middle-east-north-africa/gulf-and-arabian-peninsula/iraq/223-iraqs-tishreen-uprising-barricades-ballot-box.

78. Malcolm H. Kerr, *The Arab Cold War: Gamal 'Abd al-Nasir and His Rivals, 1958–1970* (London: Oxford University Press, 1971).

79. This is Malik Mufti's thesis in *Sovereign Creations: Pan-Arabism and Political Order in Syria and Iraq* (Ithaca, NY: Cornell University Press, 1996).

80. Toby C. Jones, "America, Oil, and War in the Middle East," *Journal of American History* 99, no. 1 (2012): 208–18.

81. Khoury, 34.

82. For details on how the Iraqi leadership perceived Kuwait, the Iraqi regime's objectives in Kuwait, and Kuwaiti resistance to the Iraqi occupation, see Joseph Sassoon and Alissa Walter, "The Iraqi Occupation of Kuwait: New Historical Perspectives," *Middle East Journal* 71, no. 4 (Autumn 2017): 607–28. For an analysis of how Iraqi soldiers viewed their mission in Kuwait, see Joseph Sassoon and Alissa Walter, "Diaries of Iraqi Soldiers: Views from Inside Saddam's Army," *International Journal of Contemporary Iraqi Studies* 12, no. 2: 183–98.

83. John J. Mearsheimer and Stephen M. Walt, "An Unnecessary War," *Foreign Policy* (January/February 2003): 52.

84. The US military dropped more than ninety tons of bombs on Iraqi cities and experimented with depleted uranium warheads to maximize the destruction of vital infrastructure targets.

85. Jones.

86. David A. Lake, "Two Cheers for Bargaining Theory: Assessing Rationalist Explanations of the Iraq War," *International Security* 35, no. 3 (Winter 2010/2011): 7–52.

87. The ground forces for the invasion involved approximately 125,000 US forces, 45,000 UK forces, 2,000 Australian forces, and 600 Czech, Polish, and Slovak forces. In addition, these countries contributed approximately 67,400 sea and air forces.

88. For a discussion of the US's controversial interpretation of international law as a basis for the occupation, see Sean D. Murphy, "Assessing the Legality of Invading Iraq," *Georgetown Law Journal* 92, no. 4 (2004).

89. Alexandre Debs and Nuno P. Monteiro, "Known Unknowns: Power Shifts, Uncertainty, and War," *International Organization* 68, no. 1 (2014): 1–31.

90. Mearsheimer and Walt.

91. Lake.

92. Elizabeth N. Saunders, *Leaders at War: How Presidents Shape Military Interventions* (Ithaca, NY: Cornell University Press, 2011).

93. Jones.

94. This is the thesis in F. Gregory Gause, III, *Beyond Sectarianism: The New Middle East Cold War* (The Brookings Institution, 2014).

95. In 1933, the nascent Iraqi army massacred hundreds of Assyrian civilians in the wake of its standoff with British-armed Assyrian forces. Today, that episode lives in infamy. But at the time, General Bakr Sidqi was heralded by many as a great Arab nationalist and invited to parade his troops through the center of Baghdad. Parliament passed the controversial conscription law shortly thereafter. In 1936, Sidqi used his newly gained prestige to lead the Arab world's first coup. Sami Zubaida, "Contested Nations: Iraq and the Assyrians," *Nations and Nationalism* 6, no. 3 (2000): 363–82.

96. The discussion of the two problems with assuming cleavage-based conflict is from Stathis N. Kalyvas and Matthew Adam Kocher, "Ethnic Cleavages and Irregular War: Iraq and Vietnam," *Politics and Society* 35, no. 2 (2007): 183–223.

97. Kalyvas and Laia Balcells, "International System and Technologies of Rebellion: How the End of the Cold War Shaped Internal Conflict," *American Political Science Review* 104, no. 3 (2010): 418.

98. It is unclear how many were affected by forced migration, especially given that policies became increasingly brutal as the insurgency continued unabated. Joost R. Hiltermann, *A Poisonous Affair: America, Iraq, and the Gassing of Halabja* (Cambridge: Cambridge University Press, 2007).

99. For a summary of Ba'thist policies in the north, see Joost R. Hiltermann, "The 1988 Anfal Campaign in Iraqi Kurdistan," *Online Encyclopedia of Mass Violence*, February 2008, https://www.sciencespo.fr/mass-violence-war-massacre-resistance/en/document/1988-anfal-campaign-iraqi-kurdistan.html.

100. Khoury, 120–21.

101. Ibid., 110.

102. Ibid., 118.

103. Human Rights Watch, *Iraq's Crime of Genocide: The Anfal Campaign against the Kurds* (New Haven, CT: Yale University Press, 1995).

104. Human Rights Watch, *Endless Torment: The 1991 Uprising in Iraq and Its Aftermath* (New York: Human Rights Watch, 1992), https://www.hrw.org /report/1992/06/01/endless-torment /1991-uprising-iraq-and-its-aftermath.

105. Khoury, 133–40.

106. Human Rights Watch, *The Iraqi Government's Assault on the Marsh Arabs*, Briefing Paper, January 2003, http://www.hrw.org/legacy/backgrounder/mena/marsharabs1.htm.

107. See Ariel I. Ahram, "Development, Counterinsurgency, and the Destruction of the Iraqi Marshes," *International Journal of Middle East Studies* 47, no. 3 (2015): 447–66.

108. While acknowledging that "little authoritative information is available," the environmental organization Greenpeace estimated that the death rate among Kurdish and Shi'a refugees and displaced persons averaged one thousand daily during April, May, and June 1991 ("Iraqi Deaths from the Gulf War as of April 1992" [Washington, DC: Greenpeace, 1992]). An estimated two million Iraqis fled from cities into the mountains along the northern borders, into the southern marshes, to refugee camps in Saudi Arabia, and to Iran and Turkey.

109. Human Rights Watch, *Iraq: State of the Evidence*, November 2004, http://www.hrw.org/reports /2004/iraq1104/.

110. Pete Moore and Christopher Parker, "The War Economy of Iraq," *Middle East Research and Information Project* 243 (Summer 2007).

111. Iraq Body Count, https://www.iraqbodycount.org/database/. The most violent month for Iraqi civilians was during the US's "Shock and Awe" campaign (March–April 2003), which killed 6,700 civilians in twenty-one days. The most sustained period of high-level violence occurred between March 2006 and March 2008, when 52,000 civilians were killed. Baghdad has borne the greatest loss of life overall, 48 percent of all deaths. Iraq Body Count, "The War in Iraq: 10 Years and Counting" (March 2013), https://www.iraqbodycount.org/analysis/numbers/ten-years/.

112. UNHCR, *Global Focus: Iraq*, 2021, https://reporting.unhcr.org/node/2547?y=2021#year.

113. Ibid.

114. In 1990, President Saddam Hussein wrote "God is great" on the Iraqi flag and called for jihad against the Western-led coalition in the First Gulf War. By the mid-1990s, the regime had declared a national Faith Campaign, built more mosques, and increased religious education. Scholars disagree on whether this shift reflected a genuine change in Ba'thists' religiosity or whether it was a more cynical strategy. For the argument that Saddam Hussein himself had become more religious and that this had radical implications for the state's approach to Islamism, see Amatzia Baram, *Saddam Husayn and Islam, 1968–2003* (Baltimore, MD: Johns Hopkins University Press, 2014). For the counterargument, see Joseph Sassoon, *Saddam Hussein's Ba'th Party: Inside an Authoritarian Regime* (New York: Cambridge University Press, 2012) and Samuel Helfont, *Compulsion in Religion: Saddam Hussein, Islam, and the Roots of Insurgencies in Iraq* (Oxford: Oxford University Press, 2018).

115. For an overview of these debates beyond Iraq, see Anna Grzymala-Busse, "Why Comparative Politics Should Take Religion (More) Seriously," *Annual Review of Political Science* 15 (2012): 421–42. For a recent debate about on Islam in politics, see *Islam and International Order* (POMEPS Studies 15, 2015).

116. For a broader articulation of this alternative, see Nathan J. Brown, "Rethinking Religion and Politics," *Islam and International Order* (POMEPS Studies 15, 2015).

117. See Chapter 4 for a discussion of the origins of the split between Shi'i and Sunni Islam.

118. Holy sites include the tombs of Shi'ism's founder, 'Ali ibn Abi Talib, the first Shi'i imam, and his son, Hussein, the third imam, who is buried in Karbala. Today, millions of pilgrims converge annually in the month of Muharram to commemorate the death of Prophet Muhammad's grandson Hussein in 680 CE at the hand of Yazid I, the second Umayyad Caliph. Historically, Iraq's centrality to Shi'ism has created a strong rivalry with neighboring Iran, especially the city of Qum, which has sought to rival Najaf as the main theological center of Shi'ism.

119. The marriage law passed during the Tanzimat reforms (1839–1876) as the Ottomans became concerned with concepts of citizenship. The conflation between "Shi'i" and "Persian," however, was confusing for many. In trying to implement the law, officials were unsure whether it applied to Sunni and non-Muslim Iranians and to non-Muslim Ottomans, and contradictory opinions were given by legal advisors (Karen M. Kern, *Imperial Citizen: Marriage and Citizenship in the Ottoman Frontier Provinces of Iraq* [Syracuse, NY: Syracuse University Press, 2011]).

120. In 1980, Saddam Hussein ordered the execution of Ayatollah Muhammad Baqir al-Sadr, along with his sister, Bint al-Huda, a theologian in her own right. In 1999, Hussein ordered the assassination of their brother Sadiq al-Sadr and two of his sons.

121. Fanar Haddad, "A Sectarian Awakening: Reinventing Sunni Identity in Iraq after 2003," *Hudson Institute*, 2014, http://www.hudson.org/research/10544-a-sectarian-awakening-einventing-sunni-identity-in-iraq-after-2003.

122. Harling, 74.

123. US Energy Information Administration, *International Energy Statistics*, 2021, https://www.eia.gov/international/overview/country/IRQ.

124. The World Bank, *World Development Indicators*, 2019, http://data.worldbank.org/indicator/NY. GDP.PETR.RT.ZS.

125. Central Intelligence Agency, *The World Factbook: Iraq, 2017,* https://www.cia.gov/the-world-factbook/countries/iraq/#economy

126. The pattern of statist development started in 1952 when the government was allowed to triple its share of oil revenue by the Iraqi Petroleum Company (IPC). State interventions before the early 1950s were limited primarily to manipulating tariffs to encourage private industry and investing in infrastructure, primarily irrigation and flood control works to regulate the rivers.

127. Joy Gordon, *Invisible War: The United States and the Iraq Sanctions* (Cambridge, MA: Harvard University Press, 2010).

128. Dobbins et al., 111.

129. Nida Alahmad, "Rewiring a State: The Techno-Politics of Electricity in the CPA's Iraq," *Middle East Research and Information Project* 266 (Spring 2013).

130. Ibid.

131. James Glanz and Robert F. Worth, "Attacks on Iraq Oil Industry Aid Vast Smuggling Scheme," *The New York Times*, June 4, 2006.

132. Yezid Sayigh, "The Crisis of the Iraqi State," *Al-Hayat*, November 23, 2017.

133. Special Inspector General for Iraq Reconstruction, *Quarterly Report and Semiannual Report to the United States Congress*, 2011.

134. Omar Dewachi, "The Toxicity of Everyday Survival in Iraq," *Jadaliyya*, August 13, 2013.

135. Omar Dewachi, "The Geopolitics of Health in the Middle East" (online presentation, London School of Economics, May 10, 2021).

136. World Bank, *Addressing the Human Development Crisis: A Public Expenditure Review for Human Development Sectors in Iraq* (Washington, DC: World Bank Group, 2014), https://documents1 .worldbank.org/curated/en/568141622306648034/pdf/Addressing-the-Human-Capital-Crisis-A-Public-Expenditure-Review-for-Human-Development-Sectors-in-Iraq.pdf.

137. International Crisis Group, "Fight or Flight: The Desperate Plight of Iraq's Generation 2000," *Middle East Report* 169, August 2016. David Siddhartha Patel, "How Oil and Demography Shape Post-Saddam Iraq," Brandeis University Crown Center for Middle East Studies, Middle East Brief 122, September 2018.

CHAPTER 13

1. Benny Gshur and Barbara S. Okun, "Generational Effects on Marriage Patterns among Israeli Jews," *Journal of Marriage and Family* 65 (May 2003): 287–310.

2. Israel Central Bureau of Statistics, http://www.cbs.gov.il/reader/cw_usr_view_SHTML?ID = 8 02.

3. *Report of the Official Commission of Inquiry into the October 2000 Events*, Jerusalem, August 2003; full text [in Hebrew] at Supreme Court of Israel, http://elyon1.court.gov.il/heb/veadot/or /inside_index.htm; official summary [in English] at Adalah, the Legal Center for Arab Minority Rights in Israel, http://www.adalah.org/fea tures/commission/orreport-en.pdf.

4. National Committee for the Heads of the Arab Local Authorities in Israel, *Future Vision of the Palestinian Arabs in Israel*, 2006; text [in Hebrew] at website of Knesset, http://www.knesset.gov.il/committees/heb/material/data/H26-12-2006_10-30-37_heb.pdf; text [in English] at website of Mossawa Center, http://www.mossawacenter.org/files/files/File/Reports/2006/Future%20Vision %20(English).pdf.

5. See https://www.cbs.gov.il/he/mediarelease/DocLib/2018/195/32_18_195b.pdf.

6. https://www.cbs.gov.il/he/mediarelease/DocLib/2017/138/01_17_138b.pdf

7. "The Electoral System in Israel," Israel Government Portal, 2010, with links to "Basic Law: The Knesset" (1958) [in English] and "The Knesset Elections Law" (Combined Version, 1969) [in Hebrew], http://www.gov.il/FirstGov/TopNavEng/EngSubjects/EngSElections/EngSEElectoral/EngSEEElectoral/.

8. World Bank data, http://data.worldbank.org/indicator/BX.KLT.DINV.WD.GD.ZS.

9. See https://ustr.gov/trade-agreements/free-trade- agreements/israel-fta.

10. See http://www.oecd.org/economy/israel-economic- forecast-summary.htm and http://data.worldbank.org/indicator/NY.GDP.MKTP.KD.ZG.

11. See http://www.oecd.org/eco/surveys/Israel-2018-OECD-economic-survey-overview.pdf.

12. "The Gaza Strip," *B'tselem*, November 11, 2017 (accessed November 9, 2018).

CHAPTER 14

1. https://data.worldbank.org/country/jordan?view=chart

2. https://data.worldbank.org/indicator/SL.UEM.TOTL.ZS?locations=JO&view=chart; https://www.worldbank.org/en/country/jordan/overview

3. https://data.worldbank.org/indicator/DT.ODA.ALLD.CD?locations=JO

4. https://databank.worldbank.org/views/reports/reportwidget.aspx?Report_Name=CountryProfile&Id=b450fd57&tbar=y&dd = y&inf=n&zm = n&country=JOR

CHAPTER 15

1. For a fuller and more detailed account of the founding of Kuwait, see Ahmed Abu Hakima, *History of Kuwait 1750–1965* (London: Luzac & Company Press, 1983); Ahmed Abu Hakima, *History of Eastern Arabia 1750–1800* (London: Probsthain, 1965).

2. For a detailed account of the politics and influence of the Ottoman Empire on the Gulf, including Kuwait, see Frederick Anscombe, *The Ottoman Gulf: The Creation of Kuwait, Saudi Arabia and Qatar* (New York: Columbia University Press, 1997).

3. For detailed accounts of the reign of Mubarak, see B. J. Slot, *Mubarak Al-Sabah: Founder of Modern Kuwait, 1896–1915* (London: Arabian, 2005); Salwa Al-Ghanim, *The Reign of Mubarak-Al-Sabah: Shaikh of Kuwait 1896–1915* (London: I. B. Tauris, 1998).

4. On the issue of expatriates and Kuwait's migration policy, see Sharon Russell and Muhammad Al-Ramadhan, "Kuwait's Migration Policy since the Gulf Crisis," *International Journal of Middle East Studies* 26 (1994): 569–87; Nasra Shah, "Foreign Workers in Kuwait: Implications for Kuwaiti Labor Force," *International Migration Review* 20, no. 4 (Winter 1986): 815–32.

5. On the history and politics of tribes and tribalism in Kuwait, see Anh Nga Longva, "Nationalism in Pre-Modern Guise: The Discourse on Hadhar and Badu in Kuwait," *International Journal of Middle East Studies* 38, no. 2 (2006): 171–87; Nicolas Gavrielides, "Tribal Democracy: The Anatomy of Parliamentary Elections in Kuwait," in ed. Linda Layne, *Elections in the Middle East: Implications of Recent Trends* (Boulder, CO: Westview Press, 1987), 187–213.

6. Graham Fuller, *The Arab Shia: The Forgotten Muslims* (New York: Palgrave, 2001), 155–77.

7. For more details on the Bidoon, see Claire Beaugrand, *Stateless in the Gulf: Migration, Nationality and Society in Kuwait* (London: I.B Tauris, 2017).

8. Amiri Decree, *Kuwait Times*, May 18, 1999, 1.

9. For analysis of the position of women in Kuwaiti society and politics, see Haya Al-Mughni, *Women in Kuwait: The Politics of Gender* (London: Saqi Books, 2001); Mary Ann Tétreault and Haya Al-Mughni, "Gender, Citizenship and Nationalism in Kuwait," *British Journal of Middle Eastern Studies* 22, no. 1 (1995): 64–80; and Mary Ann Tétreault and Haya Al-Mughni, "Modernization and Its Discontents: State and Gender in Kuwait," *Middle East Journal* 49, no. 3 (1995): 403–17.

10. Shafeeq Ghabra, "Balancing State and Society: The Islamic Movement in Kuwait," *Middle East Policy* 5 (1997): 58–72.

11. For a comprehensive account on Islamists in Kuwait, see Falah Almdarires, *Islamic Extremism in Kuwait: From the Muslim Brotherhood to Al-Qaeda and Other Islamist Political Groups* (London: Routledge, 2010).

12. For a detailed history of the Al Sabah family, see Alan Rush, *Al-Sabah: Genealogy and History of Kuwait's Ruling Family, 1752–1986* (London: Ithaca Press, 1987).

13. Abdul Reda Assiri and Kamal Al-Monoufi, "Kuwait's Political Elite: The Cabinet," *Middle East Journal* 42 (Winter 1988): 48–51.

14. Abdo Baaklini, "Legislatures in the Gulf Area: The Experience of Kuwait 1961–1976," *International Journal of Middle East Studies* 14, no. 3 (1982): 372–73.

15. On the link between the Iraqi occupation and Kuwait's democratization, see Mary Ann Tétreault, *Stories of Democracy: Politics and Society in Contemporary Kuwait* (New York: Columbia University Press, 2000), 76–100; Steve Tetiv, "Kuwait's Democratic Experiment in Its Broader International Context," *Middle East Journal* 56, no. 2 (Spring 2002): 257–71.

16. M. Khouja and P. Sadler, *The Economy of Kuwait: Development and Role in International Finance* (London: Macmillan, 1979), 7–17.

17. See Abdulkarim Al-Dekhayel, *Kuwait, Oil and Political Legitimation* (London: Ithaca Press, 2000).

18. Paul Kennedy, *Doing Business with Kuwait* (London: Kogan Page, 2004), 68–69.

19. Walid Moubarak, "The Kuwait Fund in the Context of Arab and Third World Politics," *Middle East Journal* 41, no. 4 (Autumn 1987): 539.

20. Nivin Salah, "The EU and the Gulf States," *Middle East Policy* 7, no. 1 (October 1999): 68.

21. Henner Fürtig, "GCC-EU Political Cooperation: Myth or Reality?" *British Journal of Middle Eastern Studies* 31, no. 1 (May 2004): 25.

22. On Kuwait's relationship with the United States, see Chookiat Panaspornprasit, *US-Kuwaiti Relations 1961–1992: An Uneasy Relationship* (London: Routledge, 2005).

CHAPTER 16

1. Among the thoughtful writers to examine these contradictions are Kamal S. Salibi, *A House of Many Mansions: The History of Lebanon Reconsidered* (London: I. B. Tauris, 1988); Samir Khalaf, *Lebanon's Predicament* (New York: Columbia University Press, 1987).

2. Among the best histories on Lebanon are Philip K. Hitti, *Lebanon in History* (London: Macmillan, 1957); Kamal S. Salibi, *The Modern History of Lebanon* (New York: Praeger, 1965). For more on Ottoman Lebanon, see Engin Akarli, *The Long Peace: Ottoman Lebanon, 1861–1920* (Berkeley: University of California Press, 1993); Iliya F. Harik, *Politics and Change in a Traditional Society: Lebanon 1711–1845* (Princeton, NJ: Princeton University Press, 1968); Leila Tarazi Fawaz, *An Occasion for War: Civil Conflict in Lebanon and Damascus in 1860* (London: Centre for Lebanese Studies and I. B. Tauris, 1994) and *Merchants and Migrants in Nineteenth Century Beirut* (Cambridge, MA: Harvard University Press, 1983); and Nadim Shehadi and Dana Haffar Mills, eds., *Lebanon: A History of Conflict and Consensus* (London: Centre for Lebanese Studies and I. B. Tauris, 1988).

3. To trace the evolution of these institutions and their later impact, see Abdo Baaklini, *Legislative and Political Development: Lebanon, 1842–1972* (Durham, NC: Duke University Press, 1976).

4. For more on the interwar period, see Meir Zamir, *The Formation of Modern Lebanon* (Ithaca, NY: Cornell University Press, 1985) and *Lebanon's Quest: The Road to Statehood, 1926–1939* (New York: I. B. Tauris, 1997); and Stephen H. Longrigg, *Syria and Lebanon under French Mandate* (New York: Oxford University Press, 1958), 58.

5. A good analysis of the National Pact is in Farid El Khazen, *The Communal Pact of National Identities: The Making and Politics of the 1943 National Pact,* papers on Lebanon, no. 12 (Oxford: Centre for Lebanese Studies, 1991).

6. For more on the period between independence and civil war, see Michael C. Hudson, *The Precarious Republic: Political Modernization in Lebanon* (New York: Random House, 1968); Leonard Binder, ed., *Politics in Lebanon* (New York: Wiley, 1966); and Elie A. Salem, *Modernisation without Revolution: Lebanon's Experience* (Bloomington: Indiana University Press, 1973).

7. For more on the breakdown of the state and the drift into civil war, see Farid El Khazen, *The Breakdown of the State in Lebanon, 1967–1976* (Cambridge, MA: Harvard University Press, 2001); Kamal S. Salibi, *Crossroads to Civil War: Lebanon 1958–1976* (Delmar, NY: Caravan Books, 1976).

8. For more on the civil war, see Theodor Hanf, *Coexistence in Wartime Lebanon: Decline of a State and Rise of a Nation* (London: Centre for Lebanese Studies and I. B. Tauris, 1993); Walid Khalidi, *Conflict and Violence in Lebanon: Confrontation in the Middle East* (Cambridge, MA: Harvard Center for International Affairs, 1979); Roger Owen, ed., *Essays on the Crisis in Lebanon* (London: Ithaca Press, 1976); Marius Deeb, *The Lebanese Civil War* (New York: Praeger, 1980); Thomas L. Friedman, *From Beirut to Jerusalem* (New York: Simon & Schuster, 1984); and Robert Fisk, *Pity the Nation: Lebanon at War*, 3rd ed. (New York: Oxford University Press, 2001).

9. For more on the Syrian-Israeli dynamics in Lebanon, see Adeed I. Dawisha, *Syria and the Lebanese Crisis* (London: Macmillan, 1980); Yair Evron, *War and Intervention in Lebanon: The Israeli-Syrian Deterrence Dialogue* (London: Croom Helm, 1987).

10. See Ze'ev Schiff and Ehud Ya'ari, eds., *Israel's Lebanon War* (New York: Simon & Schuster, 1984); Itamar Rabinovich, *The War for Lebanon, 1970–1983* (Ithaca, NY: Cornell University Press, 1984).

11. For a good examination of the Palestinian presence in Lebanon, see Rex Brynen, *Sanctuary and Survival: The PLO in Lebanon* (Boulder, CO: Westview Press, 1990).

12. For more on this period, see Elie Salem, *Violence and Diplomacy in Lebanon: The Troubled Years, 1982–1988* (New York: I. B. Tauris, 1995); Wadi D. Haddad, *Lebanon: The Politics of Revolving Doors* (New York: Praeger, 1985).

13. For more analysis on the Taif Accord, see Joseph Maila, *The Document of National Reconciliation: A Commentary* (Oxford: Centre for Lebanese Studies, 1992); Paul Salem, "A Commentary on the Taif Agreement," *Beirut Review* 1, no. 1 (Spring 1991): 19–72.

14. For more on this postwar period, see Deirdre Collings, ed., *Peace for Lebanon: From War to Reconstruction* (Boulder, CO: Lynne Rienner, 1994); Elizabeth Picard, *Lebanon. A Shattered Country* (New York: Holmes & Meier, 1996); and Theodor Hanf and Nawaf Salam, eds., *Lebanon in Limbo: Postwar Society and State in an Uncertain Regional Environment* (Baden-Baden: Nomos Verlagsgesellschaft, 2003).

15. There has been much scholarship about the Shi'a of Lebanon as well as Hizbullah: see, for example, Fouad Ajami, *The Vanished Imam: Musa al-Sadr and the Shia of Lebanon* (Ithaca, NY: Cornell University Press, 1986); Majid Halawi, *A Lebanon Defied: Musa al-Sadr and the Shia Community* (Boulder, CO: Westview Press, 1992); Augustus Richard Norton, ed., *Amal and the Shi'a: Struggle for the Soul of Lebanon* (Austin: University of Texas Press, 1987); Augustus Richard Norton, *Hezbollah: A Short History* (Princeton, NJ: Princeton University Press, 2007); Hala Jaber, *Hezbollah: Born with a Vengeance* (New York: Columbia University Press, 1997); and Judith Harik, *Hezbullah: The Changing Face of Terrorism* (London: I. B. Tauris, 2004).

16. Lebanon Country Profile, World Bank, 2017.

CHAPTER 17

1. Dirk Vandewalle, *Libya since Independence: Oil and State-building* (Ithaca, NY: Cornell University Press, 1998), 52.

2. Lisa Anderson, *The State and Social Transformation in Tunisia and Libya, 1830–1980* (Princeton, NJ: Princeton University Press, 1986), 259. See also Vandewalle, *Libya since Independence*, 56.

3. See Hanspeter Mattes, "Formal and Informal Authority in Libya since 1969," in *Libya since 1969: Qadhafi's Revolution Revisited*, ed. Dirk Vandewalle (New York: Palgrave, 2011).

4. See Ali Abdullatif Ahmida, *The Making of Modern Libya: State Formation, Colonization, and Resistance*, 2nd ed. (Albany: SUNY Press, 2008), chap. 2.

5. John Wright, *Libya: A Modern History* (Baltimore, MD: Johns Hopkins University Press, 1982), 39.

6. Vandewalle, *Libya since Independence*, 46.

7. Ragaei El Mallakh, "The Economics of Rapid Growth," *Middle East Journal* 23, no. 3 (1969): 308–9, 312, 316.

8. Ronald Bruce St. John, "The Libyan Economy in Transition: Opportunity and Challenges," in *Libya since 1969*, ed. Vandewalle, 128.

9. Vandewalle, *Libya since Independence*, 55.

10. Anderson, *The State and Social Transformation*, 264–65.

11. Ibid., 191.

12. See UN Development Program (UNDP), *Human Development Report 2010* (New York: United Nations, 2010).

13. Amal Obeidi, "Political Elites in Libya since 1969," in *Libya since 1969*, ed. Vandewalle, 117.

14. Anderson, *The State and Social Transformation*, 253–54. See also Jamil M. Abun-Nasr, *A History of the Maghrib in the Islamic Period* (New York: Cambridge University Press, 1987), 405.

15. See Mattes, "Formal and Informal Authority in Libya." On the lived experience of the Jamahiriyyah, see Amal Obeidi, *Political Culture in Libya* (New York: Rutledge, 2001); Mabroka Al-Werfalli, *Political Alienation in Libya: Assessing Citizens' Political Attitude and Behavior* (Reading: Ithaca Press, 2011). For a literary account of the early al-Qadhafi state, see Hisham Matar, *In the Country of Men* (New York: Viking, 2006).

16. Ahmida, *The Making of Modern Libya*, 93–95.

17. Alison Pargeter, "Prodigal or Pariah? Foreign Policy in Libya," in *Libya since 1969*, ed. Vandewalle, 83.

18. Pargeter, "Prodigal or Pariah?" 90.

19. Henry Swainson Cowper, *The Hill of the Graces* (London: Methuen & Co, 1897), 304, cited in Wright, *Libya: A Modern History.*

20. Ahmida, *The Making of Modern Libya*, 118.

21. See Geoff L. Simons, *Libya and the West: From Independence to Lockerbie* (Oxford: Centre for Libyan Studies, 2003), chap. 7–8.

CHAPTER 18

1. L. E. Sweet, "Pirates or Polities? Arab Societies of the Persian or Arabian Gulf, 18th Century," *Ethnohistory* 11, no. 3 (Summer 1964): 262–80; Peter Lienhardt, "The Authority of Shaykhs in the Gulf: an Essay in Nineteenth-Century History," in *Arabian Studies*, Vol. 2 (London: C. Hurst, 1975), 61–75.

2. James Onley, *The Arabian Frontier of the British Raj: Merchants, Rulers, and the British in the Nineteenth Century Gulf* (New York: Oxford University Press, 2007); James Onley, "The Politics of Protection in the Gulf: The Arab Rulers and the British Resident in the Nineteenth Century," *New Arabian Studies* 6 (2004): 30–92.

3. F. Gregory Gause, *The International Relations of the Persian Gulf* (New York: Cambridge University Press, 2010), 18–19.

4. Michael Herb, *All in the Family: Absolutism, Revolution, and Democracy in the Middle Eastern Monarchies* (Albany: State University of New York Press, 1999).

5. In Oman, a number of members of the wider al-Busaidi clan hold additional cabinet-level posts.

6. On Gulf labour markets and their political consequences, see Michael Herb, *The Wages of Oil: Parliaments and Economic Development in Kuwait and the UAE* (Ithaca, NY: Cornell University Press, 2014).

7. Martin Hvidt, "The Dubai Model: An Outline of Key Development-Process Elements in Dubai," *International Journal of Middle East Studies* 41, no. 3 (August 2009): 397–418.

8. Justin Gengler, *Group Conflict and Political Mobilisation in Bahrain and the Arab Gulf: Rethinking the Rentier State* (Bloomington: Indiana University Press, 2015), 96.

9. Matthew S. Hopper, "Globalisation and the Economics of African Slavery in Arabia in the Age of Empire," *Journal of African Development* 12, no. 1 (Spring 2010): 155–84.

10. Steffen Hertog, "The Sociology of the Gulf Rentier Systems: Societies of Intermediaries," *Comparative Studies in Society and History* 52, no. 2 (2010): 297–98; Lori Noora, "*Temporary Workers or Permanent Migrants? The Kafala System and Contestations over Residency in the Arab Gulf States*" (Institut Français des Relations Internationales [IFRI]), November 2012, http://www.ifri.org/fr/publications/enotes/notes-de-lifri/temporary- workers-or-permanent-migrants-kafala-system.

11. Michael L. Ross, "Does Oil Hinder Democracy?" *World Politics* 53 (April 2001): 325–61; Stephen Haber and Victor Menaldo, "Do Natural Resources Fuel Authoritarianism? A Reappraisal of the Resource Curse," *American Political Science Review* 105, no. 1 (February 2011): 1–26.

12. Gwenn Okruhlik, "Rentier Wealth, Unruly Law, and the Rise of Opposition: The Political Economy of Rentier States," *Comparative Politics* 31 (April 1999): 295–315.

13. Al-Jazeera, "*Arab States Issue 13 Demands to End Qatar-Gulf Crisis,*" 12 July 2017, https://www.aljazeera.com/news/2017/06/arab-states-issue-list-demands-qatar-crisis-170623022133024.html

14. *New York Times*, "Tiny, Wealthy Qatar Goes Its Own Way, and Pays for It," January 22, 2018, https://www.nytimes.com/2018/01/22/world/middleeast/qatar-saudi-emir-boycott.html.

15. Politico, "*Qatar Eyes Stake in Newsmax,*" May 8, 2018, https://www.politico.com/story/2018/05/08/qatar-newsmax-ruddy-al-jazeera-trump–573242; Bloomberg, "*Qatar and the Kushners: What to Watch For,*" May 17, 2018, https://www.bloomberg.com/view/articles/2018–05–17/qatar-the-kushners- and–666-fifth-avenue; *New York Times*, Kushners Near Deal with Qatar-Linked Company for Troubled Tower, May 17, 2018, https://www.nytimes.com/2018/05/17/nyregion/kushner-deal-qatar–666–5th.html.

16. Christopher M. Davidson, *The United Arab Emirates: A Study in Survival* (Boulder, CO: Lynne Rienner, 2005), 189.

17. Christopher M. Davidson, "The Emirates of Abu Dhabi and Dubai: Contrasting Roles in the International System," *Asian Affairs* 38, no. 1 (2007): 37–38.

18. Sultan Al Qassemi, "The UAE Is One Nation . . . It's Time Our Passports Said So," *Abu Dhabi National*, October 11, 2009.

19. *The Washington Post*, "In the UAE, the United States Has a Quiet, Potent Ally Nicknamed 'Little Sparta,'" November 9, 2014, https://www.washingtonpost.com/world/national-security/in-the-uae-the-united-states-has-a-quiet-potent-ally-nicknamed-little-sparta/2014/11/08/3fc6a50c–643a–11e4–836c–83bc4f26eb67_story.html?; Mustafa Gurbuz, "Turkey's Challenge to Arab Interests in the Horn of Africa," *Arab Centre Washington DC* (blog), February 22, 2018, http://arabcenterdc.org/policy_analyses/turkeys-challenge-to-arab-interests-in-the-horn-of-africa.

20. "The UAE Is Scrambling to Control Ports in Africa," *The Economist*, July 19, 2018, https://www.economist.com/middle-east-and-africa/2018/07/19/the-uae-is-scrambling-to-control-ports-in-africa; Ismail N. Telci, "*A Lost Love between the Horn of Africa and UAE,*" Aljazeera Centre for Studies, May 28, 2018, http://studies.aljazeera.net/en/reports/2018/05/lost-love-horn-africa-uae-\180528092015371.html; and Mustafa Gurbuz, "Turkey's Challenge to Arab Interests in the Horn of Africa," *Arab Centre Washington DC* (blog), February 22, 2018, http://arabcenterdc.org/policy_analyses/turkeys-challenge-to-arab-interests-in-the-horn-of-africa.

21. Dale F. Eickelman, "From Theocracy to Monarchy: Authority and Legitimacy in Inner Oman, 1935–1957," *International Journal of Middle East Studies* 17, no. 1 (February 1, 1985): 6.

22. Sarah G. Phillips and Jennifer S. Hunt. "Without Sultan Qaboos, We Would Be Yemen': The Renaissance Narrative and the Political Settlement in Oman," *Journal of International Development* 29, no. 5 (n.d.): 645–60. doi: 10.1002/jid.3290.

23. Marc Valeri, *Oman: Politics and Society in the Qaboos State* (New York: Columbia University Press, 2009), 203.

24. Many of the dates were shipped to the United States, where they were a holiday tradition. See Hopper, 'Globalisation and the Economics of African Slavery,' 164.

25. James Worrall, "Oman: The 'Forgotten' Corner of the Arab Sprin," *Middle East Policy* 19, no. 3 (2012): 98–115.

26. Marc Valeri, "The Ṣuḥār Paradox: Social and Political Mobilisations in the Sultanate of Oman since 2011," *Arabian Humanities*, no. 4 (January 12, 2015), http://cy.revues.org/2828.

27. Jure Snoj, "*Population of Qatar by Nationality - 2019 Report,*" 15 August 2019, Priya DSouza Communications, https://priyadsouza.com/population-of-qatar-by-nationality-in–2017/.

28. Ali Khalifa Al-Kuwari, ed., Al-Sha'b Yurid Al-Islah Fi *Qatar . . . aydan* (Beirut: Muntada al-Ma'arif, 2012).

29. Mehran Kamrava, *Qatar: Small State, Big Politics* (Ithaca, NY: Cornell University Press, 2013), 119, 135–136.

30. Fuad I. Khuri, *Tribe and State in Bahrain: The Transformation of Social and Political Authority in an Arab State* (Chicago: University of Chicago Press, 1980), 47–53.

31. Katja Niethammer, "Voices in Parliament, Debates in Majalis, and Banners on Streets: Avenues of Political Participation in Bahrain," *EUI Working Papers* (Robert Schuman Centre for Advanced Studies, European University Institute, 2006).

32. Clive Holes, "Dialect and National Identity: The Cultural Politics of Self-Representation in Bahraini," in Paul Dresch and James P. Piscatori, ed., *Monarchies and Nations: Globalisation and Identity in the Arab States of the Gulf* (London: I. B. Tauris, 2005), 57.

33. Gengler, *Group Conflict*, 57.

34. International Crisis Group, "Popular Protest in North Africa and the Middle East (VIII): Bahrain's Rocky Road to Reform," *Middle East/North Africa Report*, July 28, 2011.

CHAPTER 19

1. In 1998, Hassan II succeeded in convincing Abderrahman Youssoufi, leader of the largest opposition party, the USFP, to head a so-called government of *alternance*. The government was mainly drawn from opposition parties that had largely been excluded from power in the past.

2. See Clifford Geertz, *Islam Observed: Religious Development in Morocco and Indonesia* (New Haven, CT: Yale University Press, 1968).

3. Bettina Dennerlein, "Legitimate Bounds and Bound Legitimacy: The Act of Allegiance to the Ruler (Bai'a) in 19th Century Morocco," *Die Welt des Islams* 41, no. 3 (November 2001): 287–310.

4. See Abdellah Hammoudi, *Master and Disciple: The Cultural Foundations of Moroccan Authoritarianism* (Chicago: University of Chicago Press, 1997); Rahma Bourquia and Susan Gilson Miller, eds., *In the Shadow of the Sultan—Culture, Power, and Politics in Morocco* (Cambridge, MA: Harvard University Press, 1999).

5. Elaine Combs-Schilling, "Etching Patriarchal Rule: Ritual Dye, Erotic Potency, and the Moroccan Monarchy," *Journal of the History of Sexuality* 1, no. 4 (April 1991): 658–81.

6. The notion of *makhzen* has changed over time to refer to the state apparatus and to the education, health care, and economic services it provides. The people who work closely with the monarchy are also part of the *makhzen*, and the Moroccan people have generally held them in awe.

7. George Joffe, "Morocco: Monarchy, Legitimacy and Succession," *Third World Quarterly* 10, no. 1 (January 1988): 201–28.

8. See Henry Munson, *Religion and Power in Morocco* (New Haven, CT: Yale University Press, 1993).

9. Naguib Rabia, "Legitimacy and « Transitional Continuity » in a Monarchical Regime : Case of Morocco," *International Journal of Public Administration* 43, no. 5 (2020): 404–24.

10. All constitutions were submitted for ratification by popular vote.

11. It was done mainly to allow him to exercise more power within the parliament and situate himself at the top of political institutions and the representatives of the nation.

12. Elite *immobilisme* refers to a kind of stasis and lack of initiative on the part of the Moroccan elite. See also Saloua Zerhouni, "Morocco: Reconciling Continuity and Change," in *Arab Elite: Negotiating the Politics of Change*, ed. Volker Perthes (Boulder, CO: Lynne Rienner, 2004).

13. Following the 1992 constitutional revision, Morocco proclaimed its adherence to the principles, laws, and obligations that were derived from the charters of international organizations and reaffirmed its attachment to human rights as they are universally recognized. In response to international criticism, King Hassan released political prisoners, created a Ministry of Human Rights (1993), and announced the destruction of the Tazmamart death camp (1994).

14. Youssoufi refused to enter into arrangements for a change of government and left the country after a massive use of money in the indirect elections of 1993. There is also the fact that the king wanted to keep possession of the four ministries called "ministries of sovereignty"— Interior, Justice, Islamic Affairs, and Foreign Affairs. For more details, see Mohammed Tozy, "Political Changes in the Maghreb," *CODESRIA Bulletin* 1 (2000): 47–54.

15. In liberal democracies, *alternance* means the emergence of opposition parties to power as a result of their success in free and transparent elections. For *alternance* in the Moroccan context, see Abdellah Boudahrain, *Le Nouveau Maroc Politique, Quel Avenir?* (Casablanca: Al Madariss, 1999), 61–73.

16. In his first speeches, the new king affirmed his attachment to the principles of constitutional monarchy and called for a new concept of authority based on accountability.

17. The family code provided women with more rights when it came to marriage, divorce, and child custody.

18. A few weeks after his ascension to power, King Mohammed VI ordered the Consultative Council for Human Rights (CCDH) to activate an independent indemnity commission (Commission d'Arbitrage) in order to compensate former victims of forcible disappearances and detention; see Susan Slyomovics, "A Truth Commission for Morocco," *Middle East Report*, no. 218 (Spring 2001).

19. King Mohammed VI created a number of committees in charge of important dossiers such as investment, tourism, education, and reform of the family code, although designated ministries were already in charge of those issues.

20. Roger Letourneau, "Social Change in the Muslim Cities of North Africa," *American Journal of Sociology* 60, no. 6 (May 1955): 529.

21. Mohamed Ameur, "Le Logement des pauvres à Fes," *Revue Tiers Monde* 29, no. 116 (1988): 1171–81.

22. See Will D. Swearingen, *Moroccan Mirages: Agrarian Dreams and Deceptions, 1912–1986* (Princeton, NJ: Princeton University Press, 1987), 145.

23. Hassan Awad, "Morocco's Expanding Towns," *Geographical Journal* 130, no. 1 (March 1964): 49–64.

24. Laetitia Cairoli, "Garment Factory Workers in the City of Fez," *Middle East Journal* 53, no. 1 (Winter 1999): 28–43.

25. Susan Joekes, "Working for Lipstick? Male and Female Labor in the Clothing Industry in Morocco," in *Women, Work and Ideology in the Third World*, ed. Haleh Afshar (London: Tavistock, 1985), 183–214.

26. Shana Cohen, "Alienation and Globalization in Morocco: Addressing the Social and Political Impact of Market Integration," *Comparative Studies in Society and History* 45, no. 1 (January 2003): 168–89.

27. Driss Maghraoui and Saloua Zerhouni, "Searching for Political Normalization: The Party of Justice and Development in Morocco," in *Islamist Parties and Political Normalization in the Muslim World*, eds. Quinn Mecham and Julie Chernov Hwang (Philadelphia: University of Pennsylvania Press, 2014), 112–33.

28. See Amal Vinogradov and John Waterbury, "Situations of Contested Legitimacy in Morocco: An Alternative Framework," *Comparative Studies in Society and History* 13, no. 1 (January 1971): 32–59.

29. Between 1965 and 1970, King Hassan declared a state of emergency during which he concentrated all powers in his hands.

30. To encourage MPs to make use of this prerogative, at least one day per month is reserved for the examination of proposed bills, including those put forward by the opposition (Article 82).

31. The constitution established a Superior Council of Security, which is in charge of coordinating the country's internal and external security; it also aims to institutionalize norms of good governance in the security field (Article 54).

32. See Mohamed Madani, D. Maghraoui, and Zerhouni, "The 2011 Moroccan Constitution: A Critical Analysis," IDEA, 2012, http://www.idea.int/publications/the_2011_moroccan_constitution/loader.cfm? csModule=security/getfile&pageid=56782.

33. According to different studies, the majority of Moroccans do not perceive parliament as an efficient institution. MPs are perceived as serving their own interests, and media coverage of parliamentary activities reinforces this image among the population.

34. Rémy Leveau, *Le fellah marocain défenseur du trône* (Paris: Fondation Nationale des Siences Politiques, 1985).

35. See Henry Clement, *The Mediterranean Debt Crescent: Money and Power in Algeria, Egypt, Morocco, Tunisia and Turkey* (Gainesville: University Press of Florida, 1996), 135–39.

36. André Bank, "Rents, Cooptation and Economized Discourse: Three Dimensions of Political Rule in Jordan, Morocco and Syria," *Journal of Mediterranean Studies* 14, nos. 1/2 (2004): 155–79.

37. See Michel Laurent and Guilain Denoeux, "Campagne d'Assainissement au Maroc: Immunization Politique et Contamination de la Justice," *Monde Arabe-Maghreb Machrek*, no. 154 (October/December 1996).

38. Shana Cohen, "Alienation and Globalization in Morocco: Addressing the Social and Political Impact of Market Integration," *Comparative Studies in Society and History* 45, no. 1 (January 2003): 168–89.

39. The marriage contract now requires the consent and signature of the bride.

40. Some observers spoke about the "one million march," but there is no exact figure on the number of participants in this march. Overall, the demonstration was considered a success.

41. For an analysis of these obstacles, see Katja Zvan Elliott, "Reforming the Moroccan Personal Status Code: A Revolution for Whom?" *Mediterranean Politics* 14, no. 2 (2009): 213–27.

42. When the Romans arrived in North Africa, they met tough resistance and named the inhabitants of the region Barbarians, hence the word *Berber.*

43. Among others, we can cite l'Association Marocaine de la Recherche et d'Echanges Culturels and the Association Nouvelle pour la Culture et les Arts Populaires. These kinds of associations exist in both the countryside and the cities.

44. In an interview conducted by four Lebanese papers (*Al-hawadith, la Revue du Liban, Monday Morning,* and *Al-Bairak*) in March 2002, King Mohammed VI said, "Amazigh is the property of all Moroccans. It is a national wealth, a basic component of the national pluralistic identity."

45. President of the Bureau of la Confédération Tada des Associations Culturelles Amazighes du Maroc, July 2003.

46. See Maghraoui, "The Dynamics of Civil Society in Morocco."

47. Maghraoui, "Depoliticization in Morocco," 24–32.

48. It is safe to say that the social movements that are currently taking place in the MENA region have gone beyond the *khubziste* (bread seeker) demands and logics; see Larbi Sadiki, "Popular Uprisings and Arab Democratization," *International Journal of Middle East Studies* 32, no. 1 (2000): 71–95.

49. See the official Arabic *communiqué* of the movement: *al-bayan arrasmi li harkat 20 fibrayar.*

50. For instance, art initiatives such as The Theater of the *Mahgour*; *falsafa fi zanka* (philosophy in the streets), *lkraya fi zanka* (reading in the streets).

51. Hassan II was the only Arab leader to invite for a visit an Israeli head of government, Shimon Peres.

52. According to Article 31, "The King accredits ambassadors to foreign countries and international organizations. Ambassadors or representatives of international organizations are accredited to Him. He signs and ratifies treaties...." The same article stipulates that only treaties relating to the state finances require prior approval of the parliament. In addition, the king appoints the government, including the foreign minister. As commander in chief of the Royal Armed Forces, he is in direct control of national defense.

53. Abderrahim Maslouhi, "Politique Intérieure et Politique Extérieure au Maroc, Essai d'Identification de la Dynamique Interférentielle dans le Champ Politico-marocain" (unpublished dissertation, Université Mohammed V, Rabat, 1999).

54. For instance, the palace invited the political parties represented in parliament to formulate their views on the project of regionalization and autonomy of the southern provinces. The young sovereign also consulted new actors, notably members of the autonomous civil society, in matters related to foreign policy.

55. The minister is appointed by the king and must not have any political affiliation. This prerogative was maintained by the late king when the *alternance* government was established in 1998, despite protests by the opposition parties.

56. Former prime minister Abderrahmane Youssoufi was very active in international affairs and played an important part in promoting a more liberal image of Morocco. The prime minister for the 2002 government, Driss Jettou, was also strongly involved in the negotiations for an advanced status with the EU.

57. The new king reactivated the role of the Royal Advisory Council for Saharan Affairs and renewed its composition in 2006.

58. In a royal speech at the opening of the October 1982 session of the Chamber of Representatives, Hassan II encouraged the parliamentarians to develop a genuine parliamentary diplomacy.

59. As a result of the parliament's diplomatic activities, recognition of the Sahrawi Arab Democratic Republic (SADR) has been withdrawn or frozen several times. During the sixth legislature (1997–2002), a group of members of parliament representing different political sensibilities was set up to do lobbying work in the European Parliament. In the seventh legislative period, members of parliament repeatedly campaigned for the legitimacy of the Moroccan position. For instance, parliamentarians of the majority groups and the PJD organized a diplomatic tour through Africa and Latin America in 2005.

60. Moroccan parliamentarians are very active within European and Arab institutions such as the Euro-Mediterranean Parliamentary Assembly and the Arab Interparliamentary Union, working for the promotion of foreign investments in Morocco.

61. King Mohammed VI in a message to the participants of the conference organized at Rabat on the occasion of the National Day of Diplomacy, April 28, 2000.

62. King Hassan II was the head of Bayt al Qods, and Mohammed VI succeeded his father to this position.

63. In 1963, Morocco initiated negotiations with the EEC, which resulted in a trade agreement in 1969. The cooperation was later extended in 1976 by a new agreement that included not only trade regulations but also financial aid for socioeconomic development in Morocco.

64. In the context of the MEDA I program, €630 million was invested in sectors supporting economic transition and enhancing socioeconomic balance.

65. In the context of the MEDA II program, €687 million was allocated to the following domains: development of the private sector, adjustment of the financial sector, improvement of the public health and water sectors, development of trade relations, administrative reforms, and support for the northern provinces.

66. In 2004, the financial commitment reached 90 percent and actual disbursement reached 40 percent of the financial aid allocated to Morocco, which makes Morocco the foremost beneficiary of the MEDA program.

67. It is not an accident that in 1988, as crown prince, Mohammed VI did an internship of several months in the cabinet of Jacques Delors, president of the Commission of the European Communities; in 1993, he obtained his doctorate with a dissertation on "The EEC-Maghreb Cooperation."

68. King Mohammed VI (speech at the dinner given in his honor by President Jacques Chirac, Paris, March 20, 2000).

69. King Mohammed VI (speech on the occasion of the sixth anniversary of his reign).

70. The European Neighborhood Policy was approved by the European Council in June 2003.

71. See the 2021 World Press Freedom Index | RSF

CHAPTER 20

1. Jamil Hilal, "Reclaiming the Palestinian Narrative," *Al-Shabaka Commentary*, January 6, 2013, http://al-shabaka.org/commentaries/reclaiming-the- palestinian-narrative/; also see Beshara Doumani, "Palestine versus the Palestinians? The Iron Laws and Ironies of a People Denied," *Journal of Palestine Studies* 36, no. 4 (Summer 2007): 49–64.

2. For the sake of simplicity, in this chapter we are focusing on the occupied West Bank (which always include East Jerusalem) and Gaza Strip, and we use the Occupied Palestinian Territory (oPt), the Palestinian Authority (PA), and the State of Palestine as synonyms and interchangeably.

3. Statistics are acquired from the Palestinian Central Bureau of Statistics, http://www.pcbs.gov.ps/site/lang__en/881/default.aspx#Census and http://www.pcbs.gov.ps/Downloads/book2345.pdf and https://www.pcbs.gov.ps/site/512/default.aspx?lang=en&ItemID=4024; and Israel's Central Bureau of Statistics, https://www.cbs.gov.il/en/mediarelease/Pages/2020/Population-of-Israel-on-the-Eve-of-2021.aspx.

4. See footnotes below for CIA data (used in the other chapters of this book).

5. 2,402 square miles (6,220 square km); West Bank (including East Jerusalem), 2,263 square miles (5,860 square km); Gaza, 139 square miles (360 square km).

6. West Bank (including East Jerusalem), 2,949,246 (July 2021 est.); Gaza, 1,957,062 (July 2021 est.).

7. West Bank, 56.06 (2021 est.); Gaza, 64.2 (2021 est.).

8. West Bank, Muslim 80–85% (predominantly Sunni), Jewish 12–14%, Christian 1–2.5% (mainly Greek Orthodox), other, unaffiliated, unspecified.

9. West Bank, Unity Semi-presidential republic; Gaza, Unity Semi-presidential republic (disputed).

10. West Bank, $9.828 billion (2014 est.); Gaza, $2.938 billion (2014 est.).

11. Agriculture, 3% (2017 est.); Industry, 21.1% (2017 est.); Services, 75% (2017 est.).

12. Sources for CIA footnote numbers: https://www.cia.gov/the-world-factbook/countries/west-bank/, https://web.archive.org/web/20140608203237/http://www.un.int/wcm/content/site/palestine/cache/offonce/pid/12353, http://www.pcbs.gov.ps/Downloads/book2546.pdf, https://www.cia.gov/the-world-factbook/countries/gaza-strip,http://www.pcbs.gov.ps/Downloads/book2546.pdf.

13. In addition to the argument that the 1993 Oslo Peace Accords can be traced to the aftermath of the 1973 October War, it is rooted in the 1978 Camp David framework for peace. See Osamah Khalil, "Oslo's Roots: Kissinger, the PLO, and the Peace Process," Al-Shabaka Policy Brief, September 3, 2013, https://al-shabaka.org/briefs/oslos-roots-kissinger-plo-and-peace-pro cess/.

14. Ari Shavit, "The Big Freeze," *Haaretz.com*, August 10, 2004, http://www.haaretz.com/hasen/p ages/ShArt.jhtml? itemNo=485929.

15. In May 2012, Defense Minister Ehud Barak declared that Israel should abandon negotiated peace with the Palestinians but engage in unilateral decisions concerning the fate of the oPt; it further illustrates that the Israeli government is not keen on having any negotiating process with the PLO. In 2015 and during his electoral campaign, the Israeli Prime Minister Benjamin Netanyahu announced that there will never be an independent Palestinian state as long as he serves as prime minister of Israel. See http://www.washingtonpost.com/world/middle_east/on-final-day-of-campaign-netanyahu-says-no- palestinian-state-if-he-wins/2015/03/16/4f4468e8-cbdc-11e4-8730-4f473416e759_story.html.

16. Ghassan Khatib, *Palestinian Politics and the Middle East Peace Process: Consensus and Competition in the Palestinian Negotiating Team* (Oxon: Routledge, 2011).

17. Peter Lagerquist, "Privatizing the Occupation: The Political Economy of an Oslo Development Project," *Journal of Palestine Studies* 32, no. 2 (2003): 5–20.

18. Mushtaq Husain Khan, George Giacaman, and Inge Amundsen, eds., *State Formation in Palestine: Viability and Governance during a Social Transformation (Curzon Political Economy of the Middle East and North Africa series)* (London: Routledge, 2004).

19. Rashid Khalidi, *Palestinian Identity: The Construction of Modern National Consciousness* (New York: Columbia University Press, 1997).

20. UNDP, *Human Development Report 2009–2010: Occupied Palestinian Territory*, United Nations Development Program (2010), http://www.undp.ps/en/newsroom/publications/pdf/other/phd reng.pdf.

21. It should be noted, however, that the birth rate for the Israeli settlers living in (according to international law) illegal settlements in the West Bank is considerably high.

22. Shaul Mishal and Avraham Sela, *The Palestinian Hamas: Vision, Violence, and Coexistence* (New York: Columbia University Press, 2000).

23. Lamees Farraj and Tariq Dana, "The Politicization of Public Sector Employment and Salaries in the West Bank and Gaza," Al-Shabaka Policy Brief, March 14, 2021, https://al-shabaka.org/ briefs/the-politicization-of-public-sector-employment-and-salaries-in-palestine/; also see Jamil Hilal, *"The Palestinian Middle Class: A Research into the Confusion of Identity, Authority and Culture,"* Institute for Palestine Studies and Muwatin, The Palestinian Institute for the Study of Democracy, Beirut, 2006; and Jamil Hilal, "Palestinian class formation under settler colonialism," 2014, https://yplus.ps/wp-content/uploads/2021/01/Hilal-Jamil-Palestinian-Class -Formation-under-Settler-Colonialism.pdf.

24. Joost R. Hiltermann, *Behind the Intifada: Labor and Women's Movements in the Occupied Territories* (Princeton, NJ: Princeton University Press, 1991); Glenn E. Robinson, *Building a Palestinian State: The Incomplete Revolution* (Bloomington: Indiana University Press, 1997).

25. Benoît Challand, *Palestinian Civil Society: Foreign Donors and the Power to Promote and Exclude* (London: Routledge, 2009); Tariq Dana, "Palestinian Civil Society: What Went Wrong?" *Al-Shabaka Policy Brief*, April 14, 2013, https://al-shabaka.org/briefs/palestinian-civil-society-what-went-wrong/; Tariq Dana, "The Structural Transformation of Palestinian Civil Society: Key Paradigm Shifts," *Middle East Critique*, 24, no. 2 (2015): 191–210.

26. De-development is a process that forestalls development by "depriving or ridding the economy of its capacity and potential for rational structural transformation [i.e., natural patterns of growth and development] and preventing the emergence of any self-correcting measures" (Roy, 2001). De-development occurs when normal economic relations are impaired or abandoned, preventing any logical or rational arrangement of the economy or its constituent parts, diminishing productive capacity, and precluding sustainable growth. Over time, de-development represents nothing less than the denial of economic potential (Roy cited in Mandy Turner and Omar Shweiki, ed., *Decolonizing Palestinian Political Economy: De-Development and Beyond* [London: Palgrave Macmillan, 2014]). See also Sara M. Roy, *Failing Peace: Gaza and the Palestinian-Israeli Conflict* (London: Pluto, 2007).

27. Robinson, *Building a Palestinian State*.

28. Alaa Tartir, "The Palestinian Authority Security Forces: Whose Security?" *Al-Shabaka Policy Brief*, May 16, 2017, https://al-shabaka.org/briefs/palestinian- authority-security-forces-whose-security/.

29. For further information and analysis on Palestinian Christians, see *This Week in Palestine*, December 2019 Edition, Issue 260, https://thisweekinpalestine.com/

30. Jeroen Gunning, *Hamas in Politics: Democracy, Religion, Violence* (New York: Columbia University Press 2008).

31. The same fragmentation between Areas A, B, and C to protect Israeli settlements existed in the Gaza Strip from 1994 until Israel's disengagement from Gaza in 2005. It should be noted that the Gaza PA does not control its own borders, and anyone willing to enter or leave Gaza needs Israeli or Egyptian permission. On the Gaza blockade, see http://gisha.org/topic/control-over-gaza.

32. For further analysis, see *Reclaiming The PLO, Re-Engaging Youth*, An Al-Shabaka Policy Circle Report, Co-Facilitated by Marwa Fatafta and Alaa Tartir, 2020. Available at https://al-shabaka.org/focuses/reclaiming-the-plo-re-engaging-youth/

33. Tariq Dana, "The Palestinian Capitalists That Have Gone Too Far," *Al-Shabaka Policy Brief*, January 14, 2014, http://al-shabaka.org/briefs/palestinian-capitalists-have-gone-too-far/.

34. Nicolas Pelham. "Gaza's Tunnel Phenomenon: The Unintended Dynamics of Israel's Siege," *Journal of Palestine Studies* 41, no. 4 (2012): 6–31. https://doi.org/10.1525/jps.2012.xli.4.6; Björn Brenner, *Gaza under Hamas: From Islamic Democracy to Islamist Governance* (London: I.B. Tauris, 2016); and Ahmed Tannira, *Foreign Aid to the Gaza Strip between Trusteeship and De-Development* (London: Anthem Press, 2020).

35. An estimated 40% of all Palestinian men in the oPt have spent some time in Israeli prisons. See Stéphanie Latte Abdallah, 2021. *La toile carcérale. Une histoire de l'enfermement en Palestine*, Paris, Bayard.

36. Emile F. Sahliyeh, *In Search of Leadership: West Bank Politics since 1967* (Washington, DC: Brookings Institution Press, 1988).

37. Roy, *Failing Peace*.

38. Rema Hammami, "NGOs: The Professionalization of Politics," *Race and Class* 37, no. 2 (1995): 51–63.

39. Benoît Challand, *Palestinian Civil Society: Foreign Donors and the Power to Promote and Exclude* (London: Routledge, 2009).

40. Alaa Tartir, "Contentious Economics in Occupied Palestine," in *Contentious Politics in the Middle East*, ed. Fawaz A. Gerges (London: Palgrave Macmillan, 2015).

41. Jamil Hilal, ed., *Where Now for Palestine? The Demise of the Two-State Solution* (London: Zed, 2007).

42. Alaa Tartir, "Palestinians Have Been Abandoned by Their Leaders," *Foreign Policy*, https://foreignpolicy.com/2018/05/24/palestinians-have-been-abandoned-by-their-leaders/.

43. Postponement of the General Elections (30 April 2021) https://www.elections.ps/Tabld/1083/ArtMID/9183/ArticleID/2781/Postponement-of-the-General-Elections.aspx. For further analysis, see Alaa Tartir, A New Approach to Elections in Palestine, *Al-Jazeera*, May 2021 https://www.aljazeera.com/opinions/2021/5/1/why-palestinians-should-vote-no-at-the-upcoming-elections.

44. The ECFR's *Mapping Palestinian Politics* provides an interactive overview of the main Palestinian political institutions and players in Palestine, Israel, and the diaspora https://ecfr.eu/special/mapping_palestinian_politics/.

45. Anne Le More, *International Assistance to the Palestinians after Oslo: Political Guilt, Wasted Money* (London: Routledge, 2008).

46. Jeremy Wildeman and Alaa Tartir, "Unwilling to Change, Determined to Fail: Donor Aid in Occupied Palestine in the Aftermath of the Arab Uprisings," *Mediterranean Politics* 19, no. 3 (2014): 431–49. Also see Alaa Tartir and Jeremy Wildeman, "Mapping of Donor Funding to the Occupied Palestinian Territories 2012–2014/15," AidWatch Palestine, 2017, https://alaatartirdotcom.files.wordpress.com/2017/11/aidwatch-study-published.pdf; Are John Knudsen and Alaa Tartir, Country Evaluation Brief: Palestine, Chr. Michelsen Institute (CMI), 2017, https://alaatartirdotcom.files.wordpress.com/2017/06/5-17- country-evaluation-brief_palestine.pdf; J. Wildeman and A. Tartir, "*Political Economy of Foreign Aid in the Occupied Palestinian Territories: A Conceptual Framing*," in *Political Economy of Palestine. Middle East Today*, eds. A. Tartir, T. Dana, and T. Seidel (Cham: Palgrave Macmillan). https://doi.org/10.1007/978-3-030-68643-7_10.

47. Rex Brynen, *A Very Political Economy: Peacebuilding and Foreign Aid in the West Bank and Gaza* (Washington, DC: United States Institute of Peace Press, 2000).

48. Lagerquist, "Privatizing the Occupation."

49. Human Rights Watch, *Ripe for Abuse: Palestinian Child Labor in Israeli Agricultural Settlements in the West Bank* (2015), http://www.hrw.org/sites/default/files/reports/isrpal0415_forUPload_2.pdf.

50. For further insights, see Ihab Maharmeh, Israel's Violations of Palestinian Workers' Rights: COVID-19 and Systemic Abuse, *Al-Shabaka Policy Brief*, 2021 https://al-shabaka.org/briefs/israels-violations-of-palestinian-workers-rights-covid-19-and-systemic-abuse/; Lucy Garbett, *Palestinian Workers in Israel Caught between Indispensable and Disposable*, MERIP, 2020 https://merip.org/2020/05/palestinian-workers-in-israel-caught-between-indispensable-and-disposable/.

51. For further analysis on international aid, watch "Is it Time to Reform International Aid to Palestine?" *Webinar*, October 6, 2020, https://www.youtube.com/watch?v=wWWMn32HcnY&ab_channel=FoundationforMiddleEastPeace; listen to International Aid to Palestine Podcast, August 31, 2021, https://open.spotify.com/episode/3SEwquMwPtMLasVf7i3n8J. For a broader critical analysis on the political economy of Palestine, see Alaa Tartir, Tariq Dana, and Timothy Seidel, eds. *Political Economy of Palestine. Critical, Interdisciplinary, and Decolonial Perspectives* (London: Palgrave MacMillan, 2021).

52. Alaa Tartir, *Discord around the Abraham Accords*, Institut Montaigne, 2020, https://www.institu tmontaigne.org/en/blog/discord-around-abraham-accords.

53. These are figures from the UN (OCHA office): seven hundred armed Palestinians and 1,500 civilians, and sixty-six soldiers and seven civilians on the Israeli side.

54. For details, please refer to Public Opinion Poll No (80) by the Palestinian Center for Policy and Survey Research (PSR), http://pcpsr.org/en/node/845.

55. BDS, "Introducing the BDS Movement," http://www.bdsmovement.net/bdsintro.

56. The case of Ahed Tamimi from the Nabi Saleh village in the West Bank is another example of how the Israeli oppression is resisted through popular and peaceful resistance means. See Alice Speri, "How Ahed Tamimi Became the Symbol of Palestinian Resistance to Israeli Oppression," *The Intercept*, July 31, 2018, https://theintercept.com/2018/07/31/ahed-tamimi-released-palestine-child-prisoners/?platform=hootsuite.

57. Valentina Azarova, "Palestine's Day in Court? The Unexpected Effects of ICC Action," *Al-Shabaka Policy Brief*, April 1, 2015, http://al-shabaka.org/briefs/palestines-day-in-court-the-unexpected-effects-of-icc-action/.

58. Ben White, "'Jewish Nation State': How Israel Enshrines Apartheid into Law," *Middle East Eye*, July 19, 2018, http://www.middleeasteye.net/columns/how- israel-enshrines-apartheid-law -818001636.

CHAPTER 21

1. David Rundell, *Vision or Mirage* (Bloomsbury Publishing, 2020), 117.

2. Ibid., 130.

3. Ibid.

4. Ibid.

5. M. Allison, *Militants Seize Mecca*, August 2011, 2.

6. Rundell, *Vision or Mirage*, 129.

7. Ibid., 57.

8. Ibid.

9. Ibid., 63.

10. Ibid., 72.

11. Alexei Vassiliev, *The History of Saudi Arabia* (Saiqi Books, 2000), 299.

12. Sultan Al-Sughair, " Well no 7 That Established KSA on World Oil Map," *Arabnews.com*, August 1, 2015.

13. Ibid.

14. Ali Naimi, *Out of the Desert* (Penguin Publishing, 2016).

15. Rundell, *Vision or Mirage*, 159.

16. Robert Rapier, "How Much Oil Does Saudi Arabia Really Have," *Forbes.com*, February 14, 2018.

17. Rundell, *Vision or Mirage*, 158.

18. Ibid., 159.

19. Ibid.

20. Nehme, M., *"Political Development in Saudi Arabia,"* Sagepub.com, 1995, 634.

21. Rundell, *Vision or Mirage*, 161.

22. M. Nehme, *"Political Development in Saudi Arabia,"* Sagepub.com, 1995, 634.

23. Ibid., 632.

24. P. Menoret, "Kingdom of Saudi Arabia," in *The Middle East,* 15th ed., ed. Ellen Lust, 628.

25. Rundell, *Vision or Mirage*, 158.

26. Nehme, *Political Development in Saudi Arabia*, 632.

27. Ibid., 636.

28. Ibid.

29. Ibid., 633.

30. Rundell, *Vision or Mirage*, 43.

31. Ibid., 47.

32. Ibid., 157.

33. Ibid., 158.

34. Algaissi Abdullah, "Preparedness and Response to COVID-19 in Saudi Arabia," *Journal of Infection and Public Health*, Sciencedirect.com, June 2020; David Rundell, *Vision or Mirage* (Bloomsbury Publishing, 2020), 157.

35. Siddiq Allah Morad and Sahel Zreik, *Education in Saudi Arabia*, April 9, 2020, Wenr.wes.org

36. Ibid.

37. Alainna Liloia, " Saudi Women Are Going to College….," *The conversation.com*, March 25, 2019.

38. Arab Bedouin in Saudi Arabia Joshuaproject.ney.

39. Fertility rate, births/women. Data. Worldbank.org.

40. Varun Gudinho, *"Two Thirds of Saudi Arabia's Population in under 25,"* Gulfbusiness.com. August 10, 2020.

41. Rundell, *Vision or Mirage*, 72.

42. Ibid.

43. Francoise de Bel-Air. "Demography, Migration and Labor Markets in Saudi Arabia," *Gulf Research Center*, 2014, 7.

44. Helene Thiollet, "Refugees and Migrants from Eritrea to the Arab World: The Cases of Sudan, Yemen, and Saudi Arabia 1991–2007." Paper presented at conference on "Migration and Refugee Movements in the MENA," American University in Cairo, 2007, 6.

45. Rundell, *Vision or Mirage*, 127.

46. Ibid., 65.

47. Ibid., 119.

48. Ibid.

49. Ibid.

50. Saudiembassy.net on the Basic Law of Governance.

51. Rundell, *Vision or Mirage*, 201.

52. William Cleveland, *A History of the Modern Middle East* (Westview Publishing, 2016), 478.

53. Ibid.

54. Rundell, *Vision or Mirage*, 124.

55. Cleveland, *A History of the Modern Middle East*.

56. Rundell, *Vision or Mirage*, 129.

57. Ibid., 119.

58. Ibid., 133.

59. Ibid., 132.

59. Article 44.

61. Madawi Al-Rasheed, *Contesting the Saudi State: Islamic Voices from a New Generation* (Cambridge: Cambridge University Press, 2007), 57.

62. Cleveland, *A History of the Modern Middle East*, 115.

63. Ibid.

64. Rundell, *Vision or Mirage*, 103.

64. Ibid., 95.

65. Cleveland, *A History of the Modern Middle East*, 412.

66. Ibid.

67. Ibid.

68. Rundell, *Vision or Mirage*, 101.

69. Rundell, *Vision or Mirage*, 95.

70. "Mecca 1979: The Mosque Siege That Changes the Course of Saudi History," *BBC.com*, December 27, 2019.

71. Quran sura verse 191 cited in David Rundell, *Vision or Mirage* (Bloomsbury Publishing, 2020), 58.

72. M. Allison, *Militants Seize Mecca*, August 2011, 2.

73. Ibid., 5.

74. Yaroslav Trofimov, "1979: Remembering the 'Siege of Mecca,'" *Npr.org*, August 20, 2009.

75. Allison, *Militants Seize Mecca*.

76. "Mecca 1979: The Mosque Siege That Changes the Course of Saudi History," *BBC.com*, December 27, 2019.

77. Jamal Khashogi, "By Blaming 1979 for Saudi Arabia's Problems....," *Washington Post*, April 3, 2018.

78. *New York Times*, January 24, 2018.

79. Rundell, *Vision or Mirage*, 91.

80. Sebastian Maisel, *The New Rise of Tribalism in Saudi Arabia*, 2014, 103.

81. Ibid., 100.

82. Rundell, *Vision or Mirage*, cite Dickinson, 86.

83. Maisel, *The New Rise of Tribalism in Saudi Arabia*, 103.

84. Ibid.

85. Ibid.

86. Ibid., 100.

87. Ibid., 103.

88. Rundell, *Vision or Mirage*, cite Dickinson, 87.

89. Ibid., 83.

90. Maisel, *The New Rise of Tribalism in Saudi Arabia*, 106.

91. Rundell, *Vision or Mirage*, cite Dickinson, 89.

92. Ibid., 91.

93. Madawi Al-Rasheed, *A History of Saudi Arabia* (Cambridge: Cambridge University Press, 2002), p. 147.

94. Toby Craig Jones, "Rebellion on the Saudi Periphery: Modernity, Modernization and the Shi'a Uprisings of 1979," *International Journal of Middle Easter Studies* 38 (2006), 213-33, 215.

95. Laurence Louer, *Transnational Shia Politics: Religious and Political Networks in the Gulf* (New York: Columbia University Press, 2008), 233–34.

96. Al-Rasheed, *Contesting the Saudi State*, 118.

97. Ibid., 175–210.

98. L. Carl Brown, *International Politics and the Middle East, Old Rules, Dangerous Game* (London: I.B. Tauris 1984), 4.

99. Rashid Khaldi, *Sowing Crisis: The Cold War and American Dominance in the Middle East* (Boston, MA: Beacon Press, 2009), 11.

100. Ellis Goldberg and Robert Vitalis, *The Arabian Peninsula: Crucible of Globalization* (San Domenico di Fiesole: European University Institute, 2009).

101. Malcolm Kerr, *The Arab Cold War: Gamal 'Abd al Nasir and His Rivals, 1958-1970* (Oxford: Oxford University Press, 1971).

102. Khalidi, *Sowing Crisis*, 14.

103. Madawi, Al-Rasheed, ed. *Kingdom without Borders: Saudi Arabia's Political, Religious and Media Frontiers* (London: Hurst, 2008), 323–37.

104. Thiollet, "Refugees and Migrants from Eritrea to the Arab World," 5.

105. Hugh Naylor, "Yemen Conflict's Risk for Saudis: Their Vietnam," *Washington Post*, April 9, 2015.

CHAPTER 22

1. Abdul Latif Tibawi, *A Modern History of Syria* (London: Macmillan, 1969), 241–378.

2. See Philip Khoury, *Syria and the French Mandate: The Politics of Nationalism 1920–1936* (Princeton, NJ: Princeton University Press, 1987); R. Bayly Winder, "Syrian Deputies and Cabinet Ministers: 1919–1959," *Middle East Journal* 16 (August 1962): 407–29, and 17 (Winter–Spring 1963): 35–54.

3. M. Van Dusen, "Downfall of a Traditional Elite," in *Political Elite and Political Development in the Middle East*, ed. F. Tachau (Cambridge, MA: Schenkman/Wiley, 1975), 115–55.

4. Doreen Warriner, *Land Reform and Development in the Middle East* (London: Oxford University Press, 1962).

5. See Rizkallah Hilan, *Culture et developement en Syrie et dans les pays retardes* (Paris: Editions Anthropos, 1969); Steven Heydemann, *Authoritarianism in Syria: Institutions and Social Conflict* (Ithaca, NY: Cornell University Press, 1999).

6. John Devlin, *The Ba'th Party: A History from Its Origins to 1966* (Stanford, CA: Hoover Institution Press, 1976).

7. Patrick Seale, *The Struggle for Syria* (London: Oxford University Press, 1965).

8. Itamar Rabinovich, *Syria under the Ba'th, 1963–1966: The Army-Party Symbiosis* (New York: Halstead Press, 1972).

9. Tabitha Petran, *Syria* (London: Ernest Benn, 1972), 195–204, 239–48.

10. See Adeed Dawisha, "Syria under Asad, 1970–1978: The Centres of Power," *Government and Opposition* 13, no. 3 (Summer 1978); Raymond Hinnebusch, *Syria: Revolution from Above* (London: Routledge, 2001), chap. 4; and Patrick Seale, *Asad: The Struggle for the Middle East* (Berkeley: University of California Press, 1988).

11. Eyal Zisser, *Asad's Legacy: Syria in Transition* (London: Hurst, 2001), 17–36.

12. Van Dusen, "Downfall of a Traditional Elite."

13. Nikolaos Van Dam, *The Struggle for Power in Syria: Sectarianism, Regionalism, and Tribalism in Politics, 1961–1980* (London: Croom-Helm, 1981).

14. Hanna Batatu, "Syria's Muslim Brethren," *MERIP Reports* 12, no. 110 (November/December 1982): 12–20.

15. See Hinnebusch, *Syria*, chap. 5.

16. Line Khatib, *Islamic Revivalism in Syria: The Rise and Fall of Ba'athist Secularism* (London: Routledge, 2011).

17. Teije Hidde Donker, "Enduring Ambiguity: Sunni Community–Syrian Regime Dynamics," *Mediterranean Politics* 15, no. 3 (2010): 435–52.

18. Volker Perthes, *Syria under Bashar al-Asad: Modernisation and the Limits of Change*, Adelphi Papers (London: Oxford University Press for International Institute for Strategic Studies, 2004).

19. Perthes, *Syria under Bashar al-Asad.*

20. Alan George, *Syria: Neither Bread nor Freedom* (London: Zed Books, 2003).

21. Roshanak Shaery-Eisenlohr, "From Subjects to Citizens? Civil Society and the Internet in Syria," *Middle East Critique* 20, no. 2 (2011): 127–38.

22. Raymond Hinnebusch and Tina Zintl, eds., *Syria from Reform to Revolt, Volume 1: Political Economy and International Relations* (Syracuse, NY: Syracuse University Press, 2015).

23. Elizabeth Longuenesse, "The Class Nature of the State in Syria," *MERIP Reports* 9, no. 4 (1979): 3–11.

24. Raymond Hinnebusch, *Peasant and Bureaucracy in Ba'thist Syria: The Political Economy of Rural Development* (Boulder, CO: Westview Press, 1989).

25. Raymond Hinnebusch, "The Political Economy of Economic Liberalisation in Syria," *International Journal of Middle East Studies* 27 (1995): 305–20.

26. Volker Perthes, *The Political Economy of Syria under Asad* (London: I. B. Taurus, 1995).

27. Flynt Leverett, *Inheriting Syria: Bashar's Trial by Fire* (Washington, DC: Brookings Institution Press, 2005); Samer Abboud, "The Transition Paradigm and the Case of Syria," in *Syria's Economy and the Transition Paradigm*, St. Andrews Papers on Contemporary Syria (Fife: University of St. Andrews, 2009), 3–31; and Bassam Haddad, *Business Networks in Syria: The Political Economy of Authoritarian Resilience* (Stanford, CA: Stanford University Press, 2011).

28. See http://erikmeyersson.com/2015/07/01/the-staggering-economic-costs-of-the-syrian-civil-war/; http://www.globalenvision.org/2015/03/25/cost- civil-war-Syria's-economy-after-four-years-conflict.

29. Fayez Sarah, "The New Syrians," *Al Hayat*, July 16, 2011.

30. Kim Ghattas, "Syria's Spontaneously Organised Protests," *BBC News*, April 22, 2011, http://www.bbc.co.uk/news/world-middle-east-13168276.

31. Raymond Hinnebusch, "Syria: From Authoritarian Upgrading to Revolution? *International Affairs* 88 (January 2012): 95–113.

32. This section is based on Aron Lund, "Gangs of Latakia: The Militiafication of the Assad Regime," *Syria Comment*, July 24, 2013, http://www.joshualandis.com/blog/the-militiafication- of-the-assad-regime/; Rana Khalaf, "Governance without Government in Syria; Civil Society and State-building during Conflict," *Syria Studies* 7, no. 3, 2015, http://ojs.st-andrews.ac.uk/index.php/syria/article/view/1176; Kheder Khaddour, *The Assad Regime's Hold on the Syrian State,* Carnegie Middle East Centre, July 8, 2015, http://carnegie-mec.org/2015/07/08/assad-regime-s- hold-on-Syrian-state/id3k.

33. Malcolm Kerr, "Hafiz al-Asad and the Changing Patterns of Syrian Politics," *International Journal* 28, no. 4 (1975): 689–707.

34. Moshe Maoz, *Asad, the Sphinx of Damascus: A Political Biography* (New York: Grove Weidenfeld, 1988); Seale, *Asad*.

35. Eberhard Kienle, "Syria, the Kuwait War, and the New World Order," in *The Gulf War and the New World Order*, eds. Tareq and Jacqueline Ismael (Gainesville: University Press of Florida, 1994).

36. Leverett, *Inheriting Syria*, 47–48. Also note 108, 243.an.

CHAPTER 23

1. Stephanie Beswick, *Sudan's Blood Memory: The Legacy of War, Ethnicity, and Slavery in Early South Sudan* (Rochester, NY: University of Rochester Press, 2004).

2. Robert Collins, "Slavery in the Sudan in History," *Slavery & Abolition* 20, no. 3 (1999): 69–95. doi:10.1080/01440399908575286.

3. Sean Rex O'Fahey, *The Darfur Sultanate: A History* (New York: Columbia University Press, 2008).

4. Amir H. Idris, *Identity, Citizenship, and Violence in Two Sudans: Reimagining a Common Future* (Basingstoke: Palgrave Macmillan, 2013).

5. Ahmed Ibrahim Abushouk and Anders Bjørkelo, *The Principles of Native Administration in the Anglo Egyptian Sudan 1898-1956* (Omdurman and Bergen: Abdel Karim Mirghani Cultural Centre and Centre for Middle Eastern and Islamic Studies, 2004).

6. Peter Woodward, *Sudan, 1898-1989: The Unstable State* (Boulder, CO: Lynne Rienner, 1991).

7. Ahmed Ibrahim Abushouk, "The Anglo-Egyptian Sudan: From Collaboration Mechanism to Party Politics, 1898–1956," *The Journal of Imperial and Commonwealth History*, 38, no. 2 (2010): 207–36, doi:10.1080/03086531003743924.

8. Atta el-Battahani, "Ideological Expansionist Movements versus Historical Indigenous Rights in the Darfur Region of Sudan: From Actual Homicide to Potential Genocide," in *Darfur and the Crisis of Governance in Sudan*, eds. Salah M. Hassan and Carina E. Ray (Ithaca, NY: Cornell University Press, 2009): 43–67.

9. Atta El-Battahani, "The Post-Secession State in Sudan: Building Coalitions or Deepening Conflicts?" in *Sudan Divided: Continuing Conflict in a Contested State*, eds. Gunnar Sørbø and Abdel Ghaffar M. Ahmed (New York: Palgrave Macmillan, 2013).

10. Atta el-Battahani, "CPA Implementation a Complex Web: Politics and Conflict in Sudan" in *Peace by Piece: Addressing Sudan's Conflicts*, eds. Mark Simmons and Peter Dixon (Accord: An International Review of Peace Initiatives, 2006).

11. Abdel Salam Sidahmed and Alsir Sidahmed, *Sudan* (London: Routledge, 2005).

12. Ann Mosely Lesch, *Sudan: Contested National Identities* (Bloomington: Indiana University Press, 1998).

13. Haytam Karar, "The Implications of Socio-Politics and Political Economy on Education Policy in Sudan: 1900 to 2000," *Italian Journal of Sociology of Education* 11, no. 2 (2019): 428–47.

14. Abdullahi A Gallab, *The First Islamist Republic: Development and Disintegration of Islamism in the Sudan* (London: Routledge, 2008).

15. Heather J. Sharkey, "Arab Identity and Ideology in Sudan: The Politics of Language, Ethnicity, and Race," *African Affairs* 107, no. 426 (2008): 21–43. doi:10.1093/afraf/adm068.

16. Harry Verhoeven, "The Rise and Fall of Sudan's Al-Ingaz Revolution: The Transition from Militarised Islamism to Economic Salvation and the Comprehensive Peace Agreement," *Civil Wars*, 15, no. 2 (2013): 118–140. doi: 10.1080/13698249.2013.817846.

17. Sidahmed and Sidahmed, *Sudan*, 2005.

18. Alex de Waal, "Sudan: What Kind of State? What kind of Crisis? Occasional paper 2," Social Science Research Council (2007).

19. Douglas Johnson, *The Root Causes of Sudan's Civil Wars: Peace or Truce* (London: James Currey, 2011).

20. Paul Ladouceur, "The Southern Sudan: A Forgotten War and a Forgotten Peace," *International Journal: Canada's Journal of Global Policy Analysis* 30, no. 3 (1975): 406–27.

21. Sidahmed, 1996.

22. John Young, "John Garang's Legacy to the Peace Process, the SPLM/A & the South," *Review of African Political Economy*, 32, no. 106 (2005): 535–48. doi: 10.1080/03056240500467039.

23. John Young, "Eastern Sudan: Caught in a Web of External Interests," *Review of African Political Economy*, 33, no. 109 (2006): 594–601.

24. Hilde Frafjord Johnsen, *Waging Peace in Sudan, The Inside Story of the Negotiations that Ended Africa's Longest Civil War* (Chicago: Sussex Academic Press, 2011).

25. John Young, "Sudan: A Flawed Peace Process Leading to a Flawed Peace," *Review of African Political Economy*, 32, no. 103 (2005): 99–113.

26. de Waal, 2007.

27. Abdullahi El Tom, "The Black Book of Sudan: Imbalance of Power and Wealth in Sudan," *Journal of African International Affairs* 1, no. 2 (2003): 25–35.

28. Julie Flint and Alex de Waal, *Darfur: A Short History of a Long War* (London: Zed Books, 2006).

29. Sudan Peace Agreement Sudan Peace Agreement | ConstitutionNet.

30. Munzoul Assal, "Six Years after the Eastern Sudan Peace Agreement: An Assessment," in *Sudan Divided: Continuing Conflict in a Contested State*, eds. Gunnar Sørbø and Abdel Ghaffar M. Ahmed (New York: Palgrave Macmillan, 2013).

31. Luke A. Patey, "Crude Days Ahead? Oil and the Resource Curse in Sudan," *African Affairs* 109, no. 437 (October 2010): 617–36. doi:10.1093/afraf/adq043.

32. Ibid.

33. Patey, "Crude Days Ahead," 2010.

34. This paragraph builds on Alsir Sidahmed, "Oil and Politics in Sudan" in *Sudan Divided: Continuing Conflict in a Contested State*, eds. Gunnar Sørbø and Abdel Ghaffar M. Ahmed (New York: Palgrave Macmillan, 2013).

35. Ibid.

36. Mohammed Hussein Sharfi, "The Dynamics of the Loss of Oil Revenues in the Economy of North Sudan" *Review of African Political Economy* 41, no. 140 (2014): 316–22. doi:10.1080/03056244.2013.876982.

37. Sidahmed, "Oil and Politics," 2013.

38. Sørbø and Ahmed, *Sudan Divided*, 2013.

39. Integrated Food Security Phase Classification. "Sudan: Acute Food Insecurity Situation April - May 2021 and Projections for June - September 2021 and October 2021 - February 2022" Sudan: Acute Food Insecurity Situation April - May 2021 and Projections for June - September 2021 and October 2021 - February 2022 | IPC Global Platform (ipcinfo.org).

40. Susanne Jaspars, "The State, Inequality, and the Political Economy of Long-Term Food Aid in Sudan" *African Affairs* 117, no. 469 (2018): 592–612. doi:10.1093/afraf/ady030.

41. Aldan Young, *Transforming Sudan: Decolonization, Economic Development and State Formation* (Cambridge: Cambridge University Press, 2017).

42. Sørbø and Ahmed, *Sudan Divided*, 2013.

43. Young, 2017.

44. Gallab, 2008.

45. Laura Mann, "*Wasta!* The Long-Term Implications of Education Expansion and Economic Liberalisation on Politics in Sudan," *Review of African Political Economy* 41, no. 142 (2014): 561–78. doi:10.1080/03056244.2014.952276.

46. Atta El-Battahani, *The Sudan Armed Forces and Prospects of Change* (Bergen: Chr. Michelsen Institute, CMI Insight no. 2016:3) 5790-the-sudan-armed-forces-and-prospects-of-change.pdf (cmi.no).

47. Willow Berridge, "Briefing: The Uprising in Sudan," *African Affairs*, 119, no. 474 (January 2020): 164–76. doi:10.1093/afraf/adz015.

48. Inaki Albisu Ardigo, "Sudan: Overview of Corruption and Anti-corruption," U4 Anti-Corruption Resource Centre, Chr. Michelsen Institute (U4 Helpdesk Answer 2020:11) sudan-overview-of-corruption-and-anti-corruption-2020.pdf (u4.no).

49. Aljazeera, Sudan's Omar al-Bashir Sentenced to Two Years for Corruption, December 2019, Sudan's Omar al-Bashir Sentenced to Two Years for Corruption | Omar al-Bashir News | Al Jazeera.

50. Jean-Baptiste Gallopin, "Bad Company: How Dark Money Threatens Sudan's Transition," *European Council of Foreign Affairs, Policy Brief*, (June 2020) Bad company: How dark money threatens Sudan's transition (ecfr.eu).

51. Sudan now ranks as Africa's third largest country.

52. Abdel Salam Sidahmed, *Politics and Islam in Contemporary Sudan* (St.Martin's Press: New York, 1996).

53. Ibid., 1996.

54. This paragraph builds on Munzoul Assal, "Urbanization and the Future of Sudan," African Arguments, January 2008. https://africanarguments.org/2008/01/urbanization-and-the-future/.

55. Sudan Humanitarian Needs Overview 2021 (December 2020). https://reliefweb.int/report/sudan/sudan-humanitarian-needs-overview-2021-december-2020.

56. John Voll, "The Sudan after Nimeiry," *Current History*, 85, no. 511 (1986): 213–32.

57. Sidahmed and Sidahmed, 2005.

58. Justin Willis and Atta El Battahani, "We Changed the Laws: Electoral Practice and Malpractice in Sudan Since 1953," *African Affairs*, 109, no. 435 (2010): 191–212.

59. Gabriel Warburg "Democracy in the Sudan: Trial and Error," *Northeast African Studies*, 8, no. 2/3 (1986): 77–94.

60. Atta el-Battahani "Multiparty Elections & the Predicament of Northern Hegemony in Sudan," in *Multi-party Elections in Africa*, eds. Michael Cowen and Liisa Laakso (James Curry: Oxford, 2002).

61. John Voll and Sarah Potts Voll, *The Sudan: Unity and Diversity in a Multicultural State* (London: Westview Press, 1985).

62. Voll, 1986.

63. Ibid.

64. Ibid.

65. Gallab, 2008.

66. Fragile State Index, "Fragility in the World 2021," Fragile States Index | The Fund for Peace.

67. Woodward, 1991.

68. Ansar translates as "follower" and it should not be confused with the Salafist group Ansar al-Sunna.

69. Gabriel Warbur, *Islam, Sectarianism and Politics in Sudan since the Mahdiyya* (Hurst & Co., 2003).

70. Willis and El battahani, 2010.

71. Muhammad Mahmoud, "Sufism and Islamism in the Sudan," in *African Islam and Islam in Africa: Encounters between Sufis and Islamists*, eds. David Westerlund and Eva Evers Rosander (Ohio University Press, 1997).

72. Tareq Y. Ismael, *The Sudanese Communist Party: Ideology and Party Politics* (Routledge, 2013).

73. Sondra Hale, *Gender Politics in Sudan: Islamism, Socialism, and the State* (Boulder, CO: Westview Press, 1996).

74. Ibid.

75. Sidahmed, 1996.

76. Abdelwahab El-Affendi, *Turabi's Revolution: Islam and Power in Sudan* (London: Grey Seal, 1991).

77. John Esposito and John Voll, *Makers of Contemporary Islam* (Oxford University Press: Oxford, 2001).

78. Aron Layish and Gabriel Warburg, *The Reinstatement of Islamic Law in Sudan: An Evaluation of a Legal Experiment in the Light of its Historical Context, Methodology, and Repercussions* (Leiden: Brill, 2002).

79. Munzoul Assal, "Sudan's Popular Uprising and the Demise of Islamism," Bergen: Chr. Michelsen Institute (CMI Brief no. 2019:3).

80. Margaret A. Novicki, "John Garang: A New Sudan," *Africa Report*, 34, no. 4 (1989): 43. Retrieved from https://www.proquest.com/scholarly-journals/john-garang-new-sudan/docview/1304 059918/se-2?accountid=8579.

81. Hugh Vondracek, "A Single Raised Hand: Prospects for Peace in the Sudanese Rivalry," *African Security* 7, no. 4 (2014): 251–76. doi: 10.1080/19392206.2014.977171.

82. Hasan Abdel Ati, "Untapped Potential: Civil Society and the Search for Peace," in *Peace by Piece: Addressing Sudan's Conflicts*, eds. Mark Simmons and Peter Dixon (Pretoria: ACCORD, 2006).

83. Samia Al-Nagar and Liv Tønnessen, "Women's Rights and the Women's Movement in Sudan (1952–2014)," in *Women's Activism in Africa: Struggles for Rights and Representation*, eds. Balghis Badri and Aili Marie Tripp (London: Zed Books, 2017).

84. Abdel Ati, 2006.

85. Berridge, 2020.

86. Munzoul Assal, "From the Country to the Town," in John *The Sudan Handbook*, eds. Justin Willis Ryle and Jok Madut Jok (Oxford: Jamaes Currey, 2011).

87. Munzoul Assal, "Civil Society and Peacebuilding in Sudan: A Critical look," Chr. Michelsen Institute (Sudan Working Paper SWP 2016:2).

88. Assal, 2011.

89. JérômeTubiana, "Darfur after Doha," in *Sudan Divided: Continuing Conflict in a Contested State*, eds. Gunnar Sørbø and Abdel Ghaffar M. Ahmed (New York: Palgrave Macmillan, 2013).

90. Al-Nagar and Tønnessen, 2017.

91. Liv Tønnessen, "Enemies of the State: Curbing Women Activists Advocating Rape Reform in Sudan," *Journal of International Women's Studies* 18, no. 2 (2017): 143–55.

92. Assal, 2016.

93. Freedom House, "Sudan: Freedom in the World 2021," Sudan: Freedom in the World 2021 Country Report | Freedom House.

94. This paragraph on the October revolution builds on Willow Berridge. *Civil Uprisings in Modern Sudan, the Khartoum springs of 1964 and 1985* (Bloomsbury Academic, 2015).

95. Abbas Abdelkarim, Abdalla El Hassan and David Seddon, "From Popular Protest to Military Take-over: An Analytical Chronology of Recent Events in Sudan," *Review of African Political Economy*, 12, no. 33 (1985): 82–89. doi: 10.1080/03056248508703636.

96. Mahmoud Muhammad Taha, *The Second Message of Islam*. Translated by Abdullahi An-Nai'm (Syracuse University Press, 1987).

97. This paragraph on the April intifada builds on Berridge 2015.

98. Jean-Nicolas Bach and Clément Deshayes, "Sudan," in *Africa Yearbook Volume 16: Politics, Economy and Society South of the Sahara in 2019*, eds. Albert K. Awedoba, Benedikt Kamski, Andreas Mehler, David Sebududubu (Brill, 2020).

99. Berridge, 2020.

100. Ann M. Lesch, "From Fragmentation to Fragmentation? Sudan's Foreign Policy," in *The Foreign Policies of Arab States: The Challenge of Globalization*, ed. Ali al-Din Hilal (American University of Cairo Press, 2010).

101. Ibid.

102. Gunnar Sørbø, *Sudan's Transition: Living in Bad Surroundings* (Bergen: Chr. Michelsen Institute, Sudan Working Paper 2020), 4.

103. Mohammed Hussein Sharfi, "Sudan's Radical Foreign Policy Agenda in the 1990s: An Overview of Implications," *Contemporary Arab Affairs* 8, no. 4 (2015): 523–34.

104. Bach and Deshayes.

105. Sørbø, 2020.

106. Mohammed Amin, "Is Sudan Backtracking on Normalisation with Israel?" *Middle East Eye*, August 2020 Is Sudan backtracking on normalisation with Israel? | Middle East Eye.

107. Sørbø, 2020.

108. Bach and Deshayes, 2020.

109. Sørbø, 2020.

110. Ibid.

111. Nadia Sarwar, "Post-Independence South Sudan: An Era of Hope and Challenges, *Strategic Studies* 32, no. 2/3 (2012): 172–82.

112. Lesch, 2010.

113. Munzoul A sisal, "Rights and Decisions to Return: Internally Displaced Persons in Post-war Sudan," in *Forced Displacement*, eds. Grabska K. and Mehta L. (Palgrave Macmillan, 2008).

114. Suleiman Baldo, "Border Control from Hell: How the EU's Migration Partnership Legitimizes Sudan's "Militia State," *Enough Project*, April 2017 Border Control from Hell: How the EU's migration partnership legitimizes Sudan's "militia state" - The Enough Project.

115. Abdelmageed M. Yahya, "Irregular Migration or Human Trafficking? The Realities of Cross-border Population Mobility in Western Sudan" (Bergen: Chr. Michelsen Institute Sudan Brief 2020:1).

116. Jérôme Tubiana Clotilde Warin Gaffar Mohammud Saeneen, "The Impact of EU Migration Policies on Central Saharan Routes" Clingendael, CRU Report, September 2018. Effects of EU policies in Sudan | Multilateral Damage (clingendael.org).

117. Michael Asiedu, *The Construction of the Grand Ethiopian Renaissance Dam (GERD) and Geopolitical Tension between Egypt and Ethiopia with Sudan in the Mix* (Global Political Trends Center (GPoT), 2018).

118. Hanna Ramy Lofty, *Transboundary Water Resources and the Political Economy of Large-Scale Land Investments in the Nile: Sudan, Hydropolitics and Arab Food Security* (Routledge, 2016).

119. Sørbø, 2020.

120. Ibid.

121. Harry Verhoeven, "The Gulf and the Horn: Changing Geographies of Security Interdependence and Competing Visions of Regional Order," *Civil Wars*, 20, no. 3 (2018): 333–57. doi: 10.1080/13698249.2018.1483125.

122. James A. Fargher, "British Interventionism in the Red Sea Eastern Sudan and Britain's Global Defence Strategy," *War in History* 8, no. 2 (2019): 283–300.

123. Bach and Deshayes, 2020.

124. Lesch, 1998.

125. Einas Ahmad, "Political Islam in Sudan: Islamists and the Challenge of State Power (1989–2004)," in *Islam and Muslim Politics in Africa*, eds. Benjamin Soares and Rene Otayek (New York: Palgrave Macmillan, 2007).

126. Lesch, 1998.

127. Sidahmed and Sidahmed, 2005.

128. Carolyn Fluehr-Lobban, "Shari'a Law in the Sudan: History and Trends since Independence," *Africa Today*, 28, no. 2 (1981): 69–77.

129. Gallab, 2008.

130. Abdullahi Ali Ibrahim, *Manichaean Delirium: Decolonizing the Judiciary and Islamic Renewal in Sudan, 1898–1985* (Leiden: Brill, 2008).

131. Carolyn Fluehr-Lobban, *Islamic Law and Society in the Sudan* (London: Frank Cass, 1987).

132. Samia al-Nagar and Liv Tønnessen, "Sudanese Women's Demands for Freedom, Peace, and Justice in the 2019 Revolution," in *Women and Peacebuilding in Africa*, eds. Ladan Affi, Liv Tønnessen and Aili Marie Tripp (James Currey, 2021).

133. Ibid.

134. Ibid.

135. Al-Nagar and Tønnessen, 2017.

136. Salma A. Nageeb, *New Spaces and Old Frontiers: Women, Social Space, and Islamization in Sudan* (Lanham, MD: Lexington Books, 2004).

137. Al-Nagar and Tønnessen, 2021.

138. Liv Tønnessen, "Women at Work in Sudan: Marital Privilege or Constitutional Right," *Social Politics: International Studies in Gender, State and Society* 26, no. 2 (2019): 223–44.

139. Al-Nagar and Tønnessen, 2021.

140. Einas Ahmed, "Militant Salafism in Sudan," *Islamic Africa*, 6, no. 1–2 (2015): 164–84.

141. Noah Salomon, *For Love of the Prophet: An Ethnography of Sudan's Islamic State* (Princeton University Press, 2017).

142. Lesch, 1998.

143. Liv Tønnessen, "Ansar al-Sunna and Women's Agency in Sudan: A Salafi Approach to Empowerment through Gender Segregation," *Frontiers: A Journal of Women's Studies* 37, no. 3 (2016): 92–124.

144. Ahmed, 2015.

CHAPTER 24

1. This chapter draws upon the chapter in previous editions, authored by Laryssa Chomiak and Robert Parks.

2. World Bank, *Tunisia-Integration and Competitiveness Second Development Policy Loan Project* (Washington, DC: World Bank, 2010), http://documents.worldbank.org/curated/en/2010/12/1332 9800/tunisia- integration-competitiveness-second-development- policy-loan-project.

3. Specifically, see Bob Rijkers, Caroline Freund, and Antonio Nucifora, *All in the Family: State Capture in Tunisia*, Policy Research working paper no. WPS 6810 (Washington, DC: World Bank, 2014), http://elibrary.worldbank.org/doi/pdf/10.1596/1813-9450-6810; Rijkers, Leila Baghdadi, and Gael J. R. F. Raballand, *Political Connections and Tariff Evasion: Evidence from Tunisia.* Policy Research working paper no. WPS 7336 (Washington, DC: World Bank, 2015), http://documents.worldbank.org/curated/en/2015/06/24697879/political-connections-tariff - evasion-evidence-tunisia.

4. See Laryssa Chomiak, "Architecture of Resistance in Tunisia," in *Taking to the Streets: The Transformation of Arab Activism*, eds. Lina Khatib and Ellen Lust (Baltimore, MD: Johns Hopkins University Press, 2014), chap. 1.

5. See The Carter Center, "National Constituent Assembly Elections in Tunisia, October 23, 2011: Final Report," https://www.cartercenter.org/resources/pdfs/news/peace_publications/electio n_reports/tunisia-final- Oct2011.pdf.

6. For an overview of their collective struggles for democratization, see Mustapha Ben Jaafar, *Un si long chemin vers la démocratie. Entretien avec Vincent Geisser* (Tunis: Nirvana, 2014); Rachid Ghannouchi and Olivier Ravanello, *Au sujet de l'Islam* (Paris: Plon, 2015); and Pierre Piccinin da Prata, *Tunisie. Du triomphe au naufrage: Entretiens avec le Président Moncef Marzouki* (Paris: L'Harmattan, 2013).

7. See http://databank.worldbank.org/data/home.aspx.

8. See the Tunisian Ministry of Tourism website at http://www.tourisme.gov.tn/en/ achievements-and-prospects/tourism-in-figures/figures-2013.html.

9. For more on this rebellion, see Eric Gobe, "The Gafsa Mining Basin between Riots and Social Movement: Meaning and Significance of a Protest Movement in Ben Ali's Tunisia," Working Paper (2010), https://hal.archives-ouvertes.fr/file/index/docid/557826/filename/Tunisia_Th e_Gafsa_mining_basin_between_Riots_and_Social_Movement.pdf.

10. Unfortunately, current strike figures are not available in ILOSTA or LABORSTA. See http://ww w.marxist.com/tunisia-one-year-after-the-revolution-wave-of-strike-and-uprisings.htm.

11. African Economic Outlook Series, "Tunisia 2012," African Development Bank, http://www.afd b.org/fileadmin/uploads/afdb/Documents/Generic-Documents/Tunisia%20Full%20PDF%20 Country%20Note.pdf.

12. See http://www.reuters.com/article/2012/09/14/us-protests-tunisia-school-idUSBRE88D 18020120914.

13. See http://www.aljazeera.com/news/africa/2013/02/201321918739992693.html.

14. Amel Boubekeur, "The Politics of Protest in Tunisia: Instrument in Parties' Competition vs. Tool for Participation," *SWP Comments* 13 (March 2015): 1–8.

15. See http://www.nytimes.com/2014/01/29/world/africa/islamist-party-in-tunisia-hands-power-to-caretaker- government.html?_r=0.

16. See https://ecdpm.org/great-insights/north-africa-hope-in-troubled-times/deepening-democracy-transitional-tunisia/.

17. See full interview with Acharaa Al-Magharibi, https://acharaa.com/%d8%a7%d9%84% d8%b1%d8%a6%d9%8a%d8%b3%d9%8a%d8%a9/%d8%a7%d9%84%d8%b4%d8%a7%d8%b 1%d8%b9-%d8%a7%d9%84%d9%85%d8%ba%d8%a7%d8%b1%d8%a8%d9%8a-%d8%aa%d 9%86%d8%b4%d8%b1-%d8%ad%d9%88%d8%a7%d8%b1-%d9%82%d9%8a%d8%b3-%d8% b3%d8%b9%d9%8a%d8%af-%d9%83%d8%a7%d9%85/.

18. See https://www.jeuneafrique.com/1111122/politique/tunisie-conflit-ouvert-entre-kais-saied-et-hichem-mechichi/.

19. See https://www.reuters.com/world/africa/tunisia-president-takes-new-powers-says-will -reform-system-2021-09-22/.

20. See https://www.lorientlejour.com/article/1275966/dix-huit-ong-denoncent-laccaparement-du-pouvoir-par-le-president.html.

21. See, for example, https://www.hrw.org/news/2021/09/27/joint-statement-tunisia-unpreced-ented-confiscation-power-presidency; https://www.icj.org/tunisia-reverse-the-presidents-power-grab/; https://www.article19.org/resources/tunisia-greater-presidential-powers-threaten-rights-and-freedoms/.

22. Clement Henry Moore calls this the "Colonial Dialectic." See *Tunisia since Independence: The Dynamics of One-Party Rule* (Berkeley: California University Press, 1965), 25–40; Moore, "The Era of the Neo-Destour," in *Tunisia: The Politics of Modernization*, ed. Charles A. Micaud (New York: Praeger, 1963), 69–128.

23. For a firsthand account, see Ahmed Ben Salah's memoires, *Pour rétablir la vérité: Réformes et développement en Tunisie 1961–1969* (Tunis: Cérès Éditions Diffusion, 2008).

24. For more on the cooperative movement, see John L. Simmons, "Agricultural Cooperative and Tunisian Development—Part One," *The Middle East Journal* 24, no. 4 (1970): 455–65; "Agricultural Cooperative and Tunisian Development—Part Two," *The Middle East Journal* 25, no. 10 (1971): 45–57.

25. For firsthand accounts of the 1971 Congress, see Beji Caïd Essebsi, *Bourguiba: Le bon grain de livraie* (Paris: Sud Éditions, 2009); Ahmed Mestiri, *Un témoignage pour l'Histoire* (Paris: Sud Éditions, 2011).

26. See Azzam S. Tamimi, *Rachid Ghannouchi: A Democrat within Islamism* (Oxford: Oxford University Press, 2001).

27. See his memoires: Mohamed Mzali, *Un Premier minister de Bourguiba témoigne* (Paris: Éditions Jean Picollec, 2004).

28. See Eva Bellin, *Stalled Democracy: Capital, Labor, and the Paradox of State-Sponsored Development* (Ithaca, NY: Cornell University Press, 2002); Emma Murphy, *Economic and Political Change in Tunisia: From Bourguiba to Ben Ali* (London: Palgrave Macmillan, 1999).

29. Souad Bakalti, "Mouvement et organizations féminines de lutte de libération nationale en Tunisia," in *Actus du IXe colloque international sur les procésus et enjeux de la decolonization en Tunisie (1952–1964)* (Tunis: ISHMN, 1999), cited in Kenneth J. Perkins, *A History of Modern Tunisia* (New York: Cambridge University Press, 2004), 138.

30. For an overview of these issues in the post–Ben Ali era, see Doris H. Gray, "Tunisia after the Uprising: Islamist and Secular Quests for Women's Rights," *Mediterranean Politics* 17, no. 3 (2012): 285–302.

31. For an excellent overview of women's health in Tunisia, see Angel M. Foster, *Women's Comprehensive Health Care in Contemporary Tunisia* (PhD dissertation, University of Oxford, 2001).

32. Unless otherwise noted, data in this section are taken from the World Bank's World Development Indicators Database.

33. See https://nces.ed.gov/TIMSS/tables11.asp.

34. See Zaid Al-Ali, "Tunisia's President Just Gave Himself Unprecedented Powers. He Says he'll Rule by Decree," *Washington Post*, September 24, 2021. https://www.washingtonpost.com/politics/2021/09/24/tunisias-president-just-gave-himself-unprecedented-powers-he-says-hell-rule-by-decree/.

35. These are the *Commission d'Établissement des Faits sur les Abus et Violations Commis à Partir du 17 Décembre 2010*, and the *Commission Nationale d'Investigation sur la Corruption et la Malversation*.

36. See http://data.worldbank.org/indicator/MS.MIL.XPND.GD.ZS?page=1.

37. Consult the Official Journal of the Tunisian Republic for details on the law at http://www.cnudst.rnrt.tn/wwwisis/jort.06/form.htm.

38. See https://www.hrw.org/news/2014/07/07/tunisia-amend-draft-counterterrorism-law.

39. See http://www.reformes.gov.tn/%D8%AD%D8%AC%D9%85+%D8%A7%D9%84%D8%A3%D8%AC%D9%88%D8%B1+%D9%81%D9%8A+2018--3.html.

40. "Tunisia's Decentralization Reforms: The Gap Between Ideas and Implementation." In *The Dynamics of Decentralization in the MENA: Processes Outcomes and Obstacles*, Working paper No. 31/2020, Governance and Local Development Program (University of Gothenburg, May 2020).

41. Guillermo O'Donnell and Philippe C. Schmitter, *Transitions from Authoritarian Rule: Tentative Conclusions about Uncertain Democracies* (Johns Hopkins University Press, 2013), 43.

42. Anouar Boukhars, "The Fragility of Elite Settlements in Tunisia," *African Security Review* 26, no. 3 (2017): 257–70.

43. Sharan Grewal and Shadi Hamid, "The Dark Side of Consensus in Tunisia: Lessons from 2015–2019," *Brookings Institute*, 2020; Hamza Meddeb, "Tunisia's Geography of Anger: Regional Inequalities and the Rise of Populism," *Carnegie Middle East Center*, 2020.

44. "Civil Society in a Time of Transition," *EuroMed Survey of Civil Society and Social Movements in the Euro-Mediterranean Region:* Tenth edition. IEMED, January 2020.

45. During the Beylical period, Maleki and Hanafi schools of jurisprudence were legally enforced on separate communities and contractual obligations. Similar provisions applied to the Jewish and Ibadi communities.

46. For an excellent overview of the development of Salafism in Tunisia, see Fabio Merone, "The Emergence of Salafism in Tunisia," Jadaliyya (2012), http://www.jadaliyya.com/pages/index/6934/the- emergence-of-salafism-in-tunisia.

47. For the difference between the two words in the Tunisian context, see Mohamed Kerrou, *Public et Privé en Islam* (Tunis: IRMC, 2002), 17–42.

48. For an excellent overview of this period, see Susan Waltz, "Islamist Appeal in Tunisia," *Middle East Journal* 40, no. 4 (1986): 651–70.

49. Laryssa Chomiak, "The Richness of Tunisia's New Politics," *The Washington Post*, October 29, 2014, http://www.washingtonpost.com/blogs/monkey-cage/wp/2014/10/29/the-richness-of-tunisias-new-politics/.

50. Nadia Marzouki, "Tunisia's Rotten Compromise," *Middle East Research and Information Project*, July 10, 2015, http://www.merip.org/mero/mero071015.

51. US Department of State, 2009.

52. Unless otherwise indicated, all figures are taken from the World Bank World Development Indicators Databank.

53. Richards and Waterbury, citing World Development Reports of 1982 and 1987, 70.

54. IMF, *Balance of Payments Statistics Yearbook*, 2007.

55. Unless otherwise indicated, all figures from the World Bank World Development Indicators.

56. International Labor Organization, http://www.ilo.org/ilostat/faces/home/statisticaldata/Contry ProfileId?_afrLoop=287710147108920#%40%3F_afrLoop%3D287710147108920%26_adf.ctrl-state%3Dt3wx05tio_195.

57. See http://www-wds.worldbank.org/external/default/WDSContentServer/WDSP/IB/2014/03/25/000158349_20140325092905/Rendered/PDF/WPS6810.pdf.

58. See Clement M.Henry, *The Mediterranean Debt Crescent: Money and Power in Algeria, Morocco, Tunisia, and Turkey* (Gainesville: University Press of Florida, 1996); Clement M.Henry and Robert Springborg, *Globalization and the Politics of Development in the Middle East* (New York: Cambridge University Press, 2002).

59. For a more detailed list of these holdings, see http://www.confiscation.tn/ and http://www.finances.gov.tn/index.php?option=com_content&view=article&id=201:gestion-des-biens-confisques&catid=28& Itemid=577&lang=fr.

60. See Chomiak and Parks, "Repossessing the Dispossessed," *Jadaliyya* (2013), http://www.jadaliyya.com/pages/index/9485/repossessing-the-dispossessed.

61. See https://www.imf.org/external/pubs/ft/scr/2013/cr13161.pdf.

CHAPTER 25

1. Perry Anderson, *Lineages of Absolutist States* (London: Verso, 1974).

2. Karen Barkey, *Bandits and Bureaucrats: The Ottoman Route to State Centralization* (Ithaca, NY: Cornell University Press, 1994).

3. Soner Cagaptay, *Islam, Secularism and Nationalism in Modern Turkey: Who Is Turk?* (London: Routledge, 2006).

4. A. L. Macfie, *The End of the Ottoman Empire, 1908–1923* (New York: Longman, 1998); see also Gasper in this volume.

5. Feroz Ahmad, *Turkey: The Quest for Identity* (Oxford: Oneworld, 2003); Erik J. Zürcher, *Turkey: A Modern History*, 3rd ed. (London: I. B. Tauris, 2004); Bernard Lewis, *The Emergence of Modern Turkey* (New York: Oxford University Press, 1968); and Andrew Mango, *Atatürk* (London: John Murray, 1999).

6. Roderic H. Davison, "From Empire to Republic, 1909–1923," in *Turkey: A Short History*, ed. Roderic H. Davison (Englewood Cliffs, NJ: Prentice Hall, 1968).

7. Serif Mardin, "Center-Periphery Relations: A Key to Turkish Politics?" *Daedalus* 102, no. 1 (Winter 1973): 169–90.

8. Ali Riza Gürgen and Safak Erten, "Approaches of Şerif Mardin and Metin Heper on State and Civil Society in Turkey," *Journal of Historical Studies* 3 (2005): 1–14.

9. Nilüfer Narlı, "The Tension between the Center and Peripheral Economy and the Rise of a Counter Business Elite in Turkey," *Islam en Turquie: Les Annales de L'Autre Islam* 6 (1999): 5072; Berna Turam, *Between Islam and the State: The Politics of Engagement* (Stanford, CA: Stanford University Press, 2007).

10. Binnaz Toprak, "Islam and the Secular State in Turkey," in *Turkey: Political, Social and Economic Challenges in the 1990s*, eds. Ç. Balım et al. (New York: E. J. Brill, 1995); E. Fuat Keyman and Ergun Özbudun, "Cultural Globalization in Turkey: Actors, Discourse and Strategies," in *Many Globalizations: Cultural Diversity in the Contemporary World*, eds. P. L. Berger and S. P. Huntington (New York: Oxford University Press, 2002).

11. Ali Çarkoğlu, "A New Electoral Victory for the 'Pro-Islamists' or the 'New Centre-Right'? The Justice and Development Party Phenomenon in the July 2007 Parliamentary Elections in Turkey," *South European Society and Politics* 12, no. 4 (2007): 501–19; Ali Çarkoğlu and M. J. Hinich, "Spatial Analysis of Turkey's Party Preferences," *Electoral Studies* 25, no. 2 (2006): 363–92.

12. Ramin Ahmadov, "Counter Transformations in the Center and Periphery of Turkish Society and the Rise of the Justice and Development Party," *Alternatives: Turkish Journal of International Relations* 7, nos. 2/3 (2008).

13. https://data.tuik.gov.tr/Bulten/Index?p=Income-and-Living-Conditions-Survey-2020-37404

14. Eda Doğan, *Measurement of Poverty in Turkey,* The Ministry of Development Expertise Report (2014), http://www.kalkinma.gov.tr/Lists/Uzmanlk%20Tezleri/Attachments/372/Türkiyede%20Yoksulluğun%20Ölçülmesi%20Tez.pdf.

15. See http://erg.sabanciuniv.edu/sites/erg.sabanciuniv.edu/files/ERG_EMR2013.web_0.pdf; http://www.turkstat.gov.tr/PreHaberBultenleri.do?id = 18623.

16. See http://www.tuik.gov.tr/PreHaberBultenleri.do?id= 18619.

17. https://turkey.unfpa.org/sites/default/files/pub-pdf/ingilizce_web_son_pdf.pdf

18. SIS Household Surveys, Turkish Statistical Institute (TürkStat), Ankara, www.turkstat.gov.tr/.

19. https://www3.weforum.org/docs/WEF_GGGR_2021.pdf

20. http://hdr.undp.org/sites/default/files/hdr2020.pdf, 361

21. https://wid.world/country/turkey/ World Inequality index

22. See https://wid.world/country/turkey/.

23. Binnaz Toprak, "Islam and Democracy in Turkey," *Turkish Studies* 6, no. 2 (2005): 169–70.

24. Toprak, "Islam and the Secular State in Turkey," in *Turkey*, eds. Ç. Balım et al.; Keyman and Özbudun, "Cultural Globalization in Turkey," in *Many Globalizations*, eds. Berger and Huntington.

25. Nilüfer Göle, *The Forbidden Modern: The Civilization and Veiling* (Ann Arbor: University of Michigan Press, 1996).

26. Soner Cagaptay, "Turkey's Republic of Fear," *Wall Street Journal* (March 4, 2010).

27. See Binnaz Toprak et al., *Türkiye'de Farkli Olmak: Dindarlik ve Muhafazarlik ekseninde ötekile-stirilenler* [*Being Different in Turkey: Othering on the Nexus of Religion and Conservatism*] (Istanbul: Metis Yayinevi, 2008).

28. Binnaz Toprak and İlkay Sunar, "Islam in Politics: The Case of Turkey," in *Society and Democracy in Turkey*, ed. State Sunar (Istanbul: Bahçeşehir University, 2005), 155–73; Çarkoğlu, "A New Electoral Victory."

29. B. Esen and Şebnem Gumuscu, "Building a Competitive Authoritarian Regime: State–Business Relations in the AKP's Turkey," *Journal of Balkan and Near Eastern Studies* 20, no. 4 (2017): 349–72.

30. https://www.aljazeera.com/news/2021/4/26/turkey-orders-532-arrests-in-military-probe-over-gulen-links

31. Murat Somer, "Turkey's Kurdish Conflict: Changing Context, and Domestic and Regional Implications," *Middle East Journal* 58, no. 2 (Spring 2004): 235–53; Dogu Ergil, "The Kurdish Question in Turkey," *Journal of Democracy* 11, no. 3 (2000): 122–35; and Kemal Kirişci and Gareth Winrow, *The Kurdish Question and Turkey: An Example of Trans-State Ethnic Conflict* (London: Frank Cass, 1997).

32. *CIA World Factbook, 2016*, https://www.cia.gov/library/publications/the-world-factbook/geos/tu.html.

33. Ergil, "The Kurdish Question in Turkey," note 43.

34. Luigi Narbone and Nathalie Tocci, "Running around in Circles? The Cyclical Relationship between Turkey and the European Union," in *Turkey's Road to European Union Membership: National Identity and Political Change*, eds. Susannah Verney and Kostas Ifantis (London: Routledge, 2009), 30.

35. See http://www.crisisgroup.be/interactives/turkey/.

36. See https://freedomhouse.org/report/freedom-world/2018/turkey.

37. B. Esen and Şebnem Gumuscu, "Building a Competitive Authoritarian Regime: State–Business Relations in the AKP's Turkey," *Journal of Balkan and Near Eastern Studies* 20, no. 4 (2017): 349–72; Ayşe Buğra and Osman Savaşkan, *New Capitalism in Turkey: The Relationship between Politics, Religion and Business* (Cheltenham: Edward Elgar, 2014).

38. Murat Somer, "Understanding Turkey's Democratic Breakdown: Old vs. New and Indigenous vs. Global Authoritarianism," *Southeast European and Black Sea Studies* 16, no. 4 (2016): 481–503; Erdem S. Aytaç, Ali Çarkoğlu, and Kerem Yıldırım, "Taking Sides: Determinants of Support for a Presidential System in Turkey," *South European Society and Politics* 22, no. 1 (2017): 1–20.

39. E. Uğur, "Islamists and Politics of Democratization: Evidence from Turkey," *Contemporary Islam* 11, no. 2 (2017): 137–55.

40. J. McCoy, T. Rahman, and M. Somer, "Polarization and the Global Crisis of Democracy: Common Patterns, Dynamics, and Pernicious Consequences for Democratic Polities," *American Behavioral Scientist* [s. l.] 62, no. 1 (2018): 16–42.

41. Ali Çarkoğlu, Mehmet Kabasakal, Tarhan Erdem, and Omer Faruk, "Siyasi Partilerde Reform" [Reform in Political Parties] (Research Report prepared for TESEV, 2000).

42. Ersin Kalaycıoğlu, "Turkey," in *Introduction to Comparative Politics*, eds. Mark Kesselman, Joel Krieger, and William A. Joseph (New York: Houghton Mifflin 2005), 229.

43. For an overview, see William Hale, *Turkish Politics and the Military* (London: Routledge, 1994); for a critical assessment, see Ümit Cizre, "Demythologizing the National Security Concept," *Middle East Journal* 57, no. 2 (2002): 213–90. For the tensions between the AKP and the military, see Ümit Cizre, "Justice and Development Party and the Military," in *Secular and Islamic Politics in Turkey: The Making of the Justice and Development Party*, ed. Ümit Cizre (New York: Routledge, 2008).

44. J. Samuel Valenzuela, "Democratic Consolidation in Post-Transnational Settings: Notion, Process and Facilitating Conditions," in *Valenzuela—Issues in Democratic Consolidation: The New South American Democracies in Comparative Perspective*, eds. Scott Mainwaring, G. O'Donnell, and J. Samuel (South Bend, IN: Notre Dame Press, 1992).

45. Ayşe Güneş Ayata and Sencer Ayata, "Ethnic and Religious Bases of Voting," in *Politics, Parties, and Elections in Turkey*, eds. Sabri Sayarı and Yılmaz Esmer (Boulder, CO: Lynne Rienner, 2002), 137–55; Yılmaz Esmer, "At the Ballot Box: Determinants of Voting Behavior," in *Politics, Parties, and Elections in Turkey*, eds. Sayari and Esmer, 91–114; and Ersin Kalaycıoğlu, "Elections and Party Preferences in Turkey: Changes and Continuities in the 1990s," *Comparative Political Studies* 27, no. 3 (October 1994): 402–24.

46. Kalaycıoğlu, "Elections and Party Preferences in Turkey"; Kalaycıoğlu, "The Shaping of Party Preferences in Turkey Coping with the Post–Cold War Era," *New Perspectives on Turkey*, 20 (Spring 1999): 47–76.

47. Yılmaz Esmer, "Parties and the Electorate," in *Turkey*, eds. Balım et al.; Esmer, "At the Ballot Box: Determinants of Voting Behavior."

48. Ali Çarkoğlu, "Macro Economic Determinants of Electoral Support for Incumbents in Turkey, 1950–1995," *New Perspectives on Turkey* 17 (1997): 75–96; Çarkoğlu, "The Nature of Left–Right Ideological Self-Placement in the Turkish Context," *Turkish Studies* 8, no. 2 (2007): 253–71.

49. Ersin Kalaycıoğlu and Çarkoğlu, *The Rising Tide of Conservatism in Turkey* (New York: Palgrave Macmillan, 2009).

50. Ibid.

51. Ali Çarkoğlu and Mine Eder, "Developmentalism à la Turca: The Southeast Anatolia Development Project," in *Environmentalism in Turkey: Between Development and Democracy?* eds. Fikret Adaman and Murat Arsel (London: Ashgate, 2005), 167–85.

52. Sabri Sayarı, "The Changing Party System," in *Politics, Parties and Elections in Turkey*, eds. Sabri Sayarı and Yilmaz Esmer, 9–33.

53. Özbudun, *Contemporary Turkish Politics*, 75.

54. With the AKP, however, trust has risen.

55. Ziya Öniş, "Political Economy of Justice and Development Party," in *The Emergence of New Turkey: Democracy and the AK Parti*, ed. Hakan Yavuz (Salt Lake City: University of Utah Press, 2006), 207–34.

56. See for instance, Jenny White, *Islamist Mobilization in Turkey: A Study in Vernacular Politics* (Seattle: University of Washington Press, 2002).

57. Despite significant diversity among the Alevis, there are problems of measuring political behavior along sectarian lines, and there is sufficient evidence that they form a politically distinct group. See Ali Çarkoğlu, "Political Preferences of the Turkish Electorate: Reflections of an Alevi-Sunni Cleavage," *Turkish Studies* 6, no. 2 (2005).

58. https://rsf.org/en/taxonomy/term/145. Retrieved in December 25th, 2021.

59. Susan Corke, Andrew Finkel, David J. Kramer, Carla Anne Robbins, and Nate Schenkkan, *Democracy in Crisis: Corruption, Media, and Power in Turkey*, https://freedomhouse.org/sites/default/files/Turkey%20Report%20-%202-3-14.pdf.

60. Şevket Pamuk, "Economic Change in Twentieth Century Turkey: Is the Glass More Than Half Full?" in *Cambridge History of Modern Turkey*, ed. Reşat Kasaba (New York: Cambridge University Press, 2008), 266–67.

61. Ilkay Sunar, "The Politics of State Interventionism in Populist Egypt and Turkey," in *Developmentalism and Beyond: Society and Politics in Egypt and Turkey*, eds. Ayşe Öncü and Çağlar Keyder (Cairo: American University in Cairo Press, 1994).

62. Şevket Pamuk, "Intervention during the Great Depression: Another Look at the Turkish Experience," in *The Mediterranean Response to Globalization before 1950*, eds. Pamuk and Jeffrey Williamson (New York: Routledge, 2000), 326.

63. Turkey's major agricultural exports were and still are hazelnuts, figs, raisins, and tobacco.

64. Ziya Öniş, "Political Economy of Turkey in the 1980s: Anatomy of Unorthodox Liberalism," in *Strong State and Economic Interest Groups*, ed. Metin Heper (New York: Walter de Gruyter, 1991).

65. For various interpretations of this era, see Ziya Öniş and Steven B. Webb, "Turkey: Democratization and Adjustment from Above," in *Voting for Reform: Democracy, Political Liberalization, and Economic Adjustment*, eds. Stephan Haggard and Steven B. Webb (New York: World Bank and Oxford University Press, 1994), 128; Metin Heper, ed., *Strong State and Economic Interest Groups: The Post-1980 Turkish Experience* (New York: Walter de Gruyter, 1991).

66. Heper, *Strong State*, 27–40.

67. See John Waterbury, "Export-Led Growth and Center-Right Coalition in Turkey," *Comparative Politics* 24 (1992): 127–45; Ayşe Buğra, *State and Business in Modern Turkey: A Comparative Study* (Albany: State University of New York Press, 1994).

68. See Korkut Boratav, "Inter-Class and Intra-Class Relations of Distribution under Structural Adjustment: Turkey during the 1980s," in *Political Economy of Turkey: Debt, Adjustment, and Sustainability*, eds. Tosun Aricanlı and Dani Rodrik (New York: St. Martin's Press, 1990); H. Akder, "Policy Formation in the Process of Implementing Agricultural Reform in Turkey," *International Journal of Agricultural Resources, Governance and Ecology* 6, no. 4/5 (2007): 514–32; David Waldner, *State Building and Late Development* (Ithaca, NY: Cornell University Press, 1999).

69. *Global Economic Prospects and the Developing Countries* (Washington, DC: World Bank, 1996).

70. Peter B. Evans, *Embedded Autonomy: States and Industrial Transformation* (Princeton, NJ: Princeton University Press, 1995).

71. For the problem of too much autonomy of the state, see Mine Eder, "Becoming Western: Turkey and the European Union," in *Regionalism across the North-South Divide: State Strategies and Globalization*, eds. Jean Grugel and Will Hout (New York: Routledge, 1999), 79–95.

72. Daron Acemoğlu and Murat Ucer, "The Ups and Downs of Turkish Growth, 2002–2015: Political Dynamics, the European Union and the Institutional Slide," http://www.nber.org/papers/w216 08.pdf.

73. Mehmet Uğur has extensively discussed this issue in *The European Union and Turkey: An Anchor/Credibility Dilemma* (London: Ashgate, 1999). The following discussion is framed accordingly.

74. Ibid., 55–85.

75. Kemal Kirişci, "U.S.-Turkish Relations: New Uncertainties in a Renewed Partnership," in *Turkey in World Politics: The Emerging Multi-Regional Power*, eds. Barry Rubin and Kemal Kirişchi (Boulder, CO: Lynne Rienner, 2001), 169–97; also see Mustafa Aydın, "Reconstructing Turkish-American Relations: Divergence versus Convergences," *New Perspectives on Turkey* 40 (Spring 2009): 145–47; F. Stephen Larrabee, *Troubled Partnership: U.S.-Turkish Relations in an Era of Global Geopolitical Change* (Santa Monica, CA: Rand Corporation, 2010).

76. Kirişci, "A Friendlier Schengen Visa System as a Tool of 'Soft Power,'" *European Journal of Migration and Law* 7 (2005): 343–67.

77. Ibid.

78. Larrabee, "Troubled Partnership," 49.

79. Bülent Aras and Hakan Fidan, "Turkey and Eurasia: Frontiers of a New Geographic Imagination," *New Perspectives on Turkey* 40 (Spring 2009): 193–217.

80. https://en.goc.gov.tr/temporary-protection27. Retrieved on December 25th, 2021.

81. Meliha Benli Altunışık, "The New Turn in Turkish Foreign Policy in the Middle East: Regional and Domestic Insecurities," IAI papers 7 July 2020.

CHAPTER 26

1. See Asher Orkaby, *Beyond the Arab Cold War: The International History of the Yemen Civil War, 1962–68* (Oxford: Oxford University Press, 2017); Dana Adams Schmidt, *Yemen: The Unknown War* (New York: Holt, Rinehart and Winston, 1968); and Edgar O'Ballance, *The War in the Yemen* (Hamden, CT: Archon Books, 1971).

2. See Fred Halliday, *Revolution and Foreign Policy: The Case of South Yemen, 1967–1987* (Cambridge: Cambridge University Press, 2002).

3. The opening sentence of the PDRY's 1970 constitution reads, "Believing in the unity of the Yemen, and the unity of the destiny of the Yemeni people in the territory...." Cited in Michael Hudson, *Arab Politics: The Search for Legitimacy* (New Haven, CT: Yale University Press, 1977), 357.

4. For further discussion of this period, see Robert Burrowes, *The Yemen Arab Republic: The Politics of Development, 1962–1986* (Boulder, CO: Westview Press, 1987).

5. For discussion of this period, see John Ishiyama, "The Sickle and the Minaret: Communist Successor Parties in Yemen and Afghanistan after the Cold War," *Middle East Review of International Affairs* 9, no. 1 (March 2005): 7–29.

6. For more on the elite divisions leading up to the defections in 2011, see Sarah Phillips, *Yemen and the Politics of Permanent Crisis* (London: Routledge, 2011).

7. Derek B. Miller, "Demand, Stockpiles and Social Controls: Small Arms in Yemen," *Small Arms Survey*, Occasional Paper no. 9 (May 2003).

8. See Sheila Carapico, *Civil Society in Yemen: The Political Economy of Activism in Modern Arabia* (Cambridge: Cambridge University Press, 1998); Carapico, "Elections and Mass Politics in Yemen," *Middle East Report* 23, no. 6 (November/December 1993): 2–7.

9. Although there are no definitive figures regarding the size and geographical dispersion of all Yemeni tribes, the northern tribal confederations, the Hashid and the Bakil (and to a lesser extent the Madhaj), have the greatest influence on Yemen's national politics. Paul Dresch, *Tribes, Government and History in Yemen* (Oxford: Clarendon Press, 1989); Shelagh Weir, *A Tribal Order: Politics and Law in the Mountains of Yemen* (Austin: University of Texas Press, 2007); and Steven C. Caton, *"Peaks of Yemen I Summon": Poetry as Cultural Practice in a North Yemeni Tribe* (Berkeley: University of California Press, 1990) are all excellent studies of North Yemeni tribes.

10. Sarah Phillips, *Yemen's Democracy Experiment in Regional Perspective: Patronage and Pluralized Authoritarianism* (New York: Palgrave Macmillan, 2008), chap. 4.

11. International Crisis Group, "Yemen: Coping with Terrorism and Violence in a Fragile State," *ICG Middle East Report* no. 8 (January 8, 2003): 14.

12. Burrowes, *The Yemen Arab Republic*, 8.

13. For discussion of the economic decline at this time, see Robert Burrowes, "The Republic of Yemen: The Politics of Unification and Civil War, 1989–1995," in *The Middle East Dilemma: The Politics and Economics of Arab Integration*, ed. Michael Hudson (New York: Columbia University Press, 1998), 187–213.

14. See Joseph Kostiner, *Yemen: The Tortuous Quest for Unity, 1990–94* (London: Royal Institute of International Affairs, 1996), chap. 5; Robert Burrowes, "'It's the Economy, Stupid': The Political Economy of Yemen and the 1997 Elections," in *Yemen Today: Crisis and Solutions*, eds. E. G. H. Joffe, M. J. Hachemi, and E. W. Watkins (London: Caravel Press, 1997), 202–12.

15. For more on the economic decline, see Christopher Boucek, *Yemen: Avoiding a Downward Spiral* (Washington, DC: Carnegie Endowment for International Peace, 2009).

16. For more, see Phillips, *Yemen and the Politics of Permanent Crisis*, 130.

17. For more, see Steven C. Caton, "Global Water Security and the Demonization of Qat: The New Water Governmentality and Developing Countries like Yemen" in *Bioinsecurity and Vulnerability*, eds. Steven C. Caton and Nancy N. Chen (Santa Fe, NM: School for Advanced Research Press, 2014).

18. For further details, see Gregory D. Johnsen, *The Last Refuge: Yemen, al-Qaeda, and America's War in Arabia* (London: Scribe, 2012); Jeremy Scahill, *Dirty War: The World Is a Battlefield* (New York: Nation Books, 2013); Sarah Phillips, "What Comes Next in Yemen? Al-Qaeda, the Tribes and State-Building," Carnegie Paper no. 107 (Washington, DC: Carnegie Endowment for International Peace, March 2010); and Johnsen, "The Expansion Strategy of Al-Qa'ida in the Arabian Peninsula," *CTC Sentinel* 2, no. 9 (September 2009).

19. See, for example, the 2015 al-Jazeera documentary *Al Qaeda Informant*, http://www.aljazeera.com/news/2015/06/informant-yemen-saleh-helped-direct-al-qaeda-150604073415522.html.

INDEX